LET'S GO

PAGES PACKED WITH ESSENTIAL INFORM...

"Value-packed, unbeatable, accurat...

—...mes

"The guides are aimed not only ... e independent traveler; a sort of streetwise ...

—*The New York Times*

"Unbeatable; good sight-seeing advic... ...te info on restaurants, hotels,
and inns; a commitment to money-sav... ravel; and a wry style that brightens
nearly every page."

—*The Washington Post*

THE BEST TRAVEL BARGAINS IN YOUR BUDGET

"All the dirt, dirt cheap."

—*People*

"Let's Go follows the creed that you don't have to toss your life's savings to the
wind to travel—unless you want to."

—*The Salt Lake Tribune*

REAL ADVICE FOR REAL EXPERIENCES

"The writers seem to have experienced every rooster-packed bus and lunar-
surfaced mattress about which they write."

—*The New York Times*

"[Let's Go's] devoted updaters really walk the walk (and thumb the ride, and
trek the trail). Learn how to fish, haggle, find work—anywhere."

—*Food & Wine*

"A world-wise traveling companion—always ready with friendly advice and helpful hints, all sprinkled with a bit of wit."

—*The Philadelphia Inquirer*

A GUIDE WITH A SPIRIT AND A SOCIAL CONSCIENCE

"Lighthearted and sophisticated, informative and fun to read. [Let's Go] helps
the novice traveler navigate like a knowledgeable old hand."

—*Atlanta Journal-Constitution*

"The serious mission at the book's core reveals itself in exhortations to respect
the culture and the environment—and, if possible, to visit as a volunteer, a
student, or a teacher rather than a tourist."

—*San Francisco Chronicle*

LET'S GO PUBLICATIONS

TRAVEL GUIDES

Australia
Austria & Switzerland
Brazil
Britain
California
Central America
Chile
China
Costa Rica
Costa Rica, Nicaragua & Panama
Eastern Europe
Ecuador
Egypt
Europe
France
Germany
Greece
Guatemala & Belize
Hawaii
India & Nepal
Ireland
Israel
Italy
Japan
Mexico
New Zealand
Peru
Puerto Rico
Southeast Asia
Spain & Portugal with Morocco
Thailand
USA
Vietnam
Western Europe
Yucatan Peninsula

ROADTRIP GUIDE

Roadtripping USA

ADVENTURE GUIDES

Alaska
Pacific Northwest
Southwest USA

CITY GUIDES

Amsterdam
Barcelona
Berlin, Prague & Budapest
Boston
Buenos Aires
Florence
London
London, Oxford, Cambridge & Edinburgh
New York City
Paris
Rome
San Francisco
Washington, DC

POCKET CITY GUIDES

Amsterdam
Berlin
Boston
Chicago
London
New York City
Paris
San Francisco
Venice
Washington, DC

LET'S GO

EUROPE

2010

JASON MEYER BOOK EDITOR

ASSOCIATE EDITORS

RONAN DEVLIN   JUN LI
KRYSTEN KECHES   LINGBO LI
NICKCLETTE IZUEGBU

RESEARCHER-WRITERS

RACHEL BANAY   ANDREW MOORE
AMANDA MANGASER   EMILY NAPHTAL
MEGHA MAJUMDAR   ALYSSA STACHOWSKI
ASHLEY MESSINA   CATHERINE ZIELINSKI

DEREK WETZEL MAP EDITOR
VANESSA DUBE MANAGING EDITOR

EDITORS

COURTNEY A. FISKE   RUSSELL FORD RENNIE
SARA PLANA   CHARLIE E. RIGGS
OLGA I. ZHULINA

HOW TO USE THIS BOOK

Conquering the great continent that is ▓Europe is no easy task. Yes, dear reader, there are many mysteries in this Old World. That is why you have come to us. We will be your Virgil, teaching you the art of budget travel. We will guide you through Genoa's labyrinthine *vicoli* and Vilnius's breakaway artists' republic. From old-school Parisian cafes to unexplored limestone karsts on Croatia's Dalmatian Coast, this continent—like a coffee shop in Amsterdam—has it. And our gritty, dutiful researchers have fanned out to Irish shoals and Russian *stolis*, between Norway's herring pickling factories and Austria's posh ski towns, to bring you the freshest, most comprehensive travel guide ever produced. Here's how to use it:

COVERING THE BASICS. The first chapter is **Discover** (p. 1). Its purpose is to help you find the best this Earth has to offer. If you prefer people telling you what to do (or just want some ideas), check out this chapter's **suggested itineraries.** The **Essentials** (p. 13) section gets down to the nitty-gritty, detailing the info you'll need to get around and stay safe on your journey. The **Transportation** (p. 42) section will help you get to and around Europe, while the **Beyond Tourism (p. 55)** chapter suggests ways to work and volunteer your way across the Continent. Then we get to the meat of the book: **country chapters,** organized alphabetically. The **Appendix** (p. 783) has a weather chart for major cities and a handy dandy phrasebook with nine languages to help you say "I'm lost," land a bed, or find your way to a bathroom no matter where you are.

TRANSPORTATION INFO. Because you've told *Let's Go* you're traveling on budget airlines, we've created a new transportation format to help you navigate getting to where you really want to go from that random town an hour away: **Regional Hubs,** listed in the Intercity Transportation section of major cities. We've also collected info on bus, ferry, and train routes; these range from solid Spanish AVE schedules to, well, any transportation in Romania.

RANKINGS AND FEATURES. Our researchers list establishments in order of value from best to worst, with absolute favorites denoted by the *Let's Go* thumbpick ▓. Since the lowest price does not always mean the best value, we've incorporated a system of price ranges (❶-❺) for food and accommodations. Tipboxes come in a variety of flavors: warnings (▓), helpful hints and resources (▓), insider deals (▓), cheap finds (▓), and then a smattering of stuff you should know (▓,▓,▓).

AWESOMENESS. From ☎ codes to avoiding scams, from the best borscht to the boldest brews, we'll guide you through the souvenir-cluttered jungle of the old-school Europa to the most authentic food, craziest nightlife, and most mind-bendingly beautiful landscapes around. Start in Brussels, in Stockholm, in Moscow. Open this bad boy up, and select your own adventure.

A NOTE TO OUR READERS. The information for this book was gathered by Let's Go researchers from May 2008 through August 2009. Each listing is based on one researcher's opinion, formed during his or her visit at a particular time. Those traveling at other times may have different experiences since prices, dates, hours, and conditions are always subject to change. You are urged to check the facts presented in this book beforehand to avoid inconvenience and surprises.

CONTENTS

RESEARCHERS

Rachel Banay *Britain and Ireland*

After graduating from Harvard and hopping around Northern Ireland for *Let's Go Britain*, Rachel joined the Europe team for a whirlwind tour of the Republic of Ireland. She impressed us with her ability to explore big cities within a single day and still have the time and energy to hit the pubs with new friends Guinness and Jameson.

Danny Bilotti *Venice, Milan, Munich, Vienna, Amsterdam, Brussels*

Fame seemed to follow this California-born Economics major wherever he went, bumping into both John Malkovich and Furious Pete (a record-holding competitive eater). We were a little concerned about sending him off to represent Let's Go, given that he said he was most looking forward to embarrassing America abroad—but we're pretty sure he failed in that regard, and succeeded in most others, including charming us with great coverage of Munich.

Paul Katz *Lisbon, Madrid, Seville, Nice, Paris*

Paul kept us laughing in the office all summer with his enthusiastically cheesy video blogs. Having traveled extensively in Latin America, this was his first extended trip to Europe, and he braved the language barrier and the hostile Parisian nightclub bouncers with admirable courage. Always going out of his way to improve our coverage and organization, we hope he'll remember us someday when he has his own travel show and turns those cheesy video blogs into hour-long films.

Amanda Mangaser *Croatia, Turkey*

While travelling the world, perhaps only in a swimsuit, Amanda's excitement about international exploration and vivid writing style left us anxiously waiting for more. Personal adversity, ferry schedules, cardboard box surprises, weeks in Athens... nothing fazed her wit or charm. Top prize for tales from the road on our most awesome route.

Megha Majumdar *Sweden*

A native of India, Megha joined *Let's Go* eager to begin researching her route. She covered a whopping five countries in just seven weeks, smiling through it all. Despite computer troubles and a rigorous itinerary, she added new coverage, savored blood sausage, climbed medieval towers, and even outwitted a swarm of vicious insects.

RESEARCHERS

Ashley Messina
Poland, Slovakia

Ashley fearlessly traversed four countries, expertly sampling local cuisines and always finding the top-shelf tea. Whether it was partying in Prague or finding the best *pierogi* in Poland, her excellent writing and timely, flawless copy kept the office running smoothly.

Andrew Moore
Finland, Iceland, Norway

This accomplished skier was legendary for his crazy tales of roughin' it in Scandinavia—often choosing to forgo lodging expenses and sleep by the river and in a hotel lobby. Subsisting on mostly yogurt, he epitomized the B in budget. He'll soon be using his thrifty, hard-working charms as a US State Department employee.

Emily Naphtal
Austria, Switzerland, Slovenia

Packing in four countries in two months, Emily proved to be quite the fighter. She biked through Slovenian castles and caves, experienced the Eurocup Fancamp in Salzburg, and even went skydiving after a computer meltdown in the Swiss Alps. Add a steaming cup of cappuccino and it was all in day's work for this determined researcher.

Alyssa Stachowski
Belgium, Denmark, Netherlands

Ridiculous, memorable moments filled the daily travels of Alyssa. Her tales never failed to amaze with their unique twists and turns, grooves and bumps. Ask about Copenhagen, Møn, and of course, Amsterdam—she may just leave you flabbergasted and hilariously entertained.

Catherine Zielinski
Russia, Ukraine

This researcher took on the Russian giants Moscow and St. Petersburg, mastering Cyrillic in the pursuit of perfect copy. Armed with charm and enthusiasm, she managed to wrangle a free Manu Chao concert. That's traveling like a true professional.

ACKNOWLEDGMENTS

TEAM EUROPE THANKS: ◪Vanessa J. Dube for the edits, advice, and treats. Mr. Wetzel for providing clear direction and guidance. The digital saviors, InDesign tamers, and all-around playas PROD. Sam and Inés, leading the way with smiles and veteran wisdom. Laura Gordon for random fun and slosh ball. Pod-tastic award goes to Ricaloha, true audiophiles and brethren Mississippi-haters. Crunchalicious teams BRI/ITA/S&P/GER/FRA. The newly rebranded EUR Presents: Nick Traverse. Rachel, Amanda, Megha, Ashley, Andrew, Emily, Alyssa, and Catherine; thanks for blazing glorious trails of epic proportion through The Continent. Your coverage truly made this book possible, and, your stories from the road kept us entertained all summer long.

THE EDITORS THANK: First and foremost our lord (Jay-C) and savior (Starbucks, Terry's Chocolate Orange). We also owe gratitude to Barack Obama (peace be upon Him), the Oxford comma, the water cooler, bagel/payday Fridays, the HSA "SummerFun" team for being so inclusive, Rotio (wherefore art thou Rotio?), the real Robinson Crusoe, the Cambridge weather and defective umbrellas, BoltBus, Henry Louis Gates, Jr. (sorry 'bout the phone call), the office blog, gratuitous nudity, the 20-20-20 rule and bananas (no more eye twitches), the Portuguese flag, trips to the beach (ha!), sunbathing recently married Mormon final club alums, non-existent free food in the square, dog-star puns, and last but not least, America. The local time in Tehran is 1:21am.

But seriously, the MEs and RMs, our researchers (and all their wisdom on tablecloths and hipsters), LGHQ, HSA, our significant others (future, Canadian, and otherwise), and families (thanks Mom).

Research Managers
David Andersson, Jesse Barron, Andrew Fine, Beatrice Franklin, Claire Shepro
Editors
Courtney A. Fiske, Sara Plana, Russell Ford Rennie,
Charlie E. Riggs, Olga I. Zhulina
Typesetter
C. Alexander Tremblay

PRICE RANGES
EUROPE

① ② ③ ④ ⑤

Our researchers list establishments in order of value from best to worst, honoring our favorites with the Let's Go thumbs-up (👍). Because the best *value* is not always the cheapest *price*, we have incorporated a system of price ranges based on a rough expectation of what you will spend. For **accommodations,** we base our range on the cheapest price for which a single traveler can stay for one night. For **restaurants** and other dining establishments, we estimate the average amount one traveler will spend in one sitting. The table below tells you what you'll *typically* find in Europe at the corresponding price range, but keep in mind that no system can allow for the quirks of individual establishments. For country-specific information, a table at the beginning of each country chapter lists the price ranges for each bracket.

ACCOMMODATIONS	WHAT YOU'RE *LIKELY* TO FIND
❶	Campgrounds and dorm rooms, both in hostels and actual universities. Expect bunk beds and a communal bath. You may have to provide or rent towels and sheets. Be ready for things to go bump in the night.
❷	Upper-end hostels or lower-end hotels and pensions. You may have a private bathroom, or there may be a sink in your room and communal shower in the hall.
❸	A small room with a private bath or pension. Should have decent amenities, such as phone and TV. Breakfast may be included in the price of the room.
❹	Should have bigger rooms than a ❸, with more amenities or in a more convenient location. Breakfast probably included.
❺	Large hotels or upscale chains. Rooms should elicit an involuntary "wow." If it's a ❺ and it doesn't have the perks you want, you've paid too much.

FOOD	WHAT YOU'RE *LIKELY* TO FIND
❶	Street food, *gelateria*, milk bar, corner *crêperie*, or a fast-food joint, but also university cafeterias and bakeries. Soups, gyros, kebab, most *bliny* and other simple dishes in minimalist surroundings. Usually takeout, but you may have the option of sitting down.
❷	Sandwiches, *naleśniki*, *brocadillos*, appetizers at a bar, or low-priced entrees and *tapas*. Most *trattorie* or ethnic eateries are a ❷. Either takeout or a sit-down meal (sometimes with servers!), but only slightly more fashionable decor.
❸	Mid-priced entrees, pub fare, seafood, and exotic pasta dishes. A cheeseburger in Moscow. Many medieval-themed and hunting-lodge-decor establishments. Wild game. More upscale ethnic eateries. Since you'll have a waiter, tip will set you back a little extra.
❹	A somewhat fancy restaurant or *brasserie*. Entrees tend to be heartier or more elaborate, but you're really paying for decor and ambience. Few restaurants in this range have a dress code, but some may look down on T-shirts and sandals.
❺	Your meal might cost more than your room, but there's a reason—it's something fabulous, famous, or both. Slacks and dress shirts may be expected. Offers foreign-sounding food and a decent wine list.

DISCOVER EUROPE

Some things never change. Aspiring writers still spin romances in Parisian garrets; a glass of sangria at twilight on the Plaza Mayor tastes as sweet as ever; and iconic treasures, from the onion domes of St. Basil's cathedral to the behemoth slabs of Stonehenge, continue to inspire awe. But against this ancient backdrop, a freshly costumed continent takes the stage. As the European Union grows from a small clique of nations trading coal and steel to a 27-member commonwealth with a parliament and a central bank, Eastern and Western Europe find themselves more closely connected than ever before. Ease of travel between the two make it seem like the Continent is simultaneously shrinking and expanding. With improved transport links increasing the range of possible itineraries, determining the must-see destinations of 21st-century Europe has become even more difficult.

While Prague and Barcelona may have been the hot spots a few years ago, emerging cities like Kraków and Stockholm are poised to inherit the tourist money train. Newly minted cultural meccas like Bilbao's Guggenheim (p. 715) and London's Tate Modern (p. 126) have joined the ranks of timeless galleries like the Louvre (p. 251) and the Hermitage (p. 645), while a constant influx of students and DJs keep Europe's nightlife dependably hot. Whether it's Dublin's pubs, Lyon's upscale bistros, Sweden's frozen north country, Amsterdam's canals, or Croatia's dazzling beaches that call to you, *Let's Go Europe 2010* will help to keep you informed and on-budget.

TACKLING EUROPE

Anyone who tells you that there is one "best way" to see Europe should be politely ignored. This book is designed to facilitate all varieties of travel, from a few days in Paris to a breathless, continent-wide summer sprint to a leisurely year (or two) abroad. This chapter is made up of tools to help you create your own itinerary: **themed categories** let you know where to find your museums, mountains, and madhouses, while **suggested itineraries** outline various paths across Europe. Look to chapter introductions for country-specific itineraries and for more detailed information.

WHEN TO GO

While summer sees the most tourist traffic in Europe, the best mix of value and accessibility comes in late spring and early fall. To the delight of skiing and ice-climbing enthusiasts, traveling during the low season (mid-Sept. to June) brings cheaper airfares and accommodations, in addition to freedom from hordes of fannypack-toting tourists. On the flip side, many attractions, hostels, and tourist offices close in the winter, and in some rural areas local transportation dwindles or shuts down altogether. Most of Europe's best **festivals** (p. 4)

1

also take place in summer. For more advice on when to visit, see the **Weather Chart** on p. 783 and the **Essentials** section at the beginning of each chapter.

WHAT TO DO

🏛 MUSEUMS

Europe has kept millennia worth of artistic masterpieces close to home in strongholds like the Louvre, the Prado, and the Vatican Museums. European museums do not merely house art, however. They also have exhibits on erotica, leprosy, marijuana, marzipan, puppets, and secret police—in short, whatever can be captioned. A trip across Europe qualifies as little more than a stopover without an afternoon spent among some of its paintings and artifacts—whether they include the pinnacles of Western culture, or more morbid or risqué fare.

THE SUBLIME	THE RIDICULOUS
▥ **BRITAIN: THE BRITISH MUSEUM** (p. 127). Holding world artifacts like Egypt's Rosetta Stone or Iran's Oxus Treasure, the British Museum contains almost nothing British.	▥ **DENMARK: LOUISIANA MUSEUM OF MODERN ART** (p. 213). This well-rounded museum's name honors the three wives of the estate's original owner—all of them were named Louisa.
▥ **SPAIN: MUSEO DEL PRADO** (p. 675). It's an art-lover's heaven to see hell, as painted by Hieronymus Bosch. Velázquez's famous 10 by 9 ft. painting *Las Meninas* is as luminous as it is tall.	▥ **GERMANY: SCHOKOLADENMUSEUM** (p. 321). This chocolate museum, detailing the chocolate-making process, has gold fountains that spurt out samples and can be described only as magical.
▥ **FRANCE: THE LOUVRE** (p. 251). Six million visitors come each year to see 35,000 works of art, including Da Vinci's surprisingly small painting of art's most famous face, the Mona Lisa.	▥ **ITALY: PALERMO CATACOMBS** (p. 533). The withered faces and mostly empty eye sockets of 8000 posing corpses gaze enviously at living spectators in Europe's creepiest underground tomb.
▥ **GERMANY: GEMÄLDEGALERIE** (p. 304). With over 1000 works from 1200 to 1800 by the likes of Bruegel and Raphael, it's no wonder this is one of the most visited museums in Germany.	▥ **THE NETHERLANDS: CANNABIS COLLEGE** (p. 557). Cannabis College is just like college, except there are no libraries, no lectures, no studying, no liquor, no dorms, and no full-time students.
▥ **ITALY: VATICAN MUSEUMS** (p. 471). Look for the *School of Athens* here; the painting tops off a mindblowing amount of Renaissance and other art, including the incredible Raphael Rooms.	▥ **SWITZERLAND: VERKEHRSHAUS DER SCHWEIZ** (p. 746). The Swiss Transport Museum, with an IMAX theater and a wide array of cool contraptions, isn't nearly as dorky as its name implies.
▥ **THE NETHERLANDS: RIJKSMUSEUM** (p. 557). Renovations shouldn't deter visitors who come to see the pinnacles of the Dutch Golden Age, including Rembrandts and Vermeers, that line the walls.	▥ **BRITAIN: TATE MODERN** (p. 126). Organized thematically, this former power station turned modern art powerhouse is as much a masterpiece as any of the works in its galleries.

🏛 ARCHITECTURE

European architecture is a huge part of the continent's appeal. Royal lines from the early Welsh dynasties and Greek ruling families to the Bourbons, Hapsburgs, and Romanovs have all been outlasted by the emblems of their magnificence—castles, palaces, and châteaux. Monarchs had loose purse strings and were jealous of each other; Louis XIV's palace at Versailles (p. 257), which has become a byword for opulence, whet the ambition of rival monarchs and spurred the construction of competing domiciles. No expense was spared for God, either, as the many splendid cathedrals, monasteries, synagogues, temples, and mosques rising skyward from their cityscapes attest. Budapest's Great Synagogue (p. 403) is among the finest of its kind, while Chartres's Cathédrale de Notre Dame (p. 244) and Cologne's Dom (p. 320) are pinnacles of Gothic style.

ROYAL REALTY	SACRED SITES
AUSTRIA: SCHLOß SCHÖNBRUNN (p. 77). If the palace isn't impressive enough, check out the classical gardens that extend behind for four times the length of the structure.	**BRITAIN: WESTMINSTER ABBEY** (p. 118). Royal weddings and coronations take place in the sanctuary; nearby, poets and politicians from the earliest kings to Winston Churchill rest in peace.
BRITAIN: BUCKINGHAM PALACE (p. 119). Britain's royal family has lived in Buckingham Palace since 1832, guarded by everybody's favorite stoic, puffy-hatted guards.	**FRANCE: CHARTRES CATHEDRAL** (p. 258). The world's finest example of early Gothic architecture has intact stained-glass windows from the 12th century and a crypt from the 9th.
FRANCE: VERSAILLES (p. 257). Once home to the entire French court, the lavish palace, manicured gardens, and Hall of Mirrors epitomize Pre-Revolutionary France's regal extravagance.	**HUNGARY: THE GREAT SYNAGOGUE** (p. 403). Europe's largest synagogue can hold 3000. Inscribed leaves of a metal tree in the courtyard commemorate the victims of the Holocaust.
GERMANY: NEUSCHWANSTEIN (p. 343). A waterfall, an artificial grotto, a Byzantine throne room, and a Wagnerian opera hall deck out the inspiration for Disney's Cinderella Castle.	**ITALY: SISTINE CHAPEL** (p. 469). Each fresco on its famous ceiling depicts a scene from Genesis. Michelangelo painted himself as a flayed human skin hanging between heaven and hell.
ITALY: PALAZZO DUCALE (p. 501). The home of the Venetian *Doge* (mayor) could pass as a city unto itself, complete with on-site prisons that miscreants once entered via the Bridge of Sighs.	**RUSSIA: ST. BASIL'S CATHEDRAL** (p. 634). Commissioned by Ivan the Terrible to celebrate his victory over the Tatars, today its colorful, onion-shaped domes are instantly recognizable.
SPAIN: THE ALHAMBRA (p. 695). The Spanish say, *"Si mueres sin ver la Alhambra, no has vivido."* ("If you die without seeing the Alhambra, you have not lived.") We agree.	**TURKEY: AYA SOFIA** (p. 767). The gold-leafed mosaic dome of Byzantine emperor Justinian's masterful cathedral-turned-mosque appears to be floating on a bed of luminescent pearls.
SWEDEN: KUNGLIGA SLOTTET (p. 728). Still the official residence of the Swedish royal family, the *Kungliga Slottet* (Royal Palace) recently hosted lavish festivities for the Crown Princess's 30th birthday.	**UKRAINE: KYIV-CAVE MONASTERY** (p. 781). Kyiv's oldest holy site houses the Refectory Church, the 12th-century Holy Trinity Gate Church, and caves where monks lie mummified.

OUTDOORS

Europe's museums and ruins tend be a stronger draw than its mountains and rivers. But for any traveler, budget or otherwise, solo or companioned, expert or neophyte, an excursion to the outdoors can round off (or salvage, as the case may be) any journey. Fjords, volcanoes, valleys, gorges, and plateaus mark the spots where the Earth's plates collide. Waters of innumerable shades of blue wash up on uninhabited shores of black-, white-, and red-sand beaches. Mountains, whether sprawling with trees or culminating in ice, continue to challenge mankind and dwarf the man-made, just as they did when civilization began.

JUST CHILLIN'	HARDCORE THRILL-SEEKIN'
CROATIA: THE DALMATIAN COAST (p. 173). Touted as the new French Riviera, the Dalmatian Coast has some of the clearest waters in the Mediterranean. What it doesn't have is dalmatians—at least no more than any other place.	**GERMANY: DER SCHWARZWALD** (p. 332). The eerie darkness pervading this tangled evergreen, once the inspiration Brothers Grimm, lures hikers and skiers (instead of red-caped little girls.)
GREECE: DELPHI (p. 375). Journey to the beautiful mountaintop of the Oracle of Delphi, where ancient citizens went to hear cryptic prophecies. Soak in the history, and prepare to know thyself.	**ITALY: CINQUE TERRE** (p. 489). An outdoorsman's paradise, the hiking trails of Cinque Terre have opportunities for cliff diving, horseback riding, and kayaking between villages.

JUST CHILLIN'	HARDCORE THRILL-SEEKIN'
ICELAND: THERMAL POOLS (p. 418). Iceland may be expensive, but freeloaders can find naturally occurring "hotpots" outside of Reykjavík. Each thermal pool maintains its distinct character.	SPAIN: PAMPLONA (p. 712). While not outdoorsy in the traditional sense, the Running of the Bulls in Pamplona attracts runners and adrenaline junkies from all over the world.

FESTIVALS

COUNTRIES	APR. - JUNE	JULY - AUG.	SEPT. - MAR.
AUSTRIA AND SWITZERLAND	Vienna Festwochen (early May to mid-June)	Salzburger Festspiele (late July-Aug.)	Escalade (Geneva; Dec. 11-13) Fasnacht (Basel; Mar. 2-4)
BELGIUM	Festival of Fairground Arts (Wallonie; late May)	Gentse Feesten (Ghent; mid- to late July)	International French Language Film Festival (Namur; late Sept.)
BRITAIN AND IRELAND	Bloomsday (Dublin; June 16) Wimbledon (London; late June-early July)	Fringe Festival (Edinburgh; Aug.) Edinburgh Int'l Festival (mid-Aug. to early Sept.)	Matchmaking Festival (Lisdoonvarna; Sept.) St. Patrick's Day (Mar. 17)
CZECH REPUBLIC	Prague Spring Festival (May-June)	Int'l Film Festival (Karlovy Vary; July)	Int'l Organ Festival (Olomouc; Sept.)
FRANCE	Cannes Film Festival (May 13-24)	Festival d'Avignon (July-Aug.) Bastille Day (July 14)	Carnevale (Nice, Nantes; Jan 25-Feb. 5)
GERMANY	May Day (Berlin; May 1) Christopher St. Day (late June)	Rhine in Flames Festival (various locations in the Rhine Valley; throughout summer)	Oktoberfest (Munich; Sept. 19-Oct. 4) Fasching (Munich; Feb. 1-5)
HUNGARY	Danube Festival (Budapest; June)	Golden Shell Folklore (Siófok; June) Sziget Rock Festival (Budapest; Aug.)	Éger Vintage Days (Sept.) Festival of Wine Songs (Pécs; Sept.)
ITALY	Maggio Musicale (Florence; May to mid-June)	Il Palio (Siena; July 2 and Aug. 16) Umbria Jazz Festival (July)	Carnevale (late Feb.) Scoppio del Carro (Florence; Easter Su)
THE NETHERLANDS	Queen's Day (Apr. 30) Holland Festival (June)	Gay Pride Parade (early Aug.)	Flower Parade (Aalsmeer; early Sept.)
PORTUGAL	Burning of the Ribbons (Coimbra; early May)	Lisbon Beer Festival (July)	Carnaval (early Mar.) Semana Santa (Apr. 5-12)
SCANDINAVIA	Midsummer (June 19-25)	Savonlinna Opera Festival (July) Quart Music Festival (Kristiansand; early July)	Helsinki Festival (late Aug.-early Sept.) Tromsø Film Festival (mid-Jan.)
SPAIN	Feria de Abril (Sevilla; mid-Apr.)	San Fermines (Pamplona; early to mid-July)	Las Fallas (Valencia; Mar.) Carnaval (Mar.)

CHANNEL JUMPING (1 month)

Belfast (2 days)
Belfast's conflict-ridden history makes it a fascinating destination; hunt out the political murals here (p. 441).

Galway (1 day)
Sit in on a traditional Irish music "session" in one of Galway's many pubs (p. 440).

Edinburgh (3 days)
Take a tour around Edinburgh Castle, and don't forget to sample the local delicacy, haggis (p. 148).

START

Dublin (3 days)
Discover history by day and pubs by night in Dublin, where a pint is never far away (p. 427).

London (4 days)
Finish the English leg of the tour in London, where you can catch the Changing of the Guard (p. 108).

END

Brittany (2 days)
Bring it full circle and explore the Celtic side of France with a stay in Brittany (p. 259).

Paris (4 days)
You could spend years in Paris's museums without seeing everything. Cram as much as you can into a few days and grab a crepe or two (p. 233).

Loire Valley (3 days)
Meander through the Loire Valley, home to spectacular cathedrals and châteaux (p. 258).

THE BEST OF WESTERN EUROPE (2 months)

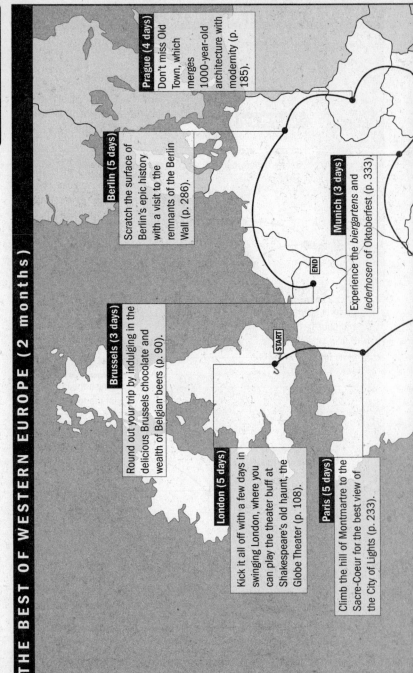

Prague (4 days)

Don't miss Old Town, which merges 1000-year-old architecture with modernity (p. 185).

Berlin (5 days)

Scratch the surface of Berlin's epic history with a visit to the remnants of the Berlin Wall (p. 286).

Munich (3 days)

Experience the *biergartens* and *lederhosen* of Oktoberfest (p. 333).

Brussels (3 days)

Round out your trip by indulging in the delicious Brussels chocolate and wealth of Belgian beers (p. 90).

London (5 days)

Kick it all off with a few days in swinging London, where you can play the theater buff at Shakespeare's old haunt, the Globe Theater (p. 108).

Paris (5 days)

Climb the hill of Montmartre to the Sacre-Coeur for the best view of the City of Lights (p. 233).

START

END

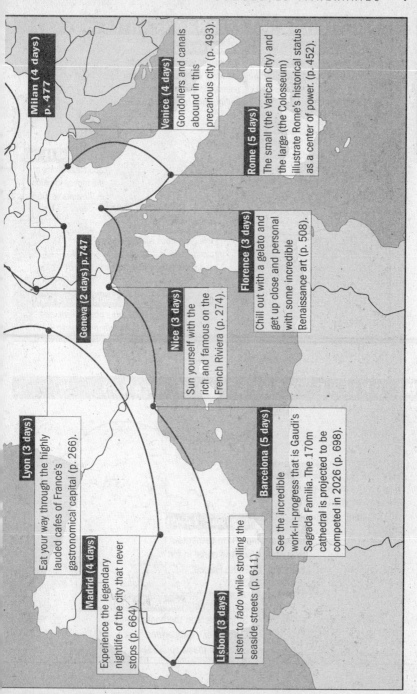

Milan (4 days) p. 477

Venice (4 days)
Gondoliers and canals abound in this precarious city (p. 493).

Rome (5 days)
The small (the Vatican City) and the large (the Colosseum) illustrate Rome's historical status as a center of power. (p. 452).

Geneva (2 days) p.747

Nice (3 days)
Sun yourself with the rich and famous on the French Riviera (p. 274).

Florence (3 days)
Chill out with a gelato and get up close and personal with some incredible Renaissance art (p. 508).

Lyon (3 days)
Eat your way through the highly lauded cafes of France's gastronomical capital (p. 266).

Madrid (4 days)
Experience the legendary nightlife of the city that never stops (p. 664).

Barcelona (5 days)
See the incredible work-in-progress that is Gaudí's Sagrada Familia. The 170m cathedral is projected to be competed in 2026 (p. 698).

Lisbon (3 days)
Listen to *fado* while strolling the seaside streets (p. 611).

DISCOVER

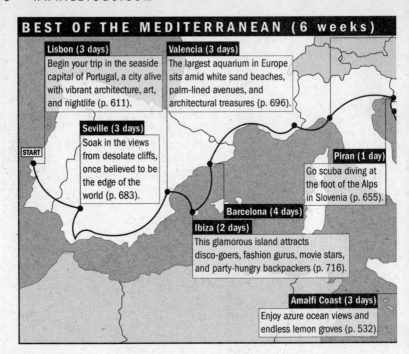

BEST OF THE MEDITERRANEAN (6 weeks)

Lisbon (3 days)
Begin your trip in the seaside capital of Portugal, a city alive with vibrant architecture, art, and nightlife (p. 611).

Valencia (3 days)
The largest aquarium in Europe sits amid white sand beaches, palm-lined avenues, and architectural treasures (p. 696).

Seville (3 days)
Soak in the views from desolate cliffs, once believed to be the edge of the world (p. 683).

Piran (1 day)
Go scuba diving at the foot of the Alps in Slovenia (p. 655).

START

Barcelona (4 days)

Ibiza (2 days)
This glamorous island attracts disco-goers, fashion gurus, movie stars, and party-hungry backpackers (p. 716).

Amalfi Coast (3 days)
Enjoy azure ocean views and endless lemon groves (p. 532).

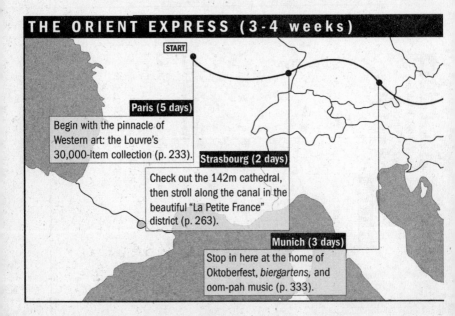

THE ORIENT EXPRESS (3-4 weeks)

START

Paris (5 days)
Begin with the pinnacle of Western art: the Louvre's 30,000-item collection (p. 233).

Strasbourg (2 days)
Check out the 142m cathedral, then stroll along the canal in the beautiful "La Petite France" district (p. 263).

Munich (3 days)
Stop in here at the home of Oktoberfest, *biergartens,* and oom-pah music (p. 333).

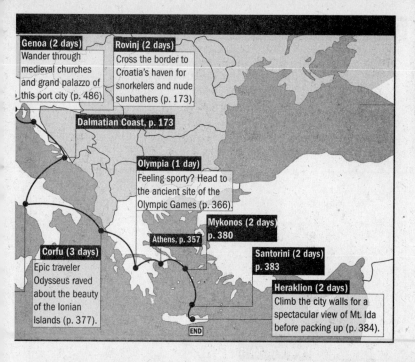

Genoa (2 days) Wander through medieval churches and grand palazzo of this port city (p. 486).

Rovinj (2 days) Cross the border to Croatia's haven for snorkelers and nude sunbathers (p. 173).

Dalmatian Coast, p. 173

Olympia (1 day) Feeling sporty? Head to the ancient site of the Olympic Games (p. 366).

Mykonos (2 days) p. 380

Athens, p. 357

Corfu (3 days) Epic traveler Odysseus raved about the beauty of the Ionian Islands (p. 377).

Santorini (2 days) p. 383

Heraklion (2 days) Climb the city walls for a spectacular view of Mt. Ida before packing up (p. 384).

END

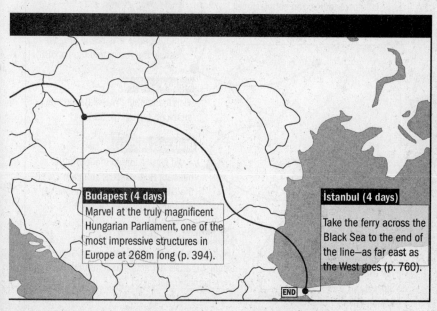

Budapest (4 days) Marvel at the truly magnificent Hungarian Parliament, one of the most impressive structures in Europe at 268m long (p. 394).

İstanbul (4 days) Take the ferry across the Black Sea to the end of the line—as far east as the West goes (p. 760).

END

THE MIDDLE ROAD (3 weeks)

St. Petersburg (3 days)
Begin your trip in Peter the Great's lavish and utterly paradoxical city-on-a-swamp (p. 639).

START

Prague (3 days)
Settle here to discover cobblestone streets, Baroque buildings, and 1000-year old alleys (p. 185).

Warsaw (3 days)
Exuberant nightlife and a cutting-edge arts scene are sure to satisfy the young and hip (p. 588).

Kraków (3 days)
Visit the looming Wawel Castle and snack on *pierogi* (p. 598).

Budapest (4 days)
Avoid getting lost in the labyrinths beneath Buda Castle, and then cross the Danube to Pest for a glimpse of Hungary's crown jewels (p. 394).

Ljubljana (2 days)
Dodge dragons as you explore Slovenia's folklore-filled capital (p. 652).

Dalmatian Coast (3 days)
Finish your tour by island-hopping in style along Croatia's dramatic coast, touted as the new French Riviera (p. 173).

END

FAR EAST (3-4 weeks)

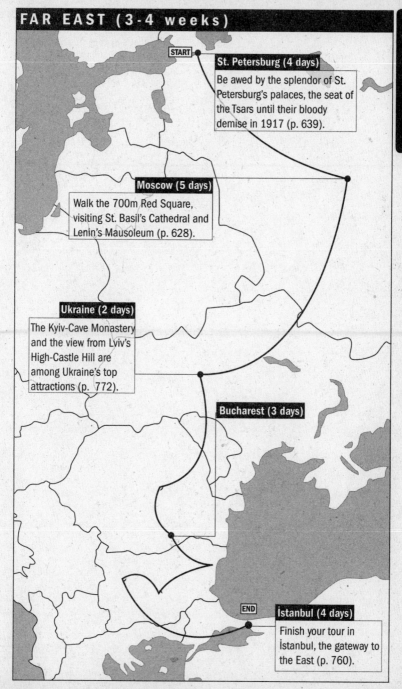

START

St. Petersburg (4 days)
Be awed by the splendor of St. Petersburg's palaces, the seat of the Tsars until their bloody demise in 1917 (p. 639).

Moscow (5 days)
Walk the 700m Red Square, visiting St. Basil's Cathedral and Lenin's Mausoleum (p. 628).

Ukraine (2 days)
The Kyiv-Cave Monastery and the view from Lviv's High-Castle Hill are among Ukraine's top attractions (p. 772).

Bucharest (3 days)

END

İstanbul (4 days)
Finish your tour in İstanbul, the gateway to the East (p. 760).

ESSENTIALS

PLANNING YOUR TRIP

AT A GLANCE
Passport (p. 13). Required for all non-EU citizens traveling in Europe.
Visa (p. 14). Not required for citizens of Australia, Canada, Ireland, New Zealand, the UK, and the US for stays shorter than 90 days in a 6-month period in most European countries.
Work Permit (p. 15). Required for all non-EU citizens planning to work in any European country.
Vaccinations (p. 23). Visitors to Europe should be up to date on vaccines for diphtheria, hepatitis A, hepatitis B, and mumps. Visitors to Eastern Europe should also be vaccinated for measles, rabies, and typhoid.

EMBASSIES AND CONSULATES

CONSULAR SERVICES

Information about European consular services abroad and foreign consular services in Europe is located in individual country chapters; it can also be found at **www.embassiesabroad.com** and **www.embassyworld.com**.

TOURIST OFFICES

Information about national tourist boards in Europe is located in individual country chapters; it can also be found at **www.towd.com**.

DOCUMENTS AND FORMALITIES

PASSPORTS

REQUIREMENTS. Citizens of Australia, Canada, Ireland, New Zealand, the UK, and the US need valid passports to enter European countries and to re-enter their home countries. Most countries do not allow entrance if the holder's passport expires within six months. Returning home with an expired passport is illegal and may result in a fine and/or delays upon re-entry.

NEW PASSPORTS. Citizens of Australia, Canada, Ireland, New Zealand, the UK, and the US can apply for a passport at their local passport office and at most post offices and courts of law. Applications must be filed at least two months before the departure date, though most passport offices offer rush services for a very steep fee. Be warned that even "rushed" passports can take up to two weeks to arrive. Citizens living abroad who need a passport or renewal should contact the nearest passport office or consulate of their home country.

PASSPORT MAINTENANCE. Photocopy the page of your passport with your photo, as well as your visas, traveler's check serial numbers, and any other important documents. Carry one set of copies in a safe place, apart from the originals, and leave another set at home. Consulates also recommend that you carry an expired passport or an official copy of your birth certificate in a part of your baggage separate from other documents.

If you lose your passport, immediately notify the local police and the nearest embassy or consulate of your home government. To expedite its replacement, you must show ID and proof of citizenship. It also helps to know all information previously recorded in the passport. In some cases, a replacement may take weeks to process, and it may be valid only for a limited time. Any visas stamped in your old passport will be lost. In an emergency, ask for temporary traveling papers that will permit you to re-enter your home country.

ONE EUROPE. European unity has come a long way since 1958, when the European Economic Community (EEC) was created to promote European solidarity and cooperation. Since then, the EEC has become the European Union (EU), a mighty political, legal, and economic institution. On May 1, 2004, 10 South, Central, and Eastern European countries—Cyprus, the Czech Republic, Estonia, Hungary, Latvia, Lithuania, Malta, Poland, Slovakia, and Slovenia—were admitted into the EU, joining 15 other member states: Austria, Belgium, Denmark, Finland, France, Germany, Greece, Ireland, Italy, Luxembourg, the Netherlands, Portugal, Spain, Sweden, and the UK. On January 1, 2007, two other countries, Bulgaria and Romania, came into the fold, bringing the tally of member states to 27.

What does this have to do with the average non-EU tourist? The EU's **freedom of movement** policy means that most border controls have been abolished and visa policies harmonized. Under this treaty, known as the **Schengen Agreement,** you're still required to carry a passport (or government-issued ID card for EU citizens) when crossing an internal border, but, once you've been admitted into one country, you're free to travel to other participating states. Most EU states are already members of Schengen (minus Bulgaria, Cyprus, Ireland, Romania, and the UK), as are Iceland and Norway. In 2009, Cyprus, Liechtenstein, and Switzerland will bring the number of Schengen countries to 27. Britain and Ireland have also formed a **common travel area,** abolishing passport controls between the UK and the Republic of Ireland.

For more information on the effects of EU policy for travelers, see **The Euro** (p. 18) and **Customs in the EU** (p. 16).

VISAS, INVITATIONS, AND WORK PERMITS

VISAS. As of August 2008, citizens of Australia, Canada, Ireland, New Zealand, the UK, or the US did not need a visa to visit the following countries for fewer than 90 days: Andorra, Austria, Belgium, Britain, Denmark, France, Germany, Greece, Ireland, Italy, Liechtenstein, Luxembourg, the Netherlands, Portugal, Spain, and Switzerland. For travelers planning to spend more than 90 days in any European country, visas cost US$35-200 and typically allow you six months in that country. Visas can usually be purchased at a consulate or at www.

itseasypassport.com/services/visas/visas.htm. Double-check entrance requirements at the nearest embassy or consulate of your destination for up-to-date info before departure. US citizens can consult http://travel.state.gov/travel.

WORK PERMITS. Admission as a visitor does not include the right to work, which is authorized only by a work permit. Entering a country in Europe to study typically requires a special study visa (which does not necessarily authorize employment), which can be fairly expensive, though many study-abroad programs are able to subsidize it. For more info, see **Beyond Tourism,** p. 55.

IDENTIFICATION

When you travel, always carry at least two forms of identification on your person, including a photo ID; a passport and a driver's license or birth certificate is usually adequate. Never carry all of your IDs together; split them up in case of theft or loss, and keep photocopies of them in your luggage and at home.

STUDENT, TEACHER, AND YOUTH IDENTIFICATION. The **International Student Identity Card** (ISIC), the most widely accepted form of student ID, provides discounts on some sights, accommodations, food, and transportation; access to a 24hr. emergency helpline; and insurance benefits for US cardholders (see **Insurance,** p. 24). Applicants must be full-time secondary or post-secondary school students. Because of the proliferation of fake ISICs, some services (particularly airlines) require additional proof of student identity.

The **International Teacher Identity Card** (ITIC) offers teachers the same insurance coverage as the ISIC and similar but limited discounts. For travelers who are under 26 years old but are not students, the **International Youth Travel Card** (IYTC) also offers many of the same benefits as the ISIC.

Each of these identity cards costs US$22. ISICs and ITICs are valid until the new year unless purchased between September and December, in which case they are valid until the beginning of the following new year. IYTCs are valid for one year from the date of issue. To learn more about ISICs, ITICs, and IYTCs, see www.myisic.com. Many travel agencies issue the cards; for more info, see the **International Student Travel Confederation** (ISTC) website (www.istc.org).

The **International Student Exchange Card** (ISE Card) is a similar identification card strictly available to students, faculty, and youths aged 12 to 26. The card provides discounts, medical benefits, access to a 24hr. emergency helpline, and the ability to purchase student airfares. An ISE Card generally costs US$25 and should be purchased well before your departure date; for more information, call in the US ☎800-255-8000, or visit online at www.isecard.com.

CUSTOMS

When you enter a European country, you must declare certain items from abroad and pay a duty on the value of those articles if they exceed a set allowance. Note that goods purchased at **duty-free** shops are not exempt from duty or sales tax; "duty-free" merely means that you need not pay a tax in the country of purchase. Duty-free allowances were abolished for travel between EU member states but still exist for those arriving from outside the EU. Upon returning home, you must likewise declare all goods and articles acquired abroad and pay a duty on the value of goods and articles in excess of your home country's allowance. In order to expedite your return, it is recommended to make a list of any valuables brought from home, and register them with customs before traveling abroad, and being sure to keep receipts for all goods acquired abroad.

ESSENTIALS

ESSENTIALS

> **CUSTOMS IN THE EU.** As well as freedom of movement of people (p. 14), travelers in the European Union can also take advantage of the freedom of movement of goods. This means that there are no customs controls at internal EU borders (i.e., you can take the blue customs channel at the airport), and travelers are free to transport whatever legal substances they like as long as it is for their own personal (non-commercial) use—up to 800 cigarettes, 10L of spirits, 90L of wine (including up to 60L of sparkling wine), and 110L of beer. Duty-free allowances were abolished on June 30, 1999, for travel between the original 15 EU member states; this now also applies to Cyprus and Malta. However, travelers between the EU and the rest of the world still get a duty-free allowance when passing through customs.

MONEY

CURRENCY AND EXCHANGE

The currency chart on the next page is based on August 2008 exchange rates between euro and Australian dollars (AUS$), Canadian dollars (CDN$), New Zealand dollars (NZ$), British pounds (UK£), and US dollars (US$). Check the currency converter on websites like www.xe.com or www.bloomberg.com, or a large newspaper, for the latest exchange rates.

As a general rule, it's cheaper to convert money in Europe than in the United States. While currency exchange will probably be available in your arrival airport, it's wise to bring enough currency to last for the first 24-72hr. of your trip, since airport rates are generally less competitive.

EURO (€)		
AUS$1 = €0.59		€1 = AUS$1.70
CDN$1 = €0.62		€1 = CDN$1.62
NZ$1 = €0.47		€1 = NZ$2.15
UK£1 = €1.26		€1 = UK£0.79
US$1 = €0.65		€1 = US$1.54

When exchanging money abroad, try to go only to banks or official exchange establishments that have at most a 5% margin between their buy and sell prices. Because you lose money with every transaction, convert large sums (unless the currency is depreciating rapidly), but no more than you'll need.

If you use traveler's checks or bills, carry some in small denominations (the equivalent of US$50 or less) for times when you are forced to exchange money at disadvantageous rates, but bring a range of denominations, as charges may be levied per check cashed. Store your money in a variety of forms; ideally, at any given time you will be carrying some cash, some traveler's checks, and an ATM and/or credit card. All travelers should also consider carrying some US dollars (about US$50 worth), which are often preferred by local tellers.

CREDIT, ATM, AND DEBIT CARDS

Where they are accepted, credit cards often offer superior exchange rates—up to 5% better than the retail rate used by banks and other currency exchange establishments. Credit cards may also offer services such as insurance or emergency help and are sometimes required to reserve hotel rooms or rental cars. **MasterCard** (a.k.a. **EuroCard** in Europe) and Visa (e.g., **Carte Bleue**) are the most frequently accepted; **American Express** cards work at some ATMs and at AmEx offices and major airports.

The use of ATM cards is widespread in Europe. Depending on the system that your home bank uses, you can most likely access your personal bank account from abroad. ATMs get the same wholesale exchange rate as credit cards, but there is often a limit on the amount of money you can withdraw per day. There is also typically a surcharge of US$1-5 per withdrawal.

Debit cards are as convenient as credit cards but withdraw money directly from the holder's checking account. A debit card can be used wherever its associated credit card company (usually MasterCard or Visa) is accepted. Debit cards often also function as ATM cards and can be used to withdraw cash from associated banks and ATMs throughout Europe.

The two major international money networks are **MasterCard/Maestro/Cirrus** (for ATM locations ☎+1-800-424-7787 or www.mastercard.com) and **Visa/PLUS** (for ATM locations ☎+1-800-847-2911 or www.visa.com). Most ATMs charge a transaction fee that is paid to the bank that owns the ATM.

PINS AND ATMS. To use a cash or credit card to withdraw money from a cash machine (ATM) in Europe, you must have a four-digit Personal Identification Number (PIN). If your PIN is longer than four digits, ask your bank whether you can just use the first four or whether you'll need a new one. Credit cards don't usually come with PINs, so, if you intend to hit up ATMs in Europe with a credit card to get cash advances, call your credit-card company before leaving to request one.

Travelers with alphabetic, rather than numerical, PINs may also be thrown off by the lack of letters on European cash machines. The following are the corresponding numbers to use: 1 = QZ; 2 = ABC; 3 = DEF; 4 = GHI; 5 = JKL; 6 = MNO; 7 = PRS; 8 = TUV; and 9 = WXY. Note that if you mistakenly punch the wrong code into the machine three times, it will swallow your card.

TRAVELER'S CHECKS

Traveler's checks are one of the safest means of carrying funds. American Express and Visa are the most recognized brands. Many banks and agencies sell them for a small commission. Check issuers provide refunds if the checks are lost or stolen, and many provide additional services, such as toll-free refund hotlines abroad, emergency message services, and assistance with lost and stolen credit cards or passports. Traveler's checks are readily accepted in most of Western Europe. Ask about toll-free refund hotlines and the location of refund centers when purchasing checks, and always carry emergency cash.

American Express: Checks available with commission at select banks, at all AmEx offices, and online (www.americanexpress.com; US residents only). Cardholders can also purchase checks by phone (☎800-528-4800).

Travelex: Thomas Cook MasterCard and Interpayment Visa traveler's checks available. For information about Thomas Cook MasterCard in Canada and the US call ☎800-223-7373, UK ☎0800 622 101; elsewhere, call UK collect ☎+44 1733 318 950. For Interpayment Visa in Canada and the US ☎800-223-7373, in the UK ☎0800 515 884; elsewhere, call UK collect ☎+44 1733 318 949. For more info, visit www.travelex.com.

Visa: Checks available (generally with commission) at banks worldwide. For office locations, call the Visa Travelers Cheque Global Refund and Assistance Center: in Australia ☎800-882-426, New Zealand ☎800-447-002, UK ☎0800 895 078, US

☎800-227-6811; elsewhere, call UK collect ☎+44 2079 378 091. Visa also offers TravelMoney, a pre-paid debit card that can be reloaded online or by phone. For more info on Visa travel services, see http://usa.visa.com/personal/using_visa/travel_with_visa.html.

THE EURO. As of January 1, 2009, the official currency of 16 members of the European Union—Austria, Belgium, Cyprus, Finland, France, Germany, Greece, Ireland, Italy, Luxembourg, Malta, the Netherlands, Portugal, Slovakia, Slovenia, and Spain—will be the euro.

The currency has some important—and positive—consequences for travelers hitting more than one euro-zone country. For one thing, money-changers across the euro-zone are obliged to exchange money at the official, fixed rate (below) and at no commission (though they may still charge a small service fee). Second, euro-denominated traveler's checks allow you to pay for goods and services across the euro-zone, again at the official rate and commission-free. At the time of printing, €1 = US$1.54 = CDN$1.62 = NZ$2.15. For more info, check an online currency converter or www.europa.eu.int.

GETTING MONEY FROM HOME

The easiest and cheapest solution for running out of money while traveling is to have someone back home make a deposit to the bank account linked to your credit card or ATM card. Failing that, consider one of the options below.

WIRING MONEY

It is possible to arrange a **bank money transfer**, which means asking a bank back home to wire money to a bank in Europe. This is the cheapest way to transfer cash, but it's also the slowest, usually taking several days or more. Note that some banks may only release your funds in local currency, potentially sticking you with a poor exchange rate; inquire about this in advance. Money transfer services like **Western Union** are faster and more convenient than bank transfers, but also much pricier. Western Union has many locations worldwide. To find one, visit www.westernunion.com, or call: Australia ☎800 173 833, Canada and US ☎800-325-6000, UK ☎0800 833 833. To wire money using a credit card (Discover, MasterCard, or Visa), call in Canada and the US ☎800-225-5227, UK ☎0800 833 833. Money transfer services are also available to **American Express** cardholders and at selected **Thomas Cook** offices.

US STATE DEPARTMENT (US CITIZENS)

In serious emergencies only, the US State Department will forward money within hours to the nearest consular office or embassy, which will then disburse it according to internal instructions for a US$30 fee. If you wish to use this service, you must contact the Overseas Citizens Service division of the US State Department (from overseas ☎202-501-4444, toll-free 888-407-4747).

COSTS

The cost of your trip will vary depending on where you go, how you travel, and where you stay. The most significant expenses will probably be your round-trip (return) airfare to Europe (see **Getting to Europe: By Plane,** p. 42) and a rail pass or bus pass (see **Getting around Europe,** p. 46).

STAYING ON A BUDGET

Your daily budget will vary greatly from country to country. A bare-bones day in Europe would include camping or sleeping in hostels and buying food in supermarkets. A slightly more comfortable day would include sleeping in hostels or guesthouses and the occasional budget hotel, eating one meal per day at a restaurant, and going out at night. Be sure to factor in emergency reserve funds (at least US$200) when planning how much money you'll need.

TIPS FOR SAVING MONEY

Some simple ways to save include searching out free entertainment, splitting accommodation and food costs with trustworthy fellow travelers, and buying food in grocery stores. Full- or multi-day local transportation passes can also save you valuable pocket change. Bring a **sleepsack** (p. 20) to save at hostels that charge for linens, and do your **laundry** in the sink (unless you're explicitly prohibited from doing so). Museums often have certain days when admission is free. If you are eligible, consider getting an ISIC or an IYTC; many sights and museums offer reduced admission to students and youths. Renting a bike is cheaper than renting a moped or scooter. Drinking at bars and clubs quickly becomes expensive. It's cheaper to buy alcohol at a supermarket and imbibe before going out. That said, don't go overboard. Though staying within your budget is important, don't do so at the expense of your health.

TIPPING AND BARGAINING

In most European countries, a 5-10% gratuity is included in the food service bill. Additional tipping is not expected, but an extra 5-10% for good service is not unusual. Where gratuity is not included, 10-15% tips are standard and rounding up to the next unit of currency is common. Many countries have their own unique tipping practices with which you should familiarize yourself before visiting. In general, tipping in bars and pubs is unnecessary. For other services such as taxis or hairdressers, a 10-15% tip is usually recommended. Watch other customers to gauge what is appropriate. Bargaining is useful in Greece, and in outdoor markets across Europe.

TAXES

The EU imposes a value added tax (VAT) on goods and services, usually included in the sticker price. Non-EU citizens visiting Europe may obtain a

TOP TEN WAYS TO SAVE IN EUROPE

1. Always ask about discounts. If **under 26,** you should rarely go a full day without being rewarded for your youth and inexperience.

2. Be aware that room prices tend to shoot up and transportation is a hassle on **festival dates** and during local holidays.

3. Consider purchasing the combination transportation and sights **discount passes** offered by many city tourist offices; they often pay for themselves many times over.

4. Get **out** of the city. A day hiking or beach-lounging provides relief for both you and your wallet.

5. Travel early; trains, buses, and ferries leaving early in the day or on weekdays (as opposed to weekends) are generally cheaper than those leaving at other times.

6. Don't expect to eat out every meal in Europe. **Street markets** are excellent places to find cheap fruits and vegetables, and most hostels have kitchens.

7. In major cities, make your base on the **outskirts** of the town, where food and beds tend to be both cheaper and less touristed.

8. Bring a **sleepsack** to avoid the occasional linens rental charge.

9. Clubbing is expensive enough without depending on overpriced mojitos; start the night off with ⊠**market-purchased booze.**

10. Be your own tour guide; sightseeing is best—and free—on your own with your **Let's Go.**

refund for taxes paid on retail goods, but not for taxes paid on services. As the VAT is 15-25%, it might be worthwhile to file for a refund. To do so, you must obtain Tax-Free Shopping Cheques, available from shops sporting the Europe Tax-Free Shopping logo, and save your receipts. Upon leaving the EU, present your goods, invoices, and passport to customs and have your checks stamped. Then, go to an ETS cash refund office on site or file for a refund once back home. Keep in mind that goods must be taken out of the country within three months of purchase, and that most countries require minimum purchase amounts per store to become eligible for a refund. See www.globalrefund.com for more info and downloads of relevant forms.

PACKING

Pack lightly. Lay out only what you absolutely need, then take half the clothes and twice the money. The **Travelite FAQ** (www.travelite.org) is a good resource for tips on traveling light. The online **Universal Packing List** (http://upl.codeq.info) will generate a customized list of suggested items based on your trip length, the expected climate, your planned activities, and other factors. If you plan to do a lot of hiking, also consult **The Great Outdoors,** p. 33.

Luggage: If you plan to cover most of your itinerary by foot, a sturdy frame backpack is unbeatable. (For backpack basics, see p. 35.) Toting a suitcase or trunk is fine if you plan to live in 1 or 2 cities, but not if you plan to move around frequently. In addition to your main piece of luggage, a daypack (a small backpack or courier bag) is useful.

Clothing: No matter when you're traveling, it's a good idea to bring a warm jacket or wool sweater, a rain jacket (Gore-Tex® is both waterproof and breathable), sturdy shoes or hiking boots, and thick socks. Waterproof sandals are a must-have for grubby hostel showers. You may also want one outfit for going out, and maybe a nicer pair of shoes. If you plan to visit religious or cultural sites, remember to dress modestly.

 DISPOSABLES. If you're tight on space and plan to give your clothes a good workout, consider buying a pack of simple cotton undershirts. A pack of plain t-shirts is cheap and light, and you won't feel bad throwing them away when they get covered in backpacker grime.

Sleepsack: Some hostels require that you either provide your own linens or rent linens from them. Save cash by making your own sleepsack: fold a full-size sheet in half the long way, then sew it closed along the long side and one of the short sides.

Adapters and Converters: In Europe, electricity is 230V AC, enough to fry any 120V North American appliance. Americans and Canadians should buy an adapter (changes the shape of the plug; US$10-30) and a converter (changes the voltage; US$10-30); don't use an adapter without a converter unless appliance instructions explicitly state otherwise. Australians and New Zealanders won't need a converter, but will need a set of adapters. For more on all things adaptable, check out http://kropla.com/electric.htm.

Toiletries: Toothbrushes, towels, soap, talcum powder (to keep feet dry), deodorant, razors, tampons, and condoms are available, but it may be difficult to find your preferred brand, so bring extras. Also, be sure to bring enough extra contact lenses and solution for your entire trip. Bring your glasses and a copy of your prescription, too, in case you need an emergency replacement. If you use heat disinfection, either switch temporarily to a chemical disinfection system (check first to make sure it's safe with your brand of lenses), or buy a converter to 220/240V. Pack minimal toiletries in your hand baggage to avoid confiscation at airport security checks.

 KEEP IT CLEAN. Multi-purpose liquid soaps will save space and keep you from smelling like last night's fish and chips. Dr. Bronner's® and Campsuds® both make soap that you can use as toothpaste, shampoo, laundry detergent, dishwashing liquid, and more. Plus, they're biodegradable.

First Aid: For a basic first-aid kit, pack bandages, a pain reliever, antibiotic cream, a thermometer, a pocket knife, tweezers, moleskin, decongestant, motion-sickness remedy, diarrhea or upset-stomach medication (Pepto Bismol® or Imodium®), an antihistamine, sunscreen, insect repellent, and burn ointment. If you will be in remote regions of less-developed Eastern European countries, consider a syringe for emergencies (get an explanatory letter from your doctor). Leave all sharp objects in your checked luggage.

Film: Digital cameras can be a more economical option and less of a hassle than regular cameras, just be sure to bring along a large enough memory card and extra (or rechargeable) batteries. Less serious photographers may want to bring a disposable camera or two. Despite disclaimers, airport security X-rays can fog film, so buy a lead-lined pouch at a camera store or ask security to hand-inspect it. Always pack film in your carry-on luggage, as higher-intensity X-rays are used on checked luggage.

Other Useful Items: For safety, bring a **money belt** and a small **padlock.** Basic **outdoors equipment** (water bottle, compass, waterproof matches, pocketknife, sunglasses, sunscreen, hat) may also prove useful. Make quick repairs with a needle and thread; also consider electrical tape for patching tears. To do laundry by hand, bring detergent, a small rubber ball to stop up the sink, and string for a makeshift clothesline. Extra plastic bags are crucial for storing food, dirty shoes, and wet clothes, and for keeping liquids from exploding all over your clothes. Other items include an umbrella, a battery-powered alarm clock, safety pins, rubber bands, a flashlight, a utility pocketknife, earplugs, garbage bags, and a small calculator. A mobile phone can be a lifesaver on the road; see p. 29 for information on acquiring one that will work at your destination.

Important Documents: Don't forget your passport, traveler's checks, ATM and/or credit cards, adequate ID, and photocopies of all of the aforementioned. Other documents you may wish to have include: hosteling membership card (p. 31); a driver's license (p. 15); travel insurance forms (p. 24); an ISIC (p. 24); a rail or bus pass (p. 47).

SAFETY AND HEALTH

GENERAL ADVICE

In any type of crisis situation, the most important thing to do is **stay calm.** Your country's embassy abroad is usually your best resource in an emergency; registering with that embassy upon arrival in the country is often a good idea. *Let's Go* lists consulates in the **Practical Information** section of large cities.

ESSENTIALS

 TRAVEL ADVISORIES. The following government offices provide travel information and advisories by telephone, by fax, or via the web:

Australian Department of Foreign Affairs and Trade: ☎+61 2 6261 1111; www.dfat.gov.au.

Canadian Department of Foreign Affairs and International Trade (DFAIT): ☎+1-800-267-8376; www.dfait-maeci.gc.ca. Visit the website for the booklet *Bon Voyage...But.*

Ireland Department of Foreign Affairs: ☎353 1 478 0822; www.foreignaffairs.gov.ie.

New Zealand Ministry of Foreign Affairs and Trade: ☎+64 4 439 8000; www.mfat.govt.nz.

United Kingdom Foreign and Commonwealth Office: ☎+44 20 7008 1500; www.fco.gov.uk.

US Department of State: ☎+1-888-407-4747; http://travel.state.gov. Visit the website for the booklet *A Safe Trip Abroad.*

DRUGS AND ALCOHOL. Drug and alcohol laws vary widely throughout Europe. "Soft" drugs are tolerated in the Netherlands, while in much of Eastern Europe drug possession may lead to a heavy prison sentence. If you carry **prescription drugs,** include both a copy of the prescriptions themselves and a note from a doctor, especially at border crossings. **Public drunkenness** is culturally unacceptable and against the law in many countries; it can also jeopardize your safety.

TERRORISM AND CIVIL UNREST. In the wake of September 11 and the war in Iraq, be vigilant near embassies and be wary of big crowds and demonstrations. Keep an eye on the news, pay attention to travel warnings, and comply with security measures. Overall, risks of civil unrest tend to be localized and rarely directed toward tourists. Tensions remain in Northern Ireland, especially around July "marching season," which reaches its height July 4-12. Notoriously violent separatist movements include the ETA, a Basque group that operates in southern France and Spain, and FLNC, a Corsican separatist group in France. The November 17 group in Greece is known for anti-Western acts, though they have not targeted tourists, to date. The box above lists offices to contact and webpages to visit to get the most updated list about travel advisories.

PERSONAL SAFETY

EXPLORING AND TRAVELING

To avoid unwanted attention, try to blend in. Respecting local customs (in many cases, dressing more conservatively than you would at home) may ward off would-be hecklers. Familiarize yourself with your surroundings before setting out, and carry yourself with confidence. Avoid checking maps on the street. If you are traveling alone, be sure someone at home knows your itinerary, and never tell anyone you meet that you're by yourself. When walking at night, stick to busy, well-lit streets and avoid dark alleyways. If you ever feel uncomfortable, leave the area as quickly and directly as you can.

There is no sure-fire way to avoid all the threatening situations you might encounter while traveling, but a good **self defense course** will give you concrete ways to react to unwanted advances. **Impact, Prepare,** and **Model Mugging** can refer you to local self defense courses in Australia, Canada, Switzerland and the US. Visit the website at www.modelmugging.org for more info.

If you are using a **car**, familiarize yourself with local driving signals and wear a seatbelt. Children under 40 lbs. should ride only in specially designed car-seats, available for a small fee from most car rental agencies. Study route maps before you hit the road and, if you plan on spending a lot of time driving, con-sider bringing spare parts. For long drives in desolate areas, invest in a mobile phone (p. 29) and a roadside assistance program. Park your vehicle in a garage or well-traveled area and use a steering wheel locking device in larger cities. **Sleeping in your car** is very dangerous, and it's also illegal in many countries. For info on the perils of **hitchhiking,** see p. 54.

POSSESSIONS AND VALUABLES

Never leave your belongings unattended; crime occurs in even the most safe-looking hostels and hotels. Bring your own padlock for hostel lockers, and don't store valuables in a locker. Be particularly careful on **buses** and **trains;** horror stories abound about determined thieves who wait for travelers to fall asleep. Carry your bag or purse in front of you. When traveling with others, sleep in alternate shifts. When alone, use good judgment in selecting a train compartment: never stay in an empty one, and use a lock to secure your pack to the luggage rack. Use extra caution if traveling at night or on overnight trains. Try to sleep on top bunks with your luggage stored above you, and keep important documents and other valuables on you at all times.

There are a few steps you can take to minimize the financial risk associated with traveling. First, **bring as little with you as possible.** Second, buy a few com-bination **padlocks** to secure your belongings either in your pack or in a hostel or train station locker. Third, **carry as little cash as possible.** Keep your traveler's checks and ATM/credit cards in a **money belt**—not a "fanny pack"—along with your passport and ID cards. Fourth, **keep a small cash reserve separate from your primary stash.** This should be about US$50 (US$ or euro are best) sewn into or stored in the depths of your pack, along with your traveler's check numbers and photocopies of your passport and other important documents.

In large cities **con artists** often work in groups and may involve children. Beware of certain classics: sob stories that require money, rolls of bills "found" on the street, mustard spilled (or saliva spit) onto your shoulder to distract you while they snatch your bag. **Never let your passport and your bags out of your sight.** Hostel workers will sometimes stand at bus and train station arrival points to try to recruit tired and disoriented travelers to their hostel; never believe strangers who tell you that theirs is the only hostel open. Beware of **pickpockets** in city crowds, especially on public transportation. Also, be alert in public tele-phone booths: if you must say your calling card number, do so very quietly; if you punch it in, make sure no one can look over your shoulder.

If you will be traveling with electronic devices, check whether your hom-eowner's insurance covers loss, theft, or damage when you travel. If not, you might consider purchasing a low-cost separate insurance policy. **Safeware** (☎+1-800-800-1492; www.safeware.com) specializes in covering computers. State rates vary, but average US$200 for global coverage up to $4000.

PRE-DEPARTURE HEALTH

In your **passport,** write the names of any people you wish to be contacted in case of a medical emergency, and list any allergies or medical conditions. Matching a prescription to a foreign equivalent is not always easy, safe, or possible, so if you take prescription drugs, carry up-to-date prescriptions or a statement from your doctor stating the medication's trade name, manufacturer, chemical name, and dosage. While traveling, be sure to keep all medication in your carry-on luggage. For tips on packing a **first-aid kit,** see p. 21.

INSURANCE

Travel insurance covers four basic areas: medical/health problems, property loss, trip cancellation/interruption, and emergency evacuation. Though regular insurance policies may well extend to travel-related accidents, you may consider purchasing separate travel insurance if the cost of potential trip cancellation, interruption, or emergency medical evacuation is greater than you can absorb. Prices for independent travel insurance generally run about US$50 per week for full coverage, while trip cancellation/interruption may be purchased separately at a rate of US$3-5 per day, depending on length of stay.

Medical insurance (especially university policies) often covers costs incurred abroad; check with your provider. **Australians** traveling in Finland, Ireland, Italy, the Netherlands, Sweden, or the UK are entitled to many of the services that they would receive at home as part of the Reciprocal Health Care Agreement. **Homeowners' insurance** often covers theft during travel and loss of travel documents (passport, plane ticket, rail pass, etc.) up to US$500.

ISIC and **ITIC** (p. 15) provide basic insurance benefits to US cardholders, including US$100 per day of in-hospital sickness for up to 100 days and US$10,000 of accident-related medical reimbursement (see www.myisic.com for details). Cardholders have access to a toll-free 24hr. helpline for emergencies. **American Express** (☎+1-800-528-4800) grants most cardholders automatic collision and theft insurance on car rentals made with the card.

USEFUL ORGANIZATIONS AND PUBLICATIONS

The American **Centers for Disease Control and Prevention** (**CDC;** ☎+1-800-311-3435; www.cdc.gov/travel) maintains an international travelers' hotline and an informative website. Consult the appropriate government agency of your home country for consular information sheets on health, entry requirements, and other issues for various countries (see **Travel Advisories,** p. 22). For quick information on health and other travel warnings, call the **Overseas Citizens Services** (M-F 8am-8pm from US ☎+1-888-407-4747, from overseas ☎+1-202-501-4444), or contact a passport agency, embassy, or consulate abroad. For information on medical evacuation services and travel insurance firms, see the US government's website http://travel.state.gov/travel/abroad_health.html or the **British Foreign and Commonwealth Office** (www.fco.gov.uk). For general health information, contact the **American Red Cross** (☎+1-202-303-4498; www.redcross.org).

STAYING HEALTHY

Common sense is the simplest prescription for good health while you travel. Drink plenty of hydrating fluids to prevent dehydration and constipation, and wear sturdy, broken-in shoes and clean socks.

 COMES IN HANDY. A small bottle of liquid hand cleanser, a stash of moist towelettes, or even a package of baby wipes can keep your hands and face germ-free and refreshed on the road. The hand cleanser should have an alcohol content of at least 70% to be effective.

ONCE IN WESTERN EUROPE

ENVIRONMENTAL HAZARDS

Heat exhaustion and dehydration: Heat exhaustion leads to nausea, excessive thirst, headaches, and dizziness. Avoid it by drinking plenty of fluids, eating salty foods (e.g., crackers), abstaining from dehydrating beverages (e.g., alcohol and caffeinated beverages), and wearing sunscreen. Continuous heat stress can eventually lead to heatstroke, characterized by a rising temperature, severe headache, delirium, and cessation of sweating. Victims should be cooled off with wet towels and taken to a doctor.

Sunburn: Always wear sunscreen (SPF 30 or higher) when spending time outdoors. If you get sunburned, drink more fluids than usual and apply an aloe-based lotion. Severe sunburns can lead to sun poisoning, a condition that can cause fever, chills, nausea, and vomiting. Sun poisoning should always be treated by a doctor.

Hypothermia and frostbite: A rapid drop in body temperature is the clearest sign of overexposure to cold. Victims may also shiver, feel exhausted, have poor coordination or slurred speech, hallucinate, or suffer amnesia. Do not let hypothermia victims fall asleep. To avoid hypothermia, keep dry, wear layers, and stay out of the wind. When the temperature is below freezing, watch out for frostbite. If skin turns white or blue, waxy, and cold, do not rub the area. Drink warm beverages, stay dry, and slowly warm the area with dry fabric or steady body contact until a doctor can be found.

High Altitude: Allow your body a couple of days to adjust to less oxygen before exerting yourself. Note that alcohol is more potent and UV rays are stronger at high elevations.

INSECT-BORNE DISEASES

Many diseases are transmitted by insects—mainly mosquitoes, fleas, ticks, and lice. Be aware of insects in wet or forested areas, especially while hiking and camping. Wear long pants and long sleeves, tuck your pants into your socks, and use a mosquito net. Use insect repellents such as DEET and soak or spray your gear with permethrin (licensed in the US only for use on clothing). **Ticks**—which can carry Lyme and other diseases—can be particularly dangerous in rural and forested regions.

Tick-borne encephalitis: A viral infection of the central nervous system transmitted during the summer by tick bites (primarily in wooded areas) or by consumption of unpasteurized dairy products. The risk of contracting the disease is relatively low, especially if precautions are taken against tick bites.

Lyme disease: A bacterial infection carried by ticks and marked by a circular bull's-eye rash of 2 in. or more. Later symptoms include fever, headache, fatigue, and aches and pains. Antibiotics are effective if administered early. Left untreated, Lyme disease can cause problems in joints, the heart, and the nervous system. If you find a tick attached to your skin, grasp the head with tweezers as close to your skin as possible and apply slow, steady traction. Removing a tick within 24hr. greatly reduces the risk of infection. Do not try to remove ticks with petroleum jelly, nail polish remover, or a hot match. Ticks usually inhabit moist, shaded environments and heavily wooded areas. If you are going to be hiking in these areas, wear long clothes and DEET.

Other insect-borne diseases: Lymphatic filariasis is a roundworm infestation transmitted by mosquitoes. Infection causes enlargement of extremities and has no vaccine. **Leishmaniasis,** a parasite transmitted by sand flies, can occur in rural areas of Western Europe. Common symptoms are fever, weakness, and swelling of the spleen, as well as skin sores. There is a treatment, but no vaccine.

FOOD- AND WATER-BORNE DISEASES

Prevention is the best cure: be sure that your food is properly cooked and the water you drink is clean. Watch out for food from markets or street vendors that may have been cooked in unhygienic conditions. Other culprits are raw shellfish, unpasteurized milk, and sauces containing raw eggs. If the region's tap water is known to be unsanitary, peel fruits and vegetables before eating them and avoid tap water (including ice cubes and anything washed in tap water). Buy bottled water, or purify your own water by bringing it to a rolling boil or treating it with **iodine tablets;** note that some parasites have exteriors that resist iodine treatment, so boiling is more reliable. Always wash your hands.

Giardiasis: Transmitted through parasites and acquired by drinking untreated water from streams or lakes. Symptoms include diarrhea, cramps, bloating, fatigue, weight loss, and nausea. If untreated, it can lead to severe dehydration. Giardiasis occurs worldwide.

Hepatitis A: A viral infection of the liver acquired through contaminated water or shellfish from contaminated water. Symptoms include fatigue, fever, loss of appetite, nausea, dark urine, jaundice, vomiting, aches and pains, and light stools. The risk is highest in rural areas and the countryside, but it is also present in urban areas. Ask your doctor about the Hepatitis A vaccine or an injection of immune globulin.

Traveler's diarrhea: Results from drinking fecally contaminated water or eating uncooked and contaminated foods. Symptoms include nausea, bloating, and urgency. Try quick-energy, non-sugary foods with protein and carbohydrates to keep your strength up. Over-the-counter anti-diarrheals (e.g., Imodium®) may counteract the problem. The most dangerous side effect is dehydration; drink 8 oz. of water with tsp. of sugar or honey and a pinch of salt, try uncaffeinated soft drinks, or eat salted crackers. If you develop a fever or your symptoms don't go away after 4-5 days, consult a doctor. Consult a doctor immediately for treatment of diarrhea in children.

Sexually transmitted infections (STIs): Gonorrhea, chlamydia, genital warts, syphilis, herpes, HPV, and other STIs are easier to catch than HIV and can be just as serious. Though condoms may protect you from some STIs, oral or even tactile contact can lead to transmission. If you think you may have contracted an STI, see a doctor immediately.

OTHER HEALTH CONCERNS

MEDICAL CARE ON THE ROAD

While healthcare systems in Western Europe tend to be quite accessible and of high quality, medical care varies greatly across Eastern and Southern Europe. Major cities such as Prague have English-speaking medical centers or hospitals for foreigners. In general, medical service in these regions is not up to Western standards; though basic supplies are usually there, specialized treatment is not. Tourist offices may have names of local doctors who speak English. In the event of a medical emergency, contact your embassy for aid and recommendations. All EU citizens can receive free or reduced-cost first aid and emergency services by presenting a **European Health Insurance Card.**

If you are concerned about obtaining medical assistance while traveling, you may wish to employ special support services. The **MedPass** from **GlobalCare, Inc.,** 6875 Shiloh Rd. East, Alpharetta, GA 30005, USA (☎800-860-1111; www.globalcare.net), provides 24hr. international medical assistance, support, and medical evacuation resources. The **International Association for Medical Assistance to Travelers (IAMAT;** US ☎+1-716-754-4883, Canada 519-836-0102; www.iamat.org) has free membership, lists English-speaking doctors worldwide, and offers detailed info on immunization requirements and sanitation. If your regular insurance policy does not cover travel abroad, you may wish to purchase additional coverage in case of emergency (see p. 24).

Those with medical conditions may want to obtain a **MedicAlert** membership (US$40 per year), which includes among other things a stainless steel ID tag and a 24hr. collect-call number. Contact the MedicAlert Foundation International, 2323 Colorado Ave., Turlock, CA 95382, USA (☎+1-888-633-4298, outside US ☎+1-209-668-3333; www.medicalert.org).

WOMEN'S HEALTH

Women traveling in unsanitary conditions are vulnerable to urinary tract **infections.** Over-the-counter medicines can sometimes alleviate symptoms, but if they persist, see a doctor. Vaginal yeast infections may flare up in hot and humid climates. Wearing loose-fitting trousers or a skirt and cotton underwear will help, as will over-the-counter remedies. Bring supplies if you are prone to infection, as it may be difficult to find the brands you prefer on the road. **Tampons, pads,** and **contraceptive devices** are widely available in most of Western Europe, but can be hard to find in areas of Eastern Europe. **Abortion** laws also vary from country to country. In much of Western Europe, abortion is legal during at least the first 10-12 weeks of pregnancy, but remains illegal in Ireland, Monaco, and Spain, except in extreme circumstances.

KEEPING IN TOUCH

BY EMAIL AND INTERNET

Email is popular and easily accessible in most of Europe. Although in some places it's possible to forge a remote link with your home server, in most cases this is a much slower (and thus more expensive) option than taking advantage of free **web-based email accounts** (e.g., www.gmail.com and www.hotmail.com). **Internet cafes** and the occasional free Internet terminal at a public library or university are listed in the **Practical Information** sections of major cities. For lists of additional cybercafes in Europe, check out www.cybercaptive.com, www. netcafeguide.com, and www.cybercafe.com.

> **WARY WI-FI.** Wireless hot spots make Internet access possible in public and remote places. Unfortunately, they also pose **security risks.** Hot spots are public, open networks that use unencrypted, unsecured connections. They are susceptible to hacks and "packet sniffing"—ways of stealing passwords and other private information. To prevent problems, disable ad hoc mode, turn off file sharing and network discovery, encrypt your email, turn on your firewall, beware of phony networks, and watch for over-the-shoulder creeps.

Travelers find that taking their **laptop computers** on the road with them can be a convenient option for staying connected. Laptop users can call an Internet service provider via a modem using long-distance phone cards specifically intended for such calls. Another option is **Voice over Internet Protocol (VoIP).** A particularly popular provider, **Skype,** allows users to contact other users for free, and to call landlines and mobile phones for an additional fee. Some Internet cafes allow travelers to connect their laptops to the Internet. Travelers with wireless-enabled computers may be able to take advantage of an increasing number of wireless "hot spots," where they can get online for free or for a small fee. Newer computers can detect these hot spots automatically; otherwise, websites like www.jiwire.com can help you find them. Bringing your laptop to a cafe can make you stand out as a (seemingly rich) tourist, so be wary of flashing that tech bling in sketchy neighborhoods.

BY TELEPHONE

CALLING HOME FROM EUROPE

Prepaid phone cards are a common and relatively inexpensive means of calling abroad. Each one comes with a Personal Identification Number (PIN) and a toll-free access number. Call the access number and then follow the directions for dialing your PIN. To purchase prepaid phone cards, check online for the best rates; www.callingcards.com is a good place to start. Online providers generally send your access number and PIN via email, with no actual "card" involved. You can also call home with prepaid phone cards purchased in Europe (see **Calling Within Europe,** p. 28).

PLACING INTERNATIONAL CALLS. All international dialing prefixes and country codes for Europe are shown in a chart on the **Inside Back Cover** of this book. To place international calls, dial:

1. The **international dialing prefix.** To call from **Australia,** dial 0011; **Canada** or the **US,** 011; **Ireland, New Zealand,** or the **UK,** 00.
2. The **country code** of the country you want to call. To call **Australia,** dial 61; **Canada** or the **US,** 1; **Ireland,** 353; **New Zealand,** 64; the **UK,** 44.
3. The **city/area code.** *Let's Go* lists the city/area codes for cities and towns in Europe opposite the city or town name, next to a ☎, as well as in every phone number. If the first digit is a zero (e.g., 020 for London), omit the zero when calling from abroad (e.g., dial 20 from **Canada** to reach **London**).
4. The **local number.**

Another option is to purchase a **calling card,** linked to a major national telecommunications service in your home country. Calls are billed collect or to your account. To obtain a calling card, contact the appropriate company listed below. Where available, there are often advantages to purchasing calling cards online, including better rates and immediate access to your account. Companies that offer calling cards include: **AT&T Direct** (US ☎800-364-9292; www.att.com); **Canada Direct** (☎800-561-8868; www.infocanadadirect.com); **MCI** (☎800-777-5000; www.minutepass.com); **Telecom New Zealand Direct** (www.telecom.co.nz); **Telstra Australia** (☎1800 676 638; www.telstra.com). To call home with a calling card, contact the operator for your service provider by dialing the appropriate toll-free access number. Placing a **collect call** through an international operator can be expensive but may be necessary in case of an emergency. You can frequently call collect without even possessing a company's calling card just by calling its access number and following the instructions. *Let's Go* lists access numbers in the **Essentials** sections of each chapter.

CALLING WITHIN EUROPE

The simplest way to call within a country is to use a public pay phone. However, much of Europe has switched to a **prepaid phone card** system, and in some countries you may have a hard time finding coin-operated phones. Prepaid phone cards (available at newspaper kiosks and tobacco stores), which carry a certain amount of phone time depending on the card's denomination, usually save time and money in the long run. Another kind of prepaid phone card comes with a PIN and a toll-free access number. Instead of inserting the card into the phone, you call the access number and follow the directions on the card. These cards can be used to make international as well as domestic calls.

MOBILE PHONES

Mobile phones are an increasingly popular option for travelers calling within Europe. In addition to greater convenience and safety, mobile phones often provide an economical alternative to expensive landline calls. Virtually all of Western Europe has excellent coverage. The international standard for mobile phones is **Global System for Mobile Communication** (GSM). To make and receive calls in Europe, you need a **GSM-compatible phone** and a **subscriber identity module (SIM) card**, a country-specific, thumbnail-sized chip that gives you a local phone number and plugs you into the local network. Many SIM cards are prepaid, and incoming calls are free. When you use up the prepaid time, you can buy additional cards or vouchers (usually available at convenience stores) to "top up" your phone. For more info on GSM phones, check out www.telestial.com, www.orange.co.uk, www.roadpost.com, or www.planetomni.com. Companies like **Cellular Abroad** (www.cellularabroad.com) rent mobile phones that work in a variety of destinations around the world.

GSM PHONES. Just having a GSM phone doesn't mean you're necessarily good to go when you travel abroad. The majority of GSM phones sold in the United States operate on a different **frequency** (1900) than international phones (900/1800) and will not work abroad. Tri-band phones work on all three frequencies (900/1800/1900) and will operate through most of the world. Additionally, some GSM phones are **SIM-locked** and will only accept SIM cards from a single carrier. You'll need a **SIM-unlocked** phone to use a SIM card from a local carrier when you travel.

TIME DIFFERENCES

All of Europe falls within 3hr. of **Greenwich Mean Time (GMT).** For more info, consult the time zone chart on the **Inside Back Cover.** GMT is 5hr. ahead of New York time, 8hr. ahead of Vancouver time, 10hr. behind Sydney time, and 12hr. behind Auckland time. Iceland is the only country in Europe to ignore Daylight Saving Time; fall and spring switchover times vary in countries that do observe Daylight Saving. For more info, visit www.worldtimeserver.com.

BY MAIL

SENDING MAIL HOME FROM EUROPE

Airmail is the best way to send mail home from Europe. From Western Europe to North America, delivery time averages about seven days. **Aerogrammes,** printed sheets that fold into envelopes and travel via airmail, are available at post offices. Write "airmail" or "*par avion*" (or *por avión, mit Luftpost, via aerea,* etc.) on the front. Most post offices will charge exorbitant fees or simply refuse to send aerogrammes with enclosures. **Surface mail** is by far the cheapest and slowest way to send mail. It takes one to two months to cross the Atlantic and one to three to cross the Pacific—good for heavy items you won't need for a while, such as souvenirs that you've acquired along the way. Check the **Essentials** section of each chapter for country-specific postal info.

SENDING MAIL TO EUROPE

To ensure timely delivery, mark envelopes "airmail" in both English and the local language. In addition to standard postage systems, **Federal Express** (Australia ☎+61 13 26 10, Canada and the US +1-800-463-3339, Ireland +353 800 535 800, New Zealand +64 800 733 339, the UK +44 8456 070 809; www.fedex.com) handles express mail services from most countries to Europe.

There are several ways to arrange pick-up of letters sent to you while you are abroad. Mail can be sent via **Poste Restante** (General Delivery, *Lista de Correos, Fermo Posta, Postlagernde Briefe*, etc.) to almost any city or town in Europe with a post office, though it can be unreliable in Eastern Europe. See individual country chapters for more info on addressing Poste Restante letters. The mail will go to a special desk in a town's central post office, unless you specify a post office by street address or postal code. It's best to use the largest post office, since mail may be sent there regardless. It's usually safer and quicker, though more expensive, to send mail express or registered. Bring your passport for pick-up; there may be a small fee. If the clerks insist that there is nothing for you, ask them to check under your first name as well. *Let's Go* lists post offices in the **Practical Information** section for each city and most towns.

American Express's travel offices throughout the world offer a free **Client Letter Service** (mail held up to 30 days and forwarded upon request) for cardholders who contact them in advance. Some offices provide these services to non-cardholders (especially AmEx Travelers Cheque holders), but call ahead to make sure. *Let's Go* lists AmEx locations for most large cities in **Practical Information** sections; for a complete list, visit www.americanexpress.com/travel.

ACCOMMODATIONS

HOSTELS

Many hostels are laid out dorm-style, often with large single-sex rooms and bunk beds, although private rooms sleeping two to four are becoming more common. They sometimes have kitchens, bike or moped rentals, storage areas, airport transportation, breakfast and other meals, laundry facilities, and Internet. There can be drawbacks: some hostels close during certain daytime "lockout" hours, have a curfew, don't accept reservations, impose a maximum stay, or—less frequently—require that you do chores. In Western Europe, a hostel dorm bed will average around US$15-30 and a private room around US$30-50.

 A HOSTELER'S BILL OF RIGHTS. There are certain standard features that we do not include in our hostel listings. Unless we state otherwise, you can expect that every hostel has free hot showers, no lockout, no curfew, some system of secure luggage storage, and no key deposit.

HOSTELLING INTERNATIONAL

Joining the youth hostel association in your own country (listed below) automatically grants you membership privileges in **Hostelling International (HI)**, a federation of national hosteling associations. Non-HI members may be allowed to stay in some hostels but will have to pay extra. HI hostels are scattered throughout Western Europe and are typically less expensive than private hostels. HI's umbrella organization's website (www.hihostel.com), which lists the web addresses and phone numbers of all national associations, can be a great place to begin researching hosteling in a specific region. Other comprehensive hosteling websites include www.hostels.com and www.hostelplanet.com.

Most HI hostels also honor **guest memberships**—you'll get a blank card with space for six validation stamps. Each night you'll pay a nonmember supplement and earn one guest stamp; get six stamps and you're a member. In some countries you may need to remind the hostel reception. A new membership benefit is the **FreeNites program**, which allows hostelers to gain points toward free rooms. Most student travel agencies (see p. 42) sell HI cards, as do all of the national hosteling organizations listed below. All prices listed below are valid for **one-year memberships** unless otherwise noted.

> **BOOKING HOSTELS ONLINE.** One of the easiest ways to ensure you've got a bed for the night is by reserving online. Click to the Hostelworld booking engine through www.letsgo.com, and you'll have access to bargain accommodations from Argentina to Zimbabwe with no added commission.

Australian Youth Hostels Association (YHA), 422 Kent St., Sydney, NSW 200 (☎02 9261 1111; www.yha.com.au). AUS$42, under 26 AUS$32.

Hostelling International-Canada (HI-C), 205 Catherine St. Ste. 400, Ottawa, ON K2P 1C3 (☎613-237-7884; www.hihostels.ca). CDN$35, under 18 free.

An Óige (Irish Youth Hostel Association), 61 Mountjoy St., Dublin 7 (☎01 830 4555; www.irelandyha.org). EUR€20, under 18 EUR€10.

Hostelling International Northern Ireland (HINI), 22-32 Donegall Rd., Belfast BT12 5JN (☎028 9032 4733; www.hini.org.uk). UK£15, under 25 UK£10.

Scottish Youth Hostels Association (SYHA), 7 Glebe Cres., Stirling FK8 2JA (☎01786 89 14 00; www.syha.org.uk). UK£8, under 16 free.

Youth Hostels Association (England and Wales), Trevelyan House, Dimple Rd., Matlock, Derbyshire DE4 3YH (☎01629 592 600; www.yha.org.uk). UK£16, under 26 UK£10.

Hostelling International-USA, 8401 Colesville Rd., Ste. 600, Silver Spring, MD 20910 (☎301-495-1240; www.hiayh.org). US$28, under 18 free.

OTHER TYPES OF ACCOMMODATIONS

YMCAS AND YWCAS

Young Men's Christian Association (YMCA) and **Young Women's Christian Association (YWCA)** lodgings are usually cheaper than a hotel but more expensive than a hostel. Not all locations offer lodging; those that do are often located in urban downtowns. Many YMCAs accept women and families; some will not lodge those under 18 without parental permission. **World Alliance of YMCAs,** 12 Clos Belmont, 1208 Geneva, SWI (☎41 22 849 5100; www.ymca.int), has more info and a register of Western European YMCAs with housing options.

YMCA of the USA, 101 North Wacker Dr., Chicago, IL 60606 (☎800-872-9622; www.
ymca.net). Provides a listing of the nearly 1000 Ys across the US and Canada, as well
as information on prices and services.

European Alliance of YMCAs (YMCA Europe), Na Porici 12, CZ-110 00 Prague 1, Czech
Republic (☎420 224 872 020; www.ymcaeurope.com). Maintains listings of European
Ys with opportunities to volunteer abroad.

HOTELS, GUESTHOUSES, AND PENSIONS

In Western Europe, **hotel singles** cost about US$30 (€20) per night, **doubles**
US$40 (€26). You'll typically share a hall bathroom; a private bathroom and
hot showers may cost extra. Some hotels offer "full pension" (all meals) and
"half pension" (no lunch). Smaller **guesthouses** and **pensions** are often cheaper
than hotels. If you make reservations in writing, note your night of arrival
and the number of nights you plan to stay. After sending you a confirmation,
the hotel may request payment for the first night. Often it's easiest to reserve
over the phone with a credit card.

BED AND BREAKFASTS (B&BS)

For a cozy alternative to impersonal hotel rooms, **B&Bs** (private homes with
rooms available to travelers) range from acceptable to sublime. Rooms generally cost about €35 for a single and €70 for a double in Western Europe, depending on the season and location. Any number of websites provide listings for
B&Bs. Check out **InnFinder** (www.inncrawler.com), **InnSite** (www.innsite.com),
or **BedandBreakfast.com** (www.bedandbreakfast.com).

UNIVERSITY DORMS

Many **colleges** and **universities** open their residence halls to travelers when school
is not in session; some do so even during term-time. Getting a room may take a
couple of phone calls and require advanced planning, but rates tend to be low
and many offer free local calls and Internet. Where available, university dorms
are listed in the **Accommodations** section of each city.

HOME EXCHANGES AND HOSPITALITY CLUBS

Home exchange offers the traveler various types of homes (houses, apartments, condominiums, villas, even castles), plus the opportunity to live like a
native and to cut down on accommodation fees. For more info, contact **HomeEx-
change.com Inc.,** P.O. Box 787, Hermosa Beach, CA 90254, USA (☎310-798-3864
or toll free 800-877-8723; www.homeexchange.com), or **Intervac International
Home Exchange** (www.intervac.com; see site for phone listings by country).

Hospitality clubs link their members with individuals or families abroad who
are willing to host travelers for free or for a small fee to promote cultural
exchange and general good karma. In exchange, members usually must be willing to host travelers in their own homes; a small membership fee may also be
required. **The Hospitality Club** (www.hospitalityclub.org) is a good place to start.
Servas (www.servas.org) is an established, more formal, peace-based organization, and requires a fee and an interview to join. As always, use common sense
when planning to stay with or host someone you do not know.

LONG-TERM ACCOMMODATIONS

Travelers planning to stay in Western Europe for extended periods of time may
find it most cost-effective to rent an **apartment.** Rent varies widely by region,

season, and quality. Besides the rent itself, prospective tenants usually are also required to front a security deposit and the last month's rent. Generally, for stays shorter than three months, it is more feasible to **sublet** than lease your own apartment. Sublets are also more likely to be furnished. Out of session, it may be possible to arrange to sublet rooms from university students on summer break. It is far easier to find an apartment once you have arrived at your destination than to attempt to use the Internet or phone from home. By staying in a hostel for your first week or so, you can make local contacts and, more importantly, check out your new digs before you commit.

CAMPING

With Europe's vast terrain encompassing beaches, mountains, and plains, **camping** always has some new adventure to offer. Furthermore, you can explore nature for prices refreshingly easy on the wallet. Most towns have several campgrounds within walking distance, occasionally offering a cheap shuttle service to reach them. Even the most rudimentary campings (campgrounds) provide showers and laundry facilities, though almost all forbid campfires. In addition to tent camping, other patrons opt to drive RVs across Europe. Campgrounds usually charge a flat fee per person (usually around €4-6) plus a few euro extra for electricity, tents, cars, or running water. Most larger campgrounds also operate on-site general stores or cafes perfect for a quick, cheap bite. In some countries, it is illegal to pitch your tent or park your RV overnight along the road; look for designated camping areas within national parks, recognized campgrounds, or ask landowners permission before setting up residency on private property. In Sweden, Finland, and Norway, the **right of public access** permits travelers to tent one night in the forests and wilderness for free.

If planning on using campgrounds as your go-to accommodation, consider buying an **International Camping Carnet** (ICC, US$45). Available through the association of **Family Campers and RVers** (☎800-245-9755; www.fcrv.org), the card entitles holders to discounts at some campgrounds and may save travelers from having to leave their passport as a deposit. National tourist offices offer more info on country-specific camping. Additionally, check out **Interhike** (www.interhike.com) which lists campgrounds by region. First-time campers may also want to peruse **KarmaBum Cafe** (www.karmabum.com) for suggested itineraries, packing lists, blogs, and camping recipes. For more info on outdoor activities in Western Europe, see **The Great Outdoors,** below.

THE GREAT OUTDOORS

Camping can be a great way to see Europe on the cheap. There are organized **campgrounds** outside most cities. Showers, bathrooms, and a small restaurant or store are common; some sites have more elaborate facilities. Prices are low, usually US$5-15 per person plus additional charges for tents and cars. While camping is a cheaper option than hosteling, the cost of transportation to and from campgrounds can add up. Some public grounds allow **free camping,** but check local laws. Many areas have additional park-specific rules. **The Great Outdoor Recreation Pages** (www.gorp.com) provides excellent general info.

ESSENTIALS

LEAVE NO TRACE. *Let's Go* encourages travelers to embrace the "Leave No Trace" ethic, minimizing their impact on natural environments. Trekkers should set up camp on durable surfaces, use cookstoves instead of campfires, bury human waste away from water supplies, bag trash and carry it out with them, and respect wildlife and natural objects. For more detailed information, contact the **Leave No Trace Center for Outdoor Ethics,** P.O. Box 997, Boulder, CO 80306 (☎800-332-4100 or 303-442-8222; www.lnt.org).

USEFUL RESOURCES

There are a variety of publishing companies that offer hiking guidebooks to meet the educational needs of the novice or the expert. For information about biking, camping, and hiking, write or call the publishers listed below to receive a free catalog. Campers heading to Europe should consider buying an **International Camping Carnet.** Similar to a hostel membership card, it's required at a few campgrounds in addition to providing discounts at others. It is available in North America from the **Family Campers and RVers Association** (www.fcrv.org) and in the UK from **The Caravan Club** (see below).

Automobile Association, Contact Centre, Carr Ellison House, William Armstrong Dr., Newcastle-upon-Tyne NE4 7YA, UK (☎08706 000 371; www.theaa.com). Publishes *Caravan and Camping Europe* and *Britain and Ireland* (UK£10) as well as road atlases for Europe as a whole and for Britain, France, Germany, Ireland, Italy, and Spain.

The Caravan Club, East Grinstead House, East Grinstead, West Sussex RH19 1UA, UK (☎01342 326 944; www.caravanclub.co.uk). For UK£36, members get access to campgrounds, insurance services, equipment discounts, maps, and a magazine.

Sierra Club Books, 85 2nd St., 2nd fl., San Francisco, CA 94105, USA (☎415-977-5500; www.sierraclub.org). Publishes general resource books on hiking and camping.

The Mountaineers Books, 1001 SW Klickitat Way, Ste. 201, Seattle, WA 98134, USA (☎206-223-6303; www.mountaineersbooks.org). Over 600 titles on hiking, biking, mountaineering, natural history, and conservation.

WILDERNESS SAFETY

Staying **warm, dry,** and **well hydrated** are the keys to a happy and safe wilderness experience. Before any hike, prepare yourself for an emergency by packing a first-aid kit, a reflector, a whistle, high-energy food, extra water, raingear, a hat, gloves, and several **extra pairs of socks.** For warmth, wear wool or insulating synthetic materials designed for the outdoors. Cotton is a bad choice as it takes a ridiculously long time to dry and loses its insulating effect when wet.

Check **weather forecasts** often and pay attention to the skies when hiking, as weather patterns can change suddenly, especially in mountainous areas. Always let someone—a friend, your hostel staff, a park ranger, or a local hiking organization—know when and where you are going. Know your physical limits and do not attempt a hike beyond your ability.

CAMPING AND HIKING EQUIPMENT

WHAT TO BUY

Good camping equipment is both sturdy and light. North American suppliers tend to offer the most competitive prices.

Sleeping Bags: Most sleeping bags are rated by season; "summer" means 30-40°F (around 0°C) at night; "four-season" or "winter" often means below 0°F (-17°C). Bags are made of down (warm and light, but expensive, and miserable when wet) or of synthetic material (heavy, durable, and warm when wet). Prices range US$50-250 for a summer synthetic and US$200-300 for a good down winter bag. Sleeping bag pads include foam pads (US$10-30), air mattresses (US$15-50), and self-inflating mats (US$30-120). Bring a stuff sack to store your bag and keep it dry.

Tents: The best tents are free-standing (with their own frames and suspension systems), set up quickly, and only require staking in high winds. Low-profile dome tents are the best all around. 2-person tents start at US$100, 4-person tents at US$160. Make sure your tent has a rain fly and seal its seams with waterproofer. Other useful accessories include a battery-operated lantern, a plastic groundcloth, and a nylon tarp.

Backpacks: Internal-frame packs mold to your back, keep a lower center of gravity, and flex to allow you to hike difficult trails, while external-frame packs are more comfortable for long hikes over even terrain, as they carry weight higher and distribute it more evenly. Make sure your pack has a hip-belt to transfer weight to your legs. Any serious backpacking requires a pack of at least 4000 cu. in., plus 500 cu. in. for sleeping bags in internal-frame packs. Sturdy backpacks cost anywhere from US$125 to US$420—your pack is an area where it doesn't pay to economize. On your hunt for the perfect pack, fill up each prospective model with something heavy, strap it on, and walk around the store to get a sense of how the model distributes weight. Either buy a rain cover (US$10-20) or store your belongings in plastic bags inside your pack.

Boots: Be sure to wear hiking boots with good ankle support. They should fit snugly and comfortably over 1-2 pairs of wool socks and a pair of thin liner socks. It is important to break in new boots over several weeks before you go to spare yourself from uncomfortable blisters. If this is your first pair of boots, get fitting advice from your local retailer.

Other Necessities: Synthetic layers, like those made of polypropylene or polyester, and a pile jacket will keep you warm even when wet. A space blanket (US$5-15) will help you to retain body heat and doubles as a groundcloth. Durable plastic water bottles are vital; however, you might want to take note of recent health concerns over the presence of BPA, used in the production of shatter- and leak-resistant bottles. Carry water-purification tablets for when you can't boil water. Virtually every organized campground in Europe forbids fires or the gathering of firewood, so you'll need a camp stove and a propane-filled fuel bottle to operate it. Keep in mind you may have to buy some equipment after you arrive because of airline restrictions. Also bring a first-aid kit, pocketknife, insect repellent, and waterproof matches or a lighter.

WHERE TO BUY IT

The online and mail-order companies listed below offer lower prices than many retail stores. A visit to a local camping or outdoors store will give you a good sense of the look and weight of certain items before you buy.

Campmor, 28 Parkway, P.O. Box 700, Upper Saddle River, NJ 07458, USA (☎800-525-4784; www.campmor.com). Wide selection of tents, packs, clothing, and other gear.

Cotswold Outdoor, Unit 11 Kemble Business Park, Crudwell, Malmesbury Wiltshire SN16 9SH, UK (☎08704 427 755; www.cotswoldoutdoor.com).

Discount Camping, 833 Main North Rd., Pooraka, SA 5095, Australia (☎08 8262 3399; www.discountcamping.com.au). Sells everything from tents to tools.

Eastern Mountain Sports (EMS), 1 Vose Farm Rd., Peterborough, NH 03458, USA (☎888-463-6367; www.ems.com). Offers GPS and electronic gear as well.

Gear-Zone, 17 Westlegate, Norwich, Norfolk NR1 3LT, UK (☎1603 410 108; www.gear-zone.co.uk) Comprehensive selection of clothing, tents, and bags.

Recreational Equipment, Inc. (REI), Sumner, WA 98352, USA (US and Canada ☎800-426-4840, elsewhere 253-891-2500; www.rei.com).

ORGANIZED ADVENTURE TRIPS

Organized adventure tours offer another way of exploring the wild. Activities include hiking, biking, skiing, canoeing, kayaking, rafting, climbing, photo safaris, and archaeological digs. Organizations that specialize in camping and outdoor equipment are also a good source for info. Some companies, like the ones below, list organized tour opportunities throughout Europe.

Specialty Travel Index, PO Box 458, San Anselmo, CA 94979, USA (US ☎888-624-4030, elsewhere 415-455-1643; www.specialtytravel.com).

Ecotravel (www.ecotravel.com). Online directory of various programs in Europe and throughout the world. Includes itineraries, guides, and articles.

NatureTrek, Cheriton Mill, Cheriton, Alresford, Hampshire, SO24 0NG (☎01962 733051; www.naturetrek.co.uk). Offers responsible travel opportunities all over the globe.

SPECIFIC CONCERNS

SUSTAINABLE TRAVEL

As the number of travelers on the road rises, the detrimental effect they can have on natural environments is an increasing concern. With this in mind, *Let's Go* promotes the philosophy of **sustainable travel.** Through sensitivity to issues of ecology and sustainability, today's travelers can be a powerful force in preserving as well as restoring the places they visit.

Ecotourism, a rising trend in sustainable travel, focuses on the conservation of natural habitats—mainly, on how to use them without exploitation or over-development. Travelers can make a difference by doing advance research, by supporting organizations and establishments that pay attention to their carbon "footprint," and by patronizing establishments that strive to be environmentally friendly. **International Friends of Nature** (www.nfi.at) has info about sustainable travel options in Europe. For more info, see **Beyond Tourism,** p. 55.

ECOTOURISM RESOURCES. For more info on environmentally responsible tourism, contact one of the organizations below:

Conservation International, 2011 Crystal Dr., Ste. 500, Arlington, VA 22202, USA (☎+1-800-406-2306 or 703-341-2400; www.conservation.org).

Green Globe, Green Globe vof, Verbenalaan 1, 2111 ZL Aerdenhout, The Netherlands (☎+31 23 544 0306; www.greenglobe.com).

International Ecotourism Society, 1333 H St. NW, Ste. 300E, Washington, D.C. 20005, USA (☎+1-202-347-9203; www.ecotourism.org).

United Nations Environment Program, 39-43 Quai André Citroën, 75739 Paris Cedex 15, France (☎+33 1 44 37 14 50; www.uneptie.org/pc/tourism).

RESPONSIBLE TRAVEL

Your tourist dollars can make a big impact on the destinations you visit. The choices you make during your trip can have potent effects on local communities—for better or for worse. Travelers who care about the destinations they explore should become aware of the social, cultural, and political implications of their choices. Simple decisions such as buying local products, paying fair prices for products or services, and attempting to speak the local language can have a strong, positive effect on the community.

Community-based tourism aims to channel tourist money into the local economy by emphasizing tours and cultural programs run by members of the host community. This type of tourism also benefits the tourists themselves, as it often takes them beyond the traditional tours of the region. The *Ethical Travel Guide*, a project of **Tourism Concern** (☎+44 20 7133 3330; www.tourismconcern. org.uk), is an excellent resource for info on community-based travel, with a directory of 300 establishments in 60 countries.

TRAVELING ALONE

Traveling alone can be extremely beneficial, providing a sense of independence and a greater opportunity to connect with locals. On the other hand, solo travelers are more vulnerable targets of harassment and street theft. If you are traveling alone, look confident, try not to stand out as a tourist, and be especially careful in deserted or very crowded areas. If questioned, never admit that you are traveling alone. Maintain regular contact with someone at home who knows your itinerary, and always research your destination before traveling. For more tips, pick up *Traveling Solo* (6th ed.) by Eleanor Berman (Globe Pequot Press; 2008), visit www.travelaloneandloveit.com, or subscribe to **Connecting: Solo Travel Network,** 689 Park Rd., Unit 6, Gibsons, BC V0N 1V7, Canada (☎+1-604-886-9099; www.cstn.org; membership US$50).

WOMEN TRAVELERS

Women exploring on their own inevitably face some additional safety concerns. Single women can consider staying in hostels which offer single rooms that lock from the inside or in religious organizations with single-sex rooms. It's a good idea to stick to centrally located accommodations and to avoid solitary late-night treks or metro rides.

Always carry extra money for a phone call, bus, or taxi. **Hitchhiking** is never safe for lone women, or even for two women traveling together. Look as if you know where you're going, and approach older women or couples for directions if you're lost or uncomfortable. Generally, the less you look like a tourist, the better off you'll be. Dress conservatively, especially in rural areas. Wearing a conspicuous **wedding band** sometimes helps prevent unwanted advances.

Your best answer to verbal harassment is no answer at all; feigning deafness, pretending you don't understand the language, or staring straight ahead will usually do the trick. The extremely persistent can sometimes be dissuaded by a firm, loud "Go away!" in the appropriate language. Seek out a police officer or a passerby if you are being harassed. Memorize the emergency numbers in places you visit, and consider carrying a whistle on your keychain. A self defense course will both prepare you for a potential attack and raise your level of awareness of your surroundings (see recommendations on self defense, p. 22). Also, it might be a good idea to talk with your doctor about the health concerns that women face when traveling (p. 27).

GLBT TRAVELERS

Attitudes toward gay, lesbian, bisexual, and transgendered (GLBT) travelers are particular to each region in Europe. On the whole, countries in Northern and Western Europe tend to be queer-friendly, while Eastern Europe harbors enclaves of tolerance in cities amid stretches of cultural conservatism. Countries like Romania that outlawed homosexuality as recently as 2002 are becoming more liberal today, and can be considered viable destinations for GLBT travelers. Listed below are contact organizations that offer materials addressing some specific concerns. **Out and About** (www.planetout.com) offers a weekly newsletter addressing travel concerns and a comprehensive site addressing gay travel concerns. The online newspaper **365gay.com** has a travel section, and the French-language site **netgai.com** (http://netgai.com/international/Europe) includes links to country-specific resources.

Gay's the Word, 66 Marchmont St., London WC1N 1AB, UK (☎+44 20 7278 7654; http://freespace.virgin.net/gays.theword). The largest gay and lesbian bookshop in the UK, with both fiction and non-fiction titles. Mail-order service available.

Giovanni's Room, 345 S. 12th St., Philadelphia, PA 19107, USA (☎+1-215-923-2960; www.queerbooks.com). An international lesbian and gay bookstore with mail-order service (carries many of the publications listed below).

International Lesbian and Gay Association (ILGA), 17 Rue de la Charité, 1210 Brussels, BEL (☎+32 2 502 2471; www.ilga.org). Provides political information, such as homosexuality laws of individual countries.

ADDITIONAL RESOURCES.
Spartacus International Gay Guide 2008 (US$22).
The Damron Men's Travel Guide 2006. Gina M. Gatta, Damron Co. (US$22).
The Gay Vacation Guide: The Best Trips and How to Plan Them. Mark Chesnut, Kensington Books (US$15).

TRAVELERS WITH DISABILITIES

European countries vary in accessibility to travelers with disabilities. Some tourist boards, particularly in Western and Northern Europe, provide directories on the accessibility of various accommodations and transportation services. If these services are not available, contact establishments directly. Those with disabilities should inform airlines and hotels of their disabilities when making reservations; some time may be needed to prepare special accommodations. Call ahead to restaurants, museums, and other facilities to find out if they are wheelchair-accessible. **Guide dog owners** should inquire as to the quarantine policies of each destination country.

Rail is the most convenient form of travel for disabled travelers in Europe. Many stations have ramps, and some trains have wheelchair lifts, special seating areas, and special toilets. All Eurostar, some InterCity (IC), and some EuroCity (EC) trains are wheelchair-accessible. CityNightLine trains, French TGV (high speed), and Conrail trains feature special compartments. In general, the countries with the most **wheelchair-accessible rail networks** are: Denmark (IC and Lyn trains), France (TGVs and other long-distance trains), Germany (ICE, EC, IC, and IR trains), Ireland (most major trains), Italy (EC and IC trains), the Netherlands (most trains), Sweden (X2000s, most IC and IR trains), and Switzerland (all IC, most EC, and some regional trains). Austria, Poland, and the UK offer accessibility on selected routes. Bulgaria, the Czech Republic, Greece, Hungary, Slovakia, and Spain's rail systems have limited wheelchair accessibility. For those who wish to rent cars, some major **car rental** agencies (e.g., Hertz) offer hand-controlled vehicles.

USEFUL ORGANIZATIONS

Access Abroad, www.umabroad.umn.edu/access. A website devoted to making study abroad available to students with disabilities. The site is maintained by Disability Services, University of Minnesota, 230 Heller Hall, 271 19th Ave. S., Minneapolis, MN 55455, USA (☎+1-612-626-7379).

Accessible Journeys, 35 W. Sellers Ave., Ridley Park, PA 19078, USA (☎+1-800-846-4537; www.disabilitytravel.com). Designs tours for wheelchair users and slow walkers. The site has tips and forums for all travelers.

Flying Wheels, 143 W. Bridge St., Owatonna, MN 55060, USA (☎+1-507-451-5005; www.flyingwheelstravel.com). Specializes in escorted trips to Europe for people with physical disabilities. Plans custom trips worldwide.

The Guided Tour, Inc., 7900 Old York Rd., Ste. 114B, Elkins Park, PA 19027, USA (☎+1-800-783-5841; www.guidedtour.com). Organizes travel programs for persons with developmental and physical challenges in Ireland, Italy, Spain, and the UK.

Society for Accessible Travel and Hospitality (SATH), 347 5th Ave., Ste. 605, New York, NY 10016, USA (☎+1-212-447-7284; www.sath.org). An advocacy group that publishes free online travel information and the travel magazine *Open World*. Annual membership US$49, students and seniors US$29.

MINORITY TRAVELERS

In general, minority travelers will find a high level of tolerance in large cities; small towns and the countryside are less predictable. The increasingly mainstream reality of anti-immigrant sentiments means that travelers of African or Arab descent (regardless of their citizenship) may be the object of unwarranted assumptions and even hostility. Anti-Semitism remains a very real problem in many countries, especially in France, Austria, and much of Eastern Europe. Discrimination is particularly forceful against Roma (gypsies) throughout much of Eastern Europe. Jews, Muslims, and other minority travelers should keep an eye out for skinheads, who have been linked to racist violence in Central and Eastern Europe, and elsewhere. **The European Union Agency for Fundamental Rights (FRA)**, Rahlgasse 3, 1060 Vienna, AUT (☎43 15 80 30; www.eumc.europa. eu), publishes a wealth of country-specific statistics and reports. Travelers can consult **United for Intercultural Action**, Postbus 413, NL-1000 AK, Amsterdam, NTH (☎31 20 683 4778; www.unitedagainstracism.org), for a list of over 500 country-specific organizations that work against racism and discrimination.

DIETARY CONCERNS

Vegetarians will find no shortage of meat-free dining options throughout most of Northern and Western Europe, although **vegans** may have a trickier time outside urban centers, where eggs and dairy can dominate traditional dishes. The cuisine of Eastern Europe still tends to be heavy on meat and gravy, although major cities often boast surprisingly inventive vegetarian and ethnic fare.

The travel section of **The Vegetarian Resource Group's** website, at www.vrg.org/travel, has a comprehensive list of organizations and websites that are geared toward helping vegetarians and vegans traveling abroad. The website for the **European Vegetarian Union (EVU)**, at www.europeanvegetarian.org, includes links to dozens of veggie-friendly organizations. For more info, consult *The Vegetarian Traveler: Where to Stay if You're Vegetarian, Vegan, Environmentally Sensitive*, by Jed and Susan Civic (Larson Publications; 1997), *Vegetarian Europe*, by Alex Bourke (Vegetarian Guides; 2000), and the indispensable, multilingual *Vegan Passport* (The Vegan Society; 2005), along with the websites www.vegdining.com, www.happycow.net, and www.vegetariansabroad.com.

Those looking to keep **kosher** will find abundant dining options across Europe; contact synagogues in larger cities for information, or consult www.kashrut.com/travel/Europe for country-specific resources. Your own synagogue or college Hillel should have access to lists of Jewish institutions across the nation. Hebrew College Online also offers a searchable database of kosher restaurants at www.shamash.org/kosher. Another good resource is the *Jewish Travel Guide*, edited by Michael Zaidner (Vallentine Mitchell; 2004). Travelers looking for **halal** groceries and restaurants will have the most success in France and Eastern European nations with substantial Muslim populations; consult www. zabihah.com for establishment reviews. Keep in mind that if you are strict in your observance, you may have to prepare your own food.

OTHER RESOURCES

TRAVEL PUBLISHERS AND BOOKSTORES

The Globe Corner Bookstore, 90 Mt. Auburn St., Cambridge, MA 02138 (☎617-497-6277; www.globecorner.com). Sponsors an Adventure Travel Lecture Series and carries a vast selection of guides and maps to every imaginable destination. Online catalog includes atlases and monthly staff picks of outstanding travel writing.

Hippocrene Books, 171 Madison Ave., New York, NY 10016 (☎718-454-2366; www. hippocrenebooks.com). Publishes foreign-language dictionaries and learning guides, along with ethnic cookbooks and a smattering of guidebooks.

WORLD WIDE WEB

Almost every aspect of budget travel is accessible via the web. In 10min. at the keyboard, you can make a hostel reservation, get advice on travel hot spots from other travelers, or find out how much a train ride costs. Listed here are some regional and travel-related sites to start off your surfing; other relevant websites are listed throughout the book. Because website turnover is high, use search engines (e.g., www.google.com) to strike out on your own.

LET'S GO ONLINE. Plan your next trip on our newly redesigned website, **www.letsgo.com.** It features the latest travel info on your favorite destinations, as well as tons of interactive features: make your own itinerary, read blogs from our trusty researcher-writers, browse our photo library, watch exclusive videos, check out our newsletter, find travel deals, and buy new guides. We're always updating and adding new features, so check back often!

Backpacker's Ultimate Guide: www.bugeurope.com. Tips on packing, transportation, and where to go. Also tons of country-specific travel information.

BootsnAll.com: www.bootsnall.com. Numerous resources for independent travelers, from planning your trip to reporting on it when you get back.

How to See the World: www.artoftravel.com. A compendium of great travel tips. Advice on everything from finding cheap flights to self defense.

Travel Intelligence: www.travelintelligence.net. A large collection of travel writing by distinguished travel writers.

Travel Library: www.travel-library.com. A fantastic set of links for general information and personal travelogues.

World Hum: www.worldhum.com. An independently produced collection of "travel dispatches from a shrinking planet."

INFORMATION ABOUT WESTERN EUROPE

BBC News: http://news.bbc.co.uk. The latest coverage from one of Europe's most reputable sources for English-language news, for free.

CIA World Factbook: www.odci.gov/cia/publications/factbook/index.html. Tons of vital statistics on countries' geography, government, economy, and people.

EUROPA: http://europa.eu/index_en.htm. English-language gateway to the European Union, featuring news articles and a citizen's guide to EU institutions.

ESSENTIALS

TRANSPORTATION

GETTING TO EUROPE

BY PLANE

When it comes to airfare, a little effort can save you a bundle. Tickets sold by consolidators, couriers, and standby seating are good deals, but last-minute specials, airfare wars, and charter flights often beat these fares. The key is to hunt around, be flexible, and ask about discounts. Students, seniors, and those under 26 should never pay full price for a ticket.

AIRFARES

Airfares to Europe peak between mid-June and early September; holidays are also expensive. The cheapest times to travel are November to mid-December and January to March. Midweek (M-Th morning) round-trip flights run US$60-$120 cheaper than weekend flights, but they are generally more crowded and less likely to permit frequent-flier upgrades. Not fixing a return date ("open return") or arriving in and departing from different cities ("open jaw") is usually significantly pricier than buying a round-trip. Flights between Europe's capitals or regional hubs (Amsterdam, London, Paris, Prague, Warsaw, Zürich) tend to be cheaper than those to more rural areas.

If your European destinations are part of a more extensive globe-hop, consider a round-the-world (RTW) ticket. Tickets usually include at least five stops and are valid for about a year; prices range from US$1600-$5000. Try **Northwest Airlines/KLM** (☎800-225-2525; www.nwa.com) or **Star Alliance** (www.staralliance.com), a consortium of 16 airlines including United.

BUDGET AND STUDENT TRAVEL AGENCIES

While agents specializing in flights to Europe can make your life easy, they may not find you the lowest possible fare—they get paid on commission. Travelers holding **ISIC**s and **IYTC**s (p. 15) qualify for big discounts from student travel agencies. Most flights from budget agencies are on major airlines, but in peak season some may sell seats on less reliable chartered aircrafts.

STA Travel, 9/89 5900 Wilshire Blvd., Ste. 900, Los Angeles, CA 90036, USA (24hr. reservations and info ☎800-781-4040; www.statravel.com). A student and youth travel organization with over 150 offices worldwide, including US offices in many college towns. Ticket booking, travel insurance, rail passes, and more.

The Adventure Travel Company, 124 McDougal St., New York, NY 10021, USA (☎1800 467 4594; www.theadventuretravelcompany.com). Offices across Canada and the US including Champaign, New York, San Francisco, Seattle, and San Diego.

FLIGHT PLANNING ON THE INTERNET. The Internet may be the budget traveler's dream when it comes to finding and booking bargain fares, but the array of options can be overwhelming. Many airline sites offer special last-minute deals online, though some require membership logins or email subscriptions. Try www.airfrance.com, www.britishairways.com, www.icelandair.com, and www.lufthansa.de. **STA** (www.sta.com) and **StudentUniverse** (www.studentuniverse.com) provide quotes on student tickets, while **Expedia** (www.expedia.com), **Orbitz** (www.orbitz.com), and **Travelocity** (www.travelocity.com) offer full travel services. **Priceline** (www.priceline.com) lets you specify a price, and obligates you to buy any ticket that meets or beats it; **Hotwire** (www.hotwire.com) offers bargain fares but won't reveal the airline or flight times until you buy. Other sites that compile deals include www.bestfares.com, www.flights.com, www.lowestfare.com, www.onetravel.com, and www.travelzoo.com. There are tools available to sift through multiple offers; **Booking Buddy** (www.bookingbuddy.com), **SideStep** (www.sidestep.com), and **Kayak** (www.kayak.com) let you enter your trip information once and search multiple sites. Spain-based **eDreams** (www.edreams.com) is convenient to book budget flights within Europe.

USIT, 19-21 Aston Quay, Dublin 2, Ireland (☎+353 1 602 1906; www.usit.ie). Ireland's leading student/budget travel agency has 20 offices throughout Northern Ireland and the Republic of Ireland. Offers programs to work, study, and volunteer worldwide.

COMMERCIAL AIRLINES

Commercial airlines' lowest regular offer is the **APEX** (Advance Purchase Excursion) fare, which provides confirmed reservations and allows "open-jaw" tickets. Generally, reservations must be made seven to 21 days ahead of departure, with seven- to 14-day minimum stay and 90-day maximum stay restrictions. These fares carry hefty cancellation and change penalties (fees rise in summer). Use **Expedia** or **Travelocity** to get an idea of the lowest published fares, then use the resources listed here to try to beat those fares. Low-season fares should be appreciably cheaper than the high-season ones listed here.

TRAVELING FROM NORTH AMERICA

Basic round-trip fares to **Europe** range from roughly US$400-1500: to **Frankfurt**, US$450-1250; **London**, US$250-550; **Paris**, US$600-1400. Standard commercial carriers like **American** (☎800-433-7300; www.aa.com), **United** (☎800-538-2929; www.united.com), and **Northwest** (☎800-225-2525; www.nwa.com) will probably offer the most convenient flights, but they may not be the cheapest. Check **Lufthansa** (☎800-399-5838; www.lufthansa.com), **British Airways** (☎800-247-9297; www.britishairways.com), **Air France** (☎800-237-2747; www.airfrance.us), and **Alitalia** (☎800-223-5730; www.alitaliausa.com) for cheap tickets from US destinations to all over Europe. You might find an even better deal on one of the following airlines if any of their limited departure points is convenient for you.

Icelandair: ☎800-223-5500; www.icelandair.com. Stopovers in Iceland for no extra cost on most flights. New York to Frankfurt Apr.-Aug. US$900-1000; Sept.-Oct. US$600-800; Dec.-Mar. US$500. For last-minute offers, subscribe to their "Lucky Fares" email list.

Finnair: ☎800-950-5000; www.finnair.com. Cheap round-trips from New York, San Francisco, and Toronto to Helsinki; connections throughout Europe. New York to Helsinki June-Sept. US$1250; Oct.-May US$830-1200.

BEFORE YOU BOOK. The emergence of no-frills airlines has made hop-scotching around Europe by air increasingly affordable. Many budget airlines save money by flying out of smaller, regional airports. A flight billed as Paris to Barcelona might in fact be from Beauvais (80km north of Paris) to Girona (104km northeast of Barcelona). For a more detailed list of these airlines by country, check out www.whichbudget.com.

easyJet: UK ☎0871 244 2366; www.easyjet.com. 104 destinations including links to Eastern Europe. Also serves Egypt, Morocco, and Turkey.

Ryanair: Ireland ☎0818 303 030, UK 0871 246 00 00; www.ryanair.com. Serves 132 destinations in Austria, Belgium, the Czech Republic, France, Germany, Ireland, Italy, Latvia, the Netherlands, Poland, Portugal, Scandinavia, Spain, the UK, and Morocco.

SkyEurope: UK ☎0905 7222 747; www.skyeurope.com. 40 destinations in 19 countries around Central and Eastern Europe, including the Czech Republic and Slovakia.

Sterling: Denmark ☎70 10 84 84, UK ☎870 787 8038. www.sterling.dk. The first Scandinavian-based budget airline. Connects Denmark, Norway, and Sweden to 40 cities across Europe.

Wizz Air: Hungary ☎06 90 181 181, Poland ☎ 03 00 50 30 10; www.wizzair.com. 50 destinations in Belgium, Bulgaria, Croatia, France, Germany, Greece, Hungary, Ireland, Italy, the Netherlands, Norway, Poland, Romania, Slovenia, Spain, Sweden, and the UK.

You'll have to buy shuttle tickets to reach the airports of many of these airlines, and add an hour or so to your travel time. After round-trip shuttle tickets and fees for checked luggage or other services that might come standard on other airlines, that €0.01 sale fare can suddenly jump to €20-100. Be particularly aware of baggage allowances, which are generally small and strictly policed. Prices for no-frills airlines vary dramatically; shop around, book months ahead, pack light, and stay flexible to nab the best fares.

TRAVELING FROM THE UK AND IRELAND

Because of the many carriers flying from the British Isles to the continent, we only include discount airlines or those with cheap specials here. The **Air Travel Advisory Bureau** in London (www.atab.co.uk) provides referrals to travel agencies that offer discounted airfares. **Cheapflights** (www.cheapflights.co.uk) publishes bargains. For more info on budget airlines like Ryanair, see p. 44.

Aer Lingus: Ireland ☎08 18 36 50 00; www.aerlingus.com. Round-trip tickets from Cork, Dublin, and Shannon to destinations across Europe (€15-300).

bmibaby: UK ☎08 712 240 224; www.bmibaby.com. Departures from throughout the UK to destinations across Europe. Fares from UK£25.

TRAVELING FROM AUSTRALIA AND NEW ZEALAND

Air New Zealand: New Zealand ☎0800 73 70 00; www.airnz.co.nz. Flights from Auckland to London.

Qantas Air: Australia ☎13 13 13, New Zealand 0800 808 767; www.qantas.com.au. Flights from Australia to London for around AUS$2400.

Singapore Air: Australia ☎13 10 11, New Zealand 0800 808 909; www.singaporeair.com. Flies from Adelaide, Auckland, Brisbane, Christchurch, Melbourne, Perth, Sydney, and Wellington to Western Europe.

Thai Airways: Australia ☎ 13 00 65 19 60, New Zealand 09 377 3886; www.thaiair.com. Major cities in Australia and New Zealand to Frankfurt and London.

AIR COURIER FLIGHTS

Those who travel light should consider courier flights. Couriers help transport cargo on international flights by using their checked luggage space for freight. Generally, couriers are limited to carry-ons and must deal with complex flight restrictions. Most flights are round-trip only, with short fixed-length stays (usually one week) and a limit of one ticket per issue. Most of these flights also operate only out of major gateway cities. Round-trip courier fares from the US to Europe run about US$200-500. Most flights leave from L.A., Miami, New York, or San Francisco in the US, and from Montreal, Toronto, or Vancouver in Canada. Generally, you must be over 18 (in some cases 21). In summer, the most popular destinations require an advance reservation. Super-discounted fares are common for "last-minute" flights (3-14 days ahead).

Air Courier Association, 1767A Denver West Blvd., Golden, CO 80401, USA (☎800-461-8556; www.aircourier.org). Departure cities throughout Canada and the US to Western Europe (US$150-650). 1-year membership US$39, plus some monthly fees.

International Association of Air Travel Couriers (IAATC; www.courier.org). Courier and consolidator fares from North America to Europe. 1-year membership US$45.

Courier Travel (www.couriertravel.org). Searchable online database. 6 departure points in the US to various European destinations. Membership US$40 per household.

STANDBY FLIGHTS

Traveling standby requires considerable flexibility in arrival and departure dates and cities. Companies dealing in standby flights sell vouchers, along with the promise to get you to your destination (or near it) within a certain window of time (typically 1-5 days). You call in before your specific window of time to hear your flight options and the probability that you will be able to board each flight. You can then decide which flights you want to try to make, show up at the right airport at the appropriate time, present your voucher, and board if space is available. Vouchers can usually be bought for both one-way and round-trip travel. You may receive a refund only if every available flight within your date range is full; if you opt not to take an available (but less convenient) flight, you can only get credit toward future travel. Read agreements and contracts carefully, as tricky fine print abounds. To check on a company's service record in the US, contact the **Better Business Bureau** (☎703-276-0100; www.bbb.org). It is difficult to receive refunds, and clients' vouchers will not be honored when an airline fails to receive payment in time.

TICKET CONSOLIDATORS

Ticket consolidators, also known as "**bucket shops,**" buy unsold tickets in bulk from commercial airlines and sell them at discounted rates. Look for tiny advertisements in the Sunday travel section of any major newspaper; call quickly, as availability is extremely limited. Not all bucket shops are reliable, so insist on a receipt that gives full details of flight restrictions, refund policies, and tickets, and pay by credit card (in spite of the 2-5% fee).

GETTING AROUND EUROPE

> **GOING MY WAY, SAILOR?** In Europe, fares are listed as either **single** (one-way) or **return** (round-trip). "Period returns" require you to return within a specific number of days; "day return" means you must return on the same day. Round-trip fares on trains and buses in Europe are simply twice the one-way fare. Unless stated otherwise, *Let's Go* always lists single fares.

TRANSPORTATION

BY PLANE

A number of European airlines offer discount coupon packets. Most are only available as add-ons for transatlantic passengers, but some are stand-alone offers. **Europe by Air's** FlightPass allows non-EU residents to country-hop to over 150 European cities for US$99 or $129 per flight, plus tax. (☎888-321-4737; www.europebyair.com.) **Iberia's** Europass allows passengers flying from the US to Spain to add a minimum of two additional destinations in Europe for $139 per trip. (US ☎800-772-4642; www.iberia.com.)

BY TRAIN

Trains in Europe are generally comfortable, convenient, and reasonably fast, although quality varies by country. Second-class compartments, which seat two to six, are great places to meet fellow travelers. However, trains can be unsafe, especially in Eastern Europe. For safety tips, see p. 22. For long trips, make sure you are on the correct car, as trains sometimes split at crossroads. Towns listed in parentheses on European train schedules require a switch at the town listed immediately before the parentheses.

You can either buy a **rail pass,** which allows you unlimited travel within a region for a given period of time, or rely on individual point-to-point tickets as you go. Almost all countries give students or youths (usually defined as anyone under 26) direct discounts on regular domestic rail tickets, and many also sell a student or youth card that provides 20-50% off all fares for up to a year.

RESERVATIONS. While seat reservations are required only for selected trains (usually on major lines), you are not guaranteed a seat without one (usually US$5-30). You should strongly consider reserving in advance during peak holiday and tourist seasons (at the very latest, a few hours ahead). You will also have to purchase a **supplement** (US$10-50) or special fare for high-speed or high-quality trains such as Spain's AVE, Switzerland's Cisalpino, Finland's Pendolino, Italy's ETR500 and Pendolino, Germany's ICE, and certain French TGVs. InterRail holders must also purchase supplements (US$3-20) for trains like EuroCity, InterCity, and many TGVs; supplements are often unnecessary for Eurail Pass and Europass holders.

OVERNIGHT TRAINS. On night trains, you won't waste valuable daylight hours traveling and you can avoid the hassle and expense of staying at a hotel. However, the main drawbacks include discomfort, sleepless nights, and the lack of scenery. The risk of theft also increases dramatically at night, particularly in Eastern Europe. **Sleeping accommodations** on trains differ from country to country. **Couchettes** (berths) typically have four to six seats per compartment (supplement about US$10-50 per person); **sleepers** (beds) in private sleeping cars offer more privacy, but are more expensive (supplement US$40-150). If you are using a rail pass valid only for a restricted number of days, inspect train schedules to maximize the use of your pass: an overnight train or boat journey often uses up only one of your travel days if it departs after 7pm.

SHOULD YOU BUY A RAIL PASS? Rail passes were designed to allow you to jump on any train in Europe, go wherever you want whenever you want, and change your plans at will. In practice, it's not so simple. You still must stand in line to validate your pass, pay for supplements, and fork over cash for seat and couchette reservations. More importantly, rail passes don't always pay off. Estimate the point-to-point cost of each leg of your journey; add them up and compare the total with the cost of a rail pass. If you are planning to spend a great deal time on trains, a rail pass will probably be worth it. But especially if you are under 26, point-to-point tickets may be cheaper.

A rail pass won't always pay for itself in the Balkans, Belgium, Eastern Europe, Greece, Iceland, Ireland, Italy, Luxembourg, the Netherlands, Portugal, or Spain, where train fares are reasonable, distances short, or buses preferable. If, however, the total cost of your trips nears the price of the pass, the convenience of avoiding ticket lines may be worth the difference.

MULTINATIONAL RAIL PASSES

EURAIL PASSES. Eurail is valid in most of Western Europe: Austria, Belgium, Denmark, Finland, France, Germany, Greece, Italy, Luxembourg, the Netherlands, Norway, Portugal, the Republic of Ireland, Spain, Sweden, and Switzerland. It is **not valid** in the UK. **Eurail Global Passes,** valid for a number of consecutive days, are best for those planning on spending extensive time on trains every few days. Other types of global passes are valid for any 10 or 15 (not necessarily consecutive) days within a two-month period, and are more cost-effective for those traveling longer distances less frequently. **Eurail Pass Saver** provides first-class travel for travelers in groups of two to five (prices are per person). **Eurail Pass Youth** provides parallel second-class perks for those under 26. Passholders receive a timetable for major routes and a map with details on bike rental, car rental, hotel, and museum discounts. Passholders also often receive reduced fares or free passage on many boat, bus, and private railroad lines. The **Eurail Select Pass** is a slimmed-down version of the Eurail Pass: it allows five to 10 days of unlimited travel in any two-month period within three, four, or five bordering European countries. **Eurail Select Passes** (for individuals) and **Eurail Select Pass Saver** (for people traveling in groups of two to five) range from US$505/429 per person (5 days) to US$765/645 (10 days). The **Eurail Select Pass Youth** (2nd class), for those ages 12-25, costs US$279-619. You are entitled to the same **freebies** afforded by the Eurail Pass, but only when they are within or between countries that you have purchased.

PICKY PASSES. In **Eastern Europe**, finding a pass is complicated. **Global passes** aren't accepted anywhere in Eastern Europe except Hungary and Romania; **Select passes** apply to Bulgaria, Croatia, and Slovenia, as well as Hungary and Romania; and **Regional passes** are available for all of those countries, with the exception of Bulgaria and the additions of the Czech Republic and Poland.

SHOPPING AROUND FOR A EURAIL. Eurail Passes can be bought only by non-Europeans from non-European distributors. These passes must be sold at uniform prices determined by the EU. However, some travel agents tack on a US$10 handling fee, and others offer certain bonuses with purchase, so shop around. Also, remember that pass prices rise annually, so if you're planning to travel early in the year, you can save cash by purchasing before January 1 (you have 3 months from the purchase date to validate your pass in Europe). It's best to buy a Eurail before leaving; only a few places in major cities sell them, and at a marked-up price. You can get a replacement for a lost pass only if you have purchased insurance on it under the **Pass Security Plan** (US$14). Eurail Passes are available through travel agents, student travel agencies like STA (p. 42), and **Rail Europe** (Canada ☎800-361-7245, US 888-382-7245; www.raileurope. com). It is also possible to buy directly from Eurail's website, www.eurail.com. Shipping is free to North America, Australia, and New Zealand.

OTHER MULTINATIONAL PASSES. If you have lived for at least six months in one of the European countries where **InterRail Passes** are valid, they are an economical option. The InterRail Pass allows travel within 30 European countries (excluding the passholder's country of residence). The **Global Pass** is valid for a given number of days (not necessarily consecutive) within a 10 day to one-month period. (5 days within 10 days, adult 1st class €329, adult 2nd class €249, youth €159; 10 days within 22 days €489/359/239; 1 month continuous €809/599/399.) The **One Country Pass** unsurprisingly limits travel to one country (€33 for 3 days). Passholders receive free admission to many museums, as well as **discounts** on accommodations, food, and many ferries to Ireland, Scandinavia, and the rest of Europe. Passes are available at www.interrailnet.com, as well as from travel agents, at major train stations throughout Europe, and through online vendors (www.railpassdirect.co.uk).

DOMESTIC RAIL PASSES

If you are planning to spend a significant amount of time within one country or region, a national pass—valid on all rail lines of a country's rail company—may be more cost-effective than a multinational pass. Many national passes are limited and don't provide the free or discounted travel on private railways and ferries that Eurail does. Some of these passes can be bought only in Europe, some only outside Europe; check with a rail agent or with national tourist offices.

NATIONAL RAIL PASSES. The domestic analogs of the Eurail pass, national rail passes are valid either for a given number of consecutive days or for a specific number of days within a given time period. Usually, they must be purchased before you leave. Though they will usually save travelers some money, the passes may actually be a more expensive alternative to point-to-point tickets, particularly in Eastern Europe. For more info, check out www.raileurope.com/us/rail/passes/single_country_index.htm.

RAIL-AND-DRIVE PASSES. Many countries (as well as Eurail) offer rail-and-drive passes, which combine car rental with rail travel—a good option for travelers who wish both to visit cities accessible by rail and to travel in the surrounding areas. Prices range US$300-2400. Children under 11 cost US$102-500, and adding more days costs US$72-105 per day (see **By Car**, p. 49).

> **FURTHER READING & RESOURCES ON TRAIN TRAVEL.**
> **Info on rail travel and rail passes:** www.raileurope.com or www.eurail.com.
> **Point-to-point fares and schedules:** www.raileurope.com/us/rail/fares_schedules/index.htm. Allows you to calculate whether buying a rail pass would save you money.
> **Railsaver:** www.railpass.com/new. Uses your itinerary to calculate the best rail pass for your trip.
> **European Railway Server:** www.railfaneurope.net. Links to rail servers throughout Europe.
> **Thomas Cook European Timetable,** updated monthly, covers all major and most minor train routes in Europe. Buy directly from Thomas Cook (www.thomascooktimetables.com).

BY BUS

In some cases, buses prove a better option than train travel. In Britain and Hungary, the bus and train systems are on par; in the Baltics, Greece, Ireland, Spain, and Portugal, bus networks are more extensive, efficient, and often more comfortable; in Iceland and parts of northern Scandinavia, bus service is the only ground transportation available. In the rest of Europe, bus travel is more of a gamble. Scattered offerings from private companies are often cheap, but sometimes unreliable. Amsterdam, Athens, London, Munich, and Oslo are centers for lines that offer long-distance rides across Europe. **International bus passes** allow unlimited travel on a hop-on, hop-off basis between major European cities, often at cheaper prices than rail passes.

Eurolines, offices in 19 countries (UK ☎8717 81 81 81; www.eurolines.co.uk or www.eurolines.com). The largest operator of Europe-wide coach services. Unlimited 15-day (high season €329, under 26 €279; low season €199/169) or 30-day (high season €439/359; low season €299/229) travel passes offer unlimited transit among 40 major European cities. Discount passes €29 or €39.

Busabout, 258 Vauxhall Bridge Rd., London, SW1V 1BS, UK (☎020 7950 1661; www.busabout.com). Offers 3 interconnecting bus circuits. 1 loop US$639; 2 loops US$1069; 3 loops US$1319. Flexipass with 6 stops $549; additional stops $59. Also sells discounted international SIM cards. (US$9; from US$0.29 per min.)

BY CAR

Cars offer speed, freedom, access to the countryside, and an escape from the town-to-town mentality of trains. Although a single traveler won't save by renting a car, four usually will. If you can't decide between train and car travel, you may benefit from a combination of the two; RailEurope and other rail pass vendors offer rail-and-drive packages. Fly-and-drive packages are also often available from travel agents or airline/rental agency partnerships. Before setting off, know the laws of the countries in which you'll be driving (e.g., both seat belts and headlights must be on at all times in **Scandinavia**, and remember to drive on the left in **Ireland and the UK**). For an informal primer on European road signs and conventions, check out www.travlang.com/signs. The **Association for Safe International Road Travel** (ASIRT) can provide more specific information about road conditions (☎301-983-5252; www.asirt.org). ASIRT considers road travel

TRANSPORTATION

(by car or bus) to be relatively safe in Denmark, Ireland, the Netherlands, Norway, Sweden, Switzerland, and the UK, and relatively **unsafe** in Turkey and many parts of Eastern Europe. Western Europeans use **unleaded gas** almost exclusively, but it's not available in many gas stations in Eastern Europe.

RENTING A CAR

Cars can be rented from a US-based firm **(Alamo, Avis, Budget, or Hertz)** with European offices, from a European-based company with local representatives (Europcar), or from a tour operator (Auto Europe, Europe By Car, or Kemwel Holiday Autos) that will arrange a rental for you from a European company. Multinationals offer greater flexibility, but tour operators often strike better deals. Ask airlines about special fly-and-drive packages; you may get up to a week of free or discounted rental. See **Costs and Insurance**, p. 50, for more info. Minimum age requirements vary but tend to fall in the range of 21-25, with some as low as 18. There may be an additional insurance fee for drivers under 25. At most agencies, to rent a car, you'll need a driver's license from home with proof that you've had it for a year or an **International Driving Permit** (p. 51). Car rental in Europe is available through the following agencies:

Auto Europe (Canada and the US ☎888-223-5555; www.autoeurope.com).

Budget (Australia ☎1300 36 28 48, Canada ☎800-268-8900, New Zealand ☎0800 283 438, UK 87 01 56 56 56, US 800-527-0700; www.budget.com).

Europcar International (UK ☎18 70 607 5000; www.europcar.com).

Hertz (Canada and the US 800-654-3001; www.hertz.com).

COSTS AND INSURANCE

Expect to pay US$200-600 per week, plus tax (5-25%), for a tiny car with a manual transmission; automatics can double or triple the price. Larger vehicles and 4WD will also raise prices. Reserve and pay in advance if at all possible. It is less expensive to reserve a car from the US than from Europe. Rates are generally lowest in Belgium, Germany, the Netherlands, and the UK, higher in Ireland and Italy, and highest in Scandinavia and Eastern Europe. National chains often allow one-way rentals, with pick-up in one city and drop-off in another. There is usually a minimum hire period and sometimes an extra drop-off charge of several hundred dollars.

Many rental packages offer unlimited kilometers, while others offer a fixed distance per day with a per-kilometer surcharge after that. Be sure to ask whether the price includes **insurance** against theft and collision. Remember that if you are driving a conventional vehicle on an **unpaved road** in a rental car, you are almost never covered by insurance. Always check if prices quoted include tax and collision insurance; some credit cards provide insurance, allowing their customers to decline the collision damage waiver. Ask about discounts and check the terms of insurance, particularly the size of the deductible. Beware that cars rented on an **American Express or Visa/MasterCard Gold** or **Platinum** credit cards in Europe might not carry the automatic insurance that they would in some other countries. Check with your credit card company. Insurance plans almost always come with an **excess** (or deductible) for conventional vehicles; excess is usually higher for younger drivers and for 4WD. This provision means you pay for all damages up to the specified sum, unless they are the fault of another vehicle. The excess you will be quoted applies to collisions with other vehicles; other collisions ("single-vehicle collisions") will cost you even more. The excess can often be reduced or waived for an additional charge. Remember to return the car with a **full tank** of gas to avoid high fuel charges. Gas prices are generally highest in Scandinavia. Throughout Europe, fuel tends to be cheaper in cities than in outlying areas.

LEASING A CAR

Leasing can be cheaper than renting, especially for more than 17 days. It is often the only option for those aged 18 to 21. The cheapest leases are agreements to buy the car and then sell it back to the manufacturer. Leases generally include insurance coverage and are not taxed. The most affordable ones usually originate in Belgium, France, or Germany. Expect to pay US$1000-2000 for 60 days. **Renault Eurodrive** leases new cars in a tax-free package to qualifying non-EU citizens (Australia ☎9299 33 44, Canada ☎450-461-1149, New Zealand ☎0800 807 778, US ☎212-730-0676; www.renault-eurodrive.com).

BUYING A CAR

If you're brave and know what you're doing, buying a used car or van in Europe and selling it just before you leave can provide the cheapest wheels for long trips. Check with consulates for import-export laws concerning used vehicles, registration, and safety and emission standards.

ON THE ROAD

Road conditions and **regional hazards** are variable throughout Europe. Steep, curvy mountain roads may be closed in winter. Road conditions in Eastern Europe are often poor as a result of maintenance issues and inadequately enforced traffic laws. Western European roads are generally excellent, but each area has its own dangers. In Scandinavia, for example, drivers should be on the lookout for moose and elk; on the Autobahn, the threat may come from cars speeding by at 150kph. In this book, region-specific hazards are listed in country introductions. Carry emergency equipment with you (see **Driving Precautions**, below) and know what to do in case of a breakdown. Car rental companies will often have phone numbers for emergency services.

DRIVING PERMITS AND CAR INSURANCE

INTERNATIONAL DRIVING PERMIT (IDP). To drive a car in **Europe**, you must **be over 18** and have an **International Driving Permit (IDP)**, though certain countries (such as the UK) allow travelers to drive with a valid American or Canadian license for a limited number of months. It may be a good idea to get an IDP anyway, in case you're in a situation (e.g., you get in an accident or become stranded in a small town) **where the police do not know English; information on the IDP is printed in 11 languages, including French, German, Italian, Portuguese, Russian, Spanish, and Swedish**. Your IDP must be issued in your home country before you depart. An application for an IDP usually requires a photo, a current license, an additional form of identification, and a fee of around US$20. To apply, contact your country's automobile association (i.e., the AAA in the US or the CAA in Canada). Be wary of buying IDPs from unauthorized online vendors.

CAR INSURANCE. If you rent, lease, or borrow a car, you will need an International Insurance Certificate, or Green Card, to certify that you have liability insurance and that it applies abroad. Green Cards can be obtained at car rental agencies, car dealerships (for those leasing cars), some travel agents, and some border crossings. Rental agencies may require you to purchase theft insurance in countries they consider to have a high risk of auto theft.

TRANSPORTATION

DRIVING PRECAUTIONS. When traveling in summer, bring substantial amounts of **water** (5L per person per day) for drinking and for the radiator. For long drives to unpopulated areas, register with police before beginning the trip, and again upon arrival at the destination. Check with the local automobile club for details. Make sure tires are in good repair and have enough air, and get good maps. A **compass** and a **car manual** can also be very useful. Always carry a **spare tire** and **jack, jumper cables,** extra **oil, flares,** a **flashlight** (torch), and **heavy blankets** (in case your car breaks down at night or in winter). A **mobile phone** may help in an emergency. If you don't know how to change a tire, learn, especially if you're traveling in deserted areas. Blowouts on dirt roads are very common. If the car breaks down, stay with your car to wait for help.

BY CHUNNEL FROM THE UK

Traversing 27 mi. under the sea, the Chunnel is undoubtedly the fastest, most convenient, and least scenic route from England to France.

BY TRAIN. Eurostar, Eurostar House, Waterloo Station, London SE1 8SE (UK ☎08 705 186 186; www.eurostar.com) runs frequent trains between London and the continent. Ten to 28 trains per day run to 100 destinations including Paris (4hr., US$75-400, 2nd class), Disneyland Paris, Brussels, Lille, and Calais. Book online, at major rail stations in the UK, or at the office above.

BY BUS. Eurolines provides bus-ferry combinations (see p. 49).

BY CAR. Eurotunnel, Customer relations, P.O. Box 2000, Folkestone, Kent CT18 8XY (UK ☎08 705 353 535; www.eurotunnel.co.uk) shuttles cars and passengers between Kent and Nord-Pas-de-Calais. Return fares for vehicle and all passengers range from UK£223-253 with car. One-way starts at UK£49, two- to five-day return for a car UK£165-298. Book online or via phone. Travelers with cars can also look into sea crossings by ferry (see below).

BY BOAT

Most long-distance ferries are quite comfortable; the cheapest ticket typically includes a reclining chair or couchette. Fares jump sharply in July and August. ISIC holders can often get student fares, and Eurail Pass holders get reductions and sometimes free trips. You'll occasionally have to pay a port tax (around US$10). The fares below are **one-way** for **adult foot passengers** unless otherwise noted. Though standard round-trip fares are usually twice the one-way fare, **fixed-period returns** (usually within 5 days) may be cheaper. Ferries run **year-round** unless otherwise noted. Bringing a **bike** costs up to US$15 in high season.

FERRIES FROM BRITAIN AND IRELAND

Ferries are frequent and dependable. The main route across the English Channel from Britain to France is Dover-Calais. The main ferry port on England's southern coast is Portsmouth, with connections to France and Spain. Ferries also cross the Irish Sea, connecting Northern Ireland with Scotland and England, and the Republic of Ireland with Wales. See the directory online at www.seaview.co.uk/ferries.html for schedules and more information.

Brittany Ferries: UK ☎0871 2440 744, France ☎825 828 828, Spain ☎942 360 611; www.brittany-ferries.com. **Cork** to **Roscoff, FRA** (14hr.); **Plymouth** to **Roscoff, FRA** (6hr.) and **Santander, SPA** (18hr.); **Poole** to **Cherbourg, FRA** (4hr.); **Portsmouth** to **St-Malo, FRA** (10hr.) and **Caen, FRA** (5hr.).

DFDS Seaways: UK ☎0871 522 9955; www.dfdsseaways.co.uk. **Harwich** to **Cuxhaven** (19hr.) and **Esbjerg, DEN** (18hr.); **Newcastle** to **Amsterdam, NTH** (16hr.), and **Haugesund, NOR** (18hr.); **Dover** to **Calais, FRA** (1-2hr.).

Irish Ferries: Northern Ireland ☎353 818 300 400; Republic of Ireland ☎08 18 30 04 00, Great Britain ☎87 05 17 17 17; www.irishferries.com. **Rosslare** to **Pembroke** (3hr.) and **Cherbourg** or **Roscoff, FRA** (18hr.). **Holyhead** to **Dublin, IRE** (2-3hr.).

P&O Ferries: UK ☎08 705 980 333; www.poferries.com. **Dover** to **Calais, FRA** (1hr., 25 per day, UK £14); **Hull** to **Rotterdam, NTH** (10hr.) and **Zeebrugge, BEL** (12hr.).

FERRIES IN SCANDINAVIA

Ferries run to many North Sea destinations. Booking ahead is not necessary for deck passage. Baltic Sea ferries sail between Poland and Scandinavia.

Color Line: Norway ☎0810 00 811; www.colorline.com. Ferries run from 6 cities and towns in Norway to **Frederikshavn** and **Hirtshal, DEN** (€24-80); **Strömsand, SWE** (€9-22); **Kiel, GER** (€98-108). Car packages from €137. Student discounts available.

Tallinksilja Line: Finland ☎09 180 41, Sweden ☎08 22 21 40; www.tallinksilja.com. Connects Helsinki and Turku to **Sweden** (€18-116) and **Stockholm, SWE** to **Tallinn, EST** (€20-33); **Rostock, GER** (€91-133); **Riga, LAT** (€22-32). Eurail passes accepted.

Viking Line: Finland ☎0600 415 77, Sweden ☎0452 40 00; www.vikingline.fi. Ferries run between **Helsinki** and **Turku, FIN** to destinations in **Estonia** and **Sweden**. M-Th and Su cruises min. age 18, F-Sa 21. One-way €33-59. Eurail discounts available.

MEDITERRANEAN AND AEGEAN FERRIES

Mediterranean ferries may be the most glamorous, but they can also be the most turbulent. Ferries run from Spain to Morocco, from Italy to Tunisia, and from France to both Morocco and Tunisia. Reservations are recommended, especially in July and August. Schedules are erratic, with varying prices for similar routes. Shop around, and beware of small companies that don't take reservations. Ferries traverse the Adriatic from Ancona, ITA to Split, CRO and from Bari, ITA to Dubrovnik, CRO. They also cross the Aegean, from Ancona, ITA to Patras, GCE and from Bari, ITA to Igoumenitsa and Patras, GCE. **Eurail** is valid on certain ferries between Brindisi, ITA and Corfu, Igoumenitsa, and Patras, GCE. Many ferry companies operate on these routes.

BY MOPED AND MOTORCYCLE

Motorized bikes and **mopeds** don't use much gas, can be put on trains and ferries, and are a good compromise between costly car travel and the limited range of bicycles. However, they're uncomfortable for long distances, dangerous in the rain, and unpredictable on rough roads. Always wear a helmet, and never ride with a backpack. If you've never ridden a moped before, a twisting Alpine road is not the place to start. Expect to pay about US$20-35 per day; try auto repair shops, and remember to bargain. **Motorcycles** are more expensive and normally require a license, but are better for long distances. Before renting, ask if the price includes tax and insurance. Avoid handing your passport over as a deposit; if you have an accident or mechanical failure you may not get it back until you cover all repairs. Pay ahead of time instead.

BY THUMB

 WARNING. Let's Go strongly urges you to consider the risks before you choose to hitch. We do not recommend hitchhiking, and none of the information presented here is intended to do so.

No one should hitch without careful consideration of the risks involved. Hitching means entrusting your life to an unknown person and risking theft, assault, sexual harassment, and unsafe driving. However, some travelers report that hitchhiking in Europe allows them to meet locals and travel in areas where public transportation is sketchy. **Britain** and **Ireland** are probably the easiest places in Western Europe to get a lift. Hitching in **Scandinavia** is slow but steady. Long-distance hitching in the developed countries of northwestern Europe demands close attention to expressway junctions, rest stop locations, and destination signs. Hitching in southern Europe is generally mediocre. In some Eastern European countries, the line between hitching and taking a taxi is virtually nonexistent. Hitchhiking at night can be particularly dangerous; experienced hitchers stand in well-lit places. For women traveling alone or even two women traveling together, hitching is simply too dangerous. A man and a woman are a safer combination, two men will have a harder time, and three will go nowhere. Experienced hitchers pick a spot outside of built-up areas, where drivers can stop, return to the road without causing an accident, and have time to look over potential passengers as they approach. Hitching on super-highways is usually illegal: one may only thumb at rest stops or at the entrance ramps to highways. Finally, success often depends on appearance.

Most Western European countries have ride services that pair drivers with riders; fees vary according to destination. **Eurostop** (www.taxistop.be/index_ils.htm), Taxistop's ride service, is one of the largest in Europe. Also try **Allostop** in France (French-language website www.allostop.net) and **Verband der Deutschen Mitfahrzentralen** in Germany (German-language website www.mitfahrzentrale.de). Not all organizations screen drivers and riders; ask ahead.

BEYOND TOURISM

A PHILOSOPHY FOR TRAVELERS

BEYOND TOURISM HIGHLIGHTS

NURTURE endangered griffon vultures on the Cres Island in **Croatia** (p. 160).

RESTORE castles in **France** (p. 227) and **Germany** (p. 281).

POLITICK as an intern at NATO in **Belgium** (p. 86).

IMMERSE yourself in film production in the **Czech Republic** (p. 180).

As a tourist, you are always a foreigner. Sure, hostel-hopping and sightseeing can be great fun, but connecting with a foreign country through studying, volunteering, or working can extend your travels beyond tourist traps. Instead of feeling like a stranger in a strange land, you can understand Europe like a local. Instead of being that tourist asking for directions, you can be the one who gives them (and correctly!). All the while, you get the satisfaction of leaving Europe in better shape than you found it (after all, it's being nice enough to let you stay here). It's not wishful thinking—it's Beyond Tourism.

As a **volunteer** in Europe, you can unleash your inner superhero with projects from building homes in Ireland to digging up ancient treasures in Italy. This chapter is chock-full of ideas to get involved, whether you're looking to pitch in for a day or run away from home for a whole new life in European activism.

The powers of **studying** abroad are beyond comprehension: it actually makes you feel sorry for those poor tourists who don't get to do any homework while they're here; quite literally the perfect combo of academics and local culture.

Working abroad immerses you in a new culture and can bring some of the most meaningful relationships and experiences of your life. Yes, we know you're on vacation, but these aren't your normal desk jobs. (Plus, it doesn't hurt that it helps pay for more globetrotting.) If you're an EU citizen, work will be far easier to come by, but there are still options for those not so blessed.

 SHARE YOUR EXPERIENCE. Have you had a particularly enjoyable volunteer, study, or work experience that you'd like to share with other travelers? Post it to our website, www.letsgo.com!

VOLUNTEERING

Feel like saving the world this week? Volunteering can be a powerful and fulfilling experience, especially when combined with the thrill of traveling in a new place. Europe offers an endless varieties of opportunities to volunteer, with exciting choices from teaching English to ecological conservation.

Most people who volunteer in Europe do so on a short-term basis at organizations that make use of drop-in or once-a-week volunteers. The best way to find opportunities that match your interests and schedule may be to check with local or national volunteer centers. As always, read up before heading out.

Those looking for longer, more intensive volunteer opportunities usually choose to go through a parent organization that takes care of logistical details and often provides a group environment and support system—for a fee. There are two main types of organizations—religious and secular—although there are rarely restrictions on participation for either. Websites like **www.volunteerabroad.com**, **www.servenet.org**, and **www.idealist.org** allow you to search for volunteer openings both in your country and abroad.

ONLINE DIRECTORIES: VOLUNTEERING

www.alliance-network.org. Various international service organizations.

www.idealist.org. Provides extensive listings of service opportunities.

www.worldvolunteerweb.org. Lists organizations and events around the world.

COMMUNITY DEVELOPMENT

If working closely with locals and helping in a hands-on fashion appeals to you, check out community development options. Many returning travelers report that working among locals was one of their most rewarding experiences.

Global Volunteers, 375 E. Little Canada Rd., St. Paul, MN 55109, USA (☎800-487-1074; www.globalvolunteers.org). A variety of 1- to 3-week volunteer programs throughout Europe. Fees range US$2000-3000, including room and board but not airfare.

Habitat for Humanity, 121 Habitat St., Americus, GA 31709, USA (☎800-422-4828; www.habitat.org). A Christian non-profit organization coordinating 9- to 14-day service trips in Britain, Germany, Greece, Hungary, Ireland, the Netherlands, Poland, Portugal, and Switzerland. Participants aid in building homes. Program around US$1000-2200.

Service Civil International Voluntary Service (SCI-IVS), 5505 Walnut Level Rd., Crozet, VA 22932, USA (☎206-350-6585; www.sci-ivs.org). Arranges placement in 2- to 3-week outdoor service camps (workcamps), or 3-month teaching opportunities throughout Europe. 18+. Registration fee US$235, including room and board.

Volunteer Abroad, 7800 Point Meadows Dr., Ste. 218 Jacksonville, FL 32256, USA (☎720-570-1702; www.volunteerabroad.com/search.cfm). Volunteer work in Europe.

CONSERVATION

As more people realize that long-cherished habitats and structures are in danger, diverse programs have stepped in to aid the concerned in lending a hand.

Club du Vieux Manoir, Ancienne Abbaye du Moncel, 60700 Pontpoint, FRA (☎33 03 44 72 33 98; http://cvmclubduvieuxmanoir.free.fr). Offers year-long and summer programs restoring castles and churches throughout France. €15 annual membership and insurance fee. Costs €14 per day, including food and tent.

Earthwatch Institute, 3 Clock Tower Pl., Ste. 100, P.O. Box 75, Maynard, MA, 01754, USA (☎978-461-0081; www.earthwatch.org). Arranges 2-day to 3-week programs promoting the conservation of natural resources. Fees vary based on program location and duration. Costs range US$400-4000, including room and board but not airfare.

The National Trust, P.O. Box 39, Warrington, WA5 7WD, UK (☎ 44 017 938 176 32; www.nationaltrust.org.uk/volunteers). Arranges numerous volunteer opportunities, including Working Holidays. From £60 per week, including room and board.

World-Wide Opportunities on Organic Farms (WWOOF), PO Box 2154, Winslow Buckingham, MK18 3WS England, UK (www.wwoof.org). Arranges volunteer work with organic and eco-conscious farms around the world. You become a member of WWOOF in the country in which you plan to work; prices vary by country.

HUMANITARIAN AND SOCIAL SERVICES

Europe's complex, war-torn history offers up opportunities to help rebuild. Numerous peace programs can prove to be fulfilling for volunteers.

Brethren Volunteer Service (BVS), 1451 Dundee Ave., Elgin, IL 60120, USA (☎800-323-8039; www.brethrenvolunteerservice.org). Peace and social justice based programs. Minimum commitment of 2 yr., must be 21 to serve overseas. US$75 fee for background check; US$500 fee for international volunteers.

Simon Wiesenthal Center, 1399 South Roxbury Dr., Los Angeles, CA 90035, USA (☎800-900-9036; www.wiesenthal.org). Fights anti-Semitism and Holocaust denial throughout Europe. Small, discretionary donation required for membership.

Volunteers for Peace, 1034 Tiffany Rd., Belmont, VT 05730, USA (☎802-259-2759; www.vfp.org). Arranges placement in camps throughout Europe. US$30 membership required for registration. Programs average US$250-500 for 2-3 weeks.

I HAVE TO PAY TO VOLUNTEER? Many volunteers are surprised to learn that some organizations require large fees or "donations," but don't go calling them scams just yet. While such fees may seem ridiculous at first, they often keep the organization afloat, covering airfare, room, board, and administrative expenses for the volunteers. If you're concerned about how a program spends its fees, request an annual report or finance account. A reputable organization won't refuse to inform you of how volunteer money is spent. Pay-to-volunteer programs might be a good idea for young travelers who are looking for more support and structure (such as pre-arranged transportation and housing) or anyone who would rather not deal with the uncertainty of creating a volunteer experience from scratch.

STUDYING

It's hard to dread the first day of school when London is your campus and exotic restaurants are your meal plan. A growing number of students report that studying abroad is the highlight of their learning careers. If you've never studied abroad, you don't know what you're missing—and, if you have studied abroad, you do know what you're missing.

Study-abroad programs range from basic language and culture courses to university-level classes, often for college credit (it's legit, Mom and Dad). In order to choose a program that best fits your needs, research as much as you can before making your decision—determine costs and duration as well as what kinds of students participate in the program and what sorts of accommodations are provided. (Since when was back-to-school shopping this fun?)

In programs that have large groups of students who speak the same language, there is a trade-off. You may feel more comfortable in the community, but you will not have the same opportunity to practice a foreign language or to befriend other international students. For accommodations, dorm life provides a better opportunity to mingle with fellow students, but there is less of a chance to experience the local scene. If you live with a family, you could potentially build lifelong friendships with natives and experience day-to-day life in more depth, but you might also get stuck sharing a room with their pet iguana. Conditions can vary greatly from family to family.

UNIVERSITIES

Most university-level study-abroad programs are conducted in the local language, although many programs offer classes in English as well as lower-level language courses. Savvy linguists may find it cheaper to enroll directly in a university abroad, although getting college credit may be more difficult. You can search online at www.studyabroad.com for various semester-abroad programs that meet your criteria, including your desired location and focus of study. If you're a college student, your friendly neighborhood study-abroad office is often a great resource, and the best place to start.

ONLINE DIRECTORIES: STUDY ABROAD

These websites are good resources for finding programs that cater to your particular interests. Each has links to various study-abroad programs broken down by a variety of criteria, including desired location and focus of study.

www.petersons.com/stdyabrd/sasector.html. Lists study-abroad programs at accredited institutions that usually offer cross credits.

www.studyabroad.com. A great starting point for finding college- or high-school-level programs in foreign languages or specific academic subjects. Also includes information for teaching and volunteering opportunities.

www.westudyabroad.com. Lists language courses and college-level programs.

AMERICAN PROGRAMS

The following is a list of organizations that can either help place students in university programs abroad or that have their own branch in Europe.

American Institute for Foreign Study, College Division, River Plaza, 9 W. Broad St., Stamford, CT 06902, USA (☎800-727-2437; www.aifsabroad.com). Organizes programs for high school and college study at universities in Austria, Britain, the Czech Republic, France, Hungary, Ireland, Italy, Russia, and Spain. Summer programs US$4900-6500; Semester-long programs US$11,000-16,000. Scholarships available.

Council on International Educational Exchange (CIEE), 7 Custom House St., 3rd fl., Portland, ME, 04101, USA (☎800-407-8839; www.ciee.org/study). Sponsors work, volunteer, academic, and internship programs in Belgium, Britain, the Czech Republic, France, Hungary, Ireland, Italy, the Netherlands, Spain, and Turkey for around US$14,000 per semester. Also offers volunteer opportunities. US$30 application fee.

International Association for the Exchange of Students for Technical Experience (IAESTE), 10400 Little Patuxent Pkwy. Ste. 250, Columbia, MD 21044, USA (☎410-997-3068; www.iaeste.org). Offers 8- to 12-week internships in Europe for college students who have completed 2 years study in a particular trade.

School for International Training, College Semester Abroad, Kipling Rd., P.O. Box 676, Brattleboro, VT 05302, USA (☎888-272-7881 or 802-258-7751; www.sit.edu/studyabroad). Programs in Europe cost around US$10,000-16,000. Also runs The Experiment in International Living (☎800-345-2929; fax 802-258-3428; www.usexperiment.org), 3- to 5-week summer programs that offer high school students homestays, community service, ecological adventure, and language training in Europe for US$5900-7000.

AUSTRALIAN PROGRAMS

The following organizations place Australian students in programs in Europe.

**World Exchange Program Australia, (☎1 300 884 733; www.wep.org.au). Places Australian high school students for 3 months to 1 year in high schools abroad. Group study tours also available. Costs for one semester in Europe are AUS$8950-6290.

**Innovative Universities European Union Centre (IUEU), (☎298 507 915 ; www.iueu. edu.au). Offers undergraduates from Flinders, La Trobe and Macquarie universities a chance to study abroad for one semester in their Global Citizenship program.

LANGUAGE SCHOOLS

Enrolling at a language school has two major perks: a slightly less rigorous courseload and the ability to learn exactly what those kids in Mainz are calling you under their breath. There can be great variety in language schools—independently run, affiliated with a large university, local, international—but one thing is constant: they rarely offer college credit. Their programs are also good for younger high-school students who might not feel comfortable with older students in a university program. Some worthwhile organizations include:

Association of Commonwealth Universities (ACU), Woburn House, 20-24 Tavistock Sq., London WC1H 9HF, UK (☎020 7380 6700; www.acu.ac.uk). Publishes information about Commonwealth Universities, including those in Cyprus and the UK.

Eurocentres, Seestr. 247, CH-8038 Zürich, SWI (☎41 1 485 50 40; www.eurocentres. com). Language programs for beginning to advanced students with homestays in Britain, France, Germany, Ireland, Italy, Spain, and Switzerland.

Language Immersion Institute, SCB 106, State University of New York at New Paltz, 1 Hawk Dr., New Paltz, NY 12561, USA (☎845-257-3500; www.newpaltz.edu/lii). 2-week summer language courses and some overseas courses in French, German, Greek, Hungarian, Italian, Polish, Portugese, Spanish, and Swedish. Around US$1000 for a 2-week course, not including accommodations.

Sprachcaffe Languages Plus, 413 Ontario St., Toronto, ON M5A 2V9, CAN (☎888-526-4758; www.sprachcaffe.com). Language classes in France, Germany, Italy, the Netherlands, and Spain for US$200-500 per week. Homestays available. Also offers French and Spanish language and travel programs for teenagers.

WORKING

Nowhere does money grow on trees (though *Let's Go*'s researchers aren't done looking), but there are still some pretty good opportunities to earn a living and travel at the same time. As with volunteering, work opportunities tend to fall into two categories. Some travelers want long-term jobs that allow them to integrate into a community, while others seek out short-term jobs to finance the next leg of their travels. In Europe, people who want to work long-term should look for jobs like teaching English, taking care of local children, and other opportunities that can be found through a bit of research and luck. People looking for short term work have options like picking fruit and working for summer programs abroad. **Transitions Abroad** (www.transitionsabroad.com) also offers updated online listings for work over any time span.

Employment opportunities for those who want short-term work may be more limited and are generally contingent upon the city or region's economic needs. In addition to local papers, international English-language newspapers, such as the International Herald Tribune (www.iht.com), often list job opportunities in their classified sections. If applicable, travelers should also consult federally run employment offices. Note that working abroad often requires a special work visa; see the box below for info about obtaining one.

> **VISA INFORMATION. EU Citizens:** The EU's 2004 and 2007 enlargements led the 15 previous member states (EU-15) to fear that waves of Eastern European immigrants would flood their labor markets. This fear caused some members of the union to institute a transition period of up to seven years during which citizens of the new EU countries may still need a visa or permit to work. EU-15 citizens generally have the right to work in the pre-enlargement countries for up to three months without a visa; longer-term employment usually requires a work permit. By law, all EU-15 citizens are given equal consideration for jobs not directly related to national security.
> **Everyone else:** Getting a work visa in Europe is difficult for non-EU citizens. Different countries have varying policies for granting work permits to those from non-EU countries. It is possible for students to work part-time without a work permit in some countries. In 2007, the EU introduced the "blue card" program, aimed at long term, skilled workers, which requires an employment contract in place before immigration.

LONG-TERM WORK

If you're planning to spend more than three months working in Europe, search for a job well in advance. International placement agencies are often the easiest way to find employment abroad, especially for those interested in teaching English. Although often only available to college students, **internships** are a good way to segue into working abroad; although they are often un- or underpaid, many say the experience is well worth it. Be wary of advertisements for companies claiming to be able get you a job abroad for a fee—often the same listings are available online or in newspapers. Some organizations include:

Escapeartist.com (jobs.escapeartist.com). International employers post directly to this website; various jobs in European countries advertised.

International Cooperative Education, 15 Spiros Way, Menlo Park, CA, 94025, USA (☎650-323-4944; www.icemenlo.com). Finds summer jobs in Belgium, Britain, Germany, and Switzerland. $250 application fee and $700 placement fee.

StepStone (www.stepstone.com, branches across Europe listed at www.stepstone.com/EN/Company/Locations). Database covering international employment in Austria, Belgium, Britain, Denmark, France, Germany, Italy, the Netherlands, Norway, Portugal, and Sweden. Several search options and a list of openings.

TEACHING ENGLISH

While some elite private American schools offer competitive salaries, let's just say that teaching jobs abroad pay more in personal satisfaction and emotional fulfillment than in actual cash. Perhaps this is why volunteering as a teacher instead of getting paid is a popular option. Even then, teachers often receive some sort of a daily stipend to help with living expenses. For countries that have a low cost of living, even though salaries at private schools may be low compared to those in the US, the low cost of living makes it much more profitable. In almost all cases, you must have at least a bachelor's degree to be a full-fledged teacher, although college undergraduates can often get summer positions teaching or tutoring. Many schools require teachers to have a **Teaching English as a Foreign Language (TEFL)** certificate. You may still be able to find a teaching job without one, but certified teachers often find higher-paying jobs.

Those who can't speak the local language don't have to give up their dream of teaching, either. Private schools usually hire native English speakers for English-immersion classrooms where no local language is spoken. (Teachers in public schools will more likely work in both English and the local language.) Placement agencies or university fellowship programs are the best resources for finding teaching jobs. The alternative is to contact schools directly or to try your luck once you arrive in Europe. In the latter case, the best time to look is several weeks before the start of the school year. The following organizations are extremely helpful in placing teachers in Europe.

International Schools Services (ISS), 15 Roszel Rd., P.O. Box 5910, Princeton, NJ 08543, USA (☎609-452-0990; www.iss.edu). Hires teachers for more than 200 international and American schools around the world; candidates should have 2 years teaching experience and/or teacher certification. 2-year commitment expected.

Teaching English as a Foreign Language (TEFL), TEFL Professional Network Ltd., 72 Pentyla Baglan Rd., Port Talbot, SA12 8AD, UK (www.tefl.com). Maintains an extensive database of openings throughout Europe. Offers job training and certification.

AU PAIR WORK

Au pairs are typically women aged 18-27 who work as live-in nannies, caring for children and doing light housework in foreign countries in exchange for room, board, and a small spending allowance or stipend. One perk of the job is that it allows you to get to know Europe without the high expenses of traveling. Drawbacks, however, can include mediocre pay and long hours. Average weekly pay will vary depending on location. Much of the au pair experience depends on the family with which you are placed. The agencies below are a good starting point for looking for employment.

Childcare International, Ltd., Trafalgar House, Grenville Pl., London NW7 3SA (☎44 020 8906 3116; www.childint.co.uk). Offers au pair and nanny placement.

InterExchange, 161 6th Ave., New York, NY, 10013, USA (☎212-924-0446; www.interexchange.org). Au pair, internship, and short-term work placement in France, Germany, the Netherlands, and Spain. US$495-595 placement fee and US$75 application fee.

Sunny AuPairs (☎44 020 8144 1635, in US 503-616-3026; www.sunnyaupairs.com). Online, worldwide database connecting au pairs with families. No placement fee.

SHORT-TERM WORK

Believe it or not, traveling for long periods of time can be hard on the wallet. Many travelers try their hand at odd jobs for a few weeks at a time to help pay for another month or two of touring around. Work options vary across the continent, but work possibilities might include picking fruit, serving, or opportunities through keeping an ear out for wherever labor is needed. Another popular option is to work several hours a day at a hostel in exchange for free or discounted room and/or board. Most often, these short-term jobs are found by word of mouth or by expressing interest to the owner of a hostel or restaurant. Due to high turnover in the tourism industry, many places are eager for help,

B E Y O N D   T O U R I S M

even if it is only temporary. Let's Go lists temporary jobs of this nature whenever possible, but recommends checking the work restrictions of your visa.

FURTHER READING ON BEYOND TOURISM

Alternatives to the Peace Corps: A Guide of Global Volunteer Opportunities, by Paul Backhurst. Food First Books, 2005.

The Back Door Guide to Short-Term Job Adventures: Internships, Summer Jobs, Seasonal Work, Volunteer Vacations, and Transitions Abroad, by Michael Landes. Ten Speed Press, 2005.

Green Volunteers: The World Guide to Voluntary Work in Nature Conservation, ed. Fabio Ausenda. Universe, 2007.

How to Get a Job in Europe, by Cheryl Matherly and Robert Sanborn. Planning Communications, 2003.

International Job Finder: Where the Jobs Are Worldwide, by Daniel Lauber and Kraig Rice. Planning Communications, 2002.

Live and Work Abroad: A Guide for Modern Nomads, by Huw Francis and Michelyne Callan. Vacation-Work Publications, 2001.

Short-Term Adventures That Will Benefit You and Others, by Doug Cutchins, Anne Geissinger, and Bill McMillon. Chicago Review Press, 2006.

Work Your Way Around the World, by Susan Griffith. Vacation-Work Publications, 2007.

BEYOND TOURISM

AUSTRIA
(ÖSTERREICH)

With Vienna's high culture and the Alps's high mountains, Austria offers different extremes of beauty. Many of the world's most famous composers and thinkers, including Mozart and Freud, called Austria home. Today, its small villages brim with locally brewed beer, jagged peaks draw hikers and skiers, and magnificent palaces, museums, and concerts are omnipresent. Stroll along the blue Danube River or relax in a Viennese coffeehouse and listen to a waltz.

DISCOVER AUSTRIA: SUGGESTED ITINERARIES

THREE DAYS Spend all three days in **Vienna** (p. 67). From the stately **Stephansdom** to the majestic **Hofburg Palace**, Vienna's many attractions will leave you with enough sensory stimulation to last you until your next trip.

ONE WEEK Begin in **Salzburg** (3 days; p. 80) to see the home of Mozart and the **Salzburger Festspiele** (p. 67). End your trip by basking in the glory of **Vienna** (4 days) and its famous streetside cafe culture.

ESSENTIALS

FACTS AND FIGURES

OFFICIAL NAME: Republic of Austria.

CAPITAL: Vienna.

MAJOR CITIES: Graz, Innsbruck, Salzburg.

POPULATION: 8,205,000.

LAND AREA: 82,400 sq. km.

TIME ZONE: GMT +1.

LANGUAGE: German.

RELIGIONS: Roman Catholic 74%, Protestant 5%, Muslim 4%, Other/None 17%.

PERCENTAGE OF AUSTRIA'S LAND AREA COVERED BY THE ALPS: 62.

WHEN TO GO

Between November and March, prices in western Austria double and travelers need reservations months in advance. The situation reverses in the summer, when the eastern half of the country fills with tourists. Accommodations are cheaper and less crowded in the shoulder seasons (May-June and Sept.-Oct.). Cultural opportunities also vary with the seasons: the Vienna State Opera, like many other theaters, has no shows in July or August, and the Vienna Boys' Choir only performs May-June and Sept.-Oct.

DOCUMENTS AND FORMALITIES

EMBASSIES. Foreign embassies in Austria are in Vienna (p. 67). Austrian embassies abroad include: **Australia,** 12 Talbot St., Forrest, Canberra, ACT, 2603 (☎02 6295 1533; www.austriaemb.org.au); **Canada,** 445 Wilbrod St., Ottawa, ON, K1N 6M7 (☎613-789-1444; www.austro.org); **Ireland,** 15 Ailesbury Ct., 93 Ailesbury Rd., Dublin, 4 (☎01 269 45 77); **New Zealand,** Level 2, Willbank House, 57 Willis St., Wellington, 6001 (☎04 499 63 93); **UK,** 18 Belgrave Mews West, London, SW1X 8HU (☎020 7344 3250; www.bmaa.gv.at/london); **US,** 3524 International Ct., NW, Washington, D.C., 20008 (☎202-895-6700; www.austria.org).

VISA AND ENTRY INFORMATION. EU citizens do not need a visa. Citizens of Australia, Canada, New Zealand, and the US do not need a visa for stays of up to 90 days, beginning upon entry into any of the countries in the EU's freedom-of-movement zone. For more info, see p. 14. For stays of longer than 90 days, all non-EU citizens need visas, available at Austrian embassies. For American citizens, visas are $80 or free of charge for students studying abroad.

TOURIST SERVICES AND MONEY

EMERGENCY	Ambulance: ☎144. Fire: ☎122. Police: ☎133.

TOURIST OFFICES. For general info, contact the **Austrian National Tourist Office,** Margaretenstr. 1, A-1040 Vienna (☎588 66 287; www.austria.info). All tourist offices are marked with a green "i"; most brochures are available in English.

MONEY. The **euro (€)** has replaced the **schilling** as the unit of currency in Austria. As a general rule, it's cheaper to exchange money in Austria than at home. Railroad stations, airports, hotels, and most travel agencies offer exchange services, as do banks. If you stay in hostels and prepare most of your own food, expect to spend €30-60 per day. Accommodations start at about €12 and a basic sit-down meal usually costs around €8. Menus will say whether service is included (*Preise inklusive* or *Bedienung inklusiv*); if it is, a tip is not expected. If not, 10% will do. Austrian restaurants expect you to seat yourself, and servers will not bring the bill until you ask them to do so. Say "*Zahlen bitte*" (TSAHL-en BIT-uh) to settle your accounts, and give tips directly to the server. Don't expect to bargain, except at street markets.

Austria has a **20% value added tax (VAT),** a sales tax applied to most purchased goods (p. 19). The prices given in *Let's Go* include VAT. In an airport upon exiting the EU, non-EU citizens can claim a refund on the tax paid for goods purchased at participating stores. In order to qualify for a refund in a store, you must spend at least €75; make sure to ask for a refund form when you pay. For more info on qualifying for a VAT refund, see p. 19.

TRANSPORTATION

BY PLANE. The only major international airport is Vienna's **Schwechat-Flughafen (VIE).** Other airports are in Innsbruck, Graz, Linz, and Salzburg. From London-Stansted, **Ryanair** (☎3531 249 7791; www.ryanair.com) flies to the latter three. For more info on flying to Austria, see p. 42.

BY TRAIN. The **Österreichische Bundesbahn** (ÖBB; www.oebb.at), Austria's state railroad, operates an efficient system with fast and comfortable **trains.** Eurail and InterRail passes are valid in Austria, but they do not guarantee a seat

without a reservation. The **Austria Rail** pass allows three to eight days of travel within any 15-day period on all rail lines. It also entitles holders to 40% off **bike rentals** at train stations (2nd-class US$148 for three days).

BY BUS. The Austrian **bus system** consists mainly of PostBuses, which cover areas inaccessible by train for comparably high prices. Buy tickets at the station or from the driver. For information, call ☎43 17 11 01 from abroad or ☎0810 222 333 within Austria from 7am-8pm.

BY CAR. Driving is a convenient way to see the more isolated parts of Austria, but gas is costly, an international license is required, and some small towns prohibit cars. The roads are well maintained and well marked, and Austrian drivers are quite careful. **Mitfahrzentralen** (ride-share services) in larger cities pair drivers with riders for a small fee. Riders then negotiate fares with the drivers. Be aware that not all organizations screen their participants; ask ahead.

BY BIKE. Bicycles are a great way to get around Austria, as roads in the country are generally smooth and safe. Many train stations rent **bikes** and allow you to return them to any participating station.

KEEPING IN TOUCH

PHONE CODES	**Country code:** 43. **International dialing prefix:** 00 (for Vienna, dial 00 431). For more info on how to place international calls, see **Inside Back Cover.**

EMAIL AND THE INTERNET. It's easy to find **Internet** cafes (€2-6 per hr.) in Austria, especially in larger cities. In small towns, however, cafes are less frequent and may charge more. Ask at a hostel or tourist office for suggestions.

TELEPHONES. Wherever possible, use a **calling card** for international phone calls, as long-distance rates for national phone services are often exorbitant. Prepaid phone cards and major credit cards can be used for direct international calls but are still less cost-efficient. For info on **mobile phones,** see p. 29. The most popular companies are A1, One, and T-mobile. Direct-dial access numbers for calling out of Austria include: **AT&T Direct** (☎0800 200 288); **British Telecom** (☎0800 890 043); **Canada Direct** (☎0800 200 217); **MCI WorldPhone** (☎0800 999 762); **Sprint** (☎0800 200 236); **Telecom New Zealand** (☎0800 200 222),

MAIL. Letters take one or two days within Austria. Airmail (€1.40) to North America takes four to seven days, and up to nine days to Australia and New Zealand. Mark all **letters** and packages *"mit Flugpost"* (airmail). Aerogrammes are the cheapest option. To receive mail in Austria, have mail delivered **Poste Restante.** Mail will go to the main post office unless you specify a subsidiary by street address. Address mail to be held according to the following example: LAST NAME, First name, Postlagernde Briefe, Postal code City, AUSTRIA.

ACCOMMODATIONS AND CAMPING

AUSTRIA	❶	❷	❸	❹	❺
ACCOMMODATIONS	under €16	€16-26	€27-34	€35-55	over €55

Always ask if your lodging provides a **guest card** *(Gästekarte)*, which grants discounts on activities, museums, and public transportation. The **Österreichischer Jugendherbergsverband-Hauptverband (ÖJH)** runs the over 80 **HI hostels** in Austria. Because of the rigorous standards of the national organization, these are usually very clean and orderly. Most charge €18-25 per night for dorms, with a €3-5 HI discount. **Independent hostels** vary in quality, but often have more personality and foster a lively backpacking culture. Slightly more expensive **Pensionen** are similar to American and British B&Bs. In small to mid-sized towns, singles will cost about €20-30, but expect to pay twice as much in big cities. **Hotels** are expensive (singles over €35; doubles over €48). Cheaper options have "Gasthof," "Gästehaus," or "Pension-Garni" in the name. Renting a **Privatzimmer** (room in a family home) is an inexpensive option. Contact the tourist office about rooms (€16-30). **Camping** in Austria is less about getting out into nature than having a cheap place to sleep; most sites are large plots glutted with RVs and are open in summer only. Prices run €10-15 per tent site and €5-8 per extra person. In the high Alps, hikers and mountaineers can retire to the well-maintained system of **Hütten** (mountain huts) where traditional Austrian fare and a good night's rest await them. Reserve ahead.

HIKING AND SKIING. Almost every town has hiking trails in its vicinity; consult the local tourist office. Trails are marked with either a red-white-red marker (only sturdy boots and hiking poles necessary) or a blue-white-blue marker (mountaineering equipment needed). Because of snow, most mountain hiking trails and mountain huts are open only from late June to early September. Western Austria is one of the world's best skiing regions; the area around Innsbruck is full of runs. High season is November to March.

FOOD AND DRINK

AUSTRIA	❶	❷	❸	❹	❺
FOOD AND DRINK	under €5	€5-10	€11-16	€17-25	over €25

Loaded with fat, salt, and cholesterol, traditional Austrian cuisine is bad for your skin, your heart, and your figure. *Wienerschnitzel* is a breaded meat cutlet (usually veal or pork) fried in butter. Natives nurse their sweet teeth with *Sacher Torte* (a rich chocolate cake layered with marmalade) and *Linzer Torte* (a light yellow cake with currant jam). Austrian beers are outstanding—try Stiegl, a Salzburg brew; Zipfer, from Upper Austria; and Styrian Gösser.

 EAT YOUR VEGGIES. Vegetarians should look on the menu for Spätzle (noodles), Eierschwammerl (yellow mushrooms), or anything with "Vegi" in it.

HOLIDAYS AND FESTIVALS

Holidays: Just about everything closes on public holidays. New Year's Day (Jan. 1); Epiphany (Jan. 6); Easter (Apr. 13); Labor Day (May 1); Ascension (May 21); Corpus Christi (June 11); Assumption (Aug. 15); Austrian National Day (Oct. 26); All Saints' Day (Nov. 1); Immaculate Conception (Dec. 8); Christmas (Dec. 25); Boxing Day (Dec. 26).

Festivals: Vienna celebrates *Fasching* (Carnival) from New Year's until the start of Lent. Austria's most famous summer music festivals are the *Wiener Festwochen* (early May to mid-June; www.festwochen.at) and the *Salzburger Festspiele* (late July-late August; www.salzburgerfestspiele.at).

BEYOND TOURISM

Austria caters more to tourism than volunteerism; there are only limited opportunities to give back, so your best bet is to find them through a placement service. Short-term work abound at hotels, ski resorts, and farms. For more info on opportunities across Europe, see **Beyond Tourism,** p. 55.

Actilingua Academy, Glorietteg. 8, A-1130 Vienna (☎431 877 6701; www.actilingua.com). Study German in Vienna (from €419) for 2 to 4 weeks, with accommodation in dorms, apartments, or with a host family.

Bergwald Projekt/Mountain Forest Project, Hauptstr. 24, 7014 Trin (☎081 630 4145; www.bergwaldprojekt.ch). Organizes week-long conservation projects in the forests of Austria, Germany, and Switzerland.

Concordia, 19 North Street, Portslade, Brighton, BN41 1DH, UK (☎012 7342 2218; www.concordia-iye.org.uk). British volunteer organization that directs community projects in Austria, which have in the past included renovating historic buildings and parks and directing a youth drama project.

VIENNA (WIEN) ☎01

War, marriage, and Hapsburg maneuvering transformed Vienna (pop. 1,700,000) from a Roman camp along the Danube into Europe's political linchpin, engendering a culture of luxury and intrigue that lingers today. Beethoven and Mozart made Vienna an everlasting arbiter of high culture, and the tradition continues with the city's prestigious orchestras and world-class museums. Freud, Klimt, and Kafka gave voice to the unique energy that drives the city's art and culture forward. Its dozens of coffeehouses radiate artistic and intellectual energy—on any given afternoon, cafes turn the sidewalks into a sea of umbrellas while bars and clubs pulse with techno and indie rock until dawn.

✈ INTERCITY TRANSPORTATION

Flights: Wien-Schwechat Flughafen (VIE; ☎01 700 70; www.viennaairport.com), 18km from the city center, is home to **Austrian Airlines** (☎01 517 89; www.aua. com). The **S-Bahn** (☎65 17 17) stops at Wien Mitte (30min., 2-3 per hr., €3). The **Vienna Airport Lines bus** (☎930 00 23 00) goes to Südbahnhof (20min.) and West-bahnhof (40min.; 2 per hr.; €6, round-trip €11). The **City Airport Train (CAT;** ☎01 25 250; www.cityairporttrain.com) takes only 16min. to reach Wien Mitte (2 per hr. 6:05am-11:35pm; online €8, round-trip €15; from a ticket machine €9, round-trip €16; on board €10, children up to 14 free; Eurail not valid).

Budget Airlines: M.R. Štefánik International Airport (BTS; ☎421 2 3303 3353; www. letiskobratislava.sk) in Bratislava, Slovakia serves as a gateway to Western Europe. In addition to domestic flights from Slovakia, budget airlines **SkyEurope** (☎48 50 11 11; www.skyeurope.com) and **Ryanair** (www.ryanair.com; see **Transportation,** p. 42) run shuttle buses to and from Vienna (1-1½hr., 7-8 per day, 363Sk). Vienna-bound **trains** (☎20 29 11 11; www.zsr.sk) depart from **Bratislava Hlavná Stanica** every hr. (1hr., round-trip 283Sk). **Buses** make a similar journey, leaving from **Mlynské nivy 31** (1hr., every hr., 400Sk). Another option is to sail to Vienna (1hr., 2 per day, 150Sk) with **Lodná osobná doprava,** Fajnorovo nábr. 2 (☎52 93 22 26; open daily 8:30am-5:30pm).

Trains: Vienna has 2 train stations with international connections. Call ☎05 17 17 or check www.oebb.at for detailed train info. Credit cards accepted.

Westbahnhof, XV, Mariahilferstr. 132. Info counter open daily 7:30am-9pm. Trains go to: **Innsbruck** (4-5hr., 7 per day, €54); **Salzburg** (2-3hr., every hr., €43); **Amsterdam, NTH** (12hr., 4 per day, €135); **Berlin, DEU** (9-11hr., every 2hr., €100-130); **Budapest, HUN** (3hr., 17 per day, €36); **Hamburg, DEU** (9-12hr., 6 per day, €80); **Munich, DEU** (5hr., 10 per day, €72); **Paris, FRA** (14-24hr., 2 per day, €70-160); **Zürich, CHE** (9hr., 3 per day, €88).

Südbahnhof, X, Wiener Gürtel 1a. Info counter open daily 7am-8pm. Trains go south and east to: **Graz** (2hr., every hr., €30); **Kraków, POL** (7hr., 4 per day, €46); **Prague, CZR** (4-5hr., 8 per day, €44); **Rome, ITA** (13-18hr., 6 per day, €75-100); **Venice, ITA** (7-11hr., 6 per day, €50-70).

Buses: Buses in Austria are rarely cheaper than trains; compare prices before buying a ticket. **Postbus** (☎0810 222 333; www.postbus.at) provides regional bus service and **Eurolines** (☎798 29 00; www.eurolines.at) connects to international destinations. Buses leave from the city stations at **Erdberg, Floridsdorf, Heiligenstadt, Hütteldorf, Kagran, Reumannplatz,** and **Wien Mitte/Landstraße.**

⚞ ORIENTATION

Vienna is divided into 23 **Bezirke** (districts). District numbering begins in the city center, **Innenstadt.** The borders of the center, the **Ringstraße** (ring road) on three sides and the Danube Canal on the fourth, were originally the location of a wall that protected the city from invaders. At the center of the Innenstadt lies **Stephansplatz** and the pedestrian district. The best way to reach Innenstadt is to take the U-bahn to Stephanspl. (U1, U3) or **Karlsplatz** (U1, U2, U4); **Schwedenplatz** (U1, U4) is close to the city's nightlife. Tram lines 1 and 2 circle the Innenstadt on the Ringstr., with line 2 heading clockwise and 1 counterclockwise.

The **Ringstraße** consists of different segments, such as Opernring and Kärnt-ner Ring. Many of Vienna's attractions lie within District I, right in the center and immediately around the Ringstr. Districts II-IX spread out from the city center following the clockwise traffic of the Ring. The remaining districts expand from yet another ring road, the **Gürtel** (Belt). Similar to the Ring, this major thoroughfare has numerous segments, including Margaretengürtel, Neu-baugürtel, and Währinger Gürtel. Like Vienna's street signs, *Let's Go* indicates the district number in Roman/Arabic numerals before the street and number.

◪ LOCAL TRANSPORTATION

Public Transportation: Wiener Linien (☎790 91 00; www.wienerlinien.at). The **U-Bahn** (subway), **Straßenbahn** (tram), **S-Bahn** (elevated tram), and **bus lines** operate on a 1-ticket system, so you can transfer between modes of transportation without having to buy a new ticket. Purchase tickets at a counter, machine, on board, or at a tobacco shop (trafik). A **single fare** (€1.70 in advance, €2.20 on board) lets you travel to any destination in the city and switch from bus to U-Bahn to tram to S-Bahn in any order, provided your travel is uninterrupted. Other ticket options include a **1-day pass** (€5.70), **3-day rover ticket** (€14), **7-day pass** (valid M 9am to the next M 9am; €14), and an **8-day pass**(valid any 8 days, not necessarily consecutive; can be split between several people, but must be validated for each person; €27). The **Vorteilscard** (Vienna Card; €19) allows for 72hr. of travel and discounts at museums and sights, and can be pur-chased at the ticket office and hotels. To avoid a €60 fine from plainclothes inspectors, **validate your ticket** by punching it in the machine. Tickets need only be stamped once. Regular trams and subway cars do not run midnight-5am. **Night buses** run 2 per hr., 12:30-4:30am, along most routes; "N" signs designate night bus stops. A night bus schedule and **discount passes** are available from Wiener Linien info offices (open M-F 6:30am-6:30pm, Sa-Su 8:30am-4pm) in the Karlspl., Stephanspl., Westbahnhof, and some other U-Bahn stations, and at the **tourist office** (see below).

Taxis: ☎313 00, ☎401 00, ☎601 60, or ☎814 00. Stands at Südbahnhof, Karlspl. in the city center, Westbahnhof, and by the Bermuda Dreieck. Rates outside the city are not regulated, and should be negotiated. **Accredited taxis** have yellow-and-black signs on the roof. Base rate M-Sa €2.50 plus €0.20 per 0.2km; base rate Su 11pm-6am €3; holidays slightly more expensive. €2.50 surcharge for calling a taxi.

Bike Rental: Pedal Power, II, Ausstellungsstr. 3 (☎01 729 72 34; www.pedalpower. at). €17 per 4hr., €28 per day, students €14/€21. Delivery available. 2½hr. guided tours in English and German. €23, students €17. Open daily May-Sept. 8am-7pm; Mar.-Apr. and Oct. 8am-6pm.

◪ PRACTICAL INFORMATION

Tourist Office: I, Albertinapl. (☎01 245 55; www.vienna.info), on the corner of Maysed-erg. Follow Operng. up 1 block from the Opera House and look for the massive sign above the corner. Books rooms with €2.90 fee. Open daily 9am-7pm.

Embassies and Consulates: Australia, IV, Mattiellistr. 2-4 (☎01 50 67 40). Open M-F 8:30am-4:30pm. **Canada,** I, Laurenzerberg 2 (☎01 531 38 30 00). Open M-F 8:30am-12:30pm and 1:30-3:30pm. **Ireland,** I, Rotenturmstr. 16-18, 5th fl. (☎01 715 42 46). Open M-F 9:30-11am and 1:30-4pm. **New Zealand,** III, Salesianerg. 15 (☎01 318 85 05). **UK,** III, Jaurèesg. 10 (☎01 716 13 53 33, after hours for UK nationals in emergencies only ☎0676 569 40 12). Open M-F 9:15am-12:30pm and 2-3:30pm. **US,** X, Boltzmanng. 16 (☎01 31 33 90). Open M-F 8-11:30am. 24hr. emergency services.

Currency Exchange and Banks: ATMs are your best bet. Nearly all accept Cirrus/MC/V. **Banks** generally give the best available exchange rate. Most open M-W and F 8am-3pm, Th 8am-5:30pm. **Train station** exchanges have long hours (daily 7am-10pm at the Westbahnhof), but charge 1% with a €6 minimum fee. Stay away from the 24hr. bill-exchange machines in Innenstadt, as they generally charge outrageous fees.

Luggage Storage: Lockers available at all train stations. €2-3.50 per 24hr.

Emergency: ☎141.

24hr. Pharmacy: ☎15 50. Consulates have lists of English-speaking doctors.

Hospital: Allgemeines Krankenhaus, IX, Währinger Gürtel 18-20 (☎01 40 40 00).

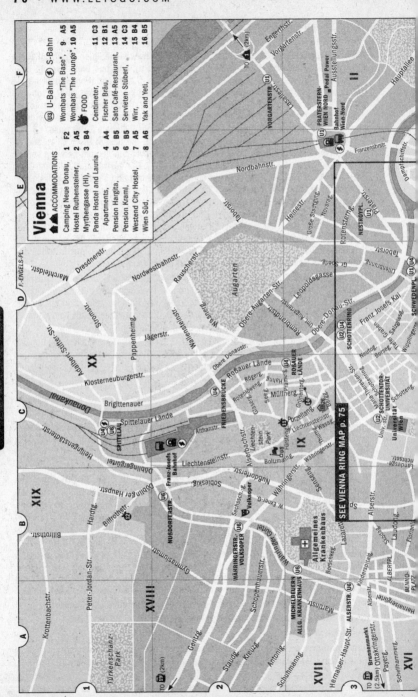

Vienna

▲▲ ACCOMMODATIONS

Camping Neue Donau,	**1** F2
Hostel Ruthensteiner,	**2** A5
Mythengasse (HI),	**3** B4
Panda Hostel and Lauria	
Apartments,	**4** A4
Pension Hargita,	**5** B5
Pension Kraml,	**6** B5
Westend City Hostel,	**7** A5
Wien Süd,	**8** A6

Ⓤ U-Bahn Ⓢ S-Bahn

Wombats "The Base",	**9** A5
Wombats "The Lounge"	**10** A5
🍴 FOOD	
Centimeter,	**11** C3
Fischer Bräu,	**12** B1
Sato Café-Restaurant,	**13** A5
Servieten Stüberl,	**14** C3
Wirr,	**15** B4
Yak and Yeti,	**16** B5

SEE VIENNA RING MAP p. 75

COFFEEHOUSES	
Café Sperl,	17 C5

WINE TAVERNS	
10er Marie,	18 A3
Buschenschank Heinrich Nierscher,	A2

NIGHTLIFE	
Chelsea,	20 A4
Felixx,	21 C5
Mango,	22 C5

MUSEUMS	
Kunst Huas Wien,	23 E4
Österreichische Galerie: Oberes Belvedere,	24 D5
Österreichische Galerie: Unteres Belvedere,	25 E5
Freud Museum,	26 C3

AUSTRIA

Internet Access: C@IICenter West, XV, Mariahilferstr. 149. €1.40 per 30min., €2.50 per hr. Open daily 9am-midnight. ARI-X, VII (☎01 9911 151 612), corner of Kaiserstr. and Lerchenfelderstr. €1 per hr. Open M-Sa 9am-11pm, Su noon-11pm.

Post Office: Hauptpostamt, I, Fleischmarkt 19 (☎01 0577 677 10 10). Open daily 6am-10pm. Branches throughout the city and at the train stations; look for yellow signs with trumpet logos. Postal Codes: A-1010 (1st district) through A-1230 (23rd district).

ACCOMMODATIONS AND CAMPING

Hunting for cheap rooms in Vienna during high season (June-Sept.) can be unpleasant; call for reservations at least five days ahead. For info on camping near Vienna, visit www.campingwien.at.

Hostel Ruthensteiner, XV, Robert-Hamerlingg. 24 (☎01 893 42 02; www.hostelru-thensteiner.com). Knowledgeable staff, spotless rooms, kitchen, and a courtyard with a massive chess set. Guitars and piano available for guest use. Breakfast €2.50. Linens €2. Internet €2 per 40min. Key deposit €10. 5-night max. stay. Reception 24hr. 8-bed dorms €18; singles €32; doubles €50, with bath €54; quads €72/80. AmEx/MC/V. ❷

Wombats City Hostel, (☎01 897 23 36; www.wombats-hostels.com) has 2 separate locations. **"The Lounge"** (XV, Mariahilferstr. 137). Exit Westbahnhof and turn right on Mariahilferstr. The bright walls and leather couches add a modern touch to the college dorm atmosphere. Loud, popular bar in the basement vault, 24hr. reception, and no curfew make this a more social hostel. **"The Base"** (XV, Grang. 6). Continue on Mariahi-lferstr., turn right on Rosinag., and left on Grang. On a quiet street farther from the train station, this wildly colorful hostel compensates with an in-house pub, guided tours, and nightly English-language movies. Breakfast €3.50 daily 7:30-10am. Laundry €4.50. Internet €2 per hr. Free Wi-Fi in the lobby. Dorms €21; doubles €50. MC/V. ❷

Westend City Hostel, VI, Fügerg. 3 (☎01 597 67 29; www.westendhostel.at), near West-bahnhof. A rose-filled courtyard and plain dorms provide travelers a peaceful place to spend the night. Breakfast included. Internet €4 per hr. Free Wi-Fi. Reception 24hr. Check-out 10:30am. Lockout 10:30am-2pm. Open from mid-Mar. to Nov. Dorms €20-23; singles €52-65; doubles €62-80. Cash only. ❷

Pension Kraml, VI, Brauerg. 5 (☎01 587 85 88; www.pensionkraml.at). U3: Zieglerg. Exit on Otto-Bauer-G., take the 1st left onto Königsegg., then 1st right. Large plush rooms in rich red. Lounge has cable TV. Breakfast included. Reception 24hr. Singles €35; doubles €56, with shower €66, with full bath €76; triples €78/€87. 3- to 5-person apartment with bath €99-135. Cash only. ❸

Camping Neue Donau, XXII, Am Kleehäufel 119 (☎01 202 40 10; www.campingwien.at/nd). U1: Kaisermühlen. Take the Schüttaustr. exit, cross the street, then take bus #91a to Kleehäufel. 4km from the city center and adjacent to Neue Donau beaches, though not directly on the water. Kitchen, showers, and supermarket. Boat and bike rental available. Laundry €4.50. Reception 8am-12:30pm and 3-6:15pm. Open Easter-Sept. €6-7 per person; €10-12 per tent. AmEx/MC/V. ❶

FOOD

Viennese food is all about meat: *Tafelspitz* (boiled beef), *Gulasch* (goulash), and *Wiener Schnitzel* (deep-fried, breaded veal or pork cutlet) are all tradi-tional. But vegetarians need not fear—there's plenty of tasty non-meat fare in this bustling metropolis. The city boasts elaborate sweets, including *Mohr in Hemd* (chocolate and hazelnut soufflé draped in hot chocolate sauce) and the renowned *Sacher Torte*. Restaurants that call themselves *Stüberln* ("little sitting rooms") or advertise *Schmankerl* serve traditional Viennese fare.

Innenstadt restaurants are expensive. The neighborhood north of the university, where Universitätsstr. and Währingerstr. meet (U2: Schottentor), is more budget-friendly. Affordable restaurants line **Burggasse** in District VII and the area around Rechte and Linke Wienzeile near Naschmarkt (U4: Kettenbrückeng). The **Naschmarkt** hosts Vienna's biggest produce market. (Open M-F 6am-6:30pm and Sa 6am-2pm.) The **Brunnenmarkt** (XVI, U6: Josefstädterstr.) has Turkish flair. There's a **kosher** supermarket at II, Hollandstr. 10. (☎01 216 96 75. Open M-Th 8:30am-6:30pm and F 8am-2pm.)

> **TIP**
>
> **B.Y.O.B.** When shopping at Austrian supermarkets, bring your own bag; most supermarkets charge €0.05-0.20 per bag. Come early, too—many supermarkets close M-Sa at around 6:30-7pm often close Su.

INSIDE THE RING

Trzesniewski, I, Dorotheerg. 1 (☎01 512 32 91). From Stephansdom, follow the signs 3 blocks down on the left side of the Graben. Once Kafka's favorite, this stand-up establishment has been serving delicious open-faced mini-sandwiches (€1) for over 100 years. They're mainly egg- and cucumber-based, but can also include salmon, onion, paprika, and herring—presumably no angsty vermin. Open M-F 8:30am-7:30pm and Sa 9am-5pm. Cash only. ❶

Smutny, I, Elisabethstr. 8 (☎01 587 13 56; www.smutny. com), U6: Karlspl. A traditional Viennese restaurant serving *Wiener schnitzel* (€15) and *Fiakergulash* (goulash with beef, egg, potato, and sausage; €12). Open daily 10am-midnight. AmEx/MC/V. ❸

Inigo, I, Bäckerstr. 18 (☎01 512 74 51; www.inigo.at). Founded by a Jesuit priest, Inigo aids the chronically unemployed by hiring them as cooks. Hearty entrees served with a complimentary salad in a cheery interior or the church square. Vegetarian entrees €8-10. Soups €4. Salads €2-7. Open M-Th and Sa 9:30am-midnight. AmEx/MC/V. ❷

OUTSIDE THE RING

Yak and Yeti, VI, Hofmühlg. 21 (☎01 595 54 52; www. yakundyeti.at). U3: Zieglerg. This Himalayan restaurant serves *momos* (Nepalese dumplings; €8-11) and other ethnic specialties. Eat meditatively under the prayer flags in their lush garden. Lunch buffet €6.50. All you can eat specials T and Th evening €10.

COFFEE CULTURE

Vienna is the world's coffee capital, but for those used to *mocha lattes* or half-caff lite soys, understanding the jumble of German words on the *Kaffeehaus* menu can be daunting. Here's a cheat sheet for deciphering the menu:

A **Mokka** or a **Schwarze** is strong, pure black espresso and nothing more. The **Kleiner Brauner** ("small brown") lightens the espresso with milk or cream while the **Verlängerter** lowers the stakes yet again with weaker coffee. The quintessential Viennese cafe drink, a **Mélange** melds black espresso with steamed milk, sometimes capping it with a dollop of whipped cream. The **Kapuziner** ("the monk") also consists of espresso with gently foamed milk but is more commonly known by its Italian name, "cappuccino." The **Einspanner** is a strong black coffee heaped with whipped cream and sometimes a dash of chocolate shavings. **Eiskaffee**, or hot coffee with vanilla ice cream, is refreshing on hot summer days.

Vienna's specialty coffee drinks combine espresso with a variety of liqueurs for caffeine with a punch. Some cafes serve the **Maria Theresia**, with orange liqueur, or the **Pharisär**, with rum and sugar. Other liqueurs include **Mariller** (apricot) and **Kirsche** (cherry). Or, for a protein boost, try the milk-less mocha **Kaisermelange**, stirred with brandy and an egg yolk. Be prepared to shell out €6-7 for an indulgent delight.

Entrees €7-13. Try a mango mousse (€4.50) for dessert. Open M-F 11:30am-2:30pm and 6-10:30pm, Sa 11:30am-10:30pm. MC/V. ❸

Fresco Grill IX, Liechtensteinstr. 10 (☎660 467 89 83; www.frescofrill.at). U2: Schottentor. Head north along Liechtensteinstr. Vienna's best burritos in a hip, relaxed atmosphere. Hang out and enjoy a 1½L pitcher of beer (€3) with free chips and salsa. Free Wi-Fi. Burritos €4.50-5.50. Open daily in summer M-F noon-9pm, in winter 11am-11pm. 5% student discount. Check website for freebies. MC/V. ❷

☕ COFFEEHOUSES

For years these venerable establishments have been havens for artists, writers, and thinkers: Vienna's cafes saw Franz Kafka brood about solitude, Theodor Herzl plan the creation of Israel, and Sigmund Freud ponder the perversity of the human mind. The only dictat of coffeehouse etiquette is that you linger; the waiter *(Herr Ober)* will serve you when you sit down and then leave you to sip your *Mélange* (coffee and steamed milk), read, and contemplate life's great questions. When you're ready to leave, ask to pay with a *"Zahlen, bitte."*

Café Central, I, Herreng. 14 (☎01 533 37 63; www.palaisevents.at), at the corner of Strauchg. With green-gold arches and live music, this luxurious coffeehouse transports patrons to a world of bygone manners and opulence. The house specialty is coffee with apricot liqueur (€5.90). Open M-Th and Sa 7:30am-10pm, F and Su 10am-10pm. AmEx/MC/V.

Kleines Café, I, Franziskanerpl. 3. Escape from the busy pedestrian streets with a *Mélange* (€3.30) and chat with locals on a leather couch in the sotthing interior or by the fountain in the square. Sandwiches €3-5. Croissants, apple *(apfel)* strudel, and curd strudel €2.10. Eggs €7. Open daily 10am-2am. Cash only.

Café Sperl, VI, Gumpendorferstr. 11 (☎01 586 41 58; www.cafesperl.at). U2: Museumsquartier. Marble tables and crystal chandeliers adorn one of Vienna's oldest, most elegant cafes. Sept.-June Su live piano 3:30-5:30pm. Open Sept.-June M-Sa 7am-11pm, Su 11am-8pm; July-Aug. M-Sa 7am-11pm. AmEx/MC/V.

🍷 WINE TAVERNS (HEURIGEN)

Those tired of high culture can find Dionysian release on the outskirts of the city in a number of wine taverns, hidden from the disapproving eyes and powdered wigs of opera ticket salesmen. Marked by a hanging branch, *Heurigen* serve *Heuriger* (wine) and Austrian delicacies, often in a relaxed outdoors setting akin to German beer gardens. The wine is from the most recent harvest; good *Heuriger* is white, fruity, and full-bodied. Open in summer, *Heurigen* cluster in the Viennese suburbs where the grapes grow. Tourist buses head to the most famous region, **Grinzing,** in District XIX; you'll find better atmosphere in the hills of **Sievering, Neustift am Walde** (both in District XIX), and **Neuwaldegg** (in XVII). True Heuriger devotees make the trip to **Gumpoldskirchen.**

Buschenschank Heinrich Nierscher, XIX, Strehlg. 21 (☎01 440 21 46). U6: Währingerstr. Tram #41 to Plötzleinsdorf (the last stop); then take bus #41A to Plötzleinsfriedhof (the 2nd stop) or walk up Pötzleinsdorfer Str., which becomes Khevenhüller Str.; go right on Strehlg. Enjoy a glass of *Heuriger* (€2.50) in the oversized country kitchen or the backyard overlooking the vineyards. Select a tray of meat, cheese, and bread for a light supper (€4-6). Open M and Th-Su 3pm-midnight. Cash only.

10er Marie, XVI, Ottakringerstr. 222-224 (☎01 489 46 47). U3: Ottakring. Turn left on Thaliastr., then right onto Johannes-Krawarik. Locals frequent the large garden behind the yellow house. Though it lacks its own vines, this wine garden is most accessible from the interior, perfect for tipsy patrons who need to take the subway home. ¼L of wine €2. Open M-Sa 3pm-midnight. MC/V.

Vienna Ring

🍴 FOOD
Smutny, 4
Trzesniewski, 8

🏛 MUSEUMS
Albertina, 15
Haus der Musik, 9
Kunsthalle Wien, 7
Kunsthistorisches Museum, 11
Leopold Museum, 3
Museum Moderner Kunst, 14

BARS
Chelsea, 12
Das Möbel, 13

COFFEEHOUSES
Café Central, 2
Café Hawelka, 6
Demel, 5
Kleines Café, 10

★ NIGHTLIFE
Flex, 1

AUSTRIA

Donaukanal
Danube Canal

Tempel Israel
Tempelg.
Kosher Supermarket

SCHOTTENRING
Franz Josefs Kai

Wien-Mitte Bahnhof
City Air Terminal
Landstr.

STUBENTOR
STADTPARK
Johann Strauss Monument
BEETHOVENPL

SCHWEDENPL
Fleischmarkt
Ruprecht
Stadttempel

Stephansdom
STEPHANSPL
HOHER MARKT
RUDOLFSPL

FRANZISKANER PL.
Franziskanerkirche
Weihburg.

PETERSPL
Peterskirche
Graben

Kärntner Str.
Staatsoper
KARLSPLATZ

AM HOF
JUDENPL
Kirche am Hof

FREYUNG
Austria Fountain
Schottenstift

HERRENG.
MICHAELER PL.
Hofburg
Hofburgkapelle

MINORITEN PL.
HELDENPL
Hofgarten
Volksgarten

SCHOTTENTOR
Dr. Karl-Renner-Ring
Dr. Karl-Lueger-Ring

Sigmund Freud Park
Votivkirche
Universität Wien

Rathauspark
Rathaus
Parlament
Burgtheater

MARIA THERESIENPL
MUSEUMS QUARTIER
Burgring
Opernring
Burggarten

VOLKSTHEATER
Technische Universität

SCHILLERPL
Bösendorferstr.
Schwarzenbergstr.
Schubertring
Stubenring

300 meters
300 yards

⊙ SIGHTS

Vienna's contrasting streets are by turns stately, residential, and decaying. Unlike nearby cities in Germany, Vienna was largely unaffected by the destruction of WWII, which means that visitors can enjoy the same buildings that Freud and Kafka wandered by. To wander on your own, grab a copy of *Vienna from A to Z* (€3.60) from the tourist office. The office also leads themed English-language walking tours (€12). Contact **Pedal Power,** II, Ausstellungsstr. 3 (☎01 729 72 34; www.pedalpower.at) for **cycling tours** (€23). **Bus tours** (€35) are given by **Vienna Sightseeing Tours,** IV, Goldegg. 29 (☎01 712 46 83; www.viennasightseeing.at).

STEPHANSDOM AND GRABEN. In the heart of the city, the massive **Stephansdom** is one of Vienna's most treasured landmarks. For a view of the old city and the church's mosaic roof, take the elevator up the North Tower. Or, to work off that strudel, climb the 343 steps of the slightly higher South Tower. *(☎01 515 52 35 26. North Tower open daily Apr.-June and Sept.-Oct. 8:30am-5:30pm; Nov.-Mar. 8:30am-5pm; July-Aug. 9am-5pm. €4.50. South Tower open daily 9am-5:30pm. €3.50.)* Downstairs, skeletons of plague victims fill the **catacombs.** The **Gruft** (vault) stores urns containing the Hapsburgs' innards. *(Tours in English. M-Sa 2 per hr. 10-11:30am and 1:30-4:30pm, Su and holidays 1:30-4:30pm. Cathedral tour daily 3:45pm. €4.50, children €1. MC/V.)* From Stephanspl., follow Graben to see Jugendstil architecture, including Otto Wagner's red marble **Grabenhof** and the underground public toilet complex designed by the fortuitously-named **Adolf Loos.**

HOFBURG PALACE. Previously a medieval castle, this imperial palace was the Hapsburgs' home until 1918. Wing by wing, it was expanded continuously over 800 years. Now home to the President's office and a few small museums, its grandest assets are in the **royal treasury.** The palace is best admired from its **Michaelplatz** and **Heldenplatz** entrances. *(☎01 533 75 70; www.hofburg-wien.at and www.kmh.at. U3: Herreng. Open daily Sept.-June 9am-5:30pm, July-Aug. 9am-8pm. €10, students €7.50.)*

HOHER MARKT AND STADTTEMPEL. Once both a market and an execution site, **Hoher Markt** was home to the Roman encampment **Vindobona.** Roman ruins lie beneath the shopping arcade across from the fountain. *(Open Tu-Su 9am-6pm. €4, students €3. MC/V.)* The biggest draw is the 1914 Jugendstil **Ankeruhr** (clock), whose figures—from Marcus Aurelius to Maria Theresa—rotate past the Viennese coat of arms accompanied by the tunes of their times. To find it, look across the square from the Roman Museum; it's in the corner, connecting two buildings on the second floor. *(1 figure appears every hr. All figures appear at noon.)* Hidden on Ruprechtspl. is the **Stadttempel,** the only synagogue in Vienna to escape destruction during Kristallnacht. *(Seitenstetteng. 4. Mandatory guided tours M and Th at 11:30am and 2pm. €2, students €1.)*

AM HOF AND FREYUNG. Once a medieval jousting square, Am Hof now houses the **Kirche am Hof** (Church of the Nine Choirs of Angels) and **Collalto Palace,** where Mozart gave his first public performance. Just west of Am Hof is **Freyung,** the square with the **Austriabrunnen** (Austria Fountain) in the center. Medieval fugitives took asylum in the **Schottenstift** (Monastery of the Scots), giving rise to the name *Freyung* or "sanctuary." Today, the annual **Christkindl market** fills the plaza with baked goods and holiday cheer (Dec. 1-24).

SCHLOSS SCHÖNBRUNN. Schönbrunn began as a humble hunting lodge, but because of Maria Theresa's efforts became a splendid palace. The **Imperial Tour** passes through the dazzling **Hall of Mirrors,** where six-year-old Mozart played. The longer **Grand Tour** also visits Maria Theresa's exquisite 18th-century rooms, including the ornate **Millions Room.** *(Schönbrunnerstr. 47. U4: Schönbrunn. ☎01 811 132 39; www.schoenbrunn.at. Open daily July-Aug. 8:30am-6pm; Apr.-June and Sept.-Oct. 8:30am-5pm; Nov.-Mar. 8:30am-4:30pm. Imperial Tour 22 rooms; 35min.; €9.50, students €8.50. Grand Tour 40 rooms; 50min.; €13/12. English-language audio tour and/or booklet included.)* As impressive as Schönbrunn itself, the **gardens** behind the palace contain a **labyrinth** and a profusion of manicured greenery, flowers, and statuary, as well as numerous other amusements, including a zoo. *(Park open daily 6am-dusk. Labyrinth open daily July-Aug. 9am-7pm; Apr.-June and Sept. 9am-6pm; Oct. 9am-5pm; Nov. closed. Park free. Labyrinth €2.90, students €2.40.)*

KARLSKIRCHE. Situated in Karlspl., **Karlskirche** (the Church of St. Borromeo) is an eclectic masterpiece. Under restoration as of 2007, it combines a Neoclassical portico with a Baroque dome. An elevator takes visitors up to a somewhat precarious platform with a dazzling new view over the church. Climb the stairs to view the city from the highest point, although the view is somewhat obscured by grates. *(IV, Kreuzherreng. 1. U1, 2, or 4 to Karlspl. ☎01 504 61 87. Open M-Sa 9am-12:30pm and 1-7pm, Su 1-7pm. €6, students €4.)*

ZENTRALFRIEDHOF. The Viennese describe the Central Cemetery as half the size of Geneva but twice as lively. **Tor II** (Gate 2) contains the tombs of Beethoven, Brahms, Schubert, Strauss, and an honorary monument to Mozart, whose true resting place is an unmarked pauper's grave in the **Cemetery of Saint Marx**, III, Leberstr. 6-8. **Tor I** (Gate 1) holds the old **Jewish Cemetery**, where many headstones are cracked and neglected. *(XI, Simmeringer Hauptstr. 234. Tram #71 from Schwarzenbergpl. or Simmering. ☎01 76 04 10; www.friedhoefewien.at. Open daily May-Aug. 7am-7pm; Mar.-Apr. and Sept.-Oct. 7am-6pm; Nov.-Feb. 8am-5pm. Free.)*

🏛 MUSEUMS

With a museum around every corner, Vienna can exhaust even the most zealous of travelers. The **Vienna Card** (€19), available at the tourist office, large U-bahn stops, and most hostels, tries to make the task a little easierl it entitles holders to museum and transit discounts for 72hr.

🖾ÖSTERREICHISCHE GALERIE (AUSTRIAN GALLERY). The grounds of **Schloß Belvedere** house the Österreichische Galerie's two museums, along with a classic Austrian garden and a carriage museum. Home to Klimt's **🖾The Kiss** and one of David's portraits of Napoleon on horseback, the **Oberes (Upper) Belvedere** supplements its magnificent collection of 19th- and 20th-century art with the Austrian Museum of Baroque Art and the Austrian Museum of Medieval Art. *(III, Prinz-Eugen-Str. 27. Walk from the Südbahnhof or take tram D from Schwarzenbergpl. to Schloß Belvedere, or take U1 to Suditorolerplatz. €9.50, students €6. MC/V.)* The **Unteres (Lower) Belvedere** hosts temporary exhibits of contemporary art. *(Unteres Belvedere, III, Rennweg 6. Tram #71 from Schwarzenbergpl. to Unteres Belvedere. €9.50, students €6. Both Belvederes ☎01 79 55 70; www.belvedere.at. Open daily 10am-6pm. Lower Belvedere open W 10am-9pm. Combo ticket €13.50, students €9.50.)*

🖾KUNST HAUS WIEN. Artist-environmentalist **Friedenreich Hundertwasser** built this museum without straight lines—even the floor bends. Arboreal "tree tenants" grow from the windowsills and the top floor. Check out his designs for a model city and a new flag for New Zealand. *(III, Untere Weißgerberstr. 13. U1 or 4 to Schwedenpl., then tram 1 to Radetzkypl. ☎01 712 04 91; www.kunsthauswien.at. Open daily 10am-7pm. Each exhibit €9, both €12; students €7/9. MC/V.)*

ÖSTERREICHISCHES MUSEUM FÜR ANGEWANDTE KUNST (MAK). This intimate, eclectic museum is dedicated to design. It examines the smooth curves of Thonet bentwood chairs, the intricacies of Venetian glass, and the steel heights of modern architecture. *(I, Stubenring 5. U3: Stubentor. ☎ 01 71 13 60; www.mak.at. Open Tu 10am-midnight, W-Su 10am-6pm. €7.90, students €5.50. Sa and holidays free. MC/V.)*

KUNSTHISTORISCHES MUSEUM (MUSEUM OF FINE ARTS). One of the world's largest art collections boasts Italian paintings, Classical art, and an Egyptian burial chamber. The main building contains works by Venetian and Flemish masters. Across the street in the Neue Burg wing of the Hofburg Palace, the **Ephesos Museum** exhibits findings from excavations in Turkey. The **Sammlung alter Musikinstrumente** includes Beethoven's harpsichord and Mozart's piano. *(U2: Museumsquartier. Across from the Burgring and Heldenpl., to the right of Maria Theresienpl. ☎ 01 525 24 41; www.khm.at. Main building open Tu-Th 10am-9pm, F-Su 10am-6pm; Ephesos and Sammlung open M and W-Su 10am-6pm. €10, students €7.50. Audio tour €3. AmEx/MC/V.)*

MUSEUMSQUARTIER. Central Europe's largest collection of modern art, the **Museum Moderner Kunst (MUMOK)** highlights Classical Modernism, Fluxus, Photo Realism, Pop Art, and Viennese Actionism in a building made from basalt lava. *(Open M-W and F-Su 10am-6pm, Th 10am-9pm. €9, students €6.50. AmEx/MC/V.)* The **Leopold Museum** has the world's largest Schiele collection. *(Open M, W-Su 10am-7pm, Th 10am-9pm. €10, students €6.50. AmEx/MC/V.)* Themed exhibits of contemporary artists fill **Kunsthalle Wien.** *(U2: Museumsquartier. ☎ 01 52 57 00; www.mqw.at. Open M-W and F-Su 10am-7pm, Th 10am-10pm. Exhibition Hall 1 €8.50; students M €7, W-Su €6. Exhibition Hall 2 €6/3.50/4.50. Both €11/7/9. "Art" combination ticket admits visitors to all 2 museums; €22. "Duo" ticket admits to Leopold and MUMOK; €17, students €11.)*

FREUD MUSEUM. See the home of the founder of psychoanalysis, Sigmund Freud. It contains bric-a-brac, like his report cards and certificate of circumcision—potential clues to all his hang-ups? Don't bring your mother along... *(IX, Bergg. 19. U2: Schottentor. ☎ 01 319 15 96; www.freud-museum.at. Open daily July-Sept. 9am-6pm; Oct.-June 9am-5pm. €7, students €4.50. MC/V.)*

🎭 ENTERTAINMENT

Many of classical music's greats lived, composed, and performed in Vienna. Beethoven, Haydn, and Mozart wrote their best-known masterpieces here. A century later, Berg, Schönberg, and Webern revolutionized the music world. Today, Vienna hosts many budget performances, though prices rise in the summer. The **Bundestheaterkasse,** I, Hanuschg. 3, sells tickets for the Staatsoper, the Volksoper, and the Burgtheater. (☎ 01 514 44 78 80. Open from June to mid-Aug. M-F 10am-2pm; from mid-Aug. to June M-F 8am-6pm, Sa-Su 9am-noon.)

Staatsoper, I, Opernring 2 (☎ 01 514 44 22 50; www.wiener-staatsoper.at). Vienna's premier opera performs nearly every night Sept.-June. No shorts. Seats €3.50-254. 500 standing-room tickets go on sale 80min. before every show (1 per person; €2-3.50); arrive 2hr. before curtain. Box office in the foyer open M-F 9am until 1hr. before curtain, Sa 9am-noon; 1st Sa of each month and during Advent 9am-5pm. MC/V.

Wiener Philharmoniker Orchestra (☎ 01 505 65 25; www.wienerphilharmoniker.at). The Philharmonic plays in the Musikverein, Austria's premier concert hall. To purchase tickets, visit the box office, Bösendorferstr. 12, well in advance of performances. Tickets also available at Lothinringerstrasse 20. MC/V.

🍸 NIGHTLIFE

With one of the highest bar-to-cobblestone ratios in the world, Vienna is a great place to party if you know where to look. Take U1 or 4 to Schwedenpl., which will drop you within blocks of the **Bermuda Dreieck** (Bermuda Triangle), a hot clubbing area. If you make it out alive, head down **Rotenturmstraße** toward Stephansdom or walk around the area between the synagogue and **Ruprechtskirche.**

Slightly outside the Ring, the streets off **Burggasse** and **Stiftgasse** in District VII and the **university quarter** in Districts XIII and IX have outdoor courtyards and hip bars. For listings, pick up the indispensable *Falter* (€2.60).

▨ **Chelsea,** VIII, Lerchenfeldergürtel 29-31. U6: Thaliastr. or Josefstädterstr. (☎01 407 93 09; www.chelsea.co.at), under the U-Bahn between the 2 stops. Austrian and international bands pack this underground club to the brim twice a week, while weekend DJs spin techno-pop. Concerts start at 10pm. ½L beer €3.50. Cover €6-13 for performances, bar free. Happy hour 4-5pm. Open M-Sa 6pm-4am, Su 4pm-3am. Cash only.

▨ **Siebensternbraeu,** VII, Siebensterngasse 19 (☎01 523 86 97; www.7stern.at), between Stiftgasse and Kirchengasse. This brewhouse has a Bavarian feel and beer garden to match. Traditional Austrian fare along with beer brewed in the massive kettles at the center of the establishment. 7 varieties of home-brewed beer €3.50 per ½L. Food €7-16. Open T-Su 11am-midnight. Garden and kitchen open until 11pm. AmEx/MC/V.

Krah Krah, I, Rabensteig. 8 (☎01 533 81 93; www.krah-krah.at). A Bermuda Dreieck bar, Krah Krah has 49 beer varieties, including many lesser-known Austrian brews. Be careful with the Kulmbach Kulminator 28, the "world's strongest beer" (0.3L, €4.90) which has been known to destroy happy-go-lucky backpackers. Happy hour M-F 3:30-5:30pm. Open M-Sa 11am-2am, Su 11am-1:30am. MC/V.

Das Möbel, VII, Burgg. 10 (☎01 524 94 97; www.das-moebel.at). U2 or 3: Volkstheater. An artsy crowd chats on metal couches and Swiss-army tables, all created by designers and for sale. Don't leave without seeing (and sullying) the post-modern bathroom. Internet free for 15min., €0.90 per 15min. thereafter. Open daily 11am-1am. Cash only.

Flex, I, Donaulände (☎01 533 75 25; www.flex.at), near the Schottenring U-Bahn station (U2 or U4) down by the Danube. Grab a beer or bring your own and sit by the river with other partiers. DJs start spinning techno, reggae, house, ska, or electronic at 11pm in the most famous dance club in the city. Beer €3.50. Cover €4-10, free after 3:30am. Open daily 8pm-4am. Cash only.

Volksgarten Disco, I, Burgring 1 (☎01 532 42 41; www.volksgarten.at). U2: Volkstheater. Pool, dance floor, and bangin' young crowd make this one of Vienna's most exclusive clubs. Cover €5-15. Open June-Aug. M 8pm-2am, Th 8pm-4am, F 11pm-6am, Sa 9pm-6am; Sept.-May M 8pm-2am, Th 8pm-4am, F and Sa 11pm-6am. AmEx/MC/V.

passage, I, the corner of Burgring. and Babenbergerstr. (☎01 961 88 00; www.sunshine.at). What used to be an underground walkway is now a collection of small but fashionable nightclubs. Getting in can be difficult—dress to impress. Club Cosmopolitan plays soul music, Club Fusion spins house, and disco blares from the Bachelor Club. Hours vary by season; check the website. Cash only.

Mango, VI, Laimgrubeng. 3 (☎01 920 47 14; www.mangobar.at). U2: Museumsquartier. Mango advertises itself as "the place where young gays meet," and easy to see why people are drawn to its casual atmosphere, golden walls, and pop music. Open daily 9pm-4am. Cash only.

Why Not, I, Tiefer Graben 22 (☎01 920 47 14; www.why-not.at). Gay and lesbian clientele dances late into the night amid 4 discoballs in Vienna's only GLBT disco. Drinks from €3. Cover after midnight €9 includes 2 drinks. Open F-Sa 10pm-4am. Cash only.

▨ FESTIVALS

Vienna hosts several important festivals, mostly musical. The **Wiener Festwochen** (May-June) has a diverse program of concerts, exhibitions, and plays. (☎01 58 92 20; www.festwochen.or.at.) In May, over 4000 people attend **Lifeball,** Europe's largest AIDS charity event and Vienna's biggest gay celebration. With the Lifeball Style Police threatening to dispose of under-dressed guests (make-up and hair-styling are musts), come looking like you deserve to mix and mingle with Bill Clinton, Elton John, and other celebrities. (☎01 595

56 77; www.lifeball.org. Tickets €75-150.) Democrats host **The Danube Island Festival** in late June, which celebrates with fireworks and concerts, hosting up to to a million partiers in years past. (☎01 535 35 35; www.donauinselfest. at. Free.) The *Staatsoper* and *Volkstheater* host **Jazzfest Wien** (☎01 503 56 47; www.viennajazz.org) during the first weeks of July.

SALZBURGER LAND AND HOHE TAUERN REGION

Salzburger Land's precious white gold, *Salz* (salt), first drew settlers more than 3000 years ago. Modern travelers instead prefer to seek the shining lakes and rolling hills of the Salzkammergut, making Salzburg an enticing destination.

SALZBURG ☎ 0662

As its Baroque architecture attests, Salzburg was Austria's ecclesiastical center in the 17th and 18th centuries. This golden age fostered a rich musical culture that lives on today in elaborate concert halls and impromptu folk performances. The city's love for its native genius, Mozart, climaxes in summer during the Salzburg Festival, when fans the world over come to pay their respects.

▐ TRANSPORTATION

Trains leave from **Hauptbahnhof**, in Südtirolerpl. (☎05 17 17) for: Graz (4hr., every hr. 8am-6:30pm, €40); Innsbruck (2hr., 1 every day, €34); Munich, GER (2-3hr., 30 per day, €27); Vienna (3hr., 26 per day, €44); Zürich, SWI (6hr., 7 per day, €73). **Buses** depart from the depot in front of the train station. Single tickets (€1.80) available at automatic machines or from the drivers. Books of 5 tickets (€8), day passes (€4.20), and week passes (€11) are available at machines. Punch your ticket when you board or risk a €36 fine.

▟ ▐ ORIENTATION AND PRACTICAL INFORMATION

Three hills and the **Salzach River** delineate Salzburg, located just a few kilometers from the German border. The **Neustadt** is north of the river, and the beautiful **Altstadt** squeezes between the southern bank and the **Mönchsberg** hill. The Hauptbahnhof is on the northern side of town beyond the Neustadt; bus #1 connects it to **Hanuschplatz**, the *Altstadt's* main public transportation hub, by the river near Griesg. and the Staatsbrücke. Buses #3, 5, and 6 run from the Hauptbahnhof to Rathaus and Mozartsteg, also in the *Altstadt*. Neustadt hubs include **Mirabellplatz, Makartplatz,** and **Mozartsteg,** the pedestrian bridge leading across the Salzach to Mozartpl. To reach the *Altstadt* on foot, turn left from the station onto Rainerstr. and follow it straight under the tunnel and on to Mirabellpl.; continue to Makartplatz and turn right to cross the **Makartsteg** bridge.

Tourist Office: Mozartpl. 5 (☎0662 88 98 73 30), in the *Altstadt*. Books rooms (€2.20 fee and 10% deposit) and gives tours of the city (daily 12:15pm, €8). It also sells the **Salzburg Card,** which grants admission to all museums and sights and unlimited public transportation. 1-day pass €23, 2-day €31, 3-day €36. Open daily 9am-6pm.

Currency Exchange: Banks offer the best rates for cash but often charge higher commissions. Banking hours M-F 8am-12:30pm and 2-4:30pm.

Luggage Storage: 24hr. lockers at the train station €2-3.50.

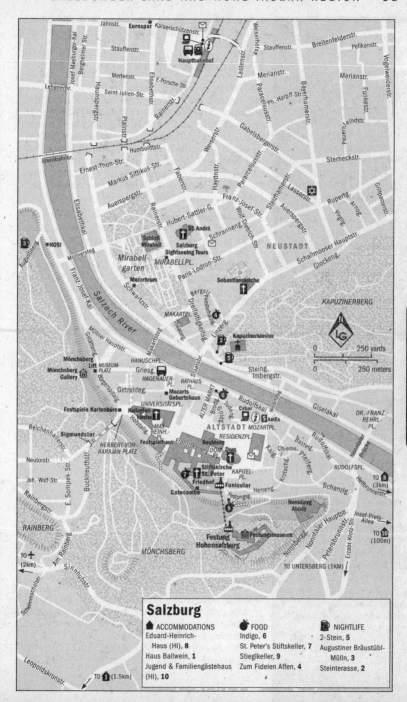

Salzburg

🏠 ACCOMMODATIONS
Eduard-Heinrich-
Haus (HI), **8**
Haus Ballwein, **1**
Jugend & Familiengästehaus
(HI), **10**

🍴 FOOD
Indigo, **6**
St. Peter's Stiftskeller, **7**
Stieglkeller, **9**
Zum Fidelen Affen, **4**

🍺 NIGHTLIFE
2-Stein, **5**
Augustiner Bräustübl-
Mülln, **3**
Steinterasse, **2**

AUSTRIA

ON THE MENU

LET THEM EAT CAKE

It comes as no surprise that the world's most famous cake-eating advocate, Marie Antoinette, came from Austria. A trip to this cake nation is not complete without indulging your sweet tooth on one of the following delicacies:

Linzer Torte: Named for the city of Linz, the Linzer Torte is allegedly "the oldest cake". Made from ground almonds, sugar, butter, flour, egg yolks, and either raspberry or red currant jam, the torte dates back to 1653. It might be surprising how late the "first cake" emerged, but the use of sugar cane did not become popular in Europe until well after Columbus reached America.

Sacher Torte: Made from chocolate, rum, and apricot preserves, the Sacher Torte has also stood the international taste-test of time. Created especially by sixteen year old Edouard Sacher, the royal pastry chef's apprentice, for Emperor Franz Josef in 1832, the torte can only be served in two pastry shops in Vienna: Sacher Café and Demels. Today, the Sacher Hotel sells around 360,000 of these tortes every year!

Strudel: introduced during the Hapsburg reign, the most popular two varieties, *Apfel* strudel and *Topfen* strudel, are made with apples and soft cheese, respectively. According to legend, the emperor's pastry chef decreed that the crust on a strudel should be so thin that a love letter could be read through it.

Post Office: At the train station (☎0662 88 30 30). Open M-F 7am-6pm, Sa 8am-2pm, Su 1-6pm. **Postal Code:** A-5020.

⛫ ACCOMMODATIONS

Within the city itself, budget hotels and hostels are few and far between. Instead, try looking for accommodations outside Salzburg that are still accessible by public transportation. For the best deal, check out *Privatzimmer* (rooms in a family home), usually located on the city's outskirts, with welcoming hosts and bargain prices. Reservations are recommended, especially in summer. For a complete list of *Privatzimmer* and booking help, see the tourist office.

Eduard-Heinrich-Haus (HI), Eduard-Heinrich-Str. 2 (☎0662 62 59 76; www.hostel-ehh.at). Spacious rooms overlook the garden. Breakfast included. Laundry €6. Internet €2.60 per 20min. Key deposit €20 or ID. Reception M-F 7am-midnight, Sa-Su 7-10am and 5pm-midnight. Dorms €16-32; singles €29, with bath €33; doubles €41/47; triples €47/55; quads €62/78. €3 HI discount. Reserve ahead. AmEx/MC/V. ❶

Jugend & Familiengästehaus (HI), Josef-Preis-Allee 18 (☎0662 84 26 700; www.jfgh.at). Take bus #5 (dir.: Birkensiedlung) to Justizgebäude, close to the Altstadt. Kids pack this family-friendly hostel in May and June when school orchestras descend on Salzburg. Breakfast included. Laundry €3. Internet €3 per 40min. Reception 7am-12:30am. Dorms €15.50-35; doubles €54, with shower and toilet €86. €1.50 HI discount. €3 discount for 2 or more nights. AmEx/MC/V. ❷

🍴 FOOD

Countless beer gardens and pastry-shop patios make Salzburg a great place for outdoor dining. Local specialties include *Salzburger nockerl* (egg whites, sugar, and raspberry filling baked into three mounds that represent the hills of Salzburg) and the world-famous *Mozartkugel* (hazelnuts coated in pistachio marzipan, nougat, and chocolate). **Supermarkets** cluster on the Mirabellpl. side of the river. **Open-air markets** in Universitätspl. sell fresh fruits and veggies, giant pretzels, meats, and cheeses. (Open M-F 6am-7pm, Sa 6am-1pm.)

Indigo, Rudolfskai 8 (☎0662 84 34 80; www.indigo-food.com), is located along the river. This tiny eatery draws a local crowd with delicious salads, bowls of steaming Asian noodles, and sushi. Salads €1.35 per 100g. Noodles €5.50-7.50. Sushi €0.70-15.50, sandwiches (€3-4), curries (€4-5), and soup (€3.40-5.70).

Open M-Th 10am-10pm, F-Sa 10am-midnight, Su noon-8pm. Free Wi-Fi 11:30am-2pm. Cash only. ❶

Zum Fidelen Affen, Priesterhausg. 8 (☎0662 87 73 61), off Linzerg. Hearty Austrian food keeps everyone coming back to Zum Fidelen Affen ("The Faithful Ape"). Try the toasted black bread with various toppings (€5-7), the farmer's salad (€9), or the Monkey Steak (roasted pork with bacon, mushrooms, and tomatoes; €10). Vegetarian options available. Open M-Sa 5pm-midnight. AmEx/MC/V. ❷

🔵 SIGHTS

FESTUNG HOHENSALZBURG. Built between 1077 and 1681 by the ruling archbishops, the imposing Hohensalzburg Fortress, which looms over Salzburg from atop Mönchsberg, is the largest completely preserved castle in all of Europe—partly because it was never successfully attacked. The **Festungsmuseum** inside the fortress has side-by-side histories of Salzburg, the fortress, and the world. An audio tour (30min., 4 per hr.) leads visitors up the **watch-tower** for an unmatched panorama of the city and to an organ nicknamed the "Bull of Salzburg" for its off-key snorting. (*☎0662 8424 3011. Take the trail or the Festungsbahn funicular up to the fortress from Festungsg. Funicular May-Aug. 9am-10pm; Sept. 9am-9pm; Oct-Apr. 9am-5pm. Open daily July-Aug. 9am-7pm; Sept. and May-June 9am-6pm; Oct.-Apr. 9am-5pm. Last museum entry 30min. before closing. €10; includes round-trip funicular ride.)*

MOZARTS GEBURTSHAUS. Mozart's birthplace and childhood home holds a collection of the child genius' belongings, including his first violin and key-

AUSTRIA

board instruments. (☎0662 084 4313. Getreideg. 9. Open daily July-Aug. 9am-7pm; Sept.-June 9am-6pm. Last entry 30min. before closing. €6.50, students €5.50. Cash only.)

STIFTSKIRCHE, CATACOMBS, AND THE DOM. The **Monastery of St. Peter** rests against the Mönchsberg cliffs. **Stiftskirche St. Peter,** a church within the monastery, features a marble portal from 1244. In the 18th century, the building was remodeled in Rococo style. (☎0662 844 5760. Open daily 9am-12:15pm and 2:30-6:30pm.) To the right of the church's entrance is the monastery's **Friedhof** (cemetery). Tiger lilies, roses, and ivy embellish the fanciful curls of the wrought-iron crosses. The entrance to the **catacombs** is on the far right, against the Mönchsberg. (Monastery open May-Sept. Tu-Su 10:30am-5pm; Oct.-Apr. W-Th 10:30am-3:30pm, F-Su 10:30am-4pm. €1, students €0.60. Cemetery open Apr.-Sept. 6:30am-7pm; Oct.-Mar. 6:30am-6pm. Free.) The exit at the other end of the cemetery leads to the immense Baroque **Dom** (cathedral), where Mozart was christened in 1756 and later worked as concertmaster and court organist. The square in front of the cathedral, **Domplatz,** features a statue of the Virgin Mary and figures representing Wisdom, Faith, the Church, and the Devil.

RESIDENZ. Home of the later Salzburg princes, this palace once boasted 180 rooms of Renaissance, Baroque, and Classical art. Most of the building is now used by the University of Salzburg, but the second floor staterooms—the **Prunkräume**—still contain their original ornate furnishing. (☎0662 804 226 90; www.salzburg-burgen.at. Residenzpl. 1. Open daily 9am-5pm. Last entry 4:30pm. €8.20, students €6.20; includes audio tour. Free with Salzburg Card.)

KOLLEGIENKIRCHE. In Mozart's backyard stands one of the largest Baroque chapels on the continent. Sculpted clouds coat the nave, while pudgy cherubim frolic over the church's immense apse. (Open daily 9am-5pm. Free.)

MIRABELL PALACE AND GARDENS. Mirabellpl. holds the marvelous **Schloß Mirabell,** which the supposedly celibate Archbishop Wolf Dietrich built for his mistress and their 15 children in 1606. (Open daily 7am-9pm. Free.) However, the main attraction is the ornate maze of flowers beds and fountains behind the palace. The **Mirabellgarten** contains the moss-covered **Zauberflötenhäuschen** ("Magic Flute Little House") where Mozart purportedly composed *The Magic Flute.*

☀ FESTIVALS

During the **Salzburger Festspiele** (July-Aug.), operas, plays, films, concerts, and tourists overrun every available public space; expect room prices to rise accordingly and plan ahead. Info and tickets for Festspiele events are available through the *Festspiele Kartenbüro* (ticket office) and *Direkt Verkauf* (daily box office) at Karajanpl. 11, against the mountain and next to the tunnel. (☎0662 804 5500; www.salzburgfestival.at. Open mid-Mar. to June M-F 9:30am-3pm, through the end of Festspiele daily 9:30am-6pm. Tickets €15-360.) In other months, head to a concert organized by the Mozarteum. Their **Mozartwoche,** a week-long celebration of Mozart, during which his sacred works are performed, occurs at the end of January. (Jan. 25-Feb. 5. ☎0662 87 31 54; www.mozarteum. at.) The Dom has a concert program in July, August, and early October. (☎0662 88 46 23 45. €20, students €7.) From May to September, the Mirabell Gardens hosts outdoor performances including concerts, folk singing, and dancing. For more info, visit www.salzburg-festivals.com.

🍺 BARS AND BEER GARDENS

Munich may be the world's beer capital, but much of its liquid gold flows south to Austria's pubs and *Biergärten* (beer gardens). These lager oases cluster in the city center along the Salzach River. The more boisterous revelers stick to Rudolfskai, between the *Staatsbrücke* and *Mozartsteg*. Elsewhere, especially along Chiemseegasse and around Anton-Neumayr-Platz, you can throw back a few drinks in a reserved *Beisl* (pub). Refined bars with middle-aged patrons can be found along Steingasse and Giselakai on the other side of the river.

☒ **Augustiner Bräustübl-Mülln,** Augustinerg. 4 (☎0662 43 12 46). Although the monks are gone, the Bäukloster they founded in 1621 continues to turn out home-brewed beer by the barrel. Follow the long halls to the end to reach the Biergärten. Beer 0.3L €2.10, 0.5L €2.60. Open M-F 3-11pm, Sa-Su 2:30-11pm; last call 10:30pm. Cash only.

2-Stein, Giselakai 9 (☎0662 87 71 79). The go-to place for Salzburg's gay and lesbian scene. Mixed drinks from €5. Open M-W and Su 6pm-4am, Th-Sa 6pm-5am. MC/V.

Steinterrasse, Giselakai 3-5 (☎0662 874 34 60; www.hotelstein.at), on the 7th fl. of the Stein Hotel. This hip cafe-bar knows that a lofty rooftop panorama doesn't have to mean equally lofty prices. A young crowd comes to flirt while admiring the lights of the Altstadt. Beer €2.60-3.90. Mixed drinks €5-10. Open daily 9am-1am. AmEx/MC/V.

BELGIUM
(BELGIQUE, BELGIË)

Surrounded by France, Germany, and The Netherlands, Belgium is a convergence of different cultures. Appropriately, the small country attracts an array of travelers: chocoholics, Europhiles, and art-lovers all come together in Belgium. Sweet-toothed foreigners flock to Brussels, the home of filled chocolate, to nibble confections from one of 2000 cocoa-oriented specialty shops and to brush shoulders with diplomats en route to European Union and NATO headquarters. In Flanders, Gothic towers surround cobblestone squares, while visitors below admire Old Masters' canvases and guzzle monk-brewed ale. Wallonie has less tourist infrastructure, but the caves of the Lesse Valley and the forested hills of the Ardennes compensate with their stunning natural beauty.

DISCOVER BELGIUM: SUGGESTED ITINERARY

THREE DAYS. While it all away in **Brussels** (p. 90), the self-styled capital of Europe. It may be expensive, but what a way to go (bankrupt)—in front of a juicy steak au poivre at one of its many Michelin-starred restaurants.

ONE WEEK. Plan for at least two days in **Brussels.** Head north to the elegant boulevards of **Antwerp** (p. 99) and historic **Ghent** (p. 100). Finish by heading west to the winding streets and canals of Romantic **Bruges** (p. 96).

ESSENTIALS

FACTS AND FIGURES

OFFICIAL NAME: Kingdom of Belgium.

CAPITAL: Brussels.

MAJOR CITIES: Antwerp, Ghent, Liège.

POPULATION: 10,584,534.

LAND AREA: 30,500 sq. km.

TIME ZONE: GMT +1.

HEAD OF STATE: King Albert II.

LANGUAGES: Dutch (60%), French (40%).

RELIGIONS: Roman Catholic (75%), Protestant (25%).

FRENCH FRIES: Invented in Belgium during the 18th century, despite what the name suggests. Served with mayonnaise.

VARIETIES OF BEER: Over 500!

WHEN TO GO

May, June, and September are the best months to visit with temperatures around 18-22°C (64-72°F) in Brussels and Antwerp, and about 6°C (10°F) higher in Liège and Ghent. July and August tend to be rainy and hot. Winters are cool, 2-7°C (36-45°F), and somewhat colder in the Ardennes.

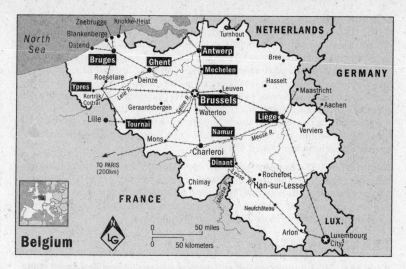

Belgium

DOCUMENTS AND FORMALITIES

EMBASSIES AND CONSULATES. Foreign embassies in Belgium are in Brussels. Belgian embassies abroad include: **Australia** and **New Zealand,** 19 Arkana St., Yarralumla, ACT 2600 (☎02 62 73 25 02; www.diplomatie.be/canberra); **Canada,** 360 Albert St., Ste. 820, Ottawa, ON, K1R 7X7 (☎613-236-7267; www.diplomatie.be/ottawa); **Ireland,** 2 Shrewsbury Rd., Ballsbridge, Dublin 4 (☎01 205 71 00; www.diplomatie.be/dublin); **UK,** 17 Grosvenor Crescent, London, SW1X 7EE (☎020 7470 3700; www.diplomatie.be/london); **US,** 3330 Garfield St., NW, Washington, D.C., 20008 (☎202-333-6900; www.diplobel.us).

VISA AND ENTRY INFORMATION. EU citizens do not need a visa. Citizens of Australia, Canada, New Zealand, and the US do not need a visa for stays of up to 90 days, beginning upon entry into any of the countries in the EU's freedom-of-movement zone. For stays longer than 90 days, all non-EU citizens need visas (around US$85), available at Belgian consulates. Visit www.diplobel.us. US citizens' visas tend to be issued a few weeks after application submission.

TOURIST SERVICES AND MONEY

EMERGENCY	Ambulance: ☎100. Fire: ☎100. Police: ☎101.

TOURIST OFFICES. Bureaux de Tourisme, marked by green-and-white or blue signs labeled "i," are supplemented by **Info Jeunes/Info-Jeugd,** info centers that help people find work and secure accommodations in Wallonie and Flanders, respectively. The **Belgian Tourist Information Center (BBB),** Grasmarkt 63, Brussels (☎025 04 03 90), has national tourist info. The weekly English-language *Bulletin* (www.thebulletin.be; €2.80 at newsstands) provides events and news info.

MONEY. The **euro (€)** has replaced the Belgian **franc** as the unit of currency in Belgium. **ATMs** generally offer the best exchange rates. **Credit cards** are used widely throughout Belgium, most notably in the country's major cities. A bare-bones day in Belgium might cost €35, while a more comfortable day runs about €50-65. Tipping is not common, though rounding up is. Restaurant bills usually include a service charge, although outstanding service warrants an extra 5-10% tip. Give bathroom attendants €0.25 and movie and theater attendants €0.50.

Belgium has a 21% **value added tax (VAT)**, a sales tax applied to most goods and services. Restaurant and taxi prices usually include VAT; at restaurants, this may be listed as *service comprise* or *incluse*. The prices given in *Let's Go* include VAT. In the airport, upon exiting the EU, non-EU citizens can claim a refund on the tax paid for goods bought at participating stores. In order to qualify for a refund, you must spend at least €125 on a single item; make sure to ask for a refund form when you pay.

BUSINESS HOURS. Banks are generally open Monday through Friday 9am-4pm but often close for lunch midday. **Stores** are open Monday through Saturday 10am-5pm or 6pm; stores sometimes close on Mondays, but may be open Sundays in summer. Most **sights** are open Sundays but closed Mondays; in Bruges and Tournai, museums close Tuesdays or Wednesdays.

TRANSPORTATION

BY PLANE. Most international flights land at **Brussels International Airport** (BRU; ☎27 53 87 98; www.brusselsairport.be), located roughly 20min. away from Brussels. Budget airlines, like **Ryanair** and **easyJet**, fly out of **Brussels South Charleroi Airport** (CRL; ☎71 25 12 11; www.charleroi-airport.com), about 1hr. south of Brussels, and Brussels International Airport. The Belgian national airline, **Brussels Airlines** (☎070 35 11 11, US ☎516-740-5200, UK ☎087 0735 2345; www.brusselsairlines.com), flies to Brussels from most major European cities.

BY TRAIN AND BUS. The extensive and reliable **Belgian Rail** (www.b-rail.be) network traverses the country. **Eurail** is valid in Belgium. A **Benelux Tourrail Pass** (US$210, under 26 US$160) allows five days of unlimited train travel in a one-month period in Belgium, the Netherlands, and Luxembourg. Travelers with time to explore Belgium's nooks and crannies might consider the **Rail Pass** (€70) or Go Pass (under 26 only; €45), both of which allow 10 single trips within the country over a one-year period and can be transferred among travelers. Because trains are widely available, buses are used primarily for local transport. Single tickets are €1.50, and are cheaper when bought in packs.

BY FERRY. P&O Ferries (☎070 70 77 71, UK ☎087 0598 03 33; www.poferries.com) from Hull, BRI to Zeebrugge, north of Bruges (12hr., 7pm, from €150).

BY CAR, BIKE, AND THUMB. Belgium honors drivers' licenses from Australia, Canada, the EU, and the US. New Zealanders must contact the New Zealand Automobile Association (☎0800 822 422; www.aa.co.nz) for an International Driving Permit. **Speed limits** are 120kph on motorways, 90kph on main roads, and 50kph elsewhere. **Biking** is popular; many roads in Flanders have bike lanes. **Hitchhiking** is illegal in Belgium. *Let's Go* does not recommend hitchhiking.

KEEPING IN TOUCH

PHONE CODES	**Country code: 32. International dialing prefix: 00.** For more info on how to place international calls, see **Inside Back Cover.**

EMAIL AND THE INTERNET. There are cybercafes in all of the larger towns and cities in Belgium. Expect to pay €2-3 per 30min. In smaller towns, Internet is generally available in hostels for €5-6 per hr.

TELEPHONE. Most pay phones require a **phone card** (from €5), available at post offices, supermarkets, and newsstands. Whenever possible, use a calling card for international phone calls, as long-distance rates for national phone services are often very high. Calls are cheapest 6:30pm-8am and weekends. **Mobile phones** are an increasingly popular and economical option. Major mobile carriers include Vodafone, Base, and Mobistar. When dialing within a city, the city code must still be dialed. For operator assistance within Belgium, dial ☎ 12 07; for international, dial ☎ 12 04 (€0.25). Direct-dial access numbers for calling out of Belgium include: **AT&T** (☎0800 100 10); **British Telecom** (☎0800 100 24); **Canada Direct** (☎0800 100 19); **Telecom New Zealand** (☎0800 100 64).

MAIL. Post offices are open Monday to Friday 9am-5pm, with a midday break. Sent within Belgium, a postcard or letter (up to 50g) costs €0.46 for non-priority and €0.52 for priority. Within the EU, costs are €0.70/0.80, and for the rest of the world €0.75/0.90. For info see www.post.be. **Poste Restante** available.

ACCOMMODATIONS AND CAMPING

BELGIUM	❶	❷	❸	❹	❺
ACCOMMODATIONS	under €10	€10-20	€21-30	€31-40	over €40

Hotels in Belgium are fairly expensive, with rock-bottom singles from €30 and doubles from €40-45. Belgium's 31 **HI youth hostels** are run by the **Flemish Youth Hostel Federation** (www.vjh.be) in Flanders and **Les Auberges de Jeunesses** (www.laj.be) in Wallonie. Expect to pay around €18 per night, including linen, for modern, basic hostels. Private hostels cost about the same but are usually nicer, although some charge separately for linen. **Hotels** are noticeably more expensive than the nicest hostel; make reservations in advance to secure accommodations. Most receptionists speak some English. Reservations are a good idea, particularly in summer and on weekends. **Campgrounds** charge about €4 per night and are common in Wallonie but not in Flanders. An International Camping Card is unnecessary in Belgium.

FOOD AND DRINK

BELGIUM	❶	❷	❸	❹	❺
FOOD	under €5	€5-9	€10-13	€14-18	over €18

Belgian cuisine, acclaimed but expensive, fuses French and German styles. An evening meal may cost as much as a night's accommodations. Fresh seafood appears in *moules* or *mosselen* (steamed mussels) and *moules frites* (steamed mussels with french fries), the national dishes, which are often tasty and reasonably affordable (€14-20). *Frites* (french fries) are ubiquitous and budget-friendly; Belgians eat them dipped in mayonnaise. Look for *friekots* ("french fry shacks") in Belgian towns. Belgian **beer** is a source of national pride, its consumption a national pastime. More varieties—over 500, ranging from ordinary pilsners (€1) to Trappist ales (€3) brewed by monks—are produced here than in any other country. Leave room for chocolate **pralines** from Leonidas or Neuhaus and Belgian **waffles** *(gaufres)*, sold on the street and in cafes.

BEYOND TOURISM

Volunteer *(benévolat)* and work opportunities in Belgium focus on its strong international offerings, especially in Brussels, which is home to both NATO and the EU. Private-sector short- and long-term employment is listed at www. jobsabroad.com/Belgium.cfm. A selection of public-sector job and volunteer opportunities is listed below. For more info on opportunities across Europe, see the Beyond Tourism chapter p. 55.

Amnesty International, r. Berckmans 9, 1060 Brussels (☎02 538 8177; www.amnesty-international.be). One of the world's foremost human rights organizations has offices in Brussels. Paid positions and volunteer work available.

The International School of Brussels, Kattenberg-Botisfort 19, Brussels (☎02 661 42 11; www.isb.be). The ISB hires teachers for positions lasting more than 1yr. Must have permission to work in Belgium.

North Atlantic Treaty Organization (NATO), bd. Leopold III, 1110 Brussels (www.nato. int). Current students and recent graduates (within 1yr.) who are nationals of a NATO member state and fluent in 1 official NATO language (English or French), with a working knowledge of the other, can apply for 6-month internships. Requirements and application details available at www.nato.int/structur/interns/index.html. Application deadlines are far ahead of start dates.

BRUSSELS (BRUXELLES, BRUSSEL)   ☎02

The headquarters of NATO and the capital of the European Union, Brussels (pop. 1,200,000) is a dish best served piping hot in your finest china at a banquet full of diplomats and functionaries. Despite their numbers, these civil servants aren't the only ones with claims to Belgium's capital; beneath the drone of parliamentary procedure bustles the spirited clamor of locals and their profound appreciation of *frites*, beer, and whimsy. In a city that juxtaposes old and new, skyscrapers and historic buildings are plastered with three-story comics by local artists. Brussels defiantly remains a colorful city of character and history, much like its symbol, the ever-streaming *Manneken Pis*.

⌐ TRANSPORTATION

Flights: Brussels Airport (BRU; ☎090 07 00 00, €0.45 per min.; www.brusselsairport. be) is 14km from the city and accessible by train. **South Charleroi Airport (CRL;** ☎02 71 25 12 11; www.charleroi-airport.com) is 46km outside the city, between Brussels and Charleroi, and serves a number of European airlines, including **Ryanair.** From the airport, **Bus A** runs to the Charleroi-ZUID train station, where you can catch a train to Brussels. There is also a bus service which goes from the airport to Brussels's Gare du Midi (1hr., buy tickets on board). Timetables can be found on the website.

Trains: (☎02 555 2555; www.sncb.be). All international trains stop at **Gare du Midi;** most also stop at **Gare Centrale** or **Gare du Nord.** Trains run to: **Antwerp** (45min., €6.10); **Bruges** (45min., €12); **Liège** (1hr., €17); **Amsterdam, NTH** (3hr., €43, under 26 €34); **Cologne, DEU** (2hr.; €26, under 26 €22); **Luxembourg City, LUX** (1hr., €28.80); **Paris, FRA** (1hr., €55-86). **Eurostar** goes to **London, ENG** (2hr., €79-224, with Eurail or Benelux pass from €75, under 26 from €60).

Public Transportation: The **Société des Transports Intercommunaux Bruxellois (STIB;** ☎090 01 03 10, €0.45 per min.; www.stib.be) runs the **Métro (M), buses,** and

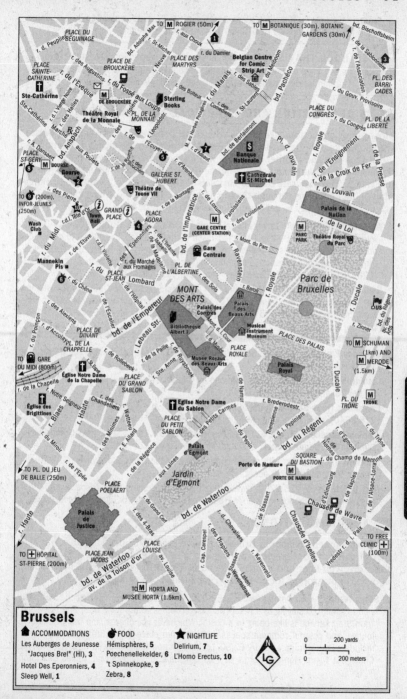

BELGIUM

Brussels

🏠 ACCOMMODATIONS
Les Auberges de Jeunesse
"Jacques Brel" (HI), **3**
Hotel Des Eperonniers, **4**
Sleep Well, **1**

🍎 FOOD
Hémisphères, **5**
Poechenellekelder, **6**
't Spinnekopke, **9**
Zebra, **8**

⭐ NIGHTLIFE
Delirium, **7**
L'Homo Erectus, **10**

0   200 yards
0   200 meters

trams daily from 5:30am-12:30am. 1hr. ticket €1.70, 1-day pass €4.50, 3-day pass €9, 5 trips €7, 10 trips €11.50. Check the website for more info.

> **HOLD THAT STUB.** Always hold on to your receipt or ticket stub to avoid steep fines on public transportation; although enforcement may appear lax, authorities do conduct spot checks and could charge you a fine.

ORIENTATION AND PRACTICAL INFORMATION

Most major attractions are clustered around **Grand-Place**, between the **Bourse** (Stock Market) to the west and the **Parc de Bruxelles** to the east. One **Métro** line circles the city and another bisects it, while efficient **3/4 trams** run north-south. Signs list street names in both French and Flemish; *Let's Go* lists all addresses in French. The concrete hills of Brussels make biking inconvenient, so don't plan on maneuvering through the bustle of the city by bike. Since cars rule the streets, the best way to get around is either by foot or tram.

Tourist Office: Brussels International Tourism and Congress (BITC; ☎02 548 0452; www.brures.com). M: Bourse. On Grand-Place in the Town Hall. The official tourist office books accommodations in the city for no charge and sells the **Brussels Card,** which provides free public transport, a city map, and access to 25 museums for 1, 2, or 3 days (€20/28/33). Open daily Easter-Dec. 9am-6pm; Jan.-Easter M-Sa 9am-6pm.

Embassies and Consulates: Australia, 6-8 r. Guimard (☎02 286 0500; www.austemb. be). **Canada,** 2 av. Tervuren (☎02 741 0611; www.international.gc.ca/brussels). **Ireland,** 50 r. Wiertz (☎02 235 6676). **New Zealand,** 1 sq. de Meeus (☎02 512 1040). **UK,** 85 r. d'Arlon (☎02 287 6211; www.british-embassy.be). **US,** 27 bd. du Régent (☎02 508 2111; www.brussels.usembassy.gov).

Currency Exchange: Travelex, Nord Station (☎02 513 2845). Open M-F 10am-5pm, Sa 10am-7pm, Su 10am-4pm.

Laundromat: Wash Club, 68 r. du Marché au Charbon. M: Bourse. Wash €3.50 per 8kg, €7 per 18kg. Open daily 7am-10pm.

Pharmacy: Neos-Bourse Pharmacie, 61 bd. Anspach at r. du Marché aux Poulets (☎02 218 0640). M: Bourse. Open M-Sa 8:30am-6:30pm.

Medical Services: St. Luc's, 10 av. Hippocrate (☎02 764 1111), near Grand-Place. **Clinique St Etienne Kliniek,** 100 r. du Meridien (☎02 225 9111).

Internet: Internet cafes with phone booths can be found on ch. de Wavre. M: Porte de Namur. Most charge €1-2 per hr.

Post Office: (☎02 226 9700; www.laposte.be). At the corner of bd. Anspach and r. des Augustins. M: De Brouckère. Open M-F 8am-7pm, Sa 10:30am-6:30pm. **Poste Restante.**

ACCOMMODATIONS

Lodging is much cheaper in Brussels than in other European capitals, but can be difficult to find, especially on weekends in summer. Overall, accommodations are well-kept and centrally located. The **BITC** (see **Practical Information,** abovee) books rooms for no fee, and sometimes offers discounts.

Sleep Well, 23 r. du Damier (☎02 218 5050; www.sleepwell.be). M: Rogier. "Star" service is similar to staying in a hotel (visitors get rooms with private bath and TV), while "non-Star" service is like being in a hostel. Whichever you choose, the bar, pool table, lounge, and colorful common spaces make it a fun place to be. Breakfast and linens included. Free storage. Laundry €2.50. Lockout for non-Star 11am-3pm. Check-in 3pm. Check-out 11am. Non-star dorms €18-23; singles €30; doubles €54; triples €72. Star singles €42; doubles €60, triples €85. Discounts after 1st night for all non-Star rooms except singles. MC/V. ❷

Les Auberges de Jeunesse "Jacques Brel" (HI), 30 r. de la Sablonnière (☎02 218 0187). M: Botanique. Spacious rooms surround a courtyard with a picturesque fountain. Breakfast and linens included. Bring lock and towel. Free laundry. Free internet 7pm-midnight. Reception 8am-1am. Lockout noon-3pm. Dorms €19-21; singles €34; doubles €52; triples and quads €63-84. €3 HI discount. MC/V. ❷

FOOD

Brussels has earned its reputation as one of the culinary capitals of Europe, although the city's restaurants are often more suited to the five-star set than to the student traveler. Inexpensive eateries cluster outside **Grand-Place**. Vendors along **Rue du Marché aux Fromages** to the south hawk cheap Greek and Middle Eastern food until late at night, while the smell of lobster and seafood permeates the air on **Rue des Bouchers**. *Frites* vendors are scattered throughout the city and offer mountains of golden fries in white paper cones for around €3. An **AD Delhaize** supermarket is on the corner of bd. Anspach and r. du Marché aux Poulets. (M: Bourse. Open M-Th and Sa 9am-8pm, F 9am-9pm, Su 9am-6pm.) **Grocery stores** such as **Carrefour** can be found throughout the city and are a great way to save while still getting quality Belgian treats like their famous chocolates and **waffles** (you can get about 10 for the price of one from vendors.)

Poechenellekelder, 5 r. du Chêne (☎02 511 9262; www.poechenellekelder.com). If the ongoing trickle of water from *Manneken Pis* makes you parched, head across the street for a drink amid hanging marionettes in this 3-story bar. Opt for outdoor seating to watch the tourists giggle at the miniscule statue while you bask in the sunlight enjoying a drink. Coffee (€2-6) is supplemented by a menu of *tartines* (open-faced sandwiches; €4-7) and *pâté* (€8). Beer €2-8. Open Tu-Su 11am-2am. Cash only. ❸

A La Mort Subite, 7 r. Montagne-aux-Herbes-Potagères (☎02 513 1318; www.alamortsubite.com). M: Gare Centrale or De Brouckère. Across from Galeries Royals St. Hubert. Feel classy—but not out of place—while ordering an omelette (€4.30-8.70) or Gueuze Mort Subite (Belgian beer; €4) brewed specifically for the restaurant. Open M-Sa 11am-1am, Su 12-11pm. MC/V. ❷

In 't Spinnekopke, 1 pl. du Jardin aux Fleurs (☎02 511 8695). M: Bourse. Tucked away near a small square with a fountain. Locals "inside the spider's head" savor the authentically Belgian menu. Entrees €15-25. Open

ON THE MENU

WAFFLING THE ISSUE

At the base of the budget tourist's food pyramid in Belgium lies an auspicious dietary group: the waffle (*gaufre* in French, *wafel* in Dutch). There are two types of Belgian waffles, both made on such particular waffle irons that they can not be made well elsewhere.

Brussels waffles are flat and more or less rectangular. They're light and airy, and bear some resemblance to ones eaten in the US (the kind served at diner brunches, not the ones that emerge from the freezer, pop out of the toaster, and beg to be drowned in high fructose corn syrup). Belgian recipes tend to use beaten egg whites and yeast as leavening agents, which give them their light, crisp texture. **De Lièges** waffles, ubiquitous on Belgian streets, are generally smaller, sweeter, and denser than their counterparts, and have a crunchy caramelized-sugar crust.

Pause at a cafe for a Brussels waffle, and savor it with a knife and fork. Approach a street vendor for a hand-held Liège waffle and continue to wander (in search of your next waffle?). Both can be topped with chocolate, fruit, or ice cream, or dusted with powdered sugar. Waffles generally cost about €1.50, though prices mount with the toppings. Since you can't visit Belgium without sampling its waffles, you might as well indulge!

M-F noon-3pm, 6pm-midnight, Sa 6pm-midnight. Kitchen closes at 11pm. AmEx/MC/V. ❺

Hémisphères, 29 r. Leopold (☎02 513 9370; www.hemispheres-resto.be). This restaurant, art gallery, and "intercultural space" serves Middle Eastern, Indian, and Asian fare. Couscous with veggies or meat €11-15. Entrees €7-15. Concerts 1 Sa per month. Open M-F noon-3pm and 6-10:30pm, Sa 6:30pm-late. MC/V. ❹

Da-Kao II, 19 r. Van Artevelde (☎02 512 6716). Offers large, budget-friendly portions of Vietnamese and Thai food. Entrees €5-12. Open M-Sa 12pm-3pm and 6pm-midnight. Cash only. ❶

Zebra, 31 pl. St-Géry. (☎02 513 5116). M: Bourse. Hipsters abound in this centrally located cafe and bar. Known for its mixed drinks. Also serves juices, milkshakes, and light but filling sandwiches (€5), salads (€6.50), and soups (€3.50). Open M-Th and Su 11am-1am, F-Sa 11am-2am. Kitchen open 11am-9pm. AmEx/MC/V over €12. ❶

Mokafe, in Galeries Royals St. Hubert (☎02 511 7870). Pause at this authentic old time coffee shop for a break from endless shopping. Pastries €1-3. Crepes €4-6. Waffles €5. Mixed drinks €6. Open daily 7am-midnight. AmEx/MC/V. ❷

Maison Antoine, 1 pl. Jourdan. M: Schuman. The Maison, a famed fast-food kiosk in the center of a parking lot, has served the best *frites* (€2-2.20) in town for 58 years. Nearby is a romantic park with sculptures where you and your *frites* can have some one-on-one time. Make sure to get a side of flavored mayo (€0.50). Open M-Th and Su 11:30am-1am, F-Sa 11:30am-2am. ❶

Gaufre de Bruxelles, Pl. Agora. (☎02 514 0171; www.belgiumwaffle.com). An outdoor seating area and hordes of hungry Belgians separate this waffle pavilion from the competition. Delicious waffles (€2.60-5.50) come topped with homemade ice cream. Add chocolate, whipped cream, strawberries, or bananas (€1.50-4.20) if you're feeling indulgent. Open daily 7am-midnight. AmEx/MC/V. ❶

NO LADIES' CHOICE. Women navigating Brussels on their own are often the target of unwanted advances from male admirers. While sexual harassment is illegal in Belgium, isolated incidents are rarely prosecuted. Consider venturing out with a companion.

👁 SIGHTS

GRAND-PLACE AND ENVIRONS. Three blocks behind the town hall, on the corner of r. de l'Étuve and r. du Chêne, is Brussels's most giggled-at sight, the 🔖**Mannekin Pis,** a fountain of a boy peeing continuously. Legend claims it commemorates a young Belgian who defused a bomb destined for the Grand-Place. The fountain was actually installed to supply the neighborhood with water during the reign of Albert and Isabelle. To close the gender gap, a statue of a squatting girl *(Jeanneken)* now pees down an alley off r. des Bouchers. Victor Hugo once called Grand-Place "the most beautiful square in the world."

During the day, be sure to visit **La Maison du Roi** (King's House), now the city museum, whose most riveting exhibit is the collection of clothes worn by *Mannekin Pis*. It's also home to the town hall, where 40min. guided tours reveal over-the-top decorations and an impressive collection of paintings. *(La Maison du Roi ☎02 279 4350. Open Tu-Su 10am-5pm. €3. Town Hall ☎02 548 0445. English-language tours Tu-W 3:15pm, Su 10:45am and 12:15pm; arrive early. €3, students €2.50.)* You'll find an extremely brief introduction to the brewing process and a quiet spot to enjoy Belgium's famed beers at the **Belgian Brewer's Museum.** *(10 Grand-Place. 2 buildings left of the town hall. ☎02 511 4987; www.beerparadise.be. Open daily 10am-5pm. €6, includes 1 beer.)* Nearby, the **Museum of Cocoa and Chocolate** tells of Belgium's other renowned edible export. Cacao fruits grow on display, and the smell of chocolate permeates the air as an expert demonstrates the art of working with chocolate. (11 r. de la Tête d'Or. ☎02 514 2048; www.mucc.be. Open July-Aug. and holidays daily 10am-5pm; Sept.-June Tu-Su 10am-4:30pm. €5.50, students €4.50.) The top floor of **Parking 58** provides a view of the entire city from the Palace of Justice to Atomium. Take the elevator to the 10th floor and enjoy a sunset fit for a bureaucrat. (1 r. de l'Eveque near St. Kateljine. Free.) In the skylit **Galeries Royals Saint-Hubert arcade,** one block behind Grand-Place, a long covered walkway is lined with shops whose wares range from *haute couture* to marzipan frogs. Just north of Gare Centrale, the **Cathédrale Saint-Michel et Sainte-Gudule** hosts royal affairs under its soaring ribbed vaults. At times, music from a pipe organ or carillon serenades visitors. (Pl. Ste-Gudule. Open M-F 7am-6pm, Sa-Su 8:30am-3pm. Free.)

MONT DES ARTS. The ◪**Musées Royaux des Beaux-Arts** encompass the **Musée d'Art Ancien,** the **Musée d'Art Moderne,** and several contemporary exhibits. The museums steward a huge collection of Belgian art, including Bruegel's famous *Landscape with the Fall of Icarus,* and pieces by Rubens. Other masterpieces on display include David's *Death of Marat* and paintings by Delacroix, Gauguin, Seurat, and van Gogh. Connected by a tunnel and requiring a separate ticket, the **Musée Magritte** houses the works of the famed Surrealist and Brussels native René Magritte. The great hall is itself a work of architectural beauty and the panoramic view of Brussels from the fourth floor of the Magritte alone justifies the price of admission. (3 r. de la Régence. M: Parc. ☎02 508 3211; www.fine-arts-museum. be. Open Tu-Su 10am-5pm. Some wings close noon-2pm. Each museum costs €8, under 26 €2, under 18 free; combination tickets costs €13, under 26 €3, under 18 free. 1st W of each month 1-5pm free. Audio tour €2.50.) The **Musical Instrument Museum (MIM)** houses over 1500 instruments; stand in front of one and your headphones automatically play a sample of its music. (2 r. Montagne de la Cour. ☎02 545 0130; www.mim.fgov.be. Open Tu-F 9:30am-4:45pm, Sa-Su 10am-5pm. €5, students €4. 1st W of each month 1-5pm free.)

BELGIAN CENTER FOR COMIC STRIP ART. Comic strips (les BD) are a serious business in Belgium. Today, a restored warehouse designed by famous architect Victor Horta pays tribute to what Belgians call the Ninth Art. Tintin and the Smurfs make several appearances, and amusing displays document comic strip history. (☎02 191 980; www. comicscenter.net. R. des Sables. M: Rogier. Open Tu-Su 10am-6pm. Students with ISIC €6.)

♫ ▨ ENTERTAINMENT AND NIGHTLIFE

The weekly *What's On*, part of the *Bulletin* newspaper and available free at the tourist office, contains info on cultural events. The **Théâtre Royal de la Monnaie,** on pl. de la Monnaie, is renowned for its opera and ballet. (M: De Brouckère. ☎02 229 1200, box office ☎02 70 39 39; www.lamonnaie.be. Tickets from €8, half-price tickets go on sale 20min. prior to the event.) The **Théâtre Royal de Toone VII,** 66 r. du Marché-aux-herbes, stages marionette performances, a distinctly Belgian art form. (☎02 513 5486; www.toone.be for show times and prices. F 8:30pm, Sa 4pm and 8:30pm; occasionally Tu-Th. €10, students €7.) On summer nights, live concerts on Grand-Place and the Bourse bring the streets to life. The *All the Fun* pamphlet, available at the tourist office, lists the newest clubs and bars. On **Place St-Géry,** patios are jammed with a laid-back crowd of students and backpackers. Choose from over 2000 beers at carefree ▨**Delirium,** 4A impasse de la Fidélité. (☎02 251 4434; www.deliriumcafe.be. Jam session Th and Su 11pm. Open daily 10am-4am.) **GBLT nightlife** in Brussels primarily centers on r. des Pierres and r. du Marché au Charbon, next to Grand-Place. **L'Homo Erectus,** 57 r. des Pierres, is an extremely popular destination. (☎02 514 7493; www.lhomoerectus.com. Open daily 3pm-3am.)

FLANDERS (VLAANDEREN)

BRUGES (BRUGGE)   ☎050

Bruges (pop. 117,000) is arguably Belgium's most romantic city. Canals carve their way through rows of pointed brick houses and cobblestone streets en route to the breathtaking Gothic Markt. The city's buildings remain some of the best-preserved examples of Northern Renaissance architecture. Though a bit crowded, Bruges is a relaxing getaway to catch your breath.

⌐ TRANSPORTATION

Trains leave from the **Stationsplein,** a 10min. walk south of the city. (Open daily 4:30am-11pm. Info desk open daily 8am-7pm.) Trains head to: Antwerp (1hr., 2 per hr., €13); Brussels (1hr., 1-3 per hr.; €12); Ghent (20min., 3 per hr., €5.60); Knokke (30min., 2 per hr., €3); Ostend (15min., 3 per hr., €3.30).

▦❷ ORIENTATION AND PRACTICAL INFORMATION

Bruges is enclosed by a circular canal, with the train station, Stationsplein, just beyond its southern extreme. The historic district is entirely accessible by foot, while bikes are popular for countryside visits. The dizzying **Belfort** looms high over the center of town, presiding over the handsome **Markt.** On the easternmost edge of the city, the beautiful, windmill-lined **Kruisvestraat** and serene **Minnewater Park** have stretches of gorgeous green land, ideal for picnicking.

Tourist Office: In and Uit, 't Zand 34 (☎050 44 46 46; www.brugge.be). From the train station, head left to 't Zand and walk for 10min.; it's in the red concert hall. Books rooms for a €2.50 fee and €20 deposit, and sells **maps** (€0.50) and ▨ **info guides** for €1. (Open M-W and F-Su 10am-6pm, Th 10am-8pm.)

Currency Exchange: Goffin, Steenstraat 2, is near the Markt and charges no commission on cash exchange (☎050 34 04 71.) Open M-Sa 9am-5:30pm.

Luggage Storage: At the train station. €2.60-3.60.

Laundromat: Belfort, Ezelstr. 51. Wash €3-6, dry €1. Open daily 7am-10pm.

Police: Hauwerstr. 7 (☎050 44 89 30).

Hospitals: A. Z. St-Jan (☎050 45 21 11; not Oud St-Janshospitaal, a museum). **St-Lucas** (☎050 36 91 11). **St-Franciscus Xaveriuskliniek** (☎050 47 04 70).

Internet: Teleboutique Brugge, Predikherenstr. 48, is one of the cheapest options. €2 per hour. Open daily 10am-10pm. Cash only.

Post Office: Markt 5. Open M and W-F 9am-6pm, Sa 9:30am-12:30pm.

⌐ ACCOMMODATIONS

▨ **Snuffel Backpacker Hostel,** Ezelstr. 47-49 (☎050 33 31 33; www.snuffel.be). Take bus #3 or 13 (€1.30) from the station to the stop after Markt, then take the 1st left. Colorful rooms decorated by local artists. On-site bar Happy hour (9-10pm, beer €1) is a favorite among locals. Guests also get a free Bruges card, which gives access to museums and offers many discounts. Kitchen. Bike rental €6 per day. Breakfast €3. Lockers available; bring lock or rent one. Linens included. Free Wi-Fi. Key deposit €5. Reception 7:30am-midnight. Dorms €14; doubles €36; quads €60-64. AmEx/MC/V. ❷

Passage, Dweersstr. 26 (☎050 34 02 32; www.passagebruges.com). Old-world, refined hostel-hotel-cafe in an ideal location. Safes available. Breakfast €5; included in private

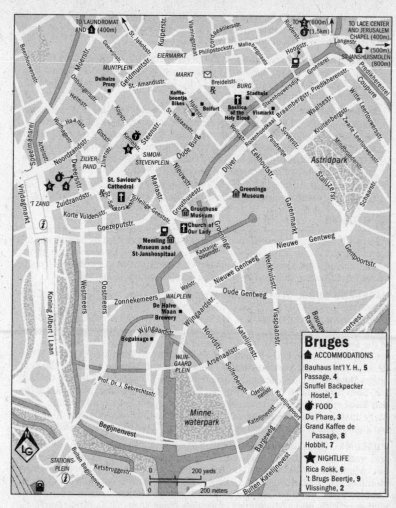

rooms. Free beer at bar with purchase of dinner. Internet €4 per hr. Reception 9am-11pm; need code to get in after close. Open mid-Feb. to mid-Jan. Dorms €14; singles €25-45; doubles €45-60; triples and quads €75-90. AmEx/MC/V. ❷

Bauhaus International Youth Hostel and Hotel, Langestr. 133-137 (☎500 34 10 93; www.bauhaus.be). Take bus #6 or 16 from the station; ask to stop at the hostel. A giant candelabra and popular bar lead the way to airy rooms. Bike rental €9 per day. Breakfast and linens included. Lockers €1.50. Internet €3 per hr. Reception 8am-midnight. Dorms €14-15; singles from €26; doubles from €40; triples from €57. AmEx/MC/V. ❷

🔲 FOOD

Inexpensive restaurants can be hard to find in Bruges. Seafood lovers should splurge at least once on the city's famous *mosselen* (mussels; €15-22) found at the **Vismarkt**, near the Burg. (Open Tu-Sa 8am-1pm.) Restaurants close early in Bruges (around 10pm); grab groceries at **Delhaize Proxy**, Noordzandstr. 4, near the Markt. (Open M-Sa 9am-7pm.)

Grand Kaffee de Passage, Dweersstr. 26-28 (☎050 34 02 32). Next to the Passage hostel. Traditional Belgian cuisine in a candlelit setting. Try the excellent Flemish stew (€11). Desserts are cheap and tasty (€2-5). Entrees €8-15. Open daily 5-11pm. Closed from mid-Jan. to mid-Feb. AmEx/MC/V. ❸

Du Phare, Sasplein 2 (☎050 34 35 90; www.duphare.be). From the Burg, walk down Hoogstr. and turn left at the canal onto Verversdijk, crossing to the right side at the second bridge. Follow the canal for 20min. to Sasplein. Bus #4 stops right outside. This jazz and blues bistro serves international fare (€11-20). Open M and W 11:30am-2:30pm and 7pm-midnight, Tu and F-Sa 11:30am-2:30pm and 6:30pm-midnight, Su 11:30am-midnight. Reservations recommended F-Sa. AmEx/MC/V. ❸

Hobbit, Kemelstr. 8-10 (☎050 33 55 20; www.hobbitgrill.be). Try filling meats and pastas off funny newsprint menus. Entrees €7-11. Open daily 6pm-1am. AmEx/MC/V. ❷

◎ SIGHTS

Filled with Gothic and neo-Gothic buildings and crisscrossed by canals, picturesque Bruges is best experienced on foot. Avoid visiting Bruges on Mondays, when museums are closed. If you plan to visit many museums, consider a cost-saving combination ticket (€15, includes admission to 5 museums).

MARKT AND BURG. The medieval **Belfort** (belfry) looms over the Markt; climb its 366 steep steps for a city view. *(Belfort open Tu-Su 9:30am-5pm. Last entry 4:15pm. €5. Bell concerts mid-June to Sept. M, W, and Sa 9pm, Su 2:15pm; Oct. to mid-June W and Sa-Su 2:15pm.)* Behind the Markt, the Burg is dominated by the finely detailed facade of the **Stadhuis** (Town Hall). Inside, wander through the gilded **Gothic Hall,** where residents of Bruges still get married. *(☎050 44 81 10. Open Tu-Su 9:30am-4:30pm. €2.50, under 26 €1.50. Audio tour included.)* This ticket will also get you into **Liberty of Bruges Museum,** which contains an ornate fireplace. *(Open M-Sa 9:30am-12:30pm and 1:30-5pm).* Tucked in a corner of the Burg next to the Stadhuis, the **Basilica of the Holy Blood** supposedly holds the blood of Christ in a spectacularly ornate sanctuary upstairs. *(Basilica open daily Apr.-Sept. 9:30am-noon and 2-6pm; Oct.-Mar. 10am-noon and 2-4pm; closed W afternoon. Holy Relic can be viewed at 11am and 2-4pm. Museum €1.50.)*

MUSEUMS. From the Burg, follow Wollestr. left and then head right on Dijver and walk through the garden to reach the **Groeninge Museum,** small for its price but overflowing with beautiful portraits and works by Jan van Eyck and Hans Memling. *(Dijver 12. ☎050 50 44 87. Open Tu-Su 9:30am-5pm. €8, under 26 €6. Audio tour included.)* Formerly a palace, the nearby **Gruuthuse Museum** houses a large collection of 16th- and 17th-century tapestries. *(Dijver 17. ☎050 44 87 62. Open Tu-Su 9:30am-5pm. €6, students €4. Audio tour included.)*

OTHER SIGHTS. Sophisticated beer aficionados will enjoy the accompanying samples at 150-year-old **De Halve Maan,** a beer museum and brewery. *(Welplein 26. ☎50 33 26 97; www.halvemaan.be. 45min. tours Apr.-Sept. 1 per hr. M-F 11am-4pm, Sa-Su 11am-5pm; Oct.-Mar. tours M-F 11am and 3pm, Sa-Su 1 per hr. 11am-4pm. €5, includes beer.)* For God-sanctioned fun, wander the grounds of the **Beguinage,** home to nuns who share their flower-covered yard with passersby. The Beguine's house displays furnishings typical of medieval Flemish households. *(From Simon Stevinplein, follow Mariastr., and turn right on Wijngaardstr.; at the canal, turn right and cross the footbridge. ☎050 33 00 11. Open Mar.-Nov. daily 10am-noon and 1:45-5pm; gate open 6:30am-6:30pm. Church and garden free; house €2, under 26 €1.)* Walk along the river to see the windmills; to enter, go down to 235-year-old windmill **St-Janshuismolen,** which still gives occasional flour-grinding demonstrations in summer. (☎ *050 33 00 44. Open May-Sept. daily 9:30am-12:30pm and 1:30-5pm. €2, under 26 €1.)*

🌸 📷 FESTIVALS AND NIGHTLIFE

Bruges plays host to the **Cactusfestival** (☎ 050 33 20 14; www.cactusfestival. be. €25 per day, €63 for 3 days), a series of alt-pop and hip-hop concerts the first full weekend in July. The city also sponsors **Klinkers,** an open-air music and film series that's free to the public during the months of July and August (☎ 50 33 20 14; www.klinkers-brugge.be).

At **'t Brugs Beertje,** Kemelstr. 5, off Steenstr., you can sample some of the 250 varieties of beer. (☎ 050 33 96 16. Open M, Th and Su 4pm-12:30am, F-Sa 4pm-2am.) Stop by Bruges's oldest pub, **Vlissinghe,** Blekersstr. 2, established in 1515. From the Burg, take Hoogstr. and turn left onto Verversdijk immediately before the canal. Cross the second bridge onto Blekersstr. (☎ 050 34 37 37. Open W-Sa 11am-midnight, Su 11am-7pm.) Steer clear of the pricey tourist-trap clubs behind the Markt. Belgian students tend to prefer the dance floor of **Rica Rokk,** 't Zand 6, where shots are €3 and a liter of beer starts at €19. (☎ 050 33 24 34; www.maricarokk.com. Open daily 9:30am-5am.)

> **⭐TIP⭐ THE LONG ARM OF THE LAW.** If you're wobbling back to your hostel with a bellyful of beer, think twice before yielding to nature's call en route. Police will fine you up to €152 if they catch you urinating in public. Keep €0.30 handy for the public toilets; many of these stalls close at 8pm.

ANTWERP (ANTWERPEN, ANVERS) ☎ 03

While Antwerp (pop. 466,000) was once known for its avant-garde fashion and jet-setting party hoppers, the hipster scene has since calmed down. But an afternoon of window-shopping in the city's diamond quarter or along the Meir reveals that Antwerp still holds an attraction for the backpaper fashionista.

📷 📷 TRANSPORTATION AND PRACTICAL INFORMATION. Antwerp has two train stations: **Berchem,** which handles most of the city's international traffic, and **Centraal,** the domestic-centered station. **Trains** leave from Berchem to: Amsterdam, NTH (2hr., 1 per hr., €21-29); Brussels (45min., 4 per hr., €6.10); and Rotterdam, NTH (1hr., 1 per hr., €13-18). Centraal ticket office is open daily 6am-10pm. Lockers are available in Centraal. The **tourist office** is downstairs. To reach Grote Markt from Berchem, take tram #8 (€1.20, €1.50 on board) to Groenpl. From Centraal take tram #2 (dir.: Linkeroever) or walk down Meir, the main pedestrian thoroughfare, to Groenpl. (☎ 03 232 0103. Open M-Sa 9am-5:45pm, Su 9am-4:45pm. English-language historical tour from Grote Markt 13 Sa-Su 11am. €5.) **Postal Code:** 2000.

📷 📷 ACCOMMODATIONS AND FOOD. The well-worn **New International Youth Hotel ❷,** Provinciestr. 256, is a 10min. walk from Centraal Station, on the corner of De Boeystr. and Provinciestr. Turn left out of the station onto Pelikaanstr., which becomes Simonsstr.; turn left Van Den Nestlei, walk under the bridge, then turn right onto De Boeystr. (☎ 03 230 0522; www.youthhotel.be. Breakfast included. Reception 8am-midnight. Dorms €19-21, under 26 with sleeping bag €15; singles €34; doubles €49-61; triples €70-79. MC/V.) Take the metro to Groenpl. for **Guesthouse 26 ❺,** Pelgrimsstr. 26, in the heart of the city. Inventive

BELGIUM

decor keeps guests returning. (☎03 289 3995; www.guesthouse26.be. Breakfast included. Reserve ahead. Singles €55-75; doubles €65-85. AmEx/MC/V.)

More than 400 religious figurines accompany your meal at █'t Elfde Gebod ❹, Torfburg 10. (☎03 289 3466 Entrees €8-20. Open daily noon-2am. Kitchen open noon-10:30pm. MC/V.) Da Giovanni ❷, Jan Blomstr. 8, off Groenpl., serves hearty pizzas (€4-10) bringing Italy to Belgium with a traditional, rich decor of wine bottles and grapes hanging from the ceiling. (☎03 226 7450; www.dagiovanni. be. Pasta €7-13. Meat Entrees €13-18. Fish €13-20. Open daily 11am-midnight. 20% student discount. AmEx/MC/V.)

█▓ **SIGHTS AND NIGHTLIFE.** The main promenades, De Keyserlei and the Meir, draw crowds to their elegant department stores and avant-garde boutiques. On the western edge of the district, the Cathedral of Our Lady, Groenpl. 21, holds Rubens's *Descent from the Cross*. (www.dekathedraal.be. Open M-F 10am-5pm, Sa 10am-3pm, Su 1-4pm. Tours 1-3 per day. English tours at 3:45pm. €4, students €2, seniors and children €1.50.) A stroll by the Schelde River leads to the 13th-century Steen Castle, Steenplein 1. The Museum Voor Schone Kunsten (KMSKA; Royal Museum of Fine Arts), Leopold De Waelpl. 1-9, possesses one of the world's finest collections of Flemish paintings. (☎03 238 7809; www. kmska.be. Open Tu-Sa 10am-5pm, Su 10am-6pm. €6, under 19 free.)

Café d'Anvers, Verversrui 15, north of Grote Markt, used to be an old church but is now a palatial club located smack in the center of the red-light district. (☎03 226 3870; www.cafe-d-anvers.com. Cover: Th free; F €5, €8 after midnight; Sa free, €10 after midnight. Open Th 11pm-6am, F-Sa 11pm-7:30am.) Bars behind the cathedral and in the trendy neighborhood around the Royal Museum of Fine Arts offer an alternative to the club scene. Step into the 15th-century cellars for a candlelit dinner at Pelgrom, Pelgrimstr. 15, before sampling the local *elixir d'Anvers* (strong herbal liqueur; €5) doled out by bartenders in traditional dress. (☎03 234 0809. Open daily noon-late.)

GHENT (GENT)   ☎09

Once the heart of Flanders's textile industry, modern Ghent (pop. 233,000) still celebrates the memory of its medieval greatness, and its more recent industrial past, with awe-inspiring buildings in the city's main square. Ghent has yet to become a major tourist destination, so enjoy making new discoveries and blending in with locals on your trip.

▐▓ **TRANSPORTATION AND PRACTICAL INFORMATION.** Trains run from St-Pietersstation (accessible by tram #1) to Antwerp (50min., 3per hr., €8.20), Bruges (25min., 3 per hr., €8), and Brussels (35min., 5 per hr., €7.40). The tourist office, Botermarkt 17A, in the crypt of the belfry, books rooms for no fee and leads walking tours. (☎09 266 5232; www.visitgent.be. Open daily Apr.-Oct. 9:30am-6:30pm; Nov.-Mar. 9:30am-4:30pm. Tours Nov.-Apr. daily 2:30pm; buy tickets by 2pm. €7.) The tourist office and most museums sell a pass for 15 museums and monuments in Ghent (€12.50). A great resource for young, budget-conscious backpackers, █Use-It, St-Pietersnieuwstr. 21, has quirky maps for self-guided tours, free Internet, and free toilets. (☎09 324 3906; www.use-it. be. Open M-F 1-6pm.) Postal Code: 9000.

▐▐ **ACCOMMODATIONS AND FOOD.** If you must spend the night on a budget in Ghent, try De Draecke (HI) ❷, St-Widostr. 11. From the station, take tram #1 (€1.20, €1.50 on board) to Gravensteen (15min.) Facing the castle, head left over the canal, then right on Gewad and right on St-Widostr. (☎09 233 7050;

www.vjh.be. Breakfast and linens included. Internet €2 per 30min. Reception 7:30am-11pm. Dorms €20; doubles €50. €3 HI discount. AmEx/MC/V.) To get to **Camping Blaarmeersen ❶**, Zuiderlaan 12, take bus #9 from St-Pietersstation toward Mariakerke and to Europabrug (Waterportbaan); cross the street and hop on bus #38 or 39 to Blaarmeersen. Take the first street on the left to its end. (☎09 266 8160. Laundry restaurant. Open Mar. to mid-Oct. €4.50 per person, €4.50 per tent; low season €3.50/3.50.)

St-Pietersnieuwstraat, by the university, has cheap kebab and pita joints that stay open until around midnight. **Magazijn ❷**, Penitenterstr. 24, has filling fare (€8.50-16) and vegetarian options. (☎09 234 0708. Kitchen open Tu-F noon-2pm and 6-11pm, Sa 6-11pm. Bar open late. Cash only.) For groceries, stop by the **Contact GB** at Hoogpoort 42. (☎09 225 0592. Open M-Sa 8:30am-6pm. MC/V.)

◙ SIGHTS. The **Leie canal** runs through the city and wraps around the **Gravensteen** (Castle of Counts), St-Veerlepl. 11, a partially restored medieval fortress. (☎09 225 9306. Open daily Apr.-Sept. 9am-6pm; Oct.-Mar. 9am-5pm. €6, under 26 €1.20.) Nearby is the historic **Partershol quarter,** with well-preserved 16th- to 18th-century houses. From Gravensteen, head down Geldmunt, make a right on Lange Steenst., and then turn right into the Old Town. From the Partershol, follow the river toward Groenten Markt and Korenmarkt. Walk across **St-Michielshelling** bridge for the best view of Ghent's skyline. From here, walk north on either of the two bridges, where you can take a 40min. boat tour (Mar.-Nov. 4 per hr., €5.50, students and over 60 €5, children €3). St-Michielshelling connects two majestic cathedrals. Facing the bridge with Graslei behind you, **St-Niklaaskerk** is on your right (☎09 225 3700. Open M 2:30-5pm, Tu-Su 10am-5pm. Free.) On the left, on Limburgstr., the elaborately decorated ◙**St-Baafskathedraal** holds Flemish brothers Hubert and Jan van Eyck's *Adoration of the Mystic Lamb* and Rubens's *St. Bavo's Entrance into the Monastery of Ghent.* (www.sintbaafskathedraal-gent.be. Open daily Apr.-Oct. 8:30am-6pm; Nov.-Mar. 8:30am-5pm. *The Ghent Alterpiece* exhibit open Apr.-Oct. M-Sa 9:30am-5pm, Su 1-5pm; Nov.-Mar. M-Sa 10:30am-4pm, Su 1-4pm. Cathedral and crypt free. The Ghent Alterpiece exhibit €3.) **Stedelijk Museum voor Actuele Kunst (SMAK),** in Citadel Park, a 30min. walk from the tourist office or a shorter ride on the #1 tram from Korenmarkt (dir.: Flanders Expo; €1.20, €1.50 on tram), regularly rotates its collection of cutting-edge modern art. (☎09 221 1703; www.smak.be. Open Tu-Su 10am-6pm. €5, students €3.80; free 1st F of each month 6-10pm.)

◙◙ NIGHTLIFE AND FESTIVALS. **Korenmarkt** and **Vrijdagmarkt** are filled with restaurants and pubs. *Use-It's* (p. 100) guide to nightlife can direct you to live music options. One popular haunt is the dimly lit **Charlatan,** Vlasmarkt 6, which features a nightly DJ. (☎09 224 2457; www.charlatan.be. Live bands Th and Su. Open Tu-Su 7pm-late.) For **GLBT nightlife,** consult *Use-It's Ghent Gay Map* or head to the **Foyer Casa Rosa,** Kammerstr. 22/Belfortstr. 39, an info center and bar. (☎09 269 2812; www.casarosa.be. Bar open M-F 3pm-1am, Sa-Su 3pm-2am; info center open M 6-9pm, W 3-9pm, Sa 3-6pm.) The **Gentse Feesten** brings performers, carnival rides, and flowing *jenever* (flavored gin) to the city center. (Mid-July. ☎09 269 4600; www.gentsefeesten.be.)

GREAT BRITAIN

After colonizing two-fifths of the globe, spearheading the Industrial Revolution, and winning every foreign war in its history but two, Britain seems intent on making the world forget its tiny size. It's hard to believe that the rolling farms of the south and the rugged cliffs of the north are only a day's train ride apart, or that people as diverse as clubbers, miners, and monks all occupy an area roughly the size of Oregon. Beyond the fairytale cottages and sheep farms of "Merry Olde England," today's Britain is a high-energy destination driven by international influence. Though the sun may have set on the British Empire, a colonial legacy survives in multicultural urban centers and a dynamic arts and theater scene. Brits now eat kebabs and curry as often as they do scones, and dance clubs in post-industrial settings draw as much attention as elegant country inns.

DISCOVER BRITAIN: SUGGESTED ITINERARIES

THREE DAYS. Spend it all in **London** (p. 108), the city of tea, royalty, and James Bond. After a stroll through **Hyde Park,** head to **Buckingham Palace** for the changing of the guard. Check out the renowned collections of the **British Museum** and the **Tate Modern.** Stop at famed **Westminster Abbey** and catch a play at Shakespeare's **Globe Theatre** before grabbing a drink in the **East End.**

ONE WEEK. Begin, of course, in **London** (3 days), then visit academia at the colleges of **Oxford** (1 day; p. 136). Travel to **Scotland** for a day in the museums and galleries of **Glasgow** (p. 156) and finish off with pubs and parties in lively **Edinburgh** (2 days; p. 148).

ESSENTIALS

FACTS AND FIGURES

OFFICIAL NAME: United Kingdom of Great Britain and Northern Ireland.

CAPITAL: London.

MAJOR CITIES: Cardiff, Edinburgh, Glasgow, Liverpool, Manchester.

POPULATION: 60,776,000.

LAND AREA: 244,800 sq. km.

TIME ZONE: GMT.

LANGUAGE: English; also Welsh and Scottish Gaelic.

RELIGIONS: Christian: Protestant and Catholic (72%), Muslim (3%).

TOTAL NUMBER OF HARRY POTTER BOOKS SOLD: 400,000,000.

WHEN TO GO

It's wise to plan around the high season (June-Aug.). Spring and fall are better times to visit; the weather is reasonable and flights are cheaper, though there may be less transportation to rural areas. If you plan to visit the cities, the low season (Nov.-Mar.) is most economical. Keep in mind, however, that sights and accommodations often close or have reduced hours. In Scotland, summer light lasts almost until midnight, but in winter, the sun may set as early as 3:45pm. Regardless of when you go, it will rain—always.

IT'S ALL BRITISH TO ME. The United Kingdom is a political union of England, Northern Ireland, Scotland, and Wales. This is also referred to as Britain, not to be confused with the island of Great Britain, which only includes England, Scotland, and Wales. *Let's Go* uses United Kingdom and Britain interchangeably. This chapter covers Great Britain. For Northern Ireland information and coverage, see p. 441.

DOCUMENTS AND FORMALITIES

EMBASSIES AND CONSULATES. Foreign embassies in Britain are in London (p. 108). British embassies abroad include: **Australia,** Commonwealth Ave., Yarralumla, ACT 2600 (☎02 6270 6666; http://bhc.britaus.net); **Canada,** 80 Elgin St., Ottawa, ON, K1P 5K7 (☎613-237-1530; www.britainincanada.org); **Ireland,** 29 Merrion Rd., Ballsbridge, Dublin 4 (☎01 205 3700; www.british-embassy.ie); **New Zealand,** 44 Hill St., Thorndon, Wellington, 6011 (☎04 924 2888; www.britain.org.nz); **US,** 3100 Mass. Ave. NW, Washington, D.C., 20008 (☎202-588-7800; www.britainusa.com).

VISA AND ENTRY INFORMATION. EU citizens do not need a visa. Citizens of Australia, Canada, New Zealand, and the US do not need a visa for stays of up to 6 months. Students planning to study in the UK for six months or more must obtain a student visa (around US$90). For a full list of countries whose citizens require visas, call your British embassy or visit www.ukvisas.gov.uk.

TOURIST SERVICES AND MONEY

EMERGENCY	Ambulance, Fire, and Police: ☎999.

TOURIST OFFICES. Formerly the British Tourist Authority, **Visit Britain** (☎020 8846 9000; www.visitbritain.com) is an umbrella organization for regional tourist boards. Tourist offices in Britain are listed under for each city and town. They stock maps and provide info on sights and accommodations.

IT'S JUST A TIC. Tourist offices in Britain are known as Tourist Information Centres, or TICs. Britain's National Parks also have National Park Information Centres, or NPICs. This chapter refers to all offices as TICs and NPICs.

MONEY. The British unit of currency is the **pound sterling** (£), plural pounds sterling. One pound is equal to 100 **pence,** with standard denominations of 1p, 2p, 5p, 10p, 20p, 50p, £1, and £2 in coins, and £5, £10, £20, and £50 in notes. **Quid** is slang for pounds. Scotland has its own bank notes, which can be used interchangeably with English currency, though you may have difficulty using Scottish £1 notes outside Scotland. As a rule, it's cheaper to exchange money in Britain than at home. ATMs offer the best exchange rates. Many British department stores, such as Marks & Spencer, also offer excellent exchange services. Tips in restaurants are often included in the bill, sometimes as a "service charge." If gratuity is not included, tip your server about 12.5%. A 10% tip is common for taxi drivers, and £1-3 is usual for bellhops and chambermaids. To the relief of budget travelers from the US, tipping is not expected at pubs and bars in Britain. Aside from open-air markets, don't expect to bargain. For more info on money in Europe, see p. 16.

The UK has a 17.5% **value added tax (VAT),** a sales tax applied to everything but food, books, medicine, and children's clothing. The tax is included in the amount indicated on the price tag. The prices stated in *Let's Go* include VAT. In the airport upon exiting the EU, non-EU citizens can claim a refund on the tax paid for goods purchased at participating stores. You can obtain refunds only for goods you take out of the country. To apply for a refund, fill out the form that you are given in the shop and present it with the goods and receipts at customs upon departure—look for the Tax-Free Refund Desk at the airport. At peak times, this process can take an hour. You must leave the UK within three months of your purchase to claim a refund, and you must apply for the refund before leaving. For more info on qualifying for a VAT refund, see p. 19. For VAT info specific to the UK, visit http://customs.hmrc.gov.uk.

BRITISH POUND (£)		
AUS$1 = £0.47	£1 = AUS$2.14
CDN$1 = £0.51	£1 = CDN$1.97
EUR€1 = £0.79	£1 = EUR€1.27
NZ$1 = £0.38	£1 = NZ$2.62
US$1 = £0.54	£1 = US$1.86

TRANSPORTATION

BY PLANE. Most international flights land at **London's Heathrow** (LHR; ☎0870 000 0123; www.heathrowairport.com) or **Gatwick (WSX;** ☎0870 000 2468; www. gatwickairport.com) airports; **Manchester (MAN)** and **Edinburgh (EDI)** also have international airports. **Budget airlines,** like Ryanair and easyJet, fly out of many locales, including **Stansted Airport** and **Luton Airport,** (p. 109). The national airline, **British Airways** (☎0870 850 9850, US ☎800-247-9297; www.britishairways. com), offers discounted youth fares for those under 24. For more info on traveling by plane around Europe, see p. 46.

BY TRAIN. Britain's main carrier is **National Rail Enquiries** (☎08457 484 950). The country's train network is extensive, crisscrossing the length and breadth of the island. Prices and schedules often change; find up-to-date information from their website (www.nationalrail.co.uk/planmyjourney) or **Network Rail** (www.networkrail.co.uk; schedules only). **Eurostar** trains run to Britain from the Continent through the Chunnel (p. 52). The **BritRail Pass,** sold only outside Britain, allows unlimited travel in England, Scotland, and Wales (www.britrail. net). In Canada and the US, contact **Rail Europe** (Canada ☎800-361-7245, US ☎888-382-7245; www.raileurope.com). Eurail passes are not valid in Britain. Rail discount cards (£20), available at rail stations and through travel agents, grant 33% off most point-to-point fares and are available to those ages 16-25 or over 60, full-time students, and families. In general, traveling by train costs more than by bus. For more info on train travel, see p. 46.

BY BUS. The British distinguish between **buses,** which cover short routes, and **coaches,** which cover long distances; *Let's Go* refers to both as buses. **National Express** (☎08705 808 080; www.nationalexpress.com) is the main operator of long-distance bus service in Britain, while **Scottish Citylink** (☎08705 505 050; www.citylink.co.uk) has the most extensive coverage in Scotland. The **Brit Xplorer Pass** offers unlimited travel on National Express buses (7-day £79, 14-day £139, 28-day £219). **NX2 cards** (£10), available online for ages 16-26, reduce fares

Great Britain

by up to 30%. Plan ahead for the cheapest rides, National Express's **Fun Fares,** which are only sold online (limited number of tickets out of London from £1).

BY CAR. To drive, you must be 17 and have a valid license from your home country; to rent, you must be over 21. Britain is covered by a high-speed system of **motorways** (M-roads) that connect London to other major cities. Visitors should be able to handle **driving on the left side** of the road and driving **manual transmission** ("stick shift" is far more common than automatic). Roads are generally well maintained, but gasoline (petrol) prices are high. In London, driving is restricted during weekday working hours, with charges imposed in certain congestion zones; parking can be similarly nightmarish.

BY FERRY. Several ferry lines provide service between Britain and the Continent. Ask for discounts; ISIC holders can sometimes get student fares, and

Eurail pass-holders are eligible for reductions and free trips. **Seaview Ferries** (www.seaview.co.uk/ferries.html) has a directory of UK ferries. Book ahead in summer. For more info on boats to Ireland and the Continent, see p. 52.

BY BIKE AND BY FOOT. Much of the British countryside is well suited to biking. Many cities and villages have rental shops and route maps. Large-scale *Ordnance Survey* maps, often available at TICs, detail the extensive system of long-distance hiking paths. TICs and NPICs can provide extra information.

BY THUMB. Hitchhiking or standing on M-roads is illegal; one may only thumb at rest stops or at the entrance ramps to highways. Despite this, hitchhiking is fairly common in rural parts of Scotland and Wales (England is tougher) where public transportation is spotty. *Let's Go* does not recommend hitchhiking.

KEEPING IN TOUCH

PHONE CODES	**Country code: 44. International dialing prefix: 00.** Within Britain, dial city code + local number, even when dialing inside the city. For more info on how to place international calls, see **Inside Back Cover.**

EMAIL AND THE INTERNET. Internet access is ubiquitous in big cities, common in towns, and sparse in rural areas. Internet cafes or public terminals can be found almost everywhere; they usually cost £2-6 per hour, but you often pay only for the time used. For more info, see www.cybercafes.com. Public libraries usually have free or inexpensive Internet access, but you might have to wait or make an advance reservation. Many coffee shops, particularly chains such as Caffe Nero and Starbucks, offer Wi-Fi for a fee.

TELEPHONE. Most public **pay phones** in Britain are run by British Telecom (BT). Public phones charge at least 30p and don't accept 1, 2, or 5p coins. A BT Chargecard bills calls to your credit card, but most pay phones now have readers where you can swipe credit cards directly (generally AmEx/MC/V). The number for the operator in Britain is ☎100, the international operator ☎155. Whenever possible, use a **calling card** for international phone calls, as long-distance rates for national phone services are often very high. **Mobile phones** are an increasingly popular and economical option. Major mobile carriers include T-Mobile, Vodafone, and O2. Direct-dial access numbers for calling out of Britain include: **AT&T Direct** (☎0800 890 011); **Canada Direct** (☎0800 096 0634 or 0800 559 3141); **Telecom New Zealand Direct** (☎0800 890 064); **Telstra Australia** (☎0800 890 061). For more info on calling home from Europe, see p. 28.

MAIL. **Royal Mail** has tried to standardize their rates around the world. Check shipment costs with the Postal Calculator at www.royalmail.com. **Airmail** is the best way to send mail home from Britain. Just write "Par Avión—Airmail" on the top left corner of your envelope or stop by any post office to get a free airmail label. Letters sent via Airmail should be delivered within three working days to European destinations and five working days to Australia, Canada, and the US. To receive mail in the UK, have mail delivered **Poste Restante.** Mail will go to the main post office unless you specify a subsidiary by street address. Address mail to be held according to the following example: First Name, Last Name, Poste Restante, post office address, Postal Code, UK. Bring a passport to pick up your mail; there may be a small fee.

ACCOMMODATIONS AND CAMPING

BRITAIN	❶	❷	❸	❹	❺
ACCOMMODATIONS	under £15	£15-20	£21-30	£31-40	over £40

Hostelling International (HI) hostels are prevalent throughout Britain. They are run by the **Youth Hostels Association of England and Wales (YHA;** ☎08707 708 868; www. yha.org.uk), the **Scottish Youth Hostels Association (SYHA;** ☎01786 891 400; www. syha.org.uk), and **Hostelling International Northern Ireland (HINI;** ☎028 9032 4733; www.hini.org.uk). Dorms cost around £12-15 in rural areas, £15-20 in larger cities, and £20-35 in London. Make reservations at least a week in advance, especially in more touristed areas on weekends and during the summer. You can book **B&Bs** by calling directly, or by asking the local TIC to help you. TICs usually charge a flat fee of £1-5 plus 10% deposit, deductible from the amount you pay the B&B proprietor. **Campgrounds** tend to be privately owned and cost £3-10 per person per night. It is illegal to camp in national parks.

FOOD AND DRINK

BRITAIN	❶	❷	❸	❹	❺
FOOD	under £6	£6-10	£11-15	£16-20	over £20

A pillar of traditional British fare, the cholesterol-filled, meat-anchored **full English breakfast** is still served in most B&Bs across the country. Beans on toast or toast smothered in Marmite (the most acquired of tastes—a salty, brown spread made from yeast) are breakfast staples. The best native dishes for lunch or dinner are roasts—beef, lamb, and Wiltshire hams—and **Yorkshire pudding,** a type of popover drizzled with meat juices. Despite their intriguing names, **bangers and mash** and **bubble and squeak** are just sausages and potatoes and cabbage and potatoes, respectively. Pubs serve savory meat pies like **Cornish pasties** (PASS-tees) or **ploughman's lunches** consisting of bread, cheese, and pickles. **Fish and chips** (french fries) are traditionally drowned in malt vinegar and salt. **Crisps,** or potato chips, come in an astonishing variety, with flavors like prawn cocktail. Britons make their desserts (often called "puddings" or "afters") exceedingly sweet and gloopy. **Sponges, trifles, tarts,** and the ill-named **spotted dick** (spongy currant cake) will satiate the sweetest tooth. To escape English food, try Chinese, Greek, or Indian cuisine. British **"tea"** refers to both a drink, served strong and milky, and to a social ritual. A high tea might include cooked meats, salad, sandwiches, and pastries, while the oft-stereotyped afternoon tea comes with finger sandwiches, scones with jam and **clotted cream** (a sinful cross between whipped cream and butter), and small cakes. **Cream tea,** a specialty of Cornwall and Devon, includes scones or crumpets, jam, and clotted cream.

HOLIDAYS AND FESTIVALS

Holidays: New Year's Day (Jan. 1, 2009); Epiphany (Jan. 6, 2009); Good Friday (Apr. 10, 2009); Easter (Apr. 13, 2009); Ascension (May 21, 2009); Pentecost (May 31, 2009); Corpus Christi (June 11, 2009); Bank Holidays (May 4, May 25, and Aug. 31, 2009); Assumption (Aug. 15, 2009); All Saints' Day (Nov. 1, 2009); Christmas (Dec. 25, 2009); Boxing Day (Dec. 28, 2009).

Festivals: Scotland's New Year's Eve celebration, *Hogmanay,* takes over the streets in Edinburgh and Glasgow. The *National Eisteddfod of Wales* (Aug. 1-8, 2009) has brought

Welsh writers, musicians, and artists together since 1176. One of the largest music and theater festivals in the world is the *Edinburgh International Festival* (Aug. 14-Sept. 6, 2009); also highly recommended is the *Edinburgh Fringe Festival* (Aug. 2009). Manchester's Gay Village hosts *Manchester Pride* (www.manchesterpride.com) in August, and London throws a huge street party at the *Notting Hill Carnival* (Aug. 23-24, 2009). Bonfires and fireworks abound on England's *Guy Fawkes Day* (Nov. 5, 2009) in celebration of a conspirator's failed attempt to destroy the Houses of Parliament in 1605.

BEYOND TOURISM

There are many opportunities for volunteering, studying, and working in Britain. As a volunteer, you can participate in projects ranging from archaeological digs to lobbying for social change. Explore your academic passions at the country's prestigious institutions or pursue an independent research project. For more info on opportunities across Europe, see **Beyond Tourism**, p. 55.

The National Trust, Volunteering and Community Involvement Office, P.O. Box 39, Warrington WA5 7WD (☎0870 458 4000; www.nationaltrust.org.uk/volunteering). Arranges numerous volunteer opportunities, including volunteer work on holidays.

The Teacher Recruitment Company, Pennineway Offices (1), 87-89 Saffron Hill, London EC1N 8QU (☎0845 833 1934; www.teachers.eu.com). International recruitment agency that lists positions across the country and provides info on jobs in the UK.

University of Oxford, College Admissions Office, Wellington Sq., Oxford OX1 2JD (☎01865 288 000; www.ox.ac.uk). Large range of summer programs (£880-3780) and year-long courses (£8880-11,840).

ENGLAND

A land where the stately once prevailed, England is now a youthful, hip, and forward-looking nation on the cutting edge of art, music, and film. But traditionalists can rest easy; for all the moving and shaking in large cities, scores of ancient towns, opulent castles, and comforting cups of tea still abound.

LONDON ☎020

London offers visitors a bewildering array of choices: Leonardo at the National Gallery or Hirst at the Tate Modern; Rossini at the Royal Opera or Les Misérables at the Queen's; Bond Street couture or Camden cutting-edge—you could spend your entire stay just deciding what to do. London is not often described as a unified city but rather as a conglomeration of villages, whose heritage and traditions are still evolving. Thanks to the feisty independence and diversity of each area, the London "buzz" is continually on the move.

✈ INTERCITY TRANSPORTATION

Flights: Heathrow (**LON;** ☎08700 000 123) is London's main airport. The **Piccadilly Line** heads from the airport to central London (1hr., 20 per hr., £4-10). **Heathrow Connect** runs to **Paddington** (20min., 2 per hr., £10), as does the more expensive **Heathrow Express**

GREAT BRITAIN

(15min.; 4 per hr.; £15.50, round-trip £29). From **Gatwick Airport** (**LGW;** ☎08700 002 468), the **Gatwick Express** heads to **Victoria** (30min.; 4 per hr., round-trip £28.90).

✈ **Regional Hubs: London Luton Airport** (**LTN;** ☎1582 405 100; www.london-luton. co.uk) serves as a hub for **easyJet, Ryanair,** and **Wizz Air.** First Capital Connect (☎0845 026 4700; www.firstcapitalconnect.co.uk) and Midland Mainline (☎0870 010 1296; www.midlandmainline.com) run **trains** between London King's Cross and Luton (30min.-1hr., 3-4 per hr., £10-20). Easybus (www.easybus.co.uk) and National Express (☎08705 808 080; www.nationalexpress.com) operate **buses** between London Victoria and Luton (1hr., 2-3 per hr., from £2). **London Stansted Airport** (**STN;** ☎0870 000 0303; www.stanstedairport.com) is the main hub for **Ryanair,** and also serves **easyJet** and **Wizz Air.** The Stansted Express (☎0845 600 7245; www.stanstedexpress.com) train shuttles between London Liverpool and Stansted (45min., 4 per hr., £15-24). Easybus runs **buses** between London Baker St. and Stansted and National Express runs **buses** from London Victoria (1hr., 3-6 per hr., from £2).

Trains: London has 8 major train stations: **Charing Cross** (southern England); **Euston** (the northwest); **King's Cross** (the northeast); **Liverpool Street** (East Anglia); **Paddington** (the west and south Wales); **St. Pancras** (the Midlands and the northwest); **Victoria** (the south); **Waterloo** (the south, the southwest, and the Continent). All stations are linked by the subway, referred to as the **Underground** or **Tube** (⊖). Itineraries involving a change of stations in London usually include a crosstown transfer by Tube. Get information at the station ticket office or from the **National Rail Enquiries Line** (☎08457 484 950; www.britrail.com).

Buses: Long-distance buses (coaches) arrive in London at **Victoria Coach Station,** 164 Buckingham Palace Rd. ⊖Victoria. **National Express** (☎08705 808 080; www.nationalexpress.com) is the largest operator of intercity services.

✳ ORIENTATION

The **West End,** stretching east from Park Lane to Kingsway and south from Oxford St. to the River Thames, is the heart of London. In this area you'll find aristocratic **Mayfair,** the shopping near **Oxford Circus,** the clubs of **Soho,** and the boutiques of **Covent Garden.** Heading east of the West End, you'll pass legalistic **Holborn** before hitting the ancient **City of London** ("the City"), the site of the original Roman settlement and home to the Tower of London. The City's eastern border encompasses the ethnically diverse, working-class **East End.**

Westminster encompasses the grandeur of **Trafalgar Square** and extends south along the Thames; this is the location of both royal and political London, with the Houses of Parliament, Buckingham Palace, and Westminster Abbey. Farther west lies rich, snooty **Chelsea.** Across the river, the **South Bank** has an incredible variety of entertainment and museums. To the south, **Brixton** is one of the hottest nightlife spots in town, besides touristy Leicester Square and Piccadilly Circus. The huge expanse of **Hyde Park** lies west of the West End; along its southern border are chic **Knightsbridge** and posh **Kensington.** North of Hyde Park is the media-infested **Notting Hill** and the B&B- and hostel-filled **Bayswater.** Bayswater, Mayfair, and **Marylebone** meet at Marble Arch, on Hyde Park's northeast corner; from there, Marylebone stretches west to meet academic **Bloomsbury,** north of Soho and Holborn. **Camden Town, Islington, Hampstead,** and **Highgate** lie to the north of Bloomsbury and the City. A good street atlas is essential. ▨**London A to Z** (£10) is available at newsstands and bookstores.

▣ LOCAL TRANSPORTATION

Public Transportation: Run by **Transport for London** (**TfL;** 24hr. info ☎020 7222 1234; www.thetube.com). The **Underground** or **Tube** (⊖) is divided into 6 concentric zones; fares depend on the number of zones crossed. Buy your ticket before you board and

GREAT BRITAIN

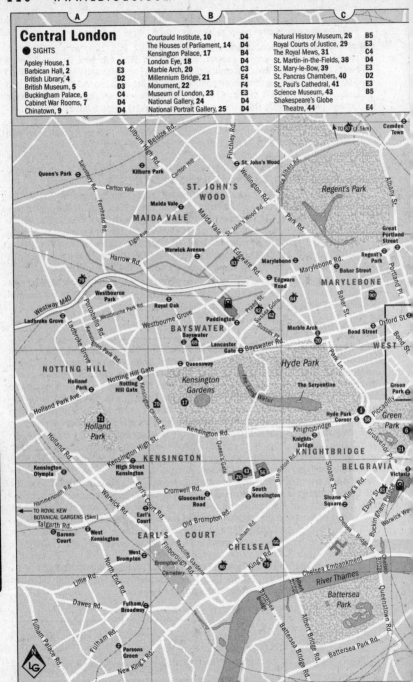

Central London

● SIGHTS

Apsley House, 1	C4
Barbican Hall, 2	E3
British Library, 4	D2
British Museum, 5	D3
Buckingham Palace, 6	C4
Cabinet War Rooms, 7	D4
Chinatown, 9	D4

Courtauld Institute, 10	D4
The Houses of Parliament, 14	D4
Kensington Palace, 17	B4
London Eye, 18	D4
Marble Arch, 20	C3
Millennium Bridge, 21	E4
Monument, 22	F4
Museum of London, 23	E3
National Gallery, 24	D4
National Portrait Gallery, 25	D4

Natural History Museum, 26	B5
Royal Courts of Justice, 29	E3
The Royal Mews, 31	C4
St. Martin-in-the-Fields, 38	D4
St. Mary-le-Bow, 39	E3
St. Pancras Chambers, 40	D2
St. Paul's Cathedral, 41	E3
Science Museum, 43	B5
Shakespeare's Globe Theatre, 44	E4

GREAT BRITAIN

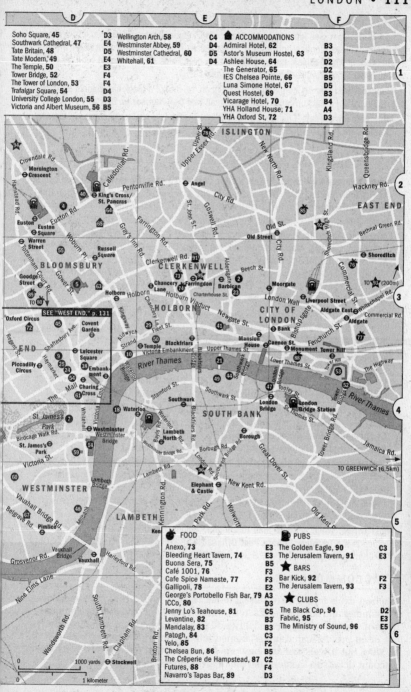

Soho Square, **45** D3
Southwark Cathedral, **47** E4
Tate Britain, **48** D5
Tate Modern, **49** E4
The Temple, **50** E3
Tower Bridge, **52** F4
The Tower of London, **53** F4
Trafalgar Square, **54** D4
University College London, **55** D3
Victoria and Albert Museum, **56** B5

Wellington Arch, **58** C4
Westminster Abbey, **59** D4
Westminster Cathedral, **60** D5
Whitehall, **61** D4

♠ ACCOMMODATIONS
Admiral Hotel, **62** B3
Astor's Museum Hostel, **63** D3
Ashlee House, **64** D2
The Generator, **65** D2
IES Chelsea Pointe, **66** B5
Luna Simone Hotel, **67** D5
Quest Hostel, **69** B3
Vicarage Hotel, **70** B4
YHA Holland House, **71** A4
YHA Oxford St, **72** D3

🍴 FOOD
Anexo, **73** E3
Bleeding Heart Tavern, **74** E3
Buona Sera, **75** B5
Café 1001, **76** F3
Cafe Spice Namaste, **77** F3
Gallipoli, **78** E2
George's Portobello Fish Bar, **79** A3
ICCo, **80** D3
Jenny Lo's Teahouse, **81** C5
Levantine, **82** B3
Mandalay, **83** B3
Patogh, **84** C3
Yelo, **85** F2
Chelsea Bun, **86** B5
The Crêperie de Hampstead, **87** C2
Futures, **88** F4
Navarro's Tapas Bar, **89** D3

🍺 PUBS
The Golden Eagle, **90** C3
The Jerusalem Tavern, **91** E3

★ BARS
Bar Kick, **92** F2
The Jerusalem Tavern, **93** F3

★ CLUBS
The Black Cap, **94** D2
Fabric, **95** E3
The Ministry of Sound, **96** E5

GREAT BRITAIN

pass it through automatic gates at both ends of your journey. Runs approximately 5am-11:30pm. See Tube map in the front of this guide. **Buses** are divided into 4 zones. Zones 1-3 are identical to the Tube zones. Buses run 5:30am-midnight, after which a network of **Night Buses,** prefixed by "N," take over. Fares £2. **Travelcard** valid on all TfL services. 1-day Travelcard from £5.30 (Zones 1-2).

Licensed Taxicabs: An illuminated "taxi" sign on the roof of a black cab signals availability. Tip 10%. For pickup (min. £2 charge), call **Taxi One-Number** (☎08718 718 710).

Minicabs: Private cars. Cheaper but less reliable—stick to a reputable company. **London Radio Cars** (☎020 8905 0000; www.londonradiocars.com) offers 24hr. pickup.

🛈 PRACTICAL INFORMATION

Tourist Information Centre: Britain Visitor Centre, 1 Regent St. (www.visitbritain.com). ⊖Piccadilly Circus. Open M 9:30am-6:30pm, Tu-F 9am-6:30pm, Sa-Su 10am-4pm. **London Information Centre,** 1 Leicester Pl. (☎020 7930 6769; www.londoninformationcentre.com). ⊖Leicester Sq. Open M-F 8am-midnight, Sa-Su 9am-6pm.

Embassies: Australia, Australia House, Strand (☎020 7379 4334). ⊖Temple. Open M-F 9am-5pm. **Canada,** MacDonald House, 1 Grosvenor Sq. (☎020 7258 6600). ⊖Bond St. Open M-F 9am-5pm. **Ireland,** 17 Grosvenor Pl. (☎020 7235 2171). ⊖Hyde Park Corner. Open M-F 9:30am-1pm and 2:15-5pm. **New Zealand,** New Zealand House, 80 Haymarket (☎020 7930 8422). ⊖Piccadilly Circus. Open M-F 9am-5pm. **US,** 24 Grosvenor Sq. (☎020 7499 9000). ⊖Bond St. Open M-F 8:30am-5:30pm.

Police: London is covered by 2 police forces: the **City of London Police** (☎020 7601 2222) for the City and the **Metropolitan Police** (☎020 7230 1212) for the outskirts. At least 1 station is open 24hr. Call ☎020 7230 1212 for the nearest station.

Pharmacies: Most pharmacies open M-Sa 9:30am-5:30pm; a "duty" chemist in each district opens Su; hours limited. **Zafash Pharmacy,** 233-235 Old Brompton Rd. (☎020 7373 2798), ⊖Earl's Ct., is 24hr. **Bliss Chemist,** 5-6 Marble Arch (☎020 7723 6116), ⊖Marble Arch, is open daily 9am-midnight.

Hospitals: Charing Cross, Fulham Palace Rd. (☎020 8846 1234), entrance on St. Dunstan's Rd., ⊖Hammersmith. **Royal Free,** Pond St. (☎020 7794 0500), ⊖Belsize Park. **St. Thomas's,** Lambeth Palace Rd. (☎020 7188 7188), ⊖Waterloo. **University College London Hospital,** Grafton Way (☎08 4515 5500), ⊖Warren St.

Internet: Don't pay more than £2 per hr. Try the ubiquitous **easyInternet** (☎020 7241 9000; www.easyeverything.com). Locations include 9-16 Tottenham Ct. Rd. (⊖Tottenham Ct. Rd.); 456/459 Strand (⊖Charing Cross); 358 Oxford St. (⊖Bond St.); 160-166 Kensington High St. (⊖High St. Kensington). Prices vary with demand, but they're usually around £1.60 per hr. Min. 50p-£1.

Post Office: When sending mail to London, include the full postal code. The largest office is the **Trafalgar Square Post Office,** 24-28 William IV St. (☎020 7484 9305), ⊖Charing Cross. Open M, W-F 8:30am-6:30pm, Tu 9:15am-6:30pm, Sa 9am-5:30pm.

🏠 ACCOMMODATIONS

The best deals in town are **student residence halls,** which rent out rooms over the summer and sometimes Easter vacations. **B&B** encompasses accommodations of varying quality, personality, and price. Be aware that in-room showers are often prefabricated units jammed into a corner. Linens are included at all **YHAs,** but towels are not; buy one from reception ($3.50). YHAs also sell discount tickets to theaters and major attractions.

BAYSWATER

▨ **The Pavilion,** 34-36 Sussex Gardens (☎020 7262 0905; www.pavilionhoteluk.com).
⊖Paddington or Edgeware Rd. With over 30 themed rooms, including "Honky Tonk Afro"
(dedicated to the 70s), "Casablanca Nights" (recalling a Moorish fantasy), and
2 James Bond inspired pads ("Gold Finger" and "Diamonds Are Forever"), this is
the place to come for a hilariously sumptuous hotel experience. Decadent decor
with funky additions like zebra print, Grecian busts, or Warhol-esque Marilyn photos accompany flatscreen TVs. Priding itself on its connection to all things art,
fashion, and rock & roll, the Pavilion has hosted a number of celebrity visitors
and fashion shoots: a naked Naomi Campbell and an impatient Kate Beckinsale
both posed here. Continental breakfast included. Parking £10 per day. Reception
24hr. Singles £60-85; doubles £100; triples £130. AmEx/MC/V. ❺

Quest Hostel, 45 Queensborough Terr. (☎020 7229 7782; www.astorhostels.com).
⊖Queensway. Night Bus #N15, 94, 148. A chummy staff operates this simple backpacker hostel with a blackboard welcoming new check-ins by name. Mostly co-ed
dorms (1 female-only room). Nearly all have bath; otherwise, facilities on every other fl.
Recently refurbished kitchen. Continental breakfast included. Under-bed luggage storage; padlocks £2 (£5 deposit). Lockers £1.50 per day; £7 per week. Linens included.
Laundry £2.50 per wash, £0.50 per dry. Wi-Fi £1 per 40min. Max stay 2 weeks in
summer; longer in winter. Reception 24hr. 4- to 9-bed dorms £16-25; doubles £35-40.
Rates increase July-Aug. and on weekends. Ages 18-35 only. MC/V. ❶

BLOOMSBURY

Many B&Bs and hostels are on busy roads, so be wary of noise levels. The area
becomes seedier closer to King's Cross.

▨ **The Generator,** 37 Tavistock Pl. (☎020 7388 7666; www.generatorhostels.com).
⊖Russell Sq. or King's Cross St. Pancras. Night Bus #N19, N35, N38, N41, N55, N91,
N243. At the ultimate party hostel in London, you'll be greeted by the "Welcome Host"
and shortly after offered a complimentary beer. Co-ed dorms (women-only available),
a bar with nightly events (6pm-2am), cheap pints (6-9pm, £1.50), a full cafeteria-style
dining area with dinner specials (from £4.50), and well-equipped lounge areas make
this one of the best places to meet fellow travelers. All rooms have sinks; private doubles have tables and chairs. New clean showers. Continental breakfast included. Lockers (padlocks £4), free towels and linens, laundry (wash £2; dry £0.50 per 10min.), cash
machine, charge station (for any phone or iPod) and an in-house travel shop that sells
Tube, train, and theater tickets. Small safes £1 per day, £5 per week.; larger safes £3/10.
Internet £1 per 30min. Wi-Fi £1.50 per hr.; £4 per 3hr. Reserve 1 week in advance for
Sa-Su. Online booking. Credit card required with reservation. 4- to 12-bed dorms £15-25;
singles £50-65; doubles with 2 twin beds £50-65; triples £60-75; quads £80-100;
6-bed private rooms £120-150. Discounts for long stays. 18+. MC/V. ❶

▨ **YHA St. Pancras International,** 79-81 Euston Rd. (☎020 7388 9998; www.yha.org.
uk). ⊖King's Cross St. Pancras. Night Bus #N10, N73, N91, 390. Opposite the British
Library and St. Pancras Tube. After a £1.6 million refurbishment, this hostel has
come out sparkling, with a sunken bar-cafe (beers from £2.20; pub style mains
£5.50) and clean, spacious rooms with plush wall-to-wall carpets and wooden
bunks. Family bunk rooms, single-sex dorms, basic doubles, and premium doubles (with bath and TV) are sparkling. Kitchen and elevators available. Breakfast
£3.50-5. Linens included. Laundry (wash and dry £4.50). Wi-Fi £1.50 per 15min.;
£3 per 30min. 1 week max. stay. Reserve dorms 1 week in advance for Sa-Su

or summer, 2 weeks for doubles. 4- to 6-bed dorms £23-32, under 18 £18-25; doubles £63, with bath £68. £3 discount with HI, ISIC, or NUS card. MC/V. ❷

George Hotel, 58-60 Cartwright Gardens (☎020 7387 8777; www.georgehotel.com). ⊖Russell Sq. Night Bus #N10, N73, N91, 390. Spacious rooms with flatscreen satellite TV, radio, tea/coffee facilities, phone, and alarm clock, plus hair dryer and iron on request. The front rooms on the 1st fl. have high ceilings and tall windows; others have bay windows. Full English breakfast included. Free internet and Wi-Fi. Reserve 3 weeks in advance for summer; 48hr. cancellation policy. Singles £50, with shower £75; doubles £69/75, with bath £89; triples £79/89/99; basic quads £89. Discounts for stays over 4 days. MC/V. ❸

KENSINGTON AND EARL'S COURT

▨ **Astor Hyde Park,** 191 Queensgate (☎020 7581 0103; www.astorhostels.co.uk). ⊖South Kensington or Gloucester Rd. Set in a recently renovated Victorian walk-up, this social backpacker's hostel offers clean, spacious rooms outfitted with full ensuite baths and decorated with modern art. Sleek lounge with flatscreen TV and dining hall with pool table. Regular F night parties. Breakfast included; occasional hostel dinners £3-4. Lockers under beds; padlock £2. Safes £1.50 per day, £7 per week. Free luggage storage before check-in and after check-out. Wash £2.50; dry 50p per 20min. Internet 50p per 15min. Free Wi-Fi. Reception 24hr. Dorms in summer £15-25, in winter £13-20; doubles £35-40/25-30. Ages 18-35 only. AmEx/MC/V. ❶

■ **Vicarage Hotel,** 10 Vicarage Gate (☎020 7229 4030; www.londonvicaragehotel.com). ⊖High St. Kensington. Night Bus #27, N28, N31, N52. Walking on Kensington Church St. from Kensington High St., you'll see 2 streets marked Vicarage Gate; take the 2nd on your right. Immaculately maintained Victorian house with ornate hallways, TV lounge, and elegant bedrooms; all have shiny wood furnishings, tea and coffee sundries, and hair dryers. Rooms with private baths have TV. Full English breakfast included. Free Wi-Fi. Best to reserve 2 months in advance with 1 night's deposit; personal checks accepted for deposit with at least 6 weeks notice. Singles £55, with private bathroom £93; doubles £93/122; triples £117/156; quads £128/172. AmEx/MC/V. ❸

OTHER NEIGHBORHOODS

■ **YHA Oxford Street (HI),** 14 Noel St. (☎020 7734 1618; www.yha.org.uk). ⊖Oxford Circus. Night Bus: more than 10 Night Buses run along Oxford St., including #N7, N8, and N207. Small, clean, bright rooms with limited facilities but an unbeatable location for nightlife. Some doubles have bunk beds, sink, mirror, and wardrobe; others have single beds and wardrobes. Clean communal toilets and showers. Spacious, comfy TV lounge. Huge, well-equipped kitchen. Laundry available. Towels £3.50. Wi-Fi £3 per hr. Travelcards sold at reception; discount tickets to popular attractions. Reserve at least 2 weeks in advance. 3- to 4-bed dorms £22-27, under 18 £17-21; 2-bed dorms £27-34. MC/V. ❷

■ **Morgan House,** 120 Ebury St. (☎020 7730 2384; www.morganhouse.co.uk). ⊖Victoria. A touch of pizzazz makes this B&B a neighborhood standout. A boistrous couple rents mid-sized rooms with floral decor and country-style furnishings. Many have fireplaces and all have TV, kettle, and phone for incoming calls (pay phone downstairs). English breakfast included. Wi-Fi available. Reserve 2-3 months in advance. 48hr. cancellation policy. Singles with sink £52; doubles with sink £72, with bath £92; triples £92/112; quads with bath £132. MC/V. ❸

IES Chelsea Pointe, (☎020 7808 9200; www.iesreshall.com), corner of Manresa Rd. and King's Rd., entrance on Manresa Rd. ⊖Sloane Sq., then Bus #11, 19, 22, 319; ⊖South Kensington, then Bus #49. Night Bus #N11, N19, N22. Brand new university residence offers clean, basic dorms. Amenities include phones, a modern kitchen, laundry service, and 5 TV/DVD lounges. Linens provided but guests must wash them. Free Wi-Fi. 1 week min. stay. Reservations recommended. 72hr. cancellation policy. Wheelchair-accessible. More availability during summer and winter school breaks. Singles £300-360 per week; doubles £394 per week. In the heart of trendy Chelsea, these prices are unheard of. AmEx/MC/V. ❸

◪ FOOD

Any restaurant charging under £10 for a main course is relatively inexpensive. For the best and cheapest ethnic restaurants, head to the source: Whitechapel for Bangladeshi baltis, Chinatown for dim sum, South Kensington for French pastries, Edgware Road for shawarma. The best places to get your own ingredients are street markets (see **Shopping, p. 129**). To buy groceries, try supermarket chains **Tesco, Safeway, Sainsbury's,** or **Marks & Spencer.**

BAYSWATER

Aphrodite Taverna, 15 Hereford Rd. (☎020 7229 2206). ⊖Bayswater or Notting Hill Gate. Zealously decorated walls feature an abundance of Aphrodite sculptures. Fabulous menu includes traditional favorites like *dolmedes* (stuffed grape leaves; £8.50), *keftedes* (Greek meatballs; £8.50), hummus, *tzaziki,* and *tambouli.* £1 cover is amply rewarded with baskets of freshly baked pita and other appetizers. Cafe Aphrodite next door offers some of Taverna's specialties at cheaper prices as well as a full sandwich menu (from £3). Takeaway available. Restaurant open M-Sa noon-midnight. Cafe open daily 8am-5pm. AmEx/MC/V. Restaurant ❷. Cafe ❶

Durbar Tandoori, 24 Hereford St. (☎020 7727 1947; www.durbartandoori.co.uk). ⊖Bayswater. Enjoy the refined dining room and revel in the inexpensive goodness of London's oldest family-owned Indian restaurant, which celebrated 50 years in 2006. Generous portions of dishes from regions throughout India. Vegetarian and meat entrees from £6. Bargain take-away lunch box £6. Chef's special dinner for 2 £25. Open M-Th and Sa-Su noon-2:30pm and 5:30-11:30pm, F 5:30-11:30 pm. AmEx/MC/V. ❷

BLOOMSBURY

▣ **Navarro's Tapas Bar,** 67 Charlotte St. (☎020 7637 7713; www.navarros.co.uk). ⊖Goodge St. Colorful, bustling tapas restaurant with blue tiled walls, brightly painted furniture, and flamenco music straight from Seville. The authenticity carries over to the excellent food—try the spicy fried potatoes (*patatas bravas;* £4.90), spinach with chickpeas (*espinacas con garbanzos;* £5) or one of the many brochettes of lamb, chicken, or prawns (£12-15). Tapas £4-15; 2-3 per person is plenty. £10 min. purchase. Reservations recommended for dinner. Open M-F noon-3pm and 6-10pm, Sa 6-10pm. AmEx/MC/V. ❸

▣ **Newman Arms,** 23 Rathbone St., (☎020 7636 1127). ⊖Tottenham Court Rd. or Goodge St. A pub with a famous upstairs pie room and restaurant. Connoisseurs at 10 sought-after tables dig into homemade pies (with potatoes and vegetables; £10). Most are filled with seasonal game, but there's always a vegetarian option. Just-as-comforting desserts like spotted dick, puddings, and crumbles. Pints from £3. Book in advance. Pub open M-F noon-12:30am. Restaurant open M-Th noon-3pm and 6-9pm, F noon-3pm. MC/V. ❷

CHELSEA

▣ **Buona Sera,** at the Jam, 289A King's Rd. (☎020 7352 8827). ⊖Sloane Sq., then Bus #19 or 319 (or a 10-15min. walk along King's). With patented "bunk" tables stacked high into the air and plants for effect, the treetop-esque dining experience alone justifies a visit; the mouth-watering Italian fare makes it practically mandatory. Waiters climb small wooden ladders to deliver generous plates of pasta (£8.20-11) along with fish and steak dishes (£12-15). Enjoy, but don't drop your fork. Open M 6pm-midnight, Tu-F noon-3pm and 6pm-midnight, Sa-Su noon-midnight. Reservations recommended F-Sa; for a higher bunk always reserve. AmEx/MC/V. ❸

Chelsea Bun, 9A Limerston St. (☎020 7352 3635). ⊖Sloane Sq., then Bus #11 or 22. Chelsea-ites spill into this spirited and casual Anglo-American diner, which serves heaping portions of everything from the "Ultimate Breakfast" (3 eggs, 3 pancakes, sausages, hash browns, bacon, burger, french toast, kitchen sink; £11) to Tijuana Benedict (eggs with chorizo sausage and tomato; £0). Also serves a plethora of sandwiches, salads, pasta, and burgers £2.80-9.20. Extensive vegetarian and vegan options. Early-bird specials available M-F 7am-noon (£2.20-3.20) and breakfast (from £4) served until 6pm. £3.50 min. per person lunch, £5.50 dinner. Open M-Sa 7am-midnight, Su 8am-7pm. MC/V. ❷

THE CITY OF LONDON

▣ **CafeSpice Namaste,** 16 Prescot St. (☎020 7488 9242; www.cafespice.co.uk). ⊖Tower Hill or DLR: Tower Gateway. Somewhat out of the way, but well worth the trek. Bright, festive decorations bring a zany feel to this old Victorian warehouse with courtyard seating. Extensive menu of Goan and Parsi specialties. Meat mains are on the pricey side (from £14.30), but vegetarian dishes (from £5.50) are tasty and affordable. Varied wine list and excellent, if expensive, desserts. Open M-F noon-3pm and 6:15-10:30pm, Sa 6:30-10:30pm. Reservations recommended. AmEx/MC/V. ❸

CLERKENWELL AND HOLBORN

▨ **The Clerkenwell Kitchen,** 31 Clerkenwell Close (☎020 7101 9959; www.theclerken-wellkitchen.co.uk). ⊖Farringdon. Hidden in a former warehouse among the twists and turns of the Close, this hip cafe specializes in sustainable food production. Every day the staff prepares 6 dishes, 2 puddings, and a selection of takeaway sanwiches, pastries, and tarts, almost all of which are made with organic and local ingredients. Dishes like spinach, onion, and feta tart and crab and fennel linguini £4.50-11. Open M-W and F 8am-5pm, Th 8am-11pm; breakfast 8-11am, lunch noon-3pm, snacks 3-5pm. MC/V. ❷

EAST LONDON

▨ **Café 1001,** 91 Brick Lane, Dray Walk (☎7247 9679; www.cafe1001.co.uk), in an alley just off Brick Ln. ⊖Aldgate East. This massive warehouse-turned-artists' den feels more like a never-ending block party than a cafe. Young students, artists and assorted hipster types lounge in couches in the spacious upstairs or at the numerous picnic tables that dominate the alleyway, while staff dole out fresh homemade food to eat in or take away. Choose from a variety of premade salads (3 for £3.50) and healthy main dishes (£5.95 including 3 side salads) at the buffet, or grab a massive sandwich (from £3.50) and pastry (from £.80) at the cafe side. Selections of wine and beer (£2-4). Outdoor barbecue weather permitting (burgers £4, with fries £4.50). Nightly DJs or live bands 8pm-close, W live jazz. Open M-Th and Su 6am-midnight, F-Sa 6am-12:30am. ❶

▨ **Chaat,** 36 Redchurch St. (☎020 7739 9595; www.chaatlondon.co.uk). ⊖Liverpool St. A sleek but cozy restaurant, tea room, and bar, Chaat is the perfect place to do just that--over delicious Bangladeshi food, served in five courses. Start with a "Chit Chaat" like samosas or tomato, ginger, and coriander soup; follow it with a veggie or meat dish; add a "Mopper" (rice or bread) and an accompaniment like dhal or pan-fried okra; and finish with a homemade dip. Doubles as an art gallery. All 5 "parts" £13.95. Reservations recommended. Open M-Sa 6:30-11pm. AmEx/MC/V. ❷

MARYLEBONE AND REGENT'S PARK

▨ **Le Relais de Venise "L'Entrecote,"** 120 Marylebone Ln. (☎020 7486 0878; www.relaisdevenice.com). ⊖Bond St. 2nd location at 5 Throgmorton St., The City (☎020 7638 6325). This wildly popular French restaurant ventures across the channel; the queue is usually down the street. There's only one dish on the menu: steak, fries, and salad (£19). Pace yourself: as soon as you're done, they'll bring you more. Delicious desserts £5. Open M-Th noon-2:30pm and 6-10:45pm, F noon-2:45pm and 6-10:45pm, Sa 12:30-3:30pm and 6:30-10:45pm, Su 12:30-3:30pm and 6:30-10:30pm. AmEx/MC/V. ❹

NORTH LONDON

▨ **Gallipoli Cafe Bistro,** 102 Upper St. (☎020 7359 0630), **Gallipoli Again,** 120 Upper St. (☎0207 359 1578), and **Gallipoli Bazaar,** 107 Upper St. (☎020 7226 5333). ⊖Angel. Three's usually a crowd, but not with this group of tasty Upper St. eateries. In fact, they only bring the crowds. Dark walls, patterned tiles, and hanging lamp and lanterns provide the background to spectacular Lebanese, Turkish, and Mediterranean delights like hummus, falafel, *kisir* (simliar to tabouleh), kebab, and *moussaka*. Try one of the set meals for 2, which come with a selection of hot and cold appetizers (£11-15 per person). Gallipoli Cafe was the original; Gallipoli Again opened in response to its immense popularity (with the added bonus of an outdoor patio); and Gallipoli Bazaar, which sits between the other two, serves up *sheesha* and food in tea-room surroundings. Again and Bazaar wheelchair-accessible. Open M-Th 10:30am-11pm, F-Sa 10:30am-midnight, Su 10:30am-11pm. Reservations recommended F-Sa. MC/V. ❷

THE WEST END

▓ **Busaba Eathai,** 8-13 Bird St. (☎020 7518 8080; www.busaba.com). ⊖Oxford St. Also at 106-110 Wardour St., Soho (☎7255 8686). Incense, floating candles, and slick wood paneling make you feel like you're dining in a Buddhist temple. Large, tightly-packed communal tables ensure a lively wait for the affordable, filling dishes. Students and locals line up for stir fry, curry, pad thai, and other wok creations (£6.20-11). Tons of vegetarian dishes. Open M-Th noon-11pm, F-Sa noon-11:30pm, Su noon-10pm. AmEx/MC/V. ❷

▓ **The Breakfast Club,** 33 D'Arblay St. (☎020 726 5454; www.thebreakfastclubsoho. com). A favorite spot for the irreverent brunch-goer, serving creative twists on classics like eggs benedict, pancakes, burritos and burgers. Large family-style tables with red-checkered table cloths. Specials like The Full Monty (bacon, sausage, beans, tomatoes, mushrooms; £6.20) or The Number wrap (goat cheese, roasted red peppers and eggplant, pesto, tomato chutney; £6). Full Metal Jacket Potatoes with a variety of toppings £4.50-5.50. Super smoothies £3.50. Open M-F 8am-6pm, Sa 9:30am-5pm, Su 10am-4pm. Cash only. ❶

OTHER NEIGHBORHOODS

▓ **George's Portobello Fish Bar,** 329 Portobello Rd. (☎020 8969 7895). ⊖Ladbroke Grove. A London institution, George's garners praise from all who enter: Naked Chef Jamie Oliver, for one, raves about the place. George opened up here in 1961, and with his daughter now at the helm, the fish and chips are still as good as ever. Cod, rockfish, plaice, and skate come with a huge serving of chunky chips (from £7) and the popular barbecue ribs (£7) are made according to a secret recipe. With only a couple outdoor tables, seating is so scarce that on Sa, a seat costs £3 per person. Open M-F 11am-11:45pm, Sa 11am-9pm, Su noon-9:30pm. Cash only. ❷

▓ **Rock and Sole Place,** 47 Endell St. (☎020 7836 3785). ⊖Covent Garden. There's a reason Rock and Sole's been around since 1871: messy and delicious fried fish in an equally no-frills environment. A self-proclaimed "master fryer" (qualifications unclear) turns out tasty haddock, cod, halibut, and sole filets (all with chips; £9 takeaway, £11 sit down), while customers gather around the crowded diner tables inside, or the large wooden picnic tables under the giant tree outside. Extras like mushy peas, baked beans, coleslaw, or curry or gravy sauce £0.50-1.50. Open M-Sa 11:30am-11:45pm, Su noon-10:30pm. MC/V. ❷

⊙ SIGHTS

WESTMINSTER

The City of Westminster, now a borough of London, has been the seat of British power for over 1000 years. William the Conqueror was crowned in Westminster Abbey on Christmas Day, AD 1066, and his successors built the Palace of Westminster, which today houses Parliament.

▓**WESTMINSTER ABBEY.** Founded as a Benedictine monastery, Westminster Abbey has evolved into a house of kings and queens both living and dead. Almost nothing remains of **St. Edward's Abbey:** Henry III's 13th-century Gothic reworking created most of the current grand structure. Britons buried or commemorated inside the Abbey include: **Henry VII; Mary, Queen of Scots; Elizabeth I;** and the scholars and artists honored in the **"Poet's Corner"** (Jane Austen, the

Brontë sisters, Chaucer, Shakespeare, and Dylan Thomas). A door off the east cloister leads to the **Chapter House,** the original meeting place of the House of Commons. Next door to the Abbey (through the cloisters), the lackluster **Abbey Museum** is in the Norman undercroft. Just north of the Abbey, **St. Margaret's Church** enjoys a strange status: as a part of the Royal Peculiar, it is neither under the jurisdiction of the diocese of England nor the archbishop of Canterbury. Since 1614, it's been the official worshipping place of the House of Commons. *(Parliament Sq. ✪Westminster. Abbey ☎ 7654 4900, Chapter House 7222 5152; www.westminster-abbey.org. No photography. Abbey open M-Tu and Th-F 9:30am-3:45pm, W 9:30am-7pm, Sa 9:30am-1:45pm, Su open for services only. Museum open daily 10:30am-4pm. Partially wheelchair-accessible. Abbey and Museum £15, students and children 11-17 £12, families of 4 £36. Services free. 1hr. tours £3 Apr.-Oct. M-F 10, 10:30, 11am, 2, 2:30pm, Sa 10, 10:30, 11am; Oct.-Mar. M-F 10:30, 11am, 2, 2:30pm, Sa 10:30, 11am. Audio tours available; free. M-F 9:30am-3:30pm, Sa 9:30am-1pm. AmEx/MC/V.)*

BUCKINGHAM PALACE. The Palace has been the official residence of the British monarchs since 1837, when a youthful Queen Victoria decamped from nearby Kensington Palace to set up housekeeping in this English Taj Mahal. With 755 rooms and a suite of state chambers decorated with Rembrandt and Vermeer, **Buckingham Palace** celebrates the splendor and power of 19th-century English monarchy. The Palace is open to visitors from late July to late September every year, but don't expect to meet the Queen—the State Rooms are the only rooms on view, and they are used only for formal occasions. "God Save the Queen" is the rallying cry at the Queens Gallery, dedicated to exhibits of absurdly valuable items from the Royal Collection. Detached from the palace and tour, the **Royal Mews** acts as a museum, stable, riding school, and working carriage house. The main attraction is the Queen's collection of coaches, including the Cinderella-like "Glass Coach" used to carry royal brides, including Princess Diana, to their weddings, and the State Coaches of Australia, Ireland, and Scotland. Another highlight is the 4 ton **Gold State Coach,** which can occasionally be seen wheeling around the streets in the early morning on practice runs for major events. To witness the Palace for free, attend a session of the **Changing of the Guard.** Show up well before 11:30am and stand in front of the Palace in view of the morning guards, or use the steps of the Victoria Memorial as a vantage point. *(✪St. James's Park, Victoria, Green Park, or Hyde Park Corner. ☎020 7766 7324; www. the-royal-collection.com. Palace open late July to late Sept. daily 9:30am-6:30pm, last admission 4:15pm. £15, students £14, children 6-17 £8.50, under 5 free, families of 5 £67. Advance booking is recommended and required for disabled visitors. Queens Gallery open daily 10am-5:30pm, last admission 4:30pm. Wheelchair-accessible. £8, students £7, families £22. Royal Mews open late July to late Sept. daily 10am-5pm, last admission 4:15pm; Mar.-July and late Sept. to late Oct. M-Th and Sa-Su 11am–4pm, last admission 3:15pm. Wheelchair-accessible. £7, seniors £6, children under 17 £4.50, families £19. Changing of the Guard Apr. -late July daily, Aug.-Mar. every other day, excepting the Queen's absence, inclement weather, or pressing state functions. Free.)*

THE HOUSES OF PARLIAMENT. Soaring like a spike against the London skyline, the **Palace of Westminster** is one of the most recognizable buildings in the city. It has been home to both the House of Lords and the House of Commons (together known as Parliament) since the 11th century, when Edward the Confessor established his court here. Standing guard on the northern side of the building is the Clock Tower, nicknamed **Big Ben,** after the robustly proportioned Benjamin Hall, a former Commissioner of Works. **Victoria Tower,** at the south end of the palace building, contains copies of every Act of Parliament since 1497. A flag flying from the top signals that Parliament is in session. When the Queen is in the building, a special royal banner is flown instead. Visitors with enough patience or luck to make it inside the chambers can hear the occa-

GREAT BRITAIN

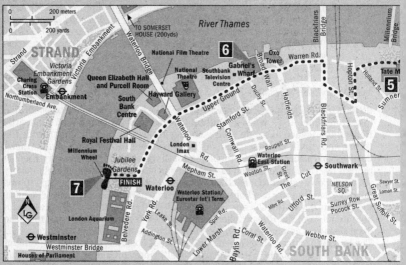

THE MILLENNIUM MILE

Stark, modern monuments to London's present—the round glass sphere of City Hall, the converted power station that is the Tate Modern—line your side of the river, while stately relics of a rich past—the Tower of London and St. Paul's Cathedral—stand on the opposite bank. Whether it's a search for Shakespeare and Picasso that brings you to the South Bank, or just a hankering for a nice walk, you will find yourself rewarded.

1. TOWER OF LONDON. Begin your trek to the Tower early to avoid the crowds. Tours given by the Yeomen Warders meet every 1½hr. near the entrance. Listen as they expertly recount tales of royal conspiracy, treason, and murder. See the **White Tower,** once a fortress and residence of kings. Shiver at the executioner's stone on the tower green and pay your respects at the Chapel of St. Peter ad Vinculum, which holds the remains of three queens. First, get the dirt on the gemstones at **Martin Tower,** then wait in line to see the **Crown Jewels.** The jewels include such glittering lovelies as the largest cut diamond in the world (p. 122). Time: 2hr.

2. TOWER BRIDGE. An engineering wonder that puts its plainer sibling, the London Bridge, to shame. Marvel at its beauty, but skip the Tower Bridge Experience. Call in advance to inquire what times the Tower drawbridge is lifted (p. 123). Time: no need to stop walking; take in the mechanics as you head to the next sight.

3. DESIGN MUSEUM. On Butler's Wharf, let the Design Museum introduce you to the latest innovations in contemporary design. See what's to come in the forward-looking Review Gallery or hone in on individual designers and products in the Temporary Gallery. From the museum, walk along the **Queen's Walk.** To your left you will find the *HMS Belfast,* which was launched in 1938 and then led the landing on D-Day in 1944. Time: 1hr.

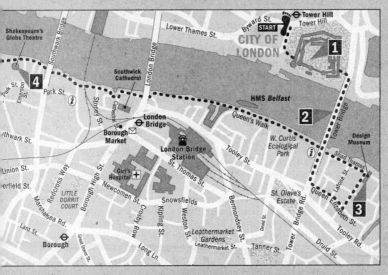

4. SHAKESPEARE'S GLOBE THEATRE. "I hope to see London once ere I die," says Shakespeare's Davy in *Henry IV.* In time, he may see it from the beautiful recreation of The Bard's most famous theater. Excellent exhibits detail the intracacies of costuming and stage effects in Shakespeare's day, as well as the more modern process of rebuilding of the theater almost 400 years after the original burned down (p. 123). You might be able to catch a matinee performance. Call in advance for tour and show times. Time: 1hr. for tour; 3hr. for performance.

5. TATE MODERN. It's hard to imagine anything casting a shadow over the Globe Theatre, but the massive former Bankside Power Station does just that. One of the world's premier modern art museums, the Tate promises a new spin on well-known favorites and works by emerging British artists. Be sure to catch one of the informative docent tours and don't forget to check out the rotating installation in the Turbine Room (p. 126). Time: 2hr.

6. GABRIEL'S WHARF. Check out the cafes, bars, and boutiques of colorful Gabriel's Wharf. If you missed the top floor of the Tate Modern, go to the public viewing gallery on the 8th floor of the **OXO Tower Wharf.** On your way to the London Eye, stop by the **South Bank Centre.** Established as a primary cultural center in 1951, it now exhibits a range of music from Philharmonic extravaganzas to low-key jazz. You may even catch one of the free lunchtime or afternoon events. Call in advance for dates and times. Time: 1½hr. for schmoozing and dinner.]

7. LONDON EYE. The London Eye, also known as the Millennium Wheel, has firmly established itself as one of London's top attractions, popular with locals and tourists alike. As Europe's tallest Ferris wheel, the Eye offers amazing 360° views from its glass pods; you may be able to see all of London lit up at sunset. Book in advance to minimize queue time (p. 124). Time: 1hr.

sional debates between members of both the Lords and the Commons. *(Parliament Sq., in Westminster. Queue for both Houses forms at St. Stephen's entrance, between Old and New Palace Yards. ⊖Westminster. ☎08709 063 773; www.parliament.uk/visiting/visiting. cfm. "Line of Route" Tour: includes both Houses. UK residents can contact their MPs for tours year-round, generally M-W mornings and F. Foreign visitors may tour Aug.-Sept. Book online, by phone, or in person at Abingdon Green ticket office (open mid-July) across from Palace of Westminster. Open Aug. M-Tu and F-Sa 9:15am-4:30pm, W-Th 1:15-4:30pm; Sept. M and F-Sa 9:15am-4:30pm, Tu-Th 1:15-4:30pm. 1¼hr. tours depart every few min. £12, students £8. MC/V.)*

> **PARLIAMENTARY PROCEDURE.** Arrive early in the afternoon to minimize waiting, which often exceeds 2hr. Keep in mind that the wait for Lords is generally shorter than the wait for Commons. To sit in on Parliament's "question time" (40min.; M-W 2:30pm, Th-F 11am) apply for tickets several weeks in advance through your embassy in London.

THE CITY OF LONDON

◪**ST. PAUL'S CATHEDRAL.** Originally built in 604 AD, the majestic St. Paul's is a cornerstone of London's architectural and historical legacy. Architect Christopher Wren's masterpiece is the fifth cathedral to occupy the site. Two years after the Great Fire of 1666, construction of the present cathedral began. Inside, the nave leads to the second-tallest freestanding dome in Europe (after St. Peter's in the Vatican), its height accentuated by the tricky perspective of the paintings on the inner surface. Climbing the 259 narrow steps is exhausting, but the views from the top of the dome are extraordinary and worth the trip: a panoramic cityscape. Circling the base of the inner dome, the **Whispering Gallery** is a perfect resounding chamber: whisper into the wall, and your friend on the other side will hear you—or, theoretically, he or she could if everyone else weren't trying the same thing. Far, far below the lofty dome, the crypt is packed wall-to-wall with plaques and tombs of great Britons and, of course, the ubiquitous gift shop. Lord Nelson commands a prime location, with radiating galleries of gravestones and tributes honoring other military heroes, from Epstein's bust of T.E. Lawrence (of Arabia) to a plaque commemorating the casualties of the Gulf War. The magnificently carved stone of the exterior is warmed and softened by the cathedral gardens which curve round the sides in a ramble of roses and clipped grass. *(St. Paul's Churchyard. ⊖St. Paul's. ☎020 7246 8350; www.stpauls.co.uk. Open M-Sa 8:30am-4pm; last entry 3:45pm. Dome and galleries open M-Sa 8:30am-4pm. Open for worship daily 7:15am-6pm. Partially wheelchair-accessible. Admission £11, students £8.50, children 7-16 £3.50, worshippers free. Group of 10 or more £0.50 discount per ticket. 1½-2hr. "Supertour" M-F 10:45, 11:30am, 1:30, 2pm; £3, students £2.50, children 7-16 £1; English only. Audio tours in English, Chinese, French, German, Italian, Japanese, Russian, and Spanish; 9am-3:30pm; £4, students £3.50.)*

> **ST. PAUL'S FOR POCKET CHANGE.** To gain access to the Cathedral's nave for free, attend an Evensong service (M-Sa 5pm, 45min). Arrive at 4:50pm to be admitted to seats in the choir.

THE TOWER OF LONDON. The turrets of this multi-functional block—serving as palace, prison, royal mint, and museum over the past 900 years—are impressive not only for their appearance but also for their integral role in England's history. A popular way to get a feel for the Tower is to join one of the theatrical ◪**Yeoman Warders' Tours.** Queen Anne Boleyn passed through Traitor's Gate just before her death, but entering the Tower is no longer as perilous as it used to be. **St. Thomas's Tower** begins the self-guided tour of the Medieval Palace. At the end of the **Wall Walk**—a series of eight towers—is **Martin Tower,** which houses an exhibit that traces the history of the British Crown and is now home to a fascinating collection of retired crowns (without the gemstones; those have been recycled into the current models); informative plaques are much better here than in the **Jewel House,** where the crown jewels are held. With the exception of the Coronation Spoon, everything dates from after 1660, since Cromwell melted down the original booty. The centerpiece of the fortress is White Tower, which begins with the first-floor ▓**Chapel of St. John the Evangelist.** Outside, Tower Green is a lovely grassy area—not so lovely, though, for those once executed there. *(Tower Hill, next to Tower Bridge, within easy reach of the South Bank and the East End. ⊖Tower Hill or DLR: Tower Gateway. ☎0870 751 5175, ticket sales 0870 756 6060; www.hrp. org.uk. Open Mar.-Oct. M and Su 10am-6pm, Tu-Sa 9am-6pm; buildings close at 5:30pm, last entry 5pm. Nov.-Feb. M and Su 10am-5pm, Tu-Sa 9am-5pm; buildings close at 4:30pm, last entry 4pm. Tower Green open only by Yeoman tours, after 4:30pm, or for daily services. £17, concessions £15, children 5-15 £9.50, children under 5 free, families of 5 £47. Tickets also sold at Tube stations; buy them in advance to avoid long queues at the door. "Yeoman Warders' Tours" meet near entrance; 45min.-1hr., every 30min. M and Su 10am-3:30pm, Tu-Sa 9:30am-3:30pm. Audio tours in 9 languages including English. £4, concessions £3.)*

TOWER BRIDGE. Not to be mistaken for its plainer sibling, London Bridge, Tower Bridge is featured in most movies set in London. A relatively new construction—built in 1894—its bright blue suspension cables connect the banks of the Thames, raising it above the cluster of other bridges in the area. The Victorian steam-powered lifting mechanism remained in use until 1973, when electric motors took over. Although clippers no longer sail into London very often, there's still enough large river traffic for the bridge to be lifted around 1000 times per year and five or six times per day in the summer. Call for the schedule or check the signs posted at each entrance. Historians and technophiles will appreciate the **Tower Bridge Exhibition,** which combines scenic 140 ft. glass-enclosed walkways with videos presenting a history of the bridge. *(Entrance to the Tower Bridge Exhibition is through the west side (upriver) of the North Tower. ⊖Tower Hill or London Bridge. ☎020 7403 3761, for lifting schedule 7940 3984; www.towerbridge.org.uk. Open daily Apr.-Sept. 10am-5:30pm; Oct.-Mar. 9:30am-5pm. Wheelchair-accessible. £7, students £5, children 5-16 £3.)*

THE SOUTH BANK

▓**SHAKESPEARE'S GLOBE THEATRE.** This incarnation of the Globe is faithful to the original, thatch roof and all. The original burned down in 1613 after a 14-year run as the Bard's preferred playhouse. Today's reconstruction had its first full season in 1997 and now stands as the cornerstone of the International Shakespeare Globe Centre. The informative exhibit inside covers the theater's history and includes displays on costumes and customs of the theater, as well as information on other prominent playwrights of Shakespeare's era. There's also an interactive display where you can trade lines with recorded Globe actors. Try to arrive in time for a tour of the theater itself. Tours that run during a matinee skip the Globe but are the only way to gain admission to the neighboring **Rose Theatre,** where both Shakespeare and Christopher Marlowe performed. For info on performances, see p. 128. *(Bankside, close to Bankside pier. ⊖Southwark or London Bridge. ☎020 7902 1400; www.shakespeares-globe.org. Open Mar. daily 9am-5pm (exhibit and tours); Apr.-Sept. M-Sa 9am-12:30pm (exhibit and Globe tour) and 12:30-5pm (exhibit and Rose Tour), Su 9-11:30am (exhibit and Globe) and noon-5pm (exhibit and Rose); Oct.-Apr. daily 10am-5pm (exhibit). Wheelchair-accessible. £11, concessions £8.50, children 5-15 £6.50, families of 5 £28.)*

For info on performances, see p. 128.

GREAT BRITAIN

LONDON EYE. At 135m (430 ft.), the British Airways London Eye, also known as the Millennium Wheel, is the biggest observational wheel in the world. The ellipsoidal glass "pods" give uninterrupted views from the top during each 30min. revolution. *(Jubilee Gardens, between County Hall and the Festival Hall. ⊖Waterloo. ☎087 990 8883; www.londoneye.com. Open daily May-June 10am-9pm; July-Aug. 10am-9:30pm; Sept. 10am-9pm; Oct.-Apr. 10am-8pm. Wheelchair-accessible. Buy tickets from the box office at the corner of County Hall before joining the queue at the Eye. Advance booking recommended, but check the weather. £17, concessions £14, children under 16 £8.50.)*

GET HIGH FOR FREE. If paying £20 for the London Eye seems a bit steep for a bird's-eye view of the city, climb the tower at the nearby Tate Modern (p. 126), which gives a similar view for free.

REGENT'S PARK. When Crown Architect John Nash designed Regent's Park, he envisioned a residential development for the "wealthy and good." Fortunately for us commonfolk, Parliament opened the space to all in 1811, creating London's handsomest and most popular recreation area. Most of the park's top attractions and activities lie near the **Inner Circle,** a road that separates the meticulously maintained **Queen Mary's Gardens** from the rest of the grounds. While the few villas in the park—The Holme and St. John's Lodge—are private residences for the unimaginably rich and are not available for public viewing, the formal **Gardens of St. John's Lodge** ("The Secret Garden"), on the northern edge of the Inner Circle, give a peek into the backyard of one such mansion. The climb up Primrose Hill, just north of Regent's Park proper, offers a splendid view of central London. *(⊖Baker St., Regent's Park, Great Portland St., or Camden Town. ☎020 7486 7905, police ☎020 7706 7272; www.royalparks.org. Open daily 5am-dusk. Free.)* The famous **Open Air Theatre,** which began in 1932, is now Britain's premier outdoor Shakespeare theater and stages performances from May to Sept. *(☎020 826 4242; www.opentheatre.org. £10-30.)*

CLERKENWELL AND HOLBORN

Clerkenwell buildings are beautiful from the outside but inaccessible to tourists; walk the **Clerkenwell Historic Trail** to see the exteriors. *(Free maps at the 3 Things Coffee Room, 53 Clerkenwell Close. ☎020 7125 37438. ⊖Farringdon. Open daily 8am-8pm.)*

THE TEMPLE. Named after the crusading Order of the Knights Templar, this complex of buildings houses legal and parliamentary offices, but it hasn't lost its clerical flavor: silent, suited barristers hurry by at all hours, clutching briefcases. The charming network of gardens and the medieval church remain open to the enterprising visitor. Make sure to see the **Inner Temple Gateway,** between 16 and 17 Fleet St., the 1681 fountain of **Fountain Court** (featured in Dickens's *Martin Chuzzlewit*), and Elm Court, tucked behind the church, a tiny yet exquisite garden ringed by massive stone structures. *(Between Essex St. and Temple Ave.; church courtyard off Middle Temple Ln. ⊖Temple or Blackfriars. Free.)*

KENSINGTON AND EARL'S COURT

Nobody took much notice of Kensington before 1689, when the newly crowned William III and Mary II moved into Kensington Palace. In 1851, the Great Exhibition brought in enough money to finance museums and colleges. Now that the neighborhood is home to expensive stores like Harrods and Harvey Nichols, it's hard to imagine the days when the area was known for taverns and highwaymen (robbers galloping on horseback).

HYDE PARK AND KENSINGTON GARDENS. Enclosed by London's wealthiest neighborhoods, **Hyde Park** has served as the model for city parks around the world, including Central Park in New York and Paris's Bois de Boulogne. **Kensington Gardens,** contiguous with Hyde Park and originally part of it, was created in the late 17th century when William and Mary set up house in Kensington Palace. *(Framed by Kensington Rd., Knightsbridge, Park Ln., and Bayswater Rd. ⊖Queensway, Lancaster Gate, Marble Arch, Hyde Park Corner, or High St. Kensington. ☎020 7298 2100; www. royalparks.org.uk. Park open daily 6am-dusk. Free. "Liberty Drive" rides available Tu-F 10am-5pm for seniors and the disabled; ☎077 6749 8096. A full program of music, performance, and children's activities takes place during the summer; see park notice boards for details.)* In the middle of the park is the **Serpentine,** officially known as the "Long Water West of the Serpentine Bridge." Doggy-paddling tourists and boaters have made it London's busiest swimming hole. Nowhere near the water, the **Serpentine Gallery** holds contemporary art and is free and open to the public daily from 10am to 6pm. *(⊖Hyde Park Corner. Boating: ☎020 7262 1330. Open Apr.-Sept. daily 10am-5pm or later in fine weather. £5 per 30min., £7 per hr.; children £2/3. Deposit may be required for large groups. Swimming at the Lido, south shore: ☎020 7706 3422. Open from June to early Sept. daily 10am-5:30pm. Lockers and sun lounges available. £4, after 4pm £3; students £3/2; children 1p/80p; families £9. Gallery open daily 10am-5pm. Free.)* At the northeast corner of the park, near Marble Arch, you can see free speech in action as proselytizers, politicos, and flat-out crazies dispense wisdom to bemused tourists at **Speaker's Corner** on Sundays, the only place in London where demonstrators can assemble without a permit.

KNIGHTSBRIDGE AND BELGRAVIA

▧APSLEY HOUSE. Named for Baron Apsley, the house later known as "No. 1, London" was bought in 1817 by the Duke of Wellington, whose heirs still occupy a modest suite on the top floor. Most visitors come for Wellington's fine art collection, much of which was given to him by the crowned heads of Europe following the Battle of Waterloo. The old masters hang in the Waterloo Gallery, where the duke held his annual Waterloo banquet around the stupendous silver centerpiece, now displayed in the dining room. *(Hyde Park Corner. ⊖Hyde Park Corner. ☎020 7499 5676; www.english-heritage.org.uk/london. Open Apr.-Oct. W-Su 11am-5pm; Nov.-Mar. W-Su 11am-4pm. Wheelchair-accessible. £5.70, students £4.80, children 5-18 £2.90. Joint ticket with Wellington Arch £7/6/3.50. Audio tours free. MC/V.)*

THE WEST END

▧TRAFALGAR SQUARE. John Nash first suggested laying out this square in 1820, but it took almost 50 years for London's largest traffic roundabout to take on its current appearance. The square is named in commemoration of the defeat of Napoleon's navy at Trafalgar—England's greatest naval victory. It has traditionally been a site for public rallies and protest movements, but it is packed with tourists, pigeons, and the ever-ubiquitous black taxis on a daily basis. Towering over the square is the 170 ft. granite **Nelson's Column,** which until recently was one of the world's tallest displays of decades-old pigeon droppings. Now, thanks to a deep clean sponsored by the Mayor, this monument to naval hero Lord Nelson sparkles once again. *(⊖Charing Cross.)*

▥ MUSEUMS AND GALLERIES

Centuries spent as the capital of an empire, together with a decidedly English penchant for collecting, have given London a spectacular set of museums. Art lovers, history buffs, and amateur ethnologists won't know which way to turn. Even better news for museum lovers: since 2002, admission to all major collections is free in celebration of the Queen's Golden Jubilee.

MAJOR COLLECTIONS

▨TATE MODERN. Sir Giles Gilbert Scott's mammoth building, formerly the Bankside power station, houses the second half of the national collection (the other set is held in the National Gallery). The Tate Modern is probably the most popular museum in London, as well as one of the most famous modern art museums in the world. The public galleries on the third and fifth floors are divided into four themes. The collection is enormous, but gallery space is limited—works rotate frequently. If you are dying to see a particular piece, head to the museum's computer station on the fifth floor to browse the entire collection. The seventh floor has unblemished views of the Thames and north and south of London. *(Main entrance on Bankside, on the South Bank; 2nd entrance on Queen's Walk. ⊖Southwark or Blackfriars. From the Southwark Tube, turn left up Union, then left on Great Suffolk, then left on Holland. ☎020 7887 8000; www.tate. org.uk. Open M-Th and Su 10am-6pm, F-Sa 10am-10pm. Free; special exhibits can be up to £10. Free tours meet on the gallery concourses: Level 3 at 11am and noon, Level 5 at 2 and 3pm. 5 types of audio tours include highlights, collection tour, architecture tour, children's tour, and tours for the visually impaired; £4, concessions £3.50. Free talks M-F 1pm; meet at the concourse on the appropriate level. Wheelchair-accessible on Holland St.)*

▨NATIONAL GALLERY. The National Gallery is an enormous gallery stuffed with masterpieces. Unless you have a few years, you will have to power past the magnificent collections of Titians, Botticellis, DaVincis, and medieval art. Don't miss the fabulously detailed *Arnolfini Wedding Portrait* by Van Eyck or Van Gogh's iconic *Sunflowers.* Founded by an Act of Parliament in 1824, the Gallery has grown to hold an enormous collection of Western European paintings, ranging from the 1200s to the 1900s. Numerous additions have been made, the most recent (and controversial) being the massive modern Sainsbury Wing, which holds almost all of the museum's large exhibitions as well as restaurants and lecture halls. If pressed for time, head to **Art Start** in the Sainsbury Wing, where you can design and print out a personalized tour of the paintings you want to see. Themed audio tours and family routes also available from the information desk. *(Main entrance (Portico Entrance) on north side of Trafalgar Sq. ⊖Charing Cross or Leicester Sq. ☎020 7747 2885; www.nationalgallery.org.uk. Wheelchair-accessible at Sainsbury Wing on Pall Mall East, Orange St., and Getty Entrance. Open M-Th and Sa-Su 10am-6pm, F 10am-9pm. Special exhibitions in the Sainsbury Wing occasionally open until 10pm. Offers themed workshops (£30-40), lectures (£3-18), and courses (£30-45) to accompany exhibitions. Free, suggested donation £5; some temporary exhibitions £5-10, seniors £4-8, students and ages 12-18 £2-5. 1hr. tours start at Sainsbury Wing information desk. Tours daily 11:30am and 2:30pm. Audio guides £3.50, students £3. AmEx/MC/V for ticketed events.)*

▨NATIONAL PORTRAIT GALLERY. Take a vast and magnificent tour of the *Who's Who* in Great Britain, beginning with priceless portraits of the Tudors and ending with today's celebrities. Try to trace family resemblances through the royal families (the Stuarts' noses) or admire the centuries of changing costume: velvet, taffeta, fabulously-patterned brocade. The famous picture of Shakespeare with an earring hangs near the Queen Elizabeth portraits in the Tudor wing. New facilities include an IT Gallery, with computers to search for pictures and print out a personalized tour, and a third-floor restaurant offering an aerial view of London, although the inflated prices will limit most visitors to coffee. To see the paintings in chronological order, take the escalator in the Ondaatje Wing to the top floor. *(St. Martin's Pl., at the start of Charing Cross Rd., Trafalgar Sq. ⊖Leicester Sq. or Charing Cross. ☎020 7312 2463; www.npg.org.uk. Open M-W and Sa-Su 10am-6pm, Th-F 10am-9pm. Wheelchair-accessible on Orange St. Free lectures Tu 3pm. Free gallery talks Sa-Su* *afternoons. Free live music F 6:30pm. General admission free; some special exhibitions free, others up to £6. Popular events require tickets, available from the information desk. Audio tours £2.)*

BRITISH MUSEUM. With 50,000 items from all corners of the globe, the magnificent collection is expansive and, although a bit difficult to navigate, definitely worth seeing. Most people don't even make it past the main floor, but they should—the galleries upstairs and downstairs are some of the best. Must-sees include the Rosetta stone, which was the key in deciphering ancient Egyptian hieroglyphs and the ancient mummies. *(Great Russell St. ⊖Tottenham Court Rd., Russell Square, or Holborn. ☎020 7323 8000; www.britishmuseum.org. Great Court open M-W and Su 9am-6pm, Th-Sa 9am-11pm (9pm in winter); galleries open daily 10am-5:30pm, selected galleries open Th-F 10am-8:30pm; library open M-W and Sa 10am-5:30pm, Th 10am-8:30pm, F noon-8:30pm. Free 30-40min. tours daily starting at 11am from the Enlightenment Desk. "Highlights Tour" daily 10:30am, 1, 3pm; advanced booking recommended. Wheelchair-accessible. Free; £3 suggested donation. Temporary exhibitions around £5, concessions £3.50. "Highlights Tour" £8, concessions £5. Audio tours £3.50, family audio tours for 2 adults and up to 3 children £10. MC/V.)*

VICTORIA AND ALBERT MUSEUM. As the largest museum of decorative (and not-so-decorative) art and design in the world, the V&A has over 9 mi. of corridors open to the public and is twice the size of the British Museum. It displays "the fine and applied arts of all countries, all styles, all periods." Unlike the British Museum, the V&A's documentation is consistently excellent and thorough. Highlights include the Glass Gallery, the Japanese and Korean areas with suits of armor and kimonos, and the Indian Gallery. Themed itineraries ($5) available at the desk can help streamline your visit, and **Family Trail** cards suggest kid-friendly routes. *(Main entrance on Cromwell Rd., wheelchair-accessible entrance on Exhibition Rd. ⊖South Kensington. ☎020 7942 2000; www.vam.ac.uk. Open M-Th and Sa-Su 10am-5:45pm, F 10am-10pm. Wheelchair-accessible. Free tours meet at rear of main entrance: introductory tours daily 10:30, 11:30am, 1:30, 3:30pm, plus W 4:30pm; British gallery tours daily 12:30 and 2:30pm. Talks and events meet at rear of main entrance. Free lunchtime talks W 1:15pm; free gallery talks Th 1pm (45-60min); F talks 7-8pm with big names in art, design and fashion industries, £8, concessions £6. Admission free.)*

TATE BRITAIN. Tate Britain is the foremost collection on British art from 1500 to the present, including pieces from foreign artists working in Britain and Brits working abroad. There are four Tate Galleries in England; this is the original Tate, opened in 1897 to house Sir Henry Tate's collection of "modern" British art and later expanded to include a gift from famed British artist J.M.W. Turner. Turner's modest donation of 282 oils and 19,000 watercolors can make the museum feel like one big tribute to the man. The annual and always controversial **Turner Prize** for contemporary visual art is still given here. Four contemporary British artists are nominated for the $40,000 prize; their short-listed works go on show from late October through late January. In 2008, the exhibition moves temporarily to the Liverpool branch of the Tate. The Modern British Art Gallery, featuring works by Vanessa Bell and Francis Bacon, is also worth a look. *(Millbank, near Vauxhall Bridge, in Westminster. ⊖Pimlico. Information ☎7887 8008, M-F exhibition booking 7887 8888; www.tate.org.uk. Open daily 10am-5:50pm, last entry 5pm. Wheelchair-accessible via Clore Wing. Free; special exhibitions £7-11. Audio tours free. See website for free tours and lectures.)*

OTHER MUSEUMS AND GALLERIES

▨ **Courtald Institute,** Somerset House, Strand, just east of Waterloo Bridge (☎020 7420 9400; www.courtauld.ac.uk). ⊖Charing Cross or Temple. Small, outstanding collection ranges from 14th-century Italian icons to 20th-century abstractions. Manet's *A Bar at the Follies Bergères,* Van Gogh's *Self-Portrait with Bandaged*

Ear, and a room devoted to Degas bronzes. Open daily 10am-6pm, last admission at 5:30pm. Wheelchair-accessible. £5, concessions £4, under 18 free.

■ **Cabinet War Rooms,** Clive Steps, far end of King Charles St. (☎020 7930 6961; www. iwm.org.uk). ❸Westminster. Churchill and his strategists lived and worked underground here from 1939 to 1945. Highlights include the room with the top-secret transatlantic hotline—the official story was that it was Churchill's personal toilet. Open daily 9:30am-6pm; last admission 5pm. £12, students £9.50, under 16 free. MC/V.

🎭 ENTERTAINMENT

Although West End ticket prices are sky high and the quality of some shows questionable, the city that brought the world Shakespeare, the Sex Pistols, and Andrew Lloyd Webber still retains its unique theatrical edge. London is a city of immense talent, full of up-and-comers, experimenters, and undergrounders.

JAZZ

■ **Jazz Café,** 5 Parkway (☎020 7534 6955; www.jazzcafe.co.uk), in North London. ❸Camden Town. Famous and popular. Crowded front bar and balcony restaurant overlook the dance floor and stage. Shows can be pricey at this nightspot, but the top roster of jazz, hip-hop, funk, and Latin performers (£10-30) explains Jazz Café's popularity. F-Sa jazzy DJs spin following the show. Box office open M-Sa 10:30am-5:30pm. Cover £5-10. Open M-Th and Su 7pm-2am, F-Sa 7pm-3:30am. 18+. MC/V.

POP AND ROCK

■ **The Monto Water Rats,** 328 Grays Inn Rd. (☎020 7813 1079; www.themonto.com), in Bloomsbury. ❸King's Cross St. Pancras. Where young indie rock bands come in search of a record deal. Bob Dylan had his UK debut here in 1962 and Oasis was signed here after their 1st London gig. Generous gastropub lunches (fish and chips £5-6) M-F noon-3pm. Tickets £6. Open for coffee M-F 8:30am-midnight. Music M-Sa 8pm-late (headliner 9:45pm). MC/V.

THEATER

London's West End is dominated by musicals and plays that run for years, if not decades. For a list of shows and discount tickets, head to the **tkts** booth in Leicester Sq. (❸Leicester Sq. www.tkts.co.uk. Most shows £20-30; up to £2.50 booking fee per ticket. Open M-Sa 10am-7pm, Su noon-3pm. MC/V.)

REPERTORY

■ **Shakespeare's Globe Theatre,** 21 New Globe Walk (☎020 7087 7398; www.shakespeares-globe.org), in the South Bank. ❸Southwark or London Bridge. Innovative, top-notch performances at this faithful reproduction of Shakespeare's original 16th-century playhouse. Choose among 3 covered tiers of hard, backless wooden benches (cushions £1 extra) or stand through a performance as a "groundling"; come 30min. before the show to get as close as you can. Should it rain, the show must go on, and umbrellas are prohibited. For tours of the Globe, see p. 123. Wheelchair-accessible. Performances from mid-May to late Sept. Tu-Sa 7:30pm, Su 6:30pm; June-Sept. Tu-Sa 2 and 7:30pm, Su 1 and 6:30pm. Box office open M-Sa 10am-6pm, 8pm on performance days; Su 10am-5pm, 7pm on performance days. New plays from £20, others from £15, yard (standing) £5.

"OFF-WEST END"

■ **The Almeida,** Almeida St. (☎020 7359 4404; www.almeida.co.uk), in North London. ❸Angel. The top fringe theater in London. Shows M-Sa 7:30pm, Sa matinees 3pm;

occasional W matinees 3pm, other weekday matinees 2:30pm. Tickets usually £8-32, occasionally as high as £46. Wheelchair-accessible. MC/V.

🔲 **The King's Head,** 115 Upper St. (☎020 7226 1916; www.kingsheadtheatre.org), in North London. ⊖Angel or Highbury and Islington. Above an attached pub, this theater focuses on new writing and rediscovered works. Alums include Hugh Grant, Gary Oldman, and Anthony Minghella. Shows Tu-Sa 8pm, Sa 3:30pm. £10-20, concessions £2.50 off; matinees £5 off. Occasional lunchtime shows and M night short-run shows; call for schedule. MC/V.

🔲 SHOPPING

London has long been considered one of the fashion capitals of the world. Unfortunately, the city features many underwhelming chain stores in addition to its one-of-a-kind boutiques. The truly budget-conscious should stick to window-shopping in Knightsbridge and on Regent Street. Vintage shopping in Notting Hill is also a viable alternative; steer clear of Oxford Street, where so-called vintage clothing was probably made in 2002 and marked up 200%.

DEPARTMENT STORES

🔲 **Selfridges,** 400 Oxford St. (☎020 0870 837 7377; www.selfridges.com). ⊖Bond St. Tourists may flock to Harrods, but Londoners head to Selfridges. You'll find all the biggies here—Gucci, Chanel, Dior—but there are also more affordable brands. Styles run the gamut from traditional tweeds to space-age clubwear. Departments specialize in every product imaginable, from antiques and scented candles, not to mention key cutting and theater tickets. With 18 cafes and restaurants, a hair salon, an exchange bureau, and even a hotel, shopaholics need never leave. Massive Jan. and July sales. Wheelchair-accessible. Open M-Sa 9:30am-9pm, Su noon-6pm. AmEx/MC/V.

Harrods, 87-135 Brompton Rd. (☎020 7730 1234; www.harrods.com). ⊖Knightsbridge. In the Victorian era, this was *the* place for the wealthy to shop; over a century later, it is less of a provider of goods than a tourist extravaganza. Given the sky-high prices, it's no wonder that only souvenir-seekers and oil sheiks actually shop here. Open M-Sa 10am-8pm; Su 11:30am-6pm, browsing only 11:30am-noon. Wheelchair-accessible. AmEx/MC/V/gold/diamonds..

STREET MARKETS

Better for people-watching than hardcore shopping, street markets may not bring you the big goods but they are a much better alternative to a day on Oxford Street. **Portobello Road Markets** (www.portobelloroad.co.uk) includes foods, antiques, secondhand clothing, and jewelry. In order to see it all, come Friday or Saturday when everything is sure to be open. (⊖Notting Hill Gate; also Westbourne Park and Ladroke Grove. Stalls set their own times.) 🔲**Camden Passage Market** (www.camdenpassageislington.co.uk) is more for looking than for buying—London's premier antique shops line these charming alleyways. (Islington High St., in North London. ⊖Angel. Turn right from the Tube; it's the alleyway that starts behind "The Mall" antiques gallery on Upper St. Stalls open W 7:30am-6pm and Sa 9am-6pm; some stores open daily, but W is the best day to go.) Its overrun sibling **Camden Markets** (☎020 7969 1500) mostly includes cheap clubbing gear and tourist trinkets; avoid the canal areas. The best bet is to stick with the **Stables Market,** farthest north from the Tube station. (Make a sharp right out of the Tube station to reach Camden High St., where most of the markets start. All stores are accessible from ⊖Camden Town. Many stores open daily 9:30am-6pm; Stables open F-Su.) **Brixton Market** has London's best selection of Afro-Caribbean fruits, vegetables, spices, and fish. It is unforgettably colorful, noisy, and fun. (Along Electric Ave., Pope's Rd., and Brixton

Station Rd., and inside markets in Granville Arcade and Market Row; in South London. ⊖Brixton. Open M-Sa 10am-sunset.) Formerly a wholesale vegetable market, **◼Spitalfields** has become the best of the East End markets. On Sundays, food shares space with rows of clothing by 25-30 independent local designers. (Commercial St., in East London. ⊖Shoreditch (during rush hour), Liverpool St., or Aldgate East. Crafts market open M-F 10am-4pm, Su 9am-5pm. Antiques market open Th 9am-5pm.) **Petticoat Lane Market** is Spitalfield's little sister market, on Petticoat Ln., off of Commercial Street. It sells everything from clothes to crafts, and is open M-F 10am-2:30pm and Su 9am-2pm. Crowds at this market can be overwhelming at times; head to the **Sunday (Up) Market** for similar items in a calmer environment. (☎020 7770 6100; www.bricklanemarket.com. Housed in a portion of the old Truman Brewery just off Hanbury St., in East London. ⊖Shoreditch or Aldgate East. Open Su 10am-5pm.)

◼ NIGHTLIFE

From pubs to taverns to bars to clubs, London has all the nightlife that a person could want. First-time visitors may initially head to the **West End,** drawn by the flashy lights and pumping music of Leicester Sq. For a more authentic experience, head to the **East End** or **Brixton.** Soho's **Old Compton Street** is still the center of GLBT nightlife. Before heading out for the evening, make sure to plan out **Night Bus** travel. Listings open past 11pm include local Night Bus routes. Night Buses in the West End are ubiquitous—head to Trafalgar Sq., Oxford St., or Piccadilly Circus to catch buses to all destinations.

PUBS

◼ **The Court London,** 108A Tottenham Court Rd. (☎087 2148 1508). ⊖Goodge St. A lighthearted pub that's all about students, with pool tables, televised sporting events, regular DJ nights, and deals on drinks and food. Pleasant outdoor picnic-style seating area. Jukebox. Burger and beer £3.75. "Screaming" burger (with bacon, cheese, onion rings, and BBQ sauce) and beer £5.75. Wine from £1; beer from £2. Mixed drinks M £2.50. Open M-Th 11am-midnight, F-Sa 11am-1am, Su noon-6pm. AmEx/MC/V.

◼ **The Jerusalem Tavern,** 55 Britton St. (☎020 7490 4281; www.stpetersbrewery.co.uk). ⊖Farringdon. Tiny and wonderfully ancient, this showcase pub for the beers of the St. Peter's Brewery has many nooks and crannies, which fill with locals at lunchtime and at night. The availability of brews changes with the seasons and is advertised on a chalkboard outside. Specialty ales (£3.40) like grapefruit or cinnamon, several organic ales, Golden Ale, Honey Porter, Summer Ale, and Suffolk Gold are available in season. Pub grub £6.50-8.50. Sourdough sandwiches £6.80. Open M-F 11am-11pm. Lunch served daily noon-3pm, dinner served Tu-Th 5-9:30pm. MC/V.

The Golden Eagle, 59 Marylebone Ln. (☎020 7935 3228). ⊖Bond St. The quintessence of "olde worlde"—both in terms of clientele and charm—this is one of the friendliest pubs around. Sidle up and join locals for the authentic pub sing-alongs (Tu and Th-F 8:30-11pm) around the piano in the corner. Beer and cider £2.40-3.50. Open M-Sa 11am-11pm, Su noon-7pm. MC/V.

BARS

◼ **Lab,** 12 Old Compton St. (☎020 7437 7820; www.lab-townhouse.com). ⊖Leicester Sq. or Tottenham Court Rd. With restroom signs for "bitches" and "bastards," the only thing this bar takes seriously is its stellar drink selection. Drink sections like "high and mighty," "short and sexy," and "streets ahead" fill the book-length menu. Licensed mixologists serve up the award-winning concoctions (£6.80-7.50), while hip 20-somethings lounge in the colorful retro atmosphere. DJs spin house and funk nightly from 8pm. Open M-Sa 4pm-midnight, Su 4pm-10:30pm. Cash only.

▨ **The Old School Yard,** 111 Long Ln. (☎020 7357 6281; www.theoldschoolyard.com). ◉Borough. Just like Cat Stevens imagined it. Blue skies and fluffy clouds adorn the ceiling, sports trophies and Teenage Mutant Ninja Turtles paraphernalia cover the walls, and old-time tunes fill the air. The drink menu comes on notebook paper, organized by subject: don't know much about history? Go for geography and try a Manhattan. Beers from £3.30. Mixed drinks from £4.90. Happy Hour Tu-Sa 5:30-8pm, Su all day; mixed drinks £4.50, beers £2.50. Occasional events like Show-ke-oke (karaoke to Westerns) and Flair bartending competition. Open Tu-Th 5:30-11:30pm, F-Sa 5:30pm-12:30am, Su 5:30-10:30pm. AmEx/MC/V.

Vibe Bar, 91-95 Brick Ln. (☎020 7426 0491; www.vibe-bar.co.uk). ◉Aldgate East or Liverpool St. Night Bus. Once the home of the Truman Brewery, this funky bar is heavy on style and light on pretension. Vibe prides itself on promoting new artists and combining music and visual displays. Dim lighting, brick interior, and mural-covered walls give the place an artsy, casual feel. In the summer, pour into the outdoor courtyard for drinking, BBQ, and general revelry. Free internet. DJs spin hip hop, garage, techno, and more M-Th and Su 11am-11:30pm. Cover F-Sa after 8pm £4. Open M-Th and Su 11am-11:30pm, F-Sa 11am-1am. AmEx/MC/V over £10.

West End Nightlife

★ CLUBS
The Edge, **3**
The End, **1**
Fitzroy Tavern, **7**
G-A-Y, **2**
Lab, **6**
Masala Zone, **4**
Rock and Sole Plaice, **5**

GREAT BRITAIN

CLUBS

▨ **Ministry of Sound,** 103 Gaunt St. (☎020 7378 6528; www.ministryofsound.com). ⊖Elephant and Castle; take the exit for South Bank University. Night Bus #N35, N133, N343. A mecca for serious clubbers worldwide—arrive before it opens or stand in line all night. Emphasis on dancing rather than decor, with a massive main room, smaller 2nd dance floor, and perpetually packed overhead balcony bar. Multiple artists often take over different venues on the same night. Dress to impress. Cover varies; usually £10-20. Hours depend on event; generally F 10pm-6am, Sa 11pm-7am, Su 10:30pm-3:30am. AmEx/MC/V.

▨ **Club Surya,** 156 Pentonville Rd. (☎020 8888 2333; www.club4climate.com/surya). ⊖King's Cross. The first ecological club in London, this nightclub seeks to enlighten (the name means Sun God). The bar area is made out of melted cell phones, the tables consist of old magazines, and downstairs, the music runs on the energy created by those on the electrifying dance floor. Also uses wind turbines and solar panels, hires local artists for the decor, and dedicates a portion of the profits to charity. Free entry for those who can prove they've traveled there by foot, bike, or public transport. Mixed drinks £7. Cover F-Sa £10-15. Open M-Th and Su 9am-11pm, F-Sa 9am-midnight. AmEx/MC/V.

GLBT NIGHTLIFE

Many venues have Gay and Lesbian nights on a rotating basis. Check *TimeOut* and look for flyers/magazines floating around Soho: *The Pink Paper* (free from newsagents) and *Boyz* (www.boyz.co.uk; free at gay bars and clubs).

▨ **The Edge,** 11 Soho Sq. (☎020 7439 1313; www.edge.uk.com). ⊖Oxford Circus or Tottenham Court Rd. A friendly "polysexual" drinking spot just off Soho Sq. offers several types of venues, complete with Häagen Dazs ice cream and £14 bottles of wine. 4 floors of stylish brick, silver, or hot pink. Relaxed bar on the ground fl., sleek black lounge bar on the 1st fl., piano bar decked out in white on the 2nd, and a newly refurbished disco dance bar, with lit up dance floor, on the top fl. Piano bar Tu-Sa. Live jazz last W of the month. DJs and dancing F-Sa. Cover Th-Sa after 10pm £2. Open M-Sa noon-1am, Su noon-11pm. MC/V.

▨ **The Black Cap,** 171 Camden High St. (☎020 7428 -2721; www.theblackcap.com). ⊖Camden Town. North London's most popular gay bar and cabaret is always buzzing and draws an eclectic male and female crowd. The rooftop patio is the highlight of the place, with plenty of tables for outside revelry. Live shows and club scene downstairs F-Su nights and some weeknights (times vary; call for details). Cover for downstairs M-Th and Su before 11pm £2, 11pm-close £3; F-Sa before 11pm £3, 11pm-close £4. Open M-Th noon-2am, F-Sa noon-3am, Su noon-1am. Kitchen open noon-10pm.

SOUTHERN ENGLAND

History and myth shroud Southern England. Cornwall, the alleged birthplace of King Arthur, was the last stronghold of the Celts in England, but traces of older Neolithic communities linger in the stone circles their builders left behind. In WWII, German bombings uncovered long-buried evidence of an invasion by Caesar, whose Romans dotted the countryside with settlements. William the Conqueror left his mark in the form of awe-inspiring castles and cathedrals. Apart from this pomp and circumstance lies a less palpable presence: the voices of British literati such as Jane Austen, Geoffrey Chaucer, Charles Dickens, and E.M. Forster echo above the sprawling pastures and seaside cliffs.

CANTERBURY ☎01227

Archbishop Thomas Becket met his demise at ◼**Canterbury Cathedral** in 1170 after an irate Henry II asked, "Will no one rid me of this troublesome priest?" Later, in his famed *Canterbury Tales*, Chaucer caricatured the pilgrims who traveled the road from London to England's most famous execution site. The steps to the nave have been worn shallow by centuries of these plodding pilgrim feet. (☎01227 762 862; www.canterbury-cathedral.org. Cathedral open Easter-Sept. M-Sa 9am-5:30pm, Su 12:30-2:30pm; Oct.-Easter M-Sa 9am-5pm, Su 12:30-2:30 pm. 1hr. tours available, 3 per day M-Sa; check nave for times. Evensong M-F 5:30pm, Sa 3:15pm, Su 3:15 and 6:15pm. £7, concessions £5.50. Tours £3.50/3. Audio tour £3.50/2.50.) The skeletons of arches and crumbling walls are all that remain of **Saint Augustine's Abbey,** outside the city wall near the cathedral—St. Augustine himself is buried under a humble pile of rocks. (☎01227 767 345. Open July-Aug. daily 10am-6pm; Sept.-Mar. Sa-Su 11am-5pm; Jan.-Mar. W-Su 10am-5pm. £0.20, concessions £3.40, child £2.10, family £10.50.) England's first Franciscan friary, **Greyfriars,** 6A Stour St., has quiet riverside gardens. (☎01227 479 364. Gardens open daily 10am-5pm. Chapel open Easter-Sept. M-Sa 2-4pm. Free.) **The Canterbury Tales,** on St. Margaret's St., recreates Chaucer's medieval England in scenes complete with ambient lighting and wax characters. Audio tours take you through the scenes in a 45min. abbreviation of Chaucer's bawdy masterpiece. (☎01227 479 227; www.canterburytales.org.uk. Open daily July-Aug. 9:30am-5pm; Mar.-June and Sept.-Oct. 10am-5pm; Nov.-Feb. 10am-4:30pm. £7.75, students £6.75, child £5.75.)

B&Bs are around **High Street** and on **New Dover Road.** Ten minutes from the city center, **Kipps Independent Hostel ❶,** 40 Nunnery Fields, is a century-old townhouse with modern amenities. (☎01227 786 121. Kitchen available. Laundry £3. Internet £2 per hr. Free Wi-Fi. If there are no vacancies, ask to set up a tent in the garden. Key deposit £10. Dorms £15. Singles £20; doubles £34. MC/V.) Share sizzling steak fajitas (£27) and grab your own margarita (£6) at **Cafe des Amis du Mexique ❷,** St. Dunstan's St., home to inspired Mexican dishes in a funky cantina setting. (☎01227 464 390. Entrees £5-10. Open M-Th noon-10pm, F-Sa noon-10:30pm, Su noon-9:30pm AmEx/MC/V.) Right next door, **Cafè Belge ❸,** 89 St. Dunstans St., is an award-winning restaurant constantly packed with students. Try the famous "fifty ways to eat fresh mussels" (£13), served up in a big silver pail. (☎01227 768 222; www.cafebelge.co.uk. Entrees £9-14. Open M-Th 11am-3pm and 6pm-late, F 11am-3pm and 6pm-late, Sa 11am-late, Su 11am-4pm and 6-9pm.) **Coffee & Corks,** 13 Palace St., is a cafe-bar with a bohemian feel.

(☎01227 457 707. Tea £1.50. Mixed drinks £4. Wine £10 per bottle. Free Wi-Fi. Open daily noon-midnight. MC/V.)

Trains run from East Station, off Castle St., to London Victoria (1hr., 2 per hr., £20.50) and Cambridge (3hr., 2 per hr., £33). Trains from West Station, Station Rd. W., off St. Dunstan's St., go to Central London (1hr., every hr., £12) and Brighton (3hr., 3 per hr., £6). National Express **buses** (☎08705 808 080) run from St. George's Ln. to London (2hr., 2 per hr., £14). The **TIC**, 12-13 Sun St., in the Buttermarket, books rooms for a £2.50 fee plus 10% deposit. (☎01227 378 100; www.canterbury.co.uk. Open Easter-Christmas M-Sa 9:30am-5pm, Su 10am-4pm; Christmas-Easter M-Sa 10am-4pm.) **Postal Code:** CT1 2BA.

SALISBURY ☎ 01722

Let's be honest—you're only here as a stopover on the way to 🪨**Stonehenge**. **Trains** run from South Western Rd., west of town across the River Avon, to London Waterloo (1hr., 2 per hr., £29.50). National Express **buses** (☎08705 808 080) go from 8 Endless St. to London (3hr., 3 per day, £14). Wilts and Dorset buses (☎01722 336 855) run to Bath (X4; every hr., £4.50) and Winchester (#68; 1hr., 8 per day, £4.65). An **Explorer** ticket is good for one day of travel on Wilts and Dorset buses (£7.50, child £4.50). The **TIC** is on Fish Row, in back of the Guildhall in Market Sq. (☎01722 334 956; www.visitsalisbury.com. Open June-Sept. M-Sa 9:30am-6pm, Su 10:30am-4:30pm; Oct.-May M-Sa 9:30am-5pm.)

🔲 **DAYTRIP FROM SALISBURY: 🪨STONEHENGE AND AVEBURY.** A ring of colossal stones amid swaying grass and indifferent sheep, Stonehenge has been battered for millennia by winds whipping at 80km per hour and visited by legions of people for over 5000 years. The monument, which has retained its present shape since about 1500 BC, was once a complete circle of 6.5m tall stones weighing up to 45 tons each. Sensationalized religious and scientific explanations for Stonehenge's purpose add to its intrigue. Some believe the stones are oriented as a calendar, with the position of the sun on the stones indicating the time of year. Admission to Stonehenge includes a 30min. audio tour. Ropes confine the throngs to a path around the outside of the monument. From the roadside or from Amesbury Hill, 2km up the A303, you can get a free view of the stones. There are also many walks and trails that pass by; ask at the Salisbury TIC. (☎01980 624 715. Open daily June-Aug. 9am-7pm; mid-Mar. to May and Sept. to mid-Oct. 9:30am-6pm; mid-Oct. to mid-Mar. 9:30am-4pm. £6.50, students £5.20.)

A question for the world: why is **Avebury's** stone circle, larger and older than its favored cousin Stonehenge, often so lonely during the day? Avebury gives an up-close and largely untouristed view of its 98 stones, dated to 2500 BC and standing in a circle with a 300m diameter. For the direct route, take the Stonehenge Tourbus, which leaves from the Salisbury train station. (Every hour, starting at 9:30am. £11 for tour, £17 with Stonehenge admission, students £14.) Wilts and Dorset **buses** (☎336 855) run daily service from the Salisbury train station and bus station (#3, 5, and 6; 30min.-2hr.; round-trip £4-8). The first bus leaves Salisbury at 9:45am, and the last leaves Stonehenge at 4:05pm. Check a schedule before you leave; intervals between drop-offs and pickups are at least 1hr. Wilts and Dorset also runs a tour bus from Salisbury (3 per day, £7.50-15). The closest lodgings are in **Salisbury** (see above).

BATH ☎ 01225

Perhaps the world's first tourist town, Bath (pop. 90,000) has been a must-see for travelers since AD 43, when the Romans built an elaborate complex of baths to house the town's curative waters. In 1701, Queen Anne's trip to the springs re-established the city as a prominent meeting place for artists, politicians, and intellectuals; it became an English social capital second only to London. No longer an upper-crust resort, today Bath plays host to crowds of tourists eager to appreciate its historic sites and well-preserved elegance.

▐▛ TRANSPORTATION AND PRACTICAL INFORMATION. Trains leave from Dorchester St. for: Birmingham (2hr., 2 per hr., £36); Bristol (15min., every 10-15min., £6); London Paddington (1.5hr., 2 per hr., £47-66.50); London Waterloo (2hr., every hr., £28.20). National Express **buses** (☎08717 818 181) run from Bath Bus Station to London (3hr., every hr., £17.50) and Oxford (2hr., 1 per day, £9.50). The train and bus stations are near the south end of Manvers St. Walk toward the town center and turn left on York St. to reach the **TIC**, in Abbey Chambers, which books rooms for £3 and a 10% deposit. (☎9067 112 000; www.visitbath.co.uk. Open June-Sept. M-Sa 9:30am-6pm, Su 10am-4pm; Oct.-May M-Sa 9:30am-5pm, Su 10am-4pm.) **Postal Code:** BA1 1AJ.

▐▐ ACCOMMODATIONS AND FOOD. B&Bs line Pulteney Rd. and Pulteney Gardens. Conveniently located **Bath Backpackers ❶**, 13 Pierrepont St., is a relaxed backpackers' lair with music-themed dorms, TV lounge, and "dungeon" bar. (☎01225 446 787; www.hostels.co.uk. Kitchen available. Internet £2 per hr. Luggage storage £2 per bag. Reception 8am-11pm. Check-out 10:30am. Reserve ahead in summer. 4-bed dorms £16-18, 8-bed £14-16, 10-bed £13-15. MC/V.) **St. Christopher's Inn ❷**, 16 Green St., has clean rooms and a downstairs pub. (☎01225 481 444; www.st-christophers.co.uk. Internet £3 per hr. Free Wi-Fi at the bar. Dorms £16-23.50. Discount for online booking. MC/V.)

Riverside Cafe ❶, below Pulteney Bridge, serves light dishes and delicious coffee. Patrons have a gorgeous view of the River Avon. (☎01225 480 532; www. riversidecafebar.co.uk. Sandwiches and soups £5-6. Open M-Sa 9am-9pm, Su 9am-5pm. MC/V.) Try the exotic vegetarian dishes, or the superb chocolate fudge cake (£5.25) at **Demuths Restaurant ❸**, 2 N. Parade Passage. (☎01225 446 059; www.demuths.co.uk. Entrees from £12. Open M-F and Su 10am-5pm and 6-10pm, Sa 9am-5pm and 6-10pm. Reserve ahead in summer. MC/V.) For groceries, head to the **Sainsbury's** supermarket on Green Park Rd. (☎01225 444 737. Open M-F 8am-10pm, Sa 7:30-10pm, Su 11am-5pm.)

▣ SIGHTS. In 1880, sewer diggers uncovered the first glimpse of an extravagant feat of Roman engineering. For 400 years, the Romans harnessed Bath's bubbling springs, where nearly 1,000,000L of 47°C (115°F) water flow every day. The **▨Roman Baths Museum**, Abbey Church Yard, shows the complexity of Roman architecture and engineering, which included central heating and internal plumbing. (☎01225 447 785; www.romanbaths.co.uk. Open daily July-Aug. 9am-10pm; Sept.-Oct. and Mar.-June 9am-6pm; Nov.-Feb. 9am-5:30pm. £10.50, concessions £9, children £6.80, families £30. Joint ticket with Museum of Costume £14/12/8.30/38. Audio tour included.)

EAST ANGLIA AND THE MIDLANDS

The rich farmland and watery flats of East Anglia stretch northeast from London, cloaking the counties of Cambridgeshire, Norfolk, Suffolk, and parts of Essex. Mention of The Midlands inevitably evokes grim urban images, but there is a unique heritage and quiet grandeur to this smokestacked landscape. Even

Birmingham, the region's much-maligned center, has its saving graces, among them a lively nightlife scene and the Cadbury chocolate empire.

OXFORD ☎01865

For nearly a millennium, the University of Oxford has been churning out talent, including 47 Nobel Prize winners, 25 British prime ministers, 86 Archbishops of Canterbury, 12 saints, six kings, and Hugh Grant. Its 38 colleges are home to impossibly intricate church ceilings, serene quads, and paintings that are older than many countries. But don't forget to come down from the ivory tower and explore the city of Oxford—a surprisingly modern metropolis of 150,000, where scaffolding creeps up ancient spires and even 11th-century buildings have been retrofitted with Wi-Fi. Those who avoid the crowds choking Cornmarket St. and explore the city's cobbled alleyways will be rewarded with historic bookshops, picturesque riverbanks, and, of course, legendary pubs inviting you to sample their brews.

TRANSPORTATION

Trains: Station on Botley Rd., down Park End. Ticket office open M-F 5:45am-8pm, Sa 7:30am-8pm, Su 7:15am-8pm. Trains (☎08457 000 125) to: **Birmingham** (1hr., 2 per hr., £23); **Glasgow** (5-7hr., every hr., £93); **London Paddington** (1hr., 2-4 per hr., £19-24); **Manchester** (3hr., 2 per hr., £57).

Buses: Station on Gloucester Green. Stagecoach (☎01865 772 250; www.stagecoach-bus.com; ticket office open M-F 9am-5pm, Sa 9:30am-1pm). National Express (☎08717 818 181; www.nationalexpress.com; ticket office open M-Th 8:30am-5:45pm, F-Sa 8:30am-6pm, Su 9am-4:30pm). The Oxford Bus Company (☎01865 785 400; www.oxfordbus.co.uk; ticket office in Debenhams Department store, at the corner of George St. and Magdalen St., open M-W 9:30am-6pm, Th 9am-8pm, F-Sa 9am-7pm).

Public Transportation: The Oxford Bus Company Cityline (☎01865 785 400) and Stagecoach Oxford (☎01865 772 250) offer frequent service to: **Abingdon Road** (Stagecoach #32, 33, Oxford Bus X3); **Banbury Road** (Stagecoach #2, 2A, 2B, 2D); **Cowley Road** (Stagecoach #1, 5A, 5B, 10, Oxford Bus #5); **Iffley Road** (Stagecoach #3, Oxford Bus #4, 4A, 4B, 4C). Fares are low (£0.60-£1.40).

Taxis: Radio Taxis (☎01865 242 424). **ABC** (☎01865 770 077). Both 24hr.

Boat Rental: Magdalen Bridge Boat House, Magdalen Bridge (☎01865 202 643; www.oxfordpunting.co.uk). Rents punts and rowboats (£14 per hr.) or chauffered punts (£20 per 30min.). Open daily 9:30am-9pm or dusk (whichever comes first).

ORIENTATION

Oxford's colleges stand around **Saint Mary's Church,** which is the spiritual heart of both the university and the greater city. The city's center is bounded by **George Street** and connecting **Broad Street** to the north and **Cornmarket** and **High Street** in the center. Directly south of the city center, the wide open spaces of **Christ Church Meadow** are surrounded by a horseshoe-shaped bend in the Thames. To the northwest, the district of **Jericho** is less touristed and is the unofficial hub of student life. Across Magdalen bridge, the corridor surrounding **Cowley Road** is a vibrant and diverse residential area that feels like its own city. **Banbury** to the north and **Abingdon** to the south are quieter, quainter towns surrounded by gorgeous countryside.

PRACTICAL INFORMATION

Tourist Information Centre: 15-16 Broad St. (☎01865 252 200; www.visitoxford.org). The busy staff books rooms for £4 plus a 10% deposit. Distributes free black-and-white maps (nicer colored maps £1.30), restaurant lists, accommodation lists, and monthly *In Oxford* guides. Open M-Sa 9:30am-5pm.

Banks: Lining Cornmarket St. The **TIC** (p. 137) has a commission-free **bureau de change**, as does **Marks & Spencer**, 13-18 Queen St. (☎01865 248 075). Open M-W and F-Sa 8am-7pm, Th 8am-8pm, Su 10:30am-5pm.

Police: St. Aldates and Speedwell St. (☎01865 505 505).

Pharmacy: Boots, Cornmarket St. (☎01865 247 461). Open M-W and F-Sa 8:30am6pm, Th 8:30am-7pm, Su 11am-5pm.

Hospital: John Radcliffe Hospital, Headley Way (☎01865 741 166). Take bus #13.

Internet Access: Free at the **Oxford Central Library** (above). **Links Communications,** 33 High St. (☎01865 204 207). £1 per 45min. Open M-Sa 10am-8:30pm, Su 11am-8:30pm.

Post Office: 102-104 St. Aldates (☎08457 223 344). **Bureau de change.** Open M and W-Sa 9am-5:30pm, Tu 9:30am-5:30pm. **Postcode:** OX1 1ZZ.

ACCOMMODATIONS

Book at least a week ahead from June to September, especially for singles. B&Bs (from £30) line the main roads out of town. Try www.stayoxford.com for affordable options.

Central Backpackers, 13 Park End St. (☎01865 242 288; www.centralbackpackers.co.uk), a short walk from the train station. Spacious rooms and clean bathrooms. Have a few drinks on the rooftop terrace—where guests frequently barbecue in the summer time. Light sleepers beware: booming bass from nearby clubs may keep you awake on weekends (but shouldn't you be out partying anyway?). Kitchen available. Female-only dorms available. Continental breakfast included. Free luggage storage and lockers. Laundry £3.50. Free internet and Wi-Fi. 12-bed dorms £16; 8-bed £17; 6-bed £18; 4-bed £19. MC/V. ❶

Oxford Backpackers Hostel, 9A Hythe Bridge St. (☎01865 721 761; www.hostels.co.uk), halfway between the bus and train stations. A self-proclaimed "funky hostel" with murals and music playing in the hallway. The bathrooms may be a little dirty, and the chairs in the common area may be losing their stuffing, but after a few drinks from the inexpensive bar, who's going to notice? Self-catering kitchen. Female-only dorm available. Continental breakfast included. Luggage storage £2. Laundry £2.50. Internet £1 per 30min. 8-bed dorms £15-16; 4-bed £17-19. MC/V. ❶

FOOD

Gloucester Green Market, behind the bus station, is full of tasty treats, fresh fruit, and assorted junk (Open W 9am-5pm). The **Covered Market** has produce and deli goods. Enter on High St. between Cornmarket St. and Turl St. (open M-Sa 8:30am-5:30pm, Su 10am-4pm). Across Magdalen Bridge, you'll find cheap restaurants on **Cowley Road** that serve international food in addition to fish and chips. For a meal on the go, try a sandwich from a **kebab van,** usually found on Broad St., High St., Queen St., or St. Aldates.

Chiang Mai Kitchen, Kemp Hall Passage (☎01865 202 233), hidden in an alley to the right of the Starbucks at 127 High St. Tasty Thai cuisine at unbeatable prices. Enjoy the fresh herbs and spices (flown in weekly from Bangkok) while soaking up the peaceful decor. Play it safe with pad thai (£9) or get exotic with jungle curry with wild venison (£9.50). Special vegetarian menu. Open M-Sa noon-2:30pm and 6-10:30pm, Su noon-2:30pm and 6-10pm. AmEx/MC/V. ❷

🎫 COLLEGES

The 🏛Tourist Information Centre sells a map (£1.25) and gives out the *Welcome to Oxford* guide, which lists the visiting hours for all of the colleges. Hours can also be accessed online at www.ox.ac.uk/visitors/colls.html. Note that those hours change without explanation or notice, so confirm in advance.

CHRIST CHURCH

COLLEGE. "The House" has Oxford's grandest quad and its most distinguished students, counting 13 past prime ministers among its alumni. Charles I made Christ Church his headquarters for three and a half years during the Civil Wars and escaped dressed as a servant when the city was besieged. Lewis Carroll first met Alice, the dean's daughter, here. The dining hall and Tom Quad serve as shooting locations for Harry Potter films. Look for rowing standings chalked on the walls and for the beautiful exterior of Christ Church's **library**. Spreading east and south from the main entrance, **Christ Church Meadow** compensates for Oxford's lack of "backs" (the riverside gardens in Cambridge). *(Down St. Aldates from Carfax. ☎01865 286 573; www.chch.ox.ac.uk. Open M-F 10:15am-11:45am and 2:15-4:30pm, Sa-Su 2:15-4:30pm. Last entry 4pm. Dining hall open 10:30am-noon and 2:30-4:30pm. Chapel services M-F 6pm; Su 8, 10, 11:15am, 6pm. £6, concessions £4.50.)*

CHRIST CHURCH CHAPEL. The only church in England to serve as both a cathedral and college chapel, Christ Church Chapel was founded in AD 730 by Oxford's patron saint, St. Frideswide, who built a nunnery here in honor of two miracles: the blinding of her persistent suitor and his subsequent recovery. A stained-glass window (c. 1320) contains a rare panel depicting St. Thomas Becket, archbishop of Canterbury, kneeling moments before his death. Many clergy are buried here, but the most aesthetically interesting tomb is the sculpture of a dead knight (John de Nowers, who died in 1386). Look for the floating toilet in the bottom right of a window showing St. Frideswide's death and the White Rabbit fretting in the windows in the hall.

ALL SOULS COLLEGE. The most prestigious of the colleges, All Souls does not even consider high school applicants. Only Oxford's best and brightest students receive an invitation-only admission offer. Candidates who survive the entrance exams are invited to a dinner, where the dons confirm that they are "well-born, well-bred, and only moderately learned." All Souls is also reported to have the most heavenly wine cellar in the city. The Great Quad may be Oxford's most serene, as hardly a living soul passes over it. *(Corner of High St. and Catte St. ☎01865 279 379; www.all-souls.ox.ac.uk. Open Sept.-July M-F 2-4pm. Free.)*

BALLIOL COLLEGE. When Lord John de Balliol insulted the Bishop of Durham, he was assigned two penances: a public whipping at Durham Cathedral and an act of charity. For charity, he bought a small house outside the Oxford city walls and gave scholars a few pence a week to study there. This community officially became Balliol College in 1266. *(Broad St. ☎01865 277 777; www.balliol. ox.ac.uk. Open daily 2-5pm. £1, students £0.50.)*

MAGDALEN COLLEGE. With extensive grounds and flower-laced quads, Magdalen (MAUD-lin) is considered Oxford's handsomest college. It has a deer park flanked by the River Cherwell and Addison's Walk, a circular path that touches the river's opposite bank. The college's most famous alumnus is playwright Oscar Wilde. *(On High St., near the Cherwell. ☎01865 276 000; www.magd.ox.ac.uk.*

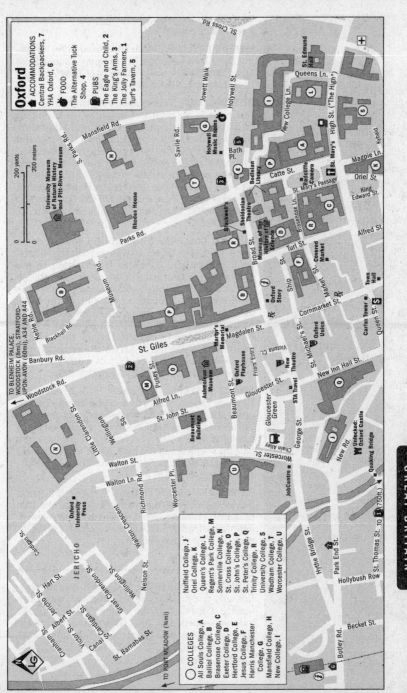

Oxford

ACCOMMODATIONS
Central Backpackers, 7
YHA Oxford, 6

FOOD
The Alternative Tuck Shop, 4

PUBS
The Eagle and Child, 2
The King's Arms, 3
The Jolly Farmers, 1
Turf's Tavern, 5

COLLEGES
All Souls College, A
Balliol College, B
Brasenose College, C
Exeter College, D
Hertford College, E
Jesus College, F
Mansfield College, H
New College, I
Nuffield College, J
Oriel College, K
Queen's College, L
Regent's Park College, M
Somerville College, N
St. Cross College, O
St. John's College, P
St. Peter's College, Q
Trinity College, R
University College, S
Wadham College, T
Worcester College, U

GREAT BRITAIN

IN RECENT NEWS

TRASHED AT OXFORD

It's summertime, the sun is shining, and you've just completed your final exam at the prestigious Oxford University. The first thing you can look forward to in your newfound freedom? A face-full of raw fish and custard.

Or, at least, a few years ago you could have. The tradition of "trashing," originating in the 1990s, refers to the practice of Oxford students throwing things at their friends upon completion of their final university exams. The items range from champagne to eggs, flour, liver, and dog food.

In 2005, the tradition started to get pretty out of hand. Street cleanups after trashing cost as much as £20,000, and one undergraduate even got an octopus thrown through his open window. Locals complained about food waste and foul-smelling streets.

As a result, the Oxford University Police clamped down on trashing. Knowing it would be impossible to eliminate the custom altogether, they cut back on the kinds of substances that could be thrown. Instead of liver and octopi, students throw much more harmless substances like confetti and glitter. So if you happen to be hit with a handful of glitter in the cobbled back alleys of Oxford in June—congratulations, you've just been trashed.

Open daily July-Sept. noon-6pm; Oct.-Mar. 1pm-dusk; Apr.--June 1-6pm. £4, concessions £3.)

MERTON COLLEGE. Tolkien lectured here, inventing the Elven language in his spare time. *(Merton St. ☎01865 276 310; www.merton.ox.ac.uk. Open M-F 2-4pm, Sa-Su 10am-4pm. Free. Library tours £2.)*

NEW COLLEGE. This is the self-proclaimed first real college of Oxford. It was here, in 1379, that William of Wykeham dreamed up an institution that would offer a comprehensive undergraduate education under one roof. The bell tower has gargoyles of the seven deadly sins on one side and the seven heavenly virtues on the other— all equally grotesque. *(New College Ln. gate in summer, Holywell St. Gate in winter. ☎01865 279 555. Open daily from Easter to mid-Oct. 11am-5pm; from Nov. to Easter 2-4pm. £2, concessions £1.)*

QUEEN'S COLLEGE. Although the college dates back to 1341, Queen's was rebuilt by Christopher Wren and Nicholas Hawksmoor in the 17th and 18th centuries in the distinctive Queen Anne style. A trumpet call summons students to dinner, where a boar's head graces the table at Christmas. That tradition supposedly commemorates a student who, attacked by a boar on the outskirts of Oxford, choked the beast to death with a volume of Aristotle—probably the nerdiest slaughter ever. *(High St. ☎01865 279 120; www.queens.ox.ac.uk. Open to Blue-Badge tours only.)*

TRINITY COLLEGE. Founded in 1555, Trinity has a Baroque chapel with a lime-wood altarpiece and cedar latticework. The college's series of eccentric presidents includes Ralph Kettell, who would come to dinner with a pair of scissors to chop anyone's hair that he deemed too long. *(Broad St. ☎01865 279 900; www.trinity.ox.ac.uk. Open daily 10am-noon and 2-4pm. £1.50, concessions £0.80.)*

UNIVERSITY COLLEGE. Built in 1249, this soot-blackened college vies with Merton for the title of oldest, claiming Alfred the Great as its founder. *(High St. ☎01865 276 602; www.univ.ox.ac.uk. Entry at the discretion of the lodge porter.)*

🏛 MUSEUMS

ASHMOLEAN MUSEUM. The grand Ashmolean— Britain's finest collection of arts and antiquities outside London and the country's oldest public museum—opened in 1683. The museum is undergoing extensive renovations until November 2009. *(Beaumont St. ☎01865 278 000. Open Tu-Sa 10am-5pm, Su noon-5pm. Free. Tours £2.)*

🍺 PUBS

🍺 **The Turf Tavern,** 4 Bath Pl. (☎01865 243 235; www.theturftavern.co.uk), hidden off Holywell St. Arguably the most popular student bar in Oxford, this 13th-century pub is tucked in an alley off an alley, but that doesn't stop just about everybody in Oxford from partaking of its 11 different ales. Bob Hawke, future prime minister of Australia, downed a yard of ale (over 2 pints) in a record 11 seconds here while at the university. The Turf is also allegedly the spot where Bill Clinton "didn't inhale" as a Rhodes Scholar. Quiz night Tu 8:30pm. Open M-Sa 11am-11pm, Su noon-10:30pm. Kitchen open noon-7pm.

The King's Arms, 40 Holywell St. (☎01865 242 369; www.kingsarmsoxford.co.uk). Oxford's unofficial student union. Until 1973, the bar was the last male-only pub in the UK. Now, the "KA" has plenty of large tables for all patrons even when it's busy. Features a rotating selection of tasty Young's cask ale. Open daily 10:30am-midnight. Kitchen open 11:30am-9pm. MC/V.

🎵 CLUBS

🎵 **Lava/Ignite,** Park End St. (☎01865 250 181; www.parkend.co.uk), across the street from Thirst. The epicenter of Oxford's student nightlife; be prepared to wait in line to get in. DJs on 3 different dance floors spin the latest techno, pop, and R&B. Look for promoters down the street handing out discount stickers. No sneakers. Cover £3-7.

🎵 **Thirst,** 7-8 Park End St. (☎01865 242 044; www.thirstbar.com). Lounge bar with a DJ and backdoor garden, where you can smoke hookah (£10) with your drinks. Arguably the most popular student hangout in Oxford. Student discount on mixed drinks (from £2.80) M-Th and Su with student ID. Open M-W and Su 7:30pm-2am, Th-Sa 7:30-3am. MC/V over £10.

STRATFORD-UPON-AVON ☎01789

Shakespeare was born here, and this fluke of fate has made Stratford-upon-Avon a major stop on the tourist superhighway. Proprietors tout the dozen-odd properties linked, however remotely, to the Bard and his extended family; shops and restaurants devotedly stencil his prose and poetry on their windows and walls. But, behind the sound and fury of rumbling tour buses and chaotic swarms of daytrippers, there lies a town worth seeing for the beauty of the Avon and for the riveting performances in the Royal Shakespeare Theatre.

📶 THENCE, AWAY! Trains (☎08457 484 950) arrive at Station Rd., off Alcester Rd., and run to: Birmingham (50min., 2 per hr., £5.90); London Marylbone (2hr., 2 per hr., £45); and Warwick (25min., 9 per day, £4.50). National Express **buses** (☎08717 818 181) go to: London (3-4hr., 4 per day, £15.80) and Oxford (1hr., 1 per day, £8). Local Stratford Blue bus #X20 stops at Wood and Bridge St., and goes to Birmingham (1hr., every hr., £4). The TIC, **Bridgefoot,** is across Warwick Rd. (☎0870 160 7930; www.shakespeare-country.co.uk. Open Apr.-Oct. M-Sa 9am-5:30pm, Su 10am-4pm; Nov.-Mar. M-Sa 9am-5pm, Su 10am-3:30pm.) Surf the **Internet** at Cyber Junction, 28 Greenhill St. (☎263 400. £4 per hr. Open M-F 10am-6pm, Sa 10:30am-5:30pm.) **Postal Code:** CV37 6PU.

📶 TO SLEEP, PERCHANCE TO DREAM. B&Bs line Evesham Place, Evesham Road, Grove Road, and Shipston Road, but reservations are a must, especially in the summer. **🏠Carlton Guest House ❸,** 22 Evesham Pl., has spacious rooms and spectacular service. (☎293 548. Singles £24-30; doubles £52; triples £60-78. Cash only.) To reach **YHA Stratford (HI) ❷,** Wellsbourne Rd., follow B4086 from the town center (35min.), or take bus #X18 or 15 from Bridge St.

(10min., every hr., £2.) This isolated hostel caters mostly to school groups and families and is a solid, inexpensive option for longer stays. (☎01789 297 093; www.stratfordyha.org.uk. Breakfast included. Internet £1 per 15min. Laundry £3. Dorms £20-25. £3 HI discount. MC/V.) Classy yet cozy, **The Oppo ❸**, 13 Sheep St., receives rave reviews from locals. (☎01789 269 980. Entrees from £9. M-Th noon-2pm and 5-9:30pm, F-Sa noon-2pm and 5-11pm, Su 6-9:30pm. MC/V.) **Hussain's ❷**, 6a Chapel St., a favorite of Ben Kingsley, offers Stratford's best Indian menu, featuring tandoori with handcrushed spices. (☎01789 276 506; www.hussainsindiancuisine. co.uk. Entrees from £6. Open daily 12:30-2:30pm and 5pm-midnight. AmEx/MC/V.) A **Somerfield** supermarket is in Town Sq. (☎292 604. Open M-Sa 8am-7pm, Su 10am-4pm.)

⬛🎭 THE PLAY'S THE THING. Stratford's Will-centered sights are best seen before 11am, when daytrippers arrive, or after 4pm, when crowds disperse. Fans can buy an **All Five Houses ticket** for admission to all official Shakespeare properties: Anne Hathaway's Cottage, Mary Arden's House, Hall's Croft, New Place and Nash's House, and Shakespeare's Birthplace. (Tickets available at all houses. £14.50, concessions £12.50.) The **Three In-Town Houses** pass covers the latter three sights. (£10.60, concessions £9.30.) **Shakespeare's Birthplace,** on Henley St., is part period re-creation and part exhibit of Shakespeare's life and works. (☎01789 201 806. Open in summer M-Sa 9am-5pm, Su 9:30am-5pm; mid-season daily 10am-5pm; winter M-Sa 10am-4pm, Su 10:30am-4pm. £8, students £7.) **New Place,** on Chapel St., was Stratford's finest home when Shakespeare bought it in 1597; now only the foundation remains, the house itself destroyed by a disgruntled 19th-century owner to spite Bard tourists. (Summer M-Sa 9:30am-5pm, Su 10am-5pm; mid-season daily 11am-5pm; winter M-Sa 11am-4pm. £4, concessions £3.50.) New Place can be viewed from **Nash's House,** on Chapel St., which belonged to the first husband of Shakespeare's granddaughter. **Hall's Croft** and **Mary Arden's House** also capitalize on connections to Shakespeare's extended family and provide exhibits on Elizabethan daily life. (Open daily 9:30am-5pm in summer, 10am-5pm in mid-season, and 10am-4pm in winter. £7, concessions £6.) Pay homage to the Bard's grave in the **Holy Trinity Church,** Trinity St. (☎01789 266 316. Open daily 8:30am-6pm. Last admission 20min. before close. Requested donation £1.50.)

The ▓Royal Shakespeare Company sells well over one million tickets each year. The Royal Shakespeare Theatre and the Swan Theatre, the RSC's more intimate neighbor, are currently undergoing a £100 million renovation and will re-open in 2010. The company will continue to perform shows down the road at The Courtyard Theatre. Visitors can get backstage tours and a glimpse at the high-tech stage to be installed at the Royal Shakespeare Theatre. Tickets are sold through the box office in the foyer of the Courtyard Theatre. (☎01789 0844 800 1110; www.rsc.org. uk. Open M and W-Sa 9:30am-8pm, Tu 10am-8pm. Tickets £10-48. Tickets £5 for ages 16-25. Standing room £5. Standby tickets in summer £15; winter £12. Disabled travelers should call ahead to advise the box office of their needs; some performances feature sign language interpretation or audio description.) The Shakespeare Birthplace Trust hosts a Poetry Festival every Sunday evening in July and August. Past participants include Seamus Heaney, Ted Hughes, and Derek Walcott. (☎01789 292 176. Tickets £7-15.) Theater crowds abound at the ▓Dirty Duck Pub, 66 Waterside, where RSC actors make appearances almost nightly. (☎01789 297 312; www.dirtyduck.co.uk. Open daily 10am-midnight. AmEx/MC/V.)

CAMBRIDGE ☎01223

Unlike museum-oriented, metropolitan Oxford, Cambridge is a town for students before tourists. It was here that Newton's theory of gravity, Watson and Crick's model of DNA, Byron's and Milton's poetry, and Winnie the Pooh were born. No longer the exclusive academy of upper-class sons, the university feeds the minds of female, international, and state-school pupils alike. At exams' end, Cambridge explodes in Pimm's-soaked glee, and May Week is a swirl of celebration on the River Cam.

▟ TRANSPORTATION

Trains: (☎08456 007 245). Station on Station Rd. (How original.) Ticket office open daily 5am-11pm. Trains to **London King's Cross** (45min., 3 per hr., £14) and **Ely** (20min., 3 per hr., round-trip £3.70).

Buses: Station on Drummer St. Ticket booth open M-Sa 9am-5pm; tickets often available onboard. **National Express** (☎08705 808 080) buses and airport shuttles pick up at stands on Parkside St. along Parker's Piece park. Buses to: **London Victoria** (2hr., every hr., £12); **Gatwick** (4hr., every hr., £31); **Heathrow** (2½hr., 2 per hr., £28); **Stansted** (1hr., every hr., £12). **Stagecoach Express** (☎01604 676 060) runs to **Oxford** (3hr., every 30min., from £11).

Public Transportation: Stagecoach (☎01223 423 578) runs **CitiBus** from the train station to the city center and around town (£5 for all-day ticket).

Taxis: Cabco (☎01223 312 444) and **Camtax** (☎01223 313 131). Both available 24hr.

Bike Rental: Station Cycles, Corn Exchange St. (☎01223 307 125). £9 per day; £50 deposit. Lock included. Open M-Sa 8am-7pm and Su 10am-6pm. AmEx/MC/V.

▓ ORIENTATION

Cambridge has two central avenues; the main shopping street starts at **Magdalene Bridge** and becomes **Bridge Street, Sidney Street, Saint Andrew's Street, Regent Street,** and **Hills Road.** The other main thoroughfare starts as **Saint John's Street,** becoming **Trinity Street, King's Parade,** and **Trumpington Street.** From the Drummer St. bus

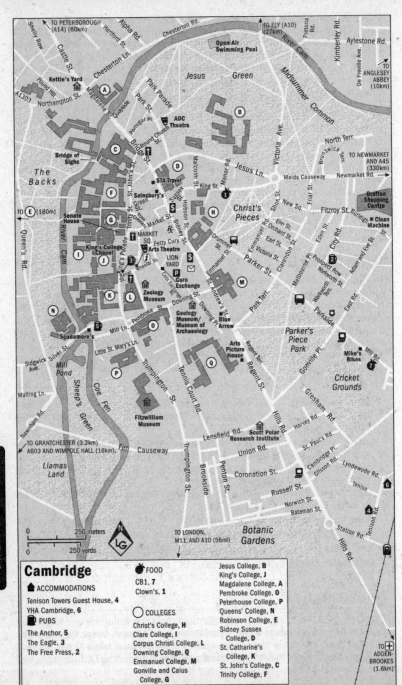

Cambridge

🏠 **ACCOMMODATIONS**

Tenison Towers Guest House, **4**
YHA Cambridge, **6**

🍺 **PUBS**

The Anchor, **5**
The Eagle, **3**
The Free Press, **2**

🍎 **FOOD**

CB1, **7**
Clown's, **1**

⭕ **COLLEGES**

Christ's College, **H**
Clare College, **I**
Corpus Christi College, **L**
Downing College, **Q**
Emmanuel College, **M**
Gonville and Caius
  College, **G**

Jesus College, **B**
King's College, **J**
Magdalene College, **A**
Pembroke College, **O**
Peterhouse College, **P**
Queens' College, **N**
Robinson College, **E**
Sidney Sussex
  College, **D**
St. Catharine's
  College, **K**
St. John's College, **C**
Trinity College, **F**

station, **Emmanuel Street** leads to the shopping district near the TIC. To get to the TIC from the train station, turn right onto Hills Rd. and follow it ¾ mi.

⚡ PRACTICAL INFORMATION

Tourist Information Centre: Wheeler St. (☎09065 268 006; www.visitcambridge.org), 1 block south of Market Sq. Books rooms for £5 and a 10% deposit. Local Secrets Card gives city-wide discounts. Sells National Express tickets. Open Easter-Oct. M-F 10am-5:30pm, Sa 10am-5pm, Su 11am-3pm; Nov.-Easter M-F 10am-5:30pm, Sa 10am-5pm.

Police: Parkside (☎01223 358 966).

Hospital: Addenbrookes Hospital, Long Rd. (☎01223 245 151). Take Cambus C1 or C2 from Emmanuel St. (£1) and get off where Hills Rd. intersects Long Rd.

Internet Access: Available at: **Jaffa Net Cafe,** 22 Mill Rd. (☎01223 308 380). From £1 per hr. 10% student discount. Open daily 10am-10pm. **Budget Internet Cafe,** 30 Hills Rd. (☎01223 362 214). 75p per 30min. Open daily 9am-11pm. AmEx/MC/V. **Web and Eat,** 32 Hills Rd. (☎01223 314 168). 70p per 30min. Open daily 8am-11pm.

Post Office: 9-11 St. Andrew's St. (☎08457 223 344). **Bureau de change.** Open M and W-Sa 9am-5:30pm, Tu 9:30am-5:30pm. **Postcode:** CB2 3AA.

🏠 ACCOMMODATIONS

John Maynard Keynes, who studied and taught at Cambridge, tells us that low supply and high demand usually mean one thing: high prices.

Tenison Towers Guest House, 148 Tenison Rd. (☎01223 363 924; www.cambridgecitytenisontowers. com). Sunny rooms and freshly baked muffins in a Victorian house. Free Wi-Fi. Singles £40; doubles £60-66; triples £84. Cash only. ❹

Warkworth Guest House, Warkworth Terr. (☎01223 363 682). Spacious ensuite rooms near the bus station in a Victorian mansion. Breakfast included. Free Wi-Fi in lounge. Singles £55; twins and doubles £75; ensuite triples £90; families £95. MC/V. ❺

🍴 FOOD

Clown's, 54 King St. (☎01223 355 711). The staff at this cozy Italian eatery will remember your name if you come more than once. Children's artwork plasters the orange walls. Huge portions of pasta and dessert (£2.50-7). Set menu includes a drink, salad, small pasta, and cake (£7.50). Open daily 8am-11pm. Cash only; accepts Euro. ❷

The Regal, 38-39 St. Andrews St. (☎01223 366 459). The largest pub in the UK. 3 floors, 2 bars, and lots of slot machines. Check out the value menu (£3-4) for classic fare. Cheap pints (£1.50-2.50) to accompany your meal. Free Wi-Fi. Open M-Th and Su 9am-midnight, F-Sa 9am-2am. AmEx/MC/V over £5. ❶

👁 SIGHTS

KING'S COLLEGE. King's College was founded by Henry VI in 1441 as a partner school to Eton: it was not until 1873 that students from other prep schools were admitted. Today, however, King's is the most socially liberal of the Cambridge colleges, drawing more of its students from state schools than any other. Its most stunning attraction is the Gothic **King's College Chapel.** From the southwest corner of the courtyard, you can see where Henry's master mason left off and the Tudors began work—the earlier stone is off-white. John Maynard Keynes, EM Forster, and Salman Rushdie all lived in King's College. *(King's Parade.* ☎01223 331 100. *Chapel and grounds open M-Sa 9:30am-5pm, Su 10am-5pm.*

Last entry 4:30pm. Contact TIC for tours. Listing of services and musical events available at porter's lodge. Choral services 10:30am, often 5:30pm. £5, students £3.50. Audio tour £2.50.)

TRINITY COLLEGE. Henry VIII intended the College of the Holy and Undivided Trinity (founded in 1546) to be the largest and richest in Cambridge. The alma mater of Sir Isaac Newton, who lived in E staircase for 30 years, the college has many other equally illustrious alumni: literati Dryden, Byron, Tennyson, and Nabokov; atom-splitter Ernest Rutherford; philosopher Ludwig Wittgenstein; and Indian statesman Jawaharlal Nehru. The **Wren Library** houses alumnus AA Milne's handwritten copies of *Winnie the Pooh* and Newton's personal copy of his *Principia.* Pass through the drab **New Court** (Prince Charles's former residence) to get to the **Backs,** where you can enjoy the view from **Trinity Bridge.** *(Trinity St. ☎01223 338 400. Chapel and courtyard open daily 10am-5pm. Easter-Oct. £2.50, concessions £1.30, children £1, families £4.40; Nov.-Easter free for all.)*

SAINT JOHN'S COLLEGE. Established in 1511 by Lady Margaret Beaufort, mother of Henry VIII, St. John's centers on a paved plaza rather than a grassy courtyard. The **Fellows' Room** in Second Court spans 93 ft. and was the site of D-Day planning. *(St. John's St. ☎01223 338 600. Open M-F 10am-5pm, Sa-Su 9:30am-5:30pm. Evensong Tu-Su 6:30pm. £3, concessions £2.)*

QUEENS' COLLEGE. Queens' College has the only unaltered Tudor courtyard in Cambridge, but the main attraction is the **Mathematical Bridge.** *(Silver St. ☎01223 335 511. Open Mar.-Oct. daily 10am-5pm. £2.)*

⬛FITZWILLIAM MUSEUM. The museum fills an immense Neoclassical edifice, built in 1875 to house Viscount Fitzwilliam's collections. Egyptian, Chinese, Japanese, Middle Eastern, and Greek antiquities downstairs are joined by 16th-century German armor. Upstairs, galleries feature works by Rubens, Monet, Van Gogh, and Picasso. *(Trumpington St. ☎01223 332 900. Open Tu-Sa 10am-5pm, Su noon-5pm. Call about lunchtime and evening concerts. Free; suggested donation £3.)*

🎵 ENTERTAINMENT

⬛PUNTING. Punting on the Cam is as traditional and obligatory as afternoon tea. Touristy and overrated? Maybe, but it's still a blast. Punters take two routes—from Magdalene Bridge to Silver St. or from Silver St. to Grantchester. The shorter, busier, and more interesting first route passes the colleges and the Backs. To propel your boat, thrust the pole behind the boat into the river-bed and rotate the pole in your hands as you push forward. Punt-bombing—jumping from bridges into the river alongside a punt to tip it—is an art form. Some more ambitious punters climb out midstream, scale a bridge while their boat passes underneath, and jump back down from the other side. Be wary of bridge-top pole-stealers. You can rent at **Scudamore's,** Silver St. Bridge. *(☎01223 359 750; www.scudamores.com. M-F £16 per hr., Sa-Su £18 per hr. £80 deposit. MC/V.)* Student-punted tours (£14, students £12) are another option.

🎵 NIGHTLIFE

The Eagle, 8 Benet St. (☎01223 505 020). Cambridge's oldest pub (in business since 1525) is in the heart of town and packed with boisterous tourists. When Watson and Crick rushed in to announce the discovery of DNA, the barmaid insisted they settle their 4-shilling tab. Check out the RAF room, where WWII pilots stood on each other's shoulders to burn their initials into the ceiling. Open M-Sa 11am-11pm, Su noon-10:30pm. AmEx/MC/V over £5.

The Anchor, Silver St. (☎01223 353 554). This jolly-looking pub, overflowing with beer and good cheer, is anchored right on the Cam. Scoff at amateur punters colliding under Silver St. Bridge or savor a pint at the same spot from which Pink Floyd's Syd Barrett drew his inspiration. Open M-Th and Su 11am-11pm, F-Sa 11am-midnight. Kitchen open M-Sa noon-10pm, Su noon-9pm. AmEx/MC/V.

FESTIVALS

May Week, actually in June—you would expect a better understanding of simple chronology from those bright Cambridge students. A celebration of the end of the term, the week is crammed with concerts, plays, and balls followed by recuperative riverside breakfasts and 5am punting. The boat clubs compete in races known as the **bumps.** Crews attempt to ram the boat in front before being bumped from behind. The celebration includes **Footlights Revue,** a series of skits by current undergrads. Past performers have included future *Monty Python* stars John Cleese and Eric Idle. £250 per person.

SCOTLAND

Half the size of England with only a tenth the population, Scotland possesses open spaces and wild natural splendor unrivaled by its neighbor to the south. The Scots revel in a distinct culture ranging from the fevered nightlife of Glasgow and the festival atmosphere of Edinburgh to the tight-knit communities of the Orkney and Shetland Islands. The Scots defended their independence for hundreds of years before reluctantly joining England to create Great Britain in 1707, and they only regained a separate parliament in 1999. The mock kilts and bagpipes of the big cities can grow tiresome: discover Scotland's true colors by venturing off the beaten path to find Gaelic-speaking B&B owners, peat-cutting crofters, and fishermen setting out in skiffs at dawn.

GETTING TO SCOTLAND

Buses from London (8-12hr.) are generally the cheapest option. National Express (☎08457 225 333; www.nationalexpress.com) **buses** connect England and Scotland via Edinburgh and Glasgow. Trains are faster (4-6hr.) but more expensive. National Express also runs **trains** (☎08457 225 333; www.nationalexpress.com) from London to Edinburgh and Glasgow. Fares vary depending on when you buy (£27-£100). A pricier option is the **Caledonian Sleeper,** run by First Scotrail (☎08456 015 929; www.firstgroup.com/scotrail), which leaves London Euston near midnight and gets to Edinburgh at 7am (£20-140). The cheapest airfares between England and Scotland are available from no-frills airlines. **easyJet** (☎0871 244 2366; www.easyjet.com) flies to Edinburgh and Glasgow from London Gatwick, Luton, and Stansted. The fares are web-only; book in advance and fly for as little as £5. Ryanair (☎08712 460 000; www.ryanair.com) flies to Edinburgh and to Glasgow Prestwick (1hr. from the city) from Dublin and London. **British Airways** (☎0844 493 0787; www.britishairways.com) sells round-trip tickets between England and Scotland from £85.

TRANSPORTATION

In the Lowlands (south of Stirling and north of the Borders), **trains** and buses run many routes frequently. In the Highlands, Scotrail and National Express trains run a few routes. Many stations are unstaffed—buy tickets on board.

A great money-saver is the **Freedom of Scotland Travelpass,** which allows unlimited train travel and transportation on most Caledonian MacBrayne ("CalMac") ferries. Purchase the pass before traveling to Britain at any BritRail distributor. **Buses** tend to be the best and cheapest way to travel. **Traveline Scotland** has the best information on all routes and services (☎0871 200 2233; www.travelinescotland.com). **Scottish Citylink** (☎08705 505 050; www. citylink.co.uk) runs most intercity routes; **Postbuses** (Royal Mail customer service ☎08457 740 740) pick up passengers and mail once or twice a day in the most remote parts of the country, typically charging £2-5 (and sometimes nothing). Many travelers find that they can be a reliable way to get around the Highlands. ▉**HAGGIS** (☎0131 557 9393; www.haggisadventures. com) and **MacBackpackers** (☎01315 589 900; www.macbackpackers.com) cater to the young and adventurous, with a number of tours departing from Edinburgh. Both run hop-on, hop-off excursions that let you travel Scotland at your own pace (usually under three months).

EDINBURGH ☎0131

A city of elegant stone amid rolling hills and ancient volcanoes, Edinburgh (ED-in-bur-ra; pop. 500,000) is the jewel of Scotland. Since David I granted it *burgh* (town) status in 1130, Edinburgh has been a haven for forward-thinking intellectuals and innovative artists. Today, world-class universities craft the next generation of Edinburgh's thinkers. Businessmen, students, and backpackers mix amidst the city's medieval architecture and mingle in lively pubs and clubs. In August, Edinburgh becomes a mecca for the arts, drawing talent and crowds from around the globe to its International and Fringe Festivals.

◀ INTERCITY TRANSPORTATION

Edinburgh lies 45 mi. east of Glasgow and 405 mi. northwest of London on Scotland's east coast, on the southern bank of the Firth of Forth.

Flights: Edinburgh International Airport (☎0870 040 0007), 7 mi. west of the city. Lothian Airlink (☎0131 555 6363) shuttles between the airport and Waverley Bridge (25min.; every 10-15min.; £3.50, children £2, round-trip £6/3). Flights to major international cities, including **New York City** (9hr.), as well as UK destinations such as **Birmingham, London Gatwick, London Heathrow,** and **Manchester.**

Trains: Waverley Station, between Princes St., Market St., and Waverley Bridge. Free bike storage beside platforms 1 and 11. Ticket office open M-Sa 4:45am-12:30am, Su 7am-12:30am. Trains (☎08457 484 950) to: **Aberdeen** (2½hr.; M-Sa every hr., Su 8 per day; £34); **Glasgow** (1hr., 4 per hr., £9.70); **Inverness** (3½hr., every 2hr., £32); **London King's Cross** (4¾hr., 2 per hr., £108); **Stirling** (50min., 2 per hr., £6.10).

Buses: The modern **Edinburgh Bus Station** is on the eastern side of St. Andrew Sq. Open daily 6am-midnight. Ticket office open daily 8am-8pm. National Express (☎08705 808 080) to **London** (10hr., 4 per day, £30). Scottish Citylink (☎08705 505 050; www.citylink.co.uk) to **Aberdeen** (2½hr., every hr., £23), **Glasgow** (1hr.; M-Sa 4 per hr., Su 2 per hr.; £6), and **Inverness** (4½hr., 8-10 per day, £25). A bus-ferry route via Stranraer goes to **Belfast** (2 per day, £28) and **Dublin, IRE** (2 per day, £32). Megabus also serves Edinburgh; for cheapest fares, book ahead online at www. megabus.com or call ☎0900 160 0900 (7am-10pm).

LOCAL TRANSPORTATION

Public Transportation: Although walking is usually the fastest and easiest way around the city center, Edinburgh has a comprehensive bus system. Lothian (☎0131 555 6363; www.lothianbuses.com) operates most buses. Exact change required (£1.10, children 70p). Buy a 1-day **Daysaver** ticket (£3, children £2.40) from any driver or in the Lothian Travelshops (☎0131 555 6363) on Waverley Bridge, Hanover St., and Shandwick Pl. Open M-Sa 8:15am-6pm. **Night buses** cover selected routes after midnight (£3). First Edinburgh (☎0870 872 7271) also operates local buses. Traveline (☎0870 608 2608; www.traveline.co.uk) has more information.

Taxis: Stands located at all train and bus stations. **City Cabs** (☎0131 228 1211). **Central Radio Taxis** (☎0131 229 2468). **Central Taxis Edinburgh** (☎0131 229 2468; www.taxis-edinburgh.co.uk).

ORIENTATION

Edinburgh's city center is divided into two halves, on either side of the train tracks, **Old Town** and **New Town**. The two are connected by three bridges: **North Bridge, Waverley Bridge,** and **The Mound.** The bridges cross over **Waverley Station,** which lies directly between Old Town and New Town. The **Royal Mile** and **Edinburgh Castle** are in Old Town and are the center of most tourist activities, while New Town plays host to upscale shopping. When reading maps, remember that Edinburgh is a multidimensional city—many streets that appear to intersect are actually on different levels. The terrain is hilly, and valleys are often spanned by bridges with streets running under them. Elevations are connected by many narrow stairway alleys known as "closes." Two miles northeast of New Town, **Leith** is the city's seaport on the Firth of Forth.

PRACTICAL INFORMATION

Tourist Information Centre: Waverley Market, 3 Princes St. (☎0845 22 55 121), north of Waverley Station. Helpful and often mobbed, the mother of all Scottish TICs books rooms for £4 plus a 10% deposit; sells bus, museum, tour, and theater tickets; and has free maps and pamphlets. **Bureau de change.** Open July-Aug. M-Sa 9am-7pm, Su 10am-7pm; Sept.-June M-Sa 9am-5pm, Su 10am-5pm.

Budget Travel: STA Travel, 27 Forrest Rd. and 72 Nicholson St. (both ☎0131 230 8569). Open M-Sa 10am-6pm, Su 11am-5pm.

Beyond Tourism: In the summer, young travelers are employed by festival organizers to help manage offices, set up, etc. Hostel notice boards often help employment agencies seeking temporary workers. **Temp Agency** (☎0131 478 5151). **Wesser and Partner** (☎01438 356 222, www.wesser.co.uk). **Kelly Services** (☎0131 220 2626).

Luggage Storage: At the Waverley train station or the bus station. £5 per item per day.

GLBT Resources: Edinburgh Lesbian, Gay, and Bisexual Centre, 58A-60 Broughton St. (☎0131 478 7069). **Gay Edinburgh**(www.visitscotland.com).

Police: Headquarters at Fettes Ave. (☎0131 311 3131; www.lbp.police.uk). Other stations at 14 St. Leonard's St. (☎0131 662 5000) and 188 High St. (☎0131 226 6966). Blue **police information boxes** are scattered throughout the city center, with tourist information and an emergency assistance button.

Pharmacy: Boots, 48 Shandwick Pl. (☎0131 225 6757) and 101-103 Princes St. (☎0131 225 8331). Open M-W and F-Sa 8am-6:30pm, Th 8am-8pm, Su 10am-6pm.

Hospital: Royal Infirmary of Edinburgh, 51 Little France Cres. (☎0131 536 1000, emergencies 536 6000).

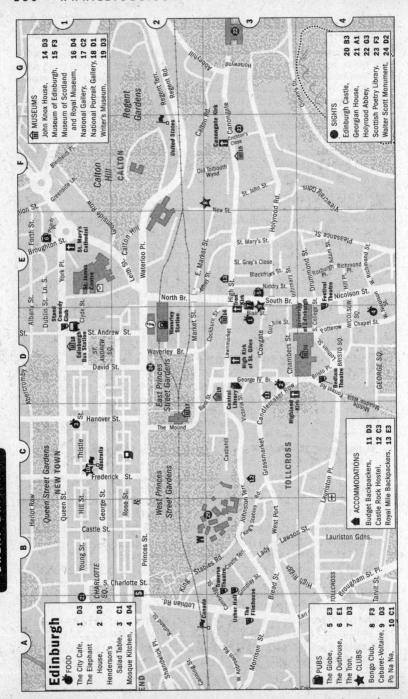

GREAT BRITAIN

Edinburgh

FOOD

The City Cafe,	1 D3
The Elephant House,	2 D3
Henderson's Salad Table,	3 C1
Mosque Kitchen,	4 D4

PUBS

The Globe,	5 E3
The Outhouse,	6 E1
The Tron,	7 D3

CLUBS

Bongo Club,	8 F3
Cabaret-Voltaire,	9 D3
Po Na Na,	10 C1

ACCOMMODATIONS

Budget Backpackers,	11 D3
Castle Rock Hostel,	12 C3
Royal Mile Backpackers,	13 E3

MUSEUMS

John Knox House,	14 D3
Museum of Edinburgh,	15 F3
Museum of Scotland and Royal Museum,	16 D4
National Gallery,	17 C2
National Portrait Gallery,	18 D1
Writer's Museum,	19 D3

SIGHTS

Edinburgh Castle,	20 B3
Georgian House,	21 A1
Holyrood Abbey,	22 G3
Scottish Poetry Library,	23 F3
Walter Scott Monument,	24 D2

Internet Access: Signs to internet cafes are on every other corner along the Royal Mile. **E-Corner,** 54 Blackfriars St. (☎0131 558 7858). £1 per 30min. with terminals and Wi-Fi. Open M-F 10am-9pm, Sa 10am-8pm, Su noon-8pm. The **Bongo Club Cafe,** 6 New St. (☎0131 558 7604), has a few free terminals. Open M-F 11am-late, Sa 12:30pm-late. Free at the **Central Library.** Many cafes throughout Old Town also offer internet access.

Post Office: St. James Centre (☎0131 556 9546). **Bureau de change.** Open M-Sa 9am-5:30pm. Branch at 46 St. Mary's St. (☎0131 556 6351). Open M-Tu and Th-F 9am-12:30pm and 1:30-5:30pm, Sa 9am-noon. **Postcode:** EH1 3SR.

ACCOMMODATIONS AND CAMPING

Hostels and hotels are the only options in the city center; **B&Bs** and **guesthouses** appear on the edges of town. Be sure to ook ahead in summer. During the Festival (from late July to early Sept.) and New Year's, prices often rise significantly. Many locals let their apartments; the TIC's booking service works magic.

HOSTELS

Scotland's Top Hostels (www.scotlands-top-hostels.com). This chain's 3 Edinburgh hostels all have a fun, relaxed environment and comfortable facilities. Also runs MacBackpacker tours in the city and around Scotland. All three run free Th pub crawls.

Royal Mile Backpackers, 105 High St. (☎0131 557 6120). The smallest of the chain's hostels. Well-kept and cozy, with a community feel (and free tea and coffee). Shared laundry facilities. Free Wi-Fi. 8-bed dorms £13-15. AmEx/MC/V. ●

Castle Rock Hostel, 15 Johnston Terr. (☎0131 225 9666, www.castlerockedinburgh.com). Just steps from the castle, with a party atmosphere and a top-notch cinema room that shows nightly movies. Ask about their haircut offer: £10 with a complimentary shot of vodka. Breakfast £2. Free Wi-Fi. Dorms £13-15; doubles £30-34; triples £45-51. AmEx/MC/V. ●

High St. Hostel, 8 Blackfriars St. (☎0131 557 3984). Ideally located just off the Royal Mile. Laid-back party environment and 16th-century architecture. Pub crawls, movie nights, and pool competitions. Free Wi-Fi. 4- to 18-bed dorms £13-15. AmEx/MC/V. ●

Budget Backpackers, 37-39 Cowgate (☎0131 226 2351; www.budgetbackpackers. co.uk). The most modern of the Old Town hostels. Spacious 2- to 12-bed rooms; female-only dorms available. Free city tour daily; pub crawl M-Sa starting at 9pm. Breakfast £2. Lockers free (bring your own padlock). Laundry £1 each for washer and dryer. Internet £1 per 30min. Reception 24hr. Key-card access. Rooms £9-24. 18+. MC/V. ❷

Globetrotter Inn, 46 Marine Dr. (☎0131 336 1030; www.globetrotterinns.com), a 15min. bus ride from Waverley train station and Edinburgh International Airport. Large grounds next to the Firth of Forth. An hourly shuttle service runs to and from the city, although a shop, TV room, gym, hot tub, and 24hr. bar make it tempting to stay put. Curtained bunks offer privacy. Light breakfast included. Free Wi-Fi and internet. Lockers free. Key-card access. Dorms £15-19; ensuite doubles and twins £46. MC/V. ●

CAMPING

Edinburgh Caravan Club Site, Marine Dr. (☎0131 312 6874), by the Firth. Take bus #27 from The Mound, get off at Silvernose, and walk 15min. down Marine Dr. Clean and family-friendly. Electricity, shop, hot water, showers, and laundry. £4.60-6 per person; £4.80-7.60 per pitch for members. £7 per pitch for non-members. MC/V. ●

Mortonhall Caravan and Camping Park, 38 Mortonhall Gate, Frogston Rd. (☎0131 664 1533; www.meadowhead.co.uk). Take bus #11 from George St. to Hyvots Bank. South of the city. Electricity, hot water, laundry. Wigwams £14-22. ❷

🔆 FOOD

Edinburgh's restaurants offer a range of cuisines. If it's traditional fare you're after, find everything from pub haggis to creative "modern Scottish" at the city's top restaurants. For food on the cheap, many **pubs** offer student and hosteler discounts in the early evening, while fast-food joints are scattered across New Town. Takeaway shops on **South Clerk, Leith Street** and **Lothian Road** have affordable Chinese and Indian fare. For groceries, try **Sainsbury's,** 9-10 St. Andrew Sq. (☎0131 225 8400; open M-Sa 7am-10pm, Su 9am-8pm) or the **Tesco** on Earl Grey St. (☎0131 221 0650; open daily 6am-11pm).

OLD TOWN

🔳 **The Mosque Kitchen,** 19A West Nicholson Street, tucked away in the courtyard of Edinburgh's central mosque. A jumble of long tables make up an outdoor cafeteria. Popular with students. Heaping plates of curry (£4) are hard to beat. Open M-Th and Sa-Su 11:30am-7pm, F noon-1pm and 1:45-7pm (closes briefly for F prayers). Cash only. ❶

🔳 **The City Cafe,** 19 Blair St. (☎0131 220 0125), right off the Royal Mile behind Tron Kirk. This perennially popular Edinburgh institution is a cafe by day and a flashy pre-club spot by night. Sip a milkshake and people-watch from the cafe's heated street-side seating. Happy hour daily 5-8pm. Open daily during the festival 11am-3am; otherwise 11am-1am. Kitchen open M-Th until 10pm, F-Su until 10pm. MC/V. ❷

Maxies Bistro and Wine Bar, 5B Johnston Terrace (☎0131 226 7770, www.maxies. co.uk). For 35 years, this institution has poured some of the world's tastiest wines on their patio overlooking Old Town. Eclectic menu with everything from pasta to Mexican (entrees £7-13). Vegetarian dishes £7. Open daily 11am-midnight. AmEx/MC/V. ❷

The Elephant House, 21 George IV Bridge (☎0131 220 5355). Harry Potter and Albus Dumbledore were born here on scribbled napkins. A perfect place to chill, chat, and read a newspaper. Exotic tea/coffee and the best shortbread in the universe. Great views of the castle. Coffee and 1hr. of internet £2.50. Open daily 8am-11pm. MC/V. ❶

NEW TOWN

🔳 **Valvonna & Crolla,** 19 Elm Row (☎0131 556 6066; www.valvonacrolla.co.uk), off Leith Walk. Beloved of foodies across the UK, this deli has been selling Italian wine, gourmet meats, and other delicious groceries since 1934. In back, the cafe serves Scottish takes on Italian specialties, complete with wine pairings. Open M-Th 8:30am-5:30pm, F-Sa 8am-6pm, Su 10:30am-3:30pm. Reservations recommended on weekends. MC/V. ❷

The Basement, 10A-12A Broughton St. (☎0131 557 0097; www.thebasement.org.uk). Menu changes daily, with plenty of vegetarian options. Energetic vibe draws students, artists, performers, and other creative types. Entrees £6-9.50, set 2-course lunch £8. Mexican night Sa-Su. Kitchen open M-Sa noon-10:30pm, Su 12:30-10:30pm. Bar open until 1am. Reservations recommended on weekends. AmEx/MC/V. ❷

Henderson's Salad Table, 94 Hanover St. (☎0131 225 2131). The flagship of Edinburgh's vegetarian scene. The bar gets going at night, offering a range of organic wines, beers, and spirits. Free Wi-Fi. Seriously good salads £2.10-7.30. Open M-Sa 8am-11pm. Kitchen open 11:30am-10pm. AmEx/MC/V. ❶

🔆 SIGHTS

CASTLE HILL AND LAWNMARKET

🔳**EDINBURGH CASTLE.** Looming over the city center atop a dormant volcano, Edinburgh Castle dominates the skyline. Its oldest surviving building is tiny

12th-century **Saint Margaret's Chapel,** built by King David I of Scotland in memory of his mother. The castle compound developed over the course of centuries; the most recent additions date to the 1920s. The central **Palace,** begun in the 1430s, was home to Stuart kings and queens and contains the room where Mary, Queen of Scots, gave birth to James VI. It also houses the **Scottish Crown Jewels,** which are older than those in London. The storied (although visually unspectacular) **Stone of Scone,** more commonly known as the Stone of Destiny, is also on permanent display. Other sections of the sprawling compound, like the Scottish National War Memorial, the National War Museum of Scotland, and the 15th-century monster cannon Mons Meg, definitely merit a visit, despite the uphill climb. The **One O'Clock Gun** fires from Monday to Saturday. Guess what time. Buy tickets online to skip the queues. (☎ *0131 225 9846; www.edinburghcastle. gov.uk. Open daily Apr.-Oct. 9:30am-6pm, Nov.-Mar. 9:30am-5pm. Last entry 45min. before closing. Free guided tours of the castle depart regularly from the entrance. £13, concessions £10.50, children £6.50. Excellent audio tour £3.50, concessions £2.50, children £1.50.)*

▧**CAMERA OBSCURA AND WORLD OF ILLUSIONS.** Climb **Outlook Tower** to see the 150-year-old camera obscura, which captures moving color images of the street below. (☎ *0131 226 3709. Open daily July 9:30am-7pm, Aug 9:30am-7:30pm, Sept.-Oct. and Apr.-June 9:30am-6pm, Nov.-Mar. 10am-5pm. Presentations every 20min., last presentation 1hr. before closing. £8.50, concessions £6.75, children £5.75.)*

▧**THE SCOTCH WHISKY EXPERIENCE.** Learn about the "history and mystery" of Scotland's most famous export at the Scotch Whisky Heritage Centre, located right next to the castle. The first portion is a barrel ride with animatronic displays that explain the process of distillation. Next, you're taught about the character of different regional whiskeys and left to choose the one that suits your fancy. (*350 Castle Hill.* ☎ *0131 220 0441; www.scotchwhiskyexperience.co.uk. Open daily June-Sept. 10am-5:30pm, Oct.-May 10am-5pm. Tours every 15min. £11, concessions £8.50.)*

HIGH STREET

▧**HIGH KIRK OF SAINT GILES.** This *kirk* is Scotland's principal church, sometimes known as **Saint Giles's Cathedral.** From its pulpit, Protestant reformer John Knox delivered the sermons that drove the Catholic Mary, Queen of Scots, into exile. Stained-glass windows illuminate the structure, whose crown spire is one of Edinburgh's hallmarks. The 20th-century ▧**Thistle Chapel** honors the Most Ancient and Most Noble Order of the Thistle, Scotland's prestigious chivalric order. (*Where Lawnmarket becomes High St.* ☎ *0131 225 9442. Open M-F 9am-7pm, Sa 9am-5pm, Su 1-5pm. Suggested donation £1.)*

HOLYROOD

PALACE OF HOLYROODHOUSE. This Stuart palace at the base of the Royal Mile remains Queen Elizabeth II's official Scottish residence. As a result, only parts of the ornate interior are open to the public. Once home to Mary, Queen of Scots, whose bedchamber is on display, the palace is every inch a kingly residence. (*At the bottom of the Royal Mile.* ☎ *0131 556 5100. Open daily Apr.-Sept. 9:30am-6pm; Nov.-Mar. 9:30am-4:30pm. Last entry 1hr. before closing. No entry while royals are in residence (often June-July). Palace £10, concessions £9, children £6, under 5 free, families £26.50. With admission to Queen's Gallery £14/12.50/8/free/38.50. Audio tour free.)*

HOLYROOD PARK. A true city oasis, Holyrood Park is filled with hills, moorland, and lochs. At 823 ft., ▧**Arthur's Seat,** the park's highest point, affords the best views of the city and Highlands. Considered a holy place by the Picts, the name "Arthur's Seat" is derived from *"Ard-na-Saigheid,"* Gaelic for "the height of the flight of arrows." From the Palace of Holyroodhouse, the walk to the summit takes about 45min.

HOLYROOD SCOTTISH PARLIAMENT BUILDING. After years of controversy and massive budget overdraws, the new Scottish Parliament Building is functional and open to visitors. (*☎ 0131 348 5200; www.scottish.parliament.uk. Open Apr.-Oct. M and F 10am-6pm, Tu-Th 9am-7pm, Sa-Su 10am-4pm; Nov.-Mar. M and F-Su 10am-4pm, Tu-Th 9am-7pm. Hours may vary; call ahead. Guided tours on non-business days £6, concessions and children £3.60, under 5 free. Free tickets to the parliamentary sessions; book in advance.*)

THE NEW TOWN

◼WALTER SCOTT MONUMENT. Statues of Sir Walter and his dog preside inside the spire of this Gothic "steeple without a church." Climb 287 narrow, winding steps past carved figures of Scott's most famous characters to reach the top. An eagle's-eye view of Princes St., the castle, and the surrounding city awaits. The journey to the top is not recommended for those who suffer from claustrophobia or vertigo. (*Princes St. between The Mound and Waverley Bridge. ☎ 0131 529 4098. Open daily Apr.-Sept. 10am-7pm, Oct.-Mar. 10am-4pm. £3.*)

🏛 MUSEUMS

◼NATIONAL GALLERY OF SCOTLAND. Housed in a grand 19th-century building designed by William Playfair, this gallery has a superb collection of works by Renaissance, Romantic, and Impressionist masters, including Raphael, Titian, El Greco, Turner, and Gauguin. Sprawling, wall-sized works illustrate important moments in Scottish history. Don't miss the octagonal room, which displays Poussin's entire *Seven Sacraments.* The impressionist room upstairs shows several works by Monet. (*On The Mound between the halves of the Princes St. Gardens.*) Next door is the **◼Royal Academy,** connected by an underground tunnel, which hosts exhibits from the National Gallery and runs a high-profile show each summer. (*At the corner of The Mound and Princes St. Special late night Th until 7pm. Exhibit prices vary, many are free; visit www.royalscottishacademy.org for information.*)

◼MUSEUM OF SCOTLAND AND ROYAL MUSEUM. The superbly designed Museum of Scotland traces the whole of Scottish history through an impressive collection of treasured objects and decorative art. Highlights include the working **Corliss Steam Engine** and the **Maiden,** Edinburgh's guillotine, used on High St. around 1565. The rooftop terrace provides a 360° view. Gallery and audio tours in various languages are free. The Royal Museum has rotating exhibits on natural history, European art, and ancient Egypt, to name a few. The **Millennium Clock,** a towering, ghoulish display of figures representing human suffering in the 20th century, chimes three times per day. Free tours, from useful intros to 1hr. circuits of the highlights, leave from the Main Hall's totem pole in the Royal Museum and the Museum of Scotland's Hawthornden Court. (*Chambers St. ☎ 0131 247 4422; www.nms.ac.uk. Both open daily 10am-5pm. Free.*)

🎦 ENTERTAINMENT

For all the latest listings and local events in Edinburgh, check out *The List* (£2.25; www.list.co.uk), available at newsstands, or *The Skinny*, a monthy music magazine with concert listings (free, available in most hostels; www.theskinny.co.uk). Watch for ads in pubs and clubs. The Fringe festival publishes its own program of activities, available in hard copy from the Fringe office and online at www.edfringe.com.

🏴 **The Stand Comedy Club,** 5 York Pl. (☎0131 558 7272; www.thestand.co.uk). Hilariously unhinged acts perform every night in front of a mural of a guy aiming a pistol at his own sombrero. Free lunchtime improv Su 1:30pm. Special program for the Fringe Festival. Call ahead. Tickets £1-13. MC/V for tickets only.

The Jazz Bar, 1A Chambers St. (☎0131 220 4298). Not just a jazz venue: you can also see blues, hip-hop, funk, and more. Classy and relaxing vibe, with stone walls and red lighting. 3 shows most days: "Tea Time" (acoustic, T-Su 5-8:30pm, free entry, free Wi-Fi), "Early Gig" (mostly jazz, daily 8:30-11pm, cover £1-5), and "Late N' Live" (daily 11:30pm-3am, or 5am during Festival, cover £1-5). Always packed on weekends. Cash only for cover. MC/V at bar over £5.

🛍 SHOPPING

From ritzy department stores to funky vintage shops, Edinburgh has something for every shopper and every wallet. If you want to get in touch with your Scottish heritage, tourist shops along the **Royal Mile** sell Highland outfits, cashmere sweaters, tartan towels, and will even trace your family history for around £10. New Town generally caters to big spenders—major chains line **Princes Street,** and **Multrees Walk** off St. Andrew's Square houses upscale designer shops like Louis Vuitton. The pedestrian **Rose Street** has smaller boutiques and plenty of pubs to whet your whistle (while you can still afford a whistle). Big malls include **St. James Shopping Centre** (off Leith St.; open M-W and F 9am-6pm, Th 9am-8pm, Sa 9am-6:30pm, Su 10am-6pm) and **Princes Mall** (Princes St.; open M-W and F-Sa 9am-6pm, Th 9am-7pm, Su 11am-5pm). For (slightly) more affordable shopping, stick to **Old Town.** The **Grassmarket, Cockburn Street,** and **Lothian Road** are all full of diverse and interesting shops.

🌙 NIGHTLIFE

Edinburgh is known internationally for its festivals, but its nightly festivities are a big draw as well. Some Festival-goers even skip the theaters altogether and spend their time doing two things—sleeping and partying. During the Fringe, the city turns into a sort of month-long Mardi Gras, with packed streets, loud revelry, and nonstop performances. The sun rises around 4am in the summer, so partying until dawn is easy.

 TOURIST TO PURIST. Don't order your Scotch on the rocks if you want to avoid looking like a tourist. Scotch whisky should be drunk neat—with no ice. Locals may mix with a splash of water—real pros ask for mineral water from the region in which the whisky was distilled.

PUBS

🏴 **The Tron,** 9 Hunter Sq. (☎0131 226 0931), behind Tron Kirk. Friendly student bar. Downstairs is a mix of alcoves and pool tables. Frequent live music. Burger and a pint £3.50 after 3pm, or get 2 meals for just £6.50. "Pound-a-pint" W. Open M-Sa noon-1am, Su 12:30pm-1am; during the Festival daily 10am-3am. Kitchen open until 9pm. AmEx/MC/V over £5.

Royal Mile Tavern, 127 High St. (☎0131 557 9681). This easygoing pub has managed to avoid the high prices and tourist gimmicks of its Royal Mile neighbors. Live music every night (don't miss "Acoustic Dave" Sa). Flash your hostel card for a £2.50 pint or to see the cheap "Backpacker food" menu. Open daily 8am-1:30pm. MC/V.

The Outhouse, 12A Broughton St. (☎0131 557 6668). Hidden up an alleyway off Broughton St. More stylish than your average pub but just as cheap. One of the best beer gardens in the city. Free Wi-Fi. Happy hour daily 5-8pm. Open daily noon-1am. Kitchen open M, W, Su 1-7pm; Tu, Th, F-Sa 1pm-late. MC/V over £5.

CLUBS

Cabaret-Voltaire, 36-38 Blair St. (☎0131 220 6176; www.thecabaretvoltaire.com). Most clubbers agree that "Cab-Volt" is the place to be in Edinburgh. Playing everything from jazz to break beat, this innovative club knows how to throw a party. Cover free-£2 on weeknights, £5-10 on weekends. Open daily 7pm-3am.

Bongo Club, 37 Holyrood Rd. (☎0131 558 7604), off Canongate. Particularly noted for its hip hop and immensely popular "Messenger" (reggae; 1 Sa per month) and "Headspin" (funk and dance; 1 Sa per month) nights. Cafe with free internet during the day. Cover £3-7. Open M-W and Su 10am-midnight, Th-F 10am-3am. MC/V.

▓ FESTIVALS

In August, Edinburgh is the place to be in Europe. What's commonly referred to as "the Festival" actually encompasses several independent events. For more info, check out www.edinburghfestivals.co.uk. The **Edinburgh International Festival** (www.eif.co.uk; early Aug.), the largest of them all, features a kaleidoscopic program of art, dance, drama, and music. Tickets (£7-58, students £3.50-29) are sold beginning in April, but a limited number of £5 tickets are available 1hr. before every event. Bookings can be made by mail, phone, fax, web, or in person at The **HUB** (☎0131 473 2000), Edinburgh's Festival center, on Castle hill. A less formal ▓**Fringe Festival** (www.edfringe.com; Aug.) has grown around the established festival. Anyone who can afford the small registration fee can perform, guaranteeing many great to not-so-good independent acts and an absolutely wild month. The **Edinburgh Jazz and Blues Festival** is in late July. (www.edinburghjazzfestival.co.uk. Tickets on sale in June.) The fun doesn't stop in winter. ▓**Hogmanay,** the traditional New Year's Eve festival, is a serious street party with a week of associated events (www.edinburghshogmanay.org).

GLASGOW ☎0141

Scotland's largest city, Glasgow (pop. 580,000), has reinvented itself countless times and retains the mark of each change. Stately architecture recalls Queen Victoria's reign, while cranes littering the River Clyde bear witness to its past as an industrial hub. By day, world-class museums give Glasgow a thriving energy, but the city truly comes alive at night.

▓▓ TRANSPORTATION AND PRACTICAL INFORMATION. Flights land at **Glasgow International Airport** (GLA; ☎8700 400 008; www.glasgowairport.com). Fairline bus #905 connects to Buchanan Station (25min., 6 per hr., £3). From **Glasgow Prestwick International Airport** (PIK; ☎0871 223 0700; www.gpia.co.uk), 52km away, express bus #X77 runs to Buchanan Station (50min., every hr., £7), and trains leave for Central Station (30min.; 2 per hr.; £5.20, with Ryanair receipt £2.60). **Trains** run from Central Station, Gordon St. (U: St. Enoch), to London King's Cross (6hr., every hr., £100) and Manchester (4hr., every hr., £50). From Queen St. Station, George Sq. (U: Buchanan St.), trains go to Aberdeen (2hr.; M-Sa every hr., Su 7 per day; £38), Edinburgh (50min., 4 per hr., £10), and Inverness (3hr., 4-7 per day, £38). A 5-10 minute walk separates the two stations. Scottish Citylink (☎08705 505 050; www.citylink.co.uk) **buses** leave Buchanan Station, on Killermont St., for Aberdeen (4hr., every hr., £22),

Glasgow

SIGHTS AND SERVICES

Buchanan Galleries,	17 E2
Centre for Contemporary Arts,	18 D2
City Chambers,	19 F3
City Hall/Ticket Centre,	20 F3
Glasgow Film Theater,	21 D2
Glasgow LGBT Centre,	22 F4
Glasgow School of Art,	23 D2
Market Square,	24 F3
Princes Sq. Shopping Centre,	25 E3
Royal Concert Hall,	26 E2
Somer eld Supermarket	27 E4
St. Enoch Shopping Ctr.	28 E4
Thomas Cook,	29 F3
Tron Theatre,	30 F4
STA Travel,	31 F3
University of Glasgow,	32 A1
Glasgow Cathedral,	33 G3

ACCOMMODATIONS

Alamo Guest House,	1 A1
Euro Hostel Glasgow,	2 E4
McLays Guest House,	3 C2
SYHA Glasgow,	4 B1

MUSEUMS

Hunterian Museum and Art Gallery,	5 A1
Kelvingrove Art Gallery and Museum,	6 A1
Provand's Lordship,	7 G3
St. Mungo Museum,	8 G3

FOOD

Grassroots Cafe,	9 C1
Stravaigin,	10 A1
Wee Curry Shop,	11 D2
Wee Curry Shop	12 D2
Willow Tea Rooms,	13 D2

PUBS

Babbity Bowster,	14 F3
Uisge Beatha,	15 B1

CLUBS

The Buff Club,	15 D2
The Polo Lounge,	16 F3

TO QUEEN'S CROSS (440yd)

TO NECROPOLIS (100yd)

TO PEOPLE'S PALACE (500yd)

GLASGOW CROSS

GLASGOW GREEN

River Clyde

TO BURRELL COLLECTION AND POLLOK PARK (3mi), GREENOCK AND GLASGOW AIRPORTS (10mi)

TO GLASGOW SCIENCE CENTRE (.5mi)

CITY CENTRE

MERCHANT CITY

COWCADDENS

GARNETHILL

BLYTHSWOOD HILL

ANDERSTON

CHARING CROSS

PARK CIRCUS

500 yards

500 meters

GIVING BACK

JPKEEP OF A SECRET

Many budget travelers rely on hostels for cheap places to spend the night but fail to realize that free accommodation can be found in many parts of the Highlands. Bothies—simple shelters in the most remote corners of the country—are left unlocked by their owners for the use of hikers passing through the area. Their locations are not well publicized due to fears of overuse and vandalism.

Despite efforts to keep locations secret, some bothies have already experienced problems with garbage and human waste buildup as more people explore rural Scotland. The Bothy Code requests that users leave the bothy in the same or better condition as they found it, but the sheer number of hikers seeking shelter has strained the honor system. To repair damage to the bothies, the **Mountain Bothies Association** organizes regular work parties of volunteers to perform tasks ranging from repainting walls to rebuilding ruins. Bothy work does not require special skills, and volunteers can participate for as long or as short a time as they wish.

The Mountain Bothies Association recommends that volunteers become members. Annual membership costs £15, with reduced rates of £7.50 for people under 26, over 60, or unemployed. Members receive a quarterly newsletter listing planned work parties and projects. For more information, visit www.mountainbothies.org.

Edinburgh (1hr., 4 per hr., £5.10), and Inverness (3hr., every hr., £21). National Express (☎08705 808 080) travels to London (8hr., 3 per day, £18).

Local transport includes the **Underground (U)** subway line (☎08457 484 950; www.spt.co.uk. M-Sa 6:30am-11pm, Su 11am-5:30pm; £1.10 one-way). A Discovery Ticket (£1.90) allows one day of unlimited travel (valid M-Sa after 9:30am, Su all day). The **TIC** is at 11 George Sq. (☎0141 204 4400; www.seeglasgow.com. U: Buchanan St. Open July-Aug. M-Sa 9am-8pm, Su 10am-6pm; June M-Sa 9am-7pm, Su 10am-6pm; Sept.-Apr. M-Sa 9am-6pm.) Surf the **Internet** at EasyInternet Cafe, 57-61 Vincent St. (☎0141 222 2365. £1 per 30min. Open daily 7am-10:45pm.) **Postal Code:** G2 5QX.

◪◩ ACCOMMODATIONS AND FOOD. Reserve ahead for B&Bs and hostels, especially in summer. B&Bs are along either side of Argyle Street, near the university, and near Renfrew Street. The former residence of a nobleman, ◪**SYHA Glasgow (HI) ❶**, 7-8 Park Terr., is now the best hostel in town. (☎0141 332 3004. U: Kelvinbridge. Ensuite rooms. Laundry available. Basement coffeehouse offers Internet £1 per hr. June-Sept. dorms £16, under 18 £12. Oct.-May rates vary, from £12. MC/V.) **The Euro Hostel Glasgow ❷**, at the corner of Clyde St. and Jamaica St., features quiet, clean rooms, and a bar, all near some of Glasgow's hippest clubs. (☎0141 222 2828; www.euro-hostels.com. U: St. Enoch. Breakfast included. Laundry £2. Free Wi-Fi. Computer access £1 per 15min. Wheelchair-accessible. Dorms £13-19; singles £40. MC/V.)

Glasgow is often called the curry capital of Britain—for good reason. The city's West End brims with kebab and curry joints, and fusion cuisine is all the rage. Throughout town, Italian and Thai eateries provide alternatives to traditional Scottish pub fare. Byres Rd. and tiny parallel Ashton Ln. overflow with affordable, trendy cafes. The ◪**Willow Tea Rooms ❷**, 217 Sauchiehall St., upstairs from Henderson Jewellers, are a cozy Glasgow landmark. (☎0141 332 0521; www.willowtearooms.co.uk. U: Buchanan St. Tea £2 per pot. 3-course afternoon tea £12. Salads and sandwiches £4-7. Open M-Sa 9am-4:30pm, Su 11am-4:15pm. MC/V.) Find great vegetarian food and creative organic dishes at the **Grassroots Cafe ❷**, 97 St. George's Rd. Try the haloumi salad—made of chickpeas, fried cheese, and fig balsamic vinegar. (☎0141 333 0534. U: St. George's Cross. Handmade pastas from £7. Open daily 10am-9:45pm. AmEx/MC/V.) **The Wee Curry Shop ❷**, 7 Buccleuch St., is the best deal in a town full of pakora and poori. (☎0141 353 0777. U: Cowcaddens. Entrees £6-10. Open

M-Sa noon-2:30pm and 5:30-10:30pm. Seats 25; reservations are a must. Cash only. Branch at 23 Ashton Ln. ☎0141 357 5280. U: Hillhead. MC/V.)

🔆 🏛 **SIGHTS AND MUSEUMS.** Glasgow is a budget traveler's paradise, with many free cathedrals and museums. *The List* (www.list.co.uk; £2.50), available at newsstands, is an essential review of exhibitions, music, and nightlife. Your first stop should be the Gothic 🔆**Glasgow Cathedral,** Castle St., the only full-scale cathedral spared by the 16th-century Scottish Reformation. (☎0141 552 6891. Open Apr.-Sept. M-Sa 9:30am-5:30pm, Su 1-5pm; Oct.-Mar. M-Sa 9:30am-4pm, Su 1-4pm. Organ recitals and concerts July-Aug. Tu 7:30pm, £7. Ask for free personal tours.) Behind the cathedral is the **Necropolis,** where tombstones lie aslant. Climb to the top of the hill for city views (open 24hr., free).

In the West End, wooded **Kelvingrove Park** lies on the banks of the River Kelvin (U: Kelvinhall). In the southwestern corner of the park, at Argyle and Sauchiehall St., the magnificent **Kelvingrove Art Gallery and Museum** features works by van Gogh, Monet, and Rembrandt. (☎0141 276 9599; www.glasgowmuseums.com. U: Kelvinhall. Open M-Th and Sa 10am-5pm, F and Su 11am-5pm. Free.) Farther west are the Gothic edifices of the **University of Glasgow.** The main building is on University Ave., which runs into Byres Rd. On campus, stop by the **Hunterian Museum,** which houses the vast and varied personal collections of William Hunter, including preserved human organs and a Pacific Islander traditional outfit. The 🔆**Hunterian Art Gallery,** across the street, displays a large Whistler collection and a variety of Rembrandts and Pissaros. (☎0141 330 4221; www. hunterian.gla.ac.uk. U: Hillhead. Both open M-Sa 9:30am-5pm. Free.) Take bus #45, 47, or 57 from Jamaica St. (15min., £1.20) to reach the famous 🔆**Burrell Collection,** in Pollok Country Park. Once the private stash of ship magnate William Burrell, the collection includes works by Cézanne and Degas, medieval tapestries, and fine china. (☎0141 287 2550. Open M-Th and Sa 10am-5pm, F and Su 11am-5pm. Tours daily 1 and 2pm. Free.)

🔆 🎭 **ENTERTAINMENT AND NIGHTLIFE.** Glaswegians have a reputation for partying hard. The infamous **Byres Road pub crawl** slithers past the University area, running from Tennant's Bar toward the River Clyde. For Scottish grub and ambience, you can't beat 🔆**Babbity Bowster,** 16-18 Blackfriars St. (☎0141 552 5055. Entrees £4-8. Open daily 11am-midnight. MC/V.) 🔆**The Buff Club,** 142 Bath Ln., with a pub and two dance floors, is the after-hours club scene in Glasgow. (☎0141 248 1777; www.thebuffclub.com. Cover £3-6, free with receipt from local bar; ask at the door for details. Open M-Th and Su 11pm-3am, F-Sa 10:30pm-3am.) **The Polo Lounge,** 84 Wilson St., is Glasgow's largest gay and lesbian club. (☎0141 553 1221. Cover £5. Open W, F-Su 5pm-3am.)

CROATIA
(HRVATSKA)

 With attractions ranging from sun-drenched beaches and cliffs around Dubrovnik to the dense forests around Plitvice, Croatia's wonders and natural beauty never cease to amaze. Unfortunately, like so many treasures of great value, Croatia has been fought over time and time again, often finding itself in the middle of dangerous political divides and deadly ethnic tensions. It was only after the devastating 1991-1995 ethnic war that Croatia achieved full independence for the first time in 800 years. And while some marked-off areas still contain landmines, the biggest threats currently facing travelers to Croatia are the ever-rising prices and tides of tourists who clog the ferryways. Despite it all, this friendly and upbeat country demands to be seen at any cost.

DISCOVER CROATIA: SUGGESTED ITINERARIES

THREE DAYS: Spend a day poking around the bizarre and fascinating architecture of **Split** (p. 174) before ferrying down the coast to the beach paradise of **Brac** island (1 day; p. 176). Aftre recovering from your sunburn, make your way to former war-zone—and what some consider Eastern Europe's most beautiful city—**Dubrovnik** (1 day; p. 176).

BEST OF CROATIA, ONE WEEK. Enjoy the East-meets-West feel of **Zagreb** (1 day; p. 165) then head to busy **Rijeka** (1 day; p. 170). Relax in gorgeous **Krk Town** (1 day; p. 171) before stopping in **Zadar** (1 day; p. 174). Have a few hours' stop in gorgeous **Plitvice National Park** (p. 169), before **Brac** (1 day; p. 176). End your journey in **Dubrovnik** (2 days; p. 176).

ESSENTIALS

FACTS AND FIGURES

OFFICIAL NAME: Republic of Croatia.

CAPITAL: Zagreb.

MAJOR CITIES: Dubrovnik, Split.

POPULATION: 4,493,000.

TIME ZONE: GMT +1.

LANGUAGE: Croatian.

RELIGIONS: Roman Catholic (88%).

POPULATION GROWTH RATE: -0.04%.

WHEN TO GO

Croatia's best weather lasts from May to September, and crowds typically show up along the Adriatic coast in July and August. If you go in late August or September, you'll find fewer crowds, lower prices, and an abundance of seasonal fruits such as figs and grapes. Late autumn is wine season. While April and October may be too cool for camping, the weather is usually nice along the coast, and private rooms are plentiful and inexpensive. You can swim in the Adriatic sea from mid-June to late September.

DOCUMENTS AND FORMALITIES

EMBASSIES AND CONSULATES. All foreign embassies in Croatia are located in Zagreb (p. 165). Embassies abroad include: **Australia,** 14 Jindalee Crescent, O'Malley ACT 2606, Canberra (☎262 866 988; croemb@dynamite.com.au); **Canada,** 229 Chapel Street, Ottawa, ON K1N 7Y6 (☎613-562-7820; www.croatiaemb.net); **Ireland,** Adelaide Chambers, Peter St., Dublin 8 (☎01 476 7181; http://ie.mfa.hr); **New Zealand,** 291 Lincoln Rd., Henderson (☎9 836 5581; croconsulate@xtra.co.nz), mail to: P.O. Box 83-200, Edmonton, Auckland; **UK,** 21 Conway Street, London, W1P 5HL. (☎020 7387 2022; http://croatia.embassy-homepage.com); **US,** 2343 Massachusetts Ave., NW, Washington, D.C. 20008 (☎202-588-5899; http://www.croatiaemb.org).

VISA AND ENTRY INFORMATION. Citizens of Australia, Canada, the EU, New Zealand, and the US do not need a visa for stays of up to 90 days. Visas cost US$26 (single-entry), US$33 (double-entry), and US$52 (multiple-entry). Apply for a **visa** at your nearest Croatian embassy or consulate at least one month before planned arrival. All visitors must **register with the police** within 48hr. of arrival—hotels, campsites, and accommodation agencies should automatically register you, but those staying with friends or in private rooms must do so themselves to avoid fines or expulsion. To register, go to room 103 on the 2nd floor of the **central police station** at Petrinjska 30, Zagreb. (☎456 3623, after hours 456 3111. Bring your passport and use form #14. Open M-F 8am-4pm.) Police may check foreigners' passports at any time and place. There is no entry fee. The easiest way of entering or exiting Croatia is by bus or train between Zagreb and a neighboring capital.

ENTRANCE REQUIREMENTS.
Passport: Required for all travelers.
Visa: see above.
Letter of Invitation: Not required for citizens of Australia, Canada, the EU, Ireland, New Zealand, the UK, and the US.
Inoculations: Recommended up-to-date DTaP (diphtheria, tetanus, and pertussis), Hepatitis A, Hepatitis B, MMR, polio booster, rabies, and typhoid.
Work Permit: Required for all foreigners planning to work in Croatia.
International Driving Permit: Required for those driving in Croatia.

TOURIST SERVICES AND MONEY

EMERGENCY	**Ambulance:** ☎94. **Fire:** ☎93. **Police:** ☎92. **General Emergency:** ☎112.

TOURIST OFFICES. Even the small towns have a branch of the resourceful state-run tourist board (*turistička zajednica*). Their staff speak English and give out maps and booklets. **Private agencies** (*turistička* or *putnička agencija*), such as **Atlas,** handle private accommodations. Local outfits are cheaper.

MONEY. The Croatian unit of currency is the **kuna (kn),** plural **kunas.** One kuna is equal to 100 **lipa. Inflation** hovers around 2.22%, so prices should stay relatively constant in the near future. Croatia became an official candidate for European Union membership in 2004, with admission projected for the end of the decade; travelers may occasionally find prices listed in euro (€), espe-

CROATIA

cially in heavily touristed areas like the Istrian Peninsula. Most tourist offices, hostels, and transportation stations exchange currency and traveler's checks; banks have the best rates. Some establishments charge a 1.5% commission to exchange **traveler's checks.** Most banks give MasterCard and Visa cash advances, and **credit cards** (namely American Express, MasterCard, and Visa) are widely accepted. Common **banks** include Zagrebačka Banka, Privredna Banka, and Splitska Banka. **ATMs** are everywhere. **Currency exchange** rate:

CROATIAN KUNA (KN)		
AUS$1 = 4.27KN	1KN = AUS$0.24
CDN$1 = 4.47KN	1KN = CDN$0.23
EUR€1 = 7.20KN	1KN = EUR€0.14
NZ$1 = 3.34KN	1KN = NZ$0.30
UK£1 = 9.11KN	1KN = UK£0.11
US$1 = 4.66KN	1KN = US$0.22

Expect to spend 300-470kn per day. Travel in Croatia is becoming more costly, with the bare minimum for accommodations, food, and transport costing 240kn. **Tipping** is not expected, although it is appropriate to round up when paying; some establishments will do it for you—check your change. Fancy restaurants often add a hefty service charge. **Bargaining** is reserved for informal transactions, such as hiring a boat for a day or renting a private room directly from an owner. Posted prices should usually be followed.

HEALTH AND SAFETY

Medical facilities in Croatia include public hospitals and clinics and private medical practitioners and pharmacies. Due to disparities in funding, private clinics and pharmacies tend to be better supplied. Both public and private facilities may demand cash payment for services; most do not accept credit cards.

Pharmacies sell Western products, including tampons and condoms (*prezervativi*). UK citizens receive free medical care with a valid passport. **Tap water** is chlorinated; though it is relatively safe, it may cause mild abdominal discomfort. Croatia's **crime rate** is relatively low, but travelers should beware of pickpockets. Travel to the former conflict areas of **Slavonia** and **Krajina** remains dangerous due to **unexploded landmines,** which are not expected to be cleared until at least 2010. In 2005, a tourist was injured by a mine on the island of Vis, which inspectors had previously declared safe. Do not stray from known safe areas, and consult www.hcr.hr for detailed info. **Women** should go out in public with a companion to ward off unwanted attention. Although incidents of **hate crime** in Croatia are rare, **minority** travelers may experience stares. **Disabled** travelers should contact Savez Organizacija Invalida Hrvatske (☎ 1 4829 394), in Zagreb, as cobblestones and a lack of ramps render it a more difficult area. Although **homosexuality** is slowly becoming accepted, discretion is recommended.

TRANSPORTATION

BY PLANE AND TRAIN. Croatia Airlines flies to and from many cities, including Frankfurt, London, Paris, Zagreb, Dubrovnik, and Split. Budget airlines like **Ryanair** fly to Zadar and Pula. **Trains** (www.hznet.hr) are slow everywhere and nonexistent south of Split. Trains run to Zagreb from Budapest, HUN; Ljubljana, SLV; Venice, ITA; and Vienna, AUT; and continue on to other Croatian destinations. *Odlazak* means departures, *Odolazak* means arrivals.

Croatia

BY BUS. Buses run faster and farther than trains at comparable or slightly higher prices and are the easiest way to get to many destinations, especially south of Split. Major companies include **Croatiabus** (www.croatiabus.hr), **Autotrans Croatia** (www.autotrans.hr), and **Austobusni Promet Varaždin** (www.ap.hr). The website of the main bus terminal in Zagreb (Austobusni Kolodvor Zagreb; www.akz.hr) provides info on timetables, although not in English.

BY BOAT. The **Jadrolinija** ferry company (www.jadrolinija.hr) sails the Rijeka-Split-Dubrovnik route, stopping at islands on the way. Ferries also go to Ancona, ITA from Split and Zadar and to Bari, ITA from Split and Dubrovnik. Though slower than buses and trains, ferries are more comfortable. A basic ticket grants only a place on the deck. Buy tickets in advance.

BY BIKE AND BY THUMB. Moped and **bike** rentals are an option in resort or urban areas. Hitchhiking is not recommended by *Let's Go*.

KEEPING IN TOUCH

PHONE CODES	**Country code: 385. International dialing** prefix: **00.** For more info on how to place international calls, see **Inside Back Cover.**

EMAIL AND INTERNET. Most towns, no matter how small, have at least one Internet cafe. Connections on the islands are slower and less reliable than those on the mainland. Internet usage typically costs 20kn per hour.

TELEPHONE. Post offices usually have **public phones;** pay after you talk. All phones on the street require a country-specific **phone card** (*telekarta*), sold at newsstands and post offices for 15-100kn. A Global Card allows calls for as cheap as 0.99kn per minute and provides the best international rates. For the international operator, dial ☎901. Croatia has two **mobile** phone networks, T-Mobile and VIP. If you bring or buy a phone compatible with the GSM 900/1800 network, SIM cards are widely available. Pressing the "L" button will cause the phone instructions to switch into English.

MAIL. The Croatian Postal Service is reliable. Mail from the US arrives within a week. Post office workers are generally helpful to foreigners. A postcard or letter to the US typically costs 3.50kn. *Avionski* and *zrakoplovom* both mean "airmail." Mail addressed to **Poste Restante** will be held for up to 30 days at the receiving post office. Address envelopes: First name LAST NAME, POSTE RES-TANTE, Pt. Republike 28, post office address, Postal Code, city, CROATIA.

LANGUAGE. Croats speak **Croatian,** a South Slavic language written in Latin script. The language has fairly recently become differentiated from Serbo-Croatian. Only a few expressions differ from Serbian, but be careful not to use the Serbian phrases in Croatia—you'll make few friends. **German** and **Italian** are common second languages among the adult population. Most Croatians under 30 will speak and understand some English.

ACCOMMODATIONS AND CAMPING

CROATIA	❶	❷	❸	❹	❺
ACCOMMODATIONS	under 150kn	150-250Kn	251-350Kn	351-450Kn	over 450Kn

For info on Croatia's youth **hostels** (in Krk, Pula, Punat, Veli Losinj, Zadar, and Zagreb), contact the **Croatian Youth Hostel Association,** Savska 5/1, 10000 Zagreb (☎1 482 9294; www.hfhs.hr/home.php?lang=en). **Hotels** in Croatia can be expensive. If you opt for a hotel, call a few days ahead, especially in the summer along the coast. Those looking to stay in either hostels or hotels in the July-August tourist season should book early, as rooms fill up quickly. Apart from hostels, **private rooms** are the major budget option for accommodations. Look for signs, especially near transportation stations. English is rarely spoken by room owners. All accommodations are subject to a tourist tax of 5-10kn (one reason the police require foreigners to register). Croatia is also one of the top camping destinations in Europe—33% of travelers stay in **campgrounds.** Facilities are usually comfortable, and prices are among the cheapest along the Mediterranean. Camping outside of designated areas is illegal. For more info, contact the Croatian Camping Union, 8. Marta 1, P.O. Box 143, HR-52440 Poreč (☎52 45 13 24; www.camping.hr).

FOOD AND DRINK

CROATIA	❶	❷	❸	❹	❺
FOOD	under 30Kn	30-60Kn	61-90Kn	91-150Kn	over 150Kn

Croatian cuisine is defined by the country's varied geography. In continental Croatia in and to the east of Zagreb, heavy meals featuring meat and creamy sauces dominate. *Purica s mlincima* (turkey with pasta) is the regional dish near Zagreb. Also popular are *burek*, a layered pie made with meat or cheese, and the spicy Slavonian *kulen*, considered one of the world's best **sausages**. *Paticada* (slow-cooked meat) is also excellent. On the coast, textures and flavors change with the presence of **seafood** and Italian influence. Don't miss out on *lignje* (squid) or *Dalmatinski prut* (Dalmatian smoked ham). The **oysters** from Ston Bay have received a number of awards at international competitions. If your budget does not allow for such treats, *slane sardele* (salted sardines) are a tasty substitute. **Vegetarian** and **kosher** eating options can be diffcult to find in Croatia, albeit not impossible. In both cases, pizza and bakeries are safe and ubiquitous options. Mix red wine with tap water to make the popular *bevanda*, and white wine with carbonated water to get *gemišt*. Karlovačko and Ožujsko are the two most popular beers.

HOLIDAYS AND FESTIVALS

Holidays: New Year's Day (Jan. 1); Epiphany (Jan. 6); Easter Sunday and Monday Easter Sunday (Apr. 12-13, 2009; Apr. 4-5, 2010); May Day (May 1); Anti-Fascist Struggle Day (June 22); National Thanksgiving Day (Aug. 5); Independence Day (Oct. 8).

Festivals: In June, Zagreb holds the catch-all festival **Cest Is D'Best** ("The Streets are the Best"). Open-air concerts and theatrical performances make the **Dubrovnik Summer Festival** (Dubrovački Ljetni; from early July to late Aug.) the event of the summer. Zagreb's **International Puppet Festival** is from late Aug. to early Sept.

BEYOND TOURISM

Coalition for Work With Psychotrauma and Peace, M. Drzica 12, 32000 Vukovar, Croatia (☎385 32 45 09 91; www.cwwpp.org). Work in education and health care related to long-term conflict stress in Croatia.

Learning Enterprises, 2227 20th St. #304, NW, Washington, D.C. 20009, USA (☎001 20 23 09 34 53; www.learningenterprises.org). 6-week summer programs place 1st-time English teachers in rural Croatia, Hungary, Romania, and Slovakia. No-fee program includes orientation and room and board with a host family.

ZAGREB ☎01

More than the stopover en route to the Adriatic coast, Croatia's capital and largest city (pop. 779,000) possesses the grand architecture, wide boulevards, and sprawling parks of a major European city. In the old city center, smartly-dressed *Zagrebčani* outnumber visitors as both enjoy the sights and smells of outdoor cafes, flower markets, and fresh produce stalls. With its welcoming, English-speaking inhabitants, growing economy, impressive cultural offerings, and unspoiled surroundings, Zagreb is an enjoyable, laid-back, and worthwhile alternative to the sun-splattered coast.

▐ TRANSPORTATION

Trains: Leave the **Glavni Kolodvor,** Trg Kralja Tomislava 12 (☎060 333 444, international info ☎378 2583; www.hznet.hr; AmEx/MC/V) for: **Ljubljana, SLN** (2 hr., 8 per day; 91kn, round-trip 235kn); **Rijeka** (4-6 hr., 3 per day, 105kn); **Split** (6-9 hr., 5 per day, 90kn); **Budapest, HUN** (7hr., 3 per day, 225kn); **Venice, ITA** (6hr., 1 per day, 320kn); **Vienna, AUT** (6hr., 2 per day, 355kn); **Zurich, SWI** (14hr., 1 per day, 647kn). There are no trains to Dubrovnik. To get to the station, take tram 2, 4, 6, 9, or 13 to the Glavni

Kolodvor stop. From the main square *(Trg Jelačića)*, take either tram 6 (toward Sopot) or tram 13 (toward Tržnica Gorica); the train station is two stops away. There are printed timetables (though not in English) for both domestic and international trains. The information booths' English-speaking staff is an extremely helpful resource.

Trams: The tram network, **Zagreb Electric Tram,** or **ZET,** covers most of the city and is the most convenient form of local transportation (☎01 356 1555; www.zet.hr). Trams are denoted by number (1-17) and run from 4am-11:20pm. **Night trams** run from 11:45pm-3:45am, but are unreliable. Buy tickets at newsstands or post offices (8kn) or from the driver (10kn). Day pass 25kn, under 6 free. Upon boarding, punch tickets in the boxes near the tram doors to avoid fines.

Buses: Leaving from the **Autobusni Kolodvor,** Avenija M. Držića bb (☎060 313 333; information and reservations from abroad ☎01 611 2789; www.akz.hr, click on "Vozni red" to search the timetables). Buses are often more efficient than trains. Trams 2, 5, 6, 7, and 8 stop at Autobusni Kolovdor. From Trg Jelačića, take tram 6 in the direction of Sopot; the bus station is six stops away. The ticketing area is upstairs. Timetables are displayed on screen in the main ticketing area and are also available online. Buses leave for: **Dubrovnik** (11hr., 8 per day, 125-253kn); **Plitvice** (2hr., 12 per day, 72-80kn); **Pula** (4hr., 17 per day, 162-216kn); **Rijeka** (3hr., 23 per day, 126-166kn); **Split** (7-9hr.; 38 per day, multiple buses every hour between 6am-midnight; 171-198kn); **Varaždin** (1.¾hr., 25 per day, 69kn); **Frankfurt, GER** (15hr., 2 per day, 660kn); **Ljubljana, SLN** (2½hr., 1 per day, 90kn); **Vienna, AUT** (7hr., 2 per day, 227kn). Large backpacks cost 7kn extra. The ticketing hall is upstairs; #14 is an information window staffed with English-speaking attendants. **Luggage storage** can be found in the *garderoba* up the staircase to the right of the ticketing hall (24hr.; 1.20kn per hr., 2.30kn per hr. for bags over 33 lbs.) **Restrooms** (3kn) are also upstairs from the ticketing hall in the waiting lounge.

PRACTICAL INFORMATION

Tourist Offices: The **Tourist Information Center (TIC),** Trg Jelačića 11, conveniently located in the main square, is a great resource for any traveler. There you'll find helpful attendants, free maps, and pamphlets the *Zagreb Info A-Z, Zagreb in Your Pocket,* and *Events and Performances.* Open M-F 8:30am-8pm, Sa 9am-5pm, Su and holidays 10am-2pm. (☎01 481 4051; www.zagreb-touristinfo.hr.) They also sell a **Zagreb Card** which covers all bus and tram rides and provides discounts in restaurants and museums (☎01 481 4052; www.zagrebcard.fivestars.hr. Valid for 1 or 3 days; 60/90kn.)

Internet: Get online at **Sublink,** Ulica Nikole Tesle (Teslina) 12 (☎481 9993; www.sublink.hr), where you'll find a friendly and welcoming English-speaking staff, cheap and fast connections, and printing and scanning services. (Open M-Sa 9am-10pm, Su and holidays 3pm-10pm. 0.245kn per min., 14.70kn per hr. 10% discount with ISIC/EURO under 26 card.) **Postal Code:** 10000.

ACCOMMODATIONS

Fulir Hostel, (☎01 483 0882; www.fulir-hostel.com), right outside of Zagreb's main square. Laidback hostel steps away from many of Zagreb's sights and nightlife. Communal kitchen. Linens and lockers included. Free Internet; Wi-Fi available. Mar.-Sept. 130kn per night, Oct.-Feb. 100kn per night. ❶

Ravnice Youth Hostel, 1 Ravnice 38d (☎01 233 2325; www.ravnice-youth-hostel.hr). Bright, clean, colorful rooms. Take tram 11 or 12 from Trg Jelačica, 4 from the train station, or 7 from the bus station to Dubrava or Dubec. The unmarked Ravnice stop is two stops past football stadium "Dinamo." Turn right on Ravnice St. and the hostel is on the second street on the left; look for a white sign marked "hostel." Laundry 50kn.

Zagreb

⌂ ACCOMMODATIONS
Evistas, 3
Fulir Hostel, 4
Ravnice Youth Hostel, 1

✦ FOOD
Dolac, 7
VIP, 5
Zvijezda Kamanjo, 6

NIGHTLIFE
Aquarius, 10
Khala, 2
KSET, 9

🏛 MUSEUMS
Ethnographic Museum, 8

300 meters
300 yards

CROATIA

TO MAKSIMIR PARK,
ZAGREB ZOO (1.5km),
(2km)

TO MIROGOJ CEMETERY (3km),
ZVIJEZDA KAMAJO (500m)

TO ŽOS (600m)

TO SAVA RIVER (1.6km),
NOVI ZAGREB (3km)

TO LAKE JARUN (1km)

Domjanićeva
Guljufova
Gotočeva
Kamaufova
Derenčinova
Vojnovićeva
Stančićeva
Ljudevita
Crvenog Križa
Pavla Šubića
Marina Držićeva
Tram
Autobusni
Kolodvor
Kvaternikov TRG
Petretićev TRG
Voćarska
Šunkovićeva
Antuna Bauera
Zvonimirova
Krešimirov TRG
Kneza Višeslava
Hrvojeva
Kraljice Jelene
Vlaška
Smičiklasova
Martićeva
Franje Račkog
TRG Žrtava Fašizma
Križanićeva
Domagojeva
Trpimirova
Šalata
ŠRC Šalata
Ribnjak
Novakova
Vončina
Mutimirova
TRG Hrvatskih Velikana
Janka
Držislava
Laundry
Misljava
Draškovićeva
Borne
New Zealand
Branjugova
Jurišićeva
Palmotićeva
Pavla Hatza
Augusta Šenoe
Movie Theater Cinestar
Tram
KAPTOL
Ribnjak Park
Cathedral of the Assumption
Amruševa
Rudera Boškovićeva
Đordićeva
Petrinjska
Vatroslav Lisinski Concert Hall
Nova Ves
Vinoteka Bornstein
Petrola Zdenka
Kaptol
Cesarčeva
TRG Nikole Šubića Zrinjskog
Trenkova
Gajeva
Glavni Kolodvor
Tram
Australia
Museum of the City of Zagreb
Opatovina
Tkalčićeva
Skalinska
Vlaška
Pod Zidom
Croatia Airlines
AmEx
TRG Kralja Tomislava
Milkovšićeva
Stone Gate
Dolac Market
Tram
TRG Bana Jelačića
Zrinjevac
Radićeva
St. Catherine's
TRG Bana Jelačića
Nikole Tesle
Berislavićeva
Preradovićeva
Haulikova
Kumičićeva
Miramarska
Opatička
Parliament
Kamenita
Bogovićeva
Preradovićeva
Andrije Hebranga
Jurjažegnjavica
Mihanovićeva
Demetrova
GORNJI GRAD
St. Mark's
Lotrščak Tower
Funicular
Jadrolinija
Jadrolinija
Gundulićeva
DONJI GRAD
Konzum
Juriažica
Jurjažegnjavica
Svačićev TRG
Mesnička
Jezuitski TRG
Croatian National Theater
TRG Maršala Tita
TRG Braće Mažuranić
Marulićev TRG
Vodnikova
Botanički Vrt
Ilica
Ilica
Kozum
Varšavska
Frankopanska
Dežmanova
Dalmatinska
Vodnikova
Runjaninova
Crnatkova
Unska
Tuškanac
Dubravkin put
Zamenhofova
Mazuranka
Medulićeva
Roosveltov TRG
Vukotinovićeva
Savska
Britanski TRG
Radićeva
Radićeva
Kačićeva
Prilaz Gjure Deželića
Klaićeva
Krišnjavoga
Vodnikova
Jukićeva
Jagićeva
Kordunska
Primorska
Krajiška
Republike Austrije
Brozova
Kranjčevićeva
Zapadni Kolodvor
Antuna Mihanovića
Pantovčak ul.
Radnički dol

ON THE MENU

CARNIVORE'S DILEMMA

Meat lovers are spoiled for choice in Croatia. Although Croatian cuisine varies by region, with strong Italian influences in Istria and an emphasis on seafood in Dalmatia, visitors to Zagreb and its surrounding areas will find most Croatian menus dominated by meat—from lamb to pork, from duck to veal. Here, *Let's Go* offers some guidance for your own meaty meal:

Pršut – Home-cured ham from the coastal highlands of Istria and Dalmatia. Try as a prelude to your meal—*pršut* served with cheese is a popular starter.

Sarma – Another starter, this dish consists of pickled cabbage leaves stuffed with minced meat.

Čevapčići – A grilled dish made with minced beef and spices, often served with onions and a paprika and eggplant relish (*ajvar*).

Mješano meso – This mixed grill entrée includes a pork or veal cutlet, minced lamb or beef, and sausage, with *ajvar* on the side.

Pašticada – Served on special occasions, this Dalmatian dish consists of a beef joint cooked in wine, vinegar, and prunes.

Gulaš – Croatia's lighter take on Hungarian goulash, this stew may be made with beef, lamb, or veal.

Internet 16kn per hr. Reception 9am-10pm. Check-out noon. Dorms 125kn. Cash only. ❶

Evistas, Augusta Senoe 28 (☎01 483 9554), right outside of Zagreb's main square. When hostels are full, try a private room at this hotel, albeit less centrally located. Call ahead. Open M-F 9am-1:30pm and 3-8pm, Sa 9:30am-5pm. ❸

🍴 FOOD

Zvijezda Kamanjo, Nova Ves 84 (☎01 466 7171). Serves up traditional Croatian cuisine on a peaceful, private outdoor patio. From Trg Jelačića, follow Kaptol past the Cathedral until it turns into Nova Ves (20min. walk). Try the delicious beef stew (*Dalmatinska pašticada*) with gnocchi—a Croatian specialty. Entrees 35-80kn. Open daily noon-11pm. ❶

VIP, Trg P. Preradovića 5 (☎01 483 0089; www.viprestoran.com). Head to the western side of the square and look for the white umbrellas. This lively bistro and internet cafe offers delectable Italian fare next to the flower market. Enjoy drinks *al fresco* with the locals, or pizza, pasta, and lasagna from 35-60kn. Internet connection 15kn per hr. Open 8am-11pm. ❶

Dolac, behind Trg Jelačića in *Gornji Grad* (Upper Town), along Pod Zidom. Open-air market selling a variety of goods. Open M-Sa 6am-3pm, Su 6am-1pm. Cash only. ❶

🏛 SIGHTS AND MUSEUMS

Zagreb is best seen on foot. Climb any of the streets extending north from Trg Jelačića to reach the historical Gornji Grad (*Upper Town*). From Trg Jelačića, take Ilica, then turn right on Tomićeva.

CATHEDRAL OF THE ASSUMPTION. The Cathedral of the Assumption (*Katredrala Marijina Uznesnja*), known simply as "the Cathedral," has graced Zagreb since the late 11th century. It's stunning during the day and enchanting when illuminated at night. (*Kaptol 1. Open daily 10am-5pm. Services M-Sa 7, 8, 9am, 6pm; Su 7, 8, 9, 10, 11:30am, 6pm. Free.*) **Mirogoj Cemetery**, Croatia's largest, just north of the Cathedral, contains 12 cream-colored towers, a garden with cypress trees, and touching epitaphs that tell the troubled history of the regions. (*Take the 106 "Mirogoj" bus from Kaptol in front of the Cathedral; 8min., 4 per hr. Open M-F 6am-8pm, Su 7:30am-6pm. No photography. Free*). Built in the 13th century, the **Stone Gate**, the last of the four original gateways to the city, remains a site to stop to pray.

ETHNOGRAPHIC MUSEUM. The Ethnographic Museum (*Etnografski Muzej*), across the street from the Mimara, displays artifacts from 19th- and

20th-century Croatian voyages to Africa, Asia, and South America, as well as a mix of traditional costumes, etchings and architecture native to Croatia. *(Mažuranicev Trg 14. ☎01 482 6220; www.etnografski-muzej.hr. English-language captions. Open Tu-Th 10am-6pm, F-Su 10am-1pm. 15kn, students and over 60 10kn; Th free. Cash only.)*

🔲**LOTRŠČAK TOWER.** The 13th-century Lotršćak Tower, part of the original city wall, offers excited visitors the most breathtaking panoramic views of Zagreb. *(At the corner of Strossmayerovo and Dverce, right at the top of the funicular. Open Mar.-Nov. Tu-Su 11am-7pm. 10kn, students 5kn.)*

🌸 📷 FESTIVALS AND NIGHTLIFE

In June, Zagreb's streets burst into life with performances for the annual Zagreb street festival **Cest is d'Best** ("The Streets are the Best,") and the **Eurokaz International Festival of New Theatre** (late June-early July). The huge **International Puppet Festival** occurs from late August to early September. In mid-December, locals flock to the colorful **Christmas Fair** for presents and holiday cheer

With a variety of clubs at **Lake Jarun** and many relaxed sidewalk cafes and bars lining lovely **Tkalčićeva,** Zagreb has an exceptional nightlife scene.

📷 **Aquarius,** Mateja Ljubeka bb (☎01 364 0231. www.aquarius.hr), on Lake Jarun. Take tram #17 to Srednjaci, the third unmarked stop after Studenski dom S. Radic. Cross the street; once at the lake, turn left and continue along the boardwalk; Aquarius is the last building. Dance and swim at this lakeside cafe/club, Zagreb's hottest nightspot, with a diverse crowd and great music selection. Cafe open daily 9am-9pm. Club open M-F and Su 10pm-4am, Sa 10pm-6am. Cover 30-40kn. Cash only.

KSET, Unska 3 (☎01 612 9999). For tastes that veer toward the alternative, join the locals flocking to edgy KSET for an eclectic mix of music,which, depending on the night, ranges from jazz to punk to electronic. Open M-F 8-11:45pm, Sa 9pm-3am.

Khala, Nova Ves 17 (☎01 486 0241), is a chic but surprisingly affordable wine bar and peaceful lounge that morphs into a house music hotspot on the weekends. Open M-Th 8am-1am, F-Su 8am-4am. Cash only.

PLITVICE LAKES NATIONAL PARK

Though it's a trek from either Zagreb or Zadar, 🔲**Plitvice Lakes National Park** *(Nacionalni Park Plitvička Jezera)* is definitely worth the transportation hassle. Some 300 sq. km of forested hills, dappled with 16 lakes and hundreds of waterfalls, Croatia's oldest and largest national park is one of the country's most spectacular sights. Declared a national park in 1949, Plitvice was added to the UNESCO World Heritage list in 1979 for the unique evolution of its lakes and waterfalls, which formed through the interaction of water and petrified vegetation and continue to evolve as the water moves along new paths. There are eight main trails around the lake (lettered A-K), all of varying difficulties.

WATCH YOUR STEP. The takeover of Plitvice Lakes National Park by the Serbs in 1991 marked the beginning of Croatia's bloody war for independence. Throughout the 1991-95 conflict, the Serbs holding the area planted landmines in the ground. Both the park's premises and surrounding area have been officially cleared of mines, and the last mine-related accident dates back to 2002. However, do not stray from the trail for any reason.

Free **shuttles** drive around the lakes (3 per hr.), and a **boat** crosses Jezero Kozjak, the largest lake (2-3 per hr., 9:30am-6:30pm). At the main entrance, local women sell delicious 🔲**strudels,** bread-cakes stuffed with cheese, spinach, nuts, apples, peaches, or cherries (15kn). If you want to enjoy the peace of the lakes by yourself, go in the early morning or the late afternoon and avoid the shortest trails. Most tourists circulate around the four lower lakes *(Donja Jezera)* to get a shot of Plitvice's famous 78m waterfall, **Veliki Slap.**

Buses run to: Rijeka (3hr., 1 per day, 120kn); Split (3hr., 7 per day, 150kn); Zadar (2hr., 6 per day, 72kn); Zagreb (2hr., 9 per day, 70kn). Most bus drivers let passengers off at the park's main entrance. **Tourist offices** offer maps and exchange currency for a 1.5% commission at each of the three entrances. (☎023 751 026; www.np-plitvicka-jezera.hr. Open daily 7am-10pm. Park open daily July-Aug. 7am-8pm; May-June 7am-7pm; Apr.-Oct. 110kn, students 55kn; Nov.-Mar. 70kn/40kn. Tour guide 700kn, min. 4hr. for groups only. MC/V.) To get to the main info center from the bus stop, walk toward the pedestrian overpass; crossing the road can be dangerous.

NORTHERN COAST

Croatia's northern coast is surrounded by cold, crystal-clear waters; covered in wild forests and low coastal hills. Part of Italy until WWII, this region mixes Italian culture with Croatian sensibilities.

RIJEKA ☎051

Life moves at a fast pace in the bustling port city of Rijeka (pop. 144,000), a major transportation center that also serves as a base for island-hopping in the Kvarner Gulf. Though less idyllic than neighboring Opatija, Rijeka's dynamism and historical attractions make it a worthwhile stop.

█🚆 TRANPORTATION AND PRACTICAL INFORMATION. The **bus** station, Trg Žabica 1, is located on the waterfront at the end of Krešimirova. (☎051 302 010. Open daily 5:30am-9:30pm.) Buses run to: Dubrovnik (12hr., 4 per day, 427kn); Krk Town (1½hr., 10-16 per day, 54kn); Pula (2.5hr, every hr., 91kn); Split (8hr., 12 per day, 236kn); Zagreb (2½hr., every hr., 140kn). To get to Korzo from the bus station, walk away from the water and turn right on Trpimirova. Cross the street to Jadranski trg and continue straight onto Korzo. The **tourist information center (TIC)**, Korzo 33, has **maps** of Rijeka's main sights. (☎051 335 882; www.tz-rijeka.hr. Open mid-June to mid-Sept. M-Sa 8am-8pm, Su and holidays 8am-2pm; mid-Sept. to mid-June M-Sa 8am-8pm.) Rijeka's tourist board turns Korzo, the city's main street, into a **Wi-Fi** hotspot in the summer.

█🔲 ORIENTATION AND SIGHTS. Daily life in Rijeka centers around **Korzo,** a wide pedestrian avenue with an abundance of stores and outdoor cafes. A stroll along Korzo takes you past the yellow **City Tower** *(Gradski toranj)*, which served as the main gate to the city when it was a Roman settlement. Behind the City Tower and through **Trg Ivana Koblera** is the **Roman Gate** *(Stara vrata)*, the oldest monument in Rijeka; through the arch are excavations with ancient Roman artifacts. Built in the 13th-century, the iconic █**Trsat fortress** stands on a hill high above the city and offers unparalleled views of the city center and harbor. To reach Trsat, visitors can follow the footsteps of centuries of pilgrims by climbing the 16th-century *Petar Kružić* 538-step stairway, beginning at Titov trg on Križanićeva or hop on bus #1 or 1a.

🔲🔲 ACCOMMODATIONS AND FOOD. Inexpensive accommodations in the city center are scarce, and no agencies officially book private rooms. **Youth**

Hostel Rijeka ❶, Šetalište XIII divizije 23, in a reno-vated villa overlooking the sea, has immaculate rooms and a friendly, helpful staff. From the bus station, walk to the waterfront and take the #2 bus toward Pećine Plumbum; the hostel is across the street from the fifth stop. (☎051 406 420; www. hfhs.hr. Breakfast included. Internet 5kn per 15min. Reception 24hr. Dorms €15.50; singles €28.40; dou-bles €18.90. HI non-members 10kn extra per night.) Those willing to pay a little extra opt for **Hotel Con-tinental ❸**, a beautiful building along the river, a 2min. walk from the city center. The simply fur-nished rooms rest inside the grand exterior. (☎051 372 008; www.jadran-hoteli.hr. Breakfast included. Singles 397kn; doubles 469kn.)

A modern take on the traditional Croatian *konoba* (in coastal towns, a small inn or cellar), **Konoba Nebuloza ❷**, Titov trg 2b, serves up regional special-ties like *žgvacet* (lamb stew) at affordable prices in an intimate dining space across from the stairway to Trsat. (☎051 372 294. Entrees 35-75kn. Open M-Sa 11am-midnight.) For a cheap meal along the waterfront, the meat dishes at **Mornar ❶**, Riva Boduli 5a, will satisfy hungry carnivores (☎051 313 257. Entrees 15-45kn. Open M-F 7am-6pm, Sa-Su 7am-3pm.) Enjoy a pastry or ice cream on the ter-race at **Cont ❶**, Šetalište A. Kačića Miošića 1, in the Hotel Continental. (☎051 372 154; www.cont.hr. Pastries and cakes 8-13kn. Open daily 7am-10pm.)

🎭🎵 **ENTERTAINMENT AND NIGHTLIFE.** Opened in 1885, the **Croatian National Theatre Ivan Zajc,** Uljar-ska 1, hosts performances during Rijeka's **Summer Nights Festival,** June and July. (☎051 355 900; www. hnk-zajc.hr.) A popular daytime café-bar **El Rio,** Jad-ranski trg 4c, comes to life when a young and hard-partying crowd flocks here for karaoke and danc-ing at night; DJs spin on the weekends. (☎051 214 428. Open M-W 7am-1am, Th-Sa 7am-5am, Su 9am-1am.) On the waterfront, catch up with Rijeka's most beautiful trendsetters under mood lighting in the Zen-inspired **Opium Buddha Bar,** Riva 12a. (☎051 336 397. Open M-W 7am-3am, Th-Su 7am-5am).

KRK TOWN ON KRK ISLAND ☎051

With its sun-drenched beach, narrow cobblestone streets, and mellow bars and cafes, peaceful Krk Town offers island charm without the crowds of nearby Baška. Along Ribarska, a well-preserved Roman **mosaic** among the ruins of thermal baths, Triton is depicted amongst dolphins and sea crea-tures. Next to the bus station, the travel agency **Autotrans ❶**, Šetalište Sv. Bernardina 3, books private accommodations, exchanges currency,

RUCKUS AND REVELRY, RIJEKA-STYLE

Though the mention of "Carnival" may conjure images of Rio rather than Rijeka, the Rijeka Carnival, Croatia's largest, attracts thou-sands of visitors every year with its own brand of glitz and spectacle. From mid-January to early Febru-ary, Rijeka bursts to life as locals and visitors alike don costumes and release their inhibitions at masked balls and glitzy parades.

2009 marks the 26th year that the Carnival has been held in Rijeka, but today's celebration is in fact a modern incarnation of a Carnival tradition that began in the Middle Ages. Like other Carnivals held around the world, the Rijeka Carnival has Christian origins. Cul-minating on the day before Lent, Shrove Tuesday (Mardis Gras or Fat Tuesday to American), the exuberant revelry serves as one last joyride before 40 days of self-restraint leading up to Easter.

Though there's rarely a dull moment during the weeks of fes-tivities, the International Parade along Korzo is the Carnival's crowning event. Replete with elab-orately-crafted floats and some 10,000 extravagantly-costumed revelers, the parade epitomizes the chaotic excitement of this port city's unforgettable party.

The City of Rijeka Tourist Asso-ciation organizes the carnival and may be contacted at ☎31 57 10 or www.ri-karneval.com.hr.

cashes travelers' checks commission-free, and offers bike rentals. (☎051 222 661; www.turizam.autotrans.hr. Jan.-June and Sept.-Dec. singles 77-88kn, doubles 126-187kn; July-Aug. singles 88-117kn, doubles 144-230kn. Stays under 4 days add 30%. Tourist tax 4.50-7kn. Registration 10kn. Bike rentals 20kn per hour, 90kn per day. Open M-Sa 9am-9pm, Su 9am-1:30pm.) A 5min. walk from the bus station, **Autocamp Ježevac ❶**, Plavnička bb, offers tree-shaded campsites near the water. (☎051 21 081; jezevac@zlatni-otok.hr. Mar.-May and Sept.-Oct. 26kn per person, 17kn per tent; June 33/22.50kn; July-Aug. 36/24kn.) Across from the bus station is supermarket **Trgovina Krk ❶**, Šetalište Sv. Bernardina bb. (☎051 222 940. Open M-Sa 7am-9pm, Su 7am-1pm. AmEx/MC/V.) **Konoba Šime ❷**, A. Mahnića 1, literally in the city wall, serves up Adriatic specialties on a harborside terrace (☎222 042. Entrees 45-75kn). The **tourist information center,** Obala hrvatske mornarice bb, provides free **maps** with a tour of Krk and directory of accommodations and restaurants (☎051 220 226; www.tz-krk.hr). The **bus** station is at Šetalište Sv. Bernardina 1 (☎051 221 111). Ticketing open M-F 6:30am-2pm, Sa-Su 7:45am-1:30pm. Buy tickets onboard for later buses. Buses run between Rijeka and Krk Town (1½hr., 10-16 per day; 54kn Rijeka-Krk Town; 50kn Krk Town-Rijeka).

PULA (POLA)   ☎52

Pula (pop. 62,000), the largest city on the Istrian Peninsula and a chaotic transportation hub, is Istria's unofficial capital. Home to some of the best-preserved Roman ruins in Croatia, Pula has a giant white-stone ▧ **Amphitheater**—the sixth-largest in the world—which is often used as a venue for summer performances. To get there from the bus station, walk straight toward the town center and take a left on Flavijevska. (Open daily 9am-9pm. 40kn, students 20kn.) From the amphitheater, walk down to the water and along the port to reach the **Forum** and **Temple of Augustus** *(Augustov hram)*, finished in the first century AD, and climb the narrow streets of the Old Town to the peaceful **Franciscan Monastery,** the **Fort** (hosting the **Historical Museum of Istria**; 10kn, students 7kn), and the ancient **Roman Theater.** From the Fort and Roman Theater on Castropola, walk down to Sergijevaca to the **Triumphal Arch of the Sergii** *(Slavoluk Sergijevaca)*. To reach the private coves of Pula's beaches, buy a bus ticket (11kn) from newsstands and take bus #1 to the Stoja campground.

Arenaturist ❶, Splitska 1, inside Hotel Riviera, arranges accommodations throughout Pula with no fee, and has a friendly, English-speaking staff. (☎52 529 400; www.arenaturist.hr. Open M-Sa 8am-8pm; also Su 8am-1pm in Aug. Accommodations 46-78kn.) If Pula's beaches are your priority, stay at the **Youth Hostel Pula (HI) ❶**, Zaljev Valsaline 4. Take bus #2 (dir.: Veruda; 11kn) to reach the hostel from the station. Get off at the second stop on Veruda (Veruda 2) and follow the HI sign; take a right off the road and walk straight, then take the first right and walk 3min. down the hill. Trampoline and pedalboats are available. (☎52 391 133; www.hfhs.hr. Breakfast included. Reception daily 8am-10pm. Reservations recommended. Bike rental 20kn per hr., 80kn per day. Internet 10am-10pm; 30kn per hr. Dorms July-Aug. 114kn; Sept. and June 93kn; Oct. and May 88kn; Nov. and Apr. 82kn. Tax 4.50-7kn.) **Pizzeria Jupiter ❶**, Castropola 42 (☎52 214 333), is the perfect spot for a bite before amphitheater concerts. From the bus station, walk past the amphitheater along Amfiteatarska, cross Sv. Ivana, and walk up Castropola, the street on the left. (Pizza 26-40kn. Open M-F 9am-11pm, Sa-Su 1-11pm. AmEx.)

Buses (☎52 502 997), the most convenient option for transport, run from Trg Istarske Brigade to Dubrovnik (15hr., 1 per day, 543kn); Zagreb (4-5hr.,18 per day, 200kn); Trieste, ITA (3hr., 4 per day, 100kn). There are no maps of the bus lines; buses #2 and #3 circle the town center in opposite directions. **Trains** (☎52

541 733) run from Kolodvorska 5 to Ljubljana, SLV (7hr., 2 per day, 138kn), and Zagreb (7hr., 3 per day, 148kn). The **tourist office** is at Forum 3 (☎52 212 987; www.pulainfo.hr. Open M-F 8am-9pm, Sa-Su 9am-9pm). **Postal Code: 52100.**

ROVINJ   ☎052

The idyllic fishing port of Rovinj (ro-VEEN; pop. 14,000), with its mild climate and cool waters, was the favorite summer resort of Austro-Hungarian emperors. Today's vacationers still bask in this Mediterranean jewel's unspoiled beauty. Rovinj is the most Italian of Istria's towns: everybody here either is or speaks Italian, and all streets have names in both languages. The 18th-century **Church of Saint Euphemia** *(Crkva Sv. Eufemije)* houses the remains of St. Euphemia, the 15-year-old martyr who was killed by circus lions in AD 304. Inside, stairs lead visitors to the ▓**bell tower** (61m) and panoramic views of this gorgeous, quintessential Mediteranean city and coast. (Open M-Sa 10am-6pm. Services M-Sa 7pm, Su 10:30am and 7pm. Free. Bell tower 10kn.) Rovinj's best beaches are on **St. Catherine's Island** *(Otok Sv. Katarine)* and ▓**Red Island** *(Crveni Otok)*, two small islands right in front of town. To get there, take the ferry from the dock at the center of town to Sv. Katarine (round-trip 30kn) and Crveni Otok (round-trip 30kn). Head through the arch in the main square and follow the signs up Grisia toward the **Church of St. Euphemia** to check out an artists' colony.

Across the street from the bus station is **Natale**, Carducci 4, a travel agency which arranges private rooms in and around the center commission-free. (☎52 813 365; www.rovinj.com. Open July-Aug. daily 7:30am-10pm; Sept.-June M-Sa 7:30am-1:30pm and 4:30pm-7pm, Su 8am-noon. Doubles July-Aug. €76 for 1 night, €57 for 2 nights, €49 for 3 nights, €38 for 4+ nights; Sept.-June €64/€54/€42/€32. Apartments July-Aug. €48-76 for 4+ nights; Sept.-June €42-66 for 4+ nights.) **Camping Polari**, 2.5km east of town, has a supermarket, several bars, and a new pool. To get there, take one of the frequent buses (6min., 9kn) from the station (☎52 801 501. Mar. 26-May 23 and Sept. 6-Oct. 3 €12 per person; May 24-July 4 and Aug. 23-Sept. 5 €16.50 per person; July 5-Aug. 22 €20.80 per person. Residence tax June-Sept. €0.95 per person per day, Mar.-May and Oct. €0.75 per person per day. Notification fee €1.20 per person upon arrival. AmEx/MC/V.) Along the waterfront below the Church of St. Euphemia, ▓**Valentino Bar**, Santa Croce 28, has elegant white tables right on the water. Patrons can also choose to sit on comfortable smooth-surfaced rock ledges, dangling their legs in the ocean. (☎52 830 683. Open daily 6pm-1am.)

To reach the **tourist office,** walk along the water past the main square to Obala Pina Budicina 12. (☎52 811 566; www.tzgrovinj.hr, www.istria-rovinj.hr. Open daily mid-June to Sept. 8am-9pm; Oct. to mid-June 8am-3pm.) Rovinj is easily explored either on foot or by bike. **Bike rental** (70kn for 24hr., 50kn for half-day or 7hr.) is available at Bike Planet, Trg na Lokvi 3, which also has **maps.** (☎52 813 396. Open M-F 7:30am-12:30pm and 5-8pm, Sa 8:30am-1pm.) With no train station, Rovinj sends **buses** to Pula (45min., 20 per day, 33kn); Zagreb (5-6hr.; M-F 8 per day, Sa-Su 10 per day; 190kn); Ljubljana, SLV (5-6hr., 1 per day, 173kn). The bus station, in the center of town, is large, has an easily decipherable timetable, helpful attendants, and luggage storage. (☎52 811 453. 0.70 lipa per hr. 10kn per day, 15kn per day for items over 30kg.) **Postal Code: 52210.**

DALMATIAN COAST

Touted as the new French Riviera, the Dalmatian Coast offers a seascape of unfathomable beauty set against a backdrop of rugged mountains. With more than 1100 islands, Dalmatia is not only Croatia's largest archipelago, but also the cleanest and clearest waters in the Mediterranean.

ZADAR   ☎ 023

Zadar (pop.71,000), crushed in WWII and the recent Balkan war, is now beautifully rejuvenated. In the *Stari Grad* (Old Town), surprisingly unaffected by earlier conflicts, time has stood still, leaving a wonderful old charm. The area's history is so well-preserved that Roman ruins serve as city benches. On the southern dock of the Old Town, concrete steps into the water form a 70m long **Sea Organ,** which plays notes as the seawater rushes in, producing a continuous and harmonious melody. In the **Roman Forum** in the center of the city, the pre-Romanesque **St. Donat's Church** *(Crkva Sv. Donata),* a rare circular church, sits atop the ruins of an ancient Roman temple. (Open daily 9am-9pm. 10kn.)

At the entrance to the Old Town, coming from Obala Kralja Tomislava, **Miatours ❷,** on Vrata Sv. Krševana, books private rooms and transportation to nearby islands. (☎023 254 400; www.miatours.hr. Open daily July-Aug. 8am-8pm; Sept.-June 8am-2:30pm. Doubles 200-300kn. AmEx/MC/V.) A short bus ride from the city, in the Borik tourist area, the popular **Youth Hostel Zadar ❶,** Obala Kneza Trpimira 76, offers easy beach access and, apart from private accommodations, is the best bet for a bed on a budget. (☎023 331 145; www.hfhs.hr. Breakfast included. Online reservations recommended. Dorms Jan.-Apr., Nov.-Dec. €10.80-12.80, May and Oct. €12.20-14.20, June *and* Sept. €12.80-12.90, July-Aug €14.90-17.80. HI non-members 10kn extra per night. Tax €0.70-1.) **Trattoria Canzona ❷,** Stomorica 8, is popular with Zadarians of all ages. (☎023 212 081. Entrees 38-70kn. Open M-Sa 10am-11pm, Su noon-11pm. Cash only.)

Buses Ante Starčevića 1 (☎023 211 555) run to: Dubrovnik (8hr., 8 per day, 177-235kn); Pula (7hr., 3 per day, 235-241kn); Rijeka (4½hr., 12 per day, 153-196kn); Split (3½hr., 2 per hr., 77-128kn); Zagreb (3½-5½hr., 2 per hr., 107-140kn); Trieste, ITA (8hr., 1 per day, 182kn). **Luggage storage** is available at the bus station (1.20kn per hr. Open 6am-10pm.) Both the **train** and bus stations are only a 15min. walk from town, but trains are less convenient. To get to the Old Town, go through the pedestrian underpass and on to Zrinsko-Frankopanska to the water. Continue straight on to Obala Krajla Tomislava; the Old Town is on the left. Alternatively, to enter through the *Kopnena Vrata* (Mainland Gate) of the Old Town, take Kralja Dmitra Zvonimira and turn right on Ante Kuzmanića. To reach the main street, **Široka ulica,** walk through the gate and straight along Špire Brusine, then turn right on M. Klaića; Široka ulica is on the left. Buses #2 and 4 run from the bus station to the Old Town. The **tourist office,** M. Klaića bb, in the corner of Narodni trg, has free **maps** and an English-speaking staff. (☎023 316 166; www.visitzadar.net. Open daily July-Aug. 8am-midnight; Jan.-June, Sept.-Dec. 8am-8pm.) **Internet** can be accessed on Varoska 3. (☎023 311 265. 30kn per hr. Open daily 10am-11pm.) **Postal Code:** 23000.

SPLIT   ☎ 021

With its rich history and rocking nightlife, the coastal city of Split (pop. 221,000) is more a cultural center than a beach resort. Here, centuries of history collide with modern life, making the city a fascinating labyrinth of perfectly preserved Roman monuments, medieval streets, and hip bars.

◨ ◪ TRANSPORTATION AND PRACTICAL INFORMATION. Buses (☎021 327 777; www.ak-split.hr) run to: Dubrovnik (4hr.; 18 per day; 113-144kn, round-trip 179-228kn); Rijeka (7½-8hr., 12 per day, 246-318kn); Zadar (3hr., approx. 2 per hr., 100kn); Zagreb (5hr., 1-4 per hr., 175-203kn); Ljubljana, SLV (11hr., 1 per day, 307kn.) **Ferries** (☎021 338 333) depart from the dock right across from the bus station to: Supetar, Brač Island (45min., 14 per day, 30kn) and Stari Grad, Hvar Island (1hr., 6-7 per day, 42kn). Ferries also leave the international harbor to Ancona, ITA (10hr., 6 per wk., €40-55) and Bari, ITA (25hr., 4 per week, €45-62). Ask help from the assistants when deciphering the ferry schedules distributed at the **Jadrolinija** office. (Open daily 7am-9pm.) The **tourist information center,** Peristil bb, has a helpful staff and provides **free maps,** including one with a walking tour of Split. (☎021 345 606; www.visitsplit.com. Open Apr.-Oct. M-Sa 8am-9pm, Su/holidays 8am-1pm; Jan.-Mar., Nov.-Dec. M-F 8am-8pm, Sa 8am-1pm.) Those who stay in town for more than three days are entitled to a free **SplitCard** that gets big discounts for sightseeing, shopping, and sleeping. Bring a hostel receipt to any tourist office to prove your stay; otherwise purchase one for 60kn. **Postal Code:** 21000.

> **!** **PASSPORT CHECK.** Keep your passport handy when traveling between Split and Dubrovnik. Most buses pass through Bosnia and Herzegovina and there are passport checkpoints on your way in and out.

 ACCOMMODATIONS AND FOOD. The small travel agency **Tour de Croatia,** Obala kneza domagoja 1, books private rooms, exchanges currency, and organizes excursions. (☎023 338 319; www.tourdecroatia.com. Open daily July-Aug. 8am-9pm; Sept.-June 9am-6pm.) At **Al's Place ❶,** Kružićeva 10, the city's first hostel, young-at-heart Al organizes daytrips and offers a wealth of expertise on Split and nearby islands. There are only 12 beds, which are usually full; reserve ahead. (☎098 918 2923; www.hostelsplit.com. Internet 5kn per 20min. Reception open daily 8:30am-1pm, 5pm-8:30pm. June-Aug.130kn; Sept.-May110kn. Cash only.) With its motto of "booze and snooze," **Split Hostel ❶,** Narodni Trg 8, is perfect for revelers. The friendly Australian staff lead nights out on the town. (☎021 342 787; www.splithostel.com. Free lockers and Wi-Fi. Reception daily 8am-10pm. Dorms Jan.-mid-Apr., Oct.-Dec. 110kn; mid-Apr.-May 125kn; June, Sept. 150kn; July-Aug. 180kn. 10% discount for pre-booking. Cash only.) Tucked away along the **narrow streets of the Old Town** are lots of snack bars and restaurants, as well as kiosks with pizzas (slices 8kn) and *bureks* (10kn). **Konoba Varos ❷,** adorned in fishnets, feeds hungry locals and curious visitors with delicious Croatian fare. Entrees 60kn-80kn (☎021 396 138).

◙ SIGHTS. The *Stari Grad* (Old Town), wedged between a mountain range and a palm-lined waterfront, sprawls inside and around the ruins of a luxurious open-air **palace,** where the Roman emperor Diocletian summered when not persecuting Christians. The **basement halls** are near the palace entrance, at the beginning of the waterfront pedestrian street *Obala hrvatskog narodnog preporoda* (known to locals as the 'Riva'); take refuge from the midday heat in the cool relief of underground Split as you lose your way in this haunting maze sprinkled with imperial artifacts. (Open M-Sa 9am-9pm, Su and holidays 9am-6pm. 25kn, students 10kn.) The view of Split from the ◙bell tower (60m) of **Cathedral of St. Domnius** *(Katedrala sv. Dujma)* is breathtaking, especially at dusk when you can see the seemingly glowing red rooftops and the Adriatic Sea sprawled around for miles; be sure to watch your head when climbing up. (Cathedral and tower open Mar.-Oct. daily 8am-8pm.10kn each.) The ◙Meštrović Gallery *(Galerija Ivana Meštrovića)*, Šetalište Ivana Meštrovića 46, houses the splendid works of Croatia's most celebrated sculptor in a gorgeous villa facing the sea. To get there from the center of town, walk right facing the water, pass the marina, and follow the road up the hill; the gallery is right past the Archaeological Museum. (☎021 340 800. Open May-Sept. Tu-Sa 9am-9pm, Su noon-9pm; Oct.-Apr. Tu-Sa 9am-4pm, Su 10am-3pm. 30kn, students 15kn.)

🎵 **NIGHTLIFE.** Revelers flock to a string of bars and clubs on **Bačvice** beach. From the Old Town, walk past the train and bus stations, cross the bridge over the train tracks, and continue left down the hill toward the beach. Farther along the waterfront, beachside club **O'Hara**, Uvala Zenta 3, blasts techno on two floors and offers potent mixed drinks to its lively clientele. (☎021 364 262. Open M-Th 8pm-3am, F-Sa 8pm-4am.) Hidden on a narrow line of steps in the Old Town, 📍**Puls**, Buvnina 1, is a popular bar with low tables, cushions directly on the pavement, and live music. DJs spin on the weekends. To get there from Obala Riva, enter Trg brače Radič, turn right at the corner snack bar, and continue straight. (Open M-F 7am-midnight, Sa 7am-1am, Su 4pm-midnight.)

BRAČ ISLAND: BOL   ☎021

Central Dalmatia's largest island, Brač (pop. 13,000) is an ocean-lover's paradise. Most visitors come to Bol (pop. 1,500) for 📍**Zlatni rat** (Golden horn), a beautiful peninsula of white-pebble beach surrounded by emerald waters and big waves perfect for windsurfing. If you prefer the "deserted island" environment, head for the less explored, calmer beaches to the east of town. The town itself is also pleasant, small enough to cross in 10min. On the eastern tip of Bol, the **Dominican monastery,** built in 1475, displays Tintoretto's altar painting *Madonna with Child* in its museum. (Museum open daily 10am-noon and 5-7pm. 10kn.) **Big Blue Sport,** Podan Glavice 2, offers windsurfing lessons and rentals, mountain bike rentals and excursions, and sea kayak rentals. (Shop ☎021 635 614, Sport Center ☎021 306 222; www.big-blue-sport.hr). There are seven **campgrounds** around Bol, three lie on Bračka cesta, the road into the western part of town. The largest is **Kito ❶**, Bračka cesta bb. (☎021 635 551; kamp_kito@inet.hr. Open May-Sept. €5 per person, tent and tax included.)

The **ferry** from Split docks at Supetar (45min., 14 per day, 30kn), the island's largest town. From there, take a **bus** to Bol (1hr.; 4-8 per day, last bus back to Supetar leaves M-Sa 4:35pm, Su 5:50pm; 35kn). The buses don't always coordinate with the ferries' arrivals; if you don't want to wait, you can take a slightly overpriced **taxi van** to Bol. (35min., 360kn, max. 7 people.) Otherwise, enjoy the wait at the beach across the street. To reach Bol's **tourist information office,** Porad bolskih pomoraca bb, walk right from the bus station to the far side of the marina. (☎021 635 638; www.bol.hr. Open daily July-Aug. 8am-10pm; Jan.-June, Sept.-Dec. 8:30am-2pm, 4:30pm-8pm.) **Postal Code:** 21420.

DUBROVNIK   ☎020

Lord Byron considered Dubrovnik (du-BROV-nik; pop. 43,800) "the pearl of the Adriatic," and George Bernard Shaw knew it as "Paradise on Earth." Although it's tough to live up to such adulation, a stroll through the torch-lit winding lanes of the *Stari Grad* (Old Town) and a sunset look into the sea from the city walls certainly justify Dubrovnik's reputation as Croatia's top destination.

🚍🎵 **TRANSPORTATION AND PRACTICAL INFORMATION.** Jadrolinija **ferries** (☎020 41 80 00; www.jadrolinija.hr) depart opposite Obala S. Radića 40 for: Korčula (3hr., 5 per week, €10-12); Rijeka (21hr., 2 per week, €29-34); Split (8.5hr., 3 per wk., €14.50-17.50); Bari, ITA (8hr., 6 per week, €40-55). The **Jadrolinija** office is opposite the dock. (Open M, W 7am-11pm; T 8am-11pm; Th-F 8am-8pm; Sa 7am-8pm; Su 8am-2:30pm and 5pm-9pm.) **Buses** (☎020 30 50 70) run from Obala Pape Ivana Pavla II, 44A, to: Rijeka (12hr., 4 per day, 415kn);

Split (4hr., 1 per hr., 132kn); Zagreb (11hr., 9-10 per day, 234kn); Trieste, ITA (15hr., 1 per day, 370kn). There's **luggage storage** at the station (open daily 4:30am-10:30pm; 5kn per bag for 1hr.; after 1hr. 1.50kn per bag per hr).

If, like most budget travelers, you're staying in either Babin Kuk or Lapad, where a number of accommodations are located, a **daypass** will be your best bet for frequent shuttling back and forth from the Old Town. (8kn at kiosks, 10kn on board. Ticket valid for 1hr. after stamped. Daypass 25kn.) To get to the Old Town's central **tourist information office**, Široka 1, from the Pile Gate, walk straight along Placa (Stradun) and turn right on Široka. (☎020 32 35 87; www. tzdubrovnik.hr. Open daily 8am-8pm.) On the same street, **the post office**, Široka 8, has **ATMs** and public telephones; it also offers Western Union services. (☎020 32 34 27. Open M-F 7:30am-9pm, Sa 10am-5pm.) **Postal Code:** 20108.

⟨⟩ ACCOMMODATIONS AND FOOD. A private room tends to be the cheapest and most comfortable option for two; arrange one through any of the indistinguishable agencies or bargain with locals at the station (doubles should go for 100-150kn per person). Take bus #6 from *Stari Grad* or #7 from the ferry and bus terminals, get off two stops past the Lapad post office, cross the street, walk uphill on Mostarska, and turn right at Dubravkina to reach **⟨⟩Apartmani Burum ❶**, Dubravkina 16, in Babin Kuk. This popular guesthouse has clean, comfortable rooms and apartments. (☎020 43 54 67; www.burumaccommodation.com. Kitchen available. Free pickup from bus station and rides to Old Town. Apr.-May 100kn; June-Sept. 150-250kn. Cash only.) **Begović Boarding House ❶**, Primorska 17, offers spacious doubles and apartments in a cozy villa. Call ahead and the owner will pick you up. (☎020 43 51 91; www.begovic-boarding-house.com. Private bathrooms. Internet first 30min. free, then 10kn per 30min. Reserve ahead July-Aug. June-Sept. singles 150-200kn; doubles 240-300kn; triples 300-360kn. Oct.-May 100-120kn, 200-240kn, 300-360kn. Cash.)

> **WELCOME! NOW, GET OUT!!** Make sure to ask for a receipt when you pay for a private room. Without a receipt, your stay won't be registered, and the accommodation will be illegal.

Harborside favorite **⟨⟩Lokanda Peskarija ❷**, Na Ponti bb, has excellent, affordable seafood. From Placa, walk to the bell tower at the end of the street, turn right on Pred Dvorum, and take the first left out of the city walls. (☎020 32 47 50. Seafood 35-60kn. Open daily 8am-1am.) Exchange books, savor smoothies, and nosh on wraps at **Fresh ❷**, Vetranićeva 4. (Wraps 28kn. Smoothies 20kn. Open daily 10am-2am.) In the center of Old Town, self-service restaurant **Express ❷**, Marojice Kaboge 1, serves up inexpensive, filling meals of pastas, soups, and salads. (☎020 32 39 94. Entrees 25-50kn. Open daily 10am-10pm.)

◯ SIGHTS. The entrance to the 2km limestone **⟨⟩City Walls** *(gradske zidine)* lies just inside the Pile Gate on the left, with a second entrance at the other end of Placa, next to the Old Port. (Open daily 8am-7:30pm. 50kn, students 20kn. Audio tour 40kn.) The baroque **Cathedral of the Assumption of the Virgin Mary** (Katedrala), Kneza Damjana Jude 1, is built on the site of a Romanesque cathedral and a 7th-century Byzantine cathedral. Its resplendent treasury (riznica) houses the "Diapers of Jesus," along with a host of golden reliquaries of St. Blaise. Above the altar, check out Titian's *Assumption of Our Lady.* (Cathedral open daily 8am-7pm; treasury open daily 8am-5pm. Cathedral free, treasury 10kn.) The 19th-century **Serbian Orthodox Church** (Srpska Pravoslavna Crkva) and its **Museum of Icons** (Muzej Ikona), Od Puča 8, together with the small yet intricate

CROATIA

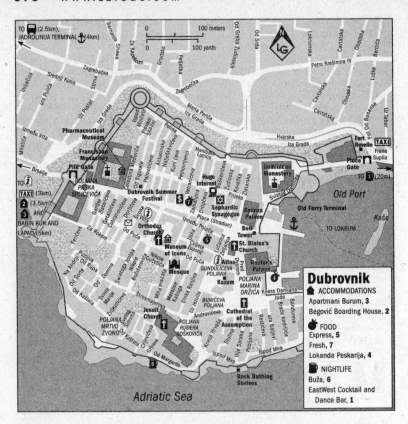

Dubrovnik

🏠 ACCOMMODATIONS
Apartmani Burum, **3**
Begović Boarding House, **2**

🍎 FOOD
Express, **5**
Fresh, **7**
Lokanda Peskarija, **4**

🍸 NIGHTLIFE
Buža, **6**
EastWest Cocktail and
Dance Bar, **1**

synagogue, Žudioska ulica 5, and **mosque**, Miha Pracata 3, stand as a symbol of Dubrovnik's tolerance. (Museum of Icons ☎020 32 32 83; open M-Sa 9am-2pm; 10kn. Synagogue and Jewish Museum ☎020 32 10 28; open May-Oct. M-F 10am-8pm; 15kn. Mosque open daily 10am-1pm and 8-9pm. Free.) Classical performances are held in many churches during summer.

🏖 **BEACHES.** Outside the fortifications of the Old Town are a number of **rock shelves** popular for sunning and swimming. To reach a beautiful but crowded **pebble beach** from the Placa's end, turn left on Svetog Dominika, bear right after the footbridge, and continue on Frana Supila. Hop on a ferry from the Old Port (daily service 9am-7pm, 10min., 2 per hr., 40kn return) to nearby **Lokrum**, which has great cliff jumping, a botanical garden, and a nude beach on its eastern end. More modest travelers can stroll (fully clothed) through the nature preserve to a smaller section of rock shelves found on the other side of the island.

 HOPSCOTCH...KABOOM?! As tempting as it may be to stroll through the hills above Dubrovnik or wander the unpaved paths on Lopud, both may still be laced with **landmines.** Stick to paved paths and beaches.

▓▓ **FESTIVALS AND NIGHTLIFE.** Dubrovnik becomes a party scene and cultural mecca from mid-July to late-August during the **Dubrovnik Summer Festival** (Dubrovački Ljetni Festival). The **festival office,** Od Sigurate 1, at the intersection of Placa and Od Sigurate, has schedules and tickets. (☎020 32 61 00; ww.dubrovnik-festival.hr. Open daily during the festival 8:30am-9pm. 50-300kn.) By night, crowds gravitate to bars in *Stari Grad* and cafes on *Buničeva Poljana,* where live bands and street performers turn up in summer. From the open-air market, climb the stairs toward the Jesuit church, veer left, and follow the signs marked "Cool Drinks" along Od Margarite to ▓**Buža,** Crijeviceva 9. Outside the city wall, perched on the rocks high above the bright blue Adriatic, this laid-back watering hole is the best place to enjoy spectacular sunsets and a midnight swim. (Beer 30-32kn. Mixed drinks 35kn. Open daily 9am-2am.) At posh **EastWest Cocktail and Dance Bar,** Frana Supila bb, a dressed-to-impress clientele reclines on white leather sofas and plush beds on the beach. (Beer 12-30kn. Mixed drinks 40-100kn. Thai massage 200kn per 30min., 300kn for 1hr. Open daily 8am-4am.)

▓ **DAYTRIPS FROM DUBROVNIK: LOPUD ISLAND**

Jadrolinija's ferries (50min., June-Aug. 4 per day, round-trip 36kn) run to Lopud and the Elafiti Islands. Purchase tickets at the Jadrolinija office, Obala S. Radića 40, across from the dock (☎ 41 80 00; www.jadrolinija.hr). Šunj Beach: from the ferry dock, face the water and turn left. Walk along the water for 5min. until you reach Konoba Barbara. Take a left on the walkway and go uphill. Bear right at the fork and follow the path to steps leading to the beach.) Fortress: from the waterfront, turn left at the town museum and follow the signs until you reach it.

In the center of the Elafiti Islands, the island of Lopud boasts one of the Adriatic's most spectacular **beaches.** Unique among the region's beaches because of its fine sand, Šunj Beach *(Plaža Šunj)* stretches along the bay and features warm, shallow water. On the opposite side of the island, the picturesque village of Lopud lies on a bay and is easily traversed in 15min. On the other end of the waterfront, uphill from the cafés and restaurants and past most of the hotels, stands a gazebo with panoramic views of the town and nearby islands. For travelers with lots of energy (and sturdy shoes), a number of **trekking trails** traverse the island; winding through deserted vineyards and olive groves, different trails lead to the ruins of medieval churches with hilltop shrines, fortresses, and monasteries. The ▓**Fortress** *(Kaštio)* has the most breathtaking vista; the **tourist office,** Obala Iva Kuljevana 12, is next to the dock and can provide maps of the island along with directions to Šunj and trekking information. (☎759 086. Open M, W, Sa-Su 8am-1pm and 5pm-7pm; T, Th 8am-3pm).

CZECH REPUBLIC
(ČESKÁ REPUBLIKA)

From the days of the Holy Roman Empire to reign of the USSR, the Czech people have stood at a crossroads of international affairs. Unlike many of their neighbors, however, the citizens of this small, landlocked country have rarely resisted as armies marched across their borders, often choosing to protest with words instead of weapons. As a result, Czech towns are among the best-preserved and the most beautiful in Europe. Today, the Czechs face another invasion, as tourists sweep in to savor the magnificent capital and some of the world's best beer.

DISCOVER CZECH REPUBLIC: SUGGESTED ITINERARIES

THREE DAYS. Voyage to the capital, **Prague** (p. 185). Stroll across the **Charles Bridge** to see **Prague Castle**, leave to explore areas like **Josefov**.

ONE WEEK. Keep exploring **Prague** (5 days; p. 185); this time, relax at the **Petřín Hill Gardens** and visit the impressive **Troja château**.

ESSENTIALS

FACTS AND FIGURES

OFFICIAL NAME: Czech Republic.

CAPITAL: Prague.

MAJOR CITIES: Brno, Olomouc, Plzeň.

POPULATION: 10,221,000.

TIME ZONE: GMT +1.

LANGUAGE: Czech.

RELIGIONS: Atheist (49%) Roman Catholic (27%), Protestant (2%).

BEER CONSUMPTION PER CAPITA: 157L per year (largest in the world).

WHEN TO GO

The Czech Republic is the most touristed country in Eastern Europe, and Prague in particular is overrun. To beat the crowds, you may want to avoid the peak season (June-Aug.), though the weather is most pleasant then.

DOCUMENTS AND FORMALITIES

EMBASSIES AND CONSULATES. Foreign embassies are in Prague (p. 186). Czech consulates abroad include: **Australia**, 8 Culoga Circuit, O'Malley, Canberra, ACT 2606 (☎02 24 18 11 11; www.mzv.cz/canberra); **Canada**, 251 Cooper St., Ottawa, ON K2P 0G2 (☎613-562-3875; www.mzv.cz/Ottawa); **Ireland,** 57 Northumberland Rd., Ballsbridge, Dublin 4 (☎016 681 135; www.msz.cz/Dublin); **New Zealand**, Level 3, BMW Mini Centre, 11-15 Great South Road and corner of Margot Street, Newmarket, Auckland (☎9 522 8736; auckland@honorary.mvz. cz); **UK**, 6-30 Kensington Palace Gardens, Kensington, London W8 4QY (☎020

73 07 51 80; www.czechcentres.cz/london); **US,** 3900 Spring of Freedom St. NW, Washington, DC 20008 (☎202-274-9100; www.mzv.cz/washington).

ENTRANCE REQUIREMENTS.
Passport: Required of all travelers. Must be valid for 90 days after visiting.
Letter of Invitation: Not required of citizens of Australia, Canada, Ireland, New Zealand, the UK, and the US.
Inoculations: Recommended up-to-date on DTaP (diphtheria, tetanus, and pertussis) hepatitis A, hepatitis B, MMR (measles, mumps, and rubella), polio booster, rabies, and typhoid.
Work Permit: Required of foreigners planning to work in the Czech Republic.
International Driving Permit: Required of foreigners. For EU citizens, a national driver's license is sufficient.

VISA AND ENTRY INFORMATION. Citizens of Australia, Canada, New Zealand, and the US don't need a visa for stays of up to 90 days; UK citizens don't need visas for stays of up to 180 days. Visas for extended stays are available at embassies or consulates. Czech visas not available at the border. Processing is 14 days when the visa is submitted by mail, seven when submitted in person.

TOURIST SERVICES AND MONEY

EMERGENCY	Ambulance: ☎155. Fire: ☎150. Police: ☎158.

TOURIST OFFICES. Municipal tourist offices in major cities provide info on sights and events, distribute lists of hostels and hotels, and often book rooms. **Tourist Information Centrum** is state-run. In Prague, these offices are often crowded and may be staffed by disgruntled employees. **CKM,** a national student tourist agency, books hostels and issues ISIC and HI cards. Most bookstores sell a national hiking map collection, *Soubor turistickch map*, with an English key.

MONEY. The Czech unit of currency is the **koruna (Kč;** crown), plural **koruny.** The government postponed its slated 2009 conversion to the euro and the earliest likely switch is in 2012. **Inflation** is around 2.6%. Relative to the rest of Eastern Europe, the Czech Republic's inflation rate is quite stable. **Banks** offer good exchange rates; **Komerční banka** is a common bank chain. **ATMs** are everywhere and offer the best exchange rates. **Bargaining** is usually acceptable, especially in heavily touristed areas, though not as much in formal indoor shops.

CZECH (KČ)		
AUS$1 = 14.45KČ		10KČ = AUS$0.70
CDN$1 = 15.61KČ		10KČ = CDN$0.64
EUR€1 = 24.38KČ		10KČ = EUR€0.41
NZ$1 = 11.76KČ		10KČ = NZ$0.85
UK£1 = 30.83KČ		10KČ = UK£0.32
US$1 = 16.59KČ		10KČ = US$0.61

HEALTH AND SAFETY

Medical facilities, especially in Prague, are of high quality, and sometimes employ English-speaking doctors. They often require cash payment, but some may accept credit cards. Travelers are urged to check with their insurance companies to see if they will cover emergency medical expenses. **Pharmacies** include *Lekarna*, and the most common chain is Droxi; pharmacies and supermarkets carry international brands of *náplast* (bandages), *tampóny* (tampons), and *kondomy* (condoms). The Czech Republic has a very low level of violent crime, but **petty crime** has increased with tourism; it is especially common in big cities, on public transportation, and near touristy areas, such as main squares in Prague. **Women** traveling alone should not experience many problems, but should exercise caution while riding public transportation, especially after dark. Hate crimes are rare in the Czech Republic, but **minorities** might experience some discrimination. This is especially true for travelers with darker skin. Travelers with **disabilities** might encounter trouble with the Czech Republic's accessibility, but there is a strong movement to make Prague's transportation system more wheelchair-friendly. Gay nightlife is taking off in Prague, and the country recently legalized registered partnerships for same-sex couples. Though tolerance is increasing, **GLBT travelers** are advised to avoid public displays of affection, especially in more rural areas.

TRANSPORTATION

BY PLANE. The main international airport is Ruzyně International Airport (**PRG**; ☎220 113 314; www.prg.aero). Many carriers, including **Air Canada, Air France, American Airlines, British Airways, CSA, Delta, KLM, Lufthansan,** and **SAS** fly into Prague. Direct flights are quite expensive; travelers might consider flying to a Western European capital and taking a train or discount airline into Prague.

BY TRAIN. The easiest and cheapest way to travel in the Czech Republic is by train. **Czech Railways** is the national train line. **Eurail** is accepted. The fastest international trains are **EuroCity** and **InterCity** (*expresní;* marked in blue on schedules). *Rychlík* trains are fast domestic trains (*zrychlený vlak;* marked in red on schedules). Avoid slow *osobni* trains, marked in white. *Odjezdy* (departures) are printed on yellow posters, *příjezdy* (arrivals) on white. Seat reservations (*mistenka*, 10Kč) are recommended on express and international trains.

BY BUS. Czech buses are often quicker and cheaper than trains in the countryside. **ČSAD** runs national and international bus lines (www.ticketsbti.csad.cz), and many European companies operate international service. Consult the timetables or buy a bus schedule (25Kč) from kiosks.

BY CAR AND BY TAXI. Roads are generally well-kept, but side roads can be dangerous, and the number of fatal car accidents is increasing in the Czech Republic. **Roadside assistance** is usually available. To drive in the Czech Republic, an **International Driver's Permit** is required. **Taxis** are a safe way to travel, though many overcharge. Negotiate the fare beforehand and make sure the meter is running during the ride. Phoning a taxi service is generally more affordable than flagging down a cab on the street. *Let's Go* does not recommend **hitchhiking.**

KEEPING IN TOUCH

PHONE CODES	**Country code:** 420. **International dialing prefix:** 00. For more information on how to place international calls, see **Inside Back Cover.**

EMAIL AND THE INTERNET. Internet is readily available throughout the Czech Republic. Internet cafes offer fast connections for about 1-2Kč per minute. Wi-Fi access is becoming more prevalent.

TELEPHONE. Card-operated phones (175Kč per 50 units; 320Kč per 100 units) are simpler to use and easier to find than coin-operated phones. You can purchase phone cards (*telefonní karta*) at most *tábaks* and *trafika* (convenience stores). To make **domestic calls,** dial the entire number. City codes no longer exist in the Czech Republic, and dialing zero is not necessary. To make an **international call** to the Czech Republic, dial the country code followed by the entire phone number. Calls run 13Kč per minute to Australia, Canada, the UK, or the US and 12Kč per minute to New Zealand. Dial ☎1181 for English info, 0800 12 34 56 for the international operator. International access codes include: **AT&T** (☎00 800 222 55288); **British Telecom** (☎00 420); **Canada Direct** (☎800 001 115); **MCI** (☎800 001 112); and **Sprint** (☎800 001 187).

MAIL. The postal system is efficient, though finding English-speaking postal employees can be a challenge. A postcard to the US costs 18Kč, to Europe 17Kč. To send airmail, stress that you want it mailed by plane (*letecky*). Go to the customs office to send packages heavier than 2kg abroad. **Poste Restante** is generally available. Address envelopes with: First Name LAST NAME, POSTE RESTANTE, post office address, Postal Code, city, CZECH REPUBLIC.

LANGUAGE. Czech is a West Slavic language, closely related to Slovak and Polish. English is widely understood, mainly among young people, and German can be useful, especially in South Bohemia. In eastern regions, you're more likely to encounter Polish. Though Russian was taught to all school children under communism, the language is not always welcome. For basic Czech words and phrases, see **Phrasebook: Czech, p. 785.**

ACCOMMODATIONS AND CAMPING

CZECH REPUBLIC	❶	❷	❸	❹	❺
ACCOMMODATIONS	under 320Kč	320-500Kč	501-800Kč	801-1200Kč	over 1200Kč

Hostels and **university dorms** are the cheapest options in July and August; two- to four-bed dorms cost 250-400Kč. **Hostels** are generally clean and safe throughout the country, but they are often rare in areas with few students. **Pensions** are the next most affordable option at 600-800Kč. **Hotels** (from 1000Kč) tend to be more luxurious and expensive. From June to September, reserve at least a week ahead in Prague, Český Krumlov, and Brno. Though staying in **private homes** is common in Eastern Europe, it is not very common in the Czech Republic. Scan train stations for *Zimmer frei* signs. Be cautious about paying in advance for this type of accomodation. There are many **campgrounds** scattered throughout the country; most are open only from mid-May to September.

FOOD AND DRINK

CZECH REPUBLIC	❶	❷	❸	❹	❺
FOOD	under 80Kč	80-110Kč	111-150Kč	151-200Kč	over 200Kč

Loving Czech cuisine starts with learning to pronounce *knedlíky* (KNED-lee-kee). These thick, wheat- or potato-based loaves of dough, feebly known in English as dumplings, are a staple. Meat, however, lies at the heart of almost all main dishes; the national meal (known as *vepřo-knedlo-zelo*) is *vepřové* (roast pork), *knedlíky*, and *zelí* (sauerkraut), frequently served with cabbage. If you're in a hurry, grab *párky* (frankfurters) or *sýr* (cheese) at a food stand. **Vegetarian** restaurants serving *bez masa* (meatless) specialties are uncommon outside Prague; traditional restaurants serve few options beyond *smaženy sýr* (fried cheese) and *saláty* (salads), and even these may contain meat products. Eating **kosher** is feasible, but beware—pork may sneak unnoticed into many dishes. *Jablkový závin* (apple strudel) and *ovocné knedlíky* (fruit dumplings) are favorite sweets, but the most beloved is *koláč*—a tart filled with poppy seeds or sweet cheese. *Vinárnas* (wine bars) serve Moravian wines and a variety of spirits, including *slivovice* (plum brandy) and *becherovka* (herbal bitter), the **national drink.** World-class local brews like *Plzeňský Prazdroj* (Pilsner Urquell), *Budvar*, and *Kruovice* dominate the drinking scene.

HOLIDAYS AND FESTIVALS

Holidays: New Year's Day (Jan. 1); Easter (Apr. 12, 2009; April 4th, 2010); May Day/ Labor Day (May 1); Liberation Day (May 8); Saints Cyril and Methodius Day (July 5); Jan Hus Day (July 6); St. Wencesclas Day (Sept. 28); Independence Day (Oct. 28); Struggle for Freedom and Democracy Day (Nov. 17); Christmas (Dec. 24-26).

Festivals: The Czech Republic hosts a number of internationally renowned festivals. If you are planning to attend, reserve tickets well in advance. In June, the **Five-Petaled Rose Festival,** a medieval festival in Český Krumlov, features music, dance, and a jousting tournament. **Masopust,** the Moravian version of Mardi Gras, is celebrated in villages across the country from Epiphany to Ash Wednesday (Jan.-Mar.).

BEYOND TOURISM

For more info on opportunities across Europe, see Beyond Tourism, p. 55.

INEX—Association of Voluntary Service, Senovážné nám. 24, 116 47 Praha 1, Czech Republic (☎ 420 222 362 715; www.inexsda.cz/eng). Ecological and historical preservation efforts, as well as construction projects, in the Czech Republic.

The Prague Center for Further Education and Professional Development, Ptrossova 19, Nové Město, 110 00 Praha 1, Czech Republic (☎420 257 534 013; www.filmstudies.cz). Teaches courses on art, filmmaking, and design in Prague.

University of West Bohemia, Univerzitní 8, 306 14 Plzeň (☎420 377 631 111; www.zcu.cz). International university centrally located in a student-friendly brewery city.

PRAGUE (PRAHA)

Home to the stately Prague Castle and Old Town Square's pastel facades, Prague (pop. 1,200,000) retains small-town charm despite its size. In the 14th century, Holy Roman Emperor Charles IV refurbished Prague with stone bridges and lavish palaces still visible today. Since the lifting of the Iron Curtain in 1989, outsiders have flooded the Czech capital. In summer, most locals leave for the countryside when the foreigner-to-resident ratio soars above nine-to-one. Despite rising prices and a hyper-touristed Staré Město (Old Town), Prague still commands the awe of its visitors.

▌ INTERCITY TRANSPORTATION

Flights: Ruzyně Airport (PRG; ☎220 111 111), 20km northwest of the city. Take bus #119 to Ⓜ A: Dejvická (12Kč, luggage 6Kč per bag); buy tickets from kiosks or machines. Airport **buses** run by Cedaz (☎220 114 296; 20-45 min., 2 per hr.) collect travelers from náměstí Republiky (120Kč); try to settle on a price before departing.

Trains: (☎221 111 122, international 224 615 249; www.vlak.cz). Prague has 4 main terminals. **Hlavní nádraží,** Ⓜ C: Hlavní nádraží (☎224 615 786) and **Nádraží Holešovice,** Ⓜ C: Nádraží Holešovice (☎224 624 632) are the largest and cover most international service. Domestic trains leave from **Masarykovo nádraží,** Ⓜ B: náměstí Republiky (☎840 112 113) and from **Smíchovské nádraží,** Ⓜ B: Smíchovské nádraží (☎972 226 150). International trains run to: **Berlin** (5hr., 6 per day, 1400Kč); **Bratislava, SLK** (5hr., 6 per day, 650Kč); **Budapest** (7-9hr., 5 per day, 1450Kč); **Kraków, POL** (7-8hr., 3 per day, 950Kč); **Moscow** (31hr., 1 per day, 3000Kč); **Munich, DEU** (7hr., 3 per day, 1400Kč); **Vienna, AUT** (4-5hr., 7 per day, 1000Kč); **Warsaw, POL** (9hr., 2 per day, 1300Kč).

Buses: (☎900 144 444; www.vlak-bus.cz). State-run **ČSAD** (☎257 319 016) has several terminals. The biggest is **Florenc,** Křižíkova 4 (☎900 149 044; Ⓜ B or C: Florenc). Info office open daily 6am-9pm. To: **Berlin** (7hr., 2 per day, 900Kč); **Budapest** (8hr., 3 per day, 1600Kč); **Paris, FRA** (15hr., 2 per day, 2200Kč); **Sofia, BGR** (24hr., 2 per day, 1600Kč); **Vienna, AUT** (5hr., 1 per day, 600Kč). 10% ISIC discount. **Tourbus** office (☎224 218 680; www.eurolines.cz), at the terminal, sells Eurolines and airport shuttle tickets. Open M-F 7am-7pm, Sa 8am-7pm, Su 9am-7pm.

▌ LOCAL TRANSPORTATION

Public Transportation: Buy interchangeable tickets for the bus, Metro, and tram at newsstands, *tabák* kiosks, machines in stations, or the DP (*Dopravní podnik;* transport authority) kiosks. Validate tickets in machines above escalators to avoid fines issued by plainclothes inspectors who roam transport lines. 3 **metro** lines run daily 5am-midnight: A is green on maps, B yellow, C red. **Night trams** #51-58 and **buses** #502-514 and 601 run after the last metro and cover the same areas as day trams and buses (2 per hr. 12:30am-4:30am); look for dark blue signs with white letters at bus stops. 18Kč tickets are good for a 20min. ride or 5 stops. 26Kč tickets are valid for 1hr., with transfers, for all travel in the same direction. Large bags and baby carriages 6Kč. DP offices (☎296 191 817; www.dpp.cz; open daily 7am-9pm), in the Muzeum stop on A and C lines, sell **multi-day passes** (1-day 100Kč, 3-day 330Kč, 5-day 500Kč).

Taxis: City Taxi (☎257 257 257) and **AAA** (☎140 14). 40Kč base, 25Kč per km, 5Kč per min. waiting. Hail a cab anywhere, but call ahead to avoid getting ripped off.

 GOING THE DISTANCE. To avoid being scammed by taxis, always ask in advance for a receipt *(Prosím, dejte mi paragon;* "please, give me a receipt")* with distance traveled and price paid.

Car Rental: Europcar, Elišky Krásnohorské 9 (☎224 811 290; www.europcar.cz). Cars from 830Kč per day. Anyone planning on renting a car must have a European driver's license. Open daily 8am-8pm. AmEx/D/MC/V.

Bike Rental: City Bike, Králodvorská 5 (☎776 180 284), rents bikes for 2, 3, or 4hr., or all day. All bikes come with a helmet, lock, map, and drink. First 2hr. 300Kč, each additional hr 50Kč up to maximum 500Kč. Open daily 9am-7pm. Cash only.

7 PRACTICAL INFORMATION

TOURIST AND FINANCIAL SERVICES

Tourist Offices: Green "i"s mark tourist offices. **Pražská Informační Služba (PIS;** Prague Information Service; ☎420 12 444; www.pis.cz) is in the **Staroměstské Radnice** (Old Town Hall). Open Apr.-Oct. daily 9am-7pm; Nov.-Mar. daily 9am-6pm. **Branches** at Na příkopě 20 and Hlavní nádraží. Open in summer M-F 9am-7pm, Sa-Su 9am-5pm; in winter M-F 9am-6pm, Sa 9am-3pm. Branch in the tower by the Malá Strana side of the Charles Bridge. Open Apr.-Oct. daily 10am-6pm.

Budget Travel: CKM, Mánesova 77 (☎222 721 595; www.ckm-praha.cz). A: Jiřího z Poděbrad. Sells budget airline tickets to those under 26. Also books accommodations in Prague from 350Kč. Open M-Th 10am-6pm, F 10am-4pm. **GTS,** Ve smečkách 27 (☎222 119 700; www.gtsint.cz). A or C: Muzeum. Offers student discounts on airline tickets (225-2500Kč in Europe). Open M-F 8am-10pm, Sa 10am-5pm.

Embassies and Consulates: See **Consular Services Abroad,** p. 13.

Currency Exchange: Exchange counters are everywhere but rates vary wildly. Train stations have high rates. Never change money on the street. **Chequepoints** are plentiful and open late, but they often charge large commissions. **Komerční banka,** Na příkopě 33 (☎222 432 111), buys notes and checks at a 2% commission. Open M and W 8:30am-5pm, Tu and Th 8:30am-5pm, F 8:30am-5:30pm. There's a 24hr. **Citibank** at Rytířska 24.

American Express/Interchange: Václavské náměstí 56 (☎222 800 224). A or C: Muzeum. AmEx **ATM** outside. Western Union services available. MC and V **cash advances** (3% commission). Open daily 9am-7pm.

 NO EASY RIDING. You might be tempted to try out one of the many bike tours offered throughout the city, but you may want to think twice: Prague's narrow streets weren't made to accommodate bikes (and drivers rarely bother), and the cobblestones may rattle your teeth out. If you really want to go on a tour, consider one of the many walking tours.

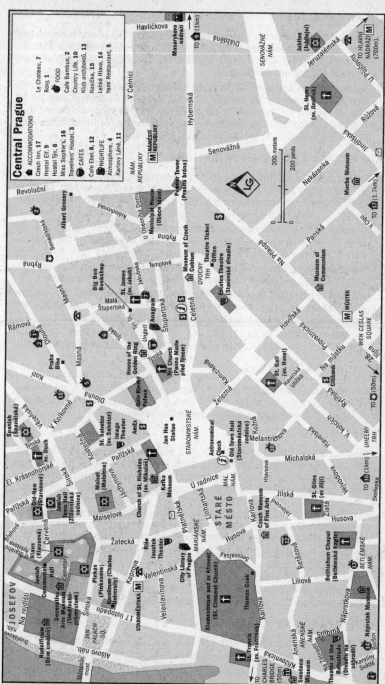

Central Prague

▲ ACCOMMODATIONS
Czech Inn, 17
Hostel Elf, 9
Hostel Týn, 6
Miss Sophie's, 16
Travellers' Hostel, 3

☕ CAFES
Cafe Ebel, 8, 12
Atmosphere, 4
Karlovy Lázně, 11

Le Chateau, 7
Roxy, 1

🍴 FOOD
Cafe Bambus, 2
Country Life, 10
Klub architektů, 13
Kosička, 15
Lehká Hlava, 14
Yami Restaurant, 5

LOCAL SERVICES

Luggage Storage: Lockers in train and bus stations take 2 5Kč coins. For storage over 24hr., use the luggage offices to the left in the basement of Hlavní nádraží. 25Kč per day, bags over 15kg 40Kč. Fine for forgotten lock code 30Kč. Open daily 6-11am, 11:30am-5:30pm, and 6pm-5:30am.

English-Language Bookstore: ◪The Globe Bookstore, Ptrossova 6 (☎224 934 203; www.globebookstore.cz). Ⓜ️B: Národní třída. Exit metro left on Spálená, take the 1st right on Ostrovní, and then the 3rd left on Pštrossova. Wide variety of new and used books and periodicals. Cafe upstairs with an expansive menu of teas, coffees, and mixed drinks. Internet 1Kč per min. Open daily 9:30am-1am.

EMERGENCY AND COMMUNICATIONS

Medical Services: Na Homolce (Hospital for Foreigners), Roentgenova 2 (☎257 271 111, after hours 257 272 146; www.homolka.cz). Bus #167. Open 24hr. **Canadian Medical Center,** Velesavínská 1 (☎235 360 133, after hours 724 300 301; www.cmc. praha.cz). Open M, W, and F 8am-6pm, Tu and Th 8am-8pm.

24hr. Pharmacy: U Lékárna Anděla, Štefánikova 6 (☎257 320 918, at night 257 324 686). Ⓜ️B: Anděl. After hours, press the button marked "Pohotovost" to the left of the main door for service.

Telephones: Phone cards sold at kiosks, post offices, and some exchange establishments for 200Kč and 300Kč. Coins also accepted (local calls from 5Kč per min.).

Internet: The post office (see below), almost any cafe, and many restaurants will have Wi-Fi. ◪**Bohemia Bagel,** Masná 2 (☎224 812 560; www.bohemiabagel.cz), Ⓜ️A: Staroměstská. 2Kč per min. Open M-F 7am-midnight, Sa-Su 8am-midnight.

Post Office: Jindřišská 14 (☎221 131 445). Ⓜ️A or B: Můstek. Internet 1Kč per min. Open daily 2am-midnight. Windows open until 7:30pm. **Postal Code:** 11000.

⌂ ACCOMMODATIONS

Hotel prices are through the roof in Prague, and hostel rates are on the rise. Reservations are a must at hotels and even at the nicer hostels in summer. A growing number of Prague residents rent affordable rooms.

STARÉ MĚSTO

Travellers' Hostel, Dlouhá 33 (☎224 826 662; www.travellers.cz). Ⓜ️B: Náměstí. Republiky. Branches at Husova 3, Střelecký Ostrov 36, and U Lanové Dráhy 3. Private kitchens for each dorm and set of single rooms means you'll always have a pretty good idea who stole your leftover goulash. Bar on the 3rd floor is a convenient alternative to the standard pub crawl (beer 25Kč). Breakfast and linens included. Laundry 150Kč. Internet and Wi-Fi. Reception 24hr. Check-in 1pm. Check-out 10am. Reserve ahead in summer. 16-bed dorms 350Kč, 6-bed 480Kč, 4-bed 500Kč; singles 1190Kč, with bath 1390Kč; doubles 1380Kč per person, with bath 1600Kč. 40Kč ISIC discount. AmEx/MC/V. ❶

Hostel Týn, Týnská 19 (☎224 828 519; www.hostel-tyn.web2001.cz). Ⓜ️B: Náměstí Republiky. Follow Týnská away from Old Town Sq. The dorms may be small, but they're never bunked. Soft beds with big pillows. Clean facilities. Kitchen access. In-room lockers. Free internet and Wi-Fi. Reception 24hr. Check-in 1pm. Check-out 10am. Quiet hours 10pm-6am. 4- and 5-bed dorms 420Kč; doubles 1240Kč. 200Kč deposit. Cash only. ❶

NOVÉ MĚSTO AND VINOHRADY

▨ **Chili Hostel,** Pštrossova 7 (☎603 119 113; www.chili.dj). Ⓜ️B: Národní třída. From the metro station, walk south on Spálená, make a right on Myslíkova, and then another right on Pštrossova. Perhaps one of the best located Nové Město hostels, though there's nothing especially spicy about it, apart from the orange and red walls and the racy anime posters that line the common area walls. The rooms, spacious and simply furnished, come in a wide range of sizes. Common room open 24 hr. Linens and towels included. Free Wi-Fi. Reception 24 hr. Check-in 2:30am. Check-out 11am. Dorms 322Kč; singles 1475Kč; doubles 966Kč. MC/V. ❶

❷ **Hostel Elf,** Husitská 11 (☎222 540 963; www.hostelelf.com). Trams 5, 9, 26, Husinecká Tram stop. From the tram stop, follow Husinecká until you reach the square and then make a left at Orebitská, which will run into Husinecká right in front of the hostel. The perfect place to stay for those who wouldn't mind crashing on a couch in a friend's apartment. The common room is the center of hostel life, with 7 enormous, thoroughly lived-in couches and a communal kitchen nearby. Clean and simply furnished dorms with shared hall baths. Bike storage available. Breakfast included. Free Wi-Fi. Reception 24hr. Check-in 2pm. Check-out 10am. Dorms from 340Kč; singles 980Kč, with private bath 1230Kč; doubles 580/730Kč. 5% discounts in dorms for students. Cash only. ❶

Golden Sickle Hostel, Vodičkova 10 (☎222 230 773; www.goldensickle.com). Ⓜ️B: Karlovo náměstí. From the metro station, cross the park and then turn left on Vodičkova; there will be small signs on the wall directing you to the hostel. In a 16th-century building within view of New Town Hall. Clean, comfortable rooms overlooking a courtyard. Each dorm has its own bath and full kitchen. Hot breakfast can be arranged in advance for 100Kč. Towels and linens included. Free Wi-Fi and internet. Pickups from the airport 590Kč for groups of 1-4. Discounts at many nearby restaurants. Reception 9am-9pm, though arrangements can be made for late arrivals. Check-out 11am. Dorms 420Kč; 2-bed apartments 1680. Cash only. ❶

CZECH REPUBLIC

Czech Inn, Francouzská 76 (☎267 267 600; www.czech-inn.com). ⓜA: Náměstí Míru. From the metro, follow Francouzská for about 2/3 km; the hostel will be on your right. As sleek and sexy as a hotel can be. From the black porcelain sinks to the large, drunk-friendly numbers painted on the doors, this place has your comfort and sense of style close to its heart. Standard dorms but with taller, more imposing bedframes; smaller rooms come equipped with chandeliers and leather chairs. Breakfast 140Kč. Towels 100Kč. Free internet and Wi-Fi. Wheelchair-accessible. Reception 24hr. Check-in 2pm. Check-out 11am. Dorms from 472Kč; single suites 1694Kč; double suites 2057Kč. AmEx/MC/V. ❷

Miss Sophie's, Melounová 3 (☎296 303 530; www.missophies.com). ⓜC: IP Pavlova. Take 1st left from subway platform, then follow Katerinská to 1st right onto Melounová. This hostel is a little less centrally located than other places in Nové Město, but it makes up for its location with style to spare. Foregoes the worn-in, cozy feel of most small hostels for sleek, ultra modern bedroom furnishings. The dimly lit brick cellar would be the perfect place to smoke expensive cigarettes and chat suavely about deconstructivism, if smoking weren't banned. Kitchen available. Linens included. Free internet and Wi-Fi. Reception 24hr. Check-in 2pm. Check-out 11am. Dorms 590Kč; singles from 2100Kč. AmEx/MC/V.❷

Hostel U Melounu (by the Watermelons), Ke Karlovu 7 (☎224 918 322; www.hostelumelounu.cz). ⓜC: I.P. Pavlova. From the metro station, walk down Legerova and make a right on Ke Karlovu. Follow it around the corner; the hostel will be on your right. A little out of the way, but with comfortable, medium-sized dorms and an inviting, TV-equipped common room. The real selling points are the cottage-like private rooms opening out onto a garden. Breakfast included. Lockers with a 100Kč deposit. Towels with a 50Kč deposit. Laundry available. Free Wi-Fi. Parking 150Kč per day. Reception 24hr. Check-in 2pm. Check-out 10am. Dorms 400Kč; private rooms in shared garden-side apartment 850Kč, with personal bath 990Kč. MC/V. ❶

OUTSIDE THE CENTER

▨ **Sir Toby's,** Dělnická 24 (☎246 032 610; www.sirtobys.com). ⓜC: Nádraží Holešovice. From the metro, take the tram to Dělnická, walk to the corner of Dělnická, and turn left. Cultivates a welcoming, social atmosphere through thrice weekly film nights and a social cellar pub (beer 30Kč) furnished with antique bazaar decor. That's not to mention the lovely barbeque-ready terrace garden or the spacious and well-equipped guest kitchen. When you do need to turn in for the evening, you'll return to big, inviting rooms, some of which have been decorated with paintings from former guests. Buffet breakfast 100Kč. Laundry service 150Kč, self-service 100Kč. Free Wi-Fi. Wheelchairs can be accommodated with advanced notice. Reception 24hr. Check-in 3pm. Check-out 11am. Dorms 380-530Kč; singles 1400Kč; doubles 1950Kč. AmEx/MC/V. ❷

Plus Prague, Přívozní 1 (☎220 510 046; www.plusprague.com). ⓜC: Nádraží Holešovice. From the metro, take Verbenského east and then turn left on Přívozní. One of the most far-out hostels you're likely to find in Prague, but also one of the most resort-like. The massive complex can house up to 540 people, while the on-site restaurant, cafe, sauna, and swimming pool keep them entertained when they don't feel like making the trek to the city center. The pastel-colored dorms are nice enough, with desks and lamps, though the close-quarters of the bunks remind you that you are still, despite appearances, staying in a hostel. Breakfast 75Kč. Free Wi-Fi in lobby, computers 20Kč per 15min. Reception 24hr. Check-in 3pm. Check-out 10am. Dorms from 250Kč; triples 1290Kč. AmEx/MC/V. ❶

🍴 FOOD

The closer you are to the city center, the more you'll pay. You will be charged for everything the waiter brings to the table, so be sure to check your bill carefully. **Tesco,** Národní třída 26, has groceries. (Open M-F 7am-10pm, Sa 8am-8pm, Su 9am-8pm.) Look for the daily **market** in Staré Město where you can grab better deals. After a night out, grab a *párek v rohlíku* (hot dog) or a *smažený sýr* (fried cheese sandwich) from a Václavské nám. vendor.

RESTAURANTS

STARÉ MĚSTO

Klub architektů, Betlémské nám. 169/5A (☎224 401 214). Metro B: Národní třída. A 12th-century cellar with 21st-century ambience. Rub elbows with the locals in this intimate cavern of vaulted brick ceilings and low-hanging black lamps. The ostrich filet (320Kč) is a must for the adventurous diner. Veggie options 70-150Kč. Meat entrees 160-320Kč. Open daily 11:30am-midnight. AmEx/MC/V. ❸

Lehká Hlava (Clear Head), Borov 2 (☎222 220 665; www.lehkahlava.cz). Metro A: Staroměstská. Cooks up vegetarian and vegan cuisine that even devout carnivores will enjoy. Entrees 95-210Kč. Open M-F 11:30am-11:30pm; Sa and Su noon-11:30pm. Kitchen closed 2:30pm-5pm. Only cold food after 10pm. MC/V. ❷

Country Life, Melantrichova 15 (☎224 213 366). Metro A: Staroměstská. 3 extensive and fresh vegetarian buffets are a welcome respite from meat-heavy Czech cuisine. Buffet 20-50Kč per 100g. Soup 25Kč. Juices from 20Kč. Open M-Th 9am-8:30pm, F 8:30am-6pm, Su 11am-8:30pm. Cash only. ❷

Kozička, Kozí 1 (☎224 818 308; www.kozicka.cz). Metro A: Staroměstská. A relaxed Old Town restaurant with a unique goat theme. Metal statues of the frolicking creatures cover the walls and floor while diners select from a menu of Czech dishes like dumplings stuffed with spiced meat and spinach or the hearty goulash (both 160Kč). Entrees 120-350Kč. Open M-F noon-4am, Sa 6pm-4am, Su 6pm-3am. AmEx/MC/V. ❸

NOVÉ MĚSTO

Dynamo, Pštrossova 29 (☎224 932 020; www.restauracedynamo.com). Ⓜ B: Národní třída. From the metro stop, walk down Ostrovní toward the river and then turn left on Pštrossova; Dynamo is on the right. A great place to take a break while exploring the shops and bookstores in the area. Serves a mix of English-speakers and cool-looking locals in an award-winning restaurant. Full menu of duck, pork, and vegetarian options (135-180Kč); the

THE BIG SPLURGE

ROLLING ON THE RIVER

Tourists flock to the Charles Bridge to take in the sights of the Vltava River, but why not enjoy the view from on the river? The **Prague Dinner River Cruise** operates year-round, and takes passengers along a slow, scenic route with prime views of the Charles Bridge, Prague Castle, Malá Strana, and Vysehrad Fortress, amongst others. Aside from the trip itself, this is an excursion that will feed and entertain you as well. Passengers nosh on an extensive buffet of classic Czech dishes whilst enjoying the repertoire of the live jazz band on deck. The cruise is an ideal location for a great date, and even better for a bad one, since your gentleman or lady friend can't desert you halfway through.

Travelers on a budget tend to avoid this sort of excursion as prices are usually quite high, but the river cruise comes at a surprisingly reasonable rate which includes the cruise, dinner buffet, and entertainment—a bargain when you consider the price of a meal in Old Town Square. Cocktail attire is appropriate, so leave your grungy backpacking clothes at home and spruce it up a bit for this worthwhile night on the town.

Cruises depart nightly at 7pm for 3hrs. Boarding point is the river embankment by the city center, near the Charles Bridge. Reservations can be made at the Prague Tourist Office in Old Town Square, online at www.pragueexperience. com. Cost is 790Kč per person.

real jewel is the tomato, mozzarella, and basil bruschetta (75Kč). Free Wi-Fi. Open daily 11:30am-midnight. AmEx/DC/MC/V. ❷

☒ **Restaurace Stará Doba,** Gorazdoba 22 (☎224 922 511; www.staradoba.cz). Ⓜ️B: Karlovo náměstí. From Karlovo náměstí, turn left on Resslova and then left again on Gorazdoba, the street directly behind the Dancing House. Melted candles line the entry and an honest-to-God beaver pelt awaits you at the bottom of the spiral stairs. Unabashedly kitschy in the best way with delicious food. Make sure you ask for the English menu so you can appreciate gems like the "Highlander's well-earned meal" (stuffed chicken breast with spinach and basil sauce; 150Kč) and the suspiciously named "Yeomanly blow-out" (stuffed steak with pepper sauce; 240Kč). Open M-F 11am-11pm, Sa 5:30-11pm. Cash only. ❸

Pizzeria di Carlo, Karlovo náměstí 30 (☎222 231 374; www.dicarlo.cz). Ⓜ️B: Karlovo náměstí. From the metro station, walk to the other side of the park and turn left on Karlovo náměstí. Head through the arcade and down the stairs. A local favorite with a relaxed atmosphere and reasonably priced pizza and pasta. The tasteful decor, complete with black-and-white portraits of nondescript relatives, will make you feel like you're back in old country. Their 30 varieties of pizza (99-155Kč) and numerous pasta entrees include some unusual offerings like the tasty Riccardo III (smoked cheese, turkey, salami, and barbecue sauce; 135Kč). Outdoor seating available. Entrees 135-195Kč. Open M-F 11am-10:30pm, Sa-Su 11:30am-10:30pm. AmEx/D/MC/V. ❷

MALÁ STRANA

☒ **Bar bar,** Všehrdova 17 (☎257 313 246; www.bar-bar.cz). Ⓜ️A: Malostranská. From the metro, take the tram to Újezd, walk north on Újezd, and then turn right on Všehrdova. It's impossible to categorize this restaurant and bar with a zeal for combining things you would never imagine together. Unexpected hits include cheese-and-spinach-stuffed pancake topped with fried egg and bacon (129Kč) and Norwegian salmon with pesto and sun-dried tomato (159Kč). The decor is a similarly strange mix of abstract art and sculptures inside television sets. We don't know; we just go for the food. Savory pancakes 115-129Kč. Sweet pancakes 74-79Kč. Pasta 115-154Kč. Entrees 125-275Kč. Beer from 20Kč. Open M-Th and Su noon-midnight, F-Sa noon-2am. MC/V. ❷

☒ **Restaurace Carmelita,** Újezd 31 (☎257 312 564; www.restauracecarmelita.cz). Ⓜ️A: Malostranská. From the metro, take the tram to Újezd. Reasonably priced (if you avoid the entrees) Italian food served in a classy, but not stuffy atmosphere that locals and visitors alike can enjoy. Greater variety than most Italian places in the area, and the indecisive will appreciate the *quattro stagioni* pizza, which contains 4 of their specialty pizzas in 1 easily divided dish (145Kč). The *gnocchi al forno* (baked gnocchi with chicken, bacon, mushrooms, cream sauce; 169Kč) is as filling as it is delicious. Appetizers 85-159Kč. Salads 98-169Kč. Pasta 109-169Kč. Entrees 175-349Kč. Wheelchair-accessible. Open M-Sa 11am-midnight. Cash only. ❸

CAFES AND TEAHOUSES

☒ **Globe Bookstore and Cafe,** Pštrossova 6 (☎224 934 203; www.globebookstore.cz). Ⓜ️B: Karlovo náměstí. From the metro, take Resslova toward the river and then turn right on Na Zderaze, which becomes Pštrossova; the cafe is on your right. Owner of the largest collection of English-language books in Central Europe, the Globe is a favorite place for Anglophone expats to congregate. Even the poet Robert Creeley was known to stop by. In the evening, the Globe hosts a variety of events, including free classic movie screenings (Su 11pm) and trivia nights. Live music most weekends. Printing available and Wi-Fi 1Kč per min. Coffee and tea 50Kč. Espresso drinks 60-95Kč. Open daily 9:30am-1am. Kitchen open 9:30am-midnight. AmEx/MC/V. ❶

🖾 **Kavárna v Sedmém Nebi,** Zborovská 68 (☎257 318 110). Trams 6, 9, 12, 20, 22, 91, Újezd tram stop. From the tram, take Vítězná toward the river, then turn right on Zborovská. Bustling cafe and popular hangout for artists, intellectuals, and those who just like the smell of cloves. Manages to keep the feel of a neighborhood establishment just off Malá Strana's main drag. A selection of tasty sandwiches (75-90Kč) keeps intense conversations well-fueled all through the afternoon. Tea 25Kč. Espresso 29Kč. Beer 38Kč. Salads 75-95Kč. Free Wi-Fi. Open M-F 10am-1am, Sa noon-1am, Su noon-midnight. Cash only. ❶

🖾 **Čajovna Pod Stromem Čajovým,** Mánesova 55 (☎776 236 314). ⓂA: Jiřho z Poděbrad. From the metro station take Mánesova west; the teahouse is on your right. There's no better place to catch up on your Kafka or check your e-mail than in the no-shoes area of this vaguely Near Eastern-themed teahouse. Peruse a (non-English) menu of more than 100 varieties of tea from all over the world. Consider the delicious pita with edam cheese (50Kč) or one of their couscous dishes (74-88Kč). Open daily 10am-11pm. Cash only. ❶

👁 SIGHTS

Escape the crowds that flock to Prague's downtown sights by venturing away from **Staroměstské náměstí,** the **Charles Bridge,** and **Václavské náměstí.** There are plenty of attractions for visitors hidden in the old Jewish quarter of Josefov, the hills of **Vyšehrad,** and the streets of **Malá Strana.**

STARÉ MĚSTO (OLD TOWN)

Navigating the 1000-year-old Staré Město—a jumble of narrow streets and alleys—can be difficult. Once the sun sets, the ancient labyrinth comes alive with the city's youth, who enliven its many bars and jazz clubs.

CHARLES BRIDGE. Thronged with tourists and the hawkers who feed on them, the Charles Bridge (Karlův Most) is Prague's most treasured landmark. The defense towers on each side offer splendid views. Five stars and a cross mark the spot where, according to legend, St. Jan Nepomuck was tossed over the side of the bridge for concealing the queen's extramarital secrets from a suspicious King Wenceslas IV in the 14th century. (Metro A: Malostranská or Staroměstská.)

OLD TOWN SQUARE. Staroměstské náměstí (Old Town Square) is the heart of Staré Město, surrounded by eight magnificent towers. (Metro A: Staroměstská; Metro A or B: Můstek.) Composed of several different architectural styles, the **Staroměstské Radnice** (Old Town Hall) has been missing a piece of its front facade since the Nazis partially demolished it in the final days of WWII. Crowds gather on the hour to watch the **astronomical clock** chime as skeletal Death empties his hourglass and a procession of apostles marches by. (Exhibition hall open in summer M 10am-7pm, Tu-F 9am-7pm, Sa-Su 9am-6pm. Clock tower open M 11am-6pm, T-Su 9am-6pm; enter through 3rd fl. of Old Town Hall. Exhibition hall 20Kč, students 10Kč. Clock tower 60/40Kč.) The spires of **Týn Church** (Chrám Matky Boží před Týnem) rise above a mass of baroque homes. Buried inside is astronomer Tycho Brahe, whose overindulgence at Emperor Rudolf's lavish dinner party in 1601 may have cost him his life. Since it was deemed improper to leave the table unless the emperor himself did so, Tycho had to remain in his chair until his bladder burst. He died 11 days later, though scholars believe mercury poisoning may have been the culprit. (Open T-Sa 10am-1pm and 3pm-5pm. Mass T, F 5pm, W, Th 5pm, Sa 8am, Su 9:30am and 9pm. Free.) The bronze statue of 15th-century theologian **Jan Hus,** the country's most famous martyr, stands in the middle of the square. Barely a surface in **St. James's Church** (Kostel sv. Jakuba) remains un-figured, un-marbleized, or unpainted. But keep your hands to yourself—legend has it that 500 years ago a thief tried to pilfer a gem from the Virgin Mary of Suffering, whereupon the figure sprang to life and yanked off his arm. *(Metro B: Staroměstská. On Malá Štupartská, behind Týn Church. Open M-Sa 10am-noon and 2-3:45pm. Mass Su 8, 9, and 10:30am.)*

NOVÉ MĚSTO (NEW TOWN)

Established in 1348 by Charles IV, Nové Město has become Prague's commercial center. The Franciscan Gardens offer an oasis from the bustling businesses.

WENCESLAS SQUARE. More a commercial boulevard than a square, **Václavské náměstí** (Wenceslas Square) owes its name to the statue of 10th-century Czech ruler and patron **Saint Wenceslas** (Václav) that stands in front of the National Museum. At his feet in solemn prayer kneel smaller statues of the country's other patron saints: St. Agnes, St. Adalbert (Vojtěch), St. Ludmila, and St. Prokop. The sculptor, Josef Václav Myslbek, took 25 years to complete the statue. The inscription under St. Wenceslas reads, "Do not let us and our descendants perish." *(Metro A or B: Můstek or Metro A or C: Muzeum.)*

FRANCISCAN GARDEN AND VELVET REVOLUTION MEMORIAL. Franciscan monks somehow manage to preserve this serene **rose garden** in the heart of Prague's commercial district. *(Metro A or B: Můstek. Enter through the arch to the left of Jungmannova and Národní, behind the statue. Open daily from mid-Apr. to mid-Sept. 7am-10pm; from mid-Sept. to mid-Oct. from 7am-8pm; mid-Oct. to mid-Apr. 8am-7pm. Free.)* Down the street on Národní, a **plaque** under the arcades and across from the Black Theatre memorializes the citizens beaten by police in a 1989 protest. A subsequent wave of protests led to the collapse of communism in Czechoslovakia.

DANCING HOUSE. American architect Frank Gehry (of Guggenheim-Bilbao fame) built the gently swaying **Tančící dům** (Dancing House) at the corner of Resslova and Rašínovo nábřeží. Since its 1996 unveiling, it has been called an eyesore by some and a shining example of postmodern design by others. *(Metro B: Karlovo nám. As you walk down Resslova toward the river, the building is on the left.)*

JOSEFOV

Josefov, Central Europe's oldest Jewish settlement, lies north of Staroměstské nám., along Maiselova. In 1180, Prague's citizens built a 4m wall around the area. The closed neighborhood bred exotic tales, many of which centered around **Rabbi Loew ben Bezalel** (1512-1609) and his legendary Golem—a mud creature that supposedly came to life to protect Prague's Jews. The city's Jews remained clustered in Josefov until WWII, when the Nazis sent the residents to death camps. Ironically, Hitler's decision to create a "museum of an extinct race" sparked the preservation of Josefov's cemetery and synagogues.

SYNAGOGUES. The **Maiselova synagoga** (Maisel Synagogue) displays artifacts from the Jewish Museum's collections, returned to the community in 1994. *(On Maiselova, between Široká and Jáchymova.)* Turn left on Široká to reach the **Pinkasova** (Pinkas Synagogue). Drawings by children interred at the Terezín camp are upstairs. Some 80,000 names line the walls downstairs, a sobering requiem for Czech Jews persecuted in the Holocaust. Backtrack along Široká and go left on Maiselova to reach Europe's oldest operating synagogue, the 700-year-old **Staronová** (Old-New Synagogue), still the religious center of Prague's Jewish community. Up Široká at Dušní, the **Španělská** (Spanish Synagogue) has an ornate Moorish interior and was first in adopting the 1830s Reform movement. *(Ⓜ A: Staroměstská. Synagogues open M-F and Su Apr.-Oct. 9am-6pm; Nov.-Mar. 9am-4:30pm. Closed Jewish holidays. Admission to all synagogues except Staronová 300Kč, students 200Kč. Staronová 200/140Kč. Combined tickets 480/320Kč. Men must cover their heads; yarmulke free. AmEx/MC/V.)*

OLD JEWISH CEMETERY. Filled with thousands of broken headstones, the Old Jewish Cemetery (Starý židovský hřbitov) stretches between the Pinkas Synagogue and the Ceremonial Hall. Between the 14th and 18th centuries, the graves were dug in layers. Rabbi Loew is buried by the wall opposite the entrance, found at the corner of Široká and Žatecká.

MALÁ STRANA

A criminals' and counter-revolutionaries' hangout for nearly a century, the streets of Malá Strana have become prized real estate. In **Malostranské Náměstí**, the towering dome of the Baroque **St. Nicholas's Cathedral** (Chrám sv. Mikuláše) is one of Prague's most prominent landmarks. Mozart played the organ here when he visited Prague, and the cathedral now hosts nightly classical music concerts. *(Malostranské náměstí 26. ⓜA: Malostranská. From the metro, take Letenská to Malostranské náměstí. ☎ 257 534 215. Open Nov.-Feb. 9am-4pm daily, Mar.-Oct. 9am-5pm daily. Last entry 15min. before closing. Concerts start around 6pm. Admission 70Kč, students 35Kč. Concerts 490/300Kč. Cash only.)* Along Letenská, a wooden gate opens into the **Wallenstein Garden** (Valdštejnská zahrada). One of the city's best-kept secrets, a beautifully tended stretch of green and a bronze Venus fountain makes a beautiful sight.*(Vadštejnské náměstí 4. ⓜA: Malostranská. From the metro, take Klárov north and then turn left on Vadštejnské. ☎ 257 072 759. Palace open Sa-Su 10am-4pm. Gardens open June-Aug. M-F 7:30am-7pm, Sa-Su 10am-5pm. Last entry 30min. before closing. Gardens wheelchair-accessible. Free.)* The **Church of Our Lady Victorious** (Kostel Panny Marie Vítězné) contains the famous wax statue of the **Infant Jesus of Prague**, said to bestow miracles on the faithful. *(Karmelitská 9. Trams 12, 20, 22, 91, Hellichova tram stop. From the tram, head north on Karmelitská. ☎ 257 533 646; www.pragjesu.info. Open M-Sa 8:30am-7pm, Su 8:30am-8pm. Museum open M-Sa 9:30am-5:30pm, Su 1-7pm. Free.)* **Petřín Gardens and View Tower,** on the hill beside Malá Strana, provide a tranquil retreat with spectacular views. Climb the steep, serene footpath, or take the funicular from above the intersection of Vítězná and Újezd. *((Open Apr.-Oct. 7am-10pm daily. Open Nov.-Mar. weekends 10am-5pm. Wheelchair-accessible. 100Kč, students 50Kč.)* While in Mala Strana, take a detour down Velkopřevorské to check out the **John Lennon wall,** a previously ordinary structure that has been covered with Lennon-related graffiti including Beatles song lyrics, peace signs, and paintings of the singer.

PRAGUE CASTLE (PRAŽSKÝ HRAD)

Prague Castle, one of the world's biggest castles, has symbolized the Czech government for over 1000 years. Since the Bohemian royal family established their residence here, the castle has housed Holy Roman Emperors, the Communist Czechoslovak government, and now the Czech Republic's president. In the **Royal Gardens** (Královská zahrada), the **Singing Fountain** spouts its harp-like tune before the **Royal Summer Palace.** *Take tram #22 or 23 from the center, get off at "Pražský hrad," and go down U Prašného Mostu past the Royal Gardens and into the Second Courtyard. Or, hike up Nerudova. ☎ 224 373 368; www.hrad.cz. Open daily Apr.-Oct. 9am-5pm; Nov.-Mar. 9am-4pm. Castle grounds open Apr.-Oct. 5am-midnight; Nov.-Mar. 9am-midnight. Ticket office and info located opposite St. Vitus's Cathedral, inside the castle walls. Tickets come in 4 different flavors. The Long Tour (350Kč, students 175Kč) gets you everything, while the Short Tour (250/125Kč) covers the most important things. Tickets valid for 2 consecutive days.*

ST. VITUS'S CATHEDRAL. Inside the castle walls stands the beautiful Gothic St. Vitus's Cathedral (Katedrála sv. Víta) which was completed in 1929 after 600 years of construction. To the right of the altar stands the silver **tomb of St. Jan Nepomuck.** In the main church, precious stones and paintings telling the saint's story line the walls of **St. Wenceslas Chapel** (Svatováclavská kaple). Climb the 287 steps of the **Great South Tower** for an excellent view, or descend underground to the **Royal Crypt** (Královská hrobka), which holds the tomb of Charles IV.

OLD ROYAL PALACE. The Old Royal Palace (Starý královský palác), to the right of the cathedral, is one of the few Czech castles where visitors can wander largely unattended. The lengthy **Vladislav Hall** once hosted jousting competitions. Upstairs in the Chancellery of Bohemia, a Protestant assembly found two Catholic governors guilty of religious persecution and threw them out the window during the 1618 Second Defenestration of Prague.

ST. GEORGE'S BASILICA AND ENVIRONS. Across from the Old Royal Palace stands St. George's Basilica (Bazilika sv. Jiří), where the skeleton of St. Ludmila is on display. The convent next door houses the National Gallery of Bohemian Art. *(Open Tu-Su 10am-6pm. 100Kč, students 50Kč.)* To the right of the Basilica, follow Jiřská halfway down and take a right on **Golden Lane** (Zlatá ulička), a former workspace of alchemists. Franz Kafka had his workspace at #22.

🏛 MUSEUMS

MUCHA MUSEUM. The museum is devoted to the work of Alfons Mucha, the Czech's most celebrated artist. Mucha, an Art Nouveau pioneer, gained fame for his poster series of "la divine" Sarah Bernhardt. *(Panská 7. Ⓜ A or B: Můstek. Walk up Václavské náměstí toward the St. Wenceslas statue. Go left on Jindřišská and left on Panská. ☎ 221 451 333; www.mucha.cz. Open daily 10am-6pm. 120Kč, students 60Kč. AmEx/MC/V.)*

FRANZ KAFKA MUSEUM. This fantastic multimedia exhibit of Kafka memorabilia uses photographs and original letters to bring visitors back to 19th-century Prague, as experienced by the renowned author. *(Cihelná 2b. Ⓜ A: Malostranská. Go down Klárov toward the river, turn right on U. Luzické Semináré and left on Cilhená. ☎ 257 535 507; www.kafkamuseum.cz. Open daily 10am-6pm. 120Kč, students 60Kč. MC/V.)*

MUSEUM OF MINIATURES. Devoted to the work of Siberian artist Anatolij Koněnko, the museum's forty exhibits all require either a magnifying glass or a microscope to view and could be carried in a purse, if they weren't bolted to the table. The collection features everything from miniature reproductions of works by Leonardo DaVinci, Matisse, and Dali to portraits of John Lennon and Václav Havel on poppy seeds. Some of the more exciting pieces include a menagerie on the wing of a mosquito and a caravan of camels passing through the eye of a needle, though the museum's greatest treasure is a 0.9mm x 0.9mm book containing the text of a Chekhov story along with illustrations. *(Strahovské nádvoří 11. ☎ 233 352 371. Tram 22, Pohořelec tram* *stop. From the tram, walk south, make a right on Dlabačov, and then make a sharp left onto Strahovské nádvoří. Wheelchair-accessible. Open daily 10am-5pm. 50Kč, students 30Kč. D/MC/V.)*

MUSEUM OF ▧COMMUNISM. Located above a McDonald's and next to a casino, this gallery attempts to explore the dream, reality, and nightmare of life under Communism in Czechoslovakia through a mix of audiovisual aids and artifacts from daily life. The museum truly outdoes itself in its elementary-school-style poster board displays. Unfortunately, the museum's gift shop and publicity posters have a much better sense of humor than the museum itself. *(Na Příkopě 10. Ⓜ️A: Můstek. ☎ 224 212 966; www.museumofcommunism.com. Open daily 9am-9pm. 180Kč, students 140Kč. Cash only.)*

♫ ENTERTAINMENT

For information on Prague's concerts and performances, consult *The Prague Post*, *Threshold*, *Do mesta-Downtown*, or *The Pill* (all free at many cafes and restaurants). Most performances start at 7 or 8pm and offer rush tickets 30min. before curtain. The majority of Prague's theaters close in July and August. Late spring and early summer usually bring an array of regular and one-off festivals. The **Prague Spring International Music Festival** (☎257 312 547; www.prague-spring. net), which runs from mid-May to early June, has weathered six decades of political and artistic turmoil yet continues to draw musicians from around the world. Every year a number of Czech and international composers and musicians debut material. Leonard Bernstein made his international debut at the festival in 1946-7. June brings all things avant-garde with the **Prague Fringe Festival** (☎224 935 183; www.praguefringe.com), featuring dancers, comedians, performance artists, and—everyone's favorite—mimes in a different venue every day. That same month, the **Prague Writers' Festival** (☎224 241 312; www.pwf.cz) brings renowned writers of all languages together for a week-long discussion covering current topics in literature and culture. At this series of public readings, rountables, and panel discussions, audience participation is welcome. Most readings are subtitled in Czech and English. Now entering its sixth year, the **United Islands of Prague** (☎257 325 041; www.unitedislands.cz) attracts more than 100 bands and a crowd of eager backpackers from across the globe. The free and open festival spans several days and multiple islands on both sides of the Vltava. For tickets to the city's shows, try **Bohemia Ticket International,** Malé náměstí 13, next to Čedok. (☎224 227 832; www.ticketsbti.cz. Open M-F 9am-5pm, Sa 9am-1pm.)

▧ NIGHTLIFE

With some of the world's best beer on tap, it's no surprise that pubs and beer halls are Prague's most popular nighttime hangouts. Tourists overrun the city center, so authentic pub experiences are largely restricted to the suburbs and outlying Metro stops. Locals prefer the many jazz and rock hangouts scattered throughout the city.

▧ **Harley's,** Dlouhá 18 (☎227 195 195; www.harleys.cz). Ⓜ️B: Náměstí Republiky. From the metro, walk north on Revoluční and then make a left on Dlouhá. A bar for travelers with a love for Harley Davidsons and Jack Daniels. The rough and tough exterior belies a surprisingly sophisticated bar, offering over 200 drink options. For Epicureans, Cuban cigars and Havana Rum are an added draw. Not surprisingly, the Prague chapter of the Hell's Angels are fans and occasionally stop by. Rock and dance DJs nightly. Beer 55Kč. Mixed drinks 100-130Kč. Open daily 7pm-6am. Cash only.

▧ **Klub Újezd,** Újezd 18 (☎257 570 873; www.klubujezd.cz). Ⓜ️A: Malostranská. From the metro, take the tram to the Újezd stop. Local gathering place for young Czech artists, poets, and punks. 3 levels provide slight variations on the same theme. The paintings, drawings, and collages that line the walls run the gamut from amusing to confusing to alarming. On warm summer nights, the ground floor opens up and the party spills onto the sidewalk. Weekend DJs spin a mix of punk, ska, and old school hip hop. Beer 35Kč. Shots 30-120Kč. Wheelchair-accessible. Open daily 2pm-4am. Cash only.

Hapu, Orlická 8 (☎775 109 331). Ⓜ️A: Flora. From the metro, walk west on Vinohradská and then make a right on Orlická. Something of a bartender's bar, this inconspicuous little place serves some of the most creative and best-mixed cocktails in Prague. The extensive and constantly changing mixed drink menu includes a ½-dozen members of the Collins drink family as well as more suspect options like "Alien Secretion" (120Kč). Beer 35Kč. Mixed drinks 80-140Kč. Open daily 6pm-2am. Cash only.

Blind Eye, Vlkova 26 (www.blindeye.cz). Trams 5, 9, 26, Husinecká tram stop. From the tram, walk east on Seifertova, then make a right on Krásova; the bar is at the corner. Named after the one-eyed Jan Žižka who lends his name to the entire neighborhood. Small, dark, rowdy, but much-loved by area expats and well-informed travelers. Regular DJs and live rock shows in an intimate atmosphere. A wide assortment of drinks you couldn't describe to your mother, including "Sex with the Bartender" (150Kč) and the appropriately named "Adios, Motherf***er" (195Kč). Beer 22Kč. Most mixed drinks 60-100Kč. Karaoke M night. Wheelchair-accessible. Open 7pm-late. Cash only.

Cross Club, Plynární 23 (☎736 535 053; www.crossclub.cz). Ⓜ️C: Nádraží Holešovice. From the metro, take Verbenského east and then turn right onto Argentinská and right onto Plynární. An impossible-to-categorize mix of bar, cafe, club, and rock venue. DJs and live acts of all stripes encourage people to get out of their comfort zones. The best part, though, may be the club itself, with its awesome, if bizarre, sense of aesthetics. Chill out in the bungalow-esque bar area before descending into the always-crowded techno-industrial-themed downstairs, lit by all manner of glowing, flashing, and spinning contraptions. Beer 20Kč. Shots 50-100Kč. Mixed drinks 85-95Kč. Cover varies, usually 75-100Kč. Open daily 4pm-late. Cash only.

Vagon Music Pub and Club, Národní třída 25 (☎221 085 599; www.vagon.cz). Ⓜ️B: Národní třída. Near the station down a flight of stairs. A favorite haunt of local musicians with spiked haircuts, this club is always friendly and never too crowded, despite what its punk-rock image may suggest. Local acts play fast and hard while their fans dance frantically in the intimate concert area. Seating and foosball tables give sweaty moshers a place to cool down. Beer 26Kč. Cover 100Kč. Open M-Sa 7pm-5am, Su 7pm-1am.

DENMARK
(DANMARK)

Straddling the border between Scandinavia and continental Europe, Denmark packs majestic castles, pristine beaches, and thriving nightlife onto the compact Jutland peninsula and its network of islands. Vibrant Copenhagen boasts the busy pedestrian thoroughfare of Strøget and the world's tallest carousel in Tivoli Gardens, while beyond the city, fairytale lovers can tour Hans Christian Andersen's home in rural Odense. In spite of the nation's historically homogenous population, its Viking past has given way to a dynamic multicultural society that draws in visitors as it turns out Legos and Skagen watches.

> ### DISCOVER DENMARK: SUGGESTED ITINERARIES

THREE DAYS. Start off in the capital of **Copenhagen** (p. 204), soaking up some sun on a bike tour (p. 208) of the city or waiting out showers in the medieval ruins beneath **Christianborg Slot.** Channel the Bard at Kronborg Slot in **Helsingør** (p. 212), where the real-life Hamlet slept.

ONE WEEK. Begin your journey in **Copenhagen** (5 days), then castle-hop to Frederiksborg Slot in nearby **Hillerød** (1 day; p. 212). Another daytrip, **Humlebæk and Rungsted** (1 day), is home to one of the best art museums you've never heard of.

ESSENTIALS

FACTS AND FIGURES

OFFICIAL NAME: Kingdom of Denmark.

CAPITAL: Copenhagen.

MAJOR CITIES: Aalborg, Århus, Odense.

POPULATION: 5,485,000.

LAND AREA: 42,400 sq. km.

TIME ZONE: GMT +1.

LANGUAGES: Danish. Pockets of Faroese, Greenlandic, and German. English is nearly universal as a second language.

TALLEST LEGO TOWER: Constructed in 2003 at Billund's Legoland; 27.22m.

WHEN TO GO

Denmark is best between May and September, when days are usually sunny and temperatures average 10-16°C (50-61°F). Winter temperatures average 0°C (32°F). Although temperate for its northern location, Denmark can turn rainy or cool at a moment's notice; always pack a sweater and an umbrella.

DOCUMENTS AND FORMALITIES

EMBASSIES AND CONSULATES. All foreign embassies are in Copenhagen (p. 205). Danish embassies abroad include: **Australia,** Gold Fields House, Level

14, 1 Alfred St., Circular Quay, Sydney, NSW, 2000 (☎02 92 47 22 24; www.
gksydney.um.dk/en); **Canada,** 47 Clarence St., Ste. 450, Ottawa, ON, K1N
9K1 (☎613-562-1811; www.ambottawa.um.dk/en); **Ireland,** Harcourt Road,
7th floor, Block E, Iveagh Court, Dublin 2 (☎01 475 6404; www.ambdublin.
um.dk/en); **New Zealand,** Forsyth Barr House, Level 7, 45 Johnston Street,
P.O. Box 10-874, Wellington, 6036 (☎04 471 0520; www.danishconsulatesnz.
org.nz); **UK,** 55 Sloane St., London, SW1X 9SR (☎020 73 33 02 00; www.
amblondon.um.dk/en); **US,** 3200 Whitehaven St., NW, Washington, D.C.,
20008 (☎202-234-4300; www.denmarkemb.org).

VISA AND ENTRY INFORMATION. EU citizens don't need visas. Citizens of Australia, Canada, New Zealand, and the US do not need a visa for stays of up to
90 days, beginning upon entry into any of the countries in the EU's freedom-
of-movement zone. For stays longer than 90 days, non-EU citizens need a residence or work permit. For more info visit www.um.dk/en.

TOURIST SERVICES AND MONEY

EMERGENCY Ambulance, Fire, and **Police:** ☎112.

TOURIST OFFICES. The **Danish Tourist Board** has offices in most cities throughout the country, with its main office in Copenhagen at Islands Brygge 43 (☎3288 9900; www.visitdenmark.dt.dk). The website offers a wealth of info as well as an online booking tool for accommodations.

MONEY. The Danish unit of currency is the **krone (kr)**, plural **kroner.** One krone is equal to 100 **øre.** The easiest way to get cash is from **ATMs**; cash cards are widely accepted, and many machines give advances on **credit cards.** Money and **traveler's checks** can be exchanged at most **banks** for a 30kr fee. Denmark has a high cost of living, which it passes along to visitors; expect to pay 100-150kr for a hostel bed, 80-130kr for a day's groceries, and 50-90kr for a cheap restaurant meal. A bare-bones day might cost 250-350kr, and a slightly more comfortable one 400-600kr. There are no hard and fast rules for **tipping.** Service at restaurants is typically included in the bill, but it's always polite to round up to the nearest 10kr, and to leave an additional 10-20kr for good service.

Denmark has a 25% **value added tax (VAT)**, a sales tax applied to most goods and services. The prices given in *Let's Go* include VAT. In the airport upon exiting the EU, non-EU citizens can claim a refund on the tax paid for goods purchased at participating stores. In order to qualify for a refund in a store, you must spend at least 300kr; make sure to ask for a refund form when you pay. For more info on qualifying for a VAT refund, see p. 19. Exchange rates:

DANISH KRONER (KR)		
	AUS$1 = 4.42KR	10KR = AUS$2.26
	CDN$1 = 4.63KR	10KR = CDN$2.16
	EUR€1 = 7.46KR	10KR = EUR€1.34
	NZ$1 = 3.49KR	10KR = NZ$2.86
	UK£1 = 9.42KR	10KR = UK£1.06
	US$1 = 4.82KR	10KR = US$2.08

BUSINESS HOURS. Shops are normally open Monday to Thursday from about 9 or 10am to 6pm and Friday until 7 or 8pm; they are always open Saturday mornings and in Copenhagen, they stay open all day Saturday. Regular banking hours are Monday to Wednesday and Friday 10am-4pm, Thursday 10am-6pm.

TRANSPORTATION

BY PLANE. International flights arrive at **Kastrup Airport** in Copenhagen (**CPH**; ☎3231 3231; www.cph.dk). Flights from Europe also arrive at **Billund Airport**, outside Århus (**BLL**; ☎7650 5050; www.billund-airport.dk). Smaller airports in Århus and Esbjerg serve as hubs for budget airline **Ryanair** (☎353 12 49 77 91; www.ryanair.com). **SAS** (Scandinavian Airlines; Denmark ☎70 10 20 00, UK 0870 60 72 77 27, US 800-221-2350; www.scandinavian.net), the national airline company, offers youth discounts to some destinations.

BY TRAIN AND BY BUS. The state-run rail line in Denmark is **DSB**; their helpful route planner is online at www.rejseplanen.dk. **Eurail** is valid on all state-run routes. The **ScanRail** pass is good for rail travel through Denmark, Finland, Norway, and Sweden, as well as many discounted ferry and bus rides. Remote towns are typically served by buses from the nearest train station. Buses are reliable and can be less expensive than trains.

DENMARK

RAIL SAVINGS. ScanRail passes purchased outside Scandinavia may be cheaper, depending on the exchange rate, and they are also more flexible. Travelers who purchase passes within Scandinavia can only use three travel days in the country of purchase. Check www.scanrail.com for more info.

BY FERRY. Several companies operate ferries to and from Denmark. **Scandlines** (☎33 15 15 15; www.scandlines.dk) arrives from Germany and Sweden and also operates domestic routes. **Color Line** (Norway ☎47 81 00 08 11; www.colorline.com) runs ferries between Denmark and Norway. **DFDS Seaways** (UK ☎08715 229 955; www.dfdsseaways.co.uk) sails from Harwich, BRI to Esbjerg and from Copenhagen to Oslo, NOR. For more info, check www.aferry.to/ferry-to-denmark-ferries.htm. Tourist offices help sort out the dozens of smaller ferries that serve Denmark's outlying islands. For more info on connections from Bornholm to Sweden, and from Jutland to Norway and Sweden, see p. 53.

BY BIKE AND BY THUMB. With its flat terrain and well-marked bike routes, Denmark is a cyclist's dream. You can rent bikes (50-80kr per day) from designated shops as well as from some tourist offices and train stations. The **Dansk Cyklist Forbund** (☎3332 3121; www.dcf.dk) provides info about cycling in Denmark and investing in long-term rentals. Pick up *Bikes and Trains* at any train station for info on bringing your bike on a train, which can cost up to 50kr. **Hitchhiking** on motorways is illegal. *Let's Go* does not recommend hitchhiking.

KEEPING IN TOUCH

PHONE CODES	**Country code: 45. International dialing prefix:** 00. For more info on how to place international calls, see **Inside Back Cover.**

EMAIL AND THE INTERNET. In Copenhagen and other cities, you can generally find at least one Internet cafe; expect to pay 15-30kr per hr. DSB, the national railroad, maintains Internet cafes in some stations as well. In smaller towns, access at public libraries is free; reserve a slot in advance.

TELEPHONE. Pay phones accept both coins and phone cards, available at post offices or kiosks in 100kr denominations. **Mobile phones** (p. 29) are a popular and economical alternative. For domestic directory info, dial ☎118; for international info, dial ☎113. International direct dial numbers include: **AT&T Direct** (☎8001 0010); **Canada Direct** (☎8001 0011); **MCI WorldPhone** (☎8001 0022); Sprint (☎8001 0877); **Telecom New Zealand** (☎8001 0064).

MAIL. Mailing a postcard or letter to Australia, Canada, New Zealand, or the US costs 8kr; to elsewhere in Europe it costs 7kr. Domestic mail costs 4.50kr.

ACCOMMODATIONS AND CAMPING

DENMARK	❶	❷	❸	❹	❺
ACCOMMODATIONS	under 100kr	100-160kr	161-220kr	221-350kr	over 350kr

Denmark's hotels are uniformly expensive, so **youth hostels** *(vandrehjem)* tend to be mobbed by budget travelers of all ages. HI-affiliated **Danhostels** are the most common and are often the only option in smaller towns. Facilities are clean, spacious, and comfortable, often attracting families as well as back-packers. Eco-conscious tourists can choose from one of the six Danhostels that have earned a **Green Key** (www.green-key.org) for their environmentally friendly practices. Room rates vary according to season and location; dorms range from 100 to 200kr per night, with a 35kr HI discount. Linens cost 40-60kr; sleeping bags are not permitted. Reserve ahead, especially in summer and near beaches. Danhostel check-in times are usually a non-negotiable 3-4hr. window. For more info, contact the **Danish Youth Hostel Association** (☎3331 3612; www.danhostel.dk). Independent hostels, found mostly in cities and larger towns, draw a younger crowd and tend to be more sociable, although their facilities are rarely as nice as those in Danhostels. Most tourist offices can book rooms for stays in **private homes** (150-250kr).

Denmark's 496 **campgrounds** (about 60kr per person) range from one star (toilets and drinking water) to three stars (showers and laundry) to five stars (swimming, restaurants, and stoves). Info is available at **DK-Camp** (☎7571 2962; www.dk-camp.dk). You'll need a **Camping Card Scandinavia** (125kr for 1yr. membership; available at www.camping.se; allow at least 3 weeks for delivery), valid across Scandinavia and sold at campgrounds as well as through the Danish Youth Hostel Association. Campsites affiliated with hostels generally do not require a card. If you plan to camp for only a night, you can buy a 24hr. pass (20kr). The **Danish Camping Council** *(Campingrådet)*, Mosedalvej 15, 2500 Valby (☎39 27 88 44; www.campingraadet.dk), sells passes and the *Camping Denmark* handbook (95kr). Sleeping in train stations, in parks, or anywhere on public property is illegal in Denmark.

FOOD AND DRINK

DENMARK	❶	❷	❸	❹	❺
FOOD	under 40kr	40-70kr	71-100kr	101-150kr	over 150kr

A "danish" in Denmark is a *wienerbrød* (Viennese bread), found in bakeries alongside other flaky treats. Traditionally, Danes have favored open-faced sandwiches called *smørrebrød* for a more substantial meal. For cheap eats, look for lunch specials *(dagens ret)* and all-you-can-eat buffets. National beers include Carlsberg and Tuborg; bottled brews tend to be cheaper than drafts. A popular alcohol is *snaps* (or *aquavit*), a clear liquor flavored with fiery spices, usually served chilled and unmixed. Many vegetarian *(vegetarret)* options are the result of Indian and Mediterranean influences, and salads and veggies *(grønsager)* can be found on most menus. Expect to pay around 120kr for a sit-down meal at a restaurant and 40-80kr in cafes and ethnic takeouts.

HOLIDAYS AND FESTIVALS

Holidays: New Year's Day (Jan. 1); Easter (Apr. 12); Queen's Birthday (Apr. 16); Worker's Day (May 1); Whit Sunday and Monday (May 11-12); Constitution Day (June 5); Mid-summer's Eve (June 23); Christmas (Dec. 24-26).

Festivals: In early Spring before the start of Lent, Danish children assault candy-filled barrels with birch branches on **Fastelavn** (Shrovetide), while adults take to the streets for carnivals. Guitar solos ring out over Roskilde during the **Roskilde Festival** (July 3-6), just before Copenhagen and Århus kick off their annual **jazz festivals,** mid-to-late July.

BEYOND TOURISM

For short-term employment in Denmark, check www.jobs-in-europe.net; For opportunities across Europe, see the **Beyond Tourism** chapter p. 55.

The American-Scandinavian Foundation (AMSCAN), 58 Park Ave., New York, NY, 10016, USA (☎212-879-9779; www.amscan.org/jobs/index.html). Volunteer and job opportunities throughout Scandinavia.

Vi Hjælper Hinanden (VHH), Aasenv. 35, 9881 Bindslev, DEN, c/o Inga Nielsen (☎98 93 86 07; www.wwoof.dk). For 50kr, the Danish branch of World-Wide Opportunities on Organic Farms (WWOOF) provides a list of farmers currently accepting volunteers.

COPENHAGEN (KØBENHAVN)

The center of Europe's oldest monarchy, Copenhagen (pop. 1,800,000) embodies a laid-back spirit. The Strøget, the city's famed pedestrian thoroughfare, now bustles with Middle Eastern restaurants and cybercafes, and neon signs glimmer next to angels in the architecture. The up-and-coming districts of Vesterbro and Nørrebro reverberate with some of Europe's wildest nightlife, while the hippie paradise of Christiania swings to a more downbeat vibe.

✈ INTERCITY TRANSPORTATION

Flights: Kastrup Airport (CPH; ☎3231 3231; www.cph.dk). **Trains** connect the airport to København H (13min., 6 per hr., 20kr or 2 clips). Ryanair flies into nearby **Sturup Airport** in Malmö, SWE **(MMX;** ☎40 613 1000; www.sturup.com) at low rates.

Trains: København H (Hovedbanegården or Central Station; domestic travel ☎7013 1415, international 7013 1416; www.dsb.dk). Trains run to: **Berlin, GER** (8hr., 9 per day, 803kr); **Hamburg, GER** (5hr., 5 per day, 537kr); **Malmö, SWE** (25min., every 20min., 71kr); **Oslo, NOR** (8hr., 2 per day, 821kr); **Stockholm, SWE** (5hr., 1 per 1-2hr., 1040kr). For international trips, fares depend on seat availability and can drop to as low as 50% of the quotes listed above; ▓**book at least 2 weeks in advance.**

✦ ORIENTATION

Copenhagen lies on the east coast of the island of **Zealand** *(Sjælland)*, across the Øresund Sound from Malmö, Sweden. The 28km **Øresund Bridge,** which opened on July 1, 2000, established the first "fixed link" between the two countries. Copenhagen's main train station, København H, lies near the city center. Just north of the station, **Vesterbrogade** passes **Tivoli** and **Rådhuspladsen,** the main square, then cuts through the city center as **Strøget** (STROY-yet), the world's longest pedestrian thoroughfare. As it heads east, Strøget goes through a series of names: **Frederiksberggade, Nygade, Vimmelskaftet, Amagertorv,** and **Østergade.** The city center is bordered to the west by five **lakes,** outside of which are the less-touristy communities of **Vesterbro, Nørrebro,** and **Østerbro.** Vesterbro and Nørrebro are home to many of the region's immigrants, while some of Copenhagen's highest-income residents live on the wide streets of Østerbro.

⊡ LOCAL TRANSPORTATION

Public Transportation: Copenhagen has an extensive public transportation system. **Buses** (☎3313 1415; www.moviatrafik.dk) run daily 5:30am-12:30am; maps are available on any bus.

S-togs (subways and suburban trains; ☎3314 1701) run M-Sa 5am-12:30am, Su 6am-12:30am. S-tog tickets are covered by Eurail, ScanRail, and InterRail passes.

Metro (☎015 1615; www.m.dk) is small but efficient. All 3 types of public transportation operate on a zone system. To travel any distance, a 2-zone **ticket** is required (19kr; additional zones 9.50kr), which covers most of Copenhagen. For extended stays, the best deal is the **rabatkort** (rebate card; 120kr), available from supermarkets, corner stores, and kiosks, which offers 10 2-zone tickets at discount. The **24hr. pass** (115kr), available at train stations, grants unlimited bus and train transport in the Northern Zealand region, as does the **Copenhagen Card.**

Night buses, marked with an "N," run 12:30-5:30am on limited routes and charge double fare; they accept the 24hr. pass.

Taxis: Københavns Taxa (☎3535 3535) and **Hovedstadens Taxi** (☎3877 7777) charge a base fare of 19kr and then 11-16kr/km. København to Kastrup Airport costs 200kr.

Bike Rental: City Bike (☎3616 4233; www.bycyklen.dk) lends bikes mid-Apr. to Nov. from 110 racks all over the city for a 20kr deposit. Anyone can return your bike and claim your deposit, so keep an eye on it.

⊠ PRACTICAL INFORMATION

Tourist Offices: Copenhagen Right Now, Vesterbrog. 4A (☎7022 2442; www.visitco-penhagen.dk). From København H, cross Vesterbrog. toward the Axelrod building. Open M-F 9am-4pm, Sa 9am-2pm. Sells the **Copenhagen Card** (1-day 199kr; 3-day 429kr), which grants free or discounted admission to most sights and unlimited travel throughout Northern Zealand; however, cardholders will need to keep up an almost manic pace to justify the cost. ▧**Use It,** Rådhusstr. 13 (☎3373 0620; www.useit.dk), has indispensable info and services for budget travelers. Offers *Playtime,* a comprehensive budget guide to the city. Provides daytime luggage storage, has free **Internet** (max. 20min.), holds mail, and finds lodgings for no charge. Open mid-June to mid-Sept. daily 9am-7pm; mid-Sept. to mid-June M-W 11am-4pm, Th 11am-6pm, F 11am-2pm.

Embassies and Consulates: Australia, Dampfærgev. 26, 2nd fl. (☎7026 3676). **Canada,** Kristen Bernikowsg. 1 (☎3348 3200). **Ireland,** Østbaneg. 21 (☎3542 3233). **New Zealand,** Store Strandst. 21, 2nd fl. (☎3337 7702). **UK,** Kastelsv. 36-40 (☎3544 5200). **US,** Dag Hammarskjölds Allé 24 (☎3555 3144). www.um.dk for complete list.

GLBT Resources: Landsforeningen for Bøsser og Lesbiske (LBL), Teglgårdstr. 13 (☎3313 1948; www.lbl.dk). Open M-F noon-2:30pm and 3-4:30pm. The monthly *Out and About,* which lists nightlife options, is available at gay clubs and the tourist office Other resources include www.copenhagen-gay-lfe.dk and www.gayguide.dk.

Police: Headquarters at Halmtorvet 20; Politigarden, Politiorvet 1 (☎3314 1448)

Medical Services: Doctors on Call (☎7013 0041 M-F 8am-4pm; ☎7020 1546 evenings/weekends; 400-600kr fee). Emergency rooms at **Amager Hospital,** Italiensv. 1 (☎3234 3234), **Frederiksberg Hospital,** Nordre Fasanv. 57 (☎3834 7711), and **Bispebjerg Hospital,** Bispebjerg Bakke 23 (☎3531 3531).

Internet: Free at Use It and **Copenhagen Hovedbibliotek (Central Library),** Krystalg. 15 (☎3373 6060). Coffee shop on 1st fl. Open M-F 10am-7pm, Sa 10am-2pm.

Post Office: In København H. Open M-F 8am-9pm, Sa-Su 10am-4pm. Address mail as follows: LAST NAME, First name, Post Denmark, Hovedbanegårdens Posthus, Hovedbanegården, 1570 Copenhagen V, DEN. **Use It** also holds mail for 2 months.

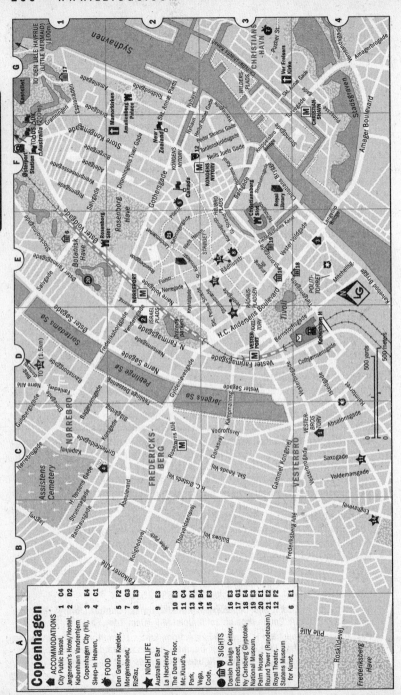

DENMARK

Copenhagen

⌂ ACCOMMODATIONS
City Public Hostel,	1 C4
Jørgensen's Hotel/Hostel,	2 D2
København Vandrehjem	
Copenhagen City (HI),	3 E4
Sleep-In Heaven,	4 C1

🍴 FOOD
Den Grønne Kælder,	5 F2
Morgenstedet,	7 G3
RizRaz,	8 E3

★ NIGHTLIFE
Australian Bar	9 E3
La Hacienda,	10 E3
The Dance Floor,	11 C4
Mc.Kluud's,	13 D1
Park,	14 B4
Vega,	15 E3
Code,	12 F2

🏛 SIGHTS
Danish Design Center,	16 E3
Frihedsmuseet,	17 G1
Ny Carlsberg Glyptotek,	18 E4
National Museum,	19 E3
Palm House,	20 E1
Round Tower (Rundetaarn),	21 E2
Royal Theater,	
Statens Museum	
for Kunst,	6 E1

ɪ ACCOMMODATIONS

Comfortable and inexpensive accommodations can be hard to find near the city center, but pedestrian-friendly streets and the great public transportation system ensure that travelers are never far from the action. Reserve well ahead in the summer. Be sure to check out early, as 10am is the standard.

Sleep-In Heaven, Struenseeg. 7 (☎3535 4648; www.sleepinheaven.com), in Nørrebro. M: Forum. Take bus 5A from the airport or from København H. (dir.: Husum; every 10-20min.) to Stengade. Go down Stengade and take your first right on Korsgade. Slight right to continue on Korsgade, left on Kapelvej, quick right onto HansTavsensGade and left into the alley. Laid-back hostel with friendly vibe with warm and helpful staff. Smoke-free. Breakfast 40kr. Linens 40kr. Lockers (refundable deposit). Free Wi-Fi. Max. 5-night stay. Reception and security guard 24hr. Dorms 145-160kr; doubles 500kr; triples 600kr. Ages 16-35. AmEx/MC/V; 5% surcharge. ●

City Public Hostel, Absalonsg. 8 (☎3331 2070). Go down Vesterbrogade and take a left on Absalonsg.. Cheap rates and great location attracts a diverse crowd of travelers. Breakfast 30kr-40kr. Locks for storage 30kr. Linens and pillow 40kr, towel 10kr. Internet. Reception 24hr. Open May-Aug. Dorms 110-150kr. Cash only. ●

Jørgensen's Hostel/Hotel Jørgensen, Rømersg. 11 (☎3313 8186; www.hoteljoergensen.dk). M: Nørreport. Small, comfortable rooms in a convenient location. Breakfast and linens included. Max. 5-night stay. Dorm lockout 11am-3pm. 6- to 14-bed dorms 150kr. Singles 475-625kr and doubles 575-750kr; both include TV and private en-suite bathrooms. Under age 35. Cash only for dorms; AmEx/MC/V for private rooms. ●

Danhostel: København Vandrerhjem Copenhagen City (HI), H.C. Andersens Bvd. 50 (☎3311 8585; www.danhostel.dk/copenhagencity). A popular 15-story resting place, only 5min. from the city center. . Linens 60kr. Internet 14kr per 20min; 29kr per hr. Bike rental 100kr per day. Reception 24hr. Check-in 2-5pm. Reserve ahead.Single-sex-dorms 145-180kr; private rooms 580-720kr. 35kr HI discount. AmEx/MC/V. ●

◖ FOOD

Stylish cafes serving delectable dishes are plentiful throughout the streets of Copenhagen, but be prepared to spend some cash. For delicious, less expensive food, try local *Schawarma* and kebab shops that line **Strøget** (full meal 40-70kr). For less authentically Danish food, budget travelers stop by the many all-you-can-eat pizza, pasta, and ethnic buffets down **Vesterbrogade** (from 70kr). Traditional cuisine includes *smørebrød* (open-faced sandwiches) and can be found on any street in Copenhagen. Green grocers in **Vesterbro** along **Istedgade** provide fresh fruits and veggies (cash only.)

RizRaz, Kompagnistr. 20 (☎3315 0575; www.rizraz.dk). M: Kongens Nytorv. This relaxed restaurant has plenty of seating, an extensive Mediterranean and Middle Eastern influenced menu with a vegetarian lunch buffet (69kr), and beautiful paintings for sale. Dinner 79kr. Grill order (includes buffet) from 119kr. Open daily 11:30am-midnight. AmEx/MC/V. Also at Store Kannikestr. 19 (☎3332 3345). ●

Den Grønne Kælder, Pilestr. 48 (☎3393 0140). M: Kongens Nytorv. Enjoy the vegetarian and vegan menu, rotated monthly and made from organic ingredients, in this cozy basement cafe. Try the local favorite "legendary hummus." Takeout 40-60kr. Lunch 50kr. Dinner starts at 105kr. Open M-Tu and Th-Sa 11am-10pm, W 1-10pm. Cash only. ●

Morgenstedet, Langgaden, Bådsmandsstr. 43 (☎3295 7770; www.morgenstedet.dk), in Christiania. Walk down Pusher St. and take a left at the end, then take a right up the concrete ramp at the bike shop and a left before the bathrooms; it will be on your right.

TIME: 4hr. With visits to Rosenborg Slot and Christianborg Slot, 6hr.

DISTANCE: About 6km.

SEASON: Year-round, although Rosenborg Slot has reduced hours Nov.-Apr.

A BIKING TOUR OF COPENHAGEN

In Copenhagen, biking is the new black. From chic women in heels to businessmen in suits, biking is the European way to travel; not to mention a great way to burn off the delicious buffets you'll be devouring. Copenhagen's flat land makes the city an ideal spot for scenic cycling as you tour fine churches, museums, and of course, castles. Rentals from **City Bike** (p. 205) are a great way to explore Copenhagen, but be sure to stake one out early. Careful: the rules require that you only ride the bikes in the city center. The eastern banks of the five western lakes are fair game, but if you cross over to the other side of the lakes, you'll face a 1000kr fine. Don't ride at night with a City Bike—and make sure you keep an eye on your City Bike when exploring the castles and museums, as anyone can take your bike, not to mention your 20kr!

When biking through the city, you should bypass pedestrian thoroughfares like Strøget to avoid strolling couples and bedazzled tourists. If you want to ride out into the beautiful countryside, ask your hostel about rental bikes. They can be a great alternative and you may get a better quality bike. You can take your bike onto an S-tog for 10kr. In Denmark, you are legally required to use lights when riding at night, and police are not shy about handing out 400kr fines to enforce this law. Helmets are recommended, but not mandatory.

The tour starts and ends in **Rådhus-Pladsen.** Begin by carefully making your way down busy Hans Christian Andersens Boulevard.

1. BOTANISK HAVE. Take a right onto Nørre Voldg. and follow it until you see the gates leading into the University of Copenhagen's lush **Botanical Gardens** (p. 211). Wander along paths lined with more than 13,000 species of plants, or hone in on the **Palm House** to view its extravagant orchids, cycads, and other tropical rarities. Explore the grounds to the **Faculty of Science of the University of Copenhagen,** located just north of the Gardens atop a hill along Øster Voldg.

2. STATENS MUSEUM FOR KUNST AND ROSENBORG SLOT. Next, head back onto Øster Voldg. At the intersection with Sølvg., you'll see the gates of the **Statens Museum for Kunst** (State Museum of Fine Arts; p. 211) to the north and the spires of **Rosenborg Slot** (p. 211) to the south. The latter served as the 16th-century summer house of King Christian IV, and the royal family took refuge here in 1801 when the British navy was shelling Copenhagen. Lock up your bike and pop inside for a look at the Sculpture Street in the museum or Denmark's crown jewels in the Slot's treasury, and don't forget to wander the King's Gardens.

3. ROUND TOWER. Backtrack down Øster Voldg. and turn left onto Gothersg. Make a right onto Landemærket and then hop off again to scale the heights of the **Round Tower** (p. 210), a onetime royal observatory that still affords a sweeping view of the city.

4. AMALIENBORG PALACE. Head back up to Gothersg. and turn right. Pass by **Kongens Nytorv,** the 1670 "new square" that turns into a skating rink each winter, and take a left onto Bredg. Keep your eyes peeled for the gilded dome of the **Marmorkirken** (Marble Church) on your left, and then turn right to enter the octagonal plaza of **Amalienborg Palace** (p. 211), a set of four Rococo mansions that the queen and her family call home. Check out the Amalienborg Museum to admire the luxurious furnishings of 19th century King Frederik VII's room.

5. NYHAVN. Continue on through the plaza, turn right on Toldbodg., and then right before the bridge onto Nyhavn. Part of the city's old waterfront, Nyhavn was known for centuries as a seedy strip for sailors to find grog, women, and a tattoo artist sober enough to wield a firm needle. Over the past 30 years, Copenhagen has embarked on a clean-up campaign, and today you're more likely to find an upscale deli serving smørrebrod than a tumbledown soup kitchen. Whenever a

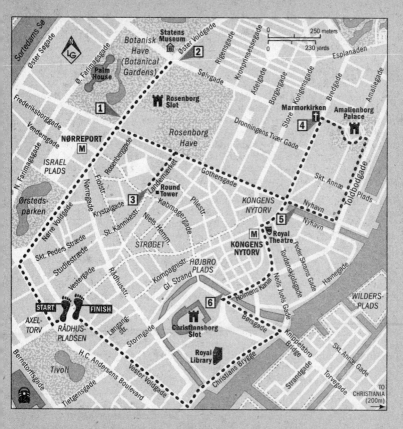

scrap of sunshine can be found, the good people of Copenhagen are soaking it up along the wharf, joined by Swedes from Malmö in search of cheap Danish beer.

6. CHRISTIANBORG SLOT. Walk your bike through Kongens Nytorv, and then thread your way between the **Royal Theater** (p. 211) and the metro station down Neils Juels G. Turn right onto Holmens Kanal and cross the bridge to reach **Christiansborg Slot** (p. 210), seat of the Danish Parliament. Look for the 103m tower; it's difficult to miss. If you arrive before 3:30pm, try to catch a tour of the **Royal Reception Rooms,** or head down into the ruins of the four previous castles underneath the present-day building. The first castle was demolished to make way for a larger one, the next two burned down in fires, and the Hanseatic League dismantled the fourth castle stone by stone after they captured the city in 1369.

7. SLIDING INTO HOME. You're in the home stretch. Head east toward the **Knippelsbro Bridge** and **Christiania** (p. 210), taking in the industrial skyline before lugging your bike down the steps to Christians Brygge below. Turn right and bike along the canal. Keep watch for the Black Diamond annex of the **Royal Library,** built in 1996 from black marble imported from Zimbabwe. Check your email at one of the free terminals inside. Make a right onto Vester Voldg. and coast back up to the Rådhus. The tour has ended; you've earned the right to call it a day. Now you can relax and watch the fireworks from Tivoli, while treating yourself to an ever--popular ice cream cone.

Sit in the enclosed outdoor dining area surrounded by lush bushes and flowerbeds and whet your appetite with the rotating menu of vegetarian cuisine. Soup with bread 45kr. Entrees 70kr. Desserts 25kr. Open Tu-Su noon-9pm. Cash only. ❷

👁 SIGHTS

Flat Copenhagen lends itself to exploration by bike (p. 208). Walking tours are detailed in *Playtime* (available at **Use It**, p. 205). Window-shop down pedestrian **Strøget** until you reach Kongens Nytorv; opposite is the picturesque **Nyhavn,** where ▣**Hans Christian Andersen** penned his first fairy tale. On a clear day, take the 6.4km walk along the five **lakes** on the western border of the city center or grab a bike and ride. Relax in the city hall square and listen to the street music as you enjoy an ice cream treat or a hot dog from local vendors. Most musuems are free and some have extended hours on Wednesdays.

CITY CENTER. ▣**Tivoli Gardens,** the famed 19th-century amusement park, features newly-built rides, an aquarium, concert hall, and theatre. Located across the street from Central Station. **Tivoli Illuminations,** an evocative light show, is staged on Tivoli Lake each night 30min. before closing. *(Vesterbrogade 3 ☎3315 1001; www.tivoligardens.com. Open mid-Sept. to mid-Apr. M-Th and Su 11am-10pm, F 11am-12:30am, Sa 11am-midnight; mid-Aug. to mid-Sept. M-Th and Su 11am-midnight, F-Sa 11am-12:30am. Admission 85kr. Rides 10-60kr. Admission with unlimited rides 285kr. AmEx/MC/V.)* From Tivoli, cross Tietgensgade to find **Ny Carlsberg Glyptotek,** home to ancient art from the 19th and 20th centuries from the Mediterranean, Denmark and France. Also features a beautiful greenhouse garden. Tickets for free guided tours go quickly. *(Dantes Pl. 7. ☎3341 8141; www.glyptoteket.dk. Open Tu-Su 10am-4pm. 50kr, students and children free. Su free. Wheelchair-accessible. Tours mid-June to Aug. W 2pm. MC/V.)* Across H.C. Andersens Bvd., aquaint yourself with the latest trends from furniture to model cars at the **Danish Design Center,** which displays exhibitions of Danish and international design. The **Flow Market Exhibition** downstairs encourages consumers to think with sustainable growth in mind, selling items such as "inner calmness" and "clean air." *(H.C. Andersens Bvd. 27. ☎3369 3369; www.ddc.dk. Open M-Tu and Th-F 10am-5pm, W 10am-9pm, Sa-Su 11am-4pm. 50kr, seniors, youth ages 12-18 and students 25kr. W after 5pm free. AmEx/MC/V.)* The ▣**National Museum's** vast collections include several large rune stones, ancient Viking art, and the permanent ethnographic exhibit, "People of the Earth." To reach the National Museum from H.C. Andersens Bvd., turn onto Stormg., take a right on Vester Volf., and go left on Ny Vesterg. *(Ny Vesterg. 10. ☎3313 4411. www.natmus.dk. Open Tu-Su 10am-5pm. Free. 1 hr. guided tours at noon, 1, 2pm on Sa, Sun, and holidays.)*

The home of Parliament *(Folketing)* and the royal reception rooms, **Christiansborg Slot** displays vivid, modernist tapestries that were designed by Bjørn Nørgård and presented to the Queen on her 50th birthday. *(Longangstraede 21. ☎3392 6300; www.ses.dk/christrainsborg. Ruins open daily May-Sept. 10am-4pm; Oct.-Apr. Tu-Su 10am-4pm. Ruins 40kr, students 30kr. Guided Castle tour daily Tu-Su at 11:30am and 1:30pm. Adults 65kr, students 55kr.)* Overlook the greater Copenhagen area from atop the impressive **Round Tower** *(Rundetaarn)*. *(Købmagerg. 52A. ☎3373 0373; www.rundetaarn.dk. Open daily May 20-Sept. 21. 10am-8pm, Sept. 21-May 20 10am-5pm. Observatory open mid-Oct.-mid-Mar. Tu,W 7-10pm. 25kr. AmEx/MC/V.)*

CHRISTIANSHAVN. In 1971, a few dozen flower children established the "free city" of **Christiania** in an abandoned Christianshavn fort. Today, the thousand-odd residents continue the tradition of artistic expression and an alternative lifestyle. Buildings surrounded by gorgeous bushes and flowerbeds are covered in ornate graffiti and murals. Vendors sell clothing and jewelry; nearby spots

DENMARK

like **Woodstock Cafe** and **Cafe Nemoland** offer cheap beer and diverse crowds. Recent government crackdowns have driven Pusher Street's once open drug trade underground, and arrests for possession have become commonplace. It's a sensitive subject so don't ask; let local people do the talking. Be careful: do not take pictures on Pusher Sreet. *(Main entrance on Prinsesseg. Take bus #66 or 2A (runs every 5min.) from København H.)*

FREDERIKSTADEN. Northeast of the city center, Edvard Eriksen's tiny **Little Mermaid** *(Lille Havfrue)* statue honors Hans Christian Andersen's beloved tale. *(S-tog: Østerport. Turn left out of the station, go left on Folke Bernadottes Allé, bear right on the path bordering the canal, go left up the stairs, and then head right along the street.)* Head back along the canal and turn left across the moat to reach **Kastellet,** a rampart-enclosed 17th-century fortress that's now a park. *(Center of Churchill Park. ☎3311 2233. Open daily 6am-10pm.)* On the other side of Kastellet, the **Frihedsmuseet** (Museum of Danish Resistance) documents the German occupation from 1940-45, when the Danes helped over 7000 Jews escape to Sweden. *(At Churchillparken. ☎3313 7714. Open May-Sept. Tu-Su 10am-5pm; Oct.-Apr. Tu-Su 10am-3pm. English-language tours July-Sept. Tu and Th 11am. Free.)* Walk south down Amalieng. to reach **Amalienborg Palace,** a complex of four enormous mansions that serve as the winter residences of the royal family. Several apartments are open to the public, including the studies of 19th-century Danish kings. The changing of the guard takes place at noon on the vast plaza. *(☎3312 0808; www.rosenborgslot.dk. Open May-Oct. daily 10am-4pm; Nov.-Apr. Tu-Su 11am-4pm. 50kr, students 30kr. Combined ticket with Rosenborg Slot 80kr. MC/V.)*

About 13,000 plant species thrive in the beautiful gardens of ▓**Botanisk Have.** *(Øster Farimagsgade 2B. ☎3532 2221 botanik.snm.ku.dk/english. Gardens open daily May-Sept. 8:30am-6pm; Oct.-Apr. daily Tu-Su 8:30am-4pm. Palm House open daily May-Dec. 10am-3pm; Jan.-Apr. daily Tu-Su 10am-3pm. Free.)* The **State Museum of Fine Arts** displays an eclectic collection of Danish and international art between its two buildings, which are linked by an impressive glass-roof gallery. *(Sølvg. 48-50. S-tog: Nørreport. Walk up Øster Voldg or take bus 6A ☎3374 8494; www.smk.dk. Open Tu and Th-Su 10am-5pm, W 10am-8pm. English-language tours July-Aug. Sa-Su 2pm. Permanent collection free. Special exhibits 80kr, students 50kr. W free. AmEx/MC/V.)*

▓▓ FESTIVALS AND ENTERTAINMENT

Whether showcasing new cinematic pictures or entertaining musical acts, Copenhagen isn't short on summer festivals. During the world-class **Copenhagen Jazz Festival** (☎3393 2013; www.festival.jazz.dk), the city teems with free outodoor concerts. For more than your average film buff, the city truly comes alive for the **NatFilm Festival** (☎3312 0005; www.natfilm.dk) during late March and early April. International and domestic releases compete for Danish distribution deals. **Zulu Sommerbio** (Summer Cinema; www.zulu.dk) holds free screenings in parks and squares across the city throughout July and August. Movies are shown in their original languages with Danish subtitles.

Royal Theater, August Bournoville Pass. 1, (☎3369 6969) is home to the world-famous Royal Danish Ballet. The box office is just off the Konges Nytorv metro and sells same-day half-price tickets. Open M-Sa 10am-6pm. Tickets online at www.billetnet.dk.

Tivoli ticket office, Vesterbrog. 3, (☎3315 1012). Sells half-price tickets for the city's theaters. Open daily mid-Apr. to mid-Sept. 11am-8pm; mid-Sept. to mid-Apr. 9am-5pm.

DENMARK

NIGHTLIFE

In Copenhagen, the real parties begin on Thursday night; many bars and clubs have cheaper drinks and reduced covers. The streets near the **city center,** as well as of **Nørrebro** and **Vesterbro,** are lined with hip, crowded bars. Look for fancier options along **Nyhavn,** where laid-back Danes bring their own beer and sit on the pier; open containers are legal within the city limits. Copenhagen has a thriving gay and lesbian scene; check out *Playtime* or *Out and About* for listings.

> **PARTNER UP.** The areas behind København H, the central train station, can be unsafe, especially at night. Explore with caution and bring a friend.

Vega, Enghavev. 40 (☎3325 7011; www.vega.dk), in Vesterbro. Bus 10. "Party time! Always crowded! Always a good time!" is what locals exclaim about this locale. One of Copenhagen's largest and most popular nightclubs, it showcases 4 floors, 5 dance rooms, 2 concert venues, and a popular bar. Dress well. Bar 18+; club 20+. Club cover after 1am 60kr. Bar open F-Sa 9pm-5am. Club open F-Sa 11pm-5am. MC/V.

Code, Radhusstraede 1 (☎3326 3626; www.code.dk), in Central Copenhagen. By day, an open cafe with a wide range of sandwiches. By night, a gay bar *and* lounge with an exotic cocktail selection. Shows 8pm-midnight. DJs on weekends 10pm-5am. MC/V.

The Australian Bar, Vesterg. 10 (☎2024 1411). M: Nørreport. Tucked away in the basement of an enclave, this relaxed bar has cheap drinks, pool tables, an arcade, and a dance-club playlist where you pick the music (8 songs/25kr). Beer 10-20kr. Mixed drinks 30kr. Reduced prices Th. Open M-W and Su 4pm-2am, Th-Sa 4pm-5am. MC/V.

La Hacienda/The Dance Floor, Gammel Torv 8 (☎3311 7478; www.la-hacienda.dk). M: Nørreport. Choose between **La Hacienda,** a laid-back lounge playing soul and hip hop, and **The Dance Floor,** a 2-story trance-driven club. Cover for men 150kr, women 130kr, 75kr before midnight; includes 1 champagne and 1 beer. Dress: Stylish and modern. 18+. Open F 11pm-8am, Sa 11pm-10am. AmEx/MC/V.

DAYTRIPS FROM COPENHAGEN

HILLERØD

At end of S-tog lines A and E. 40min., 6 per hr., 67kr or 4 clips. From train station, cross street onto Vibekev. and continue along the path until you can follow the sings; at the Torvet (main plaza), walk to the pond and bear left, following its perimeter to reach the castle entrance.

Hillerød is home to **Frederiksborg Slot,** one of Denmark's most impressive castles. Close to 90 rooms are open to the public, including the Chapel, the Rose Room, the Great Hall, and the Baroque gardens. (☎4826 0439; www.frederiksborgmuseet.dk. Gardens open daily May-Aug. 10am-9pm; Sept.-Apr. reduced hours. Castle open daily Apr.-Oct. 10am-5pm, Nov.-Mar. 11am-3pm. Gardens free. Castle 60kr, students 50kr. AmEx/MC/V.

HELSINGØR

At end of northern train line from Malmö, SWE via Copenhagen. 1hr., 3 per hr., 67kr or 4 clips.

Helsingør sits at a strategic entrance to the Baltic Sea, just 5km from Sweden. Originally built to levy taxes on passing ships, the majestic 16th-century **Kronborg Slot** is better known as **Elsinore,** the setting for Shakespeare's *Hamlet.* You'll feel like you were ttransplanted back to the 16th century. A statue of Viking chief Holger Danske sleeps in the dank, forbidding dungeon; legend holds that he will awake to defend Denmark in its darkest hour. The **tourist office,** Havnepl.

3, is in the Kulturhus, across from the station. (☎ 4921 3078; www.kronborg.dk. Open daily May-Sept. 10:30am-5pm; Apr. and Oct. Tu-Su 11am-4pm; Nov.-Mar. Tu-Su 11am-3pm. 85kr. AmEx/MC/V. Festival: www.hamletsommer.dk. Tourist office: ☎ 4921 1333; www.visithelsingor.dk. Open July M-F 10am-5pm, Sa 10am-2pm; Aug.-Jun. M-F 10am-4pm, Sa 10am-1pm.)

HUMLEBÆK AND RUNGSTED

From Copenhagen, take a Helsingør-bound train. 45min., 3 per hr., 63kr or 4 clips. From Humle-bæk Station, follow signs for 10min. or catch bus #388. From Copenhagen, take a Nivå-bound train. 30min., 3 per hr., 67kr or 4 clips. Follow the street leading out of the train station and turn right on Rungstedv., then right again on Rungsted Strandv., or take bus #388.

The gorgeous ◼**Louisiana Museum of Modern Art,** 13 Gl. Strandv., honors the three wives (all named Louisa) of the estate's original owner. It rounds out its permanent collection—including works by Lichtenstein, Picasso, and Warhol—with several major exhibitions each year. Landscape architects have lavished attention on the seaside sculpture garden and the sloping lake garden. **The Karen Blixen Museum,** Rungsted Strandv. 111, provides a chronicle of the author's life. The grounds are home to 40 species of birds. LMMA: ☎ 4919 0719; www.louisiana.dk. Open Tu-F 11am-10pm 90kr. AmEx/MC/V. KBM: ☎ 4557 1057. Open May-Sept. Tu-Su 10am-5pm; Oct.-Apr. W-F 1-4pm, Sa-Su 11am-4pm. 45kr. AmEx/MC/V.)

FINLAND
(SUOMI)

Caught in a territorial tug-of-war between Sweden and Russia since the 1400s, Finland finally secured autonomy in 1917, successfully defending its independence through both World Wars. Tarja Halonen, Finland's first female president, presides over the home of Nokia cell phones and hosts the annual World Sauna Championships. The country's lakes and boreal forest entice hikers while southern cities draw architecture students and art gurus. Finland—outside of stylish Helsinki—is more affordable than its Scandinavian neighbors.

DISCOVER FINLAND: SUGGESTED ITINERARY

THREE DAYS. Stick to the area around **Helsinki** (p. 218) by ambling along the tree-lined **Esplanadi** and checking out some of the city's great museums. Leave time for a thrilling bike ride down the Pellinge archipelago, south of **Porvoo** (p. 226). Afterward, the snowy **Lahti** is worth freezing your patootie off.

ESSENTIALS

WHEN TO GO

The long days of Finnish summer are a tourist's dream, while the two-month polar night *(kaamos)* in the country's northern regions draws winter-sports fanatics. Ski season starts in early February, continuing well into March and April. Reindeer and snowmobile safaris, along with glimpses of the rare **aurora borealis,** reward travelers willing to brave winter temperatures, which regularly drop to -20°C (-4°F). Summer tourists, celebrating Midsummer *(Juhannus)* festivities (June 21-22), can expect average temperatures of 20-25°C (68-77°F).

DOCUMENTS AND FORMALITIES

EMBASSIES AND CONSULATES. Foreign embassies in Finland are in Helsinki (p. 220). Finnish embassies abroad include: **Australia** and **New Zealand,** 12 Darwin Ave., Yarralumla, ACT 2600 (☎26 273 38 00; www.finland.org.au); **Canada,** 55 Metcalfe St., Ste. 850, Ottawa, ON K1P 6L5 (☎613-288-2233; www.finland.ca/en); **Ireland,** Russell House, Stokes Pl., St. Stephen's Green, Dublin 2 (☎01 478 1344; www.finland.ie/en); **UK,** 38 Chesham Pl., London SW1X 8HW (☎020 78 38 62 00; www.finemb.org.uk/en); **US,** 3301 Massachusetts Ave. NW, Washington, D.C. 20008 (☎202-298-5800; www.finland.org).

FACTS AND FIGURES

OFFICIAL NAME: Republic of Finland.

CAPITAL: Helsinki.

MAJOR CITIES: Oulu, Tampere, Turku.

POPULATION: 5,245,000.

LAND AREA: 338,000 sq. km.

TIME ZONE: GMT +2.

LANGUAGES: Finnish, Swedish.

NATIONAL CELEBRITY: Father Christmas, or Santa Claus, rumored to live in a northern province.

VISA AND ENTRY INFORMATION. EU citizens do not need a visa. Citizens of Australia, Canada, New Zealand, and the US do not need a visa for stays of up to 90 days, in any of the countries in the EU's freedom-of-movement zone. For more info, see p. 14. For stays longer than 90 days, all non-EU citizens need **Schengen** visas (around US$41), available at Finnish embassies and online at www.finland.org/en. Application processing takes about two weeks.

TOURIST SERVICES AND MONEY

EMERGENCY	Ambulance, Police, and Fire: ☎112.

TOURIST OFFICES. The **Finnish Tourist Board** (☎010 60 58 000; www.visitfinland. com) maintains an official online travel guide, which customizes its travel information and advice by home country.

MONEY. In 2002, the **euro** replaced the markka as the unit of currency in Finland. For more info, see p. 18. **Banks** exchange currency for a €2-5 commission, though **Forex** offices and **ATMs** offer the best exchange rates. Food from grocery stores runs €10-17 per day; meals cost around €8 for lunch and €12 for dinner. Although restaurant bills include a service charge, leaving small change for particularly good service is becoming more common. Finland has a 22% **value added tax (VAT),** a sales tax applied to services and imports. The nation has a reduced VAT of 17% for food products and 8% for public transportation, books, and medicines. The prices given in *Let's Go* include VAT. In the airport upon exiting the EU, non-EU citizens can claim a refund on the tax paid for goods purchased at participating stores. In order to qualify for a refund in a store, you must spend at least €40; make sure to ask for a refund form when you pay. For more info on qualifying for a VAT refund, see p. 19.

TRANSPORTATION

BY PLANE. Several airlines fly into Helsinki from Australia, Europe, and North America. The main airport is **Helsinki-Vantaa Airport (HEL;** ☎200 14636; www.helsinki-vantaa.fi). **Finnair** (Finland ☎0600 140 140, UK 087 0241 4411, US 800-950-5000; www.finnair.com) flies from 120 international cities and also covers the domestic market. The airline offers youth rates—inquire before purchasing. **AirÅland** (www.airaland.com) flies to Stockholm, SWE and the Åland Isles. **Ryanair** (☎353 12 49 77 91; www.ryanair.com) flies to **Tampere-Pirkkala Airport (TMP).**

BY TRAIN. The national rail company is **VR Ltd., Finnish Railways** (☎0600 41 900; www.vr.fi). Finnish rail is efficient and prices are high; seat reservations are required on **Pendolino** and recommended on **InterCity** trains (€6.40-12.60). **Eurail** is valid in Finland. A **Finnrailpass,** available only to foreigners, allows for three ($190), five ($251), or 10 travel days ($342) in a one-month period.

Finland

BY BUS. Buses are the only way to reach some smaller towns and points beyond the Arctic Circle. **Oy Matkahuolto Ab** (☎09 682 701; www.matkahuolto.fi) coordinates bus service. ISIC holders can buy a sticker (€6) for their **Matkahuolto Student Identity Card,** free from Matkahuoloto service outlets, agents, and VR (previously Suomen Valtion Rautatiet) ticket offices. The sticker gives students a 50% discount on one-way tickets purchased ahead for routes exceeding 80km. **Rail passes** are valid on buses when trains are not in service.

BY FERRY. Viking Line (Finland ☎09 123 51, Sweden 08 452 4000; www.vikingline.fi) and **Tallinksilja** (Finland ☎09 180 41, Sweden 08 666 33 30; www.tallinksilja. fi) sail from Stockholm, SWE to Helsinki, Mariehamn, and Turku. Travelers with both a **Eurail Pass** and a train ticket receive free passenger fare. Viking's "early bird" discounts are 15-50% off on ferry fares when booking trips within Finland or Sweden at least 30 days ahead. On Tallinksilja, Eurailer holders ride for free or lower rates, depending on the specific route and ticket type.

BY CAR. Finland honors foreign **driver's licenses** issued in the US, EU, and EEA countries for up to one year for drivers aged 18 years or older. Speed limits are 120kph on expressways, 30-40kph in densely populated areas, and 80-100kph on most major roads. Headlights must be used at all times. Finnish law requires all cars must have snow tires during the winter. Be wary of reindeer at night. For more info on car rental and driving in Europe, see p. 49.

BY BIKE AND BY THUMB. Finland has a well-developed network of cycling paths. **Fillari GT** route maps are available at bookstores (€10-16). Check www. visitfinland.com/cycling for pre-trip route planning. **Hitchhiking** is uncommon in Finland and illegal on highways. *Let's Go* does not recommend hitchhiking.

KEEPING IN TOUCH

PHONE CODES	**Country code: 358. International dialing prefix:** 00.
	For more info international calls, see **Inside Back Cover.**

EMAIL AND THE INTERNET. Internet cafes in Helsinki are relatively scarce compared to other European capitals, and in smaller towns they are virtually nonexistent. However, many **tourist offices** and **public libraries** offer short (15-30min.) slots of free Internet, and there is some free **Wi-Fi** access in Helsinki.

TELEPHONE. To make a long-distance call within Finland, dial 0 and then the number. **Pay phones** are rare but dependable. **Mobile phones** are extremely popular in the nation that gave the world Nokia, and prepaid mobile phone cards can be used to make international calls (cheapest 10pm-8am). For more info on mobile phones, see p. 29. For operator assistance, dial ☎118; for help with international calls, dial ☎92020. International direct dial numbers include: **ATandT Direct** (☎0800 1100 15); **Canada Direct** (☎0800 1100 11); **MCI** (☎08001 102 80); **Telecom New Zealand** (☎0800 1106 40).

MAIL. Finnish mail service is efficient. Postcards and letters under 50g cost €0.70 within Finland, €1 to the EU, and €1.40 to other destinations. International letters under 20g cost €0.70. Check www.posti.fi/english/index.html for more prices and mailing restrictions. To receive mail in Finland, have mail delivered **Poste Restante.** Mail will go to the main post office unless you specify a subsidiary by street address. Address mail according to the following format: First name, Last Name, Poste Restante, post office address, city, FINLAND.

LANGUAGES. Finnish is spoken by most of the population (92%), although children learn both **Swedish** and Finnish from the seventh grade. Three dialects of **Sámi** are also spoken by an ethnic minority in northern Finland. **English** is also widely spoken, with two-thirds of Finns reporting that they can speak at least some English; city-dwellers and those under 35 are generally the most proficient. For basic Finnish words and phrases, see **Phrasebook: Finnish, p. 786**.

ACCOMMODATIONS AND CAMPING

FINLAND	❶	❷	❸	❹	❺
ACCOMMODATIONS	under €15	€15-28	€29-50	€51-75	over €75

Finland has over 100 youth hostels (*retkeilymaja;* RET-kay-loo-MAH-yah), although only half of them are open year-round. The **Finnish Youth Hostel Association** (Suomen Retkeilymajajärjestö; ☎09 565 7150; www.srmnet.org) is Finland's HI affiliate. Prices are generally around €23 per person for a dorm room, with a €2.50 HI discount. Most have laundry facilities and a kitchen; some have saunas and rent bikes or skis. **Hotels** are generally expensive (over €50 per night); *kesähotelli* (summer hotels) are usually student lodgings vacated from June to August, and cost about €25 per night. **Camping** is common; seventy campgrounds are open year-round (tent sites €10-25 per night; small cottages from €40). The **Camping Card Scandinavia** (€6) qualifies cardholders for discounts and includes limited accident insurance. For a guide or to purchase the Camping Card, contact the **Finnish Camping Site Association.** (☎09 477 407 40; www.camping.fi. Allow three weeks for delivery of the card.) Finland's **right of public access** (*jokamiehenoikeudet*) allows travelers to temporarily camp for free in the countryside, as long as they stay a reasonable distance (about 150m) from private homes. See p. 33 for more info.

FOOD AND DRINK

FINLAND	❶	❷	❸	❹	❺
FOOD	under €8	€8-15	€16-20	€21-30	over €30

Kebab and pizza joints are cheap and popular, but the local *Kauppatori* markets and *Kauppahalli* food courts are more likely to serve recognizably Finnish fare. Traditional diet slants toward breads and sausages. In summer, however, menus feature freshly caught trout, perch, pike, and herring; a new wave of five-star chefs in Helsinki are pairing French and Mediterranean ingredients with the bounty of local fisheries. To Santa's displeasure, bowls of **reindeer stew** are a staple of Lapland, while Kuopio is known for its pillowy rye pastries. Try the strawberries—Finland is their top European producer. A surprising number of adults drink milk with meals, followed by interminable pots of coffee. You must be 18 to purchase **beer** and **wine,** 20 or older to buy liquor; the minimum age in bars is usually 18, but can be as old as 25. Alcohol stronger than light beer must be bought at state-run **Alko** liquor stores, open weekdays until at least 6pm and Saturdays until at least 4pm.

HOLIDAYS AND FESTIVALS

Holidays: New Year's Day (Jan. 1); Epiphany (Jan. 6); Good Friday (Mar. 10, 2009; Mar. 2, 2010); Easter (Apr. 12, 2009; Apr. 4, 2010); May Day (May 1); Ascension (May 1); Pentecost (May 31, 2009; May 23, 2010); Corpus Christi (May 22); Midsummer (June 21-22); Assumption (Aug. 15); All Saints' Day (Nov. 1); Independence Day (Dec. 6); Christmas (Dec. 25); Boxing Day (Dec. 26).

Festivals: Flags fly high on **Midsummer's Eve** (June 21), when the Finnish desert their cities for seaside cabins. July is the festival high-season in Finland, with gays and lesbians celebrating **Helsinki Pride,** Turku's youth taking to the mosh pits of **Ruisrock,** and Pori's residents launching their **Jazz Festival.** Savonlinna's **Opera Festival** continues into early August, while the **Helsinki Festival,** Oulu's **Music Video Festival,** and Lahti's **Sibelius Festival** close out the summer. See www.festivals.fi for more info.

BEYOND TOURISM

It is relatively difficult for foreigners to secure full-time employment in Finland, but travelers may be able to obtain summer work. Check the CIMO website (see below) or www.igapyear.com for information on work placement. The organizations below coordinate limited work and volunteer opportunities. For more info on opportunities across Europe, see Beyond Tourism, p. 55.

The American-Scandinavian Foundation (AMSCAN), 58 Park Ave., New York, NY 10016, USA (☎212-879-9779; www.amscan.org/jobs/index.html). Volunteer and job opportunities throughout Scandinavia. There are a limited number of fellowships for study in Finland available to Americans.

Centre for International Mobility (CIMO), Säästöpankinranta 2A, P.O. Box 343, 00531 Helsinki (☎2069 0501; http://finland.cimo.fi). Provides information on youth exchange programs, technical and agricultural internships, Finnish language studies, and study abroad. CIMO also organizes **European Voluntary Service Programs** (www.4evs.net)for EU citizens, who can spend a fully funded year doing service in another EU country. EVS opportunities are largely in social work. Similarly, the EU offers the European Youth in Action Program, which also offers years abroad in Finland (ec.europa.eu/youth/youth-in-action-programme/doc126_en.htm).

HELSINKI (HELSINGFORS)   ☎09

With all the appeal of a big city but without the grime, Helsinki's (pop. 570,000) attractive harbor, grand architecture, and parks make it a showcase of Northern Europe. A hub of the design world, the city also distinguishes itself with multicultural flair; here, youthful energy mingles with old-world charm.

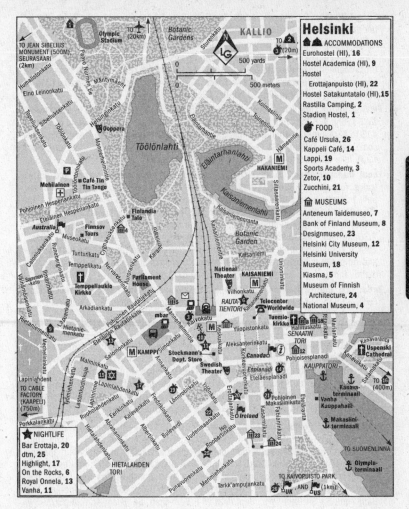

Helsinki

🏠 ACCOMMODATIONS

Eurohostel (HI), 16
Hostel Academica (HI), 9
Hostel
 Erottajanpuisto (HI), 22
Hostel Satakuntatalo (HI),15
Rastila Camping, 2
Stadion Hostel, 1

🍴 FOOD

Café Ursula, 26
Kappeli Café, 14
Lappi, 19
Sports Academy, 3
Zetor, 10
Zucchini, 21

🏛 MUSEUMS

Anteneum Taidemuseo, 7
Bank of Finland Museum, 8
Designmuseo, 23
Helsinki City Museum, 12
Helsinki University
 Museum, 18
Kiasma, 5
Museum of Finnish
 Architecture, 24
National Museum, 4

★ NIGHTLIFE

Bar Erottaja, 20
dtm, 25
Highlight, 17
On the Rocks, 6
Royal Onnela, 13
Vanha, 11

FINLAND

🖵 TRANSPORTATION

Flights: Helsinki-Vantaa Airport (HEL; ☎200 146 36; http://www.finavia.fi). Bus #615 runs from airport Platform 21 to and from the train station. (35min., buses depart roughly every 15min. weekdays 6am-9pm; every 30min. other times; from the airport M-F 6am-1am; to the airport M-F 5am-midnight. €3.80. Cash only.) A Finnair **bus** runs from airport platform 10 and from the Finnair building next to the train station (☎0600 140 140; www.finnair.com. 35min., about 3 per hr.; from the airport 5:45am-1:10am; to the airport 5am-midnight. €5.90. AmEx/MC/V.)

Trains: (☎030 072 0900, English-language info 231 999 02; www.vr.fi.) To: **Moscow, RUS** (13hr., 1 per day, from €92); **Rovaniemi** (10hr., 5 per day, from €75); **St. Peters-**

burg, RUS (5hr., 2 per day, €54.80); **Tampere** (2hr., 14 per day, €21-30); **Turku** (2hr., 7 per day, €23-34). See p. 622 for entrance requirements to Russia.

Buses: Depart from the underground Kamppi bus terminal, Narinkka 3 (☎0200 4000; www.matkahuolto.fi). From the train station, take Postik past the statue of Mannerheim. Cross Mannerheimintie onto Salomonkatu; the station will be on your left. Look for the blue sign near the stairs. Busses to **Lahti** (1-2hr., 1-2 per hr., €19), **Tampere** (2hr., 1 per hr., €22), and **Turku** (2hr., 2 per hr., €25).

Ferries: Viking Line, Lönnrotinkatu 2 (☎12 351; www.vikingline.fi), sails to **Stockholm, SWE** (16hr., 5:30pm, from €48) and **Tallinn, EST** (4hr., 11:30pm, €21). Tram #2 or bus #13 to Katajanokka terminal. Tallinksilja, Erottajankatu 19 (☎228 311; www.tallinksilja. com), sails to **Tallinn, EST** (2-3hr.; Apr.-Sept. 13 per day, Sept.-Dec. 6 per day; from €23). Take bus #15 to West terminal. For more info on Scandinavian ferries, see p. 53.

Local Transportation: (☎09 310 1071; www.hkl.fi). Most **buses, trams,** and **metro trains** run about 5:30am-11pm; major bus and tram lines, including tram #3T, run until 1:30am. Night **buses,** marked with "N," run M-Sa after 2am (€4). Single-fare tram €2; with 1hr. transfers to buses, trams, and the metro. **HKL Palvelupiste** (City Transport Office) is in the Rautatientori metro, below the train station. Open mid-June-July M-Th 7:30am-6pm, F 7:30am-5pm, Sa 10am-3pm; from Aug. to mid-June M-Th 7:30am-7pm, F 7:30am-5pm, Sa 10am-3pm. Sells the **tourist ticket** (as does the tourist office and other ticket kiosks), a good investment for unlimited access to buses, trams, the metro, and trains. 1-day €6, 3-day €12, 5-day €18. AmEx/MC/V.

Taxis: Taxi Centre Helsinki (☎0100 0700). Special airport fares with **Yellow Line** (☎0600 555 555). Reserve 1 day ahead, before 6pm. 30-55min. €22. AmEx/MC/V.

✦ 🔀 ORIENTATION AND PRACTICAL INFORMATION

Water and beaches surround Helsinki in every direction. The city's main street, **Mannerheimintie,** passes between the bus and train stations on its way south to the city center, ending at the Esplanadi. This tree-lined promenade leads east to **Kauppatori** (Market Square) and the beautiful South Harbor. Northeast of the city center lies **Kallio,** the bohemian district. Both Finnish and Swedish are used on all street signs and maps; *Let's Go* uses the Finnish names.

Tourist Offices: Pohjoisesplanadi 19 (☎3101 3300; www.visithelsinki.fi). Open May-Sept. M-F 9am-8pm, Sa-Su 9am-6pm; Oct.-Apr. M-F 9am-6pm, Sa-Su 10am-4pm. Representatives in green vests roam the city center in summer to distribute maps and answer questions. **Helsinki Card,** sold at the **Tour Shop** (☎2288 1500; www.helsinkiexpert.fi) in the tourist office, provides unlimited local transportation and free or discounted tours and admission. 1-day €33, 2-day €43, 3-day €53. Open June-Aug. M-F 9am-7pm, Sa-Su 9am-5pm; Sept.-May M-F 9am-5pm, Sa 10am-4pm. AmEx/MC/V. **Finnsov Tours,** Museokatu 15 (☎09 436 6960; www.finnsov.fi) arranges trips to Russia and expedites the visa process. Open M-F 9am-5pm. AmEx/MC/V.

Embassies: Canada, Pohjoisesplanadi 25B (☎619 228 530; www.canada.fi). Open June-Aug. M-Th 8am-noon and 1-4:30pm, F 8am-1:30pm; Sept.-May M-F 8:30am-noon and 1-4:30pm. **Ireland,** Erottajankatu 7A (☎09 646 006; helsinkiembassy@ dfa.ie). Open M-F 9am-5pm. Consular division 9am-noon by appointment. **UK,** Itäinen Puistotie 17 (☎2286 5100; www.britishembassy.gov.uk/finland). Open mid-June-late August M-F 8:30am-3:30pm, from late Aug.-mid-June M-F 9am-5pm. By appointment. **US,** Itäinen Puistotie 14A (☎6162 5730; www.usembassy.fi). Open M-F 8:30am-5pm.

Luggage Storage: Lockers in the train station €3-4 per day. The Kiasma museum and the auditorium (lower entrance) of the National Museum (p. 224) provide free same day storage even if you don't pay admission.

GBLT Resources: Seta Ry, Mannerheimintie 170A 4, 5th fl. (☎09 681 2580; www.seta.
fi). Tram #10. Organization with info on gay services. **QLife Traveler's Guide Finland** is
available at the tourist office. See the www.qlife.fi for a plethora of information.

Laundromat: Café Tin Tin Tango, Töölöntorinkatu 7 (☎2709 0972; www.tintintango.
info), an epic combination of bar, cafe, laundromat, and sauna. Wash €4, dry €2, detergent €1.20. Sandwiches €5-9. Open M-Th 7am-midnight, F 7am-2am, Sa 9am-2am, Su
10am-midnight. AmEx/MC/V.

General Emergency Number: ☎112

24 hr. Police: ☎189 4002 24hr. **Medical Hôtline:** ☎100 23.

24hr. Pharmacy: Yliopiston Apteekki, Mannerheimintie 96 (☎0203 202 00).

Hospital: 24hr. clinic **Mehiläinen,** Pohjoinen Hesperiankatu 17 (☎010 414 4444).

Telephone: Telecenter Worldwide, Vuorikatu 8 (☎09 670 612; www.woodgong.com),
offers reasonable rates. Open M-F 10am-9pm, Sa 11am-7pm, Su noon-7pm. MC/V.

Internet: Library 10, Elielinaukio 2G (☎3108 5000), upstairs in the main post office
building. Free Wi-Fi, free 30min. slots of Internet. Open M-Th 10am-8pm, F-Su noon-
6pm. Many **cafes** provide free Internet and Wi-Fi, including **mbar,** Mannerheimintie
22-24, (☎6124 5420) which offers free Wi-Fi and a DJ 3-5 times a week in the summer. M-Tu 9am-midnight, W-Th 9am-2am, F-Sa 9am-3am, Su noon-midnight. Visit www.
hel.fi/en/wlan or check the tourist office for other Internet locations.

Post Office: Elielinaukio 2F (☎2007 1000). Open summer M-F 7am-9pm, Sa-Su 10am-
6pm. **Postal Code:** 00100.

🏠🏕 ACCOMMODATIONS AND CAMPING

▩ **Hostel Erottajanpuisto (HI),** Uudenmaank. 9 (☎09 642 169; www.erottajanpuisto.
com). Well-kept rooms in a central location. Breakfast €5. Lockers €1. Laundry €7. Free
Internet and Wi-Fi. Reception 24hr. Summer dorms €23.50; singles €49; doubles €63.
Low-season singles €48; doubles €64. €2.50 HI discount. AmEx/MC/V. ❷

▩ **Hostel Satakuntatalo (HI),** Lapinrinne 1A (☎6958 5231; www.sodexho.fi/satakunta).
M: Kamppi. Spacious, well-located rooms. Breakfast and sauna included. Lockers €2,
free if you have a lock. Linens €5. Laundry €5.50, detergent €1.50. Free Internet and
Wi-Fi. Reception 24hr. Open June-Aug. Dorms €19.5; singles from €41; doubles from
€60; triples from €78; quads from €88. €2.50 HI discount. AmEx/MC/V. ❷

Hostel Academica (HI), Hietaniemenkatu 14 (☎1311 4334; www.hostelacademica.fi).
M: Kamppi. Turn right onto Runeberginkatu and left after crossing the bridge. University housing transforms into a hostel in summer months. Rooms have kitchenettes and
private bath. Sauna, linens, and towels included. Internet €2 per 30min, Wi-Fi €2 per
hr., €5 per day. Reception 24hr. Open June-Aug. Dorms €23; singles €40-55; doubles
€57-69. €2.50 HI discount. AmEx/MC/V. ❷

Stadion Hostel (HI), Pohjoinen Stadiontie 4 (☎09 477 8480; www.stadionhostel.com).
Tram #3 or 7A to Auroran Sairaala and walk down Pohj. Cheap rooms and an active
social scene. Breakfast €6. Linens included. Laundry €2.50. Free Internet. 24hr. reception. Dorms €19; singles €38; doubles €47. €2.50 HI discount. AmEx/MC/V. ❷

Eurohostel (HI), Linnankatu 9 (☎09622 0470; www.eurohostel.fi), near Katajanokka
ferry terminal. Bright rooms and free sauna. Kitchen. Breakfast €7. Linens and towels
included. Laundry €1. Internet €2 per 15min.; Wi-Fi €5 per day. Reception 24hr. Singles
€40-44, dorms €24, family room €59-68. €2.50 HI discount. AmEx/MC/V. ❸

Rastila Camping, Karavaanikatu 4 (☎107 8517; www.hel.fi/rastila). M: Rastila. Change
trains toward Vuosaari at Itäkeskus. A campground 12km from the city next to a beach.
Electricity €4.50-7. Internet €1.50/15min. at reception, some free Wi-Fi access. Reception from mid-May to mid-Sept. 24hr.; from mid-Sept. to mid-May daily 8am-10pm. €5

per person; €10 per tent site in summer, €6 in winter; Cabins in summer €45-64. **Hostel** (☎3107 1441) (HI) open from mid-June to early August. Dorms €19. MC/V. ❶

FOOD

Restaurants and cafes are easy to find on Esplanadi and the streets branching off Mannerheimintie and Uudenmaankatu. Cheaper options surround the **Hietalahti flea market** at the southern end of Bulevardi. A **supermarket** is under the train station. (Open M-Sa 7am-10pm, Su 10am-10pm.) Helsinki has many budget restaurants that serve ethnic food. Get lunch at the open-air market **Kauppatori**, where stalls sell cooked fish and local produce; a meal from a cafe will cost about €6-8. (Open June-Aug. M-Sa 6:30am-6pm; Sept.-May M-F 7am-5pm.)

Zetor, Mannerheimintie 3-5 (☎010 766 4450; www.zetor.net), in the mall opposite the train station. Cheeky menu, cheekier farm-inspired decor, a trademark tractor, and ridiculously good Finnish food. Try some of their reindeer stew (€18). Homemade beer €4-7. Entrees €11-28. Attached bar 22+. Open M 1pm-2am, T 11am-3am, W-Sa 11am-4am, Su 1pm-1am. AmEx/MC/V. ❷

Kappeli Café, Eteläesplanadi 1 (☎(010 766 3880; www.kappeli.fi). This cafe has served the bohemian and the elite since 1867. Salads and sandwiches €6-9. Open from May to mid-Sept. M-Th 9am-midnight, F-Sa 9am-2am, Su 9am-11pm; from mid-Sept. to Apr. M-Sa 10am-midnight, Su 10am-11pm. Kitchen closes 1hr. earlier. AmEx/MC/V. ❶

Café Ursula, Ehrenströmintie 3 (☎09 652 817; www.ursula.fi). This upscale cafe also has delicious budget options and an idyllic setting on the Baltic Sea. Free Wi-Fi. Sandwiches €5-6. Salad bar 11am-6pm, €10-12. Lunch buffet €9-15. Open daily in summer 9am-midnight; in spring and fall 9am-10pm; in winter 9am-8pm. AmEx/MC/V. ❷

Zucchini, Fabianinkatu 4 (☎09 622 2907), south of the tourist office. Popular vegetarian and vegan fare made with mostly organic produce. Entrees €6-10. Open from late August to late July M-F 11am-4pm. AmEx/MC/V. ❷

Lappi, Annankatu 22 (☎09 645 550; www.lappires.com). Tourists splurge on specialties like reindeer, lingonberries, fresh salmon, and Arctic char in a rustic Finnish atmosphere. Entrees from €17. Reserve ahead. Open in summer M-F 5-10:30pm, Sa 1-10:30pm; in winter M-F noon-10:30pm, Sa 1-10:30pm. AmEx/MC/V. ❸

Sports Academy, Kaivokatu 8 (☎010 766 4300; www.sportsacademy.fi). A €15 burger should hold you to snacks and beer. But you're probably not here for the food. You're here to watch the game—as is everyone else. Beer €4-6. 1st fl. open daily 10am-3pm. 2nd fl. open M-Th 11am-1am, F-Sa 11am-3am, Su noon-10pm. ❸

SIGHTS

Helsinki's Neoclassical buildings and new forms reflect Finnish architect Alvar Aalto's joke: "Architecture is our form of expression because our language is so impossible." Helsinki's **Art Nouveau** (Jugendstil) and **Modernist** structures are home to a dynamic design community. Much of the architecture of the old center, however, is the brainchild of German Carl Engel, who modeled his design after St. Petersburg. Older buildings and public squares are adorned with interesting—and, at times, imposing statues. Most sights are in the city's compact center, making it ideal for **walking tours;** pick up a walking **guide** from the tourist office for routes. Trams 3B and 3T loop around the major sights in 1hr., providing a cheap alternative to tour buses. Helsinki has many **parks** that are perfect for an afternoon stroll, including Kaivopuisto in the south, Töölönlahti in the north, and Esplanadi and Tähtitorninvuori in the center of town.

SUOMENLINNA. This **military fortification,** spanning five islands, was built by Sweden to stave off the Russian Empire. It is one of the best examples of military engineering in the 18th century. The main island path, identified by the blue street signs, leads to the **visitors center,** home of the **Suomenlinna Museum,** which details the history of the fortress. (☎ 4050 9691; www.suomenlinna.fi. Museum open daily May-Aug. 10am-6pm; Sept.-Apr. 11am-4pm. €5, students €4.30min. Film 2 per hr. AmEx/MC/V.) The islands also feature the world's only combination **church and lighthouse** and Finland's only remaining WWII **submarine.** (Submarine open from mid-May to Aug. 11am-6pm. €4, students €2. Cash only. English tours of the fortress leave from the museum June-Aug. daily 11am and 2pm; Sept. Sa-Su 1:30pm. €6.50, including admission to the Ehrensvard Museum, the Commander's residence. AmEx/MC/V.) The **Toy Museum,** on the main island, has extensive exhibits on toys from the 19th century to today. (☎ 668 417. Open July daily 11am-6pm; May-June and Aug. daily 11am-5pm; early Sept. daily 11am-4pm; Apr. Sa-Su 11am-4pm. €5. MC/V.) Southern island's smooth **rocks** are popular with swimmers and sunbathers. (City Transport ferries depart from Market St.; 15min., 1-3 per hr., round-trip €3.80. Combo ticket for military museum and submarine €6, students €3. Cash only.)

SENAATIN TORI (SENATE SQUARE). The square and its gleaming white ◙**Tuomiokirkko** (Dome Church) showcase Carl Engel's architecture and exemplify the splendor of Finland's 19th-century Russian period. The church's stunning marble reliefs house an interior so elegantly simple that every gilded detail becomes magnified. (Unioninkatu 29. ☎ 2340 6120. Open June-Aug. M-Sa 9am-noon, Su noon-8pm; Sept.-May M-Sa 9am-6pm, Su noon-6pm. Organ concerts W and F at noon.) Just south of Senate Sq., the **Helsinki City Museum** chronicles the city's 450-year history. The **City Museum** also has exhibits throughout Helsinki; pick up a list at the tourist office. (Sofiankatu 4. ☎ 3103 6630. Open M-F 9am-5pm, Sa-Su 11am-5pm. Free.) The red-brick ◙**Uspenski Orthodox Cathedral** (Uspenskinkatedraadi), the largest Orthodox church in Northern and Western Europe, evokes images of Russia with its ornate interior and 13 golden cupolas. (☎ 09 963 4267. Open M and W-F 9:30am-4pm, Tu 9:30am-6pm, Sa 9:30am-2pm Su noon-3pm. Closed M in winter.)

ESPLANADI AND MANNERHEIMINTIE. A boulevard dotted with copper patina statues and fountains, Esplanadi is a great place to people-watch. The **Designmuseo** presents the work of designers like Aalto and Eliel Saarinen alongside creations by Finnish artists and first-rate temporary exhibits. (Korkeavuorenkatu 23. ☎ 622 0540; www.designmuseum.fi. Open June-Aug. daily 11am-6pm; Sept.-May Tu 11am-8pm, W-Su 11am-6pm. €7, students €3. AmEx/MC/V.) On the same block, the small **Museum of Finnish Architecture** has temporary displays on the history and future of

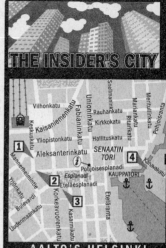

THE INSIDER'S CITY

AALTO'S HELSINKI

Finlandia Hall may be architect Alvar Aalto's most recognizable gift to Helsinki, but a number of his other Modernist creations give visitors a sense of his aesthetic breadth.

1. Rautatalo (Iron House), Keskusk. 3. The stark facade conceals an airy atrium meant to recall an Italian *piazza*, one of Aalto's favorite motifs.

2. Academic Bookstore, Pohjois-esplanadi 39. Finland's largest bookstore named its upstairs cafe after Aalto, who designed the copper and marble building in 1969.

3. Savoy Restaurant, Eteläesplanadi 14. The €40 entrees are too pricey for the budget traveler, but the decor is all Aalto's work—right down to the trademark vases.

4. Stora Enso Headquarters, Kanavak. 1. This ultramodern "sugar cube" overlooks the South Harbor and provides a provocative contrast to the two magnificent churches that flank it.

building design. *(Kasarmikatu 24. ☎8567 5100; www.mfa.fi. Open Tu and Th-F 10am-4pm, W 10am-8pm, Sa-Su 11am-4pm. €3.50, students €1.70. Free F. AmEx/MC/V.)* Across from the train station, down a block on Kaivokatu lies the **Ateneum Art Museum** (Ateneum Taidemuseo), Finland's largest, with comprehensive exhibits on Finnish art. *(Kaivokatu 2. ☎1733 6401; www.ateneum.fi. Open Tu and F 9am-6pm, W-Th 9am-8pm, Sa-Su 11am-5pm. €6, students €4; €8/6.50 during special exhibits; first W of each month free 5-8pm. AmEx/MC/V.)* A couple blocks west of the train station on Mannerheimintie is **Kiasma** (Museum of Contemporary Art), a quirky warehouse that features top-flight modern art and even calibrates the width of its doors to Fibonacci's golden ratio. *(Mannerheimintie 2. ☎1733 6501; www.kiasma.fi. Open Tu 9am-5pm, W-Su 10am-8:30pm. €7, students €5; 1st W each month free 5-8pm. AmEx/MC/V.)* Farther down the road is the grand **Parliament House,** Mannerheimintie 30. *(☎09 432 2027. Only accessible by 1hr. tours to the Session Hall, Hall of State, and the Parliament cafeteria. Open Sa 11am and 2:30pm, Su noon and 1:30pm; July and Aug. also M-F 11am and 1pm. Free.)* The next building up Mannerheimintie is Saarinen's **National Museum of Finland** (Suomen Kansallismuseo), featuring a 1928 ceiling fresco by Gallen-Kallela and many exhibits on Finnish history. *(Mannerheimintie 34. ☎40 501; www.kansallismuseo.fi. Open Tu-W 11am-8pm, Th-Su 11am-6pm. €7, students €4, under 18 free, Tu 5:30-8pm free. AmEx/MC/V.)* Head back to the city center down Mannerheimintie, turn right on Arkadiankatu, and right again on Fredrikinkatu to reach the heavily touristed **Temppeliaukio Kirkko.** This striking church is hewn out of a hill of rock with only the domed roof visible from the outside. *(Lutherinkatu 3. ☎2340 5920. English-language services Su 2pm. Usually open in summer M, Tu, Th, F 10am-8pm, W 10am-6:45pm, Sa 10am-6pm, Su 11:45am-1:45pm and 3:30-6pm.)*

OTHER SIGHTS. The **Theater Museum** contains set models and costume designs from the National Theater. *(Tallberginkatu 1. M: Ruoholahti. After exiting, walk 5 blocks down Itämerenkatu Museums are in the G entrance. ☎4763 8300; www.teatterimuseo.fi. Open Tu-Su 11am-6pm. Theater Museum closed in July. Photography Museum €6, students €4; Hotel and Restaurant Museum €2/1; Theater Museum €6/3. MC/V.)* Near the Western Harbor, the crowded **Jean Sibelius Monument** pays homage to one of the 20th century's great composers. *(On Mechelininkatu in Sibelius Park. Take bus #24, dir.: Seurasaari to Rasjasaarentie. The monument will be behind you.)* The **Helsinki Zoo,** the country's largest, includes a menagerie of 200 animal species and a boat ride around the island. *(Korkeasaari. Take the ferry from Kauppatori or Hakaniemi, or the Zoo Line Bus from Herttoniemi metro station. ☎3103 7900; www.zoo.hel.fi Open daily May-Aug. 10am-8pm; Sept. and Apr. 10am-6pm; Oct.-Mar. 10am-4pm. €12, student €7.50. Catch the boat at dock 24.)*

🔲 ENTERTAINMENT AND FESTIVALS

Helsinki's parks are always animated. In the early evening, young people sit and drink in the downtown parks. A **concert** series enlivens the Esplanadi park all summer offering shows on most days throughout the summer. Highlights of the program are **Jazz Espa** in July, and **Ethno Espa** showcasing international music (www.kulttuuri.hel.fi/espanlava). Late June's **Helsinki Pride** celebration (www.helsinkipride.fi) is Finland's largest GLBT event and lasts for a week. The two week **Helsinki Festival** (www.helsinkifestival.fi), at the end of August, wraps up the summer with cultural events ranging from music and theater to film and visual arts. At the end of September, **Helsinki Design Week** (www.helsinkidesignweek.fi) reinforces the city's image as a style capital, while the **Love and Anarchy Film Festival** (www.hiff.fi) features works from across the globe. Throughout summer, concerts rock **Kaivopuisto** (on the corner of Puistokatu and Ehrenstromintie, in the southern part of town), the **Olympic Stadium,** and **Hietaniemi Beach** (down Hesperiankatu on the western shore). Check out the **Nordic Oddity** pamphlet series, with insider advice on sights, bars, and activities.

For high culture, try the **Helsinki Philharmonic and Radio Symphony Orchestra,** the **National Opera,** or the **National Theater.** Lippupiste and Lippupalvelu, Aleksanterinkatu 52 (☎0600 900 900), in the Stockmann department store, sell tickets for most of the big venues in the city(AmEx/MC/V).

🏮 NIGHTLIFE

Bars and summer beer terraces fill up in late afternoon; most clubs don't get going until midnight and stay crazy until 4am. Bars and clubs line Mannerheimintie, Uudenmaankatu, and Iso Roobertinkatu. East of the train station, nightlife centers around Yliopistonkatu and Kaisaniemenkatu, while in bohemian Kallio, the bars around Fleminginkatu have some of the cheapest **beer** in the city. A popular night activity is heavy-metal **karaoke;** check it out Wednesday and Sunday at **Hevimesta,** Hallituskatu 3.

> **Royal Onnela,** Fredrikinkatu 46 (☎020 7759 460; www.ravintolaonnela.fi). Claims the title of biggest nightclub in Scandinavia. It has 9 dance rooms, suiting almost any musical taste from Finnish pop to disco and 80s/90s hits. Onnela dominates the Helsinki nightlife on Su. Beer €4.90, Su €1. €4 Silver card grants half-price on many drinks M,W, and Th. Sa 22+. Cover F €5 but free with Silver card, Sa €7. Club open M and W-Su 10pm-3:30am. Lapland Poro Bar open daily 6pm-4am. Karaoke bar open daily 8pm-4pm. Bars close early if not busy. AmEx/MC/V.

> **On the Rocks,** Mikonkatu 15 (☎09 612 2030; www.ontherocks.fi). This legendary bar and club offers some of the best Finnish bands. M-Sa live music. 20+. Cover free-€12. Open daily in summer noon-4am; in winter 2pm-4am. AmEx/MC/V.

> **Bar Erottaja,** Erottajankatu 13-17 (☎09 611 196). This art-student hangout is usually packed with people engaged in conversation while listening to music. Beer €3.20-580. F-Sa DJ. 22+ after 6pm. Open M-Tu and Su 2pm-1am, W-Sa 2pm-3am. AmEx/MC/V.

> **Vanha,** Mannerheimintie 3 (☎1311 4368; www.vanha.fi). A lively student crowd occasionally rents the hall as a club to party in. Check website for performance schedule. Beer €5. Cover €5. Open F-Sa 10pm-4am. AmEx/MC/V.

> **Highlight,** Fredrikinkatu 42 (☎050 409 0079). A dance club for the young and fit. 18+. Cover after 11pm €5. Open F-Sa 10pm-4am. AmEx/MC/V.

> **dtm,** Iso Roobertinkatu 28 (☎09 676 314; www.dtm.fi). This popular club claims the title of largest gay club in Scandinavia. Occasional lesbian nights F-Sa. 22+ after 10pm. Cover €2.50, Sa €5, special events €5-10. M-Th beer, shots, cider €3 and Su pints €1 after 6pm. Open M-Sa 9am-4am, Su noon-4am. AmEx/MC/V.

🏔 OUTDOOR ACTIVITIES

TÖÖLÖNLAHTI AND ELÄINTARHANLAHTI. Just north of the train station are these two city lakes and accompanying parks, which offer great walks. Northwest of the Sibelius Monument across a bridge, the island of **Seurasaari** offers a retreat from the city. It is also home to an open-air museum of farmsteads and churches. *(Take bus #24 from Erottaja to the last stop. The island is always open for hiking. Museum ☎4050 9665. Open daily June-Aug. 11am-5pm; late May and early Sept. M-F 9am-3pm, Sa-Su 11am-5pm. Tours from mid-June to mid-August daily 3pm. €6, students €4. MC/V.)*

BEACHES. Many islands south of the city feature public beaches that are accessible by ferry, including a nude beach on Pihlajasaari Island. Beyond Espoo to the west is the **Nuuksio National Park,** where flying squirrels are a common sight. *(☎0205 64 4790; www.outdoors.fi/nuuksionp. Take the train to Espoo station and bus #85 from there to Kattila in Nuuksio in summer or Nuuksionpää in winter.)*

DAYTRIPS FROM HELSINKI

PORVOO (BORGÅ). Porvoo (pop. 47,000) is along Old King Road, 50km east of Helsinki. From the bus station, walk down Lundinkatu toward the river and turn right on Runeberginkatu, following it until you see the green signs of the **Tourist Information office,** Rihkamakatu 4 (☎019 520 2316; www.porvoo.fi. Open from mid-June to Aug. M-F 9am-6pm, Sa-Su 10am-4pm; from Sept. to mid-June reduced hours.) Porvoo is known for its medieval old town and its whitewashed **hilltop cathedral** where in 1809, Tsar Alexander I granted Finland autonomy. The cathedral fell victim to an attack in May 2006; it is being rebuilt and will reopen in December 2008. The house of Finland's national poet **Johan Ludvig Runeberg,** Aleksanterinkatu 3, looks just as it did when he called it home in the mid-1800s. (☎019 581 330. Open May-Aug. daily 10am-4pm; Sept.-Apr. W-Su 10am-4pm. House and sculpture exhibit €5, students €2. Cash only.) The **Historical Museum,** in the 1764 Town Hall in Old Market Sq., features an eclectic array of artifacts but is closed for renovation until sometime in 2009. (☎019 574 7500. Check www.porvoomuseo.fi for more information.) Charming, if overpriced, cafes line the streets of Old Town. Many, such as Cafe Helmi and Cafe Fanny, sell Runeberg cakes, which the poet himself enjoyed, for about €3. The small round cakes—with almonds and cinnamon topped off with raspberry jam and a squeeze of icing—are a delicious, regional favorite. (Buses run from Helsinki (1hr., 3 per hr., €9-12). Harryn Pyörävarikko, Jokikatu 11, rents bikes to visitors heading as far south as Pellinki. ☎1965 4156.) **Postal Code:** 06100.

LAHTI. World-class winter sports facilities make Lahti (pop. 100,000) a popular destination for outdoor enthusiasts and especially snow-lovers. For trail information, call **Lahti Sports Services** (☎03 816 816). The **Ski Museum** has ski-jump and slalom simulators and a simulated shooting range. (☎038 144 523. Open M-F 10am-5pm, Sa-Su 11am-5pm. €5, students €3. MC/V.) Towering 200m above the museum, the tallest of three █**ski jumps,** accessible by a chairlift followed by an elevator, offers excellent views of the city. (Open in summer daily 10am-5pm. €5, students €3; with Ski Museum €8/€5.) The 100k of cross-country **ski trails** emanate out from the sports complex; the **tourist office** has info on the Ilvesvaellus Trail, a 30min. bus ride northwest. In Kariniemi Park, near the shore, the **Musical Fountains** combine water and music daily at 1 and 6pm in summer, 7pm in spring and fall. At the harbor, **Sibelius Hall** holds the **Sibelius Festival** in September, with performances of the composer's works. (Trains head to Helsinki (1hr., 2 per hr., from €13.20), Savonlinna (3:30hr., 6 per day, from €41.50), and Tampere (1:45hr., 1 per hr., from €25). The tourist office is at Rautatienkatu 22. ☎020 728 1750; www.lahtitravel.fi. Open M-Th 9am-5pm, F 9am-4pm; also open from mid-July to mid-Aug. Sa 10am-2pm. AmEx/MC/V.) **Postal Code:** 15110.

FRANCE

With its lavish châteaux, lavender fields, medieval streets, and sidewalk cafes, France conjures up any number of postcard-ready scenes. To the proud French, it is only natural that outsiders flock to their history-steeped homeland. Although France may no longer manipulate world events, the vineyards of Bordeaux, the museums of Paris, and the beaches of the Riviera draw more tourists than any other nation in the world. Centuries-old farms and churches share the landscape with inventive, modern architecture; street posters advertise jazz festivals as well as Baroque concerts. The country's rich culinary tradition rounds out a culture that cannot be sent home on a four-by-six.

DISCOVER FRANCE: SUGGESTED ITINERARIES

THREE DAYS. Don't even think of leaving **Paris,** the City of Light (p. 233). Explore the shops and cafes of the **Latin Quarter,** then cross the **Seine** to reach **Île de la Cité** to admire **Sainte-Chapelle** and the **Cathédrale de Notre Dame.** Visit the wacky **Centre National d'Art et de Culture Georges Pompidou** before swinging through **Marais** for food and fun. The next day, stroll down the **Champs-Élysées,** starting at the **Arc de Triomphe,** meander through the **Jardin des Tuileries,** and over to the **Musée d'Orsay.** See part of the **Louvre** the next morning, then spend the afternoon at **Versailles.**

ONE WEEK. After three days in **Paris,** go to **Orléans** (1 day), a great base for exploring the châteaux of the **Loire Valley** (1 day; p. 258). Head to **Rennes** for medieval sights and modern nightlife (1 day; p. 259), then to bubbly country (oh so tingly!) around **Reims** (1 day).

BEST OF FRANCE, THREE WEEKS. Begin with five days in Paris, then daytrip to the royal residences at **Versailles.** Whirl through the **Loire Valley** (2 days) before traveling to the wine country of **Bordeaux** (1 day; p. 271). Your inner art film will thank you for sailing through **Avignon** (p. 273) and **Aix-en-Provence** (p. 272) in sunny **Provence** (3 days). Bask in the glitter of the Riviera in **Nice** (2 days; p. 274). Then show off your tan in the Alps as you travel **Lyon** (2 days; p. 266) to revel in their wild nightlife before heading off to **Grenoble** (1 day). Spice it up with a mustard tour in **Dijon** (1 day; p. 262), and finish your trip with some German flavor in **Strasbourg** (1 day; p. 263), where trains will whisk you away to your next European adventure.

ESSENTIALS

WHEN TO GO

In July, Paris starts to shrink; by August it is devoid of Parisians, animated only by tourists and the pickpockets who love them. The French Riviera fills with Anglophones from June to September. During these months, French natives flee to other parts of the country, especially the Atlantic coast. Early summer and fall are the best times to visit Paris—the city has warmed up but not completely emptied out. The north and west have cool winters and mild summers,

while the less-crowded center and east have a more temperate climate. From December through April, the Alps provide some of the world's best skiing, while the Pyrénées offer a calmer, if less climatically dependable, alternative.

FACTS AND FIGURES

OFFICIAL NAME: French Republic.

CAPITAL: Paris.

MAJOR CITIES: Lyon, Marseille, Nice.

POPULATION: 60,880,000.

LAND AREA: 547,000 sq. km.

TIME ZONE: GMT+1.

LANGUAGE: French.

RELIGION: Roman Catholic (88%), Muslim (9%), Protestant (2%), Jewish (1%).

CHEESE VARIETIES: Over 500.

DOCUMENTS AND FORMALITIES

EMBASSIES AND CONSULATES. Foreign embassies in France are in **Paris** (p. 234). French embassies abroad include: **Australia,** Level 26, St-Martins Tower, 31 Market St., Sydney NSW 2000 (☎+61 02 92 68 24 00; www.ambafrance-au.org); **Canada,** 1501, McGill College, Bureau 1000, Montréal, QC H3A 3M8 (☎+1-878-4385; www.consulfrance-montreal.org); **Ireland,** 36 Ailesbury Rd.,

Ballsbridge, Dublin, 4 (☎+353 1 227 5000; www.ambafrance.ie); **New Zealand,** 34-42 Manners St., Wellington (☎+64 384 25 55; www.ambafrance-nz.org); **UK,** 21 Cromwell Rd., London SW7 2EN (☎+44 207 073 1000; www.consul-france-londres.org); **US,** 4101 Reservoir Rd., NW, Washington, D.C., 20007 (☎+1-202-944-6195; www.consulfrance-washington.org).

VISA AND ENTRY INFORMATION. EU citizens do not need a visa. Citizens of Australia, Canada, New Zealand, and the US do not need a visa for stays of up to 90 days, beginning upon entry into any of the countries in the EU's freedom-of-movement zone. For more info, see p. 13. For stays longer than 90 days, all non-EU citizens need Schengen visas (around US$81), available at French consulates and online at www.consulfrance-washington.org.

TOURIST SERVICES AND MONEY

EMERGENCY	Ambulance: ☎15. Fire: ☎18. Police: ☎17. General Emergency: ☎112.

TOURIST OFFICES. The **French Government Tourist Office** (**FGTO;** www.franceguide.com), also known as Maison de la France, runs tourist offices (called *syndicats d'initiative* or *offices de tourisme*) and offers tourist services to travelers abroad. In smaller towns, the **mairie** (town hall) may also distribute maps and pamphlets, help travelers find accommodations, and suggest excursions.

MONEY. The **euro (€)** has replaced the franc as the unit of currency in France. For more info, see p. 16. As a general rule, it's cheaper to exchange money in France than at home. Be prepared to spend at least €40-60 per day and considerably more in Paris. Tips are generally included in meal prices at restaurants and cafes, as well as in drink prices at bars and clubs; ask or look for the phrase *service compris* on the menu. If service is not included, tip 15-20%. Even when service is included, it is polite to leave a *pourboire* of up to 5% at a cafe, bistro, restaurant, or bar. Workers such as concierges may expect at least a €1.50 tip for services beyond the call of duty; taxi drivers expect 10-15% of the metered fare. Tipping tour guides and bus drivers €1.50-3 is customary.

France has a 19.6% **value added tax** (**VAT;** TVA in French), a sales tax applied to a wide range of goods and services. The prices included in *Let's Go* include VAT. In the airport upon exiting the EU, non-EU citizens can claim a refund on the tax paid for goods purchased at participating stores. In order to qualify for a refund in a store, you must spend at least €175; make sure to ask for a refund form when you pay. For more info on qualifying for a VAT refund, see p. 19.

TRANSPORTATION

BY PLANE. Most transatlantic flights to Paris land at **Roissy-Charles de Gaulle** (**CDG;** ☎01 48 62 22 80). Many continental and charter flights use **Orly** (**ORY;** ☎01 49 75 15 15). Aéroports de Paris (www.aeroportsdeparis.fr) has info about both. **Paris Beauvais Tillé** (**BVA;** ☎38 92 68 20 66; www.aeroportbeauvais.com) caters to budget travelers, servicing airlines like Ryanair (UK ☎0905 566 0000; www.ryanair.com). For more info on flying to France, see p. 42.

BY TRAIN. The French national railway company, **SNCF** (☎0892 35 35 35; www.sncf.fr), manages one of Europe's most efficient rail networks. Among the fastest in the world, **TGV** (www.tgv.com) trains (*train à grande vitesse;* high-speed) now link many major French cities, as well as some European destinations,

FRANCE

including Brussels, Geneva, Lausanne, and Zürich. *Rapide* trains are slower. Local Express trains are actually the slowest option. French trains offer discounts of 25-50% on tickets for travelers under 26 with the **Carte 12-25** (€52; good for 1yr.). Locate the *guichets* (ticket counters), the *quais* (platforms), and the *voies* (tracks), and you will be ready to roll. Terminals can be divided into *banlieue* (suburb) and the bigger *grandes lignes* (intercity trains). While some select trains require reservations, you are not guaranteed a seat without one (usually US$5-30). Reserve ahead during holidays and high seasons.

If you are planning to spend a great deal of time on trains, a rail pass might be worthwhile, but in many cases—especially if you are under 26—point-to-point tickets may be cheaper. **Eurail** is valid in France. Standard **Eurail Passes,** valid for a given number of consecutive days, are best for those planning on traveling long distances. **Flexipasses,** valid for any 10 or 15 (not necessarily consecutive) days within a two-month period, are more cost-effective for those traveling longer distances less frequently. **Youth Passes** and **Youth Flexipasses** provide the same second-class perks for those under 26. It is best to purchase a pass before going to France. For prices and more info, contact student travel agencies, **Rail Europe** (Canada ☎800-361-7245, US 888-382-7245; www.raileurope.com), or **Flight Centre** (US ☎866-967-5351; www.flightcentre.com)

SELF-VALIDATE=GREAT. Validate *(composter)* your ticket! Orange validation boxes lie around every station, and you must have your ticket stamped with the date and time by the machine before boarding the train.

BY BUS. Within France, long-distance buses are a secondary transportation choice, as service is relatively infrequent. However, in some regions buses are indispensable for reaching out-of-the-way towns. Bus services operated by SNCF accept rail passes. *Gare routière* is French for "bus station."

BY FERRY. Ferries across the **English Channel** (La Manche) link France to England and Ireland. The shortest and most popular route is between Dover, BRI and Calais (1hr.) and is run by **P&O Stena Line** (☎08 25 12 01 56; www.posl.com) and **SeaFrance** (☎08 25 04 40 45; www.seafrance.com). **Norfolkline** (☎44 0870 870 1020; www.norfolkline-ferries.com) provides an alternative route from Dover, BRI to Dunkerque (1hr.). **Brittany Ferries** (France ☎0825 82 88 28, UK ☎0871 244 0744; www.brittany-ferries.com) travels from Portsmouth to Caen (5¾hr.), Cherbourg (4½hr.), and St-Malo (10¾hr.). For more info on English Channel ferries, see p. 52.

BY CAR. Drivers in France visiting for fewer than 90 days must be 18 years old and carry either an **International Driving Permit (IDP)** or a valid EU-issued or American driving license. You need to also have the vehicle's registration, national plate, and current insurance certificate on hand; French car rental agencies provide necessary documents. Agencies require renters to be 20, and most charge those aged 21-24 an additional insurance fee (€20-25 per day). If you don't know how to drive stick, you may have to pay a hefty premium for a car with automatic transmission. French law requires that both drivers and passengers wear seat belts. The almost 1,000,000km of French roads are usually in great condition, due in part to expensive tolls paid by travelers. Check www.francetourism.com/practicalinfo for more info on travel and car rentals.

BY BIKE AND BY THUMB. Of Europeans, the French alone may love **cycling** more than football. Renting a **bike** (€8-19 per day) beats bringing your own if you're only touring one or two regions. Hitchhiking is illegal on French highways, although some people describe the French's ready willingness to lend a ride. *Let's Go* does not recommend hitchhiking.

KEEPING IN TOUCH

PHONE CODES	Country code: 33. **International dialing prefix:** 00. When calling within a city, dial 0 + city code + local number. For more info on how to place international calls, see **Inside Back Cover.**

EMAIL AND THE INTERNET. Internet is readily available throughout France. Only the smallest villages lack Internet cafes, and in larger towns Internet cafes are well equipped and widespread, though often pricey. In addition to the locations suggested here, check out www.cybercaptive.com for more options.

TELEPHONE. Whenever possible, use a **calling card** for international phone calls, as long-distance rates for national phone services are often very high. Publicly owned **France Télécom** pay phones charge less than their privately owned counterparts. They accept *Télécartes* (phonecards), available in 50-unit (€7.50) and 120-unit (€15) denominations at newspaper kiosks and tabacs. **Mobile phones** are an increasingly popular and economical option. Major mobile carriers include Orange, Bouyges Telecom, and SFR. *Décrochez* means pick up; you'll then be asked to *patientez* (wait) to insert your card; at *numérotez* or *composez*, you can dial. The number for general info is ☎12; for an international operator, call ☎00 33 11. International direct dial numbers include: **AT&T Direct** ☎0 800 99 00 11; **Canada Direct** ☎0 800 99 00 16 or 99 02 16; **MCI WorldPhone** ☎0 800 99 00 19; **Telecom New Zealand** ☎0 800 99 00 64; **Telstra Australia** ☎0 800 99 00 61.

MAIL. Send mail from **La Poste** offices (www.laposte.net. Open M-F 9am-7pm, Sa 9am-noon). Airmail between France and North America takes five to 10 days; writing *"prioritaire"* on the envelope should ensure delivery in about five days at no extra charge. To send a 20g airmail letter or postcard within France or from France to another EU destination costs around €0.54, to a non-EU European country €0.75, and to Australia, Canada, New Zealand, or the US €0.90. To receive mail in France, have it delivered **Poste Restante.** Mail will go to the main post office unless you specify a subsidiary by street address. Address mail to be held as follows: Last name, First name, Poste Restante, postal code, city, France. Bring a passport to pick up your mail; there may be a small fee.

ACCOMMODATIONS AND CAMPING

FRANCE	❶	❷	❸	❹	❺
ACCOMMODATIONS	under €15	€15-27	€28-38	€39-55	over €55

The **French Hostelling International (HI)** affiliate, **Fédération Unie des Auberges de Jeunesse (FUAJ;** ☎01 44 89 87 27; www.fuaj.org), operates 150 hostels within France. A dorm bed in a hostel averages €10-15. Some hostels accept reservations through the **International Booking Network** (www.hostelbooking.com). Two or more people traveling together can save money by staying in cheap hotels rather than hostels. The French government employs a four-star hotel rating system. *Gîtes d'étapes* are rural accommodations for cyclists, hikers, and other amblers in less-populated areas. After 3000 years of settlement, true wilderness in France is hard to find, and it's illegal to **camp** in most public spaces, including national parks. Instead, look for organized *campings* (campgrounds), replete with vacationing families and programmed fun. Most have toilets, showers,

FRANCE

and electrical outlets, though you may have to pay €2-5 extra for such luxuries; you'll often need to pay a fee for your car, too (€3-8).

FOOD AND DRINK

FRANCE	❶	❷	❸	❹	❺
FOOD	under €7	€7-12	€13-18	€19-33	over €33

French chefs cook for one of the world's most finicky clienteles. The largest meal of the day is *le déjeuner* (lunch), while a light croissant with or without *confiture* (jam) characterizes *le petit déjeuner* (breakfast). A complete French meal includes an *apéritif* (drink), an *entrée* (appetizer), a *plat* (main course), salad, cheese, dessert, fruit, coffee, and a *digestif* (after-dinner drink). The French drink **wine** with virtually every meal; *boisson comprise* entitles you to a free drink (usually wine) with your food. In France, the legal drinking age is 16. Most restaurants offer a *menu à prix fixe* (fixed-price meal) that costs less than ordering *à la carte*. The *formule* is a cheaper, two-course version for the hurried luncher. Odd-hour cravings between lunch and dinner can be satisfied at *brasseries* or creperies, the middle ground between cafes and restaurants. *Service compris* means the tip is included in *l'addition* (the check). It's easy to get a satisfying dinner for under €10 with staples such as cheese, pâté, wine, bread, and chocolate. For a budget-friendly **picnic,** get fresh produce at a *marché* (outdoor market) and then hop between specialty shops. Start with a *boulangerie* (bakery) for bread, proceed to a *charcuterie* (butcher) for meats, and then *pâtisseries* (pastry shops) and *confiseries* (candy shops) to satisfy a sweet tooth. When choosing a cafe, remember that major boulevards provide more expensive venues than smaller places on side streets. Prices are also cheaper at the *comptoir* (counter) than in the *salle* (seating area). For **supermarket** shopping, look for the chains **Carrefour, Casino,** and **Monoprix.**

HOLIDAYS AND FESTIVALS

Holidays: New Year's Day (Jan. 1); Good Friday (Apr. 10, 2009); Easter (Apr. 13, 2009); Labor Day (May 1); Ascension Day (May 21, 2009); Victory Day (May 8); Whit Monday (June1, 2009); Bastille Day (July 14); Assumption (Aug. 15); All Saints' Day (Nov. 1); Armistice Day (Nov. 11); Christmas (Dec. 25-26).

Festivals: Many cities celebrate a pre-Lenten Carnaval—for the most over-the-top festivities and partying, head to **Nice** (Jan. 25-Feb. 5). The **Cannes Film Festival** (May 13-24; www.festival-cannes.com) caters to the rich, famous, and creative. In 2009, the **Tour de France** will begin July 4. (www.letour.fr). The **Festival d'Avignon** (July-Aug.; www.festival-avignon.com) is famous for its theater productions.

BEYOND TOURISM

As the most visited nation in the world, France benefits economically from the tourism industry. Yet the country's popularity has adversely affected some French communities and their natural life. Throw off the *touriste* stigma and advocate for immigrant communities, restore a crumbling château, or educate others about the importance of environmental issues while exploring France. For more info on opportunities across Europe, see **Beyond Tourism**, p. 55.

Care France, CAP 19, 13 r. Georges Auric, 75019 Paris (☎01 53 19 89 89; www.
carefrance.org). An international organization providing volunteer opportunities, ranging
from combating AIDS to promoting education.

Club du Vieux Manoir, Ancienne Abbaye du Moncel, 60700 Pontpoint (☎03 44 72 33
98; cvmclubduvieuxmanoir.free.fr). Year-long and summer work restoring castles and
churches. €14 membership and insurance fee; €12.50 per day, plus food and tent.

International Partnership for Service-Learning and Leadership, 815 2nd Ave., Ste.
315, New York, NY 10017, USA (☎212-986-0989; www.ipsl.org). An organization that
matches volunteers with host families, provides intensive French classes, and requires
10-15hr. per week of service for a year, semester, or summer. Ages 18-30. Based in
Montpellier. Costs range US$7200-US$23,600.

PARIS   ☎01

Paris (pah-ree; pop. 2,153,600), a cultural and commercial center for over 2000
years, draws millions of visitors each year, from students who come to study to
tourists who snap endless pictures of the Eiffel Tower. The City of Light, Paris
is a source of inspiration unrivaled in beauty. Priceless art fills its world-class
museums and history is found in its Roman ruins, medieval streets, Renaissance hotels, and 19th-century boulevards. A vibrant political center, Paris
blends the spirit of revolution with a reverence for tradition, devoting as much
energy to preserving conventions as it does to shattering them.

▓ INTERCITY TRANSPORTATION

Flights: Some budget airlines fly into **Aéroport de Paris Beauvais Tillé (BVA),** 1hr. outside of Paris (p. 229). **Aéroport Roissy-Charles de Gaulle (CDG,** Roissy; ☎3950; www.
adp.fr), 23km northeast of Paris, serves most transatlantic flights. 24hr. English-speaking info center. The **RER B** (a Parisian commuter rail line) runs to central Paris from
Terminals 1 and 2. (35min.; every 15min. 5am-12:30am; €13). **Aéroport d'Orly (ORY;**
☎01 49 75 15 15), 18km south of Paris, is used by charters and continental flights.

Trains: Paris has 6 major train stations: **Gare d'Austerlitz** (to the Loire Valley, southwestern France, Portugal, and Spain); **Gare de l'Est** (to Austria, eastern France, Czech
Republic, southern Germany, Hungary, Luxembourg, and Switzerland); **Gare de Lyon** (to
southern and southeastern France, Greece, Italy, and Switzerland); **Gare du Nord** (to
Belgium, Britain, Eastern Europe, northern France, northern Germany, the Netherlands,
and Scandinavia); **Gare Montparnasse** (to Brittany and southwestern France on the
TGV); **Gare St-Lazare** (to). All are accessible by Métro.

Buses: Gare Routière Internationale du Paris-Gallieni, 28 av. du Général de Gaulle,
outside Paris. Ⓜ️Gallieni. Eurolines (☎08 92 89 90 91, €0.34 per min.; www.eurolines.
fr) sells tickets to most destinations in France and bordering countries.

▓ ORIENTATION

The **Seine River** (SEHN) flows from east to west through Paris with two islands,
Île de la Cité and **Île St-Louis,** situated in the city's geographical center. The Seine
splits Paris in half: the **Rive Gauche** (REEV go-sh; Left Bank) to the south and
the **Rive Droite** (REEV dwaht; Right Bank) to the north. Modern Paris is divided
into 20 *arrondissements* (districts) that spiral clockwise outward from the
center of the city. Each *arrondissement* is referred to by its number (e.g. the
Third, the Sixteenth). Sometimes it is helpful to orient yourself around central
Paris's major monuments: on Rive Gauche, the sprawling **Jardin du Luxembourg**

FRANCE

lies in the southeast; the **Eiffel Tower,** visible from many points in the city, stands in the southwest; moving clockwise and crossing the Seine to Rive Droite, the **Champs-Élysées** and **Arc de Triomphe** occupy the northwest, and the **Sacré-Coeur** stands high in the northeast. *Let's Go Europe 2010* splits Paris into five sections according to geographical grouping of *arrondissements*: the **city center** (1*er,* 2*ème,* 3*ème,* and 4*ème*); **Left Bank East** (5*ème,* 6*ème,* and 13*ème*); **Left Bank West** (7*ème,* 14*ème,* and 15*ème*); **Right Bank East** (10*ème,* 11*ème,* 12*ème,* 18*ème,* 19*ème,* and 20*ème*); **Right Bank West** (8*ème,* 9*ème,* 16*ème,* and 17*ème*).

LOCAL TRANSPORTATION

Public Transportation: The **Métro** (Ⓜ) runs from 5:30am-1:20am. Lines are numbered and are referred to by their number and final destinations; connections are called *correspondances.* Single-fare tickets within the city cost €1.60; carnet of 10 €11.40. Buy extras for when ticket booths are closed (after 10pm) and hold onto your ticket until you exit. The **RER** (Réseau Express Régional), the commuter train to the suburbs, serves as an express subway within central Paris. Keep your ticket: changing to and getting off the RER requires sticking your validated ticket into a turnstile. Watch the signboards next to the RER tracks and check that your stop is lit up before riding. Buses use the same €1.40 tickets (validate in the machine by the driver). Buses run 7am-8:30pm, **Autobus de Nuit** until 1:30am, and **Noctambus** 1 per hr. 12:30am-5:30am at stops marked with a blue "N" inside a white circle, with a red star on the upper right-hand side. The **Mobilis pass** covers the Métro, RER, and buses (€5.80 for a 1-day pass in Zones 1 and 2). A **Carte Orange weekly pass** *(carte orange hebdomadaire)* costs €16.80 and expires on Su; photo required. Refer to the front of the book for maps of Paris's transit network.

 CONSTANT VIGILANCE. The following stations can be dangerous at night: Anvers, Barbès-Rochechouart, Château d'Eau, Châtelet, Châtelet-Les-Halles, Gare de l'Est, Gare du Nord, and Pigalle. If concerned, take a taxi, or sit near the driver on a Noctilien bus.

Taxis: Alpha Taxis (☎01 53 60 63 50). **Taxi 75** (☎01 78 41 65 05). Taxis take 3 passengers (4th passenger €2-3 surcharge). **Tarif A,** daily 7am-7pm (€0.86 per km). **Tarif B,** M-Sa 7pm-7am, Su 24hr., and from the airports and immediate suburbs (€1.12 per km). **Tarif C,** from the airports 7pm-7am (€1.35 per km). In addition, there is a €2.20 base fee and min. €5.60 charge. It is customary to tip 15% and polite to add €1 extra.

Bike Rental: Vélib (www.en.velib.paris.fr). Self-service bike rental. Over 1450 terminals and 20,000 bikes in Paris. Buy a subscription (day €1, week €5, year €29) and rent bikes from any terminal in the city. Rentals under 30min. free. Available 24hr.

PRACTICAL INFORMATION

Tourist Offices: Bureau Gare d'Austerlitz, 13ème (☎01 45 84 91 70). Ⓜ Gare d'Austerlitz. Open M-Sa 8am-6pm. **Bureau Gare de Lyon,** 12ème (☎01 43 43 33 24). Ⓜ Gare de Lyon. Open M-Sa 8am-6pm. **Bureau Tour Eiffel,** Champs de Mars, 7ème (☎08 92 68 31 12). Ⓜ Champs de Mars. Open daily May-Sept. 11am-6:40pm. **Montmartre Tourist Office,** 21 pl. du Tertre, 18ème (☎01 42 62 21 21). Ⓜ Anvers. Open daily 10am-7pm.

Currency Exchange: American Express, 11 rue Scribe, 9ème (☎01 53 30 99 00; parisscribe.france@kanoofes.com). Ⓜ Opéra or RER Auber. Exchange counters open M-Sa 9am-6:30pm; member services open M-F 9am-5pm, Sa 9am-noon and 1-5pm. **Thomas Cook,** 26 av. de l'Opéra, 1er (☎01 53 29 40 00; fax 47 03 32 13). Ⓜ Georges V. Open M-Sa 9am-10:55pm, Su 8am-6pm.

GLBT Resources: SOS Homophobie, 63 rue Beaubourg, 3ème (☎01 48 06 42 41). Open M-F 8-10pm.

Laundromats: Ask at your hostel or hotel for the closest laundry facilities. **Multiservices,** 75 rue de l'Ouest, 14ème (☎01 43 35 19 51). Wash €3.50, dry €2 per 20min. Open M-Sa 8:30am-8pm. **Laverie Net A Sec,** 3 pl. Monge, 5ème. Wash €4 per 6kg, dry €1 per 9min. Soap €1. Open daily 7:30am-10pm.

Crisis Lines: Poison: ☎01 40 05 48 48. In French, but some English assistance is available. **SOS Help!** (☎01 46 21 46 46). An anonymous, confidential hotline for English speakers in crisis. Open daily (including holidays) 3-11pm. **Rape: SOS Viol** (☎08 00 05 95 95). Open M-F 10am-7pm.

Pharmacies: British and American Pharmacy, 1 rue Auber, pl. de l'Opéra, 9ème (☎01 42 65 88 29). ⓂOpéra or RER Auber. Sells hard-to-find Anglophone brands in addition to French products. English-speaking staff. Open daily 8am-8:30pm. **Pharmacie Beaubourg,** 50 rue Rambuteau, 3ème (☎01 48 87 86 37). ⓂRambuteau. Open M-Sa 8am-8pm, Su 10am-8pm. **Pharmacie des Halles,** 10 bd. de Sébastopol, 1er (☎01 42 72 03 23). ⓂChâtelet-Les Halles. Open M-Sa 9am-midnight, Su 9am-10pm. **Pharmacie Gacha,** 361 rue des Pyrénées, 20ème (☎01 46 36 59 10). ⓂPyrénées or Jourdain. Open M-F 9am-8pm, Sa 9am-7pm.

Medical Services: American Hospital of Paris, 63 bd. Victor Hugo, Neuilly (☎01 46 41 25 25). ⓂPort Maillot, then bus #82 to the end of the line. **Centre Médicale Europe,** 44 rue d'Amsterdam, 9ème (☎01 42 81 93 33). ⓂSt-Lazare. Open M-F 8am-7pm, Sa 8am-6pm. **Hôpital Bichat,** 46 rue Henri Buchard, 18ème (☎01 40 25 80 80). ⓂPort St-Ouen. Emergencies. **SOS Dentaire,** 87 bd. Port-Royal, 13ème (☎01 40 21 82 88). RER Port-Royal. No walk-ins. Open daily 9am-6pm and 8:30-11:45pm. **SOS Médecins** (☎01 48 07 77 77). Makes house calls. **SOS Oeil** (☎01 40 92 93 94). Eye care. Open daily 6am-11pm.

Internet Access: Cyber Cube, 5 rue Mignon, 6ème (☎01 53 10 30 50). ⓂSt-Michel or Odéon. €0.15 per min., €30 per 5hr., €40 per 10hr. Open M-Sa 10am-10pm. **easyInternetcafé,** 6 rue de la Harpe, 5ème (☎01 55 42 55 42). ⓂSt-Michel. €3 per hr. Open M-Sa 7:30am-8pm, Su 9am-8pm.

Post Office: There are post offices in each arrondissement. Most open M-F 8am-7pm, Sa 8am-noon. **Federal Express** (☎08 20 12 38 00). Call for pickup or dropoff at 63 bd. Haussmann, 8ème. ⓂHavre-Caumartin. Open M-F 9am-7:30pm, Sa 9am-5:30pm.

▟ ACCOMMODATIONS

Accommodations in Paris are expensive. You don't need *Let's Go* to tell you that. Expect to pay at least €20 for a hostel dorm-style bed and €28 for a hotel single. Hostels are a better option for single travelers, whereas staying in a hotel is more economical for groups. Paris's hostels skip many standard restrictions (e.g., curfews) and tend to have flexible maximum stays. Rooms fill quickly after morning check-out; arrive early or reserve ahead. Most hostels and *foyers* include the *taxe de séjour* (€0.10-2 per person per day) in listed prices.

CITY CENTER

▧ **Centre International de Paris (BVJ) Louvre,** 20 rue Jean-Jacques Rousseau (☎01 53 00 90 90; www.auberges-de-jeunesse.com). ⓂLouvre or Palais-Royal. 3-building hostel with glass-enclosed courtyard. Bright, spacious, unadorned rooms with 4-9 beds are single-sex, except for groups. Breakfast and linens included. Towels €3.50. Lockers €2. Internet €1 per 10min. Reception 24hr. Beds can be reserved in advance for a max. of 3 nights; extend your reservation

Paris Food and Accommodations

🍴 **FOOD**

Angelina's	**1 B3**
Café de l'Industrie,	**2 F4**
Chartier,	**3 D2**
Comptoir Méditerranée,	**4 D6**
Crêperie Plougastel,	**5 B6**
Georges,	**6 D4**
L'As du Falafel,	**7 E4**
La Bague de Kenza,	**8 F3**
La Victoire Suprême du Coeur,	**9 D4**

L'Ebauchoir,	**10 F6**
Le Perraudin,	**11 C6**
Palais des Thés,	**12 E4**
Piccolo Teatro,	**13 E5**
Tang Frères,	**14 E6**
Ty Yann,	**15 B3**

RER Réseau Express Régional train

🏠 ACCOMMODATIONS

Aloha Hostel,	16 A6	Hôtel de Blois, 22 B6
Auberge de Jeunesse		Hôtel Eiffel Rive
"Jules Ferry" (HI),	17 F6	Gauche, 23 A4
Centre International		Hotel Marignan, 24 D6
de Paris (BVJ):		Hotel Picard, 25 E4
Paris Louvre,	18 C4	Perfect Hôtel, 26 C1
FIAP Jean-Monnet,	19 B6	Woodstock Hostel, 27 D1
Hôtel Beaumarchais,	20 F4	Young and Happy
Hôtel Caulaincourt,	21 C1	(Y&H) Hostel, 28 D6

once there. Rooms held for only 5-10min. after stated arrival time; call if you'll be late. Under 36 only. No alcohol. Dorms €29; doubles €62. Cash only. ❷

🏨 **Hotel Picard,** 26 rue de Picardie (☎01 48 87 53 82; hotel.picard@wanadoo.fr). Ⓜ République. Welcoming, family-run hotel with superb location. Lovely rooms come in many permutations—blue, pink, with exterior window, with rooftop views—so ask ahead to see what's available. Rooms with showers also come with TV. Breakfast €5. Hall showers €3. Reserve 2 weeks ahead. Singles €44, with shower €65, with full bath €75; doubles €53/83/94; triples with full bath €114. 5% discount with *Let's Go*. MC/V. ❸

🏨 **Grand Hôtel Jeanne d'Arc,** 3 rue de Jarente (☎01 48 87 62 11; www.hoteljeannedarc.com). Ⓜ St-Paul. More like an elegant homestyle inn than a budget hotel. Cozy, stylish carpeted rooms with cable TV, toilets, and baths or showers. Stylish common room, loaded with travel guides and other books to borrow. Breakfast €7. Free internet and Wi-Fi. Wheelchair-accessible room. Reserve 2-3 months in advance, earlier for Sept.-Oct. Singles €60-84; doubles €84-97; triples €116; quads €146. MC/V. ❺

🏨 **Hôtel des Jeunes (MIJE;** ☎01 42 74 23 45; www.mije.com). 3 distinct hostels (below) in beautiful old Marais *hôtels particuliers* (mansions). Reception at all 3 locations; main welcome desk at Le Fourcy. Especially popular with school groups. Arranges airport pickup and drop-off and reservations for sights, restaurants, and shows. Restaurant in a vaulted cellar in Le Fourcy. Public phones. Breakfast and in-room shower included. Lockers free with €1 deposit. Linens included. Internet €1 per 10 min. 1-week max. stay. Reception 7am-1am. Reservations only held until noon; if you're arriving later, call ahead to confirm. Lockout noon-3pm. Quiet hours after 10pm. Reserve months ahead online and 2-3 weeks ahead by phone. No alcohol. 4- to 9-bed dorms €30-32; singles €49; doubles €72; triples €90. MIJE membership required (€2.50). Cash only. ❷

Maubuisson, 12 rue des Barres. Ⓜ Hôtel de Ville or Pont Marie. Half-timbered former convent on a silent street by a monastery. Accommodates more individual travelers than groups.

Le Fourcy, 6 rue de Fourcy. Ⓜ St-Paul or Pont Marie. Large courtyard ideal for meeting travelers.

Le Fauconnier, 11 rue du Fauconnier. Ⓜ St-Paul or Pont Marie. Ivy-covered, sun-drenched building steps away from the Seine and Île St-Louis.

LEFT BANK EAST

🏨 **Port-Royal Hôtel,** 8 blvd de Port-Royal (☎01 43 31 70 06; www.hotelportroyal.fr). Ⓜ Les Gobelins. Bright, spacious rooms, a beautiful garden courtyard, 2 comfortable sitting rooms, and a location just steps from the metro more than compensate for this elegant hotel's distance from the Latin Quarter's major sights. Hall showers €2.50. Breakfast €5.50. Wheelchair-accessible. Reserve well in advance. Singles with sink €41-53; doubles with sink €53, with full bath €79; triples with full bath €84-89. Cash only. ❹

🏨 **Hôtel Marignan,** 13 rue du Sommerard (☎01 43 54 63 81; www.hotel-marignan.com). Ⓜ Maubert-Mutualité. Hostel friendliness with hotel privacy. Clean, freshly decorated rooms with (nonfunctioning) fireplaces and classic wood moulding. Breakfast included. Kitchen for guest use, self-service laundry, and Wi-Fi. Singles €47-52, with toilet €55-60, with full bath €75; doubles €60-68/69-80/80-95; triples €80-90/90-105/105-115; quads with toilet €105-115, with full bath €120-153; quints with toilet €120-125, with full bath €145-155. AmEx/MC/V. ❹

🏨 **Hôtel de Nesle,** 7 rue du Nesle (☎01 43 54 62 41; www.hoteldenesleparis.com). Ⓜ Odéon. Every room in this wonderfully quirky hotel represents a particular figure (e.g., Molière) or locale (e.g., Africa). Some rooms with full bath; North African room with Turkish *hammam*. Adorable lobby with ceiling made of dried flowers (you'll understand when you see it). Garden with duck pond. Reserve by phone; confirm 2 days in advance with arrival time. Singles €55-85; doubles €75-100. Extra beds €15. MC/V. ❹

Centres Internationaux du Séjour de Paris: CISP "Kellermann", 17 bd. Kellermann (☎01 44 16 37 38; www.cisp.fr). Ⓜ Porte d'Italie. 363-bed hostel looks like a retro spaceship on stilts. Cafeteria (buffet €11), laundry service, and TV lounge. Breakfast included. Free Wi-Fi and parking. Reception 24hr. Check-in noon. Check-out 9:30am. Reserve 1 month ahead. 8-bed dorms €20; 2- to 4-bed €26. Singles with full bath €39; doubles with full bath €56. MC/V. ❶

LEFT BANK WEST

▨ **Hôtel de Blois,** 5 rue des Plantes (☎01 45 40 99 48; www.hoteldeblois.com). ⓜMouton-Duvernet, Alésia, or Gaîté. Flowers adorn rooms with clean bathrooms, lush carpets, hair dryers, phones, and TVs. Welcoming owner keeps scrapbook of previous guests' thank-you notes. 5 floors; no elevator. Breakfast €6.50. Wi-Fi €5 per hr., €26 per day. Reception 7am-10:30pm. Check-in 3pm. Check-out 11am. Reserve ahead. Singles and doubles with shower and toilet €55-70, with bathtub €75-85. AmEx/MC/V. ❹

▨ **FIAP Jean-Monnet,** 30 rue Cabanis (☎01 43 13 17 00, reservations 43 13 17 17; www.fiap.asso.fr). ⓜGlacière. Like a standard college dorm. 500-bed student center. Spotless rooms with bath and phones. 2 restaurants, outdoor terrace, and *discothèque* every W and F night. Breakfast included. Internet €5 per hr. Wheelchair-accessible. Reception 24hr. Check-out 9am. Curfew 2am. Reserve 2-4 weeks ahead; hostel often booked for summer before June. Be sure to specify if you want a dorm bed. 3- to 4-bed dorms €32; 5- to 6-bed €25. Singles €55; doubles €70. MC/V. ❷

▨ **Aloha Hostel,** 1 rue Borromée (☎01 42 73 03 03; www.aloha.fr). ⓜVolontaires. Frequented by international crowd. Varnished doors and cheery checkered sheets. Free city tour daily 10am. Breakfast included. Linen €3, deposit €7. Towels €3/6. Internet €2 per 30min.; free Wi-Fi. Reception 24hr. Lockout 11am-5pm. Curfew 2am. Reserve 1 week ahead. Apr.-Oct. dorms €23; doubles €50. Nov.-Mar. €4 less. Cash only. ❷

Three Ducks Hostel, 6 pl. Étienne Pernet (☎01 48 42 04 05; www.3ducks.fr). ⓜFélix Faure. Courtyard palm trees, beach-style shower sheds, airy rooms, and bar. Small 4- to 12-bed dorm rooms and a modest kitchen. Breakfast included. Linen €3.50. Towels €1. Internet €2 per 3hr. Reception 24hr. Lockout noon-4pm. Reserve online 1 week ahead, earlier for doubles. In summer 4- to 12-bed dorms €19; 3-bed €21; doubles €46. In winter 4 to 12-bed dorms €23; 3-bed €25; doubles €52. MC/V. ❶

RIGHT BANK WEST

▨ **Perfect Hôtel,** 39 rue Rodier (☎01 42 81 18 86 or 42 81 26 19; www.paris-hostel.biz). ⓜAnvers. Lives up to its name. Rooms with balcony by request. Caring staff. Well-stocked kitchen, free coffee, and a beer vending machine (€1.50). Be careful in neighborhood after dark. Breakfast included. Reception 24hr. Reserve 1 month ahead. Singles €44, with toilet €60; doubles €50/60. Extra bed €19. Cash only. ❸

▨ **Hôtel Champerret Héliopolis,** 13 rue d'Héliopolis (☎01 47 64 92 56; www.champerret-heliopolis-paris-hotel.com). ⓜPorte de Champerret. Superb staff. 22 brilliant rooms, each with hair dryer, phone, shower, and TV; several with little balconies opening onto a terrace. Breakfast €9.50. Free Wi-Fi. Wheelchair-accessible. Reception 24hr. Reserve 2 weeks ahead via email, fax, or phone. Singles €77; doubles €90, with bath €96; triples with bath €108. Check website for discounts of up to 15%. AmEx/MC/V. ❺

Woodstock Hostel, 48 rue Rodier (☎01 48 78 87 76; www.woodstock.fr). ⓜAnvers. Beatles-decorated VW Bug adorns the lobby wall. Communal kitchen and hostel (but definitely not hostile) cat. Breakfast included. Linen €2.50; €2.50 deposit. Internet and Wi-Fi €2 per 30min. 2-week max. stay. Lockout 11am-3pm. Curfew 2am. Reserve ahead. High-season 4- or 6-bed dorms €22; doubles €50. Low-season 4- or 6-bed dorms €19; doubles €22. Cash only. ❷

TOP TEN LIST

WASTE NOT, WANT NOT

While contemporary French cuisine is renowned for its sophistication, the roots of French cooking can be found in some not-so-sophisticated parts of nature's most delicious creatures.

1. Pied de Porc (pig's feet): usually chopped, seasoned, and delicately fried.

2. Tête de Veau (calf's head): rolled up, sliced, and served to the applause of French diners everywhere. A national favorite.

3. L'Os à moelle (bone marrow): served on its own with salt, parsley, and eaten with a spoon.

4. Boudin (blood sausage): mentioned as far back as Homer's *Odyssey*. Now you too, sitting "beside a great fire," can "fill a sausage with fat and blood and turn it this way and that."

5. Foie Gras ("fatty" goose liver): some American cities have banned the sale of *foie gras* but the French hold fast to tradition.

6. Whole Fish: the best meat on any fish is behind the eye. So when the whole thing arrives on a plate, carpe diem!

7. Tripe (stomach): it's pretty meta—your intestines are digesting intestines.

8. Tail: can be eaten on its own, in a stew, or you name it.

9. Groin: in French, pigs say "groin," not "oink." So when you order this, you're also imitating it.

10. Filet (muscle): who knew?

RIGHT BANK EAST

■ **Hôtel Palace,** 9 rue Bouchardon (☎01 40 40 09 45). ⓂStrasbourg-St-Denis. Clean and centrally located (for the 10ème). Breakfast €4. Reserve 2 weeks ahead, Singles €20-25, with shower €33; doubles €28-30/40; triples €55; quads €65-75. MC/V. ❶

■ **Hôtel Beaumarchais,** 3 rue Oberkampf (☎01 53 36 86 86; www.hotelbeaumarchais.com). ⓂOberkampf. Spacious hotel worth the money. Eye-popping decor. Each carpeted room has safe, shower or bath, and toilet. Suites include TV room with desk and breakfast table. A/C. Buffet breakfast €10. Reserve 2 weeks in advance. Singles €75-90; doubles €110-130; 2-person suites €150-170; triples €170-190. AmEx/MC/V. ❺

Auberge de Jeunesse "Jules Ferry" (HI), 8 bd. Jules Ferry (☎01 43 57 55 60; paris.julesferry@fuaj.org). ⓂRépublique. 99 beds. Modern, clean, and bright rooms with sinks, mirrors, and tiled floors. Party atmosphere. Kitchen. Breakfast included. Lockers €2. Linen included. Laundry €3. Internet access in lobby. 1-week max. stay. Reception and dining room 24hr. Lockout 10:30am-2pm. No reservations; arrive 8-11am to secure a bed. 4- to 6-bed dorms and doubles €22. MC/V. ❷

Centre International du Séjour de Paris: CISP "Maurice Ravel", 6 av. Maurice Ravel (☎01 43 58 96 00; www.cisp.fr). ⓂPorte de Vincennes. Large, clean rooms. Lively atmosphere. Art displays, sizable auditorium, and outdoor pool (€3-4). Guided tours of Paris. Cafeteria and restaurant available. Breakfast, linen, and towels included. Free Internet. 1-week max. stay. 24hr. reception. Curfew 1:30am. Reserve 1-2 months ahead. 8-bed dorms with shower and toilet in hall €20; 2- to 4-bed €26. Singles with full bath €39; doubles with full bath €56. AmEx/MC/V. ❶

🞑 FOOD

When in doubt, spend your money on food in Paris. Skip the museum, sleep in the dingy hotel, but **eat well.** Paris's culinary scene has been famous for centuries, and eating in the City of Light remains as exciting today as it was when Sun King Louis XIV made feasts an everyday occurrence. The city also offers delicious international dishes in addition to traditional cuisine. As an alternative to a pricey sit-down meal, stop into an *épicerie* and create a picnic lunch for Luxembourg Gardens, Parc Buttes Chaumont, or on the steps at Sacré-Coeur. *Bon appetit!*

RESTAURANTS

CITY CENTER

▩ **Berthillon,** 31 rue St-Louis en l'Île (☎01 43 54 31 61). ⓂCité or Pont Marie. This family-run institution, on l'Île since 1954, is reputed to have the best ice cream and sorbet in Paris. Flavors like blood orange and honey nougat. Single scoop €2, double €3, triple €4. Open from Sept. to mid-July W-Su 10am-8pm. When the main store is closed in summer, get your Berthillon fix at the counter located out front of the touristy Taverne du Sergeant Recruteur just down the street at 41 rue St-Louis en l'Île. Cash only. ❶

🔳 **Bistrot Victoires,** 6 rue de la Vrilliére (☎01 42 61 43 78). ⓜBourse or Palais Royal. Classic Art Nouveau bistro offers delicious fare at prices that put competition to shame. Giant salads, including the amazing *salade océane* (salmon, shirmp, oysters, and squid), €8-9. *Plats* €10-11. Open daily noon-3pm and 7-11pm. MC/V over €10. ❷

🔳 **404,** 69 rue des Gravilliers (☎01 42 74 57 81). ⓜArts et Métiers. Sophisticated family-owned Maghrebi restaurant. Enjoy your meal on the airy terrace out back or in the beautifully lit stone-walled dining room. Mouthwatering couscous (€15-24) and *tagines* (€15-19). Several vegetarian options. Open M-F noon-2:30pm and 8pm-midnight, Sa-Su noon-4pm and 8pm-midnight. AmEx/MC/V. ❹

🔳 **Briezh Café,** 109 rue Vielle du Temple (☎01 42 74 13 77; www.breizhcafe.com). ⓜFilles du Calvaire. Relaxed Breton *crêperie* uses high-quality ingredients (organic veggies, raw milk, *normand* sausage) to make simple, unpretentious, and tremendously delicious buckwheat *crêpes* and *galettes* (€3-11). Open W-Su noon-11pm. AmEx/MC/V. ❷

Chez Janou, 2 rue Roger Verlomme (☎01 42 72 28 41). ⓜChemin-Vert. Classic Provençal bistro. Lively atmosphere. Try the *ratatouille* or the goat cheese and spinach salad (both €9). Chocolate mousse (€9) brought in an enormous self-serve bowl. Over 80 kinds of *pastis*. Packed every night. Open daily noon-midnight. Kitchen open M-F noon-3pm and 8pm-midnight, Sa-Su noon-4pm and 8pm-midnight. Reservations recommended. MC/V. ❷

Chez Hanna, 54 rue des Rosiers (☎01 42 74 74 99). ⓜSt-Paul or Hôtel de Ville. Less mobbed that its more famous neighbor L'As (see below), local favorite Chez Hanna is proof that long lines do not the better falafel make. Falafel special (€5) served only at the window—eat inside and you'll have to spring for the more expensive falafel platters (€9-12). Open daily 11am-11pm. MC/V, min. €15. ❶

L'As du Falafel, 34 rue des Rosiers (☎01 48 87 63 60). ⓜSt-Paul or Hôtel de Ville. A very close 2nd to Chez Hanna, this kosher stand serves what (renowned falafel expert?) Lenny Kravitz terms "the best falafel in the world." Come lunchtime, it's got the massive lines and tourist crowd to prove it. Falafel special €5. Lemonade €4. Open M-Th and Su noon-midnight, F noon-7pm. MC/V. ❶

La Victoire Suprême du Coeur, 29-31 rue du Bourg Tibourg (☎01 40 41 95 03; www. vscoeur.com). ⓜHôtel de Ville. Run by the devotees of Indian spiritual leader and high-profile vegetarian Sri Chinmoy. Classics like seitan "steak" with mushroom sauce (€15). M-F vegan lunch buffet €13. 2-course dinner *menu* €19. Open Su-F noon-3pm and 6:30-10:30pm, Sa noon-3pm and 6:30-11pm. Cash only. ❸

LEFT BANK EAST

🔳 **Comptoir Méditerranée,** 42 rue du Cardinal Lemoine (☎01 43 25 29 08; www.savannahcafe.fr). ⓜCardinal Lemoine. Savannah Café's little sister, run by the same welcoming owner. More Lebanese deli than restaurant, serving fresh, colorful dishes. Select from 18 hot or cold options to make your own plate (€6.80-12). Sandwiches €4.40. Tantalizing pastries €1.30. Homemade lemonade €2.50. Open M-Sa 11am-10pm. T

Tang Frères, 48 av. d'Ivry, 13*ème* (☎01 45 70 80 00). ⓜPorte d'Ivry. A sensory-overload, this huge shopping center in the heart of Chinatown contains a bakery, *charcuterie*, fish counter, flower shop, and grocery store. Exotic fruits (durian €7.80 per kg), cheap Asian beers (can of Kirin €0.85, 6-pack of Tsingtao €3.72), rice wines (€3.50 per

0.5-liter), and sake (€4.95-6.80). Noodles, rice, soups, spices, teas, and tofu in bulk. Also at 174 rue de Choisy. ⓂPlace d'Italie. Open Tu-Sa 10am-8:30pm. MC/V. ❶

🍽 **Le Comptoir du Relais,** 5 carrefour de l'Odéon (☎01 44 27 07 97). ⓂOdéon. Local-heavy and hyper-crowded. Focuses on pork and other meats. *Pâté* on toast €10-12. Salads €10-22. *Plats* €14-22. Top it off with coffee-infused *crème brûlée* (€7). Open M-F noon-6pm, dinner seating 8:30pm, Sa-Su noon-11pm. Reserve ahead for weekday dinner; reservations not accepted for lunch or weekends. MC/V. ❸

🍽 **Chez Gladines,** 30 rue des 5 Diamants (☎01 45 80 70 10). ⓂPlace d'Italie. Intimate seating. Southwestern French and Basque specialties (€7.30-12). Well-deserved acclaim draws crowds; to avoid them, come before 7:30pm or after 11pm. Large salads €6.50-9. Beer €2. Espresso €1. Open M-Tu noon-3pm and 7pm-midnight, W-F noon-3pm and 7pm-1am, Sa-Su noon-4pm and 7pm-midnight. Cash only. ❷

Tang Frères, 48 av. d'Ivry (☎01 45 70 80 00). ⓂPorte d'Ivry. Also at 174 rue de Choisy. ⓂPlace d'Italie. A sensory overload, this huge shopping center in the heart of Chinatown contains a bakery, *charcuterie*, fish counter, flower shop, and grocery store. Exotic fruits (durian €7.80 per kg), cheap Asian beers (can of Kirin €0.85; 6-pack of Tsingtao €3.80), rice wines (€3.50 per 500mL), and sake (€5-6.80). Noodles, rice, soups, spices, teas, and tofu in bulk. Open Tu-Sa 10am-8:30pm. MC/V. ❶

LEFT BANK WEST

🍽 **Les Cocottes,** 135 rue St-Dominique (☎01 45 50 10 31). ⓂÉcole Militaire. A simpler, less expensive version of Christian Constant's popular haute cuisine establishments. Fresh, beautifully presented, and delicious comfort food. Try *cocottes* (cast-iron skillets filled with anything from pig's feet and pigeon to fresh vegetables; €12-16). Don't miss "La Fabuleuse" *tarte au chocolat* (€8). Open M-Th noon-2:30pm and 7-11pm, F-Sa noon-3pm and 7-10:30pm. AmEx/MC/V. ❸

🍽 **Stéphane Secco,** 20 rue Jean-Nicot (☎01 43 17 35 20). ⓂLa Tour-Maubourg. Another location at 25 bd. de Grenelle, 15ème (☎01 45 67 17 40). This delightful, pink-fronted *boulangerie-pâtisserie* is the perfect place to pick up supplies for a picnic on the nearby Seine. Creative quiches and *tartes* (€2-3 for a *petit*), rich desserts (macaroons €1-2), and bread with everything from herbs to apricots (€1-3). Open Tu-Sa 7:30am-8:30pm. Cash only. ❶

🍽 **Crêperie Plougastel,** 47 rue du Montparnasse (☎01 42 79 90 63). ⓂMontparnasse-Bienvenüe. Ambience and prompt staff set this cozy *crêperie* apart. Dessert *crêpes* feature homemade caramel. *Formule* (generous mixed salad and choice of 2 *galettes* and 5 dessert *crêpes*) €15. *Cidre* €2.90. Open daily noon-11:30pm. MC/V. ❸

Bélisaire, 2 rue Marmontel (☎01 48 28 62 24). ⓂVaugirard. Fit for aristocratic celebrations. Options on chalkboard menus rotate seasonally. Salmon and lobster ravioli are to die for. Packed daily. 3-course lunch *menu* €22. 5-course dinner *menu* €40. Open daily noon-2pm and 8-10:30pm. Reservations are a must. MC/V. ❹

RIGHT BANK WEST

🍽 **Ty Yann,** 10 rue de Constantinople (☎01 40 08 00 17). ⓂEurope. Breton chef and owner Yann cheerfully prepares outstanding *galettes* (€8-10) and *crêpes*. Decorated with Yann's mother's pastoral paintings. Chew on *La vaniteuse* (€8), with sausage sauteed in cognac, Emmental cheese, and onions. Create your own *crêpe* €6-7. Takeout 15% less. Open M-F noon-3:30pm and 7:30-10:30pm, Sa 7:30-10:30pm. MC/V. ❷

🍽 **Chez Haynes,** 3 rue Clauzel (☎01 48 78 40 63). ⓂSt-Georges. Paris's 1st African-American-owned restaurant opened in 1949. Louis Armstrong, James Baldwin, and Richard Wright enjoyed the delicious New Orleans soul food. Ma Sutton's fried honey chicken

€14. Sister Lena's BBQ spare ribs €16. Soul food Tu-Sa, Brazilian Su. Live music F-Sa nights; cover €5. Open Tu-Su 7pm-midnight; hours vary. AmEx/MC/V. ❷

🟦 **La Fournée d'Augustine,** 31 rue des Batignolles (☎01 43 87 88 41). Ⓜ️Rome. Lines out the door at lunch. Closet-size *pâtisserie* bakes an absolutely fantastic baguette (€1). Fresh sandwiches (€3-4) range from light fare like goat cheese and cucumber to the more substantial grilled chicken and veggies. *Pain au chocolat* €1.10. Lunch *formule* €5.80-7. Open M-Sa 7:30am-8pm. AmEx/MC/V over €10. ❷

Ladurée, 16 rue Royale (☎01 42 60 21 79; www.laduree.com). Ⓜ️Concorde or FDR. Also at 75 av. des Champs-Élysées, 8ème (☎01 40 75 08 75); 21 rue Bonaparte, 6ème (☎01 44 07 64 87); 62 bd. Haussmann, 9ème (☎01 42 82 40 10). Ever wanted to dine inside a Fabergé egg? Rococo decor attracts a jarring mix of well-groomed shoppers and tourists. Among the 1st Parisian *salons de thé*. Infamous mini macaroons in 16 varieties (€2). Boxes of Chocolats Incomparables from €18. Open M-Sa 8:30am-7pm, Su 10am-7pm. Lunch served until 3pm. AmEx/MC/V. ❸

Chartier, 7 rue du Faubourg-Montmartre (☎01 47 70 86 29; www.restaurant-chartier.com). Ⓜ️Grands Boulevards. Parisian fixture since 1896; the waitstaff adds up the bill on each table's paper tablecloth. Staples like *steak au poivre* (€8.50) and *langue de veau* (sheep's tongue; €9.80). Side dishes €2.50. Open daily 11:30am-10pm. AmEx/MC/V. ❷

RIGHT BANK EAST

🟦 **Le Cambodge,** 10 av. Richerand (☎01 44 84 37 70). Ⓜ️République. Inexpensive and delicious Cambodian restaurant. Good vegetarian options. *Plats* €7-10. M-Sa noon-2:30pm and 8-11:30pm. No reservations; wait up to 90min. MC/V. ❷

🟦 **Marché St-Quentin,** 85 bis bd. de Magenta. Ⓜ️Gare de l'Est or Gare du Nord. Outside: a huge construction of iron and glass, built in the 1880s, renovated in 1982, and covered by a glass ceiling. Inside: stalls of all varieties of produce, meat, cheese, seafood, and wine. Open Tu-Sa 8am-1pm and 3:30-7:30pm, Su 8am-1pm. ❶

🟦 **Le Bar à Soupes,** 33 rue Charonne (☎01 43 57 53 79; www.lebarasoupes.com). Ⓜ️Bastille. Small, bright cafe. Big bowls of delicious, freshly made soup (€5-6). 6 varieties change daily. €9.50 lunch *menu* is an astonishing deal; it comes with soup, a roll, wine or coffee, and cheese plate or dessert. Friendly staff will make your day. Gooey *gâteau chocolat* €4. Open M-Sa noon-3pm and 6:30-11pm. MC/V. ❷

🟦 **Café de l'Industrie,** 15-17 rue St-Sabin (☎01 47 00 13 53). Ⓜ️Breguet-Sabin. Happening cafe. Diverse menu. *Vin chaud* €4.50. Salads €8.50-9. Popular brunch platter (served Sa-Su; changes weekly) €12-15. Open daily 10am-2am. MC/V.

🟦 **L'Ébauchoir,** 45 rue de Citeaux (☎01 43 42 49 31; www.lebauchoir.com). Ⓜ️Faidherbe-Chaligny. Funky, lively French restaurant. Daily changing menu features delicious concoctions of seafood and meat. Vegetarian dishes upon request. Impressive wine list. *Entrées* €8-15. *Plats* €17-25. Desserts €7. Lunch *menu* €15. Open M 8-11pm, Tu-Sa noon-11pm. Kitchen open noon-2:30pm and 8-11pm. MC/V. ❸

🟦 **Ay, Caramba!,** 59 rue de Mouzaïa (☎01 42 41 23 80; http://restaurant-aycaramba.com). Ⓜ️Pré-St-Gervais. Bright yellow Tex-Mex restaurant in a drab, residential neighborhood transforms chic Parisian dining into a homegrown fiesta. Patrons salsa to live Latino singers F-Sa nights. Tacos €18. Margaritas €7. *Nachos rancheros* €7. Open Tu-Th 7:30pm-midnight, F-Su noon-3pm and 7:30pm-midnight. AmEx/MC/V. ❸

Refuge Café, 54 av. Daumesnil (☎01 43 47 25 59). Ⓜ️Gare de Lyon. Whimsical, ivy-covered cafe-restaurant seems to be out of a fairy tale. Art exhibits every month. Salads €11-15. *Plats* €15-23. *Formules* €14-22. Open M-Sa 8am-midnight. ❸

TIP **SAVE YOUR WALLET, HAVE A PICNIC.** As a major tourist attraction, Montmartre has inevitably high prices. Save a couple euro by avoiding its touristy cafes, and picnic in Paris. Buy a *croque monsieur* or ham sandwich *à emporter* and eat on the church's steps.

SIGHTS

While it would take weeks to see all of Paris's monuments, museums, and gardens, the city's small size makes sightseeing easy and enjoyable. In a few hours, you can walk from the Bastille in the east to the Eiffel Tower in the west, passing most major monuments along the way. A solid day of wandering will show you how close the medieval Notre Dame is to the modern Centre Pompidou and the funky *Latin Quarter* to the royal Louvre—the diversity of Paris is all the more amazing for the compact area in which it unfolds.

CITY CENTER

In the 3rd century BC, Paris consisted only of the **Île de la Cité,** inhabited by the Parisii, a Gallic tribe of merchants and fishermen. Today, all distance-points in France are measured from *kilomètre zéro,* a sundial in front of Notre Dame. On the far west side of the island is the **Pont Neuf** (New Bridge), actually Paris's oldest bridge—and now the city's most popular make-out spot. *(ⓂPont Neuf.)* To the east of Île de la Cité is the tiny **Île St-Louis. Rue St-Louis-en-l'Île** rolls down the center, and is a welcome distraction from busy Parisian life. There's a wealth of ice cream parlors, upscale shops, and boutique hotels, but not much to see. *(ⓂPont Marie.)* On the right bank, the **Marais** is home to some of Paris's best falafel (p. 240), museums, and bars, as well as much of Paris's Orthodox Jewish community. At the end of **rue des Francs-Bourgeois** sits the **place des Vosges,** Paris's oldest public square. Molière, Racine, and Voltaire filled the grand parlors with their *bon mots,* while Mozart played a concert here. Victor Hugo lived at no. 6, which is now a museum devoted to his life. *(ⓂChemin Vert or St-Paul.)*

FRANCE

CATHÉDRALE DE NOTRE DAME DE PARIS. This 12th- to 14th-century cathedral, begun under Bishop Maurice de Sully, is one of the world's most famous and beautiful examples of medieval architecture. After the Revolution, the building fell into disrepair—it was even used to shelter livestock—until Victor Hugo's 1831 novel *Notre Dame de Paris* (a.k.a. The Hunchback of Notre Dame) inspired citizens to lobby for the cathedral's restoration. The apocalyptic facade and seemingly weightless walls—effects produced by Gothic engineering and optical illusions—are inspiring even for the most church-weary. The cathedral's biggest draws are its enormous stained-glass rose windows that dominate the transept's northern and southern ends. A staircase inside the towers leads to a perch from which gargoyles survey the city. The best time to view the Cathedral is late at night, when you can see the full facade without mobs blocking the view. *(ⓂCité. ☎01 42 34 56 10, crypt 55 42 50 10, towers 53 10 07 00; www.notredamedeparis.fr. Cathedral open daily M-F 8am-6pm, Sa-Su 8am-7:15pm. Treasury open M-F 9:30am-6pm, Sa 9:30am-6:30pm, Su 1:30-6:30pm. Last entry 15min. before close. Crypt open Tu-Su 10am-6pm. Last entry 5:30pm. Towers open June-Aug. M-F 10am-6:30pm, Sa-Su 10am-11pm; Sept. and Apr.-May daily 10am-6:30pm; Oct.-Mar. daily 10am-5:30pm. Last entry 45min. before closing. Mass M-Sa 8, 9am, noon, 5:45, 6:15pm; Su 8:30, 9:30, 10 (high mass with Gregorian chant), 11:30am (international mass), 12:45, and 6:30pm. Free. Treasury €3, ages 12-25 €2, ages 5-11 €1. Crypt €4, over 60 €3, under 26 €2, under 12 free. Towers €8, ages 18-25 €5, under 18 free. Audio tours €5 with ID deposit; includes visit of treasury. Tours begin at the booth to the right as you enter.)*

STE-CHAPELLE, CONCIERGERIE, AND PALAIS DE JUSTICE. The Palais de la Cité contains three vastly different buildings. ■**Ste-Chapelle** remains the foremost example of flamboyant Gothic architecture and a tribute to the craft of medieval stained glass. On sunny days, light pours through the **Upper Chapel's** windows, illuminating frescoes of saints and martyrs. Around the corner is the Conciergerie, one of Paris's most famous prisons; Marie-Antoinette and Robespierre were incarcerated here during the Revolution. *(6 bd. du Palais, within Palais de la Cité. ⓜCité. ☎01 53 40 60 97; www.monum.fr. Open daily Nov.-Feb. 9am-5pm and Mar.-Oct. 9:30am-6pm, last entry 30min. before closing. €8, seniors and ages 18-25 €5, under 18 free. Cash only.)* Built after the great fire of 1776, the **Palais de Justice** houses France's district courts. *(4 bd. du Palais, within the Palais de la Cité. Enter at 6 bd. du Palais. ⓜCité. ☎01 44 32 51 51. Courtrooms open M-F 9am-noon and 1:30pm-end of last trial. Free.)*

MÉMORIAL DE LA DÉPORTATION. Commemorating the 200,000 French victims of Nazi concentration camps, the museum includes a tunnel lined with 200,000 quartz pebbles, honoring the Jewish custom of placing stones on graves. *(ⓜCité. Open daily Apr.-Sept. 10am-noon and 2-7pm; Oct.-Mar. 10am-noon and 2-5pm. Free.)*

HÔTEL DE VILLE. Paris's grandiose city hall dominates a large square filled with fountains and Belle Époque lampposts. The present edifice is a 19th-century replica of the original medieval structure, a meeting hall for the cartel that controlled traffic on the Seine. *(Info office 29 rue de Rivoli. ⓜHôtel de Ville. ☎01 42 76 43 43 or 42 76 50 49. Open M-F when there is an exhibit 9am-7pm (last entry 6:15pm); otherwise 9am-6pm. Free. Group tours available with reservations; call for available dates.)*

LEFT BANK EAST

The Latin Quarter, named for the prestigious universities that taught in Latin until 1798, lives for its ever-vibrant student population. Since the student riots in May 1968, many artists and intellectuals have migrated to the cheaper outer *arrondissements*, and the haute bourgeoisie have moved in. The 5*ème* still presents the most diverse array of bookstores, cinemas, and jazz clubs in the city. Shops and art galleries are found around **St-Germain-des-Prés** in the 6*ème*. Farther east, the residential 13*ème* doesn't have much to attract the typical tourist, but its diverse neighborhoods offer an authentic view of Parisian life.

■**JARDIN DU LUXEMBOURG.** Parisian sunbathers flock to these formal gardens. The site of a medieval monastery, and later home to 17th-century French royalty, the gardens were liberated during the Revolution. *(ⓜOdéon or RER: Luxembourg. Entrance at bd. St-Michel. Open daily sunrise-sunset. Guided tours in French depart from pl. André Honorat June every W; July-Oct. and Apr.-May 1st W of each month.)*

ODÉON. The **Cour du Commerce St-André** is one of the most picturesque walking areas in the 6*ème*, with cobblestone streets, centuries-old cafes (including Le Procope), and outdoor seating. Just south of bd. St-Germain, the Carrefour de l'Odéon, a favorite Parisian hangout, has more bistros and cafes. *(ⓜOdéon.)*

ÉGLISE ST-GERMAIN-DES-PRÉS. Paris's oldest standing church, **Église de St-Germain-des-Prés** was the centerpiece of the **Abbey of St-Germain-des-Prés,** the crux of Catholic intellectual life until it was disbanded during the Revolution. Worn away by fire and even a saltpetre explosion, the abbey's exterior looks appropriately world-weary. Its interior frescoes, redone in the 19th century, depict the life of Jesus in striking maroon, green, and gold. *(3 pl. St-Germain-des-Prés. ⓜSt-Germain-des-Prés. ☎01 55 42 81 33; www.eglise-sgp.org. Open daily 8am-7:45pm. Info office open July-Aug. M-F 10am-noon and 2-7pm; Sept.-June M 2:30-6:45pm, Tu-F 10:30am-noon and 2:30-6:45pm, Sa 3-6:45pm.)*

FRANCE

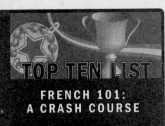

TOP TEN LIST

FRENCH 101: A CRASH COURSE

Traveling through France, you will undoubtedly encounter familiar words on signs and menus. Though these cognates will appear to help a your struggle to comprehend *le monde francophone*, beware! Some can also lead you astray. Here are some *faux amis* (false cognates; literally, "false friends") to watch out for:

Blesser has nothing to do with spirituality (or sneezing). It means **to hurt**, not to bless.

Pain is anything but misery for the French: it's their word for **bread**.

Bras is not a supportive undergarment, it's an **arm**.

Rage is not just regular anger, it's **rabies**.

Rabais, it follows, is not the disease you can catch from a dog, but a **discount**.

A *sale* is not an event with a lot of rabais; it means **dirty**.

Draguer means **to hit on**, not to drag, unless you encounter an overly aggressive flirt.

Balancer is **to swing**, not to steady oneself.

A *peste* is slightly more serious than a bothersome creature. It is a **plague**.

Puéril is not grave danger, just **childhood**.

Preservatif is not something found in packaged food, but it can be found close to packages, so to speak. This is the French word for **condom**.

Crayon means **pencil**, not crayon, and gomme is not for

PLACE ST-MICHEL AND ENVIRONS. At the center of the Latin Quarter, bd. St-Michel, which divides the 5ème and 6ème, is filled with bookstores, boutiques, cafes, and restaurants. Tourists pack pl. St-Michel, where the 1871 Paris Commune and the 1968 student uprising began. You can find many traditional bistros on nearby r. Soufflot, the street connecting the Luxembourg Gardens to the Pantheon, and smaller restaurants on r. des Fossés St-Jacques. (Ⓜ St-Michel.)

LA SORBONNE. The Sorbonne is one of Europe's oldest universities, founded in 1253 by Robert de Sorbon as a dormitory for 16 theology students. Nearby place de la Sorbonne, off bd. St-Michel, is flooded with cafes, bookstores, and during term-time, students. The **Chapelle de la Sorbonne,** which usually houses temporary exhibits on arts and letters, is undergoing renovations through 2009. (45-47 r. des Écoles. Ⓜ Cluny-La Sorbonne or RER: Luxembourg.)

PANTHÉON. Though it looks like a religious monument, the Pantheon, occupying the Left Bank's highest point, celebrates France's great thinkers. The crypt houses the tombs of Marie and Pierre Curie, Victor Hugo, Jean Jaurès, Rousseau, Voltaire, and Émile Zola. On the main level, Foucault's Pendulum confirms the rotation of the earth. (Pl. du Panthéon. Ⓜ Cardinal Lemoine or RER: Luxembourg. ☎ 01 44 32 18 04. Open daily Apr.-Sept. 10am-6:30pm, Oct.-Mar. 10am-6pm. Last entry 45min. before closing. Crypt open daily 10am-6pm. €7.50, ages 18-25 €4.80, under 18 and 1st Su of the month Oct.-Mar. free. MC/V. Conservative dress required.)

RUE MOUFFETARD. South of pl. de la Contrescarpe, r. Mouffetard plays host to one of Paris's busiest street markets, drawing a mix of Parisians and visitors. The stretch of r. Mouffetard past pl. de la Contrescarpe and onto r. Descartes and r. de la Montagne Ste-Geneviève is the quintessential Latin Quarter stroll. (Ⓜ Cardinal Lemoine, Pl. Monge, or Censier Daubenton.)

JARDIN DES PLANTES. Opened in 1640 to grow medicinal plants for King Louis XIII, the garden now features science museums, rosaries, and a zoo, which Parisians raided for food during the Prussian siege of 1871. (Ⓜ Gare d'Austerlitz, Jussieu, or Censier-Daubenton. ☎ 01 40 79 37 94; www.mnhn.fr. Jardin des Plantes and Roserie open daily in summer 7:30am-7-:45pm, in winter 7:30am-7:30pm. Free. Ménagerie Zoo, 3 quai St-Bernard and 57 rue Cuvier. Open Apr.-Sept. M-Sa 9am-6pm, Su and holidays 9am-6:30pm; Oct.-Mar. daily 10am-5pm. €7, students and ages 4-13 €5.)

BIBLIOTHÈQUE NATIONALE DE FRANCE: SITE FRANÇOIS MITTERRAND. The complex that many

Parisians refer to as "the ugliest building ever built" is the result of the last and most expensive of Mitterrand's Grands Projets. Its rotating art, literary, and photography exhibits are a welcome break from the city center's packed sights. *(Quai François Mauriac. ⓜQuai de la Gare or Bibliothèque François Mitterrand. ☎01 53 79 59 59; www.bnf.fr. Upper study library open Tu-Sa 10am-8pm, Su 1-7pm. Lower research library open M 2-8pm, Tu-Sa 9am-8pm, Su 1-7pm; closed 2 weeks in Sept. 16+. €3.30; 15-day pass €20; annual membership €35, students €18.)*

QUARTIER DE LA BUTTE-AUX-CAILLES. Historically a working-class neighborhood, the old-fashioned Butte-aux-Cailles (Quail Knoll) Quarter now attracts trend-setters, artists, and intellectuals. Funky new restaurants and galleries have cropped up in recent years. Rue de la Butte-aux-Cailles and rue des Cinq Diamants share duties as the *quartier's* main drags. *(ⓜCorvisart. Exit onto bd. Blanqui and turn onto r. Barrault, which will meet r. de la Butte-aux-Cailles.)*

LEFT BANK WEST

▣EIFFEL TOWER. Gustave Eiffel wrote of his tower: "France is the only country in the world with a 300m flagpole." Designed in 1889 as the tallest structure in the world, the Eiffel Tower was conceived as a modern monument to engineering that would surpass the Egyptian pyramids in size and notoriety. Critics dubbed it a "metal asparagus" and a "Parisian tower of Babel." Writer Guy de Maupassant ate lunch every day at its ground-floor restaurant—the only place in Paris, he claimed, from which he couldn't see the offensive thing. Nevertheless, when it was inaugurated in March 1889 as the centerpiece of the World's Fair, the tower earned Parisians' love: nearly two million people ascended it during the fair. Some still criticize its glut of tourists, trinkets, and vagrants, but don't believe the anti-hype—the tower is worth seeing. *(ⓜBir-Hakeim or Trocadéro. ☎01 44 11 23 23; www.tour-eiffel.fr. Elevator open daily from mid-June to Aug. 9am-12:45am, last entry 11pm; from Sept. to mid-June 9:30am-11:45pm, last entry 11pm. Stairs open daily from mid-June to Aug. 9am-12:45am, last entry midnight; from Sept. to mid-June 9:30am-6:30pm, last entry 6pm. Elevator to 2nd fl. €8, under 25 €6.40, under 12 €4, under 3 free; elevator to summit €13/9.90/7.50/free. Stairs to 1st and 2nd fl. €4.50/3.50/3/free.)*

▣PARC ANDRÉ CITROËN. The futuristic Parc André Citroën was created by landscapers Alain Provost and Gilles Clément in the 1990s. Hot-air balloon rides offer spectacular aerial views of Paris. *(ⓜJavel or Balard. ☎01 44 26 20 00; www.ballondeparis.com. Open in*

chewing, unless you like the taste of rubber—it is an **eraser.**

An *extincteur* is not a bazooka. It is a **fire extinguisher.**

Fesses is not a colloquial term for "coming clean." It actually means **buttocks.**

As is not another way to say *fesses* or even an insult. This is a French compliment, meaning **ace** or **champion.**

Ranger is neither a woodsman nor a mighty morpher. This means **to tidy up.**

A *smoking* has little to do with tobacco (or any other substance). It is a **tuxedo** or **dinner suit.**

Raisins are juicy **grapes,** not the dried-up snack food. Try *raisins-secs* instead.

Prunes are **plums.** *Pruneaus* are the dried fruit.

Tampons are **stamps** (for documents), not the feminine care item. If you are looking for those, ask for a *tampon hygiénique* or *napkins.* To wipe your mouth, you would do better with a *serviette.*

The *patron* is not the customer, rather, it is the **boss.**

Glacier does translate literally; however, you are more likely to see it around town on signs for **ice cream vendors;** *glace* does not mean glass, but a frozen summer treat.

If the French language seems full of deception, think again. *Deception* in French actually means **disappointment.**

summer M-F 8am-9:30pm, Sa-Su 9am-9:30pm; in winter M-F 8am-5:45pm, Sa-Su 9am-5:45pm. Guided tours leave from the Jardin Noir; €3-6.)

INVALIDES. The gold-leaf dome of the **Hôtel des Invalides,** built by Napoleon as a hospital for crippled and ill soldiers, shines at the center of the *7ème*. The grassy **Esplanade des Invalides** runs from the hôtel to the Pont Alexandre III, a bridge with gilded lampposts from which you can catch a great view of the Invalides and the Seine. Both housed inside the Invalides complex, the **Musée de l'Armée** and **Musée de l'Ordre de la Libération,** documenting the Free France movement under General de Gaulle, are worth a look; the real star, however, is the █**Musée des Plans-Reliefs,** which features dozens of enormous, detailed models of French fortresses and towns, all made around 1700. Napoleon's tomb is also here, resting in the Église St-Louis. *(127 r. de Grenelle. ⓂInvalides. Enter from either pl. des Invalides or pl. Vauban and av. de Tourville.)*

CATACOMBS. Originally excavated to provide stone for building Paris, the Catacombs were converted into a mass grave in 1785 when the stench of the city's public cemeteries became unbearable. Paris's "municipal ossuary" now has dozens of winding tunnels and hundreds of thousands of bones. *(1 av. du Colonel Henri Roi-Tanguy. ⓂDenfert-Rochereau; exit near ⓂMouton Duvernet. ☎01 43 22 47 63. Open Tu-Su 10am-4pm. €7, over 60 €5.50, ages 14-26 €3.50, under 14 free.)*

BOULEVARD DU MONTPARNASSE. In the early 20th century, avant-garde artists like Chagall, Duchamp, Léger, and Modigliani moved to Montparnasse. Soviet exiles Lenin and Trotsky talked strategy over cognac in cafes like Le Dôme, Le Sélect, and La Coupole. After WWI, Montparnasse attracted American expats like Calder, Hemingway, and Henry Miller. Chain restaurants and tourists crowd the now heavily commercialized street. Classic cafes like pricey La Coupole still hold their own, however, providing a wonderful place to sip coffee, read Apollinaire, and daydream away. *(ⓂMontparnasse-Bienvenüe or Vavin.)*

CHAMPS DE MARS. The Champs de Mars, an expanse stretching from the École Militaire to the Eiffel Tower, is named, appropriately enough, after the Roman god of war. Close to the *7ème*'s museums, the field was a drill ground for the École Militaire during Napoleon's reign. Today, despite frolicking children and a monument to international peace, the Champs can't quite hold a candle to Paris's many spectacular public parks and gardens. *(ⓂLa Motte Picquet-Grenelle or École Militaire. From the av. de la Motte-Picquet, walk toward École Militaire.)*

RIGHT BANK WEST

█**ARC DE TRIOMPHE.** Napoleon commissioned the Arc, at the western end of the Champs-Élysées, in 1806 to honor his Grande Armée. In 1940, Parisians were brought to tears by the sight of Nazis goose-stepping through the Arc. At the end of the German occupation, a sympathetic Allied army made sure that a French general would be the first to drive under the arch. The terrace at the top has a fabulous view. The **Tomb of the Unknown Soldier** has been under the Arc since November 11, 1920, and an eternal flame has been burning since 1921. *(ⓂCharles de Gaulle-Étoile. Use the pedestrian underpass on the right side of the Champs-Élysées facing the arch. Buy your ticket in the pedestrian underpass before going up to the ground level. Open daily Apr.-Sept. 10am-11pm; Oct.-Mar. 10am-10:30pm. Last entry 30min. before close. Wheelchair-accessible. €9, ages 18-25 €5.50, under 17 free.)*

█**LA DÉFENSE.** Outside the city limits, west of the *16ème*, the skyscrapers and modern architecture of La Défense make up Paris's newest (unofficial) *arrondissement*, a playground for many of Paris's biggest corporations. Its centerpiece is hard to miss: the Grande Arche de la Défense stretches 35 stories into the air and is shaped like a hollow cube. The roof of this unconventional office covers one hectare—Notre Dame could fit in its concave core. (M/ *RER: La Défense or bus #73. If you take the RER, buy your ticket before going through the turnstile.* ☎ *01 47 74 84 24. Open Apr.-Sept. daily 10am-6pm; Oct.-Mar. M-F 9:30am-5:30pm. Grande Arche open daily 10am-7pm. Last entry 6:30pm. €7.50, students, under 18, and seniors €6.)*

OPÉRA GARNIER. The exterior of the Opéra Garnier—with its newly restored multi-colored marble facade, sculpted golden goddesses, and ornate columns and friezes—is as impressive as it is kitschy. It's no wonder that Oscar Wilde once swore he saw an angel floating on the sidewalk. Inside, Chagall's whimsical ceiling design contrasts with the gold and red that dominate the theater. For shows, see **Entertainment**, p. 252. *(*M*Opéra. ☎ 08 92 89 90 90; www. operadeparis.fr. Concert hall and museum open daily 10am-5pm. Last entry 30min. before close. Concert hall closed during rehearsals; call ahead. 90min. tours in English July-Aug. daily 11:30am, 2:30pm; Sept.-June W and Sa-Su 11:30am, 2:30pm. €8, students and under 25 €4, under 10 free. Tours €12, students €9, under 10 €6, seniors €10.)*

PLACE DE LA CONCORDE. Paris's most infamous public square, built between 1757 and 1777, is the eastern terminus of the Champs-Élysées at its intersection with the Jardin des Tuileries. During the Revolution and Reign of Terror, the area became known as the *place de la Révolution*, site of the guillotine that severed the heads of 1343 aristocrats, including Louis XVI, Marie Antoinette, and Robespierre. In 1830, the square was optimistically renamed *concorde* (peace) and the 3200-year-old Obélisque de Luxor, given to Charles X by the Viceroy of Egypt, replaced the guillotine. *(*M*Concorde.)*

AVENUE DES CHAMPS-ÉLYSÉES. Extending from the Louvre, Paris's most famous thoroughfare was a piecemeal project begun under the reign of Louis XIV. The center of Parisian opulence in the early 20th century, with flashy mansions towering above exclusive cafes, the Champs has since undergone a bizarre kind of democratization. Shops along the avenue now range from designer fashion to cheap trinkets. While it may be an inelegant spectacle, the Champs offers some of the city's best people-watching—tourists, wealthy barhoppers, and even authentic Parisians crowd its broad sidewalks. *(*M*Charles de Gaulle-Étoile. Runs from the pl. Charles de Gaulle-Étoile southeast to the pl. de la Concorde.)*

BOIS DE BOULOGNE. By day, this 2000-acre park, with several gardens and two lakes, is a popular picnicking, jogging, and bike-riding spot. By night, the *bois* becomes a bazaar of crime, drugs, and prostitution. *(On the western edge of the 16ème. *M*Porte Maillot, Sablons, Pont de Neuilly, or Porte Dauphine or Porte d'Auteil.)*

RIGHT BANK EAST

■**CIMITIÈRE PÈRE LACHAISE.** This cemetery holds the remains of such famous Frenchmen as Balzac, Bernhardt, Colette, David, Delacroix, Piaf, La Fontaine, Haussmann, Molière, Proust, and Seurat within its peaceful paths and elaborate sarcophagi. Foreigners buried here include Chopin, Modigliani, Gertrude Stein, and Oscar Wilde, though the most frequently visited grave is that of Jim Morrison. French Leftists make a ceremonial pilgrimage to the **Mur des Fédérés** (Wall of the Federals), where 147 *communards* were executed in 1871. *(16 rue du Repo. *M*Père Lachaise. ☎ 01 55 25 82 10. Open from mid-Mar. to early Nov. M-F 8am-6pm, Sa 8:30am-6pm, Su and holidays 9am-6pm; from Nov. to mid-Mar. M-F 8am-5:30pm, Sa 8:30am-5:30pm, Su and holidays 9am-5:30pm. Free.)*

■**BASILIQUE DU SACRÉ-COEUR.** This ethereal basilica, with its signature shining white onion domes, was commissioned to atone for France's war crimes in the Franco-Prussian War. During WWII, 13 bombs were dropped on Paris, all near the structure, but miraculously no one was killed. *(35 rue du Chevalier-de-la-Barre.* Ⓜ*Anvers, Abbesses, or Château-Rouge.* ☎*01 53 41 89 00; www.sacre-coeur-montmartre.fr. Basilica open daily 6am-11pm. Crypt open daily 9am-5:30pm. Dome open daily 9am-6pm. Mass daily 10pm. Wheelchair-accessible. Free. Dome €5.)*

PLACE DE LA BASTILLE. This intersection was once home to the famous **Bastille Prison,** stormed on July 14, 1789, sparking the French Revolution. Two days later, the National Assembly ordered the prison demolished, but the ground plan of the prison's turrets remains embedded in the road near r. St-Antoine. At the center of the square is a monument of the winged Mercury holding a torch of freedom, symbolizing the movement towards democracy. *(*Ⓜ*Bastille.)*

OPÉRA DE LA BASTILLE. One of Mitterrand's Grands Projets, the Opéra opened in 1989 to loud protests over its unattractive design. It has been described as a huge toilet because of its resemblance to the city's coin-operated *pissoirs.* The opera has not struck a completely sour note, though; it has helped renew local interest in the arts. The guided tour offers a behind-the-scenes view of the world's largest theater. *(130 rue de Lyon.* Ⓜ*Bastille.* ☎*01 40 01 19 70; www.operadeparis. 1hr. tour almost every day, usually at 1 or 5pm; call ahead for schedule. €11, over 60 and students €9, under 18 €6. Open M-Sa 10:30am-6:30pm.)*

BAL DU MOULIN ROUGE. Along bd. de Clichy and bd. de Rochechouart, you'll find many Belle Époque cabarets, including the Bal du Moulin Rouge, immortalized by Toulouse-Lautrec's paintings, Offenbach's music, and Baz Luhrmann's 2001 blockbuster. The crowd consists of tourists out for an evening of sequins, tassels, and skin. The revues are still risqué, but the real shock is the price of admission. *(82 bd. de Clichy.* Ⓜ*Blanche.* ☎*01 53 09 82 82; www.moulin-rouge.com.)*

PARC DES BUTTES-CHAUMONT. In the south of the 19ème, Parc des Buttes-Chaumont is a mix of manmade topography and transplanted vegetation; previously a lime quarry and gallows, Napoleon III commissioned Baron Haussman to redesign the space in 1862. Today's visitors walk the winding paths surrounded by lush greenery and dynamic hills, enjoying a great view of the *quartier* from the Roman temple atop cave-filled cliffs. *(*Ⓜ*Buttes-Chaumont or Botzaris. Open daily May-Sept. 7am-10:15pm; Oct.-Apr. 7am-8:15pm; some gates close early.)*

PARC DE LA VILLETTE. Previously a meatpacking district, La Villette is the product of a successful urban renewal project. Inaugurated by President Mitterrand in 1985 as "the place of intelligent leisure," it now contains museums, libraries, and concert halls in the Cité des Sciences and the Cité de la Musique. Every July and August, La Villette holds a free open-air film festival. The Zénith concert hall hosts major rock bands, and the **Trabendo** jazz and modern music club holds an extraordinarily popular annual jazz festival. *(211 av. Jean Jaurès.* Ⓜ*Porte de Pantin. General info* ☎*01 40 03 75 75, Trabendo 42 01 12 12, Zénith 42 08 60 00; www.villette.com. Info office open M-Sa 9:30am-6:30pm. Free.)*

🏛 MUSEUMS

No visitor should miss Paris's museums, which are universally considered to be among the world's best. Cost-effective for visiting more than three museums or sights daily, the **Carte Musées et Monuments** offers admission to 65 museums in greater Paris. It is available at major museums, tourist office kiosks, and many Métro stations. A pass for one day is €15, for three days €30, for five days €45. Students with art or art history ID can get into art museums free. Most museums, including the Musée d'Orsay, are closed on Mondays.

▨MUSÉE D'ORSAY. If only the *Académiciens* who turned the Impressionists away from the Louvre could see the Musée d'Orsay. Now considered masterpieces, these "rejects" are well worth the pilgrimage to this mecca of modernity. The collection, installed in a former railway station, includes painting, sculpture, decorative arts, and photography from 1848 until WWI. On the ground floor, Classical and Proto-Impressionist works are on display, including Manet's *Olympia*, a painting that caused scandal when it was unveiled in 1865. Other highlights include Monet's *Poppies*, Renoir's *Bal au moulin de la Galette*, Dégas's *La classe de danse,* and paintings by Cézanne, Gauguin, Seurat, and Van Gogh. The top floor offers one of the most comprehensive collections of Impressionist and Post-Impressionist art in the world. In addition, the exterior and interior balconies offer supreme views of the Seine and the jungle of sculptures below. Don't miss Rodin's imperious *Honoré de Balzac.* (*62 rue de Lille.* Ⓜ*Solférino or RER: Musée d'Orsay. Enter at entrance A off 1 rue de la Légion d'Honneur.* ☎*01 40 49 48 14; www.musee-orsay.fr. Open Tu-W and F-Su 9:30am-6pm, Th 9:30am-9:45pm. Last entry 1hr. before closing. 1hr. English-language tours usually Tu-Sa 11:30am and 2:30pm; call ahead to confirm. Wheelchair-accessible; call* ☎*01 40 49 47 14 for info. €8, ages 18-25 €5.50, under 18 free. €5.50 for everyone Tu-W and F-Su after 4:15pm, Th after 6pm. Tours €7.50, ages 18-25 €5.70, under 18 free. Audio guides €5.*)

CROWDLESS CULTURE. Orsay's undeniably amazing collection draws massive crowds, marring an otherwise enjoyable museum. A Sunday morning or Thursday evening visit will avoid the tourist throngs.

■**MUSÉE DU LOUVRE.** No visitor has ever allotted enough time to thoughtfully ponder every display at the Louvre, namely because it would take weeks to read every caption of the over 30,000 items in the museum. Its masterpieces include Hammurabi's Code, Jacques-Louis David's *The Oath of the Horatii* and *The Coronation of Napoleon,* Delacroix's *Liberty Leading the People,* Vermeer's *Lacemaker,* Leonardo da Vinci's *Mona Lisa,* the classically sculpted *Winged Victory of Samothrace,* and the *Venus de Milo.* Enter through I. M. Pei's stunning glass Pyramid in the Cour Napoléon, or skip the line by entering directly from the Métro. The Louvre is organized into three different wings: Denon, Richelieu, and Sully. Each is divided according to the artwork's date, national origin, and medium. (Ⓜ*Palais Royal-Musée du Louvre.* ☎*01 40 20 53 17; www. louvre.fr. Open M, Th, and Sa 9am-6pm, W and F 9am-10pm. Last entry 45min. before closing; some galleries close up to 30min. before the museum itself closes. Free 1½hr. tours July-Aug. M-Sa in English 11am, 2, 3:45pm; in French 11:30am; sign up at the info desk. Admission €9; W and F after 6pm €6; under 18 free. Free W and F after 6pm for those under 26 and 1st Su of the month for everybody. Audio guide rental €6, under 18 €2; deposit of driver's license, passport, or credit card; available to reserve online.*)

■**CENTRE POMPIDOU.** This inside-out building has inspired debate since its 1977 opening. Whatever its aesthetic merits, the exterior's chaotic colored piping provides an appropriate shell for the Cubist, Conceptual, Fauvist, and Pop works inside. The **Musée National d'Art Moderne** is the Centre Pompidou's main attraction. (*Pl. Georges-Pompidou.* Ⓜ*Rambuteau, Hôtel de Ville, or RER Châtelet-Les Halles.* ☎*01 44 78 12 33; www.centrepompidou.fr. Centre open M and W-Su 11am-10pm; museum open M, W, and F-Su 11am-9pm; Th 11am-11pm; last ticket sales 1 hr. before closing. €12, under 26 €9, under 18 free; 1st Su of the month free.*)

■**MUSÉE RODIN.** The 18th-century Hôtel Biron holds hundreds of sculptures by Auguste Rodin, including the *The Thinker, Bourgeois de Calais,* and *La Porte d'Enfer.* Bring a book and relax amid the gracious gestures of bending flowers and flexing sculptures. (*79 rue de Varenne.* Ⓜ*Varenne.* ☎*01 44 18 61 10; www.musee-rodin.fr. Open Tu-Su Apr.-Sept. 9:30am-5:45pm; Oct.-Mar. 10am-5:45pm. Last entry*

30min. before closing. Gardens open Tu-Su Apr.-Sept. 9:30am-6:45pm; Oct.-Mar. 10am-6:45pm. €6, under 18 and 1st Su of the month free. Special exhibits €7. Permanent collections and special exhibits together €10. Garden €1. Audio tours €4.)

MUSÉE JACQUEMART-ANDRÉ. The 19th-century mansion of Nélie Jacquemart and her husband contains a world-class collection of Renaissance art, including *Madonna and Child* by Botticelli and *St. George and the Dragon* by Ucello. *(158 bd. Haussmann. ☎01 45 62 11 59. Ⓜ Miromesnil. Open daily 10am-6pm. Last entry 30min. before close. €10, students and ages 7-17 €7.30, under 7 free. 1 free child ticket per 3 purchased tickets. English headsets included.)*

MUSÉE DE CLUNY. The Musée de Cluny, housed in a monastery built atop Roman baths, holds one of the world's finest collections of medieval art. Works include **La Dame et La Licorne** (The Lady and the Unicorn), a striking 15th-century tapestry series. *(6 pl. Paul-Painlevé. Ⓜ Cluny-La Sorbonne. Info ☎01·53 73 78 00, reception 53 73 78 16. Open M and W-Su 9:15am-5:45pm; last entry at 5:15pm. Closed Jan. 1, May 1, and Dec. 25. Temporarily free; prices TBD.)*

EXPLORA SCIENCE MUSEUM. Dedicated to bringing science to young people, the Explora Science Museum is the star attraction of La Villette, in the complex's Cité des Sciences et de l'Industrie. The building's futuristic architecture only hints at the close to 300 exhibits inside. *(30 av. Corentin-Cariou. Ⓜ Porte de la Villette. ☎01 40 05 80 00; www.cite-sciences.fr. Museum open Tu-Sa 10am-6pm, Su 10am-7pm. Last entry 30min. before close. Médiathèque open Tu-Su noon-6:45pm. 1½hr. Cité des Enfants programs Tu-Su 10:30am, 12:30, 2:30, 4:30pm. €8, under 25 €6, under 7 free. Planetarium supplement €3, under 7 free. Médiathèque free. Aquarium free. Cité des Enfants €6.)*

MUSÉE CARNAVALET. Housed in Mme. de Sévigné's 16th-century *hôtel particulier*, this museum presents room after room of historical objects and curiosities from Paris's origins through the present day. *(23 rue de Sévigné. ☎01 44 59 58 58; www.paris.fr/musees/musee_carnavalet. Ⓜ Chemin Vert. Open Tu-Su 10am-6pm; last entry 5pm. Free. Special exhibits €7, under 26 €4, seniors €6, under 14 free.)*

MAISON DE BALZAC. Honoré de Balzac hid from bill collectors in this three-story hillside mansion, his home from 1840-1847. Here in this tranquil retreat, he wrote a substantial part of *La Comédie Humaine;* today's visitors can see his original manuscripts, along with his beautifully embroidered chair and desk at which he purportedly wrote and edited for 17hr. a day. *(47 rue Raynouard. Ⓜ Passy. ☎01 55 74 41 80; www.paris.fr/musees/balzac. Open Tu-Su 10am-6pm. Last entry 30min. before closing. Permanent collection free. Guided tours and temporary exhibits €4, families and seniors €3, students under 26 €2, under 12 free.)*

MUSÉE PICASSO. When Picasso died in 1973, his family paid the French inheritance tax in artwork. The French government put this collection, which includes work from his Cubist, Surrealist, and Neoclassical years, on display in 1985 in the 17th-century Hôtel Salé. *(5 rue de Thorigny. Ⓜ Chemin Vert. ☎01 42 71 25 21; www.musee-picasso.fr. Open M and W-Su Apr.-Sept. 9:30am-6pm; Oct.-Mar. 9:30am-5:30pm. Last entry 45min. before close. €8.50, ages 18-25 €6.50, under 18 and 1st Su of the month free.)*

🎵 ENTERTAINMENT

Pick up one of the weekly bibles of Parisian entertainment, *Pariscope* (€0.40) and *Figaroscope* (€1), at any newsstand or *tabac. Pariscope* includes an English-language section. For concert listings, check the free magazine *Paris Selection*, available at tourist offices. Free concerts are often held in churches and parks, especially during summer festivals. They are extremely popular, so plan to arrive early. **FNAC** stores sell concert tickets.

OPERA AND THEATER

■ **La Comédie Française,** pl. Collette, 1er (☎ 08 25 10 16 80 or 44 58 14 00; www.comedie-francaise.fr). ⓂPalais-Royal. Founded by Molière; the granddaddy of all French theaters. Generally, you don't need to speak French to understand the jokes. Box office open daily 11am-6pm and 1hr. before shows. Tickets €11-35.

Opéra de la Bastille, pl. de la Bastille, 12ème (☎08 92 89 90 90; www.operadeparis.fr). ⓂBastille. Opera and ballet with a modern spin. Subtitles in French. Rush tickets 15min. before show for students under 25 and seniors. €7-196. AmEx/MC/V.

Opéra Comique, 5 rue Favart, 2ème (☎01 42 44 45 46 or 08 25 01 01 23; www.opera-comique.com). ⓂRichelieu-Drouot. Operas on a lighter scale. €6-95. MC/V.

Opéra Garnier, pl. de l'Opéra, 9ème (☎08 92 89 90 90; www.operadeparis.fr). ⓂOpéra. Mostly ballet, chamber music, and symphonies. Tickets usually available 2 weeks ahead. Operas €7-160; ballets €6-80. Box office open M-Sa 10:30am-6:30pm. AmEx/MC/V.

JAZZ AND CABARET

Bal du Moulin Rouge, 82 bd. de Clichy, 9ème (☎01 53 09 82 82; www.moulin-rouge.com). ⓂBlanche. See **Sights,** p. 250. World-famous cabaret's reviews remain risqué. Be prepared to stand if it's a busy night. Elegant attire required; no shorts, sneakers, or sportswear permitted. Shows nightly 9pm (€99), 11pm (€89; includes champagne). 7pm dinner and 9pm show €145-175. Occasional lunch shows €95-125. MC/V.

Au Lapin Agile, 22 rue des Saules, 18ème (☎01 46 06 85 87; www.au-lapin-agile.com). ⓂLamarck-Coulaincourt. Drinks €6-7. Shows Tu-Su 9pm-2am. €24, M-F and Su students €17; includes 1 drink. MC/V.

▣ SHOPPING

In a city where Hermès scarves serve as slings for broken arms and department store history stretches back to the mid-19th century, shopping is nothing less than an art form. Consumerism is as diverse as the citizens are, from the wild club wear sold near **rue Étienne-Marcel** to the off-the-beaten path boutiques in the **18ème** or the **Marais.** The great *soldes* (sales) of the year begin after New Year's and at the very end of June, with the best prices at the beginning of February and the end of July. If at any time of year you see the word *braderie* (clearance sale) in a store window, enter without hesitation.

A true gem, **Gabrielle Geppert,** 31-34 Galerie Montpensier, 1er, is a favorite of Sharon Stone. Find an assort of gold leather and snakeskin bags, rhine-studded sunglasses in all colors, fur purses, enormous necklaces and earrings—all by vintage designers: Chanel, Louis Vuitton, Prada, and Gucci. (☎01 42 61 53 52; www.gabriellegeppert.com. ⓂPalais-Royale. Open M-Sa 10am-7:30pm. MC/V.)

Abbey Bookshop, 29 rue de la Parcheminerie, 5ème, is a laid-back shop overflows with new and used English-language titles, as well as Canadian pride courtesy of expat owner Brian. There's an impressive basement collection of anthropology, sociology, history, music, motherhood, and literary criticism titles. They're also happy to take special orders. (☎01 46 33 16 24; www.abbeybookshop.net. ⓂSt-Michel or Cluny. Open M-Sa 10am-7pm, sometimes later.)

Paris's department stores are as much sights as they are shopping destination, especially in December, when the stores go all out to decorate their windows. ■**Galeries Lafayette,** 40 bd. Haussmann, 9ème, can be chaotic but carries it all. (☎01 42 82 34 56; www.galerieslafayette.com. ⓂChaussée d'Antin-Lafayette or Havre-Caumartin. Open M-W and F-Sa 9:30am-7:30pm, Th 9:30am-9pm. AmEx/V.) **Au Bon Marché,** 24, rue de Sèvres, 7ème, is Paris's oldest, most exclusive, and most expensive, with items ranging from scarves to smoking

FRANCE

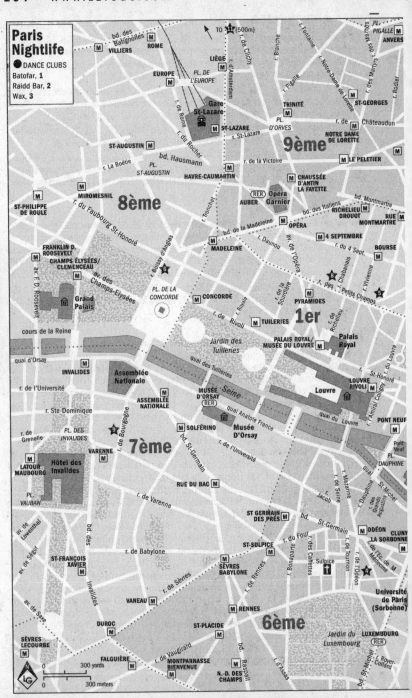

**Paris
Nightlife**

● DANCE CLUBS
Batofar, **1**
Raidd Bar, **2**
Wax, **3**

FRANCE

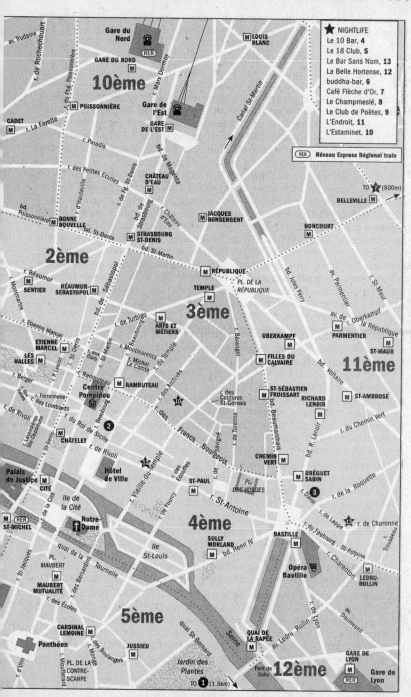

★ NIGHTLIFE
Le 10 Bar, 4
Le 18 Club, 5
Le Bar Sans Nom, 13
La Belle Hortense, 12
buddha-bar, 6
Café Flèche d'Or, 7
Le Champmeslé, 8
Le Club de Poètes, 9
L'Endroit, 11
L'Estaminet, 10

RER Réseau Express Régional train

accessories, *haute couture* to home furnishings. Across the street is ⬛**La Grande Épicerie de Paris** (38 rue de Sèvres), the celebrated gourmet food annex. (☎01 44 39 80 00. ⓜSèvres-Babylone. Store open M-W and F 9:30am-7pm, Th 10am-9pm, Sa 9:30am-8pm. *Épicerie* open M-Sa 8:30am-9pm. AmEx/MC/V.)

📻 NIGHTLIFE

In the *5ème* and *6ème*, bars draw students, while Paris's young and hip, queer and straight swarm the **Marais**, the center of Paris's GLBT life. Great neighborhood spots are springing up in the Left Bank's outlying areas, particularly in the *13ème* and *14ème*. A slightly older crowd congregates around **Les Halles**, while the outer *arrondissements* cater to locals. The **Bastille**, another central party area, is more suited to pounding shots than sipping Bordeaux.

Clubbing in Paris is less about hip DJs' beats than about dressing up and getting in. Drinks are expensive, and clubbers consume little beyond the first round. Many clubs accept reservations, so come early to assure entry on busy nights. Bouncers like tourists because they generally spend more money, so speaking English might actually give you an edge. Clubs heat up between 2 and 4am. Tune in to Radio FG (98.2 FM) or Radio Nova (101.5 FM) to find out about upcoming events. Parisian GLBT life centers around the **Marais**, comprised of the *3ème* and *4ème*. Numerous bars and clubs line **rue du Temple, rue Ste-Croix de la Bretonnerie, rue des Archives,** and **rue Vieille du Temple,** while the *3ème* boasts a lively lesbian scene. For the most comprehensive listing of organizations, consult *Illico* (free at GLBT bars and restaurants) or Zurban's annual *Paris Gay and Lesbian Guide* (€5 at any kiosk).

⬛ **Banana Café,** 13 rue de la Ferronerie (☎01 42 33 35 31; www.bananacafeparis. com). ⓜChâtelet. *Très branché* (way cool). Scantily clad men pole dance amid tropical decor. Legendary theme nights. "Go-Go Boys" Th-Sa midnight-dawn. Beer €5.50. Mixed drinks €8. Cover F-Sa €10; includes 1 drink. Happy hour 6-9pm; 2 for 1 drinks. Open daily 5:30pm-6am. AmEx/MC/V.

⬛ **Au Duc des Lombards,** 42 rue des Lombards (☎01 42 33 22 88; www.ducdeslombards.com). ⓜChâtelet. Murals of Ellington and Coltrane cover the exterior of this premier jazz joint. Still the best in French jazz. 3 sets each night. Beer €3.50-5. Mixed drinks €8-10. Music 10pm-1:30am. Cover €19-25, students €12 if you call in advance, couples €30 in advance. Open M-Sa 5pm-2am. MC/V.

⬛ **Andy Wahloo,** 69 rue des Gravilliers (☎01 42 71 20 38). ⓜArts et Métiers. Andy Warhol meets the Arab world at this Moroccan-themed lounge bar with traffic-sign tables and paint-bucket seats. Smoke hookah as live DJs spin. Beer €5-6. Mixed drinks €9-10. Happy hour 5-8pm; beer and mixed drinks €5. Open Tu-Sa 5pm-2am. AmEx/MC/V.

⬛ **Raidd Bar,** 23 rue du Temple (☎01 42 77 04 88; www.raiddbar.com). ⓜHotel de Ville. The Marais's most happening gay bar. Disco globes, sexy topless bartenders, and a lively dance floor. After 11pm, performers strip down in glass-enclosed shower stalls. Mixed drinks €8-9. Tu disco night; W 80s and house; Th DJ VIP; F-Sa club; Su 90s. Happy hour 5-11pm; buy 1 get 1 free. Enforces a strict door policy; women must be accompanied (preferably outnumbered) by men (ideally gorgeous ones). Open daily 5pm-5am. V.

L'Étoile Manquante, 34 rue Vieille du Temple (☎01 42 72 48 34; www.cafeine.com). ⓜHôtel de Ville. The brown leather banquets and concentric circles on the ceiling may seem to straddle the line between conventional and funky, but pop into the technological fantasyland of a bathroom (be sure to avoid the model trains) and you'll know not to put this quirky cafe in the normal column. Beer from €2.50. Mixed drinks €9. Salads and sandwiches €4-9. Open daily 9am-2am. Kitchen open until 1:15am. MC/V.

L'Académie de la Bière, 88 bis bd. de Port Royal (☎01 43 54 66 65; www.academie-biere.com). ⓂVavin. 12 kinds of beer on tap and over 300 more in bottles. Beer €4-9. Happy hour 3:30-7:30pm. Open M-Th and Su 10am-2am, F-Sa 10am-3am. MC/V.

Le Piano Vache, 8 rue Laplace (☎01 46 33 75 03; www.lepianovache.com). ⓂCardinal Lemoine or Maubert-Mutualité. Dim, poster-plastered bar with cow paraphernalia from its butcher-shop days. Often shown in music videos. Patrons ranges from alternative-trendy students to 30-something intellectuals to celebrities like Johnny Depp. Pints of beer €5.50, before 9pm €5. Live Jazz concerts M. Theme nights 9pm-2am. Open M-F noon-2am, Sa-Su 9pm-2am. Cash only.

Le 10 Bar, 10 rue de l'Odéon (☎01 43 26 66 83). ⓂOdéon. A classic student hangout where Parisian youth indulge in deep philosophical discussion. Either that or they're getting drunk and making fart jokes. Jukebox plays everything from Édith Piaf to Aretha Franklin. Famous *sangria* €3.50 (€3 before 8pm). Open daily 6pm-2am. MC/V.

Le Club des Poètes, 30 rue de Bourgogne (☎01 47 05 06 03; www.poesie.net). ⓂVarenne. Restaurant by day, poetry club by night (from 10pm). A troupe of readers and comedians bewitches the audience with poetry from Villon, Baudelaire, Rimbaud, and others. If you arrive after 10pm, wait to enter until you hear clapping to signal a break in the performance. Wine €4-8. Lunch *menu* €15. Open Sept.-July Tu-Sa noon-3pm and 8pm-1am. Kitchen open noon-10pm. MC/V.

buddha-bar, 8 rue Boissy d'Anglas (☎01 53 05 90 00; www.buddha-bar.com). ⓂMadeleine or Concorde. Too cool for capital letters. Perhaps the most glamorous and exclusive drinking hole in the city; Madonna drops by when she's in town. 2 dim, candlelit levels. 3-story Buddha. Creative mixed drinks €16-17. Beer €8-9. Sake €8. Wine €8-11. Open M-F noon-3pm and 6pm-2am, Sa-Su 6pm-2am. AmEx/MC/V.

Wax, 15 rue Daval (☎01 40 21 16 18). ⓂBastille. Always free and fun. In a concrete bunker with retro orange, red, yellow, and white couches. Beer €5-7. Mixed drinks €10. Disco/funk W and Su; R&B Th; house Sa-Su. Open daily 9pm-sunrise. MC/V over €15.

Batofar (☎01 53 60 17 30; www.batofar.fr), facing 11 quai François-Mauriac. ⓂQuai de la Gare or Bibliothèque Nationale de France. This 45m long, 520-ton barge/bar/club has made it big with a variety of music—mainly electronic, hip hop, reggae, and house. Attracts a friendly crowd. Live artists daily. Cover €8-15; usually includes 1 drink. Open M-Th 11pm-6am, F-Sa later; hours change for special film and DJ events. MC/V.

L'Endroit, 67 pl. du Docteur Félix Lobligeois (☎01 42 29 50 00). ⓂRome. Hip, young crowd haunts this snazzy diner-esque bar in an idyllic spot on a tree-lined *place.* The alcohol is kept on a giant rotating shelf. Wine €4-5. Beer €3-5. Mixed drinks €8-10. Open daily 10am-2am, often later F-Sa. MC/V.

Café Flèche d'Or, 102 bis rue Bagnolet (☎01 44 64 01 02; www.flechedor.fr). ⓂPorte de Bagnolet. Live concert venue. Cool, intense, and a little rough around the edges. Music ranges from reggae to hip hop to electropop to Celtic rock. Art videos, dance classes, and crazy theater on the tracks below the terrace. Beer €4-6. Mixed drinks €8-20. DJ set Th-Sa midnight-6am. Free entry for concerts 8pm-2am. Open W-Sa 10am-3am, Th-Sa 10am-6am. MC/V.

◪ DAYTRIPS FROM PARIS

▨**VERSAILLES.** Louis XIV, the Sun King, built and held court at Versailles's extraordinary palace, 12km west of Paris. The **château** embodies the Old Regime's extravagance, especially in the newly renovated **Hall of Mirrors,** the ornate State Apartments, and the fountain-filled gardens. Arrive as soon as the château opens to avoid horrendous crowds. The line to buy tickets is to the left of the courtyard, while the line to get into the château is to the right; skip the former line by buying a day pass at the Versailles tourist office, 2bis av.

TOP 10 PLACES TO FIND THE "SENTIMENT DE L'EXISTENCE"

Jean-Jacques Rousseau championed the phrase *"sentiment de l'existence,"* the fulfillment found living in the moment. So kick back in Rousseau's stomping ground and enjoy the *dolce far niente*—the sweetness of doing nothing.

1. Daydream atop of the **Denis Papin stairs** in Blois—the height may just leave you lightheaded.
2. Meditate beside the Loire from the raised **boardwalk** in Amboise.
3. Take in a sea of wheat in solitude on the way to **Beauregard.**
4. Feel on top of the world as you conquer the Loire and ascend to **Chaumont.**
5. Gawk at Napoleon's magnificent cedar in the courtyard of the **Musée des Beaux-Arts** in Tours.
6. Stroll the **quai Maynaud** and watch the sun slip behind Saumur's *château.*
7. Sink into Cathédrale St-Louis's shadow in the **Jardin de l'Evêché** and lose your senses in the view of Blois's *vieille ville.*
8. Let your desire for material goods melt away as you observe passersby in designer jeans in Le Mans's **place de la République.**
9. Sit at the bank of the moat near Sully-sur-Loire's **château** and ponder your reflection in the water traversed by Jeanne d'Arc.
10. Contemplate yin and yang as the endless tension between good and evil unfolds before you under the Tapisserie de l'Apocalypse in the **Château d'Angers.**

de Paris, or skip the latter line by buying a combo guided tour and entrance ticket to the right of the château ticket office. (☎01 30 83 78 89; www.chateauversailles.fr. *Château open Tu-Su Apr.-Oct. 9am-6:30pm; Nov.-Mar. 9am-5:30pm. Last entry 30min. before closing. Admission to palace and self-guided tour through entrance A €8, after 3:30pm €6, under 18 free. Various other passes and guided tours also available. For group discounts and reservations call ☎08 10 81 16 14.)* A shuttle (round-trip €6, 11-18 €4.50) runs through the gardens to Louis XIV's pink marble hideaway, the **Grand Trianon,** and Marie-Antoinette's **Petit Trianon,** including her pseudo-peasant Hameau, or hamlet. *(www.train-versailles.com. Both Trianons open daily Apr.-Oct. noon-6:30pm; Nov.-Mar. noon-5:30pm. Last entry 30min. before closing. Apr.-Oct. €9, 2hr. before closing €5, under 18 free; Nov.-Mar. €5, under 18 free.)* Take the RER C5 train from Ⓜ Invalides to the Versailles Rive Gauche station (30-40min., 4 per hr., round-trip €5.60). Make sure you keep your RER (not Métro) ticket to exit at the Versailles station.

▣**CHARTRES.** Chartres's phenomenal cathedral is one of the most beautiful surviving creations of the Middle Ages. Arguably the finest example of early Gothic architecture in Europe, the cathedral retains nearly all of its original 12th- and 13th-century stained-glass windows, many featuring the stunning "Chartres blue." Climb the spiral staircase to the top of the 16th-century Flamboyant Gothic left tower (Tour Jehan-de-Beauce), built 300 years after the rest of the cathedral, for dizzying views. *(☎02 37 21 75 02; www.cathedrale-chartres.com. Open daily 8:30am-7:30pm. No casual visits during mass. Mass M-F 11:45am and 6:15pm, Tu and F 9am and 6:15pm; Sa 11:45am and 6pm; Su 9:15 (Latin), 11am, 6pm (in the crypt). Call the tourist office for info on concerts in the cathedral. €10, students and children €5.)* **Trains** run from Paris's Gare Montparnasse (1hr., 1 per hr., round-trip €26). The cathedral towers are visible to the left from outside the station.

LOIRE VALLEY (VAL DE LOIRE)

The Loire, France's longest river, meanders toward the Atlantic through a valley containing vineyards that produce some of the nation's best wines. It's hardly surprising that a string of French (and English) kings chose to live in opulent châteaux by these waters rather than in the commotion of their capital cities.

⌐ TRANSPORTATION

Faced with widespread grandeur, many travelers plan overly ambitious itineraries—two châteaux per day is a reasonable goal. The city of Tours is the region's best rail hub. However, train schedules are inconvenient, and many châteaux aren't accessible by train. **Biking** is the best way to explore the region. Many stations distribute the invaluable *Châteaux pour Train et Vélo* booklet.

ORLÉANS   ☎ 02 38

A gateway from Paris into the Loire, Orléans (pop. 200,000) cherishes its historical connection to **Joan of Arc**, who marched triumphantly past the **rue de Bourgogne** in 1429 after liberating the city from a British siege. Most of Orléans's highlights are near place Ste-Croix. With stained-glass windows that depict Joan's story, the ▨**Cathédrale Sainte-Croix**, pl. Ste-Croix, is Orléans's crown jewel. (Open daily July-Aug. 9:15am-7pm; Sept.-June reduced hours.)

One block from the train station, ▨**Hôtel de L'Abeille ❹**, 64 r. Alsace-Lorraine, has been owned by the same family since 1919. Twenty-nine comfortable rooms with antique furniture and fireplaces (albeit non-functional) are worth the price. (☎02 38 53 54 87; www.hoteldelabeille.com. Continental breakfast €8.50, in bed €9.50. Wi-Fi in lobby. Singles with shower €47, with full bath €51; doubles €62-66/69-79; triples and quads €95-110. AmEx/MC/V.) Rue de Bourgogne and rue Ste-Catherine have a variety of cheap buffets and a lively bar scene at night. At ▨**Mijana ❸**, 175 r. de Bourgogne, a charming Lebanese couple prepares gourmet cuisine. (☎02 38 62 02 02; www.mijanaresto.com. Take-out sandwiches €4-6. Appetizers €7.20-8.50. *Plats* €14-17. Lunch specials, including *menu traditionel* €17.75. Open M-Sa noon-1:30pm, 7-10pm. Vegetarian options. Open M-Sa noon-1:30pm and 7-10pm. AmEx/MC/V over €15.) **Trains** leave from the Gare d'Orléans on pl. Albert I. to: Blois (40min.; at least 15 per day; €9.70 under 26 €7); Nantes (2hr.; M-F 3 per day, Sa-Su 2 per day; €35); Paris Austerlitz (1hr., every hr., €13); Tours (1hr., every 30min., €18). The **tourist office,** is located at 2 pl. de l'Étape. (☎02 38 24 05 05; www.tourisme-orleans.com. Open July-Aug. 9:30am-7pm; June 9:30am-1pm and 2-6:30pm; May and Sept. Tu-Sa 9:30am-1pm and 2-6pm; Oct.-Apr. reduced hours.) **Postal Code:** 45000.

BRITTANY (BRETAGNE)

Despite superficially French *centre-villes*, châteaux, and *creperies*, Brittany reveres its pre-Roman Celtic roots. After 800 years of Breton settlement, the province became part of France when the duke's daughter married two successive French kings. Black-and-white *Breizh* (Breton) flags still decorate buildings, however, and the Celtic language Breton remains on street signs.

RENNES   ☎ 02 99

The cultural capital of Brittany, Rennes (pop 212,000) flourishes from September to June because of its large, rowdy student population. Ethnic eateries, colorful nightspots, and crowds of university students enliven the cobblestone streets and half-timbered houses of the *vieille ville*. Medieval architecture peppers Rennes's *vieille ville*, particularly **rue de la Psalette** and **rue St-Guillaume.** At the end of r. St-Guillaume, turn left onto r. de la Monnaie to visit the **Cathédrale St-Pierre,** a 19th-century masterpiece with a solid, Neoclassical facade and frescoed, gilded interior. (Open daily 9:30am-noon and 3-6pm.) The **Musée des Beaux-Arts,** 20 q. Émile Zola, houses an excellent collection including Baroque and Breton masterpieces but few famous works. (☎02 23 62 17 45; www.mbar. org. Open Tu 10am-6pm, W-Su 10am-noon and 2-6pm. €4.30, students €2.20, under 18 free; with special exhibits €5.40/2.70/free.) Across the river and up r. Gambetta is the lush **Jardin du Thabor,** one of the most beautiful gardens in France. (☎02 99 28 56 62. Open daily June-Aug. 7:30am-8:30pm; Sept.-June 7:30am-6:30pm.) Rennes is a **partygoer's dream,** especially during term time. Look for action in **place Ste-Anne, place St-Michel,** and **place de Lices.** In a former prison, **Delicatessen,** 7 impasse Rallier du Baty, has swapped jailhouse bars for heavy beats. (Drinks €6-10. Cover €5-15. Open Tu-Sa midnight-5am.)

The **Auberge de Jeunesse (HI) ❶,** 10-12 Canal St-Martin, has simple dorms. Take the metro (dir.: Kennedy) to Ste-Anne. Follow r. de St-Malo to the right of the church downhill onto r. St-Martin; the hostel will be on the right after the bridge. (☎02 99 33 22 33; rennes@fuaj.org. Breakfast and linens included. Reception 7am-11pm. Dorms €17. MC/V.) **Rue St-Malo** has many ethnic restaurants, while the *vieille ville* contains traditional brasseries. **Le St-Germain des Champs (Restaurant Végétarien-Biologique) ❸,** 12 r. du Vau St-Germain, serves vegetarian *plats* for €10. (☎02 99 79 25 52. Open M-Sa noon-2:30pm. MC/V.)

Trains leave pl. de la Gare for: Caen (3hr., 4 per day, €33); Paris (2hr., 1 per hr., €53-65); St-Malo (1hr., 15 per day, €14.90); Tours (3hr., 4 per day, €37) via Le Mans. Buses go from 16 pl. de la Gare to Angers (2hr., 2 per day, €14) and Mont-St-Michel (1hr., 4 per day, €10). Local **buses** run Monday through Saturday 5:15am-12:30am and Sunday 7:25am-midnight. The metro line uses the same ticket (€1.10, day pass €4, carnet of 10 €11). To get from the train station to the **tourist office** is at 11 r. St-Yves. (☎02 99 67 11 11; www.tourisme-rennes.com. Open July-Aug. M-Sa 9am-7pm, Su 11am-1pm and 2-6pm; Sept.-June M 1-6pm, Tu-Sa 10am-6pm, Su 11am-1pm and 2-6pm.) **Postal Code:** 35000.

NANTES   ☎02 40

With broad boulevards, relaxing public parks, and great bistros, Nantes (pop. 280,000) knows how to take life easy. The massive **Château des Ducs de Bretagne,** built to safeguard Breton independence in the late 15th century, now houses several exhibits detailing regional history. (Château grounds open daily mid-May to mid-Sept. 9am-8pm; mid-Sept. to mid-May 10am-7pm. Museum open mid-May to mid-Sept. 9:30am-7pm; mid-Sept. to mid-May 10am-6pm. Grounds free. Exhibits each €5, 18-26 €3; both €8/4.80.) Gothic vaults soar 39m in the bright **Cathédrale St-Pierre.** (Open daily Apr.-Oct. 8am-7pm, Nov.-Mar. 8am-6pm.) The **Musée des Beaux-Arts,** 10 r. Georges Clemenceau, features a wide range of European masterpieces on the second floor. (☎02 51 17 45 00. Open M, W, F-Su 10am-6pm, Th 10am-8pm. €3.50, students €2, under 18, Th 6-8pm, and 1st Su of each month free; €2 daily after 4:30pm.)

A 15min. walk from the train station, **Auberge de Jeunesse "La Manu" (HI) ❶,** 2 pl. de la Manu, once a tobacco factory, still has an industrial feel overshadowed by bright decor and a friendly staff. (☎02 40 29 29 20; nanteslamanu@ fuaj.org. Breakfast and linens included. Luggage storage €1.50. Internet €1 per 40min. Reception daily July-Aug. 8am-noon and 3-11pm; Sept.-June 8am-noon and 5-11pm. Lockout July-Aug. 10am-4pm, Sept.-June 10am-5pm. Open Jan. to mid-Dec. 3- to 6-bed dorms €16.90. HI members only. MC/V.) Plenty of reasonably-priced eateries are between **place du Bouffay** and **place du Pilori.** One of France's most beautiful bistros, **Chez l'Huitre ❷,** 5 rue des Petites Écuries, has some of the freshest oysters. (☎51 82 02 02. 3-course *menu,* €8-12. Bucket of *huîtres* €3.50-13.60. Open daily noon-3pm and 6pm-10pm. MC/V.) For nightlife, the **Ste-Croix area,** near place du Bouffay, has bars and cafes in abundance. **Trains** leave from 27 bd. de Stalingrad for Bordeaux (4hr., 5 per day, €42), Paris (2-4hr., 1 per hr., €54-69), and Rennes (1hr., 7-15 per day, €21). The **tourist office** is at 3 cours Olivier de Clisson. (☎08 92 46 40 44; www.nantes-tourisme.com. Open M-W and F-Sa 10am-6pm, Tu 10:30am-6pm.) **Postal Code:** 44000.

NORMANDY

Rainy, fertile Normandy is a land of fields, fishing villages, and cathedrals. Invasions have twice secured the region's place in military history: in 1066, William of Normandy conquered England; on D-Day, June 6, 1944, Allied armies returned the favor, liberating France from Normandy's beaches.

ROUEN   ☎02 35

Madame Bovary—literature's most famous desperate housewife—may have criticized Rouen (pop. 106,000), but Flaubert's hometown is no provincial hamlet. Historically important as the capital of Normandy and the city where **Joan of Arc** burned at the stake in 1431, Rouen today boasts splendid Gothic cathedrals and buzzing urban energy. The most famous of Rouen's "hundred spires" belong to the �®**Cathédrale de Notre-Dame,** pl. de la Cathédrale. The central spire, standing at 495 feet, is the tallest in France. Art lovers may also recognize the cathedral's facade from Monet's celebrated studies of light. (Open Apr.-Oct. M 2-7pm, Tu-Sa 7:30am-7pm, Su 8am-6pm; Nov.-Mar. M 2-7pm, Tu-Sa 7:30am-noon and 2-6pm, Su 8am-6pm.) The **Musée Flaubert et d'Histoire de la Médicine,** 51 r. de Lecat, down r. de Crosne from pl. de Vieux-Marché, houses a large collection of bizarre paraphernalia on both subjects. (☎02 35 15 59 95; www.chu-rouen.fr. Open Tu 10am-6pm, W-Sa 10am-noon and 2-6pm. €3, 18-25 €1.50, under 18 free.) **Hotel des Arcades ❸,** 52 r. de Carmes, is down the street from the cathedral. (☎02 35 70 10 30; www.hotel-des-arcades.fr. Breakfast €6.50. Singles €29-36, with shower €40-46; doubles €30-37/41-47; triples with shower €57. AmEx/MC/V.) Cheap eateries surround place du Vieux-Marché and the Gros Horloge area. **Chez Wam ❶,** 67 r. de la République, near l'Abbatiale St-Ouen, serves delicious *kebab-frites* (kebabs with fries; €4) ideal for picnics at the nearby **Jardins de l'Hôtel de Ville.** (☎02 35 15 97 51. Open daily 10am-2am. Cash only.) **Trains** leave r. Jeanne d'Arc, on pl. Bernard Tissot, for Lille (3hr., 3 per day, €30) and Paris (1hr., 1 per hr., €19.30). The **tourist office** is at 25 pl. de la Cathédrale. (☎02 32 08 32 40; www.rouentourisme.com. Open May-Sept. M-Sa 9am-7pm, Su 9:30am-12:30pm and 2-6pm; Oct.-Apr. M-Sa 9:30am-6:30pm.) **Postal Code:** 76000.

CHAMPAGNE AND BURGUNDY

Legend has it that when Dom Perignon first tasted champagne, he exclaimed, "Come quickly! I am drinking stars!" Few modern-day visitors need further convincing as they flock to the wine cellars in Reims and Épernay. To the east, Burgundy's abbeys and cathedrals bear witness to the Middle Ages's religious fervor. Today, the region draws epicureans with its fine wines and delectable dishes like *coq au vin* and *boeuf bourguignon*.

REIMS   ☎03 26

From the 26 monarchs crowned in its cathedral to the bubbling champagne of its famed *caves* (cellars), everything Reims (pop. 191,000) touches turns to gold. The ▮**Cathédrale de Notre-Dame,** built with golden limestone taken from the medieval city walls, features sea-blue stained-glass windows by Marc Chagall, hanging chandeliers, and an impressive royal history. (☎03 26 47 55 34. Open daily 7:30am-7:30pm. Free. English-language audio tour €5.) The adjacent **Palais**

du Tau, 2 pl. du Cardinal Luçon, houses original statues from the cathedral's façade alongside majestic 16th-century tapestries. (☎03 26 47 81 79. Open May-Aug. Tu-Su 9:30am-6:30pm; Sept.-Apr. 9:30am-12:30pm and 2-5:30pm. €6.50, 18-25 €4.50, under 18 free.) **Champagne Pommery,** 5 pl. du Général Gouraud, gives the best tours of Reims's champagne caves. Its 75,000L *tonneau* (vat) is one of the largest in the world; it, along with the *maison*'s modern art exhibits, can be viewed in the lobby free of charge. (☎03 26 61 62 56; www.pommery. com. Reservations recommended, €10-17.)

> ⚠️ **STEER CLEAR.** Many of the roads in Reims's *centre-ville* are under serious construction until 2010. If you plan to drive in the city, be prepared for confusing detours and bring an up-to-date road map. The sidewalks remain open, so if you are on foot, the inconveniences will be merely aesthetic.

The ■**Centre International de Séjour/Auberge de Jeunesse (HI)** ❶, chaussée Bocquaine, has clean rooms. (☎03 26 40 52 60. Breakfast included. Free Wi-Fi. Wheelchair-accessible. Reception 24hr. Dorms €19, with toilet and shower €22; singles €28/41; doubles €21/28; triples with shower €22. €3 HI discount. MC/V.) Restaurants, and bars crowd **place Drouet d'Erlon,** Reims's nightspot. **Trains** leave bd. Joffre for Épernay (20min., 11 per day, €4.80) and Paris (1hr., 11 per day, €21). The **tourist office** is at 2 r. Guillaume de Machault. (☎03 26 77 45 00; www. reims-tourisme.com. Open mid-Apr. to mid-Oct. M-Sa 9am-7pm, Su 10am-6pm; mid-Oct. to mid-Apr. M-Sa 9am-6pm, Su 11am-6pm.) **Postal Code:** 51100.

ÉPERNAY   ☎ 03 26

Champagne's showcase town, Épernay (pop. 26,000) is rightly lavish and seductive. Palatial mansions, lush gardens, and champagne companies distinguish the aptly named ■**avenue de Champagne.** Here you'll find Moët & Chandon, 20 av. de Champagne, producers of the king of all champagnes: ■**Dom Perignon.** (☎03 26 51 20 20; www.moet.com. Reservations required. Open daily 9:30-11:30am and 2-4:30pm. Tours with several tasting options for those 18+ €13-25, 10-18 €8, under 10 free.) Ten minutes away is **Mercier,** 70 av. de Champagne, producers of the self-proclaimed "most popular champagne in France." Tours are in roller-coaster-style cars that tell the story of its Willy-Wonka-like founder, Eugène Mercier. (☎03 26 51 22 22. Open mid-Mar. to mid-Nov. daily 9:30-11:30am and 2-4:30pm; mid-Nov. to mid-Dec. and mid-Feb. to mid-Mar. M and Th-Su 9:30-11:30am and 2-4:30pm. Wheelchair-accessible. 30min. tour €8-15.) Budget hotels are rare in Épernay, but ■**Hôtel St-Pierre** ❷, 1 r. Jeanne d'Arc, offers spacious rooms at unbeatable prices. (☎03 26 54 40 80; fax 57 88 68. www.villasaintpierre.fr. Breakfast €6. Reception 7am-10pm. Singles €21, with shower €30; doubles €24/36. MC/V.) Ethnic food, as well as pricier Champagne-soaked cuisine, line **rue Gambetta,** near the tourist office. Bakeries and delis sporadically dot the area around **place des Arcades** and **place Hugues Plomb.**

Trains leave Cours de la Gare for Paris (1hr., 18 per day, €19) and Strasbourg (3hr., 3 per day, €40). From the station, walk through pl. Mendès France, head from r. Gambetta to pl. de la République, then turn left on av. de Champagne to reach the **tourist office,** 7 av. de Champagne. (☎03 26 53 33 00; www.ot-epernay. fr. Open Mar. 23 to mid-Oct. M-Sa 9:30am-12:30pm and 1:30-7pm, Su 11am-4pm; mid-Oct. to Easter M-Sa 9:30am-12:30pm and 1:30-5:30pm.) **Postal Code:** 51200.

DIJON   ☎ 03 80

Dijon (pop. 150,000) isn't just about the mustard. The capital of Burgundy, once home to dukes who wielded a power unmatched by the French monarchy,

FRANCE

counters its historic grandeur with a modern irreverence. The diverse **Musée des Beaux-Arts** occupies the east wing of the colossal Palais des Ducs de Bourgogne, on pl. de la Libération, at the center of the *vieille ville*. (☎03 80 74 52 70. Open M and W-Su May-Oct. 9:30am-6pm; Nov.-Apr. 10am-5pm. Free. Temporary exhibits €2, students €1.) Built in only 20 years, the **Église Notre-Dame,** pl. Notre Dame, is one of France's most famous churches. Its 11th-century statue of the Black Virgin is credited with having liberated the city on two occasions: in 1513 from a Swiss siege and in 1944 from the German occupation (☎03 80 41 86 76; www.notre-dame-dijon.net). Dijon's **Estivade** (☎03 80 74 53 33; tickets under €8) brings dance, music, and theater to the city throughout July. In late summer, the week-long **Fêtes de la Vigne** and **Folkloriades Internationales** (☎03 80 30 37 95; www.fetesdelavigne.com; tickets €10-46) celebrate the grape harvest with dance and music from around the world. ◼**Hotel Le Jacquemart ❸,** 32 r. Verrerie, offers florally decorated rooms and a gorgeous, old-fashioned staircase. (☎03 80 60 09 60. Breakfast €5.85. Reception 24hr. Singles €29-53; doubles €32-64. AmEx/MC/V.) **Rue Amiral Boussin** has charming cafes, while reasonably priced restaurants line **rue Berbisey, rue Monge, rue Musette,** and **place Émile Zola.** From the station at cours de la Gare, **trains** run to Lyon (2hr., 14 per day, €25), Nice (6-8hr., 6-8 per day, €88), and Paris (1-3hr., 15-19 per day, €52). The **tourist office** is at 34 r. des Forges. (☎08 92 70 05 58; www.dijon-tourism.com. Open daily May to mid-Oct. 9am-7pm; mid-Oct. to Apr. 10am-6pm.) **Postal Code:** 21000.

ALSACE-LORRAINE AND FRANCHE-COMTÉ

Influenced by its tumultuous past, the region's fascinating blend of French and German shows its dual heritage in local dialects, cuisine, and architecture. Alsatian towns display half-timbered Bavarian houses, while Lorraine's wheat fields are interspersed with elegant cities.

STRASBOURG ☎03 88

Just a few kilometers from the Franco-German border, Strasbourg (pop. 270,000) is a city with true international character. *Winstubs* (wine-bar restaurants specializing in local dishes) sit peacefully beside *pâtisseries* in the *vieille ville*, while German and French conversations mingle in the street.

> ◆**TIP** **BIG BUCKS FOR BIGWIGS.** Prices rise during EU plenary sessions. To take in the city's sights without going broke, avoid visiting (during these dates in 2009) Jan. 12-15, Feb. 2-5, Mar. 9-12 and 23-26, Apr. 21-24, May 4-7, July 14-16, Sept. 14-17, Oct. 19-22, Nov. 23-26, and Dec. 14-17.

 TRANSPORATION AND PRACTICAL INFORMATION. Trains leave from Pl. de la Gare. to Frankfurt, Germany (2-4hr., 13 per day, €52); Luxembourg (2-3hr., 10 per day, €33); Paris (4hr., 24 per day, €47; TGV 2hr., €63); Zurich, Switzerland (3hr., 4 per day, €40-47). SNCF **buses** run to surrounding towns from the station. The **Compagnie des Transports Strasbourgeois** (CTS), 14 rue de la Gare aux Marchandises (☎77 70 11, bus and tram info 77 70 70; www.cts-strasbourg.fr) has 5 tram lines which run 4:30am-12:30am. Find tickets (€1.30, round-trip €2.50) on board and *carnets* of 10 (€11.50) and day passes (€3.50)

at **CTS**, 56 rue du Jeu des Enfants. Open M-F 8:30am-6:30pm, Sa 9am-5pm.) The **tourist office** is at 17 pl. de la Cathédrale. (☎03 88 52 28 28; www.ot-strasbourg. fr. Open daily 9am-7pm. There's also a branch at pl. de la Gare. (☎03 88 32 51 49. Open M-Sa 9am-12:30pm and 1:45-7pm.) **Postal Code:** 67000.

▐▌ ACCOMMODATIONS AND FOOD. Great deals on hotels are all over the city, especially around the train station. Wherever you stay, make reservations early. Hotel prices often drop on weekends and when the EU Parliament is not in session. Near the train station, **Hôtel le Grillon ❷**, 2 r. Thiergarten, this offers the best value. (☎03 88 32 71 88; www.grillon.com. Breakfast €7.50. Internet €1 per 15min; free Wi-Fi. Reception 24hr. Singles €33, with shower €43-58; doubles €40/50-65. Extra bed €13. MC/V.) The scenic **La Petite France** neighborhood, especially along r. des Dentelles, is full of *winstubs* with Alsatian specialties.

◙ SIGHTS. The **Cathédrale de Strasbourg** is a Gothic cathedral with a tower that stretches 142m skyward; young Goethe scaled its 332 steps to cure his fear of heights. Inside, the **Horloge Astronomique** demonstrates 16th-century Swiss clockmaking wizardry. Also check out the **Pilier des Anges** (Angels' Pillar), a depiction of the Last Judgment. (Cathedral open M-Sa 7-11:40am and 12:40-7pm, Su 12:45-6pm. Tower open daily July-Aug. 9am-7:15pm; Apr.-June and Sept. 9am-6pm; Mar. and Oct. 9am-5:30pm; Nov.-Feb. 9am-4:30pm. Clock tickets sold at the northern entrance; €1. Tower €4.60, students €2.30.) The Palais Rohan houses three excellent museums. The Musée des Beaux-Arts displays 14th- to 19th-century art, including works by Botticelli, Giotto, Goya, Raphaël, and Rubens. The **Musée des Arts Décoratifs**, refurbished for Napoleon in 1805, features pistachio-green rooms encrusted with gold and marble, including the emperor's bedroom and library. The **Musée Archéologique** illustrates Alsace's history through relics and a slew of skeletons. (2 pl. du Château. All open M and W-Su 10am-6pm. €6 each, students €3; free 1st Su of every month.)

▐ NIGHTLIFE. Strasbourg specializes in friendly bars rather than throbbing clubs. **Place Kléber** attracts a student scene, while **rue des Frères** fills up quickly after 10pm with a diverse crowd. **Bar Exils**, 28 r. de l'Ail, boasts over 40 beers, leather couches, and an unflagging spirit that buzzes into the early morning. (☎03 88 35 52 70. Beer from €2; after 10pm €2.50. Open M-F noon-4am, Sa-Su 2pm-4am. MC/V min. €6.) Rock all night at **Le Tribord**, Ponts Couverts, a lively gay and lesbian club. (From pl. du Quartier Blanc, make a right onto the footpath by the canal in front of the Hotel du Départment, following it to the waterside. The club is the first boat on the right. ☎03 88 36 22 90. Beer from €2.50. Mixed drinks from €4. Open Th-Sa 10pm-4am.)

RHÔNE-ALPES AND MASSIF CENTRAL

Nature's architecture is the Alps' real attraction. The curves of the Chartreuse Valley rise to rugged crags in the Vercors range and crescendo at Europe's highest peak, Mont Blanc (4807m). From bases like Chamonix, winter skiers enjoy some of the world's most challenging slopes. In summer, hikers take over the mountains, seeking pristine vistas and clear air.

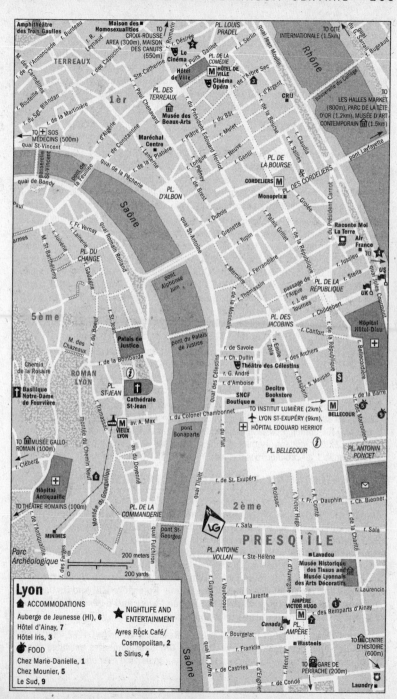

Lyon

ACCOMMODATIONS

Auberge de Jeunesse (HI), **6**
Hôtel d'Ainay, **7**
Hôtel Iris, **3**

FOOD

Chez Marie-Danielle, **1**
Chez Mounier, **5**
Le Sud, **9**

NIGHTLIFE AND ENTERTAINMENT

Ayres Rock Café/
Cosmopolitan, **2**
Le Sirius, **4**

FRANCE

LYON

☎ 04 78

Ultra-modern, ultra-friendly, and undeniably gourmet, Lyon (pop. 453,000) elicits cries of "Forget Paris!" from backpackers. Its location—at the confluence of the Rhône and Saône rivers and along an Italian road—earned Lyon (then Lugdunum) its place as Roman Gaul's capital. A transportation hub, Lyon is now better known for its beautiful parks, modern financial center, well-preserved Renaissance quarter, and fantastic restaurants.

TRANSPORTATION

Flights: Aéroport Lyon-St-Exupéry (LYS; ☎08 26 80 08 26). Satobuses/Navette Aéroport (☎72 68 72 17) **shuttles** to Gare de la Part-Dieu, Gare de Perrache, and subway stops Grange-Blanche, Jean Macé, and Mermoz Pinel (every 20min., €8.60). **Air France,** 10 q. Jules Courmont, 2ème (☎08 20 32 08 20), has 10 daily flights to Paris's **Orly** and **Charles de Gaulle airports** (from €118). Open M-Sa 9am-6pm.

Trains: The convenient **TGV,** which stops at the airport, is cheaper than daily flights to Paris. Trains passing through stop at **Gare de la Part-Dieu,** 5 pl. Béraudier (M: Part-Dieu), on the Rhône's east bank. Info desk open daily 5am-12:45am. Ticket window open M-Th and Sa 5:15am-11pm, F and Su 5:15am-midnight. Trains terminating in Lyon continue to Gare de Perrache, pl. Carnot (M: Perrache). Open daily 4:45am-12:30am. Ticket window open M 5am-10pm, Tu-Sa 5:30am-10pm, Su 7am-10pm. **SNCF trains** go from both stations to: **Dijon** (2hr., 1 per hr., €26); **Grenoble** (1hr., 1 per hr., €18); **Marseille** (1hr., 1 per hr., €44); **Nice** (6hr., 3 per day, €62); **Paris** (2hr., 17 per day, €60); **Strasbourg** (5hr., 6 per day, €49); **Geneva, SWI** (4hr., 6 per day, €23). The **SNCF Boutique** is at 2 pl. Bellecour. Open M-F 9am-6:45pm, Sa 10am-6:30pm.

Buses: On the Gare de Perrache's lowest level and at Gorge de Loup in the 9ème (☎72 61 72 61). It's almost always cheaper and faster to take the train. Domestic companies include **Philibert** (☎72 75 06 06). **Eurolines** (☎72 56 95 30; www.eurolines.fr) travels out of France; office on the main floor of Perrache open M-Sa 9am-9pm.

Local Transportation: TCL (☎08 20 42 70 00; www.tcl.fr) has information offices at both bus stations and all major metro stops. *Plan de Poche* (pocket map) available from any TCL branch. Tickets valid for all forms of mass transport. (Tickets €1.60, carnet of 10 €12.80; student discount includes 10 passes valid for 1 month €11.10. Pass valid 1hr. in 1 dir., connections included.)

ORIENTATION AND PRACTICAL INFORMATION

Lyon is divided into nine *arrondissements* (districts). The 1er, 2ème, and 4ème lie on the *presqu'île* (peninsula), which juts toward the Saône River to the west and the Rhône to the east. Starting in the south, the 2ème (the centre ville) includes the Gare de Perrache and place Bellecour. The nocturnal **Terreaux** neighborhood, with its sidewalk cafes and lively, student-packed bars, makes up the 1er. Farther north, the *presqu'île* widens into the 4ème and the famous **Croix-Rousse.** The main pedestrian roads on the *presqu'île* are **rue de la République** and **rue Victor Hugo West** of the Saône, Fourvière Hill and its basilica overlook **Vieux Lyon** (5ème). East of the Rhône (3ème and 6-8ème) lie the **Gare de la Part-Dieu** and most of the city's population.

Tourist Office: Located in the Pavilion at pl. Bellecour, 2ème (☎04 72 77 69 69; www.lyon-france.com). M: Bellecour. The **Lyon City Card** authorizes unlimited public transportation along with admission to museums, tours, and river boat cruises. 1-day pass €19; 2-day €29; 3-day €39. Open June-Sept. M-Sa 9:30am-6:30pm, Su 10am-5:30pm; Oct.-May M-Sa 10am-5:30pm. MC/V.

Police: 47 r. de la Charité, ☎04 78 42 26 56. M: Perrache.

Hospital: Hôpital Hôtel-Dieu, 1 pl. de l'Hôpital, 2*ème*, near q. du Rhône, is the most central. City hospital line ☎04 78 08 20 69.

Post Office: pl. Antonin Poncet, 2*ème* (☎04 72 40 65 22), near pl. Bellecour. **Postal Code:** 69001-69009; last digit indicates *arrondissement*.

ACCOMMODATIONS

September is Lyon's busiest month; it's easier and cheaper to find a place in summer but still wise to reserve ahead. Rooms under €30 are rare. Low-end hotels are east of place Carnot. There are inexpensive options north of place des Terraux. Watch out for budget-breaking accommodations in *vieux* Lyon.

▓ **Auberge de Jeunesse (HI),** 41-45 montée du Chemin Neuf, 5*ème* (☎04 78 15 05 50, www.fuaj.org). M: Vieux Lyon. A terrace and bar draw international backpackers. English-speaking staff. Breakfast and linens included. Laundry €4.05. Internet €5 per hr. Max. 6-night stay. Reception 24hr. Reserve ahead. Dorms €16. HI members only. MC/V. ❶

▓ **Hôtel Iris,** 36 r. de l'Arbre Sec, 1er (☎04 78 39 93 80, ☎04 72 00 89 91; www.hoteliris.freesurf.fr). M: Hôtel de Ville. This tranquil former convent is in a prime location near Terraux. Breakfast €5. Reception 8am-8:30pm. Reserve 2 weeks ahead in summer. Singles and doubles with sink €35-42, with toilet and shower €48-50. MC/V. ❸

Hôtel d'Ainay, 14 r. des Remparts d'Ainay, 2*ème* (☎04 78 42 43 42). M: Ampère-Victor Hugo. Offers spacious rooms with private bath. Travelers enjoy the great location between Perrache and Bellecour. Breakfast €4.50. Reception 24hr. Singles €27, with shower €42; doubles €32/48. Extra bed €8. MC/V. ❸

FOOD

The galaxy of Michelin stars adorning Lyon's restaurants confirms its status as the gastronomic capital of France. Equally appealing alternatives can be found on **rue St-Jean, rue des Marronniers,** and **rue Mercière** for less during lunchtime. Ethnic restaurants center on **rue de la République.** There are markets on the *quais* of the **Rhône** and **Saône** (open Tu-Su 8am-1pm).

THE BIG SPLURGE

SIPPING IN STYLE

Burgundy is known throughout the world for superb wines and country villages. The only downside of this stellar reputation is the sky-high cost of exploring these cultural treasures. However, Beaune's **Bourgogne Randonnées** offers tours of Burgundy's vineyards that—while far from cheap—are worth every penny.

Tours cost €69-250 per group, and comprehensively examine life in Beaune. The most affordable tour is a half-day extravaganza that includes a bike ride through the countryside, a tour through a local vineyard, and lunch with a *dégustation* (tasting) of six different wines. The most expensive tour is a half-day of driving, walking, or biking through a number of Côte de Beaune villages and vineyards, with a guide to explain everything from the history of the villages to how soil affects the wine's quality.

Sarah Bird, a fluent French and English speaker, leads all the tours with a contagious enthusiasm; she tailors each outing to suit travelers' particular interests. While the price tag on the tours could put quite a dent in the solo traveler's budget, the memorable day will be worth the euro, and you'll return from the vineyards with your thirsts—for wine or knowledge—quenched.

7 av. du 8 Septembre (☎03 80 22 06 03; www.bourgogne-randonnees.com).

THE PRIDE OF LYON

The pinnacle of the Lyonnais food scene is **Restaurant Paul Bocuse** ❻, 4km out of town, where the *menus* (€120-195) definitely cost more than your hotel room. (☎04 72 42 90 90; www.bocuse.fr. MC/V.) Some of these restaurants occasionally have more accessible weekend buffet brunches hovering around €30-40; check outside or call. However, gourmands need not sell their souls to enjoy Bocusian cuisine; the master has several ▧**spin-off restaurants** in Lyon, themed around the four corners of the earth: Le Nord, Le Sud, L'Est and L'Ouest. Whether heading north, south, east, or west, reserve ahead.

> **Le Sud**, 11 pl. Antonin Poncet, 2*ème* (☎04 72 77 80 00). M: Bellecour. Specializing in "la cuisine du soleil," Le Sud serves up Mediterranean fare in a casual dining room decorated with a huge metal sun. A seafood dish (from €15) is worth the splurge. Pasta dishes from €12. *Menus* €19-22. Open daily noon-2:30pm and 7-11pm, F-Sa noon-2:30pm and 7pm-midnight. AmEx/MC/V. ❶

> **Chez Mounier**, 3 r. des Marronniers, 2*ème* (☎04 78 37 79 26). M: Bellecour. Despite small portions, a friendly staff, top-notch cuisine, and great prices make this small restaurant a good choice. Afternoon *menu* €8. 4-course *menus* €11-20. Open Tu-Sa noon-2pm and 7-11pm, Su noon-1:30pm. MC/V. ❸

> **Chez Marie-Danielle**, 29 r. des Remparts d'Ainay (☎04 78 37 65 60). M: Ampère-Victor Hugo. Award-winning chef Marie-Danielle makes guests feel at home as she whips up superb *lyonnais* fare in her intimate eatery. Lunch *menu* €15. Dinner *menu* €22. Open M-F noon-2pm and 7:30-10pm. MC/V. ❹

⊙ SIGHTS

VIEUX LYON

Stacked against the Saône at the foot of the Fourvière hill, *vieux* Lyon's narrow streets are home to lively cafes, hidden passageways, and magnificent medieval and Renaissance homes. The striking *hôtels particuliers*, with their delicate carvings and ornate turrets, sprang up between the 15th and 18th centuries when Lyon was the center of Europe's silk and printing industries.

TRABOULES. The distinguishing features of vieux Lyon townhouses are their *traboules*, tunnels connecting parallel streets through a maze of courtyards, often with vaulted ceilings and exquisite spiral staircases. Although their original purpose is debated, the *traboules* were often used to transport silk from looms to storage rooms. During WWII, the passageways proved invaluable as info-gathering and escape routes for the Resistance. Many are open to the public. A 2hr. tour beginning at the tourist office is the ideal way to see them. The tourist office has a list of open *traboules* and their addresses. *(English-language tours in summer every few days at 2:30pm; winter hours vary. €9, students €5.)*

CATHÉDRALE ST-JEAN. The cathedral's soaring columns dominate the southern end of *vieux* Lyon. It was here that Henri IV met and married Maria de Médici in 1600. Inside, every hour between noon and 4pm, mechanical angels pop out of the 14th-century ▧**astronomical clock** in a reenactment of the Annunciation. *(Open M-F 8am-noon and 2-7:30pm, Sa-Su 8am-noon and 2-7pm. Free.)*

FOURVIÈRE AND ROMAN LYON

Fourvière Hill, the nucleus of Roman Lyon, is accessible via the rose-lined **Chemin de la Rosaire** (garden open daily 6am-9:30pm) and, for the more sedentary, *la ficelle* (funicular), which leaves from the *vieux* Lyon Metro station.

■BASILIQUE NOTRE-DAME DE FOURVIÈRE. During the Franco-Prussian War, the people of Lyon prayed fervently to the Virgin Mary for protection; afterward, they erected this magnificent basilica in her honor. *(Behind the esplanade at the top of the hill. Chapel open daily 7am-7pm. Basilica open daily 8am-7pm.)*

MUSÉE GALLO-ROMAIN. Taking up five mostly underground floors, this expansive museum educates and fascinates. Both history buffs and novices will appreciate a collection of mosaics and statues. *(☎72 38 81 90; www.musees-gallo-romains.com. Open Tu-Su 10am-6pm. €3.80, students €2.30; under 18 and Th free.)*

PARC ARCHÉOLOGIQUE. While the Musée Gallo-Romain provides a wonderful collection of artifacts, the Roman experience in Lyon isn't complete without a walk through this ancient park. Next to the Minimes/Théâtre Romain funicular stop, the Parc holds the well-restored 2000-year-old **Théâtre Romain** and the **Odéon,** discovered when modern developers dug into the hill. On summer evenings, relax and enjoy the show; the **Nuits de Fourvière festival** plays in both venues. *(Open daily mid-Apr. to mid-Sept. 7am-9pm; mid-Sept. to mid-Apr. 7am-7pm. Free.)*

LA PRESQU'ÎLE AND LES TERREAUX

Monumental squares, statues, and fountains are the *presqu'île's* trademarks. At its heart, **place Bellecour** links Lyon's two main pedestrian arteries. Boutique-lined **rue Victor Hugo** runs south. To the north, crowded **rue de la République,** or "la Ré," is Lyon's urban aorta. It continues through **place de la République,** ending at **place Louis Pradel** in the 1*er*, at the tip of the **Terreaux district.** Once a marshy wasteland, it was filled with soil, creating a neighborhood of dry *terreaux* (terraces) where today chic bars keep things hopping long into the night.

MUSÉE HISTORIQUE DES TISSUS. Clothing and textile fanatics will enjoy the rows of extravagant 18th-century dresses and 4000-year-old Egyptian tunics displayed here. The neighboring **Musée des Arts Décoratifs,** housed in an 18th-century *hôtel* has rooms showcasing clocks and silverware from the Renaissance to the present. *(34 r. de la Charité, 2ème. M: Ampère Victor Hugo. ☎04 78 38 42 00, www.musee-des-tissus.com. Tissus open Tu-Su 10am-5:30pm. Arts Décoratifs open Tu-Su 10am-noon and 2-5:30pm. €5, students €3.50, under 18 free; includes both museums.)*

LA CROIX-ROUSSE AND THE SILK INDUSTRY

Though mass silk manufacturing is based elsewhere today, Lyon is proud of its historical dominance of the industry in Europe. The city's **Croix-Rousse district,** a steep, uphill walk from pl.Terreaux, houses the vestiges of its silk-weaving days; Lyon's few remaining silk workers still create delicate handiwork, reconstructing and replicating rare patterns for museum and château displays.

■LA MAISON DES CANUTS. The silk industry lives on at this Croix-Rousse workshop, which provides the best intro to Lyon's *canuts* (silk weavers). Scarves cost €32 or more, but silk enthusiasts can purchase a handkerchief for €9. *(10-12 r. d'Ivry, 4ème. ☎04 78 28 62 04. Open Tu-Sa 10am-6:30pm. €5, students €2.50, under 12 free. English-language tours daily at 11am and 3:30pm.)*

EAST OF THE RHÔNE AND MODERN LYON

Lyon's newest train station and monstrous space-age mall form the core of the ultra-modern Part-Dieu district. Locals call the **Tour du Crédit Lyonnais** "le Crayon" for its unintentional resemblance to a giant pencil standing on end. Next to it, the shell-shaped **Auditorium Maurice Ravel** hosts major cultural events.

CENTRE D'HISTOIRE DE LA RÉSISTANCE ET DE LA DÉPORTATION. Housed in a building where Nazis tortured detainees during the Occupation, the museum presents documents, photos, and films about Lyon's role in the Resistance. *(14 *av. Bertholet, 7ème. M: Jean Macé. ☎04 78 72 23 11. Open W-F 9am-5:30pm, Sa-Su 9:30am-6pm. €4, students €2, under 18 free; includes audio tour in 3 languages.)*

MUSÉE D'ART CONTEMPORAIN. This extensive mecca of modern art, video, and high-tech installations resides in the futuristic **Cité International de Lyon,** a super-modern complex with shops, theaters, and Interpol's world headquarters. All of its exhibits are temporary—even the walls are rebuilt for each display. *(Q. Charles de Gaulle, next to Parc de la Tête d'Or, 6ème. Take bus #4 from M: Foch. ☎04 72 69 17 17; www.moca-lyon.org. Open W-Su noon-7pm. €5, students €3 under 18 free.)*

♫ NIGHTLIFE

At the end of June, the two-week **Festival Jazz à Vienne** welcomes jazz masters to Vienne, a sleepy river town south of Lyon, accessible by bus or train. (www.jazzavienne.com. Tickets free-€30.) In June and July, **Les Nuits de Fourvière** music festival features classical concerts, dance, movies, plays, and popular performers in the ancient Théâtre Romain and Odéon. (☎04 72 32 00 00; www.nuits-defourviere.fr. Tickets and info at the Théâtre Romain and the FNAC shop on r. de la République. Tickets from €12.) Nightlife in Lyon is fast and furious; the city's vast array of pubs, **GLBT establishments,** riverboat nightclubs, and student bars make going out an adventure. The most accessible late-night spots are a strip of riverboat clubs docked by the east bank of the Rhône. Students buzz in and out of tiny, intimate bars on **rue Ste-Catherine** (1*er*) until 1am, before hitting up the clubs. For a more mellow (and more expensive) evening, head to the jazz and piano bars on the streets off **rue Mercerie.** *Lyon Libertin* (€2) lists hot nightlife venues. For superb tips about gay nightlife, pick up *Le Petit Paumé.*

🖪 **Ayers Rock Café,** 2 r. Désirée, 1er (☎08 20 32 02 03, www.ayersrockcafe.com). M: Hôtel de Ville. This Aussie bar is a cacophony of loud rock music and wild bartenders drumming on the hanging lights for 20-somethings. Open daily 6pm-3am, summer opens at 9pm, closes at 10pm on Su. Next door slightly more chic **Cosmopolitan,** 4 r. Désirée (☎08 20 32 02 03) serves New York-themed drinks. Tu student nights; happy hour 8pm-3am. Open M-Sa 8pm-3am, opens at 9pm in summer. MC/V.

Le Sirius, across from 4 q. Augagneur, 3*ème* (☎04 78 71 78 71; www.lesirius.com). M: Guillotière. A young, international crowd packs the lower-level dance floor and bar of this cargo ship-themed riverboat. Open Tu-Sa 6pm-3am.

Q Boat, across from 17 q. Augagneur, 3*ème* (☎04 72 84 98 98, www.actunight.com). M: Guillotière. Formerly Le Fish, this club plays electronic and house music on a swanky boat. Chic Europeans crowd its 2 bars and top-floor deck. Dress well; admission at bouncer's discretion. Open W-Sa 5pm-5am, Su 2pm-5am. AmEx/MC/V.

GRENOBLE   ☎04 76

Young scholars from all corners of the globe and sizable North and West African populations meet in Grenoble (pop. 168,000), a dynamic city whose surrounding snow-capped peaks are cherished by both athletes and aesthetes. *Téléphériques* (cable cars) depart from q. Stéphane-Jay every 10min. for the 16th-century **Bastille,** a fort perched 475m above the city. (Open July-Aug. M 11am-12:15am, Tu-Su 9:15am-12:15am; Sept.-June reduced hours. €4.15 one way, 6.10 round-trip; students €3.35/4.85.) After enjoying the views from the top, you can walk down the Parc Guy Pape, through the other end of the fortress, to the **Jardin des Dauphins** (1hr.). Cross the Pont St-Laurent and go up Montée Chalemont to reach the **Musée Dauphinois,** 30 r. Maurice Gignoux, which has exhibits on the history of skiing. (Open M and W-Su June-Sept. 10am-7pm; Oct.-May 10am-6pm. Free.) The 🖪**Musée de Grenoble,** 5 pl. de Lavelette, houses one of France's most prestigious art collections. (☎04 76 63 44 44; www.museedegrenoble.fr.

Open M and W-Su 10am-6:30pm. €5, students €2, free under 18.) The biggest and most developed ski areas are to the east in Oisans; the **Alpe d'Huez** has 250km of trails. (Tourist office ☎04 76 11 44 44, ski area ☎04 76 80 30 30.) The **Belledonne region**, northeast of Grenoble, is at a lower altitude and lower prices; its most popular ski area is **Chamrousse**. Grenoble's funky night scene is found between **place St-André** and **place Notre-Dame.** International students and 20-somethings mix it up at **Le Couche-Tard,** 1 r. du Palais. (Mixed drinks €2.50. Student prices offered M-W. Open M-Sa 7pm-2am. AmEx/MC/V.)

From the tourist office, follow pl. Ste-Claire to pl. Notre-Dame and take r. du Vieux Temple on the right to reach ◧**Le Foyer de l'Étudiante ❶,** 4 r. Ste-Ursule. This stately building serves as a student dorm during most of the year, but opens its large rooms to co-ed travelers from June to August, though the shortest stay offered is one week. (☎04 76 42 00 84. Laundry €2.20. Free Wi-Fi. Singles €118 per week; doubles €80 per week per person.) Grenoblaise restaurants cater to locals around **place de Gordes** and **pl. St. Andre,** while cheap pizzerias line **quai Perrière** across the river. Pâtisseries and North African joints center on **rue Chenoise** and **rue Lionne,** between the pedestrian area and the river. Cafes cluster around place **Notre-Dame** and place **St-André,** in the heart of the *vieille ville.*

Trains leave pl. de la Gare for: Lyon (1hr., 30 per day, €18); Marseille (4-5hr., 15 per day, €37); Nice (5-6hr., 5 per day, €57); Paris (3hr., 9 per day, €70). **Buses** leave from left of the train station for Geneva, SWI (3hr., 1 per day, €26). You can find the **tourist office** at 14 r. de la République. (☎04 76 42 41 41; www.grenoble-isere.info. Open Oct.-Apr. M-Sa 9am-6:30pm, Su 10am-1pm; May-Sept. M-Sa 9am-6:30pm, Su 10am-1pm and 2-5pm.) **Postal Code:** 38000.

AQUITAINE AND PAYS BASQUE

At the geographical edge of both France and Spain, Aquitaine (AH-kee-tenn) and the Pays Basque (PAY-ee bahss-kuh) are diverse in landscape and culture. In Aquitaine, sprawling vineyards abound and in Pays Basque, closer to the Spanish border, the clinking of cowbells mixes with the scent of seafood.

BORDEAUX ☎05 56

Though its name is synonymous with wine, the city of Bordeaux (bohr-doh; pop. 235,000) has more to offer than most lushes would expect. Everyone from punks to tourists gather on the elegant streets of the shop- and cafe-filled city center, while in the surrounding countryside, the vineyards of St-Émilion, Médoc, Sauternes, and Graves are internationally renowned.

▛▟ TRANSPORTATION AND PRACTICAL INFORMATION. Trains leave Gare St-Jean, r. Charles Domercq, for: Lyon (8-10hr., 7 per day, €61-154); Marseille (6-7hr., 10 per day, €73); Nice (9-12hr., 2 per day, €105); Paris (3hr., 15-25 per day, €55); Toulouse (2-3hr., 10 per day, €32). From the train station, take tramway line C to pl. Quinconces (€1.30) and cross the street to reach the **tourist office,** 12 cours du 30 juillet, which arranges **winery tours.** (☎05 56 00 66 00; www.bordeaux-tourisme.com. Open July-Aug. M-Sa 9am-7:30pm, Su 9:30am-6:30pm; May-June and Sept.-Oct. M-Sa 9am-7pm, Su 9:30am-6:30pm; Nov.-Apr. M-Sa 9am-6:30pm, Su 9:45am-4:30pm.) **Postal Code:** 33000.

▛▛ ACCOMMODATIONS AND FOOD. A favorite among backpackers, ▧**Hôtel Studio ❷,** 26 r. Huguerie, has tiny, clean rooms with bath, phone, and TV. (☎05 56 48 00 14; www.hotel-bordeaux.com. Breakfast €5. Reserve ahead. Singles

€19-29; doubles €25-35. AmEx/MC/V.) Find rooms decorated in metallic and bright colors at **Auberge de Jeunesse Barbey (HI) ❷**, 22 cours Barbey, four blocks from the Gare St-Jean in the run-down red light district. Visitors, especially those traveling alone, should exercise caution at night. (☎05 56 33 00 70; fax 33 00 71. Breakfast and linens included. Free Internet. Max. 3-night stay. Lockout 10am-4pm. Curfew 2am. 2- to 6-bed dorms €21. MC/V.)

The Bordelais's flair for food rivals their vineyard expertise. Hunt around rue St-Remi and place St-Pierre for regional specialties: oysters, *foie gras*, and *lamproie à la bordelaise* (eel braised in red wine). Busy **🖪L'Ombrière ❸**, 13 pl. du Parlement, serves perfectly prepared French cuisine in one of the city's most beautiful squares. (Menu €15-23. Open daily noon-2pm and 7-11pm. MC/V.) Dine at **La Fromentine ❷**, 4 r. du Pas St-Georges, near pl. du Parlement, for galettes (€6-8) with imaginative names. (☎05 56 79 24 10. 3-course menu €10-15. Open M-F noon-2pm and 7-10pm, Sa 7-10pm. MC/V.)

🖪🖸 SIGHTS AND ENTERTAINMENT. Nearly nine centuries after its consecration, the **Cathédrale St-André**, in pl. Pey-Berland, sits at the heart of Gothic Bordeaux. Its bell tower, the **Tour Pey-Berland**, rises 66m. (Cathedral open M 2-7pm, Tu-F 7:30am-6pm, Sa 9am-7pm, Su 9am-6pm. Tower open June-Sept. daily 10am-1:15pm and 2-6pm; Oct.-May Tu-Su 10am-12:30pm and 2-5:30pm. €5, 18-25 and seniors €3.50, under 18 with an adult free.) For the best cityscape of Bordeaux, look down from the 114m bell tower of the **Église St-Michel.** (Open June-Sept. daily 2-7pm. €2.50, under 12 free.) Back at ground level, a lively **flea market** sells anything from Syrian *narguilas* (hookahs) to African specialties. (Open daily 9am-1pm.) Note that this area, like around the train station, should not be frequented alone at night. On pl. de Quinconces, the elaborate **Monument aux Girondins** commemorates guillotined Revolutionary leaders from towns bordering the Gironde. Bordeaux's opera house, the **Grand Théâtre,** conceals a breathtaking interior behind its Neoclassical facade and houses concerts, operas, and plays in fall and winter. (☎05 56 00 85 95; www.opera-bordeaux. com. Tours M-Sa 11am-6pm. Concert tickets from €8. Opera tickets up to €80. 50% discount for students and under 26.)

Bordeaux has a varied, vibrant nightlife. For an overview, check out the free *Clubs and Concerts* brochure at the tourist office. Year-round, students and visitors pack the bars in **Place de la Victoire, Place Gambetta,** and **Place Camille Julian.** Popular but cheesy **El Bodegon,** on pl. de la Victoire, draws students with cheap drinks, theme nights, and weekend giveaways. (Beer €3. Happy hour 6-8pm. Open M-Sa 7am-2am, Su 2pm-2am.)

PROVENCE

If Paris boasts world-class paintings, it's only because Provence inspired them. Mistral winds cut through olive groves in the north, while pink flamingoes, black bulls, and unicorn-like white horses gallop freely in the marshy south. From the Roman arena and cobblestone of Arles to Cézanne's lingering footsteps in Aix-en-Provence, Provence provides a taste of *La Vie en Rose.*

AIX-EN-PROVENCE   ☎04 42

Famous for festivals, fountains, and former residents Paul Cézanne and Émile Zola, Aix-en-Provence ("X"; pop. 141,000) caters to tourists without being ruined by them. The **chemin de Cézanne,** 9 av. Paul Cézanne, features a 2hr. self-guided tour that leads to the artist's birthplace and favorite cafes. (Open daily July-Aug. 10am-6pm; Apr.-June and Sept. 10am-noon and 2-6pm; Oct.-Mar.

10am-noon and 2-5pm. €5.50, ages 13-25 €2.) The **Fondation Vasarely,** av. Marcel-Pagnol, in nearby Jas-de-Bouffan, is a must-see for Op-Art fans. (Open Tu-Sa 10am-1pm and 2-6pm. €7, students €4.) The **Cathédrale St-Sauveur,** r. Gaston de Saporta, fell victim to misplaced violence during the Revolution; angry Aixois mistook the apostle statues for statues of royalty and defiantly chopped off their heads. The statues were re-capitated in the 19th century, but remain sans neck. (Open daily 8am-noon and 2-6pm.) In June and July, famous performers and rising stars descend on Aix for the **Festival d'Aix-en-Provence.** (☎04 42 16 11 70; www.festival-aix.com. Tickets from €8.)

July travelers should reserve rooms in March. **Hôtel Paul ❸,** 10 av. Pasteur, has relatively cheap, clean rooms and serves breakfast in a quiet garden. (☎04 42 23 23 89; hotel.paul@wanadoo.fr. Breakfast €5. Check-in before 6pm. Singles and doubles with bath €43, with garden-facing windows €53; triples €65; quads €76. Cash only.) Charming restaurants pack **rue Verrerie** and the roads north of **cours Mirabeau. Rue Verrerie,** off r. des Cordiliers, has bars and clubs.

Trains, at the end of av. Victor Hugo, run to Marseille (45min., 27 per day, €7), Nice (3-4hr., 25 per day, €35), and Paris (TGV 3hr., 10 per day, €77-131). **Buses** (☎08 91 02 40 25) leave av. de l'Europe for Marseille (30min., 6 per hr., €5). The **tourist office** is at 2 pl. du Général de Gaulle. (☎04 42 16 11 61; www.aixenprovencetourism.com. Open July-Aug. M-Sa 8:30am-9pm, Su 10am-8pm; Sept.-June M-Sa 8:30am-8pm, Su 10am-1pm and 2-6pm.) **Postal Code:** 13100.

AVIGNON   ☎04 90

Temporary home to the papacy 700 years ago, Avignon (pop. 89,500) now hosts Europe's most prestigious theater festival. For three weeks in July, the ◙**Festival d'Avignon** holds theatrical performances in over 20 venues, from cloisters to factories to palaces. (☎04 90 14 14 14; www.festival-avignon.com. Reservations accepted from mid-June. Tickets up to €45, under 25 receive discounted admission of €13 for all shows over €13.) The more experimental **Festival OFF,** also in July, is just as well established. (☎04 90 25 24 30; www.avignon-off.org. Tickets under €16. 30% discount with €10 Carte OFF.) The golden ◙**Palais des Papes,** Europe's largest Gothic palace, is a reminder of the city's brief stint as the center of the Catholic Church. Although revolutionary looting stripped the interior of its lavish furnishings and fires erased its medieval murals, its vast chambers and few remaining frescoes are still remarkable. (☎04 90 27 50 00. Open daily Aug. 9am-9pm; July to mid Sept. 9am-8pm; mid-Sept. to Oct. and Apr.-June 9am-7pm; Nov.-Mar. 9:30am-5:45pm. €10.) The French children's song "Sur le pont d'Avigon" has immortalized the 12th-century bridge **Pont St-Bénézet.** Despite its supposedly divinely ordained location, the bridge has suffered from warfare and the once-turbulent Rhône. (☎04 90 27 51 16. €4. Free audio tour. Same hours as the Palais.) Farther downstream, **Pont Daladier** makes it all the way across, offering free views of the broken bridge and the Palais.

Avignon's accommodations fill up three to four months before festival season; reserve ahead or stay in Arles or Nîmes. Rooms with many amenities, including A/C and TV, make **Hôtel Mignon ❸,** 12 r. Joseph Vernet, a good deal despite its small bathrooms. (☎04 90 82 17 30; www.hotel-mignon.com. Breakfast included. Free Internet and in-room Wi-Fi. Reception 7am-11pm. Singles €42-52, doubles €60-73, triples €72-83, quad €94. Prices increase 20% in festival season. AmEx/MC/V.) Restaurants group on **rue des Teinturiers.** Or try **Citron Pressé ❷,** 38 r. Carreterie. (☎04 90 86 09 29. 3-course *menu* with wine €12. *Plats* €3-7. Open M-Th noon-2:30pm, F-Sa noon-2pm and 7:30pm-11:30pm; during festival daily noon-2am. Cash only.) **Place des Corps Saints** has a few bars that remain busy year-round. **Trains** (☎04 90 27 81 89) run from bd. St-Roch to: Arles (20min., 1-2 per hr., €9); Lyon (2hr., 7 per day, €31); Marseille (1hr.,

1 per hr., €28); Nîmes (30min., 14 per day, €9); Paris (TGV 3-4hr., 13 per day, €97). Exit the station, **buses** are on the right, going to Arles (1hr., 5 per day, €8) and Marseille (2hr., 1 per day, €19). The **tourist office** is at 41 cours Jean Jaurès. (☎04 32 74 32 74; www.avignon-tourisme.com. Open July M-Sa 9am-7pm, Su 9:45am-5pm; Apr.-June and Aug.-Oct. M-Sa 9am-6pm, Su 9:45am-5pm; Nov.-Mar. M-F 9am-6pm, Sa 9am-5pm, Su 10am-noon.) **Postal Code:** 84000.

FRENCH RIVIERA (CÔTE D'AZUR)

Between Marseille and the Italian border, sun-drenched beaches and warm Mediterranean waters combine to form the fabled playground of the rich and famous. Chagall, F. Scott Fitzgerald, Matisse, Picasso, and Renoir all flocked to the coast in its heyday. Now, the Riviera is a curious combination of high-rolling millionaires and low-budget tourists. In May, high society makes its yearly pilgrimage to the Cannes Film Festival and the Monte-Carlo Grand Prix, while Nice's February Carnaval and summer jazz festivals draw budget travelers.

NICE   ☎04 93

Classy, colorful Nice (NIECE; pop. 340,000) is the Riviera's unofficial capital. Its non-stop nightlife, top-notch museums, and packed beaches are tourist magnets. During February Carnaval, visitors and *Niçois* alike ring in spring with revelry. When visiting Nice, prepare to have more fun than you'll remember.

▐ TRANSPORTATION

Flights: Aéroport Nice-Côte d'Azur (NCE; ☎08 20 42 33 33). Air France, 10 av. de Verdun (☎08 02 80 28 02). To: **Bastia, Corsica** (€116; under 25 and couples €59) and **Paris** (€93/50). **Buses** on the Ligne d'Azur (€4, 3-4 per hr.) leave for the airport from the train station (#99), bus station (#98); before 8am, take bus #23 (€1, 3-4 per hr.).

Trains: Gare SNCF Nice-Ville, av. Thiers (☎14 82 12). Open daily 5am-12:00am. To: **Cannes** (40min., 3 per hr., €6.30); **Marseille** (2hr., 16 per day, €28.50); **Monaco** (15min., 2-6 per hr., €2.80-4); **Paris** (5hr., 9 per day, €136.10).

Buses: 5 bd. Jean Jaurès (☎04 93 85 61 81). Info booth open M-F 8:30am-5:30pm, Sa 9am-4pm. To **Cannes** (2hr., 2-3 per hr.) and **Monaco** (1hr., 3-6 per hr.). All ligne d'Azur buses are now €1 for any destination.

Ferries: Corsica Ferries (☎04 92 00 42 93; www.corsicaferries.com). Bus #1 or 2 (dir.: Port) from pl. Masséna. To **Corsica** (€20-40, bikes €10, cars €40-65). MC/V.

Public Transportation: Ligne d'Azur, 10 av. Félix Faure (☎93 13 53 13; www.lignedazur.com), near pl. Leclerc. Buses run daily 7am-8pm. Tickets €1, 1-day pass €4, 7 day pass €15, and 10 trip pass €10. Purchase tickets and day passes on board the bus; *carnet* passes from the office. **Noctambus** (night service) runs 4 routes daily 9:10pm-1:10am. Completed in 2009, the Nice **tram** runs along Jean Médecin and Place Massena, connecting the northern reaches of the city to the eastern edge. The 8.7 km line is wheelchair-accessible, air-conditioned, and stops about every 5 minutes along its L shaped route from 6am to 2am. Prices and tickets are the same as the buses.

Bike and Scooter Rental: Holiday Bikes, 34 av. Auber (☎04 93 16 01 62; nice@holiday-bikes.com), near the train station. Bikes €18 per day, €75 per week; €230 deposit. Scooters €40/175; €500 deposit. Open M-Sa 9am-6:30pm. AmEx/MC/V.

FRANCE

Nice

ACCOMMODATIONS
Les Camélias (HI), 3
Hôtel Belle Meunière, 1
Hôtel Pastoral, 10

FOOD
Indian Lounge, 4
Lou Pilha Leva, 5
La Merenda, 7
Le Restaurant d'Angleterre, 2

NIGHTLIFE AND ENTERTAINMENT
Le Klub, 6
Tapas la Movida, 9
Thor, 11
Wayne's, 8

TO MUSÉE NATIONAL
MESSAGE BIBLIQUE
MARC CHAGALL (200m),
MUSÉE MATISSE (1km)

av. St-Jean-Baptiste
bd. Risso
St-Martin
PL. J. TOJA
r. Defly
PL. ST-FRANÇOIS
PL. St-François
Croix
Musée d'Art
Moderne et
d'Art Contemporain
Théâtre
Nationale
de Nice
r. Ed Beri
r. Giofredo
bd. Carabacel
r. Pierre Devoluy
Hôpital
St-Roch
CRU
Gare
Routière
St-Répárate
r. Delille
Palais Lascaris
Église
St-Jacques
VIEUX NICE
Théâtre du
Cours
av. Félix Faure
Ligne
d'Azur
PL.
WILSON
r. Gubernatis
r. Blacas
r. de l'Hôtel des Postes
r. Chauvain
Palais de
Justice
cours Saleya
Cité du Parc
bd. Jean Jaurès
Espace
Masséna
Flamme
et Fumée
r. Giofredo
PL.
MASSÉNA
r. Gustave Deloye
r. Pastorelli
r. de la Terrasse
Opéra de
Nice
av. Maréchal Foch
r. Gallieri
The Cat's
Whiskers
Canada
r. Lamartine
r. Biscarra
r. Spitalieri
av. Jean-Médecin
Centre
Commercial
Nice Étoile
Cyber Internet
Air France
Travelex
av. de Verdun
r. St-François de Paule
Hôtel de Ville
Suzer
r. Briea
r. Van Loo
Jardin
Albert I
av. des
Phocéens
Basilique
Notre-Dame
FNAC
Monoprix
av. Jean-Médecin
r. de Russie
r. Longchamp
r. Paradis
r. de la Liberté
r. Masséna
TO (200m)
r. de Nôtre Dame
Royal Com
Lavomatique
Nicea
r. de Belgique
Alexso
Travelex
r. d'Italie
r. Paganini
r. d'Angleterre
Karr
r. Alphonse
r. Grimaldi
r. Macarani
r. Dr. Barety
r. du Congrès
r. Halévy
av. Gustave V
r. Massenet
Galion Plage
Ruhl Plage
promenade des Anglais
Gare
Nice-Ville
Office
Provençal
Holiday
Bikes
bd. Victor Hugo
r. Rossini
av. Durante
av. Georges Clémenceau
r. Auber
r. Gounod
r. Verdi
bd. Victor Hugo
r. du Maréchal Joffre
r. de la Buffa
Espace Chaud
r. Meyerbeer
OTU Travel
r. de France
passage Méhanzone
passage Cronstad
r. de Rivoli
Jardin
Alsace-
Lorraine
bd. Gambetta
TO CATHÉDRALE ORTHODOXE RUSSIE ST-NICHOLAS (550m)
TO MUSÉE DES
BEAUX-ARTS (25m)
TO AÉROPORT
NICE-CÔTE D'AZUR (4km)
Hôtel Négresco

✚ 🛂 ORIENTATION AND PRACTICAL INFORMATION

Avenue Jean Médecin, on the left as you exit the train station, and **boulevard Gambetta,** on the right, run directly to the beach. **Place Masséna** is 10min. down av. Jean Médecin. On the coast, **promenade des Anglais** is a people-watcher's paradise. To the southeast, past av. Jean Médecin and toward the bus station, is **vieux Nice.** Everyone should exercise caution at night, around the train station, along the port, in *vieux* Nice, and on promenade des Anglais.

Tourist Office: av. Thiers (☎08 92 70 74 07; www.nicetourisme.com). Open June-Sept. M-Sa 8am-8pm, Su 9am-7pm; Oct.-May M-Sa 8am-7pm, Su 9am-6pm.

Consulates: Canada, 10 r. Lamartine (☎04 93 92 93 22). Open M-F 9am-noon. **US,** 7 av. Gustave V (☎88 89 55). Open M-F 9-11:30am and 1:30-4:30pm.

Police: 1 av. Maréchal Foch (☎04 92 17 22 22), opposite end from bd. Jean Médecin.

Hospital: St-Roch, 5 r. Pierre Dévoluy (☎04 92 03 33 75).

Post Office: 23 av. Thiers (☎04 93 82 65 22), found near the train station. Open M-F 8am-7pm, Sa 8am-noon. **Postal Code:** 06033.

⌂ ACCOMMODATIONS

Make reservations before visiting Nice; beds are elusive particularly in summer. The city has two clusters of budget accommodations: near the **train station** and near **vieux Nice.** Those by the station are newer but more remote; the surrounding neighborhood has a deservedly rough reputation, so exercise caution at night. Hotels closer to *vieux* Nice are more convenient but less modern.

▨ **Hôtel Belle Meunière,** 21 av. Durante (☎04 93 88 66 15; www.bellemeuniere.com), opposite the train station. According to legend, one of Napoleon's generals gave this stunning mansion to his mistress as a gift. Budget favorite now hosts a relaxed crowd in private rooms with baths and in 4- to 5-bed co-ed dorms, some with ensuite baths. Breakfast included in dorm prices, €3.50 for those renting private rooms. Luggage storage available after check-out (€2). Laundry from €6. Parking available. Reception 7:30am-midnight; access code after hours. Dorms in summer €17-22, in winter €15-20; doubles €44-57; triples €48-63; quads €64-84. MC/V with €1 surcharge. ❷

▨ **Villa Saint-Exupéry,** 22 av. Gravier (toll free ☎0800 30 74 09; www.vsaint.com), 5km from the *centre-ville* and less than 1km from the Comte de Falicon tram stop. One of Europe's coolest backpacker hostels, located in a former monestary. Outstanding amenities include a beatiful outdoor garden with France's longest bio-wall, canyoning and sailing tours led by staff (call ahead for prices), and cheap food and drink (nightly dinner €6.50; pizza €5.50; beer and wine €1) in the stained-glass-adorned "chapel," which morphs into a lively bar at night. Most rooms with baths, some with balconies. Breakfast, internet, and Wi-Fi included. Laundry €5. Shuttles to and from nearby tram stop run every 15min. 8am-noon and 6pm-2am. Online reservations preferred. Dorms (4-12 beds) in summer €18-30, in winter €16-22; doubles €54-90. MC/V. ❷

Hôtel Paradis, 1 rue Paradis (☎04 93 87 71 23; www.paradishotel.com). Just a block from the Mediterranean, the 7 dorm-style beds may be Nice's best deal for beachheads on a budget. Also offers airy singles, doubles, and triples with ensuite bath. A/C. Free Wi-Fi; free internet at sister hotel 5min. away. Book dorms well in advance through www.hostelbookers.com. In summer dorms €22-25; singles €75; doubles €90; triples €120. In winter singles €50; doubles €60-65; triples €90. AmEx/MC/V. ❷

Hôtel Wilson, 39 rue l'Hôtel des Postes (☎04 93 85 47 79; www.hotel-wilson-nice. com). Friendly staff, a breakfast space packed with knick knacks from around the world, and airy, well-decorated rooms set this cozy hotel apart. More expensive rooms come with showers, TVs, and thematic decor (check out the African and Asian ones). Breakfast €5.50. Free Wi-Fi. Singles from mid-Apr. to mid-Oct. €35-50, from mid. Oct.-mid. Apr. €29-43; doubles €40-65/34-58; triples €59-66/51-59; quad €82/70. MC/V. ❹

🗋 FOOD

Mediterranean spices flavor Niçois cuisine. Try crusty *pan bagnat*, a round loaf of bread topped with tuna, sardines, vegetables, and olive oil, or *socca*, a thin, olive-oil-flavored chickpea bread. Famous *salade niçoise* combines tuna, olives, eggs, potatoes, tomatoes, and a spicy mustard dressing. Save your euro for olives, cheese, and produce from the **markets** at cours Saleya and avenue Maché de la Libération (both open Tu-Su 7am-1pm). **Avenue Jean Médecin** features reasonable brasseries, panini vendors, and kebab stands.

▨ **La Merenda**, 4 rue Bosio. Savor the work of a culinary master, Dominique Le Stanc, who turned his back on one of Nice's best-known restaurants to open this 12-table gem. Outstanding *plats* (€11-16) rotate based on the availability of ingredients. *Ratatouille* and pizza €11. Wine €8 per glass. Open M-F noon-1:30pm and 7-9pm. Reserve in person for lunch and dinner. Cash only. ❸

▨ **Lou Pilha Leva**, 10-13 rue du Collet (☎04 93 13 99 08), in vieux Nice. Lively staff dishes out plate after plate of excellent local pub-style grub, including *socca* (€2.50), *pissaladière* (€3), and *salade niçoise* (€8), to patrons seated at long wooden outdoor tables. The assortment *niçois* (€8) offers a hearty sampling of the area's typical fare. Pizza €4. Lasagna €8. Open daily 10:30am-midnight. MC/V over €10. ❷

Le Restaurant d'Angleterre, 25 rue d'Angleterre (☎04 93 88 64 49), near the train station. Local favorite known for traditional French and English favorites. €16 *menù* includes starter, *plat*, side dish, and dessert. €27 gourmet *menu* includes cheese course and gourmet options like Burgundy snails. Open Tu-Sa 11:45am-2pm and 6:45-9:50pm, Su 11:45am-2pm. MC/V. ❸

Speakeasy, 7 rue Lamartine (☎04 93 85 59 50). American expat and longtime vegan cooks in Nice's only completely vegan restaurant. Testimonials from famous vegetarians from Gandhi to Brigitte Bardot line the walls of the cozy interior. Large specials (€9-11) and desserts like banana ice cream—without the cream, of course—satisfy even the staunchest carnivores. 2 courses and dessert €14. Open in summer M-F noon-2:15pm and 7-9:15pm, Sa noon-2:15pm; in winter Tu-F noon-2:15pm and 7-9:15pm, Sa noon-2:15pm. Cash only. ❸

FROM THE ROAD

LOST IN TRANSLATION

Hollywood movies and American television may have captivated a market in France, but there's often little rhyme or reason regulating the translation of their titles:

   Lolita in Spite of Myself (*Mean Girls*): Vladimir Nabokov and Lindsay Lohan: the perfect pop-culture union.

   The Counterattack of the Blondes (*Legally Blonde*): Perhaps a little aggressive for a movie about Reese Witherspoon and Harvard Law School.

   The Little Champions (*Mighty Ducks*): From the Flying V to the quack chant, the *canard* is the heart and soul of this film.

   Rambo (*Rambo*): Some words just transcend linguistic and cultural barriers.

   The Man Who Would Murmur at the Ears of Horses (*The Horse Whisperer*): Just in case there was any ambiguity in the original title.

   A Day with No End (*Groundhog Day*): If you don't get the Groundhog Day reference, this is going to be a long movie.

   La Grande Évasion (*The Great Escape*): If they didn't translate this literally, Steve McQueen would've taken everyone down.

   The Big Lebowski (*The Big Lebowski*): The French recognize that The Dude does not appreciate name changes.

   Lost in Translation (*Lost in Translation*): Apparently one title that wasn't.

                    —*Vinnie Chiappini*

⊙ SIGHTS

One look at Nice's waves and you may be tempted to spend your entire stay stretched out on the sand. As the city with the second-most museums in France, however, Nice offers more than azure waters and topless sunbathers.

■VIEUX NICE. Although vieux Nice, the oldest part of the city, lacks museums and other sights of the traditional sort, its hand-painted awnings, beautiful churches, and lively squares more than justify a meander down its winding and largely pedestrian streets. Filled with the inevitable slew of souvenir shops, vieux Nice still remains the heart of the city. Bilingual street signs introduce you to Niçard, a dialect of the Occitan language still spoken by half a million people in France. In summer, the streets of vieux Nice pulse with commerce: as shop owners ply their wares along cramped sidewalks, vendors selling fresh and dried flowers take over **cours Saleya**, and crafts merchants occupy the square fronting Nice's imposing neoclassical **Palais de Justice.***(Guided tours of vieux Nice start at the tourist office Sa 9:30am. €12, under 10 €6, under 5 free.)*

■MUSÉE D'ART MODERNE ET D'ART CONTEMPORAIN. Located just blocks from vieux Nice and spread over four levels, Nice's Museum of Modern and Contemporary Art is a true gem. Its minimalist galleries pay homage to French New Realists and American pop artists like Lichtenstein, Oldenberg, Dine, and Warhol. Particular strenghts include the museum's encyclopedic collection of statues by Niki de St-Phalle and its astounding variety of works by Yves Klein, including many in his signature shade of piercing blue. Changing contemporary exhibits showcase artists from around the world in considerable depth. *(Promenade des Arts, near av. St-Jean-Baptiste. Tram: Cathédrale. ☎ 04 93 62 61 62; www.mamac-nice.org. Open Tu-Su 10am-6pm. Tours in English available July-Aug. by reservation. Free. Tours €3, students €1.50, under 18 free. Cash only.)*

■MUSÉE NATIONAL MESSAGE BIBLIQUE MARC CHAGALL. This impressive museum was founded by Chagall to showcase an assortment of biblically themed pieces that he gave to the French government in 1966. His twelve maginifient canvases illustrating the first two books of the Hebrew Bible are arranged chromatically (rather than according to the Biblical timeline), as the artist wished. An adjacent room displays Chagall's five-piece *La cantique des cantiques* (Song of Songs) series, rendered in rich purples and deep reds. The museum includes an auditorium that hosts concerts and other events (check the schedule online); it is decorated with stained-glass panels by Chagall depicting the creation story. *(Av. du Docteur Ménard. Walk 15min. northeast from the train station or take bus #22, dir.: Rimiez, to Musée Chagall. ☎ 04 93 53 87 20; www.musee-chagall.fr. Open May-Oct. M and W-Su 10am-6pm; Nov.-Mar. M and W-Su 10am-5pm. Last entry 30min. before closing. €9.50, under 25 €7.50; art students and EU citizens free. Free 1st Su of month. Prices include permanent collection and temporary exhibitions; when there is no temporary exhibition, prices fall to €7.50/5.50.)*

LE CHÂTEAU. The remains of an 11th-century fort located on a hilltop overlooking vieux Nice, Le Château marks the city's birthplace. Celto-Ligurian tribes called the spot home until they were ousted by the Romans in 154 BC. Centuries later, Provençal nobles built a castle and the Cathédrale Ste-Marie on top of the hill as a symbol of their authority over the developing village below. Louis XIV methodically destroyed the château and fortress in 1706; all that remains today is a green park, stone ruins, and Nice's best view at the highest point, **■Terrace Nietzsche.** Those looking to avoid the lengthy but manageable walk to the summit can take an elevator most of the way, though some climbing is still required to reach the very top. *(Elevator open daily June-Aug. 9am-8pm; Sept. and Apr.-May 10am-7pm; Oct.-Mar. 10am-6pm. €0.90 one way, €1.20 round trip.)* Those overheated from the ascent should seek out the manmade waterfall just below the peak of the hill—a refreshing breeze emanates from its base. In summer, an outdoor theater hosts performances by orchestral and vocal musicians. (☎*04 93 85 62 33. Park open daily June-Aug. 9am-8pm; Sept. 10am-7pm; Oct.-Mar. 8am-6pm; Apr.-May 8am-7pm. Info booth open July-Aug. Tu-F 9:30am-12:30pm and 1:30-6pm. Free.)*

🎵 🎭 ENTERTAINMENT AND NIGHTLIFE

Nice's **Jazz Festival,** at the Parc et Arènes de Cimiez, attracts world-famous performers. (mid-July; ☎08 20 80 04 00; www.nicejazzfest.com. €31-51.) The 🎭**Carnaval** gives Rio a run for its money with three weeks of confetti, fireworks, parades, and parties. (☎04 92 14 46 46; www.nicecarnaval.com.) Bars and night-clubs around **rue Masséna** and **vieux Nice** pulsate with dance and jazz but have a strict dress code. To experience Nice's nightlife without spending a euro, head down to the **promenade des Anglais,** where street performers, musicians, and pedestrians fill the beach and boardwalk. Hard to find *Le Pitchoun* provides the lowdown on trendy bars and clubs (in French; free; www.lepitchoun.com). Exercise caution after dark; men have a reputation for harassing lone women on the promenade, in the Jardin Albert I, and near the train station, while the beach sometimes becomes a gathering place for prostitutes and thugs.

🍸 **Wayne's,** 15 rue de la Préfecture (☎04 93 13 46 99; www.waynes.fr). Huge crowd every night in and around one of vieux Nice's most popular bars. English-speaking bartend-ers serve travelers while a rowdier crew dances to pop-rock on packed tabletops and benches downstairs. Rock posters and plasma TVs complete the decor. Pints €6-7. Mixed drinks €7.50. Live music or DJ. Th Ladies Night in low season. Happy hour 5-9pm; beer €3.90. Open daily noon-2am. AmEx/MC/V.

Tapas la Movida, 2 bis rue de l'Abbaye. Once a tapas bar, this hole-in-the-wall doesn't serve food anymore. Instead, it doles out some of Nice's cheapest drinks to a young, alternative crowd. Figure out how to crawl home before attempting the 🍸 **bar-o-mètre** (€18), a meter-long box of shots. Live reggae, rock, and ska concerts M-F (M-Tu free, W-F €2). Open M-Th and Su 8:30pm-1am, F-Sa 8:30pm-2:30am. Cash only.

Smarties, 10 rue Défly (☎04 93 62 30 75; nicesmarties.free.fr). This sleek, orange-and-silver "bar electro lounge," decked out in rainbow flags, is one of Nice's trendiest spots to begin a night on the town. Open Tu-Su 5pm-12:30am. Cash only.

Le Six, 6 rue Bosio (☎04 93 62 66 64). Part nightclub and part piano bar, gay-friendly Le Six draws 20- to 40-somethings to its beautiful 19th-century space (think crystal chandeliers and elaborate moldings) to dance to drag queens belting out American top 40 hits. Climb the metal ladder to the small lounge and dance space upstairs for a great view of the antics below. Champagne €8. Mixed drinks €10. Open M-Tu and Th 10pm-4am, F-Sa 10pm-5am, Su 10pm-4am. AmEx/MC/V.

CANNES ☎04 93

Stars compete for camera time at Cannes's annual, world-famous and invite only 🎬**Festival International du Film** (May 15-26, 2009). During the rest of the year, Cannes (pop. 67,000) rolls up all but its most famous red carpet—leav-ing one at the Palais for your tacky photographic pleasure. During this down-time, it also becomes the most accessible of all the Riviera's glam towns. A palm-lined boardwalk, sandy beaches, and numerous boutiques draw the wealthy and the young. Of the town's three prestigious casinos, the least exclusive is **Le Casino Croisette,** 1 Lucien Barrière, next to the Palais des Festi-vals. (No shorts, jeans, or T-shirts. Jackets required for men in gaming rooms. 18+. Free entry. Open daily 10am-4am; table games 8pm-4am.)

Hotel Mimont ❸, 39 r. de Mimont, is Cannes's best budget hotel. English-speaking owners maintain basic, clean rooms two streets behind the train station. (☎04 93 39 51 64; canneshotelmimont65@wanadoo.fr. Free Wi-Fi. Singles €34-40; doubles €40-47; triples €60. Prices about 15% higher July-Aug. Ask about €30 petites chambres for *Let's Go* readers. MC/V.) The zone around **rue Meyna-dier** has inexpensive restaurants. Cafes and bars near the waterfront stay open all night and are a great alternative to the expense of gambling and posh clubs. Nightlife thrives around **rue Dr. G. Monod.** Try ⬛**Morrison's,** 10 r. Teisseire, for casual company in a literary-themed pub. (☎04 92 98 16 17. Beer from €5.30. Happy hour 5-8pm. Open daily 5pm-2am. MC/V.) Coastal **trains** depart from 1 r. Jean Jaurès for: Antibes (15min., €2.50); Marseille (2hr., 6:30am-11:03pm, €25); Monaco (1hr., €8); Nice (40min., €5.80); St-Raphaël (25min., €6.10). **Buses** go to Nice (1hr., 3 per hr., €6) from the pl. de l'Hôtel de Ville (☎04 93 48 70 30) and Grasse (50min., 1 per hr., €1) from the train station. The **tourist office** is at 1 bd. de la Croisette. (☎04 93 39 24 53; www.cannes.fr. Open July-Aug. daily 9am-8pm; Sept.-June 9am-7pm.) Get Internet at **Cap Cyber,** 12 r. 24 Août. (€3 per hr. Open in summer 10am-11pm; in winter 10am-10pm. MC/V.) **Postal Code:** 06400.

ST-TROPEZ
☎04 94

Hollywood stars, corporate giants, and curious backpackers congregate on the spotless streets of St-Tropez (pop. 5400), where the Riviera's glitz and glamor shines brightest. The young, beautiful, and restless flock to this "Jewel of the Riviera" to flaunt tans and designer clothing on notorious beaches and in posh nightclubs. The best beaches are difficult to reach without a car, but the *navette municipale* (shuttle) leaves pl. des Lices for Les Salins, a secluded sunspot, and **plage Tahiti** (Capon-Pinet stop), the first of the famous plages des Pampelonne. (M-Sa 5 per day, €1. Tourist office has schedule.) Take a break from the sun at the **Musée de l'Annonciade,** pl. Grammont, which showcases Fauvist and neo-Impressionist paintings. (Open M and W-Su June-Sept. 10am-noon and 2-6pm; Oct.-May 10am-1pm and 4-7pm. €6, students €4.)

Budget hotels do not exist in St-Tropez. Camping is the cheapest option, but is only available outside the city. Prices remain shockingly high, especially in July and August. To reach **Les Prairies de la Mer ❸**, a social campground on the beach, take a *bateau vert* (☎04 94 49 29 39) from the *vieux* port to Port Grimaud (Apr. to early Oct., 5min., 1 per hr., round-trip €11). Bowling, supermarkets, tennis courts and other facilities are available. (☎04 94 79 09 09; www.riviera-villages.com. Open late Mar. to early Oct. July to mid-Aug. €8 per person, €45 per tent; Apr.-June and late Aug. €3/20; Sept. to mid-Oct. €3/20. Electricity €5. MC/V.) Pricey restaurants line the streets behind the waterfront and the *vieux* port. To eat cheap, stop by the snack stands and cafes near **place des Lices,** the center of St-Tropez's wild nightlife. Sodetrav **buses** (☎04 93 97 88 51) leave av. Général Leclerc for St-Raphaël (2hr., 10-12 per day, €11.30). **Ferries** (☎04 93 95 17 46; www.tmr-saintraphael.com), at the *vieux* port, serve St-Tropez from St-Raphaël (1hr., 4-5 per day, €13 one-way, 22 round-trip). The **tourist office** is on q. Jean Jaurès. (☎04 93 97 45 21. Open daily July-Sept. 9:30am-8pm; Sept.-Oct. and mid-Mar. to June 9:30am-12:30pm and 2-7pm; early Nov. to mid-Mar. 9:30am-12:30pm and 2-6pm.) **Postal Code:** 83990.

GERMANY
(DEUTSCHLAND)

Encounters with history are unavoidable in Germany, as changes in outlook, policy, and culture are manifest in the country's architecture, landscape, and customs. Glass skyscrapers rise from concrete wastelands; towns crop up from fields and forests, interspersed with medieval castles and industrial structures. World-class music rings out from sophisticated city centers, while a grittier youth culture flourishes in quite different neighborhoods. Such divisions echo the entrenched Cold War separation between East and West. Today, nearly 20 years after the fall of the Berlin Wall, Germans have fashioned a new identity for themselves. Visitors will find flowing beer and wondrous sights from the darkest corners of the Black Forest to the shores of the Baltic Sea.

DISCOVER GERMANY: SUGGESTED ITINERARIES

THREE DAYS. Enjoy 2 days in **Berlin** (p. 286): stroll along **Unter den Linden** and the **Ku'damm,** gape at the **Brandenburger Tor** and the **Reichstag,** and explore the **Tiergarten.** Walk along the **East Side Gallery** and visit **Checkpoint Charlie** for a history of the **Berlin Wall.** Overnight it to **Munich** (p. 333) for a crazy stein-themed last day.

ONE WEEK. After scrambling through **Berlin** (3 days), head to **Hamburg** (1 day; p. 309). Take in the cathedral of **Cologne** (1 day; p. 319) before slowing down in the **Bonn** (1 day; p. 322). End your trip Bavarian-style in **Munich** (1 day).

THREE WEEKS. Begin in **Berlin** (3 days). Party in **Hamburg** (2 days), then zip to **Cologne** (1 day) and the former West German capital, **Bonn** (1 day; p. 322). Contrast the old cathedral at **Mainz** (1 day; p. 327) with glitzy **Frankfurt** (1 day; p. 323), then visit Germany's oldest university in **Heidelberg** (2 days; p. 328). Lose your way in the **Black Forest** (2 days; p. 332), before finding it again in **Munich** (2 days). See the beauty of the **Romantic Road** (2 days; p. 342). Get cultured in Goethe's **Weimar** (2 days; p. 344)—then dramatize your learnings in Faust's cellar in **Leipzig** (1 day; p. 350). End your trip in the reconstructed splendor of **Dresden** (1 day; p. 346).

ESSENTIALS

FACTS AND FIGURES

OFFICIAL NAME: Federal Republic of Germany.

CAPITAL: Berlin.

MAJOR CITIES: Cologne, Frankfurt, Hamburg, Munich.

POPULATION: 82,401,000.

LAND AREA: 349,200 sq. km.

TIME ZONE: GMT +1.

RELIGIONS: Protestant (34%), Roman Catholic (34%), Muslim (2%).

PERCENTAGE OF EUROPEAN BEER PRODUCTION: 26.5%.

BEER CONSUMED: 111.6L per capita (a whole lot of beer).

WHEN TO GO

Germany's climate is temperate. The mild months of May, June, and September are the best time to go, as there are fewer tourists and enjoyable weather. In July, Germans head en masse to summer spots. Winter sports gear up from November to April; ski season takes place from mid-December to March.

DOCUMENTS AND FORMALITIES

EMBASSIES. All foreign embassies are in Berlin (p. 286). German embassies abroad include: **Australia,** 119 Empire Circuit, Yarralumla, Canberra, ACT 2600 (☎02 6270 1911; www.germanembassy.org.au); **Canada,** 1 Waverly St., Ottawa, ON, K2P OT8 (☎613-232-1101; www.ottawa.diplo.de); **Ireland,** 31 Trimleston

Ave., Booterstown, Blackrock, Co. Dublin (☎01 269 3011; www.dublin.diplo.
de); **New Zealand,** 90-92 Hobson St., Thorndon, Wellington 6001 (☎04 473 6063;
www.wellington.diplo.de); **UK,** 23 Belgrave Sq., London, SW1X 8PZ (☎020 7824
1300; www.london.diplo.de); **US,** 4645 Reservoir Rd. NW, Washington, D.C.,
20007 (☎202-298-4000; www.germany-info.org).

VISA AND ENTRY INFORMATION. EU citizens do not need a visa. Citizens of
Australia, Canada, New Zealand, and the US do not need a visa for stays of up
to 90 days, beginning upon entry into any of the countries in the EU's freedom-
of-movement zone. For more info, see p. 13. For stays longer than 90 days, all
non-EU citizens need visas (around €100), available at German consulates.

TOURIST SERVICES AND MONEY

EMERGENCY	Ambulance and Fire: ☎112. Police: ☎110.

TOURIST OFFICES. The **National Tourist Board** website (www.germany-tourism.
de) links to regional info and provides dates of national and local festivals.
Every city in Germany has a tourist office, usually near the *Hauptbahnhof*
(main train station) or *Marktplatz* (central square). All are marked by a sign
with a thick lowercase "i," and many book rooms for a small fee.

MONEY. The **euro (€)** has replaced the **Deutschmark (DM)** as the unit of currency
in Germany. For more info, see p. 16. As a general rule, it's cheaper to exchange
money in Germany than at home. Costs for those who stay in hostels and prepare their own food may range anywhere from €25-50 per person per day. **Tipping** is not practiced as liberally in Germany as elsewhere—most natives just
round up €1. Tips are handed directly to the server with payment of the bill—if
you don't want any change, say *"Das stimmt so"* (das SHTIMMT zo; "so it
stands"). Germans rarely bargain except at flea markets. Germany has a 19%
value added tax (VAT), a sales tax applied to most goods and services. The prices
given in *Let's Go* include VAT. In the airport, non-EU citizens can claim a refund
on the tax paid for goods purchased at participating stores. In order to qualify
for a refund in a store, you must spend at least €25; make sure to ask for a
refund form when you pay. For more info on VAT refunds, see p. 19.

BUSINESS HOURS. Offices and stores are open from 9am-6pm, Monday
through Friday, often closing for an hour lunch break. Stores may be open
on Saturday in cities or shopping centers. Banks are also open from approximately 9am-6pm and close briefly in the late afternoon, but they may stay open
late on Thursday nights. Many museums are closed on Monday.

TRANSPORTATION

BY PLANE. Most international flights land at **Frankfurt Airport** (**FRA;** ☎069 6900;
www.airportcity-frankfurt.com); **Berlin (BML), Munich (MUC),** and **Hamburg (HAM)**
also have international airports. **Lufthansa,** the national airline, is not always the
best-priced option. For cheaper domestic travel by plane than by train; check
out **Air Berlin** (www.airberlin.com), among other options.

BY TRAIN. The **Deutsche Bahn** (**DB;** www.bahn.de) network is Europe's best—
and one of its most expensive. Luckily, all trains have clean and comfy second-
class compartments, and there are a wide variety of train lines to choose from.
RegionalBahn (RB) trains include rail networks between neighboring cities and

connects to **RegionalExpress (RE)** lines. **InterRegioExpress (IRE)** trains, covering larger networks between cities, are speedy and comfortable. **S-Bahn** trains run locally within large cities and high density areas. Some S-Bahn stops also service speedy **StadtExpress (SE)** trains, which directly connects city centers. **EuroCity (EC)** and **InterCity (IC)** trains zoom between major cities every 1-2hr. **InterCityExpress (ICE)** trains approach the luxury and kinetics of airplanes, barreling along the tracks at speeds up to 300kph, and service international destinations including Austria, Belgium, the Netherlands, and Switzerland. For overnight travel, choose between the first-class **DB Autozug** or cheaper **DB Nachtzug** lines.

Eurail is valid in Germany. The **German Rail Pass** allows unlimited travel for four to 10 days within a one-month period, including Basel, SWI and Salzburg, AUT. Non-EU citizens can purchase German Rail Passes at select major train stations in Germany (5- or 10-day passes only) or through travel agents (2nd class 4-day pass €169, 10-day €289; under 26 €139/199). A Schönes-Wochenende-Ticket (€33) gives up to five people unlimited travel on any of the slower trains (RE or RB) from 12:01am Saturday or Sunday until 3am the next day; single travelers often find larger groups who will share their ticket.

BY BUS. Bus service runs from the local **ZOB** (*Zentralomnibusbahnhof*), usually close to the main train station. Buses are more expensive than trains. Rail passes are not valid on buses, except for a few run by Deutsche Bahn.

BY CAR AND BY BIKE. Given generally excellent road conditions, Germans drive fast. The rumors are true: the *Autobahn* does not have a speed limit, only a recommendation of 130kph (80 mph). Watch for signs indicating the right-of-way (usually a yellow triangle). Signs with an "A" denote the *Autobahn;* signs bearing a "B" accompany secondary highways, which typically have a 100kph (60mph) speed limit. In cities and towns, speed limits hover around 30-60kph (20-35 mph). For a small fee, **Mitfahrzentralen,** and their women-only counterparts, **Frauenmitfahrzentralen,** agencies pair up drivers and riders, who then negotiate trip payment between themselves. Seat belts are mandatory, and police strictly enforce driving laws. Germany has designated lanes for **bicycles**. .

BY THUMB. Hitchhiking (or even standing) on the Autobahn is illegal. *Let's Go* does not recommend hitchhiking.

KEEPING IN TOUCH

PHONE CODES	**Country code: 49. International dialing prefix: 00.** For more info on how to place international calls, see **Inside Back Cover.**

EMAIL AND THE INTERNET. Almost all German cities, as well as a surprising number of smaller towns, have at least one Internet cafe with web access for about €2-10 per hour. Wi-Fi is often available in bigger cities; in Berlin's new Sony Center (p. 291), the Wi-Fi is completely, blissfully free. Some German universities have Internet in their libraries, intended for student use.

TELEPHONE. Most public phones will accept only a phone card (Telefonkarte), available at post offices, kiosks, and some Deutsche Bahn counters. **Mobile phones** are an increasingly popular and economical alternative (p. 29). Phone numbers have no standard length. Direct-dial access numbers for calling out of Germany include: **AT&T USADirect** (☎0800 225 5288); **Canada Direct** (☎0800 888 0014); **MCI WorldPhone** (☎0800 888 8000); **Telecom New Zealand** (☎0800 080 0064);

and **Telstra Australia** (☎0800 080 0061); most of these services require a calling card or credit card. For more info, see p. 28.

MAIL. Airmail (*Luftpost* or *par avion*) usually takes three to six days to Ireland and the UK, and four to 10 days to Australia and North America. *Let's Go* lists addresses for mail to be held **Poste Restante** (*Postlagernde Briefe*) in the **Practical Information** sections of big cities. Mail will go to the main post office unless you specify a subsidiary by street address. Address mail to be held as follows: First name Last name, *Postlagernde Briefe*, Postal code, City, GERMANY.

ACCOMMODATIONS AND CAMPING

GERMANY	❶	❷	❸	❹	❺
ACCOMMODATIONS	under €15	€15-25	€26-33	€34-50	over €50

Germany currently has more than 600 **youth hostels**—more than any other nation. Official hostels in Germany are overseen by **DJH** (*Deutsches Jugendherbergswerk*), Bismarckstr. 8, D 32756 Detmold, Germany (☎05231 740 10; www.jugendherberge.de). A growing number of **Jugendgästehäuser** (youth guesthouses) have more facilities than hostels and attract slightly older guests. DJH publishes *Jugendherbergen in Deutschland*, a guide to federated German hostels. Most charge €15-25 for dorms. The cheapest **hotel-style** accommodations are places with *Pension*, *Gasthof*, or *Gästehaus* in the name. Hotel rooms start at €20 for singles and €30 for doubles; in large cities, expect to pay nearly twice as much. *Frühstück* (breakfast) is almost always available, if not included. The best bet for a cheap bed is often a **Privatzimmer** (room in a family home), where a basic knowledge of German is very helpful. Prices can be as low as €15 per person. Reservations are made through the local tourist office or through a *Zimmervermittlung* (private booking office), sometimes for a small fee. Over 2500 **campsites** dot the German landscape. Bathrooms, a restaurant or store, and showers generally accompany a campground's well-maintained facilities. Camping costs €3-12 per tent site and €4-6 per extra person, with additional charges for tent and vehicle rental. Blue signs with a black tent on a white background indicate official sites.

FOOD AND DRINK

GERMANY	❶	❷	❸	❹	❺
FOOD AND DRINK	under €4	€4-8	€9-12	€13-20	over €20

A typical breakfast (*Frühstück*) consists of coffee or tea with **rolls** (*Brötchen*), **cold sausage** (*Wurst*), and **cheese** (*Käse*). Germans' main meal, lunch (*Mittagessen*), includes soup, broiled sausage or roasted meat, potatoes or dumplings, and a salad or vegetable. Dinner (*Abendessen* or *Abendbrot*) is a reprise of breakfast, with beer in place of coffee and a wider selection of meats and cheeses. Older Germans indulge in a daily ritual of coffee and cake (*Kaffee und Kuchen*) at 3 or 4pm. To eat cheaply, stick to a restaurant's daily menu (*Tagesmenü*), buy food in supermarkets, or head to a **university cafeteria** (*Mensa*). Fast-food stands (*Imbiß*) also offer cheap, often foreign eats. The average German beer is maltier and more "bread-like" than Czech or American beers; a common nickname for German brew is liquid bread (*flüßiges Brot*).

BEYOND TOURISM

Germany's volunteering opportunities often involve environmental preservation—working on farms or in forests and educating people—though civil service and community building prospects still exist. For more info on opportunities across Europe, see the **Beyond Tourism** chapter p. 55

World-Wide Opportunities on Organic Farms (WWOOF), Postfach 210259, 01263 Dresden, Germany (www.wwoof.de). €18 membership in WWOOF gives you room and board at a variety of organic farms in Germany in exchange for chores.

Open Houses Network, Goethepl. 9B, D-99423 Weimar (☎03 643 502 390; www.open-houses.de). A group dedicated to restoring and sharing public space (mostly in Eastern Germany), providing lodging in return for work.

BERLIN   ☎030

Berlin is bigger than Paris, up later than New York, and wilder than Amsterdam. Dizzying and electric, this city of 3.4 million has such an increasingly diverse population that it can be difficult to keep track of which *Bezirk* (neighborhood) is currently the trendiest. Traces of the past century's Nazi and Communist regimes remain etched in residents' minds, and a psychological division between East and West Germany—the problem dubbed *Mauer im Kopf* ("wall in the head")—still exists nearly two decades after the Berlin Wall's destruction. Restless and contradictory, Germany's capital shows no signs of slowing down its rapid, self-motivated reinvention. With such a dynamic character, the Berlin of next year may be radically different from the Berlin of today.

✖ INTERCITY TRANSPORTATION

Flights: The city is now transitioning from 3 airports to 1 (Flughafen Schönefeld will become the Berlin-Brandenburg International Airport, BBI), but at least until 2011, **Flughafen Tegel (TXL)** will remain West Berlin's main international airport. For info on all 3 of Berlin's airports, call ☎0180 500 0186 (www.berlin-airport.de). Take express bus #X9 from Bahnhof Zoo, bus #109 from Jakob-Kaiser-Pl. on U7, bus #128 from Kurt-Schumacher-Pl. on U6, or bus TXL from Potsdamer Pl. or Bahnhof Zoo. **Flughafen Schönefeld (BER),** southeast of Berlin, is used for intercontinental flights and travel to developing countries. Take S9 or 45 to Flughafen Berlin Schönefeld, or ride the Schönefeld Express train, which runs 2 per hr. through most major S-Bahn stations, including Alexanderpl., Bahnhof Zoo, Friedrichstr., Hauptbahnhof, and Ostbahnhof. **Flughafen Tempelhof (THF)** was slated to close October 31, 2008.

Trains: Berlin's massive new **Hauptbahnhof,** which opened in time for the 2006 World Cup, is the city's major transit hub, with many international and domestic trains continuing to **Ostbahnhof** in the East. Hauptbahnhof currently connects to the S-Bahn and a U55 line. **Bahnhof Zoologischer Garten** (a.k.a. Bahnhof Zoo), formerly the West's main station, now connects only to regional destinations. Many trains also connect to **Schönefeld Airport.** A number of U- and S-Bahn lines stop at **Oranienburg, Potsdam,** and **Spandau.** Trains in the Brandenburg regional transit system tend to stop at all major stations, as well as Alexanderpl. and Friedrichstr.

Buses: ZOB (☎030 301 03 80; www.zob-reisebuero.de), the "central" bus station, is actually at the western edge of town, by the Funkturm near Kaiserdamm. U2 to Kaiserdamm or S41/42 to Messe Nord/ICC. Open M-F 6am-9pm, Sa-Su 6am-3pm. **Gullivers,** at ZOB (☎030 890 660; www.gullivers.de), and **Berlin Linien Bus** (☎030 851 9331;

GERMANY

www.berlinlinienbus.de) often have good deals on bus fares. Open in summer daily 8am-9pm; in winter reduced hours. Check website for more information.

Mitfahrzentralen (Ride-Share): Citynetz, Joachimstaler Str. 14 (☎030 194 44; www.citynetz-mitfahrzentrale.de), has a ride-share database. U9 or 15 to Kurfürstendamm. To **Hamburg, Hanover** (€18.50), and **Frankfurt** (€31). Open M-F 9am-8pm, Sa-Su 10am-6pm. Other ride share bulletins at www.mitfahrzentrale.de and www.mitfahrgelegenheit.de. Check *030, Tip,* and *Zitty* for addresses and phone numbers.

ORIENTATION

Berlin's landmarks include the **Spree River,** which flows through the city from west to east, and the narrower **Landwehrkanal** that spills into the Spree from the south. The vast central park, **Tiergarten,** stretches between the waterways. Two radio towers loom above the city: the pointed **Funkturm,** in the west, and the globed **Fernsehturm,** rising above **Alexanderplatz** in the east. In the west, the major thoroughfare **Kurfürstendamm** (a.k.a. Ku'damm) is lined with department stores and leads to the **Bahnhof Zoologischer Garten,** West Berlin's transportation hub. Nearby is the elegant wreck of the **Kaiser-Wilhelm Gedächtniskirche,** as well as one of Berlin's few real skyscrapers, the **EuropaCenter.** Tree-lined **Straße des 17. Juni** runs east-west through the Tiergarten, ending at the **Brandenburger Tor,** the park's eastern border gate. The **Reichstag** (Parliament) is north of the gate; several blocks south, **Potsdamer Platz** bustles beneath the glittering Sony Center and the headquarters of the Deutsche Bahn. Heading east, Straße des 17. Juni becomes **Unter den Linden** and travels past most of Berlin's imperial architecture. In the east, **Karl-Marx-Allee, Prenzlauer Allee,** and **Schönhauser Allee** fan out from the central meeting point of Alexanderplatz.

Berlin is rightly considered a collection of towns, not a homogeneous city; each neighborhood has a strong sense of its individual history. **Mitte** is currently its commercial heart. The neighboring eastern districts of **Friedrichshain** and **Prenzlauer Berg** are the city's liveliest and most youthful, while **Kreuzberg** is the outpost of counterculture in the west. **Charlottenburg** in the west has a more staid, upscale character, while **Schöneberg** is in between Kreuzberg and Charlottenburg, both in geography and in spirit.

LOCAL TRANSPORTATION

Public Transportation: The **BVG** (www.bvg.de) is one of the world's most efficient transportation systems. The extensive **bus, Straßenbahn** (streetcar or tram), **U-Bahn** (subway), and **S-Bahn** (surface rail) networks will get you to your destination quickly. Almost all the reconstruction and expansion of the pre-war transit grid has been completed; service disruptions are rare, causing at most an extra 20min. wait.

Orientation and Basic Fares: Berlin is divided into 3 transit zones. **Zone A** encompasses central Berlin, including Flughafen Tempelhof. The rest of Berlin is in **Zone B,** while **Zone C** consists of the outlying areas, including Potsdam and Oranienburg. An AB ticket is the best deal, as you can buy extension tickets for the outlying areas. An **Einzelfahrausweis** (1-way ticket) is good for 2hr. after validation. Zones A and B €2.10; B and C €2.50; A, B, and C €2.80. Under 6 free with an adult; children under 14 reduced fare. Within the validation period, the ticket may be used on any S-Bahn, U-Bahn, bus, or tram. A **Tageskarte** (1-day unlimited ticket; A and B €6.10; A, B, and C €6.50) is the best deal if you're planning to travel a lot in a single day.

Night Transport: U- and S-Bahn lines generally don't run M-F 1-4am. On F-Sa nights, all trains except for the U4, S45, and S85 continue but less frequently. An extensive system of **night buses** runs 2-3 per hr. and tends to follow major transit lines; pick up the free *Nachtliniennetz* map at a Fahrscheine und Mehr office. The letter N precedes night bus numbers. Trams run at night.

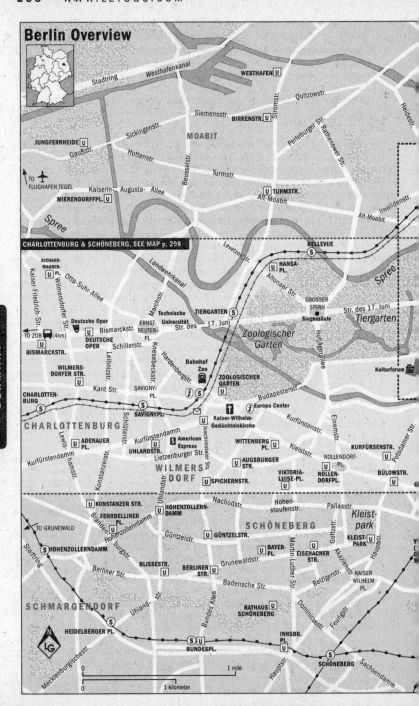

Berlin Overview

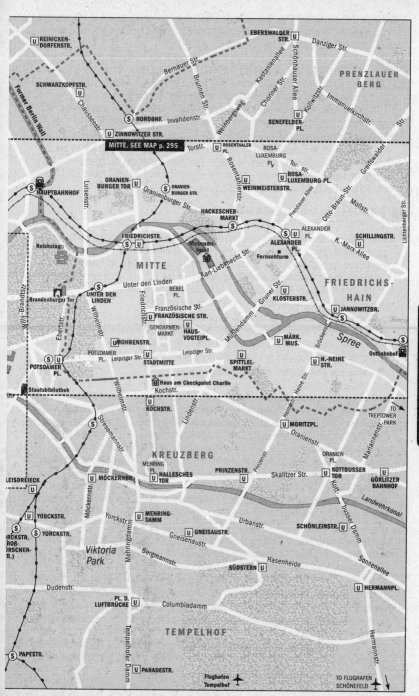

Taxis: (☎080 02 63 00 00). Call at least 15min. ahead. Female travelers can request female drivers. Trips within the city can cost up to €21. Patrons should request a *Kurzstrecke* to travel up to 2km in any direction for a flat €3 fee.

LIFE (OR, UH, DEATH) IN THE FAST LANE. When you're walking on Berlin's sidewalks, make sure you don't step onto a bike path. Lanes usually run through the middle of walkways and are marked with subtle, reddish lines. Bikers usually don't tolerate wandering tourists, so stay clear.

Bike Rental: Fahrradstation, Dorotheenstr. 30 (☎20 45 45 00; www.fahrradstation.de), near the Friedrichstr. S-Bahn station. Turn in at the parking lot next to STA. €15 per day for a standard mountain bike. Open M-F 9am-8pm, Sa 10am-6pm, Su 10am-4pm. Less central **Orange Bikes,** Kollwitzstr. 35, is a youth community project. Bikes €2.50 per 3hr., €5 per day. Open M-F 2:30-7pm, Sa 10am-7pm.

🛈 PRACTICAL INFORMATION

Tourist Offices: Euraide (www.euraide.com), in the Hauptbahnhof. Sells phone cards, rail- and walking-tour tickets. Arrive early—the office is often packed and doesn't accept phone calls. Open June-Oct. daily 8am-noon and 1-6pm; Nov.-May M-F 8am-noon and 1-4:45pm. **Berlin Tourismus Marketing (BTM),** in the EuropaCenter, on Budapester Str., in Charlottenburg. Reserves rooms (€3). Open M-Sa 10am-7pm, Su 10am-6pm. Branches at Brandenburger Tor and Alexanderpl. Fernsehturm.

City Tours: The guides at ▊**Terry Brewer's Best of Berlin** (☎177 388 1537p; www.brewersberlintours.com) are legendary for their vast knowledge and engaging personalities. 8hr. tours €12. Shorter **free tours** leave daily at 10:30am from in front of the Bandy Brooks shop on Friedrichstr. (S5, 7, 9, or 75 or U6 to Friedrichstr.)

Embassies and Consulates: Australia, Mitte, Wallstr. 76-79 (☎030 880 0880; www.australian-embassy.de). U2: "Märkisches Museum". Open M-Th 8:30am-5pm, F 8:30am- 4:15pm. **Canada,** Mitte, Leipziger Pl. 17 (☎030 20 31 20; www.canada.de). S1,2 or U2: "Potsdamer Pl." Open M-F 8:30am-12:30pm and 1:30-5pm. **Ireland,** Mitte, Friedrichstr. 200 (☎030 22 07 20; www.embassyofireland.de). U2 or 6: "Stadtmitte." Open M-F 9:30am-12:30pm and 2:30-4:45pm. **NZ,** Mitte, Friedrichstr. 60 (☎030 20 62 10; www.nzembassy.com). U2 or 6: "Stadtmitte." Open M-Th 9am-1pm and 2-5:30pm, F 9am-1pm and 2-4:30pm. Summer hours M-Th 8:30am-1pm and 2-5:30pm, F 8:30am-1pm. **UK,** Mitte, Wilhelmstr. 70-71 (☎030 20 45 70; www.britischebotschaft.de). S1-3, 5, 7, 9, 25, or 75, or U6: "Friedrichstr." Open M-F 9am-5:30pm. **US,** Clayallee 170 (☎030 832 9233; fax 83 05 12 15). U1: Oskar-Helene-Heim. Open M-F 8:30am-noon. Telephone advice available M-F 2-4pm; after hours, call ☎830 50 for emergencies. The visiting address for the United States Embassy is Pariser Pl. 2 (☎030 238 5174).

Boat Tours: The extensive canal system makes boat tours a popular option. **Reederei Heinz Riedel,** Planufer 78, Kreuzberg (☎030 693 4646; U8 to "Schönleinstr.") Tours €7-16. Open Mar.-Sept. M-F 6am-9pm, Sa 8am-6pm, Su 10am-3pm; Oct.-Feb. M-F 8am-4pm. **Stern & Kreisschiffahrt** (☎030 536 3600; www.sternundkreis.de), Puschkinallee 15, Treptow. Crusies from €5 (1hr. mini-tour). Open M-Th 9am-4pm, F 9am-2pm.

Currency Exchange: The best rates are usually found in large squares, at most major train stations, and at exchange offices with **Wechselstube** signs outside. **ReiseBank** at the *Hauptbahnhof* (open M-Sa 8am-10pm), at Bahnhof Zoo (☎030 881 7117; open daily 7:30am-10pm) and at Ostbahnhof (☎030 296 4393; open M-F 7am-10pm, Sa 8am-8pm, Su 8am-noon and 12:30-4pm), is conveniently located, but has poor rates.

Luggage Storage: In **DB Gepäck Center,** in the Hauptbahnhof, 1st floor, East Side. €4 per day. In **Bahnhof Zoo.** Lockers €3-5 per day. Max 72hr. Open daily 6am-10:30pm. 24hr. lockers also at **Ostbahnhof, Alexanderplatz** and bus station.

Crisis Lines: American Hotline (☎0177 814 1510). **Berliner Behindertenverband,** Jägerstr. 63D (☎030 204 3847), has advice for the disabled. **Frauenkrisentelefon** (☎030 615 42 43; www.frauenkrisentelefon.de) is a women's crisis line. Open M and Th 10am-noon, Tu-W and F 7-9pm, and Sa-Su 5-7pm.

Medical Services: The American and British embassies list English-speaking doctors. **Emergency doctor:** ☎31 00 31. **Emergency dentist:** ☎89 00 43 33. Both 24hr.

Internet: Inexpensive Internet cafes cluster on Oranienstr. in Kreuzberg and around U-Bahn stop Ebenswalder Str. in Prenzlauer Berg.

Post Offices: Joachimstaler Str. 7 (☎030 88 70 86 11), down Joachimstaler Str. from Bahnhof Zoo and near the Kantstr. intersection. Open M-Sa 9am-8pm. There are branches at **Tegel Airport,** open M-F 8am-6pm, Sa 8am-noon, and **Ostbahnhof,** open M-F 8am-8pm, Sa-Su 10am-6pm. **Postal Code:** 10001-14199.

ACCOMMODATIONS

Longer stays are most conveniently arranged through one of Berlin's many **Mitwohnzentrale,** which can set up house-sitting gigs or sublets (from €250 per month). **Home Company Mitwohnzentrale,** Joachimstaler Str. 17, has a useful placement website. (☎0421 792 6293; www.homecompany.de. U9 or 15 to Ku'damm. Open M-Th 9am-6pm, F 9am-5pm, Sa 11am-2pm. MC/V.)

MITTE

Mitte's Backpacker Hostel, Chausseestr. 102 (☎030 28 39 09 65; www.backpacker. de). U6 to "Zinnowitzer Str." The apex of hostel hipness, with a gregarious English-speaking staff and themed rooms, from "Aztec" to "skyline" (of Berlin, of course). The social common room is lined with antique theater sets. A pickup spot for Terry Brewer's Tours and Insider Tours bike tours. Sheets €2.50. Laundry €7. Internet €3 per hr. Bike rental €10 per day. Reception 24hr. Dorms €14-19; singles €30-34; doubles €48-54; quads €80-84. AmEx/MC/V. ❷

Circus, Weinbergsweg 1A (☎030 28 39 14 33; www.circus-berlin.de). U8 to "Rosenthaler Platz." Designed with the English-speaking traveler in mind. Nightly happy hours and W karaoke. Breakfast €2-5 until 1pm. Free laundry. Wi-Fi in rooms; internet €0.05 per min. Wheelchair-accessible. Reception and bar 24hr. 4- to 8-bed dorms €19-23; singles €40, with bath €50; doubles €56/70; triples €75. MC/V. ❷

CHARLOTTENBURG

Berolina Backpacker, Stuttgarter Pl. 17 (☎030 32 70 90 72; www.berolinabackpacker.de). S3, S5, S7, S9, or S75 to "Charlottenburg." This quiet hostel with an ivy-laced facade keeps things elegant with print art in the bunk-free dorms and daisies on the breakfast table. Surrounding cafes and proximity to the S-Bahn make up for its distance from the rush of the city. Communal and private kitchens (communal €1 per day, private €9.50) available for use. Breakfast buffet €7; "backpackers' breakfast" (a roll with cheese and coffee) €3.50. Internet €0.50 per 15min. Reception 24hr. Check-out 11am. 5-bed dorms €10-13.50; singles €29.50-35.50; doubles €37-47; triples €39-64; quads €46-60. AmEx/MC/V. ❶

SCHÖNEBERG AND WILMERSDORF

Jugendhotel Berlincity, Crellestr. 22 (☎030 7870 2130; www.jugendhotel-berlin.de). U7 to "Kleistpark" or "Yorckstr." The high ceilings and enormous windows in this former factory provide guests with spacious, airy rooms. Funky light fixtures shaped like fried eggs illuminate the hallways, which are lined with dark hard wood. Request a room with a view of the TV tower. Breakfast and linens included. Wi-Fi €1 per 20min., €5 per day. Reception 24hr. Singles €38, with bath €52; doubles €60/79; triples €87/102; quads €112/126; quints €124/150; 6-person room €146/168. MC/V. ❺

JetPAK, Pücklerstr. 54, Dahlem (☎030 8325 011; www.jetpak.de). U3 to "Fehrbelliner Pl." or U9 to "Güntzelstr.," then bus #115 (dir.: Neuruppiner Str.) to "Pücklerstr." Follow sign to Grunewald and turn left on Pücklerstr. Turn left again when the JetPAK sign directs you at the edge of the forest. Hidden in an old *Wehrmacht* military complex in the Grunewald forest, this casual hostel has a summer-camp feel that belies its history and makes up for the distance. Ping-pong table and basketball hoop outside. Common room with computers and foosball. Breakfast and linens included. Free internet. Dorms €14-18; singles €30; doubles €50. Additional €1 charge on F-Sa. Cash only. ❷

KREUZBERG

Bax Pax, Skalitzer Str. 104 (☎030 69 51 83 22; www.baxpax-kreuzberg.de). U1 or U15 to "Görlitzer Bahnhof," right across the street. Run by the same friendly people as Mitte's Backpacker Hostel. Around the corner from Oranienstr., with a pool table, roomy common spaces, walls painted with film reels, and a bed inside an antique VW Bug (ask for room 3). Kitchen facilities and an outdoor terrace. Breakfast €4.50. Linens €2.50. Internet €2 per 30min. Bike rental 1st day for €12, 2nd €10, additional days €5. Reception 24hr. Big dorms in high season €16, in low season €15; 7- to 8-bed dorms €17/15; 5- to 6-bed rooms €18/17; singles €31/30; doubles €48/46, with bath €60/56; triples €63/60; quads €76/72. AmEx/MC/V. ❷

PRENZLAUER BERG

▨ **East Seven Hostel,** Schwedter Str. 7 (☎030 93 62 22 40; www.eastseven.de). U2 to "Senefelderpl." No bunks in the well-lit, beautifully painted dorms. The grill area in the garden out back is friendly and social. Kitchen available. Linens €3. Towels €1. Laundry €4. Internet €0.50 per 20min; free Wi-Fi. Reception 7am-midnight. Dorms €13-17; singles in low-season €30, in high season €37; doubles €42/50; triples €52.50/63; quads €66/76. Cash only. ❷

▨ **Pfefferbett,** Christinenstraße 18-19 (☎030 93 93 58 58; www.pfefferbett.de). U2 to "Senefelderpl." Juxtaposing its original 19th-century brick walls with contemporary design, this hostel has a roof deck and some of the best deals in Berlin. Named after the nearby beer garden. Breakfast buffet €4. Linens €2.50. Free Wi-Fi. Reception and bar open 24hr. 6- to 8-bed dorms with shared bath from €12; 4- to 6-bed dorms with private bath from €17.50. Doubles with private bath, TV, and telephone €27. Cash only. ❶

FRIEDRICHSHAIN

▨ **Sunflower Hostel,** Helsingforser Str. 17 (☎030 44 04 42 50; www.sunflower-hostel.de). This relaxed, eclectic hostel features a vine-hung bright orange lounge. Spotless dorms are a marked contrast to the studied chaos of the common areas. The staff knows the nightlife scene well. Breakfast buffet €3. Locks and linens €3 deposit each. Laundry €4.50. Internet €0.50 per 10min.; free Wi-Fi. Reception 24hr. 7- to 8-bed dorms €10-14.50; 5- to 6-bed dorms €12.50-16.50; singles €30-36.50; doubles €38-46.50; triples €51-61.50; quads €60-79.50. 7th night free. MC/V. ❶

🗋 FOOD

Berlin's cuisine is quite diverse thanks to its Middle Eastern and Southeast Asian populations. Seasonal highlights include the beloved *Spargel* (white asparagus) in early summer, Pfifferling mushrooms in late summer, and *Federweiße* (young wine) in September. Perhaps the dearest culinary tradition is breakfast; Germans love to wake up late over a *Milchkaffee* (bowl of coffee with foamed milk) and a sprawling brunch buffet. Vendors of currywurst or bratwurst are perfect for a quick bite; or, find a 24hr. Turkish *Imbiß* (snack food stand) to satisfy any midnight craving. **Aldi, Edeka, Penny Markt,** and **Plus** are the cheapest supermarket chains (all typically open M-F 9am-8pm, Sa 9am-4pm). Stores at Ostbahnhof are an exception to Sunday closing laws. Almost every neighborhood has an **open-air market;** the market on Winterfeldtpl., is particularly busy on Saturday mornings. In Kreuzberg along Maybachufer, on the Landwehrkanal, the **Turkish market** sells cheap veggies and huge wheels of *Fladenbrot* every Tuesday and Friday. Take U8 to Schönleinstr. Also popular is the more upscale, largely **organic market** that takes over Prenzlauer Berg's Kollwitzpl. on Thursday and Friday (U2 to Senefelder Pl).

MITTE

☒ **Schwarzwaldstuben,** Tucholskystr. 48, (☎030 28 09 80 84). S-Bahn to "Oranienburger Str." Fitted out like a rustic southern German restaurant with sofas between the tables and stuffed boar heads on the wall, this is the best place for a schnitzel and Rothaus beer, made in the only state brewery left in Germany. Reserve on weekends, or drop by during the day for a *Flammkuchen* (€4.50-8), a sort of German pizza, and to read by the light of the fringed lamps. Entrees €8-18. ❹

☒ **Tadshickische Teestube,** Am Festungsgraben 1, (☎030 204 1112). S3, 5, 7, 9, or 75 to "Hackescher Markt." Dating back to the Soviet days, this Tajik teahouse is a hidden haven of oriental carpets, tea served in samovars (€2-6), and sour cream covered meat pierogi (€5). Take off your shoes before settling cross-legged onto the cushions around the low tables. Open M-F 5pm-midnight, Sa-Su 3pm-midnight. Cash only. ❷

Monsieur Vuong, Alte Schönhauser Str. 46 (☎030 99 29 69 24; www.monsieurvuong.de). U8 to "Weinmeisterstr." or U2 to "Rosa Luxembourg Pl." Gallerists, artists, and, yes, tourists perch on the red cube seats in this extremely popular Vietnamese restaurant. Fresh fruit drinks €3.40. Entrees €6-9. Open daily noon-midnight. Cash only. ❷

CHARLOTTENBURG

☒ **Schwarzes Cafe,** Kantstr. 148 (☎030 313 8038). S3, S5, S7, S9, or S75 to "Savignypl." The most popular boho cafe in the area for a reason: absinthe all night in the dimly lit, frescoed space, followed by delicious breakfast when the sun comes up. Weekly specials

ON THE MENU

THE BEST WURST

So you're finally in Germany and itching to sink your teeth into your first authentic German Wurst. With over 1500 varieties, you'll have plenty of choices. All have one thing in common: German law mandates that sausages can only be made of meat and spices. If it has cereal filling, it's not wurst.

Bockwurst: This tasty sausage is commonly roasted or grilled at street stands, and is served dripping with ketchup and mustard in a *Brötchen* (roll). Although *Bock* means billy-goat, this wurst is made of ground veal with parsley and chives. Complement your *Bockwurst* with some *Bock* beer.

Thüringer Bratwurst: Similar to the *Bockwurst*, the *Bratwurst* has a little pork too, plus ginger and nutmeg.

Frankfurter: Unlike the American variety, the German *Frankfurter* can only have this name if made in Frankfurt. It's made of lean pork ground into a paste and then cold smoked, which gives it that orange-yellow coloring.

Knockwurst: Short and plump, this sausage is served with sauerkraut. It's made of lean pork and beef, with a healthy dose of garlic.

Weißwurst: Cream and eggs give this "white sausage" its pale coloring. *Weißwurst* goes with rye bread and mustard.

Currywurst: A great late-night snack, this pork *Bratwurst* is smothered in a tomato sauce and sprinkled with paprika and curry.

served 11:30am-8pm (€7-10). Breakfast always available (€5-8.50). Open 24hr., (except Tu 3am-11am). Cash only. ❸

■ **Am Nil,** Kaiserdamm 114 (☎30 321 44 06) U2 to "Sophie-Charlotte Platz." Recline on the Oriental carpets and enjoy platters of spiced Egyptian food (€7-14). Belly dancer F and Sa 9pm. Open Tu-Su 3pm-1am. Cash only. ❸

Kuchi, Kochstr. 30 (☎030 31 50 78 15). S5, S7, S9 or S75 to "Savignypl." A bit more pricey than the sushi *Imbisse*, but you can be sure you are eating real fish in this trendy little restaurant. Sushi rolls from €4. Hot Japanese entrees. Open M-Th noon-midnight, F-Su 12:30pm-1am. Cash only. ❷

SCHÖNEBERG

■ **Café Bilderbuch,** Akazienstr. 28 (☎030 78 70 60 57; www.cafe-bilderbuch.de). U7 to "Eisenacher Str." While fringed lamps, oak bookcases, and velvety couches give this cafe a Venetian library feel, the "Bilderbuch Sudoku Puzzle" on the menu brings diners back to the twenty-first century. Daily tasty brunch baskets and sumptuous Sunday buffet (€8). Weekly dinner specials €5-8.50. Open M-Th 9am-1am, F-Sa 9am-2am, Su 10am-1am. Kitchen open 9am-11pm. Cash only. ❷

■ **Café Berio,** Maaßenstr. 7 (☎030 216 19 46; www.cafe-berio.de). U1, U2, U4, or U15 to "Nollendorfpl." Always jam-packed with locals, this 2-fl. Viennese-style cafe tempts passersby off the street with its unbeatable breakfast menu (€3-11). Entrees €5-9. Happy hour cocktails 2 for 1 M-Th and Su 7-9pm and F-Sa 7pm-midnight. Open M-Th and Su 8am-midnight, F-Sa 8am-1am. Kitchen closes at 11pm. Cash only. ❷

KREUZBERG

■ **Maroush,** Adalbertstr. 93 (☎030 69 53 61 71). U1 or U15 to Kotbusser Tor. Tourists flock to Turkish Hasir, across the street, which claims to have invented the *Döner* kebab, but this Lebanese *Imbiss* is cozier and much cheaper. Favorite choices from the menu, handwritten in Arabic and German, are chicken shawarma wrap (€2.50) and a vegetarian platter with falafel and salads (€6). Open 11am-2am. Cash only. ❷

Wirtshaus Henne, Leuschnerdamm 25 (☎030 614 7730; www.henne-berlin.de). U1, or U15 to Kottbusser Tor. Though this slightly out-of-the-way German restaurant does serve other dishes (€2.50-6), virtually everyone orders the famous *Brathähnchen* (fried chicken), arguably the best in Berlin. It has a small beer garden, but the real charm is in its dark wood interior, with plaid tablecloths and antique lanterns. Always packed, so reserve in advance. Open Tu-Sa from 7pm, Su from 5pm. Cash only. ❷

FRIEDRICHSHAIN AND PRENZLAUER BERG

■ **Hans Wurst,** Dunckerstr. 2A (☎030 41 71 78 22). U2 to "Eberswalderstr.," M10 to "Husemannstr." This cafe/restaurant-on-a-mission serves only organic, vegan foods with no flavor enhancers. Readings, DJs, and acoustic concerts in the evenings. The menu changes daily, with seasonal offerings and fresh creations (€3.70-8). Free Wi-Fi. Brunch Sa-Su 11am-5pm. Open Tu-Th noon-midnight, F-Sa noon-late. ❷

■ **Cafe-Restaurant Miró,** Raumerstr. 29 (☎030 44 73 30 13; www.miro-restaurant.de). U2 to "Eberswalder Str." A Mediterranean cafe whose candelit, pillowed back room and fresh entrees (€8-11) capture the region's essence perfectly. Breakfast €4.50-8.25. Soups €3.20-3.70. Large appetizers and salads €4-9. Open daily 10am-late. Kitchen closes at midnight. ❸

⬛ SIGHTS

Most of central Berlin's major sights lie along the **bus #100** route which runs every 5min. from Bahnhof Zoo to Prenzlauer Berg. It passes the **Siegessäule,**

GERMANY

Berlin Mitte

ACCOMMODATIONS
Circus, 5
BaxPax Downtown Hostel/Hotel, 13
CityStay Hostel, 21

FOOD & DRINK
am to pm, 41
Beth Cafe, 11
The Sixties, 42

MUSEUMS
Alte Nationalgalerie, 20
Altes Museum, 25
Bodemuseum, 18
Deutsche Guggenheim Berlin, 36
Filmmuseum Berlin, 15
Gemäldegalerie, 14
Kunst-Werke Berlin, 10
Märkisches Museum, 12
Martin-Gropius-Bau, 2
Neue Nationalgalerie, 7
Neues Museum, 22
Pergamonmuseum, 19
Topographie des Terrors, 4

BARS & NIGHTLIFE
b-flat, 9
Kaffee Burger, 8
Weekend, 16

CHURCHES
Berliner Dom, 26
Deutscher Dom, 17
Französischer Dom, 6
Marienkirche, 24
St.-Hedwigs-Kathedrale, 23

ENTERTAINMENT
Berliner Philharmoniker, 27
Deutsche Oper Berlin, 39
Deutsche Staatsoper, 38
Komische Oper, 40
Konzerthaus, 3

SIGHTS
Alte Bibliothek, 37
Berliner Rathaus, 33
Bertolt-Brecht-Haus, 1
Brandenburger Tor, 34
Checkpoint Charlie, 32
Denkmal für die ermordeten Juden Europas, 16
Deutsche Staatsbibliothek, 30
Fernsehturm, 23
Humboldt-Universität, 31
Lustgarten, 29
Reichstag, 28
Russian Embassy, 35

breathtaking **Brandenburger Tor** (p. 296) and **Unter den Linden,** the **Berliner Dom** (p. 297), and **Alexanderplatz** (p. 299). Remnants of the **Berlin Wall** still survive in a few places: in **Potsdamer Platz** (p. 296); near the **Haus Am Checkpoint Charlie** (p. 304); in **Prenzlauer Berg,** next to the sobering **Documentation Center** (p. 302); and in altered form at the **East Side Gallery** (p. 302) in Friedrichshain.

MITTE

UNTER DEN LINDEN

This famous street was named "under the linden trees" for the 18th-century specimens that still line what was the spine of Imperial Berlin and what has become the nerve center of tourist Berlin. During the DDR days, it was known as the "idiot's mile," because it was often all that visitors saw, giving them little idea of what the eastern part of the city was really like. Originating in Pariser Platz, dominated by Brandenburger Tor, the street runs east through Bebelpl. and the Lustgarten, passing most of what remains of the city's still-impressive imperial architecture. *(S1, S2, or S25 to "Unter den Linden." Bus #100 runs the length of the street every 4-6min.)*

BRANDENBURGER TOR (BRANDENBURG GATE). Don't deny yourself the obligatory photo op. Berlin's only remaining city gate and and most recognizable symbol was built by Friedrich Wilhelm II in the 18th century as a symbol of victory, although in recent years this has been rephrased as "The Victory of Peace" in a fit of political correctness. During the Cold War, when it sat along the wall and served as a barricaded gateway, it became the symbol of a divided Berlin. Today, it is the most powerful emblem of reunited Germany—in 1987, Reagan chose this spot to make his "Tear down this wall" speech. The **Room of Silence** in the northern end of the gate provides a non-denominational place for meditation and reflection. *(Open daily 11am-6pm.)*

NEUE WACHE. The combination of Prussian Neoclassicism and a copy of an Expressionist statue by Käthe Kollwitz, *Mutter mit totem Sohn* (*Mother with Dead Son*), makes for an oddly moving memorial to "the victims of war and tyranny." The "New Guardhouse" was designed by architect Karl Friedrich Schinkel, turned into a memorial to victims of "fascism and militarism," and closed after reunification. Now the remains of an unknown soldier and an unknown concentration camp victim are buried inside with earth from the camps at Buchenwald and Mauthausen and from the battlefields of Stalingrad, El Alamein, and Normandy. *(Unter den Linden 4. Open daily 10am-6pm.)*

DENKMAL FÜR DIE ERMORDETEN JUDEN EUROPAS (MEMORIAL FOR THE MURDERED JEWS OF EUROPE). Just looking at the block of concrete stelae—large rectangular columns of concrete varying in height—it is hard to know what this prominent memorial, opened in the spring of 2005 and designed by architect Peter Eisenman, represents. Most agree, however, that it is quite moving. An underground information center tells the stories of specific families murdered during the Holocaust. *(Cora-Berliner-Str. 1, at the corner of Behrenstr. and Ebertstr. near the Brandenburg Gate. ☎030 26 39 43 36; www.stiftung-denkmal.de. Open daily 10am-8pm. Last entry Apr.-Sept. 7:15pm, Oct.-Mar. 6:15pm. Free audio tour. Guided public tours Sa-Su 11am and 2pm in German and Su 4pm in English. Admission €3, students €2.50.)*

POTSDAMER PLATZ

POTSDAMER PLATZ. Both Berlin's shiniest commercial center and the site of its most high-profile architectural failures, Potsdamer Platz is amazing for the sheer speed of its construction. Built under Friedrich Wilhelm I (in imitation of Parisian boulevards) as a launch pad for troops, the area became the commercial and transportation hub of pre-war Berlin, regulated by Europe's first traffic lights (the massive clock is set into a replica of what they looked like). But the square was flattened by bombers in WWII and caught in the death strip between East and West during the Cold War. In the decade that followed reunification, a number of commercial buildings sprouted up, the most recognizable being an off-kilter glass recreation of Mt. Fuji. *(U2, or S1, S2, or S25 to "Potsdamer Pl.")*

FÜHRERBUNKER. Near Potsdamer Pl., unmarked and inconspicuous, is the site of the bunker where Hitler married Eva Braun and then shot himself. During WWII, it held 32 rooms including private apartments and was connected to Hitler's chancellery building (since destroyed). Plans to restore the bunker were shelved for fear that the site would become a pilgrimage spot for neo-Nazis; all that remains is a dirt expanse and the occasional tourist. *(Under the parking lot at the corner of In den Ministergärten and Gertrud-Kolmar-Str.)*

GENDARMENMARKT

Several blocks south of Unter den Linden, Berlin's most typically Old Europe square became the French quarter in the 18th century after the arrival of an influx of Huguenots fleeing persecution by Louis XIV. During the last week of June and the first week of July, the square becomes an outdoor stage for open-air classical concerts. *(U6 to "Französische Str." or U2 or U6 to "Stadtmitte.")*

MUSEUMSINSEL (MUSEUM ISLAND)

There are more than a handful of reasons to set aside a good chunk of time for Museum Island, the entirety of which is a **UNESCO World Heritage Sight.** After crossing the Schloßbrücke over the Spree, Unter den Linden becomes Karl-Liebknecht-Str. and cuts through the Museumsinsel, which is home to five major museums (p. 303) and the **Berliner Dom.** *(Take S3, S5, S7, S9, or S75 to "Hackescher Markt" and walk toward the Dom. Alternatively, pick up bus #100 along Unter den Linden and get off at "Lustgarten." For more information, see Museums, p. 303.)*

▨BERLINER DOM. One of Berlin's most recognizable landmarks, this elegantly bulky, multiple-domed cathedral proves that Protestants can design buildings as dramatically as Catholics. Built during the reign of Kaiser Wilhelm II in a faux-Renaissance style, the cathedral suffered severe damage in a 1944 air raid and took 20 years to fully reconstruct. Look for the Protestant icons

Charlottenburg and Schöneberg

GERMANY

SCHÖNEBERG

CHARLOTTENBURG

WILMERSDORF

Tiergarten

Zoologischer Garten

Grosser Tiergarten

Straße des 17. Juni

Straße des 17. Juni

Spree

Spreeweg

Bellevueufer

Schloßpark Bellevue

John-Foster-Dulles-Allee

TO MITTE AND PRENZLAUER BERG

TO FRIEDRICHSHAIN

GROSSER STERN

Hofjägerallee

Klingelhöferstr.

Neuer See

Großer Weg

Landwehrkanal

Lützowplatz

Tiergartenstr.

Reichpietschufer

Schöneberger Ufer

Staufenbergstr.

Potsdamer Str.

TO KREUZBERG

Pohlstr.

Bülowstr.

Nelly-Sachs-Park

Kurfürstenstr.

Frobenstr.

TO (100m), (500m)

Winterfeldtstr.

Maaßenstr. Gleditschstr.

Goltzstr.

Nollendorfpl.

Einemstr.

Martin-Luther-Str.

Kleiststr.

Fuggerstr.

Eisenacher Str.

Welserstr.

Ansbacher Str.

Motzstr.

Viktoria-Luise-Pl.

Winterfeldtstr.

A.d. Urania

Kurfürstenstr.

Budapester Str.

Tauentzienstr.

Lietzenburger Str.

Nürnberger Str.

Augsburger Str.

KaDeWe

Wittenbergpl.

Europa Center

Aquarium

Elefantentor

Breitscheid-pl.

Kurfürstendamm

Joachimstaler Str.

Bundesallee

Hardenbergpl.

ZOOLOGISCHER GARTEN

Hardenbergstr.

Fasanenstr.

Steinpl.

Uhlandstr.

Kantstr.

Grolmanstr.

Knesebeckstr.

Savignypl.

Bleibtreustr.

Leibnizstr.

Wielandstr.

Niebuhrstr.

Mommsenstr.

Lewishamstr.

Brandenburgische Str.

Konstanzer Str.

Düsseldorfer Str.

Pariser Str.

Ludwigkirchstr.

Fasanenstr.

Spichernstr.

Geisbergstr.

Technische Universität

ERNST-REUTER-PL.

Marchstr.

Einsteinufer

Salzufer

Spree

Franklinstr.

Fraunhoferstr.

Guerickestr.

Otto-Suhr-Allee

DEUTSCHE OPER

Bismarckstr.

Krumme Str.

Schillerstr.

Goethestr.

Pestalozzistr.

Wilmersdorfer Str.

Richard-Wagner-Pl.

Kaiser-Friedrich-Str.

Fritschestr.

Zillestr.

Windscheidstr.

Suarezstr.

Schloßstr.

Spandauer Damm

TO SPANDAU

Schustehrus-park

Goethe Park

Wilmersdorfer Str.

Stuttgarter Pl.

Kantstr.

Droysenstr.

Adenauerpl.

Olivaer Pl.

Württemberg Str.

Bellinerpl.

Hochmeister Platz

Westfälische Str.

Joachim-Friedrich-Str.

Holtzendorffstr.

TO FUNKTURM, (1km) AMTSGERICHT-

S BELLEVUE

S TIERGARTEN

S ZOOLOGISCHER GARTEN

S SAVIGNYPL.

S CHARLOTTENBURG

S STUTTGARTER PL.

400 yards

400 meters

(Calvin, Zwingli, and Luther) that adorn the decadent interior, or soak up the glorious view of Berlin from the top of the cupola. *(☎030 20 26 91 19; www.berlin-erdom.de. Open M-Sa 9am-8pm, Su noon-8pm, closed during services 6:30-7:30pm. Free organ recitals W-F 3pm. Frequent concerts in summer; buy tickets in the church or call ahead. Combined admission to Dom, crypt, tower, and galleries €5, students €3. Audio tour €3.)*

ALEXANDERPLATZ AND NIKOLAIVIERTEL

Formerly the heart of Weimar Berlin, **Alexanderplatz** became the center of East Berlin, an urban wasteland of fountains, pre-fab concrete apartment buildings, and—more recently—chain stores and malls. **Karl-Liebknecht-Strrasse,** which divides the Museuminsel, leads into the monolithic Alexanderplatz, a former cattle market. Behind the Marx-Engels-Forum, the preserved cobblestone streets of **Nikolaiviertel** (Nicholas' Quarter) stretch toward Mühlendamm. *(Take U2, U5, or U8, or S3, S5, S7, S9, or S75 to "Alexanderpl.")*

█FERNSEHTURM (TV TOWER). The tremendous and bizarre tower, the tallest structure in Berlin (368m0, was originally intended to prove East Germany's technological capabilities, though Swedish engineers were ultimately brought in when construction faltered. As a result, the tower has acquired some colorful, politically infused nicknames, among them "Walter Ulbricht's Last Erection." Look at the windows when the sun is out to see the cross-shaped glint pattern known as the *Papsts Rache* (Pope's Revenge), so named because it defied the Communist government's attempt to rid the city of religious symbols. An elevator whisks tourists up to the magnificent view from the spherical node (203m) and a slowly rotating cafe one floor up serves international meals for €8-16. *(☎030 242 3333; www.berlinerfernsehturm.de. Open daily Mar.-Oct. 9am-midnight, Nov.-Feb. 10am-midnight. €10, under 16 €4.50.)*

MARIENKIRCHE. The non-bombed and non-reconstructed church (Berlin's second oldest) is Gothic, the altar and pulpit Rococo, and the tower Neo-Romantic thanks to centuries of additions to the original structure. Knowledgeable guides explain the artifacts as well as the painting collection, which features works from the Dürer and Cranach schools. *(☎030 242 4467. Open daily in summer 10am-9pm, in winter 10am-6pm.)*

NEUE SYNAGOGE. This huge building, modeled after the Alhambra, was designed by Berlin architect Eduard Knoblauch in the 1850s. The synagogue, which seated 3200, was used for worship until 1940, when the Nazis occupied it and used it for storage. Amazingly, the building survived *Kristallnacht*—the SS torched it, but a local police chief bluffed his way past SS officers to order the fire extinguished. The synagogue was later destroyed by bombing, but its restoration, largely financed by international Jewish organizations, began in

---

Charlottenburg and Schöneberg

⌂ ACCOMMODATIONS

A&O Hostel, **11**
Berolina Backpacker, **8**
Jugendgästehaus am Zoo, **4**

█ BARS AND ★ NIGHTLIFE

Connection, **1**
Mister Hu, **7**
Slumberland, **19**

🍎 FOOD & DRINK

Baharat Falafel, **10**
Cafe Berio, **20**
Cafe Bilderbuch, **5**
Damas Falafel, **3**
Die Feinbäckerei, **22**
Orchidee Sushi
 Restaurant, **9**
Schwarzes Cafe, **15**
Witty's, **18**

🏛 MUSEUMS

Bauhaus-Archiv Museum Für
 Gestaltung, **13**
Gemäldegalerie, **6**
Neue Nationalgalerie, **14**
Museum Berggruen, **2**

● SIGHTS

Aquarium, **12**
Elefantentor, **16**
Kaiser-Wilhelm-Gedächtiskirche, **17**

1988 and was completed in 1995. Too big for Berlin's remaining Jewish community, the striking building is no longer used for services and instead houses an exhibit chronicling its history as well as that of the Jewish community that once thrived in the surrounding neighborhood. *(Oranienburger Str. 29. ☎ 030 88 02 83 00; www.cjudaicum.de. Open Apr.-Sept. M and Su 10am-5pm, Tu-Th 10am-6pm, F 10am-5pm; Mar. and Oct. M and Su 10am-2pm, Tu-Th 10am-8pm, F 10am-6pm; Nov.-Feb. M and Su 10am-2pm, Tu-F 10am-6pm. Last entry 30min. before closing. Permanent exhibition "Open Ye the Gates" €3, students €2. Dome €1.50/1. Temporary exhibition €3/2.)*

THE MISSING HOUSE. Across the street from the Jewish Cemetery is a 1990 art installation by Christian Boltanski in the space where a house was bombed during WWII. Boltanski researched the apartment's earlier inhabitants—Jews and non-Jews alike—and put plaques on the walls of the surrounding buildings at the approximate height of their apartment floors with their names, dates of birth and death, and professions. *(Große Hamburger Strasse.)*

TIERGARTEN

Stretching from Bahnhof Zoo in the west to the Brandenburg Gate in the east, this vast landscaped park was formerly used by Prussian monarchs as a hunting and parade ground. Today, it is frequented by strolling families, elderly couples. **Straße des 17. Juni** bisects the park from west to east, connecting Ernst-Reuter-Pl. to the Brandenburg Gate. The street is the site of many demonstrations and parades, including Barack Obama's 2008 speech, which attracted over 200,000 viewers.

THE REICHSTAG. The current home of Germany's governing body, the **Bundestag,** the Reichstag has seen some critical historical moments in its day. Philipp Scheidemann proclaimed *"Es lebe die Deutsche Republik"* ("Long live the German Republic") here in 1918. In 1933 Adolf Hitler used a fire at the Reichstag as an excuse to declare a state of emergency and seize power. In 1997, a glass dome was added to the top, built around the upside-down solar cone that powers the building. A walkway spirals up the inside of the dome, providing visitors with information about the building, panoramic views of the city, and a view of the parliament meeting inside—a powerful symbol of government transparency. Braving the line is worth it. *(☎ 030 22 73 21 52; www.bundestag.de. Open daily 8am-midnight. Last entry 10pm. Free.)*

CHARLOTTENBURG

ZOOLOGISCHER GARTEN. Germany's oldest zoo houses around 14,000 animals of 1500 species, most in open-air habitats. The southern entrance is the famous **Elefantentor** (across from Europa-Center), a decorated elephant pagoda standing at Budapester Str. 34. You had better visit the world-famous polar bear **Knut;** otherwise he might go berserk. Originally deemed the cutest polar bear alive, Knut has been diagnosed by animal specialists as a psychopath who is addicted to human attention. *(☎ 030 25 40 10; www.zoo-berlin.de. Park open daily 9am-7:30pm, animal houses open 9am-6pm; entrance closes at 6:30pm. €12, students €9, children €6. Combination ticket to zoo and aquarium €18/14/9.)*

SCHLOSS CHARLOTTENBURG (CHARLOTTENBURG PALACE). The broad Baroque palace, which was commissioned by Friedrich I in the 17th century for his second wife, Sophie-Charlotte, stands impassively at the end of a beautiful, tree-lined esplanade in northern Charlottenburg. The *Schloß*'s extensive grounds include the **Altes Schloß,** underneath the iconic dome topped with a stature of Fortuna; the **Große Orangerie,** which contains rooms filled with historic furnishings (much of it reconstructed as a result of war damage) and gratuitous gilding; the **Neuer Flügel,** which includes the marble receiving rooms and the more sober royal chambers; the **Neuer Pavillon,** a museum dedicated to Prussian architect Karl Friedrich Schinkel; the **Belvedere,** a small building housing the royal family's porcelain collection; and the **Mausoleum,** the final resting place for most of the family. Stroll the **Schloßgarten** behind the main buildings, an elysium of small lakes, footbridges, fountains, and meticulously manicured trees. *(Spandauer Damm 10-22. Take bus #M45 from Bahnhof Zoo to "Luisenpl./Schloß Charlottenburg" or U2 to "Sophie-Charlotte Pl." ☎ 030 320 9275. Altes Schloß open Tu-Su Apr.-Oct. 10am-6pm, Nov.-Mar. 10am-5pm. Neuer Flügel open M and W-Su Apr.-Oct. 10am-6pm, Nov.-Mar. 10am-5pm. Belvedere and Mausoleum open daily Apr.-Oct. 10am-6pm, Nov.-Mar. noon-5pm. Altes Schloß €10, students €7; Neuer Flügel €6/5; Belvedere €2/1.50; Mausoleum €2/1.50. Audio tours, available in English, are included.)*

OLYMPIA-STADION. This massive Nazi-built stadium comes in a close second after Tempelhof Airport in the list of monumental Third Reich buildings in Berlin. It was erected for the infamous 1936 Olympic Games, in which African-American Jesse Owens won four gold medals. Hitler refused to congratulate Owens, a legendary runner who now has a Berlin street (Jesse-Owens-Allee) named after him. Film buffs will recognize the complex from Leni Riefenstahl's terrifying film *Olympia* (1938) while others will recognize it as the sight of the 2006 World Cup final. The **Glockenturm** (bell tower) provides a great lookout point and houses an exhibit on the history of German athletics. *(S5, S7, or U2 to "Olympia-Stadion." For Glockenturm, S5 or S7 to "Pichelsburg." ☎ 030 25 00 23 22; www.olympiastadion-berlin.de. Open daily Mar. 20-May 9am-7pm, Jun.-Sept. 15 9am-8pm, Sept. 16-Oct. 31 9am-7pm, Nov.-Mar. 19 9am-4pm. €4, students €3. Tour with guide €8, students €7; children under 6 free. Audio tour €2.50.)*

KREUZBERG

SOUTHERN KREUZBERG. The cobblestone streets and pre-war ornamented apartment blocks just east of Mehringdamm form the most gentrified area of Kreuzberg—witness the outdoor organic food market on Saturdays in Chamissopl. The spine of of the area is **Bergmannstraße,** a stretch of cafes, secondhand clothing and record stores, and bookshops. West of Mehringdamm, forested Viktoria Park is the highest natural point in Berlin at 66m. A huge neo-Gothic memorial commemorating the Napoleonic Wars provides a great view of Berlin. Vineyards first planted by the Knights Templar and a number of small restaurants and beer gardens—including philosopher Georg Friedrich Hegel's favorite watering hole—are tucked away in the park near the artificial waterfall. Farther south down Mehringdamm is **Tempelhof Airport,** built by Nazi architect Albrecht Speer but most famous as the site of the Berlin Airlift, 1948-1949, one of the most dramatic crises of the Cold War. The German government closed the airport in 2008, but still visible in a flower-ringed field is a monument known as the **Hungerharke** (hunger rake) representing the three air corridors and dedicated to the 78 pilots who lost their lives in the 328 days of the airlift. *(U6 to "Platz der Luftbrücke" or U6 or U7 to "Mehringdamm.")*

EASTERN KREUZBERG. The **Landwehrkanal,** a channel bisecting Kreuzberg, is a lovely place to take a stroll, with moored boats doubling as on-the-water cafes. Its history is less pleasant: it is where the conservative, nationalist Freikorps threw the body of left-wing activist and communist revolutionary Rosa Luxemburg after murdering her in 1919. The Berlin Wall once ran near **Schlesisches Tor,** a nightlife hotspot with a huge Turkish and Balkan influence and arguably the best street art and graffiti in the city—especially around Wrangelstraße. The **Oberbaumbrücke,** an iconic double-decker brick bridge, spans the Spree River. It was once a border crossing into East Berlin, and now connects Kreuzberg to Friedrichshain. Residents of the rival neighborhoods duke it out in a "water fight" on the bridge each July 27, with up to a thousand people throwing water and rotten vegetables at one another. (U1 or U15 to "Schlesisches Tor.")

ORANIENSTRASSE. This strip's colorful mix of cafes, bars, and stores is home to the city's punk and radical elements. May Day parades, which start on Oranienpl., were the scene of violent riots in the 1980s, although May 1 has since become a family holiday complete with a big block party. The street's **Heinrichplatz** boasts, in addition to great cafes, a women-only Turkish-style bath, **Schoko Fabrik,** which doubles as a community center (www.schokofabrik.de; open M 3-11pm, Tu-Su noon-11pm). Squatters still occupy the **Bethanien Kunsthaus** in Marienplatz (www.bethanien.de), which hosts frequent exhibitions and an open-air cinema in summer. (U1 or U15 to "Kottbusser Tor" or "Görlitzer Bahnhof."

FRIEDRICHSHAIN AND LICHTENBERG

◪EAST SIDE GALLERY. The longest remaining portion of the Berlin Wall, this 1.3km stretch of cement slabs also serves as the world's largest open-air art gallery. The murals are not remnants of Cold War graffiti, but rather the organized efforts of an international group of artists who gathered here in 1989 to celebrate the end of the city's division. One of the most famous is artist Dmitri Vrubel's depiction of a wet kiss between Leonid Brezhnev and East German leader Eric Honecker. The stretch of street remains unsupervised and, on the Warschauer Str. side, open at all hours. (Along Mühlenstr. Take U1 or U15 or S3, S5-S7, S9, or S75 to "Warschauer Str." or S5, S7, S9, or S75 to "Ostbahnhof" and walk back toward the river. www.eastsidegallery.com.)

STASI MUSEUM. The Lichtenberg suburb harbors perhaps the most hated and feared building of the DDR regime: the headquarters of the East German secret police, the *Staatssicherheit* or Stasi. During the Cold War, the Stasi kept dossiers on some six million of East Germany's own citizens, an amazing feat and a testament to the huge number of civilian informers in a country of only 16 million people. On January 15, 1990, a crowd of 100,000 Berliners stormed and vandalized the building to celebrate the demise of the police state. Since a 1991 law returned the records to the people, the "Horror Files" have rocked Germany, exposing millions of informants—and wrecking careers, marriages, and friendships—at every level of German society. Officially known today as the **Forschungs- und Gedenkstätte Normannenstraße,** the building maintains its oppressive Orwellian gloom and much of its worn 1970s aesthetic. The exhibit displays the extensive offices of Erich Mielke, the loathed Minister for State Security from 1957 to 1989, a large collection of tiny microphones and hidden cameras used for surveillance by the Stasi, and a replica of a Stasi prison cell. (Ruschestr. 103, Haus 1. U5 to "Magdalenenstr." ☎ 030 553 6854; www.stasimuseum.de. Exhibits in German. English info booklet €3. Open M-F 11am-6pm, Sa-Su 2-6pm. €4, students €3.)

PRENZLAUER BERG

BERLINER MAUER DOKUMENTATIONSZENTRUM (BERLIN WALL DOCUMENTATION CENTER). A museum, a chapel, and an entire city block of the preserved Berlin Wall—two concrete barriers separated by the open *Todesstreife* (death strip)—come together in a memorial to "victims of the communist tyranny." The museum has assembled a comprehensive collection of all things Wall. Exhibits include photos, film clips, and sound bites. The collection here is both cheaper and more informative than the private museum at Checkpoint Charlie covering similar material. (Bernauer Str. 111; www.berliner-mauer-dokumentationszentrum.

de. ☎030 464 1030. *U8 to "Bernauer Str.", switch to S1 or S2 to "Nordbahnhof." Open Apr.-Oct. Tu-Su 10am-6pm, Nov.-Mar. Tu-Su 10am-5pm. Free.)*

MUSEUMS

With over 170 museums, Berlin is one of the world's great museum cities. Collections range from every epoch; the *Berlin Programm* (€1.60) lists them all.

SMB MUSEUMS

Staatliche Museen zu Berlin (SMB) runs over 20 museums in four major areas of Berlin—the **Museumsinsel, Tiergarten-Kulturforum, Charlottenburg,** and **Dahlem**—and elsewhere in Mitte and the Tiergarten. (www.smb.museum; ☎030 209 055 77.) All museums sell single-admission tickets (€8, students €4) and the three-day card (*Drei-Tage-Karte;* €19, students €9.50). Admission is free the first Sunday of every month and on Thursdays after 6pm. Unless otherwise noted, all SMB museums are open Tuesday through Sunday 10am-6pm and Thursday 10am-10pm. All offer free English-language audio tours.

MUSEUMSINSEL (MUSEUM ISLAND)

The Museumsinsel holds five separate museums on an area cordoned off from the rest of Mitte by two arms of the Spree. The museums were built in the 19th- and 20th centuries, suffered bombing during World War II and isolation and neglect afterwards, but have all been recently and extensively renovated. *(S3, S5, S7, S9, or S75 to "Hackescher Markt" or bus #100 to "Lustgarten." ☎030 266 3666. All national museums, unless otherwise noted, open Tu-W and F-Su 10am-6pm, Th 10am-10pm. Free audio tours in English. Admission to each €8, students €4. All sell a 3-day card good for admission to every museum; €14, students €7.)*

PERGAMONMUSEUM. One of the world's great ancient history museums, the Pergamon dates from the days when Heinrich Schliemann and other zealous 19th-century German archaeologists dismantled the remnants of collapsed empires the world over and sent them home for reassembly. Named for Pergamon, the city in present-day Turkey from which the enormous **Altar of Zeus** (180 BC) was taken, the museum features gargantuan pieces of ancient Mediterranean and Near Eastern civilizations from as far back as the 10th century BC. The colossal blue **Ishtar Gate** of Babylon (575 BC) and the **Roman Market Gate** of Miletus are just two more massive pieces in a collection that also includes Greek, Assyrian, and Far Eastern art. *(Bodestr. 1-3. ☎030 2090 5577. Open M-Su 10am-6pm, Th 10am-10pm. Last entry 30min. before closing. €8, students €4.)*

BODE-MUSEUM. The island's most attractive museum, which looks like it rises straight up from the water, reopened in 2006 after six years of renovations. It houses a hodgepodge of classical sculpture, Byzantine art, and oil painting. Its numismatic collection (coins and monies) is one of the world's largest. *(Monbijoubrücke. ☎030 266 3666. Open Tu-W and F-Su 10am-6pm. Th 10am-10pm. €8, students €4.)*

ALTE NATIONALGALERIE (OLD NATIONAL GALLERY). After extensive renovations, this museum is open to lovers of 19th-century art, showcasing everything from German Realism to French Impressionism. Camille Pisarro leads the all-star cast of featured artists. *(Am Lustgarten. ☎030 2090 5577. Open Tu-W and F-Su 10am-6pm. Th 10am-10pm. €8, students €4.)*

TIERGARTEN-KULTURFORUM

The Tiergarten-Kulturforum is a complex of museums at the eastern end of the Tiergarten, near the Staatsbibliothek and Potsdamer Pl. Students and local fine arts aficionados swarm throughout the buildings and on the multi-leveled courtyard in front. *(S1, S2, or S25 or U2 to "Potsdamer Pl." and walk down Potsdamer Str.; the museums will be on your right on Matthäikirchpl. ☎ 030 20 90 55 55.)*

▨ GEMÄLDEGALERIE (PICTURE GALLERY). This is the place to come in Berlin, and arguably in Germany, for painting. The city's most famous museum houses a collection of 2700 13th- to 18th-century masterpieces by Dutch, Flemish, German, and Italian masters, including works by Botticelli, Bruegel, Dürer, Gainsborough, Raphael, Rembrandt, Rubens, Titian, Velazquez, and many, many others. *(Matthäikirchplatz 4-6. ☎ 030 266 2951. Open Tu-W and F-Su 10am-6pm, Th 10am-10pm.)*

OTHER MUSEUMS IN MITTE AND TIERGARTEN

▨ HAMBURGER BAHNHOF: MUSEUM FÜR GEGENWART (MUSEUM FOR THE PRESENT). With a colossal 10,000 sq. m of exhibition space, this converted train station houses Berlin's foremost collection of contemporary art. The museum features several whimsical works by Warhol, as well as pieces by Twombly and Kiefer and some more puzzling exhibits in its vast white spaces. *(Invalidenstr. 50-51. S3, S5, S7, S9, or S75 to "Hauptbahnhof" or U6 to "Zinnowitzer Str." ☎ 030 3978 3411; www.hamburgerbahnhof.de. Open Tu-F 10am-6pm, Sa 11am-8pm, Su 11am-6pm. €8, students €4; Th 2-6pm free.)*

DEUTSCHE HISTORISCHES MUSEUM (GERMAN HISTORY MUSEUM). The oldest building on Unter den Linden, a baroque former military arsenal dating to 1730, the museum now houses a thorough exploration of German history, from Neanderthals to the Nazis to the fall of the Wall. Temporary exhibitions focus on the last 50 years, with plenty of depictions of smiling workers from the DDR era. Behind the main building stands its modern counterpart, a new wing designed by I. M. Pei that further bolster Berlin's reputation for cutting-edge architecture. *(Unter den Linden 2. S3, 5, 7, 9, or 75 to "Hackescher Markt." ☎ 030 2030 4444; www.dhm.de. Open daily 10am-6pm. €5, 18 and under free. Audio tour €3.)*

HAUS AM CHECKPOINT CHARLIE. Checkpoint Charlie, the border crossing between former East and West Berlin has become one of Berlin's most popular attractions, with tour buses, stands selling DDR memorabilia, actors clad as soldiers, and a table where you can get your passport "stamped." Perhaps the biggest rip off (those actors only charge €1 per photo) in the area is the **Haus am Checkpoint Charlie,** a two-bedroom apartment turned private museum. The exhibits detail how women curled up in loudspeakers, students dug tunnels with their fingers, and others found ingenious ways of getting into the West. Much of the same information can be gleaned for free by reading the placards along **Kochstraße,** where the wall used to run. *(Friedrichstr. 43-45. U6 to "Kochstr." ☎ 030 253 7250; www.mauer-museum.de. Museum open daily 9am-10pm. German-language films with English subtitles every 2hr. from 9:30am. €12.50, students €9.50. Audio tour €3.)*

CHARLOTTENBURG

Charlottenburg's museums range from high culture to smut and house one of the strongest collections of Picasso outside of Barcelona.

▨ MUSEUM BERGGRUEN. This intimate three-floor museum exhibits some wonderful Picassos alongside works that influenced the artist, including African masks and late French Impressionist paintings by Matisse. The top floor showcases paintings by Bauhaus teacher Paul Klee and Alberto Giacometti's surreally elongated sculptures. *(Schloßstr. 1. Near the Schloß Charlottenburg. Take bus #M45 from "Bahnhof Zoo" to "Luisenpl./Schloß Charlottenburg" or U2 to "Sophie-Charlotte-Pl." ☎ 030 3269 580. Open Tu-Su 10am-6pm. €6, students €3, children free. Audio guide free.)*

KÄTHE-KOLLWITZ-MUSEUM. Through both World Wars, Käthe Kollwitz, a member of the Berlin *Sezession* (Secession) movement and one of Germany's most prominent 20th-century artists, protested war and the condition of the working class through her haunting depictions of death, poverty, and suffering. The artist's biographical details—her son died in World War II and she withdrew into so-called inner migration during the DDR—provide context for her depictions of death, pregnancy, and starvation and for her somber self-portraits shown in what used to be a private home. *(Fasanenstr. 24. U1 to "Uhlandstr." ☎ 030 882 5210; www.kaethe-kollwitz.de. Open daily 11am-6pm. €5, students €2.50. Audio guide €3.)*

BEATE UHSE EROTIK MUSEUM. The world's largest sex museum contains over 5000 sex artifacts from around the world. Attracting a quarter of a million visitors per year, it is Berlin's fifth-most popular tourist attraction. Visitors come to see erotica ranging from naughty carvings on a 17th-century Italian deer-hunting knife to a 1955 calendar featuring Marilyn Monroe in the nude. A small exhibit describes the life of Beate Uhse, a pilot-turned-entrepreneur who pioneered Europe's first and largest sex shop chain. *(Joachimstalerstr. 4. ☎ 030 886 0666; www.erotikmuseum.de. Museum open daily 9am-midnight. €6, students €5. Gift store open M-Sa 9am-9pm, Su 1-10pm.)*

INDEPENDENT (NON-SMB) MUSEUMS

JÜDISCHES MUSEM (JEWISH MUSEUM). Architect Daniel Libeskind's design for the zinc-plated Jewish Museum is fascinating even as an architectural experience. No two walls are parallel, creating a sensation of perpetual discomfort. Underground, three symbolic hallways—the **Axis of the Holocaust,** the **Axis of Exile,** and the **Axis of Continuity**—are intended to represent the trials of death, escape, and survival. The labyrinthine "Garden of Exile" replicates the dizzying effects of dislocation and the eerie "Holocaust Tower," a giant, asymmetrical concrete room nearly devoid of light and sound, encourages reflection. Exhibits feature works by contemporary artists, memorials to victims of the Holocaust, and a history of Jews in Germany. Enter at the top of the stairs from the Axis of Continuity. *(Lindenstr. 9-14. U6 to "Kochstr.," or U1, U6, or U15 to "Prinzenstr." ☎ 030 25 99 33 00. Open M 10am-10pm, Tu-Su 10am-8pm. Last entry 1hr. before closing. €5, students €2.50. Special exhibits €4. Audio tour €2.)*

BAUHAUS-ARCHIV MUSEUM FÜR GESTALTUNG (BAUHAUS ARCHIVE MUSEUM FOR DESIGN). A must-visit for design fans, this building was conceived by Bauhaus founder **Walter Gropius** and houses rotating exhibits of paintings, sculptures, and of course, the famous furniture. *(Klingelhöferstr. 14. Bus #100, 187, 200, or 341 to "Nordische Botschaften/Adenauer-Stifteng" or U1, U2, U3, or U4 to "Nollendorfpl." ☎ 030 254 0020; www.bauhaus.de. Open M and W-Su 10am-5pm. M-Tu and Sa-Su €7, students €4; W-F €6/3. Audio tour free.)*

🎵 ENTERTAINMENT

Berlin has one of the world's most vibrant cultural scenes. Numerous festivals celebrating everything from Chinese film to West African music enrich the regular offerings; posters advertising special events plaster the city well in advance. Despite recent cutbacks, the city still generously subsidizes its art scene, and tickets are usually reasonably priced. Most theaters and concert halls offer up to 50% discounts for students who purchase tickets at the *Abendkasse* (evening box office), which generally opens 1hr. before shows. Other ticket outlets charge 15-18% commissions and do not offer student discounts. The **KaDeWe** has a ticket counter. *(☎ 030 217 7754. Open M-F 10am-8pm, Sa 10am-4pm.)* Theaters generally accept credit cards, but many ticket outlets do not—so bring cash just in case. Most theaters and operas close from mid-July to late August. The monthly pamphlets *Konzerte und Theater in Berlin und Brandenburg* (free) and *Berlin Programm* (€1.75) list concerts, film, and theater info, as do the biweekly *030*, *Kultur!news*, *Tip*, and *Zitty*.

NIGHTLIFE

Berlin's nightlife is world-renowned absolute madness—a teeming cauldron of debauchery that bubbles around the clock. Bars typically open at 6pm and get crowded around 10pm, just as the clubs open their doors. Bar scenes wind down anywhere between midnight and 6am; meanwhile, around 1am, dance floors fill up and the lights flash at clubs that keep pumping beats until dawn, when a variety of after-parties keep up the perpetual motion. In summer months it's only dark from 10:30pm to 4am, so it's easy to be unintentionally included in the early morning crowd, watching the sun rise on Berlin's landmarks and waiting for the cafes to open. From 1-4am on weekdays, 70 night buses operate throughout the city, and on Friday and Saturday nights the U- and S-Bahn run on a limited schedule throughout the night. The best sources of information about bands and dance venues are the bi-weekly magazines *Tip* (€2.70) and the superior *Zitty* (€2.70), available at all newsstands, or the free *030*, distributed in hostels, cafes, shops, and bars.

Berlin's most touristed bar scene sprawls down pricey, packed **Hackescher Markt** and **Oranienburger Straße** in Mitte. Prices fall only slightly around yuppie **Kollwitzplatz** and **Kastanienallee** in Prenzlauer Berg, but areas around Schönhauser Allee and **Danziger Straße** still harbor a somewhat edgier scene. The most serious clubbing takes place near the river in Friedrichshain, with a growing presence on the Kreuzberg side of the river. Bars line **Simon-Dach-Straße**, **Gabriel-Max-Straße**, and **Schlesiche Straße**. Businessmen and middle-aged tourists drink at bars along the Ku'damm. Gay nightlife centers on Nollendorfplatz, in the west, and lesbian nightlife has its stronghold in Kreuzberg.

MITTE

Week-End, Alexanderpl. 5 (☎030 24 63 16 76; www.week-end-berlin.de), on the 12th and 15th fl. of the building with the "Sharp" sign overlooking the city. A staple of the Berlin club scene, where techno fuels the floor until the sun rises over the block-housing of East Berlin. Wheelchair-accessible. Cover €8-12. Open F-Su 11pm-late. Cash only.

Tape, Heidestr. 14 (☎030 848 4873; www.tapeberlin.de), near a few art galleries along a strip close to the Hauptbahnhof. This converted warehouse is worth the trip. The walls, the entrance, and ravers' hands are all stamped with images of cassette tapes, the club's symbol. An artsy crowd dances in the enormous main room and hangs out on couches in the silver lounge. Cover varies. Open F-Sa 11pm-late.

Clärchen's Ballhouse, Auguststr. 24 (☎030 282 92 95; www.ballhaus.de). This odd-looking building was a ballroom before WWI, and now it is again. Older couples gather to tango and swing, while younger groups attempt to join in or enjoy beer in the flower-filled courtyard. Free introductory "swing tease" lesson W. Classical concerts and chacha brunch W. Open daily noon-late.

KREUZBERG

Club der Visionaere, Am Flutgraben 1 (☎030 69 51 89 42; www.clubdervisionaererecords.com). U1 or U15 to "Schlesisches Tor" or night bus #N65 to "Heckmannufer." Lounging around on their torch-lit raft in the canal in summer is the single most pleasant bar experience in Berlin. Legend has it that bargoers occasionally fall into the water, but more common activities include dancing to house music or downing a pizza (€5-8) along with your drink. Beer €3. Open M-F 2pm-late, Sa-Su noon-late. Cash only.

■ **Monarch Bar,** Skalitzer Str. 134. U1 or U15 to "Kotbusser Tor." Don't be put off by the urine smell in the staircase that leads up to this small, unmarked bar above Kaiser's supermarket. Some of the cheapest beer (€1 and up) around, a panoramic view of the raised S-Bahn thundering by, and a nightly DJ spinning electronica. Open 10pm-late.

PRENZLAUER BERG

■ **The Weinerei,** Veteranenstr. 14 (☎030 440 6983). The unmarked wine bar has gone from local secret to local legend, based on comfortable elegance and a strange pricin- system. Pay €1 for a glass, sample all of the wines, sample again, and again, and before leaving pay however much you think you owe. Open 10am-very late. Cash only.

■ **Klub Der Republik (KDR Bar),** Pappelallee 81. U2 to "Eberswalderstr.," M10, N2, N42. Turn into what looks like a deserted parking lot and climb the stairs of a dance studio to find a totally preserved DDR ballroom turned favorite post-wall watering hole. Cheap drinks for the neighborhood (€2-4). Open in summer from 9pm, in winter from 8pm. Cash only.

Wohnzimmer, Lettestr. 6 (☎030 445 5458). U2 to "Eberswalder Str." The name means living room, and they aren't kidding. With wood-beam floors, the bar resembles an old-fashioned kitchen, and glassware cabinets line the walls. You'll feel right at home as you settle into a velvet armchair with a matching mixed drink. Damn good mojito €5. Open daily 9am-4am. Cash only.

FRIEDRICHSHAIN

■ **Berghain/Panorama Bar,** Am Wriezener Bahnhof (☎030 29 00 05 97; www.berghain. de). S3, S5, S7, S9, or S75 to "Ostbahnhof." Heading up Str. der Pariser Kommune, take the 3rd right into what looks like a parking lot. The granddaddy of Berlin's "it" clubs deserves its reputation as a must-visit. Beneath the towering ceilings of this former power plant, spaced-out techno-fiends pulse to the reverberating music. Cover generally €12. Open F-Sa and occasionally W from midnight. Cash only.

■ **Maria am Ostbahnhof,** Am der Schillingbrücke (☎030 21 23 81 90; www.clubmaria. de). S-Bahn to "Ostbahnhof." From Stralauer Pl. exit, take Str. der Pariser Kommune to Stralauer Pl., follow it right along the wall, turn left at the bridge, and look for the red lights by the water. Tucked away by the river in an old factory, this club embodies the industrial legacy of Friedrichshain's scene. Sizable—and usually full—dance floor. Mostly electronic music, occasional punk, and reggae. Beer €2.50-3.50. Cover €10-12. Open F-Sa 11pm-late, weekdays for concerts and events only. Cash only.

GLBT NIGHTLIFE

Berlin is definitely one of Europe's most gay-friendly cities. Thousands of homosexuals flocked to Berlin during the Cold War to take part in the city's left-wing activism and avoid West Germany's *Wehrpflicht* (mandatory military service). In the gay mecca of **Schöneberg, Akazienstraße, Goltzstraße,** and **Winter-feldtstraße** have mixed bars and cafes, while the **"Bermuda Triangle"** of Eisen-acherstr., Fuggerstr., and Motzstr. is more exclusively gay. *Gay-yellowpages, Sergej,* and *Siegessäule* have GLBT entertainment listings. **Mann-o-Meter,** Bül-owstr. 106, at the corner of Else-Lasker-Schüler-Str., provides counseling, info on gay nightlife, and long-term accommodations, in addition to **Internet** access. (☎030 216 8008; www.mann-o-meter.de. Open M-F 5-10pm, Sa-Su 4-10pm.) **Spinnboden-Lesbenarchiv,** Anklamer Str. 38, has hip lesbian offerings, including exhibits, films, and other cultural info. Take U8 to "Bernauer Str." (☎030 448 5848. Open W and F 2-7pm.) The **Christopher Street Day (CSD)** parade, a 6hr. street party with ecstatic, champagne-soaked floats, draws over 250,000 participants annually in June. Nollendorfpl. hosts the **Lesbisch-schwules Stadtfest** (Lesbian-Gay City Fair) the weekend before the parade.

SCHÖNEBERG

⬛ **Hafen,** Motzstr. 19 (☎030 211 4118; www.hafen-berlin.de). U1-U4 to "Nollendorfpl." Nearly 20 years old, this bar has become a landmark for Berlin's gay community. The sign outside specifically invites in "drop dead gorgeous looking tourists," but there are plenty of locals here, too. The mostly male crowd jams the surrounding sidewalk in summer. Weekly pub quiz M 8pm (1st M of the month in English). New DJs W. Open daily 8am-4am. Cash only.

⬛ **Connection,** Fuggerstr. 33 (☎030 218 1432; www.connection-berlin.de). U1 or U2 to "Wittenbergpl." The name says it all. Find your soulmate (or one-night stand) in the disco, then go next door to the labyrinthine **Connection Garage** to get acquainted. First F of the month mixed; otherwise, men only. Cover €7, includes 1st drink. Club open F-Sa 11pm-late; Garage open M-Sa 10am-1am, Su and holidays 2pm-1am. AmEx/MC/V.

KREUZBERG

⬛ **Rose's,** Oranienstr. 187 (☎615 65 70). U1 to "Görlitzer Bahnhof." Marked only by "Bar" over the door. It's Liberace meets Cupid meets Satan. A friendly, gay and lesbian clientele packs this intense and claustrophobic party spot all night. The voluptuous dark-red interior is accessorized madness, boasting hearts, glowing lips, furry ceilings, feathers, and glitter. The small menu covers the basics with whiskey (€5) and schnapps (€2). Open M-Th and Su 11pm-6am, F-Sa 11pm-8am. Cash only.

SchwuZ, Mehringdamm 61 (☎030 629 0880; www.schwuz.de). U6 or U7 to "Mehringdamm." Enter through Melitta Sundström, a popular gay and lesbian cafe. The city's longest-running gay bar features 2 dance floors and a loungy underground area lined with pipes and its own DJ and disco lights. Crowd varies from young to very young. Lesbian night every 2nd F of the month. Cover F €5 before midnight, €6 after; Sa €6/7. Open F-Sa 11pm-late. Cash only.

▶ DAYTRIPS FROM BERLIN

KZ SACHSENHAUSEN. The small town of Oranienburg, just north of Berlin, was home to the Nazi concentration camp Sachsenhausen, where more than 100,000 Jews, communists, intellectuals, gypsies, and homosexuals were killed between 1936 and 1945. The **Gedenkstätte Sachsenhausen,** a memorial preserving the remains of the camp and recalling the imprisoned, was opened by the GDR in 1961. Some of the buildings have been preserved in their original forms, including sets of cramped barracks, the cell block where particularly "dangerous" prisoners were kept in solitary confinement and tortured daily, and a pathology department where Nazis performed medical experiments on inmates both dead and alive. However, only the foundations of **Station Z** (where prisoners were methodically exterminated) remain. A stone monolith commemorating the camp's victims stands sentinel over the wind-swept grounds. Barracks 38 and 39, the special "Jewish-only" barracks torched by neo-Nazis in 1992 and since reconstructed, feature displays on daily life in the camp during the Nazi period. The prison contains a museum housed in five original cells of the one remaining wing of the cell block. (*Str. der Nationen 22. S1 dir.: Oranienburg to the end 40min. Then either use the infrequent bus service on lines #804 and 821 to "Gedenkstätte," or take a 20min. walk from the station. Follow the signs from Stralsunder Str., turn right on Bernauer Str., left on Str. der Einheit, and right on Str. der Nationen. ☎030 301 20 00; www.gedenkstaette-sachsenhausen.de. Open daily Mar. 15-Oct. 14 8:30am-6pm; Oct. 15-Mar. 14 8:30am-4:30pm. Last entry 30min. before closing. Archive and library open Tu-F 9am-4:30pm. Visitor Information Service open M-F 8am-4:30pm. Museums closed M. Free. Audio guide €3.*)

GERMANY

NORTHERN GERMANY

Between the North Sea's western coast and the Baltic's eastern coast, the velvety plains are populated primarily by sheep and bales of hay. Farther south in Lower Saxony, cities straddle rivers and sprawl through the countryside. Hamburg, notoriously rich and radical, trades in idyllic for exciting, while the small city of Hanover charms visitors with its gardens and flourishing culture.

HAMBURG ☎040

Germany's largest port city and the second largest city in Europe, Hamburg (pop. 1,800,000) radiates an inimitable recklessness. With a skyline punctuated by ancient church towers, modern skyscrapers, and masts of ships carrying millions of containers of cargo, Hamburg is a haven for artists, intellectuals, and revelers who live it up in Germany's self-declared capital of lust.

▐ TRANSPORTATION

Trains: The **Hauptbahnhof** has connections every hour to: **Berlin** (1.5hr., €52); **Frankfurt** (5hr., €819); **Hanover** (1.5hr., €34); **Munich** (7hr., €108); **Copenhagen, DEN** (5hr., €72). DB Reisezentrum ticket office open M-F 5:30am-10pm, Sa-Su 7am-10pm; or purchase at ticket machines in the station anytime. The **Dammtor** train station is near the university; **Harburg** station is south of the Elbe; **Altona** station is to the west of the city's center; and **Bergedorf** is to the southeast.

Buses: The **ZOB** is on Steintorpl. across from the Hauptbahnhof, just past the Museum für Kunst und Gewerbe. Open M-Th and Su 5am-10pm, F-Sa 5am-midnight. **Autokraft** (☎40 280 8660) runs to **Berlin** (3hr., every 2hr. 7am-9pm, €25). **Touring Eurolines** (☎69 7903 501) runs to **Amsterdam, NTH** (8hr., M-Sa, €39); **London, UK** (daily, connecting in **Brussels,** €89); and **Paris, FRN** (11hr., daily, €69). Student discounts.

Public Transportation: HVV operates an efficient U-Bahn, S-Bahn, and bus network. One-way tickets within the downtown area €1.65; prices vary with distance and network. 1-day pass €5.10 (valid only after 9am); 3-day pass €15. Buy tickets at Automaten (machines), or consider buying a **Hamburg Card** (p. 309).

Bike Rental: Fahrradstation Dammtor/Rothebaum, Schlüterstr. 11 (☎41 46 82 77), rents bikes for just €3 per day. Open M-F 9am-6pm.

▰ ▐ ORIENTATION AND PRACTICAL INFORMATION

Hamburg's city center sits between the **Elbe River** and two lakes: **Außenalster** and **Binnenalster.** The arc of the **Alsterfleet** canal, separating the *Altstadt* on the east from the *Neustadt* on the west, echoes the arch of the impressive system of parks and gardens just above it. Most major sights lie between the **St. Pauli Landungsbrücken** port area in the west and the *Hauptbahnhof* in the east. **Mönckebergstraße,** Hamburg's most famous shopping street, runs all the way to **Rathausmarkt,** the seat of the sumptuous town hall. North of downtown, the **university** dominates the **Dammtor** area, sustaining a community of students and intellectuals. To the west of the university, the **Schanzenviertel** hums with artists, squatters, and a sizeable Turkish population, similar to the atmosphere in Altona, still further west. At the south end of town, an entirely different atmosphere reigns in **St. Pauli,** where the raucous **Fischmarkt** (fish market) is surpassed only by the wilder **Reeperbahn,** home to Hamburg's best discos.

Tourist Office: The **St. Pauli Landungsbrücken** office (☎30 05 12 03) is between piers 4 and 5 (Open Oct.-Mar. daily 10am-5:30pm; Apr.-Sept. M, Su, and W 8am-6pm, Tu

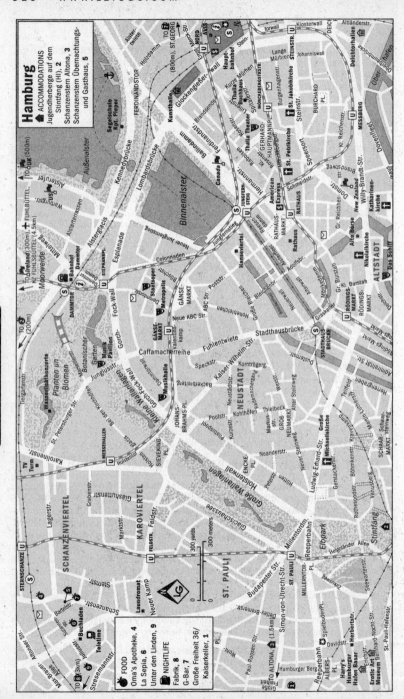

GERMANY

Hamburg

ACCOMMODATIONS
Jugendherberge auf dem
Stintfang (HI), 2
Schanzenstern Altona, 3
Schanzenstern Übernachtungs-
und Gasthaus, 5

FOOD
Oma's Apotheke, 4
La Sepia, 6
Unter den Linden, 9

NIGHTLIFE
Fabrik, 8
G-Bar, 7
Große Freiheit 36/
Kaiserkeller, 1

and Th-Sa 8am-7pm). Sells the **Hamburg Card,** which provides unlimited access to public transportation, reduced admission to museums, and discounts on restaurants, tickets, some hotels, and tours. 1-day card €8, 3-day €18, 5-day €33. The **Group Card** provides the same benefits for up to 5 people; 1-day €11.80, 3-day €29.80, 5-day €51.

Consulates: Canada, Ballindamm 35 (☎40 460 0270). S1 or 3 or U1 to Jungfernstieg; between Alstertor and Bergstr. Open M-F 9:30am-12:30pm. **Ireland,** Feldbrunnenstr. 43 (☎44 18 61 13). U1 to Hallerstr. Open M-F 9am-1pm. **New Zealand,** Domstr. 19, Zürich-Haus, block C, 3rd fl. (☎40 442 5550). U1 to Messberg. Open M-Th 9am-1pm and 2-5:30pm, F 9am-1pm and 2-4:30pm. **United Kingdom,** Harvestehuder Weg 8a (☎40 448 03 20). U1 to Hallerstr. Open M-Th 9am-4pm, F 9am-3pm. **US,** Alsterufer 27-28, 20354 Hamburg (☎40 4117 1422).

Currency Exchange: ReiseBank, on the 2nd fl. of the *Hauptbahnhof* near the Kirchenallee exit (☎40 32 34 83), has Western Union services, cashes traveler's checks, and exchanges currency. Open daily 7:30am-10pm. Watch out for steep hidden fees and consider trying one of the many exchange bureaus or banks downtown.

GLBT Resources: The neighborhood of St. Georg is the center of the gay community in the region. Pick up the free *Hinnerk* magazine and *Friends: The Gay Map* from **Cafe Gnosa** or from the tourist office. Organizations include **Hein und Fiete,** Pulverteich 21, which gives advice on health and entertainment in the area (☎40 24 03 33). Walk down Steindamm away from the *Hauptbahnhof,* turn right on Pulverteich; it's the building with the rainbow flag. Open M-F 4-9pm, Sa 4-7pm.

Internet: Internet Cafe, Adenauerallee 10 (☎28 00 38 98). €1.50 per hr. Open daily 10am-11:55pm. **Teletime,** Schulterblatt 39 (☎41 30 47 30). €0.50 per 15min. Open M-F 10am-10pm, Sa-Su 10am-7pm.

Post Office: At the Kirchenallee exit of the *Hauptbahnhof.* Open M-F 8am-6pm, Sa 8:30am-12:30pm. **Postal Code:** 20099.

ACCOMMODATIONS

Hamburg's dynamic **Schanzenviertel** area—filled with students, working-class Turks, and left-wing dissidents amid grafitti-splattered walls—houses two of the best backpacker hostels in the city. Small, relatively cheap *pensions* line **Steindamm** and the area around the *Hauptbahnhof,* where several safe hotels provide respite from the area's unsavory characters. **Lange Reihe** has equivalent lodging options in a cleaner neighborhood.

GIVING BACK

WHAT'S THE PUNKT?

Germany has a well-earned reputation as one of the world's most environmentally friendly countries. Its system of charging *Pfand,* a monetary deposit on glass and plastic bottles—which applies not only at *Biergarten* but also in grocery stores and vending machines throughout the country—is only one manifestation of this heightened awareness.

In 1990, Germany instituted a system called *Der Grüne Punkt* (The Green Dot), which has become the most widely used recycling program in Europe. The system created incentives for manufacturers to use less packaging on all their materials. Essentially, retailers have to pay for a "Green Dot" on products: the more packaging, the higher the fee. The system has led to about one million tons less garbage being processed annually.

As of 2002, the German recycling initiative was expanded and deposits were added to many bottles sold in grocery and convenience stores. Don't just throw your bottle away when you've finished. Instead, do your part to help the environment (and your wallet) by returning your bottle to one of the big machines in the supermarket to get your euros back.

☒ **Schanzenstern Übernachtungs und Gasthaus,** Bartelsstr. 12 (☎ 40 439 8441; www. schanzenstern.de). S21 or 31, or U3 to "Sternschanze." Bright, clean, and comfortable rooms. Breakfast €4-6. Reception 6:30am-2am. Free Internet between the reception area and the restaurant. Wheelchair-accessible. Laundry €4.50. Reserve ahead. Dorms €19; singles €37.50; doubles €53; triples €63; quads €77; quints €95. Cash only. ❷

☒ **Instant Sleep,** Max-Brauer-Allee 277 (☎43 18 23 10; www.instantsleep.de). S21 or 31 or U3 to "Sternschanze." Helpful, bilingual staff, communal kitchen, and long-term stays. Lockers €5 deposit. Linens €3. Reception 8am-2am. Check-out 11am. Reserve ahead. Dorms €15.50; singles €30; doubles €44; triples €60. Cash only. ❷

Jugendherberge auf dem Stintfang (HI), Alfred-Wegener-Weg 5 (☎40 31 34 88, www. djh.de/jugendherbergen/hamburg-stintfang). S1, S3, or U3 to Landungsbrücke. Newly renovated. Breakfast and linens included. Reception 24hr. Check-out 10am. Lockout 2am-6:30am. Dorms €18.80-20.30, over 27 €3 extra per night. MC/V. ❷

🍴 FOOD

Seafood is common in the port city of Hamburg. In **Schanzenviertel**, avant-garde cafes and Turkish falafel and *döner* stands entice hungry passersby. **Schulterblatt, Susannenstraße,** and **Schanzenstraße** are packed with hip, unique cafes and restaurants, while cheaper establishments crowd the **university** area, especially along **Rentzelstraße, Grindelhof,** and **Grindelallee.** In **Altona,** the pedestrian zone approaching the train station is packed with food stands and produce shops.

☒ **La Sepia,** Schulterblatt 36 (☎40 432 2484; www.lasepia.de). This Portuguese-Spanish restaurant serves delicious and reasonably-priced seafood. Lunch (11am-5pm) affords you a hearty €5 meal. Dinner €7.50-22. Open daily noon-3am. AmEx/MC/V. ❷

Unter den Linden, Juliusstr. 16 (☎40 43 81 40). Read complimentary German papers over *Milchkaffee* (coffee with foamed milk; €2.90-3.40), breakfast (€4.60-7.30). Salad or pasta (€3.70-6.90). Open daily 9:30am-1am. Cash only. ❷

Oma's Apotheke, Schanzenstr. 87 (☎40 43 66 20). Pub-like atmosphere popular with a mixed crowd. German, Italian, and American cuisine. Schnitzel €7.50. Hamburger with 1lb. fries €6.60. Open M-Th and Su 9am-1am, F-Sa 9am-2am. Cash only. ❷

👁 SIGHTS

ALTSTADT

RATHAUS. Built between 1886 and 1897, the town hall is one of *Altstadt's* most impressive buildings. The city and state governments both convene amid intricate mahogany carvings and spectacular chandeliers. In front, the **Rathausmarkt** hosts festivities ranging from demonstrations to medieval fairs. (☎428 312 470. *English-language tours every 2hrs. M-Th 10:15am-3:15pm, F 10:15am-1:15pm, Sa 10am-5pm, Su 10am-4pm. Building open daily 8am-6pm. Rooms accessible only through tours. €3, €2 with Hamburg Card.*)

GROßE MICHAELSKIRCHE. The 18th-century Michaelskirche, named after the archangel Michael, is arguably the best-recognized symbol of Hamburg. The church, battered repeatedly by lightning, fire, and allied bombs, was fully restored in 1996. A panoramic view of Hamburg awaits those who climb the 462 stairs of the spire (and those who opt for the elevator). There is daily organ music Apr.-Aug. at noon. (*U-Bahn to Baumwall, S-Bahn to Stadthausbrücke.* ☎37 67 81 00. *Church open daily May-Oct. 9am-8pm; Nov.-Apr. 10am-5pm. Crypt open June-Oct. daily 11am-4:30pm; Nov.-May Sa-Su 11am-4:30pm. Church suggested donation €2. Crypt and tower €2.50.*)

MÖNCKEBERGSTRAßE. Two spires punctuate Hamburg's glossiest shopping zone, which stretches from the *Rathaus* to the *Hauptbahnhof*. Closest to the Rathaus is **St. Petrikirche,** the oldest church in Hamburg, which also has the highest climbable tower, first dated back to 1195. (☎40 325 7400. www.samlt-petri. de. Open M-Sa 10am-6:30pm, Su 9am-9pm. Tower €2, under 15 €1, under 10 free. Frequent free concerts.) The other, **St. Jakobikirche,** is known for its 17th-century *arpschnittger* organ with almost 1000 pipes. (☎40 303 7370. Open M-Sa 10am-5pm.)

BEYOND THE ALTSTADT

PLANTEN UN BLOMEN. This huge expanse of manicured flower beds and trees includes the largest Japanese garden in Europe, complete with a teahouse built in Japan. (S21 or 31 to Dammitor. www.plantenunblomen.hamburg.de. Open May-Sept. daily 7am-11pm, Oct.-Apr. 7am-8pm. Free.) In summer, performers in the outdoor **Musikpavillon** range from Irish step-dancers to Hamburg's police choir. (May-Sept. most performances 3pm. See garden website for performance listings) At night, opt for the **Wasserlichtkonzerte,** a choreographed play of fountains and underwater lights set to music. (Daily May-Aug. 10pm, Sept. 9pm.)

KZ NEUENGAMME. An idyllic agricultural village east of Hamburg provided the backdrop for the Neuengamme concentration camp, where Nazis killed 55,000 prisoners through slave labor and imprisoned twice as many. Paths begin at the **Haus des Gedenkens,** a memorial house inscribed with the names and death dates of the victims, and winds through the camp's brick-making factory, barracks, and other memorials. (Jean-Doldier-Weg 39. S21 to Bergedorf, then bus #227 or 327. About 1hr from city. Buses run from Bergedorf M-Sa 2-3 per hr., Su 1 per hr. ☎428 131 500; www.kz-gedenkstaette-neuengamme.de. Museum and memorial open Apr.-Sept. M-F 9:30am-4pm, Sa-Su noon-7pm; Oct.-Mar. M-F 9:30am-4pm, Sa-Su noon-5pm. Path open 24hr. Tours Su noon and 2pm.)

GEDENKSTÄTTE BULLENHUSER DAMM UND ROSENGARTE. This schoolhouse is a memorial to 20 Jewish children who were subjected to extensive medical experimentation while in Auschwitz, then murdered by the SS in an attempt to destroy evidence hours before Allied troops arrived. Visitors are invited to plant a rose in the garden behind the school, where a row of memorial plaques line the fence. (Bullenhuser Damm 92. S21 to Rothenburgsort. Follow the signs to Bullenhuser Damm along Ausschläger Bildeich, over the bridge. At the intersection with Grossmannstr, the garden is on the far left; the school is 200m farther. ☎428 131 0, www.kz-gedenkstaette-neuengamme.de. Exhibit open Th 2-8pm, Su 10am-5pm. Rose garden open 24hr. Free.)

🏛 MUSEUMS

The **Hamburg Card** provides free or discounted access to nearly all museums. *Museumswelt Hamburg*, a free newspaper available at tourist offices, lists exhibits and events. Most museums are closed on Mondays and open 10am-6pm the rest of the week, and until 9pm on Thursdays.

HAMBURGER KUNSTHALLE. It would take days to fully appreciate every work in this sprawling fine arts museum. The oldest building presents the Old Masters and extensive special exhibits. In the connected four-level **Galerie der Gegenward,** contemporary art takes a stand in a mix of temporary and permanent exhibits. (Glockengieberwall 1. Turn right from Spitalerstr. City exit to the Hauptbahnhof and cross the street. ☎428 131 200; www.hamburger.kunsthalle.de. Open Tu-W and F-Su 10am-6pm, Th 10am-9pm. €8.50, students €5, families €14.)

DEICHTORHALLEN HAMBURG. Hamburg's contemporary art scene thrives inside these two airplane hangar-sized fruit markets. Inside you'll find painting and photography installations, as well as video displays. Exhibits rotate seasonally. (*Deichtorstr. 1-2. U1 to Steinstr. Follow signs from the U-Bahn.* ☎ *32 10 20; www. deichtorhallen.de. Open Tu-Su 11am-6pm. Each building €7, students €5, families €9.50. Combo ticket to both halls €12/8/16.50. Under 18 free.*)

♫ 🎭 ENTERTAINMENT AND NIGHTLIFE

The **Staatsoper**, Große Theaterstr. 36, houses one of the premier **opera** companies in Germany; the associated John Neumeier **ballet** company is one of the nation's best. (U2 to Gänsemarkt. ☎ 40 35 68 68. Open M-Sa 10am-6:30pm and 90min. before performances.) **Orchestras** all perform at the **Musikhalle** on Johannes-Brahms-Pl. (U2 to Gänsemarkt. ☎ 40 34 69 20; www.musikhalle-hamburg.de. Box office open M-F 10am-4pm.

Hamburg's unrestrained nightlife scene heats up in the **Schanzenviertel** and **St. Pauli** areas. The infamous **Reeperbahn** runs through the heart of St. Pauli; lined with sex shops, strip joints, and peep shows, it's also home to the city's best bars and clubs. Though the Reeperbahn is generally safe, it is unwise to stray alone into less crowded sidestreets. Parallel to the Reeperbahn lies **Herbertstraße**, Hamburg's official prostitution strip, where licensed sex entrepreneurs flaunt their flesh (only over the age of 18 allowed.) Students head north to the streets of the **Schanzenviertel** and west to Altona, where cafes and trendy bars create an atmosphere more leftist than lustful. The **St. Georg** district, near Berliner Tor and along Lange Reihe, is the center of Hamburg's **gay scene**. In general, clubs open and close.

🎵 **Große Freiheit 36/Kaiserkeller,** Große Freiheit 36 (☎ 40 317 7780). Big names have performed upstairs, home to popular concerts and hip club music orchestrated by DJs. **Kaiserkeller,** downstairs, caters to the rock contingent. F-Sa club nights. Cover €5-6. Concerts 7-8pm, 10pm-5am. Frequent free entry until 11pm.

Fabrik, Barnerstr. 36 (☎ 40 39 10 70; www.fabrik.de). From Altona station, head toward Offenser Hauptstr. and go right on Bahrenfelderstr. Cranks out raging beats of an eclectic mix of names in music. Every 2nd Sa of the month, "Gay Factory" attracts a mixed crowd. Live DJ 10pm most Sa; cover €7-8. Cover for live music €18-30. Cash only.

Meanie Bar/Molotow, Spielbudenpl. 5 (☎ 40 31 08 45; www.molotowclub.com), parallel to the Reeperbahn. **Meanie Bar,** upstairs, has a more relaxed atmosphere. Open daily from 9pm. No cover. The **Molotow,** in the basement of the retro Meanie Bar, keeps it hip with fashionable crowds, live bands. Molotow cover for club nights and live bands €8-15. Open from 8pm for concerts, and from 11pm F-Sa for disco. Cash only.

HANOVER (HANNOVER)   ☎ 0511

Despite its relatively small size, Hanover (pop. 523,000), is a major center in northern Germany known for hosting Oktoberfest Hannover, the second largest Oktoberfest in the world. Highlights are the three bountiful **Herrenhausen gardens.** The largest, **Großer Garten,** is one of Europe's most beautiful Baroque gardens, featuring geometric shrubbery and the **Große Fontäne,** one of Europe's highest-shooting fountains. It is also host to an annual international fireworks competition. To get there from the train station, walk to the far end of the lower shop level and take the U4 or 5 to Herrenhauser Garten. (Fountain spurts Apr.-Oct. M-F 11am-noon and 3-5pm, Sa-Su 11am-noon and 2-5pm. Garden open daily Apr. 9am-7pm; May-Aug. 9am-8pm; Sept. 9am-7pm; early Oct. 9am-6pm. Entrance €4, including admission to *Berggarten*. Concerts and performances June-Aug.; ☎ 0511 1684 1222 for schedule.) On the outskirts of the *Altstadt* is the **Neues Rathaus,** the impressive town hall built between 1901 and 1913. (Open May-Sept. M-F 9am-6pm, Sa-Su 10am-6pm. Free. Elevator M-F 9:30am-6pm, Sa-Su 10am-6pm. €2.50, students €2.) First-rate contemporary art museum, the ◪**Sprengel Museum**, Kurt-Schwitters-Pl., hosts work from some of the 20th century's greatest artists. (Open Tu 10am-8pm, W-Su 10am-6pm. €7, students €4.) North of Friederikenplatz, is the **Sculpture Mile,** a 1.5km stretch of sculpture and art exhibits.

◪**Hotel Flora ❶,** Heinrichstr. 36, is in the center of town 10min. from the station. Take the back exit and continue straight ahead onto Berliner Allee, cross the street, then turn left on Heinrichstr, a quiet street close to the *Hauptbanhof.* Rooms come with carpeting, framed Monet prints, and TVs. (☎0511 38 3910; www.hotel-flora-hannover.de. Breakfast included. Reception 8am-8pm. Singles €33-49, doubles €59-75, triples €72-96. Dogs €7.50. AmEx/MC/V.) **Jugendherberge Hannover (HI) ❶,** Ferdinand-Wilhelm-Fricke-Weg 1. Take the U3 or 7 to Fischerhof. From the stop, backtrack 10m, turn right, and cross the tracks; continue until the next stoplight at Lodemannweg, then turn right and follow the path as it curves and cross Stammestr. Turn right after going over the red footbridge. Balconies in the sun-filled rooms overlook a park. (☎0511 131 7674. Breakfast included. Internet €0.10 per min. Wheelchair-accessible. Reception 7:30am-1am. After 1am, doors open on the hr. Check-out 9am. Dorms €19.70-35.30. €3 discount under 27. MC/V.) Students fill the chic garden/bar at **The Loft,** Georgstr. 50a, off the main shopping road. (☎0511 363 1376. Happy hour M-Th, Su 9-10pm, F-Sa 8-9pm and midnight-1am. Open W-Sa from 8pm. Cash only.)

Trains leave at least every hour for: Berlin (2hr., €45-56); Frankfurt (3hr., €75); Hamburg (1hr., €38); Munich (4hr., €110); Amsterdam, NTH (4-5hr., €60-80). The **tourist office,** Ernst-August-Pl. 8, is in the Spardabank building across the street from the train station. (☎0511 1234 5111. Open Oct.-Mar. M-F 9am-7pm, Sa 9am-2pm; Apr.-Sept. also Su 9am-2pm.) The office leads **bus tours** of the city (2hr.; 1:30pm; €15) and sells the **Hannover Card** (1-day €9; 3-day €15; group ticket for up to 5 people €17/29), which covers transportation costs and reduces museum and sightseeing tour prices throughout the city. **Postal Code:** 30159.

CENTRAL AND WESTERN GERMANY

Niedersachsen (Lower Saxony), which stretches from the North Sea to the hills of central Germany, comprises agricultural plains and foggy marshland. Just south, North Rhine-Westphalia—the most economically powerful area in Germany—is so densely populated that it's nearly impossible to travel through the countryside without glimpsing the next hamlet, metropolis, or village ahead.

DÜSSELDORF ☎0211

Düsseldorf (pop. 582,000), the nation's *"Hautstadt"*—a pun on the German *"Hauptstadt"* (capital) and the French *"haute"*—is a stately metropolis with an *Altstadt* (Old Town) that features stellar nightlife and upscale shopping. In addition to glitz and glamour, Düsseldorf has an internationally recognized art school and top-notch museums that allure any creative mind.

▉▉ **TRANSPORTATION AND PRACTICAL INFORMATION. Trains** run frequently to: Amsterdam, NTH (2hr., 1 per 2hr., €32-42); Berlin (4hr., 1-2 per hr., €100); Frankfurt (2hr., 4 per hr., €70); Hamburg (4hr., 4 per hr., €80); Munich (5-6hr., 3-4 per hr., €100-122). Düsseldorf's **S-Bahn** is well-integrated into the regional **VRR** *(Verkehrsverbund Rhein-Ruhr)* system, which links most nearby

GERMANY

How are you doing Germany?

A) like a berlin party animal

B) Like a HiPPiE ...in Berlin

C) like a capital city SPACE COWBOY

D) ROCKIN' ALL OVER in BERLIN

E) flying into Frankfurt Airport

F) slxxp xasy in Munich

cities and is the cheapest way to travel between Aachen and Cologne. On the **public transportation system,** single tickets cost €1.10-2.10. *Tagestickets* (€5-21.20) allow up to five people to travel for 24hr. on any line. To reach the **tourist office,** Immermannstr. 65, head out of the train station and to the right; look for the Immermannhof building. It books rooms for free, except during trade fairs. (☎0211 172 0228. Open M-F 9:30am-1pm and 1:30-5:30pm, Sa 10am-1pm.) The **post office** is on Konrad-Adenauer-Pl. to the right of the tourist office. (Open M-F 8am-6pm, Sa 9am-2pm.) **Postal Code:** 40210.

█▐ ACCOMMODATIONS AND FOOD. Düsseldorf's hotels and hostels often double their prices during trade fairs, which take place from August to April. Clean, filled with friendly staff and patrons, and close to the center of town is █**Backpackers Düsseldorf ❷,** Fürstenwall 180. Take bus #725 (dir.: Hafen/ Lausward) from the station, and get off at Corneliusstr. (☎0211 302 0848; www.backpackers-duesseldorf.de. Kitchen available. Breakfast, lockers with mandatory deposit, linens, and towel included. Free Internet and Wi-Fi. Reception 8am-9pm. Reserve ahead F-Sa in summer. Dorms €22. MC/V.) The modern **Jugendgästehaus Düsseldorf (HI) ❷,** Düsseldorfer Str. 1, is conveniently located just over the Rheinkniebrücke from the *Altstadt.* Take U70 or 74-77 to Luegpl., then walk 500m down Kaiser-Wilhelm-Ring. Or, get off at Belsenpl., and take bus #835 or 836 to the Jugendherberge stop. (☎0211 55 73 10; www. duesseldorf-jugendherberge.de. Breakfast and linen included. Reception 6am-1am. Curfew 1am. Dorms €24.80; singles €42; doubles €62; quads €93. €3.10 HI discount. Cash only.) The *Altstadt's* numerous options for cheap eats can't be beat; rows upon rows of pizzerias, Chinese diners, and Döner, waffle, and crepe stands reach from Heinrich-Heine-Allee to the banks of the Rhine. The local outlet of the Czech brewery **Pilsner Urquell ❷,** Grabenstr. 6, specializes in Eastern-European fare. (☎0211 868 1411. Entrees €5-15. Beer €2.50-4.10. Open M-Sa 11:30-1pm, Su 4pm-midnight. MC/V.)

◪ SIGHTS. Königsallee ("the Kö"), just outside the *Altstadt,* embodies the vitality of wealthy Düsseldorf. The river running through it is serene and provides a lovely backdrop for the outdoor cafes. To reach the Kö from the train station, walk 10min. down Graf-Adolf-Str. Midway up the street is the upscale, marble-and-copper **Kö-Galerie.** Better deals in non-designer stores can be found along Flingerstr. in the *Altstadt.* To get to the Baroque **Schloß Benrath,** Benrather Schloßallee 104, in the suburbs of Düsseldorf, take tram #701. The Schloß's strategically placed mirrors and false exterior windows make the castle appear larger than it is. (☎0211 899 3832; www.schloss-benrath.de. Open Tu-Su mid-Apr. to Oct. 10am-6pm; Nov. to mid-Apr. 11am-5pm. Tours 1 per hr. €7, students €4.) At the upper end of the Kö is the beautiful **Hofgarten,** the oldest public park in Germany. To its west, the **K20 Kunstsammlung Nordrhein-Westfalen,** Grabbepl. 5, has various works by Expressionists, Surrealists, and former Düsseldorf resident Paul Klee. (U70 or 75-79 to Heinrich-Heine-Allee, and walk two blocks north. ☎838 1130; www.kunstsammlung.de. Open Tu-F 10am-6pm, Sa-Su 11am-6pm. Closed until fall 2009. €6.50, students €4.50.)

◪ NIGHTLIFE. Rumor has it that Düsseldorf's 500 pubs make up the longest bar in the world. By nightfall, it's nearly impossible to see where one pub ends and the next begins in the crowded *Altstadt.* The newsletter *Prinz* (€3) gives tips on the entertainment scene; some youth hostels give it out for free. █ **Mad Wallstreet,** Kurzestr. 6, an economist's vision of heaven, is a play on the market economy, listing values on flatscreens to show fluctuating drink prices every 300 seconds throughout the night. The law of drunken supply and demand

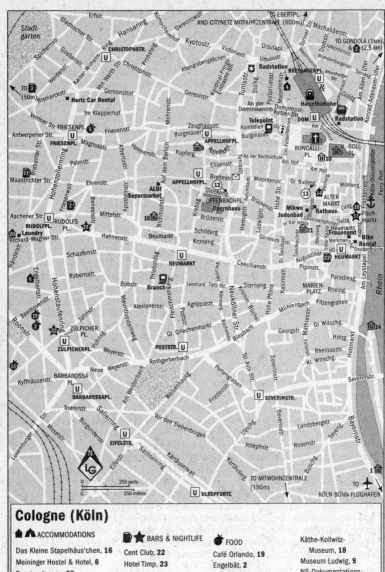

Cologne (Köln)

🏠🏕 ACCOMMODATIONS

Das Kleine Stapelhäus'chen, 16
Meininger Hostel & Hotel, 6
Pension Jansen, 20
Station Hostel for
  Backpackers, 4

🍸⭐ BARS & NIGHTLIFE

Cent Club, 22
Hotel Timp, 23
M20, 11
Papa Joe's Jazzlokal, 17
Stadtgarten, 3

🍴 FOOD

Café Orlando, 19
Engelbät, 2
Päffgen-Brauerei, 5
Restaurant Magnus, 15

**🕇 🏛 ○ CHURCHES,
MUSEUMS, AND SITES**

Dom, 7
House #4711, 12
Imhoff-Stollwerck-
  Museum, 1

Käthe-Kollwitz-
  Museum, 18
Museum Ludwig, 9
NS-Dokumentations-
  Zentrum, 8
Römisch-Germanisches
  Museum, 10
Römisches Praetorium
  und Kanal, 13
Schokoladen-
  museum, 14
Wallraf-Richartz
  Museum, 21

means prices of popular drinks soar as others plummet. (www.madwallstreet. de. Beer €0.90, shooters €1.90, mixed drinks €2.90. Open W-Sa 10pm-5am. Cash only.) **Zur Uel**, Ratinger Str. 16, is a restaurant by day and a rowdy German pub by night. (☎0211 32 53 69. Beer €2-3. M-Sa 9am-4am, Su 10am-1am. Food service M-Sa until 3pm, Su until 4pm.) **Stahlwerk**, Ronsdorfer Str. 134, located on the corner of Lierenfeldstr., is a classic 2 floor factory-turned-disco that packs in 1500 or more. Dress to impress and don't plan to leave before the city starts to wake up; most parties don't end until 7am. Take the U75 to "Ronsdorfer Str."(☎0211 73 03 50; www.stahlwerk.de. Cover €4-6. Open F-Sa and the last Su of the month from 11pm. Cash only.) **GLBT nightlife** clusters along Bismarckstr., at the intersection with Charlottenstr. *Facolte* (€2), a gay and lesbian nightlife magazine, is available at most newsstands in the city.

COLOGNE (KÖLN)   ☎0221

Although 90% of historic Cologne (pop. 991,000) crumbled to the ground during WWII, the magnificent Gothic *Dom* amazingly survived 14 bombings and remains one of Germany's main attractions. Today, the city is the largest in North Rhine-Westphalia, offering first-rate museums, theaters, and nightlife.

◤ TRANSPORTATION

Flights: Planes depart from **Köln-Bonn Flughafen (CGN)**. Flight info ☎022 03 40 40 01 02; www.koeln-bonn-airport.de. Airport shuttle S13 leaves the train station M-F, 3-6 per hr.; Sa-Su, 2 per hr. Shuttle to Berlin, 24 per day, 6:30am-8:30pm.

Trains: Cologne's **Hauptbahnhof** has trains that leave for **Berlin** (4-5hr., 1-2 per hr., €86-104); **Düsseldorf** (30min.-1hr., 5-7per hr., €10-18); **Frankfurt** (1-2hr., 2-3 per hr., €34-63); **Hamburg** (4hr., 2-3 per hr., €74-86); **Munich** (4-5hr., 2-3 per hr., €91-124); **Amsterdam, NTH** (2-3hr., 1-3 per hr., €40-56); **Paris, FRA** (4hr., 3 per hr., €87-120).

Public Transportation: KVB offices have free **maps** of the S- and U-Bahn, bus, and streetcar lines; branch downstairs in the *Hauptbahnhof*. Major terminals include the **Hauptbahnhof, Neumarkt,** and **Appellhofplatz**. Single-ride tickets from €1.50, depending on distance. Day pass from €5.20. The Minigruppen-Ticket (from €5.60) allows up to 4 people to ride M-F 9am-midnight and all day Sa-Su. Week tickets from €13.70. The WelcomeCard allows visitors to use all forms of public transportation in Cologne and Bonn (1-day €9, 2-day €14, 3-day €19).

Bike Rental: Kölner Fahrradverleih, Markmannsg. (☎0171 629 87 96), in the *Altstadt*. €2 per hr., €10 per day, €40 per wk.; €25 deposit. Open daily 10am-6pm.

◢ ☷ ORIENTATION AND PRACTICAL INFORMATION

Cologne extends across the Rhine, but the city center and nearly all sights are located on the western side. The *Altstadt* splits into **Altstadt-Nord,** near the **Hauptbahnhof,** and **Altstadt-Süd,** just south of the **Severinsbrücke** bridge.

Tourist Office: KölnTourismus, Unter Fettenhennen 19 (☎0221 22 13 04 10; www. koelntourismus.de), across from the main entrance to the *Dom*, books rooms for a €3 fee and sells the **Welcome Card** (€9), which provides a day's worth of free public transportation and museum discounts. Open daily M-F 9am-10pm, Sa and Su 10am-5pm.

Post Office: At the corner of Breitestr. and Tunisstr. in the WDR-Arkaden shopping gallery. Open M-F 9am-7pm, Sa 9am-2pm. **Postal Code:** 50667.

🏠 🏕 ACCOMMODATIONS AND CAMPING

Conventions held in Cologne fill hotels in spring and fall, and the city's hostels often sell out during these times. If you're staying over a weekend in summer, reserve at least two weeks ahead.

- 🏨 **Station Hostel for Backpackers,** Marzellenstr. 44-56 (☎0221 912 5301; www.hostel-cologne.de). Large dorms without bunks and an ideal location attract crowds of backpackers. Breakfast price varies. Free Wi-Fi. Reception 24hr. 4- to 6-bed dorms €17-21; singles €30-37; doubles €45-52; triples €72. Cash only. ❷

- 🏨 **Meininger City Hostel & Hotel,** Engelbertst. 33-35 (☎0221 355 332 014; www.meininger-hostels.de). U1, 7, 12, 15, 16, or 18 to Rudolfpl., then turn left on Habsburgerst., right on Lindenst., and left on Engelbertst. Breakfast included. Reception 24hr. Free Wi-Fi, lockers, towels, and linen. Dorms €17-22; small dorms €20-24; multi-bed room (4-6) €24-32; twins €34-44; singles €43-56; triples €28-36. Cash only. ❷

- **Pension Jansen,** Richard-Wagner-Str. 18 (☎0221 25 18 75; www.pensionjansen.de). U1, 6, 7, 15, 17, or 19 to Rudolfpl. Family-run with high-ceilinged rooms and colorful walls and decor. Breakfast included. Singles €45-80; doubles €65-90. Cash only. ❸

- **Das Kleine Stapelhäus'chen,** Fischmarkt 1-3 (☎0221 272 7777; www.koeln-altstadt.de/stapelhaeuschen). From the Rathaus, cross the Altenmarkt and take Lintg. to the Fischmarkt. An old-fashioned, richly decorated inn overlooking the Rhine. Breakfast included. Singles €39-52, with bath €52-82; doubles €64-74/90-121. MC/V. ❹

🍴 FOOD

Cheap restaurants converge on **Zülpicherstraße** to the southeast and **Eigelstein** and **Weidengasse** in the Turkish district. Ethnic restaurants line the perimeter of the *Altstadt*, particularly from **Hohenzollernring** to **Hohenstaufenring.** German eateries surround **Domplatz.** An **open-air market** on Wilhelmspl. fills the Nippes neighborhood. (Open M-Sa 8am-1pm.)

- 🍴 **Päffgen-Brauerei,** Friesenstr. 64. Take U3-5, 12, 16, or 18 to Friesenpl. A local favorite since 1883. *Kölsch* (€1.40) is brewed on the premises, consumed in the 600-seat beer garden, and refilled until you put your coaster on top of your glass. Entrees €7-15. Open daily 10am-midnight. Sa and Su until 12:30am. Cash only. ❸

- 🍴 **Café Orlando,** Engelbertstr. 7 (☎0221 23 75 23; www.cafeorlando.de). U8 or 9 to "Zülpicher Pl." Free Wi-Fi and an assortment of newspapers create a Sunday morning atmosphere at this student popular cafe. Complete breakfasts (€3.10-6), omelettes, and salads (€5.50-8), and drinks (€3.50-4.80). Open daily 9am-11pm. Cash only. ❷

- **Restaurant Magnus,** Zülpicherstr. 48 (☎0221 24 14 69). Take U8, 9, 12, 15, 16, or 18 to Zülpicher Pl. Locals steadily flock to this crowded cafe for funky tunes, artfully prepared meals (mostly Italian) from €4, and many delicious vegetarian options (€5-8). Open daily 8pm-3am. Cash only. ❷

- **Engelbät,** Engelbertst. 7. (☎0221 24 69 14). U8 or 9 to Zülpicher Pl. The best place for plentiful crepes, vegetarian and otherwise (€5-8). Breakfast (€1.50-3.50) served daily until 3pm. Open daily 11am-midnight. Cash only. ❶

👁 SIGHTS

DOM. Germany's greatest cathedral, the *Dom*, is a perfect realization of High Gothic style. Built over the course of six centuries, it was finally finished in 1880 and miraculously escaped destruction during WWII. A chapel on the inside right houses a 15th-century **triptych** depicting the city's five patron saints. Behind the altar in the center of the choir is the **Shrine of the Magi,** the cathedral's most sacred compartment, which allegedly holds the remains of the Three Kings and was once a pilgrimage site for monarchs. Before exiting the choir, stop in the **Chapel of the Cross** to admire the 10th-century **Gero crucifix,** which is the oldest intact sculpture of a crucified Christ. It takes about 15min. to scale the 509 steps of the **Südturm** (south tower); catch your breath at the **Glockenstube,** a chamber with the tower's nine bells, three-quarters of the way up. (*Cathedral open daily 6am-7:30pm. 45min. English-language tours M-Sa 10:30am and 2:30pm, Su 2:30pm. Tower open daily May-Sept. 9am-6pm; Nov.-Feb. 9am-4pm; Mar.-Apr. and Oct. 9am-5pm. Cathedral free. Tour €6, children €4. Tower €3.50, students €1.*)

🏛 MUSEUMS

Gourmands will want to head straight for the ⬛**Schokoladenmuseum,** which is best described as Willy Wonka's factory come to life. It presents every step of chocolate production, from the rainforests to the gold fountain that spurts streams of free samples. (*Rheinauhafen 1A, near the Severinsbrücke.* ☎ *0221 931 8880; www.schokoladenmuseum.de. From the train station, head for the Rhine, and walk to the right along the river; go under the Deutzer Brücke, and take the 1st footbridge. Open Tu-Sa 10am-6pm, Su 11am-7pm. €6.50, students €4.*) Masterpieces from the Middle Ages to the Post-Impressionist period are gathered in the **Wallraf-Richartz Museum.** (*Martinstr. 39. From the Heumarkt, take Gürzenichtstr. 1 block to Martinstr.* ☎ *0221 276 94; www.museenkoeln. de/wrm. Open Tu-W and F 10am-6pm, Th 10am-10pm, Sa-Su 11am-6pm. €7.50, students €5.*) The collection of the **Museum Ludwig** focuses on 20th-century and contemporary art. (*Bischofsgartenstr. 1, behind the Römisch-Germanisches Museum.* ☎ *0221 22 12 61 65. Open Tu-Su 10am-6pm, 1st F of each month 10am-10pm. €9, students €6.*) The chilling **NS-Dokumentations-Zentrum,** Appellhofpl. 23-25, includes a former Gestapo prison with inmates' wall graffiti intact. (*☎ 0221 22 12 63 32. U3-6 or 19 to Appelhofpl. Open Tu-W and F 10am-4 pm, Th 10am-6pm. €3.60, students €1.50.*)

🎵 📷 ENTERTAINMENT AND NIGHTLIFE

Cologne explodes in celebration during ⬛**Karneval** (late Jan. to early Feb.), a week-long pre-Lenten festival made up of 50 neighborhood processions. **Weiberfastnacht** (late Jan.) is the first major to-do: the mayor mounts the platform at Alter Markt and surrenders leadership to the city's women, who then hunt down their husbands at work and chop off their ties. The weekend builds to the out-of-control parade on **Rosenmontag** (Rose Monday; early Feb.), when thousands of merry participants sing and dance their way through the city center while exchanging *Bützchen* (kisses on the cheek). While most revelers nurse their hangovers on **Shrove Tuesday,** pubs and restaurants set fire to the straw scarecrows hanging out their windows.

Roman mosaics dating back to the 3rd century record the wild excesses of the city's early residents. The monthly *Kölner* (€1), sold at newsstands, lists clubs, parties, and concerts. The closer to the Rhine or *Dom* you venture, the faster your wallet will empty. After dark in **Hohenzollernring,** crowds of people move from theaters to clubs and finally to cafes in the early morning. The area around **Zülpicherpl.** is a favorite of students and the best option for an affordable good time. Radiating westward from Friesenpl., the **Belgisches Viertel** (Belgian Quarter) has slightly more expensive bars and cafes.

⬛ **Papa Joe's Jazzlokal,** Buttermarkt 37 (☎0221 257 7931). Papa Joe has a legendary reputation for providing good jazz and good times. *Kölsch* (€3.60) in 0.4L glasses. Live jazz M-Sa 10:30pm-12:30am. Su "4 o'clock Jazz"—8hours of, nonstop jazz from two bands starting at 3:30pm (not June-Sept.). Open daily 8pm-3am. Cash only.

◙ **Cent Club,** Hohenstaufenring 25-27 (www.centclub.de). Near Zülpicher Pl. Take U8 or 9 to Zülpicher. This student disco features more dance (to R&B, pop, dance classics) and less talk, with the appeal of low-priced drinks. Shots €0.50. Beer €1-2. Mixed drinks from €3. Cover W-Sa €5. Open W-Sa 9pm-3am.

◙ **Hotel Timp,** Heumarkt 25 (☎0221 258 1409; www.timp.de). Across from the Heumarkt U-Bahn stop. This club/hotel has become an institution in Cologne for travesty theater. Gay and straight crowds come for the glitter-filled cabarets. Drag shows daily 1-4am. No cover. 1st drink M-Th and Su €8, F-Sa €13. Open daily 10am-late. AmEx/MC/V.

M20, Maastrichterstr. 20 (☎0221 51 96 66; www.m20-koeln.de). U1, 6, or 7 to Rudolfpl. DJs deliver some of the city's best drum'n'bass and punk to a local crowd. Cocktails €5. Beer €1.50-3.20. Open from 8pm. Cash only.

Stadtgarten, Venloerstr. 40 (☎0221 95 29 94 33). Take U3, 5, 6, or 12 to Friesenpl. Downstairs hosts parties playing everything from soul to techno, while the upper concert hall is renowned for its jazz recordings and performances. Cover €6-15. Open M-Th 9pm-1am, F-Sa 9pm-3am. Cash only.

BONN   ☎0228

While it was the residence of Chancellor Konrad Adenauer, Bonn (pop. 314,300) served as the West German capital—and was derided as *"Hauptdorf,"* or "capital village." The city also maintains notoriety from its most famous native—Beethoven. ◙**Beethovenhaus,** Bonng. 20, Ludwig van Beethoven's birthplace, houses a fantastic collection of the composer's personal effects. The Digital Archives Studio offers recordings and scores of all of his works. (☎0228 981 7525; www.beethoven-haus-bonn.de. Open Apr.-Oct. M-Sa 10am-6pm, Su 11am-6pm; Nov.-Mar. M-Sa 10am-5pm, Su 11am-5pm. €5, students €4.) To reach Bonn's "other" palace, stroll down Poppelsdorfer Allee to **Poppelsdorfer Schloß,** which has a French facade, an Italian courtyard, and beautifully manicured botanical gardens; check out the world's largest water lilies in the greenhouses. (Gardens open Apr.-Oct. M-F and Su 9am-6pm; Oct.-Mar. M-F 9am-4pm.) Five museums line the *Museumsmeile* near the banks of the Rhine, though they're not within walking distance; take U16, 63, 66, 67, or 68 to the Heussallee/Museumsmeile stop. Around 7000 interactive exhibits examine post-WWII Germany at the ◙**Haus der Geschichte,** Willy-Brandt-Allee 14. (☎0228 916 50. Open Tu-Su 9am-7pm. Free.) One block away, the immense **Kunstmuseum Bonn,** Friedrich-Ebert-Allee 2, houses a superb collection of 20th-century German art. (☎0228 77 62 60. Open Tu and Th-Su 11am-6pm, W 11am-9pm. €5, students €2.50.)

◙**Deutsches Haus ❹,** Kasernenstr. 19-21, is on a quiet residential street within easy walking distance of the *Altstadt* and serves a decadent included breakfast to its visitors. (☎0228 63 37 77; info@hotel-deutscheshaus.net. Reception 6am-11pm. Singles €35-38, with bath €65-75; doubles €65-67, with bath €83-90; triples €110-118. AmEx/MC/V.) For the spacious but distant **Jugendherberge Bonn (HI) ❷,** Haager Weg 42, take bus #621 (dir.: Ippendorf Altenheim) to Jugendgästehaus. (☎0228 28 99 70; bonn@jugendherberge.de. Reception 7am-1am. Wheelchair-accessible. Breakfast and linens included. Laundry €4. Curfew 1am. Dorms €24; singles €40.30; doubles €60.20. MC/V.) Take a break from meaty German fare at ◙**Cassius-Garten ❷,** Maximilianstr. 28D, near the train station, which serves salad and whole-grain baked goods, all for €1.50 per 100g. (☎0228 65 24 29; www.cassiusgarten.de. Open M-Sa 8am-8pm.) *Schnüss* (€1), sold at newsstands, has club and concert listings. ◙**The Jazz Galerie,** Oxfordstr. 24, is mostly

jazz-less bar and disco popular with swanky youths. (☎0228 63 93 24. Cover €8.50; includes 2 drinks. Open Th from 9pm, F-Sa from 10pm. Cash only.)
    Trains head to Berlin (5hr., 4 per day, €87-100) and Cologne (30min., 4-5 per hr., €9-15). The **tourist office** is located at Windeckstr. 1, off Münsterpl.; follow Poststr. from the station. (☎0228 77 50 00; www.bonn.de. Open M-F 9am-6:30pm, Sa 9am-4pm, Su 10am-2pm.) The **post office** is at Münsterpl. 17. (Open M-F 9am-8pm, Sa 9am-4pm.) **Postal Code:** 53111.

KASSEL   ☎0561

Kassel's (pop. 198,000) park, the 🁢**Wilhelmshöhe,** is famed throughout Germany. To reach it, take tram #1 from Banhof Wilhelmshöhe (dir.: Wilhelmshöhe) to the last stop. Inside, **Schloß Wilhelmshöhe** is a dressed-down version of the Residenz in Würzburg; the palace houses art from the classical era to the 1700s. (☎0561 31 68 00. Open Tu-Su Mar.-Oct. 10am-5pm; Nov.-Feb. 10am-4pm. €6, students €2.) Wilhelm IX built **Schloß Löwenburg** in the 18th-century with stones deliberately missing so it would resemble a crumbling medieval castle—he was obsessed with the year 1495 and imagined himself a knight. (☎0561 31 68 02 44. Open Tu-Su Mar.-Oct. 10am-5pm; Nov.-Feb. 10am-4pm; Dec. 10am-4pm. Required tours 1 per hr.; €4, students €2, under 18 free.) Park paths lead to the statue of **Herkules** (Hercules), Kassel's emblem. A viewing pedestal provides stunning views of the park. (Pedestal open mid-Mar. to mid-Nov. Tu-Su 10am-5pm. €3, students €2.) To the east lies the city itself, whose historic sights were destroyed in WWII. The **Brüder-Grimm-Museum,** Schöne Aussicht 2, displays a handwritten copy of The Brothers Grimm's *Children's and Household Tales.* (☎0561 787 2033; www.grimms.de. Open daily 10am-5pm. €1.50, students €1.)
    To reach the flower-filled **Jugendherberge und Bildungsstätte Kassel (HI) ❷,** Schenkendorfstr. 18, take streetcar #4 from the Wilhelmshöhe station to Querallee, then turn left on Querallee, which becomes Schenkendorfstr. (☎0561 77 64 55; www.djh-hessen.de/jh/kassel. Breakfast included. Internet €2 per hr., €15 per day. Reception 8am-11:30pm. Curfew 12:30am. Floor mattresses €15; dorms €20; singles €25; doubles €40. €3.10 HI discount. Cash only.) **Friedrich-Ebert-Straße,** the upper part of **Wilhelmshöher Allee,** and the area around **Königsplatz** have markets, takeout stands, and cafes scattered among clothing stores. 🁢**Limerick ❷,** Wilhelmshöher Allee 116, has a pan-European menu boasting 237 entrees and appetizers. The 25 beers on tap (€2-3) attract loyal crowds. (☎0561 77 66 49. Open M-Th 11am-1am, F-Sa 11am-2am, Su 11am-midnight. Cash only.)
    Most trains stop only at Bahnhof Wilhelmshöhe. From Bahnhof Wilhelmshöhe to: Berlin (3hr., 2 per hr., €78); Düsseldorf (3hr., 1 per 2hrs., €44-80); Frankfurt (2hr., 3-4 per hr., €35-45); Hamburg (2hr., 3 per hr., €65); Munich (4hr., 2-3 per hr., €89). The **tourist offices** has two locations, one in the Bahnhof Wilhelmshöhe and the another in the Rathaus. (☎0561 70 77 07; www.kassel-tourist.de. Both are open M-Sa 9am-6pm.) **Postal Code:** 34117.

FRANKFURT AM MAIN   ☎069

International offices, shiny skyscrapers, and expensive cars can be found at every intersection in Frankfurt (pop. 660,000), best known as the home of the EU's Central Bank and a major international airport. Don't let Frankfurt's reputation as a transportation center fool you—from shopping to museums to great nightlife, there's always something to see and do in this international city.

TRANSPORTATION

Flights: The largest and busiest airport in Germany, Frankfurt's **Flughafen Rhein-Main (FRA; ☎01805 37 24 36)** is connected to the *Hauptbahnhof* by S-Bahn trains S8 and 9 (2-3 per hr.) Buy tickets (€3.60) from the green machines marked "Fahrkarten" before boarding. Taxis to the city center cost around €20.

Trains: Trains run from the **Hauptbahnhof** to: **Amsterdam, NTH** (4hr., 1 per 2hr., €150); **Berlin** (4hr., 2 per hr., €90-105); **Cologne** (1hr., 1 per hr., €38-60); **Hamburg** (3-5hr., 2 per hr., €78-98); **Munich** (3hr., 1 per hr., €64-81). For schedules, reservations, and info call ☎01805 19 41 95; www.bahn.de. Note: there is no English help option.

Public Transportation: Frankfurt's public transportation system runs daily 4am-1:30am. Single-ride tickets (€2.20; reduced fares available) are valid for 1hr. in 1 direction. **Eurail** is valid only on S-Bahn trains. The **Tageskarte** (day pass; €5.60) provides unlimited transportation on the S-Bahn, U-Bahn, streetcars, and buses, and can be purchased from machines in any station. S-Bahn trains leave the *Hauptbahnhof* from the lower level; U-Bahn trains are reached through the shopping passage (*Einkaufspassage*).

Taxis: ☎23 00 01, ☎23 00 33, or ☎25 00 01. From €1.40 per km.

Bike Rental: Deutsche Bahn (DB) runs the citywide service **Call a Bike** (☎0700 05 22 55 22; www.callabike.de). Bikes marked with the red DB logo can be found throughout the city for your immediate rental. To do so, call the service hotline or go online and set up an account. (€0.10 per min., €15 per day.)

ORIENTATION AND PRACTICAL INFORMATION

Frankfurt's *Hauptbahnhof* opens onto the city's red-light district; from the station, the *Altstadt* is a 20min. walk down Kaiserstr. or Münchenerstr. The tourist heavy **Römerberg** square is just north of the Main River, while most commercial stores lie farther north along **Zeil**, the city's commercial center. Cafes and services cluster near the university in **Bockenheim** (U6 or 7 to Bockenheimer Warte). Across the river, the **Sachsenhausen** area draws pub-crawlers and museum-goers (take U1, 2, or 3 to Schweizer Pl.).

Tourist Office: in the *Hauptbahnhof* (☎21 23 88 00; www.frankfurt-tourismus.de). Book rooms for a €3 fee or for free if you call ahead. Sells the **Frankfurt Card** (1-day €8, 2-day €12), which allows unlimited use of public transportation and provides discounts on many sights. Open M-F 8am-9pm, Sa-Su and holidays 9am-6pm. Branch in **Römerberg** square (open M-F 9:30am-5:30pm, Sa-Su 10am-4pm).

Currency Exchange: Cheaper exchange rates can be found outside the train station. Try **Deutsche Bank,** across the street. (Open M-F 9am-1pm, 2-5pm.)

Laundromat: SB Waschsalon, Wallstr. 8, near Haus der Jugend in Sachsenhausen. Wash €3.50 for a small machine (6 kg) or €5 for a large machine (12 kg). Dry €0.50 per 15min. Soap €0.50. Open M-Sa 6am-11pm.

Internet: In the basement of the train station. €2.50 per hr. Open M-Sa 8:30am-1am. Internet cafes are on Kaiserstr., across from the *Hauptbahnhof.*

Post Office: Goethe Pl. 7. Walk 10min. down Taunusstr. from the *Hauptbahnhof,* or take the U- or S-Bahn to Hauptwache and walk south to the square. Open M-F 7am-8pm, Sa 8am-2pm. **Postal Code:** 60313.

ACCOMMODATIONS AND CAMPING

Deals are rare and trade fairs make rooms scarce in Frankfurt; reserve several weeks ahead. The **Westend/University** area has a few cheap options.

Stay & Learn Hostel/Frankfurt Hostel, Kaiserstr. 74 (☎069 247 5130; www.frankfurt-hostel.com). Convenient, sociable hostel organizes free city tours and holds free bi-weekly dinners. 24-hr reception located on the 4th fl. Luggage storage included. Free breakfast. €2 beers at the bar. Internet €1 per hr. Free Wi-Fi. Dorms €17-20; singles €50; doubles €60; triples €66. Higher rates during trade fairs. MC/V. ❷

Haus der Jugend (HI), Deutschherrnufer 12 (☎069 610 0150; www.jugendherberge-frankfurt.de). Take bus #46 (dir.: Mühlberg) from the station to Frankensteiner Pl., or take tram #16 (dir.: Offenbach Stadtgrenze) to *Lokalbahnhof*. Great location along the Main and in front of Sachsenhausen's pubs and cafes. Breakfast and linens included. Check-in 1pm, check-out 9:30am; curfew 2am. Dorms from €21.50; under 27 from €17; singles €39-43; doubles €56-76. HI discount €3.10. MC/V. ❷

City Camp Frankfurt, An der Sandelmühle 35B (☎069 57 03 32; www.city-camp-frankfurt.de). An inexpensive option for all types of travelers. U1-3: Heddernheim. Take a left at the Kleingartnerverein sign and continue until you reach the Sandel-mühle sign. Cross the stream, turn left, and follow signs to the campground. Reception M-F 9am-1pm, 4-8pm; Sa-Su 10am-1pm, 5-8pm. Campsites €6 per person, €2.50 per child under 14; €3.50 per tent. Showers €1 per 4min. Cash only. ❶

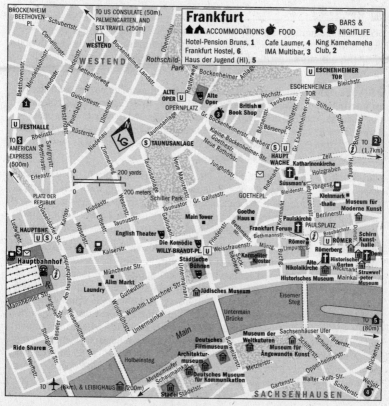

FOOD

The most reasonably priced meals can be found in **Sachsenhausen** or near the university in **Bockenheim. Kleinmarkthalle,** on Haseng. between Berlinerstr. and Töngesg., is a three-story warehouse with bakeries, butchers, fruits, nuts, cheese, and vegetable stands. (Open M-F 8am-6pm, Sa 8am-4pm.)

- **Cafe Laumer,** Bockenheimer Landstr. 67 (☎069 72 79 12). U6 or U7 to "Westend." Dine like a local on the outdoor patio or in the backyard garden of this celebrated cafe in the Westend, only blocks from the Uni. Enjoy the special of the day (€6.70) or drink coffee (€2.20). Open M-F 8am-7pm, Sa 8:30am-7pm, Su 9:30am-7pm. AmEx/V/MC. ❷

- **Adolf Wagner,** Schweizer Str. 71 (☎069 61 25 65). Saucy German dishes (€5-17) and some of the region's most renowned *Äpfelwein* (€1.40 per 0.3L) keep the patrons of this famous corner of Sachsenhausen jolly. Open daily 11am-midnight. Cash only. ❸

- **IMA Multibar,** Klein Bockenheimer Str. 14 (☎069 90 02 56 65). This fast-paced and hip bar/cafe combo, on the back streets (off Zeil), offers hungry patrons delicious smoothies (€3.50) and wraps (€4-7.30) by day, and a great selection of beer, wine, and cocktails by night. Drinks from €7. MC/V. ❷

SIGHTS

Beneath the daunting skyscrapers that define the Frankfurt landscape are several historic sights, all of which have undergone some degree of reconstruction since the old city's destruction in 1944. The **Museumsufer** along the southern bank of the Main includes some of the city's most vital cultural institutions.

STÄDEL. The *Städel's* impressive collection comprises seven centuries of art and includes notable works by Old Masters, Impressionists, and Modernists. **Holbein's,** the first floor cafe, is a widely celebrated destination for visitors. *(Schaumainkai 63, between Dürerstr. and Holbeinstr. ☎605 0980; www.staedelmuseum.de. Open Tu and F-Su 10am-6pm, W-Th 10am-9pm. €10, students €8, under 12 and last Sa of each month free. English-language audio tour €4, students €3.)*

MUSEUM FÜR MODERNE KUNST. The modern architecture of this triangular "slice of cake" building complements the art within. This museum houses a permanent collection of European and American art from the 1960s to the present and stages large-scale temporary exhibitions. *(Domstr. 10. ☎21 23 04 47; www.mmk-frankfurt.de. Open Tu and Th-Su 10am-5pm, W 10am-8pm. €7, students €3.50.)*

RÖMERBERG. This plaza, at the heart of Frankfurt's *Altstadt,* is surrounded on all four sides by tons of things to see and do. With its picturesque **Fachwerkhaeuser** (half-timbered houses) and daunting **Statue of Justice** fountain at the center of the square, the Römerberg is justifiably the most heavily-touristed spot in Frankfurt. Across from the Römerberg, **Paulskirche** (St. Paul's Church), the birthplace of Germany's 19th-century attempt at constitutional government, now memorializes the trials of German democracy with an acclaimed mural. At the west end of the Römerberg, the gables of **Römer** have marked the site of Frankfurt's city hall since 1405. *(St. Paul's Church: ☎21 23 85 26. Open daily 10am-5pm. Free. Römer enter from Limpurgerg. Open daily 10am-1pm and 2-5pm. €2. Gothic Dom: church open M-Th and Sa-Su 9am-noon and 2:30-6pm. Museum open Tu-F 10am-5pm and Sa-Su 11am-5pm. Church free. Museum €2, students €1.)*

NIGHTLIFE

Though Frankfurt lacks a centralized nightlife scene, a number of techno clubs lie between **Zeil** and **Bleichstraße**. Wait until midnight or 1am for things to really heat up. Visit www.nachtleben.de for more info on Frankfurt's clubs. For drinks, head to the cobblestone streets of the **Sachsenhausen** district, between Brückenstr. and Dreieichstr., where there are rowdy pubs and beer gardens serving specialty *Aepfelwein*.

> **Odeon,** Seilerstr. 34 (☎069 28 50 55). The party changes daily, with M night hip-hop, and Th-Sa house music. F 27+, Sa Wild Card. M and Th-F drinks half-price until midnight. Cover from €5, students €3 on Th only. Open M-Sa from 10pm. Cash only.
>
> **King Kamehameha Club,** Hanauer Landstr. 192 (☎069 48 00 370; www.king-kamehameha.de). Take the U6 to "Ostbahnhof" and walk down Hanauer Landstr. With intricate timber rafters, exposed brick, and a raging dance floor. Partygoers drink vodka and Red Bull (€8). Open Th-Sa from 10pm. Cover from €10. Cash only.

SOUTHWESTERN GERMANY

The Rhine and Mosel River Valleys are filled with much to be seen and drunk. Along river banks, medieval castles loom over vineyards. Farther south, modern cities fade slowly into the beautiful hinterlands of the Black Forest.

RHINE VALLEY (RHEINTAL)

The Rhine River carves its way through an 80km stretch of the Rhine Valley and flows north all the way from Mainz to Bonn. According to German folklore, this region of medieval castles and jagged cliffs is enchanted. Magical or not, it's certainly one of Germany's most stunning regions.

⌐ TRANSPORTATION

Two different **train** lines traverse the Rhine Valley, one on each bank; the line on the western side stays closer to the water and has better views. It's often tricky to switch banks, as train and ferry schedules don't always match up. A train crosses the river from Mainz to Wiesbaden. **Boats** are the best way to see the sights; the Köln-Düsseldorfer (KD) Line and Bingen Rüdesheim Line cover the Mainz-Koblenz stretch three to four times per day in summer (€20-40).

MAINZ ☎06131

The capital of Rheinland-Pfalz, and the proud birthplace of Johannes Gutenberg, Mainz is a small but lively city at the southern end of the Rheintal. Mainz was once the most powerful Catholic diocese in the world north of the Alps, and the **Martinsdom**, a colossal sandstone 10th-century cathedral, still stands as a relic of this legacy. (☎06131 25 34 12. Open Mar.-Oct. M-F 9am-6:30pm, Sa 9am-4pm, Su 1-2:45pm and 4-6:30pm; Nov.-Feb. M-F 9am-5pm, Sa 9am-4pm, Su 12:45-3pm and 4-5pm. Free.) On a hill south of the *Dom*, the Gothic **Stephanskirche** on Stephansberg is inlaid with stunning stained-glass windows by Russian exile Marc Chagall. (Open M-F 10am-noon and 2-5pm, Sa 2-5pm. Free.) The advent of movable type in 1455 is immortalized at the **Gutenberg Museum,** Liebfrauenpl. 5, across from the *Dom*, which has a replica of Gutenberg's original press. (Open Tu-Sa 9am-5pm, Su 11am-3pm. €5, students €3.)

To reach the plain but comfortable rooms and the surprisingly lively downstairs bistro of the **Jugendgästehaus (HI) ❷**, Otto-Brunfels-Schneise 4, take bus #62 (dir.: Weisenau) or 63 (dir.: Laubenheim) to Viktorstift/Jugendherberge, and follow the signs. (☎06131 853 32; www.diejugendherbergen.de. Breakfast included. Reception 7:30am-9:30pm. 4- to 6-bed dorms €18.40; singles and doubles add €10/5. MC/V.) Tucked along a tiny back street between the *Dom* and the Rhein, the **Weinstube Rote Kopf ❶**, Rotekopfg. 4, serves locally-produced wines and traditional regional dishes. The comfortable, welcoming ambiance comes at the right price; main dishes are €4.80 and up. (☎06131 23 10 13; www.rotekopf.de. Open M-Sa 11:30am-midnight.)

Trains run to Cologne (1hr., 2-3 per hr., €34-61); Frankfurt (40min., 4 per hr., €10-15); Hamburg (6hr., 1 per hr., €87-103); Koblenz (1hr., 3-5 per hr., €16.10-19.50). **KD ferries** (☎06131 23 28 00; www.k-d.com) depart from the wharfs on the other side of the *Rathaus* (City Hall). The **tourist office**, in Brückenturm by the river in the *Altstadt*, conducts English-language tours. From the station, walk straight down Schottstr., turn right onto Kaiserstr., and continue straight for 10min. until you reach Ludwigstr.; turn left and follow the green signs beginning at the cathedral. (☎06131 28 62 10; www.info-mainz.de/tourist. Open M-F 9am-6pm, Sa 10:30am-2pm. 2hr. English-language tours May-Oct. W and F-Sa 2pm; Nov.-Apr. Sa 2pm. €5.) **Postal Code:** 55001.

HEIDELBERG   ☎06221

With its picturesque setting along the Neckar River and its crumbling castle looming high above the town, Heidelberg (pop. 142,000) has long been one of Germany's top tourist attractions. Today, legions of visitors fill the length of *Hauptstraß*. Fortunately, Heidelberg remains home to a large and prestigious university, which enables it to keep its youthful charm.

🖪🎯 TRANSPORTATION AND PRACTICAL INFORMATION. Trains run to Frankfurt (1hr., 1-2 per hr., €14-24), Hamburg (7hr., 1 per hr., €87-101), and Stuttgart (1hr., 1-2 per hr., €18-33). Within Heidelberg, single-ride **bus** tickets cost €2.10; day passes (€5) are available on board. **Rhein-Neckar-Fahrgastschifffahrt** (☎06221 201 81; www.rnf-schifffahrt.de), in front of the *Kongresshaus*, runs **ferries** all over Germany and cruises up the Neckar to Neckarsteinach (3hr. round-trip, Easter-late Oct. 1 per hr., €10.50). Rent **bikes** at **Eldorado,** Neckarstaden 52, near the Alte Brücke. Take bus #41 or 42 from the *Hauptbahnhof* to Marstallstraße and continue for 100m. (☎06221 654 4460; www.eldorado-hd.de. Open Tu-F 9am-noon and 2-6pm, Sa 10am-6pm, Su 2-6pm. €5 per hr., €15 per day.)

Heidelberg's attractions lie mostly in the eastern part of the city, along the south bank of the Neckar. From the train station, take any bus or streetcar to Bismarckpl., then walk east down **Hauptstraße,** the city's main thoroughfare, to the *Altstadt*. The **tourist office,** in front of the station, books room for a €3 fee. (☎06221 138 8121. Open Apr.-Oct. M-Sa 9am-7pm, Su 10am-6pm; Nov.-Mar. M-Sa 9am-6pm.) The office sells the **Heidelberg Card,** which includes admission to many major sights. (1-day card €10, 2-day €14, 4-day €20.) The **post office** is at Sofienstr. 8-10. (Open M-F 9:30am-6pm, Sa 9:30am-1pm.) **Postal Code:** 69115.

🖪🎯 ACCOMMODATIONS AND FOOD. 🔊Sudpfanne Hostel ❶, Haputstr. 223, offers the only cheap, dorm-style accommodations (from €20 per night) in the heart of town. Take bus #33 (dir.: Köpfel) from the *Hauptbahnhof* to "Nekcarmünzpl." (☎06221 163 636; www.heidelberger-sudpfanne.de. Check-in 3pm-midnight. Check-out noon. Free Internet. Cash only.) To get to the **Jugendherberge (HI) ❷**, Tiergartenstr. 5, take bus #32 from the *Hauptbahnhof* to Chirurgische Klinik, then take bus #31 to Jugendherberge. Next to one of Europe's largest zoos, this hostel also teems with wild species, including *Schoolchildus germanus*, and features a discotheque in its basement. (☎65 11 90. Breakfast included. Reception until 2am. Reserve ahead. Dorms €24, under 27 €21; singles €29; doubles €34. MC/V.)

Historic student pubs outside the center have great dining options for hungry budget travelers. **T Falafel ❶**, Heug. 1., (☎06221 216 10 303) serves up delicious, piping hot Lebanese food from a small, hidden storefront in a side street off Hauptstr. Head to **Merlin ❷**, Bergheimer Str. 85, for calm cafe ambiance and a sorcery-themed breakfast for €4-10. (☎06221 65 78 56. Open M-Th and Su 10am-1am, F-Sa 10am-3:30am. AmEx/MC/V.)

◪ SIGHTS. Every summer, droves of tourists lay siege to the **◪Heidelberg Castle.** The 14th-century castle has been destroyed twice by war (1622 and 1693) and once by lightning (1764), leaving it with a unique, battered beauty and a layered architectural history. The cool, musty wine cellar houses the **Großes Faß** (with a 221,726L capacity, it is the largest wine barrel ever used). The castle **gardens** offer great views of the city below; trek up at night to enjoy the city's lights. (☎06221 53 84 21. Grounds open daily 8am-6pm; last entry 5:30pm. English-language audio tour €3.50. English-language tours every hr. M-F 11:15am-4:15pm, Sa-Su 10:15am-4:15pm; €4, students €2. Schloß, Großes Faß, and Pharmaceutical Museum €3, students €1.50.) Reach the castle by the uphill path (10min.) from the Kornmarkt or by the **Bergbahn,** one of Germany's oldest cable cars. (Take bus #33, dir.: Köpfel, to Rathaus/Bergbahn. Cable cars leave from the parking lot next to the bus stop daily Mar.-Oct. every 10min. 9am-8pm; Nov.-Feb. every 20 min. 9am-6pm. Round-trip €5.)

Heidelberg is also home to Germany's oldest (est. 1386) and most prestigious university. Over 20 Nobel laureates have been part of the faculty. Housed in the same building as the Museum der Universität Heidelberg is the **Alte Aula,** the school's oldest and most beautiful auditorium. *(Grabeng. 1. ☎06221 54 21 52.)* Before 1914, students were exempt from trials by civil authorities due to a code of academic freedom, so the faculty tried crimes from plagiarism to pig-chasing. View the irreverent, colorful graffiti of guilty students in the **◪Studentkarzer** jail. (Augustinerg. 2. ☎06221 54 35 54. Museum, auditorium, and jail open Apr.-Sept. Tu-Su 10am-6pm; Oct.-Mar. Tu-Sa 10am-4pm. €3, students €2.50.)

On the opposite side of the Neckar from the *Altstadt,* the steep **Philosophenweg** (Philosopher's Path), where famed thinkers Johann Wolfgang von Goethe, Ludwig Feuerbach, and Ernst Jünger once strolled, offers unbeatable views of the city. Follow signs to the top of **Heiligenberg** (Holy Mountain), where you'll find the ruins of the 9th-century **St. Michael Basilika,** the 11th-century **Stefanskloster,** and **Thingstätte,** an amphitheater built by the Nazis using forced labor, on the site of an ancient Celtic gathering place. (To get to the path, use the steep, stone-walled footpath 10m west of the Karl-Theodor-Brücke.) At the center of the **Altstadt** is the cobblestoned **Marktplatz,** where alleged witches and heretics were burned at the stake in the 15th century. Two of Heidelberg's oldest structures border the square. East of the Marktplatz, the **Kornmarkt** offers great views of the castle above and a beautiful central fountain. The twin domes of the **Brückentor** tower over the 18th-century Alte Brücke.

▨▨ FESTIVALS AND NIGHTLIFE. A favorite event for both tourists and residents, the **Schlossbeleuchtung** (castle lighting) occurs annually on the first Saturday in June, the second Saturday in July, and the first Saturday in September. The

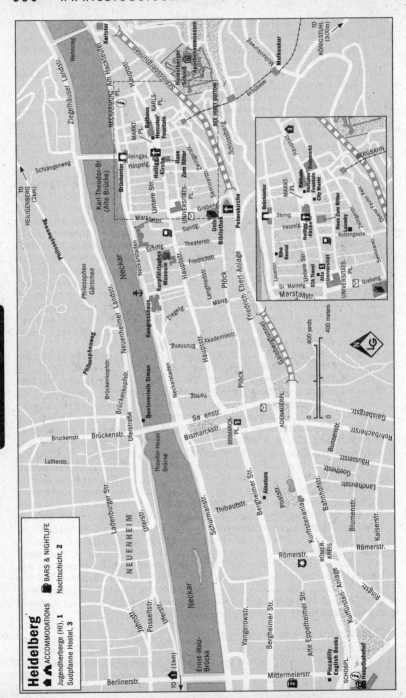

GERMANY

NEUENHEIM

Heidelberg

▲ ACCOMMODATIONS
Jugendherberge (HI), **1**
Sudpfanne Hostel, **3**

🍷 BARS & NIGHTLIFE
Nachtschicht, **2**

ceremony begins after nightfall with the "burning" of the castle; meanwhile, fireworks are set off over the *Altstadt* from the Alte Brücke. Head to Neuenheim or the Philosophenweg for the best views.

Popular nightspots fan out from the Marktpl. On the Neckar side of the Heiliggeistkirche, **⬛Untere Straße** has the most expansive collection of bars in the city, and revelers fill the narrow way until 1 or 2am. **Steingasse,** off the Marktpl. toward the Neckar, is also lined with bars attracting excited late-night crowds. At **Nachtschicht,** in the Land-fried-Komplex near the train station, university students dance in an old warehouse-turned-nightclub. (☎06221 43 85 50; www.nachtschicht.com. Cover €8; M and F students €3.50. Open W 10pm-3am, Th-F 10pm-4am, Sa 10pm-5am. Cash only.)

STUTTGART ☎0711

Daimler-Benz, Porsche, and a host of other corporate thoroughbreds keep Stuttgart (pop. 591,000) speeding along in the fast lane. In the heart of the Stuttgart lies the **Schloßplatz,** a 19th-century grassy square framed by an ornate palace and graced by the "Jubilee Column." Because almost 20% of Stuttgart is under a land preservation order, the city is known for its urban green spaces, the crown jewel of which is the palatial **Schloßgarten..** At the northern end of the gardens is Rosenstein-park, home to the **⬛Wilhelma,** a must-see for every visitor to Stuttgart. The Wilhelma is a zoo, with over 8000 different animals, and botanical garden, boasting over 6000 species of plants, housed in the ornate buildings and manicured gardens that were built by King Wilhelm as a summer retreat. Take U14 (dir.: Remseck) to "Wilhelma." (☎0711 540 20; www.wilhelma.de. Open daily 8:15am-dusk. €11.40, after 4pm and Nov-Feb. €8; ages 6-17 €5.70/4.) The superb **⬛Staatsgalerie Stuttgart,** Konrad-Adenauer-Str. 30-32, displays Dalí, Kandinsky, and Picasso in its new wing, as well as paintings from the Middle Ages to the 19th century in its old wing. (☎0711 47 04 00; www.staatsgalerie.de. Open Tu-W and F-Su 10am-6pm, Th 10am-9pm. €4.50, students €3; special exhibits add at least €2, W free.) The sleek, modern **Mercedes-Benz Museum,** Mercedesstr. 100, is a must for car-lovers. Take S1 (dir.: Plochingen) to Gottlieb-Daimler-Stadion and follow the signs. (☎0711 173 0000; www.mercedes-benz.com/museum. Open Tu-Su 9am-6pm. €8, students €4.) Stuttgart's club scene doesn't pick up until after midnight, but when it does, **Eberhardstraße, Rotebühlplatz,** and **Theodor-Heuss-Straße** are the most popular areas. **Bravo Charlie,**

LOCAL LEGEND

TREASURE AND TRYSTS

If the *Nibelungenlied* (Song of the Nibelungs) can be trusted, budget-strained backpackers in Southwestern Germany need look no farther than the nearby Rhein to replenish their supply of cash: the medieval epic claims that the greatest treasure ever known is still buried beneath the river.

According to the legend, Worms, a town near Heidelberg, was home to the Burgundian princess Kriemhild and her older brother Günther. Several versions of the narrative exist, but most agree that Siegfried, slayer of the ⬛dragon Fafnir and owner of the *Nibelungenschatz* (a treasure of unsurpassed worth), set out to court Kriemhild after hearing of her unsurpassed beauty. Günther consented to the marriage only after Siegfried helped him beguile Brünhild, the Queen of Iceland.

Much later, when the two men, along with their wives, reunited, Brünhild learned that it was Siegfried, not Günther, who bested her in combat and won her hand. Afraid that his deception would become public knowledge, Günther had Siegfried assassinated. The *Nibelungenschatz* was thrown into the Rhein outside of Worms, and both Gunther and Kriemhild perished in subsequent attempts to recover it. The Nibelung story was later made famous in Wagner's *"Ring" cycle*, and also influenced Tolkien's The Lord of the Rings.

Lautenschlagerstr. 14, is a hip cafe and restaurant by day and Stuttgart's most popular bar and nightclub after dark. (☎0711 23 16 882, www.bravo-charlie. de. Open M 8:30am-1am, Tu-W 8:30am-2am, Th 8:30am-3am, F 8:30am-5am, Sa 10am-5am, Su noon-1am.) The monthly magazine *Schwulst* (www.schwulst. de) has info on **gay and lesbian nightlife.**

The comfortable **Jugendgästehaus Stuttgart (IB) ❶**, Richard-Wagner-Str. 2, is one of the most affordable places to stay in town. Take the U15 to "Bubenbad". Delicious breakfast buffet and sheets included. (☎0711 24 11 32; jgh-stuttgart@ internationaler-bund.de. Dinner M-Th €7. Laundry facilities €1.50. Key deposit. Reception 24hr. Dorms €16.50; singles €21.50; doubles €19 per person. Bath add €5. 1-night stays add €2.50. Show your ▨*Let's Go* for a 10% discount. AmEx/ MC/V.) International clientele crash in hip rooms with funky wall paintings at **Alex 30 Hostel ❶**, Alexanderstr. 30. Take tram #15 (dir.: Ruhbank) to Olgaeck. (☎0711 838 8950; www.alex30-hostel.de. Breakfast €6. Linens €3. Dorms €22; singles €34; doubles €54, with shower €64. MC/V.) Look for mid-range restaurants in the pedestrian zone between Pfarrstr. and Charlottenstr. **San's Sandwich Bar ❶**, Eberhardstr. 47, serves sandwiches (€2.70-3.50) with plenty of vegetarian options and baked goodies. (☎0711 410 1118; www.sans-stuttgart.de. Open M-F 8:30am-10pm, Sa 10am-7pm. Cash only.)

Trains run to Berlin (6hr., 2 per hr., €122); Frankfurt (1-2hr., 2 per hr., €38-55); Munich (2-3hr., 2 per hr., €34-50); Paris, FRA (8hr., 4 per day, €95-111). **Tourist office,** Königstr. 1A, is across from the train station. (☎0711 222 80. Open M-F 9am-8pm, Sa 9am-6pm, Su 11am-6pm.) The **post office,** Arnulf-Klett-Pl. 2, is in the station. (Open M-F 8:30am-6pm, Sa 8:30am-12:30pm.) **Postal Code:** 70173.

BLACK FOREST (SCHWARZWALD)

Nestled in the southwest corner of Baden-Württemberg, with France to the west and Switzerland to the south, is the mysterious *Schwarzwald* (Black Forest), a web of small towns tucked between tree-covered hills. The eerie darkness of the Black Forest has inspired a host of German fairy tales, most notably Hansel and Gretel. Today, the trees lure hikers and skiers with their grim beauty. The gateway into the forest, tucked into its western edge, lies **Freiburg** (pop. 210,000) known for its ▨**Münster**, a 13th- to 16th-century stone cathedral. (☎0761 298 5963. Open M-Sa 9:30am-5pm, Su 1-5pm. Tours M-F 2-3pm, Sa-Su 2:30-3:30pm. Tower €1.50, students €1.) Tourists flock in summer to the tiny village of **Triberg** (pop. 5000) to see the world's largest **cuckoo clocks** or hike around the breathtaking **Gutacher Wasserfall,** a series of cascades tumbling 163m down moss-covered rocks that attracts a half-million visitors each year. (Park open 24hr.; admission 9am-7pm. €2.50, under 18 €2. Free for anyone spending the night in town–be sure to get your *Gästekarte* when you check in.)

CONSTANCE (KONSTANZ)   ☎07531

Situated between the **Bodensee** (Lake Constance) and the **Rhein,** Constance is the last German town before the Swiss and Austrian borders. Often said to be in the "German Riviera," this elegant university town was spared from destruction in WWII thanks to its proximity to non-German neighbors. Today, the city's *Altstadt* and large waterfront promenades are some of Germany's most beautiful. The **Münster** (Cathedral) in the town center displays ancient religious relics and dark tunnels beneath its soaring 76m Gothic spire. (Open M-F 10am-5pm, Sa-Su 12:30-5:30pm.) Wander down **Rheinsteig,** along the Rhine **Seestraße,** or near the yacht harbor on the lake. Constance also has a number of public **beaches;** all are free and open from May to September. Take bus #5 to **Freibad Horn,** which is the largest (and most crowded) of the beaches with a nude sunbathing section enclosed by hedges.

Though technically in Switzerland, the █**Jugendherberge Kreuzlingen (HI) ❷**, Promenadenstr. 7, is only a 15-20 min. walk from downtown. With clean, comfortable rooms that overlook the lake, a stay there is worth the trek. From the train station, head to the harbor, turn right, and walk into Switzerland along Seestr. When the road curves under a bridge, take the gravel path that veers slightly to the right. Pass through the border checkpoint "Klein Venedig" until the road curves under the bridge. (from Germany ☎+41 71 688 26 63; from Switzerland ☎071 688 26 63), Breakfast included. Reception 8-10am and 5-9pm. Closed Dec.-Feb. €20 per person per room. AmEx/MC/V.) Fall asleep to the sound of lapping waves and RVs at **Campingplatz Brudehofer ❶**, Fohrenbühlweg 50. Take bus #1 to Staad and walk for 10min. keeping the lake to your left. The campground is on the waterfront. (☎07531 313 88; www.campingkonstanz.de. Showers €1. Reception closed 1-3pm. €4 per person, €2.30 per child, €3.80-5.80 per tent, €2.80 per car, €6-8 per RV, €0.50 per bike. Cash only.)

Trains run from Constance to most cities in southern Germany; access destinations in Switzerland by walking to the Kreuzlingen station. BSB **ferries** leave hourly for ports around the lake. You can purchase tickets on board or in the building behind the train station, Hafenstr. 6. (☎05731 364 0389; www. bsb-online.com. Open Apr.-Oct. M-Th 8am-noon and 1-4pm, F 8am-noon and 1-5pm.) The **tourist office,** Bahnhofspl. 13, to the right of the train station, can help you locate private rooms for a €2.50 fee. (☎07531 133 030; www.konstanz. de. Open Apr.-Oct. M-F 9am-6:30pm, Sa 9am-4pm, Su 10am-1pm; Nov.-Mar. M-F 9:30am-12:30pm and 2-6pm.) **Postal Code:** 78462.

BAVARIA (BAYERN)

Bavaria is the Germany of Teutonic myth and Wagnerian opera. From the Baroque cities along the Danube to mad King Ludwig's castles high in the Alps, the region attracts more tourists than any other part of the country.

MUNICH (MÜNCHEN) ☎089

Bavaria's capital and cultural center, Munich (pop. 1,245,000) is a sprawling, liberal metropolis where world-class museums, handsome parks, colossal architecture, and a genial population create a thriving city.

▅ TRANSPORTATION

Flights: Flughafen München (MUC; ☎089 97 52 13 13). **Buses** S1 and 8 run from the airport to the *Hauptbahnhof* and Marienpl. (40min., 3 per hr., €8.80 or 8 strips on the *Streifenkarte*). For all-day travel, buy a **Gesaskamtnetz** day pass that covers all zones (€10). The Lufthansa **shuttle bus** goes to the *Hauptbahnhof* (40min., 3 per hr., €10) but is slower and more expensive than taking the train.

Trains: Munich's **Hauptbahnhof** (☎118 61) is the hub of southern Germany with connections to: **Berlin** (6hr., 2 per hr., €110); **Cologne** (4½hr., 2 per hr., €122); **Frankfurt** (3hr., 2 per hr., €85); **Füssen** (2hr., 2 per hr., €20); **Hamburg** (6hr., 1 per hr., €115); **Amsterdam, NTH** (7-9hr., 17 per day, €140); **Budapest, HUN** (7-9hr., 8 per day, €98); **Copenhagen, DEN** (11-15hr., 8 per day, €156); **Paris, FRA** (8-10hr., 6 per day, €124-152); **Prague, CZR** (6-7hr., 4 per day, €55); **Rome, ITA** (10-11hr., 5 per day, €126); **Salzburg, AUT** (1-2hr., 1 per hr., €29); **Venice, ITA** (7-10hr., 6 per day, €92);

Vienna, AUT (4-6hr., 1-2 per hr., €73); **Zürich, SWI** (4-5hr., 4-5 per day, €70). The train goes through Austria, so make sure you've included Austria in the list of countries the pass covers if you have a Eurail pass—otherwise pay a small nominal fee (under €10) before you board the train. Purchase a **Bayern-Ticket** (€21, 2-5 people €29) for unlimited train transit daily 9am-3am in Bavaria and to Salzburg. **EurAide**, in the station, sells tickets. **Reisezentrum** ticket counters at the station are open daily 7am-9:30pm.

Ride Share: Mitfahrzentrale, Lämmerstr. 6 (☎089 194 40; www.mifaz.de/muenchen). Arranges intercity rides with drivers going the same way. See **Transportation**, p. 283.

Public Transportation: MVV (☎089 41 42 43 44; www.mvv-muenchen.de) operates **buses, trains,** the **S-Bahn** (underground trains), and the **U-Bahn** (subway). Most run M-Th 5am-12:30am, F-Sa 5am-2am. S-Bahn trains run until 2 or 3am daily. Night buses and trams ("N") serve Munich's dedicated clubbers. Eurail, Inter Rail, and German rail passes are valid on the S-Bahn but not on buses, trams, or the U-Bahn.

Tickets: Buy tickets at the blue vending machines and validate them in the blue boxes before entering the platform; otherwise, risk a €40 fine.

Prices: Single-ride tickets €2.20 (valid 2hr.). **Kurzstrecke** (short-trip) tickets €1.10 (1hr. or 2 stops on the U- or S-Bahn, 4 stops on a tram or bus). A **Streifenkarte** (10-strip ticket; €10.50) can be used by more than 1 person. Cancel 2 strips per person for a normal ride, or 1 strip for a short trip; for rides beyond the city center, cancel 2 strips per zone. A **Single-Tageskarte** (single-day ticket; €5) for *Innenraum* (the city's central zone) is valid until 6am the next day; the **partner** day pass (€9) is valid for up to 5 people. **3-day** single pass €13; 5-person pass €21. The **XXL Ticket** (single €6.70, partner €12) gives day-long transit in Munich's 2 innermost zones, white and green. Single **Gesamtnetz** (day ticket for all zones) €10; 5-person pass €18.

Taxis: Taxi-München-Zentrale (☎089 216 10 or 089 194 10).

Bike Rental: Mike's Bike Tours, Bräuhausstr. 10 (☎089 25 54 39 87; after hours ☎0172 852 0660). €12 per 1st day; €9 per day thereafter. 50% discount with tour (below). Open daily mid.-Apr. to mid-Oct. 10am-8pm; Mar. to mid-Apr. and mid-Oct. to mid-Nov. 10:30am-1pm and 4:30-5:30pm. **Radius Bikes** (☎089 59 61 13), in the *Hauptbahnhof,* behind the lockers opposite tracks 30-36. €3-4 per hr., €15-18 per day. €50 deposit. Open daily mid-Apr. to mid-Oct. 10am-6pm. 10% student discount.

ORIENTATION

Downtown Munich is split into quadrants by thoroughfares running east-west and north-south. These intersect at Munich's central square, **Marienplatz,** and link the traffic rings at **Karlsplatz** (called Stachus by locals) in the west, **Isartorplatz** in the east, **Odeonsplatz** in the north, and **Sendlinger Tor** in the south. In the east beyond the Isartor, the Isar River flows north-south. The *Hauptbahnhof* is beyond Karlspl., to the west of the ring. To get to Marienpl. from the station, take any eastbound S-Bahn or use the main exit and make a right on Bahnhofpl., a left on Bayerstr. heading east through Karlspl., and continue straight. The **university** is to the north amid the **Schwabing** district's budget restaurants; to the east of Schwabing is the **English Garden** and to the west, **Olympiapark.** South of downtown is the **Glockenbachviertel,** filled with nightlife hot spots and gay bars. Here, travelers can find many hostels and fast food options, although the area can be dimly lit at night. Oktoberfest takes place on the large, open **Theresienwiese,** southeast of the train station on the U4 and 5 lines.

PRACTICAL INFORMATION

The most comprehensive list of services, events, and museums can be found in the English-language monthly *Munich Found* for €3 at the tourist office.

Tourist Offices: Main office (☎089 23 39 65 55) on the front side of the *Hauptbahnhof,* next to Yorma's on Bahnhofpl. Books rooms for free with a 10-15% deposit,

Munich (München)

ACCOMMODATIONS
Euro Youth Hotel, 9
Jaegers, 8
Jugendherberge Pullach Burg
  Schwaneck (HI), 14
Jugendlager Kapuzinerhölzl
  (The Tent), 7
Wombat's, 3

FOOD
Buxs, 13
Café Ignaz, 4
Dean & David, 2
Mensa, 1
News Bar, 11
Poseidon, 21
Weisses Brauhaus, 12

BEER GARDENS
Augustinerkeller, 5
Hirschgarten, 6

BARS AND BEERHALLS
Bei Carla, 18
Café Am Hochhaus, 22
Café Selig, 15
Hofbräuhaus, 10
Sausalitos, 23
Trachtenvogl, 16
Zappeforster, 17

CLUBS
Atomic Cafe, 24
Kultfabrik, 19
Muffathalle, 20

GERMANY

and sells English-language city **maps** (€0.30). Open M-Sa 9am-6pm, Su 10am-6pm. **Branch office,** on Marienpl. at the entrance to the Neues Rathaus tower, is open M-F 10am-8pm, Sa 10am-4pm, Su noon-4pm, and accepts MC/V. **EurAide** (☎089 59 38 89), counter at the Reisezentrum in the *Hauptbahnhof*, books train tickets for free, English-language city tours, and explains public transportation. Open June-Sept. M-Sa 7:45am-noon and 2-6pm, Su 8am-noon; Oct.-May reduced hours.

Tours: ▨**Mike's Bike Tours,** Bräuhausstr. 10 (☎089 25 54 39 87; www.mikesbiketours. com). If you only have 1 day in Munich, take this tour. Starting from the Altes Rathaus on Marienpl., the 4hr., 6km city tour includes a *Biergärten* break. Tours leave daily mid-Apr. to Aug. 11:30am and 4pm; Sept. to mid-Nov. and Mar. to mid-Apr. 12:30pm. €24. Look for coupons on biking tours at youth hostels.

Consulates: Canada, Tal 29 (☎089 219 9570). Open M-F 9am-noon; 2-4pm by appointment only. **Ireland,** Dennigerstr. 15 (☎089 20 80 59 90). Open M-F 9am-noon. **UK,** Möhlstr. 5 (☎089 21 10 90). Open M-Th 8:30am-noon and 1-5pm, F 8:30am-noon and 1-3:30pm. **US,** Königinstr. 5 (☎089 288 80). Open M-F 1-4pm.

Currency Exchange: ReiseBank (☎089 551 0813), at the front of the *Hauptbahnhof*. Slightly cheaper than other banks. Open daily 7am-11pm.

Laundromat: SB Waschcenter, Lindwurmstr. 124. Wash €3.50, dry €0.60 per 10min. Detergent €0.30. Open daily 7am-11pm. A **branch** is located at Untersbergstr. 8 (U2, 7, or 8 to Untersbergstraße) provides free Wi-Fi.

Medical Emergency: ☎112 or 192 22.

Post Office: Bahnhofpl. In the yellow building opposite the Hauptbahnhof exit. Open M-F 7:30am-8pm, Sa 9am-4pm. **Postal Code:** 80335.

▮▮ ACCOMMODATIONS AND CAMPING

Lodgings in Munich tend to be either seedy, expensive, or booked solid. During mid-summer and Oktoberfest, book at least a week ahead or start calling before noon; rooms are hard to find and prices jump 10% or more.

▨ **Euro Youth Hotel,** Senefelderstr. 5 (☎089 59 90 88 11; www.euro-youth-hotel.de). Friendly, well-informed staff offers helpful info and spotless rooms. Fun and noisy travelers' bar serves *Augustinerbräu* (€2.90) daily 6pm-4am, lending this alpine lodge a frat-house atmosphere. Happy hour 6-9pm, beer €2. Breakfast €3.90. Free storage lockers (€10 deposit). Larger lockers available; locks €1.50 or bring your own. Laundry: wash €3, dry €1.50. Internet €1 per 30min. Free Wi-Fi. Reception and security 24hr. Large dorms €17.50; 3- to 5-person dorms €21.50; singles €35; doubles €60-70; quads €84. AmEx/MC/V. ❷

▨ **Wombat's,** Senefelderstr. 1 (☎089 59 98 91 80; www.wombats-hostels.com). Sleek, modern, and surprisingly sophisticated. Enjoy your free welcome drink in the ultra-cool glassed-in lounge with beanbags and lounge chairs. Swanky colored walls complement the large rooms, lending this relaxed hostel a cool, laid-back feel. Breakfast buffet €3.70. Laundry: wash €2, dry €2.50. Internet €0.50 per 20min. Free Wi-Fi. Reception 24hr. Dorms from €18; singles and doubles from €35 per person. MC/V. ❷

Jugendlager Kapuzinerhölzl (The Tent), In den Kirchen 30 (☎089 141 4300; www. the-tent.com). Tram #17 (dir.: Amalienburgstr.) to "Botanischer Garten" (15min.). Follow the signs on Franz-Schrank-Str. and turn left on In den Kirchen. Join 250 international "campers" under a gigantic tent in a series of bunk beds or on the wood floor. Join this alternative backpacking community at evening campfires. Organic breakfast €2. Free lockers. Wash €2.50, dry €2. Internet access €0.50 per 15min. Free city tours in German and English on W mornings. Free kitchen facilities. Passport or €25 required as deposit. Reception 24hr. Open June to mid-Oct. €7.50 gets you a foam pad, wool blankets, and shower facilities. Beds €10.50; camping €5.50 per site plus €5.50 per person. Cash only; MC/V if you book online. ❶

Campingplatz Thalkirchen, Zentralländstr. 49 (☎089 723 1707). U3 (dir.: Fürstenried West) to "Thalkirchen," change to bus #135, and get off at the "Campingplatz" (20min.). The surrounding woods and meandering paths give the site a rural feel. TV lounge and supermarket. Showers €1 per 6min. Laundry: wash €5, dry €0.50 per 10min. Reception open 7am-11pm. €4.70 per person, under 14 €1.50; €3-8 per tent; €4.50 per car. RVs €11.50 per person. Cash only. ❶

FOOD

For a typical Bavarian lunch, spread a *Brez'n* (pretzel) with *Leberwurst* (liverwurst) or cheese. Traditional *weißwürste* (white veal sausages) are a local specialty, but are only eaten before noon. Don't eat the skin; slice them open instead. *Leberknödel* are liver dumplings. Just south of Marienpl., vendors gather in the bustling **Viktualienmarkt** to sell flowers, meats, fresh veggies, and specialty dishes, but don't expect budget groceries. (Open M-F 10am-8pm, Sa 8am-4pm.) Off **Ludwigstraße,** the university district supplies students with inexpensive yet filling meals. Many reasonably priced restaurants and cafes cluster around **Schellingstraße, Amalienstraße,** and **Türkenstraße** (U3 or 6 to Universität).

▨ **Schelling Salon,** Schellingstr. 54 (☎089 272 0788), U3 or U6 to "Universität." Bavarian *Knödel* and billiards since 1872. Rack up at tables where Lenin, Rilke, and Hitler once played (€7 per hr.). A great spot to unwind with a beer and friends after a hectic week of drinking. Breakfast €3-5. German entrees €4-11. Open M and Th-Su 6:30am-1am. Cash only. ❸

▨ **Cafe Ignaz,** Georgenstr. 67 (☎089 27 16 093; www.ignaz-cafe.de). U2 to "Josephspl." Take Adelheidstr. 1 block north and turn right on Georgenstr. Have a heart-healthy dinner of anything from crepes to stir-fry dishes (€5-9) at this rockin' eco-friendly cafe, before diving into one of its many desserts. Breakfast buffet (€7) M and W-F 8-11:30am. Lunch buffet (€7.50) M-F noon-2pm. Brunch buffet (€9) Sa-Su 9am-1:30pm. Open M and W-F 8am-10pm, Tu 11am-11pm, Sa-Su 8am-11pm. AmEx/MC/V. ❷

Weißes Bräuhaus, Tal 7 (☎089 290 1380; www.weisses-brauhaus.de). Founded in 1490, this traditional restaurant cooks up dishes like the *Münchener Voressen* (€6.50) made of calf and pig lungs. Choose from 40-50 options on the daily menu (€3-17) served by waitresses in classic Bavarian garb. Open daily 8am-12:30am. MC/V. ❸

ON THE MENU

TAP THAT

Although droves of tourists visit Germany to guzzle its renowned beer, few understand the intricacies of German *Bierkultur*. Beer is typically served by the quart (*Maß*, ask for "*Ein Maß, bitte.*") and sometimes by the pint (Halb-Maß). A *Helles* is a pale, often Bavarian, lager. Those looking for a bitter, less malty beer with more alcohol order the foam-crowned *Pilsener*, and often search far and wide for the perfect head.

A *Radler* (Bikers' Brew) is a 50-50 blend of *Helles* and sparkling lemonade, so named because the inventor sought to mitigate the inebriation of the crazed cyclists passing through his pub. In the north, this same beverage is called an *Alster*, after the river. *Weißbier* is a cloudy, strong beer made with malted wheat (*Weizen*), while *Rauchbier* acquires its distinctive smoky taste from malted barley.

Even the toasted, malty lager, *Dunkeles*, is not the strongest beer. If you're in the mood for severe inebriation, try a *Bock* (strong beer) or a *Doppelbock* (even stronger). These beers are often brewed by monks because they are rich enough to sustain them through religious fasts. Piety has never looked so enticing.

There are over 1000 German breweries producing thousands more brands of German beer each year. With a liquor pool that big, you'll have more than enough opportunities to lift a glass and shout "*Prost!*"

SIGHTS

RESIDENZ. The richly decorated Residenz is the most visible presence of the Wittelsbach dynasty, whose state rooms now make up the **Residenzmuseum.** The luxurious apartments reflect the Renaissance, Baroque, Rococo, and Neoclassical styles. Also on display are collections of porcelain, gold and silverware, and a 17th-century court chapel. Highlights include the Rococo **Ahnengalerie,** hung with over 100 family portraits tracing the royal lineage, and the spectacular **Renaissance Antiquarium,** the oldest room in the palace, replete with stunning frescoes and statuary. *(Max-Joseph-Pl. 3. U3-6 to "Odeonspl." ☎089 29 06 71; www.residenz-muenchen.de. Open daily from Apr. to mid-Oct. 9am-6pm; from late Oct. to Mar. 10am-4pm. Last admission 30min. before closing. German-language tours meet outside the museum entrance Su at 11am. €6, students €5, under 18 free.)*

HOFGARTEN. Behind the Residenz, the beautifully landscaped Hofgarten shelters a small temple where couples gather on Sunday afternoons for free swing dancing. The **Schatzkammer** (treasury), which shares the same entrance as the Residenz, contains the most precious religious and secular symbols of Wittelsbach power: crowns, swords, crosses, and reliquaries collected during the Counter-Reformation to increase the dynasty's Catholic prestige. A comprehensive free audio tour of both the Schatzkammer and the Residenz is available in five languages. A collection of **Egyptian art** is also housed on the premises. *(Treasury open same hours as Residenzmuseum. €6; students, seniors, and group members €5; under 18 free. Combination ticket to Schatzkammer and Residenzmuseum €9, students and seniors €8. Art collection ☎089 28 92 76 30. Open Tu-F 9am-5pm, Sa-Su 10am-5pm. €5, students and seniors €4, under 18 free, Su €1.)*

ENGLISCHER GARTEN. Stretching majestically along the city's western border, the Englischer Garten (English Garden) is the largest metropolitan public park in the world, dwarfing both New York's Central Park and London's Hyde Park, offering everything from nude sunbathing and bustling beer gardens to pick-up soccer games and shaded bike paths. On sunny days, all of Munich turns out to fly kites, ride horses, and tan. Nude sunbathing areas are designated **FKK** (Frei Körper Kultur, or Free Body Culture) on signs and park maps. The main park ends with the **Kleinhesseloher See,** a large artificial lake, but the park extends much further and becomes ever more wild. If you look carefully you might see a roaming flock of sheep. There are several beer gardens on the grounds as well as a Japanese tea house, a Chinese pagoda, and a Greek temple. Daring Müncheners surf the white-water rapids of the Eisbach, the artificial river that flows through the park.

MARIENPLATZ. Sacred stone spires tower above the Marienpl., a major S- and U-Bahn junction and the social nexus of the city at the center of Munich's large pedestrian zone. The plaza, formerly known as Marktplatz, takes its name from the ornate 17th-century monument to the Virgin Mary at its center, the **Mariensäule,** which was built in 1638 and restored in 1970 to celebrate the city's near-miraculous survival of both the Swedish invasion and the plague. At the neo-Gothic **Neues Rathaus** (built in medieval style at the dawn of the 20th century), a **Glockenspiel** chimes with a display of a victorious Bavarian jouster. (Chimes daily 11am and noon; summer also 5pm.) At 9pm a mechanical watchman marches out and the Guardian Angel escorts the *Münchner Kindl* ("Munich Child," a symbol of the city) to bed. All of Munich's coats of arms are on the face of the **Altes Rathaus** tower, to the right of the Neues Rathaus, with the notable exception of the Nazi swastika-bearing shield. Hitler commemorated his failed 1923 Putsch in the ballroom, which is still in use for official functions. *(Tower open daily 10am-7pm. €2, under 18 €1, under 6 free.)*

🏛 MUSEUMS

Many of Munich's museums would require days to explore completely. All state-owned museums, including the three **Pinakotheken,** are €1 on Sunday.

🎨PINAKOTHEKEN. Designed by *Münchener* Stephan Braunfels, the beautiful **Pinakothek der Moderne** is four museums in one. Subgalleries display architecture, design, drawings, and paintings by artists ranging from Picasso to contemporary masters. *(Barerstr. 40. U2 to Königspl or tram #27 to Pinakotheken. ☎ 089 23 80 53 60. Open Tu-W and Sa-Su 10am-5pm, Th-F 10am-8pm. €9.50, students €6. Audio tour free.)* Commissioned in 1826 by King Ludwig I, the **Alte Pinakothek** houses 500 years of art, works by 19th- and 20th-century artists including works by Leonardo da Vinci, Rembrandt, and Rubens. *(Barerstr. 27. ☎ 089 23 80 52 16; www.alte-pinakothek.de. Open Tu 10am-8pm, W-Su 10am-6pm. €5.50, students €4.)* Next door, the **Neue Pinakothek** displays fascinating work of famous artists including Cézanne, Monet, and van Gogh. *(Barerstr. 29. ☎ 089 23 80 51 95; www.neue-pinakothek.de. Open M and Th-Su 10am-5pm, W 10am-8pm. €5.50, students €4; includes audio tour.)*

DEUTSCHES MUSEUM. The Deutsches Museum is one of the world's most comprehensive museums of science and technology. Exhibits include an early telephone, the work bench on which Otto Hahn first split an atom, and a recreated subterranean labyrinth of mining tunnels. The museum's 50+ departments cover over 17km. An English guidebook (€4) thoroughly explains all exhibits, though many signs have English translations. *(Museuminsel 1. S1-S8 to "Isartor" or tram #18 to "Deutsches Museum." ☎ 089 21 791; www.deutsches-museum.de. Open daily 9am-5pm. €8.50, students €3, under 6 free. Flight museum: Effnerstr. 18. ☎ 089 315 71 40. S-Bahn to "Oberschleißheim," then follow signs. Open daily 9am-5pm. €5, students and seniors €3. Transportation museum: Theresienhöhe 14a. ☎ 089 500 8067 62. U4-5 to "Schwanthalerhöhe." Open daily 9am-5pm. €5, students and seniors €3. Combined admission to flight, transportation, and science museums €17.)*

🎭 ENTERTAINMENT

Munich deserves its reputation as a world-class cultural center. Sixty theaters are scattered generously throughout the city staging productions that range from dramatic classics at the **Residenztheater** and **Volkstheater** to comic opera at the **Staatstheater am Gärtnerplatz** to experimental works at the **Theater im Marstall.** Munich's numerous fringe theaters, cabaret stages, and art cinemas in Schwabing reveal its bohemian spirit. *Monatsprogramm* (free) and *Munich Found* (free at the tourist office) list schedules for festivals, museums, and performances. In July, a magnificent **opera festival** arrives at the 🎭**Bayerische Staatsoper** (Bavarian National Opera), Max-Joseph-Pl. 2. *(☎ 089 21 85 01; www. bayerische.staatsoper.de. U3-6 to Odeonspl. or tram #19 to Nationaltheater.)* For €8-10, students can buy tickets for performances marked "Young Audience Program" two weeks in advance. Snag leftover tickets—if there are any—at the **evening box office,** Max-Joseph-Pl. 2, near the theater, for €10. *(Opens 1hr. before curtain.)* Standing-room tickets are half-price and can be purchased at any time. The **daytime box** office is at Marstallpl. 5. *(☎ 089 21 85 19 20. Open M-F 10am-6pm, Sa 10am-1pm. Performances Oct.-July.)*

🌙 NIGHTLIFE

Munich's nightlife is a mix of Bavarian *Gemütlichkeit* (coziness) and chic trendiness. A typical odyssey begins at a beer hall, which usually closes around midnight. Cafes and bars close their taps at 1am (later on weekends), while discos and dance clubs, sedate before midnight, throb until 4am. Trendsetters head to **Leopoldstraße** in **Schwabing** or **Glockenbachviertel**, near Gärnterpl. Many venues require partiers to dress up.

BEER HALLS AND GARDENS

Bavaria agreed to become a part of a larger Germany on one condition: that it be allowed to maintain its beer purity laws. Since then, Munich has remained loyal to six great labels: **Augustiner, Hacker-Pschorr, Hofbräu, Löwenbräu, Paulaner**, and **Spaten-Franziskaner**, which together provide Müncheners and tourists alike with all the fuel they need for late-night revelry. Four main types of beer are served in Munich: *Helles* (standard light beer with a crisp, sharp taste); *Dunkles* (dark beer with a heavier, fuller flavor); *Weißbier* (smooth, cloudy blond beer made from wheat instead of barley); and *Radler* or *Russ'n* ("shandy" or "cyclist's brew": half beer and half lemon soda with a light, fruity taste). Munich's beer is typically 5% alcohol, though in **Starkbierzeit** (the first two weeks of Lent), Müncheners traditionally drink *Starkbier*, a dark beer that is 8-10% alcohol. Daring travelers can go for a full liter of beer, known as a ▓**Maß** (€5-7). Specify if you want a *halb-Maß* (.5L, €3-4); Weißbier is almost exclusively served in 0.5L sizes. It's traditional to bring your own food to outdoor beer halls—drinks, however, must be bought at the *Biergarten*. Bare tables usually indicate cafeteria-style *Selbstbedienung* (self-service).

▓ **Augustiner Bräustuben**, Landsberger Str. 19 (☎089 50 70 47; www.augustiner-braustuben.de). S1-S8 to "Hackerbrücke." Walk to the far side of the bridge to Landsberger Str. and take a right. In the Augustiner brewery's former horse stalls. With a candlelit interior and some of the cheapest beer in the city (*Maß*; €5.10), this relatively undiscovered beer hall is the perfect place to share laughs over heaps of Bavarian food at great prices (€5-9) either inside or on the recently completed roof terrace. Devoted carnivores should try the *Bräustüberl* (duck, two cuts of pork, *Kraut*, and two types of dumplings; €10). Open daily 10am-midnight; kitchen open daily 11am-11pm. MC/V.

Hirschgarten, Hirschgarten 1 (☎089 17 999 119, www. hirschgarten.de). Tram #17 (dir.: Amalienburgstr.) to "Romanpl." Walk south to the end of Guntherstr. The largest *Biergarten* in Europe (seating 8000), tucked away in a small park just outside the city center, is boisterous and always crowded. Families come for the grassy park and carousel, and to see the deer still kept on the premises. Entrees €6-18. *Maß* €6. Open daily 9am-midnight; kitchen open until 10:30pm. MC/V.

K & K Klub, Reichenbachstr. 22 (☎089 20 20 74 63; www.kuk-club.de). U1-U2 to "Frauenhoferstr." Subdued walls, cube seats, and a large projection screen playing art films attract a young, artsy crowd. Sip a beer (€3.40) against the orange glow of the illuminated tribal symbols and retro video games (€0.50). Local DJs play electro, indie, and house M-Sa. Open M-W and Su 8pm-2am, Th-Sa 8pm-5am. Cash only.

Cafe Am Hochhaus, Blumenstr. 29 (☎089 058 152, www.cafeamhochhaus.de). U1-U3 or U6 to "Sendlinger Tor." Sometimes a dance party, sometimes a relaxed cafe with quirky wallpaper, the mood changes nightly with the crowd. Live DJs spin everything from funk to house starting at 10pm. Open daily 8pm-3am or even later. Cash only.

GLBT NIGHTLIFE

▓ **Morizz**, Klenzestr. 43 (☎089 201 6776). U1 or U2 to "Frauenhofer Str." Subdued ambient lighting and stylish decor create an intimate interior that attracts a mixed crowd.

Settle into the chic low chairs for a mixed drink (€7.60-8.50) and upscale Thai dishes (€6-15), served until 12:30am. Open M-Th and Su 7pm-2am, F-Sa 7pm-3am. MC/V.

🏳️ **Bau,** Müllerstr. 41 (☎089 26 92 08; www.bau-munich.de). U1 or U2 to "Fraunhoferstr." Broad rainbow stripes on the door and posters of leather-clad men on the walls suit the heavy-duty construction theme of this gay club and bar. No mixed drinks—only beer (€2.70) and liquor (€2.50). Drinks buy 1 get 1 free M 8-10pm; €1 shots every Th 8-10pm and 1-3am. Open daily 8pm-4am. AmEx/MC/V.

🎪 OKTOBERFEST

Every fall, hordes of tourists make an unholy pilgrimage to Munich to drink and be merry in true Bavarian style. From the penultimate Saturday of September through early October (Sept. 19-Oct. 4, 2009), beer consumption prevails. The numbers for this festival have become truly mind-boggling: participants chug five million liters of beer, but only on a full stomach of 200,000 *Würste*. What began in 1810 as a celebration of the wedding of Ludwig I has become the world's largest folk festival. Representatives from all over Bavaria met outside the city gates for a week of horse racing on fields they named **Theresienwiese** in honor of Ludwig's bride (U4 or U5 to Theresienwiese). The bash was such fun that Munich's citizens have repeated the revelry (minus the horses) ever since. An agricultural show, inaugurated in 1811, is still held every three years.

📷 DAYTRIPS FROM MUNICH

DACHAU. *Arbeit Macht Frei* (Work Will Set You Free) was the first message prisoners saw as they passed through the **Jourhaus** gate into Dachau, where over 206,000 "undesirables" were interned between 1933 and 1945. Dachau, the Third Reich's first concentration camp, was primarily a work rather than a death camp like Auschwitz; the SS reserved it for the construction of armaments knowing the Allies would not bomb prisoners of war. Restored in 1962, the crematorium, gates, and walls now form a **memorial** to the victims. *(Open Tu-Su 9am-5pm. Free.)* In former administrative buildings, the **museum** examines pre-1930s anti-Semitism, the rise of Nazism, the establishment of the concentration camp system, and the lives of prisoners. A short **English-language film** (22min., free) screens at 11:30am, 2, and 3:30pm. Displays in the barracks, the former prison and the torture chamber chronicle prisoners' lives and SS guards' barbarism. A 2hr. English-language **tour** covers the entire camp. *(May-Sept. Tu-F at 1:30pm, Sa-Su at noon and 1:30pm; Oct.-Apr. Th-Su at 1:30pm. €3.)* A brief **introduction** (30min.) gives a general overview of the complex. *(May-Sept. Tu-F 12:30pm, Sa-Su 11am and 12:30pm; Oct.-Apr. Th-Su 12:30pm. €1.50.)* Or, purchase the worthwhile audio tour (€3, students €2) for a self-directed tour of the camp. Food and beverages are not available at Dachau; pack your own lunch. *(Take the S2 (dir.: Petershausen) to Dachau (20min.), then bus #726 (dir.: Saubachsiedlung) to KZ-Gedenkstätte (10min.); a €6.70 XXL day pass covers the trip.)*

NUREMBERG (NÜRNBERG)   ☎0911

Before it witnessed the fanaticism of Hitler's Nazi rallies, Nuremberg (pop. 501,000) hosted Imperial Diets (parliamentary meetings) in the first Reich. Today, the remnants of both regimes draw visitors to the city, which new generations have rechristened **Stadt der Menschenrechte** (City of Human Rights). Head up Königstr. for the real sights of the city. Take a detour to the

GERMANY

left for the pillared **Straße der Menschenrechte** (Avenue of Human Rights) as well as the gleaming glass **Germanisches Nationalmuseum,** Kartäuserg. 1, which chronicles German art since prehistoric times. (☎0911 133 10. Open Tu and Th-Su 10am-6pm, W 10am-9pm. Last entry 1hr. before closing. €6, students €4, W 6-9pm free.) Hidden in the fence of the **Schöner Brunnen** (Beautiful Fountain), in the Hauptmarkt, is a seamless, spinning golden ring, thought to bring good luck. Atop the hill, the **Kaiserburg** (Fortress of the Holy Roman Emperor) looms symbolically over Nuremberg. Climb the **Sinwellturm** for the best views of the city. (Open daily 9am-6pm. €6, students €5; includes a tour of the castle and museum.). On the far side of the lake is the **Zeppelintribüne,** the grandstand where Hitler addressed the masses. The *Fascination and Terror* exhibit, in the ▓**Kongresshalle** at the north end of the park, covers the Nazi era. (☎0911 231 5666. Open M-F 9am-6pm, Sa-Su 10am-6pm. €5, students €2.50; includes audio tour.) Tram #9 from the train station stops directly at the Kongresshalle *(Dokumentationszentrum)* stop. To reach the Zeppelintribüne, walk clockwise around the lake.

▓**Jugendgästehaus (HI) ❶,** Burg 2, sits in a castle above the city. From the tourist office, follow Königstr. over the bridge to the Hauptmarkt, head diagonally across to the fountain, and continue up Burgstr. (☎0911 230 9360. Reception 7am-1am. Curfew 1am. Dorms €21.40; singles €39.50; doubles €46. AmEx/MC/V.) The eccentricly-named and spacious rooms—like "Wrong Room" and "Right Room"—of **Lette'm Sleep ❶,** Frauentormauer 42, are only a short walk away from the train station. Take the first left after entering the *Altstadt* through Königpl. (☎0911 992 8128. Lockers available, bring your own lock. Linens €3. Free Internet. Reception 24hr. Dorms €16; singles €30; doubles €48-52. MC/V.) **Bratwursthäusle ❶,** Rathauspl. 1, has cheaper fare like three *Rostbratwurst* in a *Weckla* (bratwurst in a roll) for €1.80, six *Würste with kraut* for €6.20, and seasonal *Spargel* (white asparagus) for €4. (☎0911 22 76 95. Entrees €3-8. Open daily 10am-10:30pm. Cash only.) **Hauptmarkt vendors** sell cheese, sandwiches, pastries, and produce from early morning to dusk. Nuremberg's nightlife thrives in the *Altstadt.* **Hirsch,** Vogelweiherstr. 66, the city's most popular club, has multiple bars and a *Biergärten* out front. (Take nightbus #5 to Vogelweiherstr. ☎0911 429 414; www.der-hirsch.de. Mixed drinks €5.50. M-Th frequent concerts. Cover €3-15. Open M-Th 8pm-2am, F-Sa 10pm-5am. Cash only.) **Cine Città,** Gewerbemuseumspl. 3, U-Bahn to Wöhrder Wiese, packs 16 bars and cafes, 17 German-language cinemas, an IMAX theater, and a disco inside one complex. (☎0911 20 66 60. Open M-Th and Su until 2am, F-Sa until 3am.) **Cartoon,** An der Sparkasse 6, is a popular gay bar near Lorenzpl. (☎0911 22 71 70. Shots €3.80. Mixed drinks €5-7.50. Open M-Th 11am-1am, F-Sa 11am-3am, Su 2pm-1am.)

Trains go to: Berlin (4½hr., every hr., €86); Frankfurt (2hr., 2 per hr., €46); Munich (1hr., 2 per hr., €47); Stuttgart (2-3hr., every hr., €30-36). Walk through the tunnel from the train station to the *Altstadt* and take a right to reach the **tourist office,** Königstr. 93. (☎0911 233 6132. Open M-Sa 9am-7pm, Su 10am-4pm.) A second office is in the Hauptmarkt. (Open M-Sa 9am-6pm.) **Internet** is available at the immaculate **Telepoint,** on the underground level of the train station. (€1.50 per hr. Open daily 8am-midnight.) **Postal Code:** 90402.

ROMANTIC ROAD

Groomed fields of sunflowers, vineyards, and hills checker the landscape between Würzburg and Füssen. Officially christened *Romantische Straße* (the

Romantic Road) in 1950, the road is dotted with almost a hundred castles, helping to make it one of the most traversed routes in Germany.

⬛ TRANSPORTATION

Train travel is the most flexible, economical way to visit the Romantic Road. Deutsche Bahn operates a **bus** route along the Romantic Road, shuttling tourists from Frankfurt to Munich (13hr., €99), stopping in Würzburg (2hr., €22), Rothenburg (4hr., €35), and Füssen (11hr., €80). A Castle Road **bus** route connects Rothenburg with Nuremburg (3hr., €14). Both buses run once a day in each direction. For reservations and more detailed information, see www.romanticroadcoach.de. There is a 10% student and under 26 discount, and a 60% Eurail and German Rail Pass discount.

FÜSSEN   ☎ 08362

Füssen ("feet") seems an apt name for a little town at the foot of the Bavarian Alps. Füssen is the ideal basecamp for some of Germany's best daytrips; the town is mere minutes from King Ludwig's famed **Königsschlößer,** one of the best hiking, biking, and boating regions in the country. Although Füssen's best accommodations are pensions, the tourist office keeps a list of *Privatzimmer* with vacant rooms. **Jugendherberge (HI) ❷,** Mariahilfer Str. 5, lies in a residential area 15min. from the town center. Turn right from the station and follow the railroad tracks. (☎08362 77 54. Laundry €1.60. Reception daily Mar.-Sept. 7am-noon and 5-10pm; Oct. and Dec.-Apr. 5-10pm. Lockout 11pm-6:30am; keycode available. Dorms €17.50. MC/V.) Bakeries, butcher shops, and *Imbiße* (snack bars) stand among the pricey cafes on **Reichenstraße,** particularly off the Luitpold Passage. The **Plus** supermarket is on the right toward the rotary from the station. (Open M-Sa 8:30am-8pm.) **Trains** run to Augsburg (1hr., every hr., €17) and Munich (2hr., every hr., €21). To get to the **tourist office,** Kaiser-Maximilian-Pl. 1, from the train station, walk the length of Bahnhofstr. and then head across the roundabout to the big yellow building on your left. (☎938 50; www.fuessen.de. Open June-Sept. M-F 9am-6pm, Sa 10am-2pm; Oct.-May M-F 9am-5pm, Sa 10am-noon.) **Postal Code:** 87629.

⬛ DAYTRIP FROM FÜSSEN: ⬛KÖNIGSSCHLÖßER. King Ludwig II, a frenzied visionary, built fantastic castles soaring into the alpine skies. In 1886, a band of nobles and bureaucrats deposed Ludwig, declared him insane, and imprisoned him; three days later, the king was mysteriously discovered dead in a lake. The fairy-tale castles that Ludwig created and the enigma of his death captivate tourists. The glitzy **Schloß Neuschwanstein** inspired Disney's Cinderella Castle, and is one of Germany's iconic attractions. Hike 10min. to the **Marienbrücke,** a bridge that spans the gorge behind the castle. Climb the mountain on the other side of the bridge for the enchantment without the crowds. Ludwig spent his summers in the bright yellow **Schloß Hohenschwangau** across the valley. Don't miss the night-sky frescoes in the king's bedroom. While you're there, spend the extra money to see both castles; seeing the pair of them makes the experience more memorable. From the Füssen train station, take **bus** #73 or 78, marked "Königsschlößer" (10min.; 1-2 per hr.; €1.70, round-trip €3.20) or **walk** the 4km along beautiful, winding roads. Tickets for both castles are sold at the **Ticket-Service Center,** about 100m uphill from the bus stop. Arrive before 10am to escape long lines. (☎08362 93 08 30. Both castles open daily Apr.-Sept. 9am-6pm, ticket windows open 8am-5pm; Oct.-Mar. castles 10am-4pm, tickets 9am-3pm. Mandatory tours of each castle €9, students €8; 10 languages available. Combination ticket €17/15.)

EASTERN GERMANY

Saxony *(Sachsen)* and Thuringia *(Thüringen)*, the most interesting regions in eastern Germany outside of Berlin, encompass Dresden, Leipzig, and Weimar. Castles surrounding Dresden reveal Saxony's one-time wealth, while boxy GDR-era buildings recall the socialist aesthetic.

WEIMAR ☎03643

The writer Johann Wolfgang Goethe once said of Weimar (pop. 64,000), "Where else can you find so much that is good in a place that is so small?" Indeed, Weimar's diverse cultural attractions, lustrous parks, and rich history make the city a UNESCO World Heritage site and a worthwhile stop on any tour of eastern Germany. The **Goethehaus** and **Goethe-Nationalmuseum,** Frauenplan 1, preserve the chambers where the poet wrote, entertained guests, and, after a half-century in Weimar, died. The elegant abode is now stuffed with his art collection, and his fetching yellow buggy is parked under the house. (Open Apr.-Sept. Tu-F and Su 9am-6pm, Sa 9am-7pm; Oct. Tu-Su 9am-6pm; Nov.-Mar. Tu-Su 9am-4pm. €6.50, students €5. Museum only €3/2.50.) The multi-talented Goethe landscaped the vast and bushy **Park an der Ilm,** Corona-Schöfer-Str., which contains his quaint little **Gartenhaus,** a retreat he owned until his death. Take in the intense floral smell-scape, and see more of the poet's possessions. (Access from inside the park. Open daily Apr.-Oct. 10am-6pm; Nov.-Mar. 10am-4pm. €3.50, students €2.50.) With the Medieval Palace Tower out front, the **Schloßmuseum** (Palace Museum), Burgplatz 4, is one of the city's most impressive sites. (Open Apr.-Oct. Tu-Su 10am-6pm; Nov.-Mar. daily 10am-4pm. €5, students €4.)

Jugendherberge Germania (HI) ❷, Carl-August-Allee 13, is close to the train station but a 15min. walk from the city center. Small but comfortable beds at good prices make this hostel a deal. (☎03643 85 04 90; www.djh-thueringen. de. Breakfast included. First night €24, under 27 €21; €23/20 thereafter. Cash only.) Enjoy filling savory or sweet crêpes at **Crêperie du Palais ❶,** Am Palais 1, near Theaterpl. and down the street from the Hababusch hostel. (Open daily 11am-midnight. Cash only.) Both a cafe and a gallery, **ACC ❶,** Burgpl. 1-2, serves creative daily specials (€5-6.50), screens art films in the hallway, and offers free Wi-Fi to its clientele. (Open daily May-Sept. 10am-1am; Oct.-Apr. 11am-1am. AmEx/MC/V.) A **market** is on Marktpl. (Open M-Sa 6am-4pm.))

Trains run to Dresden (3hr., every hr., €43); Frankfurt (3hr., every hr., €53); and Leipzig (1hr., every hr., €24). To reach Goetheplatz, a **bus** hub at the center of the *Altstadt,* follow Carl-August-Allee downhill from the station to Karl-Liebknecht-Str. (15min.) The **Weimar Information Center,** Markt 10, is across from the *Rathaus.* (☎03643 85 74 50; www.weimar.de. Books rooms for free.) They sell **maps** (€0.20), city guides (€0.50), as well as the **Weimar Card,** which provides free admission to the *Goethehaus* and the *Schloßmuseum,* and discounts to most other sights in the city, as well as free public transportation within Weimar. Student admission is often still lower than the Weimar Card price. (72hr. €10, 72hr. extensions €5). Information center open Apr.-Oct. M-F 9:30am-6pm, Sa-Su 9:30am-3pm. Nov.-Mar. M-F 10am-6pm, Sa-Su 10am-2pm.)

EISENACH ☎03691

Birthplace of Johann Sebastian Bach, residence-in-exile of Martin Luther, and site of the famous Wartburg castle, Eisenach (pop. 44,000) has garnered national and international attention for almost a millenium. The picturesque city Martin Luther once called "my dear town," is best known as home to ▓**Wartburg Fortress,** which protected Luther in 1521 after his excommunication. It was here, disguised as a bearded noble that Luther famously fought an apparition of the devil with an inkwell by translating the New Testament into German and growing a heretical mustache. Keep your eyes peeled for the view from the **southern tower** (entrance €0.50). To reach Wartburg, walk along Schloßberg and follow the signs, or catch one of the buses (every hr. 9am-5pm; €1.50, €1.10 at the tourist office) running between the train station and the castle parking lot that stops twice along the way. (Open daily Mar.-Oct. 8:30am-8pm, last tour 5pm; Nov.-Feb. 9am-5pm, last tour 3:30pm. Castle grounds free, but to see inside the palace, you must take a tour; every 15min in German, English tour 1:30pm; €7, students €4.) Eisenach is also the birthplace of composer **Johann Sebastian Bach**. Although his exact place of birth is unknown, historical records suggest that Bach was born in 1685 in the **Bachhaus,** Frauenplan 21. Roughly every hour, a guide deftly demonstrates Bach selections on five period keyboard instruments–house organ to clavichord–and provides historical context in German. (Open daily 10am-6pm. €6, students €3.50. English translations at exhibits.) Martin Luther served as a choir-boy and Bach was baptized at the 800-year-old **Georgenkirche,** where members of Bach's family were organists for 132 years. (Open M-Sa 10am-12:30pm and 2-5pm, Su 11:30am-12:30pm and 2-5pm.)

The **Residenz Haus ❶,** Auf der Esplanade, around the corner from the tourist office, offers clean, spacious rooms. (☎21 41 33; www.residenzhaus-eisenach. de. Shared baths. Breakfast €6. €20 per person in rooms of three or more; singles and doubles €25 per person. Cash only.) To reach the Mediterranean-inspired **Jugendherberge Arthur Becker (HI) ❶,** Mariental 24, take bus #3 or 10 (dir.: Mariental) to Liliengrund Parkpl., or call a taxi (€6). To make the 35min. walk, take Bahnhofstr. from the station and stay left before the tower for Wartburger Allee, which runs into Mariental. (☎74 32 59; ww.djh-thueringen.de. Breakfast included. Reception M-F 7am-10pm, Sa-Su 7-10am and 3-10pm. Dorms €21.50, under 27 €18.50. Cash only.) **La Fontana ❶,** Georgenstr. 22, with a large fountain in front, is the best deal in town. (☎74 35 39. Pizza and pasta €3-5. Open M-Th and Su 11:30am-10:30pm, F-Sa 11:30am-11pm. Cash only.) For groceries, head to **Edeka** on Johannispl. (Open M-F 7am-5pm, Sa 7am-4pm.)

Trains run to and from Weimar (1hr., 1 per hr., €13-17). The **tourist office,** is on Markt 9. (Apr.-Oct. M-F 10:30am and 2pm, Sa-Su 3-4 per day; Nov.-Mar. Sa-Su 10am and 2pm. 2hr. €5). From the station, follow Bahnhofstr. through the tunnel and veer left, then take a right onto Karlstr. (☎03691 792 30. Open M-F 10am-6pm, Sa 10am-4pm; Apr.-Oct. also Su 10am-4pm.) **Postal Code:** 99817.

WITTENBERG   ☎03491

Martin Luther ignited the Protestant Reformation here in 1517 when he nailed his 95 Theses to the door of the **Schloßkirche;** Wittenberg (pop. 48,000) has celebrated its native heretic ever since. All major sights surround **Collegienstraße** (which becomes **Schloßstraße** toward the church). In the back of the old university courtyard, the **⧆Lutherhaus,** Collegienstr. 54, chronicles the Reformation through art, artifacts, letters, and texts. Hundreds of early printed pamphlets, for and against Luther's ideas, show that the Reformation was also a media revolution. (☎03491 420 3118; www.martinluther.de. Open Apr.-Oct. daily 9am-6pm; Nov.-Mar. Tu-Su 10am-5pm. €5, students €3.) Wittenberg's elegant **Altes Rathaus,** Markt 26, dominates the *Markt* with its arctic facade. Inside, a sleek modern room displays a terrific collection of 20th-century Christian graphic art. The departure from classical oil paintings is stark. (☎03491 401 149 www. christlichekunst-wb.de. Open Tu-Su 10am-5pm. €3, students €2.)

The **Jugendherberge im Schloß (HI)** is next to the church, Schlossstr. 14-15; enter first through the archway. Medieval on the outside, modern on the inside, the hostel couldn't be more convenient. (☎0341 505 205. Breakfast included. Rooms have shower and toilet, some are wheelchair-accessible. Linens €3.50. Reception 8am-10pm. Check-out 9:30am. Curfew 10pm. Dorms €23, under 27 €20. HI members €3 discount. MC/V.) Look for cheap meals along the Collegienstr.-Schloßstr. strip. **Zum Schwarzen Bär ❷**, Schloßstr. 2, the Wittenberger Kartoffelhaus, serves spud-centric dishes with a sense of humor. (☎0341 411 200. Entrees €4-12. Open daily 11am-1am. Kitchen open until midnight. V.)

Trains leave for Berlin (45min., 1 per hr., €21) and Leipzig (1hr., every 2hr., €10). Follow the "City" and "Altstadt" signs out of the station to the red brick path, which leads to Collegienstr., the start of the pedestrian zone. The **tourist office,** Schloßpl. 2, opposite the church, supplies **maps** in a dozen languages, including English and German (€0.50), books rooms for free, and frequently gives tours in German. **Postal Code:** 06886.

DRESDEN   ☎0351

Over the course of two nights in February 1945, Allied firebombs incinerated over three-quarters of Dresden, killing between 25,000 and 50,000 civilians. With most of the *Altstadt* in ruins, the surviving 19th-century *Neustadt* became Dresden's nerve center: today, it is still an energetic nexus of nightlife and alternative culture. Since the war, the *Altstadt* has resurrected its regal grandeur, .

⌦ TRANSPORTATION

Flights: Dresden Airport (DRS; ☎0351 881 3360; www.dresden-airport.de) is 9km from the city. S2 runs there from both train stations (13min. from *Neustadt*, 23min. from the *Hauptbahnhof*; 2 per hr. 4am-11:30pm; €1.80).

Trains: Nearly all trains stop at both the **Hauptbahnhof** in the *Altstadt* and **Bahnhof Dresden Neustadt** across the Elbe. Trains run to: **Berlin** (3hr., 1 per hr., €33-55); **Frankfurt am Main** (4hr., 1 per hr., €80); **Leipzig** (1hr., 1-2 per hr., €25); **Munich** (6hr., 1-2 per hr., €93); **Budapest, HUN** (11hr., 2 per day, €81); **Prague, CZR** (2hr., 9 per day, €20). Tickets are available at the *Reisezentrum* desk, but are cheaper at the machines located throughout the station's main hall.

Public Transportation: Much of Dresden is accessible on foot, but if jumping between districts, you may want to use **trams,** which cover the whole city. 1hr. ticket €1.80. Day pass €4.50. The €6 **Family Card,** good for 2 passengers until 4am, is probably the best deal. Weekly pass €17. Tickets are available from *Fahrkarte* dispensers at major stops and on **streetcars.** Validate on board. For info and **maps,** go to 1 of the **Service Punkt** stands in front of the *Hauptbahnhof* (open M-F 8am-7pm, Sa 8am-6pm, Su 9am-6pm) or at Postpl. (open M-F 8am-7pm, Sa 8am-6pm). Most major lines run hourly after midnight until 4am—look for the moon sign marked **Gute-Nacht-Linie.**

Taxis: ☎21 12 11 and ☎88 88 88 88 ("eight times eight"). Mercedes, BMW, and other fine German automobile taxis wait outside both train stations.

Bike Rental: Rent city bikes in either train station. In the *Hauptbahnhof,* look for **Gepaeck Center** (☎0351 461 32 62. Open daily 6:15am-9:30pm.) The **Fahrradverleih** is in the *Neustadt Bahnhof.* (☎0351 804 13 70. Open daily 6am-10pm.) €7 per day.

✴ ❼ ORIENTATION AND PRACTICAL INFORMATION

A 60-degree hook in the **Elbe** bisects Dresden, 60km northwest of the Czech border, pointing toward the **Alsdadt** in the south and separating it from the **Neustadt** above. The **Hauptbahnhof** is at the southern foot of the city center. **Prager Str.,** a pedestrian zone lined with modern glass-window shops and fountains, leads

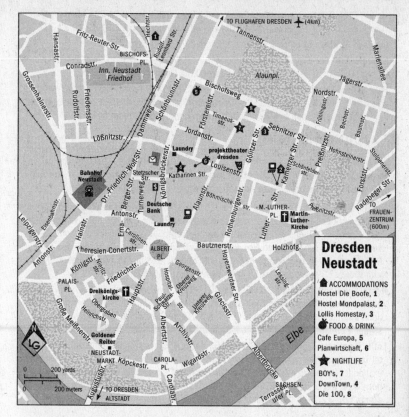

Dresden Neustadt

🏠 ACCOMMODATIONS
Hostel Die Boofe, 1
Hostel Mondpalast, 2
Lollis Homestay, 3

🍴 FOOD & DRINK
Cafe Europa, 5
Planwirtschaft, 6

★ NIGHTLIFE
BOY's, 7
DownTown, 4
Die 100, 8

from the train station to the **Altmarkt. Neumarkt,** the site of the famous **Frauen-kirche,** and the **Zwinger palace,** which now extends into the rest of the city, border the Elbe and separate the Altmarkt from the river. The central walking bridge, **Augustusbrucke,** links the *Altstadt* city center with the *Neustadt's* pedestrian **Haupstr.,** at the Golden Rider statue. Haupstr, a tree-covered promenade, ends in the north at **Albertplatz,** a transportation hub that marks the effective end of the tourist zone. Thereafter, the city morphs into Dresden's residential youth headquarters. **Antonstr.** connects the **Dresden-Neustadt train station** to Albertpl. The Albertpl. pulse with the lively energy of Dresden's young alternative scene. Five romantic bridges—**Marienbrücke, Augustbrücke, Carolabrücke, Albertbrücke,** and the **"Blue Marvel" Loschwitzbrücke**—connect the city's two halves.

Tourist Office: 2 main branches: Prager Str. 2, near the *Hauptbahnhof* in the Prager Spitze shopping center (open M-Sa 10am-7pm), and Theaterpl. in the *Schinkelwache,* a small building directly in front of the Semper-Oper (open M-F 10am-6pm, Sa-Su 10am-4pm). 2 cards provide transportation and discounted rates to Dresden museums: the **Dresden City-Card,** valid for 48hr. of transport in the city-zone (€21), and the **Dresden Regio-Card,** good for 72hr. in the Oberelbe region, including Meißen and Saxon Switzerland (€32). Call the city hotlines for general info (☎0351 49 19 21 00), room reservations (☎0351 49 19 22 22), and tours and advance tickets (☎0351 49 19 22 33).

Luggage Storage: At all train stations. Lockers €2-2.50 for 24hr.

Laundromat: Eco-Express, Königsbrücker Str. 2. Wash €1.90 6-11am, €2.40 11am-11pm. Dry €0.50 per 10min. Powder soap €0.30. Open M-Sa 6am-11pm.

Post Office: The **Hauptpostamt,** Königsbrücker Str. 21/29 (☎0351 819 1373), in the *Neustadt.* Open M-F 9am-7pm, Sa 10am-1pm. Branch in the *Altstadt* on Wallstr. at the Altmarkt Galerie. Open M-F 8am-6pm, Sa 9am-noon. **Postal Code:** 01099.

◪ ACCOMMODATIONS

The *Neustadt* is home to a number of independent hostels, close to the city's best nightlife. Quieter, though often larger, hostels are situated below the *Altstadt,* while pricier hotels are actually closer to many of the city sights.

▣ **Hostel Mondpalast,** Louisenstr. 77 (☎0351 563 4050; www.mondpalast.de). Settle into comfy beds in large, clean rooms. Bike rental €5 per 3hr., €7 per day. Breakfast (until 2pm) €5. Linens €2. Internet €2 per hr. Reception 24hr. Check-out noon. 8- to 10- bed dorms Jan.-Mar. and Nov. €13, Apr.-Oct. and Dec. €13.50; 5- to 6-bed dorms €15/16; 3- to 4- bed dorms €16/17, with shower €18.50/19.50; singles €29/34, with shower €39/44; doubles €37/44, with shower €50/52. AmEx/MC/V. ❶

Hostel Die Boofe, Hechtstr. 10 (☎0351 801 3361; www.boofe.de). Focus of this hostel is the bar downstairs. Wheelchair-accessible. Breakfast €6. Internet €1 per hr. Reception 7am-midnight. Check-in 2pm. Check-out 11am. 4-bed dorm €15, with shower €18; singles €29/39; doubles €40/50. F-Sa add €1.50 per person, singles add €2.50. ❶

Lollis Homestay, Görlitzer Str. 34 (☎0351 8108 4558; www.lollishome.de). This hostel reproduces the relaxed feel of a student flat, with free coffee, tea, and a book exchange. Old bikes available to borrow. Breakfast €3. Linens €2. Laundry €3. Internet €2.50 per hr. Dorms €13-16; singles €27-38; doubles €36-42; triples €48-57; quads €60-72. 10% ISIC discount. MC/V; €2.50 surcharge. ❶

◪ FOOD

It's difficult to find anything in the *Altstadt* that does not target tourists; the cheapest eats are at the *Imbiß* stands along **Prager Straße** and around **Postplatz.** The area in the *Neustadt* between **Albertplatz** and **Alaunpark** spawns a new bar every few weeks and is home to many quirky, student-friendly restaurants.

▣ **Cafe Aha,** Kreuzstr. 7 (☎0351 496 0673; www.ladencafe.de), across the street from Kreuzkirche in the *Altstadt.* Ecologically sound foods and abundant vegetarian options. Store open M-F 10am-7pm, Sa 10am-6pm. Cafe open daily 10am-midnight; kitchen closes at 10:30pm. AmEx/MC/V; €10 min. ❷

▣ **Planwirtschaft,** Louisenstr. 20 (☎0351 801 3187; www.planwirtschaft.de). Traditional and neo-German cuisine made with ingredients direct from local farms. Inventive soups, fresh salads (€3.50-7), entrees (€7-13), and "German tapas" (€6.80). Giant breakfast buffet (€9), daily 9am-3pm. Open M-Th and Su 9am-1am, F-Sa 9am-2am. MC/V. ❷

Cafe Europa, Königsbrücker Str. 68 (☎0351 804 4810; www.cafe-europa-dresden.de). Open 24hr. Draws a crowd of students and 20-somethings with 120 different drinks and a rack of 14 international newspapers. Breakfast menu with dishes from around the world €3.10-7.50, 6am-4pm. Pastas and more €6-10. Free Wi-Fi. AmEx/MC/V. ❶

👁 SIGHTS

Saxony's electors once ruled nearly all of central Europe from the banks of the majestic Elbe. Destroyed during WWII and partially rebuilt during Communist times, Dresden's *Altstadt* is one of Europe's undisputed cultural centers.

KREUZKIRCHE. After it was leveled three times—by fire in 1669 and 1897 and then by the Seven Years' War in 1760—the Kreuzkirche survived WWII, despite the flames that ruined its interior. Its tower offers a bird's-eye view of downtown. *(An der Kreuzkirche 6. ☎ 0351 439 39 20; www.dresdner-kreuzkirche.de. Open Apr.-Oct. M-F 10am-5:30pm, Sa 10am-4:30pm, Su noon-5:30pm; Nov.-Mar. M-Sa 10am-3:30pm, Su noon-4:30pm. Church free. Tower €2.)* The world-class **Kreuzchor** boys' choir has sung here since the 13th century. *(☎ 0351 315 3560; www.kreuzchor.de. Vespers Sa 6pm, winter 5pm. For other concerts, pick up a schedule at the church.)*

FRAUENKIRCHE. The product of a legendary 10-year reconstruction effort after crumbling to the ground on February 13, 1945, the Frauenkirche re-opened on Oct. 31, 2005, completing Dresden's skyline with its regal silhouette. On weekends, the quickly moving line can curl around the Neumarkt. *(Neumarkt. ☎ 0351 498 11 31; www.frauenkirche-dresden.de. Open M-F 10am-noon and 1-6pm. Sa-Su hours vary, check the information center on Neumarkt for details or pick up a free copy of the German-language Leben in der Frauenkirche schedule at the tourist office and look for "Offene Kirche." Entry free. Audio guides €2.50, available in English. The church holds open masses M-F at noon and 6pm, except for Th 6pm. Afterward, a short tour in German is given. Cupola open daily 10am-1pm; Apr.-Oct. also 2-6pm, Nov.-Mar. 2-4pm. €8, students €5.)*

🏛 MUSEUMS

After several years of renovations, Dresden's museums are once again ready to compete with the best in Europe. Once home to several acquisitive Saxon kings, Dresden has accrued some formidable collections. If you plan on visiting more than one in a day, consider a **Tageskarte** (€12, students €7), which grants one-day admission to the Schloß, most of the Zwinger, and more. The **Dresden City-Card** and **Dresden Regio-Card** (see **Practical Information** above) include museum admission. Info about all museums is at www.skd-dresden.de.

ZWINGER. A glorious example of Baroque design, Zwinger narrowly escaped destruction in the 1945 bombings. The palace interior has been converted into museum space for the **Saxon State Art Collection.** Through the archway from the Semper-Oper, 🖼**Gemäldegalerie Alte Meister** has a world-class collection of Dutch and Italian paintings from 1400 to 1800, including Cranach the Elder's luminous *Adam and Eve,* Giorgione's *Sleeping Venus,* and Raphael's enchanting *Sistine Madonna.* *(☎ 0351 49 14 20 00. Open Tu-Su 10am-6pm. €6, students €3.50; includes entry to the Rüstkammer.)* The 🖼**Rüstkammer,** just across the archway, shows the deadly toys of the Wettin princes in one of the greatest collections of weaponry in Europe. *(Open Tu-Su 10am-6pm. €3, students €2.)*

🎭 ENTERTAINMENT

Dresden has long been a focal point for German music, opera, and theater. Most theaters break from mid-July to early September, but open-air festivals bridge the gap. Outdoor movies screen along the Elbe during **Filmnächte am Elbufer** in July and August. (Office at Alaunstr. 62. ☎ 0351 89 93 20; www.film-naechte-am-elbufer.de. Most shows start at 8 or 9:30pm and cost €6.50.) The **Zwinger** has classical concerts in summer at 6:30pm.

Sächsische Staatsoper (Semper-Oper), Theaterpl. 2 (☎0351 491 10; www.semper-oper.de). Home to amazing opera, the city's first class orchestra performs the German symphonic canon here as well. Tickets €4.50-160. Box office at Schinkelwache, across Theaterpl. Open M-F 10am-6pm, Sa-Su 10am-4pm, and 1hr. before performances.

projekttheater dresden, Louisenstr. 47 (☎0351 810 7610; www.projekttheater.de). Cutting-edge, international experimental theater. Tickets €11, students €9. Shows start 8 or 9pm, matinees at 10am or noon. Box office open 1hr. before all shows.

◧ NIGHTLIFE

It's as if the entire *Neustadt* spends the day anticipating nightfall. A decade ago, the area north of Albertpl. was a maze of gray streets and crumbling buildings; since then, an alternative community has thrived in bars on **Louisenstraße, Goerlitzerstraße, Bischofsweg, Kamenzerstraße**, and **Albertplatz**. The German-language *Dresdener Kulturmagazin*, free at *Neustadt* hostels, describes every bar.

DownTown, Katharinenstr. 11-13 (☎0351 801 39 23; www.downtown-dresden.de). Constantly packed. Rotating pop, rock, and electronic music. Cover €4, students €3. Drinks €3-9. Open daily 7pm-5am. Club open Th-Sa 10pm-5am. Cash only.

Die 100, Alaunstr. 100 (☎0351 801 39 57; www.cafe100.de). Over 300 German, French, and Israeli wines (from €3.50 per glass, bottles from €13) on the menu. Unpolished, relaxed atmosphere in candlelit interior and intimate stone courtyard. In the cellar, there's often music. Salads and sandwiches €3-5. Open daily 5pm-3am. Cash only.

BOY's, Alaunstr. 80 (☎0351 796 88 24; www.boysdresden.de), just beyond the Kunsthof Passage. A half-naked devil mannequin guards this popular gay bar. The interior is a devilish/amorous red. Drinks €4-9. Open Tu-Th 8pm-3am, F-Su 8pm-5am. MC/V.

LEIPZIG ☎0341

Leipzig (pop. 500,000) is known as the city of music, and indeed, it's hard to walk more than a few blocks without being serenaded by a classical quartet, wooed by a Spanish guitar, or riveted by the choir music wafting from the Thomaskirche. Large enough to have a life outside its university but small enough to feel the influence of its students, Leipzig boasts world-class museums and corners packed with cafes, cabarets, and second-hand stores.

◧◪ TRANSPORTATION AND PRACTICAL INFORMATION. Leipzig lies on the Berlin-Munich line. **Trains** run to: Berlin (2½hr., 2 per hr., €40); Dresden (1½hr, every hr., €28); Frankfurt (4hr., every hr., €67); Munich (5hr., every 2hr., €84). To find the **tourist office**, Richard-Wagner-Str. 1, walk across Willy-Brandt-Pl. and take Goethestr. toward the left; the office is on the first corner. (☎0341 710 4265. Open Mar.-Oct. M-F 9:30am-6pm, Sa 9:30am-4pm, Su 9:30am-3pm; Nov.-Feb. M-F 10am-6pm.) There you can buy the **Leipzig Card**, good for free tram and bus rides within the city, discounts on city tours, and reduced admission to museums. (1-day, until 4am, €8.90; 3-day €18.50, 3-day group ticket for 2 adults and 3 children up to 14 €34.) **Postal Code:** 04109.

◪◧ ACCOMMODATIONS AND FOOD. To reach ◪**Hostel Sleepy Lion ❶**, Käthe-Kollwitz-Str. 3, take streetcar #1 (dir.: Lausen) to Gottschedstr., or, from the station, turn right and walk along Trondlinring, then left on Goerdelering and continue straight on Käthe-Kollwitz-Str. Run by young locals and close to nightlife, the **Sleepy Lion ❶** draws an international crowd. In the lounge, pool balls crackle (€1 a game) and upbeat music blasts around the clock. (☎0341 993 9480; www.hostel-leipzig.de. All rooms with shower and toilet. Bike rental €5 per day.

Breakfast €3.50. Linens €2.50. Internet €2 per hr. Reception 24hr. Dorms €14-16; singles €30; doubles €42; quads €68. Winter reduced rates. AmEx/MC/V.)

Imbiß stands, bistros, and bakeries line **Grimmaischestraße** in the Innenstadt. But life doesn't extinguish beyond the ring; the city extends a tentacle south, culminating in the student-populated Karl-Liebknecht-Str., (streetcar #10 or 11 to Südpl.), a funky refuge from downtown crowds and downtown prices. If you're itching to eat in the swarm of Barfussg. head to **Bellini's ①,** Barfußgäßchen 3-7 (☎0341 961 7681), the most reasonably priced eatery on the row. (All dishes under €10. Crispy baguettes €4-5.50. Colorful salads and pastas €7.60-9.80. Open daily noon-late. MC/V.)

🏛🌙 SIGHTS AND NIGHTLIFE. The heart of Leipzig is the **Marktplatz,** a cobblestone square guarded by the slanted 16th-century **Altes Rathaus** (old town hall). Head back to Thomasg., turn left, then turn right on Dittrichring to reach Leipzig's fascinating **🏛Museum in der "Runden Ecke,"** Dittrichring 24. Situated in former Stasi headquarters, the museum carefully preserves and displays the tools the secret police used to play Big Brother. (☎0341 961 2443; www.runde-ecke-leipzig.de. Open daily 10am-6pm. Free.) Outside the city ring, the **Völkerschlachtdenkmal,** fashioned after a Mesopotamian temple in 1913, memorializes the centennial of the 1813 Battle of Nations, when the combined forces of Austria, Prussia, Russia, and Sweden defeated Napoleon near Leipzig. Climb the 364 steps for an impressive view of the city. (Tram #15 from the station to Völkerschlachtdenkmal. Open daily Apr.-Oct. 10am-6pm; Nov.-Mar. 10am-4pm. €5, students €3.) Leipzig's rounded, glass **Gewandhaus,** Augustuspl. 8, has housed a major international orchestra, once directed by Felix Mendelssohn, since 1843. (☎0341 127 0280; www.gewandhaus.de. Open M-F 10am-6pm, Su 10am-2pm, and 1hr. before performances. Tickets €9-26 and up.)

The free magazines *Frizz and Blitz* have nightlife info, as does *Kreuzer* (€2.50 at newsstands). **Barfußgäßchen,** a street off the *Markt*, is the place to see and be seen for younger people. Leipzig University students spent eight years excavating a series of medieval tunnels so they could get their groove on in the **🏛Moritzbastei,** Universitätsstr. 9, a massive cave with bars, a cafe, and multi-level dance floors under vaulted brick ceilings. (☎0341 702 590; www.moritzbastei.de. Cover W €4, students €2.50; Sa €4.50/3. Free until 11pm. Cafe open M-F 10am-midnight, Sa noon-midnight, Su 9am-midnight. Club open W 10am-6am, Sa noon-6am. Cash only.)

GREECE
(ΕΛΛΑΔΑ)

Greece is a land where sacred monasteries are mountainside fixtures, leisurely seaside siestas are standard issue, and circle-dancing and drinking until daybreak are summer rites. Visitors explore evidence of magnificent past civilizations, as well as Greece's island beaches, spectacular gorges, and famous hospitality. The Greek lifestyle is truly a unique mix of high speed and sun-inspired lounging, encouraging tourists to adopt the natives' go-with-the-flow attitude.

DISCOVER GREECE: SUGGESTED ITINERARIES

THREE DAYS. Spend it all in **Athens** (p. 357). Roam the **Acropolis**, gaze at innumerous treasures in the **National Archaeological Museum**, and pay homage at the **Parthenon**. Visit the ancient **Agora**, then take a trip down to **Poseidon's Temple**, long since dry, at Cape Sounion.

ONE WEEK. Begin your sojourn in **Athens** (3 days). Sprint to **Olympia** (1 day; p. 366) and see where the games began. Sail to **Corfu** (1 day; p. 377) and peer into Albania from atop Mt. Pantokrator. Lastly, soak up Byzantine history in **Thessaloniki** (2 days; p. 371).

BEST OF GREECE, THREE WEEKS. Explore **Athens** (4 days) before visiting the mansions of **Nafplion** (1 day; p. 368). Race west to **Olympia** (1 day) and take a ferry to the beaches of **Corfu** (2 days). Back on the mainland, wander **Thessaloniki** (2 days), then climb to the cliff-side monasteries of **Meteora** (1 day; p. 374). Consult the gods at **Mount Olympus** (1 day; p. 374) and the Oracle of **Delphi** (1 day). On Crete (3 days; p. 384), hike Europe's largest gorge. Seek rest on **Santorini** (1 day; p. 383), debauchery on **Ios** (1 day; p. 382), and sun on **Mykonos** (1 day; p. 380).

ESSENTIALS

FACTS AND FIGURES

OFFICIAL NAME: Hellenic Republic.

CAPITAL: Athens.

MAJOR CITIES: Thessaloniki, Patras.

POPULATION: 10,723,000.

LAND AREA: 131,900 sq. km.

TIME ZONE: GMT +2.

LANGUAGE: Greek.

RELIGION: Eastern Orthodox (98%).

HIGHEST PEAK: Mt. Olympus (2917m).

VERSES IN NATIONAL ANTHEM: 158.

WHEN TO GO

July through August is peak season; it is best to visit in May, early June, or September, when smaller crowds enjoy the gorgeous weather. Visiting during low season ensures lower prices, but many sights and accommodations have shorter hours or close altogether.

DOCUMENTS AND FORMALITIES

EMBASSIES. Foreign embassies in Greece are in Athens (p. 357). Greek embassies abroad include: **Australia,** 9 Turrana St., Yarralumla, Canberra, ACT, 2600 (☎62 7330 11); **Canada,** 80 MacLaren St., Ottawa, ON, K2P 0K6 (☎613-238-6271; www.greekembassy.ca); **Ireland,** 1 Upper Pembroke St., Dublin, 2 (☎31 676 7254, ext. 5); **New Zealand,** 5-7 Willeston St., 10th fl., Wellington (☎4 473 7775, ext. 6); **UK,** 1a Holland Park, London, W11 3TP (☎020 72 21 64 67; www.greekembassy.org.uk); **US,** 2217 Massachusetts Ave., NW, Washington, DC, 20008 (☎202-939-1300; www.greekembassy.org).

VISA AND ENTRY INFORMATION. EU citizens do not need a visa. Citizens of Australia, Canada, New Zealand, and the US do not need a visa for stays of up to 90 days, beginning upon entry into any of the countries in the EU's freedom-of-movement zone. For more info, see p. 14. For stays longer than 90 days, all non-EU citizens need Schengen visas, available at Greek embassies and online at www.greekembassy.org. Processing a tourist visa takes about 20 days.

TOURIST SERVICES AND MONEY

EMERGENCY	Ambulance: ☎166. Fire: ☎199. Police: ☎100. General Emergency: ☎112.

TOURIST OFFICES. Two national organizations oversee tourism in Greece: **Greek National Tourist Organization** (GNTO; known as the EOT in Greece) and the **tourist police** (*touristiki astinomia*). The GNTO, Tsoha 7, Athens supplies general info about Grecian sights and accommodations. (☎2108 70 70 00; www.gnto.gr. Open M-F 8am-3pm.) In addition to the "Tourist Police" insignia decorating their uniforms, white belts, gloves, and cap bands help identify the tourist police. The **Tourist Police Service** and **General Police Directorate**, P. Kanellopoulou 4, Athens (☎2106 92 8510, 24hr. general emergency 171) deal with local and immediate problems concerning bus schedules, accommodations, and lost passports. Offices are willing to help, but their staff's English may be limited.

MONEY. The **euro (€)** has replaced the Greek **drachma** as the unit of currency in Greece. For more info, see p. 16. It's generally cheaper to change money in Greece than at home. When changing money in Greece, go to a bank with at most a 5% margin between its buy and sell prices. A bare-bones day in Greece costs €40-60. A day with more comforts runs €55-75. While all restaurant prices include a 15% gratuity, **tipping** an additional 5-10% for the assistant waiters and busboys is considered good form. Taxi drivers do not expect tips although patrons generally round their fare up to the nearest euro. Generally, **bargaining** is expected for street wares and at other informal venues, but when in doubt, wait and watch to avoid offending merchants. Bargaining for cheaper *domatia* (rooms to let), at small hotels, and for unmetered taxi rides is common.

Greece has a 19% **value added tax (VAT),** a sales tax applied to goods and services sold in mainland Greece and 13% VAT on the Aegean islands. Both are included in the listed price. The prices given in *Let's Go* include VAT. In the airport upon exiting the EU, non-EU citizens can claim a refund on the tax paid for goods purchased at participating stores. In order to qualify for a refund in a store, you must spend at least €120; make sure to ask for a refund form when you pay. For more info on qualifying for a VAT refund, see p. 19.

GREECE

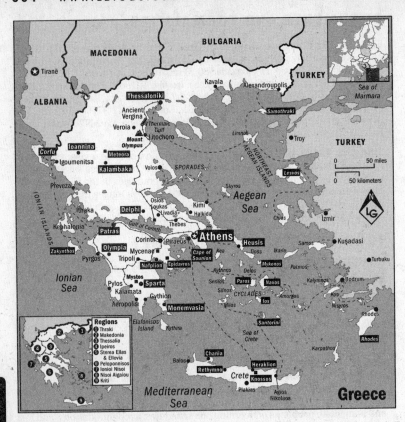

Greece

GREECE

TRANSPORTATION

BY PLANE. International flights land in **Athens International Airport (ATH; ☎21035 30 000; www.aia.gr);** some also serve Corfu (CFU), Heraklion (HER), Kos (KSG), and Thessaloniki (SKG). **Olympic Airlines,** 96 Syngrou Ave., Athens, 11741 (☎21092 691 11; www.olympicairlines.com), offers domestic service. A 1hr. flight from Athens (€60-100) can get you to many Grecian island.

BY TRAIN. Greece is served by a number of international train routes that connect Athens and Thessaloniki to most European cities. Train service within Greece, however, is limited and sometimes uncomfortable. The new air-conditioned, intercity express trains, while a bit more expensive and less frequent, are worth the price. **Eurail** is valid on all Greek trains. **Hellenic Railways Organization (OSE; ☎1110; www.osenet.gr)** connects Athens to major Greek cities.

BY BUS. Few buses run directly from European cities to Greece, except for chartered tour buses. Domestic bus service is extensive and fares are cheap. **KTEL** (www.ktel.org) operates most domestic buses; check with an official source about scheduled departures, as posted schedules are often outdated.

BY FERRY. Boats travel from Bari, ITA, to Corfu, Durres, Igoumenitsa, Patras, and Sami and from Ancona, ITA, to Corfu, Igoumenitsa, and Patras. Ferries also run from Greece to various points on the Turkish coast. There is frequent ferry service to the Greek islands, but schedules are irregular and incorrect info is common. Check schedules at the tourist office, the port police, or at www.ferries.gr. Make reservations and arrive at least 1hr. before your departure time. In addition to conventional service, **Hellenic Seaways** (☎21041 99 000; www.hellenicseaways.gr) provides high-speed vessels between the islands at twice the cost and speed of ferries. Student and children receive reduced fares; travelers buying tickets up to 15 days before intended departure date receive a 15% **Early Booking Discount** on ferries leaving Tuesday through Thursday.

BY CAR AND MOPED. You must be 18 to drive in Greece, and 21 to rent a car; some agencies require renters to be at least 23 or 25. Rental agencies may quote low daily rates that exclude the 18% tax and **collision damage waiver (CDW)** insurance. Foreign drivers must have an **International Driving Permit** and an **International Insurance Certificate.** The **Automobile and Touring Club of Greece (ELPA),** Messogion 395, Athens, 15343, provides help and offers reciprocal membership to members of foreign auto clubs like AAA. (☎21060 68 800, 24hr. emergency roadside assistance 104, infoline 174; www.elpa.gr.) **Mopeds,** while great for exploring, are extremely dangerous—wear a helmet.

KEEPING IN TOUCH

PHONE CODES	**Country code: 30. International dialing prefix:** 00. For more info on how to place international calls, see **Inside Back Cover.**

EMAIL AND THE INTERNET. The availability of the Internet in Greece is rapidly expanding. In all big cities, most small cities and large towns, and on most islands, you'll be able to find Internet cafes. Expect to pay €2-6 per hr.

TELEPHONE. Whenever possible use a calling card for international phone calls, as long-distance rates for national phone services are often very high. **Pay phones** in Greece use prepaid **phone cards,** sold at *peripteros* (streetside kiosks) and OTE offices. **Mobile phones** are an increasingly popular, economical option. Major mobile carriers include Q-Telecom, Telestet, and Vodaphone. Direct-dial access numbers for calling out of Greece include: **AT&T Direct** (☎00 800 1311); **British Telecom** (☎00 800 4411); **Canada Direct** (☎00 800 1611); **Sprint** (☎00 800 1411); **NTL** (☎00 800 4422); For info on calling home from Europe, see p. 28.

MAIL. Airmail is the best way to send mail home from Greece. To send a letter (up to 20g) anywhere from Greece costs €0.65. To receive mail in Greece, have it delivered **Poste Restante.** Mail will go to the main post office unless you specify a subsidiary by street address. Address mail to be held as follows: First name LAST NAME, Town Post Office, Island, Greece, Postal Code, POSTE RESTANTE. Bring a passport to pick up your mail; there may be a small fee.

ACCOMMODATIONS AND CAMPING

GREECE	❶	❷	❸	❹	❺
ACCOMMODATIONS	under €19	€20-28	€29-38	€98-70	over €70

Local tourist offices usually have lists of inexpensive accommodations. A **hostel** bed averages €15-30. Those not endorsed by HI are usually still safe and reputable. In many areas, **domatia** are a good option; locals offering cheap lodging may approach you as you enter town, a common practice that is illegal. It's usually a better bet to go to an official tourist office. Prices vary; expect to pay €15-35 for a single and €25-45 for a double. Always see the room and negotiate with *domatia* owners before settling on a price; never pay more than you would to stay in a hotel. **Hotel** prices are regulated, but proprietors may push you to take the most expensive room. Budget hotels start at €20 for singles and €30 for doubles. Check your bill carefully, and threaten to contact the tourist police if you think you're being cheated. Greece has plenty of official **campgrounds,** which cost €2-3 per tent plus €4-8 per person. Though common in summer, camping on beaches—sometimes illegal—may not be the safest option.

FOOD AND DRINK

GREECE	❶	❷	❸	❹	❺
FOOD	under €5	€5-9	€10-15	€16-25	over €25

Penny-pinching carnivores will thank Zeus for lamb, chicken, or pork *souvlaki*, stuffed into a pita to make **gyros** (YEE-ros). **Vegetarians** can also find cheap eateries; options include *horiatiki* (Greek salad), savory pastries like *tiropita* (cheese pie) and *spanakopita* (spinach and feta pie). Frothy iced coffee milkshakes take the edge off the summer heat. **Ouzo** (a powerful licorice-flavored spirit) is served with *mezedes* (snacks of octopus, cheese, and sausage). Breakfast, served only in the early morning, is generally very simple: a piece of toast with *marmelada* or a pastry. Lunch, a hearty and leisurely meal, can begin as early as noon but is more likely eaten sometime between 2 and 5pm. Dinner is a drawn-out, relaxed affair served late. Greek restaurants are known as *tavernas* or *estiatorios;* a grill is a *psistaria.*

HOLIDAYS AND FESTIVALS

Holidays: Feast of St. Basil/New Year's Day (Jan. 1); Epiphany (Jan. 6); Clean Monday (Mar. 10); Independence Day (Mar. 25); St. George's Day (Apr. 23); Orthodox Good Friday (Apr. 17, 2009; Apr. 2, 2010); Orthodox Easter (Apr. 19-20, 2009; Apr. 4-5, 2010); Labor Day (May 1); Pentecost (May 11-12); Day of the Holy Spirit (June 16); Assumption (Aug. 15); Feast of St. Demetrius (Oct. 26); Okhi Day (Oct. 28); All Saints' Day (Nov. 1); Christmas (Dec. 25-26).

Festivals: Three weeks of **Carnival** feasting and dancing (mid Feb. to early Mar.) precede Lenten fasting. April 23 is **St. George's Day,** when Greece honors the dragon-slaying knight with horse races, wrestling matches, and dances. The **Feast of St. Demetrius** (Oct. 26) is celebrated with particular enthusiasm in Thessaloniki.

BEYOND TOURISM

Doing more than just sightseeing on a trip to Greece is as easy (and as challenging) as offering some of one's own time and energy. Though considered wealthy by international standards, Greece has an abundance of aid organizations to combat the nation's very real problems. For more information on opportunities across Europe, see **Beyond Tourism,** p. 55.

American School of Classical Studies at Athens (ASCSA), 54 Souidias St., GR-106 76 Athens (☎21072 36 313; www.ascsa.edu.gr). Provides study abroad opportunities in Greece for students interested in archaeology and the classics. US$2950-17,000 including tuition, room, and partial board.

Archelon Sea Turtle Protection Society, Solomou 57, 10432 Athens (☎/fax 21052 31 342; www.archelon.gr). Non-profit group devoted to studying and protecting sea turtles on the beaches of Zakynthos, Crete, and the Peloponnese. Opportunities for seasonal field work and year-round work at the rehabilitation center. €100 participation fee.

ATHENS (Αθήνα) ☎210

An illustrious past invigorates Athens. The ghosts of antiquity peer down from its hilltops, instilling residents with a sense of the city's historic importance. Home to 3.7 million people—a third of Greece's population—Athens is daring and modern; its patriotic citizens pushed their capital into the 21st century with massive clean-up and building projects before the 2004 Olympic Games. International menus, hipster bars, and large warehouse performance spaces crowd Byzantine churches, traditional *tavernas*, and toppled columns.

▐ TRANSPORTATION

Flights: Eleftherios Venizelou (ATH; ☎210 353 0000; www.aia.gr). Greece's international airport operates as one massive, yet navigable terminal. Arrivals are on the ground floor, departures on the 2nd. The **Suburban Rail** services the airport from the city center in 30min. 4 bus lines run to Athens, Piraeus, and Rafina. Budget airlines **SkyEurope** (www.skyeurope.com) and **Wizz Air** (www.wizzair.com) fly to Athens.

Ferries: Most leave from the **Piraeus** port. Ferry schedule changes daily; check ahead at the tourist office (☎1440; www.openseas.gr or www.ferries.gr). Ferries sail directly to all major Greek **islands** except for the Sporades and Ionians. To Crete: **Hania** (11hr., €30-33); **Heraklion** (11hr., €27-35); **Rethymno** (11hr., €21-29). Others to: **Ios** (7hr., €25.50-32); **Kos** (13hr., €36-45.50); **Lesvos** (12hr., €26); **Mykonos** (6hr., €21); **Naxos** (6hr., €24-30); **Paros** (5hr., €25-29); **Patmos** (8hr., €33-34); **Rhodes** (14hr., €43-53); **Santorini** (9hr., €27-34). International ferries head to **Turkey** (€30).

Trains: Hellenic Railways (OSE), Sina 6 (☎1110 362 7947; www.ose.gr). **Larisis Train Station** (☎210 529 8837) serves northern Greece. Ticket office open daily 5am-midnight. Trolley #1 from El. Venizelou in Pl. Syndagma (5 per hr., €1) or the Metro to Larisis Station. Trains go to **Thessaloniki** (7hr., 5 per day, €15; express 4¼hr., 2 per day, €48).

Buses: Terminal A, Kifissou 100 (☎210 512 4910). Take blue bus #051 from the corner of Zinonos and Menandrou near Pl. Omonia (4 per hr. from 5am-midnight, €0.80). Buses to: **Corfu** (9½hr., 2-3 per day, €39.50); **Corinth** (1½hr., 1 per hr., €7.50); **Patras** (3hr., 2 per hr., €17; express 2hr., 9 per day); **Thessaloniki** (6hr., 12-13 per day, €35). **Terminal B,** Liossion 260 (☎210 831 7153). Take blue bus #024 from Amalias, outside the National Gardens (45min., 3 per hr. 5:10am-11:40pm, €0.80). Buses to **Delphi** (3hr., 6 per day, €13.60).

> **THE WHEELS ON THE BUS GO...** Getting to and from Athens by bus can be incredibly confusing as there are two intercity bus terminals (Terminal A and Terminal B) and yet another terminal (Mavromateon) serving destinations outside of Athens but within the prefecture of Attica (including Cape Sounion). The larger Terminal A is more difficult to reach than Terminal B, as the bus to the terminal departs from a random intersection in Omonia, but taking a local bus to the bus station is much cheaper than taking a taxi and is still the best bet.

Public Transportation: Yellow **KTEL** buses travel all around Attica from orange bus stops throughout the city. Other buses in Athens and its suburbs are blue and designated by 3-digit numbers. Electrical antennae distinguish **trolleys** from buses. Public transport tickets (valid for bus, trolley, tram, and metro connections) are available at blue **OASA (Athens Urban Transport Organization)** booths and some kiosks, and may be used for up to

Athens

🏠 **ACCOMMODATIONS**

Athens Backpackers, 1	B6
Hostel Aphrodite (HI), 2	A1
Hotel Orion, 4	C2
Pagration Athens Youth Hostel, 5	F6
Student and Traveller's Inn, 7	C5

🍴 **FOOD**

Chroma Chroma, 8	C4
Noodle Bar, 9	C5
O Barba Giannis, 10	C2
Thanasis, 11	B4

🍸 **NIGHTLIFE**

Bretto's, 12	B6
Hoxton, 14	A3
Wunderbar, 15	C2

🏛 **MUSEUMS**

New Acropolis Museum, 16	B5
Agora Museum, 17	A5
Byzantine & Christian Museum, 13	D4
Benaki Museum of Islamic Art, 6	A4
National Archaeolgical Museum, 3	C1

GREECE

90min. after validation. Travelers without validated tickets face a fine of 60 times the ticket price. A standard public transport ticket costs €0.80. 24hr. tickets (€3) and 7-day tickets (€10) are also available. The modern Athens **metro** consists of 3 lines running from 5:30am to midnight. The green **M1** line runs from northern Kifissia to Piraeus, the red **M2** from Ag. Antonios to Ag. Dimitrios, the blue **M3** from Egaleo to the airport via Doukissis Plakentias. Buy tickets (€0.70 for trips in 1-2 successive zones of M1, €0.80 for trips in all 3 zones of M1 and for combined trips between M1, M2, and M3) in any station.

Taxis: Ikaros (☎210 515 2800); **Hermes** (☎210 411 5200); **Kosmos** (☎1300). Base fare €1; €0.34 per km, midnight-5am €0.65 per km. €3.20 surcharge from airport, €0.86 surcharge for trips from port, bus, and railway terminals, plus €0.32 for each piece of luggage over 10kg. Minimum fare €2.65. Call for pickup (€1.60-2.65 extra).

✈ 🛈 ORIENTATION AND PRACTICAL INFORMATION

Most travelers hang around the **Acropolis** and **Agoras,** while guide-bearing foreigners flood central **Plaka,** Athens's old town. Marked by the square and flea market, **Monastiraki** (Little Monastery) is a hectic, exciting neighborhood where crowded *tavernas* and Psiri's trendy bars keep pedestrian traffic flowing late into the night. In the heart of Athens, **Syntagma Square** is the transportation center. On the opposite side of Stadiou, bustling **Omonia Square** bursts with ethnic and ideological diversity. A short walk north on **Em. Benaki** leads to the hip, student-filled neighborhood of **Exarhia,** where a young, alternative vibe enlivens graffiti-painted streets lined with relaxed cafes, independent bookshops, and record stores. The **Larisis** train station is to the northwest of town, while most museums are on **Vas Sofias** to the east. The fashionable neighborhood of **Kolonaki** attracts a posh Athenian crowd and is situated below Lycavittos Hill. Take the M1 (green line) south to its end or bus #040 from Filellinon and Mitropoleos, in Syntagma (4 per hr.), to reach Athens's port city, **Piraeus.** The metro also travels east to several beaches. If you get lost, just look for Syntagma or the Acropolis, Athens's clearest reference points.

Tourist Office: Information Office, Amalias 26 (☎210 331 0392 or 210 331 0716; www.gnto.gr). Has tons of useful literature, up-to-date bus schedules, and the most detailed city map. Open M-F 9am-7pm, Sa-Su 10am-4pm.

Budget Travel: STA Travel, Voulis 43 (☎210 321 1188). Open M-F 9am-5pm, Sa 10am-2pm. **Consolas Travel,** Eolou 100 (☎210 321 9228), on the 9th fl. above the post office. Open M and Sa 9am-2pm, Tu-F 9am-5pm.

Bank: National Bank, Karageorgi Servias 2 (☎210 334 0500), in Pl. Syntagma. Open M-Th 8am-2:30pm, F 8am-2pm; open for **currency exchange** M-F 3:30-5pm, Sa 9am-2pm, Su 9am-1pm. Commission about 5%. 24hr. currency exchange at the airport, but commissions there are usually exorbitant.

Emergencies: Poison control ☎210 779 3777. **AIDS Help Line** ☎210 722 2222.

Tourist Police: Dimitrakopoulou 77 (☎171). English spoken. Open 24hr.

Pharmacies: Check *Athens News* for a current list of 24hr. pharmacies.

Hospitals: Duty hospitals and **clinics** ☎1434. Free emergency health care for tourists. Geniko Kratiko; **Public General Hospital,** Mesogion 154 (☎210 777 8901). Near Kolonaki is the public hospital **Evangelismos,** Ypsilantou 45-47 (☎210 720 1000).

Internet: Athens has many Internet cafes. Expect to pay around €3 per hr. **Bits and Bytes,** Kapnikareas 19 (☎210 325 31; www.bnb.gr), in Plaka. 9am-midnight €5 per hr., midnight-9am €3 per hr. Open 24hr. **2nd location** in Exarhia, Akadamias 78 (☎210 381 3830). **C@FE4U,** Ippokratous 44 (☎210 361 1981; www.cafe4u.gr). Open 24hr. Free **city Wi-Fi** at Syntagma Sq., Thesseion Sq., Kotzia Sq., and across the Evangelismos Metro Station at the National Hellenic Research Foundation (SSID: athenswifi).

Post Office: Syntagma (☎210 323 7573, 210 331 9501), on the corner of Mitropoleos. Open M-F 7:30am-8pm, Sa 7:30am-2pm, Su 9am-1:30pm. **Postal Code:** 10300.

ACCOMMODATIONS

Many budget accommodations exist in Athens, but prices generally increase toward the city center at Pl. Syntagma. The reception desk at **Youth Hostel #5** (otherwise known as Pagration Youth Hostel), Damareos 75 in Pagrati, acts as the Athens branch of the **Greek Youth Hostel Association,** which has 10 other affiliated hostels in Thessaloniki, Patra, and Olympia as well as on Santorini and Crete that share common (and very reasonable) rates. (☎21075 19 530. Open M-F 9am-3pm.) The **Hellenic Chamber of Hotels,** Stadiou 24, provides info and reservations for hotels throughout Greece. (☎21033 10 022; www.grhotels.gr. Open May-Nov. M-F 8:30am-1:30pm.)

Athens Backpackers, Makri 12 (☎21092 24 044; www.backpackers.gr). ⓂAcropolis; walk down Ath. Diakou away from the Acropolis and take the 1st left onto Makri. While its proximity to the city's major sights is a huge plus, the real draw here is the spectacular view of the Acropolis from the rooftop, where cold beer (€1.50), cheap cocktails (€3), and karaoke flow nightly during summer. Plenty of space between bunks in tidy, spacious rooms. Breakfast, luggage storage, A/C, and the friendly Aussies at the front desk sweeten the deal. Some rooms have bath and patio. Also offers weekend daytrips to sites near Athens, complete with tours and lunch (€40-50). Laundry €5. Free Wi-Fi. 6- or 8-bed dorms €18-25. AmEx/MC/V. ❶

Hotel Acropolis House, 6-8 Kodrou (☎21032 22 344 or 26 241; www.acropolishouse.gr), across from Adonis Hotel. This 19th-century mansion-turned-guesthouse has been run by the same family since 1965. While the rooms are a tad small and very basic—bed, desk, TV, and not much else—the high ceilings, Neoclassical architectural detailing, and floor-to-ceiling art collection add charm. A/C. Some rooms have bath, others have a bathroom on the hall. Breakfast included. Doubles €60-79. Reservations recommended in the high season. ❹

Hotel Orion, Em. Benaki 105 (☎21033 02 387; www.orion-dryades.com). Walk up Em. Benaki toward the Strefi Hill, or take bus #230 from Pl. Syntagma. Orion's rooms might charitably be described as "cozy," but its array of amenities and funky 70s decor more than make up for the small size. All rooms have A/C and TVs. Exquisite rooftop canopy, kitchen, and killer view of the Acropo-

THE HIDDEN DEAL

ATHENS OFF THE BEATEN PATH

In a city packed with tourists, escaping the crowds may seem like an impossible feat. But there's much more to Athens than the Acropolis: arm yourself with a good map and a 24hr. public transportation ticket (€3), and explore this city on the cheap!

Antonis Tritsis Environmental Park: This expansive park in the western Athens area boasts many rare bird species. You don't need binoculars, however, to appreciate the natural beauty of this wildlife reserve and its mission to raise environmental awareness. Visitors can stock up on organic goodies at the park's shops. (☎210 231 6977; 23 Spyrou Moustaki, Ilion park.www.ornithologiki.gr.)

Fruit and vegetable markets: On any given day of the week, one or more of Athens's neighborhoods becomes a hotspot where locals stock up on fresh produce. For the best quality, go early—prices tend to drop as the selection dwindles. Try Xenokratous in Kolonaki on Friday and Kallidromiou St. in Exarhia on Saturday.

DESTE Foundation Centre for Contemporary Art: Check out the latest, hippest exhibition at this sleek building in one of Athens's northern suburbs. Open W-Th 5pm-8pm. Free. (☎210 275 8490; Filellinon 11 & Em. Pappa St., Nea Ionia. www.deste.gr.)

lis. Breakfast €6, but the bakery around the corner has great pastries for less. Internet €1 per day. Singles €30; doubles with private baths €40-45. MC/V. ❷

Pagration Athens Youth Hostel, Damareos 75 (☎21075 19 530). From Omonia or Pl. Syndagma, take trolley #2 or 11 to Filolaou (past Imittou) or walk through the National Garden, down Eratosthenous, then 3 blocks down Efthidiou to Frinis and down Frinis until you come to Damareos; it's on your right. There's no sign for this cheery, family-owned hostel—just the number 75 and a green door. The charming common spaces and ultra-helpful staff make this out-of-the-way hostel worth the 20-25min. walk to the city center. TV lounge and full kitchen. Hot showers €0.50. Laundry €4 to wash, with dryer €7; or line-dry on the roof for free. Quiet hours 2:30-5pm and 11pm-7am. High-season dorms €12. When the hostel fills up, the owner opens the roof (€10 per person) to travelers; bring a sleeping bag. Cash only. ❶

🏠 FOOD

Athens offers a mix of fast-food stands, open-air cafes, side-street *tavernas*, and upscale restaurants. On the streets, vendors sell dried fruits and nuts or fresh coconut (€1-2), and you can find *spanakopita* (cheese and spinach feta pies) at any local bakery (€1.50-2). Diners on a budget can choose from the many *souvlaki* spots in **Monastiraki**, at the end of **Mitropoleos**. Places in **Plaka** tend to advertise "authentic Greek for tourists." If you really want to eat like a local, head to the simple *tavernas* uphill on Em. Benaki in Exarhia.

🍽 **O Barba Giannis,** Em. Benaki 94 (☎21038 24 138). From Exarchia, take Metaxa to Benaki and walk 3 blocks toward the Strefi Hill; it's the yellow building on the corner with tall green doors. "Uncle John's" is informal, and that's how the locals like it—at 3pm, when other cafes sit empty, Giannis is bustling. The place has a French feel, but the food is pure Greek. So is the staff: only Tony speaks English. Stewed veal with pasta €7. Open M-Sa noon-1:30am. Cash only. ❷

🍽 **Matsoukas,** Karageorgi Servias 3 (☎21032 52 054). Shelves packed floor to ceiling with delicious sugary treats. Dried fruit, chocolate, cookies, and colorful marzipan abound. Try a chunk of nougat (€12 per kilo) or a ball of marzipan rolled in pistachios (€15 per kilo). Ouzo and *metaxa* €9-15. Open daily 8am-midnight. MC/V.❶

🍽 **Taverna Platanos,** Diogenous 4 (☎21032 20 666), near the Popular Musical Instruments Museum and Roman Agora. An oasis of cool and quiet minutes away from Plaka's most crowded streets. Fresh, traditional Greek fare. Stuffed grape leaves, grilled dishes, and foods cooked with ample amounts of olive oil, as well as a selection of fruit, cheese, and a few desserts. Enjoy it on the outdoor patio, or inside the cozy *taverna*. Spinach pie €3.80. Greek salad €6.30. Moussaka €7.40. Open M-Sa noon-4:30pm and 7:30pm-midnight, Su noon-4:30pm. Cash only. ❷

🍽 **Stamatopoulos,** Lissiou 26 (☎21032 28 722). Walking north on Adrianou, turn left at Eat at Milton's. Family-owned since 1882, this popular restaurant tucked in a corner just off 1 of Plaka's busiest streets has a bright outdoor terrace, lively Greek music, and dancing every night. Grilled *haloumi* cheese with tomatoes €5. Veal in a clay pot with white sauce €10. Open M and W-Su 7pm-3am. Cash only. ❷

Cook-cou Food, Themistokleous 66 (☎21038 31 955). This cafe's zebra-print booths and pulsing techno-pop might feel out of place in other neighborhoods, but in Exarhia it fits right in. The kitchen fashions typical Greek ingredients into creative treasures, such as lentils with mango (€5.50) and chicken breast stuffed with *manouri* cheese (€7). The menu changes daily, but the house wine (€1 per glass) is always a steal. Vegetarian entrees €4.50-€6. Meat entrees €6.80-€7.50. Open in summer M-Sa 7am-7pm, in winter M-Sa 1pm-1am. Cash only. ❷

Derlicious, Tsakalof 14 (☎21036 30 284), tucked between boutiques on the southern-most block of Tsakalof. The sign is written in Greek letters, but you'll know it by the open coals just behind the counter. Such low-priced fare is rare in Kolonaki, and although the staff might be brisk, the cheap and "derlicious" food is worth every penny. Try the *flaouto* (big tortilla) with chicken (€3.22). Open M-W and Su 1pm-4am, Th 1pm-5am, F-Sa 1pm-6am. Cash only. ❶

Taverna Kiouri,Filikis Eterias 4 (☎21036 14 033). Look for it below street level. A bastion of homespun simplicity in slick Pl. Kolonaki, Kiouri sells traditional Greek food for modest prices. Try meatballs with egg and lemon sauce (€8) or daily specials like sardines cooked with tomatoes and vegetables (€8). No matter what you choose, you'll be taken care of by the welcoming staff. M-Sa 8am-10pm. Cash only. ❷

Cucina Povera, Eforionos 13 (☎21075 66 008; www.cucinapovera.gr). Walk east from the Panathenaic Stadium (away from the Acropolis) on Vas. Konstandinou, then turn right on Eratosthenous and left onto Eforionos. Cucina Povera whips up elegant dishes from simple ingredients, such as *aubergine millefeuille* with creamy cheese (€8.50) and stuffed rooster with vegetables and Gruyère (€12.50). The menu changes daily, but the house burger stuffed with olives, *metsovone* cheese, and potatoes is always on the menu for €12. Open M-Sa noon-3pm and 8-11pm, Su noon-3pm. Cash only. ❷

SIGHTS

ACROPOLIS

The Acropolis has stood over the heart of Athens since the fifth century BC. Although each Greek city-state had an *acropolis* (high point), the buildings atop Athens's peak outshine their imitators and continue to awe visitors. Visit as early or as late in the day as possible to avoid large crowds and the broiling midday sun. *(Enter on Dionissiou Areopagitou or Theorias. ☎210 321 0219. Open daily in summer 8am-7pm; in winter 8am-2:30pm. Admission includes access to the Acropolis, the Agora, the Roman Agora, the Temple of Olympian Zeus, Keramikos, and the Theater of Dionysos, within a 4-day period; purchase tickets at any of the sights. €12, students and EU seniors over 65 €6, under 19 free. Cash only.)*

◪**PARTHENON.** The **Temple of Athena Parthenos** (Athena the Virgin), commonly known as the Parthenon, watches over Athens. Ancient Athenians saw their city as the capital of civilization; the **metopes** (scenes in the spaces above the columns) on the sides of the temple celebrate Athens's rise. The architect Iktinos successfully integrated the Golden Mean, about a four-to-nine ratio, in every aspect of the temple.

◪**NEW ACROPOLIS MUSEUM.** Recently completed after a protracted €130 million construction process, the New Acropolis Museum, 300m southeast of the Acropolis at 2-4 Makriyianni, houses a superb collection of statues, including five of the original **Caryatids** that supported the southern side of the Erechtheion. The carvings of a lion devouring a bull and of a wrestling match between Herakles and a sea monster display the ancient mastery of anatomical and emotional detail. Notice the empty space where room has been left for the British to return the missing Elgin Marbles. *(☎210 924 1043; www.newacropolismuseum.gr. Visitors can tour the ground floor 10am-noon. Expected to open early 2009.)*

TEMPLE OF ATHENA NIKE. Currently undergoing renovation, this tiny temple was first raised during the Peace of Nikias (421-415 BC), a respite from the Peloponnesian War. Ringed by eight miniature Ionic columns, it housed a winged statue of Nike, the goddess of victory. Athenians, afraid Nike might abandon them, clipped the statue's wings. The remains of the 5m thick **Cyclopean wall** that once circled the Acropolis now lie below the temple.

ERECHTHEION. Completed in 406 BC, just before Sparta defeated Athens in the Peloponnesian War, the Erechtheion lies to the left of the Parthenon,

THE HIDDEN DEAL

ATHENS FOR FREE

Reeling from the €12 Acropolis admission fee? Though crowds of tourists have inflated the city's prices, there's still fun to be had on a tight budget—or with no budget at all. Save your Euros for *souvlaki*: this is Athens for free.

Wi-Fi: Before ducking into an internet cafe, take a look around—odds are you're within walking distance of one of Athens's free hotspots. Provided by the city, the hotspots are located in and around the city center: Syntagma Sq., Thesseion Sq., Kotzia Sq., and opposite the Evangelismos Metro Station at the National Hellenic Research Foundation.

Escape the crowds: So, that epic photo you took of the Parthenon on your visit to the Acropolis was marred by the head of a random tourist? No worries! Leave the crowds behind and ascend Filopappou Hill, southwest of the Acropolis. Wander the hill's wooded paths and don't forget to stop for photos—the hill offers sweeping vistas of Attica, the Saronic Gulf and the Acropolis.

On guard: Members of the Greek Presidential Guard, *evzones*, stand before the Tomb of the Unknown Soldier, in front of Parliament. Every hour, visitors can check out the changing of the guard. For the big show, head to the city center on Sunday at 11am to watch the *evzones* parade in traditional uniform toward Synagma Sq. Get there early, or be prepared to rub elbows with every other tourist in Athens.

supported by copies of the famous Caryatids in the museum. The building is named after a snake-bodied hero, whom Poseidon speared during a dispute. When Poseidon struck a truce with Athena, he was allowed to share her temple—the eastern half is devoted to the goddess of wisdom and the western part to the god of the sea.

OTHER SIGHTS

■NATIONAL ARCHAEOLOGICAL MUSEUM. Almost every artifact in this collection is a masterpiece. The museum's highlights include the **Mask of Agamemnon,** in fact excavated from the tomb of a king who lived at least three centuries before Agamemnon, as well as the colorful 16th-century BC "Spring Fresco," from the Akrotiri settlement on Santorini (Thira), which depicts swallows floating above undulating red lilies. *(Patission 44. Take trolley #2, 4, 5, 9, 11, 15, or 18 across from the National Gardens in Syntagma, or trolley #3 or 13 from the north side of Vas. Sofias. Metro stop Victoria on the green line (M1). ☎ 210 821 7717. Open M 1-7:30pm, Tu-Su 8am-7:30pm. €7, students and EU seniors €3, EU students and under 19 free.)*

■BENAKI MUSEUM OF ISLAMIC ART. Built on the ruins of ancient Athenian fortifications, the building's glass windows, marble staircases, and white walls showcase a collection of brilliant tiles, metalwork, and tapestries documenting the history of the Islamic world until the 19th-century. Its exhibits include an inlaid marble reception room brought from a 17th-century Cairo mansion and pottery with Kufic inscriptions. *(Ag. Asomaton 22 & Dipilou, in Psiri. M: Thisso. ☎ 210 325 1311; www.benaki.gr. Open Tu and Th-Su 9am-3pm, W 9am-9pm. €5, students free. W free.)*

AGORA. The Agora served as Athens's marketplace, administrative center, and focus of daily life from the sixth century BC to the AD sixth century. Many of Athenian democracy's greatest debates were held here; Socrates, Aristotle, Demosthenes, Xenophon, and St. Paul all lectured in the Agora. The 415 BC **■Hephaesteion,** on a hill in the Agora's northwest corner, is Greece's best-preserved Classical temple, with friezes depicting Theseus's adventures. The **Stoa of Attalos,** an ancient shopping mall, played host to informal philosophers' plentiful gatherings. Reconstructed in the 1950s, it now houses the **Agora Museum.** *(Enter the Agora off Pl. Thission, from Adrianou, or as you descend from the Acropolis. ☎ 210 321 0185. Agora open daily 8am-7:30pm. Museum open Tu-Su 8am-7:20pm. €4, students and EU seniors €2, under 19 and with Acropolis ticket free.)*

🎵 📷 ENTERTAINMENT AND NIGHTLIFE

The weekly *Athens News* (€1) lists cultural events, as well as news and ferry info. Summertime performances are staged in venues throughout the city, including the ancient **Odeon of Herodes Atticus**, as part of the ▨**Athens Festival** (May-Sept.; www.greekfestival.gr). Chic Athenians head to the seaside clubs in **Glyfada**, enjoying the breezy night air. **Psiri** and **Gazi** are the bar and club districts. Get started on **Miaouli**, where young crowds gather after dark. For an alternative to bar hopping, follow the guitar-playing local teens and couples that pack **Pavlou** at night.

▨ **Psira**, Miaouli 19 (☎21032 44046), half a block from Pl. Iroön. On a street full of relaxed and funky pubs, Psira is the most relaxed and funkiest. Its tiny interior is wallpapered with images of the South Seas and hung with photos of James Dean and lots of tinsel. There's room for all on the sidewalk outside. Beer €4. Mixed drinks €6. Open daily noon-4am or later. Cash only.

Brettos, Kydatheneon 41 (☎21032 32 110). Serves its own ouzos (€3-4) straight from the barrel. Offers over 90 different varieties of Greek wine. Backlit shelves of colorful glass bottles line the walls from from counter to ceiling, converting Brettos into a cathedral of liquor for its devout clientele. Red wine €2 per glass. Ouzo €2.50-€19 per bottle. Open daily 10am-midnight. Cash only.

Wunderbar, Themistokleous 80 (☎21038 18 577), on Pl. Exarhia. A pop oasis in Exarhia's alternative desert. Late-night revelers lounge under large umbrellas outside, enjoying one of Wunderbar's signature specialty chocolate drinks (€5). Mixed drinks €8. Champagne €9. Open M-Th 9am-3am, F-Su 9am-dawn. Cash only.

Flower, Dorylaou 2 (☎21064 32 111), in Pl. Mavili. An intimate little dive, Flower offers drinks and snacks in a casual, mellow setting. Additional seating outside in the square. Shots €4. Mixed drinks €7. Open daily 7pm-late. Cash only.

📷 DAYTRIPS FROM ATHENS

▨CAPE SOUNION PENINSULA (ΑΚΡΩΤΗΡΙΟ ΣΟΥΝΙΟ).

Orange-striped KTEL buses go to Cape Sounion from Athens. Bus #1 leaves from the Mavromateon 14 bus stop (near Aeros Park, on Alexandras and 28 Oktovriou-Patission) and stops at all points on the Apollo Coast (2hr., every hr. 6:30am-6pm, €5.70). The other follows a less scenic inland route that also stops at the port of Lavrio (2hr., every hr. 6am-6pm, €4). The last coastal bus leaves Sounion at 9pm (last inland at 9:30pm). Both temples ☎22560 39 363. Open daily 9:30am-sunset except on Jan. 1, Mar. 25, Easter, May 1, Dec. 25, Dec. 26. €4, students and EU seniors over 65 €2, EU students and children under 18 free. Nov.-Mar. Su free.

A tiny tourist colony rests atop the sharp cliff of Cape Sounion, where around 440 BC ancient Greeks built the enormous ▨**Temple of Poseidon** in gleaming white marble. Legend holds that the surrounding Aegean Sea was named for King Aegeus of Athens, who leapt to his death from these cliffs when he saw his son Theseus's ship sporting a black sail—a sign of his son's demise. Unfortunately for Aegeus, Theseus was on board celebrating his triumph over the Minotaur and had forgotten to raise the victorious sail. Today, visitors flock to the site to see the 16 Doric columns that remain from Pericles's reconstruction. Hundreds of names have been carved into the monumental structure; look closely for Lord Byron's on the square column closest to the site entrance. Across the street 500m below is the somewhat deteriorated **Temple of Athena Sounias**.

THE PELOPONNESE (ΠΕΛΟΠΟΝΗΣΟΣ)

Stretching its fingers into the Mediterranean, the Peloponnese transports its visitors to another time and place. The achievements of ancient civilizations dot the peninsula's landscape, as most of Greece's significant archaeological sites—including Olympia, Mycenae, Messini, Corinth, Mystras, and Epidavros—rest in this former home of King Pelops. Away from urban transportation hubs, serene villages welcome visitors to traditional Greece.

PATRAS (ΠΑΤΡΑ) ☎2610

Located on the northwestern tip of the Peloponnese, sprawling Patras (pop. 172,000) operates as the region's primary transportation hub. Charter tourism often skips the city, favoring other nearby islands. During ▪Carnival (end of Feb. to early Mar.; ☎2610 390 925; www.carnivalpatras.gr), however, Patras transforms into a gigantic dance floor of costumed, inebriated revelers consumed by pre-Lenten madness. The biggest European festival of its kind revives ancient celebrations in honor of Dionysus—god of wine and debauchery. Entirely covered in colorful frescoes, **Agios Andreas,** 199 Ag. Andreou, is Greece's largest Orthodox cathedral. Follow the waterfront with the town to your left to get there. (☎2610 321 184. Dress modestly. Open daily 7am-9pm.) Sweet black grapes are made into Mavrodaphne wine at the ▪Achaïa Clauss Winery. Take bus #7 (30min., €1.20) toward Seravali from the intersection of Kanakari and Gerokostopoulou. (☎2610 368 100. Open daily 10am-5pm. Free.)

Across from the ferry terminal, lounge on the deck of ▪Rooms to Let Spyros Vazouras ❸, Tofalou 2, where rooftop ocean views complement brightly tiled rooms with A/C and TV. (☎2610 452 157 or 2610 742 487; www.patrasrooms.gr. Singles €30; doubles €40; extra bed €10.) Centrally located **Pension Nicos ❷,** Patreos 3, sparkles with marble and inlaid stone decor while offering comfortable, pristine rooms at affordable prices. (☎2610 623 757. Reception 3rd fl. Curfew 4am. Singles €23; doubles €33, with bath €38; triples €43/48. MC/V.)

Trains (☎2610 639 108) leave from Amalias 27, right across the port, for Kalamata (5hr., 5 per day, €5) via Pirgos (2hr., 8 per day, €2-4), where you can catch a train to Olympia. A direct railway line between Patras and Athens is currently under construction. To reach Athens from Patras, go to Kiato (2 hr., 9 per day, €2-5), where you can transfer onto the **Suburban Rail** (Proastiakos; www.proastiakos.gr) to Athens (1½hr., 4 per day). KTEL **buses** (☎2610 623 886; www.ktel.org) leave from farther down on Amalias for: Athens (3hr., 2 per hr., €17); Ioannina (4hr., 2 per day, €20); Kalamata (3hr., 2 per day, €20); Thessaloniki (7hr., 4 per day, €39.40). **Ferries** go to Corfu (7hr., M-W and F-Su midnight, €30-33), Vathy on Ithaka (2-3hr.; M-F and Su 12:30, 8:30pm, Sa 12:30pm; €15), and Sami on Kephalonia (3hr.; M-F and Su 12:30, 8:30pm; €15). Six major ferry lines also travel to Italy: Ancona (21hr.); Bari (16hr.); Brindisi (14hr.); Venice (30hr.). The ▪tourist office, Amalias 6, 50m past the bus station, provides a wealth of information about Patras, including 1-day, 3-day, and week-long itineraries, and offers free bike rental and short-term Internet access. (☎2610 461 740 or 2610 461 741; infocenterpatras.gr. Open daily 8am-10pm.) **Postal Code:** 26001.

OLYMPIA (ΟΛΥΜΠΙΑ) ☎26240

Every four years, ancient city-states would call a sacred truce and travel to Olympia for a pan-Hellenic assembly that showcased athletic ability and fostered peace and diplomacy. Modern Olympia, set among meadows and shaded by cypress and olive trees, is recognized as much for its pristine natural beauty as for its illustrious past. The ancient ▪Olympic site, whose central sanctuary was called the **Altis**, draws hordes of tourists. Toward the entrance lie the ruins of the **Temple of Zeus.** Once home to master sculptor Phidias's awe-inspiring Statue of Zeus, one of the Seven Wonders of the Ancient World, the 27m sanctuary was the largest temple completed on the Greek mainland before the Parthenon. The **Temple of Hera**, dating from the seventh century BC, is better preserved than Zeus's temple; it sits to the left facing the hill, past the temples of Metroön and the Nymphaeum. Today, the **Olympic flame** lighting ceremony takes place here before the torch travels around the world to herald the Olympic Games' commencement. Facing away from the Temple of Hera, walk through the archway to reach the ancient **Olympic stadium.** (Open June-Sept. daily 8am- 7:30pm.) The **Archaeological Museum** has an impressive sculpture collection; check out the *Nike of Paeonius* and the *Hermes, carrying the infant Dionysus* by Praxiteles. (Open M 12:30-7:30pm, Tu-Su 8am-7:30pm. Temple and museum each €6, non-EU students €3, EU students free. Both €9/5/free.) Also onsite are the **Museum of the History of the Olympic Games** and the **Museum of the History of Excavations.** (Both museums open M 12:30-7:30pm, Tu-Su 8am-7:30pm. Free.)

The centrally located **Youth Hostel ❶**, Kondili 18, across from the main square, is a cheap place to meet international backpackers and has airy rooms with narrow balconies. (☎26240 22 580. Linens €1. Limited hot showers. Check-out 10am. Lockout 10am-12:30pm. Curfew 11:45pm. Open Feb.-Dec. Dorms €10; doubles €23. Cash only.) Mini-markets, bakeries, and fast food restaurants line **Kondili**, while a walk toward the railroad station or up the hill leads to inexpensive *tavernas*. A filling meal is as Greek as it gets at **Vasilakis Restaurant ❷**, on the corner of Karamanli and Spiliopoulou. Take a right off Kohili before the Youth Hostel, walking towards the ruins. (☎26240 22 104. *Souvlaki* pita €1.50. Chicken and fries €10. Open daily 11:30am-midnight.)

Trains leave the station in the lower part of town for Pirgos (25min., 5 per day, €1), as do **buses** (1hr., 7-15 per day, €1.90). The Town Hall **info center,** at the right end of Kondili, before the turn to the sights, serves as a tourist office. (☎26240 22 262. Open M-F 9:30am-3pm.) **Postal Code:** 27065.

SPARTA (ΣΠΑΡΤΗ)   ☎27310

Though the Spartans of antiquity were renowned for their military strength and physical prowess (weak babies were abandoned on mountaintops), they left little of their fierce legacy behind. Modern Spartans, no longer producing Greek *hoplites*, make olive oil. A few stone fragments and a grove of olive trees comprise the meager ruins at **Ancient Sparta**, a 1km walk north along Paleologou from the town center. At the end of Paleologou, an imposing statue of King Leonidas stands heroically before the soccer stadium. Two blocks from the central *plateia* lies the city's **Archaeological Museum.** Opening into a garden of orange trees and headless statues, the museum displays votive masks, intricate mosaics, lead figures resembling a toy army, and Grecian vases. (☎27310 28 575. Closed indefinitely for renovations.)

Accommodations in Sparta rarely come cheap, and few attractions exist to assuage an empty wallet. **Hotel Cecil ❸**, Paleologou 125, on the corner of Thermopylon, has ordinary, spotless rooms with A/C, bath, phone, and TV in a recently renovated building. (☎27310 24 980. Reserve ahead. Singles €40; doubles €60; triples €75.) Family-run and popular with locals, **Diethnes ❷**, Paleologou 105, 2½ blocks to the right of the intersection of Lykourgou and Paleologou, serves tasty Greek food in an intimate garden with orange trees. Though it has a few vegetarian options (€5), the restaurant specializes in €7 lamb entrees. (☎27310 81 033. Open 8am-midnight.)

Buses go to Athens (3hr., 10 per day, €17) via Tripoli (1hr., €5) and Monemvasia (2hr., 3-4 per day, €9). Town center from the bus station: walk nine blocks uphill on Lykourgou; the **tourist office** is on the third floor of the glass building in the *plateia*. (☎ 27310 24 852. Open M-F 8am-2pm.) **Postal Code:** 23100.

▶ DAYTRIP FROM SPARTA: ▓MYSTRAS (ΜΥΣΤΡΑΣ). Once Byzantium's religious center and the locus of Constantinople's rule over the Peloponnese, Mystras, 6km from Sparta, is a well-preserved medieval town perched on a hillside. The **Agia Sophia** church, where the city's royalty lies buried, and the **Agios Theodoros** fresco contribute to Mystras's timelessness. Don't miss the **castle's** staggering panoramic views of the surrounding countryside. Modest dress is required to visit the functioning convent and its beautifully decorated Pantanassa Church. (*☎ 27310 83 377. Open daily Aug.-Sept. 8am-7:30pm; Oct.-July 8:30am-3pm. €5, students €3, EU students free.*) **Buses** to Mystras leave from the stop on Lykourgou before the intersection with Paleologou and from the corner of Lykourgou and Leonidou in Sparta for the ruins, returning 15min. later (20min., 4-9 per day, €1.40). **Taxis** go to Mystras from the corner of Paleologou and Lykourgou (€5).

MONEMVASIA (ΜΟΝΕΜΒΑΣΙΑ) ☎27320

On a monolithic rock that springs dramatically from the sea, Monemvasia is a Grecian treasure. No cars or bikes are allowed within the Old Town's walls, imbuing the flowered balconies and picturesque corners with a sense of medieval timelessness. Atop the rock, uphill from the *plateia* amidst the ruins of the upper town, is the beautiful **Agia Sofia**, a 12th-century Byzantine church. From Agia Sofia, paths continue uphill toward the old **citadel**, which affords sweeping views of the town and sea below. In the *plateia*, along the shop-lined main street, is the **Archaeological Collection.** (Open Tu-Su 8:30am-3pm. Free.) To get to the Old Town, cross the bridge from Gefyra and follow the road as it curves up the hill. It's an easy 20min. walk, but both the heat and crowds increase as the day wears on. It's better to go in the early morning or late evening, when the setting sun illuminates the panorama in breathtaking shades. A bus also shuttles people up and down the road and leaves from the bridge at the foot of the hill (2min., 4 per hr. 8am-midnight, €1).

Multiple pensions and waterfront *domatia* in **Gefyra** are a budget traveler's best option. Accommodation is available on the rock itself, but it's hardly "budget." With a unique, romantic ambience, dining in the Old Town is beautiful but expensive. On the main road to the right, just before the Archaeological Museum, is **Restaurant Matoula ❸**, with its vine-covered trellises and sweeping ocean views. The food is traditional, made from local ingredients, and the fresh fish is to die for. (☎27320 61 660. Entrees €8-14. *Moussaka* €8. Open daily noon-midnight. MC/V.) For those on a tight budget, there are many cheap Greek fast-food eateries and bakeries. Backpackers often picnic on the beach in New Town, soaking up the beautiful views for free. **Buses** leave from Spartis for Athens (4 per day, €26) and Sparta (2hr., €9). **Postal Code:** 23070.

NAFPLION (ΝΑΥΠΛΙΟ) ☎27520

A tiny Venetian town surrounded on three sides by sky-blue waters, Nafplion is one of the Peloponnese's most beautiful—and most popular—tourist destinations. In July and August, the town teems with more Americans and Italians than locals. After passing from the Venetians to Ottomans, Nafplion became Greece's first capital in 1821. The 18th-century **▓Palamidi fortress** crowns the city, offering spectacular views of the gulf. Climb the 999 steps from across the central *plateia*, right across from the bus station, or take a taxi up the 3km road. (☎27520 28 036. Open 8am-7pm. €4, students €2, EU students and under 18 free.) A small, pebbly beach, **Arvanitia**, is farther along Polizoidhou, past the Palamidi steps; if it's too crowded, follow the footpath to private coves, or take a taxi (€5) to sandy **Karathona** beach. To reach **Bouboulinas,** the waterfront promenade, go left from the bus station and follow Syngrou to the harbor; the **Old Town** is on your left. From Arvanitia, you can walk the short path around the promontory; keep the sea to your left and the town's walls to your right.

Old Town accommodations are often expensive, but ▨**Dimitris Bekas's Domatia ❷**, Efthimiopoulou 26, is a great budget option for travelers spending the night. This small, central pension offers cozy rooms and a roof deck. The friendly manager steadfastly refuses to raise his prices during high season. From the bus station, walk right on Fotomara until you reach the small Catholic church, then turn right on Zygomala, and left up the first set of stairs. (☎27520 24 594. Reserve ahead July-Aug. Singles €22; doubles €28, with bath €30.) ▨**Ellas ❷**, in Pl. Syntagma, has inexpensive Greek and Italian food. The cheerful staff serves people-watching patrons on the outdoor *plateia*. (☎27520 27 278. Entrees €5-7. Open daily noon-4pm and 7-11pm. MC/V.)

Buses, Syngrou 8 (☎27520 27 323; www.ktel-argolis.gr/en/index.htm), depart for: Athens (3hr., 1 per hr. 5am-8pm, €11.80); Epidavros (40min., 3-5 per day, €2.60); Mycenae (45min., 3 per day, €2.60). The **tourist office** is at 25 Martiou, located directly across from the bus station. (☎27520 24 444. Open daily 9am-1pm and 4-8pm.) **Postal Code:** 21100.

▧ DAYTRIPS FROM NAFPLION: EPIDAVROS (ΕΠΙΔΑΥΡΟΣ). Like Olympia and Delphi, **Epidavros** was once both a town and a sanctuary—first to the ancient deity Maleatas and then to Apollo. Eventually, the energies of the sanctuary were directed toward the demigod-doctor Asclepius, the son of Apollo who caught Zeus's wrath (and fatal thunderbolt) when he began to raise people from the dead. Under the patronage of Asclepius, Epidavros became famous across the ancient world as a center of medicine. Today, visitors can explore the **sanctuary,** which is undergoing heavy restoration, and visit a small museum of ancient medical equipment and other artifacts. *(☎27530 22 009. Sanctuary open daily June-Sept. 8am-7pm; Oct.-May 8am-5pm. Museum open June-Sept. M noon-7pm, Tu-Su 8am-7pm; Oct.-May M noon-5pm, Tu-Su 8am-5pm. Both open during festival F-Sa 8am-8pm. €6, students €3, EU students and under 19 free.)* The best-known structure at the site, however, is the splendidly preserved fourth-century ▨**theater,** renowned for its extraordinary acoustics: a match struck or a coin dropped in the center of the stage can be heard in the top rows. Fortunately for today's visitors, Greece's most famous ancient theater has come alive again after centuries of silence: during July and August it hosts the ▨**Epidavros Theater Festival,** with performances by international artists and modern interpretations of classical plays. *(☎27530 22 026; www.greekfestival.gr/?lang=en. Performances begin at 9pm. Tickets at the site's box office: €10-50, the Athens Festival Box Office ☎210 32 72 000, or at Nafplion's bus station.* KTEL **buses** go to Nafplion (45min., 4 per day, €2.60) and make a special trip on performance nights (7:30pm, €6), returning spectators to Nafplion 20min. after the performance ends. Buses run from Ligurio to Athens (2½hr., 2 per day).

NORTHERN AND
CENTRAL GREECE

Northern and central Greece offer an escape from tourist-packed Athens, with fantastic hiking and Byzantine and Hellenistic heritage. Scattered across the region, traditional villages host diverse attractions: the depths of the Vikos Gorge, the heights of Mount Olympus, and the serenity of Meteora's mountaintop monasteries. Greece's heartland boasts some of the country's great cities,

GREECE

Thessaloniki

ACCOMMODATIONS
Hotel Atlantis, 1
Hotel Augustos, 3
Hotel Olympic, 6

FOOD
Chatzi, 4
Derlicatessen, 5
Healthy Advice, 2
Ouzeri Melathron, 7

Thermaic Gulf

INTERNATIONAL FAIRGROUNDS

MESSEGELANDE

300 yards

300 meters

TO PELLA (38km)
TO DOME (3 km), ANCIENT VERGINA (30km)
Train Station

including Thessaloniki and Ioannina. Connected to its Balkan neighbors, the north is where multicultural Greece emerges.

THESSALONIKI Θεσσαλονίκη ☎2310

Thessaloniki (a.k.a. Salonica; pop. 364,000), the Balkans' trade center, has historically been one of the most diverse cities in Greece, and is second in size only to Athens. The city is an energetic bazaar of clothing shops and fashionable cafes, while its churches and mosques provide a material timeline of the region's restless past. Thessaloniki's current lack of tourism infrastructure and subway construction through 2012 may frustrate some travelers.

TRANSPORTATION

Flights: Macedonia Airport (SKG; ☎2310 985 000), 16km east of town. Take bus #78 from the KTEL station or Pl. Aristotelous (2 per hr., €0.50 at kiosks, €0.60 onboard) or taxi (€15). **Olympic Airlines,** Kountouriotou 3 (☎2310 368 311; www.olympicairlines. com; open M-F 8am-4pm), and **Aegean Airlines,** 1 Nikis, off Venizelou (☎2310 239 225; www.aegeanair.com; open M-F 8am-3pm, Sa 8am-2pm), fly to: **Athens** (1hr., 24 per day, €72); **Corfu** (1hr., 5 per week, €116); **Chania** (1hr., 9 per week, €144); **Ioannina** (35min., 4 per week, €130); **Heraklion** (1hr., 15 per week, €85); **Lesvos** (1hr., 15 per day, €96); **Rhodes** (2hr., 11 per week, €110).

Ferries: Buy tickets at **Karacharisis Travel and Shipping Agency,** Kountouriotou 8 (☎2310 513 005). Open M-F 8:30am-8:30pm, Sa 8:30am-2:30pm. Most destinations are pretty far from Thessaloniki (and more easily accessible via Athens), but if you must depart from this city, ferries leave once per week for: **Heraklion** (21-24hr., €38) via **Skiathos** (5hr., €19); **Mykonos** (13hr., €42); **Mytilini** (14 hr., €44); **Naxos** (14hr., €39) via **Syros** (12hr., €38); **Santorini** (17-18hr., €45).

Trains: To reach the **main terminal,** Monastiriou 28, (☎2310 517 517), in the western part of the city, take any bus down Egnatia (€0.50 at kiosks, €0.60 onboard). Trains go to: **Athens** (7hr., 3 per day, €15; express 5hr., 4 per day, €28); **Istanbul, TUR** (14hr., 1 per day, €25); **Skopje, MAC** (4hr., 2 per day, €11); **Sofia, BUL** (7hr., 2 per day, €16). Timetables are available online at www.ose.gr. All trains are run by OSE. It's wise to book a day in advance for trains to Athens.

Buses: Most **KTEL** buses leave from the central, dome-shaped **Macedonia Bus Station** 3km west of the city center (☎2310 595 408). Because Thessaloniki is a major transportation hub, each destination city has its own "platform" or parking spot, and its own ticketing booth. To: **Athens** (6hr., 8 per day, €24); **Corinth** (7hr., 1 per day, €37); **Ioannina** (6hr., 6 per day, €28); **Patras** (7hr., 4 per day, €33). Schedules are subject to change.

Local Transportation: Local buses run often throughout the city. Buy tickets at *periptera* (newsstands; €0.50) or on board (€0.60).

Taxis: (☎2310 551 525) run down Egnatia, Mitropoleos, and Tsimiski with stands at Ag. Sophia and the intersection of Mitropoleos and Aristotelous.

ORIENTATION AND PRACTICAL INFORMATION

Thessaloniki stretches along the Thermaic Gulf's northern shore from the iconic **White Tower** in the east to the prominent western **harbor.** Its rough grid layout makes it nearly impossible to get lost. Its most important arteries run parallel to the water. Closest to shore is **Nikis,** which goes from the harbor to the White Tower and is home to the city's main cafes. Farthest from shore is **Egnatia,** the city's busiest thoroughfare, a six-lane avenue; the Arch of Galerius stands at its intersection with D. Gounari. Inland from Egnatia are **Agios Dimitriou** and the **Old Town.** The city's main square, Aristotelous, has numerous banks, businesses, and restaurants.

Tourist Offices: EOT (☎23109 85 215), at the airport. Open M-F 8am-8pm, Sa 8am-2pm. **GNTO,** Tsimiski 136 (☎2310 2 21 100), at the eastern end of Tsimiski, north of the White Tower. Open M-F 8am-2:50pm, Sa 8:30am-2pm.

Banks: Citi Bank, Tsimiski 21 (☎23103 73 300). Open M-Th 8am-2:30pm, F 8am-2pm. **HSBC,** Tsimiski 8 (☎23102 86 044). Open M-Sa 8am-2:30pm, Su 8am-2pm. No bank accepts Bulgarian or Albanian currencies; travelers coming from these countries must head to the exchange booths at El. Venizelou's intersection with Ermou. All the above banks have **24hr. ATMS.**

Police: (☎23105 53 800). **Tourist police,** 5th fl., Dodekanisou 4 (☎23105 54 871). Free maps and brochures. Open daily 8am-10pm.

Hospital: Acepa Hospital, Kiriakidi 1 (☎23109 93 111). **Hippokratio General Hospital,** A. Papanastassiou 50 (☎23108 92 000). Some doctors speak English. On weekends and at night call ☎1434 to find which hospital has emergency care.

Internet Access: E-Global, Vas. Irakliou 40 (☎23102 52 780; www.e-global.gr), behind the American Consulate. Internet €2.20 per hr., min. €1. Open 24hr.

Post Office: Aristotelous 26 (☎2310 2 68 954), just below Egnatia. Open M-F 7:30am-8pm, Sa 7:30am-2pm, Su 9am-1:30pm. Poste Restante. **Postal Code:** 54101.

ACCOMMODATIONS

Budget options are available, but be prepared to get what you pay for. Thessaloniki's less expensive, slightly run-down hotels are along the western end of **Egnatia** between **Plateia Dimokratias** (500m east of the train station) and **Aristotelous.** Most face the chaotic road on one side and squalid back streets on the other. Hotels fill up quickly during high season, April through September.

Hotel Augustos, El. Svoronou 4 (☎23105 22 550; www.augustos.gr). Clean Rooms with wooden floors and high ceilings. Some have A/C and TVs. Free Wi-Fi. Reception 24hr. Singles €25, with bath €30; doubles €40/50; triples €50/60. Cash only. ❷

Hotel Kastoria, Egnatia 24 and L. Sofou 17 (☎23105 36 280). Most buses stop right outside at the Kolombou stop on Egnatia. The cheapest available option sports cracked linoleum floors and water-stained ceilings. Sinks in each room; communal bathrooms. Reception 24hr. Singles €20; doubles €30; triples €40. Cash only. ❶

Hotel Atlantis, Egnatia 14 (☎2310 5 40 131; www.atlantishotel.com.gr), by the Kolombou bus stop. Underwent renovations last year. Clean and stylish, the standard rooms have sinks and well-maintained shared baths. Only the pricier rooms have A/C and fridges. Hospitable English-speaking staff. Breakfast €4. Free Wi-Fi. Reception and bar 24hr. Singles €27, with bath €33; doubles €40; triples €50. AmEx/MC/V. ❷

FOOD

The old city overflows with *tavernas* and restaurants providing sweeping views of the gulf, while the lovely **Bit Bazaar** has characteristic *ouzeries.* Thessaloniki's restaurants have a delightful custom of giving patrons free watermelon or sweets after a meal, but if you crave anything from dried fruits to apple-sized cherries, head to the bustling public **market,** right off Aristotelous.

Ouzeri Melathron, Karypi 21-34 (☎23102 75 016). From El. Venizelou, walking toward Egnatia take the 1st right after Ermou into the cobblestone passageway. The cheeky menu at this secluded gem features a little of everything and a lot of chicken. Try the

Transvestite Lamb (actually chicken; €5.94) or Maria's Tits (smoked pork chop in mild mustard sauce; €6.16). Free drink with ISIC. Open daily 12:30pm-2:30am. MC/V. ❷

▨ **Healthy Advice,** Al. Svolou 54 (☎23102 83 255). Already missing your ecofriendly-health-food fix? The friendly French-Canadian owner will personally serve you innovative sandwiches and salads, even concocting unique creations (€3.50-7) using the freshest ingredients. Ask for Theo's salad (blue cheese with corn, jalapenos, arugula, hot sauce, and a homemade mustard dressing). Open daily 11:30am-2am. Cash Only. ❶

Delicatessen, Kouskoura 7 (☎23102 36 367). Hands down the most popular place to eat souvlaki (€2), and for good reason: after tasting it here, you won't want to eat the Greek staple anywhere else. Try lamb, chicken, or even mushroom and cheese souvlaki. Open M-W noon-4am, Th-Sa noon-5:30am. Cash only. ❶

◉ SIGHTS

Reminders of Thessaloniki's Byzantine and Ottoman might pervade its streets. The **Roman Agora,** a second-century odeon and covered market, still rests at the top of Aristotelous. Its lower square once held eight *caryatids*, sculptures of women believed to have been magically petrified. (Open daily 8am-8pm. Free.) Originally a temple honoring Jupiter, the **Rotunda** (now **Agios Georgios**) was erected by the Roman Caesar Galerius at the beginning of the AD fourth century. It later became a church honoring martyred Christians, then a mosque under the Ottomans. (☎2310 968 860. Open Tu-F 8am-7pm, Sa-Su 8:30am-3pm. Free.) At D. Gounari and Egnatia stands the striking ▨**Arch of Galerius,** known locally as *Kamara* (Arch), which constituted part of a larger gateway connecting the palace complex to the main city street. Erected by Galerius to commemorate his victory over the Persians, it now serves as a popular meeting spot for locals. Two blocks south of the arch, in Pl. Navarino, a small section of the once 150 sq. km **Palace of Galerius** is open for viewing. The weathered mosaic floors and octagonal hall, believed to have housed Galerius's throne, are particularly notable. The ▨**Archaeological Museum,** M. Andronikou 6, features some of the area's most prized artifacts, including the Derveni krater and sculptures of Greek goddesses. (☎2310 830 538. Open M 10:30am-5pm, Tu-Su 8:30am-3pm. €6, students and seniors €3, EU students and children free.) Its gruesome executions earned the **White Tower** the nickname "Bloody Tower." A walk to the top of Thessaloniki's most prominent landmark, all that remains of the 15th-century Ottoman seawall, no longer means inevitable death; instead the tower offers a view of the city and its shoreline. (Bus #3, 5, 6, 33, or 39. ☎2310 267 832. Open M 12:30pm-7pm, Tu-Su 8:30am-7pm. €2, students free.)

▨ NIGHTLIFE

Thessaloniki is a city that lives outside, with citizens packing its bars, boardwalks, and cafes. The **Ladadika** district, a two-by-three-block rectangle of *tavernas* behind the port, was the city's red-light strip until the 80s, but has since transformed into a sea of dance clubs. The heart of the city's social life during the winter, it shuts down almost entirely in summer, when everyone moves to the open-air discos around the airport. As Thessaloniki's popular clubs change frequently, ask the locals for an update. The waterfront cafes and the **Aristotelous** promenade are always packed, as is the student-territory **Bit Bazaar,** a cobblestoned square of *ouzeries* and wine and tapas bars. For a unique experience, drink and dance to music on one of the three ▨**pirate boats** that leave from behind the White Tower for 30min. harbor tours.

MOUNT OLYMPUS (ΟΛΥΜΠΟΣ ΟΡΟΣ) ☎23520

Erupting out of the Thermaic Gulf, the formidable slopes of Mt. Olympus, Greece's highest peak, mesmerized the ancient Greeks, who believed it to be their pantheon's divine dwelling place. Today, a network of well-maintained **hiking** trails makes the summit accessible to anyone with sturdy legs. Mt. Olympus has eight peaks: Ag. Andonios (2817m), Kalogeros (2701m), Mytikas (2917m), Profitis Ilias (2803m), Skala (2866m), Skolio (2911m), Stefani (the Throne of Zeus, 2909m), and Toumba (2801m). The region became Greece's first national park in 1938. From **Litochoro Town** (pop.7000, 300m), the easiest and most popular trail begins at **Prionia** (1100m), 18km from the village, and ascends 4km through a sheltered, forested ravine to 🏔**Zolotas refuge** (2100m), also known as Refuge A or—to the Greeks—as Spilios Agapitos. At the Zolotas refuge, you'll find reliable resources for all aspects of hiking: updates on weather and trail conditions, advice on routes, and reservations for any of the **Greek Alpine Club (EOS)** refuges. With years of knowledge and experience, the staff is happy to dispense info over the phone in English. (☎23520 84 544. Curfew 10pm. Open mid-May to Oct. Camping €5; dorms €10.)

To rest up before your big hike or race, head to **Hotel Park ②**, Ag. Nikolaou 23, at the bottom of the hill after the park, which has large rooms with A/C, bath, fridge, phone, TV; a few balconies. (☎23520 81 252; hotelpark_litochoro@ yahoo.gr. Breakfast €5. Reception 24hr. Singles €25; doubles €35; triples €45. Cash only.) For a meal with a view, try 🏔**Gastrodromio En Olympo ③**, off the *plateia* by the church. (☎23520 21 300. Entrees €8-14. Open daily 10am-midnight. MC/V.) Those wisely seeking water and trail snacks for the arduous hike up Olympus should stay away from the expensive supermarkets above the *plateia* and head to **Arvanitides**, Perikliko Torba 14, at the end of Odos Ermi. (☎23520 21 195. Open M-F 8am-9pm, Sa-Su 8am-8pm.)

KTEL buses (☎23520 81 271) leave from the Litochoro station, Ag. Nikolaou 20, opposite the tourist office, for Athens (5hr., 3 per day, €30), Plaka (15min., 1 per hr., €2), and Thessaloniki (1hr., 16 per day, €8) via Katerini (30min., 1 per hr., €2). The **tourist office** is on Ag. Nikolaou by the park. (☎23520 83 100. Open daily 9am-2:30pm and 4:30-9:30pm.) **Postal Code:** 60200.

METEORA AND KALAMBAKA
(ΜΕΤΕΩΡΑ AND ΚΑΛΑΜΠΑΚΑ) ☎24320

The monastic community of Meteora lies atop a series of awe-inspiring rock pinnacles. Inhabited by hermits since the 11th century, these summits were chosen as the location of a series of 21 frescoed Byzantine **monasteries** in the 14th century. Six monasteries remain in use and open to the public. Don't expect a hidden treasure—tour buses and sweaty faces are as common here as Byzantine icons, and the traditionally dressed monks drive Jeeps. For monastic silence rarely experienced during the day, visit the complex after hours, when the museums are closed. The largest, oldest, and most popular monastery, **Great Meteoron** houses a **folk and history museum** and the 16th-century **Church of the Transfiguration.** On the first level, visitors can peer through a door into the monastery's ossuary to see shelves upon shelves of deceased monks' skulls and other skeletal remains. The complex's second largest monastery, **Varlaam,** is 800m down the road. Take the right fork to reach the **Roussanou** convent, which was accessible only by rope ladder until 1897. (Modest dress required: no sleeveless shirts, long pants for men and long skirts for women. Tie-on skirts available at the monastery entrance. Hours vary by season and monastery. Great Meteoron, ☎24320 22 278 or 24320 75 398, open in summer M and W-Su 9am-5pm; Varlaam, ☎24320 22 277, open M-W and F-Su 9am-4pm; Roussanou, ☎24320 22

649, open daily 9am-6pm. Each monastery €2.) Meteora is accessible from the Kalambaka **bus** station (15min., 2-4 per day, €1.40), or visitors can walk 45min. up the hill along the **footpath** that begins at the end of Vlahava.

Meteora and Kalambaka's rocky landscapes create a **climber's** paradise; for info, equipment rental, guided excursions, and lessons, contact local climbing instructor **Kostas Liolios** (☎69725 67582; kliolios@kalampaka.com). Accommodation owners may approach you at the bus station offering lower prices for decent rooms; be aware that picking up people from the station is illegal here. At the base of Meteora, ■**Alsos House ❸**, Kanari 5, has rooms with A/C, balcony, bath, and gorgeous views. From the Town Hall and main square (Pl. Dimarhiou), follow Vlahava until it ends, then follow the signs. The owner sometimes hires students in summer in exchange for room and board. (☎24320 24 097; www.alsoshouse.gr. Breakfast included. Free Internet and Wi-Fi. Free parking. Reserve ahead. Singles €35-40; doubles €50-55; triples €70-75; 2-room apartment with kitchen €90. 10% *Let's Go* or ISIC discount. MC/V.) In the center of town, **Taverna Panellinion ❶**, Pl. Dimarhiou, serves up a wide range of traditional, delicious Greek fare on a lovely trellis-shaded patio. (☎24320 24 735. Entrees €5-8. Open daily noon-11pm.)

Trains (☎24320 22 451) leave Kalambaka for Athens (5hr., 2 per day, €21). **Buses** (☎24320 22 432) depart Kalambaka for: Athens (5hr., 7 per day, €25) via Trikala; Ioannina (3hr., 2 per day, €11.20); Patras (5hr.; Tu, Th-F, and Su 1 per day; €27.50); Thessaloniki (3hr., 6 per day, €17.50) via Trikala. Helpful staff provide maps and transportation information at the **municipal tourist office,** across the street from the fountain in Pl. Dimarhiou, at the beginning of Vlahava. (☎24320 77 734. Open M-F 8am-8pm, Sa 8am-2pm.) **Postal Code:** 42200.

DELPHI (ΔΕΛΦΟΙ)   ☎22650

Troubled denizens of the ancient world journeyed to the stunning mountain-top of the ■**Oracle of Delphi,** where the priestess of Apollo conveyed the god's cryptic prophecies. Leading up the hillside along the **Sacred Way** are the remains of the legendary **Temple of Apollo,** followed by a perfectly preserved **theater** and a **stadium** that once hosted the holy **Delphic Games.** At the entrance to the site, the **archaeological museum** exhibits an extensive collection of artifacts found near the temple, including the **Sphinxes** (the oracle's guards). Head east from Delphi to reach the temple, but go early in the morning to avoid the nonstop flow of guided groups. (Archaeological site open daily 7:30am-7:30pm. Museum open M noon-6:30pm, Tu-Su 7:30am-7:30pm. Each €6, both €9; students €3/5; EU students free.) For overnight stays, the recently renovated **Hotel Sibylla ❷**, Pavlou 9, offers wonderful views and private baths at the best prices in town. (☎22650 82 335; www.sibylla-hotel.gr. No-commission currency exchange. Singles €20-24; doubles €26-30; triples €35-40. €2 *Let's Go* discount.) In July, Delphi springs to life with a series of musical and theatrical **performances** at its Cultural Center (☎22650 331 2781; www.eccd.gr). From Delphi, **buses** go to Athens (3hr., 6 per day, €13.60). Delphi's **tourist office,** Pavlou 12 or Friderikis 11, is right up to the stairs next to the town hall. (☎22650 82 900. Open M-F 8am-2:30pm.) **Postal Code:** 33054.

ZAGOROHORIA   ☎26530

Between the Albanian border and the North Pindos mountain range, a string of 46 *horia* (little hamlets) show few signs of interference from modern society. Home to **Vikos Gorge**—the world's deepest canyon—and **Vikos-Aoös National Park,** the region is popular among nature enthusiasts. North of Vikos Gorge, the two **Papingo** villages, **Megalo** (large) and **Mikro** (small), have become vacation

LOCAL LEGEND

THE WORLD'S BELLY BUTTON

As they make the ascent up the Sacred Way at Delphi, many visitors stride unknowingly past the center of the earth—or, more specifically, its belly button.

According to ancient Greek mythology, Zeus wished to find the center of the world—its *omphalos*, or "navel." The king of the gods sent two eagles, one from the west and one from the east, to fly across the earth until they met. The two eagles encountered one another at Delphi, and there an *omphalos* stone was erected to mark the center of the world. Of course, another legend holds that the stone marks the place where Apollo slayed the serpent Python.

The Archaeological Museum at Delphi houses an *omphalos* stone, a conical object representing the earth's navel. Though the marker at the actual site is less aesthetically evocative, visitors can place their hands on the stone and enjoy a glorious moment at the center of the world—or at least its belly button. Look for a concrete, egg-shaped stone set on a square base on the Sacred Way before the Temple of Apollo.

(p. 375. Delphi archaeological sites open daily 7:30am-7:30pm. Museum open M noon-6:30pm, Tu-Su 7:30am-7:30pm. Sites €6, museum €6, both €9; students €3/5; EU students free.)

destinations for wealthy Greeks and serve as the start point for some beautiful hikes.

TRANSPORTATION AND PRACTICAL INFORMATION. Buses go to Ioannina from the Papingos (1hr., 2 per week, €5). Papingo visitors may consider hiking 3hr. to **Klidonia** to catch more frequent buses (1hr., 8 per day, €4). **Taxis** can take you to Ioannina or Konitsa (€35). The closest **banks** are in Kalpaki and Konitsa. Any trip should include a visit to the **Zagori Information Center** in the town of **Aspraggeli**. (☎26530 22 241. Open daily 9am-6pm.)

ACCOMMODATIONS AND FOOD. An increase in tourism has raised the region's lodging prices. If pensions and *domatia* are full or high-season prices are outrageous, backpackers may hike 3km to the **EOS Refuge ❶**, near Mt. Astraka. (☎26530 26 553. 60-bed dorm €10.) Freelance camping is illegal. **Pension Koulis ❸** has rooms reminiscent of an alpine ski lodge. Facing the town from where the cobblestoned road starts, take the first left after the church. The pension is on the corner of the next crossroads to the left. (☎26530 41 115. Breakfast included. Reception 24hr. Singles €35; doubles €50; triples €65. MC/V.) At **Tsoumanis Estiatorio ❷**, outside town on the road to Mikro Papingo, two brothers serve lamb from their father's flock and vegetables from their gardens. (☎26530 42 108. Entrees €5-9. Open daily 11am-1am.)

SIGHTS AND HIKING. Vikos Gorge, whose walls are 900m deep and only 110m apart, is the steepest on earth. In spring, the gorge's river rushes along the 15km stretch of canyon floor. By summer, all that is left is the occasional puddle in the dry riverbed. People have walked through the gorge's ravine since the 12th century BC, when early settlers took shelter in its caves. Today, hikers follow the well-marked **O3 domestic trail** (red diamonds on white square backgrounds) section of the Greek National E4 route through the gorge. The path stretches from the village of Kipi in the south to Megalo Papingo at its northernmost tip, winding through Zagorohoria's center. The gorge can be accessed from Kipi, Monodendri, the Papingo villages, and Vikos Village.

Zagorohoria's most spectacular hikes begin in **Mikro Papingo,** from where visitors can climb **Mount Astraka** (2436m). Most ascents take about 4hr. and are appropriate for intermediate-level hikers. More advanced hikers climb 4hr. to the pristine **Drakolimni** (Dragon Lake; 2000m), an alpine pool filled with spotted newts. Both hikes can be paired with a stay in the **EOS Refuge** (1900m), on a nearby ridge. From the refuge, a path (3km, 1hr.) descends into the blossom-dotted valley, passes **Xeroloutsa**, a shallow alpine lake, and ends at Drakolimni. Multi-day treks deep into the Pindos are possible, using the EOS hut as a starting point. For easier hikes, the family-friendly **Papingo Natural Pools** are a great option. When the main road curves right before ascending to Mikro Papingo from Megalo, you'll see a small bridge and parking lot. Opposite the parking lot, the white-rock trail begins. The pools become warmer and cleaner as you climb along, but beware of the venomous snakes when taking a dip in the lower pools.

IOANNINA   ☎26510

The capital of Epirus, Ioannina serves as the natural transportation hub for northern Greece. The city reached its height of fame after its 1788 capture by Ali Pasha, an Albanian-born visionary leader and womanizer. Legend has it that when Ali Pasha wasn't able to get the girl he wanted, he strangled all of his other lovers and threw their bodies into Ioannina's lake. The city is also the site of the **Frourio**, a monumental fortress built in the 14th century, where many of the city's residents live today. To reach the **Its-Kale** (inner citadel) from the Frourio's main entrance, veer left, and follow the signs. To the right along the wall are the remnants of Ali Pasha's **hamam** (baths). Catch a ferry from the waterfront (10min., 2 per hr. 7am-midnight, €2) to the island of **Nisi** to explore Byzantine monasteries and the **Ali Pasha Museum** (open daily 9am-9pm; €2). **Hotel Tourist ❺**, Kolleti 18, on the right a few blocks up G. Averof from the *kastro*, offers simple rooms with A/C, TV, bath, and phone. (☎ 26510 26443; www.hoteltourist.gr/en.htm. Singles €45; doubles €44; triples €66.) Portions are huge and prices reasonable at lakeside **Limni ❷**. (☎26510 78 988; www.limni-ioa.gr. Entrees €5-8.) **Buses**, Zossimadon 4, depart from the main terminal to: Athens (6hr., 7 per day, €34); Kalambaka (2hr., 2 per day, €11); Thessaloniki (5hr., 4 per day, €27). For info, call ☎26510 26 286. To reach the **tourist office**, walk down Dodonis; the office is located immediately after the school. (☎26510 46 662. Open M-F 7:30am-7:30pm.) **Postal Code:** 45110.

IONIAN ISLANDS (IONIA NHΣIA)

West of mainland Greece, the Ionian Islands entice travelers with their lush vegetation and turquoise waters. Never conquered by the Ottomans, the islands reflect the influences of British, French, Russian, and Venetian occupants. Today, they are a favorite among Western Europeans and travelers seeking the truly unconventional Greece.

CORFU (KEPKYPA)   ☎26610

Ever since Homer's Odysseus raved about Corfu's beauty, the surrounding seas have brought a steady stream of conquerors, colonists, and tourists. There is something for everyone in Corfu, with archaeological sites, beautiful beaches, and rich nightlife. Situated between the New Fortress on the east and the Old Fortress on the west, **Corfu Town** (pop. 39,500) is a jumbled labyrinth of Venetian buildings. The winding streets and hidden plazas of the Old Town, though quaint and charming, are an urban planner's nightmares. Saunter along the serene, tree-shaded pathways of the grounds at ▨**Mon Repos Estate**, which features a Doric temple, lovely gardens, and the **Museum of Paleopolis**, which displays the island's archaeological treasures. To reach the estate from the Old Town, walk away from the Old Fortress and follow Dimokratias along the waterfront to the end of the bay. Once you reach the hill, be careful walking up the road as there are no sidewalks and cars and motorcycles may emerge out of blind turns. (☎26610 30 680. Estate open daily 8am-7pm. Museum open Tu-Su 8:30am-3pm. Estate free. Museum €3, EU students €2.) **Paleokastritsa beach,** with caves perfect for exploring, lies west of Corfu Town. Take a KTEL bus to Paleokastritsa (45min., 4-7 per day, €2.10). Traditional villages encircle ▨**Mt. Pantokrator** and its sunset panorama and views into Albania and Italy.

Finding cheap accommodations in Corfu Town is virtually impossible. Plan to stay in a nearby village only a bus ride away, or book months ahead. The **Federation of Owners of Tourist Accommodation of Corfu,** Polilas 2A, is more of a local service for hostel owners than a tourist office, but can be helpful in a crunch. (☎26610 26 133; www.holidaysincorfu.com. Open M-F 9am-3pm and 5-8pm.) KTEL buses run from Corfu Town to Ag. Gordios (45min., 3-7 per day, €2), home to an impressive beach and the backpacker's legend **Pink Palace Hotel ❷.** Patrons can partake in 24/7 bacchanalia with this quintessential party hostel. Lock up your valuables in the front desk's safety deposit box before enjoying the daily events. (☎26610 53 103; www.thepinkpalace.com. Bus service to Athens €55, mid-July to mid-Aug. €65. Scooter and kayak rentals €10 per day. Bar open 24hr. Breakfast, cafeteria-style dinner, and plane/bus/ferry pickup included. Laundry €9. Internet €2 per 35min. Dorms from €18; private rooms from €25.) For more mellow digs, take bus #11 to nearby Pelekas (20min., 7 per day, €1), where ▨**Pension Martini ❷,** down the hill from the bus stop, on the left side of the street, offers sunny rooms with balconies and superb views. In the evening, join the family for wine or *ouzo* in the garden. (☎26610 94 326; www. pensionmartini.com. Singles and doubles €25-35.)

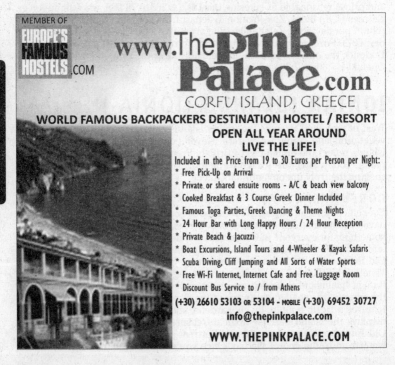

Olympic and Aegean Airlines connect Corfu's **Ioannis Kapodistrias Airport** (**CFU** or **LGKR;** ☎26610 39 040) to Athens (1hr., 2-3 per day, €64-121) and Thessaloniki (1hr., 3 per week, €85-142). **Ferries** run from Corfu Town to: Bari, ITA (10hr., 4 per week); Brindisi, ITA (8hr., 1-2 per day); Patras (8hr., 5 per week); Venice, ITA (24hr., 1 per day). Prices vary significantly. For more info, try any of the travel agencies that line the road to the port. **International Tours** (☎26610 39 007; www.intertourscorfu.com) and **Ionian Cruises** (☎26610 31 649; www.ionian-cruises.com), both across the street from the old port on El. Venizelou, book international ferries. Buy your ticket at least a day ahead and ask if it includes port tax. Green KTEL **buses** depart from the intercity bus station (☎26610 28 927) between I. Theotoki and the New Fortress for Athens (8hr., 3 per day, €40-47) and Thessaloniki (8hr., 2 per day, €38-45); prices include ferry. Blue municipal buses leave from Pl. San Rocco (☎26610 32 158; tickets €1) The **tourist office** is in Pl. San Rocco in a green kiosk. (☎26610 20 733. Open daily 9am-2pm and 6-9pm.) **Postal Code:** 49100.

ZAKYNTHOS (ΖΑΚΥΝΘΟΣ)   ☎26950

Known as the greenest Ionian Island, Zakynthos is home to thousands of species of plants and flowers, as well as a large *Caretta caretta* (loggerhead sea turtle) population. **Zakynthos Town** maintains a romantic, nostalgic air. Boats leave Zakynthos Town for many of the island's spectacular sights, including the glowing **Blue Caves** on the northeastern shore past Skinari. Southwest of the Blue Caves is ◼**Smuggler's Wreck.** A shipwrecked boat's remains have made the beach one of the most photographed in the world. **Keri Caves** and **Marathonisi** (also called Turtle Island because of its resemblance to a turtle) lie farther south. Agencies giving tours of Zakynthos advertise along Lomvardou; most excursions leave around 9:30am, return at 5:30pm, and cost €16-25. For a more intimate travel experience, skip the huge cruise ships and hire a small fishing boat from the docks in northern villages. A 10min. walk down the beach (with the water on your right) will take you to the deserted sands of ◼**Kalamaki,** a turtle nesting site, and protected **National Marine Park** (www.nmp-zak.org). At night, the turtles inhabit some of Zakynthos's most picturesque beaches, like **Gerakas,** on the island's southeastern tip.

Athina Marouda Rooms for Rent ❶, on Tzoulati and Koutouzi, has simple, clean rooms with fans, large windows, and communal baths. (☎26950 45 194. June-Sept. singles €15; doubles €30. Oct.-May €10/20. Cash only.) Dining in the *plateias* and by the waterfront is a treat. **Village Inn ❸**, Lomvardou 20, at the right end of the waterfront before Pl. Solomou, feels more like a bayou lounge and has tables facing the water. (☎26950 26 991. Entrees €6-15. Th night live Greek music. Open daily 8am-midnight. MC/V.) Getting around the island can be frustrating—taxis can be terribly overpriced and tour operators may seem like glorified tourist babysitters. Dozens of places rent **scooters** (€15 per day), but driver's license requirements are strictly enforced. **Buses** go from the station, two blocks away from the water, to Kalamaki (20min., 12 per day, €1.20) and Laganas (20min., 15 per day, €1.20). Buses also board **ferries** to the mainland and continue to Athens (6hr., 5 per day, €23), Patras (3hr., 3 per day, €7), and Thessaloniki (10hr., M-Th and Su 1 per day, €43). **Postal Code:** 29100.

CYCLADES (ΚΥΚΛΑΔΕΣ)

Sun-drenched, winding stone streets, and trellis-covered *tavernas* define the Cycladic islands, but subtle quirks make each distinct. Orange and black sands coat Santorini's shoreline, and celebrated archaeological sites testify to Delos's mythical and historical significance. Naxos and Paros offer travelers peaceful

GREECE

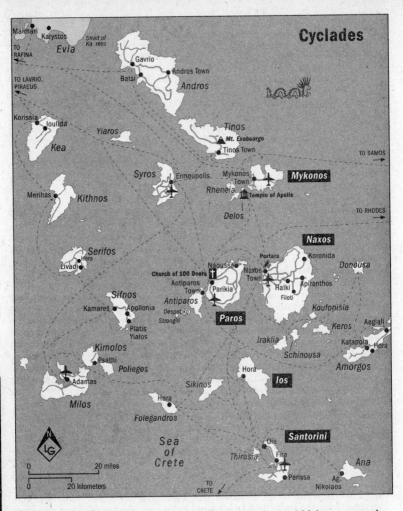

mountains and villages, while notorious party spots Ios and Mykonos uncork some of the world's wildest nightlife.

MYKONOS (ΜΥΚΟΝΟΣ) ☎22890

Coveted by 18th-century pirates, Mykonos still attracts revelers and gluttons. Although Mykonos is a fundamentally chic sophisticates' playground, you don't have to break the bank to have a good time. Ambling down **Mykonos Town's** colorful alleyways at dawn or dusk, surrounded by tourist-friendly pelicans, is the cheapest, most exhilarating way to experience the island. Drinking and sunbathing are Mykonos's main forms of entertainment. While the island's beaches are nude, bathers' degree of bareness varies; in most places, people prefer to show off their designer bathing suits rather than their birthday suits.

Platis Yialos and **Super Paradise** appeal to more brazen nudists, while **Elia** beach attracts a tamer crowd. The super-famous **Paradise** beach is so crowded with hungover Italians and overpriced sun beds that you can barely see its gorgeous water. The **Skandinavian Bar,** inland from the waterfront towards Little Venice, is a two-building party complex. (☎22890 22 669. Beer €4-6. Mixed drinks from €8. Open daily 9pm-5am.) After drinking all night, usher in a new day at █Cavo **Paradiso,** on Paradise beach. Considered one of the world's top dance clubs, it hosts internationally renowned DJs and inebriated crowds. Take the bus to Paradise beach and follow the signs; it's a 10min. walk. (☎22890 27 205. Drinks from €10. Cover €25, after 2am €40; includes 1 drink. Open daily 3-11am.)

Like everything else on Mykonos, accommodations are prohibitively expensive. Camping is the best budget option. The popular **Paradise Beach Camping ❶,** 6km from Mykonos Town, has decent facilities, plenty of services, and proximity to the beach. (☎22890 22 129; www.paradisemykonos.com. Free pickup at port or airport. Safes available. Breakfast included. Internet €4.50 per hr. €5-10 per person, €2.50-4 per small tent, €4.50-7 per large tent; 1- to 2-person cabin €15-50. 3-person tent rental €8-18.) Cozy and colorful █Kalidonios ❸, Dilou 1, off Kalogera, serves a range of Greek and Mediterranean dishes. (☎22890 27 606. Entrees €8-15. Open daily noon-12:30am. MC/V.) For a cheap meal, head to **Pasta Fresca ❶,** on Georgouli, near the Skandinavian Bar. Its streetside takeout window is the place to grab the best *gyros* (€2) and chicken pitas (€2) that Mykonos has to offer. (☎22890 22 563. Open daily 4pm-late.)

Ferries run from the New Port, west of town, to Naxos (3hr., 1 per week, €9.50), Paros (3hr., 1 per day, €8.40), and Piraeus (6hr., 1 per day, €26). The **tourist police** are at the ferry landing. (☎22890 22 482. Open daily 8am-9pm.) **Buses** run south from Mykonos Town to Platis Yialos and Paradise (20min., 2 per hr., €1.20-1.50) and to Elia (30min., 8 per day, €1.10). Windmills Travel, on Xenias, around the corner from South Station, has a number of **GLBT resources.** (☎22890 26 555; www.windmillstravel.com. Open daily 8am-10pm.) **Postal Code:** 84600.

PAROS (ΠΑΡΟΣ)
☎22840

Now a central transportation hub, Paros was once famed for its slabs of pure white marble, used to construct many of the ancient world's great statues and buildings. It's a favorite destination for families and older travelers, removed from the luxurious debauchery of Mykonos and the youth-filled streets of Ios. Behind the commercial surface of **Parikia,** Paros's port and largest city, flower-lined streets wind through archways to one of the world's most treasured Orthodox basilicas, the **Panagia Ekatontapiliani** (Church of Our Lady of 100 Doors). This white three-building complex is dedicated to St. Helen, mother of the Emperor Constantine, who reportedly had a vision of the True Cross here while traveling to the Holy Land. (Dress modestly. Open daily 7am-10pm. Mass M-Sa 7-7:30pm, Su 7-10am. Free.) About 8km north of town, **Naoussa beach** is the most popular and crowded destination on the island. On the opposite coast, █Aliki beach is much quieter, but often windy.

Turn left at the dock and take a right after the cemetery ruins to reach the well-kept, cottage-like **Rena Rooms ❷.** (☎22840 22 220; www.cycladesnet.gr/ rena. Free pickup and luggage storage. Reserve ahead. Singles €15-35; doubles €20-40; triples €30-55. 20% *Let's Go* discount. Additional discount if paid in cash. MC/V.) The funky █Happy Green Cow ❸, a block off the *plateia* behind the National Bank, serves tasty vegetarian dinners. (☎22840 24 691. Entrees €12-15. Open Apr.-Nov. daily 7pm-midnight.) At the far end of the Old Town's waterfront, 5min. past the port and bus station, Paros's nightlife pulses late into the night. A central courtyard connects three themed bar areas: **The Dubliner,** an Irish pub, **Down Under,** an Aussie bar, and **Paros Rock Cafe,** decorated with bright

GREECE

colors and the appropriate flags. Follow the spotlight and crowds to the end of the harbor. (Beer €3-5. Mixed drinks €5-6. Cover €3; includes 1 drink.)

Ferries go to: Folegandros (5hr., 3 per week, €9); Ios (3hr., 5 per week, €13); Mykonos (5hr., 5 per week, €7); Naxos (1hr., 2 per day, €7); Thessaloniki (19hr., 2 per week, €38). Check with the budget travel office **Polos Tours** (☎22840 22 092; www.polostours.gr), 50m to the right of the ferry dock gate, for ferry schedules and departure times. The **tourist police** are on the *plateia* behind the telephone office. (☎22840 21 673. Open M-F 7am-2:30pm.) **Postal Code:** 84400.

NAXOS (ΝΑΞΟΣ)   ☎22850

Ancient Greeks believed Dionysus, the god of wine and revelry, once lived on Naxos (pop. 20,000), the largest of the Cyclades. Olive groves, small villages, chalky ruins, silent monasteries, and unadulterated hikes fill its interior, while sandy beaches line its shores. **Naxos Town,** its capital, is a dense collection of labyrinthine streets, bustling *tavernas*, and tiny museums, crowned by the ▧**Kastro,** an inhabited Venetian fortress, tranquil despite the tourists. At the Kastro's entrance, the **Domus Della Rocca-Barozzi** (a.k.a. the Venetian Museum) exhibits photographs, books, and furniture belonging to a local aristocratic family still living there. (☎22850 223 87; www.naxosisland.gr/venetianmuseum. Open daily in high season 10am-3pm and 7-11pm; low season 10am-3pm and 7-10pm. €5, students €3. Nightly summer concerts at 9:15pm. €10; reserve ahead at the museum reception.) The **Archaeological Museum** occupies the former Collège Français. (Open Tu-Su 8am-5pm. €3, students €2.)

Accommodations in Naxos are available in private rooms and studios on the street between the town's center and the nearby Ag. Giorgios beach, or in campsites by the island's many beaches. Though most campgrounds vary little in price (generally €4-8 per person, €2-3 per tent), **Naxos Camping ❶** is the closest to Naxos Town (2km) and only 150m from **Ag. Giorgios** beach. (☎22850 235 00. Prices vary seasonally.) Nearby **Heavens Cafe Bar ❷** serves scrumptious Belgian waffles with delicious fresh fruit for €5. (☎22850 227 47. Internet €3 per hr.; free Wi-Fi. Open daily 8am-2am.)

Ferries go from Naxos Town to: Crete (7hr., 1 per week, €21); Ios (1hr., 1 per day, €10); Mykonos (3hr., 1 per day, €9); Paros (1hr., 4 per day, €8); Piraeus (6hr., 4 per day, €28); Rhodes (13hr., 1 per week, €25); Santorini (3hr., 3 per day, €13). A bus goes from the port to the beaches of Ag. Giorgios, Ag. Prokopios, Ag. Anna, and Plaka (2 per hr. 7:30am-2am, €1.20). **Buses** (☎22850 222 91) also run from Naxos Town to ▧**Apiranthos,** a beautiful village with narrow, marble paths (1hr., 5 per day, €2.30). The Naxos Town **tourist office** is located next to the bus station. (☎22850 229 93. Open daily 8am-11pm.) **Postal Code:** 84300.

IOS (ΙΟΣ)   ☎22860

Despite recent concerted efforts to tone down its party-animal reputation, Ios remains the Greek debauchery heaven—or hell. Life on the island revolves around its insane and non-stop party scene: breakfast is served at 2pm, drinking begins at 3pm, people don't go out before midnight, and revelers dance madly in the streets until well after dawn. The **port** of Gialos is at one end of the island's sole paved road. The town of **Hora** sits above it on a hill, but most visitors spend their days at **Mylopotas beach,** a 25min. walk downhill from Hora or a short bus ride from town (3-6 per hr., €1.20). Establishments on the beach offer snorkeling, water-skiing, and windsurfing during the day (€9-45). Sunning is typically followed—or accompanied—by drinking; the afternoon bars are no less crowded than the nighttime ones. Head up from the *plateia* to reach the **Slammer Bar** for tequila slammers (€3), then stop by **Disco 69** for some dirty dancing (beer €5; cover €6 midnight-4am). Get lost in the streetside ▧**Red**

Bull (beer €3), dance on the tables at **Sweet Irish Dream** (beer €3; cover €5 2:30-4:30am), or grind to techno at **Scorpion Disco,** the island's largest club (cover €7 2-4:30am, includes a mixed drink and shot). Most clubs close between 4 and 7am, when the drunkenness and antics spill onto the streets. A few hours later, crowds begin to re-gather at the beach.

In addition to cheap dorms, ■**Francesco's** ❶ offers stunning sunset harbor views from its terrace. Take the steps up the hill to the left in the *plateia* and then the first left at the Diesel shop. (☎22860 91 223; www.francescos.net. Breakfast 9am-2pm €2.50-5. Internet €1 per 15min. Reception 9am-2pm and 6-10pm. Check-out 11am. Dorms €11-18; 2- to 4-person rooms with A/C and bath €15-28 per person.) Back in town, ■**Ali Baba's** ❷, next to Ios Gym, serves authentic Thai food. (☎22860 91 558. Entrees €6-12. Open Mar.-Oct. daily 6pm-1am.) Off the main church's *plateia*, **Old Byron's** ❸ is an intimate wine bar and bistro with creative renditions of Greek staples. (☎697 819 2212. Entrees €9-15. Reserve ahead. Open M-Sa 6-11:30pm, Su noon-11:30pm. MC/V.) Greek fast food and creperies pack the central *plateia*. **Ferries** go to: Naxos (1hr., 1-3 per day, €9); Paros (3hr., 1-3 per day, €10); Piraeus (8hr., 2-3 per day, €35); Santorini (1hr., 3-5 per day, €7). **Postal Code:** 84001.

SANTORINI (ΣΑΝΤΟΡΙΝΗ)   ☎22860

Whitewashed towns sitting delicately on cliffs, black-sand beaches, and deeply scarred hills make Santorini's landscape nearly as dramatic as the volcanic cataclysm that created it. Wander around the town's cobbled streets in **Fira** (pop. 2500), the island's capital. At Santorini's northern tip, the town of **Oia** (*EE-ah;* pop. 700) is the best place in Greece to watch the sunset, though its fame draws crowds hours in advance. To catch a glimpse of the sun, and not of someone taking a picture of it, walk down the hill from the village and settle alone near the many windmills and pebbled walls. To get to Oia, take a **bus** from Fira (25min., 23 per day, €1.20). **Red Beach,** and the impressive archaeological excavation site of the Minoan city **Akrotiri**, entirely preserved by lava (but currently closed for repairs), lie on Santorini's southwestern edge. Buses run to Akrotiri from Fira (30min., 15 per day, €1.60). Buses also leave Fira for the black-sand beaches of **Kamari** (20min., 32 per day, €1.20), **Perissa** (30min., 32 per day, €1.90), and **Perivolos** (20min., 21 per day, €1.90). The bus stops before Perissa in Pyrgos; from there, ■**hike** (2hr.) across a rocky mountain path to the ruins of **Ancient Thira**. Stop after 1hr. on a paved road at **Profitis Ilias Monastery,** whose lofty location provides an island panorama. (Open M and W 4-5pm, Sa 4:30-8:30pm. Dress modestly. Free.)

Close to Perissa's beach, ■**Youth Hostel Anna** ❶ has colorful rooms and loads of backpackers hanging out on its streetside veranda. (☎22860 82 182. Port pickup and drop-off included. Reception 9am-5pm and 7-10pm. Check-out 11:30am. Reserve ahead. June-Aug. 10-bed dorms €12; 4-bed dorms €15; doubles €50; triples €60. Sept.-May €6/8/22/30. MC/V.) At night, head to ■**Murphy's** in Fira, which claims to be Greece's first Irish pub. (Beer €5. Mixed drinks €6.50. Cover €5 after 10pm. Open Mar.-Oct. daily 11:30am-late.)

Olympic Airways (☎22860 22 493) and **Aegean Airways** (☎22860 28 500) fly from Fira's airport to Athens (50min., 4-7 per day, €85-120) and Thessaloniki (1hr., 1-2 per day, €125). **Ferries** depart from Fira to: Crete (4hr., 4 per week, €16); Ios (1hr., 1-3 per day, €7); Naxos (3hr., 1-2 per day, €16); Paros (4hr., 1-4 per day, €17); Piraeus (10hr., 2-3 per day, €33). Most ferries depart from Athinios Harbor. Frequent **buses** (25min., €1.70) with changing daily schedules connect to Fira, but most hostels and hotels offer **shuttle** service as well. Check bus and ferry schedules at any travel agency for up-to-date

GREECE

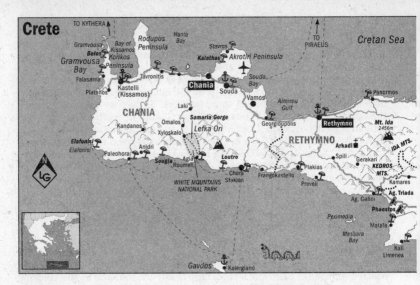

Crete

information, and be aware that the self-proclaimed **tourist offices** at the port are actually for-profit agencies. **Postal Codes:** 84700 (Fira); 84702 (Oia).

CRETE (KPHTH)

According to a Greek saying, a Cretan's first loyalty is to his island, his second to his country. Since 3000 BC, when Minoan civilization flourished on the island, Crete has maintained an identity distinct from the rest of Greece; pride in the island proves well founded. Travelers will be drawn to Crete's warm hospitality and enticing beaches, gorges, monasteries, mosques, and villages.

HERAKLION (ΗΡΑΚΛΕΙΟ)   ☎2810

Heraklion, also spelled Iraklion (pop. 138,000), Crete's capital and primary port, may not be particularly picturesque, but its importance as a transportation hub makes it a necessary stop on the way to Crete's more scenic destinations. Olympic Airways and Aegean Airlines **fly** domestically from the **Heraklion International Airport**, Nikos Kazantzakis (**HER;** ☎2810 397 129) to: Athens (50min., 4-7 per day, €80-100); Rhodes (1hr., 6 per week, €105-115); Thessaloniki (1hr., 2 per day, from €109). Budget airline Wizz Air also flies from Heraklion to Budapest, HUN (1-3hr., 1 per week, €145) and Katowice, POL (3hr., 1 per week, €280). From Terminal A, between the old city walls and the harbor, **buses** leave for Agios Nikolaos (1½hr., 19-21 per day, €6.20) and Chania (3hr., 16 per day, €12) via Rethymno (1-1½hr., €6.30). **Buses** leave across from Terminal B for Phaestos (1½hr., 1 per day, €5.70). **Ferries** also go to: Mykonos (8hr., 2 per week, €25); Naxos (8½hr., 3 per week, €23); Paros (7hr., 4 per week, €26); Santorini (4hr., 3 per week, €16). Check for travel delays online at **GNET**, Merambelou 14-16. (☎2810 221 622. Open daily 24hr.) Soothe the burn of a missed flight with drinks or a borrowed book atop the quiet rooftop garden at **Rent Rooms Hellas ❶**, Handa-

kos 24. Walk east along the waterfront and turn left onto Handakos. (☎2810 288 851. Free luggage storage. Check-out 11am. Dorms €11; doubles €25-31; triples €42.) The open-air **market** on 1866, near Pl. Venizelou, sells cheese, meat, and produce. (Open M-Sa 8am-2pm.) **Ouzeri Tou Terzaki** ❷, Loch. Marineli 17, in the center of town, serves fresh Greek meals with complimentary raki liquor and fruit. (☎2810 221 444; www.en.terzakhs.gr. *Mezedhes* €5-10. Open M-Sa noon-midnight. MC/V.) Those looking to kill time between connections should check out the ◼**Tomb of Nikos Kazantzakis**, on top of the city walls. Even visitors unfamiliar with his most famous novel, *Zorba the Greek*, should make the climb to catch a spectacular sunset over Mt. Ida. **Postal Code:** 71001.

KNOSSOS (ΚΝΩΣΟΣ)   ☎2810

◼**Knossos**, Crete's most famous archaeological site, is a must-see. Excavations have revealed the remains of the largest, most complicated of Crete's **Minoan palaces.** Legend and fact coexist at the palace of Knossos, the site of King Minos's machinations, the labyrinth with its monstrous Minotaur, and the imprisonment—and winged escape—of Daedalus and Icarus. The first palace was built around 1900 BC, but was destroyed by an earthquake around 1700 BC. Atop the ruins of the first structure was built a second, more magnificent palace, which was partially destroyed around 1450 BC and then wiped out by fire a century later. In the early 20th century, Sir Arthur Evans financed and supervised the excavations, restoring large parts of the second palace. His work often toed the line between preservation and tenuous interpretation, painting the palace's current form with controversy. Tourist crowds give the Minoan palace a Disneyland feel, but the sights are well worth navigating. Don't miss the ◼**Dolphin Fresco** on the northern wall of the Queen's Hall. Walking north from the royal quarters, you'll stumble across the grand **pithoi**—storage jars so massive that, according to legend, Minos's son met a sticky demise by drowning in one filled with honey. (☎2810 231 940. Open daily 8am-7pm. €6, students €3.) To reach Knossos from Heraklion, take **bus** #2 from Terminal A (20min., 2 per hr., €1.30).

CHANIA (XANIA)   ☎28210

Despite an avalanche of tourists, Chania (pop. 56,000), Crete's second largest city, retains a pleasantly relaxed seaside atmosphere. A day in idyllic Old Chania is easily whiled away people-watching from cafes or wandering along the waterfront. The **Venetian lighthouse** marks the entrance to the city's stunning architectural relic, the **Venetian Inner Harbor,** built in the 14th century. From the fortress's ruins, sunset views over the open sea dazzle tourists. The inlet has retained its original breakwater and Venetian arsenal, though the Nazis destroyed much of it during WWII. Nestled away on the northwestern tip of Crete, the heavenly ◪**blue lagoon** of **Balos** is the island's uncontested best beach, where bright white sand, warm shallow water, and sky melt into one. The most popular excursion from Chania is the 5-6hr. hike through ◪**Samaria Gorge** (ΦΑΡΑΓΓΙ ΤΗΣ ΣΑΜΑΡΙΑΣ), a spectacular 16km ravine extending through the White Mountains. Sculpted by 14 million years of rainwater, the gorge is the longest in Europe. (Open daily May 1-Oct. 15. 7am-3pm. €5, under 15 free.) The trail starts at Xyloskalo and ends at **Agia Roumeli,** on the southern coast; take an early bus marked OMALOS from Chania to Xyloskalo (departures at 6:15am, 7:30am, and 8:30am, 1hr., €6.20) for a day's worth of hiking. To return to Chania on the same day, take a boat to Chora Sfakion from Agia Roumeli (departures at 3:45pm and 6pm, 1hr., €8). From Chora Sfakion, catch the bus back to Chania (departures at 5:30pm and 7:15pm, 2hr., €6.80). The bus doesn't depart until after the boat's arrival.

The only backpacker-friendly accommodation in Chania is central **Eftihis Rooms ❶,** Tsouderon 21. From the bus station, walk toward the harbor on Halidon and turn right on Skrydlof, which becomes Tsouderon. (☎28210 46 829. A/C. Singles €20; doubles €30; triples €30. Cash only.) Fresh food is available at the covered municipal **market,** connecting new and old Chania, while touristy *tavernas* line the harbor. Chania's nightlife vibrantly buzzes along **Sourmeli Street,** in the heart of the old harbor.

From the port of Souda, **ferries** go to Piraeus (9hr., 2 per day, €24). Bus #13 connects from the port of Souda to Chania's municipal market on Zymvrakakidon. (☎28210 27 044; www.chaniabus.gr/eng/index.html. 20-25min.; €1.30, students €1). **Buses** (☎28210 93 052) leave from the corner of Kidonias and Kelaidi for the airport (25min., 3 per day), Heraklion (3hr., 16 per day, €12), and Rethymno (1-1½hr., 16 per day, €6). **Taxis** to the airport cost €16-18. The **tourist information center,** Kidonias 29-31, is located next to the city hall. (☎28210 36 155; www.chaniacrete.gr. Open May-Sept. M-Sa 8:30am-7pm; Oct.-Apr. M-Sa 8:30am-2pm.) **Postal Code:** 73001.

RETHYMNO (ΡΕΘΥΜΝΟ)   ☎28310

Rethymno has a reputation for bizarre power struggles. According to myth, **Zeus** was born to Rhea in the cave of Idaion Andron outside this regional capital. The titan Cronus, antsy about his infant son's approaching dominion, attempted to eat him; luckily for Greek mythological history, Rhea tricked Cronus into swallowing a stone instead, and Zeus grew up to be king of the gods. Warring humans followed Cronus's quest for power evident in Rethymno's skyline of minarets and ruined Venetian fortresses. The sprawling ◪**Venetian Fortezza,** a fortress built in 1580, is the high point of the city, and provides magnificent views of the coast and surrounding towns. Explore the series of churches and crumbling facades that comprise the ruins. (☎28310 28 101. Open daily 8am-8pm, last entry 7:15pm. €4, students free.) On the corner of Pl. Martiron, the **public gardens** provide a much-needed oasis of shade in the scorching Greek sun. Rethymno's **Wine Festival** at the end of July is a crowded, all-you-can-drink celebration. **February Carnival** is the largest celebration in all of Crete.

GREECE

The gardens and outdoor bar (beer and wine €1.50-2) buzz with backpackers at ▧Youth Hostel ❶, Tombazi 41. Outdoor beds are available in the summer. From the bus station, walk down I. Gavriil and take the first left at Pl. Martiron through the Porta Megali; Tombazi is the second right. (☎28310 22 848; www.yhrethymno.com. Breakfast €2-4. Solar-powered showers during the day. Sheets €1. Internet €3 per hr. Wi-Fi €5 per day. Reception July-Aug. 8am-noon and 5-9pm. Check-out 10am. Dorms July-Aug. €10 per night, €60 per week; Sept.-June €9/54.) An **open-air market** on El. Venizelou by the New Town marina opens Thursdays at 7am and closes around 2:30pm, though the selection dwindles by 10am. For affordable nighttime eats, tourists and locals head to **Plateia Titou Petihaki.** The bar scene in Rethymno centers on **Ioulias Petichaki, Nearhou,** and **Plateia Plasteira** near the western end of the harbor. ▧**Rock Cafe Club,** I. Petihaki 6, is popular dancing locations. The patrons are unpretentious, the DJs are savvy, and the bars remain fully stocked. (☎23810 654 325. Beer €4. Mixed drinks €7. Open M-Th and Su 11pm-4am, F-Sa 11pm-morning.)

Buy **ferry** tickets to Piraeus (daily 8pm, €30) at any travel office. **Buses** run from the Rethymno station (☎28310 22 212), overlooking the water off I. Gavriil, to: Agia Galini (1hr., 4-5 per day, €5.60); Arkadi Monastery (1hr., 2-3 per day, €2.50); Chania (1hr., 17 per day 6:15am-10:30pm, €6); Heraklion (1½hr., 18 per day 6:30am-10:15pm, €6.30); Plakias (45min., 7 per day, €4.10). The **tourist office** (☎28310 29 148; www.rethymnon.gr) is located at the far eastern end of the waterfront on El. Venizelou. (Open 8:30am-8:30pm.) **Game Net Cafe,** Koundouriotou 8, in Pl. Martiron, has **Internet** at the best rates in town. (€2.50 per hr., €1.50 after midnight.) **Postal Code:** 74100.

EASTERN AEGEAN ISLANDS

Scattered along Turkey's coast, the islands of the **Dodecanese** are marked by a history of persistence in the face of countless invasions. The more isolated islands of the **Northeast Aegean** remain sheltered from creeping globalization. The palpable cultural authenticity here is a traveler's welcome and reward.

RHODES (ΡΟΔΟΣ)   ☎22410

The undisputed tourism capital of the Dodecanese, the island of Rhodes has retained its sense of serenity in the sandy beaches along its eastern coast, the jagged cliffs skirting its western coast, and the green mountains dotted with villages in its interior. Beautiful ancient artifacts, remnants from a rich past, blanket the island. Rhodes is best known for a sight that no longer exists—the 33m **Colossus,** which was once one of the Seven Wonders of the Ancient World. The pebbled streets of the Old Town, constructed by the Knights of St. John, lend **Rhodes Town** a medieval flair. At the top of the hill, a tall, square tower marks the entrance to the **Palace of the Grandmaster,** which contains 300 rooms filled with intricate mosaic floorwork. (☎22410 25 500. €6, students €3.) The beautiful halls and courtyards of the **Archaeological Museum,** which dominates the **Plateia Argiokastrou,** shelter the exquisite first century BC statue of *Aphrodite Bathing.* (☎22410 31 048. Open Tu-Su 8:30am-3pm. €3, students €2.) On Rhodes's western shore, the ruins of **Kamiros** offer a glimpse of an ancient city grid. Daily **buses** run out of Rhodes Town. (☎22410 40 037. €4, students €2.) North of Kamiros, the Valley of Butterflies, or **Petaloudes,** attracts Jersey moths and nature enthusiasts alike. (☎22410 81 801. Open Easter-Oct. €5.) The vine-enclosed garden-bar of **Hotel Anastasia** ❷, 28 Oktovriou 46, complements bright, pastel rooms. (☎22410 28 007. Breakfast €4. Singles €35; doubles €50. V.) For cheap eateries, **Orfanidou** (popularly known as Bar St.) features venues with

GREECE

greasy food, while crepe stands (€2-5) line the streets of the Old Town. Nightlife in Rhodes's Old Town focuses around the street of **Militadou,** off Apelou. **Ferries** leave the eastern docks in Commercial Harbor, across from the Milon Gate into the Old Town, to: Halki (2hr., 2 per week, €8); Kos (2hr., 2 per day, €14); Patmos (7hr., i per day, €22); Sitia, Crete (10hr., 2 per week, €25). The Rhodes Town **tourist office** is at the intersection of Makariou and Papagou. (☎22410 44 333; www.ando.gr/eot. Open M-F 8am-2:45pm.) **Postal Code:** 8510.

LESVOS (ΛΕΣΒΟΣ)   ☎22510

Olive groves, art colonies, and a petrified forest harmonize Lesvos, or Lesbos. Born on this island, the seventh-century lyrical poet Sappho garnered a large female following. Due to her much-debated homosexuality, the word "lesbian"—once describing a native islander—developed its modern connotation. Visitors can gaze upon **Sappho's statue** at **Mytilini,** the island's capital and central port city, or walk on preserved mosaic floors excavated from ancient Ag. Kyriaki at the ▨**Archaeological Museum,** 8 Noemvriou. (Open Tu-Su 8am-3pm. €3, students €2, EU students and under 18 free.) Only 4km south of Mytilini, the village of **Varia** is home to the **Musée Tériade,** which displays lithographs by Chagall, Matisse, Miró, and Picasso, and the **Theophilos Museum,** which features work by neo-Primitivist Theophilos Hadzimichali. (☎22510 23 372. Musée Tériade open Tu-Su 9am-2pm and 5-8pm. Theophilos Museum open Tu-Su 10am-4pm. Each museum €2, students free.) Local **buses** (20min., 1 per hr.) leave Mytilini for Varia. Tell the driver you're going to the museums. **Molyvos,** a castle-crowned village, provides easy access to nearby **Eftalou's** hot springs and beaches. Abundant doubles at Mytilini *domatia* run €30-35 before July 15, and €35-50 during the high season. **Olympic** and **Aegean Airlines** fly out of the airport (**MJT;** ☎22510 61 590), 6km south of Mytilini, for Athens (1hr., 6 per day, €50-150) and Rhodes (1hr., 5 per week, €58). **Ferries** go from Mytilini to Thessaloniki (13hr., 1 per week, €35). Ticket can be purchased from **Zoumboulis Tours** (☎22510 37 755). **Postal Code:** 81100.

SAMOTHRAKI (ΣΑΜΟΘΡΑΚΗ)   ☎22510

Samothraki (also called Samothrace) was once a pilgrimage site for Thracians who worshipped Anatolian gods. When the first colonists arrived in the 10th century BC, they saw the same vista still viewable from the ferry dock today: grassy fields at the base of the Aegean's tallest peak, **Fengari** (1670m). From **Kamariotissa,** Samothraki's port town, it is easy to reach the **Sanctuary of the Great Gods at Paleopolis,** where the famous *Winged Victory of Samothrace,* now a centerpiece in the Louvre, was found in 1863. (Open daily 8:30am-8:30pm. €3, students €2, EU students free.) Above the sanctuary rest the remains of the ancient Samothraki. Therma, a charming one-road village, has natural hot springs and hosts the trailhead for the 4hr. climb up Fengari. Unmarked **waterfalls** near **Therma** are also a worthwhile trip; check with the locals for hikes suiting your schedule and abilities. **Kaviros Hotel ❷,** to the left of the grocery store in Therma, has well-lit rooms with A/C, TV, and fridges. (☎25510 98 277. Singles and doubles €30-40 depending on season.) **Sinatisi ❷,** a few doors down from the national bank in Kamariotissa, is a local favorite for fresh fish. (☎25510 41 308. Open daily noon-5pm and 7pm-1am.) **Ferries** dock on the southern edge of Kamariotissa and run to Lesvos (7hr.). **Postal Code:** 68002.

HUNGARY
(MAGYARORSZÁG)

A country as unique as its language, Hungary has much more to offer than a profusion of wine, goulash, and thermal spas. Hip Budapest remains Hungary's ascendant social, economic, and political capital. Beyond the big-city rush are towns lined with cobblestone streets and wine valleys nestled in the northern hills, while beach resorts abound in the east. Though Hungary can be more expensive than some of its neighbors, it has a value all its own.

DISCOVER HUNGARY: SUGGESTED ITINERARIES

THREE DAYS. Three days is hardly enough time for **Budapest** (p. 394). Spend a day at the churches and museums of **Castle Hill** and an afternoon in the waters of the **Kiraly Baths** before exploring the **City Park.** Get a lesson in Hungarian history at the **Parliament** before taking in the **Opera House.**

ESSENTIALS

FACTS AND FIGURES

OFFICIAL NAME: Hungary.

CAPITAL: Budapest.

MAJOR CITIES: Debrecen, Miskolc, Szeged.

POPULATION: 9,931,000.

TIME ZONE: GMT + 1.

LANGUAGE: Hungarian.

RELIGIONS: Roman Catholic (52%).

NUMBER OF MCDONALD'S RESTAURANTS: 94.

WHEN TO GO

Spring is the best time to visit; flowers are in bloom throughout the countryside and the tourists haven't yet arrived. July and August comprise Hungary's high-season, which means crowds, booked hostels, and sweltering summer weather. Autumn is beautiful, with mild, cooler weather through October. Avoid going in January and February, as temperatures average around freezing and many museums and tourist spots shut down or reduce their hours.

DOCUMENTS AND FORMALITIES

EMBASSIES AND CONSULATES. Foreign embassies are in Budapest (see p. 398). Hungary's embassies and consulates abroad include: **Australia,** 17 Beale Crescent, Deakin, ACT 2600 (☎62 82 32 26; www.matra.com.au/~hungemb); **Canada,** 299 Waverley St., Ottawa, ON K2P 0V9 (☎613-230-2717; www.mfa.gov/emb/ottawa); **Ireland,** 2 Fitzwilliam Pl., Dublin 2 (☎661 2902; www.mfa.gov.hu/emb/dublin); **New Zealand,** Consulate-General, PO Box 29-039, Wellington 6443 (☎973 7507; www.hungarianconsulate.co.nz); **UK,** 35 Eaton Pl., London SW1X

8BY (☎20 72 35 52 18; www.mfa.gov/emb/london); **US,** 3910 Shoemaker St. NW, Washington, D.C. 20008 (☎202-362-6730; www.huembwas.org).

> **ENTRANCE REQUIREMENTS.**
> **Passport:** Required for all non-EU citizens.
> **Visa:** See below.
> **Letter of Invitation:** Not required.
> **Inoculations:** Not required. Recommended up-to-date on DTaP (diphtheria, tetanus, and pertussis), hepatitis A, hepatitis B, MMR (measles, mumps, and rubella), polio booster, and typhoid.
> **Work Permit:** Required for all foreigners planning to work in Hungary.
> **Driving Permit:** International Driving Permits are recognized in Hungary, as are US and European licenses with Hungarian translations attached.

VISA AND ENTRY INFORMATION. Citizens of Australia, Canada, Ireland, New Zealand, and the US can visit Hungary without visas for up to 90 days; UK citizens can visit without a visa for up to 180 days. Consult your embassy for longer stays. Passports must be valid for six months after the end of the trip. There is no fee for crossing the Hungarian border. In general, border officials are efficient; plan on a 30min. crossing time.

TOURIST SERVICES AND MONEY

TOURIST OFFICES. Tourinform has branches in most cities and is a useful first-stop tourist service. Tourinform doesn't make accommodation reservations but will find vacancies, especially in university dorms and private *panzió.* Agencies also stock maps and provide local information; employees generally speak English and German. Most **IBUSZ** offices throughout the country book private rooms, exchange money, and sell train tickets, but they are generally better at assisting in travel plans than at providing info. Local agencies may be staffed only by Hungarian and German speakers, but they are often very helpful.

HUNGARY

HUNGARIAN FORINTS (FT)	
AUS$1 = 138.90FT	1000FT = AUS$7.20
CDN$1 = 149.95FT	1000FT = CDN$6.67
EUR€1 = 235.32FT	1000FT = EUR€4.25
NZ$1 = 113.724FT	1000FT = NZ$8.80
UK£1 = 297.00FT	1000FT = UK£3.37
US$1 = 159.09FT	1000FT = US$6.29

MONEY. The national currency is the **forint (Ft).** One forint is divided into 100 **fillérs,** which have disappeared almost entirely from circulation. Hungary has a **Value Added Tax (VAT)** rate of 20%. **Inflation** is at 7.8%. Currency exchange machines are slow but offer good rates, though banks like **OTP Bank** and **Raiffensen** offer the best exchange rates for **traveler's checks.** It is illegal to change money on the street. Try to avoid extended-hour exchange offices, which have poor rates.

Watch for scams: the maximum legal commission for cash-to-cash exchange is 1%. 24 hr. **ATMs** are common throughout Hungary. Major **credit cards** are accepted in many hotels and restaurants in large cities, but they're very rarely accepted in the countryside. Service is not usually included in restaurant bills and while **tipping** is not mandatory, it's generally appropriate. Cab fares are standard: bargaining won't help, so be sure to set a price before getting in.

HEALTH AND SAFETY

In Budapest, **medical assistance** is easy to obtain and fairly inexpensive, but it may not always be up to Western standards. In an emergency, especially outside Budapest, one might be sent to Germany or Vienna. Most hospitals have English-speaking doctors on staff. **Tourist insurance** is useful—and necessary—for many medical services. In the event of an emergency, however, even non-insured foreigners are entitled to free medical services. **Tap water** is usually clean, but the water in Tokaj is poorly purified. **Bottled water** can be purchased at most food stores. **Public bathrooms** (*férfi* for men, *női* for women) vary in cleanliness: pack soap, a towel, and 30Ft as a tip for the attendant. Carry **toilet paper,** as many hostels do not provide it and public restrooms provide only a single square. Many **pharmacies** (*gyógyszertár*) stock Western brands of common items, including tampons (*betet*) and condoms (*ovszer*).

Violent crime is rare. However, tourists are targets for petty theft and pick-pocketing. Check prices before getting in taxis or ordering food or drinks; cab drivers and servers may attempt to overcharge unsuspecting tourists. **Women** traveling alone in Hungary should take the usual precautions. **Minorities** are generally accepted, though dark-skinned travelers may encounter prejudice. In an emergency, your embassy will likely be more helpful than the police. Though Hungary is known for being open-minded, **GLBT** travelers may face serious discrimination, especially outside Budapest.

EMERGENCY	**Police: ☎107. Ambulance: ☎104 Fire: ☎105. General Emergency: ☎112.**

HUNGARY

TRANSPORTATION

BY PLANE. Many international airlines fly to Budapest. The national airline, **Malév**, flies to Budapest's airport, **Esterhazy**, from London, New York, and other major cities. Direct flights can be quite expensive, so flying to another European hub and taking a connecting plane or train may be the cheapest option. Other European airlines that fly to Hungary include **Sky Europe** (www.skyeurope.com) and **WizzAir** (www.wizzair.com).

BY TRAIN. Budapest is connected by train to most European capitals. Several types of **Eurail** passes are valid in Hungary. Check schedules and fares at www.elvira.hu. *Személyvonat* trains have many local stops and are excruciatingly slow; *gyorsvonat* trains, listed in red on schedules, move much faster for the same price. Large towns are connected by blue express lines; these air-conditioned **InterCity** trains are the fastest. A *pótjegy* (seat reservation) is required on trains labeled "R," and violators face a hefty fine.

The *peron* (platform) is rarely indicated until the train approaches the station and will sometimes be announced in Hungarian; look closely out the window as you approach a station. Many stations are not marked; ask the conductor what time the train will arrive (or simply point to your watch and say the town's name). Train reservations cost around US$5, and are recommended in summer and to get a sleeper compartment on night trains.

BY BUS AND BY FERRY. Buses tend to be efficient and well-priced. The major line is **Volanbusz,** a privately owned company. Purchase tickets on board, and arrive early for a seat. In larger cities, buy tickets at a kiosk, and punch them as you get on. Beware: plainclothes inspectors fine those caught without a ticket. A ferry runs down the Danube from Vienna and Bratislava to Budapest. For more info, contact **Utinform** (☎322 3600).

BY CAR AND BY TAXI. To **drive** in Hungary, carry your **International Driving Permit** and registration, and insurance papers. Car rental is available in most major cities but can be expensive. For 24hr. English assistance, contact the **Magyar Autóklub** (MAK; in Budapest, ☎345 1800). Taxi prices should not exceed the following: 6am-10pm base fare 200Ft per km, 60Ft per min. waiting; 10pm-6am 300Ft per km, 70Ft waiting. Beware of taxi scams. Before getting in, check that the meter works and ask how much the ride will cost. Taxis ordered by phone are more trustworthy than those hailed on the street.

BY BIKE AND BY THUMB. Biking terrain varies. Northeastern Hungary is topographically varied; the south is flat. **Bike rental** is sometimes difficult to find; tourist bureaus can help with locating rentals. Biking can be dangerous because cyclists do not have the right of way and drivers are not careful. Though it is fairly common in Hungary, *Let's Go* does not recommend **hitchhiking.**

KEEPING IN TOUCH

PHONE CODES	**Country code: 36. International dialing prefix:** 00. For more info on how to place international calls, see **Inside Back Cover.**

EMAIL AND THE INTERNET. Internet is available in major cities. Look for free Internet at hostels. Most Internet cafes charge 500-600Ft per hour. The Hungarian keyboard differs significantly from English-language keyboards.

TELEPHONE. For **intercity calls,** wait for the tone and dial slowly; "06" goes before the phone code. **International calls** require red or blue phones. The blue phones end calls after 3-9min. A 20Ft coin is required to start most calls. International calls cost around 9Ft, and you can make direct calls from Budapest's phone office. Phones often require *telefonkártya* (phone cards). International phone cards are sold by 2000Ft, and national cards are 800Ft. The best phone card for international calls is Barangolo. International access numbers include: **AT&T Direct** (☎06 800 01111); **Canada Direct** (☎06 800 01211); **MCI** (☎06 800 01411); **New Zealand Direct** (☎06 800 06411); and **Sprint** (☎06 800 01877). Mobile phones are common. Major vendors include Pannon GSM, T-Mobile, or Vodafone. Dialing a mobile from a public or private phone anywhere in Hungary is treated as a long-distance call, and it requires the entire 11-digit number.

MAIL. Hungarian mail is usually reliable; airmail *(légiposta)* takes one week to 10 days to the US and Europe. Mailing a letter costs about 36Ft domestically and 250Ft internationally. Those without permanent addresses can receive mail through **Poste Restante.** Address envelopes: First name, LAST NAME, POSTE RESTANTE, Post office address, Postal Code, city, HUNGARY.

LANGUAGE. Hungarian, a Finno-Ugric language, is distantly related to Turkish, Estonian, and Finnish. After Hungarian and German, English is Hungary's third most commonly spoken language. Almost all young people know some English. "Hello" is often used as an informal greeting. Coincidentally, "Szia!" (sounds like "see ya!") is another greeting—friends will often cry, "Hello, see ya!" For basic Hungarian words and phrases, see **Phrasebook: Hungarian,** p. 789.

ACCOMMODATIONS AND CAMPING

HUNGARY	❶	❷	❸	❹	❺
ACCOMMODATIONS	under 2500Ft	2500-4000Ft	4001-7000Ft	7001-12,000Ft	over 12,000Ft

Tourism is developing rapidly, and rising prices make hostels attractive. Hostels are usually large enough to accommodate summer crowds. Many **hostels** can be booked through **Express** (in Budapest, ☎266 3277), a student travel agency, or through local tourist offices. From June to August, many university dorms become hostels. These may be the cheapest options in smaller towns, as hostels are less common outside Budapest. Locations change annually; inquire at Tourinform and call ahead. **Guesthouses** and **pensions** *(panzió)* are more common than hotels in small towns. Singles are scarce, though some guesthouses have a singles rate for double rooms; however, it can be worth finding a roommate, as solo travelers must often pay for doubles. Check prices; agencies may try to rent you their most expensive rooms. **Private rooms** *(zimmer frei)* booked through tourist agencies are sometimes cheap. After staying a few nights, make arrangements directly with the owner to save yourself the agency's 20-30% commission. Hungary has over 300 **campgrounds,** most open from May to September. For more info, consult *Camping Hungary,* a booklet available in most tourist offices, or contact Tourinform in Budapest (see **Tourist Services and Money, p. 390**).

FOOD AND DRINK

HUNGARY	❶	❷	❸	❹	❺
FOOD	under 400Ft	400-800Ft	801-1300Ft	1301-2800Ft	over 2800Ft

HUNGARY

Hungarian food is more flavorful than many of its Eastern European culinary counterparts, with many spicy meat dishes. Paprika, Hungary's chief agricultural export, colors most dishes red. In Hungarian restaurants (*vendéglő* or *étterem*), *halászlé*, a spicy fish stew, is a traditional starter. Or, try *gyümölcsleves*, a cold fruit soup with whipped cream. The Hungarian national dish is *bográcsgulyás*, a soup of beef, onions, green peppers, tomatoes, potatoes, dumplings, and plenty of paprika. *Borjúpaprikás* is veal with paprika and potato-dumpling pasta. For **vegetarians** there is tasty *rántott sajt* (fried cheese) and *gombapörkölt* (mushroom stew). Delicious Hungarian fruits and vegetables abound in summer. Vegetarians should also look for *saláta* (salad) and *sajt* (cheese), as these will be the only options in many small-town restaurants. Keeping **kosher,** on the other hand, is fairly difficult. Avoid American food like hot dogs, which can cause food poisoning. The northeastern towns of Eger and Tokaj produce famous red and white **wines,** respectively. *Sör* (Hungarian beer) ranges from acceptable to first-rate. Lighter beers include *Dreher Pils, Szalon Sör,* and licensed versions of *Steffl, Gold Fassl,* and *Amstel.* Among the best-tasting *pálinka* (brandy-like liquor) are *barackpálinka* (an apricot schnapps) and *körtepálinka* (pear brandy). *Unicum,* advertised as the national drink, is an **herbal liqueur** containing over 40 herbs; legend has it that it was once used by the Hapsburgs to cure digestive ailments.

HOLIDAYS AND FESTIVALS

Holidays: New Year's Day (Jan. 1); National Day (Mar. 15); Labor Day (May 1); Pentecost (May 31, 2009; May 23, 2010); Constitution Day (St. Stephen's Day, Aug. 20); Republic Day (Oct. 23); All Saints' Day (Nov. 1); Christmas (Dec. 25-26).

Festivals: Central Europe's largest rock festival, **Sziget Festival,** hits Budapest for a week in late July or early August, featuring rollicking crowds and international superstar acts. Eger's fabulous **World Festival of Wine Songs** celebration kicks off in late September, bringing together boisterous choruses and world-famous vintage wines.

BEYOND TOURISM

Central European University, Nador u. 9, Budapest 1051, Hungary (☎36 13 27 30 09; www.ceu.hu). Affiliated with the Open Society Institute-Budapest. Offers international students the opportunity to take graduate-level courses. Tuition US$7775 per semester, not including personal expenses. Financial aid available.

Hungarian Dance Academy, Columbus u. 87-89, Budapest H-1145, Hungary (☎36 12 73 34 30; www.mtf.hu). Summer dance programs for students ages 11-24.

Central European Teaching Program, 3800 NE 72nd Ave., Portland, OR 97213, USA (☎503-287-4977; www.cetp.info). Places English teachers in state schools in Hungary and Romania for one semester (US$1700) or a full school year (US$2250).

BUDAPEST ☎01

While other parts of Hungary maintain a slow pace, Budapest (pop. 1.9 million) has seized upon cosmopolitan chic with a vengeance without giving up its old-time charms. Unlike in Prague, the sights of Budapest spread throughout the energetic city, giving it a life independent of the growing crowds of tourists; Turkish thermal baths and Roman ruins mix seamlessly with modern buildings and a legendary night scene. The area that constitutes Budapest was once two entities: the pasture-ruled city of Pest and the viticulture hills of Buda.

Although the city was ravaged by WWII, Hungarians rebuilt it, then weathered a Soviet invasion and 40 years of Communism. The resilient spirit of Budapest resonates as the city reassumes its place as a major European capital.

INTERCITY TRANSPORTATION

Flights: Ferihegy Airport (BUD; ☎01 296 9696). **Malév** (Hungarian Airlines; ☎01 235 3888) flies to major cities. To the center, take bus #93 (20min., every 15min. 4:55am-11:20pm, 270Ft), then Ⓜ3 to Kőbánya-Kispest (15min. to Deák tér, in downtown Budapest). Airport Minibus (☎01 296 8555) goes to hostels (2990Ft).

Trains: The major stations, **Keleti Pályaudvar, Nyugati Pályaudvar,** and **Déli Pályaudvar,** are also Metro stops (☎40 49 49 49). Most **international trains** arrive at Keleti station, but some from Prague go to Nyugati station. For schedules, check www.mav.hu, part of which is in English. To: **Berlin** (12-13hr., 4 per day, 15,800Ft); **Bucharest, ROM** (14hr., 5 per day, 23,600Ft); **Prague** (7-8hr., 5 per day, 16,300Ft); **Vienna, AUT** (3hr., 17 per day, 3600Ft); **Warsaw, POL** (11hr., 2 per day, 18,500Ft). The daily Orient Express stops on its way from **Paris, FRA** to **Istanbul, TUR.** Trains run to most major destinations in Hungary. Purchase tickets at an **International Ticket Office** (Keleti station open daily 8am-7pm; Nyugati station open M-Sa 5am-9pm; info desk 24hr.). Or try **MÁV Hungarian Railways,** VI, Andrássy út 35. (☎01 461 5500. Branches at all stations. Open Apr.-Sept. M-F 9am-6pm, Oct.-Mar. M-F 9am-5pm. Say "diák" for student or under 26 discounts.) The **HÉV commuter railway** station is at Batthyány tér, opposite Parliament. Trains head to **Szentendre** (45min., every 15min. 5am-9pm, 460Ft). Purchase tickets at the station for transport beyond the city limits.

Buses: Buses to international and some domestic destinations leave from the **Népliget station,** X, Üllői út 131. (Ⓜ3: Népliget. ☎01 382 0888. Ticket window open M-F 6am-9pm, Sa-Su 6am-4pm.) To **Berlin** (14hr., 6 per week, 19,900Ft), **Prague** (8hr., 6 per week, 11,900Ft), and **Vienna, AUT** (3½hr., 5 per day, 5900Ft). Buses going east of Budapest leave from **Népstadion station,** XIV, Hungária körút 46-48. (Ⓜ2: Népstadion. ☎01 252 4498. Open M-F 6am-6pm, Sa-Su 6am-4pm.) Buses to the **Danube Bend** and parts of the Uplands depart outside Árpád híd metro station on the Ⓜ3 line. (☎01 329 1450. Cashier open 6am-8pm.) Check www.volanbusz.hu for schedules.

LOCAL TRANSPORTATION

Commuter Railway: The **HÉV** station is across the river from Parliament, 1 Metro stop past the Danube in Buda at Batthyány tér. On the list of stops, those within the city limits are displayed in a different color. For these stops, a regular metro ticket will suffice. Purchase tickets at the counter to travel beyond the city limits. Békásmegyer is the final stop within the city limits.

Public Transportation: Subways, buses, and **trams** are convenient. The subways and trams run every few minutes. Buses are generally on-time and some run 24hr.; schedules are posted at stops. **Budapest Public Transport (BKV;** ☎ 80 40 66 86; www.bkv.hu) has info in Hungarian and an English website. The **metro** has 3 lines: M1 (yellow), M2 (red), and M3 (blue). **M1** runs west to east from downtown Pest past City Park along Andrássy út. **M2** runs west to east and connects Deli Train Station in Buda with Keleti Train Station in Pest along Rákóczi út. **M3** runs north to south through Pest and provides a transfer bus to the airport from the southern terminus (Kőbánya-Kispest). A 4th metro line is currently under construction that will connect southern Buda to northeastern Pest, though it is not expected to open until 2012. The metro runs 4:30am-11:30pm. Most buses and trams stop running at 11pm. Single-fare tickets for public transport (one-way on 1 line; 300Ft) are sold in metro stations, in Trafik shops, and by sidewalk vendors at tram stops. Punch them in the orange boxes at the gate of the metro or on

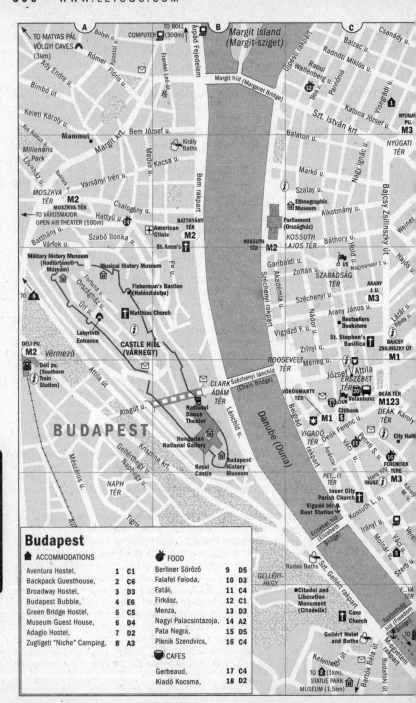

Budapest

ACCOMMODATIONS

Aventura Hostel,	1	C1
Backpack Guesthouse,	2	C6
Broadway Hostel,	3	D3
Budapest Bubble,	4	E6
Green Bridge Hostel,	5	C5
Museum Guest House,	6	D4
Adagio Hostel,	7	D2
Zugligeti "Niche" Camping,	8	A3

FOOD

Berliner Söröző	9	D5
Falafel Faloda,	10	D3
Fatál,	11	C4
Firkász,	12	C1
Menza,	13	D3
Nagyi Palacsintazoja,	14	A2
Pata Negra,	15	D5
Piknik Szendvics,	16	C4

CAFES

Gerbeaud,	17	C4
Kiadó Kocsma,	18	D2

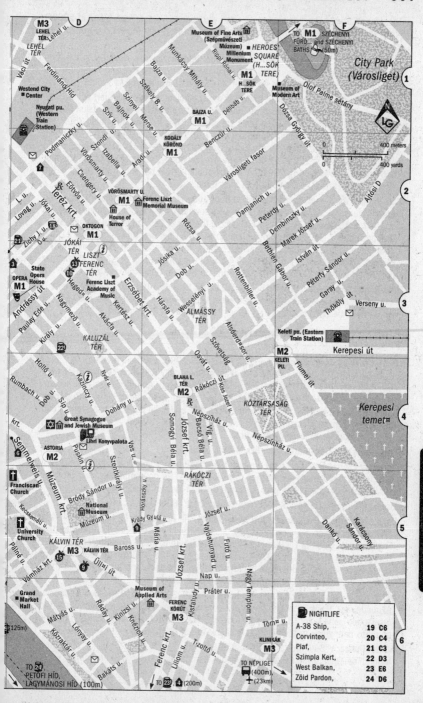

NIGHTLIFE

A-38 Ship,	19 C6
Corvinteo,	20 C4
Piaf,	21 C3
Szimpla Kert,	22 D3
West Balkan,	23 E6
Zöld Pardon,	24 D6

buses and trams; punch a new ticket when you change lines, or face a fine of 5000Ft from the undercover ticket inspectors. Day pass 1550Ft, 3-day 3850Ft, 1-week 4600Ft, 2-week 6200Ft, 1-month 9400Ft.

Night transit: After you've missed the last tram, transportation is available in the form of night (É) buses which run midnight-5am along major routes: #7É and 78É follow the Ⓜ2 route; #6É follows the 4/6 tram line; #14É and 50É follow the Ⓜ3 route.

Taxis: The Budapest public transit system is pretty efficient, so you will rarely need a cab. Beware of scams; ask how much the ride will cost and always check for yellow license plates and a running meter. Base fares are always 300Ft, with an additional 350Ft per km and 70Ft per min. waiting. **Tele5Taxi** (☎01 555 5555) is 230Ft per km by phone, 240Ft per km on the street. To the airport: 4600Ft from Pest and 5100Ft from Buda. Also try **Fötaxi** (☎01 222 2222), 225Ft per km by phone, 240Ft per km on the street or **6x6 Taxi**(☎01 666 6666), 229Ft per km by phone, 240Ft per km on the street. To the airport: 4600Ft from Pest and 5100Ft from Buda.

Car Rental: You'll need to get a certified translation of your American driver's license to drive in Hungary. Car rentals are available from several reliable agencies, though most will only rent to those over 21 (and several only to those over 25). Credit card required. **Avis,** Szabadság tér 7 (☎01 318 4240). Cars from 7900Ft per day. Drivers must be 21 and have had a license for at least 1 year. Open M-Sa 7am-6pm, Su 8am-6pm. AmEx/MC/V. **Budget,** I, Krisztina krt. 41-43 (☎01 214 0420; www.budget.hu). Cars from 7500Ft per day. Drivers must be 21. Open M-F 8am-8pm, Sa-Su 8am-6pm. AmEx/MC/V.

Bike Rental: Yellow Zebra Bikes, V, Sütő utca 2 and VI, Lázár utca 16 (☎01 266 8777), rents a wide variety of bikes at four different price levels. Also provides bike tours. Bikes 1500-2500Ft for all-day rental. Open Nov.-Mar. daily 10am-6:30pm, Apr-Oct 9:30am-7pm. MC/V.

▐ PRACTICAL INFORMATION

Tourist Offices: Tourinform, V, Sütő u. 2 (☎01 438 8080; www.hungary.com). Ⓜ1, 2, or 3: Deák tér. Off Deák tér behind McDonald's. Open daily 8am-8pm. **Vista Travel Center,** Andrássy út 1 (☎01 429 9751; incoming@vista.hu). Arranges tours and accommodations. Open M-F 9am-6:30pm, Sa 9am-2:30pm. Both offices sell the **Budapest Card** (Budapest Kártya), which provides discounts, unlimited public transportation, and admission to most museums (2-day card 6300Ft, 3-day 7500Ft). A great deal, except when museums are closed on Mondays.

Embassies and Consulates: See **Essentials,** p. 13.

Currency Exchange: Banks have the best rates. **Citibank,** V, Vörösmarty tér 4 (☎01 374 5000). Ⓜ1: Vörösmarty tér. Cashes traveler's checks for no commission and provides MC/V cash advances. Bring your passport. Open M-Th 9am-5pm, F 9am-4pm.

Luggage Storage: Lockers at all 3 train stations. 150-600Ft.

English-Language Bookstore: Libri Könyvpalota, VII, Rákóczi út. 12 (☎01 267 4843). Ⓜ2: Astoria. The best choice in the city, this multilevel bookstore has 1 fl. of up-to-date English titles. Open M-F 10am-7:30pm, Sa 10am-3pm. MC/V. **Treehugger Dan's,** VI, Csengery utca 48 (☎01 322 0774; www.treehugger.hu). Ⓜ1: Vörösmarty utca. Massive selection of secondhand English books with a hip, laid-back, and adamantly fair-trade coffee shop. Open M-F 10am-6pm, Sa 10am-5pm. Cash only.

GLBT Resources: GayGuide.net Budapest (☎06 30 93 23 334; www.budapest. gayguide.net). Posts an online guide and runs a hotline (daily 4-8pm) with info and a reservation service for GLBT-friendly lodgings. **Na Vegre!** (www.navegre.hu). Publishes an up-to-date guide to gay nightlife. Available at any gay bar.

Tourist Police: V, Sütő utca 2 (☎01 438 8080). Ⓜ1, 2, or 3: Deák tér. Inside the Tourinform office. Open 24hr. Beware of impostors demdanding to see your passport.

Pharmacies: Look for green signs labeled Apotheke, Gyógyszertár, or Pharmacie. Minimal after-hours service fees apply. **II,** Frankel Leó út 22 (☎01 212 4406). AmEx/MC/V. **VI,** Teréz körút 41 (☎01 311 4439). Open M-F 8am-8pm, Sa 8am-2pm. **VII,** Rákóczi út 39 (☎314 3695). Open M-F 7:30am-9pm, Sa 7:30am-2pm.

Medical Services: Falck (SOS) KFT, II, Kapy út 49/b (☎01 275 1535). Ambulance service US$120. **American Clinic,** I, Hattyú utca. 14 (☎01 224 9090; www.americanclinics. com). Open for appointments M-F 8am-8pm, Sa 8am-2pm. 24hr. **emergency** call line ☎01 224 9090. The US embassy (p. 13) maintains a list of English-speaking doctors.

Telephones: Cards are sold at kiosks and metro stations. 50-unit card 800Ft, 120-unit card 1800Ft. Domestic operator and info ☎198. International operator ☎190, info 199.

Internet: Cybercafes are everywhere, but they can be expensive and long waits are common. Most coffee shops and cafes have free Wi-Fi. Try **Ami Internet Coffee,** V, Váci utca. 40 (☎01 267 1644; www.amicoffee.hu). Ⓜ3: Ferenciek tér. 200Ft per 15min., 700Ft per hr. Open daily 9am-2am.

Post Office: V, Városház utca 18 (☎01 318 4811). **Poste Restante** (Postán Mar) in office around the right side of the building. Open M-F 8am-8pm, Sa 8am-2pm. Branches at Nyugati station; VI, Teréz körút. 105/107; Keleti station; VIII, Baross tér 11/c; and elsewhere. Open M-F 7am-8pm, Sa 8am-2pm. **Postal Code:** Depends on the district—postal codes are 1XX2, where XX is the district number (1052 for post office listed above).

ACCOMMODATIONS AND CAMPING

Budapest's hostels are centers for the backpacker social scene, and their common rooms can be as exciting as many bars and clubs. Many hostels are run by the **Hungarian Youth Hostels Association (HI),** which operates from an office in Keleti pu. Representatives wearing Hostelling International shirts—and legions of competitors—accost travelers as they get off the train. Beware that they may provide inaccurate descriptions of other accommodations in order to sell their own. Private rooms are more expensive than hostels, but they do offer peace, quiet, and private showers. Arrive early, bring cash, and haggle. ▧**Best Hotel Service,** V, Sütő u. 2, arranges apartment, hostel, and hotel reservations (6000Ft and up). Take M1, 2, or 3 to Deák tér. (☎318 4848; www.besthotelservice.hu. Open daily 8am-8pm.)

▧ **The Loft Hostel,** V, Veres Pálné utca 19 (☎01 328 0916; www.lofthostel.hu). Ⓜ3: Kálvin tér. From the metro, Kecskeméti út west, turn left onto Szerb utca, and then right onto Veres Pálné. Perfect for people who enjoy a relaxed, social atmosphere. Rustic-looking beams and slanted ceilings. All the wall art is by staff members or former guests. Linens included. Laundry service 1000Ft. Free Wi-Fi. Reception 24hr. 8-bed dorms 3600Ft; 6-bed dorms 4000Ft; 4-bed dorms 4500. 300Ft rate increase on weekends. Cash only. ●

▧ **Aventura Boutique Hostel,** XIII, Visegrádi utca 12 (☎239 0782; www.aventurahostel. com). Ⓜ3: Nyugati. From the metro, take Szent István körút toward the river and turn right on Visegrádi. Super-friendly, helpful staff makes you feel comfortable in 4 themed rooms. Amply pillowed India dorm has colorful linens, curtains, and lockers (1500Ft deposit) fashioned from old weapons crates. In the reception area, be sure to get a picture of yourself sitting on the couch that was once a bathtub. Massages 4500Ft. Breakfast 450Ft. Free Wi-Fi and high speed internet. Reception 24hr. Flexible check-in and check-out times. Dorms from 3300Ft; doubles from 10,900Ft. Cash only. ●

▧ **Central Backpack King,** V, Október 6 utca 15 (☎200 7184; www.centralbpk.hu). Ⓜ1: Bajcsy-Zsilinszky út. From the metro, take József Attila utca toward the river and then turn right on Október 6 ut. Upon arriving, you'll be greeted by the enthusiastic staff as well as a complimentary shot of Palinka from the manager's grandmother's village. The interior is colorful and lined with rugs of all colors and styles. Fun, social atmosphere in the center of Lipótváros means you'll never be at a loss for people to go out with. If you don't feel like going out, you can hang out in the always bustling common room, complete with a widescreen TV and movies to watch with the other bored kids. Free lockers. Linens included. Free Wi-Fi. Minimum stay of 2 nights. Reception 24hr. Check-in 2pm. Check-out 11am. Dorms from 4000Ft; doubles 8000Ft per person. Cash only. ❸

🏨 **10 Beds,** Erzsébet körút 15 (☎20 933 5965). Ⓜ2: Blaha Lujza tér. From the metro, take Erzsébet körút north for a block and a half; the hostel is on your right. A super laid-back attitude characterizes this small, intimate hostel where long-term guests sometimes become quasi-staff members. Aside from the bunk beds, the place feels more like a good friend's apartment. Free laundry service is just icing on the cake. Lockers and linens included. Free Wi-Fi. Reception 24hr. Dorms from 3000Ft. Cash only. ❷

🏨 **Home-Made Hostel,** VI, Teréz körút 22 (☎01 302 2103; www.homemadehostel.com). Ⓜ1: Oktogon. From the metro, take Teréz körút east from Oktogon; the hostel is on your left. An intimate hostel where the staff makes you feel right at home. Bond with your roommates over a homemade Hungarian dinner twice weekly. The bunkless dorms, decorated with antique TVs, radios, and rugs, make you feel like you're stepping into a 1950s Hungarian apartment. Locker deposit 1000Ft. Towels and linens included. Laundry 1000Ft. Free internet and Wi-Fi. Scooter rental available. Reception 24hr. Dorms from 3800Ft; doubles 12,000-15,000Ft. Cash only. ❷

🏨 **Carpe Noctem,** VI, Szobi utca 5 (☎20 365 8749; www.carpenoctemhostel.com). Ⓜ3: Nygati pályaudvar. From the metro, take Teréz körút east from the train station and turn left onto Szobi. Budapest's most reputable party hostel with plenty of social space. After checking in, you'll be treated to a 30min. crash course on what to do and where to drink in Budapest. Best for those looking to meet people and have a great time they'll never remember. Towels, linens, and lockers included. Laundry 1500Ft. Free internet and Wi-Fi. Reception 24hr. Dorms 4200Ft. No groups larger than 4. Cash only. ❸

🏨 **Budapest Bubble,** VIII, Bródy Sándor utca 2 (☎266 9532; budapestbubble@gmail. com). Ⓜ3: Kálvin tér. From the metro, take Múzeum körút north and turn right on Bródy Sándor. An intimate, inviting hostel near the National Museum with young, local hosts who are quick to provide information on the city. Multiple common areas, decorated with Fritz Lang posters and the occasional hookah, make you feel like you're in a sophisticated film studies major's dorm. Most evenings, the staff leads a group out to some of the area's best undiscovered bars and clubs. Free internet and Wi-Fi. Linens included. Reception 24hr. Dorms 2800-3700Ft; doubles 10,000. Cash only. ❷

🏳 HUNGARY?

Cafeterias with *"Önkiszolgáló Étterem"* signs serve cheap food (entrees 300-500Ft), and a neighborhood *kifőzés* (kiosk) or *vendéglő* (family-style restaurant) offers a real taste of Hungary. Corner markets, many open 24hr., stock the basics. The 🏛**Grand Market Hall,** IX, Fövam tér 1/3, next to Szabadság híd (M3: Kálvin tér), has acres of stalls, making it an attraction in itself. Ethnic restaurants populate the upper floor of **Mammut Plaza,** just outside the Moszkva tér metro in Buda, and **West End Plaza,** near the Nyugati metro in Pest.

RESTAURANTS

🍴 **Café Kör,** V, Sas utca 17 (☎311 0053; www.cafekor.com). Ⓜ1: Bajcsy-Zsilinszky út. From the metro, take József Attila west and turn right on Sas. Cool, classy dining caters mainly to professionals and tourists, though there are plenty of options that frugal backpackers will appreciate. Dishes like honeydew melon wrapped in prosciutto (1690Ft) set this place apart from the area's other boutique cafes. Salads 930-1890Ft. Entrees 1560-4290Ft. Wheelchair-accessible. Open daily 10am-10pm. Cash only. ❹

⬛ **Trófea Grill Étterem**, XIII, Visegrádi utca 50A (☎270 0366; www.trofeagrill.com). Ⓜ3: Nyugati. From the metro, take Szent István körút toward the river and then turn right on Visegrádi. Upscale all-you-can-eat, traditional Hungarian buffet. The large, wooden dining area is lined with the skulls of the species you'll be enjoying. All-you-can-drink beer, wine, champagne, and fountain drinks included in price. Buffet 3400Ft M-F lunch; 3800Ft M-Th dinner; 4600Ft F dinner and all day Sa-Su. Free Wi-Fi. Wheelchair-accessible. Open M-F noon-midnight, Sa 11:30am-midnight, Su 11:30am-8:30pm. Reservations recommended. MC/V. ❺

⬛ **Hummus Bar**, VII, Kertész utca 39 (☎01 321 7477). Ⓜ1: Oktogon. From the metro, take Teréz körút south, turn right at Király, and then left at Kertész. One of Budapest's true gems—a closet-sized place serving some of the city's best vegetarian and vegan food. Delicious and artfully presented hummus (800Ft) delivered to you as you relax on the floor cushions upstairs. Another location at Alkotmány utca 20 just down the street from Parliament. *Phool* 900Ft. Pita 70-250Ft. Open daily noon-11pm. Cash only. ❶

⬛ **Marquis de Salade**, VI, Hajós utca 43 (☎01 302-4086; www.marquisdesalade.hu). Ⓜ3: Arany János út. From the metro, take Bajcsy-Zsilinszky út north and then make a sharp right onto Hajós. Azerbaijani restaurant with the occasional Russian dish (or pun) thrown in for good measure. Lamb dishes, including grape leaves stuffed with minced lamb (2700Ft) and grilled lamb liver and heart (3400Ft). Marquis de Salade (chicken breast with grapefruit, shrimp, and fresh vegetables in a grapefruit dressing; 2500Ft). Salads 1300-2500Ft. Vegetarian options 2600-2800Ft. Entrees 2500-3900Ft. Not wheelchair-accessible. Open daily noon-1am. Cash only. ❺

⬛ **Giero**, Paulay Ede utca 56. Ⓜ1: Oktogon. From the metro, take Andrássy út west, turn left on Ferenc ter, and then right onto Paulay Ede; the restaurant will be on your right. With no website, telephone number, or menu, this family-run basement-cellar restaurant is about as hole-in-the-wall as it gets. With the family's children around and occasionally playing gypsy folk music, you'll feel like you've been invited into someone's home. As a guest, you don't have a lot of say over what dinner is, though you rest assured: it will be delicious. Dinner 1800Ft. Live music occasionally. Not wheelchair accessible. Open daily noon-late. Cash only. ❷

⬛ **Nagyi Palacsintazoja**, II, Hattyú utca 16 (☎01 212 4866) Ⓜ2: Moszkva tér. From the metro, walk toward the river; at the big intersection veer right on Hattyú utca. Tiny, no-frills eatery dishes out small but tasty sweet and savory crepes piled with toppings like cheese, fruit, or chocolate sauce. After a raucous night partying, there are few better ways to avoid sleep than watching the sunrise over Parliament while noshing on a marzipan-stuffed crepe (180Ft). Another location is at Batthyány tér 5. Sweet crepes 130-640Ft. Savory crepes 240-620Ft. Open 24hr. Cash only. ❶

CAFES

Once the haunts of the literary, intellectual, and cultural elite—as well as political dissidents—the cafes boast mysterious histories and delicious pastries.

⬛ **1000 Tea**, V, Váci utca 65 (☎337 8217; www.1000tea.hu). Ⓜ3: Kálvin tér. From the metro, take Vámház toward the river and turn right on Váci. Japanese-style teahouse located in a tranquil courtyard just off Váci. One thousand teas may be stretching it, though the menu is certainly impressive, containing every tea you could imagine. The indulgent may spring for tea served in traditional kung fu style (1200Ft), while bold 2-somes should consider one of the tea samplers (1400Ft). Teas 400-950Ft. Wheelchair-accessible. Open M-Sa noon-11pm, Su 1-11pm. Cash only. ❶

⬛ **Bar Ladino**, VII, Dob utca 53 (☎30 874 3733; www.ladino.hu). Ⓜ1: Oktogon. From the metro, take Teréz körút east for 3 blocks and turn right on Dob utca. Named for the near-extinct language of exiled Spanish Jews, Bar Ladino provides good food and great service in a cool atmosphere. Breakfast served M-F 9am-5pm, 490-790Ft. Salads 990-1690Ft. Entrees 990-2490Ft. Beer from 290Ft. Wine from 270Ft. Shots 390-700Ft. Open M-W and Su 9am-1:30am, Th 9am-2:30am, F-Sa 9am-3:30am. Cash only. ❷

🏵 **Ring Cafe and Bar,** Andrássy út 38 (☎01 331 5790; www.ringcafe.hu). Ⓜ2: Oktogon. From the metro, take Andrássy toward downtown; the cafe will be on your right. The best cafe for people-watching on historic and picturesque Andrássy and one of the best places in Budapest to find an affordable Western-style breakfast. Breakfast until noon 780-850Ft. Sandwiches 1090-1340Ft. Entrees 1190-1690Ft. Beer from 360Ft. Shots 650-1250Ft. Wheelchair-accessible. Open M-Th 8am-midnight, F 8am-1am, Sa 10am-1am, Su 10am-6pm. Cash only. ❷

🔆 SIGHTS

In 1896, Hungary's millennial birthday bash prompted the construction of Budapest's most prominent sights. Among the works commissioned by the Hapsburgs were **Hősök tér** (Heroes' Square), **Szabadság híd** (Liberty Bridge), **Vajdahunyad Vár** (Vajdahunyad Castle), and continental Europe's first metro system. Slightly grayer for wear, war, and occupation, these monuments attest to the optimism of a capital on the verge of its Golden Age. See the sights with **Absolute Walking and Biking Tours.** (☎01 211 8861; www.absolutetours.com. 3½hr. tours 4000Ft, students 3500ft. Specialized tours 4000-7000Ft.) For the more independent sightseer, **The Walker's Guide** provides 18 hours of entertaining commentary on the city's sights. Available for rental at tourist offices throughout the city. 3000Ft for 3hr., 4000Ft for 6hr., and 5000Ft for all-day rental. (www. walkersguide.travel). **Boat tours** leave from Vigadó tér piers 6-7, near Elizabeth Bridge in Pest. The evening **Danube Legend** costs 4900Ft, students 3700; its daytime counterpart, the **Duna Bella,** costs 3900/2900Ft for 2hr.

BUDA

On the east bank of the Danube, Buda sprawls between the base of **Várhegy** (Castle Hill) and southern **Gellérthegy** and leads into the city's main residential areas. Older and more peaceful than Pest, Buda is filled with lush parks.

CASTLE DISTRICT. Towering above the Danube on Várhegy, the Castle District has been razed three times in its 800-year history. With its winding, statue-filled streets, impressive views, and hodgepodge of architectural styles, the UNESCO-protected district now appears much as it did under the Hapsburg reign. The reconstructed **Buda Castle** (Vár) houses fine museums (p. 405). Bullet holes in the facade recall the 1956 uprising. (*Szent György tér 2.* Ⓜ*1, 2, or 3: Deák tér. From the metro, take bus #16 across the Danube. Or, from* Ⓜ*2: Moszkva tér, walk up to the hill on Várfok u. "Becsi kapu" marks the castle entrance.*) Beneath Buda Castle, the 🏵**Castle Labyrinths** (Budvári Labirinths) provide a spooky glimpse of the subterranean city. (*2 entrances, 1 at Úri utca 9 and 2nd at Lovas út 4/a.* ☎*1 212 0207; www.labirintus.com. Open daily 9:30am-7:30pm. Wheelchair-accessible through Lovas út entrance. 2000Ft, students 1500Ft. Cash only.*)

MATTHIAS CHURCH. The colorful roof of **Matthias Church** (Mátyás templom) on Castle Hill is one of Budapest's most photographed sights. The church was converted into a mosque in 1541, then renovated again 145 years later when the Hapsburgs defeated the Turks. Ascend the spiral steps to view the exhibits of the **Museum of Ecclesiastical Art.** *I, Szentháromság tér 2. www.matyas-templom.hu. Open M-F 9am-5pm, Sa 9am-2:30pm, Su 1-5pm. High mass daily 7, 8:30am, 6pm; Su and holidays also 10am and noon. Church and museum 750Ft, students 500Ft.)*

GELLÉRT HILL. After the coronation of King Stephen, the first Christian Hungarian monarch, in AD 1001, the Pope sent Bishop Gellért to convert the Magyars.

After those unconvinced by the bishop's message hurled him to his death, the hill he was thrown from was named Gellérthegy in his honor. The **Liberation Monument** (Szabadság Szobor), on the hilltop, honors Soviet soldiers who died ridding Hungary of the Nazis. At the base of the hill is **Gellért** (p. 402), Budapest's most famous Turkish bath. *(XI, Gellért Hill. The monument is at the top of the hill, near the Citadella.)*

PEST

Constructed in the 19th century, the winding streets of Pest now link cafes, corporations, and monuments. The crowded Belváros (Inner City) is based around Vörösmarty tér and the swarming pedestrian boulevard Váci utca.

PARLIAMENT. The palatial Gothic Parliament (Országház) stands 96m tall, a number that symbolizes the date of Hungary's millennial anniversary. The building was modeled after the UK's, right down to the facade and the riverside location. *(M2: Kossuth tér. ☎01 441 4000. English-language tours daily 10am, noon, 2pm; buy tickets early, as they often sell out during the summer. You can also ask permission from the guard to buy a ticket from the office at Gate X. Ticket office opens at 8am. Entrance with mandatory tour 2820Ft, students 1410Ft. Free with EU passport.)*

GREAT SYNAGOGUE. The largest synagogue in Europe and the second-largest in the world, Pest's Great Synagogue (Zsinagóga) was designed to hold 3000 worshippers. The enormous metal **Tree of Life,** a Holocaust memorial, sits in the garden above a mass grave for thousands of Jews killed near the end of the war. Each leaf bears the name of a family that perished. Next door, the **Jewish Museum** (Zsidó Múzeum) documents the storied past of Hungary's Jews. *(VII. At the corner of Dohány utca and Wesselényi utca M2: Astoria. ☎70 533 5696; www.greatsynagogue.hu. Open May-Oct. M-Th 10am-5pm, F and Su 10am-2pm; Nov.-Apr. M-Th 10am-3pm, F and Su 10am-1pm. Services F 6pm. Admissions usually start at 10:30am. Covered shoulders required. Men must cover their heads inside the synagogue; yarmulkes available at the entrance. Admission to Museum included with entrance to the Great Synagogue. Tours M-Th 10:30am-3:30pm every 30min., F and Su 10:30, 11:30am, 12:30pm. 1400Ft, students 750Ft. Tours 1900Ft/1600Ft.)*

ST. STEPHEN'S BASILICA (SZ. ISTVÁN BAZILIKA). Though seriously damaged in WWII, the neo-Renaissance facade of the city's largest church has been mostly restored. The Panorama Tower offers an amazing 360° view of the city. A curious attraction is St. Stephen's mummified right hand, one of Hungary's most revered religious relics. *(V. M Deák tér. Church open daily 7am-7pm, Chapel May-Oct. M-Sa 9am-5pm, Su 1-5pm, Nov.-Apr. M-Sa 10am-4pm, Mass M-Sa 8am and 6pm, Su 8, 9, 10am, noon, 6, 7:30pm. Free. Tower open daily Apr.-Oct. M-Sa 10am-6pm. 500Ft, students 400Ft. Elevator available to top of tower. Cash only.)*

ANDRÁSSY ÚT AND HEROES' SQUARE. Hungary's grandest boulevard, Andrássy út extends from Erzsébet tér northeast to Heroes' Sq. (Hősök tér). The **State Opera House** (Magyar Állami Operaház) is a vivid reminder of Budapest's Golden Age; its gilded interior glows on performance nights. *(Andrássy út 22. M1: Opera. ☎01 332 8197. 1hr. English-language tours daily 3 and 4pm. 2600Ft, students 1400Ft.)* At the Heroes' Sq. end of Andrássy út, the **Millennium Monument** (Millenniumi emlékmʼ) commemorates the nation's most prominent leaders.

CITY PARK (VÁROSLIGET). Budapest's park, located northeast of Heroes' Sq., is home to a zoo, a circus, an amusement park, and a castle. The castle's collage of Baroque, Gothic, and Romanesque styles chronicles the history of Hungarian design. Rent a rowboat or ice skates on the lake next to the castle. The park's main road is closed to automobiles on weekends. *(XIV. M1: Széchényi Fürdő. Zoo ☎01 273 4900; www.zoobudapest.com. Open May-Aug. M-Th 9am-6:30pm, F-Su 9am-7pm; Mar. and Oct. M-Th 9am-5pm, F-Su 9am-5:30pm; Apr. and Sept. M-Th 9am-5:30pm, F-Su 9am-6pm; Nov.-Jan. daily. 9am-4pm. 1700Ft, students 1200Ft. Park ☎01 363 8310. Open July-Aug. daily*

10am-8pm; May-June and Sept. M-F 11am-7pm, Sa-Su 10am-8pm, Apr. and Oct. M-F noon-6pm, Sa-Su 10am-7pm. 3320Ft, children 213-Ft weekdays; weekends 3510Ft, kids 2250Ft.)

🏛 MUSEUMS

▨MUSEUM OF APPLIED ARTS (IPARMŰVÉSZETI MÚZEUM). This collection of handcrafted pieces—including ceramics, furniture, metalwork, and Tiffany glass—deserves careful examination. Excellent temporary exhibits highlight specific crafts. Built for the 1896 millennium, the tiled Art Nouveau edifice is as intricate as the pieces within. *(IX. Üllői út 33-37. Ⓜ3: Ferenc körút ☎01 456 5100; www.imm.hu. Open W and F-Su 10am-6pm, Th 10am-10pm, Tu 2-6pm. Open house Th 6-10pm. Permanent collection 1000Ft, students 500Ft, Combined ticket 2500/1250Ft. Cash only. Group tours available.)*

▨TERROR HÁZA (HOUSE OF TERROR). The Nazi and Soviet regimes housed prisoners in the basement of this building near Heroes' Sq. An acclaimed museum opened here in 2002 to document life under the two reigns of terror and memorialize the victims who were tortured and killed. *(VI. Andrássy út 60. Ⓜ1: Vörösmarty tér. ☎01 374 2600; www.terrorhaza. hu. Open Tu-F 10am-6pm and Sa-Su 10am-7:30pm. 1500Ft, students 750Ft. Audioguides 1300Ft. AmEx/MC/V.)*

MUSEUM OF FINE ARTS (SZÉPMŰVÉSZETI MÚZEUM). A spectacular collection of European art is housed in this museum near Heroes' Sq. *(Ⓜ1: Hősök tere. From the metro, walk toward Heroes' Sq.; the museum is on the left. ☎01 469 7100; www.szepmuveszeti.hu. Open Tu-Su 10am-6pm. Ticket booth open Tu-Su 10am-5pm. Wheelchair-accessible. 1400Ft, students 700Ft. AmEx/MC/V.)*

NATIONAL MUSEUM (NEMZETI MÚZEUM). An exhibit on the second floor chronicles the history of Hungary from the founding of the state through the 20th century; the first floor is reserved for temporary exhibits. *(Múzeum körút. 14/16. Ⓜ3: Kálvin tér. ☎204 397 325; www.mng.hu. Open Tu-Su 10am-6pm. Last entry 30min before closing. 1040Ft, students 520Ft. MC/V.)*

MEMENTO PARK. After the collapse of Soviet rule, the open-air Statue Park Museum (Szoborpark Múzeum) was created in Buda, south of Gellérthegy, to display Soviet statues removed from Budapest's parks and squares. The indispensable English-language guidebook (1000Ft) explains the statues' histories. *(XXII, at the corner of Balatoni út and Szabadkai utca. Take express bus #7 from Keleti station. to Etele tér, then take the yellow Volán bus from terminal #7 bound for Diosd-Érd, get off at Memento Park. You'll need to buy a separate ticket from the Volánbusz ticket office. There is also a white direct bus from Deák tér (Ⓜ1, 2, or 3) every day* *at 11am (and also at 3pm during July and Aug.) for 3950Ft, students 2450Ft; includes price of admission and return ticket. www.mementopark.hu. Open daily 10am-dusk. Wheelchair-accessible. 1500Ft, students 1000Ft. AmEx/MC/V.)*

BUDA CASTLE. Buda Castle houses several museums. Wings B-D hold the huge **Hungarian National Gallery** (Magyar Nemzeti Galéria), a definitive collection of Hungarian painting and sculpture. Its treasures include works by Realist Mihály Munkácsy and Impressionist Paál László, and medieval gold altarpieces. *Buda Palace, wings A, B, C, and D. ☎01 356 0049; www.mng.hu. Open Tu-Su 10am-6pm. Last entry 30min before closing. Wheelchair accessible. Admission 900Ft, Hapsburg crypt 600Ft. MC/V.)* In Wing E, the **Budapest History Museum** (Budapesti Történeti Múzeum) displays a collection of recently unearthed medieval artifacts. *(Buda Palace, wing E. ☎01 487 8800; www.btm.hu. Open Tu-Sa 10am-8pm. Last entry 30min. before closing. Wheelchair-accessible. 1300Ft, students 650Ft. MC/V.)*

🎭 ENTERTAINMENT

Pesti Est, Budapest Program, Budapest Panorama, and *Budapest in Your Pocket* are the best English-language entertainment guides; pick them up at tourist offices, hotels, and many restaurants and bars. The Style section of the *Budapest Sun* (www.budapestsun.com; 300Ft) has film reviews and a 10-day calendar. The often entertaining and occasionally ascerbic *Pestiside* (Pestiside.hu) covers nightlife and cultural events. For event tickets, check **Ticket Express Hungary,** Andrássy út 18 (☎01 303 0999; www.tex.hu; open M-F 10am-6:30pm) or **Jegymester** (www.jegymester.hu). The box office at the **Palace of Arts** (☎01 555 3001; www.mupa.hu; open M-F 1pm-6pm, Sa-Su 10am-6pm) has tickets for many of the city's venues. Most of the city's major theaters are closed from July to September.

🏛 **State Opera House** (Magyar Állami Operaház), VI, Andrássy út 22 (☎01 353 0170; www.opera.hu). Ⓜ1: Opera. One of Europe's grandest opera houses is a must-see for classical music lovers. The building is gorgeous. (Yeah? Because classical music lovers will love the music; building-enthusiasts will love the building.) Hosts some of the continent's finest operas, ballets, and classical performances. While some tickets sell out a year in advance, rush tickets at a fraction of the normal price are sometimes available 1hr. before the performance. Tickets 1000-9000Ft. Wheelchair-accessible. Box office open M-Sa 11am-7pm, Su 4-7pm. Closes at 5pm on non-performance days. Call for show schedules, or check the poster at the gates. AmEx/MC/V.

🏛 **National Theatre** (Nemzeti Színház), IX, Bajor Gizi park 1 (☎01 476 6868; www.nemzetiszinhaz.hu). Millenniumi Kulturális Központ tram stop; trams 2, 24. The new home of Budapest's National Theatre is an architectural marvel, surrounded by sculptures and a partially submerged facade that serves as a memorial to the old National Theatre, which was blown up in order to expand the subway. The venue offers the best of Hungarian theater as well as works by Shakespeare and Shaw. Tickets 1200-4000Ft. Wheelchair-accessible. Box office open M-F 10am-6pm, Sa-Su 2-6pm. AmEx/MC/V.

🛁 BATHS

KIRALY BATHS (KIRALY FÜRDÓ). Construction began on the monumental Kiraly Baths by order of the Pasha of Buda in 1565. Unlike most of the area baths, the Kiraly baths are not connected directly to the thermal springs, instead taking water from another nearby bath. The Pasha ordered them built far from the springs so that bathing could continue even during an inevitable siege by Christian forces. Renovated and rebuilt after damage from WWII, the Kiraly baths, perhaps more than any other in the city, evoke the spirit of the old Turkish baths with their crescent-topped domes and octagonal bath surrounded by pillars. *(Fő utca 82-84. Margit hid tram stop, trams 4, 6. From the tram stop, take south Frankel Leó utca; it will become Fő utca. ☎01 202 3688; www.spasbudapest.com. Open daily M and W 8am-7pm (women only), Tu, Th-Sa 9am-8pm (men only), Su 9am-8pm. Bathing suit rental available. 2100Ft. Thermal tub 1200Ft. Cash only.)*

NIGHTLIFE

Relaxing garden "cafe-clubs," elegant after-hours scenes, and nightly "freakin'" fests make up Budapest's nightlife scene. Pubs and bars stay busy until at least 4am and more club-like venues are alive past 5am. Upscale cafes near Pest's **Ferencz Liszt tér** (M2: Oktogon) attract Budapest's hip residents in their 20s and 30s, while less-apparent sidestreets house a more relaxed setting.

- **Gödör Klub,** V, Erzsébet tér, (☎01 201 3868; www.godorklub.hu). Ⓜ1,2, or 3: Deák tér. What was once Budapest's biggest embarrassment is now one of its most popular hangouts. The conspicuously bare concrete walls give you the sense that the club, situated in the former foundation of what was supposed to be the new National Concert Hall, is still unfinished. During the week the cultural center maintains an extensive activities calendar, which includes pilates classes. Beer from 350Ft. Shots 200-800Ft. Open M-Th and Su 10am-2am, F-Sa 10am-4am. Cash only.

- **Szimpla Kert,** VII, Kazinczy utca 14 (☎01 352 4198 ; www.szimpla.hu). Ⓜ2: Astoria. From the metro, take Rákóczi út east and then turn left on Kazinczy. Budapest's original and perhaps best-loved ruin pub. 5 bars scattered across 2 floors. Most prefer to relax in the courtyard where old bathtubs and sedans have been turned into choice seating. Sip one of the bar's 16 varieties of *pálinka* (900Ft). Beer from 350Ft. Shots 600-800Ft. Mixed drinks 1400-2000Ft. Wheelchair-accessible. Open daily noon-3am. Cash only.

- **Corvintető,** VIII, Blaha Lujza tér 1-2 (☎772 2984; www.corvinteto.hu). Ⓜ2: Blaha Lujza tér. From the metro, walk toward the Corvin building; the entrance to the club is along Somogyi Béla út, up the stairs. Don't be misled by the graffiti-covered tile stairs—this club situated on top of a former state-owned department store is one of the most stylish places to party in Budapest. The coolest part is undoubtedly on the roof. Beer from 320Ft. Shots 600-900Ft. Open daily 6pm-5am. Cash only.

- **Pótkulcs,** VI, Csengery utca 65/b (☎01 269 1050; www.potkulcs.hu). Ⓜ1: Vörösmarty utca. From the metro, take Vörösmarty toward the train station and turn left at Szondi; the bar is on the corner of Csengery and Szondi. One of Budapest's most difficult-to-find ruin pubs, but well worth the effort. The terrace is full of greenery and surrounded by old brick. Every Tu a Hungarian folk band inspires spontaneous dancing in the main room. Beer from 450Ft. Wine from 190Ft. Shots from 500Ft. Live folk, rock, or gypsy music most nights. Terrace wheelchair-accessible. Open daily 5pm-2am at least. Cash only.

- **Mumus,** VII, Dob utca 18. Ⓜ2: Astoria. From the metro, take Károly körút north and then turn right onto Dob utca. What Mumus lacks in contact info and conspicuous signage it makes up for in atmosphere. A very simple, personal bar for those who like to go off the grid of Budapest nightlife. Laid-back students, artists, and backpackers relax at tables made from old oil drums while enjoying some of the cheapest drinks in town. Beer from 250Ft. Shots 250-450Ft. Wine from 200Ft. Open M-Sa 3pm-3am, Su 4pm-midnight. Cash only.

ICELAND
(ÍSLAND)

Created when the European and North American continents collided, Iceland's landscape is uniquely warped and contorted, marked by active volcanoes and the tortoise-like crawl of advancing and retreating glaciers. Nature is the country's greatest attraction, and visitors can pick their way through sunken ice kettles, bathe in natural hot springs, and bike through fishing villages on mountainous dirt roads. An emphasis on natural farming has made Icelandic produce and meat sought-after exports: Icelandic dining is a pleasure. Covered by more glaciers and highly dependent on and protective of its fishing industry, Iceland is quickly becoming a hot tourist and ecotourist destination.

DISCOVER ICELAND: SUGGESTED ITINERARY

THREE DAYS. Start off in **Reykjavík** (p. 413) and explore the city center and **Laugardalur** (p. 418) while munching on a lamb hot dog. Spend the next day hiking through a **bird reserve** (p. 419), followed by soaking it up in a **thermal pool** (p. 419). Cap it all off with a picnic in **Heiðmörk Reserve** (p. 419).

ONE WEEK. After three days in **Reykjavík,** spend a day at **Þingvellir National Park** (p. 420). Soothe your sore muscles with a day soaking in the **Blue Lagoon** (p. 421). Make sure to catch a free tour at **Nesjavelliri** (p. 421), a power plant driven by geothermal heat. Spend your last day exploring **Gullfoss and Geysir.**

ESSENTIALS

FACTS AND FIGURES

OFFICIAL NAME: Republic of Iceland.
CAPITAL: Reykjavík.
MAJOR CITIES: Akureyri, Ísafjörður, Kópavogur, Hafnarfjörður.
POPULATION: 302,000.

TIME ZONE: GMT.
LANGUAGE: Icelandic.
PERCENTAGE OF ARABLE LAND: 0.07%.
EXPORT EARNINGS PROVIDED BY THE FISHING INDUSTRY: 70%.

WHEN TO GO

Visitors should brave peak-season crowds to enjoy all Iceland has to offer. From June through August, travelers will have the most accommodation and transportation options. The sky never quite gets dark in summer months, though the sun dips below the horizon for a few hours each night. July temperatures average around 11˚C (52˚F). December and January receive four or five hours of sunlight daily, but the nights are illuminated by **aurora borealis,** the famous Northern Lights. Winter in Reykjavík averages 0˚C (32˚F), making transportation slower and less reliable.

BURNING THE MIDNIGHT OIL. During the summer months, the sun never quite sets over Iceland. While the near 24hr. sunlight makes for easy all-night partying, it can take its toll on visitors. Bring a sleeping mask and over-the-counter, non-habit-forming sleep aids to avoid sleepless nights.

DOCUMENTS AND FORMALITIES

EMBASSIES AND CONSULATES. Foreign embassies in Iceland are in Reykjavík. Icelandic embassies and consulates abroad include: **Australia,** 16 Hann St., Griffith, Canberra (☎262 95 68 19; benefitfarm@bigpond.com.au); **Canada,** 360 Albert St., Ste. 710, Ottawa, ON K1R 7X7 (☎613-482-1944; www.iceland.org/ca); **Ireland,** Cavendish House, Smithfield, Dublin (☎1 872 9299; jgg@goregrimes.ie); **New Zealand,** Sanford Ltd., 22 Jellicoe St., Auckland (☎9 379 4720); **UK,** 2A Hans St., London SW1X 0JE (☎020 72 59 39 99; www.iceland.org/uk); **US,** 1156 15th St. NW, Ste. 1200, Washington, D.C. 20005 (☎202-265-6653; www.iceland.org/us).

VISA AND ENTRY INFORMATION. EU citizens do not need a visa. Citizens of Australia, Canada, New Zealand, and the US do not need a visa for stays of up to 90 days, beginning upon entry into any of the countries in the EU's freedom-of-movement zone. For more info, see p. 13. For stays longer than 90 days, all non-EU citizens need visas, available at embassies abroad; check www.utl.is/english/visas/apply to find the nearest location.

TOURIST SERVICES AND MONEY

EMERGENCY	Ambulance, Fire, and Police: ☎112.

MONEY. Iceland's unit of currency is the **króna (ISK),** plural **krónur.** One króna is equal to 100 **aurars,** with standard denominations of 1, 5, 10, 50, and 100kr in coins, and 500, 1000, and 5000kr in notes. For currency exchange, **ATMs** are located throughout the larger cities. **Banks** are usually open M-F 9:15am-4pm. Major Icelandic banks, such as Landsbankinn, do not have sister banks in other countries that allow lower exchange fees. In general, there's no way around the high costs in Iceland. On average, a night in a hostel will cost 1700ISK, a guesthouse 3000-4000ISK, and a meal's worth of groceries 700-1200ISK. Restaurants include a service charge on the bill. **Tipping** is discouraged.

ICELANDIC KRÓNUR (ISK)		
AUS$1 = 54.36ISK		100ISK = AUS$1.84
CDN$1 = 64.31ISK		100ISK = CDN$1.56
EUR€1 = 91.84ISK		100ISK = EUR€1.09
NZ$1 = 47.42ISK		100ISK = NZ$2.11
UK£1 = 135.01ISK		100ISK = UK£0.74
US$1 = 68.16ISK		100ISK = US$1.47

Iceland has a 24.5% **value added tax (VAT),** a sales tax on goods and services purchased within the **European Economic Area** (EEA: the EU plus Iceland, Liechtenstein, and Norway). The prices given in *Let's Go* include VAT. In the airport upon exiting the EEA, non-EEA citizens can claim a refund on the tax paid for goods at participating stores. In order to qualify for a refund in a store, you

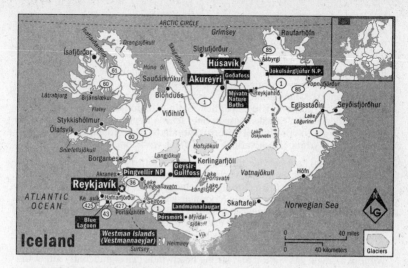

Iceland

must spend at least 4000ISK; make sure to ask for a refund form when you pay. For more info on qualifying for a VAT refund, see p. 19.

TRANSPORTATION

BY PLANE. Iceland's main international airport is **Keflavik International Airport (KEF;** ☎ 425 6000; www.keflavikairport.com), which is 50km southwest of Reykjavík. **Icelandair** (Iceland ☎505 0700, UK 0870 787 4020, US and Canada 800-223-5500; www.icelandair.net) flies to Reykjavík year-round from Europe and the US. They also provide free stop-overs of up to seven days on flights to many European cities. No-frills **Iceland Express** (Iceland ☎550 0600, UK 0870 240 5600; www.icelandexpress.com) flies to nine Western European countries on the cheap. Icelandair's domestic counterpart, **Air Iceland** (☎570 3030; www.airiceland.is), flies from Reykjavík to most major towns in Iceland and Greenland.

 SOARING PRICES. To get the most for your money, consider traveling by plane instead of bus. Discount airfare is often just as expensive, or cheaper, than terrestrial tickets. Check with Air Iceland for more info.

BY BUS. Several bus lines are organized by **Bifreiðastöð Íslands (BSÍ;** www. bsi.is); buses can be cheaper and more scenic than flights, although they run infrequently in the low-season. From mid-June to August, buses run daily on the **Ring Road (Route 1),** the highway that circles Iceland. Even then the going is slow; some unpaved stretches still exist in the east. The **Full Circle Passport** lets travelers circle the island at their own pace on the Ring Road (June-Aug.; 25,900ISK). However, it only allows travel in one direction, so travelers must move either clockwise or counter-clockwise around the country to get back to where they started. For an extra 19,200ISK, the pass provides access to the Westfjords in the extreme northwest. The **Omnibus Passport** is valid for periods of up to four weeks for unlimited travel on all scheduled bus routes, including non-Ring roads (1-week 26,900ISK, 2-week 42,000ISK, 3-week 50,000ISK; valid

May 15-Sept. 15). Travelers, especially those arriving in groups of two or more, should note that the inflexibility of the Full Circle Passport and the high cost of the Omnibus Passport make car rental a good idea for those planning on visiting rural parts of the country. Iceland has no intercity train service.

BY FERRY. The best way to see Iceland's gorgeous shoreline is on the **Norröna** ferry (☎983 5900; www.smyril-line.fo, website in Icelandic) that crosses the North Atlantic to Hanstholm, DEN; Tórshavn in the Faroe Islands; and Seyðisfjörður. From Tórshavn, you can either continue on to Bergen, NOR, or return to Seyðisfjörður. An **Eimskip Transport** liner leaves Reykjavík weekly and takes five days to get to continental ports at Thorshavn, Rotterdam, Hamburg, Fredrikstad, and Århus. (Reservations ☎525 7800; www.eimskip.com.)

BY CAR. Rental cars provide the most freedom for travelers and may even be the cheapest option for those who want to visit rural areas. Getting a car and touring Iceland's Ring Road (Rte. 1), which circles the entire island and passes many of the best destinations, is a popular way to explore the country. Book before you arrive for lower rates. Car rental *(bílaleiga)* companies charge 4000-8000ISK per day for a small car, and 10,000-25,000ISK for the **four-wheel-drive vehicles** that are imperative outside settled areas. On these routes, drivers should bring a container of extra gas, since some roads continue for 300km without a single gas station and strong headwinds can significantly affect the rate of fuel consumption. It is not uncommon for local drivers to **ford streams** in their vehicles; do not attempt this in a compact car, and cross in a convoy if possible. (24hr. reports on road conditions ☎800 6316, June-Aug. in English.) Drivers are required to wear seat belts and to keep their headlights on at all times. Iceland recognizes foreign driver's licenses, but you may need to purchase insurance for the rental vehicle (1500-3500ISK).

BY BIKE AND BY THUMB. Ferocious winds, driving rain, and gravel roads make long-distance cycling difficult. Hug the Ring Road if you prefer company; for less-traveled paths, branch out to the coastal roads that snake their way through the Eastfjords, or check **Cycling in Iceland** (http://home.wanadoo.nl/erens/icecycle.htm). Also check out the **Icelandic Mountain Bike Club**, Brekkustíg. 2, in Reykjavík, or drop by their clubhouse on the first Thursday night of each month after 8pm for some advice (☎562 0099; www.fjallahjolaklub-burinn.is). Buses will carry bikes for a 500-900ISK fee, depending on the route. Hitchhikers try the roads in summer, but sparse traffic and harsh weather exacerbate the risks. Still, rides can be found with relative ease between Reykjavík and Akureyri; flagging down a ride is harder in the east and the south. *Let's Go* does not recommend hitchhiking.

KEEPING IN TOUCH

PHONE CODES	**Country code: 354. International dialing prefix: 00.** There are no city codes in Iceland. For more info on how to place international calls, see **Inside Back Cover.**

EMAIL AND INTERNET. Internet is widespread. Seek out libraries in small towns for Internet. At cafes, a connection will cost 200-300ISK per hour.

TELEPHONE. The state-owned telephone company, **Síminn**, usually has offices in post offices, where you can buy phone cards and get the best international call rates. **Pay phones** accept prepaid phone cards, credit cards (cheapest for calls to **mobile phones**), as well as 10ISK, 50ISK, and 100ISK coins. Iceland uses two different mobile phone networks: digital GSM phones service 98% of the country's population, but only a small fraction of its land area, so hikers, fishermen, and others who travel outside of settled areas rely on analog NMT phones. Prepaid GSM phone cards are available at gas stations and convenience stores. OG Vodafone generally offers the best prepaid rates. For operator assistance, dial ☎118; for international assistance, dial ☎1811. International direct dial numbers include: **AT&T Direct** (☎800 222 55 288); **British Telecom** (☎800 89 0354); **Canada Direct** (☎800 9010); **Telecom New Zealand** (☎800 9064).

MAIL. Mailing a letter or postcard (up to 20g) from Iceland costs from 60ISK within Iceland, from 70ISK to Europe, and from 80ISK outside of Europe. Post offices *(póstur)* are generally open M-F 9am-6pm in Reykjavík and 9am-4:30pm in the countryside. Check www.postur.is for additional info. To receive mail in Iceland, have mail delivered **Poste Restante.** Mail will go to the main post office unless you specify a subsidiary by street address. Address mail to be held according to the following example (Reykjavík): First name, Last name, Poste Restante, ÍSLANDSPÓSTUR, Posthússtr. 5, 101 Reykjavík, ICELAND.

LANGUAGE. Icelandic is a Nordic language which developed in 9th-century Norway and came into its present form in 12th-century Iceland. It is a very pure form of the old Norwegian language of the vikings. Most Icelanders, especially those under 35, speak at least some English.

ACCOMMODATIONS AND CAMPING

ICELAND	❶	❷	❸	❹	❺
ACCOMMODATIONS	under 2000ISK	2000-3000ISK	3001-5000ISK	5001-10,000ISK	over 10,000ISK

Iceland's **HI youth hostels** are clean and reasonably priced at roughly 1800-2300ISK for nonmembers. HI members receive a 150-400ISK discount. Visit **Hostelling International Iceland,** Sundlaugarvegur 34, 105 Reykjavík (☎553 8110; www.hostel.is), for locations and pricing as well as for info on Iceland's seven eco-friendly Green Hostels. Expect to pay around 2100ISK for sleeping bag accommodations *(svefnpokapláss;* beds with no linens or blankets) and another 650ISK for linens. **Guesthouses** and **farmhouses** (☎570 2700; www.farmholidays.is) are a cheap, homey option outside cities. Many remote lodgings will pick up tourists in the nearest town for a small fee. Campers can choose among Iceland's 125 designated **campsites** (usually open June-Aug.). Camping outside official sites is prohibited. Official campsites range from grassy areas with cold-water taps to sumptuous facilities around Reykjavík; listings can be found at www.camping.is. Most charge around 600-800ISK, and many don't allow open flames (so be sure to bring a camp stove). Visit www.infoiceland.is/infoiceland/accommodation/camping for tips.

FOOD AND DRINK

ICELAND	❶	❷	❸	❹	❺
FOOD	under 500ISK	500-1000ISK	1001-1400ISK	1401-2000ISK	over 2000ISK

Iceland is in the middle of a culinary explosion. A history of food shortages led Iceland to value all that was pickled, dried, or smoked. But now, with more exotic methods and flavors introduced by a trickle of Asian immigrants, not everything is simply boiled and salted. Fresh **fish** and gamey free-range lamb—staples of Icelandic cuisine—remain essentials. But they're being mixed in new and delicious ways with vitamin-rich vegetables grown in greenhouse towns (such as Hveragerði) and a range of cheeses. Still, tradition is strong: *skyr*, a dairy product that tastes like a cross between yogurt and fresh cheese, and *hangikjot*, smoked lamb sandwiches, are more popular than ever. Food in Iceland is very expensive, and a cheap restaurant meal will cost at least 800ISK. **Grocery stores** are the way to go in virtually every town. **Alcohol** presents the same quandary: beer costs 500-600ISK for a large glass (0.5L, approx. 17 oz.) at pubs and cafes, while the price of hard liquor is even steeper. The country's national drink is *brennivín*, a schnapps made from potato, usually seasoned with caraway, and nicknamed "Black Death." Bootleggers in the countryside cook up batches of *landi*, a potent homemade moonshine, in protest against high liquor taxes. *Let's Go* does not recommend moonshine.

HOLIDAYS AND FESTIVALS

Holidays: New Year's Day (Jan. 1); Maundy Thursday (Apr. 9, 2009; Apr. 1, 2010); Good Friday (Apr. 10, 2009; Apr. 2, 2010); Easter (Apr. 12, 2009; Apr. 4, 2010); Sumardagurinn Fyrsti (1st day of summer; Apr. 24); Ascension (May 1); Pentecost (May 31, 2009; May 23, 2010); National Day (June 17); Tradesman's Day (Aug. 4); Christmas (Dec. 25); Boxing Day (Dec. 26).

Festivals: The month-long **Þorrablót festival** (during Feb.) is a holdover from the midwinter feasts of past centuries. Icelanders eat *svi* (singed and boiled sheep's head), *hrútspungur* (pickled ram's testicles), and *hákarl* (shark meat that has been allowed to rot underground) in commemoration of their heritage. **"Beer Day,"** celebrated in bars and restaurants, celebrates the March 1st, 1989 lifting of a 75yr. prohibition. **Sumardagurinn Fyrsti** marks the 1st day of summer with a carnival. The Reykjanes Peninsula celebrates **Sjómannadagur** (Seamen's Day) on June 4 with boat races and tug-of-war. During the 1st weekend in August, Icelanders head to the country for **Verslunarmannahelgi** for barbecues, camping, and drinking.

BEYOND TOURISM

Travelers hoping to stay in Iceland may be able to secure summer work. Check www.eurojobs.com for info on job placement. Ecotourism opportunities abound; organizations run tours on horseback to hot springs and up mountains. For more info on opportunities across Europe, see **Beyond Tourism,** p. 55.

Earthwatch Institute, 3 Clock Tower Pl., Ste. 100, Box 75, Maynard, MA, 01754 (Canada and US ☎800-776-0188, UK 44 18 65 31 88 38, Australia 03 96 82 68 28; www.earthwatch.org). For a hefty fee (€2095), Earthwatch organizes volunteers, guided by scientists, to conduct geological fieldwork in the Icelandic glaciers. They also coordinate fundraising efforts to curtail the fee.

International Cultural Youth Exchange, Große Hamburger Str. 30, Berlin, GER (☎49 30 28 39 05 50; www.icye.org). ICYE brings together volunteers and host organizations on a variety of projects worldwide, including several in Iceland. ICYE also organizes European Voluntary Service programs (http://europa.eu.int/comm/youth/program/guide/action2_en.html) for EU citizens to serve for a fully funded year in another EU country.

Volunteers for Peace (☎802-259-2759; www.vfp.org). Runs 2800 "workcamps" throughout the world, including several in Iceland. $250 per 2- to 3-week workcamp, including room and board, plus $20 VFP membership fee.

REYKJAVÍK

Home of 60% of Icelanders, Reykjavík (pop. 200,000) is a modestly sized capital with an international clubbing reputation. Bold, modern architecture along with white painted concrete structures rise above the blue waters of the Faxaflói Bay. The city's refreshingly clear air complements the clean streets and well-kept gardens. The spring rain and the endless winter night force social life indoors for much of the year, where many locals sip espresso while arguing over environmental policy in this hub of renewable energy.

▌ TRANSPORTATION

Flights: International flights arrive at **Keflavík Airport (KEF),** 55km from Reykjavík. From the main exit, catch a **Flybus** (☎562 1011; www.flybus.is) to **BSÍ Bus Terminal** (45min.; 1500ISK, round-trip 2700ISK). Flybus also offers free transport from the bus terminal to many hostels and hotels; ask or check website for more info. A public bus to the city center runs from Gamla-Hringbraut across the street from the bus terminal (M-F 7am-midnight, Sa-Su 10am-midnight; 280ISK). Flybus service to the airport departs from BSÍ, but most hostels and hotels can also arrange for bus pick-up. Nearby **Reykjavík Airport (RKV)** is the departure point for domestic flights. Take bus #15.

Buses: **Umferðarmiðstöð BSÍ** (BSÍ Bus Terminal), Vatnsmrarvegur 10 (☎562 1011; www.bsi.is), off Gamla-Hringbraut. Walk 15-20min. south along Tjörnin from the city center or take bus #1, 3, 5, or 14. (2-3 per hr., 280ISK). Open daily 4:30am-midnight.

Public Transportation: Bus service can be infrequent and roundabout; walking is often a speedier option. **Strætó** (☎540 2700; www.straeto.is) operates yellow city buses (280ISK). **Lækjartorg,** on Lækjargata, is the main bus station for the city center. Hlemmur, 1km east of Lækjartorg where Hverfisgata meets Laugavegur, is another major terminal, with more connections than Lækjartorg (open while buses run. After 8pm buy tickets at kiosk). Pick up a schedule at the terminal. Don't feel bad asking for navigational help at hostels and info desks—recent changes in the bus routes have confused even some drivers. Buy packages of 11 adult fares (2500ISK) or a day pass for 600kr, 3 day pass for 1500kr. Pay fare with coins; drivers do not give change. Ticket packages are sold at the terminal, city hall, and at swimming pools. If you need to change buses, ask the driver of the 1st bus for *skiptimiði* (free transfer ticket), valid for 1hr. after the fare has been paid. Most buses 2-3 per hr. M-Sa 7am-midnight, Su 10am-midnight.

Taxis: BSR (☎561 0000; www.bsr.is). 24hr. service. **Hreyfill** (☎588 5522; www.hreyfill.is/english). Also offers private tours for groups of 1-8.

Car Rental: **Berg,** Tangarhöfða 10 (☎577 6050; www.bergcar.is). Unlimited distance with insurance from 9000ISK per day; low-season reduced rates. Pick-up available at Keflavík and Reykjavík Airports. Berg is generally the cheapest option other than **Vaka** (567 6700, www.vakabilar.is. Reserve ahead). Fuel costs around 300ISK per L. Iceland can be a difficult country to drive in. Drivers should stick to the rim-road and exercise caution. See www.visitreykjavik.is for more information on car rental.

Bike Rental: **Reykjavík Youth Hostel** campground (p. 416). 1500ISK per 4hr., 2500ISK per day. Helmet included. **Borgarhjól,** Hverfisgata 50, is closer to the city center, down the road from Culture House. (☎551 5653; www.borgarhjol.net. Fees change frequently, though generally similar to those above.)

Hitchhiking: Many foreigners hitchhike outside of Reykjavík because of confusing bus routes, but it is never completely safe. *Let's Go* does not recommend hitchhiking.

Reykjavík

🔺 ACCOMMODATIONS
Domus Guesthouse, **5**
Guesthouse 101, **15**
Flóki Inn, **16**
Reykjavík Youth Hostel (HI)
   and Campsite, **6**
Salvation Army Guesthouse, **7**

🍴 FOOD
Á Næstu Grösum, **12**
Bæjarins Beztu, **2**

Babalú
   Coffeehouse, **14**
Kaffi Hljómalind, **9**
Nonnabiti, **1**
Santa Maria, **17**
Seabaron, **10**

⭐ NIGHTLIFE
22, **13**
Hressin
   Garskálinn, **3**
NASA, **8**
Sólon, **4**
Vegamót, **11**

ORIENTATION AND PRACTICAL INFORMATION

Lækjartorg is Reykjavík's main square and a navigational base. Lækjargata, a main street, leads southwest from Lækjartorg and becomes **Fríkirkjuvegur** when it reaches **Lake Tjörnin** (the Pond), the southern limit of the city center. Reykjavík's main thoroughfare extends eastward from Lækjartorg, changing names from Austurstræti to Bankastræti and then to **Laugavegur**, as it is commonly known. Helpful publications, including *What's On in Reykjavík*, *Reykjavík City Guide*, and *The Reykjavík Grapevine*, are available for free at tourist offices and around the city. *The Grapevine*, published by American expatriates, includes opinionated local news coverage and comprehensive listings of current music and arts events as well as some helpful tips for travelers.

Tourist Offices: Upplsingamiðstöð Ferðamanna í Reykjavík, Adalstræti 2 (☎590 1550; www.visitreykjavik.is). Open from June to mid-Sept. daily 8:30am-7pm; Sept.-May M-F 9am-6pm, Sa 9am-4pm, Su 10am-2pm. Sells the Reykjavík Card (1-day 1200ISK, 2-day 1700ISK, 3-day 2200ISK), which allows unlimited public transportation, free entry to some sights and thermal pools (p. 418), and limited **Internet** at the tourist center. Several discount coupon books are also available at the center. Tourist Information Center, Bankastræti 2 (☎522 4979; www.itm.is) is just off of Laugavegur and

ICELAND

offers solid advice. Open May-Aug. daily 8am-7pm; Sept.-May. M-F 10am-5pm. City Hall Information Center, Vonarstræti 3 (☎411 1005), is in the lobby of City Hall. Open M-F 8:30am-4:30pm and Sa-Su noon-4pm.

Embassies: Canada, Túngata 14 (☎575 6500). Open M-F 9am-noon. **UK,** Laufásvegur. 31 (☎550 5100). Open M-F 8:30am-noon. **US,** Laufásvegur 21 (☎562 9100). Open M-F 8am-12:30pm and 1:30pm-5pm.

Luggage Storage: At BSÍ Bus Terminal (☎562 1011), next to the ticket window. 400ISK for the 1st day, 200ISK per day thereafter. Open daily 4:30am-midnight.

GLBT Resources: Gay Community Center, Laugavegur 3, 4th fl. (☎552 7878; www.samtokin78.is). Open M-F 1-5pm (unofficially 9am-5pm) and Sa in winter 9am-5pm; cafe open M and Th 8-11:30pm; library open M and Th 8-11pm. More info at www.gayice.is. Be sure to check out the gay pride events in from early to mid-Aug. each year.

Police: Hverfisgata 113 (☎444 1000). **Emergency Number** ☎112.

Pharmacy: Lyfja Lágmúla, Lágmúla 5 (☎533 2300). Open daily 8am-midnight.

Hospital: National Hospital, on Hringbraut (☎543 1000), has a 24hr. emergency department. To save money try the **Heilsurverndarstödin**—the Health Center for Tourists Barónsstígur 47. (☎458 9060. Open M-F 9am-midnight.)

Internet: Reykjavík Public Library, Tryggvagur 15 (☎563 1705), is the cheapest option. Free Wi-Fi, 200ISK per hr. Open M-Th 10am-7pm, F 11am-7pm, Sa-Su 1-5pm. In winter, open M 10am-9pm, F 11am-7pm, Sa-Su 1-5pm. MC/V. **Ground Zero,** Vallarstræti 4 (☎562 7776), at Ingólfstorg Sq. 300ISK per 30min., 500ISK per hr. Open M-F 11am-1am, Sa-Su noon-1am. AmEx/MC/V.

Post Office: Íslandspóstur, Pósthússtræti 5 (☎580 1000), in a big red building, is at the intersection with Austurstræti. Open M-F 9am-6:00pm. **Poste Restante** available; send to: Central Post Office Pósthússtræti 5 I5-101 Reykjavik, Iceland.

Alcohol: The legal drinking age in Iceland is 20. Most alcohol is not sold in stores but at **Vinbuð,** the government liquor store. Open M-Th, Sa-Su 11am-6pm, F 11am-7pm. MC/V. One is located in downtown Reykjavik at Austurstræti 10a.

🏠 🏕 ACCOMMODATIONS AND CAMPING

Gistiheimili (guesthouses) offer sleeping-bag accommodations starting from 2500ISK (bed and pillow in a small room; add 300-600ISK for linens). Hotels cost at least 6500ISK. Call ahead for reservations, especially in summer.

Reykjavík Youth Hostel (HI), Sundlaugarvegur 34 (☎553 8110). Bus #14 from Lækjargata. This popular, eco-friendly hostel is east of the city center, but it's adjacent to Reykjavík's largest thermal pool and has excellent facilities. The staff gives tips for exploring the city's less touristy sights. Breakfast 900ISK. Linens 700ISK. Laundry 350ISK per token. Free Wi-Fi; Internet 300ISK per 30min, 500ISK per hr. Reception 8am-midnight; ring bell after hours. Dorms 2300ISK, HI 1850ISK; doubles 4500/3800ISK. Pre-pitched tents 1450ISK per person. AmEx/MC/V. ❷

Domus Guesthouse, Hverfisgata 45 (☎561 1200). Take bus #13, 1, 3, or 6 and get off across from the Regnboginn movie theater on Hverfisgötu. Close to the city center, the guesthouse offers spacious rooms with TVs and couches. All sleeping-bag accommodations are located across the street. Breakfast included with private rooms. Open mid-May-Sept. Reception 2pm-midnight, ring doorbell after. Sleeping-bag accommodations 3900ISK; singles 9900ISK; doubles 11,900ISK. MC/V. ❸

Flóki Inn, Flókagata 1 (☎552 1155; www.innsoficeland.is), a 15min. walk from the city center. A relaxing, intimate guesthouse. Breakfast included. Reception 24hr. Free Wi-Fi, Internet 350ISK per. 15min. Some rooms have kitchen available. Singles 8800ISK; doubles 11,500ISK. Extra bed 2500ISK. Reduced prices Oct.-May. AmEx/MC/V. ❹

Salvation Army Guesthouse, Kirkjustræti 2 (☎561 3203; www.guesthouse.is). Located near City Hall in the heart of Reykjavík, this bright yellow hostel is cozy with modest accommodations. Its prime location makes it ideal for exploring the nightlife. 24hr. reception. Breakfast 800ISK. Sleeping-bag accommodations 3000ISK; singles 6600ISK; doubles 9600ISK. Reduced prices in winter. AmEx/MC/V. ❷

Guesthouse 101, Laugavegur 101 (☎562 6101; www.iceland101.com), off Snorrabraut (29) on the third fl. This converted office building east of the city center has small, bright, modern rooms. Wheelchair-accessible. Breakfast included. Singles 7600ISK; doubles 9900ISK. Reduced prices in winter. AmEx/MC/V. ❹

Reykjavík Youth Hostel Campsite (☎568 6944), next to the hostel. Helpful staff and a sociable character make this a good alternative. Luggage storage 300ISK. Reception 24hr. Open from mid-May to mid-Sept. Tent sites 850ISK. 4-person cabins 5000ISK. Showers. Electricity 400ISK. Can use hostel's facilities as well. AmEx/MC/V. ❶

🍴 FOOD

An Icelandic meal featuring *hákarl* (shark meat that has been allowed to rot underground), lamb, or puffin generally costs 1500ISK or more, but worth the splurge at least once. Check out the harbor area outside downtown for some affordable seafood. To maintain a leaner budget, check out the lunch specials throughout the city (www.restaurant.is) and cook for yourself in the evenings. Pick up groceries at **Bónus,** Laugavegur 59. (☎562 8200. Open M-F noon-6:30pm, Sa 10am-8pm.) Other restaurants are on **Austurstræti** and **Hverfisgata.**

Á Næstu Grösum, Laugavegur 20B (☎552 8410), entrance off Klapparstígur. This 2nd fl. all-vegetarian restaurant, the 1st in Iceland, uses fresh, seasonal ingredients in creative ways. The airy dining room showcases the work of up-and-coming local artists. Soup (800ISK) comes with free refills. Daily special 1490ISK. 3 items, rice and salad 1590ISK. Vegan options. Open M-F 11:30am-10pm, Su 5-10pm. MC/V. ❷

Santa Maria, Laugavegur 22A (☎552 7775). Recently opened, this authentic Mexican restaurant has gained popularity for a menu where nothing is over 1000ISK. MC/V. ❶

Babalú Coffeehouse, Skólavördustigur 22A (☎552 2278). Near the church, the second floor cafe is a perfect place to relax. Serves savory crepes (950ISK) and smaller, sweet crepes (650ISK). Enjoy a coffee (300ISK) on the patio. Free Wi-Fi. Open daily in summer 11am-10pm; in winter noon-7:30pm. AmEx/MC/V. ❷

Kaffi Hljómalind, Laugavegur 23 (☎517 1980), east of the city center. Organic, vegetarian-friendly cafe serves big portions of soup, with free refill and bread (700ISK). Breakfast combination 1050ISK. Free Wi-Fi, vocal patrons, a box of toys, and large windows make this a great place for people-watching or passing the time. Live music or poetry reading usually W 8pm. Open M-F 9am-10pm, Sa-Su 11am-10pm. MC/V. ❷

Shalimar, Austurstræti 4 (☎551 0292). Spice it up with this traditional Indian restaurant in the heart of downtown. Get some naan (300ISK) with your dinner special (1290ISK). Open M-F 11am-10pm, Sa 4pm-11pm, Su 4pm-10pm. AmEx/MC/V. ❸

Seabaron Restaurant, Geirsgata 8 (☎553 1500). Famous for its lobster soup (950ISK), it also offers fish and whale kabobs (1200ISK-1500ISK). Try it out for lunch. Open in summer daily 11:30am-10pm; in winter 11:30am-9pm. MC/V. ❸

Nonnabiti, Hafnarstræti 11 (☎551 2312), west of Lækjartorgata toward the main tourist office. This sandwich shop is good for cheap, tasty meals. Burgers 690-1000ISK. Hot sandwiches 500-830ISK. 100ISK discount on subs M-F 9:30am-1:30pm. Open M-Th 9am-2am, F 9am-5:30am, Sa 10am-5:30am, Su noon-midnight. AmEx/MC/V. ❶

Bæjarins Beztu, corner of Tryggvagur and Pósthússtræti. This tiny stand on the harbor serves the Icelandic hot dog (230ISK) by which all others are measured. The owner proudly displays a picture of Bill Clinton eating one of her hot dogs, served up with "the works." You know you've found it when you see the perpetual line outside the small red kiosk. Weekend crowds head here to satisfy late-night cravings, often singing while they wait. Open until 12:30am, or until crowds dissipate—sometimes past 6am. MC/V. ❶

SIGHTS

CITY CENTER. Reykjavík's City Hall, on the northern shore of Lake Tjörnin, houses an impressive **three-dimensional model** of Iceland that vividly renders the country's striking topography. *(Open in summer M-F 8am-7pm, Sa-Su 10-6pm; winter M-F 8am-7pm, Sa-Su noon-6pm. Free.)* Just beyond City Hall lies **Aðalstræti,** the oldest street in the city. The recently opened 871 +/- 2 **Settlement Museum,** 16 Aðalstræti, in the basement of Hotel Reykjavik Centrum, features the preserved foundation of a Viking longhouse, with interactive displays and artifacts. By dating surrounding volcanic deposits, archaeologists theorize that the structure was built around AD 869-873. *(☎ 411 6370. Open daily 10am-5pm. 600ISK. AmEx/MC/V.)* Nearby is the oldest house in the city, **Fogetastofur,** Aðalstræti 10, built in 1762, which offers exhibits, pictures, and maps describing Reykjavík's growth since the 18th century. *(Museum open M-F 9am-6pm, Sa-Su noon-5pm. Free.)* The **Hafnarhús** (Harbor House) is the most eclectic of the three divisions of the Reykjavík Art Museum. The museum, a renovated warehouse, holds a collection of paintings by Erro, Iceland's preeminent contemporary artist. *(Tryggvagata 17, off Aðalstræti. ☎ 590 1200; www.artmuseum.is. Open daily high-season 10am-5pm, Th 10am-10pm; low-season 1-4pm. Free.)* Follow Tryggvagata to the intersection of Lækjargata and Hverfisgata and look up on the hill to see the statue of **Ingólfur Arnason,** Iceland's first settler, and revel in the view of the mountains to the north. The **Culture House** has a detailed exhibit on Iceland's ancient history and mythology, including carefully preserved vellum manuscripts of Eddas and Sagas. *(Hverfisgata 15. ☎ 545 1400. Open daily 11am-5pm. 300ISK.)*

East of Lake Tjörnin, the **National Gallery of Iceland** presents contemporary Icelandic art. The toys and cushions on the bottom floor aren't an installment piece; they're for restless children. *(Fríkirkjuvegur 7. ☎ 515 9600. Open Tu-Su 10am-5pm. Free.)* Continue eastward to the **Hallgrímskirkja** landmark church on Skólavörðustígur, designed by Guðjón Samúelsson to look like it formed from a volcanic eruption. The church will be under construction until September 2009, but you can still go up to the tower for an unparalleled view of the city. *(☎ 510 1000; www.hallgrimskirkja.is. Open daily 9am-5pm; occasionally closes later in summer. Organ concerts Th at noon, in summer also Sa at noon. Elevator to the top 400ISK.)* Across from the church, the **Einar Jónsson Museum** on Njarðargata exhibits 300 of the sculptor's imposing, allegorical works inspired by Iceland's Christian and pagan heritage. Don't miss the free **sculpture garden** in the back. *(☎ 551 3797; www.skulptur.is. Open from June to mid-Sept. Tu-Su 2-5pm; mid-Sept.-May Sa-Su 2-5pm. 400ISK. Free with ISIC.)*

> **DON'T GET FLEECED.** Visiting Reykjavík isn't cheap. Check out **Sirkus** (flea market) for deals on clothes, music, and jewelry. (In a large white building near the Harbor House on Tryggvagata. ☎ 562 5030. From noon to five on Saturdays and Sundays.) It's worth a stop just to try a free sample of the *hákarl*—rotten shark—a traditional Icelandic dish.

LAUGARDALUR. Sights cluster around Laugardalur, a large park east of the city center. The white dome of the **Ásmundarsafn** (Ásmundur Sveinsson Sculpture Museum), on Sigtún, houses works spanning Sveinsson's career in a building the artist lived in and designed. The sculpture garden around the museum features larger works, some of which are interactive pieces ideal for climbing

SURVIVING ICELAND

You might have the sixth sense—and no, not the one involving Bruce Willis and dead people. The Icelandic sixth sense allows you to see *huldufolk* (hidden people), magical creatures that 80% of Icelanders believe exist. Some *huldufolk* are friendly, upstanding citizens. Others are up to no damn good. To help you get through your trip to Iceland, *Let's Go* offers a brief survival guide:

Elves: Apparently, some look like humans, which makes picking them out a total crapshoot. **Strategy:** No cause for alarm. They're harmless and live in their Westman Islands village.

Faeries: A deceptive bunch. The beautiful faeries are known to lure you with soft, plaintive music. Then, BOOM—they'll carry you off. **Strategy:** Earplugs, or just run if you hear soft, plaintive music.

Gnomes: Small and subterranean. Strategy: Nothing to fear. Icelandic roads are often built around their settlements. They're that respected.

Trolls: Bad news if you run into one of these nocturnal beasts. Some live in Dimmuborgir, near Mývatn. Strategy: Although they're ugly, trolls fuss over hygiene. Get them dirty, mess with their hair, etc. The power plant at Nesjavelliri (p. 421), for example, maintains a shower for the trolls to enjoy so they don't meddle with Reykjavík's water supply. An A+ tactic.

or relaxing on. *(Take bus #14 to the Laugardalslaug thermal pools, turn left and walk down Reykjavegur to Sigtún.* ☎553 2155. *Open daily May-Sept. 10am-4pm; Oct.-Apr. 1-4pm. Free.)* Walking out of the museum, continue straight down Sigtún until it becomes Engjavegur and proceed to the **Reykjavík Botanic Garden,** one of the few forested areas in Iceland. *(Skúlatún 2.* ☎553 8870. *Garden open 24hr. Greenhouse and pavilion open daily Apr.-Sept. 10am-10pm; Oct.-Mar. 10am-5pm. Free.)* Just outside the garden, opposite the pavilion and greenhouse, a free outdoor exhibit outlines the history of the **Washing Springs,** Reykjavík's geothermal square, where the women of the city once came to do their cooking and their laundry. The Laugardalur region has a variety of sports facilities, but be sure to visit the city's largest thermal swimming pool, **Laugardalslaug** (see Thermal Pools, below).

OTHER SIGHTS. The **Saga Museum** rivals Madame Tussauds with its depiction of Icelandic history using life-size wax models. One figure shows a woman exposing her breast, which supposedly caused the Norwegian army to retreat during a bygone battle. *Let's Go* does not recommend flashing. *(Bus #18 south to Perlan.* ☎511 1517; *www.sagamuseum.is. Open Mar.-Oct. 10am-6pm; Nov.-Feb. noon-5pm. 1000ISK, students 800ISK.)* The renovated ◙**National Museum** has a more comprehensive overview of Iceland's past with audio/visuals and interactive exhibits that let you try on Icelandic garb. *(Suðurgata 41. Bus #14, 1, 3, or 6 from Hlemmur station.* ☎530 2200; *www.natmus.is/english. Open May-Sept. 15 daily 10am-5pm; Sept 16-Apr. Tu-Su 11am-5pm. 600ISK, students 300ISK. W free. Free guided tours summer daily 11am, winter Sa 2pm. MC/V.)* From the National Museum, take bus #12 or 19 from Hlemmur to **Árbæjarsafn,** an open-air museum that chronicles the lives of past generations of Icelanders. Check for the website for summer weekend special events, like folk dances and Viking games. *(Kistuhylur 4.* ☎411 6300; *www.reykjavikmuseum.is. Open June-Aug. daily 10am-5pm. 600ISK, F Free. Low-season tours M, W, F 1pm-2pm; call ahead.)*

◪ THERMAL POOLS

Reykjavík's thermal pools are all equipped with a hot pot (naturally occurring hot tub) and steam room or sauna, although each pool maintains a distinct character. Those searching for the cheapest option should seek out the city beach and its free hot pot at **Nauthólsvik.** Unless otherwise specified, all pools listed below charge 360ISK admission, with 10 visits for 2500ISK.

Laugardalslaug, Laugardalslaug-Sundlaugarvegur 105 (☎411 5100). Take bus #14 from the city center;

entrance is on the right. The city's largest thermal pool features indoor and outdoor facilities, a water slide, 5 hot pots, and a sauna. Swimsuit or towel rental 350ISK, admission to all 3 750kr. Open Apr.-Sept. M-F 6:30am-10:30pm, Sa-Su 8am-10pm; Oct.-Mar. M-F 6:30am-10:30pm, Sa-Su 8am-8pm. MC/V.

Vesturbaejarlaug, Hofsvallagata (☎551 5004). This pool is often recommended by locals as it has far fewer tourists and a good ice cream store just outside. Outdoor pool, 3 hot tubs, steam bath. Open May-Aug. M-F 6:30am-10pm, Sa-Su 8am-8pm; Sept.-April M-F 6:30am-9:30pm, Sa-Su 8am-7pm.

Sundhöll Reykjavíkur, Barónsstígur 101 (☎411 5350). This centrally located pool is an easy walk from city center. It offers an indoor pool as well as sunbathing areas and hot pots. Open M-F 6:30am-9:30pm, Sa-Su 8am-7pm. AmEx/MC/V.

Sundlaug Seltjarnarness, Suðurströnd 170 (☎561 1551). Take bus #11 from Hlemmur station to Sundlaug stop and follow the signs. Swimsuit and towel rental 300ISK each. Open M-F 6:30am-10pm, Sa-Su 8am-8pm. AmEx/MC/V.

Ylströndin Nauthólsvík. Take bus #119 south until the last stop. Although not considered a classic thermal pool by locals, this remote city beach is worth it. Lockers 200ISK. Free. Open May-Sept. daily 10am-8pm. Closed in rainy weather.

HIKING

Reykjavík has a range of hikes for different experience levels. Take precaution when scaling heights—conditions on hilltops can be very different compared with weather at sea level and can change quickly. For a casual stroll, take bus #18 to the Perlan stop by the Saga Museum to reach trails on the forested hill around **Perlan,** one of which features a working model of the **Strokkur Geyser** (see Gullfoss and Geysir, p. 420). At the southwest corner of the park is **Nauthólsvík beach** (see Thermal Pools, above) and a scenic trail around the airport that leads back to the city. If you get tired, catch bus #12 on Skeljanes back to the center. Pick up **maps** at the tourist office. If basking in the midnight sun on a black lava beach is what you've always dreamed of, visit the ⬛**Grótta** bird reserve on the western tip of the peninsula. Take bus #11 out to Hofgarður and walk 15min. along the sea on Byggarðstangi. Although the Grótta itself is closed during nesting season (May-June), the bird-filled sky is still an amazing sight. Check out the **lighthouse** at the edge of the peninsula: high tides make it a temporary island. South of the city lies the **Heiðmörk Reserve,** a large park with picnic spots and beginner to intermediate hiking trails. Take bus #1 or 2 from Hlemmur to Hamraborg and transfer to bus #28. Ask the driver to let you off at Lake Elliðavatn; from there, walk 3-4km south to the reserve.

TIP
DOOR-TO-DOOR. Legs aching after a long hike? The BSÍ bus drivers will generally let you off anywhere along the route upon request. You can also flag buses down like taxis and they will often stop to pick you up. Pick up by excursion buses and flybus can be made though most hotels and hostels.

Secluded and slow-paced **Viðey Island,** home to Viking structures and Iceland's second-oldest church, has been inhabited since the 10th century. The island features several sculpture exhibitions and the new, playfully postmodern "Blind Pavilion." To Viðey take the ferry from the Reykjavík harbor Miðbakki. (☎533 5055; www.ferja.is. Ferry departs daily 1, 2, 3, 7, and 9pm; June 10-Aug. 12 also 8:30am. Round-trip 800ISK.) Across the bay from Reykjavík looms **Mt. Esja,** which you can ascend via a well-maintained trail (2-3hr.). The trail is not difficult, but hikers should be prepared for rain, hail, or even a brief but powerful snow squall. Arrive early in the morning in order to make the buses there and

ICELAND

back; be especially mindful on Sundays. Take bus #15 to Háholt and transfer to bus #27 (once per 1-2 hr.) and exit at Esjuskáli or simply tell the bus driver you're heading to Esja and ask for an exchange ticket.

NIGHTLIFE

Despite being unnervingly quiet on weeknights, Reykjavík asserts its status as a wild party town each weekend. The city's thriving independent music scene centers at ▇12 Tónar, Skólavörðustígur 12, a truly unique record store. After taking in the concerts, Icelanders hit the bars and clubs until the wee hours. Most bars do not have cover charges, but bouncers tend to regulate who enters, especially after 2am. Clubs have steep drink prices, so many locals drink at home or head to the vínbuð (government liquor store) before going out. Don't bother showing up before 12:30am and plan to be out until 4 or 5am. Boisterous crowds tend to bar-hop around Austurstræti, Tryggvagata, and Laugavegur. The establishments listed below are 20+, unless otherwise noted.

22, Laugavegur 22 (☎578 7800). With 3 floors, this bar, club, and lounge has a DJ Th-Su after midnight playing a variety of popular music. The top fl. is the conversation room, offering a deck for smokers. Beer 600ISK. Mixed drinks 750-1500ISK. Open M-Th and Su 11:30am-1am, F-Sa 11am-5:30am. AmEx/MC/V.

Sólon, Bankastræti 7A (☎562 3232). This trendy cafe morphs at night into a posh club bouncing with hip hop, pop, and electronica. Cafe downstairs, large dance floor and bar upstairs. Try Iceland's famous schnapps, *brennivín* (black death), used to stave off the dark, cold winters and chase the ammonia taste of *hákarl* (550ISK). Beer 700ISK. Th live music. Open M-Th 11am-1am, F-Sa 11am-5am, Su noon-midnight. Kitchen until 10pm. Club open midnight-late. AmEx/MC/V.

Hressingarskálinn, Austurstræti 20 (☎561 2240) Plays a variety of popular music. Th-Sa live music or other free entertainment. M-Th and Su 9am-1am, F-Sa 10am-5:30am. Kitchen open in summer until 11pm; in winter 10pm. AmEx/MC/V.

Vegamót, Vegamótarstígur 4 (☎511 3040), off Laugavegur. Students and professionals head to this posh bar to flaunt it and see others do the same. Beer 700ISK. 22+. Th-Sa live DJ. Open M-Th and Su 11:00am-1am, F-Sa 11:30am-4:30am. AmEx/MC/V.

NASA, Thorraldssenstræti 4 (☎511 1313; www.nasa.is), at Austurvollur Sq. The large central dance floor draws a varied crowd, depending on the evening's band. F-Sa live bands. Cover 500-1500ISK. Open F-Sa 11am-last customer. MC/V.

DAYTRIPS FROM REYKJAVÍK

Iceland's main attractions are its natural wonders. ▇Iceland Excursions runs the popular "Golden Circle Classic" tour, which stops at Hveragerði, Kerið, Skálholt, Geysir, Gullfoss, and Þingvellir National Park. (☎540 1313; www.grayline.is. 9-10hr., 8773ISK.) Arctic Adventures is one company offering a variety of adventure tours, with the Golden Circle Rafting trip (13990ISK) a perennial favorite. (Laugavegur 11 in the Cintamani store. ☎562 7000; www.adventures.is. MC/V.) Also worth a look is a diving or snorkeling tour (see www.dive.is) as Iceland offers some of the best diving sights in the world. Highlanders offers exciting but pricey off-road tours in jeeps that can traverse rivers, crags, and glaciers. (☎588-9588; www.hl.is. From 13,900ISK.)

GULLFOSS AND GEYSIR. The glacial river Hvita plunges down 32m to create Gullfoss (Golden Falls). A dirt path passes along the falls, where many get soaked in the mist. The adjacent hill houses a small cafeteria and gift shop, and affords a stunning view of the surrounding mountains, plains, and cliffs. On the horizon you can see the tip of Longjökull, a glacier the size of Hong

Kong. The Geysir (namesake of the word "geyser") area, 10km down the road, is a teeming bed of hot springs in a barren landscape. The **Strokkur Geyser** (the Churn) erupts around every 4min., spewing sulfurous water up to 35m. Exercise caution around the thermal pools—more than one tourist has fallen into the nearby Blesi pool and been badly scalded. The small, but excellent **museum** at the visitors center offers a multimedia show on the science behind these natural phenomena. The top portion of the museum is dedicated to **Aðalbjörg Egilsdottur,** who donated her collection of early 19th-century household Icelandic artifacts. *(Open daily 10am-5pm. BSÍ runs a round-trip bus to Gulfoss and Geysir with Iceland Excursions, departing from the BSÍ Terminal in Reykjavík June-Aug. daily 8:30am; 6hr., round-trip 5200ISK. Museum 800ISK, students 650ISK.)*

ÞINGVELLIR NATIONAL PARK. The European and North American tectonic plates meet at Þingvellir National Park, a place of both geologic and cultural significance for Iceland. The Öxará River, slicing through lava fields and jagged fissures, leads to the **Drekkingarhylur** (Drowning Pool), where adulterous women were once drowned, and on to Lake Þingvallavatn, Iceland's largest lake. This lake has exceptionally clear water, making for one of the best **diving** and **snorkeling** sites in the world. *(For diving opportunities check out www.dive.is or call ☎663 2858.)* Not far from the Drekkingarhylur lies the site of the **Alþingi** (ancient parliament), where for almost nine centuries, starting in AD 930, Icelanders gathered annually in the shadow of the **Lögberg** (Law Rock) to discuss matters of law, economics, and justice. **Maps** are available at the **Þingvellir Visitors Center.** *(Info center ☎482 2660. Open June-Aug. daily 8:30am-8pm; May and Sept. daily 9am-5pm. BSÍ does not run buses to Þingvellir; the site can be reached only by taking a tour bus or driving. Check out Iceland on Your Own and Reykjavik Excursions opportunities.)*

BLUE LAGOON. The southwest corner of the Reykjanes Peninsula, only 15 minutes from Keflavík airport, harbors an oasis in the middle of a lava field: a vast pool of geothermally heated water. The lagoon has become a tourist magnet, but it's worth braving the crowds. The cloudy blue waters, rich in silica and other minerals, are famous for their healing powers. Bathers who have their fill of wading through the 36-39°C (97-102°F) waters can indulge in a steam bath, a silica facial, or an in-water massage (3600ISK for 10 min.). Stand under the waterfall for a free, all-natural **shoulder massage.** *(Open daily from mid-May to Aug. 8am-10pm; from Sept. to mid-May 9am-9pm. Towel rental 350ISK. Bathing suit rental 400ISK. Admission and locker 2300ISK. AmEx/MC/V.)* Try taking the **bus** to the Blue Lagoon on your way to or from Keflavík. Airport buses leave at 8:30am or 11am, spend a few hours at the lagoon and then take you back to the airport for the same 4400ISK fee. *(Buses run from BSÍ Bus Terminal in Reykjavík. 1hr., 6 per day 8:30am-6pm; round-trip 4400 ISK with Blue Lagoon admission. ☎420 8809; www.bluelagoon.com.)*

NESJAVELLIRI. This power plant provides Reykjavík with half of its hot water and electricity by capturing geothermal heat that escapes from the intersection of the North American and European tectonic plates. Pipes run 26km from Nesjavelliri to the capital city on rollers to avoid destruction by one of Iceland's frequent earthquakes. The geothermal energy hub is also fueled by three nearby volcanic systems. **Free tours** of the facilities are available and provide a detailed look at Iceland's latest strides in renewable energy. *(Accessible only by car or tour bus; see Iceland Excursions. ☎480 2408. Open June-Aug. M-Sa 9am-5pm, Su 1pm-6pm.)*

IRELAND

REPUBLIC OF IRELAND

The green, rolling hills of Ireland, dotted with Celtic crosses, medieval monasteries, and Norman castles, have long inspired poets and musicians, from Yeats to U2. Today, the Emerald Isle's jagged coastal cliffs and untouched mountain ranges balance the country's thriving urban centers. Dublin pays tribute to the virtues of fine brews and the legacy of resisting British rule, while Galway offers a vibrant arts scene. In the past few decades, the computing and tourism industries have raised Ireland out of the economic doldrums, and current living standards are among the highest in Western Europe. Despite fears for the decline of traditional culture, the Irish language lives on in secluded areas known as the gaeltacht, and village pubs still echo with reels and jigs.

DISCOVER IRELAND: SUGGESTED ITINERARIES

THREE DAYS. Spend it all in **Dublin** (p. 428). Wander through **Trinity College** and sample the whiskey at the **Old Jameson Distillery.** Take a day to visit the **National Museums,** shop on **O'Connell Street** and get smart at the **James Joyce Cultural Centre.** Work up your pubbing potential by night in **Temple Bar.**

ONE WEEK. After visiting the sights and pubs of **Dublin** (3 days), enjoy the wonders of **Cork** and the stone at **Blarney** (1 day). Return to the urban scene in the cultural center of **Galway** (1 day; p. 440). And yeah, we're fudging it a little to include **Belfast** (2 days), but the capital of Northern Ireland is a worthy last stop on the Emerald Isle.

ESSENTIALS

FACTS AND FIGURES

OFFICIAL NAME: Republic of Ireland.

CAPITAL: Dublin.

MAJOR CITIES: Cork, Galway, Limerick.

POPULATION: 4,109,000.

TIME ZONE: GMT.

LANGUAGES: English, Irish.

LONGEST LOCATION NAME IN IRELAND: Muckanaghederdauhaulia, in Galway County.

LEASE ON THE ORIGINAL GUINNESS BREWERY IN DUBLIN: 9000 years.

WHEN TO GO

Ireland has a consistently cool, wet climate, with average temperatures ranging from around 4°C (39°F) in winter to 16°C (61°F) in summer. Travelers should bring rain gear in any season. Don't be discouraged by cloudy, foggy mornings—the weather usually clears by noon. The southeastern coast is the driest and sunniest, while western Ireland is considerably wetter and cloudier. May and June offer the most sun; July and August are warmest. December and January have short, wet days, but temperatures rarely drop below freezing.

DOCUMENTS AND FORMALITIES

EMBASSIES AND CONSULATES. Foreign embassies in Ireland are in Dublin (p. 430). Irish embassies abroad include: **Australia**, 20 Arkana St., Yarralumla, Canberra, ACT 2600 (☎06 273 3022; irishemb@cyberone.com.au); **Canada**, Ste. 1105, 130 Albert St., Ottawa, ON K1P 5G4 (☎613-233-6281; www.irishembassyottawa.com); **UK**, 17 Grosvenor Pl., London SW1X 7HR (☎020 72 35 21 71; www.ireland.embassyhomepage.com); **US**, 2234 Massachusetts Ave., NW, Washington, D.C., 20008 (☎202-462-3939; www.irelandemb.org).

VISA AND ENTRY INFORMATION. EU citizens do not need a visa. Citizens of Australia, Canada, New Zealand, and the US do not need a visa for stays of up to 90 days, beginning upon entry into any of the countries in the EU's freedom-of-movement zone. For more info, see p. 14. For stays longer than 90 days, non-EU citizens must register with the **Garda National Immigration Bureau**, 13-14 Burgh Quay, Dublin, 2 (☎01 666 9100; www.garda.ie/gnib).

TOURIST SERVICES AND MONEY

EMERGENCY	Ambulance, Fire, and Police: ☎999. Emergency: ☎112.

TOURIST OFFICES. Bord Fáilte (Irish Tourist Board; ☎1850 23 03 30; www.ireland.ie) operates a nationwide network of offices. Most tourist offices book rooms for a small fee (around €4) and a 10% deposit, but many hostels and B&Bs are not on the board's central list.

MONEY. The **euro (€)** has replaced the **Irish pound (£)** as the unit of currency in the Republic of Ireland. For more info, p. 18. Northern Ireland uses the **pound sterling (£).** As a general rule, it is cheaper to exchange money in Ireland than at home. ATMs are the easiest way to retrieve money and are much more common than bureaux de change. MasterCard and Visa are almost universally accepted. If you stay in hostels and prepare your own food, expect to spend about €30 per person per day; a slightly more comfortable day (sleeping in B&Bs, eating one meal per day at a restaurant, going out at night) would cost €60. Most people working in restaurants do not expect a tip, unless the restaurant is targeted exclusively toward tourists. In that case, consider leaving 10-15%. Tipping is very uncommon for other services, such as taxis and hairdressers. In most cases, people are happy if you simply round up the bill to the nearest euro.

Ireland has a 21% **value added tax (VAT),** a sales tax applied to most goods and services, excluding food, health services, and children's clothing. The prices listed in *Let's Go* include VAT. In the airport upon exiting the EU, non-EU citizens can claim a refund on the tax paid for goods purchased at participating stores. While there is no minimum purchase amount to qualify for a refund, purchases greater than €250 must be approved at the customs desk before the refund can be issued. For more info on VAT refunds, see p. 19.

TRANSPORTATION

BY PLANE. A popular carrier to Ireland is national airline **Aer Lingus** (☎081 836 5000, US 800-474-7424; www.aerlingus.com), with direct flights to London,

Paris, and the US. **Ryanair** (☎081 830 3030; www.ryanair.com) offers low fares from Cork, Dublin, and Shannon to destinations across Europe. **British Airways** (Ireland ☎890 626 747, UK 0844 493 0787, US 800-247-9297; www.ba.com) flies into most major Irish airports daily.

BY FERRY. Ferries run between Britain and Ireland many times per day. Fares for adults generally cost €15-30, with additional fees for cars. **Irish Ferries** (Ireland ☎01 818 300 400, UK 8705 17 17 17, US 772-563-2856; www.irishferries.com) and **Stena Line** (☎01 204 7777; www.stenaline.ie/ferry) typically offer discounts to students, seniors, and families. Ferries run from Dublin to Holyhead, BRI; from Cork to Roscoff, FRA (p. 52); and from Rosslare Harbour to Pembroke, Wales, Cherbourg, FRA, and Roscoff, FRA.

BY TRAIN. Iarnród Éireann (Irish Rail; www.irishrail.ie) is useful for travel to urban areas. The **Eurail Global** pass is accepted in the Republic but not in Northern Ireland. The **BritRail** pass does not cover travel in anywhere in Ireland, but the **BritRail+Ireland** pass (€289-504) offers five or 10 days of travel in a one-month period as well as ferry service between Britain and Ireland.

BY BUS. Bus Éireann (☎01 836 6111; www.buseireann.ie), Ireland's national bus company, operates Expressway buses that link larger cities as well as local buses that serve the countryside and smaller towns. One-way fares between cities generally range €5-25. Bus Éireann offers the **Irish Rover** pass, which also covers the Ulsterbus service in Northern Ireland (3 of 8 consecutive days €76, under 16 €44; 8 of 15 days €172/94; 15 of 30 days €255/138). The **Emerald Card**, also available through Bus Éireann, offers unlimited travel on Expressway and other buses, Ulsterbus, Northern Ireland Railways, and local services (8 of 15 consecutive days €248, under 16 €124; 15 of 30 days €426).

Bus Éireann works in conjunction with ferry services and the bus company **Eurolines** (www.eurolines.com) to connect Ireland with Britain and the Continent. Eurolines passes for unlimited travel between major cities range €199-439. Discounts are available in the low-season and for people under 26 or over 60. A major route runs between Dublin and Victoria Station in London; other stops include Birmingham, Bristol, Cardiff, Glasgow, and Liverpool, with services to Cork, Derry/Londonderry, Galway, Limerick, and Waterford.

BY CAR. Drivers in Ireland use the left side of the road. Gasoline (petrol) prices are high. Be particularly cautious at roundabouts—give way to traffic from the right. **Dan Dooley** (☎062 53103, UK 0800 282 189, US 800-331-9301; www.dandooley.com) and **Enterprise** (☎UK 0870 350 3000, US 800-261-7331; www.enterprise.ie) will rent to drivers between 21 and 24, though such drivers must pay an additional daily surcharge. Fares are €85-200 per week (plus VAT), including insurance and unlimited mileage. If you plan to drive a car in Ireland for longer than 90 days, you must have an **International Driving Permit (IDP).** If you rent, lease, or borrow a car, you will need a **green card** or an **International Insurance Certificate** to certify that you have insurance. It is always significantly less expensive to reserve a car from the US than from within Europe.

BY BIKE, FOOT, AND THUMB. Ireland's countryside is well suited to **biking,** as many roads are not heavily traveled. Single-digit "N" roads are more trafficked and should be avoided. Ireland's mountains, fields, and hills make **walking** and **hiking** arduous joys. The **Wicklow Way,** a 132km hiking trail in the mountains southeast of Dublin, has hostels within a day's walk of each other. Some locals caution against **hitchhiking** in County Dublin and the Midlands, where it is not very common. *Let's Go* does not recommend hitchhiking.

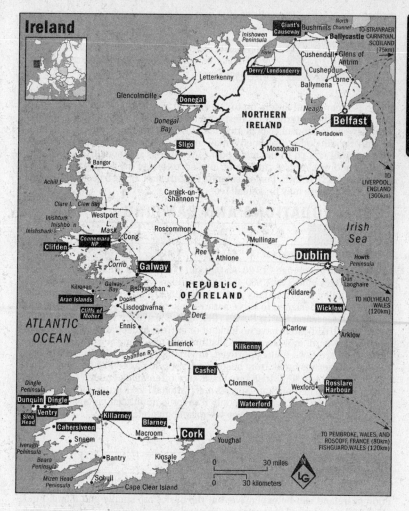

KEEPING IN TOUCH

EMAIL AND THE INTERNET. Internet access is available in most cafes, hostels, and libraries in cities and towns. One hour of web time costs about €3-6, though discounts are often available with an ISIC. Find listings of Internet cafes at www.cybercafes.com.

TELEPHONE. Whenever possible, use a calling card for international phone calls, as long-distance rates for national phone services are often very high. Mobile phones are an increasingly popular and economical option, and carriers Vodafone and O2 offer the best service. Direct-dial access numbers for calling out of Ireland include: **AT&T Direct** (☎800 550 000); **British Telecom** (☎800

890 353); **Canada Direct** (☎800 555 001); **MCI WorldPhone** (☎800 55 10 01); **Telecom New Zealand Direct** (☎800 55 00 64).

PHONE CODES	**Country code: 353. International dialing prefix:** 00. For more info on how to place international calls, see **Inside Back Cover.**

MAIL. Postcards and letters up to 50g cost €0.55 within Ireland and €0.82 to Europe and other international destinations. Airmail parcels take four to nine days between Ireland and North America. Dublin is the only place in the Republic with Postal Codes. To receive mail in Ireland, have mail delivered **Poste Restante.** Mail will go to the main post office unless you specify a subsidiary by street address. Address mail to be held according to the following example: First name LAST NAME, Poste Restante, City, Ireland. Bring a passport to pick up your mail; there may be a small fee.

ACCOMMODATIONS AND CAMPING

IRELAND	❶	❷	❸	❹	❺
ACCOMMODATIONS	under €17	€17-26	€27-40	€41-56	over €56

A **hostel** bed will average €13-20. **An Óige** (an OYJ), the **HI** affiliate, operates 27 hostels countrywide. (☎01 830 4555; www.irelandyha.org. One-year membership €20, under 18 €10.) Many An Óige hostels are in remote areas or small villages and are designed to serve nature-seekers. Over 100 hostels in Ireland belong to **Independent Holiday Hostels (IHH;** ☎01 836 4700; www.hostels-ireland. com). Most IHH hostels have no lockout or curfew, accept all ages, require no membership card, and have a less institutional feel than their An Óige counterparts; all are Bord Fáilte-approved. In virtually every Irish town, **B&Bs** can provide a luxurious break from hosteling. Expect to pay €30-35 for singles and €45-60 for doubles. "Full Irish breakfasts" are often filling enough to last until dinner. Camping in Irish State Forests and National Parks is not allowed. **Camping** on public land is permissible only if there is no official campsite nearby. Sites cost €5-13. For more info, see www.camping-ireland.ie.

FOOD AND DRINK

IRELAND	❶	❷	❸	❹	❺
FOOD	under €6	€6-10	€11-15	€16-20	over €20

Food in Ireland can be expensive, but the basics are simple and filling. Find quick and greasy staples at **chippers** (fish and chips shops) and **takeaways.** Most pubs serve Irish stew, burgers, soup, and sandwiches. Cafes and restaurants have begun to offer more vegetarian options to complement the typical meat-based entrees. **Soda bread** is delicious, and Irish **cheddars** are addictive. **Guinness,** a rich, dark stout, is revered with a zeal usually reserved for the Holy Trinity. Known as "the dark stuff" or "the blonde in the black skirt," a proper pint has a head so thick that you can stand a match in it. **Irish whiskey,** which Queen Elizabeth once said was her only true Irish friend, is sweeter than its Scotch counterpart. "A big one" (a pint of Guinness) and "a small one" (a glass of whiskey) are often ordered alongside one another. When ordering at an Irish **pub,** one individual in a small group will usually approach the bar and buy a round of drinks for everyone. Once those drinks are downed, another individual will buy the next round. It's considered poor form to refuse someone's offer to buy you a drink. The legal age in Ireland to purchase alcohol is 18.

HOLIDAYS AND FESTIVALS

Holidays: New Year's Day (Jan. 1); St. Patrick's Day (Mar. 17); Good Friday and Easter Monday (Apr. 10, 2009 and Apr. 13, 2009); and Christmas (Dec. 25). There are 4 bank holidays, which will be observed on May 4, Jun. 8, Aug. 3, and Oct. 26 in 2009. Northern Ireland also observes Orangemen's Day (July 13).

Festivals: All of Ireland goes green for St. Patrick's Day (Mar. 17). On *Bloomsday* (June 16), Dublin celebrates James Joyce's Ulysses. In mid-July, the *Galway Arts Festival* offers theater, trad, rock, and film. Many return happy from the *Lisdoonvarna Matchmaking Festival* in the Burren in early Sept.

BEYOND TOURISM

To find opportunities that accommodate your interests and schedule, check with national agencies such as Volunteering Ireland (www.volunteeringireland.com). For more info on opportunities in Europe, see **Beyond Tourism,** p. 55.

L'Arche Ireland, "Seolta," Warrenhouse Rd., Baldoyle, Dublin, 13 (☎01 839 4356; www.larche.ie). Assistants can join residential communities in Cork, Dublin, or Kilkenny to live with, work with, and teach people with learning disabilities. Room, board, and small stipend provided. Commitment of 1-2yr. expected.

Sustainable Land Use Company, Doorian, Glenties, Co. Donegal (☎074 955 1286; www.donegalorganic.ie). Offers opportunities to assist with organic farming, forestry, habitat maintenance, and wildlife in the northern county of Donegal.

Focus Ireland, 9-12 High St., Dublin, 8 (☎01 881 5900; www.focusireland.ie). Advocacy and fundraising for the homeless in Dublin, Limerick, and Waterford.

DUBLIN
☎01

In a country known for its rural landscapes, the international flavor and frenetic pace of Dublin stick out like the 120m spire in the city's heart. Ireland's capital since the Middle Ages, Dublin offers all the amenities of other world-class cities on a more manageable scale, with all buildings topping off at five stories. Prestigious Trinity College holds treasures of Ireland's past, while Temple Bar has

NO WORK, ALL PLAY

SOWING THE SEEDS OF LOVE

What started as a pragmatic matchmaking service for country boys who did not get a chance to mingle with their sophisticated female counterparts is now sold as a six-week singles' bonanza. Every September through early October, Lisdoonvarna welcomes thousands of unattached partiers who come to partake in the live music, dancing, drinking, games and lovin' of the **Matchmaking Festival.** A far cry from its modest precursor over 150 years ago, during which bachelor farmers who had recently completed their harvests earnestly sought wives, the festival now attracts fun-loving strangers who indulge in daily dances starting at noon. Despite this shift, an official matchmaker still presides over the festival. Accordingly, events cater to those looking for flings, and something a bit more meaningful. Willie Daly inherited the tradition from his family, and he continues to make romantic matches part-time—he also runs an equestrian center outside of town.

Lisdoonvarna Matchmaking Festival; www.matchmakerireland. com. Six weeks, Sept.-mid-Oct. For more information or to book accommodations, call the Hydro Hotel (☎065 707 4005). Find cheaper dormitory beds at Sleepzone Burren (☎065 707 4036). Book early, as beds fill fast.

become one of Europe's hottest nightspots. The city's musical, cultural, and drinkable attractions continue to draw droves of visitors.

▐ TRANSPORTATION

Flights: Dublin Airport (DUB; ☎01 814 1111; www.dublinairport.com). Dublin **buses** #41 and 41B run from the airport to Eden Quay in the city center (40-45min., every 10min., €1.80). Airlink **shuttle** (☎01 703 3092) runs nonstop to Busáras Central Bus Station and O'Connell St. (20-25min., every 10-20min. 5:45am-11:30pm, €6), and to Heuston Station (50min., €6). A **taxi** to the city center costs roughly €25.

Trains: The **Irish Rail Travel Centre**, 35 Lower Abbey St. (☎01 836 6222; www.irishrail. ie), sells train tickets. Open M-F 8:30am-6pm, Sa 9:30am-6pm.

Pearse Station, Pearse St. (☎01 828 6000). Ticketing open M-Sa 7:30am-9:50pm, Su 9am-9:50pm. Receives southbound trains from Connolly Station and serves as a departure point for **Dublin Area Rapid Transit (DART)** trains serving the suburbs and coast (4-6 per hr., €2-6.70).

Connolly Station, Amiens St. (☎01 703 2358), north of the Liffey and close to Busáras. Bus #20b heads south of the river and #130 goes to the city center, while the DART runs to Tara Station on the south quay. Trains to: **Belfast** (2hr.; M-Sa 9 per day, Su 5 per day; €36), **Sligo** (3hr., M-Sa 8 per day, Su 6 per day per day, €29), and **Wexford and Rosslare** (3hr., 3 per day, €20.50).

Heuston Station (☎01 703 2132), south of Victoria Quay and west of the city center (a 25min. walk from Trinity College). Buses #78 and 79 run to the city center. Trains to: **Cork** (3hr., M-Sa 15 per day, Su 11 per day, €59.50); **Galway** (2hr.; M-Sa 7 per day, Su 6 per day; €31.50 M-Th and Sa, €44 F and Su); **Limerick** (2hr.; M-Sa 10, Su 7 per day; €45.50); **Waterford** (2hr.; M-Sa 6 per day, Su 4 per day; €24.50 M-Th and Sa, €31.50 F and Su).

Buses: Intercity buses to Dublin arrive at **Busáras Central Bus Station**, Store St. (☎01 836 6111; www.buseireann.ie), next to Connolly Station. Buses to: **Belfast** (3hr., 24 per day, €15); **Cork** (4½hr., 6 per day, €12); **Derry/Londonderry** (4hr., 9 per day, €20); **Donegal** (4hr., 10 per day, €18); **Galway** (3hr., 17 per day, €15); **Limerick** (3½hr., 13 per day, €10); **Rosslare** (3hr., 13 per day, €16.80); **Sligo** (4hr., 5-6 per day, €18); **Tralee** (6hr., 9 per day, €23); **Wexford** (2hr.; M-Sa 17 per day, Su 10 per day; €13.50).

Ferries: Irish Ferries, 2-4 Merrion Row, (☎0818 300 400; www.irishferries.com) off St. Stephen's Green. Open M-F 9am-5pm, Sa 9am-1pm. Stena Line ferries arrive from Holyhead at the **Dún Laoghaire** ferry terminal (☎01 204 7777; www.stenaline.com).

Public Transportation: Info on local buses available at **Dublin Bus Office**, 59 Upper O'Connell St. (☎01 873 4222; www.dublinbus.ie). Open M 8:30am-5:30pm, Tu-F 9am-5:30pm, Sa 9am-2pm, Su 9:30am-2pm. **Rambler** passes offer unlimited rides for a day (€6) or a week (€23). Dublin Bus runs the **NiteLink** service to the suburbs (M-Th 12:30 and 2am, F-Sa every 20min. 12:30-4:30am; €5; passes not valid). The **Luas** (☎01 461 4910 or ☎1800 300 604; www.luas.ie; phone line open M-F 7am-7pm, Sa 10am-2pm), Dublin's **Light Rail Tram System,** is the city's newest form of mass transit.

Taxis: Blue Cabs (☎01 802 2222), **ABC** (☎01 285 5444), and **City Cabs** (☎01 872 7272) have wheelchair-accessible cabs (call ahead). Available 24hr.

Car Rental: Europcar, Dublin Airport (☎01 812 0410; www.www.europcar.ie). Economy around €50 per day, €200 per wk. Ages 24-70.

Bike Rental: Cycle Ways, 185-6 Parnell St. (☎01 873 4748). Rents quality hybrid or mountain bikes. €20 per day, €80 per week with €200 deposit. Open M-W and F-Sa 9:30am-6pm, Th 9:30am-8pm, Su 11am-5pm. AmEx/MC/V.

✴ ⚡ ORIENTATION AND PRACTICAL INFORMATION

Although Dublin is compact, getting lost is not much of a challenge. Street signs, when posted, are located high up on the sides of buildings at most intersections. The essential *Dublin Visitor Map* is available for free at the Dublin Bus Office. The **Liffey River** forms a natural boundary between Dublin's North

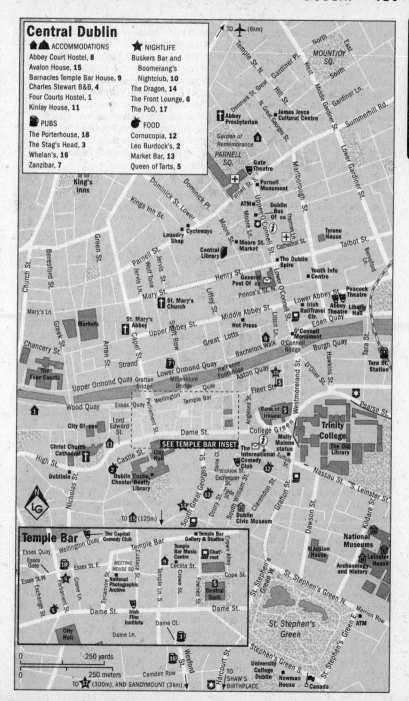

Central Dublin

ACCOMMODATIONS
Abbey Court Hostel, **8**
Avalon House, **15**
Barnacles Temple Bar House, **9**
Charles Stewart B&B, **4**
Four Courts Hostel, **1**
Kinlay House, **11**

PUBS
The Porterhouse, **18**
The Stag's Head, **3**
Whelan's, **16**
Zanzibar, **7**

NIGHTLIFE
Buskers Bar and
  Boomerang's
  Nightclub, **10**
The Dragon, **14**
The Front Lounge, **6**
The PoD, **17**

FOOD
Cornucopia, **12**
Leo Burdock's, **2**
Market Bar, **13**
Queen of Tarts, **5**

Temple Bar

and South Sides. Heuston Station and the more famous sights, posh stores, and upscale restaurants are on the **South Side,** while Connolly Station, the majority of hostels, and the bus station are on the **North Side.** The North Side is less expensive than the more touristed South Side, but it also has a reputation for being rougher, especially after dark. The streets running alongside the Liffey are called **quays** (pronounced "keys"); the name of the quay changes with each bridge. **O'Connell Street,** three blocks west of the Busáras Central Bus Station, is the primary link between northern and southern Dublin. On the North Side, **Henry** and **Mary Streets** constitute a pedestrian shopping zone, intersecting with O'Connell St. two blocks from the Liffey at the **General Post Office.** On the South Side, a block from the river, **Fleet Street** becomes **Temple Bar,** an area full of music centers and galleries. **Dame Street** runs parallel to Temple Bar and leads east to **Trinity College,** Dublin's cultural center.

Tourist Office: Main Office, Suffolk St. (☎01 605 7700; www.visitdublin.com). Near Trinity College in a converted church. Open M-Sa 9am-5:30pm, Su 10:30am-3pm; July-Aug. M-Sa 9am-7pm; Su 10:30am-5pm. **Northern Ireland Tourist Board,** 16 Nassau St. (☎01 679 1977 or ☎1850 230 230). Open M-F 9:15am-5:30pm, Sa 10am-5pm.

Embassies: Australia, Fitzwilton House, Wilton Terr., 7th fl. (☎01 664 5300; www.ireland.embassy.gov.au); **Canada,** 7-8 Wilton Terr. (☎01 234 4000; www.canada.ie); **UK,** 29 Merrion Rd. (☎01 205 3700); www.britishembassy.ie); **US,** 42 Elgin Rd. (☎01 668 8777; http://dublin.usembassy.gov).

Luggage Storage: Connolly Station: Small lockers €4, large lockers €6. Open daily 5am-midnight. **Busáras:** Lockers €6/8. Open 24hr.

Police (Garda): Dublin Metro Headquarters, Harcourt Terr. (☎01 666 9500); Store St. Station (☎01 666 8000); Fitzgibbon St. Station (☎01 666 8400); Pearse St. Station (☎01 666 9000). **Police Confidential Report Line:** ☎800 666 111.

Pharmacy: Hickey's, 56 Lower O'Connell St. (☎01 873 0427). Convenient to bus routes. Open M-F 7:30am-10pm, Sa 8am-10pm, Su and bank holidays 10am-10pm. Other branches scattered about the city, including locations on Grafton St. and Henry St.

Hospital: St. James's Hospital, James St. (☎01 410 3000). Bus #123. **Mater Misericordiae Hospital,** Eccles St. (☎01 803 2000). Buses #3, 10, 11, 16, 22 36, 121. **Beaumont Hospital,** Beaumont Rd. (☎01 809 3000). Buses #103, 104, 27b, 42a.

Internet: The Internet Exchange at Cecilia St. (☎01 670 3000) in Temple Bar. €3 per hr. Open M-F 8am-2am, Sa-Su 10am-2am. There are numerous other Internet cafes with comparable rates around the city.

Post Office: General Post Office, O'Connell St. (☎01 705 7000). **Poste Restante** pickup at the Poste Restante window (see Mail, p. 29). Open M-Sa 8am-8pm. Smaller post offices, including one on Suffolk St. across from the tourist office, are typically open M-Tu and Th-F 9am-6pm, W 9:30am-6pm. **Postal Codes:** Dublin is the only place in the Republic that uses postal codes. The city is organized into regions numbered 1-18, 20, 22, and 24; even-numbered codes are for areas south of the Liffey, while odd-numbered ones are for the north. The numbers radiate out from the city center: North City Centre is 1, South City Centre is 2.

▐ ACCOMMODATIONS

Because Dublin is an incredibly popular destination, it is necessary to book accommodations at least one week in advance, particularly around holidays and in the summer. If the following accommodations are full, consult Dublin Tourism's annual *Sleep!* Guide (€2.50), or ask hostel staff for referrals.

▧ **Four Courts Hostel,** 15-17 Merchants Quay (☎01 672 5839). On the south bank of the river. Bus #748 from the airport stops next door. 230-bed hostel with pristine, well-lit rooms and hardwood floors. Quiet lounge and a combination TV/game room provide plenty of space to wind down. Continental breakfast included. In-room lockers. Free Wi-Fi; computer use €1 per 15min. Laundry €7.50. 8- to 16-bed dorms €17-21.50; 4- to 6-bed €25-38; doubles €64-72; triples around €90. ❶

▨ **Abbey Court Hostel,** 29 Bachelor's Walk (☎01 878 0700; www.abbey-court.com). Corner of O'Connell St. and Bachelor's Walk near bridge. Hostel boasts clean, narrow rooms overlooking the Liffey. Hidden apartments each have lounge, TV, and courtyard. Internet €1 per 15min., €2 per 40min. Continental breakfast at **NYStyle cafe** next door included. Free luggage storage; security box €1. Full-service laundry €8. 12-bed dorms €19-23; 6-bed €24-27; 4-bed €27-31; doubles €78-89. Long-term rate €108-126 per week includes breakfast. Apartments from €89 per night. ❷

Parkway Guest House, 5 Gardiner Pl. (☎01 874 0469; www.parkway-guesthouse.com). Sports fans bond with the proprietor, a former hurling star, while those less athletically inclined still appreciate his great eye for interior design, sound advice, and all-star breakfasts. Singles €40; doubles €60-80, €80-100 with bath. MC/V. ❸

Avalon House (IHH), 55 Aungier St. (☎01 475 0001; www.avalon-house.ie). Performers get free accommodation if they spend 1hr. teaching other guests. Wheelchair-accessible with elevator. Light continental breakfast included. Lockers and smaller lock boxes €1 per day; €8-10 deposit. Laundry €7. Free Wi-Fi. 24hr. reception. Large dorms €14-20; 4- to 6-bed dorms €24-31; singles €32-41; doubles €30-39. MC/V. ❶

Barnacles Temple Bar House, 19 Temple Ln. (☎01 671 6277). Patrons can nearly jump into bed from Temple Bar pubs, including the actual Temple Bar, next door. Spacious, sky-lit lounge with fireplace and TV. Breakfast included. Free luggage storage. Laundry €7. Free Wi-Fi; Internet on house computers €1 per 15min. 11-bed dorms €19-21; 6-bed €27-29.50; quads €28.50-31.50; doubles €80-87. ❶

Kinlay House (IHH), 2-12 Lord Edward St. (☎01 679 6644). Great location a few blocks from Temple Bar. If you don't get a room with a view of the Christ Church Cathedral, at least you can watch the plasma TV. Continental breakfast included. Lockers €1 with €5 deposit. Laundry €8. Free Internet. 4- to 6-bed dorms €22-33; 16- to 24-bed €18-24; doubles €30-38; triples €32-41. Min. stay 2 nights on weekend. ❶

▍ FOOD

Dublin's many **open-air markets** sell fresh food at relatively cheap prices. The later in the week, the livelier the market. Bustling **Moore St. Market,** between Henry St. and Parnell St., is a great place to get fresh veggies. (Open M-Sa 10am-5pm.) The **Thomas Street Market,** along the continuation of Dame St., is a calmer alternative. (Generally open Th-Sa 11am-5pm, although some stalls are open during the week.) Produce can be found every day along Wexford Sreet. The best value for supermarkets around Dublin is in the **Dunnes Stores** chain, with full branches at St. Stephen's Green (☎01 478 0188; open M-W and F 8:30am-8pm, Th 8:30am-9pm, Sa 8:30am-7pm, Su 10am-7pm), the ILAC Centre off Henry St., and N. Earl St. off O'Connell.

▨ **Queen of Tarts,** Dame St. (☎01 670 7499), across from City Hall (and new, bigger location on Cow's Lane, Temple Bar). Pastries, light meals, and coffee in a supremely feminine hideaway. Delectable tarts €10 (savory) and €5.50 (sweet). Breakfast €3.50-10. Sandwiches €8. Open M-F 7:30am-7pm, Sa-Su 9am-7pm. MC/V. ❶

▨ **Market Bar,** Fade St. (☎01 613 9094; www.tapas.ie). Right off S. Great Georges after Lower Stephen St. Huge sausage factory given a classy makeover; now serves tapas in heaping portions. Small tapas €8; large tapas €12. Kitchen open M-Th noon-11:30pm, F-Sa noon-12:30am, Su 3-11pm. ❶

Cornucopia, 19 Wicklow St. (☎01 671 9449). If there's space, sit down in this cozy spot for a delicious meal (€11-12) or a cheaper salad smorgasbord (€4.25-9.25 for choice of 2, 4, or 6 salads). Accommodates many dietary restrictions. Open M-F 8:30am-9pm, Sa 8:30am-8pm, Su noon-7pm. ❷

Leo Burdock's, 2 Werburgh St. (☎01 454 0306), behind The Lord Edward Pub across from Christ Church Cathedral. Additional location on Lower Liffey St. Fish and chips served the right way—in brown paper. A nightly pilgrimage for many Dubliners. Takeaway only. Fish €4.50-7; chips €3. Open daily noon-midnight. ❶

🄖 SIGHTS

TRINITY COLLEGE. The British built **Trinity College** in 1592 as a Protestant seminary that would "civilize the Irish and cure them of Popery." The college became part of the path on which members of the Anglo-Irish elite trod on their way to high positions: it has educated such luminaries as Jonathan Swift, Robert Emmett, Thomas Moore, Oscar Wilde, and Samuel Beckett. The Catholic Church deemed it a cardinal sin to attend Trinity until the 1960s; when the Church lifted the ban, the size of the student body tripled. Today, it's a celebrated center of learning, located steps away from the teeming center of a cosmopolitan capital, and an unmissable stop on the tourist trail. (Between Westmoreland and Grafton St., South Dublin. Main entrance fronts the traffic circle now called College Green. Pearse St. runs along the north edge of the college, Nassau St. the south. ☎01 608 1724; www.tcd.ie. Grounds always open. Free.)

KILDARE STREET. Just southeast of Trinity College, the museums on Kildare St. offer scientific and artistic wonders. The **National Gallery's** extensive collection includes paintings by Brueghel, Goya, Caravaggio, Vermeer, and Rembrandt. (Merrion Sq. W. ☎01 661 5133; www.nationalgallery.ie. Open M-W and F-Sa 9:30am-5:30pm, Th 9:30am-8:30pm, Su noon-5:30pm. Free guided tours Sa 3pm, Su 2, 3, 4pm; July also daily 3pm. Admission free. Temporary exhibits €10, students and seniors €6.) The **National Museum of Archaeology and History,** Dublin's largest museum, has incredible artifacts spanning the last two millennia to illustrate the history of Ireland, including the **Tara Brooch.** (Kildare St., next to Leinster House. ☎01 677 7444; www.museum.ie. Open Tu-Sa 10am-5pm, Su 2-5pm. Guided tours €2; call for times. Museum free.)

DAME STREET AND THE CATHEDRALS. Norman King John built **Dublin Castle** in 1204 on top of the Viking settlement Dubh Linn ("black pool"); more recently, a series of structures from the 18th and 19th centuries has covered the site, culminating in an uninspired 20th-century office complex. Next door, the intricate inner dome of **Dublin City Hall** shelters statues of national heroes like **Daniel O'Connell.** (Dame St., at the intersection of Parliament and Castle St. ☎01 677 7129; www.dublincastle.ie. State Apartments open M-F 10am-5pm, Sa-Su and holidays 2-4:45pm; closed during official functions. €4.50, students and seniors €3.50, children €2. Grounds free.) At the **Chester Beatty Library,** behind Dublin Castle, visitors can see the treasures bequeathed to Ireland by American mining magnate Alfred Chester Beatty. (☎01 407 0750; www.cbl.ie. 45min. tours W 1pm, Su 3 and 4pm. Open May-Sept. M-F 10am-5pm, Sa 11am-5pm, Su 1-5pm; Oct.-Apr. Tu-F 10am-5pm, Sa 11am-5pm, Su 1-5pm. Free.) Across from the castle sits the historic **Christ Church Cathedral.** Stained glass sparkles above the raised crypts, one of which supposedly belongs to Strongbow. The entrance fee includes admission to the **"Treasure of Christ Church,"** a rotating exhibit that displays the church's hoard of medieval manuscripts, gleaming gold vessels, and funereal busts. (At the end of Dame St., uphill and across from the Castle. A 10min.

walk from O'Connell Bride, or take bus #50 from Eden Quay or 78A from Aston Quay. ☎01 677 8099. Open daily 9am-5pm except during services. €6, students and seniors €4.) **St. Patrick's Cathedral,** Ireland's largest, dates back to the 12th century, although Sir Benjamin Guinness remodeled much of the building in 1864. Jonathan Swift spent his last years as Dean of St. Patrick's; his grave is marked on the floor of the south nave. *(From Christ Church, Nicholas St. runs south and downhill, eventually becoming Patrick St. Take bus #49, 49A, 50, 54A, 56A, 65, 65B, 77, or 77A from Eden Quay. ☎01 475 4817; www.stpatrickscathedral.ie. Open Mar.-Oct. daily 9am-6pm; Nov.-Feb. Sa 9am-5pm, Su 9am-3pm. Church closed to visitors Su half hr. before services which begin 8:30am, 11:15am, 3:15pm, although visitors are welcome to attend. €5.50, students and seniors €4.20.)*

GUINNESS BREWERY AND KILMAINHAM.

Guinness brews its black magic at the St. James' Gate Brewery, right next door to the **Guinness Storehouse.** The abundance of stout-stamped paper bags hanging from the arms of tourists are a good indication of Ireland's number one tourist attraction. Forward-looking Arthur Guinness ensured the success of his original 1759 brewery by signing a 9000-year lease, which is dramatically set into the floor of the massive reception hall. The self-guided tour ends with a complimentary pint in the top floor's **Gravity Bar,** a modern, light-filled space that commands a stunning panoramic view of the city. *(St. James's Gate. From Christ Church Cathedral, follow High St. west through its name changes—Cornmarket, Thomas, and James. Or, take bus #51B or 78A from Aston Quay or #123 from O'Connell St. ☎01 408 4800; www.guinness-storehouse.com. Open daily July-Aug. 9:30am-7pm; Sept.-June 9:30am-5pm. €14, students over 18 and seniors €10, students under 18 €8, ages 6-12 €5, under 6 free.)* Almost all the rebels who fought in Ireland's struggle for independence between 1792 and 1921 spent time at **Kilmainham Gaol.** The ghastly, compelling stories of the prisoners are dealt out in two doses, first in the comprehensive museum that sets the jail in the context of its sociopolitical history, and then in a 1hr. tour of the dank chambers that ends in the haunting wasteland of an execution yard. *(Inchicore Rd. Take bus #51b, 51c, 78a, or 79 from Aston Quay. ☎01 453 5984. Open Apr.-Sept. daily 9:30am-6pm; Oct.-Mar. M-Sa 9:30am-5:30pm, Su 10am-6pm. Last admission hr. before close. Tours every 30min. €5.30, seniors €3.70, students €2.10, families €11.50. Small museum, separate from tour, is free of charge.)*

O'CONNELL STREET AND PARNELL SQUARE.

Once Europe's widest street, O'Connell St. on the North Side now holds the less prestigious distinction of being Dublin's biggest shopping thoroughfare. The city's rich literary heritage comes to life at the **Dublin Writers' Museum,** which documents Dublin's rich literary heritage and the famous figures who played a part. Manuscripts, rare editions, and memorabilia of giants like Swift, Shaw, Wilde, Yeats, Beckett, Behan, Kavanagh, and O'Casey share space with caricatures and paintings. *(18 Parnell Sq. N. ☎01 872 2077; www.writersmuseum.com. Open June-Aug. M-F 10am-6pm, Sa 10am-5pm, Su 11am-5pm; Sept.-May M-Sa 10am-5pm, Su 11am-5pm. €7.25, students and seniors €6.10, children €4.55, families €21. Combined ticket with the Shaw birthplace €12.50, students and seniors €10.30.)* The **Irish Writers Centre,** adjacent to the museum, is the hub of Ireland's living community of writers, providing today's aspiring writers with frequent fiction and poetry readings. It is not a museum, but it does provide information about Dublin's literary happenings. *(19 Parnell Sq. N. ☎01 872 1302; www.writerscentre.ie. Open M-F 10am-5:30pm.)* Mock-ups at the **James Joyce Cultural Centre** reveal insight into Joyce's life, love, and labor, while intriguing items like the original door to his home at 7 Eccles St., a map tracing Stephen Daedalus' and Leopold Bloom's relative movements, and a 1921 Ulysses schema pique literary interest. *(35 N. Great Georges St., up Marlborough St. and past Parnell Sq. ☎01 878 8547; www.jamesjoyce.ie. Open year-round Tu-Sa 10am-5pm; Apr.-Oct. additionally Su noon-5pm. Guided tour every Sa 11am and 2pm; July-Aug. additionally Tu and Th 11am and 2pm; €10, students and seniors €8. Admission to the center €5, students and seniors €4.)*

OTHER SIGHTS. Dublin's greatest architectural triumph, the **Custom House** was designed and built in the 1780s by London-born James Gandon, who gave up the chance to be Russia's state architect so that he could settle in Dublin. The Roman and Venetian columns and domes give the cityscape a taste of what the city's 18th-century Anglo-Irish brahmins wanted Dublin to become. Carved heads along the frieze represent the rivers of Ireland; the sole woman is the Liffey. *(East of O'Connell St. at Custom House Quay, where Gardiner St. meets the river. ☎01 878 7660. Visitors Centre open mid-Mar.-Oct. M-F 10am-5pm, Sa-Su 2-5pm; Nov. to mid-Mar. W-F 10am-5pm, Su 2-5pm. €1, families €3, students free.)* The modest **St. Michan's Church,** dating back to 1095, is noteworthy for its ancient, creepy limestone vaults, which may have inspired Bram Stoker's *Dracula.* Everything in here is real, from the mummified corpses dating back 800 years to the grisly execution order of two 1798 rebels. *(Church St. ☎01 872 4154. Open Mar.-Oct. M-F 10am-12:45pm and 2-4:45pm, Sa 10am-12:45pm; Nov.-Mar. M-F 12:30-3:30pm, Sa 10am-12:45pm. Crypt tours €4, students and seniors €3.50, under 16 €3, families (2 adults, 2 children) €12. Church of Ireland services Su 10am.)* At the **Old Jameson Distillery,** learn how science, grain, and tradition come together to form liquid gold. The tour walks visitors through the creation of whiskey, although the stuff is really distilled in Co. Clare. Not to disappoint those hankering for a taste after all that talking, the tour ends at the bar with a free drink (or soft drinks for the uninitiated). Volunteer in the beginning to get the chance to taste-test a tray of six different whiskeys from around the world. *(Bow St. From O'Connell St., turn onto Henry St. and continue straight as the street narrows to Mary St., then Mary Ln.; the warehouse is on a cobblestone street on the left. Buses #68, 69, and 79 run from city center to Merchant's Quay. ☎01 807 2355. Tours daily 9:30am-6pm, typically every 45min. €12.50, students and seniors €9, children €6.)*

🎵 ENTERTAINMENT

Whether you seek poetry, punk, or something in between, Dublin is ready to entertain. The free *Event Guide* is available at music stores and hotels throughout the city. The glossier *In Dublin* (free at Tower Records, the tourist office) comes out every two weeks with feature articles and listings for music, theater, art exhibitions, comedy shows, clubs, museums, and movie theaters. Go to www.visitdublin.com for the latest hot spots.

- 🎭 **Abbey Theatre,** 26 Lower Abbey St. (☎01 878 7222; www.abbeytheatre.ie). The theater was founded by W.B. Yeats and Lady Gregory in 1904 to promote the Irish cultural revival and Modernist theater, a combination that didn't go over well with audiences. The Abbey's 1907 premiere of J.M. Synge's *Playboy of the Western World* led to storms of protest. Today, the Abbey (and Synge) have gained respectability. Ireland's National Theatre is on the cutting edge of international drama. Tickets €22-35; Sa 2:30pm matinee €18-22, students and seniors with ID €14. Box office open M-Sa 10:30am-7pm.

- **Peacock Theatre,** 26 Lower Abbey St. (☎01 878 7222). The Abbey's experimental downstairs studio theater. Evening shows, plus occasional lunchtime plays, concerts, and poetry. Doors open M-Sa at 7:30pm. Tickets €15-22; Sa 2:30pm matinees €18, students/seniors €15. Available at Abbey box office.

- **Gate Theatre,** 1 Cavendish Row (☎01 874 4045; www.gate-theatre.ie). Contemporary Irish and classic international dramas in intimate, elegant setting. Wheelchair-accessible. Box office open M-Sa 10am-7:30pm. Tickets €16-30; M-Th student ticket at curtain €15 with ID, subject to availability.

◤ PUBLIN

James Joyce proposed that a "good puzzle would be to cross Dublin without passing a pub." When a local radio station once offered £100 to the first person

IRELAND

to solve the puzzle, the winner explained that any route worked—you'd just have to stop in each one along the way. Dublin's pubs come in all shapes, sizes, and specialties. Ask around or check the publications *In Dublin*, *Hot Press*, or *Event Guide* for music listings. Normal pub hours in Ireland end at 11:30pm Sunday through Wednesday and 12:30am Thursday through Saturday. The laws that dictate these hours are subject to yearly changes—patrons often get about a half-hour after "closing" to finish off their drinks. An increasing number of pubs have late permits that allow them to remain open until at least 2am; drink prices tend to rise around midnight to cover the permit's cost (or so they claim). Bars that post their closing time as "late" mean after midnight and, sometimes, after what is legally mandated. ID-checking almost always happens at the door rather than at the bar. A growing number of bars are blurring the distinction between pub and club by hosting live music and staying open late into the night on weekdays.

◼ **The Stag's Head,** 1 Dame Ct. (☎01 679 3687). Atmospheric Victorian pub with stained glass, marble-topped round tables, and evidence of deer decapitation front and center above the bar. Student crowd dons everything from T-shirts to tuxes. Pub grub, like bangers and mash, runs €6-12. Kitchen open M-Sa noon-4pm. Bar open M-Th 10:30am-11:30pm, F-Sa 10:30am-12:30am, Su 12:30-11pm.

◼ **The Porterhouse,** 16-18 Parliament St. (☎01 679 8847). Way, way more than 99 bottles of beer on the wall, including 9 self-brewed porters, stouts, and ales. The Porterhouse Red is a must. 3 floors fill nightly with great crowd for trad, blues, and rock. Open M-W 11:30am-11:30pm, Th-F 11:30am-2am, Sa 11:30am-2:30am, Su 12:30-11pm.

Whelan's, 25 Wexford St. (☎01 478 0766; www.whelanslive.com). Pub hosts big-name trad, rock, and everything in between in attached music venue. Live music nightly starting at 8:30pm (doors open at 8pm). Th DJ takes the floor. Cover for shows next door €8-16. Open for lunch (€8-12) 12:30-2pm. Open M-W until 2am and Th-Sa until 3am.

Zanzibar, at the Ha'penny Bridge (☎01 878 7212). Dances between club and pub with explosive results. Unique private rooms on the balcony, one overlooking the Liffey. Th-Su DJ plays R&B, blues, and chart-toppers. Cover after 11pm F €5, Sa €7. Kitchen open until 10pm. 21+. Open Th-Sa 5pm-2:30am, Su noon-11:30pm.

◪ CLUBLIN

As a rule, clubs open at 10 or 10:30pm, but they don't heat up until the pubs empty around 12:30am. Clubbing is an expensive end to the evening; covers run €5-20 and pints can surpass €5. To save some money, find a club with an expensive cover but cheap drink prices and stay all night. A handful of smaller clubs on Harcourt and Camden Streets are basic but fun. Most clubs close between 1:30 and 3am, but a few have been known to stay open until daybreak. To get home after 11:30pm, take the **NiteLink bus** (M-W 12:30am and 2am, Th-Sa every 20min. from 12:30am to 4:30am; €5), which runs designated routes from the corner of Westmoreland and College St. to Dublin's suburbs. Taxi stands are sprinkled throughout the city, the most central being in front of Trinity, at the top of Grafton St. Be prepared to wait 30-45min. on weekend nights. For the most up-to-date information on clubs, check the *Event Guide*.

◼ **The PoD,** 35 Harcourt St. (☎01 476 3374; www.pod.ie), corner of Hatch St., in an old train station. Stylishly futuristic, orange interior. Serious about its music. Upstairs is **The Red Box** (☎478 0225), a huge, separate club with brain-crushing music and a crowd at the bar so deep it seems designed to winnow out the weak. Mellow train-station-turned-bar **Crawdaddy** hosts musical gigs, including some world stars. Cover €10-20; Th students €5; can rise fast when big-name DJs perform. Open until 2:30am on weekends.

▨ **The Mezz (The Hub),** 21-25 Eustace St. (☎01 670 7655). Live bands rock nightly right inside the entrance of this poster-plastered, atmospheric club—try not to knock over a drum set as you make your way toward the bar. Quiet pub by afternoon (M-Sa 5pm-2:30am, Su 5pm-1am) transforms into a loud, live-music cauldron at night. No cover. It shares the building with **The Hub,** which, as one of the only 18+ clubs in Temple Bar, attracts the younger crowd. Cover at The Hub €5-10 or more, depending on the band—doors 8pm, dancing 11:30pm. Open Tu-Sa until 2:30am.

▨ **The Dragon,** S. Great Georges St. (☎01 478 1590), a few doors down from The George. Opened in May 2005 as Dublin's newest gay club, although everyone is welcome. It's packed to its trendy rafters on weekend nights. Quieter lounge area in front gives way to a DJ spinning house by the dance floor in back. 18+. Open M and Th 5pm-2:30am, Tu-W 5-11:30pm, F-Sa 5pm-3:30am, Su 5-11pm. The upstairs bar is the drinking quarters for the Emerald Warriors, Ireland's gay rugby team.

The Village, 26 Wexford St. (☎01 475 8555). Posh ground-floor bar. Occasional live music below a popular upstairs weekend club. Th-Sa bands play 7-10:30pm (about €15), then DJs spin chill-out, jungle, and house downstairs. Tickets for live bands available next door. Club F €8, Sa €10. Bar open until 1:30am; club open Th-Sa until 3am.

SOUTHWESTERN IRELAND

The dramatic landscape of southwestern Ireland ranges from lakes and mountains to stark, ocean-battered cliffs. Rebels once hid among the coves and glens, but the region is now dominated by tourists taking in the stunning scenery of the Ring of Kerry and Cork's southern coast.

CORK ☎021

Cork (pop. 119,000) hosts most of the cultural activities in the southwest. The county gained the nickname "Rebel Cork" from its residents' early opposition to the British Crown and 20th-century support for Irish independence. Today, Cork's river quays and pub-lined streets reveal architecture both grand and grimy, evidence of the city's dual legacy of resistance and reconstruction.

▰ TRANSPORTATION

Trains: Kent Station, Lower Glanmire Rd. (☎021 455 7277; www.irishrail.ie), across the North Channel from the city center. Open M-Sa 6am-8pm, Su 8am-8:50pm. To: **Dublin** (3hr., 10-15 per day, €59.50) via **Limerick** (1hr., 7-10 per day, €23.50); **Killarney** (2hr., 6-9 per day, €23.50); **Tralee** (2hr., 6-9 per day, €31).

Buses: Parnell Pl. (☎021 450 8188), on Merchant's Quay. Info desk open M-Sa 9am-6pm. Bus Éireann to: **Dublin** (4½hr., 6 per day, €10.80); **Galway** (4hr., 12 per day, €15.30); **Killarney** (2hr., 10-15 per day, €15.70); **Limerick** (2hr., 12 per day, €12.60); **Rosslare Harbour** (4hr., 3-4 per day, €19.40); **Sligo** (7hr., 3 per day, €23.40); **Tralee** (2hr., 12-15 per day, €15.20); **Waterford** (2hr., 13-14 per day, €15/50).

Ferries: Brittany Ferries, 42 Grand Parade, sails from Cork to Roscoff, FRA. (☎021 427 7801. 12hr., Sa only, from €117.)

Public Transportation: Downtown **buses** run 2-6 per hr. M-Sa 7:30am-11:15pm, with reduced service Su 10am-11:15pm. Fares from €1.20. Catch buses and pick up schedules along St. Patrick's St., across from the Father Matthew statue.

◈🛈 ORIENTATION AND PRACTICAL INFORMATION

The center of Cork is compact and pedestrian-friendly, framed by the North and South Channels of the River Lee. From the bus station along the North Channel, **Merchant's Quay** leads west to **Saint Patrick's Street**, which curves through the center of the city and becomes **Grand Parade.** On the other side of the North Channel, across St. Patrick's Bridge, **MacCurtain Street** runs east to **Lower Glanmire Road** before becoming the N8 to Dublin. Downtown shopping and nightlife concentrates on **Washington, Oliver Plunkett,** and St. Patrick's Streets.

Tourist Office: Tourist House, Grand Parade (☎021 425 5100; www.discoverireland. ie), near the corner of South Mall, books accommodations (10% deposit plus €4) and provides a free city guide and **map.** Open June-Aug. M-Sa 9am-6pm, Su 10am-4pm; Sept.-May M-Sa 9:15am-5pm.

Police (Garda): Anglesea St. (☎021 452 2000).

Pharmacies: Regional Late-Night Pharmacy, Wilton Rd. (☎021 434 4575), opposite the hospital. Bus #8. Open M-F 9am-10pm, Sa-Su 10am-10pm.

Hospital: Cork University Hospital, Wilton Rd. (☎021 454 6400). Bus #5 and #8.

Internet: ▨**Wired To The World Internet Cafe,** 6 Thompson House, MacCurtain St., north of River Lee (☎021 453 0383; www.wiredtotheworld.ie). Internet €1 per hr. Cash only. Open M-Th 9am-midnight, F-Sa 9am-2am, Su 10am-midnight.

Post Office: Oliver Plunkett St. (☎021 485 1032). Open M, W-Sa 9am-5:30pm, Tu 9:30am-5:30pm.

⚑ ACCOMMODATIONS

Cork's fine array of busy hostels should put a smile on any budget traveler's face, but rooms go fast, so call ahead. For a full Irish breakfast and a little more privacy, head to one of the many B&Bs on **Western Road,** near the University.

Sheila's Budget Accommodation Centre (IHH), 4 Belgrave Pl. (☎021 450 5562; www. sheilashostel.ie). Friendly staff take great pride in ensuring their guests feel safe and have fun. 24hr. reception desk doubles as general store. Kitchen. Free luggage storage, small lock boxes €1 and staff hold valuables at desk for free. Free Wi-Fi. Breakfast €3. Laundry €6.50. Check-out 10:30am. Dorms €15-19; doubles €46-54. AmEx/MC/V. ❷

Kinlay House (IHH), Bob and Joan's Walk (☎021 450 8966; www.kinlayhousecork.ie), down the alley to the right of St. Anne's Church. Bright colors and warm atmosphere; some rooms have great views of the city. Plush lounge with TV and sunny Internet room. Kitchen. Continental breakfast included. Free valuables safe and luggage storage at reception. Laundry €8. Free Wi-Fi; Internet €4 per hr. Free parking. 8- to 15-bed dorms €13-16; doubles €44-48. Ensuite rooms available (additional €2). AmEx/MC/V. ❷

Brú Bar and Hostel, 57 MacCurtain St. (☎021 455 9667; www.bruhostel.com), north of the river. A lively place to stay up late and hang out at the attached bar (open 4pm-late). Continental breakfast included. Towels €2. Laundry €5. Free Internet. Check-in 1pm. Check-out 10am. 6-bed dorms €16.50-17.50; 4-bed dorms €21-22.50; doubles €50-60. MC/V. Book online for a discount. ❷

Cork International Hostel (An Óige/HI), 1-2 Redclyffe, Western Rd. (☎021 454 3289), near University College and a 20min. walk from Grand Parade. Offers clean, spacious rooms with bath. Kitchen and TV room. Continental breakfast €5. Luggage storage available. Internet €1 per 15min. Reception 8am-midnight. Check-in 1-10pm. Check-out 10:30am. Dorms €16-18.50; doubles €50-54. €2 HI discount. MC/V. ❶

FOOD

Cork's famous international flavor is reflected in its countless great eateries. For more traditional Irish cuisine, hit the small towns, or make your own with local ingredients in the expansive **English Market,** accessible from Grand Parade, Patrick, and Oliver Plunkett St. Get groceries at **Tesco,** on Paul St. inside the Paul St. Shopping Centre. (☎021 427 0781. Open M-Sa 8am-10pm, Su 8am-8pm.)

Ginos, 7 Winthrop St. (☎021 427 4485). Heaping scoops of heavenly gelato flavors like honeycomb and hazelnut could be an entire meal. Small pizza €5.50. Ice cream €1.40 per scoop. Open daily noon-10pm. MC/V. ❶

Tribes, 8 Tuckey St. (☎021 427 4446), off Oliver Plunkett St. Late-night, low-light java shop serves sandwiches, full meals and tea into the wee hours. Food served until 30min. before closing. 18+ after 8pm. Open M 10:30am-7:30pm, Tu-Th 10:30am-11pm, F-Sa 10:30am-3:30am, Su noon-11pm. Cash only. ❶

Amicus, St. Paul St. (☎021 427 6455), across from Tesco. Artistically presented dishes taste as delicious as they look. Lunch €8-12. Dinner €12-25. Open M-Th 8am-10pm, F-Sa 8am-11pm, Su 8am-9pm. AmEx/MC/V. ❸

Café Paradiso, 16 Lancaster Quay (☎021 427 7939), near the University campus. Celebrated chefs make the most of what Mother Earth has to offer, serving up award-winning vegetarian meals. Menu changes often. Lunch €8-16. Dinner €24-25. Open Tu-Sa noon-3pm and 6:30-10:30pm. MC/V. ❸

SIGHTS

Cork's sights are concentrated in three areas: the old town, the Shandon neighborhood to the north, and the university to the west. All sights can be reached by foot, although the university and gaol are farther. Hop on and off the **Cork City Tour,** a 1hr. bus ride that leaves from the tourist office and stops at locations all over town. (July-Aug. 2 per hr., Apr. and Oct. every hr.; €13, students and seniors €11. Cash only.) John Collins also begins his **Historic Walking Tour,** loaded with insider's tidbits, at the tourist office. (☎085 100 7300. Apr.-Sept. M-F 10am, 2, 4pm. €10, students and seniors €5. Cash only.)

THE OLD TOWN. In a city lacking greenery, the area around **Christ Church** provides a quiet refuge and is packed with sunbathers in summer. The site suffered a Protestant torch three times between its 1270 inception and final renovation in 1729. *(Off Grand Parade just north of Bishop Lucy Park. Free.)* Across the South Channel, there's a decent view of Cork from Keyser Hill. At the top of the stairs leading up the hill, **Elizabeth Fort** stands as an ivy-covered remnant of English domination. *(Follow S. Main St. away from the city center, cross the South Gate Bridge, turn right on Proby's Quay, and turn left on Keyser Hill. Free.)* Looming over nearby Proby's Quay, **St. Finbarr's Cathedral** is a testament to the Victorian obsession with the neo-Gothic and a trademark of the city. The cathedral houses art exhibits in the summer. *(Bishop St. ☎021 963 387. Open M-F 10am-12:45pm and 2-5pm. €3, students €1.50.)*

SHANDON AND EMMET PLACE. Like Christ Church, **St. Anne's Church** was ravaged by 17th-century English armies; the current church was built in 1722. The steeple houses the **Bells of Shandon,** which you can ring before climbing to the top. Its four clock faces are notoriously out of sync, earning the church its nickname, "the four-faced liar." *(Walk up John Redmond St. and take a right at the Craft Centre; St. Anne's is on the right. ☎021 450 5906; www.shandonbells.org. Easter-Nov. M-Sa 10am-5pm, Dec.-Easter M-Sa 10am-3pm. €6, students and seniors €5, families €12. Cash only.)* Across the North Channel, the giant brick-and-glass **Opera House** was erected two decades ago after the older, more elegant opera house went down in flames. *(Emmet Pl.,* *near Lavitt's Quay. ☎021 427 0022.)* The nearby **Crawford Art Gallery** has impressive collections of Greek and Roman sculpture casts and 19th-century Irish art. *(Emmet Pl., off Paul St. ☎021 490 7855. Open M-Sa 10am-5pm. Free.)*

WESTERN CORK. Built in 1845, ⬛**University College Cork's** campus is a collection of Gothic buildings, manicured lawns, and sculpture-studded grounds. The classic Stone Corridor is lined with Oghan stones, ancient gravestones marked with inscriptions representing an early example of pagan Irish language. The campus is also home to the architecturally striking **Lewis Glucksman Gallery,** which draws innovative, must-see exhibits. *(Main gate on Western Rd. ☎021 490 3000; www.ucc.ie. Gallery open Tu-W and F-Sa 10am-5pm, Th 10am-8pm, Su noon-5pm.)* ⬛**Fitzgerald Park** has beautiful rose gardens, a pond, and art exhibits, courtesy of the Cork Public Museum. *(From the front gate of UCC, follow the signs across the street. ☎021 427 0679. Open M-F 11am-1pm and 2:15-5pm, Sa 11am-1pm and 2:15-4pm, Su 3-5pm. Free.)* Don't miss the **Cork City Gaol** across the river from the park. Furnished cells, sound effects, and videos illustrate the experience of inmates at the 19th-century prison. *(☎021 430 5022; www.corkcitygaol.com. Open daily Mar.-Oct. 9:30am-6pm; Nov.-Feb. 10am-5pm. €7, students €6. 1hr. audio tour.)*

🅝 NIGHTLIFE

Oliver Plunkett Street, Union Quay, Washington Street, and **South Main Street** have pubs, clubs, and live music. Check out the free *WhazOn?* Cork pamphlet or the Thursday "Downtown" section in the *Evening Echo* newspaper.

🅩 **The Old Oak,** 113 Oliver Plunkett St. (☎021 427 6165), across from the General Post Office. "Best Traditional Pub in Ireland" repeated winner. Huge, packed, and great for the 20- and 30-somethings. Pints around €4. Varied live music nightly from 10:30pm-close. Open M-W noon-1:30am, Th-Sa noon-1:45am, Su noon-1am. Kitchen open daily noon-5:30pm. **Cyprus Avenue,** a music venue upstairs, is open nightly hosting various acts and a DJ on weekends. €10-20 cover for Cyprus Ave. Cash only.

🅩 **An Spailpín Fánac** (on spal-PEEN FAW-nuhk), 28 South Main St. (☎021 427 7949), across from Beamish Brewery. One of Cork's oldest (est. 1779) and favorite pubs. Visitors and locals come for live trad and bluegrass six nights a week. No cover. Cash only. Open M-Th noon-11:30pm, F-Sa noon-12:30am, Su 12:30-11pm.

An Brog, 72-73 Oliver Plunkett St. (☎021 427 0074), at the corner of Oliver Plunkett St. and Grand Parade. For those who crave good alternative rock and feel at home among students and eyebrow rings. Tends to get busy later. Pints €3 before 9pm, €4.50 after. Open M-Sa 11:30am-2am, Su 4pm-2am.

🅢 DAYTRIP FROM CORK

BLARNEY. Those impressed by the Irish way of speaking should head to Blarney Castle and its legendary Blarney Stone. The legend goes that the Earl of Blarney cooed and cajoled his way out of giving up his abode to Queen Elizabeth I, and his smooth-talking skills were imparted to the stone, which when kissed passes on the "gift of Irish gab." After stealing a smooch, enjoy the views from the top and take a walk around the dreamlike rock garden. *(Buses run from the bus station or Merchants Quay, Cork to Blarney. 13-22 per day, round-trip €5.10. Open May M-Sa 9am-6:30pm, Su 9:30am-5:30pm; June-Aug. M-Sa 9am-7pm, Su 9:30am-5:30pm; Sept. M-Sa 9am-6:30pm, Su 9:30am-sunset; Oct.-Apr. M-Sa 9am-sunset, Su 9:30am-sunset. Last entry 30min. before close. €10, €8 student.)*

WESTERN IRELAND

Even Dubliners will say that the west is the "most Irish" part of Ireland; in remote areas you may hear Irish being spoken almost as often as English. The potato famine was most devastating in the west—entire villages emigrated or died—and the current population is still less than half of what it was in 1841.

GALWAY ☎ 091

With its youthful, exuberant spirit, Galway (pop. 80,000) is one of the fastest growing cities in Europe. Performers dazzle crowds on the appropriately named Shop St., locals and tourists lounge in outdoor cafes, and hip crowds pack the pubs and clubs at night. In addition to its peaceful quay-side walks, Galway is only a short drive away from beautiful Connemara.

■ ☑ ORIENTATION AND PRACTICAL INFORMATION. Galway's train and bus stations are on a hill to the northeast of **Eyre Square,** a recently renovated block of lawns and monuments. A string of small, cheap B&Bs are north of the square along **Prospect Hill.** The western corner of the square is the gateway to the pedestrian center, filled with shoppers seeking cups of coffee or pints of stout. From the square, **Shop Street** becomes **High Street,** which then becomes **Quay Street.** The **Wolfe Tone Bridge** spans the River Corrib and connects the city center to the bohemian left bank. The **tourist office** is on Forster St. near the train and bus stations. (☎091 537 700; www.irelandwest.ie. Open Apr.-Oct. daily 9am-5:45pm; Nov.-Mar. M-Sa 9am-5:45pm.) For **Internet,** head to **Chat'rnet,** 5 Eyre St, across from The Hole in the Wall pub. (☎091 539 912. €4 per hr. Open M-Sa 9am-11pm, Su 10am-11pm. Cash only.) The **post office** is at 3 Eglinton St. (☎091 534 727. Open M and W-Sa 9am-5:30pm, Tu 9:30am-5:30pm.)

☂ ▢ ACCOMMODATIONS AND FOOD. The number of accommodations in Galway has recently skyrocketed, but reservations are still necessary in summer. Most B&Bs are concentrated in **Salthill** or on **College Road.** ◙**Barnacle's Quay Street House (IHH) ❶,** 10 Quay St., is the most conveniently located hostel in Galway. Its bright, spacious rooms are perfect for crashing after a night on the town. (☎091 568 644; www.barnacles.ie. Light breakfast included. Laundry €8. Kitchen. Free towels. Free Wi-Fi. Computer use €1 per 15min. Single-sex dorms available. Check-in 11am; check-out 10:30am. 4- to 12-bed dorms €13-20.50; doubles €56-68. MC/V.) **Sleepzone ❷,** Bóthar na mBán (BO-her na-MAHN), Woodquay, a left off Prospect Hill, has large rooms and top-notch facilities. (☎091 566 999; www.sleepzone.ie. Laundry €7. Free Wi-Fi. Single-sex dorms available. Dorms from €16-24; singles €30-55; doubles €50-76. Weekend and low-season rates vary. MC/V.) **Kinlay House ❶,** at the corner of Eyre Sq. and Merchant's Rd., has 220 beds in a convenient and clean location. From the bus station, walk down Station Rd. towards Square and turn left. (☎091 565 244; www.kinlaygalway.ie. Breakfast included. Free luggage room and safe. Towels €1. Free Wi-Fi; computer use €3 per hr. Reception 24hr. Check-out 10:30am. Dorms €15.50-22, doubles €56-63. MC/V.)

The cafes and pubs around Quay, High, and Shop Streets are good options for budget dining. An **open-air market** on Market St. sells fruit and ethnic foods. (Open Sa 8am-4pm.) How the stylish ◙**Gourmet Tart Co. ❶,** 7 Lower Abbeygate St., manages to sell its sumptuous creations at such low prices remains a mystery, but be sure to take advantage of the best deal in Galway. (Sandwiches under €4, salad buffet €13 per kg., pastries €1-2. Open daily 7:30am-7pm. Cash only.) At ◙**The Home Plate ❷,** on Mary St., diners enjoy large sandwiches (€7) and entrees (€7.50-10) on tiny wooden tables. (☎091 561 475. Open M-Sa noon-9pm, Su noon-6:30pm. Cash only.) **Zatsuma ❶**, 27 Shop St., produces delicious crepes (€3.25-6.75) with a skilled assembly line as salivating customers look on. (☎091 895 877; www.zatsuma.ie. Open daily 11am-3am. MC/V.)

◙▣ SIGHTS AND ENTERTAINMENT. The best *craic* in Galway is people-watching: Eyre Sq. and Shop St. are full of street performers, some unknowing. At the **Church of Saint. Nicholas** on Market St., a stone marks the spot where Columbus supposedly stopped to pray to the patron saint of travelers before sailing the ocean blue. (Open daily Apr.-Sept. 8:30am-8pm, Oct.-Mar. 9am-5pm. Free.) On Shop St., **Lynch's Castle** is a well-preserved 16th-century merchant's residence than now houses a bank. From Quay St., head across Wolfe Tone Bridge to the **Claddagh**, an area that was an Irish-speaking, thatch-roofed fishing village until the 1930s. The famous **Claddagh rings** are today's mass-produced reminders of yesteryear. The **Nora Barnacle House,** 8 Bowling Green, off Market St., has hardly changed since James Joyce's future wife Nora lived there with her family at the turn of the 20th century. Check out Joyce's love letters to his life-long companion. (☎091 564 743 www.norabarnacle.com. Open mid-May to mid-Sept. M-Sa 10am-1pm and 2-5pm, or by appointment. €2.50, students €2.) Hang with sea creatures for an afternoon at the **National Aquarium of Ireland,** on the Salt Hill Promenade. (☎091 585 100; www.nationalaquarium.ie. Open Apr.-Sept. M-F 9am-6pm, Sa-Su 9am-7pm; Oct.-Mar. M-F 9am-5pm, Sa-Su 9am-6pm. €9.75, students €7. MC/V.) Event listings are published in the free *Galway Advertiser*, available at the tourist office and most accommodations. In mid-July, the **Galway Arts Festival** (☎091 566 577) attracts droves of filmmakers, rock groups, theater troupes, and trad musicians.

NORTHERN IRELAND

The calm tenor of everyday life in Northern Ireland has long been overshadowed by headlines about riots and bombs. While the violence has subdued, the divisions in civil society continue to some extent. Protestants and Catholics usually live in separate neighborhoods, attend separate schools, and patronize separate stores and pubs. The 1998 Good Friday Accord began a slow march toward peace, and all sides have renewed their efforts to make their country as peaceful as it is beautiful.

BELFAST (BÉAL FEIRSTE)   ☎028

The second-largest city on the island, Belfast (pop. 276,000) is the center of Northern Ireland's cultural, commercial, and political activity. **Queen's University** testifies to the city's rich academic history—luminaries such as Nobel Laureate Seamus Heaney once roamed its halls, and Samuel Beckett taught the young men of **Campbell College.** The Belfast pub scene ranks among the best in the world, combining the historical appeal of old-fashioned watering holes with more modern bars and clubs. While Belfast has suffered from the stigma of its violent past, it has rebuilt itself, surprising most visitors with its neighborly, urbane feel. Progress is slow to take root in the still-divided West Belfast area, home to separate communities of Protestants and Catholics.

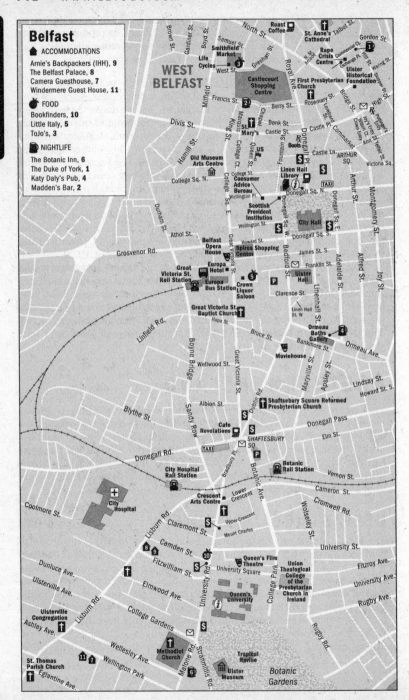

TRANSPORTATION

Flights: Belfast is served by 2 airports.

Belfast International Airport (☎028 9448 4848; www.belfastairport.com) in Aldergrove. **Aer Lingus** (☎087 0876 5000; www.aerlingus.com); **Air Transat** (☎028 9031 2312; www.airtransat.com); **BMI** (☎087 0264 2229; www.flybmi.com); **Continental** (☎012 9377 6464; www.continental.com); **easyJet** (☎087 1244 2366; www.easyjet.com); **Flyglobespan** (☎087 0556 1522; www.flyglobespan.com); **Jet2** (☎087 1226 1737; www.jet2.com); **Manx2** (☎087 0242 2226; www.manx2.com); **Wizz Air** (☎482 2351 9499; www.wizzair.com) operate from here. Translink Bus 300 has 24hr. **bus** service from the airport to Europa bus station in the city center M-F every 10min. 6:50am-6:15pm, every 15-40min. otherwise; Sa every 20min. 7:35am-6:40pm, at least once per hr. otherwise; Su every 30min. 8:15am-10:40pm, at least once per hr. otherwise. Call ☎9066 6630 or visit www.translink.co.uk for full timetables. £6, round-trip £9 if you return within 1 month. **Taxis** (☎028 9448 4353) get you there for £25-30.

Belfast City Airport (☎028 9093 9093; www.belfastcityairport.com), is located at the harbor. **Flybe** (☎087 1700 0535; www.flybe.com); **BMI** (☎087 0607 0555; www.flybmi.com); **Ryanair** (☎00353 1249 7791; www.ryanair.com); **Aer Arann** (☎080 0587 2324; www.aerarann.ie); **Manx2** (☎087 0242 2226; www.manx2.com) operate from here. To get from City Airport to Europa bus station, take **Translink Bus 600.** M-F every 20-30min., 8:35am-10:05pm, Sa every 20-30min. 8:05am-9:50pm, Su every 45min. 7:30am-9:50pm. Single £1.30, return £2.20.

Trains: For **train** and **bus** info, contact **Translink** (☎028 9066 6630; www.translink.co.uk; inquiries daily 7am-8pm). Trains depart from several of Belfast's stations **(Great Victoria Street, City Hospital, Botanic, Central)** for Derry/Londonderry (2hr.; M-F 9 per day, Sa 8 per day, Su 4 per day; £10.50 single, £15 return) and leave **Central Station,** E. Bridge St. to Dublin (2hr.; M-Sa 8 per day, Su 5 per day; £25 single, £36 return). The **Metro** buses are free with rail tickets.

Buses: Europa Bus Terminal, off Great Victoria St., (☎028 9043 4424; ticket office open M-Sa 7:35am-8:05pm, Su 9:15am-6:15pm). Buses to Derry/Londonderry (1hr.; M-F 39 per day, Sa 20 per day, Su 11 per day; £10 single, £15 return) and Dublin (3hr.; 24 per day; buses at midnight, 1, 2, 3, 4, 5am depart Glengall St.; £10 single, £14 return). The **Centrelink bus** connects the station with the city center.

Ferries: Norfolk Ferries (☎01 819 2999; www.norfolkline-ferries.co.uk) operates out of the **SeaCat** terminal and runs to Liverpool, England (8hr., fares seasonal, starting at £99 with car and £20 without). Book online and before the day of travel to avoid a £10 booking fee. **Stena Line** (☎028 087 0570 7070; www.stenaline.com), up the Lagan River, has the quickest service to Scotland, docking in Stranraer (1hr.; book online, fares seasonal, starting at £55).

ORIENTATION

Buses arrive at the **Europa Bus Station** on Great Victoria Street. To the northeast is **City Hall** in Donegall Sq. Donegall Pl. turns into Royal Avenue and runs from Donegall Sq. through the shopping area. To the east, in Cornmarket, pubs in narrow entries (small alleyways) offer an escape. The stretch of Great Victoria St. between the bus station and Shaftesbury Sq. is known as the **Golden Mile** for its highbrow establishments and Victorian architecture. Botanic Avenue and Bradbury Pl. (which becomes University Road) extend south from Shaftesbury Sq. into **Queen's University** turf. The city center, Golden Mile, and the University are relatively safe areas. Although locals advise caution in the east and west, central Belfast is safer for tourists than most European cities.

Westlink Motorway divides working-class West Belfast, more politically volatile than the city center, from the rest of Belfast. The **Protestant district** stretches along Shankill Rd., just north of the **Catholic neighborhood,** centered around Falls Rd. The River Lagan splits industrial East Belfast from Belfast proper.

IRELAND

The shipyards and docks extend north on both sides of the river as it grows into Belfast Lough. During the week, the area north of City Hall is essentially deserted after 6pm. Streets remain quiet even during the weekend, belying the boisterous pub/club scene. Although muggings are infrequent in Belfast, it's wise to use taxis after dark, particularly near pubs and clubs in the northeast.

▓ PRACTICAL INFORMATION

Tourist Information Centre: Belfast Welcome Centre, 47 Donegall Pl. (☎028 9024 6609; www.gotobelfast.com). Offers comprehensive free booklet on Belfast and info on surrounding areas. Books reservations in Northern Ireland (£2) and the Republic (£3). Open M-Sa 9am-5:30pm, Su 11am-4pm, and June-Sept. M-Sa 9am-7pm.

Laundromat: Globe Drycleaners and **Launderers,** 37-39 Botanic Ave. (☎028 9024 3956). £5 per load. Open M-F 8am-9pm, Sa 8am-6pm, Su noon-6pm.

Police: 6-18 Donegall Pass and 65 Knock Rd. (☎028 9065 0222).

Hospital: Belfast City Hospital, 91 Lisburn Rd. (☎028 9032 9241). From Shaftesbury Sq., follow Bradbury Pl. and take a right at the fork for Lisburn Rd.

Internet: Belfast Central Library, 122 Royal Ave. (☎028 9050 9150). Open M-Th 9am-8pm, F 9am-5:30pm, Sa 9am-4:30pm. £1.50 per 30min. for nonmembers.

Post Office: Central Post Office, on the corner of High St. and Bridge St. (☎084 5722 3344). Open M-Sa 10am-5:30pm. **Postal Code:** BT2 7FD.

▓ ACCOMMODATIONS

Despite fluctuating tourism and rising rents, Belfast provides a healthy selection of hostels for travelers. Almost all are near Queen's University, close to the city's pubs and restaurants, and a short walk or bus ride to the city center. Note that reservations are necessary during the summer.

▓ Arnie's Backpackers (IHH), 63 Fitzwilliam St. (☎028 9024 2867; www.arniesbackpackers.co.uk). Look for a cutout sign of a sky-gazing backpacker. Arnie, the jovial owner, may greet you with a cup of tea and check on you daily. The hostel offers bunk beds in small, clean rooms, a kitchen, common room with television and fireplace, and back garden. Reception 8:30am-9pm. 8-bed dorms £9; 4-bed £11. Cash only. ❶

The Belfast Palace (Paddy's Palace), 68 Lisburn Rd. (☎028 9033 3367; www.paddyspalace.com). This sociable new hostel offers free Wi-Fi, continental breakfast, a kitchen, and laundry. Reception M-Th and Su 8am-8pm, F-Sa 8am-10pm. Dorms £9.50-13.50. Singles £27, doubles £37. Pay for 4 nights and stay free on the 5th. MC/V. ❶

Windermere Guest House, 60 Wellington Park (☎028 9066 2693; www.windermereguesthouse.co.uk). Leather couches provide comfy seating in the living room of this Victorian house. Singles £31-34; doubles £56-60. Cash only. ❸

Camera Guesthouse, 44 Wellington Park (☎028 9066 0026; www.cameraguesthouse.com). Quiet, serene and pristine Victorian house makes an appealing choice. Breakfasts offer wide selection of organic foods and herbal teas that cater to specific dietary concerns. Singles £34, with bath £48; doubles £45/52. 3% commission. MC/V. ❹

▓ FOOD

Dublin Road, Botanic Avenue, and the **Golden Mile** around **Shaftesbury Square** have the most restaurants. The **Tesco** supermarket is at 2 Royal Ave. (☎028 9032 3270. Open M-W and Sa 8am-7pm, Th 8am-9pm, F 8am-8pm, Su 1-5pm.)

Little Italy, 13 Amelia St. (☎028 9031 4914). A little Mediterranean kitchen tucked in Belfast's city center. Customers watch at the brick counter as the industrious staff make their pizzas to order and savor the aromas of the Italiano, Vegetarian Special, Fabio, and Hawaiian pizzas. 9" £4-6, 10" £4-7, 12" £5-8. Open M-Sa 5pm-midnight. ❶

Tojo's, Smithfield Market (☎028 9032 4122). Offers some of Belfast's lowest prices for honest food. While it may look like a simple cafeteria, the chalkboard full of sandwich options, like the Tunatastic (tuna, corn, peppers; £3), fulfills its bold promise of "home-made food with a modern twist." Open M-F 8am-4pm and Sa 8am-5pm. Cash only. ❶

Bookfinders, 47 University Rd. (☎028 9032 8269). Find it one block from the University, on the corner of Camden St. A favorite with the University crowd because of its proximity, low prices, and disheveled character. Vegan soup and bread £3; sandwiches £3. Open M-Sa 10am-5:30pm. ❶

🅖 SIGHTS

DONEGALL SQUARE. The most dramatic and impressive piece of architecture in Belfast is also its administrative and geographic center. Dominating the grassy square that serves as the locus of downtown Belfast, **City Hall's** green copper dome is recognizable from nearly any point in the city. (☎028 9027 0477. Free.)

THE DOCKS AND EAST BELFAST. The poster child of Belfast's riverfront revival, the **Odyssey** packs five distinct sights into one entertainment center. (2 Queen's Quay. ☎028 9045 1055; www.theodyssey.co.uk.) The **W5 Discovery Centre** (short for "whowhatwherewhenwhy?") is a playground for curious minds and hyperactive schoolchildren. (☎028 9046 7700; www.w5online.co.uk. Workshops run throughout the summer. Wheelchair-accessible. Open M-Sa 10am-6pm; closes at 5pm when school is in session, Su noon-6pm; last admission 1hr. before closing. £7, children £5. Family discounts available.) Designed to accommodate the hordes of sinning sailors landing in Belfast port, the quirky **Sinclair Seaman's Church** does things its own way—the minister delivers his sermons from a pulpit carved in the shape of a ship's prow, collections are taken in miniature lifeboats, and the choir uses an organ from a Guinness barge with port and starboard lights. (Corporation St., down from the SeaCat terminal. ☎028 9071 5997. Open W 2-5pm; Su service at 11:30am and 7pm.)

CORNMARKET AND ST. ANNE'S. North of the city center, this shopping district consists of eight blocks around Castle Street and Royal Avenue. Relics of the old city remain in entries, or tiny alleys. Construction on **St. Anne's Cathedral,** also known as the Belfast Cathedral, was begun in 1899, but to keep from disturbing regular worship, it was built around a smaller church already on the site. Upon completion of the new exterior, builders extracted the earlier church brick by brick. (Donegall St., a few blocks from the city center. Open M-Sa 10am-4pm, Su before and after services at 10am, 11am, 3:30pm.)

GRAND OPERA HOUSE. The opera house was cyclically bombed by the IRA, restored to its original splendor at enormous cost, and then bombed again. Visitors today enjoy its grandeur, and tours offer a look behind the ornate facade and include a complimentary coffee and danish at the cafe, **Luciano's.** (☎028 9023 1919; www.goh.co.uk. Office open M-F 8:30am-9pm, Sa 8:30am-6pm. Tours begin across the street at the office W-Sa 11am. Times vary, so call ahead. £3, seniors/students/children £2.)

WEST BELFAST. West Belfast is not a tourist site in the traditional sense, although the walls and houses along the streets display political murals which speak to Belfast's religious and political divide. Visitors should definitely take a **black cab tour** of the murals, easily booked at most hostels. **Black Taxi Tours** offer witty, objective presentations. (☎077 2106 7752. 1hr. tour from £10 per person.) The **Catholic neighborhood** is centered on **Falls Road,** where the Sinn Féin office is easily spotted: one side of it is covered with an advertisement for the Sinn Féin newspaper, An

Phoblacht. On Divis St., **Divis Tower** was formerly an IRA stronghold. Farther north is Shankill Rd. and the **Protestant neighborhood.** Between the Falls and Shankill is the **Peace Line.** The side streets on the right guide you to the **Shankill Estate** and more murals. Crumlin Rd., through the estate, has the oldest Loyalist murals.

> **LIGHT TOURISM.** It's safest to visit the Falls and Shankill during the day, when the neighborhoods are full of locals and the murals are visible. Do not visit the area during **Marching Season** (the weeks around July 12) when the parades are characterized by mutual antagonism.

ENTERTAINMENT AND NIGHTLIFE

Pubs in Belfast are the place to experience the city's *craic* and meet its color-ful characters. Pubs were targets for sectarian violence at the height of the Troubles, so most are new or restored, although many retain their historic charm. Those in the city center and university area are now relatively safe. *Bushmills Irish Pub Guide*, by Sybil Taylor, relates the history of Belfast pubs (£7; available at local bookstores). For a full list of entertainment options, grab a free copy of *The Big List* or *Fate*, available in tourist centers, hostels, and certain restaurants and pubs.

- **The Duke of York,** 7-11 Commercial Ct. (☎028 9024 1062). Take first left off Hill St. Rebuilt after it was bombed by the IRA in the 60s, today it is one of Belfast's favorite pubs. Serves the city's largest selection of Irish whiskeys and draws a diverse crowd with cheer and live music. Kitchen serves sandwiches and toasties daily until 2:30pm. Open M 11:30am-11pm, Tu-F 11:30am-1am, Sa 11:30am-2am, Su 2-9pm.

- **Madden's Bar,** 74 Berry St. (☎028 9024 4114; www.maddensbarbelfast.com). You might hear Gaelic among the local crowd, and you'll definitely hear live music. W lan-guage class, 8:30pm, beginners' Irish step-dancing, 9:30pm. Th piping class followed by pipers' session and open mike. F folk night downstairs, trad upstairs. Sa blues, jazz, or electric folk downstairs, trad upstairs. Lunch M-F noon-2pm. Open daily 11am-1am.

- **Katy Daly's Pub,** 17 Ormeau Ave. (☎028 9032 5942; www.the-limelight.co.uk). Behind City Hall, head toward Queen's, take a left on Ormeau Ave., and you'll find this stalwart of the Belfast music and nightlife scene. Students and young people, tourists included, congregate in this ultimate party spot (the Limelights, Spring, and Airbrake clubs are connected). Open M-Sa 3pm-1am, Su 8pm-midnight.

- **The Botanic Inn,** 23 Malone Rd. (☎028 9050 9740). Standing in as the unofficial student union, the hugely popular "Bot" is packed nightly with raucous groups of friends and die-hard sports fans. Kitchen serves pub grub daily noon-8pm. Open M-Sa 11:30am-1am, Su noon-midnight. MC/V.

ITALY
(ITALIA)

With offspring from Michelangelo to Armani, Italy has carved a distinct path through the centuries, consistently setting a world standard for innovation and elegance. Steep Alpine peaks in the north, lush olive trees in the interior, and aquamarine waters along the Riviera provide only a few of the country's breathtaking vistas. Indulging in daily *siestas* and frequently hosting leisurely feasts, Italians seem to possess a knowledge of and appreciation for life's pleasures, while their openness lets travelers ease into Italy's relaxed lifestyle.

 DISCOVER ITALY: SUGGESTED ITINERARIES

THREE DAYS. Don't even think about leaving **Rome,** *La Città Eterna* (p. 452). Go back in time at the **Ancient City:** become a gladiator in the **Colosseum,** explore the **Roman Forum,** and stand in the well-preserved **Pantheon.** Spend a day to admiring the fine art in the **Capitoline Museums** and the **Galleria Borghese,** and then satiate your other senses in a *discoteca.* The next morning, redeem your debauched soul in **Vatican City,** gazing at the glorious ceiling of the **Sistine Chapel,** gaping at **St. Peter's Cathedral,** and enjoying the **Vatican Museums.**

ONE WEEK. Spend 3 days taking in the sights in **Rome** before heading north to **Florence** (2 days; p. 508) to immerse yourself in Italy's amazing Renaissance art at the Uffizi Gallery. Move to **Venice** (2 days; p. 493) to float along the canals.

BEST OF ITALY, 3 WEEKS. Begin by savoring the sights and history of **Rome** (3 days). Seek out the medieval houses of **Siena** (1 day; p. 520), and then move to **Florence** (3 days). Head up the coast to **Camogli** (1 day; p. 488), and the beautiful **Cinque Terre** (2 days; p. 489). Visit cosmopolitan **Milan** (2 days; p. 477) for shopping and **Lake Como** for hiking (1 day; p. 484). Join the star-crossed lovers Romeo and Juliet in **Verona** (1 day; p. 506). Paddle through labyrinthine canals and peer into delicate blown-glass in **Venice** (2 days) before flying south to **Naples** (2 days; p. 525). Be sure to check out the ash casts and preserved frescoes at ancient **Pompeii** (1 day; p. 530). Finally, hike and swim along the **Amalfi Coast** (1 day; p. 532) and revel in the shimmering waters of the Blue Grotto on the island of **Capri** (1 day; p. 530).

ESSENTIALS

FACTS AND FIGURES

OFFICIAL NAME: Italian Republic.

CAPITAL: Rome.

MAJOR CITIES: Florence, Milan, Naples, Venice.

POPULATION: 58,145,000.

TIME ZONE: GMT +1.

LANGUAGE: Italian; some German, French, and Slovene.

RELIGION: Roman Catholic (90%).

LONGEST SALAMI: Made by Rino Parenti in Zibello, displayed on Nov. 23, 2003; 486.8m in length.

WHEN TO GO

Traveling to Italy in late May or early September, when the temperature averages a comfortable 77°F (25°C), will ensure a calm, cool vacation. When planning, keep in mind festival schedules and weather patterns in northern and southern areas. Tourism goes into overdrive in June, July, and August: hotels are booked solid and prices know no limits. In August, Italians flock to the coast for vacationing, but northern cities are filled with tourists.

DOCUMENTS AND FORMALITIES

EMBASSIES AND CONSULATES. Foreign embassies in Italy are in Rome (p. 460). Italian embassies abroad include: **Australia,** 12 Grey St., Deakin, Canberra ACT 2600 (☎61 262 733 333; www.ambcanberra.esteri.it); **Canada,** 275 Slater St., 21st fl., Ottawa, ON K1P 5H9 (☎613-232-2401; www.ambottawa.esteri.it); **Ireland,** 63/65 Northumberland Rd., Dublin 4 (☎353 16 60 17 44; www.ambdublino.esteri.it); **New Zealand,** 34-38 Grant Rd., Wellington (☎64 44 735 339; www.ambwellington.esteri.it); **UK,** 14 Three Kings Yard, London, W1K 4EH (☎44 20 73 12 22 00; www.embitaly.org.uk); **US,** 3000 Whitehaven St., NW, Washington, DC 20008 (☎202-612-4400; www.ambwashingtondc.esteri.it).

VISA AND ENTRY INFORMATION. EU citizens do not need a visa. Citizens of Australia, Canada, New Zealand, and the US do not need a visa for stays of up to 90 days, beginning upon entry into any of the countries within the EU's freedom-of-movement zone. For more info, see p. 13. For stays longer than 90 days, all non-EU citizens need visas (around €60), available at Italian consulates. For more info on obtaining a visa visit www.esteri.it/visti/home_eng.asp.

TOURIST SERVICES AND MONEY

EMERGENCY	Ambulance: ☎118. Fire: ☎115. Police: ☎112. General Emergency: ☎113.

TOURIST OFFICES. The **Italian Government Tourist Board** (**ENIT;** www.italiantourism.com) provides useful info about many aspects of the country, including the arts, history, and activities. The main office in Rome (☎06 49 71 11; sedecentrale@cert.enit.it) can help locate any local office that is not listed online.

MONEY. The **euro (€)** has replaced the **lira** as the unit of currency in Italy. For more info, see p. 16. At many restaurants, a **service charge** (*servizio*) or **cover** (*coperto*) is included in the bill. Most locals do not tip, but it is appropriate for foreign visitors to leave an additional €1-2 at restaurants. Taxi drivers expect a 10-15% tip. Bargaining is common in Italy, but use discretion. It is appropriate at markets, with vendors, and unmetered taxi fares (settle the price before getting in). Haggling over prices elsewhere is usually inappropriate.

Italy has a 20% **value added tax** (**VAT,** or **IVA** in Italy), a sales tax applied to most goods and services. The prices given in *Let's Go* include VAT. In the airport upon exiting the EU, non-EU citizens can claim a refund on the tax paid for goods purchased at participating stores. In order to qualify for a refund in a store, you must spend at least €155; make sure to ask for a refund form when you pay. For more info on qualifying for a VAT refund, see p. 19.

BUSINESS HOURS. Nearly everything closes around 1-3pm for *siesta*. Most museums are open 9am-1pm and 3-6pm; some are open through lunch, however. Monday is often a *giorno di chiusura* (day of closure).

Italy

TRANSPORTATION

BY PLANE. Most international flights land at Rome's international airport, known as both **Fiumicino** and **Leonardo da Vinci** (**FCO**; ☎06 65 951; www.adr.it). Other hubs are Florence's **Amerigo Vespucci** airport (**FLR**) and Milan's **Malpensa** (**MXP**) and **Linate** (**LIN**) airports. **Alitalia** (☎800-223-5730; www.alitalia.com) is Italy's national airline. Budget airlines **Ryanair** (☎353 12 49 77 91; www.ryanair. com) and **easyJet** (☎0871 244 2366; www.easyjet.com) offer inexpensive fares to cities throughout the country; reserve ahead to get the best deals.

BY FERRY. Sicily, Sardinia, Corsica, and smaller islands along the coast are connected to the mainland by **ferries** (*traghetti*) and **hydrofoils** (*aliscafi*). Italy's largest private ferry service, **Tirrenia** (www.tirrenia.it), runs ferries to Sardinia,

Sicily, and Tunisia. Other lines, such as the **SNAV** (tickets and special offers available online at www.aferry.to/snav-ferry.htm), have hydrofoil services from major ports such as Ancona, Bari, Brindisi, Genoa, La Spezia, Livorno, Naples, and Trapani. Ferry service is also prevalent in the Lake Country. Reserve well ahead, especially in July and August.

BY TRAIN. The Italian State Railway **Ferrovie dello Stato**, or **FS** (national info line ☎89 20 21; www.trenitalia.com), offers inexpensive, efficient service and Trenitalia passes, the domestic equivalent of the Eurail Pass. There are several types of trains: the *locale* stops at every station on a line, the *diretto* makes fewer stops than the *locale*, and the *espresso* stops only at major stations. The air-conditioned *rapido*, an **InterCity (IC)** train, zips along but costs more. Tickets for the fast, pricey **Eurostar** trains require reservations. Eurail Passes are valid without a supplement on all trains except Eurostar. Always validate your ticket in the orange or yellow machine before boarding to avoid a €120 fine.

BY BUS. Bus travel within Italy has its own benefits and disadvantages; in remote parts of the country private companies offer cheap fares and are often the only option, though schedules may be unreliable. Intercity buses serve points inaccessible by train. For city buses, buy tickets in *tabaccherie* or kiosks. Validate your ticket immediately after boarding to avoid a €120 fine. Websites www.bus.it and www.italybus.it are helpful resources for trip planning.

BY CAR. To drive in Italy, you must be 18 or older and hold an **International Driving Permit (IDP)** or an EU license. There are four kinds of roads: *autostrada* (superhighways; mostly toll roads; usually 130km per hr. speed limit); *strade statali* (state roads); *strade provinciali* (provincial); and *strade communali* (local). Driving in Italy is frightening; congested traffic is common in large cities and in the north. On three-lane roads, the center lane is for passing. **Mopeds** (€30-40 per day) can be a great way to see the more scenic areas but can be disastrous in the rain and on rough roads. Always exercise caution. Practice in empty streets and learn to keep up with traffic. Drivers in Italy—especially in the south—are notorious for ignoring traffic laws.

BY BIKE AND BY THUMB. While cycling is a popular sport in Italy, bike trails are rare. Rent bikes where you see a *noleggio* sign. Hitchhiking can be unsafe in Italy, especially in the south. *Let's Go* does not recommend hitchhiking.

KEEPING IN TOUCH

PHONE CODES	**Country code: 39. International dialing prefix: 00.** For more info on how to place international calls, see **Inside Back Cover.**

EMAIL AND THE INTERNET. While **Internet** is a relatively common amenity throughout Italy, **Wi-Fi** is not, and as a general rule, the prevalence of both decreases the further you travel from urban areas. A new Italian law requires a passport or driver's license to use an Internet cafe. Rates are €2-6 per hr. For free Internet access, try local universities and libraries.

TELEPHONE. Almost all **public phones** require a prepaid card (*scheda*), sold at *tabaccherie*, Internet cafes, and post offices. Italy has no area codes, only regional prefixes that are incorporated into the number. **Mobile phones** are widely used in Italy; buying a prepaid SIM card for a GSM phone can be a good, inexpensive option. Of the service providers, **TIM** and **Vodafone** have the best networks. International direct dial numbers include: **AT&T Direct** (☎800 17 24 44); **Canada Direct** (☎800 17 22 13); **Telecom New Zealand Direct** (☎800 17 26 41); **Telstra Australia** (☎800 17 26 10).

MAIL. Airmail letters sent from Australia, North America, or the UK to Italy take anywhere from four to 15 days to arrive. Since Italian mail is notoriously unreliable, it is usually safer to send mail priority *(prioritaria)* or registered *(raccomandata)*. It costs €0.85 to send a letter worldwide. To receive mail in Italy, have mail delivered **Poste Restante.** Mail will go to the main post office unless you specify a subsidiary by street address. Address mail to be held according to the following example: First name LAST NAME, *Fermo Posta,* City, Italy. Bring a passport to pick up your mail; there may be a small fee.

ACCOMMODATIONS AND CAMPING

ITALY	❶	❷	❸	❹	❺
ACCOMMODATIONS	under €16	€16-25	€26-40	€41-60	over €60

Associazione Italiana Alberghi per la Gioventù (AIG), the Italian hostel federation, is a **Hostelling International (HI)** affiliate. A full list of AIG hostels is available online at www.ostellionline.org. Prices in Italy average around €15-25 per night for **dorms.** Hostels are the best option for solo travelers (single rooms are relatively scarce in hotels in the country), but curfews, lockouts, distant locations, and less-than-perfect security can detract from their appeal. Italian **hotel** rates are set by the state. A single room in a hotel *(camera singola)* usually starts at €25-50 per night, and a double *(camera doppia)* starts at €40-90 per room. A room with a private bath *(con bagno)* usually costs 30-50% more. Smaller **pensioni** are often cheaper than hotels. Be sure to confirm charges before checking in; Italian hotels are notorious for tacking on additional costs at check-out time. **Affittacamere** (rooms for rent in private houses) are an inexpensive option for longer stays. For more info, inquire at local tourist offices. There are over 1700 **campgrounds** in Italy; tent sites average €4.20. The **Federazione Italiana del Campeggio e del Caravaning** (www.federcampeggio.it) has a complete list of sites.

FOOD AND DRINK

ITALY	❶	❷	❸	❹	❺
FOOD	under €7	€7-15	€16-20	€21-25	over €25

Breakfast is the simplest meal in Italy: at most, *colazione* consists of coffee and a *cornetto* or *brioche* (croissant). For *pranzo* (lunch), locals grab panini or salads, or dine more calmly at an inexpensive *tavola calda* (cafeteria-style snack bar), *rosticceria* (grill), or *gastronomia* (snack bar with hot dishes for takeout). *Cena* (dinner) usually begins at 8pm or later. In Naples, it's not unusual to go for a midnight **pizza.** Traditionally, dinner is the longest meal of the day, usually lasting much of the evening and consisting of an *antipasto* (appetizer), a *primo piatto* (starch-based first course like pasta or risotto), a *secondo piatto* (meat or fish), and a *contorno* (vegetable side dish). Finally comes the *dolce* (dessert or fruit), then *caffè* (espresso), and often an after-dinner liqueur.

Lunch is usually the most important meal of the day in rural regions where daily work comes in two shifts and is separated by a long lunch and **siesta.** Many restaurants offer a fixed-price *menù turistico* including *primo, secondo,* bread, water, and wine. While food varies regionally, the importance of relaxing

ITALY

and having an extended meal does not. **La bella figura** (a good figure) is another social imperative, and the after-dinner **passeggiata** (walk) is as much a tradition as the meal itself. **Gelato** is a snack, a dessert, and even a meal in itself. **Coffee** and **wine** are their own institutions, each with their own devoted followers.

 THE UGLY DUCKLING. Before shelling out the euro for a *piccolo cono* (small cone), assess the quality of an establishment by looking at the banana gelato: if it's bright yellow, it's been made from a mix. If it's slightly gray, real bananas were used. *Gelati* in metal bins also tend to be homemade, whereas plastic tubs indicate mass-production.

HOLIDAYS AND FESTIVALS

Holidays: New Year's Day (Jan. 1); Epiphany (Jan. 6); Good Friday (Apr. 10, 2009); Easter Sunday and Monday (Apr. 12-13, 2009); Liberation Day (Apr. 25); Labor Day (May 1); Feast of the Assumption (Aug. 15); All Saints' Day (Nov. 1); Immaculate Conception (Dec. 8); Christmas (Dec. 25); St. Stephen's Day (Dec. 26).

Festivals: The most common reason for a local festival in Italy is the celebration of a religious event—everything from a patron saint's holy day to the commemoration of a special miracle counts. **Carnevale,** a country-wide celebration, is held during the 10 days leading up to Lent. In Venice, costumed Carnevale revelers fill the streets and canals. During **Scoppio del Carro,** held in Florence's P. del Duomo on Easter Sunday, Florentines set off a cart of explosives in keeping with medieval tradition. The **Spoleto Festival** (known as the Festival dei Due Mondi, or Festival of Two Worlds) is one of the world's most prestigious international arts events. Each June and July it features concerts, operas, ballets, film screenings, and modern art shows (www.spoletofestival.it). For a complete list of festivals, contact the Italian Government Tourist Board (p. 448).

BEYOND TOURISM

From harvesting grapes on vineyards in Siena to restoring and protecting marine life in the Mediterranean, there are diverse options for working for a cause. Those in search of a more lucrative experience might consider working as an intern for the Italian press or teaching English in Italian schools. For more info on opportunities across Europe, see **Beyond Tourism,** p. 55.

Associazione Culturale Linguista Educational (ACLE), V. Roma 54, 18038 San Remo, Imperio (☎01 84 50 60 70; www.acle.org). Non-profit association that works to bring theater, arts, and English language instruction to Italian children. Employees create theater programs in schools and teach English at summer camps.

Cook Italy, (☎34 90 07 82 98; www.cookitaly.com). Region- or dish-specific cooking classes. Venues include Bologna, Cortona, Florence, Lucca, Rome, and Sicily. Courses 3- to 6- nights from €950. Housing, meals, and recipes included.

Aegean Center for the Fine Arts, Paros 84400, Cyclades, Greece (☎30 22 84 02 32 87; www.aegeancenter.org). Italian branch located in Pistoia. Instruction in arts, literature, creative writing, voice, and art history. Classes taught in English. Fees cover housing in 16th-century villa, meals, and excursions. 14-week program in the fall €8500.

ROME (ROMA)   ☎06

Rome (pop. 2.8 million), *La Città Eterna*, is a concentrated expression of Italian spirit. Whether flaunting the Italian 2006 World Cup victory or retelling the mythical story of the city's founding, Romans exude a fierce pride for the Rome that was and the Rome that will be. Crumbling pagan ruins form the backdrop for the center of Christianity's largest denomination, and hip clubs and bars border grand cathedrals. Augustus once boasted that he found Rome a city of brick and left it a city of marble. No matter how you find it, you'll undoubtedly leave with plenty of memories and a new appreciation for *la dolce vita*.

✴ INTERCITY TRANSPORTATION

Flights: Da Vinci International Airport (FCO; ☎06 65 21 01), known as **Fiumicino**, handles most flights. The **Termini** line runs nonstop to Rome's main station, **Stazione Termini** (30min., 2 per hr., €11). After hours, take the blue COTRAL **bus** (☎06 80 01 50 008) to Tiburtina from outside the main doors after customs (4 per day, €5). From Tiburtina, take bus #175 or 492, or metro B to Termini. A few domestic and budget flights, including Ryanair, arrive at **Ciampino** (**CIA**; ☎06 65 951). To get to Rome, take the COTRAL bus (2 per hr., €1) to **Anagnina** station, or the **Terravision Shuttle** (www.terravision.it) to V. Marsala at the Hotel Royal Santina (40min., €8).

Trains: Trains leave Stazione Termini for: **Bologna** (2-3hr., €33-42); **Florence** (1-3hr., €14-33); **Milan** (4-8hr., €30-50); **Naples** (1-2hr., €10-25); **Venice** (4-5hr., €33-50). Trains arriving in Rome between midnight and 5am arrive at **Stazione Tiburtina** or **Stazione Ostiense,** which are connected to Termini by bus #175.

✴ ORIENTATION

Because Rome's winding streets are difficult to navigate, it's helpful to orient yourself to major landmarks and main streets. The **Tiber River,** which snakes north-south through the city, is also a useful reference point. Most trains arrive at Stazione Termini east of Rome's historical center. **Termini** and **San Lorenzo** to the east are home to the city's largest university and most of its budget accommodations. **Via Nazionale** originates two blocks northwest of Termini Station in **Piazza della Repubblica** and leads to **Piazza Venezia,** the focal point of the city, recognizable by the immense white **Vittorio Emanuele II monument.** From P. Venezia, **Via dei Fori Imperiali** runs southeast to the Ancient City, where the **Colosseum** and the **Roman Forum** attest to former glory. **Via del Corso** stretches north from P. Venezia to **Piazza del Popolo,** which has an obelisk in its center. The **Trevi Fountain, Piazza Barberini,** and the fashionable streets around **Piazza di Spagna** and the **Spanish Steps** lie to the east of V. del Corso. **Villa Borghese,** with its impressive gardens and museums, is northeast of the Spanish Steps. West of V. del Corso is the *centro storico,* the tangle of streets around the **Pantheon, Piazza Navona, Campo dei Fiori,** and the old **Jewish Ghetto.** West of P. Venezia, **Largo Argentina** marks the start of **Corso Vittorio Emanuele II,** which runs through the *centro storico* to the Tiber River. Across the river to the northwest is **Vatican City** and the **Borgo-Prati** neighborhood. South of the Vatican is **Trastevere** and residential **Testaccio.** Pick up a free **map** in English at the tourist office (see **Practical Information,** p. 460).

⊏ LOCAL TRANSPORTATION

Public Transportation: The A and B **Metropolitana subway** lines (www.metroroma.it) meet at Termini and usually run 5:30am-11:30pm; however, due to construction on the forthcoming C line, the subway now closes at 10pm. **ATAC buses** (www.atac.roma.it) run 5am-midnight (with limited late-night routes); validate your ticket in the machine when you board. Buy tickets (€1) at *tabaccherie*, newsstands, and station machines; they're valid for 1 metro ride or unlimited bus travel within 1hr. of validation. **BIG**

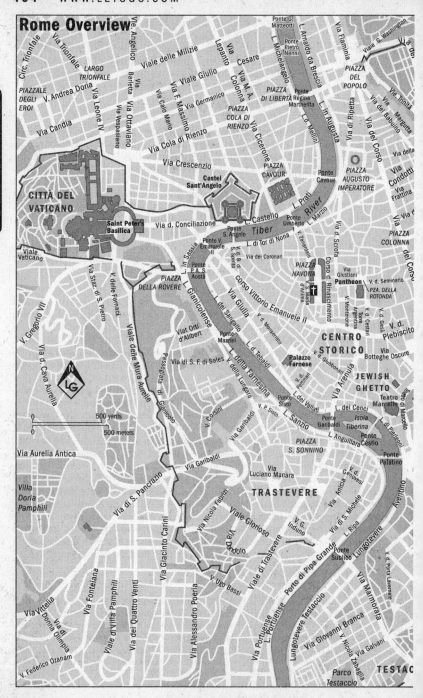

Rome Overview

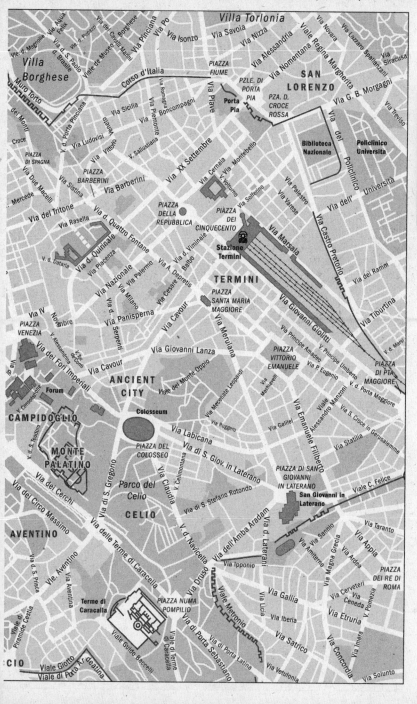

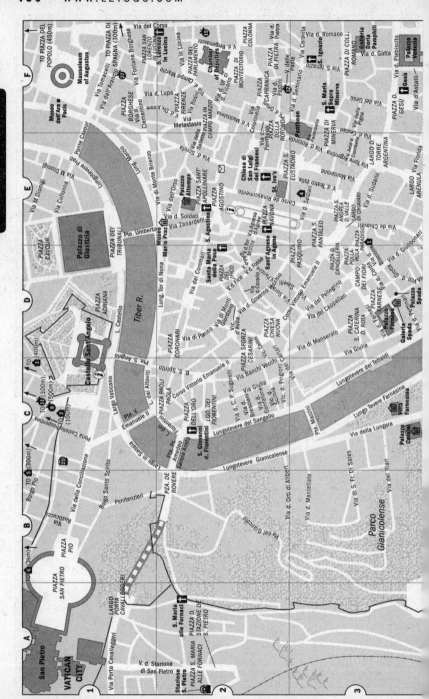

ITALY

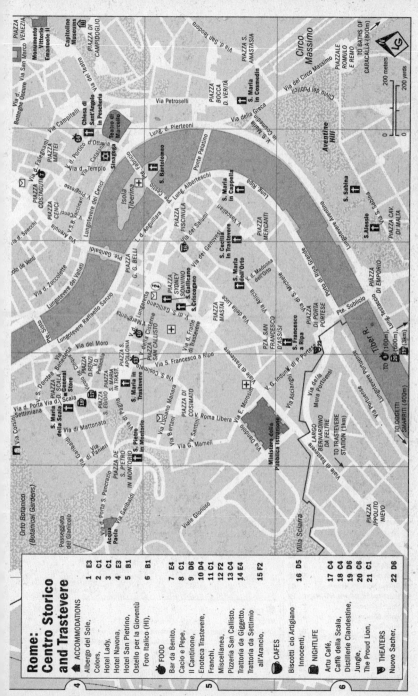

**Rome:
Centro Storico
and Trastevere**

🛏 ACCOMMODATIONS

Albergo del Sole,	1 E3
Colors,	2 C1
Hotel Lady,	3 C1
Hotel Navona,	4 E3
Hotel San Pietrino,	5 B1
Ostello per la Gioventù	
Foro Italico (HI),	6 B1

🍴 FOOD

Bar da Benito,	7 E4
Cacio e Pepe,	8 C1
Il Cantinone,	9 D6
Enoteca Trastevere,	10 D4
Franchi,	11 C1
Miscellanea,	12 F2
Pizzeria San Callisto,	13 C4
Trattoria da Gigetto,	14 E4
Trattoria da Settimio	
all'Arancio,	15 F2

☕ CAFES

Biscotti cio Artigiano	
Innocenti,	16 D5

🎵 NIGHTLIFE

Artu Café,	17 C4
Caffè della Scala,	18 C4
Distillerie Clandestine,	19 D6
Jungle,	20 C6
The Proud Lion,	21 C1

🎭 THEATERS

Nuovo Sacher,	22 D6

ITALY

Rome: Termini, San Lorenzo, and Via del Corso

ACCOMMODATIONS

Affittacamere Aries,	1	D1
Alessandro Downtown,	2	D4
Alessandro Legends,	3	D2
Alessandro Palace,	4	E2
Domus Nova Bethlehem,	5	C3
Hotel and Hostel des Artistes,	6	E2
Hotel Boccaccio,	7	B2
Hotel Bolognese,	8	E1
Hotel Cervia,	9	E2
Hotel Fontanella Borghese,	10	A1
Hotel Papa Germano,	11	D2
Hotel Scott House,	12	D4
Pensione Panda,	13	A1
Pensione Rosetta,	14	B4

FOOD

Africa,	15	E2
L'Antica Birreria Peroni,	16	B2
Arancia Blu,	17	F5
Il Brillo Parlante,	18	A1
I Buoni Amici,	19	D6
Enoteca Cavour 313,	20	B4
Hostaria da Bruno,	21	E3
Hostaria Romana da Dino,	22	E2
Luzzi,	23	C5
Trimani Wine Bar,	24	D2
Vini e Buffet,	25	A1

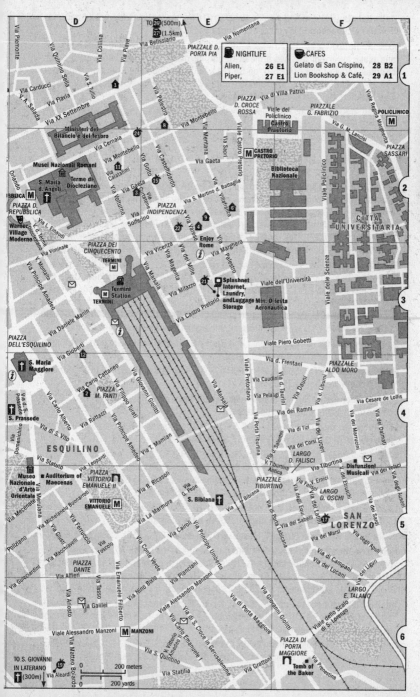

ITALY

TO 26 (500m)
27 (1.5km)

NIGHTLIFE
| Alien, | **26** E1 |
| Piper, | **27** E1 |

CAFES
| Gelato di San Crispino, | **28** B2 |
| Lion Bookshop & Café, | **29** A1 |

daily tickets (€4) and **CIS weekly tickets** (€16) allow for unlimited public transport. Beware: **pickpocketing** is rampant on buses and trains.

Taxis: Radiotaxi (☎06 35 70). Taxis are expensive. Ride only in yellow or white taxis, and make sure your taxi has a meter (if not, negotiate the price before riding). **Surcharges** apply at night (€2.60), on Su (€1), and when heading to or from Fiumicino (€7.25) or Ciampino (€5.50). Fares run about €11 from Termini to Vatican City, around €35 between the city center and Fiumicino.

Bike and Moped Rental: Bikes generally cost €5 per hr. or €10 per day while scooters cost €35-55 per day. Try **Bici & Baci,** V. del Viminale 5 (☎06 48 28 443; www.bicibaci.com). 16+. Open daily 8am-7pm. AmEx/MC/V.

ⓘ PRACTICAL INFORMATION

Tourist Office: ◼ **Enjoy Rome,** V. Marghera 8/A (☎06 44 56 890; www.enjoyrome.com). From the middle concourse of Termini, exit right, with the trains behind you; cross V. Marsala and follow V. Marghera for 3 blocks. The helpful, English-speaking staff makes reservations at museums, shows, and accommodations. They also lead walking tours (€27, under 26 €22). Pick up their detailed map and a *When in Rome* booklet. Open Apr.-Oct. M-F 8:30am-7pm, Sa 8:30am-2pm; Nov.-Mar. M-F 9am-6pm, Sa 9am-2pm.

Embassies: Australia, V. Antonio Bosio 5 (☎06 85 27 21; www.italy.embassy.gov.au). Open M-F 9am-5pm. **Canada,** V. Zara 30 (☎06 85 44 41; www.canada.it). Open M-F 9am-5pm. **Ireland,** P. di Campitelli 3 (☎06 69 79 121). **New Zealand,** V. Zara 28 (☎06 44 17 171). Open M-F 8:30am-12:45pm and 1:45-5pm. **UK,** V. XX Settembre 80a (☎06 42 20 00 01). Consular section open M-F 9:15am-1:30pm. **US,** V. Vittorio Veneto 119/A (☎06 46 741; www.usembassy.it/mission). Open M-F 8:30am-5:30pm.

Currency Exchange: Banca di Roma and **Banca Nazionale del Lavoro** have good rates, but the ubiquitous **ATMs** are an even better option. Open M-F 8:30am-1:30pm.

American Express: P. di Spagna 38 (☎06 67 641; lost cards 800 87 20 00). Open M-F 9am-5:30pm, Sa 9am-12:30pm.

Luggage Storage: In Termini Station, underneath track #24. €3.80 for first 5hr., €0.60 per hr. up to 12hr., €0.20 per hr. thereafter.

Lost Property: Oggetti Smarriti (☎06 58 16 040). On buses (☎06 58 16 040); Metro A (☎06 48 74 309); Metro B (☎06 57 53 22 65).

GLBT Resources: ARCI-GAY, V. Goito 35/B (☎06 64 50 11 02; www.arcigayroma.it). Open M-F 4-8pm. **Circolo Mario Mieli di Cultura Omosessuale,** V. Efeso 2/A (☎06 54 13 985; www.mariomieli.org). **Libreria Babele,** V. d. Banchi Vecchi. (☎06 68 76 628; www.libreriababeleroma.it). Library focusing on gay literature. Open M-Sa 11am-7pm.

Laundromat: ◼**Splashnet,** V. Varese 33 (☎06 49 38 04 50; www.splashnetrome.com), 3 blocks from Termini. *Let's Go* discount. Open daily 8:30am-11pm.

Pharmacies: Farmacia Piram, V. Nazionale 228 (☎06 48 80 754). Open 24hr. MC/V.

Hospitals: International Medical Center, V. Firenze 47 (☎06 48 82 371; www.imc84.com). Call ahead. Referral service to English-speaking doctors. General visit €100. Open M-Sa 9am-8pm; on-call 24hr. **Rome-American Hospital,** V.E. Longoni 69 (24hr. service ☎06 22 551, appointments 06 22 55 290; www.rah.it). Visits average €100-200.

Internet: Splashnet (see above). €1.50 per hr. **Yex Internet Points,** C. V. Emmanuele 106 (☎06 45 42 98 18). €2.90 per half hr., €4.80 per hr. Also offers wire transfer and currency exchange. Open daily 8am-9pm.

Post Office: Main Post Office (Posta Centrale), P. San Silvestro 19. Open M-F 8am-7pm, Sa 8am-1:15pm. Branch at V. d. Terme di Diocleziano 30, near Termini.

 ACCOMMODATIONS

Rome swells with tourists around Easter, May through July, and in September. Prices vary widely with the seasons, and proprietors are sometimes willing to negotiate rates. Termini swarms with hotel scouts. Many are legitimate and have IDs issued by tourist offices; however, beware of impostors with fake badges directing travelers to run-down locations charging exorbitant rates.

CENTRO STORICO AND ANCIENT CITY

Pensione Rosetta, V. Cavour 295 (☎06 47 82 30 69; www.rosettahotel.com), past the Fori Imperiali. Buzz at the large, wooden front doors and walk through the Vespa and palm-filled courtyard. Affordable for the location. Spacious rooms have baths, TVs, phones, and fans. A/C €5-10. Free Wi-Fi in lounge. Singles €50-60; doubles €85; triples €95; quads €120. AmEx/MC/V. ❸

Rome Student House, V. Merulana 117. From the Colosseum, walk down V. Labicana and make a left at V. Merulana. Buzz at the front and take Scala II to the 3rd floor. Make reservations beforehand so the owner, who occasionally cooks guests dinner, is not out when you arrive. Colorful rooms with fans, linens, and Wi-Fi. Check-out 10:30am. Reserve online (www.hostelworld.com). 4- to 6-person dorms €20-25. Cash only. ❷

VATICAN CITY

▨ **Colors,** V. Boezio 31 (☎06 68 74 030; www.colorshotel.com). Ⓜ A-Ottaviano. True to its name, Colors offers 18 beds in rooms painted with a verve that would put Raphael to shame. 2 hostel floors and a 3rd floor with private rooms. A/C. Kitchens and tranquil terraces on all floors. Breakfast included. Internet access €2 per hr. Reserve dorms by 9pm the night before; wise to book earlier. Dorms €27; singles €90, with bath €105; doubles €100/130; triples €120. Low season discount up to 30%. Cash only. ❷

Orange Hotel, V. Crescenzio 86 (☎06 68 68 969; www.orangehotelrome.com). Stylish, eco-friendly boutique hotel offers a lovely terrace with a solarium and a panoramic view over the cupola of San Pietro. Points for guessing the color scheme. Delightful amenities include a rooftop restaurant, parking garage, terrace hot tub, and in-hotel laundromat. All rooms with bathtubs, A/C, TVs, internet, safes, and minibars. Breakfast included. Doubles €93-174, junior suites 154-214; triples 158-218; extra beds available. AmEx/MC/V. ❺

TERMINI AND ENVIRONS

Welcome to budget traveler central. The accommodations around the **Termini station** are some of the least expensive and most centrally located in Rome. They also play host to the most backpackers and students, so look no further if a fun atmosphere is what you crave.

▨ **Alessandro Palace,** V. Vicenza 42 (☎06 44 61 958; www.hostelalessandropalace.com). From Termini's track 1, turn left on V. Marsala and right on V. Vicenza. Renovated dorms with baths and A/C. Fun bar with flatscreen TV and cheap drinks (happy hour; €3 beers daily 10-11pm). Fantastic English-speaking staff. Breakfast and pizza dinners included. Lockers free; supply your own lock. Internet (computer lounge and Wi-Fi) free 30min. per day; €1 per hr. thereafter. Check-in 3pm. Check-out 10am. 4- to 8-person dorms €25-35; doubles €110; triples and quads €44 per person. MC/V. ❷

▨ **Hotel Papa Germano,** V. Calatafimi 14/A (☎06 48 69 19; www.hotelpapagermano. com). From Termini, turn left on V. Marsala, which becomes V. Volturno, and take 4th right on V. Calatafimi. Clean, simple rooms with TVs. Helpful, English-speaking staff. Continental breakfast included. A/C €5; free fans. Free internet on 3 computers. Reception 24hr.

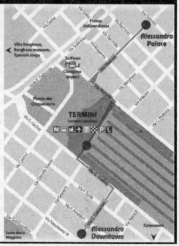

4-bed dorms €21-28; singles €35-50; doubles €50-80, with bath €60-105; triples €60-90/80-120; quads €85-120/95-140. AmEx/D/MC/V. ❷

The Yellow, V. Palestro 44 (☎06 49 38 26 82; www.the-yellow.com). From Termini, exit on V. Marsala, head down V. Marghera, and take the 4th left. Look no farther if you want to party hearty with people from all over the world. Huge rooms with stenciled *Blues Brothers* and *Pussy Wagon* logos accent this modern, chic youth hostel. Rocking hostel bar next door caters to guests. Lockers, linens, luggage storage, and fans included. A/C in rooms with bath. Breakfast €2. Free Wi-Fi in lounge. 4- to 12- person dorms with shared bath €10-30; 4- and 6-person dorms with private bath €10-34. €5 cash discount. AmEx/D/MC/V. ❶

Fawlty Towers Hotel and Hostel, V. Magenta 39, 5th fl. (☎06 44 50 374; www.fawltytowers.org). From Termini, cross V. Marsala onto V. Marghera and turn right on V. Magenta. Relaxed, bohemian feel. Brightly colored rooms. Comfortable common room with stained glass, TV, A/C, DVD player, book exchange, and free internet on 1 computer. Most rooms have A/C—ask for it when reserving, at no extra cost. Free lockers, linens, and towels. Kitchen with stocked fridge available for snacking. Free BBQs 2-3 F per month in summer on the sweet outdoor terrace. Reception 24hr. 3-bed dorms €25-30; 4-bed dorms €18-25; singles €30-55, with shower or full bath €35-60; doubles €45-70/50-85; triples €70-95/75-99; quads €80-100/80-110. Cash only; pay in advance. ❷

◪ FOOD

Traditional Roman cuisine includes *spaghetti alla carbonara* (egg and cream sauce with bacon), *spaghetti all'amatriciana* (thin tomato sauce with chiles and bacon), *carciofi alla giudia* (deep-fried artichokes, common in the Jewish Ghetto), and *fiori di zucca* (stuffed, fried zucchini flowers). Pizza is often a good and inexpensive option; like elsewhere in Italy, it is eaten with a fork and knife. Try *pizza romana*, which is like foccaccia: a flat bread with olive oil, sea salt, rosemary, and sometimes more toppings. Lunch is typically the main meal of the day, though some Romans now enjoy panini on the go during the week. Restaurants tend to close between 3 and 6:30pm.

CENTRO STORICO AND ANCIENT CITY

The area around the Forum and the Colosseum is home to some of Italy's finest tourist traps. Avoid the main streets.

▨ **Cul de Sac,** P. Pasquino 73 (☎06 68 80 10 94), off P. Navona. One of Rome's first wine bars. Substantial list of reasonably priced wines by the glass (from €2.50). At aperitif time, pair your pick with a snack like tuna, tomato and green bean salad, or the tasty *baba ghanoush*. Primi €7-8. Secondi €7-9. Open daily noon-4pm and 6pm-12:30am. AmEx/MC/V. ❷

▨ **L'Antica Birreria Peroni,** V. San Marcello 19 (☎06 67 95 310; www.anticabirreriap-eroni.it). From the Vittorio Emmanuele monument, turn right on V. Cesare Battisti and left into P. dei Santissimi Apostoli. 2 blocks down on the left. Energetic *enoteca* with a German twist and backlit beers tempting you from a ledge on the wall. Wash down a *wurstel* (€6-7) with 1 of 4 delicious Peroni beers on tap (€2-5). Fantastic *fiori di zucca* €1. Primi €6-7. Cover €1. Open M-Sa noon-midnight. AmEx/D/MC/V. ❷

Luzzi, V. San Giovanni in Laterano 88 (☎06 70 96 332), just down V. dei Fori Imperiali from the Colosseum. No-fuss *osteria* packed with locals. Specials like *pennette al sal-mone* (€7) will leave you wanting more. Enjoy inexpensive seafood (shrimp and prawns €10) and enough cheap wine to scuttle a liner (€4 per L). Primi €5-7. Secondi €7-11. Dessert €4. Open M-Tu and Th-Su noon-3pm and 7pm-midnight. AmEx/MC/V. ❷

Pizza Art, V. Arenula 76 (☎06 68 73 16 03 78). From C. V. Emanuele II, cut through Largo di Torre Argentina and walk toward the river. Counter seating only. Thick focaccia pizza topped with arugula, goat cheese, and fried treats including *suppli* (fried rice balls) and *crochette*. Most pizza €11-13 per kg; average slice €2.50. Open daily 8am-10pm. Cash only. ❶

VATICAN CITY

Cacio e Pepe, V. Giuseppe Avezzana 11 (☎06 32 17 268). From ⓜA-Ottaviano, take the V. Barletta exit; right onto V. de Milizie, then left onto V. Avezzana. Worth the walk. In summer, rub elbows with locals at the close-packed tables outside. Namesake specialty is perfectly *al dente*, topped with olive oil, grated cheese, and fresh-ground pepper (€6). Open M-F 12:30-3pm and 7:30-11pm, Sa 12:30-3pm. Cash only. ❷

La Tradizione, V. Cipro 8/e (☎06 39 72 03 49; www.latradizione.it). This gourmet store, steps from ⓜA-Cipro, has been educating palates for nearly 3 decades with a broad selection of fine meats, wines, and over 300 cheeses. Beautifully-prepared foods (including regional specialties) sold by the kg. A large meal €15. Open M 3-8:15pm, Tu-Sa 8am-2pm and 4:30-8:15pm. AmEx/MC/V. ❷

TRASTEVERE

🏛 **Giorgiagel,** V. di San Francesco a Ripa 130 (☎32 01 65 02 66 or 33 32 70 59 18). Turn right on V. de San Francesco a Ripa from Vle. Trastevere. Large portions of amazing Sicilian pastries and gelato that is right up there with Rome's best. Unbelievably decadent *cioccolato fondente* (dark chocolate) and intense *frutti di bosco* (forest fruit) make a great pair. Ingredients listed. Gelato €1.50-3. *Frappè* €2.50. Open daily 1pm-9pm. Cash only. ❶

🏛 **Da Simone,** V. Giacinto Carini 50 (☎06 58 14 980). From Acqua Paola on the Gianicolo hill, walk behind the fountain and down V. Giacomo Medici to the end of the street. Turn right, walk under the arches to V. Carini; it's behind the bus stop to the left. Treats you to fantastic pizza and prepared foods with only the best ingredients—fine extra virgin olive oil, buffalo mozzarella, and no animal fat. Priced by weight. Open M-Sa 7:30am-8:15pm. Cash only. ❶

Siven, V. di San Francesco a Ripa 137 (☎06 58 97 110). Northwest on V. de San Francesco a Ripa from Vle. Trastevere. A hole in the wall that sells tasty pizza and prepared pastas and meats (priced by weight) to a constant stream of locals, all of whom treat the chefs like old friends. Amazing spicy chicken and lasagna. Sizeable portion around €4. No seating. Open M-Sa 9am-10pm. Cash only. ❶

TERMINI AND ENVIRONS

San Lorenzo offers inexpensive food with local character to the budget-conscious student with a discriminating palate. There's a **Conad** supermarket on the lower floor of Termini Station (open daily 6am-midnight).

 LET'S NOT GO. Termini and the surrounding areas are unsafe at night. Stay alert and avoid walking alone in the neighborhood after dark.

Hostaria da Bruno, V. Varese 29 (☎06 49 04 03). Take V. Milazzo from V. Marsala and turn right on V. Varese. A bastion of authenticity in a sea of tourist traps. Try *tortellini al sugo* (meat tortellini) or *fettuccine alla gricia* (white amatriciana; €7) as you check out the pictures of founder Bruno with Pope John Paul II hanging on the wall. Open M-F noon-3pm and 7-10pm, Sa 7-10pm. AmEx/MC/V. ❷

Hostaria Romana da Dino, V. dei Mille 10 (☎06 49 14 25). From Termini's track 1, turn left on V. Marsala, right on V. Vicenza, and left on V. dei Mille. Delicious dishes for dirt-cheap prices. Loyal local following. Delectable pizza €5-7. Pasta €5-5.50. House wine €1.50 per ¼L. Open M-Tu and Th-Su 11:30am-3pm and 6:30-11pm. MC/V. ❶

AVENTINE AND TESTACCIO

P. Testaccio is just past V. Luca della Robbia. In the *piazza*, you will find **Testaccio Market,** a small market set up in metal huts. Numerous vendors offer fresh fruit, vegetables, meat, fish, pasta, candy, nuts, and a variety of prepared foods. (Prices vary, most by weight. Open M-Sa 6am-2pm. Cash only.)

◼ **Il Volpetti Più,** V. Alessandro Volta 8 (☎06 57 44 306; www.volpetti.com). Turn left on V. A. Volta, off V. Marmorata. Relive high school as you slide down the lunch line at this *tavola calda* (cafeteria)—but replace day-old sloppy joes with authentic Italian fare. Primi €6-7.50. Secondi €4-7.50. Fresh fish F €6-8. Desserts €4. Open M-Sa 10:30am-3:30pm and 5:30-9:30pm. AmEx/D/MC/V. ❷

Giacomini, V. Aventino 104-106 (☎06 57 43 645). Ⓜ️B-Circo Massimo. South on V. Aventino from the metro stop, past V. Licinia. Inside this *alimentari,* owner Claudio, certified *Maestro Salumiere Gastronomio,* prepares indescribably wonderful *panini* to order (€4-8) with the highest quality ingredients, as he has done for over 50 years. Wide selection of hand-picked meats and cheeses from only the best producers, priced by weight. Next door, his wife and daughter create similarly wonderful pizza. Open M-Sa 7:30am-2pm and 4:45-6:30pm. AmEx/MC/V. ❶

👁 SIGHTS

From ancient temples, medieval churches, and Renaissance basilicas to Baroque fountains and modern museums, *La Città Eterna* bursts with masterpieces. Travelers planning to visit many Roman monuments should consider the **Archeologica Card** (☎06 39 96 77 00; 7-day €22), valid at the Colosseum, Palantine Hill, and Baths of Caracalla, among other sites.

ANCIENT CITY

COLOSSEUM. This enduring symbol of the Eternal City—a hollowed-out marble structure that dwarfs every other ruin in Rome—once held as many as 50,000 spectators. Within 100 days of its AD 80 opening, some 5000 wild beasts perished in the arena. The floor once covered a labyrinth of brick cells, ramps, and elevators used to transport animals from cages up to arena level. Men were also infamously pitted against each other in gladiator competitions. (Ⓜ️B-Colosseo or bus 75 from Termini. ☎06 70 05 469. Open daily 8:30am-7:15pm. Last entry 6:15pm. ◼ Tour with archaeologists in Italian Sa-Su, English and Spanish daily every 30 min.-1 hr. 9:45am-5:15pm. Tours €4. Audio tour €4.50. Video tour €5.50. Combined tickets with Palatine Hill and Roman Forum €12, EU citizens 18-24 €7.50, EU citizens over 65 or under 18 free. Cash only.)

PALATINE HILL. Legend has it that the Palatine Hill was home to the she-wolf who suckled brothers Romulus and Remus, the mythical founders of Rome. The best way to attack the Palatine is from the stairs near the Forum's **Arch of Titus** (where ticket lines are shorter than at the Colosseum), which lead to gardens and lookouts. On the southwest side of the hill is an ancient village with the **Casa di Romulo,** alleged home of Romulus, and the podium of the **Temple of Cybele.** The stairs to the left lead to the **Casa di Livia,** home of Augustus's wife, which once connected to the **Casa Augusto** next door. Around the corner, the spooky **Cryptoporticus** tunnel ties Tiberius's palace to nearby buildings. **Domus Augustana** was the emperors' private space; sprawling **Domus Flavia,** to its right, held a gigantic octagonal fountain. Between them stands the **Stadium Palatinum,** or hippodrome, a sunken space once used as a riding school that is now a museum with artifacts excavated from the hill. (*South of the Forum. Same hours and prices as Colosseum. Guided English-language tour daily 12:15pm. €3.50.*)

> **IMBIBE THIS!** Remember that Rome's water is *potabile* (drinkable), and many fountains or spigots run throughout the city. Take a drink, or fill up your water bottle from these free sources of cold, refreshing *acqua naturale.*

ROMAN FORUM. Etruscans and Greeks used the Forum as a marketplace before early Romans founded a thatched-hut shanty town here in 753 BC. Enter through **Via Sacra,** Rome's oldest street, which leads to the **Arch of Titus.** The broad space in front of the Curia was the **Comitium,** where male citizens came to vote and representatives gathered for public discussion. Bordering the Comitium is the large brick **Rostra** (speaker's platform), erected by Julius Caesar in 44 BC. The **market square** holds a number of shrines and sacred precincts, including the *Lapis Nìger* (Black Stone), where Romulus was supposedly murdered by Republican senators; below are the underground ruins of a 6th-century BC altar and the oldest known Latin inscription in Rome. In the square, the **Three Sacred Trees of Rome**—olive, fig, and grape—have been replanted. The **Lower Forum** holds the 5th-century BC **Temple of Saturn,** which achieved mythological status during Rome's Golden Age, when it hosted Saturnalia, a raucous winter party. At the end of Vicus Tuscus stands the **Temple of Castor and Pollux,** built to celebrate the 499 BC Roman defeat of the Etruscans. The **Temple of Vesta,** where Vestal Virgins kept the city's sacred fire lit for more than 1000 years, is next to the **House of the Vestal Virgins,** where they lived for 30 secluded years beginning at the ripe old age of seven. *(Main entrance on V. dei Fori Imperiali, at Largo Corrado Ricci, halfway between P. Venezia and the Colosseum. ⓂB-Colosseo or bus to P. Venezia. Open in summer daily 8:30am-6:15pm; hours reduced in winter. Audio tour €4. Cash only.)*

FORI IMPERIALI. Closed indefinitely for excavations, the **Fori Imperiali,** across the street from the Ancient Forum, is a complex of temples, basilicas, and public squares constructed in the first and second centuries, still visible from the railing at V. dei Fori Imperiali. Built between AD 107 and 113, the **Forum of Trajan** included a colossal equestrian statue of Trajan and an immense triumphal arch. At one end of the now-destroyed Forum, 2500 carved legionnaires march their way up the almost perfectly preserved **Trajan's Column,** one of the greatest specimens of Roman relief-sculpture. The crowning statue is St. Peter, who replaced Trajan in 1588. The gray rock wall of the **Forum of Augustus** commemorates Augustus's victory over Caesar's murderers in 42 BC. The only remnant of **Vespasian's Forum** is the mosaic-filled **Chiesa della Santi Cosma e Damiano** across V. Cavour, near the Roman Forum. *(Reservations ☎06 67 97 702. English tour given Su at 4:30pm. €7. Inquire within the visitor's information center on V. dei Fori Imperiali.)*

CAPITOLINE HILL. Home to the original capitol, **Monte Capitolino** still serves as the seat of the city government. Michelangelo designed its **Piazza di Campidoglio,** now home to the **Capitoline Museums** (p. 472). Stairs lead up to the rear of the 7th-century **Chiesa di Santa Maria in Aracoeli.** *(Santa Maria open daily 9am-12:30pm and 3-6:30pm. Donation requested.)* The gloomy **Mamertine Prison,** consecrated as the **Chiesa di San Pietro in Carcere,** lies down the hill from the back stairs of the Aracoeli. Imprisoned here, St. Peter baptized his captors with the waters that flooded his cell. *(Prison open daily in summer 9am-7pm; in winter 9am-12:30pm and 2-5pm. Donation requested.)* At the far end of the *piazza,* opposite the stairs, lies the turreted **Palazzo dei Senatori,** the home of Rome's mayor. *(Take any bus to P. Venezia. From P. Venezia, walk around to P. d'Aracoeli and take the stairs up the hill.)*

VELABRUM. The Velabrum area is in a Tiber flood plain, south of the Jewish Ghetto. At the bend of V. del Portico d'Ottavia, a shattered pediment and a few columns are all that remain of the once magnificent **Portico d'Ottavia.** The **Teatro**

di Marcello next door was the model for the Colosseum's facade. One block south along V. Luigi Petroselli, the **Chiesa di Santa Maria in Cosmedin,** currently undergoing renovations, harbors the **Bocca della Verità,** a drain cover made famous by the film *Roman Holiday. (Chiesa open daily 9:30am-5:50pm.)*

DOMUS AUREA. Take a break from the relentless sun and enjoy the cacophony of birds chirping in the shady trees. Joggers, wild flowers, and ruins of a palatial estate now occupy Oppian Hill. This park houses a portion of Nero's "Golden House," which once covered a huge chunk of Rome. After deciding that he was a god, Nero had architects build a house worthy of his divinity. The Forum was reduced to a vestibule of the palace; Nero crowned it with the 35m *Colossus,* a huge statue of himself as the sun. *(Open daily 6:30am-9pm. Free.)*

CENTRO STORICO

VIA DEL CORSO AND PIAZZA VENEZIA. Shopping thoroughfare **Via del Corso,** so named because of its days as Ancient Rome's premier race course, runs between P. del Popolo and busy P. Venezia. **Palazzo Venezia** was one of the first Renaissance *palazzi* built in the city. Mussolini used it as an office and delivered his famous orations from its balcony, but today it's little more than a glorified roundabout dominated by the massive **Vittorio Emanuele II monument.** Off V. del Corso, the picturesque **Piazza Colonna** was named for the **Colonna di Marco Aurelio,** which imitated Trajan's column. Off the northwestern corner of the Piazza Colonoa is the **Piazza di Montecitorio,** home to Bernini's **Palazzo Montecitorio,** which is now the seat of the Chamber of Deputies.

THE PANTHEON. Architects still wonder how this 2000-year-old temple was erected. Its dome—a perfect half-sphere made of poured concrete without the support of vaults, arches, or ribs—is the largest of its kind. The light that enters the roof was used as a sundial; it also indicates the dates of equinoxes and solstices. In AD 606, it was consecrated as the **Chiesa di Santa Maria ad Martyres.** *(In P. della Rotonda. Open M-Sa 8:30am-7:30pm, Su 9am-6pm. Free.)*

PIAZZA NAVONA. Originally an AD first-century stadium, the *piazza* hosted wrestling matches, track and field events, and mock naval battles in which the stadium was flooded and filled with fleets. Each of the river god statues in Bernini's **Fountain of the Four Rivers** represents one of the four continents of the globe (as known in 1651): Ganges for Asia, Danube for Europe, Nile for Africa, and Río de la Plata for the Americas. *(Open daily 9am-noon and 4-7pm.)* C. V. Emanuele II runs to **Il Gesu,** inside which Andrea Pozzo's **Chapel of S. Ignazio** and Bernini's **Monument to S. Bellarmino** are must-sees. *(Open daily 6:45am-12:45pm and 4-7:45pm.)*

CAMPO DEI FIORI. Across C. Vittorio Emanuele II from P. Navona, Campo dei Fiori hosts a bustling, colorful, and quintessentially Italian open-air market. At night, the area transforms into a hot spot. You can find the Renaissance **Palazzo Farnese,** built by Alessandro Farnese (the first Counter-Reformation pope) in nearby P. Farnese, south of the Campo.

THE JEWISH GHETTO

Rome's Jewish community is the oldest in Europe—Israelites came in 161 BC as ambassadors from Judas Maccabei, asking for help against invaders. The Ghetto, a tiny area to which Pope Paul IV confined the Jews in 1555, was dissolved in 1870, but it still remains the center of Rome's Jewish population. In the center are **Piazza Mattei** and the 16th-century **Fontana delle Tartarughe.** Nearby is the **Chiesa di Sant'Angelo in Pescheria,** where Jews forced to attend mass resisted by stuffing wax in their ears. *(V. de Funari, after P. Campitelli. Church under restoration indefinitely.)* The **Sinagoga Ashkenazita,** on the Tiber near the Theater of

Marcellus, was bombed in 1982; guards now search all visitors. Inside is the **Jewish Museum,** which has ancient copies of the Torah and Holocaust artifacts. *(Synagogue open for services only. Museum open Oct.-May M-Th and Su 10am-10pm, F 10am-4pm; June-Sept. M-Th and Su 10am-7pm, F 9am-4pm. €7.50, students €3.)*

PIAZZA DI SPAGNA AND ENVIRONS

▓FONTANA DI TREVI. The bombastic **Fontana di Trevi** has enough presence to turn even the most jaded visitor into a romantic mush. Legend has it that a traveler who throws a coin into the fountain is ensured a speedy return to Rome; one who tosses two will fall in love there. Opposite is the Baroque **Chiesa dei Santi Vincenzo e Anastasio.** The crypt preserves the hearts and lungs of popes who served from 1590 to 1903. *(Open daily 7am-noon and 4-7pm.)*

SCALINATA DI SPAGNATHE (SPANISH STEPS). Designed by an Italian, paid for by the French, named for the Spaniards, occupied by the British, and currently featuring the American great Ronald McDonald, the **Spanish Steps** exude worldliness. The house to the right is where John Keats died; it's how the **Keats-Shelley Memorial Museum.** *(Open M-F 9am-1pm and 3-6pm, Su 11am-2pm and 3-6pm. €3.50.)*

PIAZZA DEL POPOLO. In the center of the "people's square"–once the venue for the execution of heretics–is the 3200-year-old **Obelisk of Pharaoh Ramses II** that Augustus brought back from Egypt in AD 10. The **Church of Santa Maria del Popolo** contains Renaissance and Baroque masterpieces. *(Open M-Sa 7am-noon and 4-7pm, Su 8am-1:30pm and 4:30-7:30pm.)* Two exquisite Caravaggios, *The Conversion of St. Paul* and *Crucifixion of St. Peter,* are in the **Cappella Cerasi,** which Raphael designed. *(Open M-Sa 7am-noon and 4-7pm, Su 7:30am-1:30pm and 4:30-7:30pm.)*

VILLA BORGHESE. To celebrate his purchase of a cardinalship, Scipione Borghese built the **Villa Borghese** north of P. di Spagna and V. V. Veneto. Its huge park houses three fantastic art museums: world-renowned **Galleria Borghese** (p. 471), airy **Galleria Nazionale d'Arte Moderna,** and intriguing **Museo Nazionale Etrusco di Villa Giulia.** North of the Borghese are the **Santa Priscilla catacombs** and the **Villa Ada** gardens. *(M: A-Spagna. Open M-F 9:30am-6pm, Sa-Su 9:30am-7pm. €8.50.)*

VATICAN CITY

Once the mightiest power in Europe, the administrative and spiritual center of the Roman Catholic Church now lies on 108 autonomous acres within Rome. The Vatican has symbolically preserved its independence by minting coins, running a separate press and postal system, maintaining an army of Swiss Guards, and hoarding art in the **Musei Vaticani.** *(M: A-Ottaviano. Or catch bus #64, 271, or 492 from Termini or Largo Argentina, #62 from P. Barberini, or #23 from Testaccio.)*

BASILICA DI SAN PIETRO (ST. PETER'S). A famous colonnade by Bernini leads from **Piazza San Pietro** to the church. The **obelisk** in the *piazza*'s center is framed by two fountains; stand on the round discs set in the pavement and the quadruple rows of the colonnade will visually resolve into one perfectly aligned row. Above the colonnade are 140 statues of saints; those on the basilica represent Christ, John the Baptist, and the Apostles (except for Peter). The pope opens the **Porta Sancta** (Holy Door) every 25 years by knocking on the bricks with a silver hammer; on warm Wednesday mornings, he holds papal audiences on a platform in the *piazza.* The basilica itself rests on the reputed site of St. Peter's tomb. Inside, metal lines mark the lengths of other major world churches. To the right, Michelangelo's *Pietà* has been protected by bullet-proof glass since 1972, when an axe-wielding fiend smashed Christ's nose and broke Mary's hand. The climb to the top of the **dome** might very well be worth the heart attack it could cause. An elevator will take you up about 300 of the 350 stairs. *(Modest dress required. Multilingual confession available. Church: open daily Apr.-Sept. 7am-7pm; Oct.-Mar. 7am-6pm. Mass M-Sa 8:30, 9, 10, 11am, noon, 5pm; Su 9, 10:30, 11:30am, 12:15, 1, 4, 5, 5:30pm. Free. Dome: From inside the basilica, exit the building and re-enter the door to the far left. Open daily Apr.-Sept. 8am-5pm; Oct.-Mar. 8am-4pm. Stairs €4, elevator €7.)*

SISTINE SIGHTSEEING. The Sistine Chapel is at the end of the standard route through the Vatican Museums (p. 471), and it's usually extremely crowded. Go straight to the Sistine Chapel to enjoy Michelangelo's masterpiece, and then backtrack. It's relatively empty early in the morning.

SISTINE CHAPEL. Since its completion in the 16th century, the Sistine Chapel (named for its founder, Pope Sixtus IV) has served as the chamber in which the College of Cardinals elects new popes. Michelangelo's glorious ceiling, which depicts stories from Genesis, gleams post-restoration. *The Last Judgment* fills the altar wall; the figure of Christ, as judge, sits in the upper center surrounded by saints and Mary. Michelangelo painted himself as a flayed human skin hanging between heaven and hell. The cycle was completed in 1483 by artists under Perugino, including Botticelli, Ghirlandaio, Roselli, Pinturicchio, Signorelli, and della Gatta. The frescoes on the side walls predate Michelangelo's ceiling. *(Admission included with Vatican Museums, p. 471.)*

CASTEL SANT'ANGELO. Built by Hadrian (AD 117-138) as a mausoleum for himself and his family, this mass of brick and stone has been a fortress, prison, and palace. When the plague struck Rome, Pope Gregory the Great saw an angel at its top; the plague soon abated, and the edifice was rededicated to the angel. The fortress offers an incomparable view of Rome. *(Walk along the river from St. Peter's toward Trastevere. Open daily 9am-7pm. €5. Audio tour €4.)*

TRASTEVERE

Right off the **Ponte Garibaldi** stands the statue of the famous dialect poet G. G. Belli. On V. di Santa Cecilia, through the gate and beyond the courtyard, is the **Basilica di Santa Cecilia in Trastevere.** Carlo Maderno's famous statue of Santa Cecilia lies under the altar. *(Open daily 9:30am-12:30pm and 4-6:30pm. Donation requested. Cloisters open M-F 10:15am-12:15pm, Sa-Su 11:15am-12:15pm. Cloisters €2.50. Crypt €2.50.)* From P. Sonnino, V. della Lungaretta leads west to P. S. Maria in Trastevere, home to stray dogs, expatriates, and the **Chiesa di Santa Maria in Trastevere,** built in the 4th century. *(Open M-Sa 9am-5:30pm, Su 8:30-10:30am and noon-5:30pm.)* North of the *piazza* are the Rococo **Galleria Corsini,** V. della Lungara 10, and the **Villa Farnesina** (p. 472), once home to Europe's wealthiest man. Atop the Gianicolo Hill is the **Chiesa di San Pietro in Montorio,** built on the spot believed to be the site of St. Peter's upside-down crucifixion. The church contains del Piombo's *Flagellation.* Next door is Bramante's tiny ◪**Tempietto,** characterized by a combination of ancient and Renaissance architecture; it commemorates St. Peter's martyrdom. Rome's **botanical gardens** have a rose garden that holds the bush from which all the world's roses are supposedly descended. *(Church and Tempietto open Tu-Su May-Oct. 9:30am-12:30pm and 4-6pm; Nov.-Apr. 9:30am-12:30pm and 2-4pm. Gardens open M-Sa Oct.-Mar. 9:30am-5:30pm; Apr.-Oct. 9:30am-6:30pm.)*

NEAR TERMINI

◪**PIAZZA DEL QUIRINALE.** At the southeast end of V. del Quirinale, this *piazza* occupies the summit of one of Ancient Rome's seven hills. In its center, the enormous statues of Castor and Pollux stand on either side of an obelisk from the Mausoleum of Augustus. The President of the Republic resides in the **Palazzo del Quirinale,** its Baroque architecture by Bernini, Maderno, and Fontana. Farther along the street lies the facade of Borromini's **Chiesa di San Carlo alle Quattro Fontane.** Bernini's ▓**Four Fountains** are built into the intersection of V. delle Quattro Fontane and V. del Quirinale. *(Palazzo closed to the public. Chiesa open daily 8:30am-12:30pm and 3:30-6pm.)*

BASILICA OF SANTA MARIA MAGGIORE. Crowning the Esquiline Hill, this gigantic basilica is officially part of Vatican City. To the right of the altar beneath the stunning coffered ceiling, a marble slab marks **Bernini's tomb.** The 14th-century mosaics in the **loggia** *(open daily with guided tour at 1pm; €5)* depict the August snowfall that showed the pope where to build the church; the snowstorm is re-enacted each August with white flower petals. *(Modest dress required. Open daily 7am-7pm. Museum open 9:30am-6:30pm. Suggested donation €4. Audio tour €4.)*

SOUTHERN ROME

The area south of the center, a mix of wealthy and working-class neighborhoods, is home to the city's best nightlife and some of its grandest churches.

▓**APPIAN WAY.** The Appian Way was the most important thoroughfare of Ancient Rome. Early Christians secretly constructed maze-like catacombs under the ashes of their persecutors. On Sundays, when the street is closed to traffic, take a break from the city to bike through the countryside. *(M: B-S. Giovanni to P. Appio; take bus #218 from P. di S. Giovanni to V. Appia Antica and get off at the info office.)* **San Callisto** is the largest catacomb in Rome. Its four levels once held 16 popes, St. Cecilia, and 500,000 other Christians. *(V. Appia Antica 126, entrance on road parallel to V. Appia. Open M-Tu and Th-Su 9am-noon and 2-5pm. €5.)* Catacomb **Santa Domitilla** houses an intact 3rd-century portrait of Christ and the Apostles. *(V. delle Sette Chiese 282. Facing V. Ardeatina from the San Callisto exit, cross the street and walk right up V. Sette Chiese. Open Feb.-Dec. M and W-Su 9am-noon and 2-5pm. €5. Cash only.)*

CAELIAN HILL. Southeast of the Colosseum, the Caelian was the hill where elite Romans made their home in ancient times. The ▓**Chiesa di San Giovanni in Laterano** was the seat of the papacy until the 14th century; founded by Constantine in AD 314, it is Rome's oldest Christian basilica. Outside to the left, **Scala Santa** has what are believed to be the 28 steps used by Jesus outside Pontius Pilate's home. *(Modest dress required. M: A-S. Giovanni or bus #16. Open daily 7am-6:30pm. €2, students €1.)* The **Chiesa di San Clemente** is split into three levels, each from a different era. A fresco cycle by Masolino dating from the 1420s graces its **Chapel of Santa Caterina.** *(M: B-Colosseo. Turn left down V. Labicana away from the Forum. Open M-Sa 9am-12:30pm and 3-6pm, Su 10am-12:30pm and 3-6pm. €5, students €3.50.)*

AVENTINE HILL. The **Roseto Comunale,** a public rose garden, is host to the annual Premio Roma, the worldwide competition for the best blossom. *(V. d. Valle Murcia, across the Circus Maximus from the Palatine Hill. Open May-June daily 8am-7:30pm.)* Just before the crest of the hill, stroll among orange trees at **Giardini degli Aranci.** *(Open daily dawn-dusk.)* The top left-hand panel of the wooden front doors at nearby **Chiesa di Santa Sabina** is one of the earliest-known representations of the Crucifixion. V. S. Sabina runs along the crest of the hill to **Piazza dei Cavalieri di Malta,** home of the order of the Knights of Malta. Look through the ▓**keyhole** in the arched gate: there is a perfectly framed view of the dome of St. Peter's Cathedral.

EUR. South of the city is a residential area that remains as a memento of the second Roman Empire that never was. EUR (AY-oor) is the Italian acronym for Universal Exposition of Rome, the 1942 World's Fair that Mussolini intended to be a showcase of Fascist achievement—apparently, this involved the ability to build lots of identical square buildings. **Via Cristoforo Colombo,** EUR's main street, runs north from the metro station to **Piazza Guglielmo Marconi** and its 1959 **obelisk.** There is also a scenic artificial lake surrounded by jogging paths. The nearby hills are a popular lounging spot. *(M: B-EUR Palasport or take bus #714.)*

🏛 MUSEUMS

Etruscans, emperors, and popes have been busily stuffing Rome with artwork for several millennia, leaving behind a city teeming with collections. Museums are generally closed on Mondays, Sunday afternoons, and holidays.

GALLERIA BORGHESE. Upon entering, don't miss Mark Antonio's **ceiling,** which depicts the Roman conquest of Gaul. **Room I,** on the right, houses Canova's steamy statue of **Paolina Borghese** portrayed as Venus triumphant, reclining with Paris's golden apple. The next rooms display some of Bernini's most monumental sculptures: a striking **David,** crouching with his slingshot; **Apollo and Daphne;** the weightless body in **Rape of Proserpina;** and weary-looking Aeneas in **Eneo e Anchise.** The dark paintings in the **Caravaggio Room** include *Self Portrait as Bacchus* and *David and Goliath.* The collection continues in the **pinacoteca** upstairs, which is accessible from the gardens around the back by a winding staircase. **Room IX** holds Raphael's ▧**Deposition** while Sodoma's *Pietà* graces **Room XII.** Look for del Conte's *Cleopatra and Lucrezia,* Rubens's *Pianto sul Cristo Morto,* and Titian's *Amor Sacro e Amor Profano. (Vle. del Museo Borghese. M: A-Spagna; take the Villa Borghese exit. ☎ 06 32 810. Open Tu-Su 8:30am-7:30pm. Entrance every 2hr. Reserve ahead, especially for large groups. Tickets €8.50. Audio tour €5.)*

VATICAN MUSEUMS. The Vatican Museums constitute one of the world's greatest art collections; plan to spend at least four hours exploring them. Ancient, Renaissance, and modern statues and paintings are rounded out with papal odds and ends. The **Museo Pio-Clementino** has the world's greatest collection of antique sculpture. Two Molossian hounds guard the entrance to the **Stanza degli Animali,** a marble menagerie. Other gems include the ▧**Apollo Belvedere** and **Hercules.** From the last room, the Simonetti Stairway climbs to the **Museo Etrusco,** filled with artifacts from Tuscany and northern Lazio. Back on the landing of the Simonetti Staircase is the **Stanza della Biga** (ancient marble chariot room) and the **Galleria della Candelabra** (chandelier). The long trudge to the Sistine Chapel begins here, passing through the **Galleria degli Arazzi** (tapestries),

TOP TEN PLACES TO SMOOCH IN ROMA

While you may be close enough to pucker up with strangers on the subway, save your saliva for these dreamy destinations.

1. Stroll through **Villa Borghese** (p. 471), find a secluded, shaded spot, and go in for the kill.
2. Bottle of red. Bottle of white. **Trevi Fountain** (p. 468) at night.
3. With the sun setting behind St. Peter's and the swirling Tiber beneath you, **Ponte Sisto** is the perfect place to lay it on. Hard.
4. St. Peter's Square (p. 468). Just try and keep it PG—his Holiness may be watching.
5. Look out over **Circus Maximus** (p. 465) from Palatine Hill and imagine thousands of fans cheering on you and your sweetie.
6. The terrace of the **Vittorio Emanuele II** monument. There's a reason people call this spot the "wedding cake."
7. Top of the **Spanish Steps** (p. 468). If it fails, you can always push the person down them.
8. Waiting for the **Metro.** You'd be surprised—it can get pretty steamy. Plus you'll make a stranger's day.
9. Chiesa di Santa Maria in Cosmedin (p. 481). Forget chocolates and roses; the skull and relics of St. Valentine are the key ingredient in any love potion.
10. Over a shared bowl of spaghetti, *Lady and the Tramp* style.

the **Galleria delle Mappe** (maps), the **Apartamento di Pio V** (where there is a sneaky shortcut to *la Sistina*), the **Stanza Sobieski**, and the **Stanza della Immaculata Concezione**. A door leads into the first of the four ▇**Stanze di Rafaele**, apartments built for Pope Julius II in the 1510s. One *stanza* features Raphael's **School of Athens**, painted as a trial piece for Julius, who was so impressed that he fired his other painters and commissioned Raphael to decorate the entire suite. From here, there are two paths: a staircase leading to the brilliantly frescoed Borgia Apartments, which house the **Museum of Modern Religious Art,** and another route leading to the Sistine Chapel (p. 469). On the way out of the Sistine Chapel, take a look at the **Room of the Aldobrandini Marriage**, which contains a series of rare, ancient Roman frescoes. Finally, the Vatican's painting collection, the **pinacoteca,** spans eight centuries and is one of the best in Rome. It includes Perugino's *Madonna and Child*, Titian's *Madonna of San Nicoletta dei Frari*, and Raphael's *Transfiguration*. *(Walk north from P.S. Pietro along the wall of the Vatican City for 10 blocks. ☎06 69 88 49 47; www.vatican.va. Open M-Sa 8:30am-6pm. Last entrance 2hr. before closing. €13, with ISIC €8. Also open last Su of the month 8:30am-12:30pm. Free.)*

> **ARE WE THERE YET?** Lines for the Vatican Museums begin forming around 6:30am and become increasingly unbearable as the hours pass. It's not a bad idea to drag yourself out of your rock-hard hostel bed at an ungodly hour if you want to avoid the long wait.

MUSEI CAPITOLINI. This collection of ancient sculpture is the world's first public museum of ancient art. Pope Clemente XII bought the *palazzo* in 1733 to exhibit Cardinal Alessandro Albani's ancient sculptures. The Palazzo dei Conservatori's courtyard contains fragments of the frightening **Colossus of Constantine.** The original statue of **Marcus Aurelius,** Bernini's interesting **Head of Medusa,** and the famous **Capitoline Wolf**—a statue that has symbolized the city of Rome since antiquity—occupy the first floor. At the top of the stairs, the **pinacoteca's** masterpieces include Bellini's *Portrait of a Young Man,* Caravaggio's *St. John the Baptist and Gypsy Fortune-Teller,* Rubens's *Romulus and Remus Fed by the Wolf,* and Titian's *Baptism of Christ. (On Capitoline Hill behind the Vittorio Emanuele II monument. ☎06 82 05 91 27. Open Tu-Su 9am-8pm. €6.50-8, students with ISIC €4.50-6.)*

VILLA FARNESINA. The villa was the sumptuous home of Europe's one-time wealthiest man, Agostino "il Magnifico" Chigi. To the right of the entrance lies the breathtaking **Sala di Galatea,** a vault displaying astrological signs and showing the stars as they were at 9:30pm on November 29, 1466, the moment of Agostino's birth. The room's masterpiece is Raphael's **Triumph of Galatea.** The ceiling of the **Loggia di Psiche** depicts the marriage of Cupid and Psyche. Returning to the entrance, a stucco-ceilinged stairway, with gorgeous perspective detail, ascends to Peruzzi's **Salone delle Prospettive,** which incorporates five different colored marbles in the floor design and offers views of Rome between columns. The adjacent bedroom, known as the **Stanza delle Nozze** (Marriage Room), is a highlight. A maze of stolen commissions between Raphael and Il Sodoma led to the latter's creating a masterful fresco of Alexander the Great's marriage to Roxane. *(V. della Lungara 230. Across from Palazzo Corsini on Lungotevere della Farnesina. Bus #23, 271, or 280; get off at Lungotevere della Farnesina or Ponte Sisto. ☎06 68 02 72 67. Open M-Sa 9am-1pm; 1st Su of the month 9am-1pm. Last entry 12:40pm. €5.)*

MUSEO NAZIONALE D'ARTE ANTICA. This collection of 12th- through 18th-century art is split between Palazzo Barberini and Palazzo Corsini. **Palazzo Barberini** contains paintings from the medieval through Baroque periods, and **Palazzo Corsini** features works by Caravaggio, El Greco, and Raphael. *(V. Barberini 18. M:*

A-Barberini. Bus #62 or 492. ☎06 48 14 591. Open Tu-Su 8:30am-7:30pm. €5.) **Galleria Corsini** holds works by 17th- and 18th-century painters, from Rubens to Caravaggio. *(V. della Lungara 10. Opposite Villa Farnesina in Trastevere. Take bus #23 to between Ponte Mazzini and Ponte Sisto. ☎06 22 58 24 93. Open Tu-Su 8:30am-7:30pm. €4.)*

GALLERIA SPADA. Cardinal Bernardino Spada bought an imposing assortment of paintings and sculpture and commissioned an even more impressive set of rooms to house them. Time and good luck have left the palatial 17th-century apartments nearly intact; a visit to the gallery offers a glimpse of the luxury surrounding Baroque courtly life. In **Room 1,** the modest cardinal hung portraits of himself by Cerini, Guercino, and Reni. In **Room 2,** look for paintings by Venetians Tintoretto and Titian and a frieze by Vaga, originally intended for the Sistine Chapel. **Room 4** has three canvases by the father-daughter team of Orazio and Artemisia Gentileschi. *(P. Capo d. Ferro 13, in the Palazzo Spada. Bus #64. ☎06 68 32 409. Open Tu-Su 8:30am-7:30pm. Guided tour Su 10:45am from museum bookshop. €5.)*

MUSEI NAZIONALI ROMANI. The fascinating **Museo Nazionale Romano Palazzo Massimo alle Terme** is devoted to the history of art during the Roman Empire, and features the *Lancellotti Discus Thrower* and a rare Nero-era mosaic. *(Largo di V. Peretti 1, in P. dei Cinquecento. Open Tu-Su 9am-7:45pm.)* Nearby, the **Museo Nazionale Romano Terme di Diocleziano,** a beautifully renovated complex partly housed in the huge **Baths of Diocletian,** has exhibits on ancient epigraphy (writing) and a Michelangelo cloister. *(V. Enrico de Nicola 78. Open Tu-Su 9am-7:45pm.)* The **Aula Ottogonale** holds classical sculptures. *(V. Romita 8. Open daily 9am-1pm. Free.)* Across town, the **Museo Nazionale Romano Palazzo Altemps** displays the 5th-century *Ludovisi Throne.* *(P. Sant'Apollinare 44, just north of P. Navona. Open Tu-Su 9am-7:45pm. €5. Audio tour €4. Combo ticket for Diocleziano, Crypta Balbi, and Palazzo Altemps €9.)*

🎵 ENTERTAINMENT

The weekly *Roma C'è* and *Time Out,* both available at newsstands, have comprehensive and up-to-date club, movie, and event listings.

THEATER AND CINEMA

The **Festival Roma-Europa** (www.romaeuropa.net) in late summer brings a number of world-class acts to Rome. **Teatro Argentina,** Largo di Torre Argentina 52, is the matriarch of all Italian theater venues, with year-round performances. (☎06 684 00 01 11. Box office open M-F 10am-2pm and 3-7pm, Sa 10am-2pm. Tickets €14-26, students €12-21. AmEx/MC/V.) **Teatro Colosseo,** V. Capo d'Africa 5/A, usually features work by foreign playwrights translated into Italian, but also hosts an English-language theater night. (☎06 70 04 932. M: B-Colosseo. Box office open Sept.-Apr. Tu-Sa 6-9:30pm. Tickets €10-20, students €8.)

Most English-language films are dubbed in Italian; for films in their original languages, check newspapers for listings marked **v.o.** or **l.o.** The theater of Italian director Nanni Moretti, **Nuovo Sacher,** Largo Ascianghi 1, shows independent films. (☎06 58 18 116. Films in the original language M-Tu. €7, matinee €4.50.)

MUSIC

Founded by Palestrina in the 16th century, the **Accademia Nazionale di Santa Cecilia,** V. Vittoria 6, off V. del Corso (☎06 36 11 064 or 800 90 70 80; www.santacecilia.it), remains the best in classical music performance. Concerts are held at the **Parco della Musica,** V. Pietro di Coubertin 30, near P. del Popolo (www.musicaperroma.it. Tickets at Parco della Musica. Regular season runs Sept.-June. €15, students €8.) Known as one of Europe's best jazz clubs, **Alexanderplatz Jazz Club,** V. Ostia 9, is decorated with messages left on its walls by old greats. The club moves outside to the Villa Celimontana during summer. (☎06 39 74 21 71; www.alexanderplatz.it. M: A-Ottaviano. Required membership €10. Open daily Sept.-May 9pm-2am. Shows start at 10pm.) The **Cornetto Free Music Festival Roma Live** (www.cornettoalgida.it) has attracted the likes of Pink Floyd and the Black Eyed Peas; it takes place at various venues during the summer.

SPECTATOR SPORTS

Though May brings tennis and equestrian events, sports revolve around *calcio*, or football. Rome has two teams in *Serie A*, Italy's prestigious league: **S.S. Lazio** and **A.S. Roma**. Matches are held at the **Stadio Olimpico**, in Foro Italico, almost every Sunday from September to June. Tickets (from €16) can be bought at team stores like **A.S. Roma**, P. Colonna 360 (☎06 67 86 514; www.asroma.it. Tickets sold daily 10am-6:30pm. AmEx/MC/V), and **Lazio Point**, V. Farini 34/36, near Termini. (☎06 48 26 688. Open daily 9am-7pm. AmEx/MC/V.) Tickets can also be obtained at the stadium before games, but beware of long lines. If you're buying last minute, watch out for overpriced or fake tickets.

▣ NIGHTLIFE

Romans find nighttime diversion at the pubs of San Lorenzo, the clubs of Testaccio, and everywhere in between. Pick up *Roma C'è* for updates on clubs' openings and closings. *Time Out* covers Rome's sparse but solid collection of gay nightlife listings, many of which require an **ARCI-GAY pass** (1 year. €10). Also check with **Circolo di Cultura Omosessuale Mario Mieli** (☎06 54 13 985).

ANCIENT CITY

Oppio Caffè, V. delle Terme de Tito 72 (☎06 47 45 262; www.oppiocaffe.it). ⓂB-Colosseo. Step into a neon paradise. Color-changing lights and funky art surround a pit with translucent tables in this hip bar overlooking one of history's bloodiest arenas. Check out your dreads in the reflective metal ceiling and get your thump on as DJs pump out indie-electronic beats. Mixed drinks €7. M, W, F-Su DJs. Live music 1 Th per month. Wheelchair-accessible. Open daily 7am-2am. AmEx/D/MC/V over €15.

Tree Folk's, V. Capo d'Africa 29 (☎ 06 97 61 52 72). ⓂB-Colosseo. The music and decor is a cocktail of American, German, and British classics in this creative pub that caters to your inner beer connoisseur with 10 delectable taps (€5). You'll have to be drunk to understand why the special Summer Lightning beer is only imported during the winter. Mutton €7-12. Massively delicious salads €7-10. Wine €5 per glass. Wheelchair-accessible. Open daily 7pm-2am. D/MC/V.

CENTRO STORICO

Société Lutèce, Vco. di Montevecchio 17 (☎06 68 30 14 72). Take V. di Parione from V. del Governo Vecchio; bear straight and then make a left onto Vco. di Montevecchio. Effortlessly hip. The perfect place for a pre- or post-dinner drink. Wine €6 per glass. Mixed drinks €7-8. The vaguely Middle Eastern apertif buffet is fresh, yummy, substantial, and included. Wheelchair accessible. Open daily 6pm-2am. MC/V.

Sloppy Sam's, P. Campo dei Fiori 9 (☎06 68 80 26 37). This popular pub is packed with visiting students even on a Tuesday. Numerous drink specials and a window on the action on Campo dei Fiori. Wheelchair accessible. Happy hour M-F 4pm-8pm; bottled beer and pints €4, mixed drinks €6.50, house win €3 per glass. Other specials nightly, some requiring student ID. Open daily 4pm-2am. AmEx/MC/V.

Rialto Santambrogio, V. de Sant' Ambrogio 4 (☎06 68 13 36 40; www.rialto.roma.it). Easiest to approach from V. del Portico. Tucked away in the Jewish Ghetto in a more or less unmarked building; pay close attention to the street numbers. Rialto isn't a bar,

ITALY

pub, club, or *discotheque:* it's a *centro sociale,* where serious scenesters meet to hear music, dance to visiting DJs, see art, and talk left politics. No such thing as regular hours—your best bet's to check the website for a schedule of events.

TRASTEVERE

▨ **Bir & Fud,** V. Benedetta 23 (☎06 58 94 016; www.birefud.it), behind the P. Trilussa fountain. Delicious, frequently changing Italian craft beers flow from about 20 taps and all organic food graces plates in this taste bud heaven. Co-owner and brewmaster Leonardo takes a break from perfecting his own highly original and uniformly amazing beers at the Birra del Borgo brewery (birradelborgo.it) to come by and engage other beer connoisseurs on weekends. Try the Ke-To Re-Porter (a lighter porter spiced with fermented Kentucky tobacco), the My Antonia (a savory brew originating from a partnership between Leonardo and the Dogfish Head brewmaster), the Rubus (a refreshing raspberry beer with all the fruit but none of the heaviness of a lambic), or the Opperbacco Tripllpa (a cross between a Belgian triple and an IPA with amarillo accents). Beer €5-70. Pizza €5-12. Open daily 7pm-2am. AmEx/D/MC/V.

Ma Che Siete Venuti A Fà, V. Benedetta 25 (☎06 97 27 52 18; www.football-pub. com), behind the P. Trilussa fountain. Owned by the same beer luminaries as Bir & Fud, this smaller counterpart across the street specializes in unpasteurized, unfiltered beers hand-picked from international breweries on beer scouting trips. There is absolutely nothing but the 16 taps, 100+ bottled beers, and their fans in the tiny wooden shack of an interior, filled with soccer memorabilia and kegs, and no loud music to take the focus off of malt beverages and good conversation. Try the Montegioco Makkestout, a dry stout with excellent mouth feel brewed especially for the bar. Pints and 33cl bottles €5, 75cl bottles €15. Open daily 3pm-2am. Cash only.

TESTACCIO AND OSTIENSE

▨ **L'Oasi della Birra,** P. Testaccio 38/41 (☎06 57 46 122; www.ristorantidiroma.com/oasi. htm). From V. Marmorata, turn left on V. A. Manuzio and right on P. Testaccio. You'll think it's a mirage in the middle of the club desert until you pay the bill. Enjoy affordable, incredibly delicious drinks and food before getting sloshed on expensive, bad selections on the dance floors in the area. The beer catalog boasts over 500 types from all over the world, arranged by region and type (most bottles €4.50), and there is a selection of wines (€10+ per bottle) and grappa in the quadruple digits. Gourmet meats and cheeses are similarly numerous and delectable (try 6 types for €15.50, 8 for €18.50). Happy hour daily 5-8:15pm; food and a drink €10. Open daily 5pm-midnight. AmEx/D/MC/V.

▨ **Akab,** V. di Monte Testaccio 69 (☎06 57 25 05 85; www.akabcave.com). One of Rome's most famous clubs has the potential for entirely different scenes every night on each of 3 dance floors. Advanced ventilation and an expensive permit allow smoking on the primary floor, a large area covered by a metal roof and flanked by a blue-lit bar on one side and a red-lit private table area on the other. Tu techno; Th hip-hop, R&B, and rap; F-Sa pop and mix. If you get in, get ready to rub elbows with tons of Rome's hippest club-goers doing their thing and possibly some famous musical talents (50 Cent and Fabolous performed here in 2009). Drinks €10. Cover €10-15 includes 1 drink. Open Tu and Th-Sa 10:30pm-4:30am. AmEx/D/MC/V.

▨ DAYTRIP FROM ROME: TIVOLI

From M: B-Rebibbia, exit the station, turn right, and follow signs for Tivoli through an underpass to reach the other side of V. Tiburtina. Take the blue COTRAL bus to Tivoli. Tickets (€1.60) are sold in the metro station or in the bar next door. Once the bus reaches Tivoli (35-45min.), get off at Ple. delle Nazioni Unite. The return bus to Rome stops across the street from the tourist office, which has maps and bus schedules. (☎07 74 31 12 49. Open Tu-Su 10am-6pm.) There is also an information kiosk in Ple. delle Nazioni Unite with free maps.

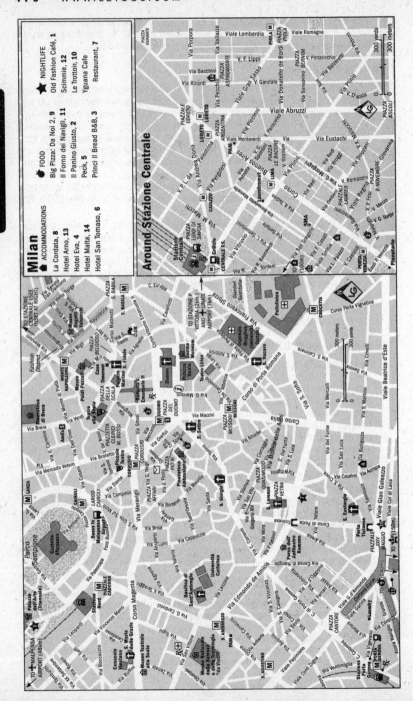

Milan

★ ACCOMMODATIONS

La Cordata, 8
Hotel Arno, 13
Hotel Eva, 4
Hotel Malta, 14
Hotel San Tomaso, 6

◆ FOOD

Big Pizza: Da Noi 2, 9
Il Forno dei Navigli, 11
Il Panino Giusto, 2
Peck, 5
Princi Il Bread B&B, 3

★ NIGHTLIFE

Old Fashion Café, 1
Scimmie, 12
Le Trottoir, 10
Yguana Cafe
Restaurant, 7

Around Stazione Centrale

Tivoli is a beautifully preserved medieval town boasting villas once owned by Latin poets Horace, Catullus, and Propertius. The tourist office provides a **map** detailing sites such as a 15th-century castle and Gothic-style houses, all within walking distance of the bus stop. **Villa d'Este,** a castle with spectacular terraced gardens, was intended to recreate an ancient Roman *nymphaea* and pleasure palace. (☎07 74 31 20 70; www.villadestetivoli.info. Open Tu-Su May-Aug. 8:30am-6:45pm; Sept. 8:30am-6:15pm; Oct. 8:30am-5:30pm; Nov.-Jan. 8:30am-4pm; Feb. 8:30am-4:30pm; Mar. 8:30am-5:15pm; Apr. 8:30am-6:30pm. €9. Audio tour €4.) **Villa Gregoriana,** at the other end of town, is a park with extensive hiking trails and great views of Tivoli's well-preserved **Temple of Vesta.** (☎06 39 96 77 61. Open daily Apr. to mid-Oct. 10am-6:30pm; mid-Oct. to Nov. and Mar. 10am-2:30pm; Dec.-Feb. by reservation only. €4. Audio tour €4.) On the way back from Tivoli, visit the vast remains of **Villa Adriana,** the largest and most expensive villa built under the Roman Empire. (☎07 74 38 27 33. Take bus #4 from P. Garibaldi's newsstand next to the playground. Open daily 9am-7:30pm; last entry 6pm. €6.50. Archaeological tour €3.50, audio tour €4.)

LOMBARDY (LOMBARDIA)

Part of the industrial triangle that drives Italy's economy, home to fashion mecca Milan, and producer of rice fields as lush as China's, Lombardy is one of the most prosperous regions of Italy. The Lombards who ruled the area after the fall of the Romans had close relations with the Franks and the Bavarians, which explains why the region's modern culture has much in common with the traditions of its northern neighbors.

MILAN (MILANO)   ☎02

Unlike Rome, Venice, or Florence, which wrap themselves in veils of historic allure, Milan (pop. 1,400,000), once the capital of the western half of the Roman Empire, presents itself simply as it is: rushed, refined, and cosmopolitan. This urban center also hides many artistic treasures, including da Vinci's *Last Supper*. Milan owes much of its heritage to the medieval Visconti and Sforza families, and its culture to Austrian, French, and Spanish occupiers. Now that Italians run the show, the city flourishes as the country's producer of cutting-edge style, hearty risotto, and die-hard football fans.

▉ TRANSPORTATION

Flights: Malpensa Airport (MXP), 48km from the city, handles intercontinental flights. **Malpensa Express** train leaves from Stazione Nord for the airport. Accessible via Cadorna Metro station (40min., onboard €11/13). **Linate Airport (LIN),** 7km away, covers domestic and European flights. From there, take **Starfly buses** (20min., €2.50) to Stazione Centrale, which is quicker than bus #73 (€1) to San Babila Metro station.

Regional Hubs: Orio al Serio Airport (BGY; ☎035 32 63 23; www.sacbo.it) in Bergamo is a hub for budget airlines **Ryanair, SkyEurope,** and **Wizz Air.**

Trains: Stazione Centrale (☎02 89 20 21; www.trenitalia.com), in P. Duca d'Aosta on M2. Trains run hourly to: **Bergamo** (1hr., €4.10); **Florence** (3hr., €15-36); **Rome** (7hr., €52-73); **Turin** (2hr., €8.75); **Venice** (2hr., €29.50).

Buses: Stazione Centrale. Intercity buses tend to be less convenient and more expensive than trains. **Autostradale, SAL, SIA,** and other carriers leave from P. Castello (M1: Cairoli) and Porta Garibaldi for **Bergamo,** the **Lake Country, Trieste,** and **Turin.**

Public Transportation: The **Metro** (Metropolitana Milanese, or **M**) runs 6am–midnight. Line #1 (red) stretches from the *pensioni* district east of Stazione Centrale through the center of town. Line #2 (green) connects Milan's 3 train stations. Use the **bus** system for trips outside the city proper. Metro tickets can be purchased at *tabaccherie*, ticket booths, and station machines. Single-fare tickets €1, 1-day pass €3, 10 trips €9.20.

⚡ 🚻 ORIENTATION AND PRACTICAL INFORMATION

Milan resembles a giant bull's-eye, defined by its ancient concentric city walls. In the outer rings lie suburbs built during the 50s and 60s to house southern immigrants. In the inner circle are four squares: **Piazza del Duomo**, where **Via Orefici, Via Mazzini,** and **Corso Vittorio Emanuele II** meet; **Piazza Castello** and the attached **Largo Cairoli,** near the Castello Sforzesco; **Piazza Cordusio,** connected to Largo Cairoli by **Via Dante;** and **Piazza San Babila,** the entrance to the business and fashion district. The **duomo** and **Galleria Vittorio Emanuele** are roughly at the center of the circles. The **Giardini Pubblici** and the **Parco Sempione** radiate from the center. From the huge **Stazione Centrale,** northeast of the city, take M3 to the *duomo*.

Tourist Office: IAT, P. Duomo 19A. (☎02 72 52 43 01; www.milanoinfotourist.com), in P. del Duomo. Pick up helpful *Hello Milano*. Open M-Sa 8:45am-1pm and 2-6pm, Su 9am-1pm and 2-5pm. **Branch** in Stazione Centrale (☎02 77 40 43 18) has shorter lines. Open M-Sa 9am-6pm, Su 9am-1pm and 2-5pm.

American Express: V. Larga 4 (☎02 72 10 41), on the corner of V. Larga and S. Clemente. Exchanges currency, handles wire transfers, and holds mail for up to 1 month for AmEx cardholders for free. Open M-F 9am-5:30pm, Sa 9am-12:30pm.

Lost Property: Ufficio Oggetti Smarriti Comune, V. Fruili 30 (☎02 88 45 39 00). Open M-F 8:30am-4pm.

Hospital: Ospedale Maggiore di Milano, V. Francesco Sforza 35 (☎02 55 031).

24hr. Pharmacy: (☎02 66 90 735). In Stazione Centrale's 2nd fl. *galleria*.

Internet: Internet Enjoy, Vle. Tunisia 11 (☎02 36 55 58 05). M1: Porta Venezia. €2-3 per hr. Open M-Sa 9am-midnight, Su 2pm-midnight.

Post Office: P. Cordusio 4 (☎02 72 48 21 26), near P. del Duomo. Currency exchange and **ATM.** Open M-F 8am-7pm, Sa 8:30am-noon. **Postal Code:** 20100.

🏠 ACCOMMODATIONS

Every season is high season in fashionable Milan—except during August, when many hotels close. Prices rise in September, November, March, and April due to theater season and business conventions. For the best deals, try the hostels on the city periphery or in the areas east of Stazione Centrale.

▥ **Hotel Eva and Hotel Arno,** V. Lazzaretto 17, 4th fl. (☎02 67 06 093; www.hotelevamilano.com or www.hotelarno.com). M1: Pta. Venezia. Follow V. Felice Casati, then take a right on V. Lazzaretto. Ring bell. Quirky, mirrored decor and spiral staircases make for an intriguing and inviting atmosphere. Note the life-size porcelain snow leopard. 18 large rooms with wood floors, TV, and phone. Shared bathroom. Free luggage storage. Free Internet. Singles €30-45; doubles €50-100; triples €65-90. AmEx/MC/V. ❸

▥ **La Cordata Ostello,** V. Burigozzo 11 (☎02 58 31 46 75; www.ostellimilano.it). M3: Missori. From P. Missori, take tram #15 2 stops to Italia San Luca; continue in the same direction for 1 block and turn right on V. Burigozzo. Entrance around the corner on V. Aurispa. Close to the Navigli area, a lively crash pad for a young, international crowd ready to party. Colorful, plant-filled common rooms with TV and large kitchens. Laundry €3. Free Internet and Wi-Fi. 7-night max. stay. Reception 24hr. except 1-2:30pm. Check-out 11am. Closed Aug. 10-20 and Dec. 23-Jan 2. Single-sex dorms €21-25; doubles €70-100; triples €90-110; quads €100-140. MC/V. ❷

Hotel Cà Grande, V. Porpora 87 (☎02 26 14 52 95; www.hotelcagrande.it), 7 blocks from Ple. Loreto. Tram #33 stops 50m from the hotel. Though a bit far, it is a pleasant option with English-speaking owners and a pleasant garden. All rooms have A/C, TV, sink, and phone. Breakfast included. Singles €40-65, with bath €45-80; doubles €55-85/60-110. AmEx/D/MC/V. ❹

Albergo Villa Mira, V. Sacchini 19 (☎02 29 52 56 18). Despite the barbed wire over the entrance, the small rooms in this family-run hostel are colorful. A few of the rooms overlook the garden patio. Singles €26-35; doubles €45-62; triples €70-85. Cash only. ❷

Hotel San Tomaso, Vle. Tunisia 6, 3rd fl. (☎02 29 51 47 47; www.hotelsantomaso.com). M1: Porta Venezia. Exit at C. Buenos Aires; turn left on Vle. Tunisia. Rooms with TV and phone. Elevator. Singles €30-65; doubles €50-100; triples €70-150. AmEx/MC/V. ❸

◖ FOOD

Choose between chowing down on focaccia with the lunch-break crowd, clinking crystal glasses, or taking your palate on a world tour through the city's ethnic neighborhoods. Old-style trattorie still follow Milanese culinary traditions with *risotto alla milanese* (rice with saffron), *cotoletta alla milanese* (breaded veal cutlet with lemon), and *osso bucò* (lamb, beef, or veal shank). Many local bars offer happy-hour buffets of focaccia, pasta, and risotto that come free with drink purchase. In the *centro*, weary tourists near the *duomo* often succumb to P. del Duomo's pricey and mediocre offerings, but cheap and delicious rewards await those who look a little harder.

▩ Big Pizza: Da Noi 2, V. Giosué Borsi 1 (☎02 83 96 77). Takes its name seriously. Beer and house wine flow liberally at this riverfront location, which has a restaurant feel but the prices of a small pizza joint. The *pizza della casa* is topped with pasta (€8). If not in the mood for pizza, try the crab pasta (€5). Calzoni €5-7. Pizza €4-8.50. Cover €1. Open M-Sa 10am-2:30pm and 7pm-midnight. MC/V. ❶

▩ Il Forno dei Navigli, Alzaia Naviglio Pavese 2 (☎02 83 23 372). Some of the most delicious pastries in the city, fresh out of "the oven of Navigli." The *cestini* (pear tart with Nutella; €2.25) defines decadence. Pastries and breads €0.50-6. Open M-Sa 7am-2pm and 6pm-1am, Su 6pm-1am. Cash only. ❶

▩ Princi, V. Speronari 6 (☎02 87 47 97; www.princi.it), off P. del Duomo. Take V. Torino and make 1st left. Stone walls and glass countertops make this more zen than you imagined an Italian bakery could be. Local favorite for authentic food on-the-go. Pastries €1-4. Pizza €3.50-5. Primi and secondi €5. Open M-Sa 7am-8pm. Cash only. ❶

Z2, Corso di Porta Ticinese 32 (☎02 89 42 02 41). Savvy, minimalist decor contributes to a relaxing and elegant atmosphere. Watch chefs in glassed-in kitchen prepare dishes such as *gnocchi agli spinaci* (€10). Primi €9-10. Secondi €10-19. Dessert €7-8. ❸

Fratelli la Bufala, Corso di Porta Ticinese 16 (☎02 83 76 529; www.fratellilabufala. com). Relax in the lively atmosphere of this buffalo-meat inspired pizzeria. Don't miss out on the lunch *menù*, with 2 courses, 1 side, and water (€10). Pizza €5.50-9.50. ❷

Trattoria Milanese, V. S. Marta 11 (☎02 86 45 19 91). M1/3: Duomo. From P. del Duomo, take V. Torino; turn right on V. Maurilio and again on V. S. Marta. Serves *costolette alla milanese* (breaded veal; €18) and *mondeghili milanesi* (breaded meatballs; €14) under brick arches. Primi €6-11. Secondi €8-23. Cover €2. Open M-F noon-3pm and 7-11:30pm. Closed last 2 weeks of July. AmEx/MC/V. ❸

Peck, V. Spadari 9 (☎02 80 23 161; www.peck.it). Aromas from the ground floor spread from the wine cellar in the basement to the deli and cafe above. Open M 3:30-7:30pm, Tu-F 9:15am-7:30pm, Sa 8:45am-7:30pm. AmEx/MC/V. ❷

IN RECENT NEWS

SLOW FOOD SPREADS FAST

The Slow Food movement sprung up in 1986 when Carlo Petrini of Bra, Italy decided enough was enough with grab-n-go fast-food chains. In a mere 22 years, his movement has grown to 80,000 members from all points of the globe who are attempting to counteract consumers' dwindling interest in the food they eat. Where is it from? What does it taste like? Sometimes we eat so quickly that we can't even remember.

Slow Food's requirements are three-fold; the food must be good, clean, and fair. In other words, it must taste good, not harm the environment, and food producers must receive fair compensation for their work. Ultimately, their view is that when you lift your fork to swirl that first bite of linguine, you are not just a consumer, but also an informed co-producer.

Keep an eye out for Slow Food's snail symbol on the doors of many restaurants in Italy for assured quality. They even opened a University of Gastronomical Sciences in 2004, offering Bachelor's and Master's degrees, along with many cultural seminars.

So before you grab that panini *"da portare via"* ("to go"), take a moment to step back and remember where your food is coming from. Even a little acknowledgement is a start.

SIGHTS

NEAR THE DUOMO AND IN THE GIARDINI PUBBLICI

DUOMO. The geographical and spiritual center of Milan and a good starting point for any walking tour of the city, the *duomo*—the third-largest church in the world—was begun in 1386 by **Gian Galeazzo Visconti,** who hoped to persuade the Virgin Mary to grant him a male heir. Work proceeded over the next centuries and was completed in 1809 at Napoleon's command. The marble tomb of **Giacomo de Médici** in the south transept was inspired by the work of Michelangelo. Climb (or ride) to the ▨roof walkway for prime views of the city and the Alps. *(M1/3: Duomo. Cathedral open daily 7am-7pm. Modest dress required. Free. Roof open daily 9:30am-9:30pm. €5, elevator €7.)*

PINACOTECA AMBROSIANA. The 23 palatial rooms of the Ambrosiana display exquisite works from the 14th through 19th centuries, including Botticelli's circular *Madonna of the Canopy,* Caravaggio's *Basket of Fruit* (the first Italian still life), Raphael's wall-sized *School of Athens,* Titian's *Adoration of the Magi,* and da Vinci's *Portrait of a Musician.* The statue-filled courtyard is enchanting. *(P. Pio XI 2. M1/3: Duomo. Open Tu-Su 10am-5:30pm. €8, under 18 and over 65 €5.)*

TEATRO ALLA SCALA. Founded in 1778, La Scala has established Milan as the opera capital of the world. Its understated Neoclassical facade and lavish interior set the stage for premieres of works by Mascagni, Puccini, Rossini, and Verdi, performed by virtuosos like Maria Callas and Enrico Caruso. The **Museo Teatrale alla Scala** is replete with portraits, pianos, and porcelain figurines. Look for the compelling and highly personal—if somewhat rapturous—account of Maria Callas' contribution to modern opera. *(Access through the Galleria Vittorio Emanuele from P. del Duomo. www.teatroallascala.org. Museum on left side of building. Open daily 9am-12:30pm and 1:30-5:30pm. €5, students €4.)*

MUSEO POLDI PEZZOLI. Poldi Pezzoli, an 18th-century nobleman and art collector, bequeathed his house and its eclectic collection to the city in 1879. Today, masterpieces hang in the Golden Room overlooking the garden. Smaller collections fill Pezzoli's former private chambers, where the decor reflects his fine taste. Particularly impressive is a tiny but interesting display of Italian military armaments. *(V. Manzoni 12. Open Tu-Su 10am-6pm. €8, students and seniors €5.50.)*

CASTELLO SFORZESCO AND ENVIRONS

■CASTELLO SFORZESCO. The Castello Sforzesco was constructed in 1368 as a defense against Venice. Later, it was used as army barracks, a horse stall, and a storage house before da Vinci converted it into a studio. Restored after WWII damage, the complex houses 10 **Musei Civici** (Civic Museums). The **■Museum of Ancient Art** contains Michelangelo's unfinished *Pietà Rondanini* (1564), his last work, and the **Museum of Decorative Art** has ornate furnishings and Murano glass. The underground level has a small Egyptian collection. *(M1: Cairoli or M2: Lanza. Open Tu-Su 9am-5:30pm. Combined admission €3, students €1.50, F 2-5:30pm free.)*

CHIESA DI SANTA MARIA DELLE GRAZIE. The church's Gothic nave is dark and patterned with frescoes, contrasting the airy Renaissance tribune Bramante added in 1497. To the left of the church entrance is the **Cenacolo Vinciano** (Vinciano Refectory), home to Leonardo da Vinci's **■Last Supper.** *(P di S. Maria delle Grazie 2. M1: Conciliazione. From P. Conciliazione, take V. Boccaccio and then go right onto V. Ruffini for about 2 blocks. Reservations ☎02 89 42 11 46. Reservation fee €1.50. Church open M-Sa 7am-noon and 3-7pm, Su 7:30am-12:15pm and 3:30-9pm. Modest dress required. Refectory open Tu-Su 8:15am-6:45pm. €6.50, EU residents 18-25 €3.25, under 18 and over 65 free.)*

PINACOTECA DI BRERA. The Brera Art Gallery presents a collection of 14th- to 20th-century paintings, with an emphasis on the Lombard School. Works include Bellini's *Pietà*, Mantegna's *Dead Christ*, and Raphael's *Marriage of the Virgin*. *(V. Brera 28. M2: Lanza. Wheelchair-accessible. Open Tu-Su 8:30am-7:15pm. €5.)*

NAVIGLI AND CORSO DI PORTA TICINESE

BASILICA DI SANT'EUSTORGIO. Founded in the 4th century to house the bones of the Magi, the church lost its original function when the dead sages were spirited off to Cologne in 1164. A great masterpiece of early Renaissance art is the **Portinari Chapel**, to the left of the entrance. Frescoes below the rainbow dome illustrate the life of St. Peter. The chapel stands on a **Paleochristian cemetery;** pagan and early Christian tombs are down the steps before the chapel entrance. *(P. S. Eustorgio 3. M2: S. Ambrogio. Basilica open M and W-Su 8:30am-noon and 3:30-6pm. Free. Cappella open Tu-Su 10am-6:30pm. €6, students and seniors €3.)*

NAVIGLI DISTRICT. Often called the Venice of Lombardy, the Navigli district, complete with canals, elevated footbridges, open-air markets, cafes, alleys, and trolleys, comes alive at night. The area was part of a medieval canal system that transported thousands of tons of marble to build the *duomo* and linked Milan to various northern cities and lakes. *(From M2: Porta Genova, take V. Vigevano.)*

▣ SHOPPING

In a city where clothes really do make the man (or woman), fashionistas arrive in spring and summer to watch models dressed in the newest styles glide down the runway. When the music has faded and the designers have bowed, world-famous **saldi** (sales) in July and January usher the garb into the real world. The **Quadrilatero della Moda** (fashion district) has become a sanctuary in its own right. This posh land, where limos transport poodles dressed to impress and jean jackets can sell for €2000, is formed by **Via Monte Napoleone, Borgospresso, Via della Spiga,** and **Via Gesu.** On these streets, Giorgio and Donatella not only sell their styles, they live in the suites above their stores and nightclubs. Even though most stores close at 7:30pm, have no fear; you can shop around the clock at the touch screens outside the Ralph Lauren Store, so long as you don't mind waiting for delivery until the next morning. Designer creations are available to mere mortals at the trendy boutiques along **Corso di Porta Ticinese.**

Small shops and affordable staples from brand names can be found on **Via Torino** near the *duomo* and on **Corso Buenos Aires** near M1: Porta Venezia. Those who don't mind being a season behind can purchase famous designer wear from *blochisti* (stocks or wholesale clothing outlets), such as the well-known **Il Salvagente**, V. Bronzetti 16, off C. XXII Marzo (M1: S. Babila), or **Gruppo Italia Grandi Firme**, V. Montegani #7/A (M2: Famagosta), which offers designer duds at 70% off. True bargain hunters cull the bazaars on **Via Faucé** (M2: Garibaldi; Tu and Sa) and **Viale Papinian** (M2: Agnostino; Sa mornings).

NIGHTLIFE

The nightlife in **Navigli** is popular with students and centers around V. Sforza. The **Brera** district invites tourists and Milanese to test their singing skills while sipping mixed drinks at one of its piano bars. **Corso di Porta Ticinese** is the sleek land of the all-night happy hour buffet, where the price of a mixed drink (€6-8) also buys dinner. A block of **Corso Como** near **Stazione Garibaldi** is home to the most exclusive clubs. Bars and clubs cluster around **Largo Cairoli**, where summer brings Milan's hottest outdoor dance venues. Southeast of **Stazione Centrale** is home to an eclectic mix of bars and much of Milan's gay and lesbian scene.

- **Yguana Café Restaurant,** V. Papa Gregorio XIV 16 (☎89 40 41 95), just off P. Vetra, a short walk down V. E. de Amicis and V. Molino delle Armi. Beautiful people sip fruity mixed drinks (€8-10). Lounge on a couch outside, or groove to hip hop downstairs. Su brunch noon-4pm. Happy-hour buffet (M-Sa 5:30-9:30pm, Su 5:30-10pm) with 50 rotating dishes makes other bars' offerings look downright pedestrian. Open M-Th and Su 5:30pm-2am, F-Sa 5:30pm-3am. Kitchen open M-F 12:30-3pm.

- **Le Trottoir,** P. XXIV Maggio 1 (☎/fax 02 83 78 166; www.letrottoir.it). Located in the center of P. XXIV Maggio as its own island in a sea of roads. This self-proclaimed *"Ritrovo d'Arte, Cultura, e Divertimento"* (House of Art, Culture, and Diversions) may be the Navigli's loudest, most crowded bar and club. A young, alternative crowd comes nightly to get down to live underground music 10:30pm-3am on ground fl., while upstairs features a DJ or jazz (M and W). Check schedule for weekly roster and other music nights. Mixed drinks €6-9. Pizza and sandwiches €8. Cover depends on act; usually €8, includes 1 drink. Happy hour daily 6-8pm with beer €4. Open daily 11am-3am. AmEx/MC/V.

- **Old Fashion Café,** Vle. Emilio Alemagna 6 (☎02 80 56 231; www.oldfashion.it). M1/2: Cadorna F. N. Walk up V. Paleocapa next to the station, and turn right on Vle. Alemagna before the bridge. Club is to left of Palazzo dell'Arte along a dirt path. Summer brings stylish clubgoers to couches encircling an outdoor dance floor and stage, with live music and DJ. Tu is the most popular night, with mixed music. Su brunch noon-6pm; €20. Appetizer buffet 7:30-10pm; €13. Open M-Tu and Th-Sa 10:30pm-4:30am, W 10:30pm-4am, Su 11am-4pm and 7:30pm-midnight.

- **L'elephant,** V. Melzo 22 (☎02 29 51 87 68; www.lelephant.it). M2: Pta. Venezia. From C. Buenos Aires turn right on V. Melzo and walk 5 blocks. An almost entirely male crowd socializes at tables under chandeliers, and on the street corner. Gay- and lesbian-friendly. Mixed drinks €7-8. Happy hour 6:30-9:30pm; €6. Open Tu-Su 6:30pm-2am.

- **Club 2,** V. Formentini 2 (☎02 86 46 48 07), down V. Madonnina from V. Fiori Chiari. This bar sets the mood with red lights and a grand piano on the ground floor and a maze of cushions in its dark downstairs "discopub." Loud bass downstairs. F-Sa DJ and karaoke. Basement open daily in winter. Beer €6. Mixed drinks €10. Open daily 8:30pm-3am.

- **Loolapaloosa,** C. Como 15 (☎02 65 55 693). Guests are invited to dance on the bar while the bartenders entertain by swinging lamps and ringing bells. Mixed drinks €6-8. Cover from €6. Buffet 6:30-10:30pm. Open M-Sa noon-4am, Su 2pm-4am.

▐BERGAMO
☎**035**

Home to the **Orio al Serio International Airport** (**BGY;** ☎035 32 63 23; www.sacbo.it), Bergamo (pop. 120,000) is a hub for budget airlines **Ryanair, SkyEurope,** and **Wizz Air. Airport buses** go to the train station in Bergamo (10min., €1.60). **Trains** (☎035 24 79 50) run from Ple. Marconi to Milan (1hr., 1 per hr., €4.10). **Buses** run from the train station to Como (6 per day, €4.40) and Milan (2 per hr., €4.40).

For overnight layovers or missed flights, head to the art-filled ▧**Ostello Città di Bergamo (HI)** ❷, V. G. Ferraris 1. From the airport, take bus 1C to Porta Nuova and change to bus #6; the hostel is at the next-to-last stop. (☎035 36 17 24; www. ostellodibergamo.it. 6- and 8-bed dorms €17; singles €30; doubles €42; 3-6 person rooms €18 per person. €3 HI discount.) Another option is the B&B **La Torretta Città Alta** ❹, Via Rocca 2. (☎035 57 61 59; www.latorrettabergamoalta.com. Singles €60-70; doubles €80-95; triples €90-110.) Dine at ▧**Trattoria Casa Mia** ❷, V. S. Bernardino 20, which makes up for its out-of-the-way location with local flavor. (☎035 22 06 76. Lunch *menù* €10. Dinner *menù* €12. Open M-Sa noon-2pm and 7-10pm. Cash only.) Supermarket **Pellicano** is at Vle. V. Emanuele II 17; walk from the station past Ple. Repubblica. (Open M 8:30am-1:30pm, Tu-F 8:30am-1:30pm and 3:30-8pm, Sa 8:30am-8pm. MC/V.) **Postal Code:** 24122.

MANTUA (MANTOVA)
☎**0376**

Though Mantua (pop. 47,000) did not become a dynamic cultural haven until the Renaissance, the arts have shaped the city's history since the birth of the poet Virgil in 70 BC. Today, the huge **Festivaletteratura** brings writers from John Grisham to Salman Rushdie to the city in early September. Mantua's grand *palazzi*, including the opulent **Palazzo Ducale,** P. Sordello 40, were built by the powerful Gonzaga family, who ascended to power in 1328, ruled for 400 years, and commissioned well-known artists to leave their marks on the town's mansions and churches. The **New Gallery** houses dozens of locally produced altarpieces from the 16th-18th centuries, removed from monasteries during the Hapsburg and Napoleonic eras. (Open Tu-Su 8:45am-7:15pm. €6.50.) Music lovers first filled the balconies of the ▧**Teatro Bibiena,** V. Accademia 4, when 14-year-old Mozart inaugurated the building in 1769. (Open Tu-Su 9:30am-12:30pm and 3-6pm. €2, under 18 €1.20.) In the southern part of the city, down V. P. Amedeo (which becomes V. Acrebi), through P. Veneto, and down Largo Parri, lies the **Palazzo del Te,** built by Giulio Romano in 1534 for Federico II Gonzaga. It is widely considered the finest building in the Mannerist style. The entirely frescoed ▧**Room of Giants** depicts the demise of the rebellious Titans at the hands of Jupiter. The hidden garden and grotto at the far end are often overlooked. (Open M 1-6pm, Tu-Su 9am-6pm. €8, students €2.50.)

Hotel ABC ❹, P. D. Leoni 25-27, across from the train station, is a modern hotel with comfortable rooms. (☎0376 32 23 29; www.hotelabcmantova.it. Breakfast included. Reserve ahead. Singles €44-165; doubles €66-165; triples €77-222; quads €88-250.) **Ostello del Mincio** ❷, V. Porto 23/25, 10km from Mantua, is the only youth hostel in the area. (☎0376 65 39 24; www.ostellodelmincio. org. Dorms €16-18, with breakfast €17-22.) To get to **Trattoria con Pizza da Chiara** ❸, V. Corridoni 44/A, from P. Cavallotti, follow C. Libertà and turn left on V. Roma, then right on the narrow V. Corridoni. Young professionals dine in this chic but unpretentious restaurant. (☎0376 22 35 68. Pizza and *primi* €4.50-9. *Secondi* €9-14.50. Cover €2. Open M and W-Su noon-2:30pm and 7-10:30pm. MC/V.) **Supermarket Sma,** V. Giustiziati 11, is behind the Rotonda di San Lorenzo on P. d'Erbe. (Open M-Sa 8:30am-7:30pm. AmEx/MC/V.)

Trains go from P. D. Leoni to Milan (2hr., 9 per day, €8.60) and Verona (40min., 20 per day, €2.60). From the train station, turn left on V. Solferino, then right on Via Bonomi to the main street, **Corso Vittorio Emanuele II.** Follow it to P. Cavallotti, across the river to C. Umberto I, which leads to P. Marconi, P. Mantegna, and the main *piazze*, **Piazza dell'Erbe** and **Piazza Sordello.** The **tourist office** is at P. Mantegna 6; follow V. Solferino until it becomes V. Fratelli Bandiera, then go right on V. Verdi. (☎0376 32 82 53; www.aptmantova.it. Open daily 9am-7pm.) **Internet** is available at Bit and Phone, V. Bertinelli 21. **Postal Code:** 46100.

THE LAKE COUNTRY

When Italy's monuments start blurring together, escape to the clear waters and green mountains of the northern Lake Country, which encompasses part of Piedmont and part of Lombardy. The mansion-spotted coast of Lake Como welcomes the rich and famous, palatial hotels dot Lake Maggiore's sleepy shores, and a young crowd descends upon Lake Garda for its watersports and bars.

LAKE COMO (LAGO DI COMO)

As the numerous luxurious villas on the lake's shores attest, the well-to-do have been using Lake Como as a refuge since before the Roman Empire. Three lakes form the forked Lake Como, joined at the three central towns: Bellagio, Menaggio, and Varenna. These smaller towns offer a more relaxing stay than Como. For a taste of the Lake's true beauty, hop on a bus or ferry, and step off whenever a castle, villa, vineyard, or small town beckons.

⬛ TRANSPORTATION. The only towns on the lake accessible by **train** are Como and Varenna, though the latter has only a very small station with limited hours. Trains go from Stazione San Giovanni (☎031 89 20 21) to Milan (1hr., 1-2 per hr., €3.50) and Zürich, SWI (4hr., 5 per day, €46). From P. Matteotti, **bus** C46 goes to Bergamo (2hr., 5 per day, €4.40), and C10 goes to Menaggio (1hr., 1 per hr., €3.20). From the train station, bus C30 goes to Bellagio (1hr., 16 per day, €2.80). Spend the day zipping between the boutiques, gardens, villas, and wineries of the lake by **ferry** (day pass €20), leaving from the piers at P. Cavour.

COMO. Situated on the southwestern tip of the lake, vibrant Como (pop. 86,000) is the lake's largest town. **Ostello Villa Olmo (HI) ❷**, V. Bellinzona 2, has clean rooms and a friendly staff. From the train station, walk 20min. down V. Borgo Vico to V. Bellinzona. (☎031 57 38 00. Breakfast included. Reception 7-10am and 4pm-midnight. Lockout 10am-4pm. Strict curfew midnight. Open Mar.-Nov. Reserve ahead. Dorms €18. €3 HI discount. Cash only.) Chic cafes fill Como's historic center, south of Piazza Cavour. **Gran Mercato** supermarket is at P. Matteotti 3. (Open M and Su 8:30am-1pm, Tu-F 8:30am-1:30pm and 3:30-7:30pm, Sa 8am-7:30pm.) The **tourist office** is at P. Cavour 17. From the station, go left on V. Fratelli Recchi and right on Vle. Fratelli Rosselli, which turns into Lungo Lario Trento and leads to the *piazza*. (☎031 26 97 12. Open M-Sa 9am-1pm and 2:30-6pm, Su 9:30am-12:30pm.) **Postal Code:** 22100.

MENAGGIO. Halfway up Lake Como's western shore are the terra-cotta rooftops of Menaggio (pop. 3200). The town's beauty and excellent **ferry** connections make it the perfect base for exploring the lake. Daytrips by ferry to the gardens and villas of **Bellagio** and **Varenna** (both 10-15min., 1-2 per hr., €3.50) are extremely popular. The **Rifugio Menaggio** mountain station is the starting point for a 2hr. round-trip hike to **Monte Grona** (1736m) that offers views of the pre-Alps and the lakes. Alternatively, the 2hr. hike to **Chiesa di San Amate** (1623m) takes you over a mountain ridge to sneak a peak at alpine pastures. A number of shorter hikes start in Menaggio. **Vecchia Menaggio ❶**, V. al Lago 13, offers hotel rooms at great prices in a fantastic location right next to the *centro*. There is also an affordable Italian restaurant downstairs. (☎0344 32 082. Doubles €40, with bath €60.) Just up the street from the ferry dock, **Super Cappa Market,** V. IV Novembre 107, stocks groceries and hiking supplies. (Open M 8-12:30pm, Tu-Sa 8am-12:30pm and 3-7pm.) In the *centro* at P. Garibaldi 4, the helpful **tourist office** has info and maps on lake excursions. **Postal Code:** 22017.

LAKE MAGGIORE (LAGO MAGGIORE)

A translation of Stendhal reads: "If it should befall that you possess a heart and shirt, then sell the shirt and visit the shores of Lake Maggiore." Though writers have always been seduced by the lake's beauty, Lake Maggiore remains less touristed than its neighbors. **Stresa** is a perfect stepping-stone to the gorgeous **Borromean Islands.** Stay at the ▨**Albergo Luina ❸**, V. Garibaldi 21, to the right past the ferry dock. (☎032 33 02 85. Breakfast €3.50. Reserve ahead in summer. Singles €35-52; doubles €55-80; triples €56-80. MC/V.) Daily excursion tickets allow you to travel between Stresa and the three islands. **Trains** run from Stresa to Milan (1hr., 2 per hr., €4.60). To reach the *centro* and the **IAT Tourist Office,** P. Marconi 16, from the ferry dock, exit the train station, turn right on V. P. d. Piemonte, take a left on Vle. D. d. Genova, and walk toward the water. Turn right at the water and walk 5-10min to reach P. Marconi and the tourist office.

◤**THE BORROMEAN ISLANDS.** Beckoning visitors with lush greenery and stately villas, the beauty of the Borromean Islands is one of the lake's major attractions. On **Isola Bella,** the opulent **Palazzo e Giardini Borromeo** showcases priceless tapestries and paintings. (Open Mar. 21-Oct. 21 daily 9am-5:30pm. €11.) From Isola Bella, ferries go to **Isola Superiore dei Pescatori,** which has a quaint fishing village with a rocky beach and ice-cold water. **Isola Madre** is the greenest island, most favored by the locals. The 16th-century ▨**Villa Taranto** surprisingly houses several puppet theaters, and its gardens overflow with exotic flowers and white peacocks. (Open daily 8:30am-6:30pm. €8.50. Combined ticket with the Palazzo e Giardini Borromeo €16.)

LAKE GARDA (LAGO DI GARDA)

Garda has staggering mountains and breezy summers. **Desenzano,** the lake's southern transport hub, is only 1hr. from Milan and 2hr. from Venice. Sirmione and Limone are best explored as daytrips. **Riva del Garda,** at the lake's northern tip, has an affordable hostel to use as a base. Exploring **Sirmione's** 13th-century castle and Roman ruins can fill a leisurely day or busy afternoon. In **Limone,** windsurfing, swimming, and eating all revolve around the unbelievable view of the lake as it winds through the mountains. Uphill from the center near the water, **La Limonaia del Castèl,** V. IV Novembre 25, transports tourists into the world of a functioning 18th-century citrus house. Trees bearing clementines, grapefruits, lemons, and limes are spread over 1633 sq. yd. of terraces. (☎0365 95 40 08; www.limone-sulgarda.it. €1.) Riva del Garda's calm and beautiful pebble beaches are Lake Garda's restitution for the budget traveler put off by steep local prices. Sleep at backpacker hot spot **Ostello Benacus (HI) ❶**, P. Cavour 10. (☎0464 55 49 11. Breakfast included. Laundry €4. Internet €2 per hr. Reception 7-9am and 3-11pm. Reserve ahead. Dorms €16. AmEx/MC/V.)

Sirmione's **tourist office** is at V. Guglilmo Marconi 6. (☎030 91 61 14; www.commune.sirmione.bs.it. Open Apr.-Oct. daily 8am-8pm; Nov.-Mar. M-F 9am-1pm and 2-6pm, Sa 9am-12:30pm.) Limone's tourist office is at V. IV Novembre 29. (☎0365 91 89 87. Open daily 8:30am-9pm.) Riva del Garda's tourist office is at Largo Medaglie d'Oro 5. (☎0464 55 44 44; www.gardatrentino.it. Open M-Sa 9am-noon and 3-6:30pm, Su 9am-noon and 3:30-6:30pm.) **Buses** run from Sirmione and Riva del Garda to Verona (1hr., 1 per hr., €4). **Ferries** (☎030 91 49 511; www.navigazionelaghi.it) run from Limone to Desenzano (4 per day, €10-13), Riva (17 per day, €3.40-5.20), and Sirmione (8 per day, €10-13). **Postal Codes:** 25019 (Sirmione), 25087 (Limone), 38066 (Riva del Garda).

ITALIAN RIVIERA (LIGURIA)

The Italian Riviera stretches 350km along the Mediterranean between France and Tuscany, forming the most touristed area of the Italian coastline. Genoa anchors the luminescent Ligurian coastal strip between the **Riviera di Levante** (rising sun) to the east and the **Riviera di Ponente** (setting sun) to the west. Lemon trees, almond blossoms, and turquoise waters greet visitors along the elegant coast, where glamor mixes with seaside relaxation. The **Cinque Terre** area (p. 489), just west of **La Spezia**, is especially worth the journey.

GENOA (GENOVA)   ☎010

Genoa (pop. 640,000), a city of grit and grandeur, has little in common with its resort neighbors. As a Ligurian will tell you, *"si deve conoscerla per amarla"* (you have to know her to love her). Once home to Liguria's most noble families, Genoa's main streets are lined with *palazzi* and *piazze;* wander through medieval churches and maze-like pathways to discover this port city.

█ TRANSPORTATION. **Colombo Internazionale Airport (GOA;** ☎010 60 15 461), services European destinations. Volabus #100 runs to Stazione Brignole from the airport (3 per hr., €3.70). Most visitors arrive at one of Genoa's two train stations: **Stazione Principe**, in P. Acquaverde, or **Stazione Brignole**, in P. Verdi. **Trains** go to Rome (5-6hr., 12 per day, €27-50), Turin (2hr., 2-3 per hr., €8-12), and points along the Italian Riviera. AMT **buses** (☎010 55 82 414) run through the city (€1.60; day pass €4). **Ferries** to Olbia, Sardinia, and Palermo, Sicily depart from Terminal Traghetti in the Ponte Assereto section of the port.

█▐ ORIENTATION AND PRACTICAL INFORMATION. From Stazione Principe, take V. Balbi to V. Cairoli, which becomes V. Garibaldi. Turn right on V. XXV Aprile at P. delle Fontane Marose to get to **Piazza de Ferrari** in the center of town. From Stazione Brignole, turn right out of the station, then left on V. Fiume and right onto V. XX Settembre. Or, take bus #18, 19, or 30 from Stazione Principe, or bus #19 or 40 from Stazione Brignole. The **tourist office**, GenovaInforma, has several locations, including a kiosk in P. Matteotti. (☎010 86 87 452. Open daily 9am-1pm and 2-6pm.) **Internet** is available at **Number One Bar/Cafe**, P. Verdi 21R. (☎010 54 18 85. €4 per hr. Open M-Sa 7:30am-11:30pm.) **Postal Code:** 16121.

> **! WATCH WHERE YOU WANDER.** The shadowy streets of the *centro storico* are riddled with drug dealers and prostitutes. Avoid the area around Stazione Principe, as well as those around V. della Maddalena, V. Sottoripa, and V. di Prè when shops are closed and streets are empty.

 ACCOMMODATIONS AND FOOD. Delight in views of the city below at **Ostello per la Gioventù (HI) ❶**, V. Costanzi 120. From Stazione Principe, take bus

#35 to V. Napoli and transfer to #40, which runs to the hostel. From Stazione Brignole, take bus #40 (last bus 12:50am) all the way up the hill. (☎010 24 22 457. Breakfast included. Dorms €16. HI members only.) Conveniently located **Albergo Argentina ❷**, V. Gropallo 4, near Stazione Brignole, has nine large, clean, comfortable rooms. (☎010 83 93 722. Singles €30-40; doubles €50-65, with bath €60-75; triples €75-90; quads €85-100. MC/V.) For camping, try **Genova Est ❶**, on V. Marcon Loc Cassa. (☎010 34 72 053; www.camping-genova-est.it. Laundry €3.50. €5.90 per person, €5.60-8.60 per tent. Electricity €2.20.) **Trattoria da Maria ❷**, V. Testa d'Oro 14R, off V. XXV Aprile, has authentic Genovese specials. (☎010 58 10 80. 2-course *menù* €9. Open M-Sa 11:45am-3pm. MC/V.)

◪♫ SIGHTS AND ENTERTAINMENT. Centro storico, the eerie and beautiful historical center bordered by Porto Antico, V. Garibaldi, and P. Ferrari, is a mass of winding streets. The area contains some of Genoa's most memorable sights, including the asymmetrical **San Lorenzo Duomo,** down V. San Lorenzo from P. Matteotti (open daily 9am-noon and 3-6pm; free), and the medieval **Torre Embraici.** Go down V. S. Lorenzo toward the water, turn left on V. Chiabrera, and left on V. di Mascherona to reach the **◪Chiesa Santa Maria di Castello,** in P. Caricamento, a labyrinth of chapels, courtyards, and crucifixes. (Open daily 9am-noon and 3:30-6:30pm. Closed to tourists during Su Mass. Free.) Don't miss the enigmatic **◪Palazzo Spinola di Pellicceria,** P. di Pellicceria 1, between V. Maddalena and P. San Luca, a late 16th-century palace which represents centuries of varying architectural styles. (☎010 27 05 300. Open Tu-Sa 8:30am-7:30pm, Su 1:30-7:30pm. €4, ages 18-25 €2.) From P. de Ferrari, take V. Boetto to P. Matteotti for a glimpse of the ornate interior and paintings by Rubens in **Chiesa di Gesù.** (Church open M-Sa 7am-12:45pm and 4-7:30pm, Su 8am-12:45pm and 5-9:45pm. Closed to tourists during Su Mass. Free.) Head past the church down V. di Porta Soprana to V. Ravecca to reach the **Porta Soprana,** one of the four gates into the city, near the boyhood home of **◪Christopher Columbus.** (Porta and Columbus' home open daily 10am-6pm. Combo ticket €7.) Genoa's multitude of *palazzi* were built by its merchant families. Follow V. Balbi through P. della Nunziata and continue to L. Zecca, where V. Cairoli leads to **Via Garibaldi,** called "Via Aurea" ("Golden Street") after the wealthy families who inhabited it. The interior of the 17th-century **Palazzo Reale,** V. Balbi 10, west of V. Garibaldi, is bathed in gold. (Open Tu-W 9am-1:30pm, Th-Su 9am-7pm. €4, ages 18-25 €2.)

Corso Italia, an upscale promenade, is home to much of Genoa's nightlife. Most people drive to get to clubs, as they are difficult to reach on foot and the city streets can be dangerous. Italian and international students flock to bars in **Piazza Erbe** and along **Via San Bernardo.** The swanky bar **Al Parador,** P. della Vittoria 49R, is easy and fairly safe to reach from Stazione Brignole. It's in the northeast corner of P. Vittoria, near the intersection of V. Cadorna and V. B. Liguria. (☎010 58 17 71. Mixed drinks €4.50. Open M-Sa 24hr. Cash only.)

FINALE LIGURE   ☎019

A beachside plaque proclaims Finale Ligure (pop. 12,000) the place for *"il riposo del popolo"* ("the people's rest"). From bodysurfing to browsing through chic boutiques to scaling the 15th-century ruins of **Castello di San Giovanni,** *riposo* takes many forms. The nearby towns of **Borgio** and **Verezzi** are also worth exploring. Walk east along V. Aurelia to find a free **beach,** less populated than those closer to town. Enclosed by ancient walls, **Finalborgo,** Finale Ligure's historic center, is a 1km walk or 2min. ACTS bus ride up V. Bruneghi from the station.

With clean rooms and incomparable views, **◪Castello Wuillerman (HI) ❶**, V. Generale Caviglia, is well worth the hike up its daunting steps. From the train station, cross the street and turn left onto V. Raimondo Pertica. After passing a church on the left, turn left onto V. Alonzo and climb the stairs to the *castello*. (☎019 69 05 15. Breakfast included. Reception 7-10am and 5-10pm. Curfew midnight. Dorms €14. HI members only. Cash only.) **Camping Del Mulino ❶**, on V. Castelli, has a restaurant and mini-market. (☎019 60 16 69; www.campingmulino.it. Reception 8am-8pm. Open Apr.-Sept. Tent sites €9.50-14. MC/V.) Fill up on huge portions of pasta at **Spaghetteria Il Post ❷**, V. Porro 21. Bring a friend—each dish is made for two. (☎019 60 00 95. Entrees €7. Cover €1. Open Tu-Su 7:30-11pm. Closed for 2 weeks in Mar. Cash only.) Cafe and night spot **Pilade ❶**, V. Garibaldi 67, has live music on Fridays. (☎019 69 22 20. Beer from €3. Pizza €2 per slice. Open daily 10am-2am. MC/V.) **Di per Di Express** supermarket is at V. Alonzo 10. (Open M-Sa 8:15am-1pm and 4:30-7:30pm, Su 9am-1pm. MC/V.)

   Trains leave from P. V. Veneto for Genoa (1hr., 2 per hr., €4). SAR **buses** run from the train station to Borgo Verezzi (10min., 4 per hr., €1). The city is divided into **Finalpia** to the east, **Finalmarina** in the center, and **Finalborgo**, farther inland. The IAT **tourist office** is at V. della Concezione 27. (☎019 68 10 19; www.inforiviera.it. Open M-Tu and Th-Su 7am-7pm.) **Postal Code:** 17024.

CAMOGLI   ☎0185

Postcard-perfect Camogli shimmers with color. Sun-faded peach houses crowd the hilltop, and red and turquoise boats bob in the water. Turn right out of the train station and keep walking until V. Repubblica turns into V. P. Schaffino to reach the handsomely furnished **Hotel Augusta ❸**, V.P. Schaffino 100. (☎0185 77 05 92; www.htlaugusta.com. Buffet breakfast included. Free Internet for 15min. Singles €40-78; doubles €55-115. AmEx/MC/V.) The creamy gelato from **Gelato e Dintorni ❶**, V. Garibaldi 104/105, puts nationally ranked rivals to shame. (☎0185 77 43 53. 2 scoops €1.70. *Granita* €2. Open daily 11:30am-11pm. Cash only.) **Trains** run on the Genoa-La Spezia line to Genoa (40min., 38 per day, €1.60) and La Spezia (1hr., 24 per day, €4). Golfo Paradiso **ferries**, V. Scalo 3 (☎0185 77 20 91; www.golfoparadiso.it), near P. Colombo, go to Cinque Terre (round-trip €20) and Portofino (round-trip €13). Buy tickets on the dock; call ahead for the schedule. Turn right from the station to find the **tourist office**, V. XX Settembre 33. (☎0185 77 10 66. Open M-Sa 9am-12:30pm and 3-6:30pm, Su 9am-12:30pm; reduced hours in low-season.) **Postal Code:** 16032.

SANTA MARGHERITA LIGURE   ☎0185

Santa Margherita Ligure was a calm fishing village until the early 20th century, when it fell into favor with Hollywood stars. Today, glitz paints the shore, but the serenity of the town's early days still lingers. If you find gardens more enticing than beaches, take the paths off V. della Vittoria uphill to the **Villa Durazzo**, surrounded by flora, and home to many 16th-century paintings. (Gardens open daily July-Aug. 9am-8pm; May-June and Sept. 9am-7pm; Apr. and Oct. 9am-6pm; Nov.-Dec. 9am-5pm. Villa open daily 9am-1pm and 2:30-6pm.)

   Cozy beds and private showers make **Hotel Conte Verde ❹**, V. Zara 1, a good choice. (☎0185 28 71 39; www.hotelconteverde.it. Breakfast included. Singles €50-120; doubles €65-150; triples €90-210; quads €100-230. AmEx/MC/V.) **Trattoria Da Pezzi ❷**, V. Cavour 21, is popular with the locals for its homestyle cuisine and jovial atmosphere. (☎0185 28 53 03. *Primi* €4-7.50. *Secondi* €6-15. Cover €1. Open M-F and Su 10am-2:15pm and 5-9:15pm. MC/V.)

   Trains along the Pisa-Genoa line go from P. Federico Raoul Nobili, at the top of V. Roma, to Genoa (50min., 2-4 per hr., €2.30) and La Spezia (1hr., 1-2 per hr., €4). Tigullio **buses** (☎0185 28 88 34) go from P. V. Veneto to Camogli (30min., 1-2 per hr., €1.10) and Portofino (20min., 3 per hr., €1). Tigullio **ferries**, V. Palestro

8/1B (☎0185 28 46 70), run tours to Cinque Terre (early May-late Sept. 1 per day, round-trip €22) and Portofino (Sa-Su 1 per hr., €4.50). To find the **tourist office,** V. XXV Aprile 2/B, turn right out of the train station, go left on C. Rainusso, and take the first left on V. Gimelli. (☎0185 28 78 17. Open M-Sa 9:30am-12:30pm and 3-7:30pm, Su 9:30am-12:30pm and 4:30-7:30pm.) **Postal Code:** 16032.

CINQUE TERRE   ☎0187

Cinque Terre is paradise for an outdoorsman—or, maybe more accurately, an outdoorsman on Spring Break. Strong hikers can cover all five villages—Corniglia, Manarola, Monterosso, Riomaggiore, and Vernazza—in about five hours, but word on the cliff is that it's been done in three. There are numerous opportunities for kayaking, cliff jumping, and horseback riding along the way. Rather than rushing, take the time to wander through the villages' tiny clusters of rainbow-colored houses amid hilly stretches of olive groves and vineyards.

TRANSPORTATION AND PRACTICAL INFORMATION. **Trains** run along the Genoa-La Spezia (Pisa) line. A **Cinque Terre Card** (1-day €8.50, 2-day €14.70, 3-day €19.50, 7-day €36.50) allows for unlimited train, bus, and path access among the five villages, La Spezia, and Levanto; it can be purchased at the **train stations** and **Cinque Terre National Park.** Monterosso is the most accessible village by train. From the station on V. Fegina, in the northern end of town, **trains** run to: Florence (3hr., 1 per hr., €9); Genoa (90min., 1 per 2hr., €5); La Spezia (20min., 2 per hr., €1.40); Pisa (2hr., 1 per hr., €5.50); Rome (7hr., 1 per 2hr., €24). **Ferries** run from La Spezia to Monterosso (2hr., 4 per day, €18). The five villages stretch along the shore between Levanto and La Spezia, connected by trains (5-20min., every 45min., €1.40), **roads** (although cars are not allowed inside the towns), and coastal and inland **footpaths. Monterosso** is the westernmost town and the largest, containing most of the services for the area, followed by higher-end **Vernazza,** rocky-shored **Corniglia,** swimming-cove-dotted **Manarola,** and affordable **Riomaggiore.** The Monterosso **park office** is at P. Garibaldi 20. (☎0187 81 78 38. Open daily 8am-8pm.) The Pro Loco **tourist office,** V. Fegina 38, Monterosso, is below the train station. (☎0187 81 75 06. Open daily 9:30am-6:30pm.) **Postal Codes:** 19016 (Monterosso); 19017 (Manarola and Riomaggiore); 19018 (Corniglia and Vernazza).

ACCOMMODATIONS. Most hotels are in Riomaggiore, and they fill quickly in summer. The tourist office offers info on the plentiful *affittacamere* (private rooms). For help finding a room in Riomaggiore, call **Edi,** V. Colombo 111. (☎0187 92 03 25.) Popular with students, **Hotel Souvenir ❷,** V. Gioberti 30, Monterosso, has 47 beds and a friendly staff. (☎0187 81 75 95. Student rooms with shared bath €26; private rooms €44. Cash only.) **Ostello Cinque Terre ❷,** V. B. Riccobaldi 21, in Manarola, has a sweeping roof terrace. Turn right from the train station and continue up the hill. (☎0187 92 02 15; www.hostel5terre. com. Bike, kayak, and snorkeling equipment rental. Breakfast €4. Laundry €6. Lockout 10am-5pm. Curfew 1am in summer, midnight in winter. Closed Nov.-Feb. Dorms €20-23; doubles €55-65; quads €88-100. MC/V.)

FOOD. Meals at **Il Ciliegio ❷,** Località Beo, in Monterosso, near P. Garibaldi, feature ingredients from the owner's garden. (☎0187 81 78 29. *Primi* €7-10.50. *Secondi* €8-15. Open Tu-Su 12:30-2:30pm and 7:30-10:30pm. AmEx/MC/V.) Grab pesto or onion focaccia (€1-1.50) at **Fratelli Cinque Terre ❶,** V. Roma 2a, Vernazza. Steps from the beach, **Bar Centrale,** P. Garibaldi 10, in Monterosso, has gelato, pizza, focaccia, panini, and drinks. (☎0187 81 76 90. Snacks from €1.50. Gelato from €2, available only after 1pm. Open daily 11am-11pm.) **Ripa del Sole ❸**, V. de Gasperi 282, Riomaggiore, serves some of the area's best seafood. (☎0187 92 07 43. *Primi* €10-13. *Secondi* €12-24. Open Tu-Su noon-2pm and 7-10pm. AmEx/ MC/V.) Get groceries at **SuperCONAD Margherita**, P. Matteotti 9, Monterosso. (Open June-Sept. M-Sa 8am-1pm and 5-8pm, Su 8am-1pm. MC/V.)

⚠️📷 OUTDOOR ACTIVITIES AND NIGHTLIFE. The best sights in Cinque Terre are the five villages themselves, and the gorgeous paths that connect them. Monterosso has Cinque Terre's largest free **beach,** in front of the historic center, sheltered by a cliff cove. The **hike** between Monterosso and Vernazza (1hr.) is considered the most difficult, with steep climbs winding past terraced vineyards. From there, the trip to Corniglia (1hr.) offers breathtaking views of the sea and olive groves, with scents of rosemary, lemon, and lavender. Near Corniglia, the secluded **Guvano Beach** is popular with students and adventurous types willing to make the trek down the mountain. Take the stairs down to the station from V. della Stazione in Corniglia and turn left, following the path along the railroad tracks to the public beach; the hike to youthful Manarola (1hr.) begins just past the beach, and is easier, though less picturesque. The most famous Cinque Terre hike, the **Via dell'Amore,** from Manarola to Riomaggiore, the smallest of the five towns, is a 20min. slate-paved walk that features a stone 📷**tunnel of love** decorated in graffiti with romantic scenes.

At night, the liveliest towns are Monterosso and Riomaggiore. **Il Casello,** V. Lungo Fessario 70, Monterosso, lures backpackers with its beachside location. (Wine from €3. Open daily noon-midnight. Cash only.) **Bar Centrale,** V. C. Colombo 144, Riomaggiore, caters to a young, international crowd. (Beer €3-5.50. Mixed drinks €5.50-7. Open daily 7:30am-1am. Cash only.)

EMILIA-ROMAGNA

Go to Florence, Venice, and Rome to sightsee. Come to Emilia-Romagna to eat. Italy's wealthy wheat- and dairy-producing region spans the fertile plains of the Po River Valley and fosters some of the finest culinary traditions of the Italian peninsula, freeing visitors from the binds of the elsewhere omnipresent *menù turistico*. But Emilia-Romagna deserves more than just a quick stopover for some *Bolognese;* combining a rich history with modern cities, it's an essential destination for any Italian traveler.

BOLOGNA ☎051

Affectionately referred to as the *grassa* (fat) and *dotta* (learned) city, Bologna (pop. 370,000) has a legacy of excellent food, education, and art. Bologna's museums and churches house priceless artistic treasures, and the city is also home to Europe's oldest university. After experiencing Bologna's many free sights and student-friendly nightlife, travelers leave more than satisfied with their taste of *la dolce vita*. Be as cautious in Bologna as in a big city; guard your wallet and don't travel solo at night.

📷📷 TRANSPORTATION AND PRACTICAL INFORMATION. Trains leave the northern tip of Bologna's walled city for: Florence (1hr., 38 per day, €5.10); Milan (3hr., 40 per day, €19); Rome (3hr., 46 per day, €32); Venice (2hr., 30 per day, €8.20). **Buses** #11, 20, and 27 run from the train station up V. Indipendenza and down V. Rizzoli to Strada Maggiore (€1). Alternatively, head through P. XX Settembre to V. dell'Indipendenza, which leads to P. del Nettuno and P. Maggiore. The **tourist office,** P. Maggiore 1, is in Palazzo del Podestà. (☎051 23 96 60; www.bolognaturismo.info. Open daily 9:30am-7:30pm.) **Postal Code:** 40100.

ꝑ ACCOMMODATIONS AND FOOD. Bologna's hotels, mostly located around V. Ugo Bassi and V. Marconi, are pricey; reserve ahead, especially in summer and early fall. Take V. Ugo Bassi from P. del Nettuno, then take the third left to reach **Albergo Panorama ❹,** V. Livraghi 1, 4th fl., where sunny rooms look out over V. Ugo Bassi. Three sparkling bathrooms serve all 10 rooms, each with sink and TV. (☎051 22 18 02; www.hotelpanoramabologna.it. Breakfast included. Reception 7am-10pm. Singles €50; doubles €60-70, with bath €80; triples €80-85; quads €90-95. AmEx/MC/V.) Six kilometers northeast of the *centro,* **Ostello due Torre San Sisto (HI) ❷,** V. Viadagola 5, has a basketball court and a reading room with satellite TV. Take bus #93 (301 on Su) from V. Marconi 69 (M-Sa 2 per hr.); ask the driver for the San Sisto stop. The hostel is the yellow building on the left. (☎051 50 18 10. Breakfast included. Internet €3.50 per hr. Lockout 10am-2pm. Dorms €16; doubles €38. €3 HI discount. AmEx/MC/V.)

Scout **Via Augusto Righi, Via Piella,** and **Via Saragozza** for traditional *trattorie* offering Bologna's signature *spaghetti alla Bolognese.* The small, student-populated eatery █**Terra del Sole ❶,** Via Petroni 3/B, offers delicious Bolognese plates with a healthy twist. The rotating menu consists of fresh pasta dishes and couscous, bean, and fruit salads. (☎051 26 26 08. Pasta *primi* €4-4.40, calzones €2.20, salads €3.80. Open M-F 11am-8pm. Cash only.) **Osteria dell'Orsa ❶,** V. Mentana 1/F, is a casual joint close to nightlife that caters to students with its fresh, simple dishes and social, communal seating. (☎051 23 15 76. *Piadini* €4-5. 0.5L wine €4. Open daily noon-1am. Cash only.) Some of the best gelato in Italy is churned at █**Il Gelatauro ❶,** V. S. Vitale 98B, where creamy flavors like almond and pine nut are sinfully rich. (☎051 23 00 49. 2 flavors €2.10, 3 flavors €2.40. Open M 8am-8pm, Tu-Th 8am-11:30pm, F-Su 8am-11pm. Closed Aug. Cash only.) A **PAM** supermarket, V. Marconi 28/A, is at the intersection with V. Riva di Reno. (Open M-Sa 7:45am-8pm, Su 9am-8pm. AmEx/MC/V.)

◖█ SIGHTS AND NIGHTLIFE. The ancient *palazzi* and expensive boutiques in █**Piazza Maggiore** are dwarfed by the Romanesque **Palazzo del Podestà,** and nearby **Basilica di San Petronio,** P. Maggiore 3. The basilica hosted both the Council of Trent (when it wasn't meeting in Trent) and the 1530 ceremony in which Pope Clement VII gave Italy to the German King Charles V. (Basilica open daily 7:45am-12:30pm and 3-6pm. Free.) The **Palazzo Archiginnasio,** behind S. Petronio, was the first home of Bologna's modern university. (V. Archiginnasio 1. Open M-F 9am-6:45pm, Sa 9am-1:45pm. Free.) **Piazza del Nettuno** contains Giambologna's 16th-century fountain, **Neptune and Attendants.** Two towers rise from P. Porta Ravegana, at the end of V. Rizzoli; the **Torre degli Garisenda** leans violently to one side, but the nearly 98m **Torre degli Asinelli** is climbable. (Open daily 9am-6pm. €3.) From V. Rizzoli, follow V. S. Stefano to P. S. Stefano, where the Romanesque █**Chiesa Santo Stefano** contains the basin where Pontius Pilate absolved himself of responsibility for Christ's death. (☎051 22 32 56. Modest dress required. Open daily 7am-noon and 3:30-6:45pm. Free.)

Bologna's disproportionate number of bars, clubs, and pubs ensure raucous late night fun for hip students and travelers alike, especially around V. Zamboni. As its name implies, █**College Bar,** Largo Resphigi 6/D, caters to a young crowd, with live music—ranging from jazz to techno—performed daily. (☎349 003 7366. 10am-5pm any 2 drinks €3.50. Open daily 10am-3am. Cash only.)

THE ICEMAN COMETH

In September 1991, Erica and Helmut Simon were hiking through the Tyrolean region of northeastern Italy, enjoying the scenery and getting some exercise. In between their photo ops and trail mix stops, they discovered something a little out of the ordinary: a fully-clothed but completely frozen human being.

As it turned out, the body belonged to a man from the late Neolithic Age (3300-3100 BCE), whom bolzanini have nicknamed Ötzi and taken under their wing in Bolzano's South Tyrol Museum of Archaeology. Though some too-cool locals insist that only tourists are interested in this human artifact, most take a sense of pride in the fact that Ötzi has made his way to their town.

In his real form, Ötzi isn't much to look at: he's a skeleton in a refrigerator. Plus, he's a little guy—at the time of his death, he stood only 5 feet, 2 inches tall and weighed only 132 pounds. His shoe size was 5½! (It turns out that this was about normal size in those days.)

But the museum has taken special care to portray him in a more flattering light, creating a replica on which a soft spotlight shines. Ötzi's no Prince Charming, but he's armed with a heavy coat, trusty tools, and a look of determination.

To see Ötzi, head to Bolazno's South Tyrol Museum of Archaeology (p. 528).

Cassero, located in a 17th-century salt warehouse in the Porta Saragozza, is popular with the gay community, but all are welcome. (☎051 64 94 416. Drinks €3-7. ARCI-GAY card required, available at ARCI-GAY, V. Don Minzoni 18, €8 for 1 month. W, F and Sa nights feature special *discoteca* events. Open in summer daily 9pm-4/6am; in winter W-Sa/Su 9pm-4/6am.) Every year from mid-June to mid-September, the city commune sponsors a ▢festival of art, cinema, dance, music, and theater. Many events are free, and few cost more than €5.

RIMINI   ☎0541

The Ibiza of the Adriatic, Rimini is the party town of choice for young European fashionistas. Beaches, nightclubs, and boardwalks crammed with boutiques, fortune tellers, and artists characterize a city where it is perfectly acceptable—and admirable—to collapse into bed and bid the rising sun good night. Rimini's most treasured attraction is its remarkable **beach** with fine sand and mild Adriatic waves. Rimini's nightlife heats up around the **lungomare** in southern Rimini and near the port. Bus #11 fills with rowdy partygoers as it traverses the strip of clubs. At ▢**Coconuts,** Lungomare Tintorin 5, a diverse crowd gathers until the wee hours for the tropical decor and two outdoor dance floors, (☎0541 52 325; www.coconuts.it. Mixed drinks €8. Open daily 6pm-5am.) *Discoteca* **T Life,** Vle. Regina Margherita 11, draws hoards of young partygoers to its bar and expansive dance floor. (☎0541 37 34 73. Shots €3-4. Mixed drinks €5-7.50. Cover €7-12, includes 1 drink. Open daily 11pm-4am. Cash only.)

Hostel Jammin' Rimini (HI) ❷, Vle. Derna 22, is at stop 13 on bus #11. Seconds from the beach, this hip hostel accommodates the Rimini partying lifestyle with a bar, no lockout, and breakfast until 10:30am. (Breakfast and linens included. Open Feb.-Dec. Dorms €21. AmEx/MC/V.) Stock up on groceries at the **STANDA** supermarket, V. Vespucci 13. (Open daily 8am-10:30pm. AmEx/MC/V.)

Trains (☎0541 89 20 21) run to Bologna (1hr., 44 per day, €6.80); Milan (3hr., 23 per day, €28); Ravenna (1hr., 23 per day, €3.10). The **tourist office** is at P. Fellini 3, stop 10 on bus #11. (Open in summer M-Sa 8:30am-7:15pm, Su 8:30am-2:15pm; in winter M-F 9am-1pm and 3:30-7pm, Sa 9am-1pm.) **Postal Code:** 47900.

THE VENETO

From the rocky foothills of the Dolomites to the fertile valleys of the Po River, the Veneto's geography is as diverse as its history. Once loosely united under the Venetian Empire, its towns have retained their cultural independence; in fact, visitors are more likely to hear regional dialects than standard Italian during neighborly exchanges. The tenacity of local culture and customs will come as a pleasant surprise for those expecting only mandolins and gondolas.

VENICE (VENEZIA) ☎041

In Venice (pop. 60,000), palaces stand tall on a steadily sinking network of wood, and the waters of age-old canals creep up the mossy steps of abandoned homes. People flock here year-round to float down labyrinthine canals, peer into delicate blown-glass, and gaze at the masterworks of Tintoretto and Titian. While dodging hoards of tourists and pigeons will prove inevitable, the city is nonetheless a worthwhile wonder.

TRANSPORTATION

The **train station** is on the northwest edge of the city; be sure to get off at **Santa Lucia**, not at Mestre. Buses and boats arrive at **Piazzale Roma,** across the Canal Grande from the train station. To get from either station to **Piazza San Marco,** take *vaporetto* (water bus) #1, 2, 51, or 52 or follow signs for a 25-30min. walk.

Flights: Aeroporto Marco Polo (VCE; ☎041 26 09 260; www.veniceairport.it), 10km north of the city. Take the **ATVO shuttlebus (☎**042 13 83 671) from the airport to Ple. Roma on the main island (30min., 1 per hr. 8am-midnight, €3).

Trains: Stazione Santa Lucia (☎041 89 20 21). Ticket windows open M-F 8:30am-7:30pm, Sa-Su 9am-1:30pm and 2-5:30pm. **Information office (☎**041 89 20 21) to the left as you exit the platforms. Trains go to: **Bologna** (2hr., 32 per day, €8.20); **Florence** (3hr., 19 per day, €23.50); **Milan** (3hr., 26 per day, €13.75); **Rome** (4hr., 23 per day, €41.50). **Luggage storage** by track #14.

Buses: Local **ACTV** buses (☎041 24 24; www.hellovenezia.it), in Ple. Roma. Open daily 7:30am-8pm. **ACTV long-distance carrier** runs buses to **Padua** (1hr., 2 per hr., €4).

Public Transportation: The **Canal Grande** can be crossed on foot only at the Scalzi, Rialto, and Accademia *ponti* (bridges). **Traghetti** (gondola ferry boats) traverse the canals at 7 locations, including Ferrovia, San Marculola, Cà d'Oro, and Rialto (€0.50). **Vaporetti** (V; water buses) provide 24hr. service around the city, with reduced service midnight-5am (single-ride €6.50; 24hr. *biglietto turistico* pass €16, 3-day €31). Buy tickets at *vaporetti* stops. Stock up on tickets by asking for a pass *non timbrato* (unvalidated), then validate before boarding by inserting tickets into one of the yellow boxes at each stop. **Lines #1** (slow) and **2** (fast) run from the station down Canal Grande and Canale della Giudecca; lines **#41** and **51** circumnavigate Venice from the station to Lido; **#42** and **52** do the reverse; line **LN** runs from F. Nuove to Burano, Murano, and Lido, and connects to Torcello.

ORIENTATION

Venice is composed of 118 islands in a lagoon, connected to the mainland by a thin causeway. The city is a veritable labyrinth and can confuse even natives, most of whom simply set off in a general direction and patiently weave their way. If you unglue your eyes from the map and go with the flow, you'll discover some unexpected surprises. Yellow signs all over the city point toward the following landmarks: **Ponte di Rialto** (in the center), **Piazza San Marco** (central south), **Ponte Accademia** (southwest), **Ferrovia** (the train station, in the northwest), and **Piazzale Roma** (south of the station). The **Canal Grande** winds through the city, creating six *sestieri* (sections): **Cannaregio** is in the north and includes

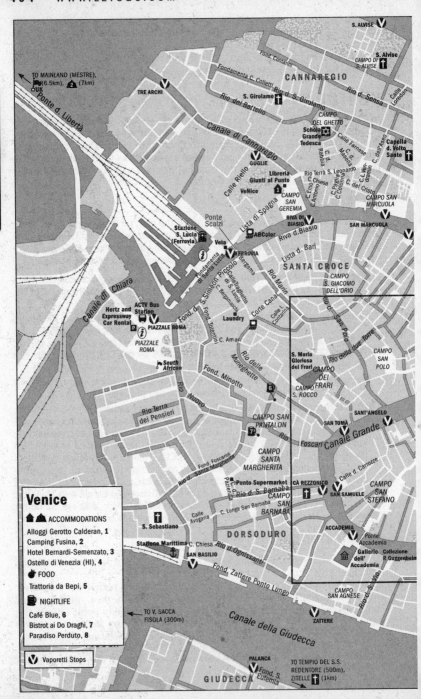

ITALY

TO MAINLAND (MESTRE), (6.5km), (7km)

Ponte d. Libertà

TRE ARCHI

Fondamenta C. Colletti

Fond. Contarini

CANNAREGIO

S. Girolamo

Rio d. S. Girolamo

Rio del Battello

Canale di Cannaregio

Rio d. Sensa

Calle Loredan

S. ALVISE

S. Alvise

CAMPO DI S. ALVISE

CAMPO DEL GHETTO

Schola Grande Tedesca

Calle Farnese

C. d. Rabbia

C. d. Masena

Calle dell'Aseo

Capella d. Volto Santo

GUGLIE

Calle Riello

Libreria Giunti al Punto

VeNice

Rio Terrà S. Leonardo

C. d. Chiesa

C. d. Antiomo

C.Emo

C.Farsetti

C. Paglia

C. Colombo

C. del Cristo

C.L.Ven-dramin

CAMPO SAN MARCUOLA

CAMPO SAN GEREMIA

Canale di Chiara

Ponte Scalzi

Lista di Spagna

ABColer

RIVA DI BIASIO

Riva d. Biasio

SAN MARCUOLA

Stazione S. Lucia (Ferrovia)

Vela

FERROVIA

Lista di Bari

SANTA CROCE

Fondamenta di Santa Lucia

Fond. de S. Simeon Piccolo

Calleteghetto di S.Lucia

C. Bergamaschi

Calle Bergama

Rio Marin

CAMPO S. GIACOMO DELL'ORIO

ACTV Bus Station

PIAZZALE ROMA

Corte Canal

Calle Cotarini

Rio de San Polo

Hertz and Expressway Car Rental

PIAZZALE ROMA

C. Amai

Laundry

CAMPO SAN POLO

South African

Fond. Minotto

Rio delle Muneghette

S. Maria Gloriosa dei Frari

Rio della due Torre

CAMPO DEI FRARI

CAMPO S. ROCCO

Rio Nuovo

Rio della

Rio Terrà dei Pensieri

CAMPO SAN PANTALON

Rio

SANT'ANGELO

SAN TOMA

Foscari

Canale Grande

Fond. Foscarini

CAMPO SANTA MARGHERITA

Rio d. S. Margherita

Calle d. Carrozze

Punto Supermarket

CÀ REZZONICO

CAMPO SAN SAMUELE

CAMPO SAN STEFANO

Rio d. S. Barnaba

CAMPO SAN BARNABA

C. Lunga San Barnaba

Calle Avogaria

Fond. Pazienza

S. Sebastiano

DORSODURO

ACCADEMIA

Ponte Accademia

Collezione P. Guggenheim

Stazione Marittima

C. Chiesa

SAN BASILIO

Rio d'Ognissanti

Galleria dell' Accademia

Fond. Zattere Ponto Lungo

CAMPO SAN AGNESE

Rio d. S. Vio

TO V. SACCA FISOLA (300m)

ZATTERE

Canale della Giudecca

PALANCA

Fond. S. Eufemia

GIUDECCA

TO TEMPIO DEL S.S. REDENTORE (500m), ZITELLE (1km)

Venice

🏠🏕 ACCOMMODATIONS

Alloggi Gerotto Calderan, **1**
Camping Fusina, **2**
Hotel Bernardi-Semenzato, **3**
Ostello di Venezia (HI), **4**

🍴 FOOD

Trattoria da Bepi, **5**

🍸 NIGHTLIFE

Café Blue, **6**
Bistrot ai Do Draghi, **7**
Paradiso Perduto, **8**

Ⓥ Vaporetti Stops

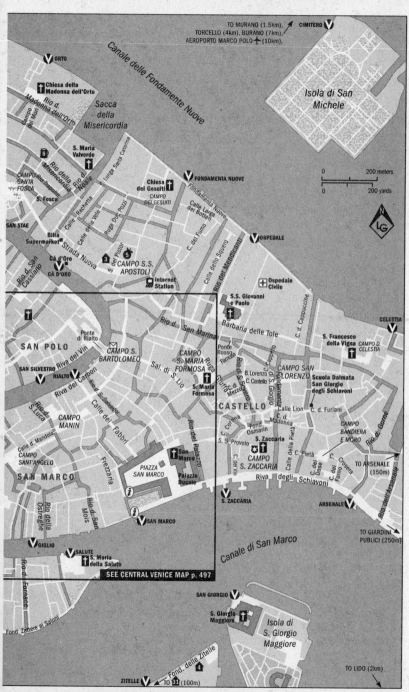

TO MURANO (1.5km),
TORCELLO (4km), BURANO (7km),
AEROPORTO MARCO POLO (10km),

CIMITERO

Isola di San
Michele

ORTO

Chiesa della
Madonna dell'Orto

Sacca
della
Misericordia

Canale delle Fondamente Nuove

Rio d.
Madonna dell'Orto

Rio della Misericordia

S. Maria
Valverde

Campo dei Mori

CAMPO
SANTA
FOSCA

Rio della Sensa

S. Fosca

FONDAMENTA NUOVE

Chiesa
dei Gesuiti

CAMPO
DEI GESUITI

Calle Lunga Santa Caterina

Calle Racchetta

Fondamenta Nuove

Calle Larga
dei Botteri

SAN STAE

Billa
Supermarket

Strada Nuova

Rio d. San
Cassiano

Cà d'Oro

CÀ D'ORO

Rio d. Noale

Calle delle Vele

Ruga Due Pozzi

S. di Pistor

CAMPO S.S.
APOSTOLI

Internet
Station

C. dei Fumo

Calle dello Squero

Rio dei Mendicanti

OSPEDALE

200 meters
200 yards

Ospedale
Civile

S.S. Giovanni
e Paolo

Calle delle Cappuccine

CELESTIA

Ponte
di Rialto

SAN POLO

Riva del Vin

Rio d. San Marina

Barbaria delle Tole

C. d. Cappuccine

S. Francesco
della Vigna

CAMPO D.
CELESTIA

SAN SILVESTRO

RIALTO

Riva del Carbon

CAMPO S.
BARTOLOMEO

CAMPO
S. MARIA
FORMOSA

Ponte
Rosso

Ruga Giuffa

Rio di S. Severo

Calle S. Lio

S. Maria
Formosa

Sal. di S. Lio

B. Lorenzo

S. Castello

Rio di S. Lorenzo

CAMPO SAN
LORENZO

Scuola Dalmata
San Giorgio
degli Schiavoni

Calle Lion

C. d. Furlani

Calle del Fabbri

CAMPO
MANIN

Calle d. Mandola

CAMPO
SANT'ANGELO

SAN MARCO

Calle Salizzada

Rio del Palazzo

CASTELLO

Corona

S. Provolo

C. Corona

Fond.
Osmarin

S. Zaccaria

CAMPO
S. ZACCARIA

Calle della Pietà

S. Pietà

C. d.
Madonna

C. d.
Bose

C. d.
Forno

C. Crosera

CAMPO
BANDIERA
E MORO

Rio di Gorne

Rio dell'Arsenale

TO ARSENALE
(150m)

Frezzaria

PIAZZA
SAN MARCO

San
Marco

Palazzo
Ducale

Rio della
Ostreghe

Rio di San
Mois

Riva degli Schiavoni

SAN MARCO

S. ZACCARIA

ARSENALE

TO GIARDINI
PUBBLICI (250m)

GIGLIO

SALUTE

S. Maria
della Salute

SEE CENTRAL VENICE MAP p. 497

Rio d.
Fornace

Canale di San Marco

SAN GIORGIO

S. Giorgio
Maggiore

Isola di
S. Giorgio
Maggiore

TO LIDO (2km)

Fond. Zattere ai Saloni

ZITELLE

Fond. delle Zitelle

TO 31 (100m)

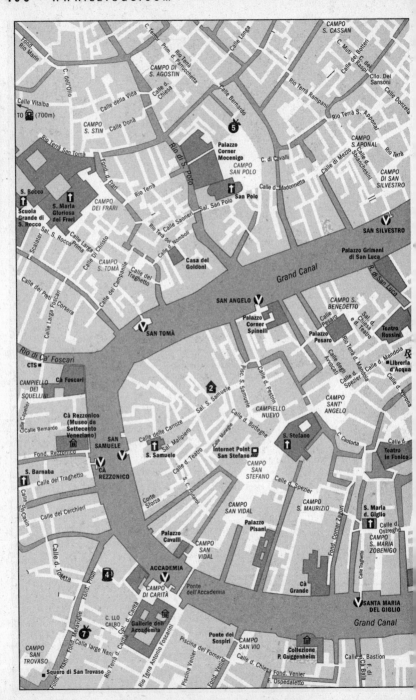

ITALY

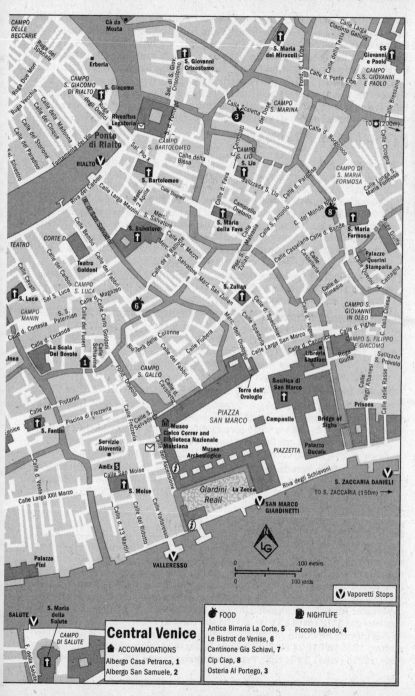

Central Venice

🏠 **ACCOMMODATIONS**

Albergo Casa Petrarca, **1**
Albergo San Samuele, **2**

🍎 **FOOD**

Antica Birraria La Corte, **5**
Le Bistrot de Venise, **6**
Cantinone Gia Schiavi, **7**
Cip Ciap, **8**
Osteria Al Portego, **3**

🌙 **NIGHTLIFE**

Piccolo Mondo, **4**

V **Vaporetti Stops**

the train station, Jewish ghetto, and Cà d'Oro; **Castello** extends east toward the Arsenale; **Dorsoduro**, across the bridge from S. Marco, stretches the length of Canale della Giudecca and up to Campo S. Pantalon; **Santa Croce** lies west of S. Polo, across the Canal Grande from the train station; **San Marco** fills in the area between the Ponte di Rialto and Ponte Accademia; and **San Polo** runs north from Chiesa S. Maria dei Frari to the Ponte di Rialto. In each *sestiere*, addresses are not specific to a particular street—every building is given a number, and jumps between numbers are unpredictable. If *sestiere* boundaries prove too vague, Venice's **parrochie** (parishes) provide a more defined idea of where you are.

PRACTICAL INFORMATION

Tourist Office: APT, Cal. della Ascensione, S. Marco 71/F (☎041 52 98 740; www.doge. it), directly opposite the basilica. Open daily 9am-3:30pm. Avoid the mobbed branches at the train and bus stations. The **Rolling Venice Card** (€4) offers discounts on transportation and at over 200 restaurants, cafes, hotels, museums, and shops for ages 14-29. Cards are valid for 1 year from date of purchase and can be purchased at APT, which provides a list of participating vendors, or at the **ACTV VeLa** office (☎041 27 47 650) in Ple. Roma. Open daily 7am-8pm. **VeneziaSi** (☎800 84 30 06), next to the tourist office in the train station, books rooms for a €2 fee. Open daily 8am-9pm. Branches in Ple. Roma (☎041 52 28 640) and the airport (☎041 54 15 133).

Budget Travel: CTS, F. Tagliapietra, Dorsoduro 3252 (☎041 52 05 660; www.cts.it). From Campo S. Barnaba, cross the bridge closest to the church and follow the road through the *piazza*. Turn left at the foot of the large bridge. Sells discounted plane tickets and issues ISICs. English spoken. Open M-F 9:30am-1:30pm and 2:30-6pm. MC/V.

Pharmacy: Farmacia Italo-Inglese, Cal. della Mandola, S. Marco 3717 (☎041 52 24 837). Follow Cal. Cortesia out of Campo Manin. Open Apr.-Nov. M-F 9am-1:30pm and 2:30-7:30pm, Sa 3:30-7:30pm; Dec.-Mar. M-F 9am-12:30pm and 3:45-7:30pm, Sa 3:30-7:30pm. MC/V. Pharmacies rotate late-night and weekend hours; check the list posted in the window of any pharmacy.

Hospital: Ospedale Civile, Campo S. S. Giovanni e Paolo, Castello (☎041 52 94 111).

Internet: ABColor, Lista di Spagna, Cannaregio 220 (☎041 52 44 380). Look for the "@" symbol on a yellow sign, left off the main street heading from the train station. €6 per hr., students €4. Printing €0.15 per page. Open M-Sa 10am-8pm. **Internet Station,** Cannaregio 5640. Just over the bridge toward S. Marco from C. Apostoli. €4 per 30min., €7 per hr. 20% student discount with ID. Open M-Sa 10am-1pm and 3-8pm.

Post Office: Poste Venezia Centrale, Salizzada Fontego dei Tedeschi, S. Marco 5554 (☎041 27 17 111), off Campo S. Bartolomeo. Open M-Sa 8:30am-6:30pm. **Postal Codes:** 30121 (Cannaregio); 30122 (Castello); 30123 (Dorsoduro); 30135 (S. Croce); 30124 (S. Marco); 30125 (S. Polo).

ACCOMMODATIONS AND CAMPING

Hotels in Venice are often more expensive than those elsewhere in Italy, but savvy travelers can find cheap rooms if they sniff out options early in summer. Agree on a price before booking, and reserve one month ahead. **VeneziaSi** (see **Tourist Offices**, p. 498) finds rooms on the same day, but not cheap ones. If you're looking for a miracle, try religious institutions, which often offer rooms in summer for €25-110. Options include: **Casa Murialdo,** F. Madonna dell'Orto, Cannaregio 3512 (☎041 71 99 33); **Domus Cavanis,** Dorsoduro 896 (☎041 52 87 374), near the Ponte Accademia; **Istituto Canossiano,** F. delle Romite, Dorsoduro 1323 (☎041 24 09 713); **Istituto Ciliota,** Cal. Muneghe S. Stefano, San Marco 2976 (☎041 52 04 888); **Patronato Salesiano Leone XIII,** Cal. S. Domenico,

Castello 1281 (☎041 52 87 299). For **camping,** plan on a 20min. boat ride from Venice. In addition to camping options listed here, Litorale del Cavallino, on the Lido's Adriatic side, has multiple beach campgrounds.

Alloggi Gerotto Calderan, Campo San Geremia, Cannaregio 283 (☎041 71 55 62 or 041 71 53 61; www.283.it). From the train station, turn left on Lista di Spagna; continue for 5min. until you reach C.S. Geremia. Half hostel, half hotel in a great location. All rooms have bath. Internet €4 per hr. Wi-Fi available, 1st 15min. free. Check-in 2pm. Lockout for dorms 10:30am-2pm. Curfew 1am. 4- to 6-person dorms €23-25; singles €35-60; doubles €50-90; triples €75-105. Rolling Venice discount 10%; discounts for longer stays. Cash only. ❷

Albergo San Samuele, Salizada S. Samuele, San Marco 3358 (☎041 52 28 045; www.albergosansamuele.it). Follow C. delle Botteghe from Campo Santo Stefano and turn left on Salizada San Samuele. Spacious and simple rooms on a quiet street 10min. from P. S. Marco, including several family suites with kitchens. Smaller rooms only have fan. Breakfast (€5) served 5min. away at Ribo Restaurant. Free Wi-Fi. 24hr reception. Reserve 1-2 months ahead. Singles with shared bath €45-65; doubles €65-85, with bath €85-120. Check website as prices change often. AmEx/MC/V. ❹

Hotel Arcadia, Cannaregio 1333/D (☎041 717 355 www.hotelarcadia.net). From Campo Geremia, cross Ponte delle Guglie and follow the road. Look for the sign on the left. Housed in a 17th-century palace, this hotel offers luxurious rooms 5min. from the train station. Rooms are equipped with private baths, TV, and safe, but (sigh) no A/C. Breakfast included. Free Wi-Fi. Singles €45-80; doubles €80-120; triples €80-150; quads €90-160. MC/V. ❹

Best B&B, Calle del Capeler, S. Polo 1575 (☎349 00 70 508). From Ponte Rialto walk northwest on Ruga D. Oresi, turn left on Calle D. Boteri and left again on Calle Del Capeler. Simple B&B in the center of the city with dorm-style rooms and a super friendly owner. Breakfast included. Reservations required. Dorms €18-28 per person; doubles €60-80; triples €100-120. Cash only. ❷

Pensione Seguso, Fondamente Zattere ai Saloni, Dorsoduro 779 (☎041 52 86 858; www.pensioneseguso.com). From V: Zattere, walk right. Great real estate right on the canal. Antique decor. Breakfast included; ½- and full-pension available. Reception open 8am-9pm. Open Jan. and Mar.-Nov. Singles €40-122, with bath €50-160; doubles €65-180/70-190; triples €150-235/160-245; quads €190-255. Prices vary seasonally. AmEx/MC/V. ❺

Foresteria Valdese, Castello 5170 (☎041 52 86 797; www.diaconiavaldese.org/venezia). From Campo Santa Maria Formosa, take Calle Lunga Santa Maria Formosa; it's over the 1st bridge. An 18th-century house run by a Protestant church. Ornately decorated with a gorgeous fresco on the ceiling and river views to match. Breakfast included. Reception 8:30am-8pm. Lockout 10am-1pm. Reservations required for bedrooms, though not possible for dorms. Dorms €27 for 1-night stays, €24 otherwise; doubles €78-88, with kitchen €85-91; triples €90-99, with bath €96-102; quads with bath €114-126; quints with bath €132-147. Rolling Venice discount €1. MC/V. ❺

La Residenza, Campo Bandiera e Moro, Castello 3608 (☎041 52 85 315; www.venicelaresidenza.com). From V: Arsenal, turn left on Riva degli Schiavoni and right on C. del Dose into the *campo.* Live like a prince: lavish carpets and paintings and a sunny terrace overlooking the *campo* greet guests in this renovated 15th-century *palazzo.* Spacious and elegantly furnished rooms with TV, A/C, private bathroom, safe, and minibar. Breakfast included. Free Wi-Fi. Reception 24hr. Singles €50-100; doubles €80-180. Extra bed €35. MC/V. ❹

◻ FOOD

With few exceptions, the best restaurants lie in alleyways, not along the canals around San Marco that advertise a *menù turistico*. Venetian cuisine is dominated by fish, like *sarde in saor* (sardines in vinegar and onions), available only in Venice and sampled cheaply at most bars with other types of *cicchetti* (tidbits of seafood, rice, and meat; €1-3). **Wines** of the Veneto and Friuli regions include the whites *Prosecco della Marca*, *Bianco di Custoza*, and dry *Tocai*, as well as the red *Valpolicella*. Venice's renowned Rialto **markets** spread between the Canal Grande and the San Polo foot of the Rialto every Monday through Saturday morning. A **BILLA supermarket,** Str. Nuova, Cannaregio 5660, is near Campo S. Fosca. (Open M-Sa 8:30am-8:30pm, Su 9am-8:30pm. AmEx/MC/V.

◪ **Le Bistrot de Venise,** C. dei Fabbri, San Marco 4685 (☎041 52 36 651; www.bis-trotdevenise.com). From P. San Marco, head through 2nd Sottoportego dei Dai under the awning. Follow road over two bridges and turn right. Scrumptious Venetian dishes and over 50 wines, based on medieval and Renaissance recipes. Only restaurant with an in-house librarian scouring for *renascimento* delicacies. Share the tasting *menù* (€45) or try dishes like marinated *umbrine* in black grape sauce with yellow garlic and almond pudding (€28). Check the website for cultural events and wine tastings on the schedule. *Enoteca:* cicchetti €3-4, meat/cheese plates €12-24. Restaurant: primi €12-24; secondi €18-32. Wine from €5 per glass. Open daily 10:30am-midnight. Rolling Venice discount 10%. AmEx/MC/V. ❹

◪ **Trattoria da Fiore,** Santo Stefano 3461 (☎041 52 35 310; www.trattoriadafiore.com). Take Calle de le Boteghe from Campiello San Stefano. Neighbors claim this is the only true *bacaro* left in San Marco. Serves a simple menu with wine (from €2 per glass) and tasty *cicchetti* (from €0.50). Try *spaghetti pinoli* with fresh tomatoes and basil (€10). Brush up on your Italian; this place is filled with locals. Plates €9-15. Open M and W-Su 8:30am-12:30am. Cash only. ❷

◪ **Gam Gam,** Canale di Cannaregio, Cannaregio 1122 (☎041 71 52 84). From Campo S. Geremia, cross the bridge and turn left. Canal-side tables, friendly owners, and a unique mix of Italian and Jewish cuisines. Bars from the old Jewish ghetto preserved for all to see. Try their *Pasticcio Gam Gam* (vegetable lasagna; €9) or their special Israeli appetizer plates (€9.80). Main courses €7.50-15. Kosher. Open M-Th and Su noon-10pm, F noon-4pm. *Let's Go* discount 10%. Cash only. ❷

◪ **Antica Birraria La Corte,** Campo S. Polo, San Polo 2168 (☎041 27 50 570; www.birrarialacorte.it). The expansive interior of this former brewery houses a large restaurant and bar as well as outdoor tables on the large peaceful *campo*. Head inside for a fun beer-hall atmosphere. Filling salads (€10) hit the spot in the summer heat. Pizza €5.50-9. Primi €11-15. Secondi €13.50-19. Cover €2. Restaurant open daily noon-2:30pm and 7-10:30pm. Pizzeria open summer 10am-midnight. AmEx/MC/V. ❸

◪ **Cantinone Gia Schiavi,** Fondamenta Meraviglie, Dorsoduro 992 (☎041 52 30 034). From the Frari, follow signs for the Accademia bridge. Just before Ponte Meraviglie, turn toward the Chiesa di San Trovaso. Cross the 1st bridge. Choose from hundreds of wines (€2-5) and dozens of fresh *cicchetti* (€1) with toppings like pumpkin cream in this old *enoteca*. Standing room only. Open M-Sa 8am-11pm, Su 8am-noon. Cash only. ❶

Cip Ciap, C. del Mondo Novo, Castello 5799/A (☎041 52 36 621). From Campo S. Maria Formosa, follow C. del Mondo Novo. Perhaps Venice's best value pizzeria. Uses fresh ingredients on Sicilian slices sold by weight (€1.20 per 100g). Their best deals are the huge prosciutto-filled calzones and margherita pies (€2.50). No seating; nab a bench in the nearby *campo*. Open M and W-Su 9am-9pm. Cash only. ❶

Frary's, Fondamenta dei Frari, San Polo 2559 (☎041 72 00 50). Across from entrance to S. Maria Gloriosa dei Frari. Right on the river. Serves Greek and Arab cuisine with many vegetarian options. Try the lunch *menù* (€12), which includes 1 appetizer and 1 main course, or the tasting *menù* (€9). Appetizers €4-6. Main courses €8.50-14. Cover €1.50. Open M and W-Su noon-3:15pm and 6-10:30pm. AmEx/MC/V. ❷

Gelati Nico, Zattere, Dorsoduro 922 (☎041 52 25 293). From V: Zattere, walk west along the waterfront. Grab a quick, freshly made gelato (€1.20) before a long walk along the waterfront. Open M-Sa 6:45am-12pm and 7:30-11:30pm. Cash only. ❶

Pizza and Kebab Toletta, Dorsoduro 1215 (☎041 24 13 324). From Ponte Accademia head west on C. Contarini Corfu, cross the bridge and follow C. Tolleta. Skip overpriced restaurants next to the museums and grab a huge slice of pizza (€1.80) or falafel sandwich (€3) at this simple pizzeria just a few blocks away. Pies €3.50-7. Open daily 11am-4pm and 5:30pm-midnight. Cash only. ❶

👁 SIGHTS

Venice's layout makes sightseeing a disorienting affair. Most sights center around the **Piazza San Marco.** Museum passes (€18, students €12), sold at participating museums, grant one-time admission to each of 10 museums over the course of six months. The Foundation for the Churches of Venice (☎041 27 50 462; www.chorusvenezia.org) sells the **Chorus Pass** (€9, students €6), which provides admission to all of Venice's churches.

AROUND PIAZZA SAN MARCO

Venice's only official *piazza*, **Piazza San Marco** is an un-Venetian expanse of light, space, and architectural harmony. Enclosing the *piazza* are rows of cafes and expensive shops along the Renaissance **Procuratie Vecchie.** The 96m brick **campanile** (bell tower; open daily 9am-9pm, €6) provides one of the best views of the city; on clear days, the panorama spans Croatia and Slovenia.

▓BASILICA DI SAN MARCO. The symmetrical arches and incomparable mosaics of Venice's crown jewel grace Piazza San Marco. To avoid the long lines at Basilica di San Marco, visit early in the morning; still, late afternoon visits profit from the best natural light. Begun in the 9th century to house the remains of St. Mark, which had been stolen from Alexandria by Venetian merchants, the church now sparkles with 13th-century Byzantine and 16th-century Renaissance mosaics. Behind the altar, the **Pala d'Oro** relief frames a parade of saints in gem-encrusted gold. The rose-adorned tomb of St. Mark rests at the altar. The **tesoro** (treasury) contains precious relics from the Fourth Crusade. Steep stairs in the atrium lead to the **Galleria della Basilica,** which affords intimate views of the tiny golden tiles in the basilica's vast ceiling mosaics, as well as the original bronze **Cavalli di San Marco** (Horses of St. Mark). A balcony overlooks the *piazza.* (*Basilica open M-Sa 9:45am-5pm, Su 2-4pm. Modest dress required. Free. Pala d'Oro and treasury open in summer M-F 9:45am-5pm, Sa-Su 2-4:30pm, in winter M-F 9:45am-4pm, Sa-Su 2-4pm. €3/2. Galleria open M-Sa 9:45am-4:45pm. €4.*)

▓PALAZZO DUCALE (DOGE'S PALACE). Once the home of Venice's *doge* (mayor), the Palazzo Ducale is now a museum. Veronese's *Rape of Europa* is among its spectacular works. In the courtyard, Sansovino's enormous sculptures, *Mars* and *Neptune*, flank the **Scala dei Giganti** (Stairs of the Giants), upon which new *doges* were crowned. The Council of Ten, the *doge's* administrators, would drop the names of suspected criminals into the **Bocca di Leone** (Lion's Mouth), on the balcony. Climb the **Scala d'Oro** (Golden Staircase) to the **Sala delle Quattro Porte** (Room of the Four Doors) and the **Sala dell'Anticollegio** (Antechamber of the Senate), whose decorations depict myths about Venice.

Courtrooms of the Council of Ten and the Council of Three lead to the **Sala del Maggior Consiglio** (Great Council Room), dominated by Tintoretto's *Paradise*, the largest oil painting in the world. Near the end, thick stone lattices line the **Ponte dei Sospiri** (Bridge of Sighs), named after the mournful groans of prisoners who walked it on their way to the prison's damp cells. *(Wheelchair-accessible. Open daily Apr.-Oct. 9am-7pm; Nov.-Mar. 9am-5pm. €16, students €10.)*

CHIESA DI SAN ZACCARIA. Designed in the late 1400s by Coducci and others, and dedicated to John the Baptist's father, this Gothic-Renaissance church holds S. Zaccaria's corpse in a sarcophagus along the nave's right wall. Nearby is Bellini's *Virgin and Child Enthroned with Four Saints*, a Renaissance masterpiece. *(S. Marco. V: S. Zaccaria. Open daily 10am-noon and 4-6pm. Free.)*

AROUND THE PONTE RIALTO

THE GRAND CANAL. The Grand Canal is Venice's "main street." Over 3km long and nearly 50m wide, it loops through the city and passes under three bridges: the **Ponte Scalzi, Rialto,** and **Accademia.** The *bricole*, candy-cane posts used for mooring boats on the canal, are painted with the colors of the family whose *palazzo* adjoins them. *(For great facade views, ride V. #1 or 2 from the train station to P. S. Marco. The facades are lit at night and produce dazzling reflections.)*

RIVOALTUS LEGATORIA. Step into the book-lined Rivoaltus shop on any given day and hear Wanda Scarpa greet you from the attic, where she has been sewing leatherbound, antique-style **journals** for an international cadre of customers and faithful locals for more than three decades. Though Venice is now littered with shops selling journals, Rivoaltus was the first and remains the best. *(Ponte di Rialto 11. Notebooks €19-39. Photo albums €37-79. Open daily 10am-7:30pm.)*

PONTE RIALTO. This structure is named after Rivo Alto, the first colony built in Venice. The original wood bridge collapsed in the 1500s; the stone replacement is strong enough to support the plethora of shops that line it today.

SAN POLO

The second-largest *campo* in Venice, **Campo San Polo** once hosted bloody bull-baiting matches during *Carnevale*. Today, the *campo* is dotted with elderly women and trees, and there is no blood spilled on the ground—only gelato.

BASILICA DI SANTA MARIA GLORIOSA DEI FRARI. Titian's corpse and two of his paintings reside within this Gothic church, known as *I Frari* and begun by Franciscans in 1340. ▨**Assumption** (1516-18), on the high altar, marks the height of the Venetian Renaissance. The golden Florentine chapel, to the right of the high altar, frames Donatello's gaunt wooden sculpture, **St. John the Baptist.** Titian's tomb is an elaborate lion-topped triumphal arch with bas-relief scenes of Paradise. *(S. Polo. V: S. Tomà. Open M-Sa 9am-6pm, Su 1-6pm. €3.)*

CHIESA DI SAN GIACOMO DI RIALTO. Between the Rialto and nearby markets stands Venice's first church, diminutively called "San Giacometto." Across the *piazza*, a statue called *Il Gobbo* (The Hunchback) supports the steps, once used for announcements. At the foot of the statue, convicted thieves would collapse after being forced to run naked from P. S. Marco. *(V: Rialto. Cross bridge and turn right. Church open M-Sa 10am-6pm. Free.)*

DORSODURO

▨**COLLEZIONE PEGGY GUGGENHEIM.** Guggenheim's Palazzo Venier dei Leoni displays works by Dalí, Duchamp, Kandinsky, Klee, Magritte, Picasso, and Pollock. The Marini sculpture *Angel in the City*, in front of the *palazzo*, was designed with a detachable penis so that Ms. Guggenheim could avoid offending her more prudish guests. *(F. Venier dei Leoni, Dorsoduro 701. V: Accademia. Turn left and follow the yellow signs. Open M and W-Su 10am-6pm. €10; students and Rolling Venice €5.)*

▨**GALLERIE DELL'ACCADEMIA.** The Accademia houses the world's most extensive collection of Venetian art. Among the enormous altarpieces in **Room II,** Giovanni Bellini's *Madonna Enthroned with Child, Saints, and Angels* stands out with its soothing serenity. **Rooms IV** and **V** have more Bellinis plus Giorgione's enigmatic *La Tempesta.* In **Room VI,** three paintings by Tintoretto, *The Creation of the Animals*, *The Temptation of Adam and Eve*, and *Cain and Abel*, grow progressively darker with age. **Room X** displays Titian's last painting, a *Pietà* intended for his tomb. In **Room XX,** works by Bellini and Carpaccio depict Venetian processions and cityscapes so accurately that scholars use them as "photos" of Venice's past. *(V: Accademia. Open M 8:15am-2pm, Tu-Su 8:15am-7:15pm. €6.50. English-language tours F-Su 10am and 3:30pm, €7.)*

CHIESA DI SANTA MARIA DELLA SALUTE. The *salute* (Italian for "health") is a hallmark of the Venetian skyline: perched on Dorsoduro's peninsula just southwest of San Marco, the church and its graceful domes are visible from everywhere in the city. In 1631, the city had **Baldassarre Longhena** build the church for the Virgin Mary, who they believed would end the current plague. Next to the *salute* stands the *dogana*, the customs house, where ships sailing into Venice were required to pay duties. *(Dorsoduro. V: Salute. ☎041 52 25 558. Open daily 9am-noon and 3-5:30pm. Free. The inside of the dogana is closed to the public.)*

CASTELLO

CHIESA DI SANTISSIMI GIOVANNI E PAOLO. This brick structure, also called San Zanipolo, is built primarily in the Gothic style but has a Renaissance portal and an arch supported by Greek columns. Inside, monumental walls and ceilings enclose the tombs and monuments of the *doges*. An altarpiece by Bellini depicts St. Christopher, St.Sebastian, and St. Vincent Ferrer. The equestrian statue of local mercenary Bartolomeo Colleoni stands on a marble pedestal outside; he left Venice his inheritance on the condition that his monument stand in San Marco, but the city chose this more modest spot. *(Castello. V: Fond. Nuove. Turn left, then right on Fond. dei Mendicanti. ☎041 52 35 913. Open M-Sa 9am-6:30pm, Su noon-6:30pm. €2.50, students €1.25.)*

CHIESA DI SANTA MARIA DEI MIRACOLI. The Lombardi family designed this small Renaissance jewel in the late 1400s. Inside the tiny pink-, white-, and blue-marble exterior sits a fully functional parish with a golden ceiling and pastel walls interrupted only by the vibrant window above the apse. *(Cross the bridge directly in front of S. Giovanni e Paolo, and continue down Cal. Larga Gallina over 2 bridges. Open July-Aug. M-Sa 10am-5pm; Sept.-June M-Sa 10am-5pm, Su 1-5pm. €3.)*

CANNAREGIO

JEWISH GHETTO. In 1516, the *doge* forced Venice's Jewish population into the old cannon-foundry area, creating the first Jewish ghetto in Europe and coining the word "ghetto," the Venetian word for foundry. In the Campo del Ghetto Nuovo, the **Schola Grande Tedesca** (German Synagogue), the area's oldest synagogue, and the **Museo Ebraica di Venezia** (Hebrew Museum of Venice) now share a building. *(Cannaregio 2899/B. V: S. Marcuola. Museum open M-F and Su June-Sept. 10am-7pm; Oct.-May 10am-4:30pm. Enter synagogue by 40min. tour every hr. daily June-Sept. 10:30am-5:30pm; Oct.-May 10:30am-4:30pm. Museum €3, students €2. Museum and tour €8.50/7.)*

CHIESA DELLA MADONNA DELL'ORTO. Tintoretto's 14th-century parish church, the final resting place of the painter and his children, contains 10 of his largest paintings, as well some works by Titian. Look for Tintoretto's *Last Judgment* and *The Sacrifice of the Golden Calf* near the high altar. There is a light switch for illuminating the works. *(V: Madonna dell'Orto. Open M-Sa 10am-5pm. €3.)*

ISLANDS OF THE LAGOON

LIDO. The breezy resort island of Lido provided the setting for Thomas Mann's haunting novella, *Death in Venice*. Visonti's film version was also shot here at the Hotel des Bains, Lungomare Marconi 17. Today, people flock to Lido to enjoy the surf at the popular public beach. An impressive shipwreck looms at one end, while a casino, horseback riding, and the fine Alberoni Golf Club add to the island's charm. *(V #1 and 2: Lido. Beach open daily 9am-8pm. Free.)*

MURANO. Famous since 1292 for its glass (Venice's artisans were forced off Venice proper because their kilns started fires), the six-island cluster of Murano affords visitors the opportunity to witness resident artisans blowing crystalline creations for free. Quiet streets are lined with shops and boutiques with jewelry, vases, and delicate figurines for a variety of prices; for demonstrations, look for signs directing to the *fornace*, concentrated around the Colona, Faro, and Navagero *vaporetto* stops. Some studios let visitors blow their own glass creations. The collection at the **Museo Vetrario** (Glass Museum) ranges from funereal urns to a sea-green octopus presumably designed by Carlo Scarpa in 1930. *(V #DM, LN, 5, 13, 41, 42: Faro from either S. Zaccaria or F Nuove. Museo Vetrario, F. Giustian 8. Open M-Tu and Th-Su Apr.-Oct. 10am-6pm; Nov.-Mar. 10am-5pm. €5.50, students and Rolling Venice €3. Basilica open daily 8am-7pm. Modest dress required. Free.)*

BURANO. Postcard-pretty Burano is a traditional fishing village where hand-tatted lace has become a community art. The small and somewhat dull **Scuola di Merletti di Burano** (Lace Museum), once the home of the island's professional lace-making school, features strips from the 16th century and yellowing lace-maker diplomas. From October to June, ask to see the lace-makers at work. *(40min. by boat from Venice. V #LN: Burano from F. Nuove. Museum in P. Galuppi.)*

TORCELLO. Torcello, a safe haven for early fishermen fleeing barbarians on the mainland, was the most powerful island in the lagoon before Venice usurped its inhabitants and its glory. The island's cathedral, **Santa Maria Assunta**, contains *Psychosis*, a mosaic in the nave, which depicts both a peaceful heaven and a scorching hell. The *campanile* affords splendid views of the outer lagoon. *(45min. by boat from Venice. V #T: Torcello from Burano. Cathedral open daily 10:30am-6pm; ticket office closes at 5:30pm. Modest dress required. €3; church, campanile, and museum €8.)*

ISOLA DI SAN MICHELE. You'll face only small crowds on Venice's cemetery island, San Michele, home to Coducci's tiny **Chiesa di San Michele in Isola,** the first Renaissance church in Venice. Enter the grounds through the church's right-hand portal and look up to see a relief depicting St. Michael slaying the dragon. Poet and fascist sympathizer Ezra Pound is buried in the Protestant cemetery, while Russian composer Igor Stravinsky and choreographer Sergei Diaghilev are entombed in the Orthodox graveyard. *(V: Cimitero from F. Nuove. Church and cemetery open daily Apr.-Sept. 7:30am-6pm; Oct.-Mar. 7:30am-4pm. Free.)*

🎵 🎭 ENTERTAINMENT AND FESTIVALS

Admire Venetian houses and *palazzi* via their original canal pathways. **Gondola** rides are most romantic about 50min. before sunset and most affordable if shared by six people. The rate that a gondolier quotes is negotiable, but expect to pay €80-100 for a 40min. ride. The most price-flexible gondoliers are those standing by themselves rather than those in groups at "taxi-stands."

Banned by the church for several centuries, Venice's famous **Carnevale** was successfully reinstated in the early 1970s. During the 10 days preceding Ash Wednesday, masked figures jam the streets while outdoor performances spring up all over. For **Mardi Gras,** the population doubles. Contact the tourist office for details, and make lodging arrangements well ahead. Venice's second-most colorful festival is the **Festa del Redentore** (3rd weekend in July), originally held to celebrate the end of the 16th-century plague. On Sunday, craftsmen build a bridge across the Giudecca Canal, connecting **Il Redentore** to the **Zattere.**

🎭 NIGHTLIFE

While pubs and bars are not uncommon in Venice, most residents agree that a vibrant nightlife is virtually nonexistent. The majority of locals prefer an evening spent sipping wine in a *piazza* to grinding in a disco, but the island's fluctuating population means that new establishments spring up (and wither and die) regularly. Student nightlife is concentrated around **Campo Santa Margherita** in Dorsoduro, and tourists swarm **Lista di Spagna** in Cannaregio.

▨ **Café Blue,** Campo S. Pantalon, Dorsoduro 3778 (☎041 52 27 613, www.cafebluevenezia.com). Popular, laid-back local hangout that is busy any time of day. Grab a glass of wine (€1.50-3.20) or a distinctly Venetian "sex on the bridge" (€6). F live jazz and blues. Free Wi-Fi. Open M-F 10am-2am, Sa-Su 6pm-2am. Cash only.

▨ **Orange,** Campo S. Margherita, Dorsoduro 3054/A (☎041 52 34 740; www.orangebar.it). The painted bar seems to be on fire at this crowded spot, where an attentive staff serves everything from *panini* (€4) to mixed drinks (€3.50-7). Humming during the day and hopping later. For a break from the orange, retreat to the quiet garden out back or the white umbrella seats in front. Beer €3-6. Wine from €2.50. Open daily 9am-2am. Cash only.

Bistrot ai Do Draghi, Campo S. Margherita 3665 (☎041 52 89 731). Maybe not as fierce as the name implies ("Bistro of the Two Dragons" in Venetian dialect), but certainly more artsy than its neighbors. A cozy spot for a late night drink with old-fashioned, wood decor and dim lighting. Extensive wine list (€1.20-1.80). Famous spritz €1.20. Open daily 8am-2am. Cash only.

Sotto Sopra, Dorsoduro 3740/1 (☎041 52 42 177). From C. Santa Margherita, follow C. della Chiesa, cross bridge and continue towards the right until you reach C. San Pantalon. Keep going until you hear the music. Funky bar features 2 fl. of stained-glass windows, Pop art, and rock music near student nightlife. Bar downstairs. Cozy upstairs seating. Beers €2-5.50. Mixed drinks €5. Wine €1.20. Open M-Sa 10am-2am. MC/V.

VERONA   ☎045

Hopeless romantics delight in the bright gardens and lifelike sculptures of Verona (pop. 245,000). The setting of Shakespeare's drama Romeo and Juliet, Verona is a popular spot for star-crossed lovers and lone travelers alike. From the winding river Adige to the city's dizzying towers, Verona offers the perks of a large city while maintaining a reputation for authentic local cuisine, rich wines, and an internationally renowned opera.

TRANSPORTATION AND PRACTICAL INFORMATION. Trains (☎89 20 21) go from P. XXV Aprile to: **Bologna** (2hr., 22 per day, €6); **Milan** (2hr., 34 per day, €7); **Trent** (1hr., 25 per day, €4.70); **Venice** (1hr., 41 per day, €8). From the station walk 20min. up **Corso Porta Nuova** or take bus #11, 12, 13, 51, 72, or 73 (Sa-Su take #91, 92, or 93) to Verona's center, the **Arena** in **P. Brà**. The **tourist office** is next to the *piazza* at V. d. Alpini 9. (☎806 86 80. Open M-Sa 9am-7pm, Su 9am-3pm.) Check email at **Internet Train,** V. Roma 17/A. (☎801 33 94. €2.50 per 30min. Open M-F 10am-11pm, Sa-Su 2-8pm. MC/V.) **Postal Code:** 37100.

ACCOMMODATIONS AND FOOD. Reserve hotel rooms ahead of time, especially during opera season (June-Aug.). The **Ostello della Gioventù ●,** Villa Francescatti, Salita Fontana del Ferro 15, is in a renovated 16th-century villa with a central courtyard, located a ways from the heart of the city. From the station, take bus #73 or night bus #90 to P. Isolo, turn right, and follow the yellow signs uphill. (☎045 59 03 60. Breakfast included; dinner €8. Curfew 11:30pm; extended to 1:30am for opera-goers. Dorms €17; family rooms €19. Cash and traveler's checks only.) To get to the romantic, conveniently located **Bed and Breakfast Anfiteatro ●,** V. Alberto Mario 5, follow V. Mazzini toward P. Brà until it branches to the right to become V. Alberto Mario. (☎347 24 88 462; www.anfiteatro-bedandbreakfast.com. TV and private bath. Breakfast buffet included. Singles €60-90; doubles €80-130; triples €100-150.) **Osteria al Duomo ●,** V. Duomo 7/a, offers a small menu but serves authentic, simple cuisine like *tagliatelle* with shrimp and zucchini. (☎045 80 04 505. *Primi* €6.50-7. *Secondi* €7-15. Cover €1. Open M-Sa 11am-3pm and 7-11pm. MC/V.) A **PAM** supermarket is at V. dei Mutilati 3. (Open M-Sa 8am-8:30pm, Su 9am-8pm.)

SIGHTS AND ENTERTAINMENT. The heart of Verona is the first-century **Arena** in P. Brà. (☎045 80 03 204. Open M 1:30-7:30pm, Tu-Su 8:30am-7:30pm. Closes 4:30pm on opera night. Ticket office closes 1hr. before Arena. €4, students €3. Cash only.) From late June to early September, tourists and singers from around the world descend on the Arena for the city's annual **Opera Festival.** (☎045 80 05 151; www.arena.it. Box office open on opera night 10am-9pm, non-performance days 10am-5:45pm. General admission M-Th and Su €17-25, F-Sa €19-27. AmEx/MC/V.) From P. Brà, V. Mazzini leads to the bustling markets and impressive architecture of **Piazza delle Erbe.** The **Giardino Giusti,** V. Giardino Giusti 2, is a 16th-century garden with a thigh-high hedge maze, whose cypress-lined avenue gradually winds up to balconies with stunning views of Verona. (☎045 80 62 611. Open daily Apr.-Sept. 9am-8pm; Oct.-Mar. 9am-7pm. €5.) The della Scala family fortress, **Castelvecchio,** down V. Roma from P. Brà, boasts a courtyard garden and an art collection that includes Pisanello's *Madonna della Quaglia.* (☎045 80 62 611. Open M 1:30-7:30pm, Tu-Su 8:30am-7:30pm.

€4, students €3. Cash only.) The balcony at **Casa di Giulietta** (Juliet's House), V. Cappello 23, overlooks a courtyard of couples waiting to rub the statue of Juliet and add their vows to the graffitied walls. The Capulets never lived here, so save your money for another scoop of gelato. (☎045 80 34 303. Open M 1:30-7:30pm, Tu-Su 8:30am-7:30pm. €4, students €3. Courtyard free.)

PIEDMONT (PIEMONTE)

More than just the source of the Po River, Piedmont has long been a fountainhead of nobility and fine cuisine. The area rose to prominence when the Savoys briefly named Turin capital of their reunited Italy in 1861. Today, European tourists escape Turin's whirlwind pace on the banks of Lake Maggiore, while hikers and skiers conquer Alpine mountaintops.

TURIN (TORINO)   ☎011

A century and a half before Turin (pop. 910,000) was selected to host the 🗓2006 **Winter Olympics,** it served as the first capital of a unified Italy. Renowned for its chocolate and cafe culture, Turin also lays claim to numerous parks and contemporary art pieces, as well as some of the country's best nightlife offerings, all while avoiding the pollution and crime problems of a big city.

▇🗓 **TRANSPORTATION AND PRACTICAL INFORMATION. Trains** (☎011 66 53 098) run from **Porta Nuova,** in the center of the city, on C. V. Emanuele II to: Genoa (2hr., 1 per hr., €8.75); Milan (2hr., 1 per hr., €8.75); Rome (6-7hr., 26 per day, from €64); Venice (5hr., 20 per day, €21.50). A new **metro line** was recently installed and Turin's transportation system will continue to change in the next few years. Eventually, **Porta Susa** will be the main train station; for now, it is a departure point for trains to Paris via Lyon, FRA (5-6hr., 4 per day). Contact the **Turismo Torino,** P. Castello 161, for ▇**brochures** with art, literary, and walking tours. (☎011 53 51 81; www.turismotorino.org. Open M-Sa 9:30am-7pm, Su 9:30am-3pm.) Unlike in other Italian cities, streets in Turin meet at right angles, so it's relatively easy to navigate. V. Roma is the major north-south thoroughfare. It runs to P. Castello, from which V. Pietro Micca extends southwest to the Olympic Atrium. **Postal Code:** 10100.

▇🗓 **ACCOMMODATIONS AND FOOD.** Turin's budget options are scattered around the city, though a few cluster near Stazione Porta Nuova. To get to comfortable **Ostello Torino (HI) ❶,** V. Alby 1, take bus #52 (#64 on Su) from Porta Nuova. After crossing the river, get off at the Lanza stop at V. Crimea and follow the "Ostello" signs to C. G. Lanza, before turning left at V. L. Gatti. (☎011 66 02 939; www.ostellotorino.it. Breakfast and linens included. Internet and Wi-Fi €1. Laundry €4. Reception M-Sa 7am-12:30pm and 3-11pm, Su 7-10am and 3-11pm. Lockout 10am-3pm. Curfew 11pm; ask for key if going out. Closed Dec. 21-Jan. 14. Single-sex or co-ed 3- to 8-bed dorms €15; doubles €31-38; triples €51; quads €68. MC/V.) The new **Open 011 ❷,** C. Venezia 11, near the V. Chiesa della Salute stop on bus #11, has a bar, library, restaurant, TV, and Wi-Fi. (☎011 51 62 038; www.openzero11.it. Dorms €16.50; singles €30; doubles €42.)

Spend the day at ▇**Eataly,** via Nizza 224, Turin's new 10,000 sq. ft. culinary amusement park. Wine and beer tastings are just the beginning: classrooms feature cooking classes by famous guest chefs and museum-quality exhibits demonstrate various food preparation techniques. Take bus #1, 18 or 35 to the

Biglieri stop, near the Lingotto Expo Center. (☎011 19 50 68 01; www.eataly.
it. Reserve ahead for classes and wine tasting. Open daily 10am-10:30pm.)
Chocolate has been the city's glory ever since Turin nobles began taking an
evening cup of it in 1678. *Gianduiotto* (hazelnut chocolate) turns up in candies and gelato. Sample *bicerin* (Turin's hot coffee-chocolate-cream drink;
€4), craved by Nietzsche and Dumas, at **Caffè Cioccolateria al Bicerin ❶**, Piazza
della Consolata 5. (☎011 43 69 325. Open M-Tu and Th-F 8:30am-7:30pm, Sa-Su
8:30am-1pm and 3:30-7:30pm.) If Eataly doesn't have everything you need,
head to **Porta Palazzo**, P. della Repubblica, perhaps Europe's largest open-air
market. (M-F 7:30am-2pm, Sa 7:30am-sunset.)

🎫🎭 **SIGHTS AND NIGHTLIFE.** The **Torino Card** (48hr. €18; 72hr. €20) is the
best deal in the city: it provides entrance to more than 140 castles, monuments,
museums, and royal residences in Turin, many of which are worth a visit. Once
the largest structure in the world built using traditional masonry, the 🏛**Mole
Antonelliana**, V. Montebello 20, a few blocks east of P. Castello, was originally a
synagogue. It's home to the eccentric **Museo Nazionale del Cinema**, which plays
hundreds of movie clips. (Museum open Tu-F and Su 9am-8pm, Sa 9am-11pm.
€5.20, students €4.20.) The **Holy Shroud of Turin,** said to be Jesus' burial cloth,
is housed in the **Cattedrale di San Giovanni,** behind the **Palazzo Reale**. With rare
exceptions, a photograph of the shroud is as close as visitors will get. (Open
daily 8am-noon and 3-6pm. Free.) The **Museo Egizio**, in the **Palazzo dell'Accademia
delle Scienze**, V. dell'Accademia delle Scienze 6, has a world-class collection of
Egyptian artifacts. (Open Tu-Su 8:30am-7:30pm. €6.50, ages 18-25 €3.)

🎭**I Murazzi** is the center of Turin's social scene and consists of two stretches of
boardwalk, one between Ponte V. Emanuele I and Ponte Umberto, and another
smaller stretch downstream. Most people show up between 7:30 and 9:30pm
and spend the next five hours sipping drinks, maneuvering among crowds at
the waterfront, or dancing in the clubs. **The Beach,** V. Murazzi del Po 18-22, has
the best dance floor in Turin. (☎011 88 87 77. Mixed drinks €6. Open W and Su
5-11pm, Th-Sa 11pm-5am.) **Quadrilatero Romano,** between P. della Repubblica and
V. Garibaldi, attracts those who would rather sit, drink, and chat until 4am.

TUSCANY (TOSCANA)

Recently, pop culture has glorified Tuscany as a sun-soaked sanctuary of art,
nature, and civilization, and this time pop culture has it right. Every town
claims a Renaissance master, every highway offers scenic vistas, every celebration culminates in parades, festivals, and galas, and every year brings more
tourists to the already beaten Tuscan path.

FLORENCE (FIRENZE)   ☎055

Florence (pop. 400,000) is the city of the Renaissance. By the 14th century, it
had already become one of the most influential cities in Europe. In the 15th
century, Florence overflowed with artistic excellence as the Medici family
amassed a peerless collection, supporting masters like Botticelli, Donatello,
and Michelangelo. These days, the tourists who flood the streets are captivated
by Florence's distinctive character, creative spirit, and timeless beauty.

TRANSPORTATION

Flights: Aeroporto Amerigo Vespucci (FLR; main line ☎055 30 615, 24hr. automated flight info line 30 61 700; www.aeroporto.firenze.it) in the suburb of Peretola. Mostly domestic and charter flights.

Trains: Stazione Santa Maria Novella, across from S. Maria Novella. Trains run 1 per hr. to: **Bologna** (1hr., €20); **Milan** (2½hr., €47); **Rome** (3hr., €44); **Siena** (1½hr., €14); **Venice** (3hr., €44).

Buses: SITA, V. S. Caterina da Siena 17 (☎800 37 37 60; www.sita-on-line.it), runs buses to **San Gimignano** (1hr., 14 per day, €5.90) and **Siena** (1hr., 2 per day, €6.50). **LAZZI,** P. Adua 1-4R (☎35 10 61; www.lazzi.it), runs to **Pisa** (1 per hr., €6.30). Both offices are near S. Maria Novella.

Public Transportation: ATAF (☎800 42 45 00; www.ataf.net), outside the train station, runs orange city buses 6am-1am. Tickets 1hr. €1.30; 24hr. €5; 3-day €12. Buy them at any newsstand, *tabaccheria,* or ticket dispenser. You cannot purchase tickets on the bus. Validate your ticket using the orange machine on board or risk a €50 fine.

Taxis: ☎43 90, 47 98, or 42 42. Outside the train station.

ORIENTATION

From the train station, a short walk on V. Panzani and a left on V. dei Cerretani leads you to the **duomo,** in the center of Florence. The bustling **Via dei Calzaiuoli** runs south from the *duomo* to **Piazza della Signoria.** V. Roma leads from the *duomo* through **Piazza della Repubblica** to the **Ponte Vecchio** (Old Bridge), which crosses from central Florence to **Oltrarno,** the district south of the **Arno River.** Note that most streets change names unpredictably.

PRACTICAL INFORMATION

Tourist Office: Informazione Turistica, P. Della Stazione 4 (☎055 21 22 45; turisimo3@ comune.fi.it), across the *piazza* from the station's main exit. Info in major foreign languages on tourist attractions, events, directions, available tours, and general emergency information. Open M-Sa 8:30-7pm, Su and holidays 8:30am-2pm.

Laundromats: Wash and Dry (☎055 58 04 480; www.washedry.it). Self-service locations throughout the city. Wash and dry €3.50 each. Detergent €1.

Emergency: ☎113 or ☎055 31 80 00

Police: Tourist Police, Ufficio Stranieri, V. Zara 2 (☎055 49 771). For visa or work-permit problems. Open M-F 9:30am-1pm. To report lost or stolen items, go around the corner to **Ufficio Denunce,** V. Duca d'Aosta 3 (☎055 49 771). Open M-Sa 8am-8pm.

Municipal Police: ☎055 32 831, in emergency ☎055 32 85.

Pharmacies: Farmacia Comunale (☎055 28 94 35), by track 16 at the train station.

Medical Services: Tourist Medical Services, V. Lorenzo il Magnifico 59 (☎055 47 54 11). English-, German-, and French-speaking doctors with 70 specialists. In P. Duomo (☎055 21 22 21). Open M-F 8am-8pm, doctors on-call 24hr. **Ospedale Santa Maria Nuova,** P. Santa Maria Nuova 1 (☎055 27 581), near the Duomo.

Internet Access: Internet Train, V. Guelfa 54/56 (☎055 26 45 146), V. dell'Oriolo 40r (☎055 26 38 968), Borgo San Jacopo 30r (☎055 265 7935), V. Giacomini 9 (☎055 50 31 647), V. de'Benci 36r (☎055 26 38 555), V. Alamanni 5a (☎055 28 69 92), V. Porta Rossa 38r (☎055 27 41 037), Lungarno B. Cellini 43r (☎055 38 30 921). Internet €3.20-4.30 per hr. Wi-Fi €2.50 per hr. Open daily 10am-10:30pm.

ITALY

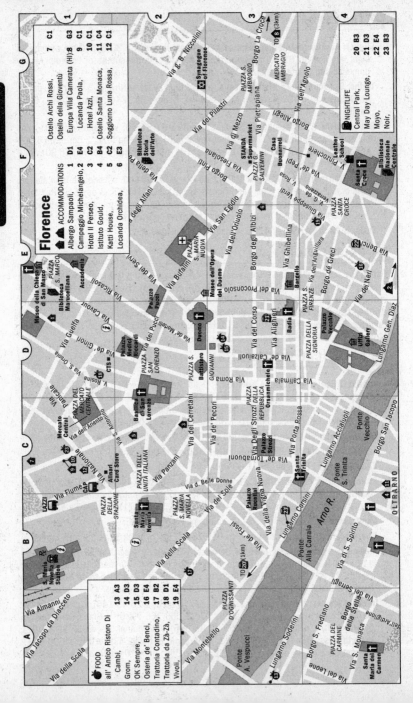

Florence

ACCOMMODATIONS
Albergo Sampaoli, 1	D1
Campeggio Michelangelo, 2	E4
Hotel II Perseo, 3	C2
Istituto Gould, 4	B4
Katti House, 5	C2
Locanda Orchidea, 6	E3
Ostello Archi Rossi, 7	C1
Ostello della Gioventù	
Europa Villa Camerata (HI),8	G3
Locanda Paola, 9	C1
Hotel Azzi, 10	C1
Ostello Santa Monaca, 11	C4
Soggiorno Luna Rossa, 12	C1

FOOD
all' Antico Ristoro Di	
Cambi, 13	A3
Grom, 14	D3
OK Sempre, 15	D3
Osteria de' Benci, 16	E4
Trattoria Contadino, 17	B2
Trattoria da Zà-Zà, 18	D1
Vivoli, 19	E4

NIGHTLIFE
Central Park, 20	B3
May Day Lounge, 21	D3
Moyo, 22	E4
Noir, 23	B3

Post Office: V. Pellicceria 3 (☎055 27 36 480), off P. della Repubblica. Open M-F
8:15am-7pm, Sa 8:15am-12:30pm. **Postal Code:** 50100.

ACCOMMODATIONS

Lodging in Florence doesn't come cheap. **Consorzio ITA,** in the train station by
track #16, can find rooms for a €3-8.50 fee. (☎066 99 10 00. Open M-Sa 8am-
8pm, Su 10am-7pm.) Make a *prenotazioni* (reservation) ahead, especially if
you plan to visit during Easter or summer. If you have any complaints, first
talk to the proprietor and then to the **Tourist Rights Protection Desk,** V. Cavour 1R
(☎055 29 08 32 33), or **Servizio Turismo,** V. Manzoni 16 (☎055 27 60 552).

■ **Ostello Archi Rossi,** V. Faenza 94r (☎055 29 08 04; www.hostelarchirossi.com). You'll
feel the Florentine creative vibe as soon as you see the frescoes painted in the reception by local art students. Each of the 30 spotless rooms comes with a PC, locker, and
shared bathroom. Archi Rossi boasts a romantic garden, free Wi-Fi, computer use, and
a free walking tour every morning with an English-speaking guide. Breakfast included;
features bacon and eggs. Complimentary pasta dinners also occasionally served. Luggage storage available. Reception 24hr. Dorms €18-25; singles €25-35. MC/V. ❶

■ **Hotel Consigli,** Lungarno Amerigo Vespucci 50 (☎055 21 41 72; www.hotelconsigli.com).
Once the playground of a Renaissance prince, this riverside palace is a sunlit sanctum
of vaulted ceilings, sweeping frescoes, and marble stairs. The rooms are enormous, cool,
and quiet, and the balcony and breakfast room look out over postcard-perfect views of
the Arno. A/C. Breakfast included. Wi-Fi €3 per hr., €5 per 2hr., €7 per 3hr. Parking €15
per day. Singles €60-90; doubles €60-150. AmEx/MC/V. ❸

■ **Holiday Rooms,** V. Nazionale 22 (☎055 28 50 84; www.marcosplaces.com). Owner Marco
has been known to meet guests at the train station to help them with their baggage—a small
taste of the conveniences and perks to come. Hardwood beds and satin curtains adorn 8
quiet rooms equipped with satellite flatscreen TVs, computers, Wi-Fi, and laundry access.
Kitchen available. Rooms €25-40 per person. Discounts at some local restaurants. ❶

■ **Soggiorno Luna Rossa,** V. Nazionale 7, 3rd fl. (☎328 62 51 017; www.marcosplaces.com).
From the Piazza Stazione near Santa Maria Novella Station, walk to V. Nazionale until you
reach Marco's other place. Wake up in a brightly-decorated room to the morning sun stream-
ing through the spectacular stained-glass windows of this centrally located hostel. 18 private
rooms available, 3 with shared bathrooms. Each with Wi-Fi, computer, satellite flatscreen TV,
and free international calls. Kitchen available. Rooms €25-40 per person. ❷

Hotel Medici, V. dei Medici 6 (☎055 28 48 18). A 6-story student favorite. Top-floor
terrace looks out over unbelievable views of the Duomo and Campanile. Breakfast
included; we recommend dining on the aforementioned terrace. No A/C. Singles €50;
doubles €75; quads €100. MC/V. ❸

Hotel Abaco, V. dei Banchi 1 (☎055 23 81 919; www.abaco-hotel.it). Convenient
location, helpful staff, and extravagant rooms. Each room is a masterpiece named
after a Renaissance great. Each with phone and TV. Breakfast included. Wi-Fi. Singles
€60; doubles €70-95; triples €110. MC/V. ❸

Hostel AF19, V. Ricasoli 9 (☎055 23 98 665; www.academyhostels.com). A bright and
spacious hostel with multi-floor suites and a location literally steps from the Duomo.
A/C. Safety lockers. Laundry €5. Free Wi-Fi in the lobby. Lockout 11am-2pm. 2- to
6-bed dorms €28-36. Cash preferred. AmEx/MC/V. ❶

FOOD

Florentine specialties include *bruschetta* (grilled bread soaked in oil and garlic and topped with tomatoes, basil, and anchovy or liver paste) and *bistecca
alla Fiorentina* (thick sirloin). The best local cheese is *pecorino*, made from

sheep's milk. A liter of house wine usually costs €3.50-6 in a *trattoria*, but stores sell bottles of chianti for as little as €2.50. The local dessert is *cantuccini di prato* (almond cookies) dipped in *vinsanto* (a rich dessert wine). Florence's own Buontalenti family supposedly invented gelato; extensive sampling is a must. For lunch, visit a *rosticceria gastronomia*, peruse the city's pushcarts, or pick up fresh produce and meats at the **Mercato Centrale**, between V. Nazionale and S. Lorenzo. (Open June-Sept. M-Sa 7:30am-2pm; Oct.-May M-F 7am-2pm, Sa 7am-2pm and 4-8pm.) To get to **STANDA** supermarket, V. Pietrapiana 1R, turn right on V. del Proconsolo, take the first left on Borgo degli Albizi, and continue straight through P. G. Salvemini. (Open M-Sa 8am-9pm, Su 9am-9pm. MC/V.)

☒ **Grom**, V. del Campanile (☎055 21 61 58), off P. del Duomo to the left of the Campanile. The kind of gelato you'll be talking about in 50 years. As fresh as it gets; sublimely balanced texture. Large store is standing-room only and flooded with tourists and locals. Cups €2-5, cones €2-4. Open daily Apr.-Sept. 10:30am-midnight, Oct.-Mar. 10:30am-11pm. ❶

☒ **Trattoria Le Mossacce**, V. del Proconsolo 55r (☎055 29 43 61; www.trattorialemossacce.it). The sort of place that you just don't expect near the Duomo, Mossacce seats strangers shoulder-to-shoulder and whips out Tuscan specialties. Primi €5-8.50. Secondi €5.50-10. Cover €1. Open daily noon-2:30pm and 7-9:30pm. ❷

☒ **Gelateria del Neri**, V. dei Neri 20-22r (☎055 21 00 34). Follow the street between Uffizi and Palazzo Vecchio. Just big enough for a counter and the waiting line, this gelateria is the locals' favorite. Serves generous scoops of creative flavors like *crema giotto* (a blend of coconut, almond, and hazelnut) and equally delicious classics like pistachio. Cones and cups from €1.50. Open daily 11am-midnight. Cash only. ❶

☒ **Teatro del Sale**, V. dei Macci 111r (☎055 20 01 492). It's "members only" at this private club, but the slight fee and mission statement ensure that the pretensions end here. In a high-arched, hardwood theatre, Fabio Picchi picks the freshest ingredients and announces each delicious course from his open kitchen. Once the last piece of mouthwatering dessert has been snatched off the plate, the entertainment begins, ranging from music lessons to theatrical performances—but many shows are in Italian, so plan ahead. Breakfast €7; lunch €20. Membership fee €5. Open Tu-Sa 9-11am, noon-2:15pm, and from 7:30pm until the end of the show. Reservations required. AmEx/MC/V. ❹

☒ **Ruth's Kosher Vegetarian Restaurant**, V. Luigi Carlo Farini 2A (☎055 24 80 888). Carnivorous Christians, be not afraid! There are plenty options for you, as well. Photos of Woody Allen and Kafka look on as wise owner Simcha makes everyone feel part of the community, serving hummus (€6), pasta (€7), and couscous (€13-15). Students enjoy special dinners W nights for €10. Free Wi-Fi. Open M-Th and Su noon-2:30pm and 7:30-10:30pm, F noon-2:30pm. AmEx/MC/V. ❷

Buongustai, V. dei Cerchi 15 (☎055 29 13 04). Walk north from Palazzo Vecchio . After a day at the nearby Duomo, Bargello, and P. della Signoria, relax at this quirky and casual spot. Make sure to try the house special *Piatto del Buongustai* (Tuscan salami, cheese, and pickled vegetables; €10). Primi €4.50-6.50. Secondi €6.50-10. Open M-Th 9:30am-3:30pm, F-Sa 8:30-11pm. Cash only. ❷

Amon Specialità e Panini Egiziani, V. Palazzuolo 26-28r (☎055 29 31 46). This Egyptian alleyway take-out whips up kebabs (€3.50-3.90), falafel (€3), hummus (€2.80), and kofta for hungry Florentines on the go. Kebab sandwiches are stuffed with generous heaps of juicy shaved meat. Open daily noon-3pm and 6-11pm. Cash only. ❶

Trattoria Mario, V. Rosina 2r, near P. del Mercato Centrale. Despite the 45min. wait, this family-run restaurant has proven its worth. Be prepared to share tables with other parties. ½ portions are available on select dishes, and all courses are created with entirely fresh ingredients; there isn't a freezer in the whole place. Try the *ribollita* (soup with beans, bread, vegetables; €4.50), the *pollo fritto* (fried chicken) on M, or come for fish F.

Be sure to arrive early in the afternoon before ingredients run out and some dishes stop being served. Open M-Sa 12-3:30pm. Cover €0.50. Cash only. ❷

Antica Gelateria Florentina, V. Faenza 2A. Every day, some of the best gelato in the Duomo area is prepared at this *gelateria* using fresh milk and fruit. The painted walls and the knowledgeable staff impart some of the treat's rich history. Enjoy nearly 30 flavors like *nocciola* (hazelnut) and *napole,* a fruit native to Italy. Cones and cups €1.60-4. Open daily noon-1am. Cash only. ❶

🜲 SIGHTS

For a list of museum openings, check out www.firenzeturismo.it. For museum reservations, call **Firenze Musei** (☎055 29 48 83; www.firenzemusei.it). There are **no student discounts** at museums and admission can be expensive. Choose destinations carefully and plan to spend a few hours at each landmark.

THE DUOMO

🜲**DUOMO (CATTEDRALE DI SANTA MARIA DEL FIORE).** In 1296, the city fathers commissioned Arnolfo di Cambio to erect a cathedral so magnificent that it would be "impossible to make it either better or more beautiful with the industry and power of man." Di Cambio succeeded, designing a massive nave with the confidence that by the time it was completed (1418), technology would have advanced enough to provide a solution to erect a dome. **Filippo Brunelleschi** was called in for this task: after studying long-neglected classical methods, he came up with his double-shelled, interlocking-brick construction. The *duomo* claims the world's third longest nave, trailing only St. Peter's in Rome and St. Paul's in London. *(Open M-W and F 10am-5pm, Th 10am-4pm, Sa 10am-4:45pm, Su 1:30-4:45pm. Mass daily 7am, 12:30, 5-7pm. Free.)* Climb the 463 steps inside the dome to **Michelangelo's lantern,** which offers an expansive view of the city from the 100m high external gallery. *(Open M-F 8:30am-7pm, Sa 8:30am-5:40pm. €6.)* The climb up the 82m **campanile** next to the *duomo,* also called "Giotto's Tower," reveals views of the *duomo,* the city, and the **battistero** (baptistry), whose bronze doors, forged by Ghiberti, are known as the 🜲**Gates of Paradise.** Byzantine-style mosaics inside the baptistry inspired details of the *Inferno* by Dante, who was christened here. *(Campanile open daily 8:30am-7:30pm. €6. Baptistry open M-Sa noon-7pm, Su 8:30am-2pm. €3.)* Most of the *duomo*'s art resides behind the cathedral in the **Museo dell'Opera del Duomo.** Up the first flight of stairs is a late *Pietà* by Michelangelo; according to legend, he broke Christ's left arm in a fit of frustration. *(P. del Duomo 9, behind the duomo. ☎055 23 02 885. Open M-Sa 9am-6:50pm, Su 9am-1pm. €6.)*

🜲**ORSANMICHELE.** Built in 1337 as a granary, the Orsanmichele became a church after a fire convinced officials to move grain operations outside the city. The ancient grain chutes are still visible outside. Within, tenacious visitors will discover Ghiberti's *St. John the Baptist* and *St. Stephen,* Donatello's *St. Peter and St. Mark,* and Giambologna's *St. Luke.* *(V. Arte della Lana, between the duomo and P. della Signoria. Open Tu-Su 10am-5pm. Free.)*

PIAZZA DELLA SIGNORIA

From P. del Duomo, **Via dei Calzaiuoli,** one of the city's oldest streets, runs south past crowds, street vendors, *gelaterie,* and chic shops to **Piazza della Signoria,** a 13th-century *piazza* bordered by the Palazzo Vecchio and the Uffizi. With the construction of the Palazzo Vecchio in 1299, the square became Florence's civic and political center. In 1497, religious zealot Girolamo Savonarola lit the **Bonfire of the Vanities** here, barbecuing some of Florence's best art. Today P. della Signoria fills daily with photo-snapping tourists who later return for drinks and dessert in its upscale cafes. Monumental sculptures stand in front of the *palazzo* and inside the 14th-century **Loggia dei Lanzi.** *(Free.)*

> **NO ART FOR YOU.** To avoid disappointment at the Uffizi, keep in mind that a few rooms are usually closed each day and famous pieces often go on temporary loan, so not all works are always on display. A sign outside the ticket office lists the rooms that are closed for the day.

THE UFFIZI. Giorgio Vasari designed this palace in 1554 for the offices *(uffizi)* of Duke Cosimo's administration; today, the gallery holds one of the world's finest art collections. Beautiful statues overlook the walkway from niches in the columns; play "spot the Renaissance man" and try to find Leonardo, Machiavelli, Petrarch, and Vespucci among them. Botticelli, Caravaggio, Cimabue, Duccio, Fra Angelico, della Francesca, Giotto, Michelangelo, Raphael, del Sarto, Titian, da Vinci, even Dürer, Rembrandt, Rubens—you name it, it's here. Be sure to look at the rare sketches in the **Cabinet of Drawings and Prints** on the first floor before confining yourself to the U-shaped corridor of the second floor. A few rooms are usually closed each day, and some works may be on loan. A sign at the ticket office lists the rooms that are closed. *(From P. B. S. Giovanni, take V. Roma past P. della Repubblica, where the street turns into V. Calimala. Continue until V. Vaccereccia and turn left. ☎055 23 88 651. Open Tu-Su 8:15am-6:35pm. €10; EU citizens 18-25 €5. Reserve ahead for €4 fee. Audio tour €4.70.)*

> **MAKE FRIENDS WITH THE UFFIZI.** If you plan on visiting 3 or more museums in Florence, consider obtaining an **Amici degli Uffizi card.** Students under 26 pay €25 for the card (regularly €60) and receive free admission to the Uffizi and all state museums in Florence (including the Accademia and Bargello). It includes one visit to each of the museums and gets you to the front of the line. For more information, call Amici degli Uffizi, V. Lorenzo il Magnifico 1, ☎055 47 94 422, or email amicidegliuffizi@waf.it.

PALAZZO VECCHIO. Arnolfo del Cambio designed this fortress-like *palazzo* in the late 13th century to be the seat of government. It included apartments which functioned as living quarters for members of the city council while they served two-month terms. After the *palazzo* became the Medici's home in 1470, Michelozzo decorated the courtyard. The **Monumental Apartments,** which house the *palazzo*'s extensive art collections, are now an art and history museum. The worthwhile **Activities Tour** includes the "Secret Routes," which reveal hidden stairwells and chambers tucked behind exquisite oil paintings. The ceiling of the **Salone del Cinquecento,** where the Grand Council of the Republic met, is so elaborately decorated that the walls can hardly support its weight. The tiny **Studio di Francesco I** is a treasure trove of Mannerist art. *(☎055 27 68 224. Open M-W and F-Sa 9am-7pm, Su 9am-1pm. Palazzo and Monumental Apartments each €6, ages 18-25 €4.50. Activities tour €8/5.50. Courtyard free. Reserve ahead for tours.)*

BARGELLO. The heart of medieval Florence is in this 13th-century fortress, once the residence of the chief magistrate and later a brutal prison with public executions in its courtyard. It was restored in the 19th century and now houses the largely untouristed **Museo Nazionale.** Donatello's bronze *David*, the first free-standing nude since antiquity, stands opposite the two bronze panels of the *Sacrifice of Isaac*, submitted by Ghiberti and Brunelleschi in the baptistry door competition. Michelangelo's early works, including *Bacchus*, *Brutus*, and *Apollo*, are on the ground floor. *(V. del Proconsolo 4, between the duomo and P. della Signoria. ☎ 055 23 88 606. Open daily 8:15am-6pm. Closed 2nd and 4th M of each month. €7.)*

PONTE VECCHIO. From the Uffizi, follow V. Georgofili left and turn right along the river to reach the Ponte Vecchio, Florence's oldest bridge, built in 1345. In the 1500s, the Medici gentrified: they kicked out the butchers and tanneries and installed goldsmiths and diamond-carvers in their place. Today, the boutiques of the shop owners' descendants make the bridge glitter with chic necklaces, brooches, and charms; tourists and street performers make up the bulk of its traffic. Don't miss the ◙**sunset view** from neighboring **Ponte alle Grazie.**

BADIA. The site of medieval Florence's richest monastery, the Badia church is now buried in the interior of a residential block. Filippino Lippi's *Apparition of the Virgin to St. Bernard*, one of the most famous paintings of the 15th century, hangs in eerie gloom to the left of the church. Be sure to glance up at the intricately carved dark wood ceiling. Some say Dante may have first glimpsed his beloved Beatrice here. Visitors are asked to walk silently among the prostrate, white-robed worshippers. *(Entrance on V. Dante Alighieri, off V. Proconsolo. ☎ 055 26 44 02. Open to tourists M 3-6pm, but visitors can walk through at any time.)*

SANTA MARIA NOVELLA

The largest open space in Florence, the P. della Repubblica teems with crowds, overpriced cafes, restaurants, and *gelaterie*. In 1890, it replaced the Mercato Vecchio as the site of the city market, but has since traded stalls for more fashionable vendors. The inscription "*antico centro della città, da secolare squalore, a vita nuova restituito*" ("ancient center of the city, squalid for centuries, restored to new life") makes a derogatory reference to the *piazza*'s location in the old Jewish ghetto. The area around Mercato Nuovo and V. Tornabuoni was Florence's financial capital in the 1400s. Now it's residential, but still touristy.

◙**CHIESA DI SANTA MARIA NOVELLA.** The chapels of the wealthiest 13th- and 14th-century merchants are part of this church. Santa Maria Novella was home to an order of Dominicans, or *Domini canes* (Hounds of the Lord), who took a bite out of sin and corruption. The facade of the *chiesa* is made of Florentine marble and is considered one of the great masterpieces of early Renaissance architecture. The Medicis commissioned Vasari to paint new frescoes over the 13th-century ones on the walls, but the painter spared Masaccio's ◙**Trinity,** the first painting to use geometric perspective. In the **Gondi Chapel** is Brunelleschi's *Crucifix*, designed in response to Donatello's, in Santa Croce, which Brunelleschi found too full of "vigorous naturalism." Donatello was supposedly so impressed by his rival's creation that he dropped the bag of eggs he was carrying. *(Open M-Th 9am-5pm, F-Su 1-5pm. €2.70.)*

CHIESA DI SANTA TRINITÀ. Hoping to spend eternity in elite company, the most fashionable *palazzo* owners commissioned family chapels in this church. The facade, designed by Bernardo Buontalenti in the 16th century, is almost Baroque in its elaborate ornamentation. Scenes from Ghirlandaio's *Life of St. Francis* decorate the **Sassetti Chapel** in the right arm of the transept. The famous altarpiece, Ghirlandaio's *Adoration of the Shepherds*, resides in the Uffizi—this one is a copy. *(In P. S. Trinità. Open M-Sa 7am-noon and 4-7pm, Su 7-noon. Free.)*

MERCATO NUOVO. The *loggie* (guilds) of the New Market have housed gold and silk traders since 1547. Today, faux designer gear dominates vendors' wares. Rubbing the snout of Pietro Tacca's plump statue, *Il Porcellino* (The Little Pig), is reputed to bring luck, but don't wait for that purse you covet to become real leather. *(Off V. Calimala, between P. della Repubblica and the Ponte Vecchio. Open dawn-dusk.)*

SAN LORENZO

⬛ACCADEMIA. It doesn't matter how many pictures of him you've seen—when you come around the corner to see Michelangelo's triumphant **⬛David** towering in self-assured perfection, you will be blown away. The statue's base was struck by lightning in 1512, the figure was damaged by anti-Medici riots in 1527, and David's left wrist was broken by a stone, after which he was moved here from P. della Signoria in 1873. In the hallway leading to *David* are Michelangelo's four *Slaves* and a *Pietà*. The master purposely left these statues unfinished, staying true to his theory of "releasing" figures from the living stone. Botticelli's Madonna paintings and Uccello's works are worth seeing. *(V. Ricasoli 60, between the churches of S. Marco and S. S. Annunziata. ☎ 055 23 88 609. Open Tu-Su 8:15am-6:50pm. Reserve ahead €4 extra. May-Sept. €10; Oct.-Apr. €7.)*

BASILICA DI SAN LORENZO. Because the Medicis lent the funds to build this church, they retained artistic control over its construction and decided to add Cosimo dei Medici's grave to Brunelleschi's spacious basilica. They cunningly placed it in front of the high altar to make the entire church his personal mausoleum. Michelangelo began the exterior, but, disgusted by Florentine politics, he abandoned the project, leaving the plain facade. *(Open M-Sa 10am-5pm, Mar.-Oct. also Su 1:30-5pm. €2.50.)* While the **Cappelle dei Medici** (Medici Chapels) offer a rare glimpse of the Baroque in Florence, the **Cappella dei Principi** (Princes' Chapel) emulates the baptistry in P. del Duomo. Michelangelo sculpted the **Sacrestia Nuova** (New Sacristy) to hold two Medici tombs. On the tomb of Lorenzo he placed the female Night and the muscular male Day; on Giuliano's sit the more androgynous Dawn and Dusk. *(Walk around to the back entrance in P. Madonna degli Aldobrandini. Open daily 8:15am-5pm. Closed 1st and 3rd M and 2nd and 4th Su. €6.)*

PIAZZA SANTA CROCE

CHIESA DI SANTA CROCE. The Franciscans built this church as far as possible from their Dominican rivals at S. Maria Novella. Ironically, the ascetic Franciscans produced what is arguably the most splendid church in the city. Luminaries buried here include Galileo, Machiavelli, Michelangelo (whose tomb was designed by Vasari), and humanist Leonardo Bruni. Check out Donatello's *Crucifix* (so irksome to Brunelleschi) in the Vernio Chapel, and his gilded *Annunciation*, by Bruni's tomb. At the end of the cloister next to the church is the perfectly proportioned **Cappella Pazzi**, whose decorations include Luca della Robbia's *tondi* of the apostles and Brunelleschi's moldings of the evangelists. *(Open M-Sa 9:30am-5:30pm, Su 1-5:30pm. €5.)*

SYNAGOGUE OF FLORENCE. This synagogue, also known as the **Museo del Tempio Israelitico**, is resplendent with arches and Sephardic domes. David Levi, a wealthy Florentine Jewish businessman, donated his fortune in 1870 to build "a monumental temple worthy of Florence," recognizing the Jews' new freedom to live and worship outside the old Jewish ghetto. *(V. Farini 4, at V. Pilastri. ☎ 055 24 52 52. Free tours every hr.; reserve ahead. Open M-Th and Su 10am-6pm, F 10am-2pm. €4.)*

CASA BUONARROTI. This museum houses Michelangelo memorabilia and two of his crucial early works, *The Madonna of the Steps* and *The Battle of the Centaurs*. Both works were completed when he was 16, and indicate his shift from relief to sculpture in the round. *(V. Ghibellina 70. ☎ 055 25 17 52. From P. S. Croce, follow V. dei Pepi and turn right on V. Ghibellina. Open M and W-Su 9:30am-2pm. €6.50, students €4.)*

OLTRARNO

Historically disdained by downtown Florentines, the far side of the Arno remains a lively and unpretentious quarter, filled with students and relatively few tourists. Head back on Ponte S. Trinità after dallying in P. San Spirito.

PALAZZO PITTI. Luca Pitti, a 15th-century banker, built his *palazzo* east of P. S. Spirito against the Boboli hill. The Medicis acquired the *palazzo* in 1550 and expanded it in every way possible. Today, it houses six museums, including the **Galleria Palatina**. Florence's most important art collection after the Uffizi, the gallery has works by Caravaggio, Raphael, Rubens, and Titian. Other museums display Medici family costumes, porcelain, and **Royal Apartments**—reminders of the time when the *palazzo* was the living quarters of the royal House of Savoy. The **Galleria d'Arte Moderna** hides one of Italian art history's big surprises, the proto-Impressionist works of the Macchiaioli group. *(Open Tu-Su 8:15am-6:50pm. Ticket for Galleria Palatina, Royal Apartments, and Galleria d'Arte Moderna €8.50.)*

SAN MINIATO AL MONTE. An inlaid marble facade and 13th-century mosaics provide a prelude to the floor inside, patterned with doves, lions, and astrological signs. Visit at 5:40pm to hear the monks chant. *(Take bus #13 from the station or climb the stairs from Piazzale Michelangelo. ☎ 055 23 42 731. Open daily Mar.-Nov. 8am-7pm; Dec.-Feb. 8am-1pm and 2:30-6pm. Free.)*

BOBOLI GARDENS. With geometrically sculpted hedges, contrasting groves of holly and cypress trees, and bubbling fountains, the elaborate gardens are an exquisite example of stylized Renaissance landscaping. A large oval lawn is just up the hill from the back of the Palazzo Pitti, with an Egyptian obelisk in the middle and marble statues dotting the perimeter. Spend an afternoon wandering through the grounds and the small on-site museums. *(Open daily June-Aug.*

8:15am-7:30pm; Apr.-May and Sept.-Oct. 8:15am-6:30pm; Nov.-Mar. reduced hours. €6.)

PIAZZALE MICHELANGELO. A visit to Piazzale Michelangelo is a must. At sunset, waning light casts a warm glow over the city. Views from here are even better (and certainly cheaper) than those from the top of the *duomo*. Make the challenging uphill trek at around 8:30pm during the summer to arrive at the *piazzale* in time for sunset. Unfortunately, the *piazzale* doubles as a large parking lot, and is home to hordes of tour buses during summer days. *(Cross the Ponte Vecchio to the Oltrarno and turn left, walk through the piazza, and turn right up V. de Bardi. Follow it uphill as it becomes V. del Monte alle Croci. A staircase to the left heads to the piazzale.)*

🎵 NIGHTLIFE

For info, consult the city's entertainment monthly, *Firenze Spettacolo* (€2). **Piazza Santo Spirito** has live music in summer. When going to bars that are far from the *centro*, keep in mind that the last bus may leave before the fun winds down, and taxis are rare in the area with the most popular discos.

🏴 **Mago Merlino Tea House,** V. Pilastri 31r (☎055 24 29 70). Always ready to share his wisdom, expert Rocco serves steaming cups of sophisticated tea in his Moroccan-inspired cafe. Choose from a variety of specialty brews (€7-9 a pot) containing everything from amber and saffron to homemade orange water and fresh mint. Take your shoes off and lounge among the floor pillows in the back room, or hit the hookah (€15 per group) in the small courtyard. Come during Happy hour (6:30-9pm) and have organic vegetarian food as you sip on a tea cocktail (€5); Rocco will make it with absinthe if you ask. Open daily 6:30pm-2am. Cash only.

Las Palmas, P. Ghiberti (☎347 27 60 033). Each summer, P. Ghiberti is transformed into a neighborhood block party with the help of Las Palmas. Drinks, live music, and an outdoor dance floor ensure fun-filled nights. Serves tasty dishes. Tables fill quickly, so make reservations. Happy hour 6:30-9pm; drinks €4. Beer €4. Mixed drinks €7. Shots €3. Open daily from the 2nd week of May to the 2nd week of Aug. 6:30pm-1:30am.

Caffè Sant'Ambrogio, P. Sant'Ambrogio 7 (☎055 24 10 35). Hip red lights and pulsating techno pop. People begin pouring in for *aperitivi* 6-9pm, but during the rest of the night, most just come in to buy their drinks before heading back into the warm night air of the *piazza*. Wine €4-6. Beer €2.50-5. Open M-Sa 10am-2am, Su 6pm-2am. MC/V.

TOP TEN LIST

WORD UP

You bought the bilingual dictionary, and you've probably got the Italian curse words down, but to *really* get in with locals, you've got to know some Tuscan slang. From picking up *una bella Italiana* in a club to respectfully telling street peddlers to scram, local lingo escapes translation and goes beyond clichéd idioms. Here are the top ten you'll need to fit in under the Tuscan sun.

1. Ganzo/a! (adj.) Cool. She/He is cool! *Lei é ganza!*

2. Bono (adj.) Hot. Zack/Kelly is hot! *Zack/Kelly é bono/a!*

3. M'attizza (v.) I'm hot for X. I'm hot for Lisa! *Lisa m'attizza.*

4. Mannaggia! (int.) Oh no. Oh no! I lost my *Let's Go!* Now I can't find that popular restaurant, The Max! *Mannaggia! Ho perso il mio* Let's Go! *Ora non posso vedere il ristorante popolare,* The Max!

5. Secchione (n.) Nerd. Screech is a nerd. *Screech è un secchione.*

6. Accipicchia! (int.) Wow. Wow, check out that dragon! *Accipicchia, che dragone!*

7. Incasinato (adj.) Screwed. I'm screwed. *Io sono incasinato(a).*

8. Donnaiolo (n.) Playboy. Slater is a playboy. *Slater è un donnaiolo.*

9. Spettagolare (v.) Gossip. Let's gossip about Skinner! *Spettagoliamo su Skinner!*

10. Cicciobomba (n.) Fatso. Jessie is a Fatso. *Jessie è un cicciobomba.*

Central, V. del Fosso Macinante 2 (☎055 35 35 05), in Parco delle Cascine. Four open-air dance floors pulse with hip-hop, reggae, and Italian "dance rock." Favored by teens and university students. Well-dressed bouncers and management keep things under control. All drinks €10. Cover €20, foreign students €3 until 1am. Open in summer Tu-Sa 8pm-3am. AmEx/MC/V.

Aquarama Meccanò, Vle. degli Olmi 1 (☎055 33 13 71), near Parco delle Cascine. One of Florence's most popular discos; caters to a slightly older crowd than Central. Open-air dance floors and sparkling grounds make for sophisticated fun. Drinks €10. Cover €10-16; includes 1 drink. Open Tu-Sa 11pm-4am. AmEx/MC/V.

SIENA   ☎0577

Siena's (pop. 49,000) vibrant character and local energy make it a distinctly Tuscan city. Locals are fiercely proud of their town's history, which dates back to the 13th century when the first Sienese began to craft a sophisticated metropolis, rich in wealth and culture. These days, the Sienese celebrate their heritage with festivals like the semi-annual *Palio*, a riotous display of pageantry in which jockeys race bareback horses around the central square.

TRANSPORTATION AND PRACTICAL INFORMATION. Trains run from P. Rosselli to Florence (1hr., 16 per day, €5.90) and Rome (3hr., 20 per day, €12.60) via Grosseto. TRA-IN/SITA **buses** (☎0577 20 42 46) run from P. Gramsci and the train station to Florence (1 per hr., €6.70) and San Gimignano (31 per day, €5.20). Across from the train station, take TRA-IN buses #3, 4, 7-10, 17, or 77 (€0.95) to Piazza del Sale or Piazza Gramsci, then follow signs to **Piazza del Campo,** Siena's *centro storico,* also known as **Il Campo.** The central **tourist office** is at P. del Campo 56. (☎0577 28 05 51; www.terresiena.it. Open mid-Mar. to mid-Nov. daily 9:30am-1pm and 2:30-6pm; mid-Nov. to mid-Mar. M-Sa 8:30am-1pm and 3-7pm, Su 9am-1pm.) Check email at **Cafe Internet,** Galleria Cecco Angiolieri 16. (€1.80 per hr. Open M-Sa 8:30am-11pm, Su 9am-11pm.) **Postal Code:** 53100.

ACCOMMODATIONS AND FOOD. Finding a room in Siena can be difficult in July and August. Reserve at least a month ahead for *Il Palio.* **Prenotazioni Alberghi e Ristoranti,** in P. S. Domenico, finds rooms for a €2 fee. (☎0577 94 08 09. Open M-Sa 9am-7pm, Su 9am-noon.) **Casa Laura ❸,** V. Roma 3, is in the less touristy university area; sacrifice immediate access to downtown Siena for spacious, well-priced rooms. Ring the doorbell, labeled "Bencini Valentini." (☎0577 22 60 61. Kitchen available. Singles €35-40; doubles €65-67; triples €70; quads €75. MC/V.) Bus #10 and 15 from P. Gramsci stop at the spotless **Ostello della Gioventù "Guidoriccio" (HI) ❶,** V. Fiorentina 89, in Località Lo Stellino. (☎0577 52 212. Curfew midnight. Dorms €14.45. Cash only.)

Sienese bakeries prepare *panforte,* a confection of honey, almonds, and citron, sold at Bar/Pasticceria **Nannini ❶,** V. Banchi di Sopra 22-24, the oldest pasticceria in Siena. (€2.10 per 100g. Open M-Th 7:30am-9pm, F-Sa 7:30am-10pm, Su 8am-9pm.) **Osteria La Chiacchera ❷,** Costa di S. Antonio 4, has delicious pasta. (☎0577 28 06 31. *Primi* €5-6. *Secondi* €8-12. Open M and W-Su noon-3:30pm and 7pm-midnight. AmEx/MC/V.) A **CONAD** supermarket is in P. Matteoti. (Open M-Sa 8:30am-8:30pm, Su 9am-1pm and 4-8pm.)

SIGHTS AND ENTERTAINMENT. Siena radiates from **Piazza del Campo (Il Campo),** a shell-shaped brick square designed for civic events. At the top of the slope by Il Campo is the **Fonte Gaia,** a marble fountain that has refreshed Siena since the 1300s. At the bottom, the **Torre del Mangia** bell tower looms over the graceful **Palazzo Pubblico.** Inside the *palazzo* is the **Museo Civico,** best appreciated for its late medieval and early Renaissance collection of Sienese-style paintings. (*Palazzo*, museum, and tower open daily Mar.-Oct. 10am-6:15pm; Nov.-Feb. 10am-5:30pm. Museum €7, students €4.50. Tower €6. Combo with entrance to the *duomo*, the Museum, the Facciatone, the Crypt, the Baptistery, and the Oratory €10.) From the *palazzo* facing Il Campo, take the left stairs and cross V. di Città to get to Siena's hilltop **duomo.** To prevent the apse from being left hanging in mid-air, the lavish **baptistry** was constructed below. (Open daily Mar.-Sept. 9:30am-8pm; first two weeks in Mar. and all of Oct. 9:30am-7:30pm; Nov.-Feb. 10am-5pm. €3-5.50.) The decorated underground rooms of the **cripta** (crypt) were used by pilgrims about to enter the *duomo*. (Check hours at the *duomo*. €6, students €5.) The **Museo dell'Opera della Metropolitana,** to the right of the *duomo*, houses its overflow art. (Open daily Mar.-Sept. 9:30am-7:30pm; Oct. 9:30am-7pm; Nov.-Feb. 10am-4:30pm. €6.) Every year on July 2 and August 16, horses speed around the edge of the Campo as part of **Il Palio.** Arrive three days early to watch the trial runs and to pick a favorite *contrada* (team).

LUCCA   ☎0583

Lucca (LOO-ka; pop. 9000) dabbles successfully in every area of tourist enjoyment: bikers rattle along the tree-lined promenade atop the town's medieval walls, fashionistas shop at trendy boutiques, and art lovers admire the architecture of the *centro*. No tour of the city is complete without seeing the perfectly intact city walls, or **baluardi** (battlements). The **Duomo di San Martino** was begun in the 6th century and finished in the 15th century. Nearby, the **Museo della Cattedrale** houses religious objects from the *duomo*. (*Duomo* open M-F 9:30am-5:45pm, Sa 9:30am-6:45pm, Su between masses. Free. *Museo* open Apr.-Oct. daily 10am-6pm; Nov.-Mar. M-F 10am-2pm, Sa-Su 10am-5pm. €4.) Climb the 227 stairs of the narrow **Torre Guinigi**, V. Sant'Andrea 41, for a view of the city and the hills beyond. (☎0583 31 68 46. Open daily June-Sept. 9am-11pm; Oct.-Jan. 9am-7pm; Feb.-May 10am-5pm. €5, students €3.50.) In the evening, *Lucchese* pack the **Piazza Napoleone.**

Family-run **Bed and Breakfast La Torre ❸**, V. del Carmine 11, offers large, bright rooms. (☎0583 95 70 44; www.roomslatorre.com. Breakfast included. Free Internet. Singles €35, with bath €50; doubles €50/80. MC/V.) From P. Napoleone, take V. Beccheria, then turn right on V. Roma and left on V. Fillungo. After six blocks, turn left into P. San Frediano and right on V. della Cavallerizza to reach the **Ostello per la Gioventù San Frediano (HI) ❶**, V. della Cavallerizza 12. (☎0583 46 99 57; www.ostellolucca.it. Breakfast €3. Dinner €10. Linens included. Towels €1.50. Laundry available. Reception 7:30-10am and 3:30pm-midnight. Lockout 10am-3:30pm. Dorms €18-19.50; 2- to 6-person rooms with bath €50-135. €3 HI discount. Cash only.) **Ristorante da Francesco ❷**, Corte Portici 13, off V. Calderia between P. San Salvatore and P. San Michele, offers patio seating and light meals. (☎0583 41 80 49. *Primi* €6. *Secondi* €7-11.50. 1L wine €7.20. Cover €1.50. Open Tu-Su noon-2:30pm and 8-10:30pm. MC/V.)

Trains (☎0583 89 20 21) run hourly from Ple. Ricasoli to Florence (1½hr., €5), Pisa (30min., €2.30), and Viareggio (20min., €2.30). **Buses** (☎0583 46 49 63) leave hourly from Ple. Verdi, next to the tourist office, for Florence (1hr., €4.70), Viareggio (30min., €2.20) and Pisa (50min., €2.50). The **tourist office** is in Ple. San Donato. (☎0583 58 31 50. Open daily 9am-7pm.) Rent bikes at **Cicli Bizzari**, P. Santa Maria 32. (☎0583 49 60 31. €2.50 per hr., €13 per day. Open daily 9am-7:30pm. Cash only.) **Postal Code:** 55100.

PISA

☎**050**

Millions of tourists arrive in Pisa (pop. 85,400) each year to marvel at the famous "Leaning Tower," forming a gelato-slurping, photo-snapping mire. Commanding a beautiful stretch of the Arno River, Pisa has a diverse array of cultural and artistic diversions, as well as three universities. The **Piazza del Duomo**, also known as the **Campo dei Miracoli** (Field of Miracles), is a grassy expanse that contrasts with the white stone of the tower, baptistry, *duomo*, and surrounding museums. Begun in 1173, the famous ■**Leaning Tower** began to tilt when the soil beneath it suddenly shifted. The tilt intensified after WWII, and thanks to the tourists who climb its steps daily, the tower slips 1-2m each year, though it's currently considered stable. Tours of 30 visitors are permitted to ascend the 294 steps once every 30min. (Tours depart daily June-Aug. 8:30am-11pm; Sept.-May 8:30am-7:30pm. Assemble next to info office 10min. before tour. €15. Cash only.) Also on the Campo is the ■**Battistero** (Baptistry), whose precise acoustics allow an unamplified choir to be heard 2km away. An acoustic demonstration occurs every 30min. (Open daily Apr.-Sept. 8am-7:30pm; Oct. 9am-5:30pm; Nov.-Feb. 9am-4:30pm; Mar. 9am-5:30pm. €5.) The dazzling **duomo** next door, considered one of the finest Romanesque cathedrals in the world, has a collection of splendid art, including a mosaic by Cimabue. (Open daily Apr.-Sept. 10am-8pm; Oct. and Mar. 10am-7pm; Nov.-Feb. 10am-1pm and 3-5pm. €2.) An **all-inclusive ticket** to the Campo's sights costs €10.50 and is available at the two *biglietterie* (ticket booths) on the Campo (at the Museo del Duomo and next to the tourist office adjacent to the tower).

Two minutes from the *duomo*, the **Albergo Helvetia ❸**, V. Don Gaefano Boschi 31, off P. Archivescovado, has large, clean rooms, small shared baths, a multilingual staff, and a welcoming downstairs bar. (☎050 55 30 84. Reception 8am-midnight. Reserve ahead. Singles €35, with bath €50; doubles €45-62. Cash only.) Steer clear of the countless touristy pizzerias near the tower and head to the river for a bite to eat, where the restaurants offer a more authentic ambience and consistently high quality. Try one of the many *primi* offerings, including various *sfogliate* (quiche) at ■**Il Paiolo ❶**, V. Curtatone e Montanara 9, near the university. (*Primi* and *secondi* €5-8. Open M-F 12:30-3pm and 8pm-1am, Sa-Su 8pm-2am. MC/V.) Get groceries at **Pam**, V. Giovanni Pascoli 8, just off C. Italia. (Open M-Sa 7:30am-8:30pm, Su 9am-1pm. Cash only.)

Trains (☎89 20 21) run from P. della Stazione, in the southern end of town, to Florence (75min., 2 per hr., €5.40), Genoa (2hr., 1 per hr., €8), and Rome (4hr., 1-2 per day, €23-29). To reach the **tourist office,** walk straight out of the train station and go left in P. Vittorio Emanuele. (☎050 42 291; www.turismo.toscana. it. Open M-F 9am-7pm, Sa 9am-1:30pm.) Take bus marked LAM ROSSA (€0.85) from the station to the Campo. **Postal Code:** 56100.

UMBRIA

Umbria is known as the "green heart of Italy" due to its wild woods, fertile plains, craggy gorges, and gentle hills. Cobblestone streets and active international universities give the region a lively character rooted in tradition and history. Umbria holds Giotto's greatest masterpieces and was home to medieval master painters Perugino and Pinturicchio.

PERUGIA

☎**075**

In Perugia (pop. 160,000), visitors can experience the city's renowned jazz festival, digest its decadent chocolate, and meander through its two universities.

The city's most popular sights frame **Piazza IV Novembre,** the heart of Perugia's social life. At its center, the **Fontana Maggiore** is adorned with sculptures and bas-reliefs by Nicolà and Giovanni Pisano. At the end of the *piazza* is the rugged, unfinished exterior of the Gothic **Cattedrale di San Lorenzo,** also known as the *duomo,* which houses the purported wedding ring of the Virgin Mary. (Open M-Sa 8am-12:45pm and 4-5:15pm, Su 4-5:45pm. Free.) The 13th-century **Palazzo dei Priori,** on the left when looking at the fountain, contains the impressive **Galleria Nazionale dell'Umbria,** C. Vannucci 19, which displays magnificent 13th- and 14th-century religious works. (Open Tu-Su 8:30am-7:30pm. €6.50.)

🛏**Ostello della Gioventù/Centro Internazionale di Accoglienza per la Gioventù ❶,** V. Bontempi 13, is a welcoming and well-located hostel with kitchen access, a reading room, and a terrace. (☎075 57 22 880; www.ostello.perugia.it. Linens €2. Lockout 9:30am-4pm. Curfew 1am, midnight in winter. Closed mid-Dec. to mid-Jan. Dorms €15. AmEx/MC/V.) 🛏**Ostello Ponte Felcino ❷,** V. Maniconi 97, is located 5km from central Perugia but is easily accessible by bus #8. Set amongst gardens in a small town, this hostel has well-equipped common areas, a friendly staff, and complimentary breakfast. (☎075 59 13 991; www.ostellopontefelcino.com. Dinner €10. Dorms €16; double and triples €18; singles €22.) Locals flock to 🍴**Ferrari ❶,** V. Scura 1, off Corso Vannucci, for its variety of made-to-order pizzas large enough for two. (€5.50-7. Open daily 8am-2am.) Don't miss Perugia's famous chocolate store, **Perugina,** C. Vannucci 101. (Open M 2:30-7:45pm, Tu-Sa 9:30am-7:45pm, Su 10:30am-1:30pm and 3-8pm.)

Trains leave Perugia FS in P. Vittorio Veneto, Fontiveggio, for: Assisi (25min., 1 per hr., €2.05); Florence (2hr., 6 per day, from €8); Orvieto (1hr., 11 per day, €7); Rome (2hr., 7 per day, €11) via Terontola or Foligno. From the station, take the new **minimetro** (€1) to Pincetto off Piazza Mazeotti or take **bus** #6, 7, 9, 11, 13D, or 15 to the central P. Italia (€1); then walk down C. Vannucci, the main shopping street, to P. IV Novembre and the *duomo.* The **tourist office** is at P. Matteotti 18. Grab a *Perugia Little Blue,* a guide written in English with a student's perspective. (☎075 57 36 458. Open daily 8:30am-6:30pm.) **Postal Code:** 06100.

ASSISI ☎075

Assisi owes its tranquil character to the legacy of St. Francis, patron saint of Italy and the town's favorite son. The undeniable jewel of Assisi (pop. 25,000) is the 13th-century 🏛**Basilica di San Francesco.** The subdued art of the lower church celebrates St. Francis's modest lifestyle, while Giotto's renowned fresco cycle in the upper church, the *Life of St. Francis,* pays tribute to the saint's consecration. (Lower basilica open daily 6am-6:45pm. Upper basilica open daily 8:30am-6:45pm. Modest dress required. Free.) Hike up to the looming fortress 🏛**Rocca Maggiore** for panoramic views of the countryside. From P. del Comune, follow V. S. Rufino to P. S. Rufino. Continue up V. Porta Perlici and take the first left up a narrow staircase. (Open daily 9am-8pm. €3.50, students €2.50.) On the way to Rocca Maggiore, explore the enchanting trails of **Colle del Paradiso,** V. della Rocca 3. (Open daily May-Oct. 10am-8pm. 6 tours per day. Free.) The pink-and-white **Basilica di Santa Chiara** houses the crucifix that is said to have spoken to St. Francis. It is surrounded by a dazzling courtyard with a fountain and lovely views of Umbrian scenery. (Open daily 6:30am-noon and 2-6pm.)

🛏**Camere Martini ❷,** V. Antonio Cristofani 6, has sunny rooms with spectacular views and balconies surrounding a central courtyard. (☎075 81 35 36; cameremartini@libero.it. Singles €25-27; doubles €40; triples €55; quads €65. Cash only.) **Ostello della Pace (HI) ❶,** V. d. Valecchi 177, offers bright rooms with two or three bunk beds and shared baths. From the train station, take the bus to P. Unità d'Italia; then walk downhill on V. Marconi, turn left at the sign, and walk for 500m. (☎075 81 67 67; www.assisihostel.com. Breakfast included. Laundry €3.50. Reception 7-9:30am and 3:30-11:30pm. Lockout 9:30am-3:30pm. Curfew 11pm. Reserve ahead. Dorms €16, singles with bath €18. HI card required; buy at hostel. MC/V.) Grab a personal pizza (€5-7) at **Pizzeria Otello ❶**, V. San Antonio 1. (Open daily noon-3pm and 7-10:30pm. AmEx/MC/V.)

From the station near the Basilica Santa Maria degli Angeli, **trains** go to Florence (2.5hr., 7 per day, €9), Perugia (30min., 1-2 per hr., €1.80), and Rome (2.5hr., 7 per day, €9). From P. Matteotti, follow V. del Torrione to Rufino, **Piazza del Commune**, the city center, and the **tourist office**. (☎81 25 34. Open M-Sa 8am-2pm and 3-6pm, Su 9am-1pm.) **Postal code:** 06081.

ORVIETO ☎0763

A city upon a city, Orvieto (pop. 20,700) was built in layers: medieval structures stand over ancient subterranean tunnels that Etruscans began burrowing into the hillside in the 8th century BC. **Underground City Excursions** offers the most complete tour of the city's twisted bowels. (☎0763 34 48 91. English-language tours leave the tourist office daily 11:15am and 4:15pm. €5.50, students €3.50.) It took 600 years, 152 sculptors, 68 painters, 90 mosaic artisans, and 33 architects to construct Orvieto's **🖾duomo.** The **Capella della Madonna di San Brizio,** off the right transept, houses the dramatic apocalypse frescoes of Luca Signorelli. Opposite it, the **🖾Cappella Corporale** holds the gold-encrusted chalice-cloth reputedly soaked with the blood of Christ. (Open M-Sa 7:30am-12:45pm and 2:30-7pm, Su 2:30-6:45pm. Modest dress required. *Duomo* free. *Capella* €5.) Two blocks down from the *duomo*, V. della Piazza del Popolo leads to the luxurious **Grand Hotel Reale ❸**, P. del Popolo 27, an opulent 13th-century palazzo with real old-world flair. (☎0763 34 12 47. Breakfast €8. Singles with bath €66; doubles €90; triples €117; quads €140. V.) **Nonnamelia ❸**, V. del Duomo 25, offers creative dishes and a wide variety of pizzas. (☎0763 34 24 02. Pizza €3.50-6. *Primi* €5.50-8. *Secondi* €7.50-14. Open daily 11:30am-3:30pm and 7-11pm. Cash only.) **Trains** run every hour to Florence (2hr., €11) and Rome (1hr., €7.10). The funicular travels up the hill from the train station to the center, **Piazza Cahen,** and a shuttle goes to the **tourist office,** P. del Duomo 24. (☎0763 34 17 72. Open M-F 8:15am-1:50pm and 4-7pm, Sa-Su 10am-1pm and 3-6pm.) **Postal Code:** 05018.

THE MARCHES (LE MARCHE)

In the Marches, green foothills separate the shores of the Adriatic from Apennine peaks, and umbrella-dotted beaches from traditional hill towns. Inland villages, easily accessible by train, rely on agriculture and preserve the region's historical legacy in the architectural remains of the Gauls and Romans.

URBINO ☎0722

The birthplace of Raphael, Urbino (pop. 15,500) charms visitors with stone dwellings scattered along its steep streets. Most remarkable is the Renaissance **Palazzo Ducale,** in P. Rinascimento, a turreted palace that ornaments the skyline. Inside, a stairway leads to the **Galleria Nazionale delle Marche,** in the former residence of Duke Frederico da Montefeltro. Look for Raphael's *Portrait of a Lady*, and don't miss the servants' tunnels. (☎0722 32 26 25. Open M 8:30am-2pm, Tu-Su 8:30am-7:15pm. Ticket office closes 1hr. before museum. €8, EU students 18-25 €4, under 18 and over 65 free.) Walk back across P. della Repubblica onto V. Raffaello to the site of Raphael's 1483 birth, the **Casa Natale di Raffaello,** V. Raffaello 57, now a museum containing period furniture, works by local masters, and the *Madonna col Bambino*, attributed to Raphael himself. (☎0722 32 01 05. Open M-Sa 9am-1pm and 3-7pm, Su 10am-1pm. €3. Cash only.)

Just doors down from Raphael's home is **Pensione Fosca** ❷. (☎0722 32 96 22. Singles €21; doubles €35; triples €45. Cash only.) At **Pizzeria Le Tre Piante** ❷, V. Voltaccia della Vecchia 1, a cheery staff serves pizzas (€3.50-6.50) on a terrace overlooking the Apennines. (☎0722 48 63. *Primi* €6.80-7.50. *Secondi* €8-15. Open Tu-Su noon-3pm and 7-11:30pm. Cash only.) **Supermarket Margherita** is on V. Raffaello 37. (Open M-Sa 7:30am-2pm and 4:30-8pm. MC/V.)

Bucci **buses** (☎0721 32 401) run from Borgo Mercatale to Rome (4hr., 2 per day, €25). The **tourist office** is at V. Puccinotti 35. (☎0722 26 13. Open M and Sa 9am-1pm, Tu-F 9am-1pm and 3-6pm.)

ANCONA   ☎071

Ancona (pop. 102,000) is the center of transportation for those heading to Croatia, Greece, and Slovenia. The P. del Duomo, a vigorous hike up a series of stairways, offers a view of the red rooftops and sapphire port below. Across the *piazza* is the **Cattedrale di San Ciriaco**, a Romanesque church with its namesake saint shrouded in velvet in the crypt. (☎071 52 688. Open in summer daily 8am-noon and 3-7pm; in winter daily 8am-noon and 3-6pm. Free.) **Pasetto Beach** seems far from the port's industrial clutter, though its "beach" is concrete.

From the train station, cross the *piazza*, turn left, take the first right, and then make a sharp right behind the newsstand to reach the **Ostello della Gioventù (HI)** ❶, V. Lamaticci 7. (☎071 42 257. Lockout 11am-4:30pm. Dorms €17. AmEx/MC/V.) **La Cantineta** ❷, V. Gramsci, offers specialties like *stoccafisso* (stockfish) at reasonable prices. (☎071 20 11 07. *Primi* €4-13. *Secondi* €5-15. Cover €1.50. Open Tu-Su noon-2:40pm and 7:30-midnight. AmEx/MC/V.)

Ferries leave Stazione Marittima for Croatia, Greece, and northern Italy. Jadrolinija (☎071 20 43 05; www.jadrolinija.hr) runs to Split, CRO (9hr., €48-53). ANEK (☎071 20 72 346; www.anekitalia.com) ferries go to Patras, GCE (22hr., €60-80). Schedules and tickets are available at the Stazione Marittima. Get up-to-date info at www.doricaportservices.it. **Trains** leave P. Rosselli for: Bologna (2hr., 36 per day, €11); Milan (4-5hr., 18 per day, €36); Rome (3-4hr., 11 per day, €14); Venice (5hr., 22 per day, €27.50). The train station is a 25min. walk from Stazione Marittima. **Buses** #1, 1/3, and 1/4 (€1) head up C. Stamira to P. Cavour, the city center. Ancona has no central tourist office, but brochures, maps, and accommodation listings can be found at Via Gramsci 2/A. (☎320 019 6321. Open May-Oct. daily 10am-1pm and 4-8pm.) **Postal Code:** 60100.

CAMPANIA

Sprung from the shadow of Mt. Vesuvius, Campania thrives in defiance of disaster. The submerged city at Baia, the relics at Pompeii, and the ruins at Cumae all attest to a land resigned to harsh natural outbursts. While Campania is one of Italy's poorest regions, often eclipsed by the prosperous North, the vibrant city of Naples and the emerald waters of the Amalfi Coast attract tourists.

NAPLES (NAPOLI)   ☎081

Naples (pop. 1 million), Italy's third largest city, is also its most chaotic—Naples moves a million miles per minute. Locals spend their waking moments out on the town, eating, drinking, shouting, laughing, and pausing in the middle of busy streets to finish conversations. The birthplace of pizza and the modern-day home of tantalizing seafood, Naples boasts unbeatable cuisine. Once you submit to the city's rapid pulse, everywhere else will just seem slow.

TRANSPORTATION

Flights: Aeroporto Capodichino, V. Umberto Maddalena (**NAP;** ☎081 78 96 259; www. gesac.it). Connects to major Italian and European cities. **Alibus** (☎081 53 11 706) goes to P. Municipio and P. Garibaldi (20min., 6am-11:30pm, €3.10).

Trains: Trenitalia (www.trenitalia.it) goes from Stazione Centrale in P. Garibaldi to **Milan** (8hr., 15 per day, €39-50) and **Rome** (2hr., 31 per day, €11-38). **Circumvesuviana** (☎800 05 39 39) runs to **Herculaneum** (€1.80) and **Pompeii** (€2.40).

Ferries: Depart from **Stazione Marittima,** on Molo Angioino, and **Molo Beverello,** at the base of P. Municipio. From P. Garibaldi, take the R2, 152, 3S, or the Alibus to P. Municipio. **Caremar,** Molo Beverello (☎081 55 13 882), runs frequently to **Capri** and **Ischia** (both 1hr., €4.80-10). **Tirrenia Lines,** Molo Angioino (☎199 12 31 199), goes to **Cagliari** (16hr.) and **Palermo** (11hr.). **Hydrofoils** are generally faster and more expensive. The daily newspaper *Il Mattino* (€1) lists up-to-date ferry schedules.

Public Transportation: The **UnicoNapoli** (www.napolipass.it) ticket is valid on the buses, funicular, Metro, and trains in Naples (€1.10 per 90min., full-day €3.10). Route info for the **Metro** and funiculars is at www.metro.na.it.

Taxis: Consortaxi (☎081 20 20 20); **Napoli** (☎081 44 44 44). Only take metered taxis, and always ask about prices up front. Meter starts at €3; €0.05 per 65m thereafter. €2.50 surcharge added 10pm-7am.

ORIENTATION AND PRACTICAL INFORMATION

The main train and bus terminals are in the immense **Piazza Garibaldi** on the east side of Naples. From P. Garibaldi, a left on **Corso Garibaldi** leads to the waterfront district; **Piazza Guglielmo Pepe** is at the end of C. Garibaldi. Access **Piazza Plebiscito,** home to upscale little restaurants and shops, by walking down **Via Nuova Marina** with the water on your left. **Via Toledo,** a chic pedestrian shopping street, links the waterfront to the Plebiscito district, where the well-to-do hang out, and the maze-like **Spanish Quarter.** Along V. Toledo, **Piazza Dante** lies on the western extreme of the **Spaccanapoli** *(centro storico)* neighborhood. Walking away from the waterfront, a right on any of the streets leads to the historic district. While violent crime is rare, theft is fairly common, so exercise caution.

Tourist Offices: EPT (☎081 26 87 79; www.eptnapoli.info), at Stazione Centrale. Free maps. Grab **▌Qui Napoli,** a bimonthly publication full of listings and events. Open M-Sa 9am-7pm, Su 9am-1pm. **Branch** at P. Gesù Nuovo (☎081 55 12 701).

Consulates: Canada, V. Carducci 29 (☎081 40 13 38). **UK,** V. dei Mille 40 (☎081 42 38 911). **US,** P. della Repubblica (☎081 58 38 111, emergency 033 79 45 083).

Currency Exchange: Thomas Cook, at the airport and in P. Municipio 70 (☎081 55 18 399, branch 081 55 18 399). Open M-F 9:30am-1pm and 3-7pm.

Police: ☎113. **Ambulance:** ☎118.

Hospital: Incurabili (☎081 25 49 422). M: Cavour (Museo).

Post Office: P. Matteotti (☎081 552 42 33), at V. Diaz on the R2 line. Unreliable *fermo-posta.* Open M-F 8:15am-6pm, Sa 8:15am-noon. **Postal Code:** 80100.

ACCOMMODATIONS

Although Naples has some fantastic bargain accommodations, especially near **Piazza Garibaldi,** be cautious when choosing a room. Avoid hotels that solicit

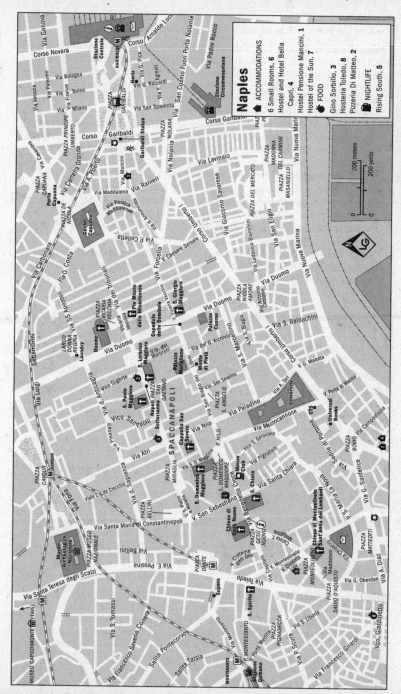

Naples

▲ ACCOMMODATIONS
6 Small Rooms, 6
Hostel and Hotel Bella Capri, 4
Hostel Pensione Mancini, 1
Hostel of the Sun, 7

♦ FOOD
Gino Sorbillo, 3
Hosteria Toledo, 8
Pizzeria Di Matteo, 2

☆ NIGHTLIFE
Rising South, 5

customers at the station, never give your passport until you've seen the room, agree on the price before unpacking, and be alert for hidden costs.

Hostel Pensione Mancini, V. P. S. Mancini, 33 (☎081 55 36 731; www.hostelpension-emancini.com). Bright, tidy, and spacious rooms, with new common room and kitchen. Breakfast and Wi-Fi included. Free luggage storage and lockers. Reception 24hr. Check-in and check-out noon. Reserve 1 week ahead. Mixed and female dorms €15-18; singles €30-40, with bath €45-55; doubles €45-55/50-65; triples €65-75/80-90; quads €72-80/80-90. 5% *Let's Go* discount. AmEx/MC/V. ❶

Hostel and Hotel Bella Capri, V. Melisurgo 4 (☎081 55 29 494; www.bellacapri.it). Top-notch hostel offers clean rooms with A/C and TV. Breakfast included. Free luggage storage, lockers, and Wi-Fi. Reception 24hr. With *Let's Go* discount, mixed and female dorms €15-19; singles €35-45, with bath €50-60; doubles €45-55/50-70; triples €60-70/70-90; quads €70-80/90-100; family rooms €100-140. AmEx/MC/V. ❸

Hostel of the Sun, V. Melisurgo 15 (☎081 42 06 393; www.hostelnapoli.com). Buzz #51. Dorms and private rooms are spacious, clean, and equipped with free lockers. Kitchen available. Breakfast included. Laundry €3, free load with 4-day stay. Free Wi-Fi. Reserve ahead in summer. Dorms €18-20; doubles €50-55, with bath €60-70; triples €75-80/70-90; quads €80-90. 10% *Let's Go* discount. MC/V. ❷

6 Small Rooms, V. Diodato Lioy 18 (☎081 79 01 378; www.6smallrooms.com). No sign; look for the call button. Friendly Australian owner and larger rooms than the name suggests. Kitchen available. Free lockers and Wi-Fi. Key (€5 deposit) for returning after midnight curfew. Dorms €18-20; singles with bath €30-40; doubles €40-45, with bath €55-60; triples €65-75; quad 85-95. 10% *Let's Go* discount. MC/V. ❷

🍴 FOOD

If you have ever doubted that Neapolitans invented pizza, Naples's *pizzerie* will take that doubt, knead it into a ball, throw it in the air, spin it on their collective finger, cover it with sauce and mozzarella, and serve it *alla margherita.*

Gino Sorbillo, V. dei Tribunali 32 (☎081 44 66 43; www.sorbillo.it). Basic *marinara* (€3), and *margherita* (€3.50) never tasted so good. Pizza €4.30-7.30. Service 10%. Open M-Sa noon-4pm and 7pm-1am. Closed 3 weeks in Aug. AmEx/MC/V. ❶

Pizzeria Di Matteo, V. dei Tribunali 94 (☎081 45 52 62), near V. Duomo. Pies, like the *marinara,* burst with flavor, while the building bursts with pizza aficionados. Expect a short wait. Pizza €2.50-6. Open M-Sa 9am-midnight. Cash only. ❶

Hosteria Toledo, Vicolo Giardinetto 78A (☎081 42 12 57), in the Spanish Quarter. Prepare yourself for Neopolitan comfort food. The *gnocchi* (€6) is hearty enough to be a meal on its own. If you're feeling adventurous or indecisive, try the chef's surprise. *Primi* €6-12. *Secondi* €5-10. Open M and Th-Su noon-4pm and 7pm-midnight. MC/V. ❷

Donna Margherita, Vico II Alabardieri 4/5/6 (☎081 40 01 29), in Chiaia. This place offers high quality food in a location close to city nightlife. Simple and elegant decor. Pizza €3.50-7. *Primi* €6-15. Open daily noon-4pm and 7pm-1am. MC/V. ❷

👁 SIGHTS

MUSEO ARCHEOLOGICO NAZIONALE. Situated in a 16th-century *palazzo* and former military barracks, the archaeological museum contains treasures from Pompeii and Herculaneum. The mezzanine has a mosaic room; one design features a fearless Alexander the Great routing the Persian army. Check out the Farnese Bull, the largest extant ancient statue. The *Gabinetto Segreto* (secret cabinet) of Aphrodite grants glimpses into the goddess's life. (*M: P. Cavour. Turn right* *from the station and walk 2 blocks.* ☎ *081 44 22 149. Open M and W-Su 9am-7:30pm. €6.50, EU students €3.25, under 18 and over 65 free. Audio tour in English, French, or Italian €4.)*

◪MUSEO AND GALLERIE DI CAPODIMONTE. Housed in another 16th-century *palazzo*, the museum resides inside a park often filled with locals. A plush royal apartment and the Italian National Picture Gallery lie within the palace. Among its impressive works are Bellini's *Transfiguration*, Masaccio's *Crucifixion*, and Titian's *Danae*. *(Take bus #178, C64, R4, M4, or M5 from the Archaeological Museum and exit at the gate to the park, on the right. 2 entrances: Porta Piccola and Porta Grande.* ☎ *081 74 99 109. Open M-Tu and Th-Su 8:30am-7:30pm. €7.50, after 2pm €6.50.)*

PALAZZO REALE AND MASCHIO ANGIONO. The 17th-century Palazzo Reale contains opulent royal apartments, the **Museo di Palazzo Reale,** and a view from the terrace of the **Royal Chapel.** *(P. Plebescito 1. Take the R2 bus from P. Garibaldi to P. Trieste e Trento and walk around the palazzo to the entrance on P. Plebiscito.* ☎ *081 40 05 47; www.pierreci.it. Open M-Tu and Th-Su 9am-7pm. €4, EU students €2, under 18 and over 65 free.)* The **Biblioteca Nazionale** stores 1½ million volumes. *(*☎ *081 78 19 231. Open M-F 10am-1pm. Reservations required.)* The **Teatro San Carlo**'s acoustics are reputed to top those of Milan's La Scala. *(Theater entrance on P. Trieste e Trento.* ☎ *081 79 72 331; www.teatrosancarlo.it. Open daily 9am-7pm.)* **Maschio Angiono's** five turrets shadow the bay. Built in 1284 by Charles II of Anjou as his royal residence, the fortress's most stunning feature is its entrance, with reliefs of Alphonse I of Aragon in 1443. *(P. Municipio. Take the R2 bus from P. Garibaldi.* ☎ *081 42 01 241. Open M-Sa 9am-7pm. €5.)*

NAPOLI SOTTERRANEA (CATACOMBS AND THE UNDERGROUND). The catacombs of S. Gennaro, S. Gaudioso, and S. Severo all date back to the early centuries AD. Tours of the subterranean alleys beneath the city are fascinating: they involve crawling through narrow underground passageways, spotting Mussolini-era graffiti, and exploring Roman aqueducts. *(P. S. Gaetano 68. Take V. dei Tribunali and turn left right before S. Paolo Maggiore.* ☎ *081 29 69 44; www.napolisotterranea.org. Tours every 2hr. M-F noon-4pm, Sa-Su 10am-6pm. €9.30, students €8.)*

DUOMO. Begun in 1315 by Robert of Anjou, the *duomo* has been redone over the centuries. Its main attraction is the **Capella del Tesoro di San Gennaro,** decorated with Baroque paintings. A 17th-century bronze grille protects the high altar, which houses the saint's head and two vials of his blood. Visitors can also view the newly opened underground **excavation site,** a tangle of Greek and Roman roads. *(Walk 3 blocks up V. Duomo from C. Umberto I or take bus #42 from P. Garibaldi.* ☎ *081 44 90 97. Open M-Sa 8:30am-noon and 4:30-6:30pm. Free. Excavation site €3.)*

◪ NIGHTLIFE

Content to groove at small clubs and discos during the winter, Neapolitans take to the streets and *piazze* in summer. **Piazza Vanvitelli** is accessible by the funicular from V. Toledo or the bus C28 from P. Vittoria. **Via Santa Maria La Nova** is another hot spot. Outdoor bars and cafes are a popular choice in **Piazza Bellini**, near P. Dante. ◪**Rising South,** V.S. Sebastiano 19, nearby Gesù Nuovo, has everything from a bar to a cinema. (Drinks €2-6. Bar open daily Sept.-May 10pm-3am.) At ◪**S'Move,** Vco. dei Sospiri 10, DJs spin techno nightly. (Beer from €3. Mixed drinks from €5. Open daily 6pm-4am. Closed 2 weeks in Aug.) **ARCI-GAY/Lesbica** (☎ 081 55 28 815) has info on gay and lesbian club nights.

◪ DAYTRIPS FROM NAPLES

◪HERCULANEUM. Buried by volcanic ash, Herculaneum is less excavated than its famous neighbor, Pompeii. A modern city sits on the remains of the ancient town. Don't miss the **House of Deer**. (Open daily 8:30am-7:30pm. €11.) As its name suggests, the **House of the Mosaic of Neptune and Amphitrite** is famous for its mosaics. The **tourist office** (☎081 78 81 243) is at V. IV Novembre 84. *(Take the Circumvesuviana train, ☎081 77 22 444, from Naples to the Ercolano Scavi stop, dir.: Sorrento. 20min. The city is 500m downhill from the stop.)*

POMPEII. On the morning of August 24, AD 79, a deadly cloud of volcanic ash from Mt. Vesuvius settled over the Roman city of Pompeii, catching the 12,000 prosperous residents by surprise and engulfing the city in suffocating black clouds. Mere hours after the eruption, stately buildings, works of art, and human bodies were sealed in hardened casts of ash. These natural tombs would remain undisturbed until 1748, when excavations began to unearth a stunningly well-preserved picture of daily Roman life. Walk down V. della Marina to reach the colonnaded **Forum**, which was once the civic and religious center of the city. Exit the Forum through the upper end by the cafeteria and head right on V. della Fortuna to reach the **House of the Faun**, where a bronze dancing faun and the spectacular Alexander Mosaic (today in the Museo Archeologico Nazionale) were found. Continue on V. della Fortuna and turn left on V. dei Vettii to reach the **House of the Vettii** and the most vivid frescoes in Pompeii. Backtrack on V. dei Vettii, cross V. della Fortuna to V. Storto, turn left on V. degli Augustali, and take a quick right to reach a small frescoed brothel (the *Lupenare*). V. dei Teatri, across the street, leads to the oldest standing **amphitheater** in the world (80 BC). To get to the ◪**Villa of the Mysteries,** the ancient city's best-preserved villa, head west on V. della Fortuna, right on V. Consolare, and all the way up Porta Ercolano and V. della Tombe. *(Take the Circumvesuviana train from Naples to the Pompeii Scavi stop, dir.: Sorrento. 40min., 2 per hr., round-trip €2.30. Archaeological site open daily Apr.-Oct. 8:30am-7:30pm; Nov.-Mar. 8:30am-5pm. €11.)*

BAY OF NAPLES

SORRENTO   ☎081

Cliff-side Sorrento makes a convenient base for daytrips around the Bay of Naples. **Ostello Le Sirene** ❷, V. degli Aranci 160, is located near the train station. (☎081 80 72 925. Dorms €16-25; doubles €40-70. Cash only.) Seaside campground **Villaggio Campeggio Santa Fortunata** ❶, V. del Capo 39, has a private beach, pool, market, and restaurant. (☎081 80 73 579. €6-10 per person; tents €5-7. Dorms €13-19.) Try the *gnocchi* (€5) or the *linguini al cartoccio* (linguini with mixed seafood; €7) at **Ristorante e Pizzeria Giardiniello** ❷, V. dell'Accademia 7. (☎081 87 84 616. Cover €1. Open Apr.-Nov. daily 11am-midnight; Dec.-Mar. M-W and F-Su 11am-midnight. AmEx/MC/V.) **Ferries** and **hydrofoils** depart for the Bay of Naples islands. Linee Marittime Partenopee (☎081 80 71 812) runs hydrofoils to Capri (20min., 17 per day, €14.50.) The **tourist office**, L. de Maio 35, is off P. Tasso, in the C. dei Forestieri compound. (☎081 80 74 033. Open M-Sa Apr.-Sept. 8:30am-6:30pm; Oct.-Mar. 8:30am-4:10pm.) **Postal Code:** 80067.

◪CAPRI   ☎081

Augustus fell in love with Capri in 29 BC, and since then, the "pearl of the Mediterranean" has become a hot spot for the rich and famous. There are two towns on the island—**Capri** proper, near the ports, and **Anacapri**, high on the hills. The best times to visit are in late spring and early fall: crowds and prices increase in summer. Visitors flock to the **Blue Grotto**, a sea cave where the water shimmers a vivid neon blue. (Short boat ride from Marina Grande €10. Tickets at Grotta Azzurra Travel Office, V. Roma 53. Tours until 5pm.) **Buses** departing from V. Roma make the trip up the mountain to Anacapri every 15min. until 2am; buses leave Anacapri for most tourist attractions. Away from pricey Capri, Anacapri is home to less expensive hotels, lovely vistas, and quiet mountain paths. Upstairs from P. Vittoria in Anacapri, **Villa San Michele** has lush gardens, ancient sculptures, and summer concerts. (☎081 83 71 401. Open daily 9am-6pm. €6.) Take the chairlift up 🏔**Monte Solaro** from P. Vittoria for great views. (Chairlift open daily Mar.-Apr. and Oct. 9:30am-4:45pm; July-Sept. 9am-6pm. Round-trip €7.) For those who prefer cliff to coastline, walk 1hr. to the **Faraglioni**, three massive rocks, or undertake the steep 1hr. hike to the ruins of Emperor Tiberius's **Villa Jovis.** The view from the **Cappella di Santa Maria del Soccorso,** built onto the villa, is unrivaled. (Open daily 9am-6pm. €2.)

Hotel Bussola ❹, V. Traversa La Vigna 14, in Anacapri, is a new building with mythological statues and mosaics. Call from P. Vittoria in Anacapri for pickup. (☎081 83 82 010; www.bussolahermes. com. Reserve ahead. Doubles €70-130. MC/V.) For convenient access to the beach and Capri's center, stay at **Vuotto Antonio ❹,** V. Campo di Teste 2. The simple rooms are devoid of modern distractions like TV and A/C, leaving guests to contemplate the coastline from their terraces. (☎081 83 70 230. Doubles €70-105. Cash only.) 🍴**Al Nido D'Oro,** Vle. T. de Tommaso 32, in Anacapri, has fresh food at low prices. (☎081 83 72 148. *Primi* €5-8. Open M-Tu and Th-Su 11am-3:30pm and 7pm-midnight.) The **supermarket,** V.G. Orlandi 299, in Anacapri, is well-stocked. (Open M-Sa 8:30am-1:30pm and 5-8:30pm, Su 8:30am-noon.)

Caremar (☎081 83 70 700) **ferries** run from Marina Grande to Naples (1hr., 3 per day, €9.60). LineaJet (☎081 83 70 819) runs **hydrofoils** to Naples (40-50min., 11 per day, €17) and Sorrento (25min., 12 per day, €14.50). Boats to other destinations run less frequently. The Capri **tourist office** sits at the end of Marina Grande. (☎081 83 70 634; www. capritourism.com. Open June-Sept. daily 9am-1pm and 3:30-6:45pm; Oct.-May reduced hours.) In Anacapri, it's at V. Orlandi 59; turn right when leaving the bus stop. (☎081 83 71 524. Open M-Sa 9am-3pm; Oct.-May reduced hours.) **Postal Codes:** 80073 (Capri); 80071 (Anacapri).

ON THE MENU

HOW DO YOU LIKE THEM LEMONS?

In the home of *limoncello*, *delizia limone*, and lemon gelato, no tourist can avoid sampling the famous limone Costa d'Amalfi (Amalfi Coast lemon). Far larger than the average supermarket variety, the ubiquitous citrus fruit resembles a grapefruit in size and in the thickness of its rind, but one bite reveals its lemony character through and through.

Lemon imagery in mosaics and frescoes at Pompeii and Herculaneum confirms the presence of these limone even in Roman times. The towns of Maiori and Minori have been famous producers of the *sfusato* lemon variety since the 11th century.

To make the cut as a *limone* Costa d'Amalfi, lemons must be grown on chestnut wood frames for at least two years, weigh more than 100 grams, and possess a thick and aromatic zest.

Given its lasting presence, the lemon has been absorbed into virtually every aspect of Amalfi cuisine. In cream for cakes, over seafood dishes, and in chocolates an confections, this sour citrus is a dear ingredient in the Amalfitano diet. So pucker up—you may be sweetly surprised.

Rigorous standards are upheld by the Consorzio Tutela Limone della Costa d'Amalfi IGP, Via Lama, Minori (☎089 87 32 11; www. igplimonecostadamalfi.it).

THE AMALFI COAST   ☎089

It happens almost imperceptibly: after the tumult of Naples and the grit of Sorrento, the highway narrows to a two-lane coastal road, and the horizon becomes illuminated with lemon groves and bright village pastels. Though the coastal towns combine simplicity and sophistication, the region's ultimate appeal rests in the tenuous balance it strikes between man and nature.

▛ TRANSPORTATION. Trains run to Salerno from Naples (45min., 40 per day, €5-10). SITA **buses** (☎089 26 66 04) connect Salerno to Amalfi (1hr., 20 per day, €2). From Amalfi, buses also go to Positano (40min., 25 per day, €2) and Sorrento (1½hr., 1 per hr., €2). Travelmar (☎089 87 29 50) runs **hydrofoils** from Amalfi to Positano (25min., 7 per day, €6) and Salerno (35min., 6 per day, €6), and from Salerno to Positano (1hr., 6 per day, €6).

AMALFI AND ATRANI. Jagged rocks, azure waters, and bright lemons define Amalfi. Visitors crowd P. del Duomo to admire the elegant 9th-century **Duomo di Sant'Andrea** and the nearby **Fontana di Sant'Andrea.** The hostel **A'Scalinatella ❶**, P. Umberto 6, runs dorms, private rooms, and camps all over Amalfi and Atrani. (☎089 87 14 92; www.hostelscalinatella.com. Tent sites €5 per person. Dorms €21; doubles €50-60, with bath €73-83. Cash only.) Amalfi's many *paninoteche* (sandwich shops) are perfect for a tight budget. The **AAST Tourist Office** is at C. Repubbliche Marinare 27. On the same street, a tunnel leads to beach town Atrani, 750m down the coast. The 4hr. **Path of the Gods** follows the coast from **Bomerano** to **Positano,** with great views along the way. The hike from **Atrani** to **Ravello** (1-2hr.) runs through lemon groves and green valleys. **Postal Code:** 84011.

RAVELLO. Perched atop cliffs, Ravello has been claimed by artists and intellectuals and its natural beauty seeps into their works. The Moorish cloister and gardens of **Villa Rufolo,** off P. del Duomo, inspired Boccaccio's *Decameron* and Wagner's *Parsifal.* (Open daily in summer 9am-8pm. €5.) The villa puts on a **summer concert series** in the gardens; tickets are sold at the Ravello Festival box office, V. Roma 10-12 (☎089 85 84 22; www.ravellofestival.com). Don't miss Ravello's **duomo** and its bronze doors; follow V. S. Francesco out of P. Duomo to the impressive **Villa Cimbrone,** whose floral walkways and gardens hide temples, grottoes, and magnificent views. (Open daily 9am-sunset. €6.) **Palazzo della Marra ❸**, V. della Marra 3, offers four immaculate rooms with terraces and kitchen access. (☎089 85 83 02; www.palazzodellamarra.com. Breakfast included. Reserve ahead. Doubles €60-80. MC/V.) **Postal Code:** 84010.

POSITANO. Today, Positano's most frequent visitors are the wealthy few who can afford its high prices, but the town still has its charms for the budget traveler. To see the large *pertusione* (hole) in the mountain **Montepertuso,** hike 45min. uphill or take the bus from P. dei Mulini. The three **Isole dei Galli,** islands off Positano's coast, were allegedly home to Homer's mythical Sirens. The beach at **Fornillo** is a serene alternative to **Spiaggia Grande,** the area's main beach. Buses to Amalfi stop at nearby ▧**Praiano beach,** a unique escape from commercial Positano. ▧**Ostello Brikette ❷**, V. Marconi 358, with two large terraces and free Wi-Fi, is accessible by the orange Interno or SITA bus; exit at the Chiesa Nuova stop and walk 100m to the left of Bar Internazionale. (☎089 87 58 57. Dorms €22-25; doubles €65-100. MC/V.) A backpacker favorite, **C'era una volta ❶**, V. Marconi 127, serves a special daily pasta and €4 margherita pizza. (☎089 81 19 30. *Primi* €6-9. Open daily May-Jan. noon-2:30pm and 7pm-midnight. AmEx/ MC/V.) The four small bars on the beach at Fornillo serve simple, fresh food.

The **tourist office** is at V. del Saraceno 4. (☎089 87 50 67. Open M-Sa 8am-2pm and 3-8pm; low-season reduced hours.) **Postal Code:** 84017.

SICILY (SICILIA)

Sicily owes its cultural complexity to Phoenicians, Greeks, Romans, Arabs, and Normans, all of whom invaded and left their mark. Ancient Greeks lauded the golden island as the second home of the gods. Now, tourists seek it as the home of *The Godfather*. While the Mafia's presence lingers in Sicily, its power is waning. Active volcano Mt. Etna ominously shadows chic resorts, archaeological treasures, fast-paced cities, and sleepy towns.

⌨ TRANSPORTATION

From southern Italy, take a train to Reggio di Calabria, then a Trenitalia **hydrofoil** (25min., €2.80) to Messina, Sicily's transport hub. **Buses** (☎090 77 19 14) serve destinations throughout the island and also make the long trek to mainland cities. **Trains** head to Messina (via ferry) from Rome (9hr., 6 per day, €43), then connect to Palermo (3hr., 22 per day, €11) and Syracuse (3hr., 16 per day, €8.75).

PALERMO ☎091

In gritty Palermo (pop. 680,000), the shrinking shadow of organized crime hovers over the twisting streets lined with ruins. While poverty, bombings, and centuries of neglect have taken their toll on much of the city, Palermo is currently experiencing a revival. Operas and ballets are performed year-round at the ◪**Teatro Massimo,** where the climactic opera scene of *The Godfather: Part III* was filmed. (Open Tu-Su 10am-3pm. Tours 25min., 2 per hr., €5.) The ◪**Cappella Palatina,** full of incredible mosaics, is in **Palazzo dei Normanni.** (Open M-Sa 8:30am-noon and 2-5pm, Su 8:30am-12:30pm. €6.) At the haunting **Cappuccini Catacombs,** P. Cappuccini 1,8000 corpses in various states of decay line the underground tunnels. Take bus #109 or 318 from Stazione Centrale to P. Indipendenza, then transfer to bus #327. (Open daily 9am-noon and 1-5pm. €2.)

Homey **Hotel Regina ❷,** C. Vittorio Emanuele 316, is near the intersection of V. Maqueda and C. V. Emanuele. (☎091 61 14 216; www.hotelreginapalermo.it. Singles €28; doubles €54, with bath €64. AmEx/MC/V.) The best restaurants in town are between Teatro Massimo and the Politeama.

Trains leave Stazione Centrale in P. Giulio Cesare at the southern end of V. Roma and V. Maqueda, for Rome (12hr.; 3 per day; €42). All **bus** lines run from V. Balsamo, next to the train station. Pick up a combined metro and bus map from an **AMAT** or **metro** info booth. To reach the **tourist office,** P. Castelnuovo 34, at the west end of the *piazza,* walk or take a bus from the station to P. Politeama, at the end of V. Maqueda. (☎091 60 58 351; www.palermotourism.com. Open M-F 8:30am-2pm and 2:30-6pm.) **Postal Code:** 90100.

SYRACUSE (SIRACUSA) ☎0931

With the glory of its Grecian golden days behind it, the city of Syracuse (pop. 125,000) takes pride in its extraordinary ruins and in the beauty of its offshore island, **Ortigia.** Syracuse's role as a Mediterranean superpower is still evident in the **Archaeological Park,** on the northern side of town. Aeschylus premiered his *Persians* before 16,000 spectators in the park's enormous **Greek theater.** (Open daily 9am-6pm; low-season 9am-2pm. €8.) On V. S. Giovanni is the ◪**Catacomba di San Giovanni,** 20,000 now-empty tombs carved into the remains of a Greek aqueduct. (Open daily 9:30am-12:30pm and 2:30-5:30pm. Mandatory guided tours every 30 min. €5. AmEx/MC/V.) More ruins lie over the Ponte Umbertino on **Ortigia,** the serene island where the attacking Greeks first landed. The **Temple of Apollo** has a few columns still standing, but those of the **Temple of Athena** inside the *duomo* are much more impressive. For those who prefer tans to temples, take bus #21 or 22 to **Fontane Bianche,** a glitzy beach with soft sand and refreshing blue water. Recently opened **lolhostel ❶,** V. Francesco Crispi 94, is becoming a true Syracuse gem as the city's first youth hostel. (☎0931 46 50 88; www.lolhostel.com. A/C. Internet €3 per hr. Free Wi-Fi. Dorms €18-20; singles €35-40; doubles €60-64. Cash only.) **◪Ristorante Porta Marina ❸,** V. dei Candelai 35, offers a great selection of seafood in a sleek modern setting. (☎0931 22 553. *Primi* €7-16. *Secondi* €8-18. AmEx/MC/V.) Get the best deals on food around the station and Archaeological Park, or at Ortigia's **open-air market,** V. Trento, off P. Pancali. (Open M-Sa 8am-1pm.) On the mainland, C. Umberto links Ponte Umbertino to the train station, passing through P. Marconi, from which C. Gelone extends through town to the Archaeological Park. **Trains** leave V. Francesco Crispi for Messina (3hr., 9 per day, €9.50) and Rome (10-13hr., 2 per day, €44). To get from the train station to the **tourist office,** V. Malta 106, take V. Crispi to P. Marconi, then follow V. Malta towards Ortigia. (☎0931 46 88 69; www.provincia.siracusa.it. Open M-F 9am-1pm.) **Postal Code:** 96100.

AEOLIAN ISLANDS (ISOLE EOLIE) ☎090

Homer believed these islands to be a home of the gods, while residents consider them *Le Perle del Mare* (Pearls of the Sea). The rugged shores, pristine landscapes, volcanoes, and mud baths might as well be divinely inspired; however, living among the gods isn't cheap, and prices rise steeply in summer.

◧ TRANSPORTATION. The archipelago lies off the Sicilian coast, north of **Milazzo,** the principal and least expensive departure point. **Trains** run from Milazzo to Messina (30min., 21 per day, €3.10) and Palermo (3hr., 12 per day, €11.60). An orange **AST bus** runs from Milazzo's train station to the port (10min., 2 per hr., €1). Ustica (☎0923 87 38 13; www.usticalines.it), Siremar (☎090 92 83 242; www.siremar.it), and Navigazione Generale Italiana (NGI; ☎090 92 84 091) **ferries** depart for Lipari (2hr., 3 per day, €7) and Vulcano (1hr., 3 per day, €6.50). **Hydrofoils** run twice as fast as ferries and more frequently, but for twice the price. Ticket offices are on V. dei Mille in Milazzo.

◩ LIPARI. Lipari, the largest and most developed of the islands, is renowned for its beaches. Visitors descend upon its shores each summer, just as pirates did centuries ago. To reach the beaches of the **Spiaggia Bianca** and **Porticello,** take the Lipari-Cavedi **bus** to **Canneto.** Lipari's best sights—aside from its beautiful shores—are all in the hilltop *castello,* where a **fortress** with ancient Greek foundations dwarfs the surrounding town. Nearby is the **◪Museo Archeologico Eoliano,** whose collection includes Greek and Sicilian pottery. (Open May-Oct. M-Sa 9am-1pm and 3-6pm; Nov.-Apr. reduced hours. €6.) *Affittacamere* (private rooms) may be the best deals, but ask to see the room and get a price in writing before accepting. Relax on your private terrace away from the bustle in one of the eight rooms with bath and A/C at **Villa Rosa ❷,** V. Francesco Crispi 134. (☎090 98 12 217; www.liparivillarosa.it. Doubles €30-60.) Camp at **Baia Unci ❶,** V. Marina Garibaldi 2, at the entrance to the hamlet of Canneto, 2km from Lipari. (☎090 98 11 909. Open mid-Mar. to mid-Oct. €8-15 per person with tent. Cash only.) **◪Da Gilberto e Vera ❶,** V. Marina Garibaldi 22-24, is renowned for its sandwiches. (☎090 98 12 756; www.gilbertoevera.it. Panini

€4.50. Open daily Mar.-Oct. 7am-4am; Nov.-Feb. 7am-2am. AmEx/MC/V.) Shop at **UPIM** supermarket, C. V. Emanuele 212. (Open M-Sa 8am-9:30pm, Su 8am-1:30pm. AmEx/MC/V.) The **tourist office**, C. V. Emanuele 202, is near the dock. (☎090 98 80 095; www.aasteolie.info. Open M-F 8:30am-1:30pm and 4:30-7:30pm; July-Aug. also open Sa 8am-2pm and 4-9pm.) **Postal Code:** 98055.

🐾 **VULCANO.** Black beaches, bubbling seas, and sulfuric mud spas attract international visitors to Vulcano. A steep 1hr. **hike** (€3) to the inactive 🏔**Gran Cratere** (Grand Crater), at the summit of Fossa di Volcane, snakes between the volcano's *fumaroli* (emissions of yellow, noxious smoke). On a clear day, you can see all the other islands from the top. The allegedly therapeutic **Laghetto di Fanghi** (mud pool) is up V. Provinciale to the right from the port (€2). This spa's pungent odor is impossible to miss. If murky gray-brown muck isn't your thing, step into the scalding waters of the **acquacalda,** where underwater volcanic outlets make the shoreline bubble like a hot tub, or visit the nearby black sands of **Sabbie Nere** (follow the signs off V. Ponente). To get to Vulcano, take the **hydrofoil** from the port at Lipari (10min., 17 per day, €5.80). Ferries and hydrofoils dock at **Porto di Levante,** on the eastern side of **Vulcanello,** the youngest volcano. V. Provinciale heads toward Fossa di Vulcane from the port. The **tourist office** is at V. Provinciale 41 (☎090 98 52 105. Open Aug. daily 8am-1:30pm and 3-5pm), or get info at the Lipari office. **Postal Code:** 98050.

SARDINIA (SARDEGNA)

An old Sardinian legend says that when God finished making the world, He had a handful of dirt left over, which He took, threw into the Mediterranean, stepped on, and—behold—created the island of Sardinia. African, Spanish, and Italian influences have shaped the architecture, language, and cuisine of this truly unique island, whose jewel-toned waters and ample beaches are widely considered some of the most beautiful in the world.

▐ TRANSPORTATION

Alitalia **flights** link Alghero, Cagliari, and Olbia to major Italian cities; recently, Ryanair and easyJet have started to serve Sardinia's airports as well. Several **ferry** companies, among them Tirrenia ferries (☎89 21 23; www.tirrenia.it), run to Olbia from Civitavecchia, just north of Rome (5-7hr., 2 per day, €22-91), and Genoa (13hr., 6 per week, from €23-50), and to Cagliari from Civitavecchia (14hr., 1 per day, €29-44), Naples (16hr., 1 per week, €29-44), and Palermo (13hr., 1 per week, €28-42). **Trains** run from Cagliari to Olbia (4hr., 1 per day, €15), Oristano (1hr., 17 per day, €5.20), and Sassari (4hr., 4 per day, €14). From Sassari, trains run to Alghero (35min., 11 per day, €2.20). **Buses** connect Cagliari to Oristano (1hr., 2 per day, €6.50) and run from Olbia to Palau (12 per day, €2.50), where ferries access the protected beaches of La Maddalena.

CAGLIARI   ☎070

Exploring Cagliari, the charming and vibrant *capoluogo* of the region of Sardinia, will take you from fascinating Roman ruins to thoroughly modern resorts and clubs along endless stretches of beach. The **Roman amphitheater** comes alive with concerts, operas, and plays during the **arts festival** in July and August. Cross V. Roma from the train station or ARST station and turn right to get to the spacious rooms of 🏠**B&B Vittoria ❸,** V. Roma 75. (☎070 64 04 026; www.bbvittoria.com. Singles €48; doubles €78. Shared bath. 10% *Let's Go* discount. Cash only.) The B&B's owners also run **Hotel aer Bundes Jack ❹**, in the same building. (☎070 66 79 70; hotel.aerbundesjack@libero.it. Breakfast €7. Reserve ahead. Singles €48-58; doubles €70-88; triples €114. Cash only.) The **tourist office** is a kiosk in P. Matteotti facing V. Roma. (☎070 66 92 55. Open M-F 8:30am-1:30pm and 2-8pm, Sa-Su 8am-8pm; low-season reduced hours.) **Postal Code:** 09100.

ALGHERO   ☎079

Vineyards, ruins, and horseback rides are just a short trip away from Alghero's parks and palms. Between massive white cliffs, 654 steps plunge downward at ▓**Grotte di Nettuno,** 70-million-year-old, stalactite-filled caverns in Capo Caccia. Take the **bus** (50min., 3 per day, round-trip €3.50) or a **boat.** (1hr.; 3-8 per day; round trip €13, includes tour but not cave entrance. Caves open daily Apr.-Sept. 9am-7pm; Oct. 9am-5pm; Nov.-Mar. 9am-4pm. €10.) Outside of Alghero proper, **Hostal de l'Alguer ❶**, V. Parenzo 79, is the cheapest option in the area. (☎079 93 20 39. Breakfast included. Large dorms €18; 4- to 6-bed dorms €18-20; doubles €21-25. €3 HI discount.) Toward Fertilia, 2km from Alghero, **La Mariposa ❶** campground, V. Lido 22, has a bar, beach access, bikes, diving excursions, and a restaurant. (☎079 95 03 60; www.lamariposa.it. Hot showers €0.50. Mar.-Oct. €8-11 per person, €4-13 per tent; 4-person bungalows €47-78. Apr.-June no charge for tents and cars. AmEx/MC/V.) The **tourist office,** P. Porta Terra 9, is to the right of the bus stop. (☎079 97 90 54. Open Apr.-Oct. M-Sa 8am-8pm, Su 10am-1pm; Nov.-Mar. M-Sa 8am-8pm.) **Postal Code:** 07041.

▓PALAU   ☎0789

Situated on the luminous waters of Sardinia's northern coast, Palau (pop. 4200) is both a gorgeous destination and a convenient base for exploring La Maddalena. Check out the **Roccia dell'Orso,** a rock that resembles a bear, from which you can enjoy stunning views of the countryside and port. (Buses to "Capo d'Orso"; 20min.; 4 per day 9:45am-6pm, last return 6:20pm; round-trip €1.50.) **Hotel La Roccia ❺**, V. dei Mille 15, has a lobby built around an enormous boulder and themed rooms, like *"Il Faro"* (the lighthouse). All 22 rooms have balcony, A/C, TV, and bath. (☎0789 70 95 28; www.hotellaroccia.com. Breakfast included. Singles €48-84; doubles €78-130. AmEx/MC/V.) Campgrounds on Palau provide a stellar budget option. **Baia Saraceno ❶**, Localit Puna Nera 1, offers three picturesque beaches 500m outside Palau. (☎0789 70 94 03; www. baiasaraceno.com. €8-17.50 per person, ages 4-12 €5.50-13. Electricity €3. 2-person bungalows €26-48, with bath €32-64. AmEx/MC/V.) After a day at the beach, try gelato or crepes at **Sicily Creperie ❶**, V. Nazionale 45. (☎33 16 44 67 72. Open 9:30am-1pm and 4-10:30pm. Cash only.) Palau's **tourist office,** P. Fresi, sits to the right of V. Nazionale when approaching from Stazione Maritime. (☎0789 70 70 25; www.palau.it. Open daily 9am-1pm and 4:30-7:30pm.) **Postal code:** 07020.

▓LA MADDALENA ARCHIPELAGO   ☎078

An ancient land bridge that once connected Corsica and Sardinia, L'Arcipelago della Maddalena was declared Sardinia's first national park in 1996. The nearby island of **Razzoli** has magnificent swimming holes, and sightseers can set out by boat to islands like Santa Maria and Spargi. ▓**Marinella IV** (☎0789 73 68 41; www.marinellagite.it) runs tour boats from Palau, located on Sardinia's northern coast. They make two or three stops at beaches and normally serve lunch. (Boats leave 10-11am and return 5-6pm. €35. Purchase tickets 1 day ahead.) **Panoramica Dei Comi** is a paved road circling the island—bike or motor along it for spectacular sea views, and then pause for a bit of sunbathing.

Charming **Hotel Arcipelago ❹**, V. Indipendenza 2, is a good deal but a 20min. walk from the *centro*. (☎0789 72 73 28. Breakfast included. Reservation required July-Aug. Singles €45-55; doubles €60-85. V.) Young locals flock to **Garden Bar ❸**, V. Garibaldi 65, for its tasty, varied cuisine and cool aquatic decor. (☎0787 73 88 25. Pizza €3.50-8. *Primi* €6-15. *Secondi* €6-20. Cover €1.50. Open daily 11:30am-3pm and 5-11pm. MC/V.)

EneRmaR and Saremar run **ferries** between Palau and La Maddalena (EneRmaR ☎0789 73 54 68 or 0789 70 84 84. www.enermar.it. 15min.; every 30min. 5:45am-11pm. Round-trip €10. Saremar ☎0789 70 92 70. 15min.; every 30min. 7am-7pm. €10.) Though there is no tourist office on the archipelago, Palau's **tourist office** usually has brochures on La Maddelena's attractions. (☎0789 70 70 25. www.palau.it. Open daily 9am-1pm and 4:30-7:30pm.) **Postal Code:** 07024.

ITALY

THE NETHERLANDS
(NEDERLAND)

The Dutch take great pride in their country, in part because they created vast stretches of it, claiming land from the ocean using dikes and canals. With most of the country's land below sea level, the task of keeping iconic tulips and windmills on dry ground has become something of a national pastime. Over the centuries, planners built dikes higher and higher to hold back the sea, culminating in a new "flexible coast" policy that depends on spillways and reservoirs to contain potentially disastrous flood waters. For a people whose land constantly threatens to become ocean, the staunch Dutch have a deeply grounded culture and down-to-earth friendliness. Time-tested art, ambitious architecture, and dynamic nightlife make the Netherlands a priority destination in Europe.

DISCOVER THE NETHERLANDS: SUGGESTED ITINERARIES

THREE DAYS. Go no farther than the canals and coffee shops of **Amsterdam** (p. 543). **Museumplein** is home to some of the finest art collections in Europe, while the houses of ill repute in the **Red Light District** are shockingly lurid.

ONE WEEK. Begin in **Amsterdam** (4 days), then move on to the stately monuments of **The Hague** (2 days; p. 564) and end the week in youthful **Rotterdam** (1 day).

10 DAYS. You can't go wrong starting off in **Amsterdam,** especially if you detour to the flower trading in **Aalsmeer** (5 days total). Take time to recover your energy with the history of **Haarlem** (1 day; p. 563). Next are **The Hague** (2 days) and **Rotterdam** (1 day). Explore the museums and perhaps visit a friend in the college town of **Utrecht** (1 day)—or maybe just go back to Amsterdam.

ESSENTIALS

FACTS AND FIGURES

OFFICIAL NAME: Kingdom of the Netherlands.

MAJOR CITIES: The Hague, Rotterdam, Utrecht.

POPULATION: 6,571,000.

LAND AREA: 41,500 sq. km.

TIME ZONE: GMT +1.

LANGUAGE: Dutch; English is spoken almost universally.

RELIGIONS: Catholic (31%), Protestant (20%), Muslim (6%).

LAND BELOW SEA LEVEL: One-third of the country, kept dry by an extensive network of dikes 2400km (1500 miles) long.

WHEN TO GO

July and August are lovely for travel in the Netherlands, which results in crowded hostels and lengthy lines. If you fancy a bit more elbow room, you may prefer April, May, and early June, as tulips and fruit trees furiously bloom

The Netherlands

and temperatures hover around 12-20°C (53-68°F). The Netherlands is famously drizzly year-round, so travelers should bring raingear.

DOCUMENTS AND FORMALITIES

EMBASSIES AND CONSULATES. Foreign embassies and consulates are in The Hague (p. 564). Both the UK and the US have consulates in Amsterdam (p. 544). Dutch embassies abroad include: **Australia,** 120 Empire Circuit, Yarralumla Canberra, ACT, 2600 (☎262 20 94 00; www.netherlands.org.au); **Canada,** 350 Albert St., Ste. 2020, Ottawa, ON, K1R 1A4 (☎613-237-5030; www.netherlandsembassy. ca); **Ireland,** 160 Merrion Rd., Dublin, 4 (☎12 69 34 44; www.netherlandsembassy. ie); **New Zealand,** P.O. Box 840, at Ballance and Featherston St., Wellington (☎044 71 63 90; www.netherlandsembassy.co.nz); **UK,** 38 Hyde Park Gate, London, SW7 5DP (☎20 75 90 32 00; www.netherlands-embassy.org.uk); **US,** 4200 Linnean Ave., NW, Washington, DC, 20008 (☎202-244-5300; www.netherlands-embassy.org).

VISA AND ENTRY INFORMATION. EU citizens do not need a visa. Citizens of Australia, Canada, New Zealand, and the US do not need a visa for stays of up to 90 days, beginning upon entry into any of the countries in the EU's freedom of movement zone. For more info, see p. 14. For stays longer than 90 days, all non-EU citizens need visas (around US$80), available at Dutch embassies and consulates or online at www.minbuza.nl/en/home, the website for the Dutch Ministry of Foreign Affairs. It will take approximately two weeks after application submission to receive a visa.

TOURIST SERVICES AND MONEY

| **EMERGENCY** | Ambulance, Fire, and Police: ☎112. |

TOURIST OFFICES. VVV (vay-vay-vay) tourist offices are marked by triangular blue signs. The website www.visitholland.com is also a useful resource. The **Holland Pass** (www.hollandpass.com, €25) grants free admission to five museums or sites of your choice and discounts at restaurants and attractions.

MONEY. The **euro (€)** has replaced the **guilder** as the unit of currency in the Netherlands. For more info, see p. 16. As a general rule, it's cheaper to exchange money in the Netherlands than at home. A bare-bones day in the Netherlands will cost €35-40; a slightly more comfortable day will run €50-60. Hotels and restaurants include a service charge in the bill; additional tips are appreciated but not necessary. Taxi drivers are generally tipped 10% of the fare.

The Netherlands has a 19% **value added tax (VAT)**, a sales tax applied to retail goods. The prices given in *Let's Go* include VAT. In the airport upon exiting the EU, non-EU citizens who have stayed in the EU fewer than 180 days can claim a refund on the tax paid for purchases at participating stores. In order to qualify for a refund in a store, you must spend at least €130; make sure to ask for a refund form when you pay. For more info on VAT refunds, see p. 19.

TRANSPORTATION

BY PLANE. Most international flights land at **Schiphol Airport** in Amsterdam (AMS; ☎800 72 44 74 65, info ☎900 724 4746; www.schiphol.nl). Budget airlines, like **Ryanair** and **easyJet**, fly out of **Eindhoven Airport (EIN;** ☎314 02 91 98 18; www.eindhovenairport.com), 10min. away from Eindhoven, and **Schiphol Airport,** to locations around Europe. The Dutch national airline, **KLM** (☎020 474 7747, US ☎800-447-4747, UK ☎08705 074 074; www.klm.com), offers student discounts. For more info on traveling by plane around Europe, see p. 46.

BY TRAIN. The national rail company is the efficient **Nederlandse Spoorwegen (NS;** Netherlands Railways; www.ns.nl). **Sneltreinen** are the fastest, while **stoptreinen** make many local stops. One-way tickets are called *enkele reis.* Same-day, round-trip tickets *(dagretour)* are valid only on the day of purchase, but are roughly 15% cheaper than normal round-trip tickets. *Weekendretour* tickets are not quite as cheap, but are valid from 7pm Friday through 4pm Monday. A day pass *(dagkaart)* allows unlimited travel throughout the country for one day, for the price equivalent to the most expensive one-way fare across the country. **Eurail** and **InterRail** have passes that are valid in the Netherlands. **Holland Rail** passes are good for three or five travel days in any one-month period. The Holland Rail pass is cheaper in the Netherlands at DER Travel Service or RailEurope offices. Overall, train service tends to be faster than bus service.

BY BUS. With transportation largely covered by the extensive rail system, bus lines are limited to short trips and travel to areas without rail lines. A **nationalized fare system** covers city buses, trams, and long-distance buses. The country is divided into zones: a trip between destinations in the same zone costs two strips on a *strippenkaart* (strip card); a trip in two zones will set you back three strips. On buses, tell the driver your destination and he or she will cancel the correct number of **strips;** on trams and subways, stamp your own in either a yellow box at the back of the tram or in the subway station. Drivers sell cards with two, three, and eight strips, but it's cheaper to buy 15-strip or 45-strip cards at tourist offices, post offices, and some newsstands. Day passes *(dagkaarten)* are valid for travel throughout the country and are discounted as special summer tickets *(zomerzwerfkaarten)* June through August.

BY CAR. Normally, tourists with a driver's license valid in their home country can drive in the Netherlands for fewer than 185 days. The country has well-maintained roadways, although drivers may cringe at high fuel prices, traffic, and scarce parking near Amsterdam, The Hague, and Rotterdam. The yellow cars of the **Royal Dutch Touring Club** (**ANWB;** toll-free ☎08 00 08 88) patrol many major roads, and offer roadside assistance in the case of a breakdown.

BY BIKE AND BY THUMB. Cycling is the way to go in the Netherlands—distances between cities are short, the countryside is absolutely flat, and most streets have separate bike lanes. Bike rentals run €6-10 per day and €30-40 per week. For a database of bike rental shops and other cycling tips and information, visit www.holland.com/global/discover/active/cycling. **Hitchhiking** is illegal on motorways but common elsewhere. *Let's Go* does not recommend hitchhiking.

KEEPING IN TOUCH

EMAIL AND THE INTERNET. Internet cafes are plentiful throughout the Netherlands. Travelers with Wi-Fi-enabled computers may be able to take advantage of an increasing number of hot spots, which offer Wi-Fi for free or for a small fee. Websites like www.jiwire.com, www.wi-fihotspotlist.com, and www.locfinder.net can help locate hot spots.

PHONE CODES	**Country code:** 31. **International dialing prefix:** 00. For more info on how to place international calls, see **Inside Back Cover.**

TELEPHONE. Some pay phones still accept coins, but **phone cards** are the rule. KPT and Telfort are the most widely accepted varieties, the former available at post offices and the latter at train stations (from €5). Whenever possible, use a calling card for international phone calls, as long-distance rates for national phone services are often very high. **Mobile phones** are an increasingly popular and economical option. Major mobile carriers include Vodafone, KPN, T-Mobile, and Telfort. For directory assistance, dial ☎09 00 80 08, for collect calls ☎08 00 01 01. Direct-dial access numbers for calling out of the Netherlands include: **AT&T Direct** (☎0800 022 9111); **British Telecom** (☎0800 022 0444); **Canada Direct** (☎0800 022 9116); **Telecom New Zealand** (☎0800 022 4464). For more info on calling home from Europe, see p. 28.

MAIL. Post offices are generally open Monday through Friday 9am-5pm, Thursday or Friday nights, and Saturday mornings in some larger towns. Amsterdam and Rotterdam have 24hr. post offices. Mailing a postcard or letter within the EU costs €0.69 and up to €0.85 outside of Europe. To receive mail in the Netherlands, have mail delivered **Poste Restante.** Mail will go to the main post office unless you specify a subsidiary by street address. Address mail to be held according to the following example: First Name, Last Name, Poste Restante, followed by the address of the post office. Bring a passport to pick up your mail. There may be a small fee.

THE NETHERLANDS

ACCOMMODATIONS AND CAMPING

NETHERLANDS	❶	❷	❸	❹	❺
ACCOMMODATIONS	under €36	€36-55	€56-77	€78-100	over €100

VVV offices around the country supply travelers with accommodation listings and can almost always reserve rooms for a €2-5 fee. **Private rooms** cost about two-thirds the price of a hotel, but are harder to find; check with the VVV. During July and August, many cities add a tourist tax (€1-2) to the price of all rooms. The country's 30 **Hostelling International (HI) youth hostels** are run by **Stayokay** (www.stayokay.com) and are dependably clean and modern. There is camping across the country, although sites tend to be crowded during the summer months; **CityCamps Holland** has a network of 17 well-maintained sites. The website www.strandheem.nl has camping information.

FOOD AND DRINK

NETHERLANDS	❶	❷	❸	❹	❺
FOOD	under €8	€8-12	€13-17	€18-22	over €22

Traditional Dutch cuisine is hearty, heavy, and meaty. Expect bread for breakfast and lunch, topped with melting *hagelslag* (flaked chocolate topping) in the morning and cheese later in the day. Generous portions of meat and fish make up dinner, traditionally the only hot meal of the day. Seafood, from various grilled fish and shellfish to fish stews and raw herring, is popular. For a truly authentic Dutch meal (most commonly available in May and June), ask for *spargel* (white asparagus), served with potatoes, ham, and eggs. Light snacks include *tostis* (hot grilled-cheese sandwiches, sometimes with ham) and *broodjes* (light, cold sandwiches). The Dutch colonial legacy has brought Surinamese and Indonesian cuisine to the Netherlands, bestowing cheaper and lighter dining options and a wealth of falafel stands in cities. Wash down meals with brimming glasses of Heineken or Amstel.

HOLIDAYS AND FESTIVALS

Holidays: New Year's Day (Jan. 1); Epiphany (Jan. 6); Good Friday (Apr. 11, 2009; Apr. 2, 2010); Easter (Apr. 4, 2009; Apr. 5, 2010); Queen's Day (Apr. 30); Ascension (May 1); WWII Remembrance Day (May 4); Liberation Day (May 5); Pentecost (May 11-12, 2009; May 23-24, 2010); Corpus Christi (May 22); Assumption (Aug. 15); All Saints' Day (Nov. 1); Saint Nicholas' Eve (December 5); Christmas (Dec. 25); Boxing Day (Dec. 26).

Festivals: Koninginnedag (Queen's Day; Apr. 30) turns the country into a huge carnival. The **Holland Festival** (June; www.hollandfestival.nl) has been celebrating performing arts in Amsterdam since 1948. In the **Bloemencorso** (Flower Parade; early Sept.), flower-covered floats crawl from Aalsmeer to Amsterdam. Historic canal houses and windmills are open to the public for **National Monument Day** (May 4). The **High Times Cannabis Cup** (late Nov.) celebrates pot.

BEYOND TOURISM

Volunteer and work opportunities often revolve around international politics or programs resulting from liberal social attitudes. Studying in the Netherlands can entail in-depth looks at sex and drugs. For more info on opportunities across Europe, see the **Beyond Tourism** chapter p. 55.

COC Amsterdam, Rozenstr. 14, Amsterdam (☎626 3087; www.cocamsterdam.nl). The world's oldest organization dedicated to the support of homosexuals and their families. Contact for involvement in support groups, gay pride activities, and publications.

University of Amsterdam, Spui 21, Amsterdam (☎525 8080 or 525 3333; www.uva.nl/english). Amsterdam's largest university offers a full range of degree programs in Dutch. Open to college and graduate students. Tuition €1445-10,000 per year, depending on the program. Discounts offered for EU citizens.

AMSTERDAM   ☎020

Amsterdam's reputation precedes it—and what a reputation it is. Born out of a murky bog and cobbled together over eight centuries, the "Dam on the River Amstel" (pop. 743,000) tempts visitors with its blend of hedonism and grandeur. Thick clouds of marijuana smoke waft from subdued coffee shops, and countless bicycles zip past blooming tulip markets. Yet there's much more to Amsterdam than its stereotypes. Against the legacy of Vincent van Gogh's thick swirls and Johannes Vermeer's luminous interiors, gritty street artists spray graffiti in protest. Politicians have sought to curb some of Amsterdam's excesses in recent years, closing over 700 coffee shops and half of the famous red-lit windows, yet the city's rebellious attitudes seems to have grown more pronounced in response.

✈ INTERCITY TRANSPORTATION

Flights: Schiphol Airport (AMS; ☎0800 72 447 465, flight info ☎0900 724 4746; www.schiphol.nl). **Sneltraihen** connects the airport to Centraal Station (20min., €5.40).

Trains: Centraal Station, Stationspl. 1 (☎0900 9292, €0.50 per min.; www.ns.nl). To: **Groningen** (2-3hr., 2 per hr., €26.60); **Haarlem** (20min., 6 per hr., €3.80); **The Hague** (50min., 1-6 per hr., €10.10); **Rotterdam** (1hr., 1-5 per hr., €13.30); **Utrecht** (30min., 3-6 per hr., €6.70); **Brussels, BEL** (2-3hr.; every hr.; €32, under 26 €24).

✴ ORIENTATION

Let the canals guide you through Amsterdam's cozy but confusing neighborhoods. In the city center, water runs in concentric half-circles, beginning at Centraal Station. The **Singel** runs around **Centrum,** which includes the **Oude Zijd** (Old Side), the infamous **Red Light District,** and the **Nieuwe Zijd** (New Side), which, oddly enough, is older than the Oude Zijd. Barely a kilometer in diameter, the Centrum overflows with bars, brothels, clubs, and tourists wading through wafts of marijuana smoke. The next three canals—the **Herengracht,** the **Keizersgracht,** and the **Prinsengracht**—constitute the **Canal Ring.** Nearby **Rembrandtplein** and **Leidseplein** are full of classy nightlife, spanning from flashy bars to traditional *bruin cafes.* Just over the **Singelgracht, Museumplein** is home to the city's most renowned art museums. The verdant, sprawling **Vondelpark** also houses more of the city's reputable art musuems. Farther out lie the more residential Amsterdam neighborhoods: to the north and west, the **Scheepvaartbuurt, Jordaan, Westerpark,** and **Oud-West;** to the south and east, **Jodenbuurt, Plantage, De Pijp,** and far-flung **Greater Amsterdam.** These districts are densely populated and boast excellent restaurants and museums.

▐ LOCAL TRANSPORTATION

Public Transportation: GVB (☎020 460 6060; www.gvb.nl), on Stationspl. in front of Centraal Station. Open M-F 7am-9pm, Sa-Su 10am-6pm. **Tram, metro,** and **bus** lines radiate from Centraal Station. Trams are the most convenient for city-center travel; the metro leads into the area's many outlying neighborhoods. Both run daily 6am-12:30am. **Night buses** traverse the complex city roads 12:30am-7:30am; pick up a schedule and map at the GVB (€3 per trip). Two strips (€1.60) gets you to nearly every sight within the city center and includes unlimited transfers for 1hr.

Buses: Trains are much quicker, but the GVB will direct you to a bus stop for domestic destinations not included on a rail line. **Muiderpoort** (2 blocks east of Oosterpark) sends buses east; **Marnixstation** (at the corner of Marnixstr. and Kinkerstr.) west; and the **Stationsplein** head both north and south.

Bike Rental: ■**Frédéric Rent a Bike,** Brouwersgr. 78 (☎020 624 5509; www.frederic.nl), in the Scheepvaartbuurt. Bikes €10 per day, €40 per week. Passport or credit card deposit. Lock and theft insurance included. **Maps** and advice are liberally dispensed by the attendants. Open daily 9am-6pm. Cash only. **Bike City,** Bloemgr. 68-70 (☎020 626 3721; www.bikecity.nl). €13.50 per day, €43.50 for 5 days. Bring a government-issued ID. Deposit €25. Open daily 9am-6pm.

GETTING AROUND. The best way to get around Amsterdam is by bike. Get a single-speed bike that has lights in the front and back—you can be ticketed for not using both at night. Get 2 locks—one for each wheel—and secure your bike to something sturdy. You'll inevitably see people biking down the wrong side of a street, running red lights, and playing chicken with trucks, but that doesn't mean you should join in the fun. Always bike perpendicular to tram rails (so your wheels don't get caught in them) and, finally, use hand signals. Canal boats are another great way to get around Amsterdam. Try taking advantage of the "Hop on, Hop off" tours where you can ride and check out different museums at the stops all day.

☑ PRACTICAL INFORMATION

Tourist Office: VVV, Stationspl. 10 (☎0900 400 4040; www.amsterdamtourist.nl), opposite Centraal Station. Books rooms and sells maps for €2. Internet €0.40 per min. Open daily 8am-9pm. Branches at Stadhouderskade 1, Schiphol Airport, and inside Centraal. Sells **Amsterdam card,** which gives you free public transit, parking, boat trip, and discounts. 24hr. pass €33, 48hr. pass €43, 72hr. pass €53.

Consulates: All foreign embassies in the Netherlands are based in **The Hague. UK,** Koningslaan 44 (☎020 676 4343). Open M-F 8:30am-1:30pm. **US,** Museumpl. 19 (☎020 575 5309; http://amsterdam.usconsulate.gov). Open M-F 8:30-11:30am. Closed last W of every month. Passport issues can be addressed at the Amsterdam offices.

Currency Exchange: American Express, Damrak 66 (☎020 504

Amsterdam

🏠 **ACCOMMODATIONS**
City Hotel, **1**
Durty Nelly's Hostel, **2**
Flying Pig Downtown, **3**
Frédéric Rent a Bike, **4**
Freeland, **5**
The Golden Bear, **6**
Hemp Hotel, **7**
Hotel Adolesce, **8**
Hotel Bema, **9**
Luckytravellers
  Fantasia Hotel, **10**
Shelter City, **11**
The Shelter Jordan, **12**
Stayokay Amsterdam
  Stadsdoelen, **13**
Stayokay Amsterdam
  Vondelpark, **14**
St. Christopher's Inn, **15**

🍴 BEST OF FOOD
Cafe-Restaurant Amsterdam, **16**
Cafe De Pijp, **17**
Cafe Latei, **18**
De Binnen Pret, **19**
In de Waag, **21**
Lanskroon, **22**
Loetje, **23**

☕ BEST OF COFFEE SHOPS
Amnesia, **24**
Kadinsky, **25**

⭐ BEST OF NIGHTLIFE
Alto, **26**
Café de Jaren, **27**
Café Zool, **28**
Dulac, **29**
Kingfisher, **30**

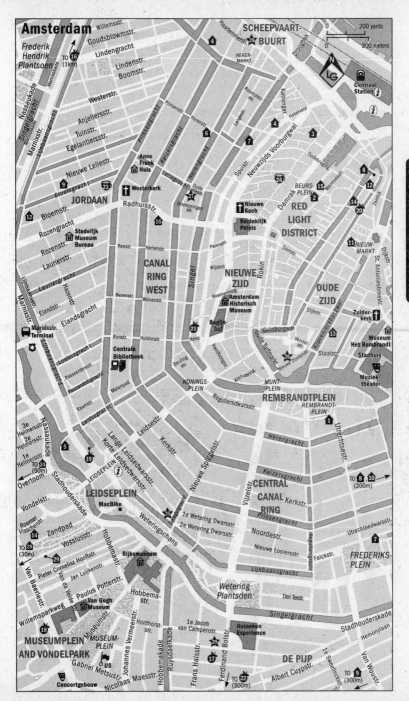

Amsterdam

THE NETHERLANDS

8777). Offers the best rates, no commission on American Express Traveler's Cheques, and a €4 flat fee for all non-Euro cash and non-AmEx traveler's checks. Open M-F 9am-5pm, Sa 9am-noon.

Library: Openbare Bibliotheek Amsterdam, Prinsengr. 587 (☎020 523 0900). Reserve free internet for 30min. at the information desk. Adequate English selection. Open Apr.-Sept. M 1-9pm, Tu-Th 10am-9pm, F-Sa 10am-5pm; Oct.-Mar. M 1-9pm, Tu-Th 10am-9pm, F-Sa 10am-5pm, Su 1-5pm.

GLBT Resources: Pink Point (☎020 428 1070; www.pinkpoint.org). A kiosk located in front of the Westerkerk. Provides info on GLBT life in Amsterdam. Open daily noon-6pm. **Gay and Lesbian Switchboard** (☎020 623 6565; www.switchboard.nl) takes calls M-F noon-10pm, Sa-Su 4-8pm.

Laundromat: Rozengracht Wasserette, Rozengr. 59 (☎020 638 5975), in the Jordaan. You can do it yourself (wash €6, with dry €7 per 5kg load) or have it done for you (€8 for 5kg). Open daily 9am-9pm. Cash only.

Police: Headquarters at Elandsgr. 117 (☎020 559 9111). The national non-emergency line, ☎0900 8844, connects you to the nearest station or the rape crisis department.

Crisis Lines: General counseling at **Telephone Helpline** (☎020 675 7575). Open 24hr. Rape crisis hotline (☎020 612 0245) staffed M-F 10:30am-11pm, Sa-Su 3:30-11pm. Drug counseling at the **Jellinek Clinic** (☎020 570 2378). Open M-F 9am-5pm.

24hr. Pharmacy: A **hotline** (☎020 694 8709) gives you the nearest 24hr. pharmacy.

Medical Services: For hospital care, **Academisch Medisch Centrum,** Meibergdreef 9 (☎020 566 9111), is easily accessible on subway #50 or 54 (dir.: Gein; stop: Holendrecht). **Tourist Medical Service** (☎020 592 3355) offers 24hr. referrals for visitors.

Internet: Many of the city's coffee shops and hostels offer internet for customers and guests. **easyInternetcafé,** Damrak 33 (☎020 320 8082). €1 per 22min., €6 per day, €10 per week, €22 for 20 days. Open daily 9am-10pm. **The Mad Processor,** Bloemgracht 82 (☎020 421 1482). Provides a relaxed setting to those hoping to surf the net. €2 per hr. Open Tu-Su 2pm-midnight.

Post Office: Singel 250, at Raadhuisstr. Open M-W and F 9am-6pm, Th 9am-8pm, Sa 10am-1:30pm.

ACCOMMODATIONS

The chaos of the **Red Light District** prompts accommodations in the **Centrum** to enforce strong security measures, while hostels and hotels in the **Canal Ring** and the **Singelgracht** are more carefree. Lodgings in the Red Light District are often bars with beds over them. Before signing up, consider how much noise and drug use you can tolerate from your neighbors. Places near the train station may be a convenient walk, but are often expensive and lacking in facilities. Amsterdam's canal-side accommodations offer affordable hotels and hostels with beautiful views, though they can be a bit cramped.

CENTRUM

Flying Pig Downtown, Nieuwendijk 100 (☎020 420 6822; www.flyingpig.nl). Knockout location and stylish decor matched with a welcoming party environment. A perennial favorite among young, energetic backpackers. Stoner-friendly lounge in reception area and drinking matches every Tu, Th, and Sa. Pitchers €10. Breakfast and linens included. Free Internet. Key deposit with locker €5. Dorms €28-29. Queen-sized dorms (holds 2 people): 32-bed €44.80, 20-bed €43.40. Weekends rates go up €3 per night. ISIC holders get a free beer in summer and a 5% discount in winter. Online booking up to a week in advance is recommended. AmEx/MC/V. ❶

Shelter City, Barndesteeg 21 (☎020 625 3230; www.shelter.nl). In the heart of the Red Light District, this clean Christian youth hostel, staffed by volunteers, is a comforting resting place for any backpacker. Activities organized by staff most nights. Breakfast and linens included. Travelers can choose to clean for 1 month for free room and board. Lockers €5 deposit. Internet €0.30 for 10min. Dorms June-Aug. €24-30. ❶

St. Christopher's Inn/Winston Hotel, Warmoesstr. 129 (☎020 623 2380; www.winston.nl). Each room is decorated by a different artist. Popular outdoor garden for those looking to imbibe. Be sure to head to **Club Winston** next door for live music. Free Wi-Fi. Dorms €29-35; singles €75-87. MC/V. ❶

Stayokay Amsterdam Stadsdoelen, Kloveniersburgwal 97 (☎020 624 6832; www.stayokay.com/stadsdoelen). This branch of the chain sleeps 176 and provides clean, drug-free lodgings in a (relatively) quiet environment. Great temporary housing choice for large younger groups. Breakfast, lockers, and linens included. Locker deposit €20 or passport. Internet €10 per 3hr. Rent bikes €10 per day. Reception 24hr. Co-ed or single-sex 8- to 20-bed dorms €19-30; singles €76. €2.50 HI discount. AmEx/MC/V. ❶

Hotel Brouwer, Singel 83 (☎020 624 6358; www.hotelbrouwer.nl). 8 gorgeously restored rooms, each with private bath and canal view. Breakfast included. Free Wi-Fi. Singles €63; doubles €100. No smoking. Cash or traveler's checks only. ❸

Hotel Royal Taste, Oudezijds Achterburgwal 47 (☎020 623 2478; www.hotelroyaltaste.nl). You'll find clean, comfortable, almost fancy accommodations at reasonable prices at Hotel Royal Taste in the heart of the red-light district. Breakfast €7.50. Free internet. Singles €50, with bath €60, with canal view €120; triples €150-165; quads €190. AmEx/MC/V. ❷

Hotel The Crown, Oudezijds Voorburgwal 21 (☎020 626 9664; www.hotelthecrown.com). Dependable rooms in a fun, if rowdy, environment. Loads of British tourists call this a

THE LOCAL STORY

THE RED LIGHT SPECIAL

Prostitution has always been legal in the Netherlands, but brothels were illegal for most of the 20th century. Since October 2000, it has been legal for a business to employ men or women as prostitutes as long as they are over the legal age of consent (16) and work voluntarily. The owner of a brothel must have a license from the government and adhere to specific regulations, set by local authorities. These require the payment of a tax by both prostitutes and employers, mandate the upkeep of a certain size workspace, and suggest that prostitutes get medical checkups four times per year.

The Netherlands has 12 red-light districts with window prostitution, but the majority of prostitutes work in brothels and sex clubs; many also work as escorts. While previous statistics indicated a majority were foreigners, the Dutch government has recently officially licensed prostitutes, making it legal for only Dutch citizens to rent rooms. Many foreigners who sold their services, particularly eastern European women, have resorted to underground clubs and escort agencies.

Windows are generally rented to prostitutes for 8hr. shifts which cost them €60-150; they make back the payment by charging €40-50 for 15-20min. of sex. Negotiations occur between prostitutes and potential customers through a propped-open door. Prostitutes have the final say about who gets admitted.

temporary home because of its proximity to the action. Canal views available upon request. Singles €50-85; doubles €70-115. AmEx/MC/V. ❷

CANAL RING AND REMBRANDTPLEIN

Hemp Hotel, Frederikspl. 15 (☎020 625 4425; www.hemp-hotel.com). Take tram line #4 to Frederiksplein. Each room is designed and decorated according to a different cultural theme. Revel in all things hemp including wines, beers, and candies. Breakfast—featuring yummy hemp bread—included. Singles €60; doubles €70, with private shower €75. MC/V with 5% surcharge. ❷

Nadia Hotel, Raadhuisstr. 51 (☎020 620 1550; www.nadia.nl). Each comfortable room includes fridge, safe, and TV. Nice interior garden. Breakfast included. Free Wi-Fi. Weekday high-season singles €65; doubles €90-120; triples €135-165. Higher prices for balcony or rooms with canal views, and on weekends. AmEx/MC/V. ❸

City Hotel, Utrechtsestr. 2 (☎020 627 2323; www.city-hotel.nl). Take tram #4 to Rembrandtplein. Clean, spacious, and above a pub on vibrant Rembrandtpl. Breakfast €5. Reception 24hr. 2- to 8-bed rooms €45 per person; singles and doubles €100; triples €135. MC/V. ❷

The Golden Bear, Kerkstr. 37 (☎020 624 4785; www.goldenbear.nl). Claim to fame as Amsterdam's oldest openly gay hotel. Rooms include a phone, safe, fridge, TV, VCR, and DVD. Continental breakfast included. Free Wi-Fi. Internet €2 per 30min. Reception 8am-10pm; ask for a key. Singles from €63 (furnished with double beds), with bath €103; doubles €73-118. ❸

WEST OF TOWN

Frédéric Rent a Bike, Brouwersgr. 78 (☎020 624 5509; www.frederic.nl). 3 cheerful rooms in the back of a bike shop—each named after a different painter. Bikes €10. Reception 9am-6pm. Singles €40-50; doubles €60-100; houseboats for 2-4 people €100-160. Apartments available for short-term stays from €140 for 2 people to €225 for 6. Cash only; AmEx/MC/V required for reservation. See **Local Transportation,** p. 543. ❶

The Shelter Jordan, Bloemstr. 179 (☎020 624 4717; www.shelter.nl). Well-run Christian hostel in the upscale Jordaan district. No obligation to participate in any of the hostel's religious activities. Best suited to those under 35. Breakfast included. Lockers with padlocks for sale. Cafe with internet (€1 per 20min.) and a piano. 1-month max. stay. Free room and board for those willing to clean; inquire at the desk. Dorms June-Aug. €24-28, Nov.-Feb. €17-21, Sept.-Oct. and Mar.-May €19-23. No drugs or alcohol. MC/V. ❶

Hotel Abba, Overtoom 122 (☎020 618 3058; www.abbabudgethotel.com), near Leidsepl. You can dance, you can jive, having the time of your life. Small, clean rooms, each with TV, table, and chairs. Breakfast included. Wi-Fi €3 per hr. Reception 8am-11pm. Rooms €25-40 per person. during high season. Cash only. ❶

Hotel de Filosoof, Anna Vondelstr. 6 (☎020 683 3013; www.hotelfilosoof.nl). The name gives away the theme—each room is dedicated to a different philosopher or culture. There is a library as well as several gorgeous gardens (including nearby Vondelpark) just a few steps away. All rooms come with cable TV, Wi-Fi, phone, and bath. Breakfast €15. Singles €80-125; doubles €95-150. AmEx/MC/V. ❹

LEIDSEPLEIN AND MUSEUMPLEIN

▨ **Hotel Bema**, Concertgebouw 19B (☎020 679 1396; www.bemahotel.com). Luxury at an affordable price. Friendly staff and beautifully decorated, airy rooms, right off the Museumplein. Breakfast included. Reception 8am-midnight. Singles €40-45; doubles and twins €65-70, with shower €85-90; triples €85-90/95-105; quads with shower €110-120. AmEx/MC/V with 5% surcharge. ❶

Flying Pig Downtown, Vossiusstr. 46-47 (☎020 400 4187; www.flyingpig.nl). Communal feeling in a tranquil setting. Bar open from 3pm. Ample breakfast included (8:30-10:30am). Free linens, internet, and Skype. Computers available for loan with deposit. Fully equipped kitchen. Reception 24-hr. High-season dorms €27-28; doubles €40. For long-term stays, ask about working in exchange for rent. Reserve ahead for discounts. AmEx/MC/V. ❶

Freeland, Marnixstr. 386 (☎020 622 7511; www.hotelfreeland.com). This GLBT-friendly establishment boasts exceptionally clean and cheery rooms. Rooms have DVD player; most have A/C and private bath. Breakfast included. Free internet in lobby, and Wi-Fi throughout the hotel. Singles €60-75; doubles €90-120; triples €150. Book early. AmEx/MC/V. ❸

Stayokay Amsterdam Vondelpark, Zandpad 5 (☎020 589 8996; www.stayokay.com/vondelpark). Between music in the lobby, a pool table (€1), foosball (€0.50), and a bar, this spotless hostel is a favorite with younger travelers. Well-suited for large groups and school trips. Breakfast and linens included; towels €3. Internet €1.50 per 15min. or €3 per hr. 7-night max stay. Reception 24hr. Dorms €24-34; doubles €80-93; quads €130-146. €2.50 HI discount. MC/V. ❶

DE PIJP, JODENBUURT, AND PLANTAGE

▨ **Hotel Adolesce**, Nieuwe Keizersgr. 26 (☎020 626 3959; www.adolesce.nl). Pristine, quiet, unique, and completely angst-free 10-room hotel in an old canal house. All rooms come with sinks, TVs, and phones; many have sofas, desks, and views of the canal. Coffee, tea, chocolate, fruit, and biscuits served all day. Reception 8:30am-1am. Singles €60-70; doubles €85-100; triples €130. No drugs allowed. MC/V. ❷

Bicycle Hotel, Van Ostadestr. 123 (☎020 679 3452; www.bicyclehotel.com). Clean digs with a large, airy, common room and a leafy garden in the beautiful De Pijp area make this a favorite among backpackers. Sink and TV in all rooms. Breakfast included. Free safe and internet. Bike rental €7.50 per day. 3-night min. weekend stay. Singles €40-70; doubles €50-85, with private shower toilet €80-115; triples €80-105/100-150. 4-person canal house in the Plantage €130. AmEx/MC/V; 4% surcharge. ❷

▣ MUNCHIES

Cheap restaurants cluster around **Leidseplein, Rembrandtplein**, and **De Pijp**. Cafes, especially in the **Jordaan**, serve inexpensive sandwiches (€2-5) and good Dutch fare (€6-10). Bakeries line **Utrechtsestraat**, south of **Prinsengracht**. Fruit, cheese, flowers, and even live chickens are sold at markets on **Albert Cuypstraat** in De Pijp (open M-Sa 9am-5pm). **Albert Heijn** supermarkets are plentiful; two of the most popular can be found in Dam Sq. and underneath Museumpl. **Lange Leidsedwarsstracht** and **Korte Leidsedwarsstracht** have a line of inexpensive pizzerias. You'll also find a good variety of spicy Indonesian restaurants and delightful Greek cuisine. Just to the left of Centraal Station on **Zeedijk**, Asian buffets offer filling yet budget-friendly meals.

CENTRUM

Cafe Latei, Zeedijk 143 (☎020 625 7485; www.latei.net), near Nieuw Markt. At this unique cafe and curiosity shop, everything except the stray cat is for sale—even your plate. Sandwiches around €3. All-day continental breakfast €7.50. Fresh juices €2-4. Th-Sa home-style Indian food. Vegetarian dishes €8. Filling meaty meals €12. Open M-F 8am-6pm, Sa 9am-6pm, Su 11am-6pm. Cash only. ❶

Greenwoods, Singel 103 (☎020 623 7071). Known for its cakes and breads, this restaurant serves high tea every Su for those looking for low-priced elegance with a canal view (€13). Breakfast (€8) served all day. Sandwiches €5. Open M-Th 9:30am-6pm, F-Su 9:30am-7pm. Cash only. ❶

Aneka Rasa, Warmoesstr. 25-29 (☎020 626 1560; www.finerestaurant.nl). Palm trees and murals make this relaxing restaurant a wonderful oasis on a rainy Dutch afternoon. Partake of the fruits of the Netherland's colonial past with dishes combining Dutch technique and Indonesian ingredients. Vegetarian plates €9-11. Meat dishes €12-14. Dinner for 2 €17-33.50. Open daily 5-10:30pm. AmEx/MC/V. ❷

In de Waag, Nieuwmarkt 4 (☎020 422 7772; www.indewaag.nl). Eat by candlelight in this upscale restaurant, an old weigh house from 1488, complete with stone walls, long wooden tables, and sleek stainless steel decor. Comfortable outdoor seating available in the Nieuwmarkt. Lunch sandwiches €5-10. Vegetarian dishes €19-21. Main courses €21-23. Complete 3-course meal €34.50. Open daily 10am-1am. Kitchen open 10am-10:30pm. MC/V. ❹

Pannenkoekenhuis Upstairs, Grimburgwal 2 (☎020 626 5603). Adorned with vintage photos of Dutch royalty. Traditional pancakes (€11), said to be among the best in Amsterdam. Open F noon-7pm, Sa noon-6pm, Su noon-5pm. ❷

Eat Mode, Zeedijk 105-107 (☎020 330 0806; www.eatmode.nl). Delicious Asian restaurant serving veggie entrees €3-6. Sushi €1.50. Rice dishes €6.50-11. Noodles €8-10. Open M-Th and Su noon-10pm, F-Sa noon-midnight. MC/V. ❶

Grekas Greek Deli, Singel 311 (☎020 620 3890). Take a break from the busy city and dine at this cozy, old-fashioned deli on the Singel canal. Starters €3-6. Salads €4-7. Entrees €12-15. Take-out items €2-10. Open W-Su 1-9pm. Cash only. ❸

CANAL RING AND REMBRANDTPLEIN

Lanskroon, Singel 385 (☎020 623 7743). Traditional Dutch pastries like *stroopwafels* (honey-filled cookies; €2), fresh fruit pies (€3.50), and exotic flavors of sorbet made on-site. Open M-F 8am-5:30pm, Sa 9am-5:30pm, Su 10am-5:30pm. Cash only. ❶

Ristorante Pizzeria Firenze, Halvemaansteeg. 9-11 (☎020 627 3360; www.pizzeria-firenze.nl). Delightful Italian restaurant and pizzeria, complete with murals of the Italian countryside, friendly service, and unbeatable prices. 25 types of pizza (€4.60-13) and pasta (€5.30-11). Lasagna €9. Glass of house wine €2.50. Open daily 1-11pm. MC/V. ❶

Foodism, Oude Leliestr. 8 (☎020 627 6424; www.foodism.nl). Bright green walls, red tables, and an alternative air. The warm staff encourages second helpings of healthy snacks and tasty smoothies (€4). Panini €5. Omelettes €6. Vegetarian and pasta platters €10-13. Breakfast (served all day) €9.50. Open M-Sa noon-10pm, Su noon-6pm. MC/V. ❷

Eetsalon Van Dobben, Korte Reguliersdwarsstr. 5-9 (☎020 624 4200; www.vandobben.com), right off Rembrandtplein. No-frills food on the go in a diner. Choose from the large selection of sandwiches (under €4), including roast beef and ham. Open M-Th 9:30am-1am, F-Sa 9:30am-2am, Su 11:30am-8pm. Cash only. ❶

WEST OF TOWN

Those who venture just west of the train station along Haarlemmerstr. will find bountiful dining opportunities with higher quality, lower prices, and better ambience than the smoke-filled interiors suggest.

▓ **Harlem: Drinks and Soulfood,** Haarlemmerstr. 77 (☎020 330 1498). Down-home soul food infused with a unique mix of Cajun and Caribbean flavors. The outdoor seating is perfect for a lazy Sunday. Lunch €5-9. Dinner entrees €11-17. Open M-Th 10am-1am, F-Sa 10am-3am, Su 11am-1am. Kitchen open 10am-10pm. Cash only. ❸

Vennington, Prinsenstr. 2 (☎020 625 9398). Dirt-cheap, delicious food in low-key setting just outside the Centrum. Let a real fruit shake (€3.50) accompany your towering club sandwich (€6.50). Sandwiches €2.50-6.50. Open daily 8am-5:30pm. Cash only. ❶

Cafe-Restaurant Amsterdam, Watertorenpl. 6 (☎020 682 2667; www.cradam.nl). A great lunch spot, this surprisingly casual restaurant with high ceilings and a spacious dining room has a seasonal menu of meat, fish, and vegetable entrees (€13-23). Free Wi-Fi. Open M-Th 11am-midnight, F-Sa 11am-1am. Kitchen open M-Th 11am-10:30pm, F-Sa 11am-11:30pm. AmEx/MC/V. ❸

De Vliegende Schotel, Nieuwe Leliestr. 162-168 (☎020 625 2041; www.vliegendeschotel.com). Organic vegetarian food. Look for the delicious daily specials (under €10). Soups and starters from €3.50. Entrees from €9.40. Open daily 6-11:30pm. Kitchen open 6-9:30pm. AmEx/MC/V. ❷

LEIDSEPLEIN AND MUSEUMPLEIN

▓ **Loetje,** Johannes Vermeerstr. 52 (☎020 662 8173). Known to have the juiciest steak in all of Amsterdam. Typical Dutch decor with wood furnishings, chalkboard menus, and crowds of hungry professionals. Hamburger €6.50. Steaks €16. Beer €4. Open M-F 11am-10pm, Sa 5:30pm-10pm. Cash only. ❷

Eat at Jo's, Marnixstr. 409 (☎020 638 3336; www.eatatjos.com). Locals rave about the the freshly prepared fusion food on the menu. Bands often grab a bite to eat after a performance at Melkweg, located inside. Menus change weekly. Open W-Su noon-9pm. Dinner starts at 5:30pm. Cash only. ❷

Bombay Inn, Lange Leidsedwarsstr. 46 (☎020 624 1784). Delicately spiced dishes at excellent value. Generous "tourist menu" includes 3 courses (chicken

BICYCLE BUILT FOR YOU

Even if you've experienced the Red Light District or clouded yourself in smoke at all of Amsterdam's coffeeshops, you can't say you've truly conquered this city unless you've ridden a bike here. The red bike lanes and special bike lights, as well as a multitude of cheap and convenient rental companies, permit tourists to whiz around as if they were locals.

A horseshoe-shaped path along any of the canals of the Central Canal Ring—Prinsengracht is prettiest—passes near the Anne Frank Huis, the Rijksmuseum, the van Gogh Museum, and the Heineken Brewery. Westerpark has wide-open biking lanes and smaller crowds than Vondelpark.

Take advantage of your mobility to explore farther afield. Leave Amsterdam to ride along the Amstel River, glimpsing windmills, houseboats, and quintessentially Dutch rolling hills. Cycle east along green trails to the seaside town of Spaarndam (20-25km). Or, use the canals as racetracks, leaving mellow locals in the dust.

MacBike, Weteringsschans 2 (☎528 76 88; www.macbike.nl), in Leidseplein, rents bikes and sells reliable bike-tour maps.

Holland-Rent-A-Bike, Damrak 247 (☎622 32 07), near Centraal Station, rents unmarked bikes to help you blend in with the locals.

menu €8.50; lamb menu €9.50). Veggie sides €5.50. Open daily 5-10pm. AmEx/MC/V. ❷

Village Bagels, Vijzelstr. 137 (☎020 468 5286; www.vilagebagels.nl). Enjoy a quiet brunch with a wide assortment of bagels and bagel sandwiches. The avocado-chicken bagel (€5.35) makes a hearty lunch. Bagels sandwiches €3.30-5.60. Open M-F 7:30am-6pm, Sa-Su 9am-6pm. Cash only. ❶

De Binnen Pret, Amstelveenseweg 134 (☎020 679 0712; www.binnenpret.org). Take tram 1 to end of Vondelpark. The menu changes every day at this one-of-a-kind restaurant where it's all you can eat for €5. Plenty of vegetarian and vegan options. Reservations are a must. Hours vary depending on volunteer participation, reduced during summer. ❶

DE PIJP, JODENBUURT, AND PLANTAGE

▨ **Bazar,** Albert Cuypstr. 182 (☎020 664 7173; www.bazaramsterdam.nl). Fantastic Turkish decor housed in the open space of a former church. Extensive menu features inexpensive cuisine from North Africa, Lebanon, and Turkey. Lunch special €10 per person (min. 2 people). Breakfast (Algerian pancakes and Turkish yogurt) and lunch start from €5. Open M-Th 9am-1am, F-Sa 9am-2am, Su 9am-midnight. Reserve ahead for dinner. ❷

Cafe De Pijp, Ferdinand Bolstr. 17-19 (☎020 670 4161). A hip and sociable restaurant in the heart of De Pijp with sleek black tables against a faux-wood background and a terrace. Mediterranean-influenced food and a laid-back atmosphere. Popular tapas €2.50-8. Mixed drinks €6. Open M-Th 4pm-1am, F 3:30pm-3am, Sa noon-2am; Su noon-1am. Cash only. ❸

Eetkunst Asmara, Jonas Daniel Meijerpl. 8 (☎020 627 1002). Enjoy specially prepared East African specialties, like beef with an assortment of mild herbs (€9). Served on *injera*, a spongy bread. Vegetarian options. Open daily 6-11pm. Cash only. ❷

Soup En Zo, Jodenbreestr. 94A (☎020 422 2243; www.soupenzo.nl). Let your nose guide you to the amazing broth at this tiny soupery, great for snacks on-the-go. Several soups and sizes (€2.70-6) with free bread and delicious toppings like coriander, dill, cheese, and nuts. Salads under €7. Open M-F 11am-8pm, Sa-Su noon-7pm. Another take-out only location in Leidseplein at Nieuwe Spiegelstraat 54 (☎020 330 7823). ❶

◉ SIGHTS

Amsterdam is not a city of traditional sights; if you want to join the sweating masses in endless lines to catch a glimpse of a postcard monument, you've come to the wrong place. But don't be fooled. This city—a collection of nearly 100 interlocking islands—is a sight in itself. Amsterdam is fairly compact, so tourists can easily explore on foot or by bike. When you get tired, the tram system will get you to any of the city's major sights within minutes. For a peaceful view of the city from the water, contract the **Saint Nicolaas Boat Club** (www.amsterdamboatclub.com), which organizes tours that offer unique views of the canal system.

CENTRUM

▨**DAM SQUARE AND KONINKLIJK PALEIS.** Next to the Nieuwe Kerk on Dam Sq. is one of Amsterdam's most impressive architectural accomplishments, the Koninklijk Paleis, . The building's exterior bursts with history, while the interior tells the story of Amsterdam's rise as a commercial power. The building was opened in 1655 and fully completed 10 years later. It originally served as the town hall, but it was no ordinary municipal building. In a city at the center of burgeoning worldwide trade, governed by a group of magistrates, the town hall became the most important government building in the region. The interior

THE NETHERLANDS

holds the opulent history of Amsterdam, including government offices and the Balcony Room where death sentences were proclaimed to the public. Architect Jacob van Campen aimed to replace the entrenched Amsterdam Renaissance style with a more Classic one. Across Dam Sq. is the Dutch **Nationaal Monument,** unveiled on May 4, 1956, to honor Dutch victims of WWII. Inside the 22m white stone obelisk is soil from all 12 of the Netherlands's provinces and the Dutch East Indies. Along the back of the monument, you'll find the provinces' crests bordered by the years 1940 and 1945. In addition to this reminder of Dutch suffering during the war, the monument is one of Amsterdam's central meeting and people-watching spots. *(Tram #5, 13, 17, or 20 to Dam. Paleis. ☎ 020 620 4060; www. paleisamsterdam.nl. Open daily June-Aug. 11am-5pm, Sept-May Tu-Su noon-5pm. €7.50, reduced €6.50. Audio tour included. AmEx/MC/V.)*

NIEUWMARKT. Nieuwmarkt is one of Amsterdam's most beloved squares. It is lined with cafes, restaurants, markets, and coffee shops. On warm summer days, crowds pack the area late into the evening. Be sure to stop and take a look at the **Waag,** Amsterdam's largest surviving medieval building. Dating back to the 15th century, then known as *Sint Antoniespoort,* the Waag came into existence as one of Amsterdam's fortified city gates. As Amsterdam expanded, it was converted into a house for public weights and measures. At the end of the 17th century, the Surgeon's Guild built an amphitheater at the top of the central tower to house public dissections as well as private anatomy lessons—famously depicted in **Rembrandt van Rijn's** *The Anatomy Lesson of Dr. Tulp.* The Waag has also housed a number of other sites, including the Jewish Historical Museum and the Amsterdam Historical Museum. *(Metro to Nieuwmarkt.)*

 FLESH PHOTOGRAPHY. As tempting as it may be, do not take pictures in the Red Light District, especially of prostitutes. Taking pictures is considered incredibly rude and can land the photographer in trouble.

OUDE KERK. Located right in the middle of the otherwise lurid Red Light District, the Old Church may be the only church in the world completely bounded by whorehouses. Erected in 1306, the Oude Kerk was the earliest parish church built in Amsterdam. It is now a cultural center that hosts photography and modern art exhibits. At the head of the church is the massive **Vater-Müller organ,** built in 1724, and still played for public concerts. The massive Gothic church has seen hard times: it was stripped of its artwork and religious artifacts during the Alteration. The Protestant church has since served a number of functions: a home for vagrants, a theater, a market, and a space for fishermen to mend broken sails on the rough hewn cobblestones that make up the church's floor. Today, there is still an empty, spare feeling inside the building, but the church is nevertheless one of the most impressive and prominent structures in the city. *(Oudekerkspl. 23. ☎ 020 625 8284; www. oudekerk.nl. Open M-Sa 11am-5pm, Su 1-5pm. €5, students and over 65 €4, under 12 free. I Amsterdam cardholders free. Tower €6. Additional charge for exhibits.)*

SINT NICOLAASKERK. Above the impressive columned altar, a burst of color emanates from the stained-glass windows of this relatively new Roman Catholic church that resembles the interior of a massive sailing vessel. Completed in 1887 to honor the patron saint of sailors, it replaced a number of Amsterdam's secret Catholic churches from the era of the Alteration. The walls of the church are art themselves, lined with magnificent murals depicting the life and story of St. Nicolaas. *(Prins Hendrikkade 73. ☎ 020 624 8749. Daily service 12:30pm; Su mass 10:30am Dutch, 1pm Spanish. Organ festi-*

val July-Sept. Sa 8:15pm. Contemporary and classical organ concerts occasionally Sa 3pm—call ahead. Open M 1-4pm, Tu-F 11am-4pm, Sa noon-3pm. Organ festival €6.)

SPUI. Pronounced "spow," this square was originally a body of water that constituted the southernmost point of the city until 1420. In 1882, the Spui was filled in and became the tree-lined, cobblestone square—perfect for quiet lounging on summer afternoons. The area, surrounded by bookstores, is home to an art market on Sundays and a book market on Fridays. Look out for **Het Lievertje** (The Little Urchin), a small bronze statue by Carel Kneulman that became a symbol for the Provos, a Dutch counter-culture movement of the 1960s. *(Tram #1, 2, 4, 5, 9, 14, 16, 24, or 25 to Spui.)*

CANAL RING AND REMBRANDTPLEIN

WESTERKERK. This stunning Protestant church was designed by Roman Catholic architect Hendrick de Keyser and completed in 1631. The blue and yellow imperial crown of Maximilian of Austria—the Hapsburg ruler of the Holy Roman Empire in the late 15th century—rests atop the 87m tower, which has become a patriotic symbol for the citizens of Amsterdam. Rembrandt is believed to be buried here, but no one knows for sure, because he was moved when his family could no longer pay his debts. In contrast to the decorative exterior, the Protestant church remains properly sober and plain inside; it is still used by a Presbyterian congregation. Make sure to climb the **Westerkerkstoren** as part of a 30min. guided tour for an awe-inspiring view of the city. *(Prinsengr. 281. ☎ 020 624 7766. Open Apr.-Sept. M-F 11am-5:30pm, July-Aug. M-Sa 11am-3pm. Tower tours Apr.-Sept. every 30min. 10am-5:30pm. €6.)*

HOMOMONUMENT. Since 1987, the Homomonument has stood as a testament to the strength and resilience of the homosexual community in Amsterdam. Conceived by Karin Daan, the monument consists of pale-pink granite triangles that allude to the symbols homosexuals were required to wear in Nazi concentration camps. The raised triangle points to the **COC**, the oldest gay rights organization in the world; the ground-level triangle points to the **Anne Frank Huis;** and the triangle with steps into the canal points to the **Nationaal Monument** on the Dam, a reminder that homosexuals were among those sent to concentration camps. On Queen's Day (Apr. 30) and Liberation Day (May 5), celebrations surround the monument. *(Next to Westerkerk. www.homomonument.nl.)*

CENTRAL CANAL RING. You haven't seen Amsterdam until you've spent some time wandering in the Central Canal Ring, the city's most expensive district and arguably its most beautiful. The **Prinsengracht** (Prince's Canal), **Keizersgracht** (Emperor's Canal), and **Herengracht** (Gentleman's Canal) are collectively known as the *grachtengordel* (canal girdle). In the 17th century, residents of Amsterdam were taxed according to the width of their homes, and houses could not be more than one plot (a few meters) wide. To encourage investment in construction, the city government allowed its elite to build homes that were twice as wide on a stretch now known as the **Golden Bend,** on Herengr. between Leidsegr. and Vijzelstr. Across the Amstel is the **Magere Brug** (Skinny Bridge), which sways precariously above the water. It is the oldest of the city's many pedestrian drawbridges and the only one still operated by hand.

REMBRANDTPLEIN. Rembrandtpl. is a disorganized grass rectangle surrounded by haphazard flower beds, criss-crossed by pedestrian paths, and populated with half-dressed locals lazing about (when weather permits, of course). A bronze likeness of the famed master Rembrandt van Rijn and a 3D version of his famous painting *Night Watch* overlook the scene. By night, Rembrandtpl. competes with Leidsepl. for Amsterdam's hippest nightlife, with a particularly rich concentration of GLBT hot spots in the area. South and west of the square lies **Reguliersdwarsstraat,** dubbed by locals "the gayest street in Amsterdam." *(In the northeast corner of the Canal Ring, just south of the Amstel.)*

LEIDSEPLEIN AND MUSEUMPLEIN

◪**VONDELPARK.** With meandering walkways, green meadows, and several ponds, this leafy park—the largest within the city center—is a lovely meeting place, constantly full of skaters, bikers, and sunbathers. In addition to a few good outdoor cafes, Vondelpark has an open-air theater where visitors can enjoy free music and dance concerts Thursday through Sunday during the summer. Every Friday, the **Friday Night Skate** takes place at the round bench by the Filmmuseum. It starts around 8:30pm and continues for 15-20km until about 10:30pm. *(www.fridaynightskate.com.)* Rent skates at Snoephuisje (near Amstelveenseweg entrance). For the less daring, try wandering around the beautifully maintained rose gardens or have a picnic lunch on any of the park's expanses of grass. *(In the southwestern corner of the city, outside the Singelgr. www.vondelpark.org. Theater ☎ 020 673 1499; www.openluchttheater.nl.)* If you get the munchies, try the pub-slash-restaurant **'t Blauwe Treehuis,** Vondelpark 5, a cylindrical tower situated inside the park that is surrounded by trees and lush greenery. *(☎020 662 0254. Lunch sandwiches €5. Dinner entrees €13. Finger food €4. Open 9am-1am. MC/V.)*

LEIDSEPLEIN. Leidsepl. is a clash of cacophonous street musicians, blaring neon lights, and clanging trams. During the day, the square is packed with countless shoppers, smokers, and drinkers lining the busy sidewalks. When night falls, tourists and street performers flock here. A slight respite is available just east of Leidsepl. along Weteringschans at **Max Euweplein.** The square sports a giant chess board with oversized pieces where older men hang out all day pondering the best moves. One of Amsterdam's more bizarre public spaces, it is notable both for the tiny park across the street (where bronze iguanas provide amusement) and for the motto inscribed above its pillars: Homo sapiens non urinat in ventum ("a wise man does not pee into the wind").

DE PIJP, JODENBUURT, AND PLANTAGE

HORTUS BOTANICUS. With over 6000 plants and 4000 species, this outstanding botanical garden is the perfect place to get lost. Originally a medicinal garden founded in 1638, visitors can now wander past lush palms, flowering cacti, and working beehives. Take an enlightening stroll through simulated ecosystems, a rock garden, a rosarium, an herb garden, a three-climate greenhouse, and a butterfly room. Many of the garden's more exceptional specimens, including a smuggled Ethiopian coffee plant whose clippings spawned the Brazilian coffee empire, were gathered during the 17th and 18th centuries by several members of the Dutch East India Company. *(Plantage Middenlaan 2A. ☎020 625 9021; www.dehortus.nl. Open Sept.-June M-F 9am-5pm, Sa-Su 10am-5pm.; July-Aug. M-F 9am-7pm, Sa-Su 10am-7pm. Guided tours in English Su 2pm, €1. €7, ages 5-14, City card holders, and seniors €3.50. Cafe open M-F 10am-5pm, Sa-Su 11am-5pm; in summer also daily until 7pm.)*

HEINEKEN EXPERIENCE. Since Heineken stopped producing here in 1988, it has turned the factory into an altar devoted to the green bottle. Visitors guide themselves past holograms, virtual-reality machines, and other multimedia treats in this orgy of brand loyalty. Some of the attractions can get absurd, but it's all in fun—after a few drinks. A visit includes two beers (or soft drinks), a tasting, and a wristband. To avoid the crowds, come before 11am and take your alcohol before noon like a true fan. New attractions will include a mini brewery, tasting bar, and the "Stable Walk," where visitors can access the nearby stables and view Heineken's iconic Shire horses. (*☎020 523 9222; www.heinekenex-perience.com. Open daily 11am-5:30pm. €15, €11.25 with I Amsterdam Card. AmEx/MC/V.)*

MUSEUMS

Whether you crave Rembrandts and van Goghs, cutting-edge photography, WWII history, or erotica, Amsterdam has a museum for you. The useful www.amsterdammuseums.nl has plenty of info for easy planning.

> **TIP**
>
> **MAJOR MOOCHING ENCOURAGED.** Visitors planning to see even a handful of museums may want to invest in a ▓**Museumjaarkaart.** The pass (€35, under 25 €20) entitles the holder to admission at most of the major museums in the Netherlands. Cards are good for a year, but are still a value for those staying only for a week. To purchase the pass, bring a passport photo to any participating museum. For more information, check the Dutch-langugage-only www.museumjaarkaart.nl.

CENTRUM

NIEUWE KERK. The New Church, an extravagant 15th-century brick-red cathedral at the heart of the Nieuwe Zijde, now plays three roles as religious edifice, historical monument, and art museum. **Commemorative windows** have been given to the church to honor royal inaugurations and other events. The church, which has been rebuilt several times after fires, is still used for weddings and other ceremonial events. Check the website before you go; the church closes for two weeks between art exhibits. (*Adjacent to Dam Sq., beside Koninklijk Paleis. ☎638 6909; www.nieuwekerk.nl. Open daily 10am-5pm. Organ recitals June-Sept. Th 12:30pm, Su 8pm. Call ahead for exact times. €4, I Amsterdam Card holders free.)*

AMSTERDAMS HISTORISCH MUSEUM. Even though nothing beats a walk around the city itself, this archival museum offers an eclectic introduction to Amsterdam's historical development by way of ancient archaeological findings, medieval manuscripts, Baroque paintings, and multimedia displays. The section of the museum that features artistic accounts of gory Golden Age anatomy lessons is particularly interesting. Catch one of the Historical Museum's hidden surprises: in the covered passageway between the museum and the Begijnhof, there is an extensive collection of large 17th-century paintings of Amsterdam's civic guards that used to hang in the Palais. (*Kalverstr. 92 and Nieuwezijds Voorburgwal 357. ☎020 523 1822; www.ahm.nl. Open M-F 10am-5pm, Sa-Su 11am-5pm; closed Queen's Day. €10, seniors €7.50, ages 6-18 €5.)*

MUSEUM AMSTELKRING "ONS' LIEVE HEER OP SOLDER." The continued persecution of Catholics after the Alteration led Jan Hartmann, a wealthy Dutch merchant, to build this secret church in 1663. The chapel is housed in the attics of three separate canal houses and includes a fantastic 18th-century Baroque altar. The large antique organ, specially designed in 1794 to maintain this secret church's covertness, is equally impressive. Small exhibitions and period rooms re-create life during the Dutch Reformation, augmented by the museum's small collection of Dutch painting and antique silver. The church is still active, holding mass six times per year and performing marriages on request; check the website for information on either. (*Oudezijds Voorburgwal 40, at Heintje Hoekssteeg. ☎020 624 6604; www.opsolder.nl. Open M-Sa 10am-5pm, Su and holidays 1-5pm. €7, students €5, ages 5-18 €1, under 5 and I Amsterdam Card holders free. AmEx/MC/V.)*

CANNABIS COLLEGE. Don't let the word college ward you off; this staggering think tank is informative and totally non-academic. The staff of volunteers is unbelievably friendly, knowledgeable, and eager to answer any questions about the establishment. If you think you're enough of an expert and want to spread your reefer know-how, don't be afraid to ask about lending a hand (or a lighter). *(Oudezijds Achterburgwal 124. ☎020 423 4420; www.cannabiscollege.com. Open daily 11am-7pm. Free. €3 to see the weed garden downstairs.)*

AMSTERDAM SEX MUSEUM. This almost requisite museum will likely disappoint those looking for a sophisticated examination of sexuality, but it does claim to be the first and oldest sex museum. The first of four floors features amusing life-size mannequins of pimps, prostitutes, and even a flasher. The museum also has ancient artifacts such as a stone phallus from the Roman age, but the exhibits are hardly informative; the majority is composed of photograph after photograph of sexual acts, some more familiar than others. The gallery of fetishes, however, is not for the weak of stomach. *(Damrak 18. ☎020 622 8376; www.sexmuseum-amsterdam.com. Open daily 9:30am-11:30pm. €3.)*

CANAL RING AND WEST OF TOWN

◼ANNE FRANK HUIS. In 1942, the Nazis began deporting all Jews to ghettos and concentration camps, forcing Anne Frank's family and four other Dutch Jews to hide in the *Achterhuis*, or annex, of this warehouse on the Prinsengracht. All eight refugees lived in this secret annex for two years, during which time Anne kept her famous diary, which can be found at the end of the tour. Displays of various household objects, text panels mounted with pages from the diary, and video footage of the rooms as they looked during WWII give some sense of life in that tumultuous time. The original bookcase used to hide the entrance to the secret annex remains, cracked open for visitors to pass through. The endless line stretching around the corner attests to the popularity of the Anne Frank Huis: your best bet is to arrive before 10am or after 7pm, or to book tickets online. *(Prinsengr. 267. ☎020 556 7100; www.annefrank.nl. Open daily Mar.-Jun. 9am-9pm; Jul.-Aug. 9am-10pm; Sept.-Mar. 9am-7pm; closed on Yom Kippur. Last entry 30min. before closing. €8.50, 10-17 €3, under 10 free. Reservations can be made online. MC/V.)*

MUSEUMPLEIN

◼RIJKSMUSEUM AMSTERDAM. Even though the main building of the museum is closed for reno-

IN RECENT NEWS

COFFEE ONLY?

Amsterdam is commonly identified as the world capital of tolerance. Chilled-out people puff thick clouds of smoke filling infamous coffeeshops, while popular smartshops sell everything from sex stimulants to mushrooms. Recent governmental trends, however, may soon dampen this international perception.

Customers must be 18 to enter a coffeeshop and may only buy 5g per visit per shop. The shops themselves cannot advertise, sell hard drugs, export soft drugs, or have more than 500g on stock. In April 2007, shops had to declare themselves a "bar" or a "coffeeshop," forcing them to make a choice between selling cannabis or alcohol. And, because of the ambiguity of how much THC is in smoothies and other food/drink items, the only legal "space" items available for purchase are cakes. Most recently (July 2008), mushrooms were banned by the government, which was a huge blow to smartshop shelves.

This may not be the end to the controversial decrees being passed in the Netherlands. Rumors over banning the purchase of cannabis by foreigners have been widespread ever since France, Germany, and other nearby countries have complained of their citizens crossing the border predominantly to buy drugs.

Will Amsterdam's tolerant reputation fade? Only time will tell, so puff away... for now.

vations, the Rijksmuseum is still a mandatory Amsterdam excursion. Originally opened in 1885, the Rijks—or "state"—museum settled into its current monumental quarters, designed by the architect of Centraal Station. It houses masterpieces by Rembrandt van Rijn, Johannes Vermeer, Frans Hals, and Jan Steen. Of this tour-de-force collection, **Rembrandt's** gargantuan and complicated militia portrait *Night Watch* is the crème de la crème. Equally astounding is the museum's collection of paintings by Vermeer. *(Stadhouderskade 42. Visitors must enter instead through the Philips Wing, around the corner at the intersection of Hobbemastr. and Jan Luijkenstr. ☎020 674 7000; www.rijksmuseum.nl. Open M-Th and Sa-Su 9am-6pm, F 9am-8:30pm. Maps available at the ticket counters. €10, students and I Amsterdam Card holders €8, under 18 free. Audio tour €4.)*

VAN GOGH MUSEUM. The Van Gogh Museum is one of Amsterdam's biggest cultural tourist attractions. Suffer the shortest wait and go around 10:30am or after 4pm. The permanent collection, including many of Van Gogh's masterpieces, is on the first floor. The second and third floors hold a substantial collection of important 19th-century art by Impressionist, post-Impressionist, Realist, and Surrealist painters and sculptors. The partially subterranean exhibition wing is the venue for the museum's top-notch traveling exhibitions. *(Paulus Potterstr. 7 ☎020 570 5200; www.vangoghmuseum.nl. Open M-Th and Sa 10am-6pm, F 10am-10pm. €10, ages 13-17 €2.50, under 12 free. Audio tours €4. AmEx/MC/V over €25.)*

> **TIP TGIF.** The Rijksmuseum and the Van Gogh Museum are open late on Fridays. Take advantage of the relative lack of tourists and spend some personal time with the world's greatest painters.

JODENBUURT AND PLANTAGE

MUSEUM HET REMBRANDT. Dutch master Rembrandt van Rijn's house at Waterloopl. has become the happy home of the artist's impressive collection of 250 etchings (of which only a selection are on display). In the upstairs studio, Rembrandt produced some of his most important works. You'll also find some of his tools and plates, including a pot he used to mix paint. *(Jodenbreestr. 4, at the corner of Oude Schans. ☎020 520 0400; www.rembrandthuis.nl. Open daily 10am-5pm. €8, students €5.50, ages 6-15 €1.50, under 6 free. Special exhibits more expensive. AmEx/MC/V.)*

VERZETSMUSEUM. The Resistance Museum traces life under the Nazi occupation and the steps the Dutch took to oppose the German forces. Visitors can track the occupation and resistance chronologically, from an exhibit on Dutch colonial resistance to one on post-war Dutch regeneration. *(Plantage Kerklaan 61. ☎020 620 2535; www.verzetsmuseum.org. Open M, Sa, and Su 11am-5pm, Tu-F 10am-5pm, public holidays 11am-5pm. €6.50; ages 7-15 €3.50; under 7, Museum Card holders free. Tour of neighborhood available by phone or email appointment; €9 per person.)*

JOODS HISTORISCH MUSEUM. In the heart of Amsterdam's traditional Jewish neighborhood, the Jewish Historical Museum connects four different 17th- and 18th-century Ashkenazi synagogues. Through exhibits by Jewish artists and galleries of historically significant Judaica, the museum presents the Netherlands's most comprehensive picture of Jewish life. *(Jonas Daniel Meijerpl. 2-4. ☎020 531 0310; www.jhm.nl. Open daily 11am-5pm, Th 11am-9pm; closed on Yom Kippur and Rosh Hashanah. Free audio tour. €7.50; seniors, ages 7-16, ISIC holders €4.50; I Amsterdam Cardholders and under 13 free.)*

GREATER AMSTERDAM

COBRA MUSEUM. This museum pays tribute to the 20th-century CoBrA art movement: the name is an abbreviation of the capital cities of the group's founding members (Copenhagen, Brussels, and Amsterdam). The beautiful, modern museum presents the movement's work from Karel Appel's experimentation with sculpture to Corneille's developing interest in color and non-Western worlds. *(Sandbergpl. 1-3, south of Amsterdam in Amstelveen. Tram #5 or bus #170, 171, or 172. The tram stop is a 10min. walk from the museum; after a 15min. ride, the bus will drop you off in bus depot adjacent to the museum. ☎020 547 5050, tour reservations ☎020 547 5045; www.cobra-museum.nl. Open Tu-Su 11am-5pm. €9.50, students, seniors, and 6-18 discounted prices. AmEx/MC/V.)*

☕ COFFEE SHOPS

"Soft" drugs, including marijuana, are tolerated in the Netherlands. **Let's Go does not recommend drug use (or hitchhiking),** though many travelers report having a great time smoking with their friends.

> **DON'T BOGART OUR CITY.** On July 1, 2008, Amsterdam banned smoking indoors. This means that marijuana consumption is only permitted in certain designated rooms inside of coffee shops. Please secure your own jay before attempting to roll one for a friend, and keep all joints, spliffs, bongs, spoons, apples, edibles, one-hitters, and Sherlock Holmes pipes inside the designated areas at all times. Thank you and enjoy your flight.

Amsterdam's coffee shops sell hashish, marijuana, and "space" goodies. As a general rule, the farther you travel from the touristed spots, the better value and higher quality the establishments you'll find. Look for the green-and-white **BCD** sticker that certifies a shop's credibility. When you move from one coffee shop to another, you must buy a drink in the next shop, even if you already have weed. While it's alright to smoke on the outdoor patio of a coffee shop, don't go walking down the street smoking a joint: it is considered déclassé. Not only is this an easy way for pickpockets and con artists to pick out a tourist, but locals also consider it offensive. Note that Europeans only smoke joints. When pipes or bongs are provided, they are usually for tourists.

Coffee shop menus have more variety than most might assume. **Hashish** comes in three varieties: blonde (Moroccan), black (Indian), and Dutch (Ice-o-Lator), all of which can cost €4-35 per gram. Typically, cost is proportional to quality and strength. Black hash hits harder than blonde, and Ice-o-Lator can send even a seasoned smoker off his or her head.

Centrum coffee shops are notorious for higher prices and poor quality product. Avoid the super touristy and commercialized places in Amsterdam and opt for smaller, more cozy shops.

Amnesia, Herengr. 133 (☎020 427 7874, www.myspace.com/amnesiahigh). Slightly larger and significantly more elegant than other coffee shops. Wide selection of drinks, milkshakes, and snacks. Buy 5 joints (€4-6 each) and get 1 free. For an extra treat, try the Amnesia Haze (€13 per g), a 2004 Cannabis Cup winner. Open daily 9:30am-1am. Cash only.

Rusland, Rusland 16 (☎020 627 9468). More than just a drug store: choose from over 40 varieties of herbal tea or refreshing yogurt shakes (€4). Pre-rolled joints €2.50-4.50. Tasty

Afghan bud €7 per g. Space muffins €5. White space muffins €1.80. Milkshakes €4. Mixed drinks with fresh fruit €2. Open M-Th and Su 10am-midnight, F-Sa 10am-1am. Cash only.

Kadinsky, Rosmarijnstg. 9 (☎020 624 7023; www.kadinsky.nl). One of the city's friendliest, hippest, and most comfortable stoneries. Joints €3.40-4. Weed €7-11 per g. 20% off 5g purchases. Open daily 9:30am-1am. Cash only.

Paradox, 1e Bloemdwarsstraat 2 (☎020 623 5639, www.paradoxcoffeeshop.com). Get blazed in this relaxed coffee shop that locals call home. The African-themed interior and steady influx of regulars provides an authentic coffee-shop experience. Pre-rolled joints €3. Hash €6.50-10. Open daily 10am-8pm. Cash only.

Yo Yo, 2e Jan van der Heijdenstr. 79 (☎020 664 7173). One of the few coffee shops where neighborhood non-smokers can relax. Apple pie (€1.80), *tostis* (grilled sandwiches), soup, and (normal) brownies served. All weed is organic and sold in bags for €5 or €10, with a monthly €3.50 special. Joints €2.50. Open M-Sa noon-8pm.

Grey Area, Oude Leliestr. 2 (☎020 420 4301; www.greyarea.nl). Last American-run coffee shop in Amsterdam. A single sticker-adorned room that is usually packed, this locale has a good reputation and a friendly staff more than happy to help novices. Borrow a glass bong or vaporizer to smoke, or hit one of Amsterdam's cheapest pure marijuana joints (€3.50). Juice (€1.50) is also available. Open daily noon-8pm.

Siberië, Brouwersgr. 11 (☎020 623 5909; www.siberie.nl). Over 25 years old, Siberie has an extensive menu of coffees and an assortment of teas. Pre-rolled joints (€2-5) are especially popular. Features unique art exhibitions, arcade, and internet. Hash €3-11. Cannabis €3-11. Open M-Th and Su 11am-11pm, F and Sa 11am-midnight. Cash only.

The Dolphins, Kerkstr. 39 (☎020 774 3336). Smoke with the fishes at this underwater-themed coffee shop. Free Wi-Fi. Pre-rolled joints €4. Try the White Dolphin reefer (€10 per g; pure joint €6.50) for an uplifting high. Vaporizers and bongs available with €10 deposit. Open M-Th and Su 10am-1am, F-Sa 10am-1am.

Abraxas, Jonge Roelensteeg 12-14 (www.abraxasparadise.nl). Try this upscale coffeeshop right in the heart of Amsterdam for potent space cakes and muffins (€3.90). Glass floors and winding staircases makes this well-decorated 2-story shop a great place to chill out. The helpful staff will tell you what type of high you will get with each strain. Highs range from "friendly" to "clear-stoned." Pre-rolled joints €3-8. Pure €4.50. Get 3 joints for €10. Open 10am-1am.

🎵 ENTERTAINMENT

The **Amsterdams Uit Buro (AUB),** Leidsepl. 26, is stuffed with free monthly magazines, pamphlets, and tips to help you sift through seasonal offerings. It also sells tickets and makes reservations for just about any cultural event in the city for a commission. **Last Minute Ticket Shop,** part of the AUB, offers some of the best deals for half-off tickets. Visit the office for a list of same-day performances at 50% off. (☎0900 0191; www.amsterdamsuitburo.nl or www.lastminuteticketshop.nl. AUB open M-Sa 10am-7:30pm, Su noon-7:30pm. Last Minute Ticket Shop begins selling tickets daily at noon.) The theater desk at the **VVV,** Stationspl. 10, can also make reservations for cultural events. (☎0900 400 4040, €0.40 per min.; www.amsterdamtourist.nl. Open F-Sa 9am-8pm.)

Filmmuseum, Vondelpark 3 (☎020 589 1400; www.filmmuseum.nl). At least 4 screenings per day, many of them older classics. Also houses an extensive information center, with 1900 periodicals and over 30,000 books on film theory and history as well as screenplays. Box office open daily 9am-10:15pm.

Boom Chicago, Leidsepl. 12 (☎020 530 0232; www.boomchicago.nl). For a laugh, head to the English-language improv comedy show M-Th and Su 8:15pm (€20). Dinner (appetizers from €5, entrees around €15) starts at 6:30pm. Open M-Th and Su 10am-1am, F-Sa 10am-3am.

Concertgebouw, Concertgebouwpl. 2-6 (☎020 671 8345; www.concertgebouw.nl). Home to the Royal Concertgebouw Orchestra. Hosts 650 events per year in its 16 beautiful venue halls. Su morning concerts with guided tours before the performance are cheaper options (€12; tours 9:30am, €3.50). Rush tickets for persons age 26 and under from €7.50. Free lunchtime concerts during fall, winter, and spring W 12:30pm. Ticket office open daily 10am-7pm; until 8:15pm for same-day ticketing. Telephone reservations until 5pm. AmEx/MC/V.

⬛ NIGHTLIFE

Leidseplein and **Rembrandtplein** remain the busiest areas for nightlife, with coffee shops, loud bars, and tacky clubs galore. Amsterdam's most traditional spots are the old, dark, wood-paneled *bruin cafes* (brown cafes). The concept of completely "straight" versus "gay" nightlife does not really apply; most establishments are gay-friendly and happily attract a mixed crowd. Rembrandtpl. is the hub for gay bars geared almost exclusively toward men. For an authentic Dutch experience, you should venture beyond the tourist bars of the Centrum.

CENTRUM

- ⬛ **Club NL,** Nieuwezijds Voorburgwal 169 (☎020 622 7510; www.clubnl.nl). Posh seating under dim red lighting in this smoky club, reminiscent of the movie *Sin City*. Celebs like Kate Moss, P. Diddy, and Mick Jagger are said to have partied at this joint. Enjoy the pricey mixed drinks while listening to the latest house music. Strict door policy to keep ratio of men to women equal. 21+. Cover F-Su €7, includes coat check. Open M-Th and Su 10pm-3am, F-Sa 10pm-4am. AmEx/MC/V.

- ⬛ **Café de Jaren,** Nieuwe Doelenstr. 20-22 (☎020 625 5771). The air of sophistication and beautiful river patio at this 2-floor riverside cafe don't quite mesh with its budget-friendly prices. Popular with students and staff from the nearby University of Amsterdam. Mixed drinks and beer €3.10). Open M-Th and Su 10am-1am, F-Sa 10am-2am. Kitchen open M-Th and Su 10am-10:30pm, F-Sa 10am-midnight. AmEx/MC/V.

- **Kingdom,** Warmoesstr. 129 (☎020 625 3912; www.winston.nl). Small eclectic club with a packed crowd and deceptively large dance floor. Live music and DJs every day of the week. Cover varies but usually €3-7. Open M-Th 9pm-3am, F-Su 9pm-4am. MC/V.

CANAL RING AND REMBRANDTPLEIN

- **Escape,** Rembrandtpl. 11 (☎020 622 1111; www.escape.nl). One of Amsterdam's hottest clubs, with 6 bars, a breezy upstairs lounge, and a hip cafe on the 1st fl. Lines grow long through 2am. Beer €2.70. Mixed drinks €6.60. Cover Th-Sa €10-16, students Th €6. Club open Th 11pm-4am, F-Sa 11pm-5am, Su 11pm-4:30am. Cash only.

- **Cafe Hoppe,** Spui 18-20 (☎020 420 4420; www. cafehipe.com). Built in the 1670s, Hoppe serves traditional Dutch drinks from barrels straight out of a Rembrandt painting. Friendly owner will happily talk about Amsterdam for hours. Open M-Th 8pm-1am, F-Su 8pm-2am. MC/V.

- **Arc...,** Reguliersdwarsstr. 44 (☎020 689 7070; www.bararc.com). This gay-friendly establishment in the heart of Amsterdam's GLBT area hosts a young, trendy crowd that overtakes the bar weekend nights. DJs spin nightly to an eager crowd that gets started around 6pm on the weekends. Mixed drinks €7.50-9. Open M-Th and Su 4pm-1am, F-Sa 4pm-3am. MC/V.

- **Montmartre,** Halvemaanstg. 17 (☎020 625 5565,). Voted best gay bar by local gay mag *Gay Krant* 8 years in a row, but the crowd is straight-friendly. Trendy and popular, with transgendered revelers on any night. Open M-Th and Su 5pm-4am, F-Sa 5pm-3am. Cash only.

WEST OF TOWN

Festina Lente, Looiersgr. 40 (☎020 638 1412; www.cafefestinalente.nl). Charming bar and cafe that continues to attract a young, fashionable, and friendly crowd. Multi-level old-fashioned interior filled with books. Ask the staff for board games on Su afternoons. Wine and beer from €2.20. Open M noon-midnight, Tu-Th 10:30am-1am, F 10:30am-3am, Sa 11am-3am, Su noon-1am. AmEx/MC/V.

Dulac, Haarlemmerstr. 118 (☎020 624 4265). Popular with locals and university students. with its pool table, booths, ample nooks, and dimly-lit interior. Entrees €7.50-17; half-price with student ID. Pint €3.90. Mixed drinks €7. DJ spins Th-Sa 8pm-3am. Open M-Tu 4pm-1am, W and Su noon-1am, F-Sa noon-3am. Kitchen open daily until 10:30pm. AmEx/MC/V.

LEIDSEPLEIN

Alto, Korte Leidsedwarsstr. 115. (☎020 626 3249). The vibe is subdued, but the live jazz performances are sizzling. Arrive early to get a table up front or listen from the bar. Cover W €5. Free jazz on other nights (and occasionally blues) M-Th and Su 10pm-2am, F-Sa 10pm-3am. Open M-Th and Su 9pm-3am, F-Sa 9pm-4am. Cash only.

The Waterhole, Korte Leidsedwarsstr. 49 (☎020 620 8904; www.waterhole.nl). Shoot a round of pool with the locals over a lager (€4.80) in this live-music bar with a southern theme. Music varies by night, with performances ranging from reggae to classic rock. M-W and Su are jam nights, and Th-Sa mostly feature local bands. Music starts around 9pm. Happy Hour 6-9pm, pints €3. Open M-Th and Su 4pm-3am, F-Sa 4pm-4am. Cash only.

DE PIJP, JODENBUURT, AND PLANTAGE

Canvas, Wibautstr. 150, 7th fl. (☎020 716 3817; www.canvasopde7e.nl). Right across from the Wibautsraat Metro stop. From the metro, cross the street and enter the high-rise and take the elevator to the 7th floor. This (figuratively) underground bar inhabits the 7th floor of an abandoned newspaper office. Provides pristine views of the sunset over Amsterdam from the rooftop terrace and an alternative vibe (astroturf and neon flamingos). Beer €2. Mixed drinks €6.50. Open M-Th 10am-1am, F-Sa 10am-3am. AmEx/MC/V.

 ULTIMATE PARTY. For a touristy good time, try Amsterdam's most famous Pub Crawl. The staff always gets the crowd going, taking you to 6 different bars, with a free drink and shot at each local hotspot along the trail. M-F and Su 8:30pm. Tram 1, 2, 5, 6, 7, 10 to Leidseplein. €20.

⬢ DAYTRIPS FROM AMSTERDAM

AALSMEER

Take bus #172 across from the Victoria Hotel near Centraal Station to the flower auction (Bloemenveiling Aalsmeer) and then on to the town of Aalsmeer. The first bus leaves at 5am (45min.; every 15min.; 6 strips to the flower auction, 2 more to the town).

The reason to visit Aalsmeer is the **Bloemenveiling Aalsmeer** (Aalsmeer flower auction). This massive warehouse and trading floor hosts thousands of traders every day representing some of the world's largest flower-export companies. Nineteen million flowers and over two million plants are bought and sold daily, with an annual turnover of almost US$2 billion. All of the flowers, often flown overnight from across the globe, go through Aalsmeer's massive trading floor (the largest commercial trading space in the world) in a beautifully choreographed dance of global commerce. Since the flowers have to make it to their final destination by the end of the day, almost all the trading is finished by 11am. To see the most action, go between 7 and 9am. Thursday is the least busy day, with trading finishing as early as 8am. The trading floor is visible to tourists via a large catwalk along the ceiling. This self-guided tour takes approximately an hour to complete. (*Legmeerdijk 313, ☎020 739 2185; www.aalsmeer.com. Open M-F 7-11am. €5, ages 6-11 €3, €4 per person for groups of 15+. Guides available to hire for €75.*)

TIP **MARCH MADNESS.** Visit the Netherlands between March and May to experience *Keufkenhof:* the millions of colorful tulips in bloom are just as pretty as they sound. (www.keukenhof.nl.)

HAARLEM ☎023

Haarlem's (pop. 150,000) narrow cobblestone streets, rippling canals, and fields of tulips in spring make for a great escape from the urban frenzy of Amsterdam. Still, the city beats with a relaxed energy that befits its size.

🖪🔢 TRANSPORTATION AND PRACTICAL INFORMATION. Trains depart for Amsterdam every few minutes (20min., €3.60). The VVV, Stationspl. 1, sells **maps** (€2) and finds accommodations for a €5 fee. It also sells discounted passes to museums. (☎0900 616 1600, €0.50 per min.; www.vvvzk.nl. Open Oct.-Mar. M-F 9:30am-5pm, Sa 10am-3pm; Apr.-Sept. M-F 9am-5:30pm, Sa 10am-4pm.)

🖪🔢 ACCOMMODATIONS AND FOOD. The best place to stay is the **Stayokay Haarlem ❶,** Jan Gijzenpad 3, 3km from the train station. Rooms are spare (but cheery) and clean with bath. (☎023 537 1176; www.stayokay.com/haarlem. Breakfast included. Wheelchair-accessible. Dorms in high-season €29; doubles €102. €2.50 HI discount. AmEx/MC/V.) Ideally located right in the town square is **Hotel Carillon ❷,** Grote Markt 27. Bright, clean rooms all have TV, shower, and phone. (☎023 531 0591; www.hotelcarillon.com. Breakfast included. Reception and bar daily in summer 7:30am-1am; in winter daily 7:30am-midnight. Singles €40, with bath €60; doubles €65/80; triples €102; quads €110. MC/V.)

The Indonesian **🖪Toko Nina ❶,** Koningstr. 48, has delicious prepared foods behind the deli counter. (☎023 531 7819; www.tokonina.nl. Combo meals €5.80-8.80. Open M 11am-7pm, Tu-F 9:30am-7pm, Sa 9:30am-6pm, Su 1-6pm. Cash only.) **Fortuyn ❶,** Grote Markt 23, one of the smaller grandcafes in Grote Markt, has more personal service. Sandwiches (€5-8) and snacks are served until 5pm, dinner (€18-23) until 10pm. (☎023 542 1899; www.grandcafefortuyn. nl. Open M-W and Su 10am-midnight, Th-Sa 10am-1am. Cash only.)

🖪 SIGHTS. The action in Haarlem centers on Grote Markt, its vibrant main square. Its main attraction is the **🖪Grote Kerk,** whose interior glows with light from the enormous stained-glass windows and houses the splendid, mammoth **Müller organ,** once played by both Handel and Mozart. Also known as St. Bavo's, it holds many historical artifacts and the graves of Jacob van Ruisdael, Pieter Saenredam, and Frans Hals. (☎023 553 2040; www.bavo.nl. Open Nov.-Feb. M-Sa 10am-4pm, Mar.-Oct. Tu-Sa 10am-4pm. €2, children €1.30. Guided tours by appointment €0.50. Organ concerts Tu 8:15pm, June-Sept. also Th 3pm; www.organfestival.nl. €2.50.) These painters' masterpieces can be found in the **🖪Frans Hals Museum,** Groot Heiligland 62. Spread through recreated period rooms, the paintings are displayed as they might have been in the Golden Age.

THE NETHERLANDS

Hals's work reveals casual brush strokes that are now understood as an early move toward Impressionism. (☎023 511 5775; www.franshalsmuseum.com. Wheelchair-accessible. Open Tu-Sa 11am-5pm, Su noon-5pm. €7, under 19 free, groups €5.30 per person.) The ▓**Corrie ten Boomhuis,** Barteljorisstr. 19, served as a secret headquarters for the Dutch Resistance in WWII. It is estimated that Corrie ten Boom saved the lives of over 800 people by arranging to have them hidden in houses, including her own. (☎023 531 0823; www.corrietenboom. com. Open daily Apr.-Oct. 10am-4pm, last tour 3:30pm; Nov.-Mar. 11am-3pm, last tour 2:30pm. Tours every 30min., alternating between Dutch and English; call or check the clock outside for times. Free, but donations accepted.)

▓ **DAYTRIP FROM HAARLEM: ZANDVOORT AND BLOEMENDAAL AAN ZEE.**
From Zandvoort, take a train to Amsterdam (30min., 3 per hr., €4.70) or Haarlem (10min., round-trip €3.20). Bloemendaal is a 30min. walk north of Zandvoort. You can also take bus #81 to Haarlem from both.

A mere 11km from Haarlem, the seaside town of Zandvoort aan Zee draws sun-starved Dutch and Germans to its miles of sandy beaches. You can stake out a spot on the sand for free, but most locals catch their rays through the comfort of beach clubs, wood pavilions that run along the shore with enclosed restaurants and outdoor patios. These clubs open early each morning, close at midnight, and are only in service during the summer. Nearby Bloemendaal aan Zee does not even qualify as a town; instead, it's a purely hedonistic collection of fashionable and fabulous beach clubs. Local club **Woodstock 69** is the granddaddy of them all, clocking in at almost 15 years old. There is a distinct hippie feel here with hammocks, tiki torches, and lots of loose clothing. (☎023 573 8084.) **Bloomingdale** tends to be the favorite of most locals. (☎023 573 7580; www.bloomingdaleaanzee.com. Open daily 10am-midnight.) Zandvoort's **VVV,** Schoolpl. 1, is about eight minutes from the beach and train station. The friendly staff can provide a guide to the beaches and accommodations, a map of hiking and biking trails in nearby **Kennemerland National Park,** and lots of information on the city. (☎023 571 7947; www.vvvzk.nl. Open Oct.-Mar. M-F 9am-12:30pm and 1:30-4:30pm, Sa 10am-2pm; Apr.-Sept. M-F 9am-12:30pm and 1:30-4:30pm, Sa 10am-4pm.)

THE HAGUE (DEN HAAG) ☎070

Whereas Amsterdam is the cultural and commercial center of the Netherlands, The Hague (pop. 480,000) is without a doubt its political nucleus; all of the Netherlands's important governmental institutions are housed here. World-class art museums (the stunning Mauritshuis in particular), a happening city center, high-class shopping, and a tons of open green space combine to make this political hub anything but boring.

▓▓ **TRANSPORTATION AND PRACTICAL INFORMATION. Trains** run from Amsterdam (55min., 1-6 per hr., €10) and Rotterdam (30min., 1-6 per hr., €4.30) to both of The Hague's major stations, Den Haag Centraal and Holland Spoor. The **VVV,** Hofweg 1, across from the Parliamentary buildings next to Dudok, has an extensive selection of city guides, bicycle **maps,** and guidebooks for sale in their shop, and the desk can arrange canal, carriage, and city tours. (☎070 340 3505; www.denhaag.com. Open M-F 10am-6pm, Sa 10am-5pm, Su noon-5pm.)

▓▓ **ACCOMMODATIONS AND FOOD.** ▓**Stayokay City Hostel Den Haag ❷,** Scheepmakerstr. 27, near Holland Spoor, is one of the best hostels in the Netherlands, with sparkling rooms, private baths, spacious lounging areas, and library. From Centraal Station take tram 1, 9, 12 or 16 to Spoor or tram 17 to

Rijswijkseplein. Or walk 20 minutes down Lekstr., making a right on Schen-kviaduct. The hostel is behind the pink building. (☎070 315 7888; www.stayo-kay.com/denhaag. Breakfast included 7:30-9:30am. Lockers €2 per 24hr. Linens included. Internet €5 per hr. Reception 7:30am-10:30pm. Wheelchair-accessible4- to 8-bed dorms €27.50; singles €56; doubles €67-78; quads €122. €2.50 HI discount. €2.50 weekend surcharge. MC/V.) **Hotel 't Centrum ❹**, Veenkade 5-6, has simple, airy, and elegant rooms. From either station take tram 17 (dir: Staten-kwartier) to Noodrwal. (☎070 346 3657; www.hotelhetcentrum.nl. Check-in 2-11:30pm. Breakfast buffet €12.50; with champagne €15. Singles €49, Su €39, with bath €75/€65; doubles with bath €95/85; 1-person apartments including breakfast €90/85; 2-person €115/105; 3-person €125/115. AmEx/MC/V.) **❺HNM Café ❶**, Molenstr. 21A, has floor-to-ceiling windows, brightly colored chairs and walls, and a large bowl of Thai noodle soup (€7) on the menu. (☎070 365 6553. Salads €8.50. Dinner €10-14. Open M-W noon-midnight, Th-Sa noon-1am, Su noon-6pm. Cash only.) The excellent **Tapaskeuken Sally ❷**, Oude Molstr. 61, is great for tapas (☎070 345 1623. Open W-Sa 5:30-10:30pm. Cash only.)

⬛🎭 SIGHTS AND ENTERTAINMENT.
The opulent home of the International Court of Justice and the Permanent Court of Arbitration, the ⬛**Peace Palace**, Carnegiepl. 2, has served as the site of international arbitrations, peace-treaty negotiations, and high-profile conflict resolutions. Take a walk around the gardens and enjoy the magnificence of the Grand Hall. Although the Permanent Court of Arbitration is closed to the public, hearings of the International Court of Justice are free to attend (☎070 302 4242, guided tours ☎070 302 4137; www.vredespaleis.nl. Tours M-F 10, 11am, 2, 3, 4pm. Book one week ahead. No tours when the court is in session. €5, under 13 €3. Cash only.) With only two modest stories, the ⬛**Mauritshuis**, Korte Vijverberg 8, is one of the most beautiful small museums anywhere, with a near-perfect collection of Dutch Golden Age art. Not counting the precious selection of paintings by Peter Paul Rubens, Jacob van Ruisdael, and Jan Steen, the museum has several excellent Rembrandts, including his famous *The Anatomy Lesson of Dr. Tulp*. Their showstopping pieces are *Girl with a Pearl Earring* and *View of Delft*, both by Johannes Vermeer. (☎070 302 3456; www.mauritshuis.nl. Open Tu-Sa 10am-5pm, Su 11am-5pm. Free audio tour. €9.50, under 18 and Museum Card holders free. AmEx/MC/V.) Show up at the **Binnenhof**, Binnenhof 8A, for a guided tour that covers both the historic **Ridderzaal** (Hall of Knights) and the **Second Chamber of the States-General,** the Netherlands's main legislative body. Tours don't run when Parliament is in session. The Binnenhof's courtyard is one of The Hague's best photo-ops. Take tram 2, 3, 6 or 10 to Binnenhof or walk about 15min. from Centraal; follow the signs. (☎070 364 6144; www.binnenhofbezoek.nl. Open M-Sa 10am-4pm. Last tour 3:45pm. Parliament is often in session Tu-Th. You can enter the Second Chamber only with a passport or driver's license. Entrance to courtyard free. Admission to Hall of Knights or Second Chamber €6; €8 for both. Tours €5, seniors and children €4.30. Cash only.)

In late June, the Hague hosts what the Dutch consider the largest free public pop concert in Europe, ⬛**Parkpop**, on 3 large stages in Zuiderpark with top big-name acts. (☎070 523 9064; www.parkpop.nl.) ⬛**De Paas,** Dunne Bierkade 16A, has 11 unusually good beers on tap, about 170 available in bottles, and nearly as many friendly faces around the bar. (☎070 360 0019; www.depaas.nl. Beer from €1.70. Open M-Th and Su 3pm-1am, F-Sa 3pm-1:30am. MC/V.)

🎭 DAYTRIP FROM THE HAGUE: DELFT.
Lily-lined canals and stone foot-bridges still line the streets of picturesque Delft (pop. 100,000), the birthplace of the 17th-century Dutch painter **Johannes Vermeer** and the home of the famous blue-and-white ceramic pottery known as ⬛**Delftware**. The best of the three

factories that produce it is **De Candelaer,** Kerkstr. 13, where everything is made from scratch, and visitors can listen to a free explanation of the process. (☎*070 213 1848; www.candelaer.nl. Open daily 9am-6pm. Will ship to the US. AmEx/MC/V.)* William of Orange, father of the Netherlands, used ◼**Het Prinsenhof,** St. Agathapl. 1, as his headquarters during the Dutch resistance to Spain in the 16th century. The gorgeous old building now houses a museum chronicling his life as well as a collection of paintings, Delftware, and other artifacts from the Dutch Golden Age. (☎*070 260 2358; www.prinsenhof-delft.nl. Open Tu-Sa 10am-5pm, Su 1-5pm. €6, ages 12-16 €5, under 12 and Museum card holders free.)* A long stretch of a canal leads up to the 27 stained-glass windows at the monumental ◼**Oude Kerk,** Heilige Geestkerkhof 25. The three antique organs are worth an examination, and the church is also Vermeer's final resting place. Its tower is about 75m high and leans a staggering— and slightly unnerving—1.96m out of line. (☎*070 212 3015; www.oudekerk-delft.nl. Open Apr.-Oct. M-Sa 9am-6pm; Nov.-Mar. M-F 11am-4pm, Sa 10am-5pm. Entrance to both Nieuwe Kerk and Oude Kerk €3, seniors €2, ages 3-12 €1.50.)* You can catch the **train** to either of the two train stations in The Hague (8min., 5 per hr., €2.30) or to Amsterdam (1hr., 5 per hr., €11.30) The **Tourist Information Point,** Hippolytusbuurt 4, has free **Internet** terminals as well as free **maps** and information on sights and events. You can also purchase a "hop-on, hop-off" city pass for the Hague and Delft, allowing you to use public transit. €13 for 24hr., €20 for 48hr. (☎*070 215 4051; www.delft.nl. Open M 10am-4pm, Tu-F 9am-6pm, Sa 10am-5pm, Su 10am-3pm.)*

ROTTERDAM   ☎010

Marked by a razor-sharp skyline, countless steamships, and darting high-speed trains, Rotterdam (pop. 590,000) is the busiest port in Europe. It's also the country's most exciting multicultural capital, with the largest traditional immigrant population in the Netherlands. Festivals, art galleries, and an extremely dynamic nightlife make Rotterdam a busy center of cultural activity and the hippest, most up-and-coming city in the Netherlands.

◼◻ **TRANSPORTATION AND PRACTICAL INFORMATION. Trains** roll out of Rotterdam Centraal to Amsterdam (1hr., 1-5 per hr., €13) and The Hague (30min., 1-5per hr., €4.30). Rotterdam has a network of **buses, trams,** and **two Metro lines** (**Calandlijn** and **Erasmuslijn**) that intersect in the center of the city at Beurs station. Metro tickets, equivalent to two strips, are valid for two hours. The **VVV,** Coolsingel 5, has free **maps** of public transportation as well as maps of the city. (☎0900 271 0120, €0.40 per min.; from abroad ☎010 414 0000; www. vvvrotterdam.nl. Open M-Th 9:30am-6pm, F 9:30am-9pm, Sa 9:30am-5pm.) Stop by the backpacker-oriented ◼**Use-it Rotterdam,** Conradstr. 2, where you will find great money-saving tips and useful info. (☎010 240 9158; www.use-it.nl.)

◻◻ **ACCOMMODATIONS AND FOOD.** For true backpackers, the clean, simple, and fun hostel ◼**Sleep-in De Mafkees ❶,** Schaatsbaan 41-45, is a great place to stay. A "honeymoon suite" is available for guests in love and willing to kiss in public. (☎010 281 0459; www.only10euroanight.nl. Dorms available end of June-Aug. €10. Breakfast included. Personal locker €1 per day. Internet €0.80 per 15min. Must bring own sleeping bag or sheets; limited rentals. Reception closed 5:15pm-11:30am. Check-in at Use-It and store luggage in lockers.) Expect knowledgeable staff and clean, comfortable rooms at the commercial **Stayokay Rotterdam ❶,** Rochussenstr. 107-109, a hostel that's great for large groups. (☎010 436 5763; www.stayokay.com/rotterdam. Internet €5 per hr. Reception 24hr. Dorms €20-31; singles €40-45; doubles €56-65. €2.50 HI discount. AmEx/MC/V.) ◼**Bazar ❷,** attracts nightly crowds with glittering colored lights, bright blue tables, and satisfying Mediterranean and Middle Eastern fusion cuisine. (☎010 206 5151. Sandwiches €4. Special dinner €8. Breakfast and lunch served all day. Reservations recommended for dinner. Open M-Th 8am-1am, F 8am-2am,

Sa 10am-2am, Su 10am-midnight. AmEx/MC/V.) ■**Bagel Bakery** ❶, Schilderstr. 57A-59A, a popular stop for students, serves artfully-topped bagels in a well-lit, hip environment. Try their freshly-baked *liefdesbrood*, "true love bread." (☎010 412 1413. Open Tu-Th 9am-9pm, F-Sa 9am-10pm, Su 10am-9pm. Cash only).

◨◪ SIGHTS AND ENTERTAINMENT. Only the extremely ambitious should attempt to see all of the ■**Museum Boijmans van Beuningen**, Museumpark 18-20, in one day. On the ground floor, you'll find post-war work by artists like Andy Warhol. The second floor is home to a large selection of Surrealist paintings as well as Expressionist pieces, plus several Monets and an impressive collection of Dutch and Flemish art by the like of Hans Memling, Anthony van Dyck, Jan Steen, Frans Hals, and Rembrandt van Rijn. (☎010 441 9400; www.boijmans.nl. Open Tu-Su 11am-5pm. €9, students €4.50, under 18 and Museum Card holders free. Wheelchair-accessible. Library open Tu-Su 11am-4:30pm; free with entrance ticket.) The ■**Nederlands Architectuurinstituut (NAI)**, Museumpark 25, boasts one of the most extraordinary designs in all of Rotterdam. The multi-level glass and steel construction—which traverses a manmade pool and looks out onto Museumpark—is home to several exhibition spaces, a world-class archive, and 39,500 books. (☎010 440 1200; www.nai.nl. Open Tu-Sa 10am-5pm, Su 11am-5pm. Library and reading room open Tu-Sa 10am-5pm, Su 11am-5pm. €8, age 12-18, students, and seniors €5, ages 4-12 €1, Museum Card holders free.) Ascending the tallest structure in the Netherlands, the popular **Euromast**, Parkhaven 20, is the best way to take in a panoramic view of Rotterdam's jagged skyline. From the 112m viewing deck, you can take an elevator to the 185m mark, where you'll see all the way to Delft and The Hague. (☎010 436 4811; www.euromast.nl. Open daily Apr.-Sept. 9:30am-11pm; Oct.-Mar. 10am-11pm. Platforms open until 10pm. €8.30, ages 4-11 €5.40.)

Coffee shops line **Oude** and **Nieuwe Binnenweg**. At **Off_Corso**, Kruiskade 22, art exhibitions share the bill with regular dance parties and live DJs at this very popular club. (☎010 280 7359; www.offcorso.nl.) ■**Dizzy**, 's-Gravendijkwal 127, Rotterdam's premier jazz cafe for 25 years, hosts frequent jam sessions. (☎010 477 3014; www. dizzy.nl. Take tram 4 to Dijkzicht. Beer €1.80. Whiskey €5.20. Open M-Th noon-1am, F-Sa noon-2am, Su noon-midnight. AmEx/MC/V.)

UTRECHT ☎030

Smack-dab in the center of the Netherlands lies Utrecht (pop. 290,000), a mecca for history buffs, thesis writers, and student revelers. The swarms of fraternity boys that fill the city's outdoor cafes are a visible testament to Utrecht's status as the Netherlands's largest university town. Utrecht is also a cultural hub: visitors come here for action-packed festivals, nightlife, and tree-lined canals.

◧◪ TRANSPORTATION AND PRACTICAL INFORMATION. Take **train** to Amsterdam (30min., 3-6 per hr., €6.60). The **VVV**, Dompl. 9, is in a building called the RonDom, a **visitor's center** for cultural history, across from the Domkerk. Pick up a free **map** of the city and a complete listing of museums and sights. (☎0900 128 8732, €0.50 per min.; www.utrechtyourway.nl. Open Apr.-Sept. M-Sa 10am-5pm, Su noon-5pm; Oct.-Mar. M-F and Su noon-5pm, Sa 10am-5pm.)

◪◩ ACCOMMODATIONS AND FOOD. ■**Strowis Hostel** ❶, Boothstr. 8, has a laid-back staff, a convenient location, and unbeatable prices. This former squat feels more like a welcoming country villa. (☎030 238 0280; www.strowis. nl. Breakfast €6. Free lockers. Linens and blanket €1.25. Free Internet. Bike rental €6 per day. Curfew M-Th and Su 2am, F-Sa 3am. Max. 2-week stay. 14-bed dorms €15; 8-bed €16; 6-bed €17; 4-bed €18; singles/doubles €57.50; triples €69.) The three-story **B&B Utrecht City Centre** ❶, Lucasbolwerk 4, is geared towards free-spirited backpackers looking for a welcoming community. Hostel includes beds, a fully-stocked kitchen with edible food (open 24hr.), a music corner full of instruments, and an extensive movie collection. Take bus # 3, 4 or 11 to Stadsschouwburg or walk down Lange Viestr. for 10min.; it's to the left on the corner of Lucasbolwerk and Nobelstr. (☎065 043 4884; www.hostelutrecht. nl. Mandatory sheet rental €2.50. Towel €1. Free Wi-Fi and plenty of computers. Bike rental €5 per day. Private rooms located in separate building. Dorms €17.50; singles €55; doubles €65; triples €90; quads €120. MC/V.) ◪**Het Nachtrestaurant ❷**, Oudegr. 158, has a decadent, pillow-lined cellar dining room, while the flashier clientele crowd the canal-side terrace. (☎030 230 3036. Tapas €3-6. Nightclub Sa 11pm-close. Open M-W 11am-midnight, Th-F 11am-1am, Sa 11am-10:30pm. Su noon-midnight. AmEx/MC/V.)

◪◪ **SIGHTS AND NIGHTLIFE.** ◪**Utrecht's Domtoren,** Achter de Dom 1, is impossible to ignore: the city's most beloved landmark is also the highest church tower in the Netherlands. The 112m tower presides over the province with magnificent spires and 26,000kg of bronze bells. The brick-red *Domkerk* was attached to the tower until an errant tornado blew away the nave in 1674. During the tour, you'll learn about the history of the church and get a glimpse of the church's bells. (☎030 231 0403. Open Oct.-Apr. M-F 11am-4:30pm, Sa 11am-3:30pm, Su 2-4pm; May-Sept. M-F 10am-5pm, Sa 10am-3:30pm, Su 2-4pm. Free concert every Sa 3:30pm. *Domtoren* accessible only through 1hr. tours daily Oct.-Mar. M-F noon, 2, 4pm, Sa 1 per hr. 10am-5pm, Su 1 per hr. noon-5pm; Apr.-Sept. M-Sa 1 per hr. 10am-5pm, Su 1 per hr. noon-5pm. Domkerk free. Domtoren €7.50, students and over 65 €6.50, ages 4-12 €4.50.) At the **Centraal Museum,** Nicolaaskerkhof 10, visitors enter a labyrinth of pavilions to experience Dutch art. The museum oversees the world's largest collection of work by De Stijl designer Gerrit Rietveld, but many of these objects have been transferred to the avant-garde **Rietveld Schroderhuis,** a UNESCO World Heritage Site. The museum is accessible only by guided tour, so call ahead for reservations. (☎030 236 2362; 030 236 2310 for Rietveld Schroderhuis; www.centraalmuseum.nl. Open Tu-Su 11am-5pm, F noon-9pm. Audio tour free. €8, students, over age 65 and ages 13-17 €6, under 12 €2.)

At ◪**'t Oude Pothuys,** Oudegr. 279, uninhibited patrons have been known to jump off the bar's terrace into the canal after a long night of festivities. (☎030 231 8970. Beer €2. Live music nightly 11pm. Open M-W and Su 3pm-2am, Th-Sa 3pm-3am. AmEx/MC.) A former squat turned political and cultural center, ◪**ACU Politiek Cultureel Centrum,** Voorstr. 71, hosts live music (W, F cover €5-6), a political discussion group (M 8pm-2am), and a Su movie night. (☎030 231 4590; www.acu.nl. Beer €1.70. Vegetarian Tu, Th, Su 6pm-8:30pm. Organic and vegan dining W 3-5pm. Cash only. Open M-Th and Su 5pm-2am. F-Sa 9pm-4am.) Utrecht's theater school, ◪**Hofman,** Janskerkhof 17A, is packed with students and twentysomethings throughout the week. Take advantage of student-friendly events and live music nights. (☎030 230 2470; www.hofman-cafe.nl. Beer €2. Open M-Th and Su 11am-2am, F-Sa 11am-3:30am. Cash only.)

NORWAY
(NORGE)

Norway's rugged countryside and remote mountain farms gave birth to one of the most feared seafaring civilizations of pre-medieval Europe: the Vikings. Modern-day Norwegians have inherited their ancestors' independent streak, voting against joining the EU in 1994 and drawing the ire of environmental groups for their refusal to ban commercial whaling. Because of high revenues from petroleum exports, Norway enjoys one of the highest standards of living in the world. Its stunning fjords and miles of coastline make the country a truly worthwhile destination—but sky-high prices and limited public transportation in rural areas may challenge even the best-prepared budget traveler.

 DISCOVER NORWAY: SUGGESTED ITINERARY

THREE DAYS. Fjords don't have anything on **Oslo** (p. 575), the best place to spend all your Norwegian time. Enjoy the city's museums, like the **Munch Museum** (p. 579), and various ethnic eateries.

ESSENTIALS

FACTS AND FIGURES

OFFICIAL NAME: Kingdom of Norway.

CAPITAL: Oslo.

MAJOR CITIES: Bergen, Stavanger, Tromsø, Trondheim.

POPULATION: 4,628,000.

LAND AREA: 307,500 sq. km.

TIME ZONE: GMT +1.

LANGUAGES: Bokmål and Nynorsk Norwegian; Sámi; Swedish and English are both widely spoken.

WINTER OLYMPIC MEDALS WON SINCE THE FIRST GAMES IN 1924: 280; more than any other nation.

WHEN TO GO

Oslo averages 18°C (63°F) in July and -4°C (24°F) in January. The north is the coldest and wettest region, though Bergen and the surrounding mountains to the south are also rainy. For a few weeks around the summer solstice (June 21), the area north of Bodø basks in the midnight sun. The **Northern Lights** are a top attraction—many come to see the spectacular nighttime displays formed when solar flares produce plasma clouds that run into atmospheric gases, which peak from November to February. Skiing is best just before Easter.

DOCUMENTS AND FORMALITIES

EMBASSIES AND CONSULATES. Foreign embassies in Norway are in Oslo. Norwegian embassies abroad include: **Australia**, 17 Hunter St., Yarralumla,

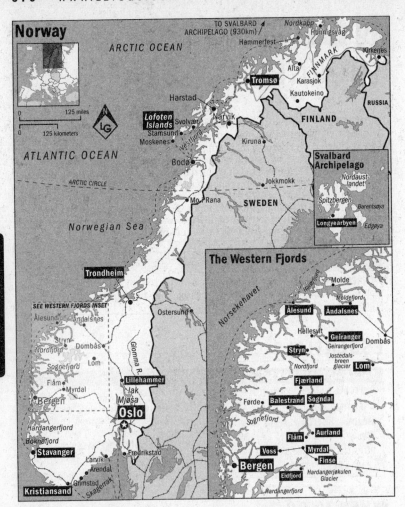

ACT 2600 (☎262 73 34 44; www.norway.org.au); **Canada,** 90 Sparks St., Ste. 532, Ottawa, ON K1P 5B4 (☎613-238-6571; www.emb-norway.ca); **Ireland,** 34 Molesworth St., Dublin 2 (☎16 62 18 00; www.norway.ie); **UK,** 25 Belgrave Sq., London SW1X 8QD (☎20 75 91 55 00; www.norway.org.uk); **US,** 2720 34th St., NW, Washington, D.C., 20008 (☎202-333-6000; www.norway.org).

VISA AND ENTRY INFORMATION. EU citizens do not need a visa. Citizens of Australia, Canada, New Zealand, and the US do not need a visa for stays of up to 90 days, beginning upon entry into any of the countries within the EU's freedom of movement zone. For more info, see p. 13. For stays longer than 90 days, all non-EU citizens need visas, available at Norwegian consulates. For more info on obtaining a visa, go to www.norway.org/visas.

TOURIST SERVICES AND MONEY

EMERGENCY	Ambulance: ☎113. Fire: ☎110. Police: ☎112.

TOURIST OFFICES. Virtually every town and village has a **Turistinformasjon** office; look for a white "i" on a square green sign. From the latter half of June through early August, most tourist offices are open daily; expect reduced hours at other times. Check www.visitnorway.com for a directory of local offices. More info on traveling in Norway is available at www.norway.no.

MONEY. The Norwegian unit of currency is the **krone (kr)**, plural kroner. One krone is equal to 100 **øre**. Banks and large post offices change money, usually for a small commission. It's generally cheaper to exchange money in Norway than at home. **Tipping** is not expected, but an extra 5-10% is always welcome for good service. It is customary to leave coins on the counter or table rather than putting the tip on a credit card. Hotel bills often include a 15% service charge.

Norway has a 25% **value added tax (VAT)**, a sales tax applied to goods and services. The prices given in *Let's Go* include VAT. Upon exiting the EU, non-EU citizens can claim a refund on the tax paid for goods purchased at participating stores. In order to qualify for a refund in a store, you must spend at least 315kr in a single store; be sure to ask for a refund form when you pay. For more info on qualifying for a VAT refund, see p. 19.

NORWEGIAN KRONER (KR)		
AUS$1 = 4.74KR		10KR = AUS$2.11
CDN$1 = 5.61KR		10KR = CDN$1.78
EUR€1 = 8.01KR		10KR = EUR€1.25
NZ$1 = 4.14KR		10KR = NZ$2.41
UK£1 = 11.78KR		10KR = UK£0.85
US$1 = 5.95KR		10KR = US$1.68

NORWAY

TRANSPORTATION

BY PLANE. The main international airport is **Oslo Airport Gardermoen (OSL;** ☎06 400; www.osl.no), though some flights land at **Bergen Airport Flesland (BGO;** ☎55 99 81 55) and **Trondheim Airport Værnes (TRD;** ☎74 84 30 00). **SAS** (Scandinavian Airlines; Norway ☎91 50 54 00, UK 08 71 52 12 772, US 800-221-2350; www.flysas.com), **Finnair,** and **Icelandair** fly to Norway. Students and those under 25 qualify for youth fares when flying domestically on SAS. Budget airlines **Norwegian** (☎21 49 00 15; www.norwegian.no) and **Widerøe** (☎75 11 11 11; www.wideroe.no) have internal fares under €100 and cheap prices to European destinations. **Ryanair** (☎353 12 49 77 91; www.ryanair.com) flies to **Sandefjord Airport Torp,** near Oslo, and **Haugesund,** near Bergen. Book early for the best fares on all airlines, or try your luck with SAS domestic standby tickets *(sjanse billetter),* purchased at the airport on the day of travel for around 400kr.

BY TRAIN. Norway's train system includes a commuter network around Oslo and long-distance lines running from Oslo to Bergen and to Stavanger via Kristiansand. Contact **Norwegian State Railways** (NSB) for timetables and tickets (☎81 50 08 88; www.nsb.no). The unguided **Norway in a Nutshell** tour combines a ride along the Flåm Railway, a cruise through Aurlandsfjord and Nærøyfjord to the port of Gudvangen, and a bus ride over the mountains to Voss. Tickets can be purchased from tourist offices or train stations in Bergen and Oslo. (☎81 56 82 22; www.norwaynutshell.com. Round-trip from Voss 595kr, from Bergen 895kr, from Oslo 1730kr.) Overnight trains may be the best option for travel as far north as Bodø and Trondheim; from there, you'll need buses or ferries to get farther north. **Eurail Passes** are valid in Norway. The **Norway Railpass,** available only outside Norway, allows three to five days of unlimited travel in a one-month period (from US$187).

> **RAIL SAVINGS.** Booking rail tickets at least a day ahead is vital, saving you hundreds of krone. For rail travel within Norway, the **Minipris** offered by NSB is a great deal. A limited number of seats are made available on regional trains for 199kr and 299kr, including on expensive routes. Go to www.nsb.no to purchase tickets; when asked to choose the type of ticket, select Minipris. (If it is not on the menu, tickets are sold out.) Minipris tickets purchased outside Norway are 50kr cheaper than those purchased in the country.

BY BUS. Buses can be quite expensive but they are the only land travel option north of Bodø and in the fjords. **Nor-way Bussekspress** (☎81 54 44 44; www. nor-way.no) operates most of the bus routes and publishes a timetable *(Rute-hefte)*, available at bus stations and on buses. Students with ISIC are eligible for a 25-50% discount—be insistent, and follow the rules listed in the *Nor-way Bussekspress* booklet. Bus passes, valid for 10 or 21 consecutive travel days (1300/2400kr), are good deals for those exploring the fjords or the north.

BY FERRY. Car ferries *(ferjer)* are usually cheaper (and slower) than the passenger express boats *(hurtigbåt* or *ekspressbåt)* cruising the coasts and fjords; both often have student and InterRail discounts. The **Hurtigruten** (☎81 03 00 00; www.hurtigruten.com) takes six to 11 days for the incredible cruise from Bergen to Kirkenes on the Russian border. Discounts for rail pass holders are limited to 50% off the Bergen-Stavanger route, but some lines also offer a 50% student discount. The common ports for international ferries are Oslo, Bergen, Kristiansand, and Stavanger. **DFDS Seaways** (☎21 62 13 40; www.dfdsseaways. com) sails from Oslo and Kristiansand to Copenhagen, DEN and Gothenburg, SWE. **Color Line** (☎22 94 42 00; www.colorline.com) runs ferries between Norway and Denmark, plus several domestic routes.

BY CAR. Citizens of Australia, Canada, the EU, New Zealand, and the US can drive in Norway for up to one year with a valid **driver's license** from their home country. Vehicles are required to keep **headlights** on at all times. Roads in Norway are in good condition, although blind curves are common and roads are narrow in some places. Drivers should be cautious, especially on mountain roads and in tunnels, as reindeer and sheep can make unexpected appearances. Driving around the fjords can be frustrating, as only Nordfjord has a road completely circumnavigating them. Insurance is required and usually included in the price of rental. Though expensive, renting a car can be more affordable than trains and buses when traveling in a group. There are numerous car ferries, so check schedules in advance. For more info on driving in Europe, see p. 49.

BY BIKE AND BY THUMB. The beautiful scenery around Norway is rewarding for **cyclists,** but the hilly terrain can be rough on bikes. Contact **Syklistenes Landsforening** (☎22 47 30 30; www.slf.no) for maps, suggested routes, and info. **Hitchhiking** is difficult in mainland Norway, but easier on the Lofoten and Svalbard Islands. Some travelers successfully hitchhike beyond the rail lines in northern Norway and the fjord areas of the west, while many others try for hours without success. Hitchhikers suggest bringing several layers of clothing, rain gear, and a warm sleeping bag. *Let's Go* does not recommend hitchhiking.

KEEPING IN TOUCH

PHONE CODES	**Country code: 47. International dialing prefix:** 095. For more info on how to place international calls, see **Inside Back Cover.**

EMAIL AND THE INTERNET. Oslo and Bergen have many Internet cafes. Expect to pay about 1kr per min. Smaller cities might have one or two Internet cafes, and most have a public library open on weekdays that offers 15-30min. of free Internet. Free **Wi-Fi** connections for travelers with laptops are also readily available. For more info on the Internet in Europe, see p. 27.

TELEPHONE. There are three types of **public phones:** black and gray phones accept 1, 5, 10, and 20kr coins; green phones accept only phone cards; red phones accept coins, phone cards, and major credit cards. **Phone cards** (*telekort;* 40, 90, or 140kr at post offices and Narvesen kiosks) are the cheapest option, especially when prices drop between 5pm and 8am. **Mobile phones** are increasingly popular and cheap in Norway; buying a prepaid SIM card for a GSM phone can be a good, inexpensive option. Of the service providers, **Netcom** and **Telenor** have the best networks. For help with domestic calls, dial ☎ 117. International direct access numbers include: **AT&T Direct** (☎80 01 90 11); **Canada Direct** (☎80 01 91 11); **MCI WorldPhone** (☎80 01 99 12); **Telecom New Zealand** (☎80 01 99 64).

MAIL. Mailing a first-class postcard or letter (under 20g) within Norway costs 7kr; outside Norway 9-11kr. To receive mail in Norway, have mail delivered **Poste Restante.** Mail will go to the main post office unless you specify a subsidiary by street address. Address mail to be held according to the following format: First name LAST NAME, Poste Restante, City, Norway. Bring a passport to pick up your mail; there may be a small fee.

LANGUAGE. Norwegian is universal; some people speak English and Swedish. The indigenous people of northern Norway speak different dialects of Sámi. For basic Norwegian words and phrases, see **Phrasebook: Norwegian** (p. 790).

ACCOMMODATIONS AND CAMPING

NORWAY	❶	❷	❸	❹	❺
ACCOMMODATIONS	under 160kr	160-260kr	261-400kr	401-550kr	over 550kr

Norske Vandrerhjem (☎23 12 45 10; www.vandrerhjem.no) operates **HI youth hostels** (*vandrerhjem*). Beds run 100-400kr, and HI members receive a 15% discount. Linens typically cost 45-60kr per stay, and sleeping bags are forbidden. Few hostels have curfews. Most hostels open in mid- to late June and close after the third week in August. Many **tourist offices** book private rooms and hotels for a fee (usually 30kr). Norwegian **right of public access** allows camping anywhere on public land for fewer than three nights, as long as you keep 150m from buildings and leave no trace. **Den Norske Turistforening** (DNT; Norwegian Mountain Touring Association) sells maps (60-70kr), offers guided hiking trips, and maintains more than 350 mountain huts (*hytter*) throughout Norway. A one-year membership (465kr; under 26, 265kr) entitles the holder to discounts on DNT lodgings (☎40 00 18 68; www.dntoslo.no). The 42 staffed huts are open

NORWAY

in summer; most have showers and serve dinner. Unstaffed huts are open mid-February to mid-October; a sizable minority have basic provisions for sale on the honor system. Members can leave a 100kr deposit at any tourist office to borrow a key. Prices vary according to age, season, and membership; official campgrounds ask 25-140kr for tent sites, 300-600kr for cabins. For more info on camping in Norway, visit www.camping.no.

FOOD AND DRINK

NORWAY	❶	❷	❸	❹	❺
FOOD	under 60kr	60-100kr	101-150kr	151-250kr	over 250kr

Many restaurants have an inexpensive *dagens ret* (dish of the day; 70-80kr). Otherwise, you'll rarely spend less than 150kr for a full meal. **Fish**—cod, herring, and salmon—is fresh and relatively inexpensive. Other specialties include cheese *(ost)*, Jarlsberg being the most popular; pork-and-veal meatballs *(kjøttkaker)* with boiled potatoes; and, for more adventurous carnivores, reindeer, ptarmigan, and whale meat *(hval)*. Christmas brings a meal of dried fish soaked in water and lye *(lutefisk)*. **Beer** is expensive in bars (45-60kr for ½L); purchase cheaper bottles from the supermarket. Try the local favorite, Frydenlund, or go rock-bottom with Danish Tuborg. You must be 18 to buy beer and wine, and 20 to buy liquor at the aptly named *Vinmonopolet* (wine monopoly) stores.

HOLIDAYS AND FESTIVALS

Holidays: New Year's Day (Jan. 1); Maundy Thursday (Apr. 9, 2009; Apr. 1, 2010)); Good Friday (Apr. 10, 2009; Apr. 2, 2010); Easter (Apr. 12, 2009; Apr. 4, 2010); Labor Day (May 1); Ascension (May 1); Pentecost (May 31, 2009; May 23, 2010); Constitution Day (May 17); Christmas (Dec. 25); Boxing Day (Dec. 26).

Festivals: Norway throws festivals virtually year-round, from the **Tromsø International Film Festival** (Jan. 15-20; www.tiff.no) to Bergen's operatic **Festpillene** (May 21-June 4; www.fib.no). The **Norwegian Wood Festival** in Frognerbadet (mid-June; www.norwegianwood.no) features pop, folk, and classic rock. Heavy metal enthusiasts flock to **Inferno**, held in Oslo on Easter weekend (www.infernofestival.net). For more info, check www.norwayfestivals.com.

BEYOND TOURISM

Citizens of the 40 signatory countries of the **Svalbard Treaty**, including Australia, Canada, New Zealand, the UK, and the US, can work on the Svalbard archipelago, including at the **University Center in Svalbard (UNIS)** (☎02 33 00; www.unis. no). For more info on opportunities, see **Beyond Tourism**, p. 55.

The American-Scandinavian Foundation (AMSCAN), 58 Park Ave., New York, NY 10016, USA (☎212-879-9779; www.amscan.org/jobs). Volunteer and job opportunities throughout Scandinavia. Fellowships for study in Norway available to Americans.

Study in Norway (www.studyinnorway.no). Education and research opportunities throughout the country for summer and term-time study. Scholarships available.

OSLO
☎ **21, 22, 23**

Scandinavian capitals consent to being urban without renouncing the landscape around them and Oslo (pop. 550,000) is no exception. The Nordmarka forest to the north and Oslofjord to the south bracket the city's cultural institutions, busy cafes, and expensive boutiques. While most of Norway remains homogeneous, Oslo has a vibrant immigrant community in its eastern and northern sections. But even as globalization moves Oslo towards greater cosmopolitanism, Norwegian history and folk traditions still shape the city. Olso is a rather pricey destination, but also an essential stop on any trip to Scandinavia.

▐▀ TRANSPORTATION

Flights: Oslo Airport Gardermoen (OSL; ☎06 400; www.osl.no), 45km north of the center. The high-speed FlyToget train (☎81 50 07 77; www.flytoget.no) runs between the airport and downtown (20min.; 3-6 per hr.; 160kr, students 80kr). White SAS Flybussen run a similar route. (☎22 80 49 70; www.flybussen.no. 40min.; 2-3 per hr.; 140kr, students 75kr; round-trip 240kr) Some budget airlines fly into **Sandefjord Airport Torp,** south of Oslo as well as the newest airport, **Rygge.** Buses and trains (50 min. 131kr) leave from Oslo S daily. **Sandefjord Airport Torp (TRF;** ☎55 42 70 00; www.torp.no), 120km south of Oslo, is a budget airline hub for Ryanair, Widerøe, and Wizz Air. Trains (☎81 50 08 88) run to **Oslo** (1hr.; 1 per hr.). Buses (2 per hr.) and taxis shuttle between the train station and airport. Buses also go to **Oslo** (1-2 per hr., 180kr) and coordinate with Ryanair arrivals and departures. See www.torpekspressen.no.

Trains: Oslo Sentralstasjon (Oslo S), Jernbanetorget 1 (☎81 50 08 88). To: **Bergen** (6.5hr., 4 per day, 739kr); **Trondheim** (7hr., 4 per day, 813kr); **Copenhagen, DEN** via **Gothenburg, SWE** (8hr., 2 per day); **Stockholm, SWE** (6hr., 2 per day). Mandatory seat reservations for domestic trains 41-71kr. Check *mini pris* tickets and book ahead.

Buses: Nor-way Bussekspress, Schweigårds gt. 8 (☎81 54 44 44; www.nor-way.no). Follow the signs from the train station through the Oslo Galleri Mall to the Bussterminalen Galleriet. Student discounts (25-50%) on most long-distance trips.

Ferries: The **Stenaline** (stenaline.no) operates to **Frederikshavn, DEN** (12hr., 7:30pm, from 160kr one way). **Color Line** (☎55 81 00 08 11; www.colorline.com) runs to **Kiel, GER** (19hr., 2pm, from 1210kr). **DFDS Seaways** (☎21 62 13 40; www.dfds.com) runs to **Copenhagen, DEN** (16hr.) daily at 5pm (930kr, 25% student discount).

Public Transportation: Buses, ferries, subways, and **trams** cost 30kr per ride or 22kr in advance. Tickets include 1hr. of unlimited transfers. If you are caught traveling without a valid ticket, you can be fined up to 900kr. **Trafikanten** (☎177; www.trafikanten.no), in front of Oslo S, sells the Dagskort (day pass 60kr), Flexicard (8 trips 160kr), and 7-day Card (210kr). Open M-F 7am-8pm, Sa-Su 8am-6pm (same as tourist office). Tickets also at Narvesen kiosks and Automat machines in the metro. All **public transit** free with Oslo Pass. Pick up most buses outside Oslo S.

Bike Rental: The city's bike-share system allows visitors to borrow one of the 1000+ bikes available at racks throughout the city center. Both the main tourist office and the Oslo S branch sell system **enrollment cards** (70kr per day). Note that bikes must be returned to a rack every 3hr. and cards must be returned to the tourist office.

Hitchhiking: Hitchhiking is not common in this area of Norway because of the extensive transportation network—however, some travelers report hitching rides to major cities at truck terminals. *Let's Go* does not recommend hitchhiking.

NORWAY

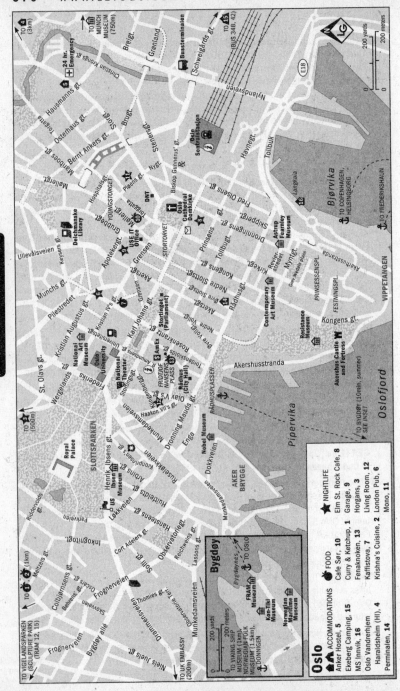

NORWAY

Oslo

ACCOMMODATIONS
Anker Hostel, **5**
Ekeberg Camping, **15**
MS Innvik, **16**
Oslo Vandrerhjem
  Haraldsheim (HI), **4**
Perminalen, **14**

🍴 **FOOD**
Cafe Sør, **10**
Curry & Ketchup, **1**
Fenaknoken, **13**
Kaffistova, **7**
Krishna's Cuisine, **2**

★ **NIGHTLIFE**
Elm St. Rock Cafe, **8**
Garage, **9**
Horgans, **3**
Living Room, **12**
London Pub, **6**
Mono, **11**

Bygdøy

ORIENTATION AND PRACTICAL INFORMATION

In Oslo center, the garden plaza **Slottsparken** (Castle Park) lies beside Oslo University and the **Nationaltheatret** (National Theater) and surrounds the Royal Palace. The city's main street, **Karl Johans gate,** runs through the heart of town from Slottsparken to the train station **Oslo Sentralstasjon** (Oslo S) at its eastern end. **Ferries** depart from the harbor, southwest of Oslo S near Akershus Castle. Many museums and beaches are southwest on the **Bygdøy peninsula.** Ferries to Bygdøy depart from the dock behind **Rådhus** (City Hall). Massive construction projects are currently reshaping the harbor, an initiative marked by the new opera house—its elaborate architecture and great fjord views from the roof make it worth a visit. **Parks** are scattered throughout Oslo, especially north of the Nationaltheatret. Of note is **Saint Hanshaugen,** a hilly park north of the city center up Akersgata as it becomes Ullevålsveien. A network of public trams, buses, and subways makes transit through the outskirts quick and easy. **Grünerløkka** to the north and **Grønland** to the east—home to many of Oslo immigrants—are often cheaper than the city's other neighborhoods, while their boutiques, cafes, and parks showcase some of the latest urban trends. Despite some concern, the area generally has few safety problems.

Tourist Offices: Fridtjof Nansenspl. 5 (☎81 53 05 55; www.visitoslo.com). Sells the **Oslo Pass,** offering unlimited public transport and admission to most museums. 1-day pass 220kr, 2-day 320kr, 3-day 410kr. Open June-Aug. daily 9am-7pm; Sept. and Apr.-May M-Sa 9am-5pm; Oct.-Mar. M-F 9am-4pm. **Oslo Central Station Tourist Info,** Jernbanetorget 1, outside Oslo S in the same building as the trafekanten. Open M-F 7am-8pm, Sa-Su 8am-6pm. █Use-It, Møllergt. 3 (☎24 14 98 20; www.use-it.no), helps find beds for no fee, offers free Internet and baggage storage, supplies information on studying and working in Oslo, and publishes the invaluable *Streetwise Budget Guide to Oslo.* Open July-Aug. M-F 9am-6pm; Sept.-June M-F 11am-5pm. Check out http://use-it.unginfo.oslo.no/sider/practical.php.

HAPPENING OSLO. Use-It organizes summer events and "happenings" for youth and foreign travelers in Oslo. Check at the office for details.

Embassies and Consulates: Australia, contact the embassy in Denmark (p. 205). **Canada,** Wergelandsv. 7, 4th fl. (☎22 99 53 00; www.canada.no). Open June-Aug. M-F 8am-4pm; Sept.-May M-F 8:30am-4:30pm. **Ireland,** Haakon VII's gt. 1 (☎55 22 01 72 00; osloembassy@dfa.ie). Open M-F 8:30am-4:30pm. **UK,** Thomas Heftyes gt. 8 (☎23 13 27 00; www.britain.no). Open in M-F 9am-noon. **US,** Henrik Ibsens gt. 48 (☎22 44 85 50; www.usa.no). Open M-F 9am-5pm.

Currency Exchange: At any major bank: Christiania, Den Norske, Landsbanker, DnB NOR, and Forebu Oslo, the Post Office, or **Forex,** in Oslo S, which offers better deals.

Luggage Storage: Lockers at Oslo S and at the **Nationaltheatret station.** 20-45kr per 24hr. Max. 7 days. Available 4:30am-1:10am. Office open M-F 9am-3pm. You can leave bags in the Use-It office (see above) for an afternoon or night.

Library and Internet: Free terminals at the **Deichmanske Library,** Arne Garborgs pl., ☎23 43 29 00. Sign up for 1hr. or drop in for 15-30min. Open Sept.-May M-F 10am-7pm, Sa 11am-2pm; June-Aug. M-F 10am-6pm, Sa 11am-2pm. Or head to the National Library, Drammensveinen 42, www.nb.no. Open M-F 9am-7pm, Sa 9am-2pm. For Internet later in the evening, find places in **Storgata** north of the train station.

GLBT Resources: Landsforeningen for Lesbisk og Homofil fri gjøring (LLH), Kongensgt. 12 (☎55 23 10 39 39; www.llh.no). Also see tourist office and www.blikk.no.

Laundromat: Look for the word *"myntvaskeri."* **Selva AS**, Ullevålsveien 15 (☎41 64 08 33). Wash 40kr, dry 30kr. Open M-F 8am-9pm, Sa 10am-3pm.

Police: ☎02800 to bypass dispatch and connect directly.

24hr. Pharmacy: Jernbanetorvets Apotek (☎23 35 81 00), opposite Oslo S.

Hospital: Oslo Kommunale Legevakt, Storgt. 40 (☎22 93 22 93).

Post Office: Main branch at Dronningensgate 15 (☎23 35 86 90). Address **Poste Restante** mail to be held in the following format: First name, LAST NAME, Poste Restante, Oslo Central Post Office, N-0101 Oslo, NORWAY. Open M-F 9am-6pm, Sa 10am-3pm. The post office at Oslo S is open M-F 9am-8pm.

Alcohol: The drinking age is 18 but 20 for liquor, so nearly all bars are 20+ throughout the country. Vsit the state liquor store, **Vinmonopolet**, in Oslo S, for cheaper alcohol.

ACCOMMODATIONS AND CAMPING

Hostels in Oslo fill up in summer. Reservations are essential. The private rooms available through **Use-It** (see tourist offices) start from below 200kr. *Pensjonater* (pensions) are well-located but can be more expensive. Check with the tourist office for last-minute accommodation deals. Travelers can **camp** for free in the forest north of town; try the end of the **Sognsvann line #3.** Young Norwegians often drink at home before heading out because of high bar prices, but most hostels, including HI, prohibit alcohol consumption on their premises.

Perminalen, Øvre Slottsgt. 2 (☎23 09 30 81; www.perminalen.no). 15min. walk from Oslo S to Christianian Torv. Backpackers head to this central hotel/hostel. Spacious rooms equipped with A/C and cable TV. Breakfast included. Internet 5kr per 5min. Free Wi-Fi. Reception 24hr. Dorms 345kr; singles 595kr; doubles 795kr. AmEx/MC/V. ❸

Anker Hostel, Storgt. 55 (☎22 99 72 00; www.ankerhostel.no). It's an easy walk north from Oslo S, but if you're coming from elsewhere, take tram #11, 13, or 17 to Hausmanns gt. Rooms with kitchenettes and bath. Breakfast 85kr. Linens 50kr. Internet 10kr per 10min. Free Wi-Fi. Reception in summer 24hr., in winter 7am-11pm. Check in at the Best Western next door if you arrive late. Dorms 235kr; doubles 525kr. AmEx/MC/V. ❷

Oslo Vandrerhjem Haraldsheim (HI), Haraldsheimvn. 4 (☎22 22 29 65; www.haraldsheim.oslo.no). Take tram #17 toward Grefson to Sinsenkrysset and walk up the hill through the park. Standard bunk dorms in a quiet, residential neighborhood. Breakfast included. Free Wi-Fi. Internet 1kr per min. Linens 50kr. Reception 24hr. Dorms 235kr; singles 395kr, with bath 450kr; doubles 520/600kr. 15% HI discount. MC/V. ❷

MS Innvik, Langkaia 49 (☎22 41 95 00; www.msinnvik.no). From Oslo S, cross the highway E18 overpass and head right along the harbor. This theater boat and BandB is on Bjørvika Bay. Cabins come with bath. Breakfast included. Reception 24hr. No kitchen. Free Wi-Fi. Cafe. Concerts free for guests. Singles 425kr; doubles 750kr. MC/V. ❹

Ekeberg Camping, Ekebergveien 65 (☎22 19 85 68; www.ekebergcamping.no), 3km from town. Bus #34 or 74. 24hr. security. Grocery store open daily 8am-10pm. Showers 10kr per 6min. Laundry 40kr. Reception 7:30am-11pm. Open June-Aug. 2-person tent sites 170kr, 4-person 245kr; 55kr per extra person. AmEx/MC/V. ❶

FOOD

Visitors can choose between hearty, often bland Norwegian fare and a variety of ethnic dishes. Either way, they usually feel robbed blind once the check arrives. Smart backpackers stock up at the city's grocery stores perhaps even buying a very cheap grill and heading to one of Oslo's many parks (a popular Norwegian activity). Look for the chains **ICA, Kiwi**, and **Rema 1000** (generally open M-F 9am-9pm, Sa-Su 9am-6pm), or pick up fresh produce at the Youngstorget **open-**

air market (M-Sa 7am-2pm). In the budget-friendly **Grønland district,** east of Oslo S, vendors hawk cheap kebabs, pizza, sushi, burgers, and falafel (from 40kr), while halal butchers can provide travelers with cooking meat.

Cafe Sør, Torggata 11 (☎41 46 30 47). This artsy, relaxing cafe attracts a young crowd with an array of teas and coffees (26-31kr). Sandwiches 93kr. At night, it's a popular hangout with nightly DJ's and weekly live acoustic performances. Beer 51kr. Free Wi-Fi. Open M-Th 11am-12:30am, F-Sa 11am-3am, Su 1pm-12:30am. AmEx/MC/V. ❷

Kaffistova, Rosenkrantz gt. 8 (☎23 21 41 00). Posh, airy eatery with modest portions of Norwegian fish, meat, and porridges. Vegetarian options. Lunch from 89kr. Dinner 123-173kr. Open M-F 10am-9pm, Sa-Su 11am-7pm. AmEx/MC/V. ❸

Krishna's Cuisine, Kirkeveien 59B (☎22 60 62 50), on the 2nd fl. Large plates of cheap Indian food. Exclusively vegetarian fare prepared with fresh seasonal ingredients. Lunch served all day 75kr. Entrees 50-110kr. Open M-Sa noon-8pm. Cash only. ❷

Curry and Ketchup, Kirkeveien 51 (☎22 69 05 22). A neighbor of Krishna's, this restaurant has a relaxed, sit-down feel. Generous helpings of Indian mainstays. Entrees 84-109kr. Open daily 2-10:30pm. Cash only. ❷

Fenaknoken, Matkultur i Tordenskidsgt. 12 (☎22 42 34 57). Gourmet Norwegian food store with seafood and free samples of delicacies like smoked elk or reindeer sausage. Fresh snack rolls 25kr, but this is mostly a shopping center, not an eatery. Open M-F 10am-5pm, Sa 10am-2pm. AmEx/MC/V. ❷

 DINING FOR POCKET CHANGE. Oslo's sky-high food prices can bring travelers to tears. For a bite on the (relatively) cheap, be sure to steer clear of the west side and main drags and head instead to Gronland or elsewhere north or east of the city.

🅖 SIGHTS

◾VIGELANDSPARKEN. Sculptor **Gustav Vigeland** (1869-1943) designed this 80-acre expanse west of the city center. The park is home to over 200 of his mammoth works, depicting all stages of the human life cycle. His controversial, puzzling art is worth deciphering. **Monolith** is a towering granite column of intertwining bodies in the middle of the park. *(Entrance on Kirkeveien. Take bus #20 or tram #12 or 15 to Vigelandsparken. Open 24hr. Free.)* While wandering through the park, stop at the **Oslo Bymuseum** (Oslo City Museum) for art and photography collections, displays on the city's history, and restored pavilions. *(☎23 28 41 70; www.oslomuseum.no. Open Tu-Su 11am-4pm. Free.)* Next to the park, the **Vigelandmuseet** (Vigeland Museum) traces the artist's development from his early works to the monumental pieces of his later years. The museum is housed in the building Vigeland used as his apartment and studio. *(Nobelsgt. 32. ☎23 49 37 00. Open June-Aug. Tu-Su 10am-5pm; Sept.-May Tu-Su noon-4pm. 50kr, students 25kr. Oct.-Mar free. MC/V.)*

ART MUSEUMS. Renovations at **Munchmuseet** (Munch Museum) improved its security system after a 2004 theft of two paintings, including a version of *The Scream,* Munch's most famous work. The paintings have been recovered, albeit with some damage. The museum has a collection of Munch's other abstract works along with temporary Impressionist exhibits. *(Tøyengt. 53. Take the metro to Tøyen or bus #20 to Munchmuseet. ☎23 49 35 00; www.munch.museum.no. Open June-Aug. daily 10am-6pm, English tours 1pm; Sept.-May Tu-F 10am-4pm, Sa-Su 11am-5pm. 65kr, students 35kr; free with Oslo Pass. AmEx/MC/V.)* The definitive version of *The Scream* is at the **Nasjonalmuseet** (National Art Museum), which also has a collection of works by Cézanne, Gauguin, van Gogh, Matisse, and Picasso, as well as renowned

UP FOR SOME KUBB?

A funny thing might happen walking through Oslo's parks. Out of nowhere, you may stumble upon people throwing wooden sticks at figurines. What's going on here? Are they vandalizing those poor, defenseless figurines?

Closer inspection reveals a whole world of fun you never knew existed—Kubb. No, not the obscure British band of the same name. Kubb is a game, nicknamed "Viking Chess," that combines bowling, chess, and horseshoes. The objective is to knock down your opponent's ten kubbs (rectangular wooden blocks). After taking these down, you move on to eliminate the king kubb—marked by a carved crown—for the win.

Kubb dates back to AD 1000 and was likely played by Vikings. It spread throughout Europe during the Norman conquests. Morbidly, some maintain that the Vikings played with the skulls and bones of their victims rather than wooden blocks. When rampant plundering and using your victims for games went out of fashion, the transition to wooden blocks began. Others believe that wooden blocks have always been used. They are common in Scandinavia, after all, and it would be unfortunate to postpone a game of kubb due to lack of skulls. Talk about a gathering gone badly wrong.

The game involves a surprising amount of strategy. Try your luck, but don't bet your life savings.

Norwegians like Dahl and Sohlberg. *(Universitetsgt. 13. ☎21 98 20 00; www.nasjonalmuseet.no. Open Tu-W and F 10am-6pm, Th 10am-7pm, Sa-Su 10am-5pm. Free.)* Next door at Oslo University's **Aulaen** (Assembly Hall), several of Munch's dreamy, idealistic murals show his interest in bringing art to the masses. *(Enter through the door by the ionic columns off Karl Johans gt. Open June 27-Aug. 3 M-F 10am-4pm. Free.)*

The **Museet for Samtidskunst** (Contemporary Art Museum) displays works by Norwegian artists and rotates its collection frequently. If you can find it, check out Inner Space V, a steel staircase leading to a mysterious corridor with a true "light at the end of the tunnel." *(Bankplassen 4. Take bus #60 or tram #10, 12, 13, or 19 to Kongens gt. ☎22 86 22 10. Open Tu-W and F 11am-5pm, Th 11am-7pm, Sa-Su midnight-5pm. From June to early Sept. English tour Su 2pm. Free.)* Nearby, the private **Astrup Fearnly Museum** of Modern Art has a more international collection, with some striking installations and video pieces. *(Dronningens gt. 4. ☎22 93 60 60; www.afmuseet.no. Open Tu-W and F 11am-5pm, Th 11am-7pm, Sa-Su noon-5pm. Free.)*

AKERSHUS CASTLE AND FORTRESS. Originally constructed in 1299, this waterfront complex was rebuilt as a Renaissance palace after Oslo burned in 1624. Norway's infamous traitor, Vidkun Quisling, was imprisoned here prior to his execution for aiding the 1940 Nazi invasion. *(Tram #12 to Rådhusplassen. ☎23 09 39 17. Complex open daily 6am-9pm. Castle open May-Aug. M-Sa 10am-4pm, Su 12:30-4pm. Sept.-Oct. Th guided tours only in English at noon and 1pm. English and Norwegian guided tours from mid-June to early Aug. Sa-Su 3pm. Grounds free. Castle 65kr, students 45kr; free with Oslo Pass. MC/V.)* The castle grounds include the powerful **Resistance Museum,** which documents Norway's campaign against the Nazi occupation. *(☎23 09 31 38. Open June-Aug. M-F 10am-5pm, Sa-Su 11am-5pm; Sept.-May M-F 10am-4pm, Sa-Su 11am-4pm. 30kr, students 15kr; free to all military personnel. Free with Oslo Pass. MC/V.)* On the other side of the complex is the **Armed Forces Museum** which offers exhibits on the history of Norway's military from the Viking age on into the Cold War. A current temporary exhibit deals with Norwegian UN Peacekeeping. *(☎23 09 35 82. Open May-Aug. M-F 10am-5pm, Sa-Su 11am-5pm; Sept.-Apr. M-F 11am-4pm, Sa-Su 11am-5pm. Free.)*

BYGDØY. Bygdøy peninsula, across the inlet from central Oslo, is mainly residential, but its beaches and museums make it worth a visit. In summer, a public **ferry** leaves from Pier 3, Råhusbrygges, in front of City Hall. *(☎23 35 68 90; www.boatsightseeing.com. 10min.; Apr.-Sept. and from late May to mid-Aug. 2-3 per hr.; 22kr, 30kr on board. Or take bus #30 from*

Oslo S to Folkemuseet or Bygdøynes.) The open-air **Norsk Folkemuseum,** near the ferry's first stop at Dronningen, recreates historical Norway, (especially that of the 18th century) with restored thatch huts, knowledgable actors in period costume, and special performances and demonstrations. *(Walk uphill from the dock and follow signs to the right for 10min., or take bus #30 from Nationaltheatret.* ☎ *22 12 37 00; www. norskfolkemuseum.no. Open mid-May to mid-Sept. daily 10am-6pm; mid-Sept. to mid-May M-F 11am-3pm, Sa-Su 11am-4pm. Fold Dance show June-Aug. Su 2pm. In summer 95kr, students 70kr; in winter 70/50kr. MC/V.)* Down the road (5min.), the **Vikingskipshuset** (Viking Ship Museum) showcases the stunning remains of three well-preserved burial vessels. *(*☎ *22 13 52 83; www.khm.uio.no. Open daily May-Sept. 9am-6pm; Oct.-Apr. 11am-4pm. 50kr, students 35kr; free with Oslo Pass. AmEx/MC/V.)* Then walk down to Bygdøynes, the ferry's second stop, and check out the ◨**Kon-Tiki Museet,** named after a displayed balsa wood raft used on a journey from Lima, Peru to the Polynesian Islands, by Oscar-winning documentarian Thor Heyerdahl. The museum hold all sorts of artifacts from his journeys and efforts to demonstrate the potential for early cross-continental transportation. *(Bygdøynesveien 36.* ☎ *23 08 67 67; www.kon-tiki.no. Open daily June-Aug. 9:30-5:30, April, May, and Sept. 10am-5pm, Mar. and Oct. 10:30am-4pm, and Nov-Feb. 10:30am-3:30pm. 50kr, students 35kr; free with Oslo Pass. AmEx/MC/V.)* Next door, the **Norsk Sjøfartsmuseum** (Norwegian Maritime Museum) is home to a video on Norway's stunning coastline and the country's oldest boat, among other nautical exhibits. Learn about the nation's seafaring history, from log canoes to cruise ships, and enjoy a view of Oslofjord. *(Bygdøynesveien 37.* ☎ *24 11 41 50. Open mid-May to Aug. daily 10am-6pm; Sept. to mid-May M-W and Sa-Su 10:30am-4pm, Th 10:30am-6pm. 40kr, students 25kr. Free with Oslo Pass. MC/V.)* The Arctic exploration vessel **FRAM,** adjacent to the museum, was used on three expeditions in the early 20th century and has advanced farther north and south than any other vessel. Visitors can roam through the well-preserved interior. *(Bygdøynesveien 36.* ☎ *23 28 29 50. Open daily June to Aug. 9am-6:00pm; May and Sept. daily 10am-5pm. Mar., Apr., Oct. daily 10am-4pm. Nov.-Feb. M-F 10am-3pm, Sa-Su 10am-4pm. 50kr, students 20kr; free with Oslo Pass. MC/V.)* The southwestern side of Bygdøy is home to two popular beaches: **Huk** appeals to a younger crowd, while **Paradisbukta** is more family-oriented. The shore between them is a **nude beach.** *(Take bus #30 or walk south for 25min. left along the shore from the Bygdøynes ferry stop.)*

OTHER SIGHTS. The **Royal Palace,** in Slottsparken, is open for guided tours, although tickets sell out ahead. Since it's not included in the Oslo pass, it may be enough just to view the daily changing of the guard at 1:30pm in front of the palace. *(Tram #12, 13, 19, or bus #30-32 to Slottsparken. Open from late June to mid-Aug. English-language tours M-Th, Sa noon, 2, 2:20pm; F and Su 2, 2:20, and 4pm. Buy tickets at post and tourist offices. 95kr, students 85kr.)* The nearby **Ibsenmuseet** (Henrik Ibsen Museum) documents the notoriously private playwright's life with a dramatic exhibition space and guided tours of his last apartment. *(Henrik Ibsens gt. 26.* ☎ *22 12 35 50; www.ibsenmuseet.no. Open from mid-May to mid-Sept. Tu-Su 11am-6pm; from mid-Sept. to mid-May Tu-W and F-Su 11am-4pm, Th 11am-6pm. English- and Norwegian-language tours 7 per day; in winter 3 per day. 45kr; with tour 85kr, students 60kr; free with Oslo Pass. AmEx/ MC/V.)* The **Domkirke,** next to Stortorvet in the city center, is hard to miss. The Lutheran cathedral has a colorful ceiling with biblical motifs. *(Karl Johans gt. 11.* ☎ *23 31 46 00; www.oslodomkirke.no. Open M-Th 10am-4pm, F 10am-4pm and 10pm-midnight, Sa 10am-4pm and 9-11pm. Free.)* The **Nobel Peace Center,** by the harbor, features profiles on all laureates, information on the award and the ceremony, and traveling exhibitions on the main floor dealing with the issues of peace in the world. *(Brynjulf Bulls Plass 1. Tram #12 to Aker Brygge.* ☎ *48 30 10 00; www.nobelpeacecenter.org. Open June-Aug. daily M-W and F-Su 10am-6pm; Th 10am-7pm; Sept.-May Tu, W, F 10am-4pm, Th 10am-7pm, Sa-Su 11am-5pm; 80kr, students 55kr; free with Oslo Pass. MC/V.)* For much of

2009, the facility will be closed for the construction of a new jump in time for trials before it hosts the 2011 World Championships. Take the 1st Subway line toward Frognerseteren to reach the world famous ski stadium **Holmenkollen**. The complex also features the world's oldest ski museum and special exhibitions on Arctic and Antarctic expeditions, A simulator recreates a leap off a ski jump and a blisteringly swift downhill run. *(Kongeveien 5. From the subway, follow the signs uphill 10min. ☎ 22 92 32 00; www.skiforeningen.no. Open daily June-Aug. 9am-8pm; Sept. and May 10am-5pm; Oct.-Apr. 10am-4pm. Museum and tower 70kr, students 60kr; free with Oslo Pass. Simulator 50kr, with Oslo Pass 40kr. AmEx/MC/V.)* **Historical Museum of the University of Oslo** has a variety of exhibits on the history of Norway. *(Frederiks Gate. ☎ 22 85 19 00; www.khm.uio.no. Open from mid-Sept. to mid-May daily 11am-6pm, from mid-May to mid-Sept. Tu-Su 10am-5pm. Free.)* Finally, for those weary of the city, there's the outdoors. **Bike trails** run through the city and along the river Akerelva. In winter, **skiing** (alpine and nordic) is a favorite activity. Supposedly, Norwegians are born with skis on their feet. Check the tourist office for the nearest trails and ski rental.

🎵 🎭 ENTERTAINMENT AND NIGHTLIFE

The monthly *What's On in Oslo*, free at tourist offices and most accommodations, follows the latest in opera, symphony, and theater. **Filmens Hus,** Dronningens gt. 16, is the center of Oslo's indie film scene. (☎22 47 45 00. Check schedule online at www.nfi.no/cinemateket. 75kr per movie, members 45kr; 6 month registration 100kr.) Jazz enthusiasts head to town for the **Oslo Jazz Festival** in mid-August. (☎22 42 91 20, booking ☎81 53 31 33; www.oslojazz. no). Buy tickets to this and other events online at billettservice.no and pick up at any post office. Countless bars along **Karl Johans gate** and in the **Aker Brygge harbor complex** attract a hard-partying crowd, while a mellow mood prevails at the cafe-by-day, bar-by-night lounges along **Thorvald Meyers gate** in Grüner Løkka. Alcohol tends to be expensive out on the town, so young Norwegians have taken to the custom of the *Vorspiel*—gathering at private homes to sip comparatively cheap, store-bought liquor before staggering out to the streets and then reconvening later for a little *nachspiel* (afterparty).

Mono, Pløens gt. 4 (☎22 41 41 66; www.cafemono.no). Jam to classic rock at this popular, funky club. Backyard area is a cafe for drinks during the day. Beer 56kr, 46kr before 6pm. M-Th and Su 20+, F-Sa 22+. 250 concerts a year (not on F). Cover for concerts 80-130kr. Frequent free concerts Sa at 6pm. Open M-Sa 11am-3:30am, Su 1pm-3:30am. Inside club opens around 6pm. MC/V.

Garage, Grensen 9 (☎22 42 37 44; www.garageoslo.no). Live music from across the globe. Rock F-Su. Beer 56kr at night, 46kr during the day. M-Th and Su 20+, F-Sa 22+. Cover for concerts 50-300kr. Open M-Sa 3pm-3:30am, Su 6pm-3:30am. MC/V.

Living Room, Olav V's gt. 1 (☎22 83 63 54; www.living-room.no). Popular lounge morphs into dance floor on weekends. Fairly strict dress code. Beer 61kr. 24+. Cover F-Sa 100kr. Open W-Su 11pm-3am. AmEx/MC/V.

Horgans, Hegdehaugsv. 24 (☎22 60 87 87). Sports bar with plenty of TVs showing the latest games, especially football matches. Also becomes a club on weekends. Beer 48kr Tu-F, 63kr after 9pm F and Sa. 23+. Cover 50kr Sa after midnight. Open Tu-Th 4pm-midnight, F-Sa 5pm-3am, Su 4pm-midnight. AmEx/MC/V.

London Pub, C.J. Hambros pl. 5 (☎22 70 87 00; www.londonpub.no). Entrance on Rosenkrantz gt. Oslo's "gay headquarters" since 1979. Large upstairs dance floor plays a mix of beats. Basement pool tables and bars draws an older crowd. Beer 36-56kr. 20+. Cover F-Sa 40kr. Open daily 3pm-3am. AmEx/MC/V.

Elm Street Rock Cafe, Dronningens gate 32 (☎22 42 14 27). Provides a good place to have a burger (84-136kr) with a lot of free sides and a beer (47kr) before a movie or concert in Oslo. Open M-Sa 11am-3:30am, Su 1pm-3:30am. Kitchen until 9pm. Live music most F and Sa in the summer. Concerts usually 50-100kr.

POLAND
(POLSKA)

Poland is a sprawling country where history has cast a long shadow. Plains that stretch from the Tatras Mountains in the south to the Baltic Sea in the north have seen foreign invaders time and time again. Meanwhile, the contrast between Western cities like Wrocław and Eastern outposts like Bialystok is a remnant of Poland's subjection to competing empires. Ravaged during WWII, and later, viciously suppressed by the USSR, Poland is finally self-governed, and the change is marked. Today's Poland is a haven for budget travelers, where the rich cultural treasures of medieval Kraków and bustlin Warsaw are complemented by wide Baltic beaches, rugged Tatras peaks, and tranquil Mazury lakes.

DISCOVER POLAND: SUGGESTED ITINERARIES

THREE DAYS. In **Kraków** (p. 598), enjoy the stunning **Wawel Castle,** medieval **Stare Miasto,** and bohemian nightlife of the **Kazimierz area.** Daytrip to **Auschwitz-Birkenau** concentration camp (p. 604).

ONE WEEK. After three days in **Kraków** and one daytripping to **Auschwitz,** go to **Warsaw** (3 days; p. 588), where the **Uprising Museum** and **Russian Market** shouldn't be missed.

ESSENTIALS

FACTS AND FIGURES

OFFICIAL NAME: Republic of Poland.

CAPITAL: Warsaw.

MAJOR CITIES: Katowice, Kraków, Łódź.

POPULATION: 38,518,000.

TIME ZONE: GMT +1.

LANGUAGE: Polish.

ANNUAL PORK CONSUMPTION PER CAPITA: 83.2 lbs.

WHEN TO GO

Poland has snowy winters and warm summers, though all weather can be unpredictable. Tourist season runs from late May to early September, except in mountain areas, which also have a winter high-season (Dec.-Mar.). Though rain is a risk in the late spring and early autumn, these months are mild, so travelers may want to consider visiting in late April, September, or early October. Many attractions are closed from mid-autumn to mid-spring.

DOCUMENTS AND FORMALITIES

EMBASSIES AND CONSULATES. Foreign embassies to Poland are in Warsaw and Kraków. For Polish embassies and consulates abroad, contact: **Australia,** 7 Turrana St., Yarralumla, Canberra, ACT 2600 (☎02 62 73 12 08; www.poland.

org.au); **Canada,** 443 Daly Ave., Ottawa, ON K1N 6H3 (☎613-789-0468; www.
polishembassy.ca); **Ireland,** 5 Ailesbury Rd., Ballbridge, Dublin 4 (☎01 283 0855;
www.dublin.polemb.net); **New Zealand,** 51 Granger Rd., Howick, Auckland 1705
(☎09 534 4670; www.polishheritage.co.nz); **UK,** 47 Portland Pl., London W1B
1JH (☎870 774 2700; www.polishembassy.org.uk); **US,** 2640 16th St. NW, Washington, D.C. 20009 (☎202-234-3800 ext. 2140; www.polandembassy.org).

ENTRANCE REQUIREMENTS.
Passport: Required for all travelers.
Visa: Not required for stays of under 90 days for citizens of Australia, Canada, New Zealand, and the US; not required for stays of under 180 days for citizens of the UK.
Letter of Invitation: Not required for most travelers.
Inoculations: Recommended up-to-date DTaP (diphtheria, tetanus, and pertussis), hepatitis A, hepatitis B, MMR, rabies, polio booster, and typhoid.
Work Permit: Required for all non-EU citizens planning to work in Poland.
International Driving Permit: Required for all non-EU citizens.

VISA AND ENTRY INFORMATION. Citizens of Australia, Canada, and the US need a visa for stays of over 90 days. EU citizens do not require a visa but will need to apply for temporary residence after 90 days. Visas for US citizens are free. Processing may take up to two weeks, but express visas can be processed within 24hr. You must be ready to present ample documentation concerning your stay, including verification of accommodation reservations, sufficient funds, and confirmation of health insurance coverage.

TOURIST SERVICES AND MONEY

TOURIST OFFICES. City-specific tourist offices are the most helpful and generally provide free info in English. Most have reliable free **maps** and sell more detailed ones. **Orbis,** the state-sponsored travel bureau, operates hotels in most cities and sells transportation tickets. **Almatur,** a student travel organization with offices in 15 major cities, offers ISICs. The state-sponsored **PTTK** and **IT** bureaus, found in nearly every city, are helpful for basic traveling needs. Try **Polish Pages,** a free guide available at hotels and tourist agencies.

POLISH ZŁOTYCH (ZŁ)		
	AUS$1 = 2.29ZŁ	1ZŁ = AUS$0.44
	CDN$1 = 2.77ZŁ	1ZŁ = CDN$0.36
	EUR€1 = 3.96ZŁ	1ZŁ = EUR€0.25
	NZ$1 = 1.94ZŁ	1ZŁ = NZ$0.52
	UK£1 = 5.74ZŁ	1ZŁ = UK£0.17
	US$1 = 3.09ZŁ	1ZŁ = US$0.32

MONEY. The Polish currency is the **złotych** (zł), plural is **złoty** (zwah-tee). **Inflation** is around 2%. **ATMs** *(bankomaty)* are common, and generally offer the best rates; MasterCard and Visa are widely accepted at ATMs. Budget accommodations rarely accept **credit cards,** but some restaurants and upscale hotels do. **Tipping** varies, but generally a few additional złoty is acceptable.

Poland *Baltic Sea*

HEALTH AND SAFETY

EMERGENCY | **Ambulance:** ☎999. **Fire:** ☎150. **Police:** ☎158. **General Emergency Number:** ☎112.

Medical clinics in major cities have private, **English-speaking doctors.** Expect to pay at least 50zł per visit. **Pharmacies** are well-stocked, and some stay open 24hr. Tap water is theoretically drinkable, but bottled mineral water will spare you from some unpleasant metals and chemicals. **Crime** rates are low, but tourists are sometimes targeted. Watch for muggers and pickpockets, especially on trains and in lower-priced hostels. Cab drivers may attempt to cheat those who do not speak Polish, and "friendly locals" looking to assist tourists are sometimes setting them up for scams. **Women** traveling alone should take the usual precautions. Those with darker skin may encounter discrimination due to long-standing prejudice against **Roma** (gypsies). There may be lingering prejudice against **Jews,** despite governmental efforts; casual anti-Semitic remarks are often heard. Like many Eastern European nations, Poland is not widely **wheelchair-accessible** but special-interest groups, newly armed with EU funds, are working to change that. Warsaw in particular, with its many steep, winding steps, is difficult to access.

Homosexuality is not widely accepted; discretion is advised. GLBT travelers might find www.gaypoland. pl a useful resource.

TRANSPORTATION

BY PLANE. Warsaw's modern **Okęcie Airport (WAW;** ☎22 650 4220; www.lotnisko-chopina.pl) is the hub for intl. flights. **LOT** (☎080 170 3703; www.lot.com), the national airline, flies to major cities in Poland.

BY TRAIN AND BUS. Trains are preferable to buses, since buses are slow and uncomfortable. For a timetable, see www.pkp.pl. *Odjazdy* (departures) are in yellow, *przyjazdy* (arrivals) in white. Inter-City and *ekspresowy* (express) trains are listed in red with an "IC" or "Ex" in front of the train number. *Pośpieszny* (direct; in red) are almost as fast and a bit cheaper. Low-priced *osobowy* (in black) are the slowest and have no restrooms. If you see a boxed "R" on the schedule, ask the clerk for a *miejscówka* (reservation). Students and seniors should buy *ulgowy* (half-price) tickets instead of normal tickets. Beware: foreign travelers are not eligible for discounts on domestic buses and trains. **Eurail** is not valid in Poland. Look for **Wasteels** tickets and **Eurotrain** passes, sold at **Almatur** and **Orbis** for discounts. Stations are not announced and are often poorly marked. In the countryside, PKS markers (yellow steering wheels that look like upside-down Mercedes-Benz symbols) indicate stops. Buses have no luggage compartments. **Polski Express** (☎022 854 02 85; www.polskiexpress.pl), a private company, offers more luxurious service, but does not run to all cities.

Theft frequently occurs on overnight trains; avoid night trains, especially Kraków-Warsaw and Prague-Kraków.

BY CAR AND TAXI. Rental cars are readily available in Warsaw and Kraków. Road conditions are poor and drivers can be aggressive and reckless. For **taxis,** either arrange the price before getting in (in Polish, if possible) or be sure the driver turns on the meter. Arrange cabs by phone, if possible.

BY BIKE AND BY THUMB. Roads in Poland can be difficult for **bikes** to navigate. For more information on cycling, see www.rowery.org.pl. Though legal, **hitchhiking** is rare and dangerous for foreigners. Hand-waving is the accepted sign. *Let's Go* does not recommend hitchhiking.

KEEPING IN TOUCH

PHONE CODES	**Country code: 48. International dialing prefix:** 00. For more information on how to place international calls, see **Inside Back Cover.**

EMAIL AND INTERNET. Internet access is available for about 5-15zł per hr.

TELEPHONE. You can purchase a long distance phone card at many places, including grocery stores. To operate the phone, start dialing the numbers you're given or insert the magnetic card. International access numbers include: **AT&T Direct** (☎00 800 111 111); **Canada Direct** (☎0 800 111 4118); **MCI** (☎00 800 111 2122); **Sprint** (☎00 800 11 3115).

MAIL. Mail in Poland is admirably efficient. Airmail *(lotnicza)* takes two to five days to Western Europe and seven to 10 days to Australia, New Zealand, and the US. Mail can be received via **Poste Restante.** Address mail as follows: First name, LAST NAME, POSTE RESTANTE, post office address, Postal Code, city, POLAND. Letters cost about 2.40zł. To pick up mail, show a passport.

LANGUAGE. **Polish** is a West Slavic language written in the Latin alphabet, and is closely related to **Czech** and **Slovak.** The language varies little across Poland. The two exceptions are in the region of **Kaszuby,** where the distinctive Germanized dialect is sometimes classified as a separate language, and in **Karpaty,** known for highlander accents. In western Poland and Mazury, **German** is the most common foreign language, although many Poles in big cities, especially young people, speak **English.** One more thing: the English word "no" means "yes" in Polish. For basic Polish words and phrases, see **Phrasebook: Polish,** p. 791.

ACCOMMODATIONS AND CAMPING

POLAND	❶	❷	❸	❹	❺
ACCOMMODATIONS	under 45zł	45-65zł	66-80zł	81-120zł	over 120zł

Hostels *(schroniska młodzieżowe)* abound and cost 30-60zł per night. They are often booked solid by tour groups; call at least a week ahead. **PTSM** is the national hostel organization. **University dorms** become budget housing in July and August; these are an especially good option in Kraków. The **Almatur** office in Warsaw arranges stays throughout Poland. PTTK runs hotels called **Dom Turysty,** which have multi-bed rooms and budget singles and doubles. These hotels generally cost 80-180zł. **Pensions** are often the best deal: the owner's service more than makes up for the small sacrifice in privacy. **Private rooms** *(wolne pokoje)* are available most places, but be careful what you agree to; they should only cost 20-60zł. **Homestays** can be a great way to meet locals; inquire at the tourist office. **Campsites** average 10-15zł per person or 20zł with a car. Campgrounds may also rent out **bungalows;** a bed costs 20-30zł. *Polska Mapa Campingów,* available at tourist offices, lists campsites. Almatur runs a number of sites in summer; ask them for a list. Camping outside of official campsites is illegal.

FOOD AND DRINK

POLAND	❶	❷	❸	❹	❺
FOOD	under 8zł	8-17zł	18-30zł	31-45zł	over 45zł

POLAND

Polish cuisine derives from French, Italian, and Slavic traditions. Meals begin with **soup**, usually *barszcz* (beet or rye), *chłodnik* (cold beets with buttermilk and eggs), *ogórkowa* (sour cucumbers), or *kapuśniak* (cabbage). Main courses include *gołąbki* (cabbage rolls with meat and rice), *kotlet schabowy* (pork cutlets), *naleśniki* (crepes), and *pierogi* (dumplings). **Kosher** eating is next to impossible, as most Jewish restaurants are not actually kosher. Poland offers a wealth of **beer, vodka,** and **spiced liquor. Żywiec** is the most popular beer. Even those who dislike beer will enjoy sweet **piwo z sokiem,** beer with raspberry syrup. *Wyborowa, Żytnia,* and *Polonez* are popular *wódka* (vodka) brands, while *Belweder* (Belvedere) is a major alcoholic export. *Żubrówka* vodka, also known as "Bison grass vodka," comes packaged with a blade of grass from the Bialowieża forest. It's often mixed with *z sokem jabłkowym* (apple juice). *Miód* (beer made with honey) and *krupnik* (mead) are old-fashioned favorites; as is *nalewka na porzeczce* (black currant vodka).

HOLIDAYS AND FESTIVALS

Holidays: Easter (Apr. 13, 2009; Apr. 4, 2010); May Day (May 1); Constitution Day (May 3); Pentecost (May 31, 2009; May 23, 2010); Corpus Christi (June 11, 2009; May 23, 2010); Assumption Day (Aug. 15); All Saints' Day (Nov. 1); Independence Day (Nov. 11); Christmas (Dec. 25).

Festivals: Unsurprisingly, many of the festivals revolve around Catholic holidays. Uniquely Polish festivals include all-night bonfire merrymaking before **St. John's Day** in June, also known as midsummer, as well as an annual August **folk festival** in Kraków.

BEYOND TOURISM

Auschwitz Jewish Center, Auschwitz Jewish Center Foundation, 36 Battery Pl., New York, NY 10280, USA (☎646-437-4276; www.ajcf.org). Offers fully paid 6-week programs for college graduates and graduate students in Oswiecim. Program focuses on cultural exchange and the study of pre-war Jewish life in Poland, with visits to the Auschwitz-Birkenau State Museum and other sites.

Jagiellonian University, Centre for European Studies, ul. Garbarska 7a, 31-131 Kraków, Poland (☎481 24 29 62 07; www.ces.uj.edu.pl). University founded in 1364 offers undergraduates summer- and semester-long programs in Central European studies and Polish language. One semester of tuition is US$3800. Scholarships available.

WARSAW (WARSZAWA)   ☎022

Massive rebuilding is nothing new for Warsaw (pop. 1,700,000). At the end of World War II, two-thirds of its population had been killed and 83% of the city was destroyed by the Nazis as revenge for the 1944 Warsaw Uprising. Having weathered the further blow of a half-century of communist rule, Warsaw has sprung back to life as a dynamic center of business, politics, and culture— evidenced by the gleaming new skyscrapers popping up next to crumbling concrete. With Poland's recent accession into the European Union, the city is transforming its culture and landscape at an even faster pace. Now is the time to visit this compelling and underrated city.

TRANSPORTATION

Flights: Port Lotniczy Warszawa-Okęcie ("Terminal 1"), Żwirki i Wigury (info desk ☎022 650 4100, reservations ☎0 801 300 952). Take bus #175 to the city center (after 10:40pm, bus #611); buy tickets at the Ruch kiosk at the top of the escalator in the arrivals hall. (Open M-F 5:30am-10:30pm.) If you arrive past 10:30pm, buy tickets from the bus driver for a 3zł surcharge (students 1.50zł). The IT *(Informacja Turystyczna)* office is in the arrivals hall (see **Tourist Offices, p. 591**). Open M-F 8am-8pm.

Trains: Warszawa Centralna, al. Jerozolimskie 54 (☎022 94 36; www.intercity.pkp.pl), is the most convenient of Warsaw's 3 major train stations. Most trains also stop at **Warszawa Zachodnia (Western Station)**, Towarowa 1, and **Warszawa Wschodnia (Eastern Station)**, Lubelska 1, in Praga. Yellow signs list departures *(odjazdy);* white signs list arrivals *(przyjazdy).* English is rarely understood; write down when and where you want to go, then ask *"Który peron?"* ("Which platform?"). Prices listed are for IC (intercity) trains and normale (2nd class) fares. To: **Gdańsk** (4hr., 20 per day, 47-90zł); **Kraków** (3-5hr., 30 per day, 47-89zł); **Łódz** (1-2hr., 13 per day, 31zł); **Lublin** (2-3hr., 17 per day, 35zł); **Poznań** (2-3hr., 20 per day, 46-89zł); **Wrocław** (4-6hr., 12 per day, 50-96zł); **Berlin, GER** (6hr., 6 per day, €29-45); **Budapest, HUN** (10-13hr., 1 per day, 280zł); **Prague, CZR** (9-12hr., 2 per day, 270-310zł).

Buses: Both **Polski Express** and **PKS** buses run out of Warsaw.

Polski Express, al. Jana Pawła II (☎022 854 0285), in a kiosk next to Warszawa Centralna. Faster than PKS. Kiosk open daily 6:30am-10pm. To: **Gdansk** (6hr., 2 per day, 60zł); **Kraków** (8hr., 2 per day, 69zł); **Łódz** (2hr., 7 per day, 25zł); **Lublin** (3hr., 7 per day, 41zł).

PKS Warszawa Zachodnia, al. Jerozolimskie 144 (☎022 822 4811, domestic info ☎03 00 30 01 30, from cell phones ☎720 8383; www.pks.warszawa.pl), connected by tunnels to the Warszawa Zachodnia train station. Cross to far side al. Jerozolimskie and take bus #127, 130, 508, or E5 to the center. To: **Gdansk** (5-7hr., 18 per day, 35-51zł); **Kraków** (5-7hr., 8 per day, 40zł); **Lublin** (3hr., 9 per day, 22-30zł); **Torun** (4hr., 12 per day, 32zł); **Wrocław** (6-8hr., 4 per day, 43zł); **Kyiv, UKR** (14hr., 1 per day, 155zł); **Vilnius, LIT** (9hr., 3 per day, 115zł).

Centrum Podróży AURA, Jerozolimskie 144 (☎022 659 4785; www.aura.pl), at the Zachodnia station, left of the entrance. Books international buses to: **Amsterdam, NTH** (23hr., 2 per day, 209-279zł); **Geneva, SWI** (27hr., 2 per day, 269-320zł); **London, GBR** (27hr., 3 per day, 280-450zł); **Paris, FRA** (25hr., 1-3 per day, 220-334zł); **Prague, CZR** (28hr.; 3 per week; 115-145zł); **Rome, ITA** (28hr., 1 per day, 249-418zł).

Public Transportation: (info line ☎022 94 84; www.ztm.waw.pl). Warsaw's public transit is excellent. Daytime **trams** and **buses** 2.40zł, with ISIC 1.25zł; day pass 7.20/3.70zł; weekly pass 26/12zł. Punch the ticket in the yellow machines on board or face a 120zł fine. If you find that you're the only one validating your ticket, remember that many locals carry 90-day passes. Bus, tram, and subway lines share the same tickets, passes, and prices. There are also 2 **sightseeing bus routes:** #180 (M-F) and #100 (Sa-Su). Purchase an all-day ticket and you can hop on and off the bus. Night buses cost double, have "N" prefixes, and run 11:30pm-5:30am. If you need to use one, ask at a tourist bureau or accommodation to explain the system for ordering them; without an order, they won't stop. Warsaw's **Metro** is not particularly convenient for tourists.

Taxis: The government sets cab fare at 2zł per km; with privately run cabs, stated prices may be lower but the risk of overcharging is greater. State-run: **ME.RC. Taxi** (☎022 677 7777), **Wawa Taxi** (☎96 44). Privately run: **Euro Taxi** (☎96 62), **Halo Taxi** (☎96 23).

ORIENTATION

The most prominent section of Warsaw lies west of the **Wisla River.** The city's grid layout and efficient public transportation make it very accessible. **Aleje Jerozolimskie** is the main east-west thoroughfare. **Warszawa Centralna,** the main train station, is at the intersection of al. Jerozolimskie and **al. Jana Pawła II,** the

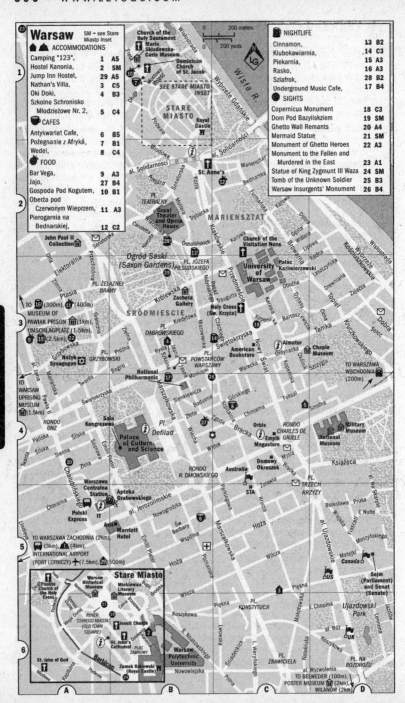

Warsaw SM = see Stare Miasto Inset

🏠🏠 ACCOMMODATIONS

Camping "123",	1	A5
Hostel Kanonia,	2	SM
Jump Inn Hostel,	29	A5
Nathan's Villa,	3	C5
Oki Doki,	4	B3
Szkolne Schronisko		
Młodzieżowe Nr. 2,	5	C4

☕ CAFES

Antykwariat Cafe,	6	B5
Pożegnanie z Afryką,	7	B1
Wedel,	8	C4

🍴 FOOD

Bar Vega,	9	A3
Jajo,	27	B4
Gospoda Pod Kogutem,	10	B1
Oberża pod		
Czerwonym Wieprzem,	11	A3
Pierogarnia na		
Bednarskiej,	12	C2

🎵 NIGHTLIFE

Cinnamon,	13	B2
Klubokawiarnia,	14	C3
Piekarnia,	15	A3
Rasko,	16	A3
Szlafrok,	28	B2
Underground Music Cafe,	17	B4

👁 SIGHTS

Copernicus Monument	18	C3
Dom Pod Bazyliszkiem	19	SM
Ghetto Wall Remants	20	A4
Mermaid Statue	21	SM
Monument of Ghetto Heroes	22	A3
Monument to the Fallen and		
Murdered in the East	23	A1
Statue of King Zygmunt III Waza	24	SM
Tomb of the Unknown Soldier	25	B3
Warsaw Insurgents' Monument	26	B4

POLAND

north-south street one block west of Marsza kowska. The northern boundary of pl. Defilad is **Świętokrzyska,** another east-west thoroughfare. Intersecting al. Jerozolimskie one city block east of Marsza kowska and the city center, the **Trakt Królewski (Royal Way)** takes different names as it runs north-south. This elegant promenade begins as **Nowy Swiat** in the city center and then turns into **Krakowskie Przedmiescie** as it leads into Stare Miasto (Old Town; just north of al. Solidarnosci overlooking the Wisla). Going south, the road becomes **al. Ujazdowskie** as it runs past embassy row, palaces, and Łazienki Park, all to the south the city center. **Praga,** the part of the city on the east bank of the Wisla, is accessible by tram via **al. Jerozolimskie** and **al. Solidarnosci.** In Praga, the two most trafficked north-south thoroughfares are **Targowa,** near the zoo, and **Francuska,** south of al. Jerozolimskie.

▞ PRACTICAL INFORMATION

Tourist Offices: Informacji Turystyczna (IT), al. Jerozolimskie 54 (☎94 31; www.warsawtour.pl), inside Centralna train station. Provides **maps** and arranges accommodations (no fee). Their free booklets list popular restaurants and special events. Open daily May-Sept. 8am-8pm; Oct.-Apr. 8am-6pm. **Branches:** Krakowskie Przedmieście 39. Open daily, same hours. In the airport, open daily, same hours. Pl. Zamkowy 1/13 (outside the Stare Miasto). Open M-F 9am-6pm, Sa 10am-6pm, Su 11am-6pm.

Budget Travel: Almatur, Kopernika 23 (☎022 826 3512). ISIC 69zł. Open M-F 9am-7pm, Sa 10am-3pm. AmEx/MC/V. **Orbis,** Bracka 16 (☎022 827 7140), entrance on al. Jerozolimskie. Open M-F 9am-6pm, Sa 10am-6pm. MC/V.

Embassies: Most are near al. Ujazdowskie. **Australia,** Nowogrodzka 11 (☎022 521 3444; ambasada@australia.pl). Open M-F 9am-1pm and 2-5pm. **Canada,** ul. Jana Matejiki 1/5 (☎022 584 3100; wsaw@international.gc.ca). Open M-F 8:30am-4:30pm. **Ireland,** Mysia 5 (☎022 849 6633; ambasada@irlandial.pl). Open M-F 9am-1pm. **UK,** al. Róz (☎022 311 0000). Open M-F 8:30am-4:30pm. **US,** ul. Piękna 12 (☎022 625 1401 or ☎022 504 2784). Open M, W, F 9am-noon, Tu, Th 9am-3pm.

Currency Exchange: Except at tourist sights, *kantory* (exchange booths) have the best rates. 24hr. at Warszawa Centralna or at al. Jerozolimskie 61.

Luggage Storage (Kasa Bagażowa): At Warszawa Centralna train station. 7zł per item per day, plus 3zł per 50zł of declared value if you want insurance. To sidestep the language barrier and to retain more control over your bag, choose a locker (8zł). Open 24hr.

GLBT Resources: Lambda, (☎022 628 5222; www.lambda.org.pl), in English and Polish. Open Tu-W 6-9pm, F 4-10pm. Info at the English-language site http://warsaw.gayguide. net. The GLBT scene in Warsaw is discreet and lacks widespread political support.

24hr. Pharmacy: Apteka Grabowskiego "21" (☎022 825 6986), upstairs at the Warszawa Centralna train station. AmEx/MC/V.

Medical Services: Centrum Medyczne LIM, al. Jerozolimskie 65/79, 9th fl. (24hr. **emergency line** ☎022 458 7000, 24hr. **ambulance** ☎430 3030; www.cm-lim.com.pl), at the Marriott. There are English-speaking doctors available. Open M-F 7am-9pm, Sa 8am-4pm, Su 9am-6pm, holidays 9am-1pm. Find another branch at **Domaniewski 41** (☎022 458 7000). Open M-F 7am-9pm, Sa 8am-8pm. **Central Emergency Station,** Hoża 56 (☎999) has a 24hr. ambulance on call.

Telephones: Directory assistance ☎022 118 913.

Post Office: Main branch, Świętokrzyska 31/33 (☎022 827 0052). Take a number at the entrance. For stamps and letters push "D"; for packages, "F." For **Poste Restante,** inquire at window #42. Open 24hr. *Kantor* open daily 8am-10pm. Most other branches open 8am-8pm. **Postal Code:** 00001.

ACCOMMODATIONS

Although accommodation options are rapidly improving, demand still outpaces supply, so reserve ahead, especially in summer. **Informacji Turystyczna** (IT; p. 591) maintains a list of accommodations in the city, including **private rooms,** and also arranges stays in **university dorms** (25-30zł) July through September.

Oki Doki, pl. Dabrowskiego 3 (☎022 826 5112; www.okidoki.pl). From Marszałkowska, turn right onto ul. Rysia, the hostel will be on your right., Each room of this chic hostel was designed by a different Warsaw artist and has a unique theme. Beer (6zł) and breakfast (10zł) in the dining room/bar (open until 1am or later). Laundry 10zł. Free Internet and Wi-Fi. Bike rental 25zł per day, 6zł per hr. 24hr. reception. Check-in 3pm. Check-out 11am. Reserve ahead. May-Aug. dorms 45-60zł; singles 110zł; doubles 135zł, with baths 185zł. Sept.-Apr. prices tend to decrease by around 5zł. MC/V. ❷

Jump Inn Hostel, Prokuratorska 2 (☎022 825 1167; www.jumpinnhostel.com) From pl. Defilad, head south on Marszałkowska for 10 minutes, take a right on Wawelska, then a right on Prokuratorska—the hostel is on your right. Located in a peaceful residential area, Jump Inn provides a home away from home with its warm, spacious rooms and extensive amenities, including free Internet, laundry, and kitchen access. Hostel guests give particular props to the free afternoon soup. Breakfast and linens included. Reception 24hr. Dorms 40-65zł, singles 100-150zł. MC/V. ❷

Nathan's Villa, Piękna 24/26 (☎050 935 8487; www.nathansvilla.com). From pl. Defilad, take any tram south on Marszałkowska to pl. Konstytucji. Go left on Piękna; the hostel is on the left. Nathan's matches a fun-loving, intimate atmosphere with unparalleled facilities and services. Though guests have been known to pass out on the lawn of this relentlessly hard-partying hostel, the rooms gleam with bright colors and brand-new furniture. Breakfast included. Free laundry. Free Internet and Wi-Fi. Reception 24hr. Dorms 40-60zł; private rooms 120-140zł. MC/V. ❷

Hostel Kanonia, ul. Jezuicka 2 (☎022 635 0676; www.kanonia.pl). Tucked into an alley right in the thick of Stare Miasto, this hostel's romantic decor and riverfront views soften the spartan rooms. Kitchen and common area. Breakfast 20zł. Free Internet and Wi-Fi. Check-in 2pm. Check-out 10am. Dorms 40-60zł; doubles 150zł. ISIC discount. ❷

Szkolne Schronisko Młodzieżowe nr. 2, Smolna 30 (☎022 827 8952), 2 blocks up Smolna from Nowy Swiat, on the left. From Centralna Station, take any tram east on al. Jerozolimskie and get off at Rondo Charles de Gaulle. The well-kept rooms of this sunny hostel exude respectability, and the central location can't be beat. Large kitchen. A/C. Free lockers and linen. Reception 24hr., but front doors locked midnight-6am. Lockout 10am-4pm. Curfew midnight. Dorms 36zł; singles 65zł. Cash only. ❶

Camping "123," Bitwy Warszawskiej 15/17 (☎022 823 3748). From Warszawa Centralna, take bus #127, 130, 508, or 517 to Zachodnia bus station. Cross to the far side of al. Jerozolimskie and take the pedestrian path west to Bitwy Warszawskiej; turn left. The campground is on the right. This tranquil campground is close to the center. Guarded 24hr. Open May-Sept. 12zł per person, 14zł per tent, 55.-65zł for campsites with electricity (labeled "stream," a literal translation of the Polish word for electricity). Singles 45zł; doubles 70zł; triples 100zł; quads 120zł. AmEx/MC/V. ❶

POLAND

FOOD

At roadside stands, the food of choice is the *kebab turecki,* a pita with spicy meat, cabbage, and pickles (5-10zł). The **Kebab Bar,** ul. Nowy Świat 31, is a stand that serves up an excellent version. **MarcPol,** on ul. Marszałkowska, is a conveniently located grocery store (M-Sa 10am-7pm, Su 10am-5pm).

RESTAURANTS

▨ **Gospoda Pod Kogutem,** Freta 48 (☎022 635 8282; www.gospodapodkogutem. pl). A rare find in touristy Stare Miasto: generous portions of delectable local food. The place to try something shamelessly traditional, like Polish-style *golonka* (pig's knuckle; 21zł) or *smalec*, surprisingly tasty fried bits of lard. Entrees 17-45zł. Open M noon-midnight, Tu-Su 11am-midnight. MC/V. ❷

Oberża pod Czerwonym Wieprzem, Żelazna 68 (☎022 850 3144; www.czerwonywieprz. pl). Donning a beret and a military-style mini-dress, an ironically cheerful hostess welcomes diners to this playful exploitation of Poland's communist past. The satire continues with a menu offering separate, cheaper dishes "for the proletariat" and more expensive selections "for dignitaries and the bourgeoisie." Entrees 11-24zł for the proletariat, 26-55zł for dignitaries and the bourgeoisie. Daily 11am-midnight. MC/V/AmEx. ❸

Jajo, ul. Zgoda 3 (☎022 826 4493). In the heart of Warsaw's commercial district, this Italian bistro combines an array of entrees (18-32zł) in a refreshingly sophisticated setting. The 3-course lunch menu, including a starter, entree, and a glass of wine, is a steal at just 20zł. Open M-Sa 10am-midnight, Su noon-9pm. AmEx/MC/V. ❷

Pierogarnia na Bednarskiej, ul. Bednarka 28/30 (☎022 828 0392), on a side street west of ul. Krakówscie Przedmiescie. Locals get their pierogi fix at this tiny, pleasant, and tavernesque shop; you don't even have to wait—they keep new pierogi boiling constantly. 3 pierogi 6zl. Open daily 11am-9pm. Cash only. ❶

Bar Vega, al. Jana Pawła II 36c (☎022 652 2754), near the former Ghetto. Secluded from the bustle of al. Jana Pawła II street vendors, the colorful Bar Vega serves a full vegetarian Indian meal for about the price of a coffee on Nowy Świat (small or big plate; 8 or 12zł, respectively). Bar Vega also funds a nonprofit to feed Warsaw's homeless children. Open M-F 11am-8pm, Sa-Su noon-7pm. Cash only. ❶

CAFES

▨ **Pożegnanie z Afryką** (Out of Africa), Freta 4/6. (☎501 383 094). This Polish chain of cafes brews consistently incredible coffee (9-15zł). Perfect for artsy romancing. In warm weather, enjoy the Stare Miasto sidewalk seating and the iced coffee (9zł). Branches throughout the city. Open daily 8am-10pm. Cash only.

▨ **Antykwariat Cafe,** Żurawia 45 (☎022 629 9929). Extending far into the courtyard beyond, Antykwariat ("Antiquarian") provides a coffee shop for all tastes. Each of its 4 rooms presents a different theme, from the "library room" with its shelves of rare books to the Japanese-inspired nook in the back. Delicate cups of coffee (5-17zł) and many varieties of tea (5zł) served with a wrapped chocolate. Also serves beer, wine, and desserts. Open M-Sa 4pm-11pm. Cash only.

Wedel, Szpitalna 17 (☎022 827 2916). The Emil Wedel house, built in 1893 for the Polish chocolate tycoon, was one of the few buildings in Warsaw to survive WWII. Its 1st fl. now houses an elegant dessert cafe. The glass chandeliers and dark marble columns of this chocolate-themed cafe offer a rare glimpse of pre-war Warsaw. Enjoy the suspicion that you've traveled back in time, along with a cup of miraculously rich hot chocolate (11zł) served alongside Wedel's selection of delectable cakes and ice cream concoctions. The adjacent **Wedel Chocolate** company store serves an array of brightly-wrapped truffles and chocolates. Open M-Sa 8am-10pm, Su 11am-8pm. AmEx/MC/V.

⊙ SIGHTS

To sightsee, trying using the bus. The bus routes #100 and 180 are convenient; they begin at pl. Zamkowy and run along pl. Teatralny, Marszalkowska, al. Ujazdowskie, and Lazienki Park. The routes then run back up the Royal Way, and go through Praga before returning to pl. Zamkowy.

STARE AND NOWE MIASTO. Warsaw's postwar reconstruction shows its finest face in Stare Miasto (Old Town), which features cobblestoned streets and colorful facades. *(Take bus #175 or E3 from the city center to Miodowa.)* The landmark **Statue of King Zygmunt III Waza,** constructed in 1644 to honor the king who moved the capital from Kraków to Warsaw, towers over the entrance. To its right stands the impressive **Royal Castle** *(Zamek Królewski)*, the royal residence from the 16th to 19th century. When the Nazis plundered and burned the castle in 1939, many Varsovians risked their lives hiding its priceless works. Today, the ◧**Royal Castle Museum** houses these rescued treasures. It also has artifacts, paintings, and the stunning Royal Apartments. The massive spherical ballroom and the river-front courtyard are particularly beautiful. *(Pl. Zamkowy 4. ☎022 355 5170; www.zamek-krolewski.art.pl. Tickets and guides inside the courtyard. Open M and Su 11am-6pm, Tu-Sa 10am-6pm. 20zl, students 13zl. Free highlights tour Su 11am-6pm. English-language tour M-Sa, 85zl per group. AmEx/MC/V.)* Across Świętojańska sits Warsaw's oldest church, **St. John's Cathedral** *(Katedra św. Jana)*, which was destroyed in the 1944 Uprising but rebuilt after the war. *(Open daily 10am-1pm and 3-5:30pm. Crypts 1zl.)*

Świętojańska leads to the restored Renaissance and Baroque **Rynek Starego Miasta** (Old Town Square); the statue of the **Warsaw Mermaid** *(Warszawa Syrenka)* marks the center. According to legend, a greedy merchant kidnapped the mermaid from the Wisła River, but local fishermen valiantly rescued her. In return, she swore to defend the city, protecting it with a shield and raised sword. Ul. Krzywe Koło runs from the northeast corner of the Rynek to the restored **Barbican** (barbakan), a rare example of 16th-century Polish fortification. It's also popular spot to relax. The Barbican opens onto Freta, the edge of **Nowe Miasto** (New Town). Nobel Prize-winning physicist and chemist **Marie Curie** was born at Freta 16 in 1867. The house is now a museum. *(☎022 831 8092. Open Tu-Sa 10am-4pm, Su 10am-3pm. 6zl, students 3zl.)*

TRAKT KRÓLEWSKI. The Trakt Królewski (Royal Way) begins at the entrance to Stare Miasto on pl. Zamkowy and stretches 4km south toward Kraków, the former capital. On the left after pl. Zamkowy, the 15th-century **St. Anne's Church** *(Kościół św. Anny)* features a striking interior with its onyx statues, gilded chandeliers, and towering paintings. *(Open daily dawn-dusk.)* ◧**Frederick Chopin** grew up near Krakówskie Przedmieście and gave his first public concert in **Pałac Radziwiłłów,** now the Polish presidential mansion guarded by four stone lions and the military police. A block down the road, set back from the street behind a grove of trees, the **Church of the Visitation Nuns** (Kościół Wizytówek) once rang with Chopin's Romantic chords. *(Open daily dawn-1pm and 3pm-dusk.)* Though the composer died abroad, his heart belongs to Poland; it now rests in an urn in **Holy Cross Church.** *(Kosciól sw. Krzyża. Krakówskie Przedmiescie 3. Open daily dawn-dusk.)*

The Royal Way continues down fashionable **Nowy Świat.** Turn left at Rondo Charles de Gaulle to reach Poland's largest museum, the **National Museum** (Muzeum Narodowe), which holds 16th- to 20th-century paintings in addition to a large collection of ancient and medieval artifacts. *(Al. Jerozolimskie 3. ☎022 022 629 3093, English-language tours 022 629 5060; www.mnw.art.pl. Open Tu-Su 10am-5pm. Permanent exhibits 12zl, students 7zl. Special exhibits 17/10zl. English-language tours 50zl; call 1 week ahead. AmEx/MC/V.)* Farther down, the Royal Way becomes al. Ujazdowskie and runs alongside **Łazienki Park** (Palac Łazienkowski), which houses the striking Neoclassical **Palace on Water** (Pałac na Wodzie). Buildings in the park feature rotating art exhibits. *(Bus #116, 180, or 195 from Nowy Świat or #119 from pl. Defilad to Bagatela. Park open daily dawn-dusk. Palace open Tu-Su 9am-4pm. 12zl, students 9zl.)* Just north of the park, off ul. Agrykola, the **Center of Contemporary Art** (Centrum Sztuki Wspólczesnej), al. Ujazdowskie 6, hosts multimedia exhibitions in the reconstructed 17th-century Ujazdowskie Castle. (☎ 022 62 81 27 13; www.csw.art.pl. Open Tu-Th and Sa-Su 11am-7pm, F 11am-9pm. 12zł, students 6zł. Cash only.)

FORMER GHETTO AND SYNAGOGUE. Walled **Muranów**, Warsaw's former ghetto, holds few traces of the nearly 400,000 Jews who made up one-third of the city's pre-war population. Built in the 1830s, the **Museum of Pawiak Prison** (Muzeum Więzienia Pawiaka) exhibits former inmates' photography and poetry. Over 100,000 Polish Jews were imprisoned here from 1939 to 1944. A dead tree outside bears the names of over 30,000 prisoners killed during WWII. (Dzielna 24/26. ☎ 022 831 92 89. Open W 9am-5pm, Th and Sa 9am-4pm, F 10am-5pm, Su 10am-4pm. Donation requested.) Follow al. Jana Pawła II, take a left on Anielewicza, and walk five blocks to reach the **Jewish Cemetery** (Cmentarz Żydowski). The thickly wooded cemetery holds the remains of socialist Ferdinand Lasalle, the families of physicist Max Born and chemist Fritz Haber, and writer Thomas Mann's wife. (Ślężna 37/39. Tram #9 to Ślężna. ☎ 022 791 5904. Open Apr.-Oct. daily 9am-6pm. 5zł, students 3zł. Free English- and Polish-language tours Su noon.) The restored **Nożyk Synagogue** (Synagoga Nożyka) was the city's only synagogue to survive WWII and now serves as the spiritual home for the 500 observant Jews remaining in Warsaw. (Twarda 6. From the center, take any tram along al. Jana Pawła II to Rondo Onz. Turn right on Twarda and left at Teatr Żydowski, the Jewish Theater. ☎ 022 620 3496. Open M-F and Su Apr.-Oct. 10am-5pm; Nov.-Feb. 10am-3pm. Closed Jewish holidays. Morning and evening prayer daily. 5zł.)

ELSEWHERE IN WARSAW. Warsaw's commercial district, southwest of Stare Miasto, is dominated by the 52-story Stalinist **Palace of Culture and Science** (Pałac Kultury i Nauki, PKiN) on Marszałkowska, which contains a string of popular shops on the ground floor and offices on the higher floors. Locals claim the view from the top is the best in Warsaw—largely because you can't see the building itself. (☎ 022 656 6000. Open daily 9am-8pm, with a special night viewing F-Sa from 8pm-11pm. Observation deck on 33rd fl. 20zł, students 15zł.) Though a bit far from the city center, the new ⬛**Warsaw Uprising Museum** is a must-see. Educational without being pedantic and somber without being heavy-handed, it recounts the tragic 1944 Uprising with full-scale replica bunkers and ruins haunted by the sound of approaching bombs. (Grzybowska 79, enter on Przyokopowa. From the center, take tram #12, 20, or 22 to Grzybowska; the museum is on the left. ☎ 022 539 79 01; www.1944.pl. Multimedia presentations have English-language subtitles. Open M, W, F 8am-6pm, Th 8am-8pm, Sa-Su 10am-6pm. 4zł, students 2zł; Su free. Cash only.)

PRAGA. Across the Wisla River from central Warsaw, the formerly run-down district of Praga is undergoing a renaissance and becoming increasingly more touristed. The gleaming onion domes and cupola of the **St. Mary Magdalene Cathedral** hint at the pre-Soviet Russian presence in Warsaw. (Al. Solidarnosci 52. From Russian Market, take tram #2, 8, 12, or 25 to the intersection of Targowa and al.Solidarnosci; church is across the street on the left. ☎ 022 619 8467. Open M and Su 1-4pm, Tu-Sa 11am-3pm.) With two tall spires, the pointed arches, and the long nave reconstructed in 1972, the **St. Michael** and **St. Florian Cathedral** is less restrained than Stare Miasto's churches. (Florianska 3, 1 block from St. Mary Magdalene. ☎ 022 619 0960; www.katedra-floriana.wpraga.opoka.org.pl.) Across the street, **Praski Park** contains the **Island of Bears**, a manmade island on which bears have been kept since 1949. (Free.)

WILANÓW. In 1677, King Jan III Sobieski bought the sleepy village of Milanowo and rebuilt the existing mansion into a Baroque palace. Since 1805, **Pałac Wilanowski**, south of Warsaw, has served as a public museum and a residence for the Polish state's highest-ranking guests. Surrounded by elegant gardens, the palace is filled with frescoed rooms, portraits, and extravagant royal apartments. (Take bus #180 from Krakówskie Przedmiesce, #516 or 519 from Marszałkowska south to Wilanów. From the bus stop, cross the highway and follow signs. ☎ 022 842 8101; www.wilanow-

POLAND

palac.art.pl. Open May 1 to mid-Sept. M,W, Sa 9:30am-6:30pm, Tu,Th, F 9:30am-4:30pm, and Su 10:30am-6:30pm; mid-Sept. to mid-Dec. and late Feb.-Apr. 30 M and W-Sa 9:30am-4:30pm, Su 10:30am-4:30pm. Last entry 1hr. before closing. Gardens open M and W-F 9:30am-dusk. Wilanów 23zł, students 15zł; Su free. Gardens 5/3zł. Cash only.)

🎭 ENTERTAINMENT AND NIGHTLIFE

Warsaw offers a variety of live music options, and free outdoor concerts abound in summer. Classical music performances rarely sell out; standby tickets cost as little as 10zł. Inquire at the **Warsaw Music Society** (Warszawskie Towarzystwo Muzyczne), ul. Morskie Oko 2 (☎022 849 5651). Take tram #4, 18, 19, 35, or 36 to Morskie Oko from ul. Marszałkowska. Nearby Łazienki Park has free Sunday performances at the **Chopin Monument** (Pomnik Chopina; concerts mid-May to Sept. Su noon, 4pm). Jazz Klub **Tygmont** (☎022 828 3409; www.tygmont.com. pl. Open daily 4pm-4am.), ul. Mazowiecka 6/8, hosts free concerts on weekday evenings. From July through September, the Old Market Square of Stare Miasto swings with free jazz nightly at 7pm.

Teatr Dramatyczny, in the Pałac Kultury, has a stage for big productions and a theater for avant-garde works. (☎022 656 6865; www.teatrdramatyczny.pl. 20-40zł; standby tickets 12-18zł.) The **Montownia Artistic Theater,** ul. Konopnickiej 6, shows a number of independent productions and frequent plays in English. (☎022 339 0760; www.montownia.art.pl. **Kinoteka** (☎022 826 1961), in the Pałac Kultury, features Hollywood blockbusters. **Kino Lab,** ul. Ujazdowskie 6 (☎022 628 1271), shows independent films. See **Center for Contemporary Art,** p. 594.

Warsaw buzzes with activity during the evenings. *Kawiarnie* (cafes) around Stare Miasto and ul. Nowy Świat are open late, and pubs with live music attract crowds. In summer, outdoor beer gardens complement the pub scene. Several publications, including *Gazeta Wyborcza,* list gay nightlife.

🏛 **Piekarnia,** Młocinska 11 (☎022 636 4979; www.pieksa.pl). Take the #22 tram to Rondo Babka and backtrack on Okopowa. Make a right on Powiazkowska, a right on Burakowa, and a right on Młocinska. The unmarked club will be down the road on your left. This Warsaw institution is so well-known that it needs neither a sign over the door nor a central location to woo the throngs of techno-lovers that flock here. Piekarnia was one of the first modern clubs in Poland and these days the so-hip-it-hurts scene picks up around 4am. If you can get past the selective bouncer and the swarm of youths outside, you're in for a fun night. Cover F 20zł, Sa 25zł. Open F-Sa 10pm-late.

Klubokawiarnia, Czeckiego 3 (www.klubo.pl). An authentic communist-era sign advertising "coffee, tea, and cold beverages" hangs over the bar, while portraits of Lenin gaze down from the bright red walls in this ironic imitation of the bad old days. Despite the nostalgic decor, Klubokawiarnia's DJs spin the hottest new tracks for a stylish young crowd. Special events on occasion, such as a "Pirate Night" or "Caribbean Night" with imported sand. Cover varies. Open daily 10pm-late. Cash only.

Underground Music Cafe, Marszałkowska 126/134 (☎022 826 7048; www.under.pl). Walk down the steps behind the large McDonald's. This 2-level dance club is a guaranteed weeknight party. A casual, young crowd of students and backpackers keep the smoky dance floor completely packed until 4am. M-Tu and Su old-school house; W and Sa hip-hop; Th 70s and 80s. Beer 5zł 11pm-midnight. Cover W-F 10zł, students 5zł; Sa 20/10zł. No cover M-Tu and Su. Open M-Sa 1pm-late, Su 4pm-late.

Szlafrok, Wierzbowa 9 (☎022 828 6477). From Marszałkowska, take a right on Senatorska, and another right on Wierzbowa; the club is on your right. This centrally-located club has all the class of a high-end establishment without the exclusivity. A sophisticated clientele mill about the gold and black columns whilst sipping from a selection of martinis and cosmopolitans. No sandals or sneakers. Cover varies. Open daily 5pm-4am.

Cinnamon, Pilsudskiego 1 (☎022 323 7600), in the Metropolitan Building across pl. Pilsudskiego from the National Opera. At this bar with attitude, one of Warsaw's strictest door policies ensures that Cinnamon is favored only by the hottest locals and expats. The lunar-themed interior and pink accents complement the suave and impeccably dressed staff who keep the martinis flowing all night long. Don't be surprised if you pop in for an elegant lunch and emerge at dawn the next day. Open daily 9am-late. MC/V.

Rasko, Krochmalna 32A (☎022 890 0299; www.rasko.pl). 1 block north of Grzybowska, turn left on Krochmalna; the bar is 2 blocks down on your right near a small sign and blue unmarked door. Rasko is a small, secluded, and artsy establishment that serves Warsaw's largely underground GLBT scene. Laid-back but cautious bouncer ensures that Warsaw's less tolerant elements stay out. The friendly staff are quick to mingle with club-goers and even join in for a round of karaoke. Beer 7zł. Open daily 6pm-2am. MC/V.

KRAKÓW ☎012

Although Kraków (KRAH-koof; pop 758,000) only recently emerged as a trendy international capital, it has long been Poland's darling. The regal architecture, cafe culture, and palpable sense of history that now bewitch throngs of visitors have drawn Polish kings, artists, and scholars for centuries. Unlike most Polish cities, Kraków emerged from WWII and years of socialist planning unscathed. The maze-like Old Town and the old Jewish quarter of Kazimierz hide scores of museums, galleries, cellar pubs, and clubs; 130,000 students add to the spirited nightlife. Still, the city's gloss and glamor can't completely hide the scars of the 20th century: the nearby Auschwitz-Birkenau Nazi death camps provide a sobering reminder of the atrocities committed in the not-so-distant past.

⌐ TRANSPORTATION

Flights: Balice Airport (John Paul II International Airport; Port Lotniczy im. Jana Pawła), Kapitana Medweckiego 1 (**KRK;** ☎012 411 1955; http://lotnisko-balice.pl/strona_en.html), 18km from the center. Connect to the main train station by bus #192 (40min.) or 208 (1hr.). Or take the **airport train** that leaves from the train platform #1 on W and F-Sa, at least once per hour. A taxi to the center costs 60-70zł. Carriers include British Airways, Central Wings, German Wings, LOT, Lufthansa, and Sky Europe. Open 24hr.

Trains: Kraków Główny, pl. Kolejowy 1 (☎012 393 5409, info ☎ 012 393 1580; www.pkp.pl). Ticket office open 5am-11pm. Go to Kasa Krajowej for domestic trains and Kasa Międzynarodowa for international trains. AmEx/MC/V. To: **Gdańsk** ("Gdynia"; 7-10hr., 12 per day, 60-100zł); **Warsaw** (3-4hr., 15 per day, 81-127zł); **Zakopane** (3-5hr., 19 per day, 30-50zł); **Bratislava, SLK** (8hr., 1 per day, 188zł); **Budapest, HUN** (11hr., 1 per day, 159-208zł); **Kyiv, UKR** (22hr., 1 per day, 240zł); **Odessa, UKR** (21hr., 1 per day, 240zł); **Prague, CZR** (9hr., 2 per day, 128-165zł); **Vienna, AUT** (8hr., 2 per day, 157-194zł). Let's Go does not recommend traveling on night trains.

Buses: Bosacka 18 (☎300 300 150). Open daily 5am-11pm. To: **Lódz** (5hr., 5 per day, 50zł); **Warsaw** (6hr., 3 per day, 50zł); **Wrocław** (5hr., 2 per day, 43zł). AmEx/MC/V.

Public Transportation: Buy **bus** and **tram** tickets at Ruch kiosks (2.50zł) or from the automatic ticket machines throughout the city and punch them on board. Large packs need their own tickets. Night buses after 11pm 5zł; day pass 11zł; there is an 100zł fine if you or your bag are caught ticketless.

Taxis: Reliable taxi companies include: **Barbakan Taxi** (☎96 61, toll-free ☎08 00 40 04 00); **Euro Taxi** (☎96 64); **Radio Taxi** (☎919, toll-free ☎08 00 50 09 19); **Wawel Taxi** (☎96 66). It is up to 30% cheaper to call a taxi than to hail one.

POLAND

Kraków: Stare Miasto

ACCOMMODATIONS
Greg & Tom, 6
Hostel Gardenhouse, 9
Hotel Polonia, 2
Kadetus, 15
Mama's Hostel, 11
Nathan's Villa Hostel, 16
The Stranger, 1
Elephant on the Moon, 21
Ars Hostel, 20

FOOD
Bagelmama, 17
Bar Mleczny Pod
  Temida, 14
Dym, 8
Fabryka Pizzy, 18
Ipanema, 3
Kuchina U Babci
  Maliny, 5
Vega Bar Restaurant, 7
Zapiecek, 22

NIGHTLIFE
Alchemia, 19
Cieó, 4
Faust, 10
Kitsch, 12
Prozak, 13

✈ 🛈 ORIENTATION AND PRACTICAL INFORMATION

The heart of the city is the **Rynek Główny** (Main Marketplace), the center of **Stare Miasto** (Old Town). Stare Miasto is encircled by the Planty gardens and, a bit farther out, a broad ring road, which is confusingly divided into sections with different names: Basztowa, Dunajewskiego, Podwale, and Westerplatte. South of Rynek Główny looms the **Wawel Castle**. The **Wisła River** snakes past the castle and borders the old Jewish district of **Kazimierz**. The train station sits northeast of Stare Miasto. A well-marked underpass cuts beneath the ring road and into the Planty gardens; from there several paths lead into the Rynek (10min.).

Tourist Office: City Tourist Information, Szpitalna 25 (☎012 432 0110; www.krakow. pl/en). The official tourist office arranges accommodations, tours, and sells guides (7-12zł). English spoken. Open daily 9am-7pm. Private tourist offices throughout town.

Budget Travel: Orbis, Rynek Główny 41 (☎012 619 2447; www.orbis.krakow.pl). Sells train tickets and arranges trips to Wieliczka and Auschwitz (each 120zł, both 238zł; up to 50% ISIC discount). Also cashes **traveler's checks** and **exchanges currency**. Open M-F 9am-7pm, Sa 9am-5pm. There are many travel agencies in Stare Miasto.

Consulates: UK, sw. Anny 9 (☎012 421 5656 or ☎012 421 7030; ukconsul@bci.krakow.pl). Open M-F 9am-4pm. **US,** Stolarska 9 (☎012 424 5100; krakow.usconsulate.gov). Open M-F 9am-4:30pm; citizen services until 3pm.

Currency Exchange and Banks: ATMs, found all over the city, offer the best rates. Bank **BPH,** Rynek Główny 4, has **Western Union Services.** Many banks require those receiving money from abroad to change it into złotych at a bad rate. Open M-F 8am-6pm.

Bike Rental: Rentabike (☎888 029 792; www.rentabike.pl). Bikes 30zł for 5hr., 55zł for first day, 45zł for each additional day. Open 24hr.

Luggage Storage: At the train station. 1% of value per day plus 5zł for the 1st day and 3zł for each additional day. Lockers near the exit. Open 5am-11pm. Lockers also available at bus station. Small bag 4zł, large bag 8zł. Open 24hr.

English-Language Bookstore: Massolit, Felicjanek 4 (☎012 432 4150; www.massolit.com). Cozy atmosphere. Open mic night 3rd Su each month at 7pm. Open M-Th and Su 10am-8pm; F-Sa 10am-9pm.

Laundromat: Piastowska 47 (☎012 622 3181), in the basement of **Hotel Piast.** Take tram #4, 13, or 14 to WKS Wawel and turn left on Piastowska. Wash 15zł, dry 15zł, detergent 3zł. Open M-Sa 10am-7pm.

Pharmacy: Apteka Pod Żółtym Tygrysem, Szczepańska 1 (☎012 422 9293), off Rynek Główny. Posts list of 24hr. pharmacies. Open M-F 8am-8pm, Sa 8am-3pm. MC/V.

Medical Services: Medicover, Krótka 1 (☎012 616 1000). **Ambulance** services available. English spoken. Open M-F 7am-9pm, Sa 9am-2pm.

Telephones: At the post office and throughout the city.

Internet: Koffeina Internet Cafe, Rynek Główny 23. 2zł per 30min., 3zł per hr. Open 10am-10pm. **Klub Garinet,** Floriańska 18 (☎012 423 2233, ext 23). 4zł per hr. Open daily 9am-midnight. **Telekomunikacja Polska** offers free Internet.

Post Office: Westerplatte 20 (☎012 422 3991). **Poste Restante** at counter #1. Open M-F 7:30am-8:30pm, Sa 8am-2pm. **Postal Code:** 31075.

ACCOMMODATIONS

New hostels frequently open in Kraków to meet the growing demand, but budget accommodations fill up quickly in summer. Be sure to call ahead. University dorms open up in June, July and August; *Kraków in Your Pocket* has a list.

Nathan's Villa Hostel, ul. św. Agnieszki 1 (☎012 422 3545; www.nathansvilla.com), south of *Stare Miasto,* near the Jewish quarter. Famous for its social atmosphere, the hostel has spacious rooms and a lively cellar pub. Breakfast, laundry, and Wi-Fi included. Reception 24hr. Dorms 45-60zł. MC/V; 3% surcharge. ❷

Elephant on the Moon, ul. Biale Wzgorze 8 (☎ 695 949 604), a 15 min. walk or short tram ride from the center of town. Enjoy being fussed over at this extremely guest-oriented hostel, where the owners are friends first and staff second. Travelers cluster in the cozy living-room of this converted residential house and enjoy the hospitality—and baked goods—provided by the tight-knit staff. Breakfast and Internet included. Reception 24hr. Flexible check-in, check-out 10:30am. Dorms 45-60zł. Cash only. ❷

Ars Hostel, ul. Kolotek 7 (☎ 012 422 3659; www.arshostel.com), south of *Stare Miasto,* next to the Castle. A veritable haven for solo travelers, Ars not only offers a comfortable bed, but also provides nightly entertainment. The staff's seasoned travelers lead vodka tastings by night and mountain hikes by day, making for an extremely social crowd that parties on until the sun comes up. Breakfast and Internet included. Check-in 1:30pm, flexible check-out. Dorms 45-60zł. AmEx/MC/V. ❷

The Stranger, ul. Dietla 97/5 (☎ 012 432 0909; www.thestrangerhostel.com), situated in a new location near the Jewish Quarter. With its new digs comes more space, featuring large, newly-furbished dorm rooms, common area, and a bar/cafe downstairs. Breakfast included. Free Internet and laundry. Reception 24hr. Dorms 32-45zł. Cash only. ❷

Mama's Hostel, ul. Bracka 4 (☎ 012 429 5940; www.mamashostel.com.pl), off Rynek Główny. The most centrally located hostel in town, Mama's garners praise for its eager staff and clean facilities. Its party-friendly location, however, means it can get noisy. Breakfast, laundry and Internet included. Reception 24hr. Flexible check-in and check-out. 12-bed dorms 40zł; 6-bed dorms 60zł. MC/V; 3% surcharge. ❶

Hostel Gardenhouse, ul. Floriańska 5 (☎ 012 431 2824; www.gardenhousehostel.com), in a courtyard off Rynek Główny. Serene dorms decorated in floral. Breakfast, laundry, and Internet included. Reception 24hr. Dorms 55-65zł; doubles 160zł. AmEx/MC/V. ❷

Hotel Polonia, Basztowa 25 (☎ 012 422 1233; www.hotel-polonia.com.pl), across from the train station. Neoclassical exterior, modern rooms, and see-through bathtubs. Breakfast 18zł, included for rooms with bath. Reception 24hr. Check-out noon. Singles 100zł, with bath 295zł; doubles 119/360zł; triples 139/429zł; suites 526zł. MC/V. ❹

Greg and Tom, ul. Pawia 12/17(☎ 012 422 4100; www.gregtomhostel.com). In addition to its convenient location near the center of Old Town, the hospitable staff and creature comforts of this hostel make it hard to leave. Breakfast, dinner, laundry, and Internet included. Reception 24hr. Dorms 50zł; doubles 75zł. AmEx/MC/V. ❷

Kadetus, ul. Zwierzyniecka 25 (☎ 012 422 3617; www.kadetus.com), southwest of Rynek Główny. Colorful dorms with modern furnishings. Breakfast, laundry, Internet, and Wi-Fi included. Reception 24hr. Dorms 40zł-45zł; doubles 65-70zł. Cash only. ❷

⬛ FOOD

Many restaurants, cafes, and grocery stores are located on and around Rynek Główny. More grocery stores surround the bus and train stations.

Bagelmama, ul. Podbrzezie 2 (☎ 012 431 1942; www.bagelmama.com), in Kazimierz, facing the Temple Synagogue. Poland is the mother of the bagel; here the blessed food returns home in triumph (3.50zł, with cream cheese or hummus 6-9zł). Strangely, it also has Kraków's best burritos (12-15zł). Open daily 10am-9pm. Cash only. ❶

Kuchina U Babci Maliny, ul. Szpitalna 38 (☎ 012 421 4818). Hearty Polish food served in quarters resembling a wooden stable upstairs and, incongruously, a Victorian drawing room below. Soup 5zł. Pierogi 8-15zł. Open daily 11am-10pm. AmEx/MC/V. ❶

Ipanema, św. Tomasza 28 (☎ 012 422 5323). Toucan figurines, bright paint, and hanging plants create a rainforest vibe to go along with the superb Brazilian cuisine. Entrees 16-50zł. Open M-Th and Su 1-11pm, F-Sa 1pm-midnight. AmEx/MC/V. ❸

Dym, św. Tomasza 13 (☎ 012 429 6661). A hub for sophisticated locals, Dym (meaning "smoke") earns high praise for its coffee (5zł), though many prefer to enjoy the relaxed vibe over beer (6-8zł). Open M-F 10am-midnight. Cash only. ❶

Fabryka Pizzy, Józefa 34 (☎ 012 433 8080). This popular Kazimierz pizza place lives up to its hype, preparing pizzas that are unusual and delicious. Browse from a menu of cleverly-named specials like the Donkey with a Sombrero (salami, red beans, hot pepper and tabasco) or the Diver's Party (shrimp, crab, mussels, olives and onions). Pizzas 15-30zł. Open M-Th and Su 11am-11pm, F-Sa noon-midnight. MC/V. ❷

Zapiecek, ul. Sławkowska 32 (☎ 012 422 7495). Every Polish city has its local pierogi institution, and Zapiecek is Kraków's. Combine the authentic yet affordable Polish fare (6-10zł) which will whet your appetite, add the Old Town location, and you've got the perfect afternoon lunch spot. Open daily 10am-9pm. Cash only. ❶

Vega Bar Restaurant, Krupnicza 22 (☎ 012 430 0846), also at św. Gertrudy 7 (☎422 3494). Fresh flowers and a colorful interior set the mood for delightful veggie cuisine—a rarity in Kraków. (4-12zł). 32 varieties of tea (2.50zł). Open daily 9am-9pm. MC/V. ❶

Bar Mleczny Pod Temida, ul. Grodzka 43 (☎ 012 422 0874). Conveniently located between Rynek Główny and Wawel Castle, this milk bar is dirt-cheap and a crowd-pleasing lunch spot. Entrees 2.50-10zł. Open daily 9am-8pm. ❶

🔘 SIGHTS

STARE MIASTO. At the center of *Stare Miasto* is the **Rynek Główny,** the largest market square in Europe, and at the heart of the *Rynek* stands the **Sukiennice** (Cloth Hall). Surrounded by multicolored row houses and cafes, it's a convenient center for exploring the nearby sights. The **Royal Road** (Droga Królewska), traversed by medieval royals on the way to coronations in Wawel, starts at St. **Florian's Church** (Kościół św. Floriana), crosses pl. Matejki, passes the **Academy of Fine Arts** (Akademia Sztuk Pieknych), and crosses Basztowa to the **Barbakan.** The Gothic-style Barbakan, built in 1499, is the best preserved of the three such defensive fortifications surviving in Europe. *(Open daily 10:30am-6pm. 6zł, students 4zł.)* The royal road continues through **Floriańska Gate,** the old city entrance and the only remnant of the city's medieval walls. Inside *Stare Miasto,* the road runs down Floriańska, past the *Rynek* and along Grodzka. A map marking all the points can be found in front of Florianska Gate. Every hour at 🔲**St. Mary's Church** (Kościół Mariacki), the blaring Hejnał trumpet calls from the taller of St. Mary's two towers and cuts off abruptly to recall the near-destruction of Kraków in 1241, when invading Tatars shot down the trumpeter as he attempted to warn the city. A stunning interior encases the world's oldest Gothic altarpiece, a 500-year-old treasure dismantled, but not destroyed, by the Nazis. *(At the corner of the Rynek closest to the train station. Cover shoulders and knees. Church open daily 11:30am-6pm. Tower open Tu, Th, and Sa 9-11:30am and 1-5:30pm. Tower 6zł, students 4zł. Altar 4/2zł.)*

Collegium Maius of Kraków's Jagiellonian University (Uniwersytet Jagielloński) is the third-oldest university in Europe, established in 1364. Alumni include astronomer **Mikołaj Kopernik** (Copernicus). The Collegium became a museum in 1964 and now boasts an extensive collection of historical scientific instruments. *(ul. Jagiellońska 15. ☎012 663 1307; www.uj.edu.pl/muzeum. Open Apr.-Oct. M,W,F 10am-2:20pm, Tu, Th 10am-5:20pm, Sa 10am-1:20pm, Nov.-March M-F 10am-2:20pm, Sa 10am-1:20pm. Closed Sundays and holidays. Guided visits only; tours 3 per hr. English-language tour daily 1pm. 12zł, students 6zł, Sa free.)* **Ulica Floriańska** runs from the *Rynek* to the Barbakan and the Floriańska Gate, which formed the entrance to the old city; they are now the only remnants of the medieval fortifications. The **Czartoryskich Museum** has letters by Copernicus and paintings by Matejko, da Vinci, and Rembrandt. *(św. Jana 19. ☎012 422 5566. Open T-Sa 10am-6pm, Su 10am-4pm; closed last Su of each month. 10zł; students 5zł; Su free.)* From the *Rynek,* walk down Grodzka and turn right to reach the brightly colored **Franciscan Church** (Kościół Franciscańska), decorated with vibrant colors and Stanisław Wyspiański's amazing stained-glass window *God the Father. (Pl. Wszystkich Swiętych 5. ☎012 422 5376. Open daily until 7:30pm. English-language tours free; donations requested.)*

WAWEL CASTLE AND SURROUNDINGS. 🔲**Wawel Castle** (Zamek Wawelski), one of Poland's top attractions, is an architectural masterpiece overlooking the Wisła River. Begun in the 10th century and remodeled in the 16th, the castle contains 71 chambers, including the **Komnaty** (state rooms) and the **Apartamenty** (royal chambers). Among the treasures are a magnificent sequence of 16th-century tapestries commissioned by the royal family and a cache of armor, swords, spears, and ancient guns. The **Lost Wawel** exhibit traces Wawel Hill's evolution from the Stone Age, displaying archaeological fragments of ancient Wawel. You can also visit the **Oriental Collection** of Turkish military regalia and Asian porcelain. *(Open Apr.-Oct. M 9:30am-1pm, Tu-F 9:30am-5pm, Sa-Su*

11am-6pm, Nov.-Mar. Tu-Sa 9:30am-4pm, Su 10am-4pm. Royal Private Apartments and Oriental Collection closed M. Wawel Castle Apr.-Oct.15zł, students 8zł, Nov.-Mar. 14/7zł, M free. Lost Wawel and Oriental Collection 7/4zł each. Royal Apartments 22/17zł, Treasury and Armory 15/8zł.) Next door is **Wawel Cathedral** (Katedra Wawelska), which once hosted the coronations and funerals of Polish monarchs. Famed poet Adam Mikiewicz lies entombed here, and Kraków native Karol Wojtyła served as archbishop before becoming Pope John Paul II. Steep stairs from the church lead to **Sigismund's Bell** (Dwon Zygmunta); the view of the city is worth the climb. *(Cathedral open M-Sa 9am-5pm, Su 12:30pm-5pm. Buy tickets at the kasa across the castle courtyard. 10zł, students 5zł.)* In the complex's southwest corner is the entrance to the **◪Dragon's Den** (Smocza Jama), a small cavern. The real treat is down the path that borders the castle walls: a wonderfully ugly metal statue of the fire-breathing dragon. *(Open daily Sept.-Apr. 10am-5pm, July-Aug. 10-6pm. 3zł.)*

KAZIMIERZ. South of *Stare Miasto* lies Kazimierz, Kraków's 600-year-old **Jewish quarter.** On the eve of WWII, 68,000 Jews lived in the Kraków area, most of them in Kazimierz, but the occupying Nazis forced many out. The 15,000 remaining were deported to death camps by March 1943. Only about 100 practicing Jews now live here, but Kazimierz is a favorite haunt of Kraków's artists and intellectuals, and it is the center of a resurgence of Central European Jewish culture. *(From the Rynek, go down ul. Sienna, which turns into Starowiślana. After 1km, turn right onto Miodowa, then left onto Szeroka.)* The **Galicia Jewish Museum** documents the past and present of Galicia, a region in southern Poland that was once the heart of Ashkenazi Jewish culture. *(Dajwór 18. ☎012 421 6842; www.galiciajewishmuseum.org. Open daily 9am-7pm. 12zł, students 6zł.)* The tiny **Remuh Synagogue** is surrounded by **Remuh's Cemetery,** which has graves dating to the plague of 1551-1552 and a wall constructed from tombstones recovered after WWII. For centuries, the cemetery was covered with sand, protecting it from 19th-century Austrian invaders and from the Nazis, who used the area as a garbage dump. *(Szeroka 40. Open May-Oct. M-F and Su 9am-6pm, Nov.-Apr. M-F and Su 9am-4pm. Services F at sundown and Sa morning. 5zł, students 2zł.)* Also on Szeroka, the **Old Synagogue** is Poland's earliest example of Jewish religious architecture and now houses a museum of Jewish history and traditions. *(Szeroka 24. ☎012 422 0962. Open Apr.-Oct. M 10am-2pm, Tu-Su 10am-5pm; Nov.-Mar. M 10am-2pm, W-Th and Sa-Su 9am-4pm, F 10am-5pm. 7zł, students 5zł, M free.)* The **Center for Jewish Culture** organizes cultural events and arranges heritage tours. *(Meiselsa 17. ☎012 430 6449; www.judaica.pl. Open M-F 10am-6pm, Sa-Su 10am-2pm.)*

▣ ENTERTAINMENT

The **Cultural Information Center,** św. Jana 2, sells the monthly guide *Karnet* (4zł) and directs visitors to box offices. (☎012 421 7787. Open M-Sa 10am-6pm.) The city jumps with jazz; check out **U Muniaka,** Florianska 3 (☎012 423 1205; open daily 7pm-2am) and **Harris Piano Jazz Bar,** Rynek Główny 28 (☎012 421 5741; shows 9pm-midnight; Tu-Sa and Su 1pm-2am.) Classical music-lovers will relish the **Sala Filharmonia** (Philharmonic Hall), Zwierzyniecka 1. (☎012 422 9477, ext. 31; www.filharmonia.krakow.pl. Box office open Tu-F 11am-7pm, Sa-Su 1hr. before curtain; closed June 20-Sept. 10.) The **opera** performs at the **Słowacki Theater,** sw. Ducha 1. (☎012 424 4525. Box office open M-Sa 9am-7pm, Su 4hr. before curtain. 30-50zł, students 25-35zł.) The **Stary Teatr** (Old Theater) has a few stages that host films, plays, and exhibits. (☎012 422 4040. Open Tu-Sa 10am-1pm and 5-7pm, Su 5-7pm. 30-60zł, students 20-35zł.)

▣ NIGHTLIFE

Kraków in Your Pocket has up-to-date info on the hottest club and pub scenes, while the free monthly English-language *KrakOut* magazine has day-by-day listings of events. Most dance clubs are in Stare Miasto, while bohemian pubs and cafes cluster in Kazimierz. For tips on Kraków's **GLBT nightlife**, see www.gayeuro.com/krakow or www.cracow.gayguide.net.

Alchemia, Estery 5 (☎516 095 863; www.alchemia.com.pl). Candles twinkle in this pleasantly disheveled bar, which includes bizarre and fascinating decor—one of the many rooms is decorated to look like a 1950s kitchen. Frequented by artists, Brits, and students downing beer (Żywiec; 6.5zł) until dawn. During the day, this Kazimierz bar masquerades as a smoky cafe. Open daily 9am-4am.

Prozak, Dominikanska 6 (☎012 429 1128; www.prozak.pl). With a shisha bar, and more dance floors, bars, and intimate nooks than you'll be able to count, Prozak is one of the top clubs in town. Hipster students, porn star look-alikes, and music aficionados lounge on low-slung couches. Pass on the undersized mixed drinks (7-20zł) for pints of beer (7-10zł). No sneakers or sandals. Cover F-Sa 10zł. Open daily 7pm-late.

Kitsch, ul. Wielopole 15 (☎012 422 5299; www.kitsch.pl), located between the Rynek and Kazimierz. This gay-friendly establishment offers a great dancing atmosphere. 6-8zl beer, mixed drinks from 8zl. T Girls' night, W Boys' night, Th Student night, with beer at 5zl for women, men, and students, respectively. Open daily 7pm-late.

Cien, sw. Jana 15 (☎012 422 2177; www.cienklub.com). Posing becomes a spectator sport in the vaults of "Shadow," so dress to impress. The club plays house techno for Krakow's beautiful people, and party-goers take advantage of the red nooks along the walls to formulate a plan of approach. Mixed drinks 10-25zł. No sneakers or sandals. Open Tu-Th 8pm-5am, F-Sa 8pm-6am. MC/V.

Faust, Rynek Główny 6 (☎012 423 8300), entrance off of Sienna St. Sell your soul in this underground labyrinth, where a raucous, friendly crowd sits at massive wooden tables or dances unabashedly to pop and techno hits. Beer 4-8zł. Disco W-Sa. Open M-Th and Su noon-1am, F-Sa 3pm-4am. Cash only.

◨ DAYTRIPS FROM KRAKÓW

AUSCHWITZ-BIRKENAU. An estimated 1½ million people, mostly Jews, were murdered and thousands more suffered unthinkable horrors in the Nazi concentration camps at **Auschwitz** (in Oświęcim) and **Birkenau** (in Brzezinka). The gates over the smaller *Konzentrationslager Auschwitz I* are inscribed with the ironic dictum *"Arbeit Macht Frei"* (Work Will Set You Free). Tours begin at the museum at Auschwitz. As you walk past the remainders of thousands of lives, the enormity of the atrocity becomes apparent. A 15min. English-language film, with footage shot by the Soviet Army that liberated the camp on January 27, 1945, is shown every 30 min. Children under 14 are strongly advised not to visit the museum. (☎844 8102. Open daily June-Aug. 8am-7pm; Sept. and May 8am-6pm; Oct. and Apr. 8am-5pm; Nov. and Mar. 8am-4pm; Dec.-Feb. 8am-3pm. English-language tour 4 per day at 10am, 11am, 1pm, and 3pm. Museum free. Film 3.50zł. Guided 3hr. tour 39zł, students 30zł; film and bus included. English-language guidebook 3zł.)

The larger, starker **Konzentrationslager Auschwitz II-Birkenau** is in the countryside 3km from the original camp, a 30min. walk along a well-marked route or a short **shuttle** ride from the Auschwitz museum parking lot (1 per hr., free). Birkenau was built later in the war and hosted much of the apparati of mass extermination. Little is left of the camp today; most was destroyed by retreating Nazis to conceal the genocide. Reconstructed train tracks lead to the ruins of the crematoria and gas chambers. Near the monument lies a pond still gray from the ashes deposited there over 60 years ago. (Open mid-Apr. to Oct. 8am-dusk. Free.) **Auschwitz Jewish Center and Synagogue** features exhibits on pre-war Jewish life in the town of Oświęcim, films based on survivors' testimonies, genealogy resources, and a reading room. Take a **taxi** for about 20zł, or take **bus** #1, 3-6, or 8 from the train station in the town center, get off at the first stop after the bridge and backtrack. *(Pl. Ks. Jana Skarbka 3-5. ☎ 844 70 02; www.ajcf.pl. Open M-F and Su Apr.-Sept. 8:30am-8pm; Oct.-Mar. 8:30am-6pm. Donation requested.)*

Buses from Kraków's central station go to Oświęcim (1½-2hr., every 30 min., 7-10zł). Return buses leave frequently from the stop on the other side of the parking lot; turn right out of the museum. PKS buses depart from the stop outside the premises. Less convenient **trains** leave from Kraków Plaszów, south of the town center (10zł). Buses #2-5, 8-9, and 24-29 connect the Oświęcim train station to the Muzeum Oświęcim stop; or, walk a block to the right out of the station, turn left onto ul. Więźniów Oświęcimia, and continue 1.6km.

WIELICZKA. The tiny town of Wieliczka, 13km southeast of Kraków, is home to a 700-year-old **salt mine.** Pious Poles carved the immense underground complex of chambers out of salt; in 1978, UNESCO declared the mine one of the world's 12 most priceless monuments. The most spectacular cavern is **St. Kinga's Chapel,** complete with an altar, relief works, and salt chandeliers. Most hostels and travel companies, including **Orbis** (p. 584), organize trips to the mines, but it's cheapest to take a private **minibus** like Contrabus that departs near the train and bus stations (30min., 4 per hr., 3.50zł). Look for "Wieliczka" marked on the door. In Wieliczka, head along the path of the former tracks, then follow signs marked *"do kopalni."* The only way to see the mines is by taking a lengthy **guided tour,** so allot at least 3hr. for the daytrip. *(ul. Daniłowicza 10. ☎ 278 73 02; www. kopalnia.pl. Wheelchair-accessible. Open daily Apr.-Oct. 7:30am-7:30pm; Nov.-Mar. 8am-4pm; closed holidays. Polish-language tours Apr.-June 47zł, students 32zł, July-Dec. 48/33zł, Jan.-Mar. 45/30zł. English-language tours June and Sept. 8 per day, July and Aug. every 35 people. 8:30am-6pm. Apr.-June 63zł, students 48zł, July-Dec. 64/49zł, Jan.-Mar. 61/46zł. MC/V.)*

PORTUGAL

While Portugal is small, its imposing forests and mountains, scenic vineyards, and almost 2000km of coastline rival the attractions of Spain. Portugal's capital, Lisbon, offers marvelous museums, castles, and churches. The country experienced international glory and fabulous wealth 400 hundred years ago during the Golden Age of Vasco da Gama. Despite suffering under the dictatorship of Salazar for 30 years in the 20th century, Portugal has reemerged as a European cultural center with a growing economy. Extremes of fortune have contributed to the unique Portuguese concept of *saudade*, a yearning for the glories of the past and a dignified resignation to the fact that the future can never compete. Visitors may experience *saudade* through a *fado* singer's song or over a glass of port, but Portugal's attractions are more likely to inspire delight than nostalgia.

 DISCOVER PORTUGAL: SUGGESTED ITINERARIES

THREE DAYS. Spend it all making your way through **Lisbon** (p. 611); venture through its famous Moorish district, the Alfama, Castelo de São Jorge, and the Parque das Nações. By night, listen to *fado* and hit the clubs in Bairro Alto.

ESSENTIALS

FACTS AND FIGURES

OFFICIAL NAME: The Portuguese Republic.

CAPITAL: Lisbon.

MAJOR CITIES: Coimbra, Porto.

POPULATION: 10,463,000.

TIME ZONE: GMT.

LANGUAGES: Portuguese, Mirandese.

RELIGION: Roman Catholic (85%).

NUMBER OF GRAPE VARIETALS AUTHORIZED FOR MAKING PORT: 48.

WHEN TO GO

Summer is high-season, but the southern coast draws tourists between March and November. In the low-season, many hostels slash their prices, and reservations are seldom necessary. While Lisbon and some of the larger towns (especially the university town of Coimbra) burst with vitality year-round, many smaller towns virtually shut down in winter, and sights reduce their hours.

DOCUMENTS AND FORMALITIES

EMBASSIES AND CONSULATES. Foreign embassies in Portugal are in Lisbon. Portuguese embassies abroad include: **Australia,** 23 Culgoa Circuit, O'Malley, Canberra, ACT 2606 (☎612 6290 1733); **Canada,** 645 Island Park Dr., Ottawa, ON K1Y 0B8 (☎613-729-2270); **Ireland,** Knocksinna Mews, 7 Willow Park, Foxrock, Dublin, 18 (☎353 289 4416); **UK,** 11 Belgrave Sq., London, SW1X 8PP (☎020

7235 5331); **US,** 2012 Massachusetts Ave. NW, Washington DC, 20036 (☎202-350-5400). **NZ** citizens should contact the embassy in Australia.

VISA AND ENTRY INFORMATION. EU citizens do not need a visa. Citizens of Australia, Canada, New Zealand, the UK, and the US do not need a visa for stays up to 90 days, beginning upon entry into any of the countries within the EU's freedom-of-movement zone. For more info, see p. 13. For stays longer than 90 days, all non-EU citizens need visas (around $100), available at Portuguese consulates.

TOURIST SERVICES AND MONEY

TOURIST OFFICES. For general info, contact the Portuguese Tourism Board, (☎+1 646 723 02 00; www.portugal.org). When in Portugal, stop by municipal and provincial tourist offices, listed in the Practical Information section of each city and town.

EMERGENCY	General Emergency: ☎112.

MONEY. The **euro (€)** has replaced the **escudo** as the unit of currency in Portugal. For more info on the euro, see p. 16. Generally, it's cheaper to exchange money in Portugal than at home. **ATMs** have the best exchange rates. Credit cards also offer good rates and may sometimes be required to reserve hotel rooms or rental cars; **MasterCard** (known in Portugal as **Eurocard**) and **Visa** are the most frequently accepted. Tips of 5-10% are customary only in fancy restaurants or hotels. Some cheaper restaurants include a 10% service charge; if they don't and you'd like to leave a tip, round up to the nearest euro and leave the change. Taxi drivers do not expect tips except for especially long trips. **Bargaining** is not customary in shops, but you can give it a shot at the local market (*mercado*) or when looking for a private room (*quarto*). Portugal has a 21% **value added tax (VAT),** a sales tax applied to retail goods. The prices given in *Let's Go* include VAT. In the airport upon exiting the EU, non-EU citizens can claim a refund on the tax paid for goods purchased at participating stores. In order to qualify for a refund in a store, you must spend at least €50-100, depending on the shopkeeper; make sure to ask for a refund form when you pay. For more info on qualifying for a VAT refund, see (p. 19).

BUSINESS HOURS. Shops are open M-F from 9am to 6pm, although many close for a few hours in the afternoon. Restaurants serve lunch from noon to 3pm and dinner from 7 to 10pm—or later. Museums are often closed on Monday, and many shops are closed over the weekend. Banks usually open around 9am M-F and close in the afternoon.

TRANSPORTATION

BY PLANE. Most international flights land at **Portela Airport** in Lisbon (**LIS;** ☎218 41 35 00); some also land at **Faro** (**FAO;** ☎289 80 08 00) or **Porto** (**OPO;** 229 43 24 00). **TAP Air Portugal** (Canada and the US ☎800-221-7370, Portugal ☎707 20 57 00, UK ☎845 601 0932; www.tap.pt) is Portugal's national airline, serving domestic and international locations. **Portugália** (☎218 93 80 70; www.flypga.pt) is smaller and flies between Faro, Lisbon, Porto, major Spanish cities, and other Western European destinations. For more information, see p. 46.

BY TRAIN. Caminhos de Ferro Portugueses (☎213 18 59 90; www.cp.pt) is Portugal's national railway. Lines run to domestic destinations, Madrid, and Paris. For travel outside of the Braga-Porto-Coimbra-Lisbon line, buses are better. Lisbon,

PORTUGAL

where local trains are fast and efficient, is the exception. Trains often leave at irregular hours, and posted schedules *(horários)* aren't always accurate; check ticket booths upon arrival. Fines for riding without a ticket *(sem bilhete)* are high. Those under 12 or over 65 get half-price tickets. Youth discounts are only available to Portuguese citizens. Train passes are usually not worth buying, as tickets are inexpensive. For more information on train travel, see p. 46.

BY BUS. Buses are cheap, frequent, and connect to just about every town in Portugal. **Rodoviária** (☎212 94 71 00), formerly the national bus company, has recently been privatized. Each company name corresponds to a particular region of the country, such as Rodoviária Alentejo or Minho e Douro, with a few exceptions such as EVA in the Algarve. Private regional companies, including **AVIC, Cabanelas,** and **Mafrense,** also operate buses. Beware of non-express buses in small regions like Estremadura and Alentejo, which stop every few minutes. Express service *(expressos)* between major cities is good, and inexpensive city buses often run to nearby villages. Portugal's main Euroline (p. 49) affiliates are Internorte, Intercentro, and Intersul. **Busabout** coaches stop in Portugal at Lisbon, Lagos, and Porto. Every coach has a guide on board to answer questions and to make travel arrangements en route.

BY CAR. A **driver's license** from one's home country is required to rent a car; no International Driving Permit is necessary. Portugal has the **highest automobile accident rate** per capita in Western Europe. The highway system *(itinerarios principais)* is easily accessible, but off the main arteries, the narrow roads are difficult to negotiate. Speed limits are ignored, recklessness is common, and lighting and road surfaces are often inadequate. Parking space in cities is non-existent. In short, buses are safer. The national automobile association, the **Automóvel Clube de Portugal (ACP),** (☎800 50 25 02; www.acp.pt), has breakdown and towing service, as well as first aid.

BY THUMB. In Portugal, **hitchhiking** is rare. Beach-bound locals occasionally hitchhike in summer, but more commonly stick to the inexpensive bus system. Rides are easiest to come by between smaller towns and at gas stations near highways and rest stops. *Let's Go* does not recommend hitchhiking.

KEEPING IN TOUCH

EMAIL AND THE INTERNET. Internet cafes in cities and most towns charge around €1.20-4 per hr. for Internet access. When in doubt, try a library, where there is often at least one computer equipped for Internet access.

TELEPHONE. Whenever possible, use a calling card for international phone calls, as long-distance rates

for national phone services are often very high. Mobile phones are an increasingly popular and economical option. Major mobile carriers include: TMN, Optimus Telecom SA, and Vodafone. Direct-dial access numbers for calling out of Portugal include: **AT&T Direct** (☎800 80 01 28); **British Telecom** (☎800 80 04 40); **Canada Direct** (☎800 80 01 22); **Telecom New Zealand Direct** (☎800 80 06 40); **Telstra Australia** (☎800 80 06 10). For more info on calling home from Europe, see p. 28.

PHONE CODES	**Country code: 351. International dialing prefix: 00.** Within Portugal, dial city code and then the local number. For more info on placing international calls, see **Inside Back Cover.**

MAIL. Mail in Portugal is somewhat inefficient. **Airmail** *(via aerea)* takes one to two weeks to reach Canada or the US, and more to get to Australia and New Zealand. **Surface mail** *(superficie)*, for packages only, takes up to two months. **Registered** or blue mail takes five to eight business days for roughly three times the price of airmail. **EMS** or **Express Mail** will most likely arrive overseas in three to four days, though it costs more than double the blue mail price. To receive mail in Portugal, have mail delivered **Poste Restante.** Mail will go to the main post office unless you specify a subsidiary by street address. Address mail to be held according to the following example: Last Name, First Name, Posta Restante, Postal code City, PORTUGAL; AIRMAIL.

ACCOMMODATIONS AND CAMPING

PORTUGAL	❶	❷	❸	❹	❺
ACCOMMODATIONS	under €16	€16-20	€21-30	€31-40	over €40

Movijovem, R. Lúcio de Azevedo 27, 1600-146 Lisbon (☎707 20 30 30; www.pousadasjuventude.pt), the **Portuguese Hostelling International** affiliate, oversees the country's HI hostels. All bookings can be made through them. A bed in a *pousada da juventude* costs €9-15 per night, including breakfast and linens, slightly less in the low-season. Though often the cheapest option, hostels may lie far from the town center. To reserve rooms in the high-season, get an **International Booking Voucher** from Movijovem (or your country's HI affiliate) and send it to the desired hostel four to eight weeks in advance. In the low-season (Oct.-Apr.), double-check to see if the hostel is open. **Hotels** in Portugal tend to be pricey. Rates typically include breakfast and showers, and most rooms without bath or shower have a sink. When business is slow, try bargaining in advance—the "official price" is just the maximum. **Pensões,** also called **residencias,** are a budget traveler's mainstay, cheaper than hotels and only slightly more expensive (and much more common) than crowded youth hostels. Like hostels, *pensões* generally provide linens and towels. Many do not take reservations in high-season; for those that do, book ahead. **Quartos** are rooms in private residences, similar to Spain's casas particulares. These may be the the cheapest option in cities and the only option in town; tourist offices can help find one. Prices are flexible and bargaining expected. Portugal has 150 **official campgrounds** *(parques de campismo)*, often beach-accessible and equipped with grocery stores and cafes. Urban and coastal parks may require reservations. Police are cracking down on illegal camping, so don't try it. Tourist offices stock *Portugal: Camping and Caravan Sites*, a free guide to official campgrounds.

PORTUGAL

FOOD AND DRINK

PORTUGAL	❶	❷	❸	❹	❺
FOOD	under €6	€6-10	€11-15	€16-20	over €20

Portuguese dishes are seasoned with olive oil, garlic, herbs, and sea salt, but few spices. The fish selection includes *choco grelhado* (grilled cuttlefish), *linguado grelhado* (grilled sole), and *peixe espada* (swordfish). Portugal's renowned *queijos* (cheeses) are made from cow, goat, and sheep milk. For dessert, try *pudim flan* (egg custard). A hearty *almoço* (lunch) is eaten between noon and 2pm; *jantar* (dinner) is served between 8pm and midnight. *Meia dose* (half-portions) cost more than half-price but are often more than adequate. The *prato do dia* (special of the day) and the set *menú* of appetizer, bread, entree, and dessert, are also filling choices. Cheap, high-quality Portuguese *vinho* (wine) is astounding. Its delicious relative, *vinho do porto* (port), is a dessert in itself. Coffees include *bica* (black espresso), *galão* (with milk, in a glass), and *café com leite* (with milk, in a cup). *Mini-Preço* and *Pingo Doce* have cheap groceries.

 NO SUCH THING AS A FREE LUNCH. Waiters in Portugal will put an assortment of snacks, ranging from simple bread and butter to sardine paste, cured ham, or herbed olives, on your table before the appetizer is served. But check the prices before you dig in: you nibble, you buy.

HOLIDAYS AND FESTIVALS

Holidays: New Year's Day (Jan. 1); Epiphany (Jan. 6); Good Friday (Apr. 10, 2009); Easter (Apr. 11-12); Liberation Day (Apr. 25); Ascension (May 21); Labor Day (May 1); Corpus Christi (Jun. 11, 2009); Portugal Day (June 10); Assumption (Aug. 15); Republic Day (Oct. 5); All Saints' Day (Nov. 1); Restoration of Independence Day (Dec. 1); Immaculate Conception (Dec. 8, 2009); Christmas (Dec. 25); New Year's Eve (Dec. 31).

Festivals: All of Portugal celebrates *Carnaval* (Feb. 24, 2009) and Holy Week (Apr. 5-12, 2009). Coimbra holds the *Queima das Fitas* (Burning of the Ribbons) festival in early May, celebrating the end of the university school year. In June, Batalha holds a *Feira International* celebrating the food, wine, and traditional handicrafts of the region, and Lisbon hosts the *Festas da Cidade,* honoring the birth of St. Anthony with music, games, parades, and street fairs. For more information on festivals, see www.portugal.org.

BEYOND TOURISM

As a volunteer in Portugal, you can contribute to efforts concerning environmental protection, social welfare, or political activism. While not many students think of studying abroad in Portugal, most Portuguese universities open their gates to foreign students. Being an au pair and teaching English are popular options for long-term work, though many people choose to seek more casual—and often illegal—jobs in resort areas. *Let's Go* does not recommend any type of illegal employment. For more info on opportunities across Europe, see **Beyond Tourism**, p. 55.

Volunteers for Peace, 1034 Tiffany Road, Belmont, VT 05730 USA (☎+1-801-259-2759; www.vfp.org). Organizes 2-3 week group projects in Spain, Portugal, and Morocco on a wide range of social and environmental issues. Average project cost $300.

Teach Abroad (www.teachabroad.com). Brings you to listings around the world for paid or stipend positions teaching English.

Universidade de Lisboa, Rectorate Al. da Universidade, Cidade Universitária, 1649-004 Lisbon, POR (☎217 96 76 24; www.ul.pt). Allows foreign students to enroll directly.

Volunteer Abroad (www.volunteer-abroad.com/Portugal.cfm). Offers opportunities to volunteer with conservation efforts around Portugal.

LISBON (LISBOA)

At sunset, the scarlet glow cast over the Rio Tejo is matched by the ruby red shimmer inside your glass of *vinho do porto.* Welcome to Lisbon. A magnificent history has left its mark upon this ancient city: illustrious bronze figures stand proud in open plazas, Roman arches and columns inspire reverence in visitors, and a towering 12th-century castle keeps watch from atop one of the city's infamous seven hills. Lisbon is quickly becoming one of the most talked-about capitals in Europe, driven by cutting-edge fashion, flourishing art and music scenes, and enthusiastic nightlife.

✴ INTERCITY TRANSPORTATION

Flights: All flights land at **Aeroporto de Lisboa** (☎218 41 35 00 or 41 37 00 for departures and arrivals) near the city's northern edge. Major **airlines** have offices at Pr. Marquês de Pombal and along Av. da Liberdade. The cheapest way into town is by bus: walk out of the terminal, turn right, and go straight across the street to the bus stop, marked by yellow metal posts with arrival times of incoming buses. Take bus #44, 45, or 745 (15-20min., every 12-25min. 6am-12:15am, €1.40) to Pr. dos Restauradores; the bus stops in front of the tourist office, located inside the Palácio da Foz. The express AeroBus #91 runs to the same locations (15min.; every 20min. 7am-11pm; €3.50, TAP passengers free); it's a good option during rush hour. The bus stop is in front of the terminal exit. A **taxi** downtown costs about €10-15 (plus a €1.60 baggage fee) at low traffic, but you're billed by time, not distance.

 PRE-PAY YOUR WAY. Ask at the airport tourist office (☎218 450 660; open 7am-midnight) about the voucher program, which allows visitors to prepay for cab rides from the airport (€21).

Trains: Train service in and out of Lisbon routinely confuses newcomers, as there are four stations in Lisbon and one across the river in Barreiro, each serving different destinations. Portugal's affordable, express **Alfa Pendular** line offers the easiest connections between Lisbon and Braga, Porto, Coimbra, and Faro. Regional trains make frequent stops; buses, although more expensive and lacking toilets, are faster and more comfortable. Suburban train lines, which offer service to Cascais and Sintra (and stops along the way), are efficient and reliable. Contact **Caminhos de Ferro Portugueses** for further info. (☎808 20 82 08; www.cp.pt.)

Estação do Barreiro, across the Rio Tejo. Southbound trains. Accessible by ferry from the Terreiro do Paço dock off Pr. do Comércio (30min., 2 per hr., €2.10).

Estação Cais do Sodré, just beyond the end of R. do Alecrim, beside the river; a 5min. walk from Baixa. M: Cais do Sodré or take any tram 28E from Bairro Alto or Alfama. Serves the southwestern suburbs.

Estação Rossio, M: Rossio. Cross the *praça* for 2 blocks until you see the station on your right. Alternatively, you can get off at M: Restauradores and walk down Av. da Liberdage; the station will be on your right. Serves the northwestern suburbs.

Estação Santa Apolónia, Av. Infante Dom Henrique. M: Santa Apolónia. Runs international, northern, and eastern lines. All trains stop at **Estação Oriente** (see below).

Estação Oriente, M: Oriente, by the **Parque das Nações.** Offers service to the south.

Buses: The **bus station** in Lisbon is close to the Jardim Zoológico metro stop, but it can be tricky to find. Once at the metro stop, follow the exit signs to Av. C. Bordalo Pinheiro. Exit the metro and go around the corner. Walk ahead 100m and then cross left in front of Sete Rios station. The stairs to the station are on the left.

▐ LOCAL TRANSPORTATION

CARRIS, Lisbon's efficient public transportation system, runs subways, buses, trams, funiculars throughout Lisbon and its surroundings (☎213 61 30 00; www.carris.pt). Short-term visitors should consider a 24-hour **bilhete combinado** (€3.50), good for unlimited travel on all CARRIS transports. Those planning a longer stay, or who intend to take the metro, should acquire a rechargeable **viva viagem** card. The pass itself costs €0.50 and can be purchased and charged in all metro stations. When entering buses, trams, or the metro, hold the card against the magnetic reader; your trip will cost only €0.79. CARRIS booths, located in most train and major metro stations (including Baixa-Chiado, Restauradores, and Marquês de Pombal), sell day passes and dispense information. (Open daily 6:30am-1pm.)

Buses: €1.40 within the city, or €0.79 with a viva viagem card. Pay on the bus; exact change not required.

Metro: (☎213 50 01 00; www.metrolisboa.pt). €0.79 with a viva viagem card (required for travel on the metro). 4 lines traverse downtown and the business district. A red "M" marks metro stops. Trains run daily 6:30am-1am, though some stations close earlier.

Trams: €1.40, or €0.79 with a viva viagem card. Many vehicles date from before WWI. Line 28E runs through Graça, Alfama, Baixa, Chiado, and Bairro Alto. Line 15E heads from Pr. do Comércio and Pr. da Figueira to Belém, passing the clubs of Alcântara along the way.

Taxis: Cabs can be hailed on the street throughout the historic center. Restauranteurs and club bouncers will gladly call you a cab after dark. **Rádio Táxis de Lisboa** (☎218 11 90 00), **Autocoope** (☎217 93 27 56), and **Teletáxis** (☎218 11 11 00). Luggage €1.60.

✳ ORIENTATION

Lisbon's historic core has four main neighborhoods: commercial **Baixa** (the low district), museum-heavy **Chiado,** nightlife-rich **Bairro Alto** (the high district), and hilly, labyrinthine **Alfama.** The last, Lisbon's famous medieval Moorish neighborhood, was the lone survivor of the 1755 earthquake. The city's oldest district is a maze of narrow alleys, unmarked alleyways, and *escandinhas,* stairways that seem only to lead to more unindentifiable streets. **Graça** is another one of the oldest neighborhoods in Lisbon, and in addition to great views of the city and river, offers several impressive historical sights that keep tourists trekking up its hilly streets day after day. Lisbon calms down as you move west from Bairro Alto into **Estrela** and **Prazeres,** where cobblestone streets give way to leafy parks and peaceful manicured cemeteries. South of these neighborhoods, the docks of riverfront **Alcântara** house Lisbon's most vibrant club scene. Several kilometers downriver, architecturally stunning **Belém** celebrates the glory of Portugal's imperial past. Northeast of the historic core, the **Parque das Nações,** built to host the 1998 World Exposition, is home to a fantastic oceanarium and Santiago Calatrava's soaring Gare do Oriente.

Lisbon

ACCOMMODATIONS
Brasileira, 8
Casa de Hospedes Globo, 15
Easy Hostel, 11
Goodnight Backpacker's Hostel, 10
Lisbon Lounge Hostel, 12
Luar Guest House, 14
Oasis Backpackers Mansion, 6
Pensão Beira Mar, 13
Pensão Ninho das Águias, 9

FOOD
Á Minha Maneira, 1
Ali-a-papa, 2
Calcuta, 3
Casa-Brasileira, 4
Churrasqueira Gaúcha, 5
Ristorante Pizzeria Valentino, 7

PORTUGAL

Expect to get lost repeatedly without a detailed map. The street-indexed *For Ways* maps (including Sintra, Cascais, and Estoril) are good, though expensive (sold at newsstands; â,¬5). The maps at the tourist offices are also reliable and free. Visitors exhausted from treks up and down the historic center's many hills can hop aboard tram 28E, which runs East-West through these neighborhoods, connecting most of their major sights. The *bairros* extending in both directions along the river are some of the fastest-growing sections of the city, offering pulsing nightlife and stunning architectural beauty, both ancient and contemporary.

⚡ PRACTICAL INFORMATION

Tourist Office: Palácio da Foz, Pr. dos Restauradores (Portugal info ☎213 46 63 07, Lisbon info ☎213 46 33 14). M: Restauradores. The largest tourist office, with info for all of Portugal. Open daily 9am-8pm. The **Welcome Center,** Pr. do Comércio (☎210 31 28 10), is the main office for the city. Sells tickets for sightseeing buses and the **Lisboa Card,** which includes transportation and entrance to most sights, for a flat fee (1-day €16, 2-day €27, 3-day €33.50; children age 5-11 €9.50/14/17). Open daily 9am-8pm.

Budget Travel: Tagus Travel, Pç. de Londres, 9C (☎218 49 15 31; www.taguseasy.pt).

Embassies: See **Embassies and Consulates,** p. 606.

Currency Exchange: Banks are open M-F 8:30am-3pm. Exchange money at **Nova Câmbios,** Praça D. Pedro IV, 42 (☎213 24 25 53). **Western Union,** Pr. Dom Pedro IV, 41 (☎213 22 04 80), inside **Cota Câmbios,** performs money transfers. Open daily 8pm-10pm. The main post office, most banks, and travel agencies also change money, and exchanges line the streets of Baixa. Ask about fees first—they can be exorbitant.

Police: Tourism Police Station, Palácio Foz in Restauradores (☎213 42 16 24), and at R. Capelo, 13 (☎213 46 61 41 or 42 16 34). English spoken.

Late-Night Pharmacy: 24hr. pharmacy rotates, check the listings in the window of any pharmacy. Look for a lighted green cross, or check listings at **Farmácia Azevedos,** Pr. Dom Pedro IV, 31 (☎213 43 04 82), at the base of Rossio in front of the metro. Regular hours 8:30am-7:40pm.

Medical Services: ☎112 in case of emergency. **Hospital de Saint Louis,** R. Luz Soriano, 182 (☎213 21 65 00) in Bairro Alto. Open daily 9am-8pm. **Hospital de São José,** R. José António Serrano (☎218 84 10 00 or 261 31 28 57).

Internet Access: Portugal Telecom (see above). **The Instituto Portuges da Juventude,** Av. Liberdade 194 (☎213 17 92 00; juventude.gov.pt). 30min. of free internet and assistance for students. Open Tu-Sa 9am-8pm. **Web C@fé,** R. Diário de Notícias 126 (☎213 421 181) in Bairro Alto. Doubles as a bar. €0.75 per 15min. Open daily 7pm-2am.

Post Office: Main office, Pr. dos Restauradores (☎213 23 89 71). Open M-F 8am-10pm, Sa-Su 9am-6pm. To avoid the lines, go to the branch at Pr. do Comércio (☎213 22 09 20). Open M-F 8:30am-6:30pm. Cash only. **Postal Code:** 1100.

🏠 🏕 ACCOMMODATIONS AND CAMPING

Lisbon has seen an explosion of tourism in recent years, and with it, a rapid growth in accommodations catering to student travelers on a budget. The result is a remarkable selection of fresh, funky, comfortable, and even occasionally elegant hostels, all at prices travelers to Paris or Madrid could only dream of.

Camping is reasonably popular in Portugal, but campers can be prime targets for thieves. Stay at an enclosed campsite and ask ahead about security. There are 30 campgrounds within a 45min. radius of the capital. The most popular, **Lisboa Camping,** is inside the 900-acre *parque florestal,* and has a four-star rating.

(☎217 62 82 00; www.lisboacamping.com. €6, children under 12 €3, tents €6-7, cars €4. Prices fall in winter. Bungalows available.)

■ **Kitsch Hostel,** Pr. Dos Restauradores 65 (☎213 46 73 32; www.kitschhostel.com). M: Restauradores. Opened in March 2009, this centrally located hostel is every bit as quirky as the name would suggest. Enter through the Tabacaria Restauradores into an energetic world of reflective ceilings, celebrity collages, and delightfully tacky furniture. All rooms with shared bath. Breakfast included. Towels €1. Free internet and Wi-Fi. Key deposit €10. 4- to 12-bed dorms M-Th and Su €14-16, F-Sa €16-18; doubles from €50; triples from €60. AmEx/MC/V. ●

■ **Oasis Backpackers Mansion,** R. de Santa Catarina, 24 (☎213 47 80 44; www.oasislisboa.com). M: Baixa-Chiado. Facing the river, turn to your right; the hostel is the yellow house at the bottom of the hill. True to its name, funky Oasis is a backpacker's haven. A diverse range of travelers gather for home-cooked dinners in the classy dining room (M-Sa, €5) or for drinks in the patio bar (open daily 6pm-midnight). Breakfast included. Laundry €7. Free internet and Wi-Fi. Key deposit €5. Co-ed dorms €18-20; doubles with private bath €44. AmEx/MC/V. ●

■ **Pensão Ninho das Águias,** Costa do Castelo, 74 (☎218 85 40 70). Perched at the top of Alfama, Ninho das Águias towers above Lisbon's other *pensões,* literally and metaphorically. Beautiful common spaces, garden patio, family vibe, and fantastic views, especially from rooms 5, 6, 12-14, and the small tower at the top of the stairs. English and French spoken. Reserve ahead in summer. Singles €30; doubles €45, with bath €50; triples (some with bath) €60. Sept.-Apr. prices drop by €10. Cash only; prices may be flexible with bargaining. ❸

Living Lounge Hostel, R. do Crucifixo 116 (☎213 46 10 78; www.lisbonloungehostel.com), and **Lisbon Lounge Hostel**, R. de São Nicolau 41 (213 462 061; www.lisbon-loungehostel.com). M: Baixa-Chiado (Baixa exit). Under joint ownership, both of these hostels feature excellent contemporary design, with bold colors and cool touches like chandeliers made from teacups. Free city tours Tu and F. Nightly dinners (€8) include wine and dessert. All rooms with shared bath; singles at Living Lounge only. Breakfast included. Laundry €7. Free internet and Wi-Fi. Key deposit €5. 4- to 8-bed dorms Oct. 15-Apr. 14 €18, Apr. 15-May 31 and Sept. 16-Oct. 14 €20, June 1-Sept. 15 €22; singles €30/35/35; doubles €50/60/60. AmEx/MC/V. ●

Lisbon Poets Hostel, R. Nova da Trinidade 2 (☎213 46 10 58; www.lisbonpoetshostel.com), on the 5th fl. Decked out in soothing earth tones and beanbag chairs, this ideally located newcomer to Lisbon's hostel scene features a small book exchange and spacious 2- to 6-bed dorms named for famous writers. Breakfast included. Laundry €7. Free internet and Wi-Fi. Key deposit €5. Co-ed dorms mid-Oct. to mid-Apr. €18, mid-Apr. to June €20, Jul. to mid-Oct. €22; doubles mid-Oct to mid-Apr. €42-65, mid-Apr. to mid-Oct. €45-70. MC/V over €50. ❷

Pensão Beira Mar, Largo Terreiro do Trigo, 16 (☎218 86 99 33; www.guesthousebeiramar.com), near the Sta. Apolonia train station. Avoid the 4-story climb by entering through the back where there are only 2 flights of stairs. 7 brightly decorated rooms with showers and sinks, some with TVs. Living room and kitchen for guest use. Breakfast included. Free internet. Singles €20-25; doubles €35-45; triples €60; quads €70. Oct.-May prices drop by €5. Cash only. ❷

▐ FOOD

Calorie-counters beware: Lisbon has some of the cheapest, most irresistible restaurants of the western European capitals, not to mention the best wine. A full dinner costs about €9-11 per person and the *prato do dia* (daily special) is often only €5-7. Between lunch and dinner, snack on cheap, filling, and addictive Portuguese pastries. The city abounds with seafood specialties such as *pratos de caracois* (snail dishes), *creme de mariscos* (seafood chowder with tomatoes), and *bacalhau cozido com grão e batatas* (cod with chickpeas and boiled potatoes, doused in olive oil). For a more diverse selection of international cuisine, head up to the winding streets of Bairro Alto.

🅰 **noo bai café,** Miradouro de Santa Catarina (☎213 46 50 14; www.noobaicafe.com). Its sandwiches (€3-5) may be excellent and its coffee (€1-2.50) and beer (€2-4) surprisingly affordable, but it's the patio's commanding view of the Tagus and the dramatic, burnt-orange 25 de Abril bridge that draws a crowd. If you see an open table by the railing, spring for it—and stay the whole day. Internet €3 per hr., free with €5 purchase. Open M-Sa noon-midnight, Su noon-10pm. MC/V over €5. ❶

Ristorante-Pizzaria Valentino, R. Jardim do Regedor 37-45 (☎213 46 17 27). A slice of Italy on the Pr. Dos Restauradores. Watch chefs prepare Italian classics in the open kitchen, and keep your eyes peeled for the Portuguese soccer stars known to swing by. Try the crunchy-crusted Pizza Caprese (€8.50). Homemade pasta €7-15. Pizzas €4-9. Open daily noon-midnight. MC/V. ❷

Casa Brasileira, R. Augusta 267-269. A great place to grab a pastry and a drink while sightseeing. Huge selection of baked goods €1-3.50. Large salads and basic entrees (hamburgers, omlettes, etc.) all €8. Open M-Sa 7am-1am, Su 8am-1am. Cash only. ❷

A Brasileira, R. Garrett 120-22 (☎213 46 95 41). This beautiful wood- and marble-filled cafe has been a Lisbon institution since poet Fernando Pessoa started coming here in the early 20th century. (He's still hanging around—that's his statue planted on the patio.) Light sandwiches and croissants €2-4; entrees €8-20. Open daily 8am-2am. Kitchen open noon-3pm and 7-11pm. AmEx/MC/V. ❷

Flôr da Sé, Largo Santo António da Sé, 9-11 (☎218 87 57 42), next to the Santo Antonio church. This *pastelaria* is clean, brightly lit, and serves quality food at notably low prices. The lunchtime *prato do dia* (€4.50) is scrumptious, and homemade desserts and candies taste as good as they look. Open M-F and Su 7am-8pm. Cash only. ❶

À Minha Maneira, Largo do Terreiro do Trigo 1 (☎218 86 11 12; www.a-minha-maneira. pt). Once a bank, the old vault has been revamped into a wine closet. Various meat and fish dishes with little choice for vegetarians. Free Wi-Fi. Entrees €8-15. Open daily noon-3pm and 7-11:30pm. Cash only. ❷❶ **Pitéu,** Lg. da Graça, 95-6 (☎218 87 10 67). *Azulejo*-lined walls and wine-inspired decorations. Serves a few Brazilian dishes in addition to traditional Portuguese dishes of fish, chicken, pork, and steak. Entrees €8-12. Open M-F noon-3pm and 7-10pm, Sa noon-3pm. Cash only. ❷

👁 SIGHTS AND MUSEUMS

BAIXA

AROUND THE ROSSIO. The **Rossio** (Pr. Dom Pedro IV) was once a cattle market, the site of public executions, a bull ring, and carnival ground. Now, the *praça* is the domain of ruthless local motorists who circle a statue of Dom Pedro IV. A statue of Gil Vicente, Portugal's first great dramatist, sits at the top of the **Teatro Nacional de Dona Maria II** at one end of the *praça*. Adjoining the Rossio is the elegant **Praça da Figueira,** on the border of Alfama.

AROUND PRAÇA DOS RESTAURADORES. Just past the Rossio train station, an obelisk and a bronze sculpture of the "Spirit of Independence" commemorate Portugal's break from Spain in 1640. Numerous shops line the *praça* and C. da Glória, the hill that leads to Bairro Alto. **Avenida da Liberdade,** Lisbon's most elegant promenade, also begins at Pr. dos Resatauradores. Modeled after the wide boulevards of Paris, this shady thoroughfare ends at **Praça do Marquês de Pombal,** where an 18th-century statue of the Marquês himself overlooks the city.

BAIRRO ALTO

■**MUSEU ARQUEOLÓGICO DO CARMO.** Located under the skeletal arches of an old church destroyed in the 1755 earthquake, this partially outdoor museum allows visitors to get very close to historical relics like mummies. *(On Lg. do Carmo. ☎ 213 47 86 29. Open M-Sa Oct.-May 10am-6pm, Apr.-Feb. 10am-7pm. €2.50, students and seniors €1.50, under 14 free.)*

■**CEMITÁRIO DOS PRAZERES.** Lisbon's most famous cemetery is not only the final resting place of some of Lisbon society's biggest names, but one of the most pleasant places to spend a peaceful afternoon. Thousands of elaborate mausoleums constitute a veritable city of the dead, replete with tree-lined "avenues" and its own small chapel and museum of death-related artifacts. *(Pr. S. João Bosco. ☎ 213 96 15 11. Take tram 28E (but only cars labeled "Prazeres") from Pr. Do Comércio or Pr. Luís de Camões to the end of the line; the large granite structure in front of you is the entrance. Cemetery open daily May-Sept. 9am-6pm, Oct.-Apr. 9am-5pm. Museum open Tu-Su 10am-4:30pm. Free.)*

ALFAMA

■**CASTELO DE SÃO JORGE.** Built by the Moors in the 11th century, the castle was conquered by Don Alfonso Enriquez, first king of Portugal. The castle was again improved and converted into the royal family's playground between the 14th and 16th centuries. Today, the Castelo consists of little more than stone ramparts, but the towers provide spectacular views of Lisbon. Wander around the ruins or explore the ponds. *(☎ 218 80 06 20; www.egeac.pt. Open daily Mar.-Oct. 9am-9pm; Nov.-Feb. 9am-6pm. Last entry 30min before closing. €5, students €2.50, with Lisboa card €3.50, under 10 or over 65 free.)*

LOWER ALFAMA. The small white **Igreja de Santo António** was built in 1812 over the saint's alleged birthplace. The construction was funded with money collected by the city's children, who fashioned altars bearing saintly images to place on doorsteps. The custom is reenacted annually on June 13, Lisbon's biggest holiday, which draws out thousands and involves a debaucherous festival the night before. The church is located on R. da Alfândeo, which begins two blocks away from Pr. do Comércio and connects Baixa and lower Alfama. *(Veer right when you see Igreja da Madalena in Lg. da Madalena on the right. Take R. de Santo António da Sé and follow the tram tracks. ☎ 218 86 91 45. Open daily 8am-7pm. Mass daily 11am, 5, and 7pm.)* In the square beyond the church is the 12th-century ■**Sé de Lisboa.** The cathedral's age, treasury (a collection of religious objects and manuscripts), and cloister (an archeological site and small museum) make it a worthwhile visit. *(☎ 218 86 67 52. Open daily 9am-7pm except during mass, held Tu-Sa 6:30pm, Su 11:30am and 7pm. Free. Treasury open M-Sa 10am-1pm and 2-5pm. €2.50, students €1.50. Cloister open M-Sa 10am-6:30pm, Su 2-6:30pm. €2.50, students €1.25.)*

GRAÇA

■**PANTEÃO NACIONAL.** The massive building that is now the Panteão Nacional (National Pantheon) was originally meant to be the Igreja da Santa Engrácia. The citizens of Graça started building the church in 1680 to honor their patron saint, but their ambitions soon outstripped their finances. Salazar's military regime eventually took over construction, completing the project and dedicating it in 1966 as the Panteão Nacional, a burial ground for important statesmen. When democracy was restored in 1975, the new government relocated the remains of prominent anti-fascist opponents to this building. The building also houses the honorary tombs of explorers like Vasco da Gama and Pedro Cabral.

(To reach the Panteão, take any #28E tram from R. Do Loreto or R. Garrett. ☎ 218 85 48 20. Open Tu-Su 10am-5pm. €2.50, seniors €1.25, under 14 free. Free Su and holidays until 2pm.)

SÃO SEBASTIÃO

▨**MUSEU DO ORIENTE.** Just opened in 2008, this new museum documents Portugal's more than five centuries of involvement in the East with detailed permanent exhibitions of artifacts from across Asia. Not to be missed are the room-sized Indian Altar to Durga and the dramatic Indonesian Barong, included in the "Gods of Asia" exhibit. *(Av. Brasilia at the Doca de Alcântara. ☎ 213 58 52 00; www. museudooriente.pt. Take tram 15E in the direction of Belém; get off when you see a large warehouse covered in black cloth on your left. Open M, W-Th, Sa-Su 10am-6pm; F 10am-10pm. €4, seniors €2.50, ages 6-12 and students €2, under 6 free. Free F 6-10pm.)*

BELÉM

To reach Belém, take tram #15 from Pr. do Comércio (15min.) and get off at the Mosteiro dos Jerónimos stop, one stop beyond the regular Belém stop. Alternatively, take the train from Estação Cais do Sodré. Exit the station by the overpass near the Padrão dos Descobrimentos. To reach the Mosteiro dos Jerónimos, exit the overpass to the right, then go through the public gardens to R. de Belém.

▨**MOSTEIRO DOS JERÓNIMOS.** Established in 1502 to commemorate Vasco da Gama's expedition to India, the Mosteiro dos Jerónimos was granted UNESCO World Heritage status in the 1980s. The country's most refined celebration of the Age of Discovery, the monastery showcases Portugal's native Manueline style, combining Gothic forms with minute Renaissance detail. Note the anachronism on the main church door: Prince Henry the Navigator mingles with the Twelve Apostles on both sides of the central column. The symbolic tombs of Luís de Camões and navigator Vasco da Gama lie in opposing transepts. *(☎ 21 362 0034. Open May-Sept. Tu-Su 10am-6:30pm; Oct.-Apr. Tu-Su 10am-5:30pm. Church free. Cloister €6, over 65 €2, students free.)*

▨**PADRÃO DOS DESCOBRIMENTOS.** Directly across from the Mosteiro is the 52m Monument to the Discoveries, built in 1960 to commemorate the 500-year anniversary of Prince Henry the Navigator's death. The white monument is shaped like a narrow cross and depicts Henry and his celebrated compatriots, Vasco da Gama and Diogo Cão. An short film about the history of Lisbon is shown inside. *(Across the highway from the Mosteiro ☎ 21 303 1950. Open May-Sept. Tu-Su 10am-6:30pm; Oct.-Apr. 10am-5:30pm. €3, students and seniors €1.50.)*

▨**PARQUE DAS NAÇÕES.** The Parque das Nações (Park of Nations) lies on the site of the former Expo '98 grounds. Until the mid-1990s, the area was a muddy wasteland with a few run-down factories and warehouses along the banks of the Tejo. However, the government transformed it to prepare for the World Exposition and afterward spent millions converting the grounds into a park. The entrance leads through the Centro Vasco da Gama shopping mall to the center of the grounds, where kiosks provide maps. *(M: Oriente. Park ☎ 21 891 9333; www.parquedasnacoes.pt.)*

▨ ♫ FESTIVALS AND ENTERTAINMENT

Those who love to mingle with locals will want to visit Lisbon in June. Open-air *feiras*—festivals of eating, drinking, live music, and dancing—fill the streets. After savoring *farturas* (huge Portuguese pastries whose name means "abundance") and Sagres beer, join in traditional Portuguese dancing. On the night of June 12, the streets explode into song and dance in honor of St. Anthony during the **Festa de Santo António.** Banners are strung between streetlights and confetti falls in buckets during a parade along Av. da Liberdade. Young crowds pack the streets of Alfama and the neighborhoods of Bairro Alto and Santa Catarina, and grilled *sardinhas* (sardines) and *ginja* (wild cherry liqueur) are sold everywhere. Lisbon also has a number of commercial *feiras*. From late May to early June, bookworms burrow for three weeks in the outdoor **Feira do Livro** in Parque Eduardo VII, behind Pr. Marquês de Pombal.

Agenda Cultural and *Follow Me Lisboa*, free at the tourist office and at kiosks in the Rossio on R. Portas de Santo Antão, have information on concerts, *fado*, movies, plays, and bullfights as well as lists of museums, gardens, and libraries.

FADO

A mandatory experience for visitors, Lisbon's trademark entertainment is the traditional *fado*, an expressive art combining elements of singing and narrative poetry. *Cantadeiras de fado*, cloaked in black dresses and shawls, relate emotional tales of lost loves and faded glory.

■ **Café Luso**, Travessa da Queimada, 10 (☎213 42 22 81; www.cafeluso.pt). Pass below the club's glowing neon-blue sign to reach *fado* nirvana. Open since 1927, Lisbon's premier *fado* club combines the best in Portuguese music, cuisine, and atmosphere. Fixed menu €25. Entrees €22-39. Min. €25. *Fado* and folkloric dance 8:30-10pm; the *fado* continues until 2am. Make reservations for F and Sa nights. Open daily 7:30pm-2am. AmEx/MC/V.

■ **O Faia**, R. Barroca, 54-56 (☎213 42 67 42; www.ofaia.com). Performances by famous *fadistas* like Anita Guerreiro and Lenita Gentil, as well as very fine Portuguese cuisine, make O Faia worth your time and money. 4 singers. Entrees €20-35. Min. €20, includes 2 drinks. *Fado* starts at 9:30pm. 2nd show starts at 11:45pm. Open M-Sa 8pm-2am. AmEx/MC/V.

BULLFIGHTING

Portuguese bullfighting differs from the Spanish variety in that the bull is typically not killed in the ring, but butchered afterwards, a tradition that dates back to the 18th century. These spectacles take place most Thursdays from late June to late September at ■**Praça de Touros de Lisboa**, Campo Pequeno. (☎217 93 21 43; www.campopequeno.com.)

FUTEBOL

Futebol is the lifeblood of many a Portuguese citizen. Lisbon's two main teams are ■**Benfica** and **Sporting**, both of which feature some of the world's finest players. (Benfica at Estádio da Luz. ☎707 200 100; www.slbenfica.pt. M: Colégio Militar-Luz. Ticket office open daily 10am-7pm. Sporting at Alvalade Stadium. ☎707 20 44 44; www.sporting.pt. M: Campo Grande. Ticket office open M-F 10am-7pm.)

■ NIGHTLIFE

Bairro Alto, where small bars and clubs fill side streets, is the premier destination for nightlife in Lisbon. **Rua do Norte, Rua do Diário Notícias,** and **Rua da Atalaia** have many small clubs packed into three short blocks. Several gay and lesbian clubs are between **Praça de Camões** and **Travessa da Queimada,** as well as in the **Rato** area near the edge of Bairro Alto. The **Docas de Santo Amaro** hosts waterfront clubs and bars, while **Avenida 24 de Julho** and **Rua das Janelas Verdes** in the **Santos** area have the most popular clubs and discos. Another hot spot is the area along the river opposite the **Santa Apolónia** train station. Jeans, sandals, and sneakers are generally not allowed. Beer runs €3-5 at clubs. Crowds flow in around 2am and stay until dawn. The easiest option to reach most clubs is to take a taxi.

■ **Pavilhão Chinês**, R. Dom Pedro V 89 (☎213 424 729). Ring the doorbell and a red-vested waiter will usher you into this delightful cross between classic and kitsch. Sip a drink or play pool in lounges dripping with Chinese paper fans, model airplanes, and anything else that happened to strike the owner's eclectic fancy. Huge range of teas (€4) and throwback mixed drinks like the Tom Collins and Sidecar (€7.50 each) presented in a 50+ page menu-cum-graphic novel. Open M-Sa 6pm-2am, Su 9pm-2am. AmEx/MC/V.

■ **op art,** Doca de Santo Amaro (☎213 95 67 87; www.opartcafe.com). During the week, trendy op art is a relaxed spot to grab a light meal or a drink; on F and Sa, it morphs from cafe to club as guest DJs pack the small all-glass structure to capacity. Beer €2.50, mixed drinks €5. Cover typically €5-10, includes 1 drink, €10-20 for special events. Open Tu-Th 3pm-2am, F 3pm-6am, Sa 1pm-6am, Su 1pm-2am. AmEx/MC/V.

■ **Restô,** R. Costa do Castelo, 7 (☎218 86 73 34). Don't be surprised to see a flying trapeze or tightrope act—Restô is on the grounds of a government-funded clown school, Chapitô. Upstairs serves Argentine steaks (€17-30) and Spanish tapas (€4-8). Huge, colorful patio with a carnival atmosphere. Downstairs bar open W-Su 10pm-2am. Shows most evenings; check the schedule online. Open M-F noon-3pm and 7:30pm-1:30am, Sa-Su noon-1:30am. Cash only.

■ **Lux,** Av. Infante D. Henrique A, (☎218 82 08 90; www.luxfragil.com). Across from the Sta. Apolónia train station; take a taxi (€5-6 from Baixa or Bairro Alto). One-of-a-kind view from the roof of this enormous 3-story complex, which many deem the best club in Lisbon. Lounge at the bar upstairs or descend into the maelstrom of light, sound, and dancing downstairs. Bouncers are very selective and tend not to look kindly on pushy tourists, so smile, be polite, speak in Portuguese if possible, and dress well—the stylish hipster look works better than suiting up. Arrive after 2am. Cover is typically €12, though you get an equivalent amount in free drinks. Open Tu-Sa 11pm-6am. AmEx/MC/V.

Portas Largas, R. da Atalaia 105 (☎213 46 63 79). Thanks to daily live music, this Bairro Alto classic is a safe bet any night of the week, even during the low-season. Gay-friendly with a mixed, welcoming crowd. Beer €2-4. *Caipirinhas* €4. Open daily July-Sept. 7pm-2am, Oct.-June 8pm-2am. Cash only.

RUSSIA
(РОССИЯ)

Over a decade after the fall of the USSR, mammoth Russia still struggles to redefine itself. Between fierce, worldly Moscow and graceful, majestic St. Petersburg lies a gulf as wide as any in Europe—and a swath of provincial towns that seem frozen in time. Mysterious and inexpensive, with good public transportation and scores of breathtaking sights, Russia is in many ways ideal for the adventurous budget traveler. While the legacy of Communism endures in bureaucratic headaches and the political situation in Chechnya raises tensions, Russia remains the epitome of Eastern European grandeur.

DISCOVER RUSSIA: SUGGESTED ITINERARIES

BEST OF MOSCOW, ONE WEEK. Queue up for the **Lenin Mausoleum** (p. 634) in the morning, then visit Russia's most recognizable landmark, **St. Basil's Cathedral** (p. 634). Check out the minarets and armory inside the **Kremlin** (p. 633) and play spy on a private tour through the old **KGB Building** (p. 637). Don't miss the collections of Russian art at the **State and New Tretyakov Galleries** (p. 636), or the shrines to literary success at museums for **Pushkin, Tolstoy, and Mayakovsky** (p. 637).

BEST OF ST. PETERSBURG, ONE WEEK. Begin with a stroll down **Nevskiy Prospect** (p. 646), St. Petersburg's main drag, then stop at the city's most famous church, the **Church of Our Savior on Spilled Blood** (p. 645). Head to the bell tower of **St. Isaac's Cathedral** (p. 645) for an incomparable view of the city. Visit an attic of aristocracy, the **Hermitage** (p. 645), where the riches are displayed in unthinkable abundance. Then wander the **canals** that make St. Petersburg "the Venice of the North."

ESSENTIALS

FACTS AND FIGURES

OFFICIAL NAME: Russian Federation.

CAPITAL: Moscow.

MAJOR CITIES: St. Petersburg, Nizhniy Novgorod, Novosibirsk, Yekatarinburg.

POPULATION: 140,702,000.

TIME ZONE (WEST RUSSIA): GMT +3.

LANGUAGE: Russian.

CHESS GRANDMASTERS: 194.

OIL EXPORTS: 5,080,000 bbl. per day (213,360,000 gallons).

WHEN TO GO

It may be wise to plan around the peak season (June-Aug.). Fall and spring (Sept.-Oct. and Apr.-May) are more appealing times to visit, since the weather is mild and flights are cheaper. If you intend to visit the large cities and linger indoors at museums and theaters, the bitter winter (Nov.-Mar.) is most economical. Keep in mind, however, that some sights and accommodations close or run reduced hours. Another factor to consider is the number of hours of daylight—in St. Petersburg, summer light lasts almost to midnight, but in winter the sun sets at around 3:45pm.

DOCUMENTS AND FORMALITIES

EMBASSIES AND CONSULATES. Foreign embassies are in Moscow (p. 631); consulates are in St. Petersburg (p. 642). Russian embassies abroad include: **Australia,** 78 Canberra Ave., Griffith, ACT 2603 (☎662 959 033; www.australia. mid.ru); **Canada,** 285 Charlotte St., Ottawa, ON K1N 8L5 (☎613-235-4341; www. rusembcanada.mid.ru); **Ireland,** 184-186 Orwell Rd., Rathgar, Dublin 14 (☎14 92 20 48; www.ireland.mid.ru); **New Zealand,** 57 Messines Rd., Karori, Wellington (☎44 76 61 13, visas 476 9548; www.russianembassy.co.nz); **UK,** 6/7 Kensington Palace Gardens, London W8 4QP (☎20 72 29 64 12), visa 229 8027; www. great-britain.mid.ru); **US,** 2650 Wisconsin Ave., NW, Washington, D.C. 20007 (☎202-298-5700; www.russianembassy.org).

ENTRANCE REQUIREMENTS.
Passport: Required for all travelers.
Visa: Required for all travelers.
Letter of Invitation: Required for all travelers.
Inoculations: Recommended up-to-date on DTaP (diphtheria, tetanus, and pertussis), Hepatitis A, Hepatitis B, MMR (measles, mumps, and rubella), polio booster, rabies, and typhoid.
Work Permit: Required of all foreigners planning to work in Russia.
International Driving Permit: Required of those planning to drive in Russia.

VISA AND ENTRY INFORMATION. Almost every visitor to Russia needs a **visa.** The standard tourist visa is valid for 30 days, while a business visa is valid for up to three months. Both come in single-entry and double-entry varieties. All applications for Russian visas require an **invitation** stating dates of travel. If you have an invitation from an authorized travel agency or Russian organization and want to get a visa on your own, apply for the visa in person or by mail at a Russian embassy or consulate. For same-day processing you must apply in person. Download an application form at www.ruscon.org. (Single-entry visas US$131-300; double-entry US$131-350, except on 10-day processing; multiple-entry US$131-450. Prices change constantly, so check with the embassy) **Visa services** and **travel agencies** can also provide visa invitations (US$30-80), as well as secure visas in a matter of days (from US$160). Some agencies can obtain visas overnight (up to US$450-700). **Host Families Association** (www.hofa.ru), arranges homestays, meals, and transport. Visa invitations for Russia, Ukraine, and Belarus cost US$30-40; www.travelcentre.com.au provides invitations to Russia, sells rail tickets, and arranges tours. **VISAtoRUSSIA.com,** 2502 North Clark Street, Suite 216, Chicago, IL 60614, USA (☎800-339-2118, in Europe ☎749 59 56 44 22), provides invitations from US$30. Students and employees may be able to obtain student visas from their school or host organization.

The best way to cross the **border** is to fly directly into Moscow or St. Petersburg. Another option is to take a train or bus into one of the major cities. Expect delays and red tape. Upon arrival, travelers must fill out an **immigration card** (part of which must be kept until departure from Russia) and to **register** their visa within three working days. Registration can be done at your hostel or hotel, or for a fee at a travel agency. As a last resort, head to the central **OVIR** (ОВИР) office to register. Do not skip this nuisance, as taking care of it will leave one less thing for bribe-seeking authorities to hassle you about—fines for visa

Western Russia

non-registration run about US$150. When in Russia, carry your passport at all times; give it to no one except hotel or OVIR staff during registration.

TOURIST SERVICES AND MONEY

EMERGENCY   Ambulance: ☎03. Fire: ☎01 Police: ☎02.

TOURIST OFFICES. There are two types of Russian tourist offices—those that only arrange tours and those that offer general travel assistance. Offices of the former type are often unhelpful with general questions, but general information offices are usually eager to assist, particularly with visa registration. Big hotels often house tourist agencies with English-speaking staff. The most accurate maps are sold by street kiosks. A great web resource is www.waytorussia.net.

RUSSIA

MONEY. The Russian unit of currency is the рубль (ruble; R), plural рубли (ru-BLEE). One ruble is equal to 100 копейки (kopecks; k), singular копейка, which comes in denominations of 1, 5, 10 and 50. Rubles have banknote denominations of 5, 10, 50, 100, 500, and 1000 and coin denominations of 1, 2, and 5. Government regulations require that you show your passport when you exchange money. Find an Обмен Валта (Obmen Valyuta), hand over your currency—most will only exchange US dollars and euro—and receive your rubles. **Inflation** runs around 12%. Do not exchange money on the street. **Banks** offer the best combination of good rates and security. ATMs (банкоматы; bankomaty) linked to major networks can be found in most cities. Banks, large restaurants, and currency exchanges often accept major **credit cards,** especially Visa. Main branches of banks will usually accept **traveler's checks** and give **cash advances** on credit cards. It's wise to keep a small amount of money (US$20 or less) on hand. Most establishments don't accept torn, written-on, or crumpled bills, and old bills are often declined. Keep in mind, however, that establishments that display prices in dollars or euro also tend to be much more expensive.

RUSSIAN RUBLES (R)	AUS$1 = 21.72R	10R = AUS$0.46
	CDN$1 = 24.07R	10R = CDN$0.42
	EUR€1 = 34.85R	10R = EUR€0.29
	NZ$1 = 19.27R	10R = NZ$0.52
	UK£1 = 51.57R	10R = UK£0.19
	US$1 = 25.45R	10R = US$0.39

HEALTH AND SAFETY

In a medical emergency, either leave the country or go to the American or European Medical Centers in Moscow or St. Petersburg; these clinics have English-speaking, Western doctors. Water is drinkable in much of Russia, but not in Moscow or St. Petersburg, so use **bottled water.** The 0.5-5R charge for **public toilets** generally gets you a hole in the ground and maybe some toilet paper.

Crimes against foreigners are on the rise, particularly in Moscow and St. Petersburg. Although it is often difficult to blend in, try not to flaunt your nationality. Seeming Russian may increase your chances of police attention, but keeps you safer among the citizenry. It is unwise to take pictures of anything related to the military or to act in a way that might attract the attention of anyone in uniform. Avoid interaction with the police unless an emergency necessitates it. It is legal for police to stop anyone on the street (including foreigners) to ask for documentation, so **carry your passport and visa with you at all times.** If you do not (and sometimes even if you do), expect to be taken to a police station and/or to be asked to pay a fine. *Let's Go* does not endorse bribery, but some travelers report that such "fines" are negotiable and, for minor infractions, should not amount to more than 500-1000R. Do not let officials go through your possessions, as travelers have reported incidences of police theft. If police try to detain you, threaten to call your embassy (*"ya pozvonyu svoyu posolstvu"*). It may be simpler and safer to go ahead and pay.

Sexual harassment can still be a problem in Russia. Local men will try to pick up lone **women** and will get away with offensive language and actions. The routine starts with an innocent-sounding *"Devushka..."* (young lady); say *"Nyet"* (No) or simply walk away. Women in Russia tend to dress quite formally. Those who do not speak Russian will also find themselves the target of unwanted attention. The authorities on the Metro and police on the street will frequently stop dark-skinned individuals, who may also receive rude treatment in shops and restaurants. Although **violent crime** against foreigners is generally rare, anti-Semitic and racist hate crimes—including murder—are on the rise. **Homosexuality** is still taboo even in the larger cities; it is best to be discreet.

TRANSPORTATION

BY PLANE. Most major international carriers fly into **Domodedovo** (DME, ☎095 933 6666, www.domodedovo.ru/en) in Moscow or **Pulkovo-2** (LED, ☎812 572 1272, www.pulkovoairport.ru/eng) in St. Petersburg. **Aeroflot**, (Leningradskiy Prospect 37, Building 9, Moscow 125167 ☎495 753 5555; www.aeroflot.org) is the most popular domestic carrier. Aeroflot has come a long way since the fall of communism, and its much-maligned safety record in fact bears comparison with most European airlines. From London, Aeroflot offers cheap flights into Russia. A number of European budget airlines land in **Tallinn, EST; Riga, LAT;** or **Helsinki, FIN,** from which you can reach Russia by bus or train.

BY TRAIN AND BY BUS. In a perfect world, all travelers would fly into St. Petersburg or Moscow, skipping customs officials who tear packs apart and demand bribes, and avoiding Belarus entirely. Nevertheless, many travelers find themselves headed to Russia on an eastbound train. If that train is passing through **Belarus,** you will need a **US$100 transit visa** to pass through the country. If you wait until you reach the Belarusian border to get one, you'll likely pay more and risk being pulled off the train for an unexpected weekend getaway in Minsk. **Trains,** however, are a cheap and relatively comfortable way to travel to Russia from **Tallinn, EST; Riga LAT;** and **Vilnius, LIT.** Domestically, trains are generally the best option. Weekend or holiday trains between St. Petersburg and Moscow sometimes sell out a week in advance. The best class is *lyuks,* with two beds, while the 2nd-class *kupeyny* has four bunks. The next class down is *platskartny,* an open car with 52 shorter, harder bunks. Aim for bunks 1-33; they're farthest from the bathroom. Day trains sometimes have a very cheap fourth class, "*opshiya,*" which typically only provides hard wooden benches. Hotels and tourist offices are invaluable resources for those who don't speak Russian; almost no train station officials speak English, and train schedules are impossibly complicated. **Women** traveling alone can try to buy out a *lyuks* compartment or can travel *platskartny* and depend on the crowds to shame would-be harassers. *Platskartny* is a better idea on the theft-ridden St. Petersburg-Moscow line, as you are less likely to be targeted in that class. Try to board trains on time; changing your ticket carries a fee of up to 25%.

BY BUS. Buses, cheaper than trains, are better for very short distances. Russian roads are in poor condition, making for bumpy trips. They are often crowded and overbooked. Be assertive in ousting people who try to sit in your seat.

BY BOAT. Cruise ships stop in the main Russian ports: St. Petersburg, Murmansk, and Vladivostok. However, they usually allow travelers less than 48hr. in the city. **Ferries** run from Vladivostok to both Japan and Korea, while Kaliningrad is served by links to Sweden and Lithuania. A river cruise runs between Moscow and St. Petersburg.

BY CAR AND BY TAXI. Although it is sometimes necessary to reach Russia's more remote regions, **renting a car** is both expensive and difficult; poor road conditions, the necessity of bribing traffic inspectors, dangerous driving practices, and the frequency of automobile crime make the experience particularly stressful. If you must drive, however, remember to bring your **International Driv-**

ing Permit. **Avis, Budget,** and **Hertz** rent cars in Russia. Hailing a **taxi** is indistinguishable from **hitchhiking**, and should be treated with equal caution. Though it is technically illegal, most drivers who stop will be private citizens trying to make a little extra cash; even cars labeled taxis may not be official. Those seeking a ride should stand off the curb and hold out a hand into the street, palm down; when a car stops, riders tell the driver the destination before getting in; he will either refuse altogether or ask "Сколько?" (Skolko?; How much?), leading to negotiations. Non-Russian speakers will get ripped off unless they manage a firm agreement and are well-aware of the fair price—if the driver agrees without asking for a price, you must ask "*skolko?*" yourself (sign language works too). Never get into a car that has more than one person in it. *Let's Go* does not recommend hitchhiking.

KEEPING IN TOUCH

PHONE CODES	**Country code:** 7. **International dialing prefix:** 8, await a second tone, then 10. For more information on placing international calls, see **inside back cover.**

EMAIL AND INTERNET. Internet cafes are prevalent throughout St. Petersburg and Moscow, but aren't as popular elsewhere, where connections are slower. Internet typically costs 35-70R per hr. Many Internet cafes are open 24hr.

TELEPHONE. Most public telephones take **phonecards**, which are sold at central telephone offices, Metro stations, and newspaper kiosks. When you are purchasing phonecards from a telephone office or Metro station, the attendant will often ask, "На улицу?" (Na ulitsu?; On the street?) to find out whether you want a card for the phones in the station or for outdoor public phones. Be careful: phone cards in Russia are very specific, and it is easy to purchase the wrong kind. For five-digit numbers, insert a "2" between the dialing code and the phone number. Make direct **international calls** from telephone offices in St. Petersburg and Moscow: calls to Europe run US$1-1.50 per min., to the US and Australia about US$1.50-2. **Mobile phones** have become a popular accessory among Russians and are a comforting safety blanket for visitors. Most new phones are compatible with Russian networks and cell phone shops are common, but service can be costly. On average, a minute costs US$0.20 and users are charged for incoming calls. For longer stays consider purchasing a SIM card ($10), but take care that your phone is not locked before buying. Major providers Megafon, BeeLine GSM, and MTS have stores throughout the cities, as do rental chains like Euroset and Svyaznoy. International access codes include: **AT&T** (which varies by region: see www.usa.att.com/traveler/access_numbers/index.jsp for specific info); **British Telecom** (http://www.thephonebook.bt.com); **Canada Direct** (www.infocanadadirect.com); **Sprint** (www.sprint.com/traveler).

MAIL. Mail service is more reliable leaving the country than coming in. Letters to the US arrive one to two weeks after mailing, while letters to other destinations take two to three weeks. Airmail is "авиа" (aviya). Send mail "заказное" (zakaznoye; certified; 40R) to reduce the chance of it being lost. Since most post office employees do not speak English it can be helpful to say "*banderoley*," which signifies international mail, and to know the Russian name of the country of destination. **Poste Restante** (mail held for collection at the post office) is Pismo Do Vostrebovaniya. Address envelopes: LAST NAME, first name, Postal Code, city, Письмо До Востребования, оссия.

RUSSIA

LANGUAGE. Russian is an East Slavic language written in the Cyrillic alphabet. Once you get the hang of the Cyrillic alphabet, you can pronounce just about any Russian word, even if you sound like an idiot. Although English is increasingly common among young people, learn at least a few helpful Russian phrases. For basic Russian words and phrases see **Phrasebook: Russian, p. 792**.

ACCOMMODATIONS AND CAMPING

RUSSIA	❶	❷	❸	❹	❺
ACCOMMODATIONS	under 500R	501-750R	751-1200R	1201-2000R	over 2000R

The **hostel** scene in Russia is limited mostly to St. Petersburg and Moscow and averages US$18-25 per night. Some hostels, particularly those in smaller towns, will only accept Russian guests. Reserve in advance. **Hotels** offer several classes of rooms. "Лкс" (Lyux), usually two-room doubles with TV, phone, fridge, and bath, are the most expensive. "Поли-лкс" (Polu-lyux) rooms are singles or doubles with TV, phone, and bath. The lowest-priced rooms are "без удобств" (bez udobstv), which means one room with a sink. Expect to pay 300-450R for a single in a budget hotel. As a rule, only cash is accepted. In many hotels, **hot water**—and sometimes all water—is only turned on for a few hours each day.

University dorms offer cheap rooms; some accept foreign students for about US$5-10 per night. The rooms are livable, but don't expect sparkling bathrooms or reliable hot water. Make arrangements through an educational institute from home. In the larger cities, private rooms and apartments can often be found for very reasonable prices (about 200R per night). Outside major train stations, there are usually women offering **private rooms** to rent—bargain with them and ask to see the room before agreeing. **Camping** is very rare in Russia.

FOOD AND DRINK

RUSSIA	❶	❷	❸	❹	❺
FOOD	under 80R	81-150R	151-300R	301-500R	over 500R

Russian cuisine is a medley of dishes both delectable and unpleasant; tasty борщ (borshch; beet soup) can come in the same meal as сало (salo; pig fat). The largest meal of the day, обед (obed; lunch), includes: салат (salat; salad), usually cucumbers and tomatoes or beets and potatoes with mayonnaise or sour cream; суп (sup; soup); and курица (kuritsa; chicken) or мясо (myaso; meat), often called котлеты (kotlety; cutlets). Other common foods include щи (shchi; cabbage soup) and блины (bliny; potato pancakes). Vegetarians and kosher diners traveling in Russia will probably find it easiest to avoid rural cuisine and to eat in foreign restaurants. On the streets, you'll see a lot of шашлыки (shashliki; barbecued meat on a stick) and квас (kvas), a slightly alcoholic dark-brown drink. Beware of any meat products hawked by sidewalk vendors; they may be several days old. Kiosks often carry alcohol such as imported cans of beer, which are warm but safe. Beware makeshift labels in Russian—you have no way of knowing what's really in the bottle. Усский Стандарт (Russkiy Standart) and Флагман (Flagman) are the best vodkas; the much-touted Stolichnaya is made mostly for export. Among local beers, Балтика (Baltika; numbered 1-7 according to brew and alcohol content) is the most popular and arguably the best. *Baltika 1* is the weakest (5%), *Baltika 7* the strongest (7%). *Baltikas 4* and *6* are dark; the rest are lagers.

RUSSIA

HOLIDAYS AND FESTIVALS

Holidays: New Year's (Jan. 1-2); Orthodox Christmas (Jan. 7); Orthodox New Year (Jan. 14); Defenders of the Motherland Day (Feb. 23); Orthodox Easter Holiday (Apr. 19th, 2009; April 4th 2010); Labor Day (May 1); Victory Day (May 9); Independence Day (June Accord and Reconciliation Day; Nov. 7); Constitution Day (Dec. 12).

Festivals: The country that perfected the "workers' rally" may have lost Communism but still knows how to Party. Come April, St. Petersburg celebrates **Music Spring**, an international classical music festival, with a twin festival in Moscow. In June, the city stays up late to celebrate the sunlight of **White Nights** (Beliye Nochi; mid-June to early July). The **Russian Winter Festival** is celebrated in major cities from late Dec. to early Jan. with folklore exhibitions and vodka. People eat pancakes covered in honey, caviar, fresh cream, and butter during **Maslyanitsa** (Butter Festival; end of Feb.).

BEYOND TOURISM

For more info on opportunities across Europe see **Beyond Tourism**, p. 55

Kitezh Children's Community (http://atschool.eduweb.co.uk/ecoliza/files/kitezh.html). Teach English to Russian orphans in a rural setting. Young people taking a "gap year" between high school and college are especially common as volunteers.

The School of Russian and Asian Studies, 175 E. 74th St. 21B, New York, NY 10021 (☎1-800-557-8774; www.sras.org). Provides study-abroad opportunities at language schools and degree programs at universities. Also arranges work, internship, and volunteer programs throughout Russia.

MOSCOW (МОСКВА) ☎(8)495

On the 16th-century sidestreets of Moscow (pop. 12,600,000) it is still possible to glimpse centuries-old golden domes squeezed between drab Soviet housing complexes and countless Lenin statues. Visiting Europe's largest city is a thrilling, intense experience, flashier and costlier than St. Petersburg, and undeniably rougher too. Very slowly, Moscow is re-creating itself as one of the world's most urbane capitals, embracing innovation with the same sense of enterprise that helped it command and then survive history's most ambitious social experiment.

⌐ TRANSPORTATION

Flights: International flights arrive at **Sheremetyevo-2** (Шереметыево-2; ☎495 956 4666). Take the **van** under the "автолайн" sign in front of the station to M2: Rechnoy Vokzal (еной Вокзал), or take bus #851 to M2: Rechnoy Vokzal or bus #517 to M8: Planyornaya. **Taxis** to the center of town tend to be overpriced; bargain down to at most 1000R. Yellow Taxi (☎495 940 8888) has fixed prices (base fare usually 400R). **Cars** outside the departures level charge 500-800R; agree on a price before getting in.

Trains: Moscow has 8 train stations arranged around the M5 (circle) line. Tickets for longer trips are sold at the **Moskovskoye Zheleznodorozhnoye Agenstvo** (Московскоые Железнодорожноые Агенство; Moscow Train Agency; Russian destinations ☎495 266 9333, international ☎495 262 0604; www.mza.ru; MC/V), on the far side of Yaroslavskiy Vokzal from the Metro station. **Train** schedules and station names are posted in Cyrillic on both sides of the hall. (Tickets available at the *kassa*, open M-F 8am-1pm and 2-7pm, Sa 8am-1pm and 2-6pm. 24hr. service available at the stations.)

Belorusskiy Vokzal (Белорусский), pl. Tverskoy Zastavy 7 (Тверской Заставы; ☎495 266 0300). M2: Belorusskaya (Белорусская). To: **Berlin, GER** (27hr., 1 per day, 5,550R); **Prague, CZR** (32hr., 1 per day, 3800R); **Vilnius, LIT** (14hr., 1 per day, 1360-2240R); **Warsaw, POL** (21hr., 8 per day, 4 direct, 2200R).

Kazanskiy Vokzal (Казанский), Komsomolskaya pl. 2 (Комсомольская; ☎495 266 2300). M5: Komsomolskaya. Opposite Leningradskiy Vokzal. To **Kazan** (10-12hr., 9 per day, 2 direct, 750-1800R).

Leningradskiy Vokzal (Ленинградский), Komsomolskaya pl. 3 (☎495 262 9143). M1 or 5: Komsomolskaya. To **St. Petersburg** (8hr., 10-20per day, 500-2100R); **Helsinki, FIN** (14hr., 1 per day, 3500R); and **Tallinn, EST** (16hr., 1 per day, 1300-2300R).

Rizhskiy Vokzal (Рижский), pr. Mira 79/3 (пр. Мира; ☎495 631 1588). M6: Rizhskaya (ижская). To **Riga, LAT** (16hr., 2 per day, 1000-4500R) and destinations in **Estonia**.

Yaroslavskiy Vokzal (Ярославский), Komsomolskaya pl. 5a (☎495 921 5914). M1 or 5: Komsomolskaya. Starting point for the **Trans-Siberian Railroad**. To Novosibirsk (48hr-72 hours., every other day, 1900-4900R), **Yaroslavl** (4hr., 1-2 per day, 220-500R), **Siberia**, and the **Far East**.

Public Transportation: The **Metro** (Метро) is fast, clean, and efficient. Metro **trains** and **buses** run daily 5:30am-1am. A station serving multiple lines may have multiple names. Buy token-cards fare cards (19R; 5 trips 75R, 10 trips 180R) from the kassy in stations. Buy **bus** and **trolley tickets** from kiosks labeled "проездные билеты" (15R) or from the driver (25R). Punch your ticket when you get on, or risk a fine.

METRO MADNESS. *Let's Go* has tried to simplify navigation by numbering each Metro line; for a key, see this guide's color map of the Moscow Metro. When speaking to Russians, use the color or name, not our number.

Taxis: Most **taxis** do not use meters and tend to overcharge. Agree on a price before getting in (150-200R across town). **Yellow Taxis** (☎495 940 8888) have fixed rates (base fare 400R). It is common and cheaper to hail a **private car** (called gypsy cabs; частники; chastniki), done by holding your arm out horizontally. Never get into a taxi or car with more than 1 person already in it. Let's Go does not recommend hitchhiking.

➕🚺 ORIENTATION AND PRACTICAL INFORMATION

A series of concentric rings spread outward from the **Kremlin** (Кремль; Kreml) and **Red Square** (Красная Площадь; Krasnaya Ploshchad). The outermost **Moscow Ring Road** marks the city limits, but most sights lie within the **Garden Ring** (Садовое Кольцо; Sadovoe Koltso). Main streets include **Tverskaya Ulitsa** (Тверская), which extends north along the Metro's green line, as well as the **Arbat** (Арбат) and **Novyy Arbat** (Новый Арбат), which run west, parallel to the blue lines. Some kiosks sell English-language and Cyrillic maps; hostels and hotels also have English tourist **maps**. Be careful when crossing streets, as drivers are oblivious to pedestrians; for safety's sake, most major streets have an underpass (переход; perekhod).

Tours: Tourist Information Centre, Ilyinka 4. Enter through the door on the western-most side. (☎495 232 5657; www.moscow-city.ru). M: Gostinyy Dvor. Open daily 10am-7pm. **Capital Tours**, ul. Ilyinka 4 (☎495 232 2442; www.capitaltours.ru), in Gostinyy Dvor. Offers 3hr. English-language bus tours of the city. Tours daily 11am and 2:30pm; 750R. 3hr. tours of the Kremlin and armory M-W, F-Su 10:30am and 230pm (1400R). **Patriarshy Dom Tours**, Vspolny per. 6 (Вспольный; from the US ☎650 678 7076, in Russia ☎495 795 0927; www.russiatravel-pdtours.netfirms.com). M5 or 7: Barrikadnaya (Баррикадная). English-language tours (510-2380R) include "Stalin's Moscow" and "Retrace the Steps of Dr. Zhivago." Open M-F 9am-6pm. No tours Th.

Budget Travel: Student Travel Agency Russia (STAR), located at Baltiyskaya 9, 3rd fl. (Балтийская; ☎495 797 9555; www.startravel.ru). M2: Sokol (Сокол). Offers dis-

MOSCOW

FOOD
Guria, 11
Korchma Taras Bulba, 3
Lyudi Kak Lyudi, 8
Moo-Moo, 9
Kruzhka, 14

NIGHTLIFE
Art-Garbage, 7
B2, 1
FAQ Art Club, 6
Karma Bar, 4
Propaganda, 5
Club Zona, 15
16 Tons, 16

ACCOMMODATIONS
Godzilla's Hostel (HI), 2
Galina's Flat, 17
Sweet Moscow, 10
Nova Hotel, 12
Comrade Hostel, 13

RUSSIA

TO OVIR, 7
TO SAKHAROV MUSEUM (1km)
TO COSMONAUT MUSEUM (6.4km), PAN-RUSSIAN EXPOSITION CENTER
TO NIKULIN MOSCOW CIRCUS (150m)
TO 2 (100m), 3 (200m), CENTRAL MUSEUM OF THE ARMED FORCES (1.2km)
TO AMERICAN (100m)
TO FINLAND TCHAIKOVSKY HALLS (100m)
TO PRESNYA NA PRESNYE 6 (100m), BANI
TO BORODINO MUSEUM (3km)
TO VICTORY PARK (0.8km)
TO NOVODEVICHY MONASTERY (3km), NEW TRETYAKOV MUSEUM (400m)
TO CHURCH OF ST. NICHOLAS IN THE WEAVERS (1km)
TO DANILOV MONASTERY (3.6km)
TO UGLY (5km)

Moscow Zoo
Moscow Choral Synagogue
Bibilo-Globus
Mayakovsky Museum
KGB Museum
Rozhdestvenka
Sanduovskiye Bani
Neglinnaya
Bolshoy Theater
Maly Theater
Metropol Hotel
Dom Inostrannykh Knig
Operetta Theater
Museum of Contemporary Art
Central Telephone & Telegraph
Time Online
Okhotnyy Ryad Underground Mall
State Historical Museum
Lenin's Mausoleum
St. Basil's Cathedral (Pokrovskiy Sobor)
RED SQUARE (KRASNAYA PL.)
KREMLIN
Alexander Gardens (Aleksandrovskiy Sad)
Residence of the President of Russia
Manezh
Moscow Hotel
Kazan Cathedral
Capital Tours
GUM
Hotel Rossiya
State Tretyakov Gallery
Stanislavsky Theater
Museum of Modern Russian History
Young Spectators' Theater
Mossovet Theater
Eliseevsky Gastronom
Ukraine
Gorky Museum House
European Medical Center
New Zealand
Patriarshiy Prud (Patriarch's Pond)
Chaliapin Museum-House
Canada
Stanislavsky Young Spectators' Theater
Pushkin Museum of Fine Arts
Cathedral of Christ the Savior (Khram Khrista Spasitelya)
Pushkin Museum
Tolstoy Museum
Smolenskiy Gastronom
Smolensk

Bol. Ustinskiy Bridge
Mal. Ustinskiy Bridge
Kotelnicheskaya nab.
Bol. Dvinayy Bridge
Kosmodamianskaya nab.
Raushskaya nab.
Sadovnicheskaya nab.
Moskvoretskaya nab.
Bol. Moskvoretskiy Bridge
Bol. Ordynka
Kremlevskaya nab. (Moskva Reka)
Bol. Kamenny Bridge
Prechistenskaya nab.
Moscow River (Moskva Reka)
Smolenskaya nab.
Rostovskaya nab.

THE ARBAT
ul. Novyy Arbat
Starokonyushennyy per.
Plotnikov Per.
Denezhyy per.
Protochnyy per.
Smolenskiy bul.
Novinskiy bul.
Nikitskiy bul.
Gogolevskiy bul.
Sivtsev Vrazhek
Kalashnyy per.
Kislovskiy per.
Vozdvizhenka
Mokhovaya
ul. TVERSKAYA
Tverskaya per.
Bryusov per.
Gazetnyy per.
Nikitskaya ul.
Bolshaya Nikitskaya
Malaya Nikitskaya
Bol. Nikitskaya
Spiridonovka
Bol. Bronnaya
Malaya Bronnaya
Bolshaya Bronnaya
Granatnyy per.
Sadovaya Kudrinskaya
PUSHKINSKAYA
CHEKHOVSKAYA
Petrovka
Dmitrovka
Bolshaya Dmitrovka
Stoleshnikov per.
Myasnitskaya ul.
Lubyanskiy proyezd
Novaya pl.
Staraya pl.
Nikolskaya ul.
Rybnyy per.
Bolshoy Cherkasskiy per.
ul. Varvarka
ul. Ilinka
SLAVYANKA
KITAI GOROD
Pyatnitskay
Bolshaya Ordynka
Serafimovicha ul.
ul. Volkhonka
Znamenka
Romanov per.
Bolshoy Znamenskiy per.
Prechistenka
Ostozhenka
Bolshoy Afanasievskiy per.
Filipovskiy per.
Bogoslovskiy per.
Krivoarbatskiy per.
Gagarinskiy per.
Trubnikovskiy per.
Povarskaya ul.
Malaya Nikitskaya ul.
Merzlyakovskiy per.
Khlebny per.
Skaterny per.
Spiridonyevskiy per.
Bogoslovskiy per.
Bryanskaya
Zoologicheskaya ul.
Bol. Gruzinskaya ul.
KRASNO-PRESNENSKAYA
BARRIKADNAYA
Sadovaya Kudrinskaya ul.
Trifonovskiy per.
Denezhnyy per.
Plyushchikha
Smolenskaya

200 metres
200 yards

count plane tickets, ISICs, and worldwide hostel booking. Branch at Mokhovaya 9 (Моховая), near the Kremlin. Open M-F 10am-7pm, Sa 11am-4pm; June-Aug. also Su 11am-4pm.

Embassies: Australia, Podkolokolnyy per. 10/2 (Подколокольный; ☎495 956 6070; www.australianembassy.ru). M6: Kitai Gorod (Китай Город). Open M-F 9am-12:30pm and 1:10-5pm. **Canada**, Starokonyushennyy per. 23 (Староконюшенный; ☎495 105 6000; www.canadianembassy.ru). M1: Kropotkinskaya (Кропоткинская) or M4: Arbatskaya (Арбатская). Open daily 9am-3pm. **Ireland**, Grokholskiy per. 5 (Грохольский; ☎495 937 5911). M5 or 6: Prospect Mira (Проспект Мира). Open M-F 9:30am-5:30pm. **New Zealand**, Povarskaya 44 (Поварская; ☎495 956 3579). M7: Barikadnaya (Барикадная). Open M-F 9am-12:30pm and 1:30-5:30pm. **UK**, Smolenskaya nab. 10 (Смоленская; ☎495 956 7200; www.britemb.msk.ru). M3: Smolenskaya. Open M-F 9am-1pm, 2-5pm. **US**, Novinskiy 21 (Новинскийй ☎495 728 5000; www.usembassy.ru). M5: Krasnopresnenskaya (Краснопресненская). Open M-F 9am-6pm. American Citizen Services (☎495 728 5577, after hours ☎495 728 5000) lists English-speaking establishments. Open M-F 9am-noon and 2-4pm.

Currency Exchange: Banks are everywhere. Typically only main branches cash **traveler's checks** or issue **cash advances.** Many banks and hotels have **ATMs.** Avoid withdrawing cash from machines on busy streets, as it may make you a target for muggers. The majority of ATMs dispense only ruble.

American Express: ul. Usacheva 33 (☎495 933 8400). M1: Sportivnaya. Exit at the front of train, turn right, and then right again on Usacheva. Open M-F 9am-5pm.

English-Language Bookstore: **Anglia British Bookshop**, Vorotnikovskiy per. 6 (Воротникщвский; ☎495 699 7766; www.anglophile.ru). M2: Mayakovskaya. Open M-F 10am-7pm, Sa 10am-6pm; Su 11am-5pm. AmEx/MC/V.

24hr. Pharmacies: Look for signs marked "круглосуточно" (kruglosutochno; always open). Locations include: Tverskaya 17 (Тверская; ☎495 629 6333), M2: Tverskaya and Zemlyanoy Val 1/4 (Земляной Вал; ☎495 917 0434), M5: Kurskaya (Курская).Новослободская; M9: Novoslobodskaya). 24-100R per hr. Open 24hr. MC/V.

Medical Services: American Clinic, Grokholskiy per. 31 (☎495 937 5757; www.americanclinic.ru). M5 or 6: Prospect Mira (Проспект Мира). American board-certified doctors that practice family and internal medicine. Consultations US$120. Open 24hr., including house calls. AmEx/MC/V. **European Medical Center**, Spiridonievsky per. 5 (☎495 933 6655; www.emcmos.ru). M3: Smolenskaya. Consultations 4320R.

THE BIG SPLURGE

A NEW SORT OF CHEMISTRY CLASS

If you have an extra several thousand rubles handy, you also have the chance to try the newest and perhaps strangest gastronomic experience to hit Moscow since the creation of okroshka, a soup flavored with kvas (a weakly alcoholic drink). These days, chef Anatoly Komm has introduced Russians—the people of hearty meals—to tiny creations in the newest fad: molecular cuisine.

With four high-class restaurants in Moscow, Komm holds tasting events with such suggestive titles as "The Alchemy of Taste" and "Frost and Sea Molecular Spectacle." Diners are asked to turn off their cell phones, to leave cigarettes behind, and to keep their minds open before being presented with between 10 and 20 courses of visionary taste treasures.

The basic principle behind Komm's meals is purely scientific: by breaking food down into its smallest components, one can later put these particles back together in combinations that will excite the tastebuds in new ways. For a fistfull of rubles, you can try a Russkaya Zakuska (Russian Appetizer), a liquid combining the tastes of every traditional Russian appetizer—a thought that is at once disturbing and intriguing.

Check out www.anatolykomm.ru.

Telephones: Local calls require **phone cards,** sold at kiosks and some Metro stops.

Internet: Timeonline (☎495 223 9687), at the bottom of the Okhotnyy Ryad (Охотный Ряд) underground mall. M1: Okhotnyy Ryad. At night, enter through the Metro underpass. Wi-Fi 50-90R per hr. Open 24hr. Cash only. **Cafemax** (www.cafemax.ru) has 4 locations: Pyatnitskaya 25/1 (Пятницкая; M2: Novokuznetskaya); Akademika Khokhlova 3 (Академика Хохлова; M1: Universitet), on the territory of MGU; Volokolamskoye shosse 10 (Волоколамское шоссе; M2: Sokol); and Novoslobodskaya 3 (Новослободская; M9: Novoslobodskaya). 24-100R per hr. Open 24hr. MC/V.

Post Office: Moscow Central Telegraph, Tverskaya ul. 7 (Тверская), uphill from the Kremlin. M1: Okhotnyy Ryad (Охотный яд). **International mail** at window #23. Faxes at #11. Bring packages unwrapped; they will be wrapped and mailed for you. Open M-F 8am-2pm and 3-8pm, Sa-Su 7am-2pm and 3-7pm. **Postal Code:** 125009.

ACCOMMODATIONS

Nova House, 4 Devyatkin pereulok. (Девяткин переулок; ☎495 623 4659. Apt. 6 M1: Kitai Gorod. Go down Maroseika from Kitai Gorod, past McDonald's, and turn left onto Devyatkin Pereulok. Go 30m, and the door will be under an arch. No signs are displayed; ring buzzer 6. This guesthouse has an incredibly hospitable owner named Alex who will make you feel at home in the big city. Only 7min. from Red Square, you can take advantage of free Internet, Wi-Fi, laundry, and a kitchen before relaxing in the living room and watching a soccer game after a hectic day in the city. English spoken. Reception 24hr. Dorms 680R. Cash only. ❷

Godzilla's Hostel (HI), Bolshoy Karetniy 6/5 (Большой Каретний; ☎495 699 4223; www.godzillashostel.com). M9: Tsvetnoy Bulvar (Цветной Бульвар). Fun, social hostel with great location, 7min. from Pushkin Square and 20min. from the Kremlin. English spoken. Female-only dorm available. Kitchen available. Free Internet. Reception 24hr. Check-out noon. Dorms 725R; doubles 1740R. ❷

Sweet Moscow, Stariy Arbat ul. 51, 8th fl. #31 (☎495 241 1446; www.sweetmoscow. com). M4: Smolenskaya. Turn right on Smolenskaya pl., then left at the McDonald's onto the Stariy Arbat. The hostel is located across from Hard Rock Cafe; no signs are displayed, so ring the buzzer. In the middle of the city's most famous pedestrian street. Laundry 150R. Free Internet. Extremely helpful English-speaking reception 24hr. 6-, 8-, and 10-bed dorms US$25. Cash only. ❶

Galina's Flat, 8 Chaplygina St, apt. 35, 5th fl. (☎495 621 6038; email galinas.flat@ mtu-net.ru.) One of the best locations for one of the cheapest prices in all of Moscow, Galina owns the apartment and rents out dorm beds to guests. The kitchen is open to all guests, and since there are only 6 beds email Galina in advance. English spoken. Reception 24hr. Dorms 400R. Cash only. ❶

Comrade Hostel, Maroseyka 11/4. Enter the courtyard, go left to building 5 and up to the third floor. (☎495 628 3126.) This centrally located hostel has a friendly, young, English-speaking staff and a calm atmosphere. Free Wi-Fi. 24hr check-in. 5-bed mixed dorm May-Sept. 840R, Oct.-Apr. 690R Laundry 200R. ❸

FOOD

Many restaurants offer "business lunch" specials (бизнес ланч; typically noon-4pm; US$5-10). For fresh produce, head to a **market.** Some of the best are by the **Turgenevskaya** and **Kuznetskiy Most** Metro stations. (Open daily 10am-8pm.) To find grocery stores, look for "продукты" (produkty) signs or look for big pictures of produce, bread, and sausages on the walls of buildings.

🔳 **Lyudi Kak Lyudi** (Люди как Люди; "People like People"), Solyanskiy Tupik 1/4 (☎495 921 1201). M1: Kitai Gorod. Enter from Solyanka. Fun, dimly-lit cafe is a favorite of young Russians. Business lunch 130R. Sandwiches 100R. English menu. Open M-Th 8am-11pm, F 8am-6am, Sa 11am-6am, Su 11am-10pm. Cash only. ❶

🔳 **Korchma Taras Bulba** (Корма Тарас Бульба), Sadovaya-Samotechnaya 13 (Садовая-Самотуоная; ☎495 694 0056, 24hr. 778 3430; www.tarasbulba.ru). M9: Tsvetnoy Bulvar (Цветной Бульвар). From the Metro, turn left and walk up Tsvetnoy bul. Delicious Ukrainian specialities served by waitresses in folk dress. English-language menu with pictures for extra guidance. Entrees 50-550R. Open 24hr. 12 locations. MC/V. ❸

Kruzhka. Over 20 locations, including 13/1 Myasnitskaya street. Visit www.kruzhka.com for all locations (☎495 411 9445). This bargain chain saves many a poor Muscovite student from starvation. With illustrated menus to help guide your order, sit back and enjoy a pint as you dine on cheap shawarma or chicken kebabs. Entrees 80-230R. Beer from 50R. Open M-Th and Su noon-midnight. F-Sa noon-4pm. Cash only. ❷

Guria (Гуриа), Komsomolskiy pr. 7/3 (Комсомольский; ☎495 246 0378), opposite St. Nicholas of the Weavers. M1 or 5: Park Kultury (Парк Культуры). Walk behind 7/3 until you reach the restaurant. Near Gorky Park and art galleries. Classy and traditional restaurant serves authentic Georgian fare at some of the city's lowest prices. Locals prefer the private, green-roofed gazebo tables in the garden. Enjoy the company of stuffed bears and moose heads if you choose to dine indoors. English-language menu. Entrees 150-500R. Open daily noon-midnight. MC/V. ❸

Moo-Moo (My-My), Koroviy Val 1 (Коровый Вал), ☎495 237 2900), M5: Dobryninskaya (Добрынинская); and Arbat 45/42 (Арбат; ☎495 241 1364), M4: Smolenskaya (Смоленская). Look for the signature cow statue outside. Moo-Moo's many locations offer cheap continental and Russian home cooking, served cafeteria-style inside leaf-covered walls. English-language menu. Salads 30-60R. Entrees 80-130R. Beer from 35R. Open daily 10am-11pm. Cash only. ❶

🔵 SIGHTS

Moscow's sights reflect the city's interrupted history; because St. Petersburg was the seat of the tsardom for 200 years, there are 16th-century churches and Soviet-era museums, but little in between. Though Moscow has no grand palaces and 80% of its pre-revolutionary splendor was demolished by the Soviet regime, the city's museums house the very best of Russian art and history.

THE KREMLIN. The Kremlin (Кремль; Kreml) is the geographical and historical center of Moscow, with origins that date back to the 12th century. In the Kremlin's Armory and its magnificent churches, the glory and the riches of the Russian Empire are on display. Besides the sights listed below, the only other place in the triangular complex visitors may enter is the **Kremlin Palace of Congresses,** the white marble behemoth built by Khrushchev in 1961 for the Communist Party, and since converted into a theater. Tourists were banned from entering the Kremlin until the 1960s; now English-speaking guides offer **tours** of the complex starting at around 1200R. Consider a prearranged tour through **Capital Tours** (see **Tours**, p. 629) or haggle to reduce the price. (☎495 202 3776; www.kreml.ru. M1, 3, 4, or 9: Aleksandrovskiy Sad (Александровский Сад). Open M-W and F-Su 10am-5pm. Buy tickets at the kassa in the Alexander Gardens 9:30am-4:00pm. Kassa closed Th. No large bags. 300R, students 150R. Audio tour 220R. MC/V.)

ARMORY MUSEUM AND DIAMOND FUND. At the southwest corner of the Kremlin, the Armory Museum (Оружейная Палата; Oruzheynaya Palata) shows the opulence of the Russian court and includes coronation gowns, crowns, and the best collection of carriages in the world. Each of the **Fabergé Eggs** in Room 2 reveals an intricate jeweled miniature. The **Diamond Fund** (Выставка Алмазного Фонда; Vystavka Almaznovo Fonda) has even more glitter, including the world's largest chunks of platinum. Consider hiring a guide, as most exhibits are in Russian. (☎ 495 921 4720. *Open M-W and F-Su. Armory lets in groups for 1hr. visits at 10am, noon, 2:30, 4:30pm. 350R, students 70R. Diamond Fund lets in groups every 20min. 10am-1pm and 2-6pm. 350R, students 250R. Bags and cameras must be checked.*)

CATHEDRAL SQUARE. A plethora of golden domes from nine different cathedrals fills the skyline of this square. The church closest to the Armory is the **Annunciation Cathedral** (Благовещенский Собор; Blagoveshchenskiy Sobor), the former private church of the tsars, which guards luminous **icons** by Andrei Rublev and Theophanes the Greek. The square **Archangel Michael Cathedral** (Архангельский Собор; Arkhangelskiy Sobor), which gleams with metallic coffins, is the final resting place for many tsars who ruled before Peter the Great, including Ivans III (the Great) and IV (the Terrible), and Mikhail Romanov. The colorful 15th-century **Assumption Cathedral** (Успенский Собор; Uspenskiy Sobor), located in the center of the square, was used to host tsars' coronations and weddings. It also housed Napoleon's cavalry in 1812. To the right lies the **Ivan the Great Bell Tower** (Колокольная Ивана Великого; Kolokolnaya Ivana Velikovo), once the highest point in Moscow; the tower is currently under renovation. Directly behind it is the 200-ton **Tsar Bell** (Царь-колокол; Tsar-kolokol), the world's largest bell. It has never rung and probably never will—a 1737 fire caused an 11-ton piece to break off.

RED SQUARE. The 700m long Red Square (Красная Площадь; Krasnaya Ploshchad) has hosted everything from farmer's markets to public hangings, from Communist parades to renegade Cessna landings. Across Red Square, northeast of the Kremlin, is **GUM**, once the world's largest purveyor of Soviet "consumer goods," now an upscale shopping mall fit to satisfy the shopping needs of the Russian elite. Also flanking the square are the **Lenin Mausoleum, Saint Basil's Cathedral,** the **State Historical Museum,** and the pink-and-green **Kazan Cathedral.** (*Combo ticket for St. Basil's and Historical museum available at either location. 230R, students 115R.*)

LENIN'S MAUSOLEUM. Lenin's likeness can be seen in bronze all over the city, but he appears in the eerily luminescent flesh in Lenin's Mausoleum (Мавзолей В.И. Ленина; Mavzoley V. I. Lenina). In the Soviet era, this squat red structure was guarded fiercely, with a long wait. Today's line is still long, and the guards remain stone-faced, allowing only a short glimpse of the former ruler as they move people along briskly. Exit along the **Kremlin wall,** where Stalin, Brezhnev, and John Reed, founder of the American Communist Party, are buried. The line to see Lenin forms between the Historical Museum and the Kremlin wall; arrive by noon to have a chance of making it through. (*Open Tu-Th and Sa-Su 10am-1pm. Free. No cameras or cell phones; check them at the bag check in the Alexander Gardens.*)

SAINT BASIL'S CATHEDRAL. Moscow has no more familiar symbol than the colorful onion-shaped domes of St. Basil's Cathedral (Собор Василия Блаженного; Sobor Vasiliya Blazhennovo). Ivan the Terrible built it to celebrate his victory over the Tatars in Kazan in 1552, and it was completed in 1561. "Basil" is the English equivalent of Vasily, the name of a fool who correctly predicted that Ivan would murder his own son. St. Basil's labyrinthine interior is filled with decorative and religious frescoes. Listen out for the choral groups that often perform in the upper chambers. (*МЗ: Ploshchad Revolyutsii (Плщщфдь Зувщлши). ☎ 495 698 3304. Open daily 11am-6pm; kassa closes 5:30pm. 100R, students 50R. English-language audio tour 120R. Tours 1000R; call 2 weeks ahead. Photo 100R, video 130R.*)

NORTH OF RED SQUARE

Just outside the main gate to Red Square is an elaborate gold circle marking **Kilometer 0**, the spot from which all distances from Moscow are measured. Don't be fooled by this tourist attraction—the real Kilometer 0 lies underneath the Lenin Mausoleum. Just a few steps away, the **Alexander Gardens** (Александровский Сад; Aleksandrovskiy Sad) are a respite from the pollution of central Moscow. At the northern end of the gardens is the **Tomb of the Unknown Soldier** (Могила Неизвестного Солдата; Mogila Neizvestnovo Soldata), where an eternal flame burns in memory of the losses suffered in the "Great Patriotic War" (WWII). To the west is **Manezh Square** (Манежная Площадь; Manezhnaya Ploshchad), a recently converted pedestrian area; nearby lies the smaller **Revolution Square** (Площадь Револции; Здщырсрфв Кумщдднгеьшш). Both squares are connected in the north by **Okhotnyy Ryad** (Охотный Ряд; Hunters' Row), once a market for wild game, now an underground mall. Across Okhotnyy Ryad is the **Duma**, the lower house of Parliament. Opposite Revolution Square is **Theater Square** (Театральная Площадь; Teatralnaya Ploshchad), home of the **Bolshoi Theatre** (see **Entertainment**, p. 637). More posh hotels, chic stores, and government buildings line Tverskaya Ulitsa, Moscow's main thoroughfare.

CHURCHES, MONASTERIES, AND SYNAGOGUES

CATHEDRAL OF CHRIST THE SAVIOR. Moscow's most controversial landmark is the enormous gold-domed Cathedral of Christ the Savior (Храм Христа Спасителз; Khram Khrista Spasitelya). Stalin demolished Nicholas I's original cathedral (built in 1839 to commemorate Russia's 1812 victory in the Patriotic War), on this site to make way for a gigantic Palace of the Soviets, but Khrushchev abandoned the project and built a heated outdoor pool instead. In 1995, after the pool's vapors damaged paintings in the nearby Pushkin Museum; Mayor Yury Luzhkov and the Orthodox Church won a renewed battle for the site and built the US $250 million cathedral in only five years. *(Volkhonka 15 (Волхонка), near the Moscow River. M1: Kropotkinskaya (Кропоткинская, ☎ 495 202 4734). www.xxc.ru. Open M-Sa 10am-6pm, Su 8:30am-6pm. Closed last M of the month. Cathedral and museum free. No cameras, shorts, or hats.)*

NOVODEVICHY MONASTERY AND CEMETERY. A serene escape from the city, Moscow's most famous monastery (Новодевиий Монастырь; Novodevichiy Monastyr) is hard to miss thanks to its high brick walls, golden domes, and tourist buses. In the center, the **Smolensk Cathedral** (Смоленский Собор; Smolenskiy Sobor) displays icons and frescoes. The cemetery (кладбище; kladbishche) is a pilgrimage site that holds the graves of such famous figures as Khrushchev, Chekhov, and Shostakovich. *(M1: Sportivnaya (Спортивная) ☎ 495 246 8526. Open M and W-Su 10am-5:30pm; kassa closes 4:45pm; closed 1st M of month. Cathedral closed on rainy and humid days. Cemetery ☎ 495 246 0832. Open daily 10am-5:30pm. Cathedral and special exhibits each 150R, students 60R. Photo 80R, video 170R.)*

MOSCOW CHORAL SYNAGOGUE. Over 100 years old, the synagogue provides a break from the city's ubiquitous onion domes. Though the synagogue remained open during Soviet rule, all but the bravest Jews were deterred by KGB agents who photographed anyone who entered. More than 200,000 Jews now live in Moscow, and services are increasingly well attended, but the occasional graffiti is a sad reminder that anti-Semitism is not dead in Russia. *(M6 or 7: Kitai-Gorod (Китай-Город). Go north on Solyanskiy Proyezd (Солянский Проезд) and take the 1st left. Open M-F 10am-6pm for visitors. Services M-F 8:30am, Sa-Su 9am; evening services daily at 7pm.)*

CHURCH OF ST. NICHOLAS IN KHAMOVNIKI. (Церковь Николая в Хамовниках; ul. Lva Tolstogo) This small late 17th-century church makes you feel like you've stumbled into a fairytale from the hub-bub of Moscow's busy streets. The church is free to enter, and was built by a community of Muscovite weavers. Its glowing candles cast shadows upon the intricate artwork that lines the walls. Former parishoners include Leo Tolstoy. *(M1: Sportinavya.)*

AREAS TO EXPLORE

▨MOSCOW METRO. Most cities put their marble above ground and their cement below, but Moscow's love of opulence means the glitz and glamour extends hundreds of feet underground. The metro (Московское Метро) is worth a tour of its own. See the Baroque elegance of **Komsomolskaya,** the stained glass of **Novoslobodskaya,** and the statues of revolutionary archetypes from farmer to factory worker in **Ploshchad Revolyutsii**—all for the price of a metro ticket.

THE ARBAT. Now a pedestrian shopping arcade, the Arbat was once a showpiece of *glasnost* and a haven for political radicals, Hare Krishnas, street poets, and *metallisty* (heavy metal rockers). Some of that eccentric flavor remains, thanks to street performers and guitar-playing teenagers. Nearby runs the bigger, newer, and uglier **Novyy Arbat,** lined with gray high-rises and massive modern stores. *(M3: Arbatskaya; Арбатская.)*

VICTORY PARK. On the left past the **Triumphal Arch,** which celebrates the 1812 defeat of Napoleon, lies Victory Park (Парк Победы; Park Pobedy), a monument to WWII. It includes the **Museum of the Great Patriotic War** *(Музей Отеественной Войны; Muzey Otechestvennoy Voyny; open Tu-Su 10am-7pm, closed last Th of each month),* the **Victory Monument,** and the gold-domed **Church of St. George the Victorious** (Храм Георгия Победаносного; Khram Georgiya Pobedonosnovo), which honors the 27 million Russians who died in battle during WWII. *(M3: Park Pobedy.)*

▥ MUSEUMS

Moscow's museums are by far the most patriotic part of the city. Government museums and small galleries alike proudly display Russian art, and dozens of historical and literary museums are devoted to the nation's past.

▨STATE TRETYAKOV GALLERY. With over 130,000 works of 11th- to early 20th-century Russian art, the Tretyakov Gallery (Государственная Третьяковская Галерея; Gosudarstvennaya Tretyakovskaya Galereya) could absorb an art lover for quite some time. A superb collection of **icons,** including works by Andrei Rublev and Theophanes the Greek is also on display. *(Lavrushinskiy per. 10 (Лаврушинский). ☎ 495 230 7788; www.tretyakov.ru. M8: Tretyakovskaya. Turn left out of the Metro, left again, then take a right on Bolshoy Tolmachevskiy per.; turn right after 2 blocks onto Lavrushinskiy per. Open Tu-Su 10am-7:30pm; kassa closes 6:30pm. 250R, students 150R.)*

▨NEW TRETYAKOV GALLERY. Where the first Tretyakov chronologically leaves off, this new gallery (Новая Третьяковская Галерея; Novaya Tretyakovskaya Galereya) begins. The collection starts on the third floor with early 20th-century art and moves through the neo-Primitivist, Futurist, Suprematist, Cubist, and Social Realist schools. The second floor holds temporary exhibits; go on weekday mornings to avoid crowds. Leaving the front door, turn left to find a statue gallery that is a real gem. The dumping ground for decapitated Lenins and Stalins and other Soviet-era statues, it now also contains sculptures of Gandhi, Einstein, Niels Bohr, and Dzerzhinsky, the founder of the Soviet secret police. *(Krymskiy Val 10 (Крымский Вал). ☎ 495 283 1378; www.tretyakov.ru. M5: Oktyabraskaya (Октябрьская). Open Tu-Su 10am-7:30pm; kassa closes at 6:30pm. 250R, students 150R. Sculpture garden open daily 9am-10pm. 100R.)*

PUSHKIN MUSEUM OF FINE ARTS. Moscow's most important collection of non-Russian art, the Pushkin Museum (Музей Личннх Колечцц. А.С. Пушкина; Muzey Izobrazitelnykh Iskusstv im. A.S. Pushkina) contains major Classical, Egyptian, and Renaissance works, boasting originals from Botticelli, Monet, Cezanne and Van Gogh. *(Volkhonka 12 (Волхонка).* ☎ *495 203 9578; www.gmii.com. M1: Kropotkinskaya (Кропоткинская). Open Tu-Su 10am-6pm; kassa closes 6pm. 60R, students 30R.)* The building to the right (Volkhonka 10) of the entrance houses the **Museum of Private Collections** (Veзtй Линых Rjллtций; Muzey Lichnych Kolletsiy), with artwork by Kandinsky, Rodchenko, and Stepanov. *(Open W-Su noon-7pm; kassa closes 6pm. 100R, students 50R.)*

STATE HISTORICAL MUSEUM. This English-language exhibit (Государственный Историеский Музей; Пщыгвфкыемуттнн Шыещкшсруылшн Ьгяун) on Russian history runs from the Neanderthals through Kyivan Rus to modern Russia. Each hall's decoration reflects the era it houses. *(Krasnaya pl. 1/2. M1: Okhotnyy Ryad (Охотный Ряд).* ☎ *495 692 3731; www.shm.ru. Open M and W-Sa 10am-6pm, Su 11am-8pm; kassa closes 1hr. earlier; closed 1st M of month. 150R, students 60R.)*

KGB MUSEUM. Documenting the history and strategies of Russian secret intelligence from Ivan the Terrible to Putin, the KGB Museum (Музей КГБ; Muzey KGB) gives punters the chance to quiz a current FSB agent. *(Bul. Lubyanka 12 (Лубянка). M1: Lubyanka.* ☎ *495 299 6724 . By pre-arranged tour only. Patriarshy Dom Tours, p. 629, leads 2hr. group tours; 550R per person.)*

HOMES OF THE LITERARY AND FAMOUS. The ▓**Mayakovsky Museum** (Музей им. В. В. Маяковского; Muzey im. V. V. Mayakovskovo) is a biographical walk-through of the futurist poet's life and art. Mayakovsky lived and died in a communal apartment on the fourth floor of this building. *(Lubyanskiy pr. 3/6 (Лубянский). M1: Lubyanka.* ☎ *495 921 9560 Open M-Tu and F-Su 10am-6pm, Th 1-9pm; kassa closes 1hr. earlier; closed last F of month. 90R, students 50R.)* If you've never seen Pushkin-worship firsthand, the **Pushkin Literary Museum** (Литературный Музей Пушкина; Literaturnyy Muzey Pushkina) with its large collection of Pushkin memorabilia, will either convert or frighten you. Either way, the sheer amount of Pushkinalia merits the small entrance price. *(Prechistenka 12/2 (Преистенка). Entrance on Khrushchevskiy per (Хрущевский). M1: Kropotkinskaya (Кропоткинская). Open Tu-Su 10am-6pm; kassa closes 5:30pm; closed last F of month. 60R.)* The **Tolstoy Museum** (Музей Толстого; Muzey Tolstovo), in the author's first Moscow neighborhood, displays original texts, paintings, and letters related to his masterpieces. *(Prechistenka 11 (Пречистенка). M1: Kropotkinskaya (Кропоткинская).* ☎ *495 637 7410; www.tolstoymuseum.ru. Open Tu-Su 10am-6pm; kassa closes 30min. earlier; closed last F of month. 150R, students 50R.)*

🎭 ENTERTAINMENT

From September through June, Moscow boasts some of the world's best **ballet, opera,** and **theater** performances. Tickets are often cheap (from 130R) if purchased ahead and can be bought from the theater *kassa* or from kiosks in town. **Bolshoi Theater** (Большой Театр), Teatralnaya pl. 1, is home to the opera and the ballet company. Though the main stage is under renovation, and not due to reopen until November 2009, performances continue on the secondary stage. (Театральная; ☎ 495 250 7317; www.bolshoi.ru. M2: Teatralnaya. *Kassa* on Petrovska ul., open daily 11am-3pm and 4-8pm. Performances Sept.-June daily 7pm, occasional matinees. 50-5000R. AmEx/MC/V.) The **Moscow Operetta Theater,** Bolshaya Dmitrovka 6, stages operettas. (Большая Дмитровка; ☎495 692 1237; www.mosoperetta.ru. *Kassa* open daily 11am-3pm and 4-7:30pm. Performances daily, 6 or 7pm. 300-1500R.)

NIGHTLIFE

Moscow's nightlife is the most varied, expensive, and debaucherous in Eastern Europe. Many clubs flaunt their exclusivity, but the city's incessant insomnia and love of house music make finding a full dance floor easy. Check the weekend editions of *The Moscow Times* or *The Moscow Tribune* for club reviews, music listings, and information on upcoming concerts.

> **SAVE FACE.** When navigating the hostile, exclusive world of Moscow nightlife, our researchers have found that there is only one proven technique to ensure that "face control" (the bouncer) doesn't ruin the night before it starts: become a wealthy, tall, waifish, blonde model in high Russian style. More realistically, try to find friends with connections, dress up, go early, and get ready to have your face controlled.

Propaganda, (Пропаганда), Bolshoy Zlatoustinskiy per. 7 (Большой Златоустинский; ☎495 624 5732; www.propogandamoscow.com). M6 or 7: Kitai Gorod (Китай-Город). Exiting the Metro, walk down Maroseyka and take a left on Bolshoy Zlatoustinsky per. Come before midnight to sip on reasonably priced drinks, then go downstairs for some quality house music and dance until dawn. Go early to eat (and avoid strict face control). Dancing after midnight. Th DJ night. Beer from 80R, after 11pm from 60R. Open daily noon-6am.

FAQ Art Club, Gozetniy per. 9/2 (☎495 629 0827; www.faqclub.ru). M2: Teatralnaya. Chill with Moscow's young, alternative crowd on the tented patio or in 1 of 4 house-themed rooms—drawings for the pre-school playhouse are appreciated. Jazz concerts Su 8pm, 300R. Call to reserve a table. Entrees 115-420R. Beer from 115R. Mixed drinks from 130R. Hookahs from 500R. Free Wi-Fi available. Open daily 7pm-6am.

Karma Bar, Pushechnaya 3 (Пушечная; ☎495 624 5633; www.karma-bar.ru). M1 or 7: Kuznetzkiy Most (Кузнетский Мост). With your back to the Metro, walk through the arch on your left and turn right on Pushechnaya. Crowd-pleasing Latin beats keep the party alive. English spoken. Beer 110-170R. Vodka 150-160R. Mixed drinks 260-320R. Su hiphop. Cover F-Sa after 11pm men 240R, women 200R. Open Th-Sa 9pm-6am, Su 11pm-6am. Sportswear strictly prohibited.

Art-Garbage, Starosadskiy per. 5/6 (Старосадский; ☎495 628 8745; www.art-garbage.ru). M6 or 7: Kitai Gorod (Китай-Город). Art gallery, club, and restaurant, Art-Garbage is refreshingly more laid-back than many of the chic and trendy Moscow establishments. Better for drinking on the inviting patio than for dancing. Hard liquor from 60R. Beer from 70R. Cover F-Sa 150-500R. Open F-Su 11am-6am.

B2, Bolshaya Sadovaya 8 (Большая Садовая; ☎495 209 9918; www.b2club.ru). M5: Mayakovskaya. This multi-story complex has it all, and without the face control: a quiet beer garden, billiard room, several dance floors, jazz club, karaoke, restaurant, sushi bar, and weekend disco. Beer 80-180R. Hard liquor from 100R. F-Sa Concerts from 200R; some free with ISIC; check website. Open daily noon-6am. MC/V.

Club Zona (Зона), ul. Leninskaya sloboda, 19/2. (ул. Ленинская слобода; ☎495 675 6975; www.zonaclub.ru.) M3: Avtozavodskaya. Dance until dawn with Moscow's young and restless in the city's largest nightclub. Once you get past the barbed wires and steel gates of this prison-themed club, you'll be faced with a feast of spectacles aimed to surprise even those who have seen it all. 5 floors. Come early to eat and avoid strict face control. English spoken. Dress to impress. Beer from 90R. Mixed drinks 120-250R. Cover 500-1,000R. F-Sa 11pm-7am.

Sixteen Tons, Presnensky Val 6/1. (☎495 253 0530; www.16tons.ru.) M2: Ulitsa 1905 Goda. Resembles an English pub on the main floor with a quirky dance floor upstairs.

This pub/restaraunt/club hosts local Russian acts. Great for getting to know some Muskovites gnoshing on pub grub. Cover Th-Sa. 100-400R. Open daily 11am-6am.

ST. PETERSBURG
(САНКТ-ПЕТЕРБУРГ)   ☎(8)812

Saint Petersburg combines the Russian high-life with a strong literary intellectual vibe. Peter the Great's penchant for gilded facades and the legacy of Russian literary giants ensure that splendor and culture are never far away. However, due to its location and Russian visa requirements, this majestic city serves more as a shrine to Russia's superb architecture, art, and literature than as an international tourist hotspot. Take advantage of this during the winter, when the snow-covered city still has many cultural events, or during the summer, when the city's white nights are truly worth losing some sleep over.

▐ TRANSPORTATION

Flights: The main airport, **Pulkovo** (Пулково), 18/4 Pilotov str. (www.pulkovo.ru) has 2 terminals: Pulkovo-1 (☎812 704 3822) for domestic flights and Pulkovo-2 (☎812 704 3444) for international flights. To get to the town center from the airport, go to the 1st bus stop on your left when exiting the airport, and grab **bus** #13 to Movskovskaya metro station. Go 7 stops over on the **metro** to Nevskiy Pr. to land in the center of town. Alternatively, hostels can also arrange **taxis** for about US$35-40. To get to the airport from the Moskovskaya (Московская) train station: take bus #13 to Pulkovo-1 (20min.) or to Pulkovo-2 (25min.).

Trains: Tsentralnye Zheleznodorozhny Kassy (Центральные Железнодорожные Кассы; Central Railroad Ticket Offices), Canal Griboyedova 24 (Грибоедовфа; ☎067).Bring cash and expect about a 20 minute wait to buy tickets from any of the open tickets windows (marked *kassy*) on your left and right.

Finlyandskiy Vokzal (Финляндский; Finland Station.), 6 Lenina pl. (Пл. Ленина; ☎812 768 7539). M1: Pl. Lenina. Sells tickets to destinations in the suburbs of St. Petersburg. Ticket counters #9 and #10 also sell tickets to **Helsinki, FIN**, (6hr., 2 per day, 2000-6000R). Luggage storage; look for signs. Also sells domestic airline tickets. ▶Interesting fact! Lenin arrived here from Finland disguised as a railway worker on April 3rd, 1917 to start the October Revolution.

Moskovskiy Vokzal (Московский; Moscow Station), 2 Vosstaniya pl. (Восстания; ☎812 168 4597). M1: Pl. Vosstaniya. 24hr. luggage storage; look for signs. From 50R. To: **Moscow** (5-9hr., 15-20 per day, 515-2500R); **Novgorod** (electrichka 3-4hr., 1 per day, 320R); **Siberia**, and **Sevastopol, UKR** (35hr., 1 per day, 1520-2700R).

Vitebskiy Vokzal (Витебский; Vitebsky Station; ☎812 168 5939 ☎812 168 3918). M1: Pushkinskaya. To: **Kyiv, UKR** (24hr., 1 per day, 990-1450R); **Odessa, UKR** (36hr.; June-Sept. 1 per day, Oct.-May 4 per week; 1100-2330R); **Riga, LAT** (13hr., 1 per day, 1700-2600R); **Tallinn, EST** (8hr., 1 per day, 640-1600R); **Vilnius, LIT** (14hr., 1 every other day, 1070-1790R); **Warsaw, POL** (1 day, 9 hr., 1 per day, 1100-1900 R). Luggage storage 51R per day.

Buses: Автовокзал (Bus Station), nab. Obvodnogo Kanala 36 (Обводного Канала; ☎812 766 5777; www.avokzal.ru). M4: Ligovsky Prospect. Take bus #3, 24, 34, 74 or trolleybus #42 to the canal. Facing the canal, turn right and walk 2 long blocks. The station will be on your right. 10R surcharge for advance tickets. Domestic and international desinations. Ticket office open daily 8am-8pm.

Local Transportation: St. Petersburg's **Metro** (Метро) is the deepest in the world and runs daily 5:45am-12:30am. You need a **zheton** (жетон; token) to enter, which costs 17R. Passes available for 7, 15, 30, or 90 days. 4 lines cover much of the city. **Buses, trams, and trolleys** (14R) run fairly frequently (6am-midnight). Licensed **private mini-**

0 ___ 300 meters
0 ___ 300 yards

N
LG

PETROGRAD SIDE

Kropotkina

Malaya Posadskaya.

Malaya Monetnaya
Malaya Monetnaya

Bolshaya Zelenina

Voskova

Markina

Sytninskaya

Vvedenskaya

Bolshoy pr.

Bolshaya Pushkarskaya

Lizy Chaikinoy

Alexandrovskiy Park

■ Synt. Market

Ⓜ GORKOVSKAYA

Mosque

Museum of Russian Political History

Kuybysheva

Kamennoostrovskiy pr.

Peter's Cabin Museum

Sezzhinskaya

Talarsky per.

Military History Museum

Zverinskaya

Blokhina

■ Zoo

Peter and Paul Cathedral

Petrovskaya nab.

Kronverkskaya nab.

Kronverkskiy pr.

Yablochkova

Tuchkov most

SPORTIVNAYA

Dobrolyubova

Mythninskaya

Fortress of Peter and Paul

■ **Nevskiy Gate**

Trubetskoy Bastion

Troitskiy most

nab.

Malaya Neva

Birzhevoy most

Rostral Column

nab. Makarova

The Marble Palace

Tuchkov Volkhovskiy Pr.

Birzhevoy Pr.

Birzhevaya

Central Naval Museum 血

VASILEVSKIY ISLAND

Mendeleyevskaya

Zoological Museum

Rostral Column

Aptekarsky per.

Millionnaya

Dvortsovaya nab.

Pushkin Museum

Akademicheskaya Kapella

1-ya Linii

2-3-ya Linii

Repina

Filologicheskiy Pr.

Kunstkamera Anthropological and Ethnographic Museum

Dvortsovyy most

⚓

Hermitage

Finnair

nab. Kan. Griboyedova

St. Petersburg State University

Winter Palace

DVORTSOVAYA PLOSHCHAD

BA

Menshikov Palace ■

ⓘ

Alexander Column

Bolshaya Konyushennaya

Malaya Konyushennaya

Academy of Arts ■

Universitetskaya nab.

Bolshaya Neva

Admiralteyskaya nab.

The Admiralty

Admiralty Proezd

☎

Australi

Nevsky Prospect

7 10

$

Dom Knigi

Lufthansa

Aur
Air

Bronze Horseman ■

Alexandrovskiy Garden

Admiralty

Bolshaya Morskaya

℞

Stroyanar Palace

SAS

Kazansky Cathedral

Angliyskaya nab.

KLM/Air France

AmEx $

Malaya Morskaya

Central Railroad Ticket Office

6

Manezh 血

✝ **St. Isaac's Cathedral**

Delta Airlines/ CSA Czech Airlines

nab. Reki Moyki

Pochtamtskiy per.

Konnogvardeyskiy bul.

Yakubovicha

✉

Pochtamtskaya

nab. Reki Moyki

11

Gorsova Pr.

Griboyedov Canal

Bankovsky per.

Galernaya

Truda

Moyka River

Kazanskaya

3

Sadovaya ul.

Gorokhovaya

Apraksin Pr.

New Holland

Voznesenskiy Pr.

✚ **American Medical Center**

Dekabristov

ul. Pisareva

SENNAYA

Big Market: 24 Hours Ⓜ

SADOVAYA

Ⓜ

Kirov Opera and Ballet/ Mariinskiy Theater

8

SENNAYA PL.

Stolярny Pr.

Sadovaya ul.

Conservatory

Great Choral Synagogue ✡

9

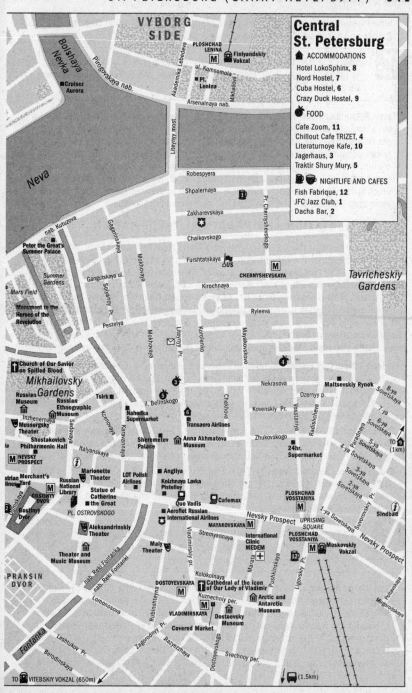

VYBORG SIDE

Bolshaya Nevka

Prigovskaya nab.

Akademika Lebedeva

ul. Komsomola

PLOSHCHAD LENINA
Ⓜ

Finlyandskiy Vokzal

Pl. Lenina

Mikhailova

Arsenalnaya nab.

Cruiser Aurora

nab. Kutuzova

Neva

Peter the Great's Summer Palace

Summer Gardens

Mars Field

Monument to the Heroes of the Revolution

Robespyera

Shpalernaya

Zakharevskaya

Chaikovskogo

Furshtatskaya

Kirochnaya

Ryleeva

Nekrasova

Ozernyy p.

Gagarinskaya

Gangutskaya ul.

Solyanoy Pr.

Pestelya

Mokhovaya

Pr. Chernyshevskogo

BUS

Ⓜ **CHERNYSHEVSKAYA**

Mayakovskovo

Kovenskiy Pr.

Vosstaniya

Radishcheva

Tavricheskiy Gardens

Maltsevskiy Rynok

8-ya Sovetskaya
7-ya Sovetskaya
6-ya Sovetskaya
5-ya Sovetskaya
4-ya Sovetskaya
3-ya Sovetskaya
2-ya Sovetskaya
1-ya Sovetskaya

Paradnaya

Suvorovskiy Pr.

TO Ⓘ ⑨ (1km)

Sindbad Ⓘ

Church of Our Savior on Spilled Blood

Mikhailovsky Gardens

Russian Museum

Russian Ethnographic Museum

Inzhenernaya

Mussorgsky Theater

Shostakovich Philharmonic Hall

Ⓜ **NEVSKY PROSPECT**

Merchant's Yard

GOSTINYY DVOR

Gostinyy Dvor

PL. OSTROVSKOGO

Aleksandrinskiy Theater

Theater and Music Museum

PRAKSIN DVOR

Tsirk

Sadovaya

Italyanskaya

Karavannaya

Ksenofya

Nahodka Supermarket

Sheremetev Palace

Russian National Library

Marionette Theater

Statue of Catherine the Great

LOT Polish Airlines

Angliya

Knizhnaya Lavka Pisteiley

il. Belinskogo

Liteyny Pr.

Korolenko

Chekhova

③

④

⑤

⑥

Transaero Airlines

Anna Akhmatova Museum

Zhukovskogo

24hr. Supermarket

PLOSHCHAD VOSSTANIYA
Ⓜ

Quo Vadis

Aeroflot Russian International Airlines

Cafemax

Nevsky Prospect

UPRISING SQUARE

1-ya Sovetskaya

Nevskiy Prospect

Mars Field

Mokhovaya

Liteyny most

Prigovskaya nab.

Maly Theater

Stremyannaya

Vladimirskiy pr.

MAYAKOVSKAYA
Ⓜ

International Clinic MEDEM ✚

PLOSHCHAD VOSSTANIYA
Ⓜ

Moskovskiy Vokzal

Marata

Pushkinskaya

Ligovskiy Pr.

⑫

nab. Reki Fontanki

DOSTOYEVSKAYA
Ⓜ

Kolokolnaya

Cathedral of the Icon of Our Lady of Vladimir

Kuznechniy per.

VLADIMIRSKAYA
Ⓜ

Dostoevsky Museum

Arctic and Antarctic Museum

Covered Market

Rubinshteyna

Zagorodnyy pr.

Razyezzhaya

Dostoyevskogo

Svechnoy per.

Lomonosova

Leshtukov Pr.

Fontanka

Berodinskaya

TO 🚉 VITEBSKIY VOKZAL (650m)

🚉 (1.5km)

Mirgorodskaya

Poltavskaya

Central St. Petersburg

🏠 **ACCOMMODATIONS**
Hotel LokoSphinx, 8
Nord Hostel, 7
Cuba Hostel, 6
Crazy Duck Hostel, 9

🍅 **FOOD**
Cafe Zoom, 11
Chillout Cafe TRIZET, 4
Literaturnoye Kafe, 10
Jagerhaus, 3
Traktir Shury Mury, 5

☕ **NIGHTLIFE AND CAFES**
Fish Fabrique, 12
JFC Jazz Club, 1
Dacha Bar, 2

RUSSIA

buses (маршрутки; ьфкыркгелш; 15-17R) move more quickly and stop on request (routes and prices are displayed on windows in Cyrillic).

 SMILE FOR THE POLICE: Beware of taking photos in the metro! This is prohibited both in St. Petersburg and Moscow, and will result in fines of up to 300 ruble.

Taxis: Both marked and private cabs operate in St. Petersburg. **St. Petersburg Taxi** is the city's umbrella service. (☎068 from a land line, ☎324 7777 from a mobile phone; 20R per km.) Marked cabs have a metered rate of 15-20R per km but most cabs want to set prices without the meter. Because taxis are notorious for overcharging tourists, always confirm the price before your trip. Ask "*skolka*?" which means "how much," and always barter below the given price. Instead of taking a taxi, many locals hail **private cars,** which is usually cheaper but unsafe for travelers new to the area. Never get in a car with more than 1 person in it. *Let's Go* does not recommend hitchhiking.

⚑ ORIENTATION AND PRACTICAL INFORMATION

St. Petersburg sits at the mouth of the **Neva River** (Нева) on 44 islands among 50 canals. The heart of the city lies on the mainland, between the south bank of the Neva and the **Fontanka River.** Many of St. Petersburg's major sights, including the **Hermitage,** are on or near **Nevskiy Prospect** (Невский проспект), the city's main street, which extends from the **Admiralty** to the **Alexander Nevskiy Monastery;** the **Moscow Train Station** is near the midpoint. Trolleys #1, 5, 7, 10, 17, and 22 run along Nevskiy Pr. northwest of the center and across the Neva lies **Vasilevskiy Island** (Vasilevskiy Ostrov), the city's largest island. On the north side of the Neva is the **Petrograd Side** archipelago, where the **Peter and Paul Fortress** stands.

Tourist Office: City Tourist Information Center, ul. Sadovaya 14 (Садовая; ☎812 310 2822; www.saintpetersburgvisit.ru). M3: Gostinyy Dvor. English-language advice, brochures, and guidebooks. Open M-F 10am-7pm, Sa noon-8pm. *St. Petersburg in Your Pocket* and *St. Petersburg Times* (www.sptimes.ru), free in tourist offices, hotels, and hostels, provide culture, entertainment, and nightlife listings.

Tours: Peter's Walking Tours, 3-ya Sovyetskaya 28 (3-я Советская; www.peterswalk. com), in the International Youth Hostel. Tours, including the "Dostoevsky Murder Route Pub Crawl," (June-Sept.) 430-800R. Specialty tours (4-6hr.) available on request.

Budget Travel: Sindbad Travel (FIYTO), 2-ya Sovetskaya 12 (2-я Советская; ☎812 332 2020; www.sindbad.ru). M1: pl. Vostanniya. Books plane, train, and bus tickets. Student discounts on flights, partnered with STA Travel. English spoken. Open M-F 10am-10pm, Sa-Su 10am-6pm.

 WATER WATER EVERYWHERE. St. Petersburg lacks an effective water purification system, making exposure to giardia (p. 26) very likely, so boil tap water, buy bottled water, or use iodine.

Consulates: Australia, Italyanskaya 1 (Итальянская; ☎/fax 812 325 7333; http:// www.russia.embassy.gov.au). M2: Nevskiy Prospect. Open M-F 9am-6pm. **Canada,** St Petersburg, Malodetskoselsky prosp. #32. (☎812 275 0502.) In an emergency, citizens of **Ireland** and **New Zealand** can call the UK consulate. **UK,** Pl. Proletarskoy Diktatury 5 (Пролетарской Диктатурыж ☎812 320 3200, emergency ☎812 937 6377; www. britain.spb.ru). M1: Chernyshevskaya. Open M-F 9am-1pm, 2-5pm. **US,** Furshtatskaya 15 (Фурштатская; ☎812 331 2600, emergency ☎812 331 2888; www.stpetersburg-usconsulate.ru). M1: Chernyshevskaya. M-F 9am-5:30 pm. Closed US and Russian holidays. Phone inquiries M-Tu, Th-F 10am-1pm, W 3-5pm.

Currency Exchange: ATMs are ubiquitous downtown and occasionally dispense dollars or euros. For **exchange booths** look for "обмен валюты" (obmen valyuti) signs everywhere, and don't forget your passport.

English-Language Bookstore: Angliya British Bookshop (Англия), nab. Reki Fontanka 38 (Реки Фонтанки; ☎812 579 8284). M2: Nevskiy Prospect. Open daily 10am-8pm. MC/V. **Dom Knigi** (Дом Книги; House of Books), Nevskiy pr. 28 (☎812 448 2355; www.spbdk.ru). M2: Nevskiy Prospect. Open daily 9am-midnight. MC/V.

Emergency: Police: ☎02. **Ambulance:** ☎03. **Fire:** ☎01. **Police Services for Foreigners:** ☎812 702 2177.

24hr. Pharmacy: PetroFarm, Nevskiy pr. 22 (☎812 314 5401), stocks Western medicines and toiletries. Pharmacist daily 9am-10pm. MC/V. Pharmacies are ubiquitous throughout the city, just look for an "Аптека" sign—many are open until late at night.

Medical Services: American Medical Center, nab. Reki Moyki 78 (Реки Мойки; ☎812 740 2090; www.amclinic.com). M2: Sennaya Pl. English-speaking doctors provide comprehensive services, including house calls and a helicopter ambulance. Insurance billing available. Consultation US$75. Open 24hr. AmEx/MC/V.

Internet Access: Quo Vadis, Nevskiy pr. 76 (☎812 333 0708; www.quovadis.ru). Enter from Liteynyy pr. and go to the 2nd fl.; it's the door on the left. Internet and Wi-Fi 70R per 30min., with ISIC 50R; 130R per hr., with ISIC 90R. Open 9am-11pm. MC/V. **Cafe-Max,** Nevskiy pr. 90 (☎812 273 6655), 2nd fl. Internet 65-150R per hr. Open 24hr. **F.M. Club,** ul. Dostoyevskogo 6 (Достоевского ул.; ☎812 764 3673; www.fmclub.spb.ru). With a full bar inside, grab a drink and surf the net. 60R per hr. Open 24hr.

Post Office: Почта оссии (Pochta Rossii). Main branch at Pochtamtskaya 9 (Почтамтская; ☎812 312 3954). From Nevskiy pr., turn onto Malaya Morskaya (Малая Морская), which becomes Pochtamtskaya. Currency exchange at window 1, information at window 2. Telephone service. Internet 50R per 30min. International mail at windows 8 and 9. Open 24hr. **Postal Code:** 190 000.

ACCOMMODATIONS

Travelers can choose from a variety of hostels, hotels, and private apartments, though hotels tend to be outrageously expensive. Hotels and hostels will register your visa upon arrival and in most cases can provide you with the necessary invitation for a fee, usually about 1000-2000R (see p. 622).

Crazy Duck Hostel, Moskovsky pr 4 (Московский проспект; ☎812 310 1304; www.crazyduck.ru). M1: Sennaya Ploschad (Сенная площадь). Take a left coming out of the metro and take a left on Moskovsky Pr. Go to the door by the "ФОТО" (photo) sign and ring apt. 7. This new hostel is a perfect mix of a clean, homey atmosphere and a great social vibe. Living room has comfy couches and a large TV, while the impressive kitchen comes stocked with free tea and coffee. Check-in 2pm. May-Oct. 550-750R. Jan.-Apr. 500-700 R. Free kitchen, Internet, and Wi-Fi. Cash only. ❶

Hotel LokoSphinx, (Локосфинкс), Canal Griboyedova 101 (Грибоедовфа; ☎812 314 8890; www.lokosphinxhotel.ru). Overlooking the canal, this 18th century building is the former cottage of Prince DeKonde. Offers a lot of privacy. Regal furnishings. Make reservations well in advance during the summer. All rooms equipped with phone and TV. English spoken. Sauna free for guests. Breakfast included. Laundry US$1-2 per item. Free Wi-Fi. Check-in 2pm. Singles 3000R; doubles 2400-3000R; apartments 2760-5640R. MC/V. ❹

Cuba Hostel, Kazanskaya 5, (☎812 921 7115; www.cubahostel.ru). M2: Nevskiy Prospect. This Latin-themed hostel sits right off Nevskiy Prospect and offers basic dorms ranging from 4 to 10 beds. What it lacks in glamor, however, is more than made up for by its vivacious ambiance. Many guests gather in the common room at night to drink, mingle, and be merry. English spoken. Check-in noon. May-Oct 550-700R. Nov.-Apr. 500-650R. Free lockers, kitchen, luggage storage, and Internet. Cash only. ❷

Nord Hostel, Bolshaya Morskaya 10 (Большая Морская; ☎812 571 0342; www. nordhostel.com). M2: Nevskiy Prospect. Centrally located in a beautiful building, Nord Hostel has much to offer: kitchen, lounge, TV, and even a piano. Staff and many of the guests speak English. Some small but airy dorms, usually co-ed. Breakfast included. Free luggage storage and laundry. Free Internet. Check-out 11am. 6- or 10-bed dorms Apr.-Jan. €24; Feb.-Mar. €18. Cash only. ❸

▣ FOOD

The **covered market,** Kuznechnyy per. 3, just around the corner from M1: Vladimirskaya (Владимирская; open M-Sa 8am-8pm, Su 8am-7pm) and the **Maltsevskiy Rynok** (Мальцевский Рынок), Nekrasova 52 (Некрасова), at the top of Ligovskiy pr. (Лиговский; M1: Pl. Vosstaniya; open daily 9am-8pm), are St. Petersburg's largest outdoor markets. The cheapest supermarkets are **Dixie,** indicated by orange and yellow square signs, but **Nakhodka** (Находка) supermarkets, nab. Reki Fontanki 5 (Реки Фонтанки), are considered the best. There are **24hr convenience stores** on the side streets off Nevskiy pr. Look for "24 часа" signs.

▨ **Cafe Zoom,** Gorokhovaya 22 (Гороховая; ☎812 448 5001; www.cafezoom.ru). "Tell me what you're reading and I'll tell you where you are," read the placemats of this chic literary themed cafe, popular with the young intelligentsia. English-language menu. Vegetarian options. Entrees 100-300R. Open M-Sa 11am-midnight, Su 1pm-midnight. Kitchen open M-Sa 11am-10:30pm, Su 1-10:30pm. 20% lunch discount. MC/V. ❷

Literaturnoye Kafe (Литературное Кафе), 18 Nevskiy pr. (☎812 312 6057). M2: Nevskiy Prospect. In its former incarnation as a confectioner's shop, this cafe attracted luminaries from Dostoevsky to Pushkin (who came here the night before his fatal duel with Dantes). Now caters to tourists, serving traditional Russian fare. English-language menu. Entrees 250-500R. Open daily 11am-11pm. AmEx/MC/V. ❸

Chillout Cafe TRIZET (Уилайт Кафе ТИЗЕТ), ul. Vosstaniya 30/7 (Восстания; ☎812 579 9315). M1: Cherneshevskaya. Perfect for a relaxing lunch, a good evening spent with friends, or a nighttime sortie. Helpful staff serve European and Middle Eastern food to patrons lounging on the wall-to-wall couches. Business lunch noon-6pm 160R. Entrees 200-350R. Beer and liquor from 80R. Hookah (pronounced "kal-yan") 300-500R. DJ F-Su 9pm-2am, F-Su 9pm-5am. Open M-Th 11am-2am, F-Su 11am-5am. ❸

Traktir Shury Mury (Трактир Шуры Муры), ul. Belinskogo 8 (Белинского; ☎812 279 8550). M2: Gostinyy Dvor. Russian and European cuisine served to locals in a traditional *dacha* (countryhouse) by traditionally costumed waitresses. English-language menu. Entrees 140-300R. Open 11am-4am. MC/V.

Knelpe Jager Haus, ul. Gorozovya 24 ул. (Гороховая, д.34 ☎812 310 8270. M1: Sennaya Ploschad (Сенная площадь). Remniscent of a dark alpine cabin, this fun young restaurant, popular with the locals, is lit by candles made out of Jager bottles sitting at every table. Flowing bread baskets and a live accordion player are free perks. English-language menu. Entrees 120-340R. Beer and liquor from 80R. Hookah from 300R. Open 24 hours. MC/V.

◉ SIGHTS

Museums and sights often charge foreigners several times more than Russians. Avoid paying the higher price by handing the cashier the exact amount for a Russian ticket and saying "adeen" (one). Walk with confidence, as if you know where you are going, and do not keep your map, camera, or *Let's Go* in plain sight.

THE HERMITAGE. Originally a collection of 255 paintings bought by Catherine the Great in 1764, the State Hermitage Museum (Эрмитаж; Ermitazh) houses the world's largest art collection; it rivals the Louvre and the Prado in architectural, historical, and artistic significance. The collection is housed in the **Winter Palace** (Зимний дворец; Zimniy Dvorets), commissioned in 1762. Tsars lived in the complex until 1917, when the museum was nationalized. Only 5% of the 3 million-piece collection is on display at a time; even so, a full tour would cover a distance of 24 mi. English-language floor plans are available at the info desk. Arrive early during the summer, when lines can be over two hours long. Also, avoid paying the photography fee by keeping your camera in your bag when buying your entrance—once inside no one checks if you've paid for the photo privileges. *(Nab. Dvortsovaya 36 (Дворцовая).* ☎ *812 571 3420; www.hermitagemuseum. org. M2: Nevskiy pr. Open Tu-Sa 10:30am-6pm, Su 10:30am-5pm. 350R, students free. English-language tours 200R. Audio tour 300R. Photography 100R. Free entrance 1st Th of month.)*

■ST. ISAAC'S CATHEDRAL. Intricately carved masterpieces of iconography are housed under the awesome 19th-century dome of St. Isaac's Cathedral (Исаакиевский Со,ор; Isaakievskiy Sobor). On a sunny day, the 100kg of gold that coats the dome is visible for miles. The 360° view of the city from atop the **colonnade** is worth the 260-step climb. *(*☎ *812 315 9732. M2: Nevskiy pr. Turn left on Nevskiy pr., then left on ul. Malaya Morskaya. Cathedral open M-Tu and Th-Su in summer 10am-7pm; in winter 11am-7pm. Colonnade open M-Tu and Th-Su 10am-4am in summer; 11am-3pm in winter. Cathedral 300R, students 170R; colonnade 150/100R. Photography 50R museum, 30R colonnade.)*

■CHURCH OF OUR SAVIOR ON SPILLED BLOOD. This church's colorful forest of elaborate "onion" domes was built between 1883 and 1907 over the site of Tsar Alexander II's 1881 assassination. Also known as the Church of Christ's Resurrection and the Church of the Bleeding Savior, the cathedral (Спас На Крови; Spas Na Krovi) took 27 years to restore after it was used as a vegetable warehouse and morgue during the Communist crackdown on religion. It is equally impressive on the inside, housing the largest display of tile mosaic in the world, with each wall depicting a particular theme from the bible. *(*☎ *812 315 1636; www.cathedral. ru; Open M-Tu and Th-Su 11am-7pm. Kassa closes 1hr. earlier. 300R, students 170R. Photography 50R.)*

THE LOCAL STORY

THE CATS THAT SAVED ART HISTORY

While cats have historically served as popular pets for Russians, they served as something else during the 900-day siege of Leningrad in World War II. As food supplies dwindled and growing numbers of citizens died of starvation, cats suffered the brutal indignity of being added to the menus of the desperate.

The obliteration of cats led to a revitalization of the city's rodent population. Any naturalist will tell you that such an upset to the ecological balance has disastrous results. The colossal vermin population infiltrated the Hermitage and began to nosh on the paintings that had been stored in its basement to protect them from the relentless German bombing. When the siege finally ended, hundreds of furry felines were purchased by the state and set free in the Hermitage to help eliminate the rats. The program was successful, and it is said that today, there are still 150 cats on staff at the Hermitage patrolling the storage areas.

This legend accounts in part for cats' ubiquitous presence in the city. In fact, the pedestrian stretch of Mikhailovskaya ul. beside Eliseevskiy is lined with small cat statues paying tribute to the rodent-hunters. For good luck, throw a coin up on these figurines, many of which are located on platforms one story above street-level.

SMOLNY CATHEDRAL. In striking blue and gold, this 94m high cathedral is over 200 years old. Said to be the perfect architectural fusion of European and Russian architectural styles, the cathedral is surrounded by four other blue-and-white churches that form a cross. Many symphonic and chamber orchestras give **concerts** here, making the church a significant venue for the classical music scene of the city. During the summer the breathtaking **view** from the belfry is worth the climb. *(3 Rastrelli Pl., M3 Chernyshevskaya. ☎812 314 2186; open Th-Tu 11am-6pm in the winter, 10am-6pm in the summer. Kassa closes 1 hr. earlier. 200R, students 100R.)*

PALACE SQUARE. (Дворцовая Площадь; Dvortsovaya Ploshchad) This huge, windswept expanse in front of the Winter Palace has witnessed many turning points in Russia's history. Catherine took the crown here after overthrowing her husband, Tsar Peter III. Much later, Nicholas II's guards fired into a crowd of protestors on "Bloody Sunday," precipitating the 1905 revolution. Finally, Lenin's Bolsheviks seized power from the provisional government during the storming of the Winter Palace in October 1917. The 700-ton **Alexander Column** took two years to cut from a cliff. At 47m it is the largest freestanding monument in the world, commemorating Russia's defeat of Napoleon in 1812.

PETER AND PAUL FORTRESS. Across the river from the Hermitage stand the walls and golden spire of St. Petersburg's first settlement, the Peter and Paul Fortress (Петропавловская Крепость; Petropavlovskaya Krepost). Originally built as a defense against the Swedes in 1703, the fortress was later used as a prison for political dissidents. Inside, the **Peter and Paul Cathedral** (Петропавловский Собор; Petropavlovskiy Sobor) glows with rosy marble walls and a Baroque partition covered with intricate iconography. The cathedral holds the remains of Peter the Great and his successors. Turn right upon entering to view the **Chapel of St. Catherine the Martyr.** The remains of the last Romanovs—Tsar Nicholas II and his family—were moved here from the Artists' Necropolis on July 17, 1998, the 80th anniversary of their murder by the Bolsheviks. Condemned prisoners awaited their fate at **Trubetskoy Bastion** (Трубецкой Бастон), where Peter the Great tortured his son, Aleksei. Dostoevsky and Trotsky served time here. *(M2: Gorkovskaya. ☎812 230 6431; www.spbmuseum.ru. Fortress open M and W-Su 6am-10pm, Tu 11am-4pm. Cathedral open daily 10am-10pm. Roof walk across the Nevskaya panorama 10am-6pm 70R students 3R. A single ticket covers most sights. Purchase at the central kassa or in the smaller one inside the main entrance. 250R, students 130R.)*

ALEXANDER NEVSKIY MONASTERY. Alexander Nevskiy Monastery (Александро-Невская Лавра; Aleksandro-Nevskaya Lavra) is a major pilgrimage site and peaceful strolling ground. The **Artists' Necropolis** (Некрапол Мастеров Искусств; Nekropol Masterov Iskusstv) is the resting place of Dostoevsky and composers Mussorgsky, Rimsky-Korsakov, Glinka, and Tchaikovsky. The **Church of the Annunciation** (Благовещенская Церков; Blagoveshchenskaya Tserkov), along the stone path on the left, holds the remains of war heroes. At the end of the path is the **Holy Trinity Cathedral** (Свято-Тройтский СоБор; Svyato-Troytskiy Sobor), teeming with devout *babushki* kissing Orthodox icons. This is an active monastery, so there is a **strict dress code** in the cathedral: no shorts, and women must cover their shoulders and heads. *(M3/4: Pl. Aleksandra Nevskovo. ☎812 274 1612. Grounds open daily 6am-11pm. Artists' Necropolis open daily 11am-7pm. Cathedral open daily 6am-9pm. Kassa closes 5pm. Cemetery 100R, students 50R; cathedral grounds 100/50R.)*

ALONG NEVSKIY PROSPECT. Many sights are clustered around the western end of bustling Nevskiy pr., the city's 5km main thoroughfare. Unfortunately, there is no metro station immediately nearby; one was built, but after the station was completed, construction of an entrance or exit connecting it to the surface was not approved, due to concerns about crime and vagrancy. The

Admiralty (Адмиралтейство; Admiralteystvo), across the street from the Winter Palace, towers over the surrounding gardens and most of Nevskiy pr. Originally intended for shipbuilding by Peter the Great, it was a naval headquarters until recently, when it became a naval college. In the park to the left of the Admiralty stands the **Bronze Horseman** statue of Peter the Great, one of the most widely recognized symbols of the city. (*M2: Nevskiy pr.*) Walking east on Nevskiy pr., the enormous, Roman-style **Kazansky Cathedral** (Казанский Собор; Kazanskiy Sobor) looms to the right. It houses the remains of General Kutuzov, commander of the Russian army in the war against Napoleon. (☎*812 314 4663. M2: Nevskiy pr. Open daily 8:30am-7:30pm. Free.*) The 220-year-old **Merchants' Yard** (Гостиный Двор; Gostinyy Dvor), one of the world's oldest indoor shopping malls, is to the right (*M3: Gostinyy Dvor. Open M-Sa 10am-10pm, Su 10am-9pm*). Nearby **Ostrovskovo Square** (Островского) houses the Aleksandrinskiy Theater (see **Festivals and Entertainment,** p. 647), a massive statue of Catherine the Great, and the **public library,** which contains Voltaire's private library, purchased in its entirety by Catherine the Great. (*Foreigners can obtain a library card for free; bring passport, visa, and 2 photographs. Library open daily 9am-9pm.*) Turn left before the Fontanka canal on nab. Reki Fontanka and look down before crossing the bridge at ul. Pestelya to find the **Smallest Monument in the World.** According to lore, landing a coin on the platform of the tiny bird statue brings good luck.

SUMMER GARDENS AND PALACE. Trezzini built the long, shady paths of the Summer Gardens and Palace (Летний Сад и Дворец; Letniy Sad i Dvorets) for Peter the Great in 1710. Peter's modest **Summer Palace,** in the northeast corner, reflects his cosmopolitan taste, with furnishings ranging from Spanish and Portuguese chairs to Dutch tile and German clocks. **Mars Field** (Марсово Поле; Marsovo Pole), a memorial to the victims of the Revolution and Civil War (1917-19), extends out from the Summer Gardens. (*M2: Nevskiy pr. Turn right on nab. Kanala Griboyedova (Канала Грибоедова), cross the Moyka, and turn right on ul. Pestelya (Пестеля).* ☎*812 314 0374. Garden open W-Su 10am-6pm, free. Palace open M 10am-4pm, Tu-Su 10am-6pm; closed last M of the month; kassa closes 5pm. Palace 300R, students 150R.*)

OTHER MUSEUMS. Spread over several buildings, the ■**State Russian Museum** (усский Музей; Russkiy Muzey) boasts the world's second-largest collection of Russian art. Exhibits are displayed in three other locations throughout the city. (*M3: Nevskiy Prospect;.* ☎*812 595 4248; www.rusmuseum.ru. Open M 10am-5pm, W-Su 10am-6pm. 300R, students 150R. Tickets to all museum sites 600R/300R. Photography 100R.*) **Dostoevsky's House** (Дом Достоевского; Dom Dostoevskovo) is where the author penned *The Brothers Karamazov* and spent the last two years of his life. (*Kuznechnyy per. 5/2 (Кузненый). M1: Vladimirskaya. On the corner of ul. Dostoevskovo.* ☎*812 311 4031. Open Tu-Su 11am-5pm. 120R, students 70R. Photography 40 R.*)

▓ ♫ FESTIVALS AND ENTERTAINMENT

From mid-May to mid-July, the city holds a series of outdoor concerts as part of the **White Nights Festival,** celebrating the long summer nights. Bridges over the Neva River go up at 1:30am and don't come back down until 4:30 or 5:30am, so be wary of partying on one side if your hostel is on the other. The home of Tchaikovsky, Prokofiev, and Stravinsky still lives up to its reputation as a mecca for the performing arts. The **Mariinskiy Theater** (Мариийнский; or Kirov), Teatralnaya pl. 1 (Театральная), M4: Sadovaya, houses perhaps the world's most famous ballet company. Tchaikovsky's *Nutcracker* and *The Sleeping Beauty*, along with works by Baryshnikov and Nijinsky premiered here. Tickets can be purchased in Gostinyy Dvor or at the theatre's box office at 1 Theatre Square from 11am-7pm. (☎812 326 4141; www.mariinsky.ru; tickets 320-4800R. *Kassa* open Tu-Su 10am-7pm.) **Aleksandrinskiy Teatr** (Александринский

Teaтp), pl. Ostrovskovo 6, M3: Gostinyy Dvor, attracts famous Russian actors and companies. (☎812 312 1546. Tickets 100-2500R.) **Mussorgsky Opera and Ballet Theater** (Театр Имени Муссоргского; Еуфек Шьутш Ьгыыщкпылщмщ), pl. Iskusstv, is open all summer, whereas the Mariinskiy closes for several weeks. (☎812 595 4284; www.mikhailovsky.ru. Bring your passport. Tickets 300-1500R. *Kassa* open 11am-3pm, 4-7pm.) **Shostakovich Philharmonic Hall**, ul. Mikhailovskaya 2, M3: Gostinyy Dvor, opposite the Russian Museum, is over 200 years old, and was the site of some Beethoven premieres. (☎812 312 9871; www.philharmonia.spb.ru. Tickets 750-2000R. *Kassa* open daily 11am-3pm and 4-7pm.) The Mussorgsky and Shostakovich theaters both lie around the **Square of the Arts.** The Friday issue of the *St. Petersburg Times* has comprehensive listings of entertainment and nightlife. Book tickets to various performances online in English at **www.kassir.ru.**

▨ NIGHTLIFE

▨ **Griboedov,** Ul. Voronezhskaya 2 (Воронежская; ☎812 764 4355; www.griboedovclub. ru). M3: Ligovsky Pr. Dance the night away underground in a former Soviet bomb shelter. Famous for its themed celebrations, Griboedov has more of a house-party feel than giant club glamor. Cheap vodka and low ceilings create a genuine retro-Soviet feel. Open daily 9pm-6am. Cover free-400R. Beer from 70R. Cash only.

▨ **Fish Fabrique,** Ligovskiy 53 (Лиговский; ☎812 764 4857; www.fishfabrique.spb.ru). M1: pl. Vosstaniya. Walk in through the courtyard, into the black door directly in front, and follow the corridor and stairs to the bar. An almost hidden location and a tight-knit, young clientele make this the perfect chill hangout. Fried bread called *grenki* is perfect at 3am. Th-Sa concerts 11pm. Beer 50-90R. Hard liquor 40-130R. Cover 150-250R. Open M-Th and Su 5pm-6am. F-Sa 5pm-8:30pm and 9pm-6am. Cash only.

Dacha, (Дача), Dumskaya ul. 9 (Думская). M2: Gostiny Dvor. Cheap beer contributes to a cheerful vibe in this bar with leather couches and young university students. Right next to two other similar bars, young people come here in search of a place to relax and socialize. Open daily 6pm-6am. Beer from 70R, hard liquor from 60R. DJ every night from 11pm-6am. Cover F-Sa 100R, includes a free drink. Cash only.

JFC Jazz Club, Shpalernaya 33 (Шпалерная; ☎812 272 9850; www.jfc.sp.ru). M1: Chernyshevskaya. This friendly club offers a wide variety of quality jazz and holds occasional classical, folk, and funk concerts. Beer from 100R. Hard liquor from 50R. Live music nightly 8-10pm. Cover 200-700R. Reserve table ahead. Open daily 7-11pm.

▣ DAYTRIP FROM ST. PETERSBURG

PETERHOF. Bent on creating his own Versailles, Peter started building the **Grand Palace** (Большой Дворец; Bolshoy Dvorets) in 1709. Catherine the Great later expanded and remodeled it, creating an absolutely stunning palace surrounded by hundreds of fountains and golden statues. Though Peterhof was burned to the ground during the Nazi retreat, it was reconstructed from various maps and photographs, and lost none of its former splendor. Today, the **Lower Gardens** are a perfect place for a picnic along the shores of the Gulf of Finland. *(Open daily 11am-6pm, 300R, students 150R. Grand Palace ☎812 450 6223. Open Tu-Su 10:30am-6pm; closed last Tu of month. 500R, students 250R. Fountains operate May-Oct. 11am-5pm.)* There are 17 museums on the grounds. Roaming the nearby **Upper Gardens** is free. *(Upon exiting, go across the street and catch bus #424, whose final destination is Peterhof. 45R.)*

SLOVENIA
(SLOVENIJA)

The first and most prosperous of Yugoslavia's breakaway republics, tiny Slovenia revels in republicanism, peace, and independence. With a historically westward gaze, Slovenia's liberal politics and high GDP helped it gain early entry into the European Union, further eroding its weak relationship with Eastern Europe. Fortunately, modernization has not adversely affected the tiny country's natural beauty and diversity: it is still possible to go skiing, explore Slovenia's stunning caves, bathe under the Mediterranean sun, and catch an opera—all in a single day.

DISCOVER SLOVENIA: SUGGESTED ITINERARIES

THREE DAYS. In **Ljubljana** (p. 652), the charming cafe culture and nightlife—especially in eclectic, Soviet-chic Metelkova—is worth at least two days. Then relax in tranquil, fairytale **Bled** (1 day; p. 656).

ONE WEEK. After 3 days in the capital city **Ljubljana** (see previous itinerary), enjoy the alpine air and peaceful hiking in **Bled** (1 day). Head down the coast to the mini-Venice of **Piran** (2 days; p. 655).

ESSENTIALS

FACTS AND FIGURES

OFFICIAL NAME: Republic of Slovenia.

CAPITAL: Ljubljana.

MAJOR CITIES: Maribor, Celje, Kranj.

POPULATION: 2,009,000.

TIME ZONE: GMT + 1.

LANGUAGE: Slovenian.

RELIGION: Roman Catholic (58%).

TRACTORS PER 100 PEOPLE: 6.

WHEN TO GO

July and August are the peak months in Slovenia; tourists flood the coast, and prices for accommodations rise. Go in spring or early autumn, and you will be blessed with a dearth of crowds and great weather for hiking and exploring the countryside. Skiing is popular from December to March.

DOCUMENTS AND FORMALITIES

EMBASSIES AND CONSULATES. Foreign embassies to Slovenia are in Ljubljana (p. 653). Embassies and consulates abroad include: **Australia,** Level 6, 60 Marcus Clarke St., Canberra, ACT 2601 (☎262 434 830; vca@gov.si); **Canada,** 150 Metcalfe St., Ste. 2101, Ottawa, ON K2P 1P1 (☎613-565-5781; www.gov.si/mzz-dkp/veleposlanistva/eng/ottawa/embassy.shtml); **Ireland,** Morrison Chambers, 2nd fl., 32 Nassau St., Dublin 2 (☎1 670 5240; vdb@mzz-dkp.gov.si); **UK,** 10 Little College St., London SW1P 3SJ (☎020 72 22 57 00; www.gov.si/mzz-dkp/veleposlanistva/eng/london/events.shtml); **US,** 1525 New Hampshire Ave. NW, Washington, DC 20036 (☎202-667-5363; www.gov.si/mzz-dkp/veleposlanistva/eng/washington). Citizens of **New Zealand** should contact the embassy in Australia.

VISA AND ENTRY INFORMATION. Citizens of the European Union, Australia, Canada, Ireland, New Zealand, the UK, and the US do not need **visas** for stays of up to 90 days. Visas take from four to seven business days to process and are not available at the border.

ENTRANCE REQUIREMENTS.

Passport: Required for all travelers (except EU citizens).

Visa: Not required for stays of under 90 days for citizens of Australia, Canada, Ireland, New Zealand, the UK, and the US.

Letter of Invitation: Not required.

Inoculations: Recommended up-to-date on DTaP (diphtheria, tetanus, and pertussis), hepatitis A, hepatitis B, MMR (measles, mumps, and rubella), polio booster, rabies, and typhoid.

Work Permit: Required of all foreigners planning to work in Slovenia.

International Driving Permit: Required of those driving in Slovenia.

TOURIST SERVICES AND MONEY

EMERGENCY Ambulance and Fire: ☎112. Police: ☎113.

There are **tourist offices** in most major cities and tourist destinations. Staff members generally speak English or German and, on the coast, perfect Italian. They can usually find accommodations for a small fee and generally give advice and maps for free. Kompas is the main tourist organization.

The **euro (€)** has replaced the **tolar** in Slovenia. SKB Banka, Ljubljanska Banka, and Gorenjska Banka are common **banks.** American Express Travelers Cheques and Eurocheques are accepted almost everywhere, but major credit cards are not consistently accepted. MasterCard and Visa **ATMs** are everywhere.

HEALTH AND SAFETY

Medical facilities are of high quality, and most have English-speaking doctors. EU citizens receive free medical care with a valid passport; other foreigners must pay cash. **Pharmacies** are stocked according to Western standards; ask for *obliž* (band-aids), *tamponi* (tampons), and *vložki* (sanitary pads). **Tap water** is safe to drink. **Crime** is rare in Slovenia. **Women** should, as always, exercise caution and avoid being out alone after dark. There are few **minorities** in Slovenia, but minorities generally just receive curious glances. Navigating Slovenia with a **wheelchair** can be difficult and requires patience and caution on slippery cobblestones. **Homosexuality** is legal, but may elicit unfriendly reactions.

TRANSPORTATION

BY PLANE. Flights arrive at **Ljubljana Airport (LJU)**. Most major airlines offer connections to the national carrier, **Adria Airways** (www.adria-airways.com). To save money, consider flying into Vienna, AUT, and taking a train to Ljubljana.

BY TRAIN AND BUS. First and second class differ little on **trains.** Those under 26 get a 20% discount on most international fares. ISIC holders should ask for the 30% *popust* (discount) off domestic tickets. Schedules often list trains

by direction. *Prihodi vlakov* means arrivals; *odhodi vlakov* is departures; *dnevno* is daily. **Eurail** is not accepted in Slovenia. Though usually more expensive than trains, **buses** may be the only option in mountainous regions. The bus is also a better choice than the train to Bled, as the train station is far from town. Buy tickets at stations or on board.

BY CAR, FERRY, BIKE, AND THUMB. Car rental agencies in Ljubljana offer reasonable rates, and Slovenia's roads are in good condition. A regular **ferry** service connects Portorož to Venice, ITA, in summer. Nearly every town in Slovenia has a bike rental office. While those who hitchhike insist that it is safe and widespread in the countryside, hitchhiking is not recommended by *Let's Go*.

KEEPING IN TOUCH

PHONE CODES	**Country code: 386. International dialing prefix: 00.** For more info on placing international calls, see **Inside Back Cover.**

EMAIL AND INTERNET. Internet access is fast and common. Though free Internet is hard to find anywhere but in the biggest cities, there are Internet cafes in most major tourist destinations. Expect to pay approximately €2-4 per hour.

TELEPHONE. All phones take **phone cards,** sold at post offices, kiosks, and gas stations. Dial ☎115 for collect calls and ☎1180 for the international operator. Calling abroad is expensive without a phone card (over US$6 per min. to the US). Use the phones at the post office and pay when you're finished.

MAIL. Airmail *(letalsko)* takes from one to two weeks to reach Australia, New Zealand, and the US. Address **Poste Restante** as follows: first name, LAST NAME, Poste Restante, post office address, Postal Code, city, SLOVENIA.

LANGUAGE. Slovenian is a South Slavic language written in the Latin alphabet. Most young Slovenes speak at least some English, but the older generations are more likely to understand German or Italian. The tourist industry is generally geared toward Germans, but most tourist office employees speak English.

ACCOMMODATIONS AND CAMPING

SLOVENIA	❶	❷	❸	❹	❺
ACCOMMODATIONS	under €15	€15-21	€22-27	€28-33	over €33

All establishments charge a nightly tourist tax. Youth hostels and student dormitories are cheap (€15-20), but generally open only in summer (June 25-Aug. 30). Hotels fall into five categories (L, deluxe; A; B; C; and D) and are expensive. Pensions are the most common form of accommodation; usually they have private singles as well as inexpensive dorms. Private rooms are the only cheap option on the coast and at Lake Bohinj. Prices vary, but rarely exceed US$30. Campgrounds can be crowded, but most are in excellent condition. Camp in designated areas to avoid fines.

FOOD AND DRINK

SLOVENIA	❶	❷	❸	❹	❺
FOOD	under €3	€3-5	€6-8	€9-10	over €10

For homestyle cooking, try a *gostilna* or *gostišče* (country-style inn or restaurant). Traditional meals begin with *jota*, a soup with potatoes, beans, and sauerkraut. Pork is the basis for many dishes, such as *Svinjska pečenka* (roast pork). **Kosher** and **vegetarian** eating is therefore very difficult within the confines of Slovenian cuisine. Those with such dietary restrictions might find pizza and bakery items their best options. Slovenia's **winemaking** tradition dates from antiquity. Renski, Rizling, and Šipon are popular whites, while Cviček and Teran are favorite reds. Brewing is also centuries old; Lako and Union are good beers. For something stronger, try *žganje*, a fruit brandy, or Viljamovka, distilled by monks who guard the secret of getting a whole pear inside the bottle.

HOLIDAYS AND FESTIVALS

Holidays: New Year's Day (Jan. 1); Culture Day (Prešeren Day; Feb. 8); Easter Holiday (Apr. 12-13); National Resistance Day (Apr. 27); Labor Day (May 1-2); Independence Day (June 25); Reformation Day (Oct. 31); Christmas Day (Dec. 25).

Festivals: Slovenia embraces its alternative artistic culture as much as its folk heritage. Hitting Ljubljana in July and Aug., the International Summer Festival is the nation's most famous. The Peasant's Wedding Day *(Kmecka ohcet)*, a presentation of ancient wedding customs held in Bohinj at the end of July, and the Cow's Ball *(Kravji Bal)* in mid-Sept., which celebrates the return of the cows to the valleys from higher pastures, are a couple of the country's many summertime folk exhibitions.

LJUBLJANA ☎01

The average traveler only stops in Ljubljana (loob-lee-AH-na; pop. 275,000) for an hour en route from Venice to Zagreb, but those who stay longer become enchanted by Slovenia's lively capital city. Bridges guarded by ▨dragons span the graceful canals, while street performances liven up summer nights. Its fortified castles, frescoed churches, and modern high-rises, reveals the city's richly layered history. It has persevered through medieval existence and communism and soon aspires to be the seat of the EU presidency.

TRANSPORTATION

Trains: Trg OF 6 (☎01 291 3332). To: **Bled** (1hr., 12 per day, €4.12); **Koper** (2hr., 3 per day, €9); **Budapest, HUN** (9hr., 6 per day, €29); **Sarajevo, BOS** (11hr., 3 per day, €840) via **Zagreb, CRO** (2hr., 8 per day, €12); **Venice, ITA** (5hr., 5 per day, €25).

Buses: Trg OF 4 (☎01 090 4230; www.ap-ljubljana.si). To: **Bled** (1hr., hourly until 9pm, €6.40); **Koper** (2hr., 5-10 per day, €12); **Maribor** (3hr., 10 per day, €12); **Zagreb, CRO** (3hr., 1 per day, €14).

Public Transportation: Buses run until 10:30pm. Drop €1 (exact change only) in the box beside the driver or buy cheaper €0.80 žetoni (tickets) at post offices, kiosks, or the main bus terminal. Day passes (€3.80) sold at **Ljubljanski Potniški Promet,** Celovška c. 160 (☎01 582 2426 or ☎01 205 6045). Open M-F 6:45am-7pm, Sa 6:45am-1pm. Pick up a bus map at the **Tourist Information Center (TIC).**

ORIENTATION AND PRACTICAL INFORMATION

The train and bus stations are side-by-side on **Trg Osvobodilne Fronte** (Trg OF or OF Sq.). To reach the center, turn right on Masarykova and left on Miklošičeva c.; continue to **Prešernov trg,** the main square. After crossing the **Tromostovje** (Triple Bridge), you'll see Stare Miasto at the base of Castle Hill. The tourist office is on the left at the corner of Stritarjeva and Adamič-Lundrovo nab.

Tourist Office: Tourist Information Center (TIC), Stritarjeva 1 (☎01 306 1215, 24hr. English-language info ☎090 939 881; www.ljubljana.si). Helpful staff speak excellent English. Pick up **free maps** and the free, useful *Ljubljana from A to Z.* Open daily June-Sept. 8am-10pm; Oct.-May 9am-7pm. Box office in TIC open M-F 9am-6pm, Sa-Su 9am-1pm. AmEx/MC/V.

Embassies: Australia, Durajska c. 50 (☎01 588 3108). Open M-F 9am-1pm. **Canada,** Durajska c. 22 (☎01 430 3570). Open M-F 9am-1pm. **Ireland,** Poljanski nasip 6 (☎01 300 8970). Open M-F 9am-noon. **UK,** Trg Republike 3 (☎01 200 3910). Open M-F 9am-noon. **US,** Prešernova 31 (☎01 200 5500). Open M-F 9am-noon and 2-4pm.

Currency Exchange: Menjalnice (private exchange) booths abound. **Ljubljanska banka** branches throughout town exchange currency for no commission and cash **traveler's checks** for a 1.5% commission. Open M-F 9am-noon and 2-7pm, Sa 9am-noon.

Luggage Storage: *Garderoba* (lockers) at train station. Luggage €2-3 per day.

Pharmacy: Lekarna Miklošič, Miklošičeva 24. Open 7:30am-5:30pm most days, 7:30am-1pm on Sat. (☎01 230 6252).

Internet: Most hostels in town offer free Internet. **Cyber Cafe Xplorer,** Petkovško nab. 23 (☎01 430 1991; www.sisky.com), has Wi-Fi. €2.50 per 30min., students €2.38. 20% discount 10am-noon. Open M-F 10am-10pm, Sa-Su 2-10pm.

Post Office: Trg OF 5 (☎01 433 0605). Open M-F 7am-midnight, Sa 7am-6pm, Su 9am-noon. **Poste Restante,** Slovenska 32 (☎01 426 4668), *atizročitev pošiljk* (outgoing mail) counter. Open M-F 7am-8pm, Sa 7am-1pm. **Postal Code: 1000.**

ACCOMMODATIONS

In the busier months of July and August, **Hostelling International Slovenia** (PZS; ☎01 231 2156) helps travelers easily find accommodations. The **TIC** finds private rooms (singles €27-45; doubles €40-75). There is a daily **tourist tax** (€0.62-1.25) at all establishments.

Fluxus, Tomšičeva 4 (☎01 251 5760; www.fluxus-hostel.com). In addition to having a strategic main square location and funky decor, this small gem offers travelers a real sense of community. 1 bath for 16 beds. Kitchen and laundry. Free Internet and printer. Reception 24hr. Reserve ahead. Dorms €21; double €63. Cash only. ❷

Hotel/Hostel Park, Tabor 9 (☎01 300 2500; www.hotelpark.si). The large size and central location of Hotel/Hostel Park makes finding a room easy even if booking on short notice. Rooms are cleaned daily. Towels and sheets included. Free Internet. Breakfast provided for hotel guests only. Dorms €18. ❶

Celica, Metelkova 8 (☎01 230 9700; www.hostelcelica.com). With your back to the train station, walk left down Masarykova, then right on Metelkova; blue signs lead the way. Local and foreign artists transformed this former prison into modern art. Bar, cafe, free Internet, and cultural arts programs. Breakfast included. Reception 24hr. Reserve ahead. Dorms €16-20; cells €18-25. Cash-only deposit €10 per person. MC/V. ❷

Ljubljana Resort: Hotel and **Camping,** Dunajska 270 (☎01 568 3913; www.ljubljanaresort.si). Take bus #6 or 8 to Ježica. From bus stop, continue down road, turn right into the resort's long drive way, and follow signs. Both campground and spacious rooms with TVs and showers are available. Reception 24hr. Flexible check out 1pm. Pool and snack bar. Reservations recommended. June 20-Aug. 20 camping €13 per person; Aug. 21-June 19 €9. Singles €90-110; doubles €130-150. Tourist tax €1.02. MC/V. ❶

◪ FOOD

Maximarket, Trg Republike 1, has a **Mercator** in the basement. (Open M-Th 9am-8pm, F 9am-10pm, Sa 8am-3pm.) There is an **open-air market** next to St. Nicholas's Cathedral. (Open June-Aug. M-Sa 6am-6pm; Sept.-May 6am-4pm.)

▨ **Zvezda Cafe,** Wolfova 14 (☎01 421 9090). This small cafe has fantastic gelato with flavors like chocolate hazelnut and jaffa. Even Mozart has his own flavor, based on chocolates with pistachio candies from Salzburg (€2-3). Sip one of the 38 specialty teas (€2), or try a cake or sandwich. Cash only for gelato, MC/V in cafe. ❷

POMF, 40 Trubarjeva cesta (☎04 186 8582). This small restaurant features indoor and outdoor seating and a variety of flavorful Slovenian favorites for low prices. Vegetarian options available. Entrees €2-6. Open M-Th 10am-11pm, F 10am-noon, Sa noon-midnight, Su noon-11pm. MC/V. ❶

Cafe Romeo, Stari trg 6. Popular with local hipsters, this is one of the few places in town that serves food on Su. Riverside outdoor seating supplements a fashionable black-and-red leather interior. Snack-oriented menu features burritos (€4.50), nachos (€3.50), and dessert crepes (€3.50). Open daily 10am-1am. Kitchen open M-Sa 11am-midnight, Su 11am-11pm. Cash only. ❷

◉ SIGHTS

A good way to see the sights is a walking tour, which departs from the *rotovž* (city hall), Mestni trg 1. (2hr. July-Aug. M-F 10am, Su 11am; May-Sept. daily 10am; Oct.-Apr. F-Su 11am. €10. Buy tickets at the tour or at the TIC.)

▨ **SAINT NICHOLAS' CATHEDRAL** (STOLNICA SV. NIKOLAIA). This dazzling cathedral's beautifully preserved frescoes are a must-see. (*Dolničarjeva 1.* ☎*01 231 0684. Open daily 6am-noon and 3-7pm. Free.*)

▨ **NATIONAL MUSEUM** (NARODNI MUSEI). Contains exhibits on archaeology, culture, and local history from the prehistoric era to the present. Upstairs, the Natural History Museum features an impressive taxidermy collection. (*Muzejska 1.* ☎*01 241 4400. Open M-W, F, and Su 10am-6pm, Th 10am-8pm. National Museum and Natural History Museum each €3, students €2. Both €4/3. 1st Su of month free.*)

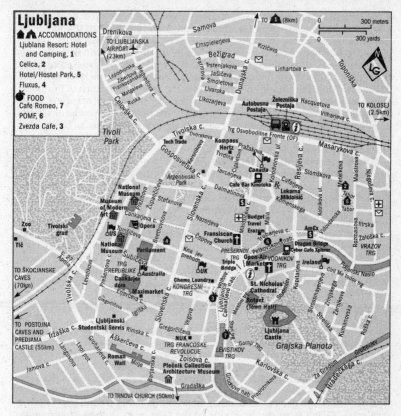

Ljubljana

🏠🏠 ACCOMMODATIONS
Ljubljana Resort: Hotel
    and Camping, 1
Celica, 2
Hotel/Hostel Park, 5
Fluxus, 4

🍴 FOOD
Cafe Romeo, 7
POMF, 6
Zvezda Cafe, 3

🐉 DRAGON BRIDGE (ZMAJSKI MOST). Head to Vodnikov trg, where this famous dragon-guarded bridge stretches across the Ljubljanica River.

PREŠERNOV TRG. Close to city hall, down Stritarjeva, and across the *Tromostovje* (Triple Bridge) is the central square of Ljubljana, with its pink 17th-century Franciscan church. (*Prešernov trg 4. ☎01 242 9300. Free.*)

LJUBLJANA CASTLE (LJUBLJANSKI GRAD). The narrow Studentovska leads uphill to the Ljubljana Castle, which has a breathtaking view. A trolley leaves every hour from 9am to 7pm for €3 from Stritarjeva ul. near the tourist office. However, the walk is only 10min. and offers more views. (*Grajska planota 1. ☎01 232 9994. Open daily May-Oct. 10am-6pm; Nov.-Apr. 10am-6pm. Access to the top tour and 20min. presentations are offered every 30min. 9am-9pm. €3.*)

PIRAN   ☎05

Unlike more modern towns on the Istrian Peninsula, Piran—chartered in 1384—has retained its Venetian charm with beautiful churches, winding cobblestone streets, and dilapidated medieval architecture. A short walk uphill from behind the red building at **Tartinijev trg**, the town's central square, leads to the Gothic **Church of Saint George** (Cerkev sv. Jurija) and the 17th-century **Saint George's Tower,** with a view of Piran and the Adriatic. (Open daily mid-

June to Sept. 10am-1pm and 4-7pm; Oct. to mid-June 11am-5pm. Free.) From the tower, head away from the church and continue uphill to the medieval **city walls** to see Piran, in all its red-tile-roofed, Mediterranean glory. (Open Apr.-Oct. 8am-9pm; Nov.-Mar. 9am-5pm. Free.) On the way down from the city walls and St. George's Church, take a left and explore St. Francis' monastery. The central gallery now features art exhibits. Piran's real attraction, however, is the **sea**. While the closest sand beach is in the neighboring town of Portorož, it's possible to go swimming off Piran's own rocky shores, and excellent **scuba diving** can be arranged through Sub-net, Prešemovo nab. 24, which runs certi-fication classes and guided dives. (☎05 673 2218; www.sub-net.si. €30 guided dive, €40 to explore a wreck. €60 per rental piece. €220 beginner's open water dive. Open Tu-Su 9am-7pm. Cash only.)

■**Youth Hostel Val (HI)**, Gregorčičeva 38A, has two- to four-bed suites. From the bus station, follow the coast past Tartinijev trg as it curves away from the harbor; the hostel is three blocks up. (☎05 673 2555; www.hostel-val.com. Breakfast included. Reception 8am-6pm. Dorms mid-May to mid-Sept. €25; mid-Sept. to mid-May €20.) ■**Tri Vdove ❸** has standout seafood dishes—try one of the value meals (€12-14). (☎05 673 0290. Entrees €5-38. Open daily 11am-midnight. AmEx/MC/V.) **Buses** go to Ljubljana (7-8 per day; €12). A **minibus** runs the length of Obala, from Lucija through Portorož and on to Piran (3 per hr., 5:30am-midnight, €1). Alternatively, a 25min. walk takes you from Piran to Portorož; facing the sea, head left. The friendly, English-speaking staff at the **tourist office**, Tartinijev trg 2., in the central square, provides bus schedules. (☎05 673 4440. 9am-5pm; later in summer.) **Postal Code:** 6330.

BLED   ☎04

Snow-covered peaks, a turquoise lake, and a stately medieval castle make Bled (pop. 11,000) one of Slovenia's most striking, visited destinations. But its beauty is only slightly diminished by popularity: more crowds show up each summer to swim, hike, paraglide, shop, or just enjoy the air.

The **Church of the Assumption** (*Cerkev Marijinega Vnebovzetja*) rises from the only Slovenian island in the center of the lake. To get there, either rent a boat (1st hr. €12, €6.30 per hr. thereafter), hop on a gondola (round-trip €12), or just swim (500m from the west side of the lake, next to the campground). Entrance to the church and museum costs €3. Built in 1011, **Bled Castle** (*Blejski Grad*) rules the lake from atop a huge rock face cliff on its shores. The fast-est way to ascend is from the small marked path branching off to the right of Riklijeva c., near St. Martin's Church. ■**Soteska Vintgar**, a 1.6km gorge carved by the waterfalls and rapids of the Radovna River, winds through the rocks of the **Triglav National Park** (*Triglavski Narodni*) and culminates with the 16m **Šum Waterfall** (down the stairs behind the second ticket booth). The **park info office** is at Kidričeva c. 2. (☎04 574 1188. €4, students €3.) To get there, go over the hill on Grajska c., away from the town center, and take a right at the bottom of the hill. Turn left after 100m and follow signs for Vintgar. Alternatively, hop on one of the frequent buses to Podhom (10min., M-Sa 10 per day, €1.30) and follow the 1.5km route. From mid-June through September, **Alpetour** (☎04 532 0440) runs a bus to the trailhead (15min., 10am; one-way €2.50, round-trip €4.50).

The spotless new **Traveller's Haven ❷**, Riklijeva c. 1. offers a great experience with a kitchen, free laundry, free Internet, free DVD rental, and free bike rental. (☎04 139 6545; travellers-haven@t2.net. Dorms €19. Cash only.) Big portions, high-quality regional food, and excellent service distinguish **Gostilna pri Planincu ❶**, Grajska c. 8, near the bus station. Try the flavorful beef goulash (€3.80). (☎04 574 1613. Open daily 9am-11pm.) **Pizzeria Rustika ❷**, Riklijeva c., offers a variety of gourmet pizzas (€5.40-7.90), sandwiches (€2.50-6.60), and salads (€3-

6). (☎04 576 8900. Open M 3-11pm, Tu-Su noon-11pm.) Pick up groceries at the **Mercator.** One is located in the central area Ljubljanska c. 4; another is across from Traveller's Haven hostel on Riklijeva c. (Open M-F 7am-7pm, Sa 7am-3pm, Su 8am-noon.)

Trains leave from the Lesce-Bled station, about 4km from Bled, for Ljubljana. (1hr., 7 per day, €4.) **Buses,** a more convenient option, go from Bled to Bohinjsko Jezero (45min., every hr. 7:20am-8:20pm, €3.60), Ljubljana (1hr., every hr. 5am-9:30pm, €6.30), and Vintgar (1 per day June 14-Sept. 30; €2.50). The lakeside **tourist office,** on the corner of the c. Svobode 10 building, gives out free maps of Bled and sells hiking **maps** (€4-10). (☎04 574 1122; www.bled.si. Open June-Sept. M-Sa 8am-7pm; Mar.-May 9am-7pm; Nov.-Feb. 9am-5pm.) **Internet** is available at the **Apropo Cocktail Bar/Internet Cafe,** Ljubljanska c. 4. (☎04 574 4044. €2 for 30min. Free Wi-Fi. Open daily 8am-midnight.) **Postal Code:** 4260.

MARIBOR   ☎02

Surrounded by the wine-growing Piramida Hill, the slow Drava River, and the adventuresome ski haven of Pohorje, Maribor (MAHR-ee-bohr; pop. 110,000) brims with youthful energy. As an important trade post between Vienna and the Adriatic, Maribor saw lots of international traffic during the middle ages. With a keen eye, observers can spot remnants of its history. Starting from the tourist office, glance down Partizanska/Slovenska c., the key merchant road beginning in the Middle Ages. Next, behold the **Franciscan Church,** Maribor's one and only basilica. Continuing down Partizanska c., enter the old town and visit **Maribor Castle** and its museum. Unfortunately, the castle is under renovation until 2015. Stop just before the castle and turn to the right to see **Freedom Square** *(Trg svobode)* and **Castle Square** *(Grajski Trg).* From Grajski Trg, continue down Slovenska ul. and make a left onto Gledaliska ul. This will lead to **Slomskov Trg.** Make sure to peek inside the beautiful **Maribor Cathedral,** Slomškov trg 20. (Open daily 6:30am-7pm. Free.) Take Postna ul. down towards the river to reach Maribor's main square, **Glavni Trg,** seat of the government buildings and the perfect place for a photo. Finally, continue down to the **Drava River.** Don't miss the oldest vine in the world *(Stara trta)*—400 years old and still bearing fruit. Finish up at the **museum,** Vojašniška 8, behind the vine, to learn more about Maribor's wine making traditions. (☎02 251 5100. Open Tu-Su 10am-6pm. Free.)

Across the river from the old town, about a 15min. walk from the center lays **Dijaški Dom (HI) ❶,** 26 Junij, Železnikova 12. From the local bus station, take bus #3 *(Brezje)* to the "Pokopališče" stop. Cross the street and walk a few paces to the right, then take the first left and follow the road as it curves. Past the Mercator supermarket, you'll see a building with "12" painted on the side. Tidy rooms and quiet environs make this the best deal in town. (☎02 480 1710. Free Internet. Open June 25-Aug. 25. Singles €15, doubles €25.) **Toti Rotov ❷,** Glavni trg 14, serves savory meals (€7) in a 16th century townhouse. (☎02 228 7650; Entrees €3-15. Open M-Th 8am-midnight, F-Sa 8am-2pm. AmEx/MC/V.)

From the train station, Partizanska c. 50 (☎02 292 2100), **trains** run to Ljubljana (2½ hr., 12 per day; €7.47-8.91) and Ptuj (1hr., 9 per day, €2.71). The bus station, Mlinska 1, sends **buses** to Ljubljana (2½-3hr., 10 per day, €12) and Ptuj (40min., 2 per hr. until 9pm, €3.60). Pick up a map from the train station or at the **tourist office** on Partizanska c. 6a. (☎02 234 6611; www.maribor-tourism.si. Rooms €25-35. 90min. city tours W and F 10am, Su 11am; €5. Open M-F 9am-7pm, Sa 9am-5pm, Su 9am-noon.) From the train station, turn left and follow Partizanska past the large Franciscan **Church of Saint Mary** to Grajski trg, where you'll see the **Florian Column.** Turn left down Vetrinska, and then turn right on Koroska c. to reach Glavni trg. From the main bus station turn right on Mlinska, follow it to Partizanska, and take a left.

SPAIN
(ESPAÑA)

The fiery spirit of flamenco; the energy of artistic genius; the explosive merging of urban style and archaic tradition—this is Spain. Here, dry golden plains give way to rugged coastline, and modern architectural feats rise from ancient plazas. Explore winding medieval alleyways that lead to bustling city centers, or watch from a cafe as mulleted youths pass by. In Spain, there is always a reason to stay up late, and there is always time for an afternoon *siesta*.

DISCOVER SPAIN: SUGGESTED ITINERARIES

THREE DAYS. Soak in **Madrid's** (p. 664) art and culture as you walk through the **Retiro's** gardens and peruse the halls of the **Prado, Thyssen-Bornemisza,** and **Nacional Centro de Arte Reina Sofía.** By night, move from the *tapas* bars of Santa Ana to Malasaña and Chueca. Daytrip to **Segovia** (p. 680) or **Toledo** (p. 679).

ONE WEEK. Begin in southern Spain, exploring the **Alhambra's** Moorish palaces in **Granada** (1 day; p. 691) and the nightlife in **Seville** (1 day). After two days in **Madrid,** travel northeast to **Barcelona** (2 days) and try to outrun the the bulls in **Pamplona** (1 day; p. 712).

ESSENTIALS

FACTS AND FIGURES

OFFICIAL NAME: Kingdom of Spain.

CAPITAL: Madrid.

GOVERNMENT: Parliamentary monarchy.

MAJOR CITIES: Barcelona, Granada, Seville, Valencia.

POPULATION: 40,448,000.

LAND AREA: 500,500 sq. km.

TIME ZONE: GMT +1.

LANGUAGES: Spanish (Castilian), Basque, Catalan, Galician.

RELIGION: Roman Catholic (94%).

LARGEST PAELLA EVER MADE: 20m in diameter, this giant *paella* fed 100,000 people in 1992.

WHEN TO GO

Summer is high season in Spain, though in many parts of the country, *Semana Santa* and other festivals are particularly busy. Tourism peaks in August, when the coastal regions overflow while inland cities empty out. Winter travel has the advantage of lighter crowds and lower prices, but sights reduce their hours.

DOCUMENTS AND FORMALITIES

EMBASSIES. Foreign embassies in Spain are in Madrid. Spanish embassies abroad include: **Australia:** 15 Arkana St., Yarralumla, ACT 2600; mailing

Spain

Bay of Biscay

COSTA VERDE

La Coruña Oviedo Cangas de Onís Guernica San Sebastián FRANCE

Santiago de Compostela CORDILLERA CANTÁBRICA Bilbao Pamplona PYRENEES ANDORRA

Astorga León Burgos Jaca Vielha Figueres Cadaqués

Miño Sierra de la Cabrera Valladolid Torla Girona COSTA BRAVA

Zamora Duero Montserrat Sitges Barcelona

Segovia Sigüenza Zaragoza COSTA DORADA

Salamanca CORDILLERA IBÉRICA Menorca

Ávila El Escorial Tajo Ciudadela Mahón

Béjar MADRID TO MENORCA →

PORTUGAL CORDILLERA CENTRAL Cuenca Balearic Sea

Cáceres Trujillo Toledo Aranjuez Golfo de Valencia Mallorca

Guadiana Buñol Valencia Palma

Badajoz Mérida Ibiza ISLAS BALEARES

Zafra Júcar Elvissa

SIERRA MORENA Alicante Formentera

Guadalquivir Córdoba SIERRA DE SEGURA COSTA BLANCA

Seville Granada Mediterranean Sea

Golfo de Cádiz Jerez de la Frontera Ronda Málaga

COSTA DE LA LUZ Arcos de la Frontera COSTA DE ALMERÍA

Cádiz Marbella

ATLANTIC OCEAN Algeciras Gibraltar COSTA DEL SOL ALGERIA

Tarifa Cueta

Strait of Gibraltar

MOROCCO

N

0   100 miles
0   100 kilometers

address: P.O. Box 9076, Deakin ACT 2600 (☎+612 6273 35 55; www.mae.es/Embajadas/Canberra/es/Home). **Canada:** 74 Stanley Ave., Ottawa, ON K1M 1P4 (☎+1-613-747-2252; www.embaspain.ca). **Ireland:** 17 Merlyn Park, Ballsbridge, Dublin 4 (☎+353 1 269 1640; www.mae.es/embajadas/dublin). **New Zealand:** 56 Victoria Street, P.O.B. 24-150, Wellington 6142 (☎+64 4 913 1167; emb.wellington@maec.es). **UK:** 39 Chesham Pl., London SW1X 8SB (☎ +44 207 235 5555; embaspuk@mail.mae.es). **US:** 2375 Pennsylvania Ave. NW, Washington, D.C. 20037 (☎+1-202-728-2330; www.spainemb.org).

VISA AND ENTRY INFORMATION. EU citizens do not need a visa. Citizens of Australia, Canada, New Zealand, the US, and many Latin American countries do not need a visa for stays of up to 90 days, beginning upon entry into the EU's freedom-of-movement zone. For more info, see p. 13. For stays over 90 days, all non-EU citizens need visas, available at Spanish consulates (€100).

TOURIST SERVICES AND MONEY

TOURIST OFFICES. For general info, contact the **Instituto de Turismo de España**, Jose Lazaro Galdiano 6, 28071 Madrid (☎913 433 500; www.tourspain.es).

SPAIN

EMERGENCY	Ambulance: ☎061. Fire: ☎080. Local Police: ☎092. National Police: ☎091. General Emergency: ☎112.

MONEY. The **euro (€)** has replaced the **peseta** as the unit of currency in Spain. For more info, see p. 16. As a general rule, it's cheaper to exchange money in Spain than at home. **ATMs** usually have good exchange rates. In restaurants, all prices include a service charge. Satisfied customers occasionally toss in some spare change—usually no more than 5%—and while it is purely optional, **tipping** is becoming increasingly widespread in restaurants and other places that cater to tourists. Many people give train, airport, and hotel porters €1 per bag, while taxi drivers sometimes get 5-10%. **Bargaining** is only common at flea markets and with street vendors.

Spain has a 7% **value added tax** (**VAT**; in Spain, **IVA**) on restaurant meals and accommodations and a 16% VAT on retail goods. The prices listed in *Let's Go* include VAT. In an airport upon exiting the EU, non-EU citizens can claim a refund on the tax paid for goods purchased at participating stores. In order to qualify for a refund in a store, you must spend at least €50-100, depending on the shop; make sure to ask for a refund form when you pay. For more info on qualifying for a VAT refund, see p. 19.

BUSINESS HOURS. Almost all museums, shops, and churches close from 2-4pm or longer for an afternoon ▧**siesta**. Most Spaniards eat lunch during their *siesta* (as well as nap), so restaurants open in the late afternoon. Shops and sights reopen at 3pm, and some may stay open until 8pm. Most restaurants will start serving dinner by 9pm, although eating close to midnight is very common in Spain. After midnight, the clubhopping commences. Increasingly, some large chains and offices are open all day, in large part due to an effort by the Spanish government to encourage a stronger economy and more "normal" business hours. It's still a safe bet that nearly every store will be closed on Sundays.

TRANSPORTATION

BY PLANE. Flights land mainly at **Barajas Airport** in Madrid (**MAD;** ☎913 93 60 00) and the **Barcelona International Airport** (**BCN;** ☎932 98 39 25). Contact AENA (☎902 40 47 04; www.aena.es) for info on flight times at most airports. See p. 42 for info on flying to Spain.

BY FERRY. Spain's islands are accessible by ferry; see the **Balearic Islands** (). Ferries are the least expensive way of traveling between Spain and Tangier or the Spanish enclave of **Ceuta** in Morocco. For more info see p. 52

BY TRAIN. Direct trains are available to Madrid and Barcelona from several European cities, including Geneva, CHE; Lisbon, POR; and Paris, FRA. Spanish trains are clean, relatively punctual, and reasonably priced. However, most train routes do tend to bypass small towns. Spain's national railway is **RENFE** (☎902 24 02 02; www.renfe.es). When possible, avoid *transvía, semidirecto,* or *correo* trains, as they are very slow. *Estrellas* are slow night trains with bunks and showers. *Cercanías* (commuter trains) go from cities to suburbs and nearby towns. There is no reason to buy a Eurail Pass if you plan to travel only within Spain. Trains are cheap, so a pass saves little money; moreover, buses are the most efficient means of traveling around Spain. Several Rail Europe passes cover travel within Spain. See www.raileurope.com for more info on the following passes. The **Spain Flexipass** ($186) offers three days of unlimited travel in a two-month period. The **Spain Rail 'n' Drive Pass**

($343) is good for three days of unlimited first-class train travel and two days of unlimited mileage in a rental car. The **Spain-Portugal Pass** offers three days or more of unlimited first-class travel in Spain and Portugal over a two-month period (from $341). For more info, see p. 46.

> **JUST SAY NO.** If you are planning on traveling only within Spain (and Portugal), do not buy a **Eurail Pass.** Bus travel is usually the best option, and trains are less expensive than in the rest of Europe. A Eurail Pass makes sense only for those planning to travel in other European countries as well.

BY BUS. In Spain, buses are cheaper and have far more comprehensive routes than trains. Buses provide the only public transportation to many isolated areas. For those traveling primarily within one region, **buses are the best method of transportation.** Spain has numerous private companies and the lack of a centralized bus company may make itinerary planning difficult. Companies' routes rarely overlap, so it is unlikely that more than one will serve your intended destination. **Alsa** (☎913 27 05 40; www.alsa.es) serves Asturias, Castilla y León, Galicia, and Madrid, as well as international destinations including France, Germany, Italy, and Portugal. **Auto-Res** (☎902 02 00 52; www.auto-res.net) serves Castilla y León, Extremadura, Galicia, Valencia, and Portugal.

BY CAR. Spain's highway system connects major cities by four-lane *autopistas*. Speeders beware: police can "photograph" the speed and license plate of your car and issue a ticket without pulling you over. If you are pulled over, fines must be paid on the spot. **Gas** prices, €0.80-1.10 per liter, are lower than in many European countries but high by North American standards. Renting a car is cheaper than elsewhere in Europe. Spain accepts Canadian, EU, and US driver's licenses; otherwise, an International Driving Permit (IDP) is required. Try **Atesa** (☎902 10 01 01; www.atesa.es), Spain's largest rental agency. The automobile association is **Real Automóvil Club de España** (RACE; ☎902 40 45 45; www.race.es). For more on renting and driving a car, see p. 50.

BY THUMB. Hitchhikers report that Castilla and Andalucía are long, hot waits, and hitchhiking out of Madrid is virtually impossible. The Mediterranean coast and the islands are more promising; remote areas in the Balearics, Catalonia, or Galicia may be best accessible by hitchhiking. Although approaching people for rides at gas stations near highways and rest stops purportedly gets results, *Let's Go* does not recommend hitchhiking.

KEEPING IN TOUCH

> **PHONE CODES**
>
> **Country code:** 34. **International dialing prefix:** 00. Within Spain, dial city code + local number, even when dialing inside the city. For more info on how to place international calls, see **Inside Back Cover.**

EMAIL AND THE INTERNET. Email is easily accessible within Spain. Internet cafes are listed in most towns and all cities, and generally charge as little as €2 per hr. In small towns, if Internet is not listed, check the library or the tourist office for listings. For a list of internet cafes in Spain, consult www.cybercafes.com.

TELEPHONE. Whenever possible, use a prepaid phone card for international phone calls, as long-distance rates for national phone service are often very high. Find them at tobacconists. However, some public phones will only accept

SPAIN

change. Mobile phones are an increasingly popular and economical option, costing as little as €30 (not including minutes). Major mobile carriers include **Movistar** and **Vodafone**. Direct-dial access numbers for calling out of Spain include: **AT&T Direct** (☎900 990 011); **British Telecom** (☎900 96 4495); **Canada Direct** (☎900 990 015); **Telecom New Zealand Direct** (☎900 990 064).

MAIL. Airmail *(por avión)* takes five to eight business days to reach Canada or the US; service is faster to the UK and Ireland and slower to Australia and New Zealand. Standard postage is €0.78 to North America. Surface mail *(por barco)* can take over a month, and packages take two to three months. Certified mail *(certificado)* is the most reliable way to send a letter or parcel and takes four to seven business days. Spain's overnight mail is not actually overnight, not worth the expense. To receive mail in Spain, have it delivered **Poste Restante.** Mail will go to the main post office unless you specify a subsidiary by street address. Address mail to be held according to the following example: Last Name, First Name; *Lista de Correos;* City; Postal Code; SPAIN; AIRMAIL.

ACCOMMODATIONS AND CAMPING

SPAIN	❶	❷	❸	❹	❺
ACCOMMODATIONS	under €18	€18-24	€25-34	€35-45	over €45

The cheapest and most basic options are *refugios, casas de huéspedes,* and *hospedajes,* while *pensiones* and *fondas* tend to be a bit nicer. All are essentially boarding houses with basic rooms, shared bath, and no A/C. Higher up the ladder but not necessarily more expensive, *hostales* generally have sinks in bedrooms and provide linens and lockers, while *hostal-residencias* are similar to hotels in overall quality. The government rates **hostales** on a two-star system; even establishments receiving one star are typically quite comfortable. The system also fixes **hostal** prices, posted in the lounge or main entrance. Prices invariably dip below the official rates in the low season (Sept.-May), so bargain away. **Red Española de Albergues Juveniles** (REAJ; www.reaj.com), the Spanish **Hostelling International** (HI) affiliate, runs more than 200 hostels year-round. Prices vary, but are generally €9-15 for guests under 26 and higher for those 26 and over. Breakfast is usually included; lunch and dinner are occasionally offered at an additional charge. Hostels usually have lockouts around 11am and have curfews between midnight and 3am. As a rule, don't expect much privacy—rooms typically have 4-20 beds in them. To reserve a bed in the high season (July-Aug. and during festivals), call at least a few weeks in advance. **Campgrounds** are generally the cheapest choice for two or more people. Most charge separate fees per person, per tent, and per car; others charge for a *parcela* (a small plot of land), plus per-person fees. Tourist offices can provide more info; pick up the *Guía de Campings* for a comprehensive guide.

FOOD AND DRINK

SPAIN	❶	❷	❸	❹	❺
FOOD	under €6	€6-10	€11-15	€16-20	over €20

Fresh, local ingredients are still an integral part of Spanish cuisine, varying according to each region's climate, geography, and history. The old Spanish saying holds true: *"Que comer es muy importante, porque de la panza, ¡nace la danza!"* (Eating is very important, because from the belly, dance is born!)

Spaniards start the day with a light breakfast *(desayuno)* of coffee or thick hot chocolate and a pastry. The main meal of the day *(comida)* consists of several courses and is typically eaten around 2 or 3pm. Dinner at home *(cena)* tends to be light. Dining out begins anywhere between 8pm and midnight. Bar-hopping for *tapas* is an integral part of the Spanish lifestyle. Some restaurants are "open" from 8am until 1 or 2am, but most serve meals only from 1pm or 2pm to 4pm and 8pm to midnight. Many restaurants offer a *plato combinado* (main course, side dish, bread, and sometimes a beverage) or a *menú del día* (two or three set dishes, bread, beverage, and dessert) for roughly €5-9. If you ask for a *menú*, this is what you may receive; *carta* is the word for menu.

Tapas (small dishes of savory meats and vegetables cooked according to local recipes) are quite tasty, and in most regions they are paired with beer or wine. *Raciones* are large *tapas* served as entrees; *bocadillos* are sandwiches. Spanish specialties include *tortilla de patata* (potato omelet), *jamón serrano* (smoked ham), *calamares fritos* (fried squid), *arroz* (rice), *chorizo* (spicy sausage), *gambas* (shrimp), *lomo de cerdo* (pork loin), *paella* (steamed saffron rice with seafood, chicken, and vegetables), and *gazpacho* (cold tomato-based soup). Vegetarians should learn the phrase *"yo soy vegetariano"* (I am a vegetarian) and specify this means no *jamón* (ham) or *atún* (tuna). A normal-sized draft beer is a *caña de cerveza;* a *tubo* is a little bigger. A *calimocho* is a mix of Coca-Cola and red wine, while *sangria* is a drink of red wine, sugar, brandy, and fruit. *Tinto de verano* is a lighter version of *sangria:* red wine and Fanta. *Café solo* means black coffee; add a touch of milk for a *nube;* a little more and it's a *café cortado;* half milk and half coffee makes a *café con leche.*

HOLIDAYS AND FESTIVALS

Holidays: New Year's Day (Jan. 1); Epiphany (Jan. 6); Maundy Thursday (Apr. 9, 2009); Good Friday (Apr. 10, 2009); Easter (Apr. 11-12); Labor Day (May 1); Assumption (Aug. 15); National Day (Oct. 12); All Saints' Day (Nov. 1); Constitution Day (Dec. 6); Feast of the Immaculate Conception (Dec. 8); Christmas (Dec. 25); New Year's Eve (Dec. 31).

Festivals: Almost every town in Spain has several festivals. In total, there are more than 3000. Nearly everything closes during festivals. All of Spain celebrates *Carnaval* the week before Ash Wednesday (Feb. 25, 2009); the biggest parties are in Catalonia and Cádiz. During the annual festival of *Las Fallas* in mid-Mar., Valencia honors St. Joseph with parades, fireworks, and the burning of effigies. The entire country honors the Holy Week, or *Semana Santa* (Mar. 16-22). Seville's *Feria de Abril* has events showcasing many different Andalusian traditions, including bullfighting and flamenco (Apr. 28-May 3, 2009). *San Fermín* (The Running of the Bulls) takes over Pamplona July 6-14 (see p. 712). For more information, see www.tourspain.es or www.gospain.org/fiestas.

BEYOND TOURISM

Spain offers volunteer opportunities from protecting dolphins on the Costa del Sol to fighting for immigrants' rights. Those seeking long-term work in Spain should consider teaching English. Short-term jobs are available in the restaurant, hotel, and tourism industries, and are typically held by those without permits. For info on opportunities across Europe, see **Beyond Tourism**, p. 55.

Enforex, Alberto Aguilera, 26, 28015 Madrid, Spain (☎915 943 776; www.enforex. com). Offers 20 Spanish programs in Spain, ranging from 1 week to a year in duration. Opportunities in 12 Spanish cities, including Granada, Sevilla, Barcelona, and Madrid.

Ecoforest, Apdo. 29, Coin 29100 Málaga, Spain (☎661 07 99 50; www.ecoforest. org). Fruit farm and vegan community in southern Spain that uses environmental education to develop a sustainable lifestyle for residents. Visitors are welcome to stay, contributing €5-15 per day towards operating costs.

MADRID ☎91

After Franco's death in 1975, young *Madrileños* celebrated their liberation from totalitarian repression with raging all-night parties across the city. This revelry became so widespread that it defined an era, and *la Movida* (the Movement) is now recognized as a world-famous nightlife renaissance. The newest generation has kept the spirit of *la Movida* alive—Madrid is truly a city that never sleeps. While neither as funky as Barcelona nor as charming as Seville, Madrid is the political, intellectual, and cultural capital of Spain, balancing its history and heritage with the festive insomnia it has come to embrace.

✕ INTERCITY TRANSPORTATION

Flights: All flights land at **Aeropuerto Internacional de Barajas** (☎902 404 704; www.aena.es.), 16km northeast of Madrid. The **Bus-Aeropuerto #200** leaves from the national terminal T2 and runs to the city center via the metro station Avenida de América. (☎902 50 78 50. Look for "EMT" signs just outside the airport doors. Daily every 10-15min. 5:20am-11:30pm. €1.) **Line 204** leaves from T4 and goes to Avenida de América as well. **Line 101** leaves from T1, 2, and 3 and goes to Canillejas. Fleets of **taxis** swarm the airport. Taxi fare to central Madrid should cost €35-40, including the €5.50 airport surcharge, depending on traffic and time of day.

Trains: Two largo *recorrido* (long-distance) **RENFE** stations, **Atocha** and **Chamartín,** connect Madrid to surrounding areas and the rest of Europe. Both stations are easily accessible by metro. Call RENFE (☎902 24 02 02; www.renfe.es) for reservations and info. Buy tickets at the station or online.

Estación Atocha, Av. Ciudad de Barcelona (☎915 066 137). M: Atocha Renfe. The cast-iron atrium of the original station has been turned into an urban rainforest, with lush plants, a small marsh with a colony of turtles, and the occasional bird. Galleries, boutiques, and restaurants provide more commercial diversions. There is a **tourist office** (☎913 15 99 76) in the station. Open M-Sa 8am-8pm, Su 9am-2pm. **RENFE information office** (☎902 24 02 02) located in the main terminal. Open daily 7am-11pm. **Luggage storage** (*consignas automáticas;* €2.40-4.50), at the back right corner of the atrium. Open daily 6:30am-10pm. Ticket windows open daily 6:30am-9pm; buy tickets at vending machines outside these hours. No international service. **AVE** (☎91 506 63 29) offers high-speed service to southern Spain, including **Barcelona** (3hr., 20-26 per day 5:45am-9pm, €110-130), **Sevilla** (2½hr., 24-20 per day 6:30am-11pm, €70-78) via **Córdoba** (1¾hr., €58-64), and **Valladolid** (1hr., 14-15 per day 6:35am-9pm, €21-34).

Estación Chamartín, C. Agustín de Foxa (☎913 00 69 69). M: Chamartín. Bus #5 runs to and from **Puerta del Sol** (45min.); the stop is just beyond the lockers. Alternatively, get off at M: Atocha Renfe and take a red Cercanías train (15min., every 5-10min., €1.20) to Chamartín. Be sure to keep your ticket, or you won't be able to exit the turnstiles. Chamartín is a mini-mall of useful services, including a **tourist office** (*Vestíbulo,* Puerta 14; ☎913 15 99 76; open M-Sa 8am-8pm, Su 9am-2pm), **currency exchange, accommodations service, post office, car rental, police,** and **luggage storage** (*consignas;* €2.40-4.50; open daily 7am-11pm). Call RENFE at ☎902 24 34 02 for international destinations and ☎902 24 02 02 (Spanish only) for domestic. Ticket windows open daily 6:30am-9pm; buy tickets at vending machines outside these hours. Chamartín serves both international and domestic destinations to the northeast and south. Most Cercanías (local) trains stop at both Chamartín and Atocha. Major destinations include: **Barcelona** (9½hr., daily 10pm, €41); **Bilbao** (5hr., 1-2 per day, €47); **Lisboa** (9hr., daily 10:25pm, €59); **Paris, FRA** (13½hr., 7pm, €115-130).

Buses: Numerous private companies serve Madrid, each with its own station and set of destinations. Most buses pass through **Estación Sur de Autobuses** or **Estación de Moncloa,** both easily accessible by metro. The Pl. Mayor tourist office and any other branch in the city has information on the most relevant intercity buses.

Estación Sur de Autobuses: C. Méndez Álvaro (☎914 68 42 00; www.estacionautobusesmadrid. com). M: Méndez Álvaro; inside station. Info booth open daily 6:30am-1am. **ATMs, food,** and **luggage storage** (€1.30 per bag per day; open M-F 6:30am-10:30pm, Sa 6:30am-3pm). Serves 40+ private bus companies. National destinations include: **Algeciras, Alicante, Aranjuez, Benidorm, Cartagena, A Coruña, Gijón, Lugo, Murcia, Oviedo, Santiago de Compostela,** and **Toledo.** Check at the station or online or call for specific info on routes and schedules.

▐ LOCAL TRANSPORTATION

Metro: Safe, speedy, spotless, and almost always under *obras* (improvements), Madrid's Metro puts most major subway systems to shame. Free Metro maps (available at any ticket booth) and the wall maps showing surrounding streets are clear and helpful. Fare and schedule info is posted in every station; trains run daily 6am-2am, with the last inbound train leaving most terminal stations around 1:30am. An individual metro ticket costs €1, or €2 if you leave the city limits; children under the age of four travel free. Frequent riders opt for the ▧**Metrobus** (10 rides valid for both the Metro and bus system; €7.40). Buy them at machines in Metro stops, *estancos* (tobacco shops), or newsstands. Remember to keep your ticket until you leave the metro--riding without one can subject you to outrageous fines. In addition, **abonos mensuales,** or monthly passes, grant unlimited travel within the city proper for €46, while **abonos turísticos** (tourist passes) come in various lengths (1, 2, 3, 5, or 7 days) and sell for €5-24. These are available at all metro stations or online. For information, call **Metro Info** (☎902 44 44 03) or visit www.metromadrid.es.

Bus: Buses cover areas inaccessible by Metro and are a great way to see the city. Bus and Metro fares are equivalent, and tickets are interchangeable. Buses run 6am-11pm, generally every 10 to 15 minutes. From midnight-6am, the **Búho** (owl), or night bus, travels from Pl. de Cibeles and other marked routes to the outskirts of the city (M-Th and Sa every 30min. midnight-3am, every hr. 3-6am; F-Sa every 20min.) These buses, marked on the essential *Red de autobuses nocturnos,* available at any tourist office or from www.emtmadrid.es, run along 26 lines covering regular daytime routes. For info, call **Empresa Municipal de Transportes.** (☎902 50 78 50 or 914 06 88 10; www.emtmadrid.es. Open M-F 8am-2pm.)

Taxi: Call **Radio Taxi Madrid** (☎915 47 32 32), **Radio-Taxi Independiente** (☎914 05 55 00 or 914 05 12 13; www.radiotaxiindependiente.com), or **Teletaxi** (☎913 71 21 31; www.tele-taxi.es). A *"libre"* sign or a green light indicates availability. Base fare is €2.05 (or €2.20 M-F after 10pm and €3.10 Sa-Su after 10pm), plus €0.98 per km 6am-10pm and €1.15 10pm-6am. **Teletaxi** charges a flat rate of €1 per km. Fare supplements include airport (€5.50) and bus and train stations (€2.95). Official taxis are white with a red stripe on the door; avoid impostors.

✦ ORIENTATION

Marking the epicenter of both Madrid and Spain, **Kilómetro 0** in **Puerta del Sol** ("Sol" for short) is within walking distance of most sights. To the west are the **Plaza Mayor,** the **Palacio Real,** and the **Ópera district.** East of Sol lies **Huertas,** the heart of cafe, museum, and theater life. The area north of Sol is bordered by **Gran Vía,** which runs northwest to **Plaza de España.** North of Gran Vía are three club- and bar-hopping

SPAIN

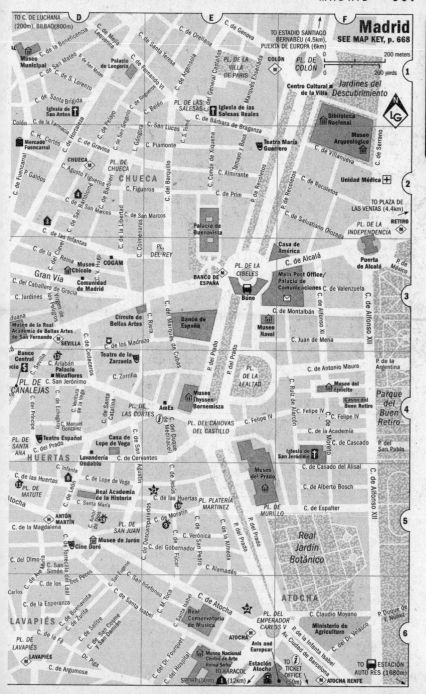

Madrid
SEE MAP KEY, p. 668

TO C. DE LUCHANA
(200m), BILBAO(800m)

Museo
Municipal

Palacio
de Longoria

PL. DE LA
VILLA
DE PARIS

COLÓN

PL. DE
COLÓN

TO ESTADIO SANTIAGO
BERNABÉU (4.5km),
PUERTA DE EUROPA (6km)

0   200 meters
0   200 yards

Centro Cultural
de la Villa

Jardines del
Descubrimiento

Iglesia de
San Anton

PL. DE LAS
SALESAS

Iglesia de las
Salesas Reales

Biblioteca
Nacional

Museo
Arqueológico

Mercado
Fuencarral

CHUECA

PL. DE
CHUECA

CHUECA

Teatro María
Guerrero

Unidad Médica

TO PLAZA DE
LAS VENTAS (4.4km)

PL. DE LA
INDEPENDENCIA

RETIRO

Museo
Chicote

COGAM

Comunidad
de Madrid

Palacio de
Buenavista

PL.
DEL REY

PL. DE LA
CIBELES

Casa de
América

C. de Alcalá

Puerta
de Alcalá

P. de
México

Gran Vía

BANCO DE
ESPAÑA

Main Post Office/
Palacio de
Comunicaciones

Buño

Museo de la Real
Academia de Bellas Artes
de San Fernando

SEVILLA

Círculo de
Bellas Artes

Banco de
España

Museo
Naval

Banco
Central

SEVILLA

Palacio
Miraflores

Teatro de la
Zarzuela

PL. DE
CANALEJAS

PL. DE LA
LEALTAD

Parque
del
Buen
Retiro

Museo del
Ejército

Casón del
Buen Retiro

Teatro Español

Casa de
Lope de Vega

Museo
Thyssen-
Bornemisza

AmEx

PL. DEL CÁNOVAS
DEL CASTILLO

PL. DE
SANTA
ANA

HUERTAS

PL. DE
LAS CORTES

Iglesia de
San Jerónimo

Lavandería
Ondablu

Real Academia
de la Historia

PL. DE
MATUTE

ANTÓN
MARTÍN

Museo de Jarón

Cine Doré

PL. DE
SAN JUAN

Museo
del Prado

PL. PLATERÍA
MARTÍNEZ

PL. DE
MURILLO

Real
Jardín
Botánico

LAVAPIÉS

PL. DE
LAVAPIÉS

Real
Conservatorio
de Música

ATOCHA

ATOCHA

PL. DEL
EMPERADOR
CARLOS V

Ministerio de
Agricultura

Avis and
Europcar

TICKET
OFFICE

Museo Nacional
Centro de Arte
Reina Sofía

Estación
Atocha

TO KARACOL
SPORT (50m)   (12km)

TO ESTACIÓN
AUTO RES (1680m)

ATOCHA RENFE

Madrid

SEE MAP, p. 666

🏠🏠 ACCOMMODATIONS

Camping Alpha,	1	E6
Cat's Hostel,	2	C5
Hostal Don Juan,	3	D2
Hostal R. Arantza,	4	D2
Hostal Oriente,	5	B3
Hostal Santillan,	6	B2
Hostel Miguel Ángela,	7	C4
La Posada de Huertas,	8	D5

🍴 FOOD

Arrocería Gala,	9	E5
Café-Botillería Manuela,	10	C1
Casa Alberto,	11	D5
El Estragón Vegetariano,	12	A5
La Finca de Susana,	13	D4
La Granja de Said,	14	C1
Inshala,	15	A4
El Mejillón de Madrid,	16	C4
Restaurante Casa Granada,	17	C5
La Sanabresa,	18	D5
Taberna Maceira,	19	E5

⭐ NIGHTLIFE

Joy Eslava,	20	B4
Teatro Kapital,	21	E5
Trocha,	22	E6

districts, linked by Calle de Fuencarral: **Malasaña, Bilbao,** and **Chueca.** Modern Madrid is beyond Gran Vía and east of Malasaña and Chueca. East of Sol, the tree-lined thoroughfares **Paseo de la Castellana, Paseo de Recoletos,** and **Paseo del Prado** split Madrid in two, running from **Atocha** in the south to **Plaza Castilla** in the north, passing the Prado, the fountains of **Plaza de Cibeles,** and **Plaza de Colón.** Madrid is safer than many European cities, but Sol, Pl. de España, Pl. Chueca, and Pl. Dos de Mayo are still intimidating at night. Travel in groups, avoid the parks and quiet streets after dark, and watch for thieves and pickpockets in crowds.

The free *Plano de Madrid* (street map) and *Plano de Transportes* (public transport map) are fantastic. Pick them up at any tourist office. Public transportation info is also available by phone (☎012) or on the web (www.ctm-madrid.es). **El Corte Inglés** offers a free one-page map of Madrid. For a comprehensive map with a street index, pick up an *Almax* map (€2-8 depending on level of detail) at any newsstand or bookstore.

🛈 PRACTICAL INFORMATION

STAYING SAFE IN MADRID. Madrid is just as safe as most major European cities, but Pta. del Sol, Pl. de España, Pl. Chueca, C. Gran Vía, and southern Malasaña can be intimidating late at night. As a general rule, avoid parks and quiet residential streets after dark and always watch out for thieves and pickpockets in crowds.

Tourist Offices: English and French are spoken at most tourist offices. Those planning trips outside the Comunidad de Madrid can visit region-specific offices within the city; ask for their addresses at any tourist office.

Regional Office of the Comunidad de Madrid, C. del Duque de Medinaceli, 2 (☎914 29 49 51, info 902 10 00 07; www.turismomadrid.es). M: Banco de España. Brochures, transportation info, and maps for the Comunidad. Extremely helpful; if you are planning to travel beyond the city itself, make this your first stop. Open M-Sa 8am-8pm, Su 9am-2pm.

Madrid Tourism Centre, Pl. Mayor, 27 (☎915 88 16 36; www.esmadrid.com). M: Sol. Hands out indispensable city and transportation maps and a complete guide to accommodations as well as *In Madrid,* a monthly activity and information guide in English. Branches at Estación Chamartín (p.664), Estación Puerta de Atocha (p. 664), and the airport (p. 664), also at Plaza de Cibeles, Plaza de Callao, and Plaza de Felipe II. All open daily 9:30am-8pm.

General Info Line: Línea Madrid (☎010). Info on all things Madrid, from police stations to zoo hours. Ask for *inglés* for an English-speaking operator.

Tours: Tours can be informative but pricey, so read the fine print before signing on. The *Ayuntamiento* offers walking tours, in English and Spanish called **Descubre Madrid** (☎915 88 29 06. €3.90; students, children, and seniors €3.12); the tours leave from the municipal tourist office, where you can get more info. **Madrid Vision** (☎917 79 18 88; www.madridvision.es) operates double-decker bus tours. There are 2 routes (Madrid Histórico and Moderno) each of which makes 15-20 stops around the city, featuring monuments and museums. Get on and off the bus as you please. €19, ages 7-16 and seniors €10; discounts available online.

Budget Travel: TIVE, C. Fernando el Católico, 88 (☎915 43 74 12). M: Moncloa. Walk straight down C. Arcipreste de Hita (one street over, parallel to C. Princesa) and turn left on C. Fernando el Católico. A great resource for long-term visitors. Lodging, tourism, and student residence info. Organizes group excursions as well as language classes and cheap trips to other European cities. Some English spoken. Some services only for Spanish nationals. Sells cheap **ISIC** cards (€6) and **Hostelling International (HI)** memberships (€21), along with discount memberships for teachers and people above 26. Open M-F 9am-2pm. Arrive early to avoid lines. Another smaller branch is located at Paseo de Recoletos, 7 (☎917 20 13 24). M: Banco de España. Open M-F 9am-2pm.

Embassies: Australia, Pl. del Descubridor Diego de Ordás 3, 2nd fl. (☎91 353 6600; www.spain.embassy.gov.au). **Canada,** Núñez de Balboa 35 (☎91 423 3250; www.canada-es.org). **Ireland,** Po. Castellana 46, 4th fl. (☎91 436 4093). **New Zealand,** Pl. de la Lealtad 2, 3rd fl. (☎91 523 0226). **UK,** Po. de Recoletos 7-9 (☎91 524 9700; www.ukinspain.com). **US,** C. Serrano 75 (☎91 587 2200; www.embusa.es).

Luggage Storage: At the airport (€3.70 for the 1st day, €4.78 per day for the next 2 weeks) and bus and train stations (€2.40-4.50 per bag per day).

Women's Resources: For general information on women's services in Spain or to report an incident, call **Instituto de la Mujer,** C. Genova, 11 (24hr. information line ☎900 19 10 10; www.mtas.es/mujer). M: Colón or Alonso Martinez. Open M-F 9am-2pm.

GLBT Resources: Most establishments in Chueca carry *Shangay*, a free guides to gay nightlife in Spain, also available online at www.shangay.com. The guide also offers detailed listings and maps of the many gay establishments in and around Madrid. Alternatively, you can purchase *Zero* magazine (€5) at any kiosk, or check it out for free online at www.zero-web.com.

Colectivo de Gais y Lesbianas de Madrid (COGAM), C. Puebla, 9 (☎915 22 45 17; www.cogam. org). M: Callao. Provides a wide range of services and organizes activities; call or check the website for a schedule. Reception open M-Th 10am-2pm and 5-8pm, F 10am-2pm.

GAY-INFORM/Línea Lesbos (☎915 23 00 70). A gay info line and hotline provides counseling from 5-9pm every night. Th 7-9pm in English. F staffed by and for lesbians, but takes all calls. Also provides information about gay associations, activities, health issues, sports, and dinners.

Laundromat: Central Madrid is tragically devoid of self-service laundromats. Try to arrange for laundry service through your hotel, or call **Tintorería La Plancha Veloz,** C. Doctor Esquerdo, 96 (☎915 73 36 76; www.laplanchaveloz.com); they'll pick up and return your clothing right to your door for no additional charge. M: Conde de Casal. Open M-F 9am-2pm and 5-8pm, Sa 9am-2pm.

Police: C. de los Madrazo, 9 (☎913 22 11 60 or 900 15 00 00). M: Sevilla. Largely administrative. English forms available. Open daily 9am-2pm. **Policía Municipal,** C. Montera 18, has staff 24hr. **Servicio de Atención al Turista Extranjero (SATE),** C. Leganitos, 19, are police who deal exclusively with tourists; they help with administrative formalities, reporting crimes, canceling credit cards, contacting embassies and family members, finding lost objects, and finding counseling. (☎915 48 85 37 for the office or ☎902 102 112 to report a crime. M: Plaza de España. Open daily 9am-midnight.)

24hr. Pharmacy: Farmacia Ortopedia, C. Mayor, 13 (☎913 664 616), off Pta. del Sol. Dial ☎098 for additional rotating locations.

Hospitals: Emergency rooms are the best option for immediate attention. US insurance is not accepted, but if you get a receipt your insurance may pay. For non-emergency concerns, **Unidad Médica Angloamericana,** C. del Conde de Aranda, 1, 1st fl. (☎914 35 18 23; www.unidadmedica.com). M: Serrano or Retiro. Regular English-speaking personnel on duty M-F 9am-8pm, Sa 10am-1pm. English-speaking specialists in every branch of medicine do non-urgent consultations. Appointments required. AmEx/MC/V. Embassies and consulates keep lists of English-speaking doctors.

Emergency Clinics: In a medical emergency, dial ☎061 or 112. **Hospital de Madrid,** Pl. del Conde del Valle Suchil, 16 (☎914 47 66 00; www.hospitaldemadrid.com). M: Bilbao. **Hospital Ramón y Cajal,** Ctra. Colmenar Viejo, km 9100 (☎913 36 80 00). M: Begoña or Bus #135 from Pl. de Castilla. **Red Cross** (☎915 22 22 22, info 902 22 22 92). **Centro Sanitorio Sandoval,** C. Sandoval, 7 (☎914 48 57 58). M: Bilbao. Free, confidential government clinic specializing in HIV/AIDS and other STIs; call ahead to arrange a visit.

Telephones: Directory services ☎11822. (See **Keeping in Touch,** p. 661.)

Internet Access: Hundreds of internet cafes are spread across the city, and most hostels provide free internet access as well. Rates are generally consistent (roughly €1-1.50 per 30min. and €2 per hr.). **Kioscocity,** C. Montera 47. Internet and Wi-Fi €1 for 15min., €1.50 for 30min., €2 per hr. Domestic and international fax services available. Open daily 24hr.

Post Office: Palacio de Comunicaciones, C. Alcalá, 51, on Pl. de Cibeles (☎902 19 71 97). M: Banco de España. Enormous palace on the far side of the plaza from the metro. Info (main vestibule) open M-Sa 8:30am-9:30pm. Windows open M-Sa 8:30am9:30pm, Su 8:30am-2pm for stamp purchases. To find a more convenient location near you, check the website at www.correos.es. **Postal Code:** 28080.

ACCOMMODATIONS

Make reservations for summer visits. Expect to pay €15-50 per person, depending on location, amenities, and season.

EL CENTRO: SOL, ÓPERA, AND PLAZA MAYOR

Miguel Ángel Residencia Comunitaria, Pl. Celenque, 1, 4th fl. (☎915 22 23 55; www.hostelmiguelangel.com), 1 block up off C. Arenal. The cleanest, classiest "backpacker hostel" around and the best deal in the *centro*. Immaculate air-conditioned rooms have bright curtains and comforters. Communal bathrooms are big and very clean. English spoken. Breakfast included. Free internet and Wi-Fi. Reserve in advance. Dorms €17-21; triples €78. ❶

Hostal Oriente, C. de Arenal, 23, 1st fl. (☎915 48 03 14). Rooms have magnificently clean white tile and creamy peach walls and bedspreads. Balconies at this elegant *hostal* add breeze but unexciting views. 17 rooms have TV, phone, A/C, and bath. Free internet. Reserve ahead. Singles €45; doubles €65; triples €85. MC/V. ❹

HUERTAS

Way Hostel, C. Relatores 17 (☎914 20 05 83; reservas@wayhostel.com). M: Tirso de Molina. The sleek black-and-white lounge and inviting kitchen at this cozy, 70-bed hostel lend it a relaxed, friendly feel. Clean, spacious 6- to 10-bed dorms are a fantastic value; most come with A/C. Breakfast included. Towels €1. Free internet and Wi-Fi. Dorms €15-22. AmEx/MC/V. ❶

Cat's Hostel, C. Cañizares, 6 (☎913 69 28 07; www.catshostel.com). M: Antón Martín. This renovated 18th-century palace stands among Europe's most beautiful hostels, although some travelers complain that its size (200 beds) makes for an institutional vibe and its unfriendly staff make for a less than pleasant stay. Basic dorms (2-14 beds) and small doubles with private baths open onto a restored Moorish patio replete with plants, fountain, and luxurious cushions. Wood-paneled pub and cave-like basement bar draw crowds, especially after the courtyard closes at midnight. No kitchen. A/C and breakfast included. Laundry €5. Free internet and Wi-Fi. Reserve ahead, as it often fills quickly. Dorms M-Th and Su €17-20, F-Sa 18-22; doubles with bath €38-42. MC/V. ❶

GRAN VÍA

Hostal Santillan, Gran Vía, 64, 8th fl. (☎915 48 23 28; www.hostalsantillan.com). M: Pl. de España. Take the glass elevator to the top of this gorgeous building. Leaf-patterned curtains and wooden furniture give rooms a homey feel. All have shower, sink, TV, and fan. A little more cash can you get you a bath and much bigger room; explore the options. Laundry €1-3 per piece. Free Wi-Fi. Singles €30-35; doubles €50-55; triples €70-75. MC/V. ❸

Hostal Concepción Arenal, C. Concepción Arenal, 6, 3rd fl. (☎915 22 68 83). M: Callao. Breezy and just far enough from Gran Vía to be tranquil. Brown decor. Quiet rooms have short but soft beds and well-scrubbed showers. Rooms come with shower and TV, some with full bath. Free Wi-Fi. Singles €29, with full bath €35; doubles €40/50; triples with ½-bath €60. MC/V. ❸

MALASAÑA AND CHUECA

🏨 **Hostal Don Juan,** Pl. Vasquez de Mella, 1, 2nd fl. (☎915 22 31 01). M: Chueca. Luxury fit for the romancing namesake himself. Chinese vases, tapestries, and antique candlesticks fill the lobby and adjacent common room. Rooms come with beautiful wooden flooring and hand-carved furniture, A/C, TV, and gleaming bath; many have small balconies. Free internet and Wi-Fi. Singles €38; doubles €53; triples €71. AmEx/MC/V. ❹

Hostal Condestable, C. Puebla, 15, 2nd fl. (☎915 31 62 02; www.hostalcondestable.com). M: Callao. Pastel-hued, fully-carpeted lobby fronts tranquil rooms with tall ceilings, solid-wood furniture, TV, and A/C; some with full bath. Communal baths are clean and bright. Singles €30, with bath €38; doubles €40/48; triples with bath €60. ❸

🍴 FOOD

In Madrid, it's not hard to fork it down without forking over too much. Most restaurants offer a *menú del día* (€9-11), which includes bread, one drink, and a choice of appetizer, main course, and dessert. Many small eateries cluster on **Calles Echegaray, Ventura de la Vega,** and **Manuel Fernández González**

ON THE MENU

TAPAS A TO Z

Food on toothpicks and in small bowls? The restaurant isn't being stingy, and your food isn't shrinking; you're experiencing an integral part of the Spanish lifestyle. The *tapas* tradition is one of the oldest in Spain. These tasty little dishes are Spain's answer to hors d'oeuvres, but they have more taste, less pretension, and they're eaten instead of meals.

To the untrained tourist, *tapas* menus are often indecipherable, if the bar has even bothered to print any. In order to avoid awkward encounters with tentacles or parts of the horse you rode in on, keep the following things in mind before *tapeando* (eating tapas).

Servings come in three sizes: *pinchos* (eaten with toothpicks), *tapas* (small plate), and *raciónes* (meal portion). On any basic menu you'll find: *Aceitunas* (olives), *albóndigas* (meatballs), *callos* (tripe), *chorizo* (sausage), *gambas* (shrimp), *jamón* (ham), *patatas bravas* (fried potatoes with spicy sauce), *pimientos* (peppers), *pulpo* (octopus), and *tortilla española* (onion and potato omelette). The more adventurous should try *morcilla* (blood sausage), or *sesos* (cow's brains). Often, bartenders will offer tastes of *tapas* with your drink and strike up a conversation. Ask for a *caña* (glass) of the house *cerveza* (beer) to guarantee the full respect of the establishment.

in Huertas. **Chueca** is filled with *bars de cañas* (small beer from the tap), which serve complimentary *tapas*. The streets west of **Calle Fuencarral** in Gran Vía are lined with cheap restaurants, while **Bilbao** has affordable ethnic cuisine. Linger in Madrid's cafes to absorb the sights of the city; you won't be bothered with the check until you ask. Keep in mind the following words for quick, cheap *madrileño* fare: *bocadillo* (a sandwich on half a baguette; €2-3); *ración* (a large *tapa* served with bread; €3-6); and *empanada* (a puff pastry with meat fillings; €1.30-2). The *Guía del Ocio* has a complete listing of Madrid's vegetarian options under the section "Otras Cocinas." **Día%** and **Champion** are the cheapest supermarket chains; smaller markets are open later but are more expensive.

🍽 **El Estragón Vegetariano,** Pl. de la Paja, 10 (☎913 65 89 82). M: La Latina. This unobtrusive restaurant, with its quiet decor and patio feel, would blush at any superlatives we might give it, but its vegetarian delights could convince even the most die-hard carnivores to switch teams. Lunch *menús* M-F €8-12. Sa-Su special entrees €9. Open M-F 1:30-4pm and 8pm-midnight, Sa-Su 8pm-midnight. AmEx/MC/V. ❸

🍽 **La Finca de Susana,** C. Arlaban, 4 (☎913 69 35 57; www.lafinca-restaurant.com). M: Sevilla. Simple, elegant dining at jaw-droppingly low prices. The beef and arugula sushi (€7.80) is one of countless top-notch plates. M-F lunch *menú* with wine an amazing €9.50. Arrive early to avoid the ever-present line down the street. Open daily 1-3:45pm and 8:30-11:45pm. AmEx/MC/V. ❷

🍽 **Arrocería Gala,** C. de Moratín, 22 (☎914 29 25 62; www.paellas-gala.com). M: Antón Martín. Pastoral Spanish scenes of bulls on hillsides are gracefully overlaid in vine and shadows from the gorgeous chandeliers. The specialty made-to-order paellas (€15-20 per person, minimum 2 people) are 2nd to none. Tasty sangria €10 per pitcher. Reserve ahead on weekends. Open Tu-Su 1-5pm and 9pm-1:30am. Cash only. ❸

🍽 **La Granja de Said,** C. de San Andrés, 11 (☎915 32 87 93). M: Tribunal or Bilbao. Moorish designs in the doorways, beautiful tiling, and the dim glow of light through lamps and tapestries bring the Middle East to Malasaña. Dine well, then puff peacefully on hookah (€8). *Tabouleh* salad €6. Delicious falafel plate €7. Open Tu-Su 1pm-5pm and 8pm-2am. MC/V. ❷

🍽 **Olokun,** C. Fuencarral, 105 (☎914 45 69 16). M: Bilbao. From the Gl. de Bilbao exit, walk south on Fuencarral. Beach scenes, tropical mixed drinks (€5-7), and delicacies like *tostones* (fried plantains; €6) served on wooden barrels bring Cuba to Malasaña. *Menú* €11.90. Salsa Th 5:30pm. Open daily noon-5pm and 9pm-2am; kitchen open until 1am. MC/V. ❷

🍽 **Bazaar,** C. de la Libertad, 21 (☎915 23 39 05; www.restaurantbazaar.com). M: Chueca. Another fantastic and shockingly affordable bistro from the team behind La Finca de Susana. Bright dining room with white leather banquettes and funky wine glasses. Elegant entrees an amazing €6-9. M-F lunch *menú* €10. Open daily 1:15-4pm and 8:30-11:45pm. MC/V. ❸

🍽 **Subiendo al Sur,** C.Ponciano, 5 (☎915 48 11 47; www.subiendoalsur.org). M: Noviciado. From the colorful Central American decor to the warm, friendly waitstaff to the knowledge that 100% of proceeds from your meal will go to support development projects in the global South, it's hard not to feel good eating at this fair-trade cafe and restaurant. Lunch *menú* €9.50. *Caña* €1. Open M 1:45-4:30pm, Tu-Sa 1:45-4:30pm and 9pm-midnight. Cash only. ❷

El Mejillón de Madrid, Pasaje de Matheu, 4, just off Espoz y Mina. No-frills seafood under umbrellas right on Madrid's shellfish row. Try the heaping plate of mussels (€8), the restaurant's namesake, or the plate of paella (€25) for 2 or more. Order 4 *raciones* (€4-11) and you'll get a free jug of sangria for up to 4 people—the best deal in the *centro*. Open M-Th, Su 11:30am-12:30am, F-Sa 11:30am-1:30am. Cash only. ❷

Sobrino del Botín, C. Cuchilleros, 17 (☎913 66 42 17; www.botin.es), off Pl. Mayor. Advertising itself as the oldest restaurant in the world, Sobrino del Botín has seen its share of the famous since it opened in 1725. Goya washed dishes here when he was

19, and Hemingway, a regular customer, mentions it by name in *The Sun Also Rises* (as the sign out front won't let passers-by forget). Ancient wooden doors and patterned red walls with gold filigree lend the kind of class that only age can bring. Entrees €8-20. Suckling pig €22.50. Open daily 1-4pm and 8pm-midnight. AmEx/MC/V. ❹

TAPAS BARS AND CAFES

▨ **Chocolatería San Ginés,** Pl. San Ginés (☎913 66 54 31). M: Sol. Tucked into a small plaza behind Joy Eslava, this beautifully-tiled *chocolatería* is a legend among early-risers and clubgoers alike, both for its unbeatable *chocolate con churros* (€4) and for its steadfast refusal to close. Open daily 24hr. Cash only. ❶

▨ **Restaurante Casa Granada,** C. Doctor Cortezo, 17, 6th fl. (☎914 20 08 25). The door (on the left side of C. Doctor Cortezo as you head downhill) is unmarked; ring the bell for the 6th fl. and then head up the elevators at the back of the modest lobby. Though easy to miss, the experience of a sunset meal on the rooftop terrace is hard to forget. Put your name on the outdoor seating list when you arrive; you'll be vying with lots of other *madrileños*-in-the-know for a table. *Cañas* of beer (€2.40) come with tapas. *Raciones* €6.50-14. Open daily noon-1am. MC/V. ❷

▨ **Casa Alberto,** C. de las Huertas, 18 (☎914 29 93 56; www.casaalberto.es). M: Antón Martín. The manual-wash bar and shanks hanging from the walls are throwbacks to the early days of this bar, founded in 1827. Very popular; getting a table during bus-tling meal hours can be difficult. Sweet vermouth (€1.70) is served with original house tapas. Try the delicious cod and lamb omelette (€4) or the *patatas ali-oli* (garlic pota-toes; €4.50). Open Tu-Sa noon-5:30pm and 8pm-1:30am. MC/V. ❷

▨ **Lolina Vintage Cafe,** C. Espíritu Santo, 9 (☎667 20 11 69; www.lolinacafe.com). This quirky cafe's mismatched armchairs, geometric wallpaper, and eccentric lamps could have come from a Brooklyn thrift store, but they fit perfectly into the trendy Malasaña scene. Great selection of teas (try the Green Earl Grey) in super-cool pots that detach to reveal cups hidden underneath (€2). Large salads €8. Hot dogs €5. Keeps bustling into the night, when mojitos are €6. Wi-Fi available. Open M-Tu and Su 9:30am-1am, W-Th 9:30am-2am, F-Sa 9:30-2:30am. MC/V. ❶

◉ SIGHTS

Two dynasties, a dictatorship, and a cultural rebirth have bequeathed Madrid a broad, diverse, and fantastic collection of parks, palaces, plazas, cathedrals, and art museums. While Madrid is small enough to walk in a day, its sights are enough to keep you for weeks. Soak it all in, strolling from Sol to Cibeles and Pl. Mayor to the Palacio Real.

HAPSBURG MADRID

In the 16th century, Hapsburgs of the Austrian dynasty funded the construc-tion of **Plaza Mayor** and the **Catedral de San Isidro.** After moving the seat of Castilla from Toledo to Madrid (then only a town of 20,000) in 1561, Felipe II and his descendants commissioned the court architects (including **Juan de Herrera,** the master behind El Escorial) to update many of Madrid's build-ings, creating a distinctive set of churches and palaces with wide central patios and scrawny black towers—the "Madrid style."

PLAZA MAYOR. Juan de Herrera, the architect of **El Escorial,** also designed this plaza. Its elegant arcades, spindly towers, and open verandas, built for Felipe III in 1620, are defining elements of the "Madrid style," which inspired architects nationwide. Toward evening, Pl. Mayor awakens as *Madrileños* resurface, tour-ists multiply, and cafes fill up. Live *flamenco* performances are a common treat.

NAKED TRUTH

Civil liberties have come a long way in Spain since Franco died; a fact that became clear to me as I walked through the Plaza de Oriente one day.

Traffic stopped, and a din arose from down C. Bailén, which runs in front of the Palacio Real. Then hundreds—perhaps thousands—of naked protesters rode by slowly on bicycles. What they wanted was unclear at first. Some chanted "Gasolina es asesina" (gas is an assassin), others merely "Coches = mierda" (cars are shit). Whatever it was, they were out in force, with their children, wives, and co-workers, drinking beer and taking pictures as they rode.

I stopped and talked to a few of the unclad riders. "We're protesting for urban transport," one said, patting his bicycle. He told me that riding your bicycle in Madrid is often dangerous because drivers don't care about cyclists. The protestors rode on, followed by a police escort, ostensibly protecting the group from traffic.

Enjoying the irony, I paused and saw the mass of naked riders being escorted past one of the most beautiful royal palaces in the world, an image that will stay with me. Riding naked in my puritanical country, much less past the Capitol or the home of the President, would not be tolerated. Madrileños cherish their rights, and that's the naked truth.

- Russell Rennie

While the cafes are a nice spot for a drink, food is overpriced. *(M: Sol. Walk down C. Mayor. The plaza is on the left.)*

BOURBON MADRID

Weakened by plagues and political losses, the Hapsburg era in Spain ended with the death of Carlos II in 1700. Felipe V, the first of Spain's Bourbon monarchs, ascended to the throne in 1714 after the 12-year War of the Spanish Succession. Bankruptcy, economic stagnation, and disillusionment compelled Felipe V to embark on a crusade of urban renewal, and his successors pursued the same ends with astounding results. Today, their lavish palaces, churches, and parks are the most spectacular (and touristed) in Madrid.

PALACIO REAL. Palacio Real. The luxurious Palacio Real lies at the western tip of central Madrid, overlooking the Río Manzanares. Felipe V commissioned Giovanni Sachetti to replace the Alcázar, which burned down in 1734, with a palace that would dwarf all others—he succeeded. Today, King Juan Carlos and Queen Sofía use the palace only on special occasions. The **Salón del Trono** (Throne Room) contains the two magnificent Spanish thrones, supported by golden lions. The room also features a ceiling fresco painted by Tiepolo, outlining the qualities of the ideal ruler. The **Salón de Gasparini,** site of the king's ceremonial dressing before the court, houses Goya's portrait of Carlos IV. Perhaps most beautiful is the **Chinese Room,** whose walls swirl with green tendril patterns. The **Real Oficina de Farmacia** (Royal Pharmacy) has crystal and china receptacles used to hold royal medicine. Also open to the public is the **Real Armería** (Armory), which has an entire floor devoted to knights' armor. *(From Pl. de Isabel II, head toward the Teatro Real. M: Ópera. ☎914 54 87 88. Open Apr.-Sept. M-Sa 9am-6pm, Su 9am-3pm; Oct.-Mar. M-Sa 9:30am-5pm, Su 9am-2pm. Arrive early to avoid lines. Changing of the guard Sept.-May 1st W of every month at noon. €8, with tour €10; students, seniors, and children ages 5-16 €3.50/6; under 5 free. EU citizens free W.)*

CATEDRAL DE NUESTRA SEÑORA DE LA ALMUDENA. Begun in 1879 and inaugurated more than a century later in 1993, this cathedral's simple forms and abstracted stained glass windows stand in stark contrast to the cherub-filled frescoes and gilded marble of most major Spanish churches. Even today, the building remains controversial, as gray stone walls clash with the ceiling panels of brilliant colors and sharp geometric shapes that verge on Art Deco. *(C. Bailén, 10. Left of the Palacio Real* *on C. Bailén. M: Ópera.* ☎ *915 422 200. Open daily Sept.-June 9am-8:30pm,; July-Aug. 10am-2pm and 5-9pm. Closed during mass. €1 donation requested. Call* ☎ *807 220 022 for a telephonic guided tour of the church.*) The blindingly white **crypt** below is worth a visit, but make sure you aren't interrupting any nuptials—oddly enough, it's a popular wedding spot. *(C. Mayor, 92; enter from the side facing away from the Palacio. Open daily 10am-1pm and 5-8pm. €2)* Visitors can also take in a **museum** that details the construction of the church; admission includes a trip up into the cupola, which affords spectacular views of the Campo del Moro, the Palace, and the city below. *(Behind the church, on the side facing the Palacio.* ☎ *915 592 894; www.archimadrid.es. Open M-Sa 10am-2:30pm. €4.)*

OTHER SIGHTS

PARQUE DEL BUEN RETIRO. Join an array of vendors, palm-readers, football players, and sunbathers in the area Felipe IV converted from a hunting ground into a *buen retiro* (nice retreat). The 300-acre park is centered around a magnificent monument to King Alfonso XII and a lake, the **Estanque Grande.** Around the lake, all manner of mimes, puppeteers, and street performers show off for the benefit of the crowd (and a few coins). *(The Estanque can be reached by following Av. de Méjico from the park's Pl. de la Independencia entrance. Boats for up to 4 people €4.55 per 45min.)*

EL RASTRO (FLEA MARKET). For hundreds of years, *El Rastro* has been a Sunday-morning tradition in Madrid. The market begins in La Latina at Pl. Cascorro off C. Toledo and ends at the bottom of C. Ribera de Cortidores. El Rastro sells everything from zebra hides to jeans to antique tools to pet birds. Whatever price you're thinking (or being offered), it can probably be bargained in half. The flea market is a pickpocket's paradise, so leave your camera behind, bust out the money belt, and turn that backpack into a frontpack. Police (p. 669) are available if you need them. (Open Sundays and holidays 9am-3pm.)

MUSEUMS: AVENIDA DEL ARTE

Considered to be among the world's best art galleries, the Museo del Prado, Museo Thyssen-Bornemisza, and the Museo Nacional Centro de Arte Reina Sofía form the impressive "Avenida del Arte."

MUSEO DEL PRADO. One of Europe's finest centers for 12th- to 17th-century art, the Prado is Spain's most prestigious museumhome to the world's greatest collection of Spanish paintings. Its 7000 pieces are the result of hundreds of years of collecting by the Hapsburgs and Bourbons. The museum provides an indispensable guide for each room. English-language **audio tours** are available for €3. On the first floor, keep an eye out for the unforgiving realism of **Diego Velázquez** (1599-1660). His technique of "illusionism" is on display in the magnificent **Las Meninas,** considered by some art historians to be the best painting ever made. Deaf and alone, **Goya** painted the *Pinturas Negras* (Black Paintings), so named for the darkness of both their color and their subject matter. The Prado also displays many of **El Greco's** religious paintings, characterized by luminous colors, elongated figures, and mystical subjects. On the second floor are works by other Spanish artists, including **Murillo** and **Ribera.** *(Po. del Prado at Pl. Cánovas del Castillo. M: Banco de España or Atocha.* ☎ *91 330 2800; www.museoprado.es. Open Tu-Su 9am-8pm €6, students €3, under 18 and over 65 free. Tu-Sa 6-8pm and Su 5-8pm free.)*

MUSEO NACIONAL CENTRO DE ARTE REINA SOFÍA. Since Juan Carlos I decreed this renovated hospital a national museum in 1988, the Reina Sofía's collection of **twentieth-century art** has grown steadily. Rooms dedicated to **Salvador Dalí, Juan Gris,** and **Joan Miró** display Spain's vital contributions to the Surrealist movement. **Picasso's** masterpiece, **Guernica,** is the highlight. *(Pl. Santa*

TO ⊞ (200m)
TO PL. DE TOROS (400m)
TO 🚌 (300m)

Av. de Carlos III
P. Canónigos
GLORIETA DE LA RECONQUISTA
C. Alfonso VI
P. del Circo Romano
P. del Cristo de la Vega
Puerta de Bisagra
Puerta de Alfonso VI
Alimentación Pantoja
C. Real del Arrabal
C. de los Azacanes
C. de Gerardo Lobo
TO 🛈
Subida a la Granja
P. Miradero
P. del Circo Romano
Av. de la Cava
Puerta de Cambrón
P. de Recaredo
C. Buzones
C. de la Merced
PL. SAN AGUSTÍN
P. de San Martín
PL. SANTA TERESA DE JESUS
C. Real
Cta. de Sta. Leocadia
Colegio de Doncellas
Museo de los Concilios y de la Cultura Visigótica
PL. DE PADILLA
Esteban Illán
C. Navarro Ledesma
PL. DE S. VICENTE
los Alfileritos
Clérigos Menores
C. de la Plata
Locutorio El Casco
PL. DE SAN NICOLÁS
C. Toledo de Ohio
PL. SAN AGUSTÍN
C. Cervantes
C. Sante Fe
PL. DE ZOCODOVER
CAMBRÓN
PL. VIRGEN DE GRACIA
C. de las Bulas
PL. STA. EULALIA
Iglesia de San Román (Museo de los Concilios)
S. Ginés
C. Nuncio Viejo
PL. DE LA MAGDALENA
Monasterio de San Juan de los Reyes
C. Cava Baja
Hospedería S. Bernando
San Pedro Mártir
Museo de Arte Contemporáneo
PL. MAYOR
Market
Alcázar
Sinagoga de Santa María la Blanca
C. de los Reyes Católicos
C. del Ángel
PL. DEL SALVADOR
C. de la Trinidad
PL. DEL AYUNTAMIENTO
Catedral
PL. ABDÓN DE PAZ
PL. SECO
Red Cross
C. Gen. Moscardó
Iglesia de Santo Tomé
C. Santo Tomé
Salvador
Cisneros
PL. SAN JUSTO
Conservatorio
Casa-Museo de El Greco
Sinagoga del Tránsito
Museo del Taller del Moro
S. Marcos
PL. STA. ISABEL
P. del Tránsito
Cta. de la Reina
Convento Sta. Isabel
Palacio Rey Dom Pedro
PL. DE LAS FUENTES
PL. SAN LUCAS
C. de los Descalzos
P. San Cristóbal
C. San Torcuato
S. Bartolomé
C. de la Plata
Iglesia de San Andrés
Seminario
PL. DON FERNANDO
Cabestreros
Río Tajo
C. San Cipriano
PL. DEL CALVARIO
PL. DEL CERRO DE LAS MELOJAS
Carreras de San Sebastián

Toledo

🏠 ACCOMMODATIONS
Hostal Alfonso XII, **5**
Residencia Juvenil Castillo
San Servando (HI), **1**
🍴 FOOD
La Adabía, **2**
Restaurante Gambrinus, **4**
⭐ NIGHTLIFE
Café Teatro Pícaro, **3**

Isabel 52. ☎ 91 774 1000; www.museoreinasofia.es. M: Atocha. Open M and W-Sa 10am-9pm, Su 10am-2:30pm. €3, students €1.50. Sa after 2:30pm, Su, holidays, under 18, over 65 free.)

🔲**MUSEO THYSSEN-BORNEMISZA.** The Thyssen-Bornemisza exhibits works ranging from 14th-century paintings to 20th-century sculptures. The museum's collection constitutes the world's most extensive private showcase. The top floor is dedicated to the **Old Masters** collection, which includes such notables as Hans Holbein's austere *Portrait of Henry VIII* and El Greco's *Annunciation*. The Thyssen-Bornemisza's Baroque collection, with pieces by Caravaggio, Claude Lorraine, and Ribera, rivals the Prado's. The **Impressionist** and **Post-Impressionist** collections demonstrate the evolution toward modern art forms. The ground floor of the museum houses the extensive twentieth-century collection. The showcased artists include Chagall, Dalí, Hopper, O'Keeffe, Picasso, Pollock, and Rothko. (*Paseo del Prado, 8, on the corner of Po. del Prado and C. Manuel González. M: Banco de España or Atocha.* ☎ 91 369 0151; www.museothyssen.org. Open Tu-Su 10am-7pm. Last entry 6:30pm. €6, students with ISIC and seniors €4, under 12 free. Audio guides €4.)

🎵 ENTERTAINMENT

FÚTBOL

Real Madrid plays at **Estadio Santiago Bernabéu,** Av. Cochina Espina, 1. (☎914 57 11 12. M: Santiago Bernabéu.) In the summer, the club offers tours of the stadium. (☎902 29 17 09; www.realmadrid.com. Tours on non-game days, M-Sa 10am-7pm, Su 10:30am-6:30pm. €15, under 14 €10.) Atlético de Madrid plays at **Estadio Vicente Calderón,** Po. de la Virgen del Puerto, 67. (☎913 64 22 34; www.clubatleticodemadrid.com. M: Pirámides or Marqués de Vadillos.) Getafe plays at **Coliseum Alfonso Pérez,** Av. Teresa de Calcuta s/n. (☎916 95 97 71. M: Los Espartales.) Tickets for Real games sell out well in advance and will probably run €50-100; tickets for Atlético are a little cheaper, and lower still for Getafe.

BULLFIGHTS

Some call it animal torture, others tradition; either way, bullfighting remains one of Spain's most cherished traditions, and it is at its brightest (or its darkest) at the **Plaza de las Ventas,** C. Alcalá, 237, the most important bullfighting arena in the world since its opening in 1931. (☎913 56 22 00; www.las-ventas.com or www.taquillatoros.com. M: Ventas.) The ring plays host to the real professionals; you can also catch a summer *Novillada* (beginner) show, when a younger and less experienced bullfighter takes on smaller bulls. Seats costs €2-115, depending on their location in the *sol* (sun) or *sombra* (shade).

Tickets are available, in person only, the Friday and Saturday before and Sunday of a bullfight. There are bullfights every Sunday from March to October and less frequently during the rest of the year. From early May to early June, the **Fiestas de San Isidro** in Pl. de las Ventas stages a daily *corrida* (bullfight) with top *toreros* and the fiercest bulls. Look for posters in bars and cafes for upcoming *corridas* (especially on C. Victoria, off C. San Jerónimo). **Plaza de Toros Palacio de Vistalegre** also hosts bullfights and cultural events. (☎914 22 07 80. M: Vista Alegre. Call for schedule and prices.) To watch amateurs, head to the **Escuela de Tauromaquia de Madrid,** a training school with its own *corridas* on Saturdays at 7:30pm. (At the Casa de Campo, Avda. de Portugal Lago. ☎914 70 19 90. Open M-F 10am-2pm. €7, children €3.50.)

🎇 NIGHTLIFE

Indulging in Madrid's world-renowned, mind-melting nightlife, especially in the summer months, is not an optional part of your visit—it's required. This city does nightlife bigger and better, later and harder, with more bars, clubs, and discos than nearly anywhere else on earth. People hit the streets around 10 or 11 when music and liquor begin pouring out of bars and *cervecerías*, and revelers don't go to bed until they've "killed the night" and, usually, a good part of the following morning. Proud of their nocturnal offerings, *madrileños* will tell you with a straight face that they were bored in Paris or New York—how can a city be truly exciting if the traffic isn't as heavy at 2am on a Saturday as it is at 5pm on a Monday?

■ **Cool,** C. Isabel la Católica, 6 (☎902 49 99 94). M: Santo Domingo. Madrid's aptly named club-of-the-moment draws a beautiful, fashionable crowd of gay and straight people with its crisp design and pounding house beats. Small lounge and dance floor upstairs overlook the main room below. Men dominate "Royal Club" Sa, Madrid's best gay night. Lines can be long and the bouncers particularly difficult, so dress well and be polite. Cover €12-18, includes 1 drink. Call ahead to add youself to the list for dicounted entry. Open Th and Su midnight-5:30am, F-Sa midnight-6am. AmEx/MC/V.

▨ **Cuevas de Sésamo,** C. del Príncipe, 7 (☎914 296 524). M: Antón Martín. "Descend into these caves like Dante!" (Antonio Machado) is one of the many colorful literary tidbits that welcome you to this packed, smoky, underground gem. Charmingly worn plush seats, live jazz from an unassuming upright piano (Tu-Su), and strong, cheap sangria (large pitcher €10, small pitcher €6) bring in Madrid's bohemian youth. Open daily 7pm-2am. Cash only.

▨ **Why Not?,** C. de San Bartolomé, 7. M: Chueca. A super-hip, wood-paneled underground bunker playing Europop and salsa. Well-dressed patrons sip drinks under a domed ceiling and the gazes of black-and-white Hollywood stars of olden days. Beer €7. Mixed drinks €10-15. Cover €10 when crowded, includes 1 drink. Open daily M-Th and Su 9pm-3:30am, F-Sa 9pm-6am. MC/V.

▨ **Café-Botillería Manuela,** C. de San Vicente Ferrer, 29 (☎915 31 70 37). M: Tribunal. Gleaming marble, mirrors, and antique brass fixtures fill this Old World Parisian cafe. Player piano stacked high with classic board games. Enjoy conversation over a glass of *rioja* (€2.50). Tapas €3-8. Mixed drinks €6. Live music last Sa of every month at 9:30pm. Open June-Aug. daily 6pm-2am; Sept.-May daily 4pm-2am. Cash only.

Reinabruja, C. Jacometrezo, 6 (☎915 42 81 93). M: Callao. A sinuous, subterranean jungle of stenciled pillars and curving, color-changing illuminated honeycombed walls surrounding a bumping central dance floor packed with trendy 20- to 30-year-olds. Come ready and raring to dance to house music—there's practically nowhere to sit down. Wine €7. Mixed drinks €9. Cover €12, includes 1 drink. Open Th-Sa 11pm-6am. MC/V.

Teatro Kapital, C. de Atocha, 125 (☎91 420 29 06). M: Atocha. 7 fl. of justly famed *discoteca* insanity. From hip hop to house, cinemas to karaoke, Kapital offers countless ways to lose yourself, your dignity, and your money in the madness. Special-effects insanity on the massive main dance floor (converted from an old theater) include digital projections and a giant nitrogen-spray cannon. For a change of pace, ascend up through the surrounding 4-story maze of balconies to the palm- and fountain-filled rooftop *terraza*, where you can relax with a hookah (€30) or a game of pool under the open sky. Drinks €11. Cover Th €15, F €18, Sa €22, all with 1 drink included; keep your eyes peeled for flyers that will get you a 2nd drink free. Open Th midnight-5:30am, F-Sa midnight-6am. AmEx/MC/V.

El Café de Schérezad, C. Santa Maria, 18 (☎ 913 694 140). M: Antón Martín. Young *madrileños* lie on plush cushions smoking hookah and relaxing to soothing Moroccan music. Delicious herbal teas come with fresh fruit and small pastries. Tea €3.50; hookah €7-10. Open daily 5pm-3am. Cash only.

Bar Nike, C. Augusto Figueroa, 22 (☎915 21 07 51). M: Chueca. A colorless *cafetería* where half of Chueca comes to drink before clubbing. Absolutely packed from wall to wall. Fight your way to the bar for an enormous, sticky *calimocho* (red wine and cola; €4.50). Beer €4.80. Sangria €5. Open daily noon-3am. Cash only.

CASTILLA LA MANCHA

Land of austere plains and miles of empty landscapes, Castilla La Mancha has played host to bloody conflicts and epic heroes both real and imaginary. The region is one of Spain's least developed and provokes the imagination with its solitary crags, gloomy medieval fortresses, and whirling windmills.

TOLEDO ☎925

Cervantes called Toledo (pop. 75,000) "the glory of Spain and light of her cities." The city is a former capital of the Holy Roman, Visigoth, and Muslim Empires, and its churches, synagogues, and mosques share twisting alleyways. Toledo is known as the "City of Three Cultures," symbol of a time when Spain's three religions coexisted peacefully, although as one might expect, locals will tell you the history is somewhat romanticized.

TRANSPORTATION AND PRACTICAL INFORMATION. From the station on Po. de la Rosa, just over Puente de Azarquiel, **trains** (RENFE info ☎902 24 02 02) run to Madrid (30min., 9-11 per day, €9). **Buses** run from Av. Castilla La Mancha (☎925 21 58 50), 10min. from **Puerta de Bisagra** (the city gate), to Madrid (1hr., 2 per hr., €4.53) and Valencia (5hr., 1 per day, €25). Within the city, buses #8.1 and #8.2 serve the bus station and buses #1-7 run from the Pl. de Zocodóver to points outside the old city. Buses (€1; at night €1.30) stop to the right of the train station, underneath and across the street from the bus station. Though Toledo's streets are well labeled, it's easy to get lost; pick up a map at the **tourist office**, at Pta. de Bisagra. (☎925 22 08 43. Open July-Sept. M-F 9am-7pm, Sa 10am-6pm, Su 10am-2pm; Oct.-June M-F 9am-6pm, Sa 10am-6pm, Su 10am-2pm.) **Postal Code:** 45001.

ACCOMMODATIONS AND FOOD. Toledo is full of accommodations, but finding a bed in summer can be a hassle, especially on weekends. Reservations are strongly recommended. Spacious rooms among suits of armor await at the **Residencia Juvenil San Servando (HI) ❶**, Castillo San Servando, uphill on Subida del Hospital from the train station, in a 14th-century castle with a pool, TV room, and Internet. (☎925 22 45 54. Dorms €11, with breakfast €15; under 30 €9.20/11. MC/V.) To get to **Hostal Alfonso XII ❹**, C. Alfonso XII, 18 (☎925 25 25 09; www.hostal-alfonso12.com), turn off C. Santo Tomé up Campana and follow it to C. Alfonso XII. Scented herbs and flowers fill the halls and rooms with good aromas. Wooden beams traverse the ceilings and add the finishing note to an elegant, deceptively rustic place with modern amenities. Rooms have TV, A/C, and Wi-Fi. (Singles €40; doubles €55; triples €70. MC/V.) *Pastelería* windows beckon with *mazapán* (marzipan) of every shape and size. For the widest array, stop by the **market** in Pl. Mayor, behind the cathedral. (Open M-Sa 9am-8pm.) To reach **La Abadía ❷**, Pl. de San Nicolás 3, bear left when C. de la Sillería splits; Pl. de San Nicolás is on the right. Dine on the regional lunch *menú* (€10) in a maze of underground rooms. Combo *tapas* plates €5-10.(☎925 25 11 40. Open daily 8am-midnight. AmEx/MC/V.) **Restaurante Gambrinus ❸**, C. Santo Tomé, 10 offers the shadiest outdoor seating in the old city, which is perfect for people-watching as you slowly conquer a hearty traditional Spanish plate. There are big soups (€6) for the hungry. (☎925 21 44 40. Meat dishes €10-11. Open daily 11am-4pm and 8pm-midnight. MC/V.)

SIGHTS AND NIGHTLIFE. At Arco de Palacio, up C. del Comercio from Pl. de Zocodóver, Toledo's **cathedral** boasts five naves, delicate stained glass, and unapologetic ostentation. The **sacristía** holds 18 works by *El Greco* (including *El Espolio*), as well as paintings by other notable Spanish and European masters. (☎925 22 22 41. Open M-Sa 10am-6:30pm, Su 2-6:30pm. €8, students €6. Audio tour €3. Dress modestly.) Greek painter Doménikos Theotokópoulos, better known as **El Greco**, spent most of his life in Toledo. A great introduction to his work is the **Casa Museo de El Greco**, on C. Samuel Leví 2, which contains 19 of his works. (☎925 22 44 05. Open in summer Tu-Sa 10am-2pm and 4-9pm,

Su 10am-2pm; in winter Tu-Sa 10am-2pm and 4-6pm, Su 10am-2pm. €2.40; students, under 18, Sa afternoon, and Su free. Closed for renovations until at least 2009.) Up the hill and to the right is the **Iglesia de Santo Tomé**, which still houses one of his most famous and recognized works, **El Entierro del Conde de Orgaz** (The Burial of Count Orgaz). Arrive early to beat the tour groups. Pl. del Conde, 4. (☎925 25 60 98; www.santotome.org. Open daily Mar.-Oct. 15 10am-7pm; Oct.16-Feb. 10am-6pm. €2.30, students and over 65 €1.80.)

On the same street as Museo El Greco is the **Sinagoga del Tránsito,** one of two remaining synagogues in Toledo's *judería* (Jewish quarter). Inside, the **Museo Sefardí** documents early Jewish history in Spain. Look up at the Hebrew letters carved into the *mudéjar* plasterwork and a stunning coffered wood ceiling. (☎711 35 52 30; www.museosefardi.net. Open Mar.-Nov. Tu-Sa 10am-2pm and 4-9pm, Su 10am-2pm; Dec.-Feb. Tu-Sa 10am-2pm and 4-6pm, Su 10am-2pm. €2.40, students, seniors, and under 18 free. Sa after 4pm and Su free.) Nestling in the middle of the city, the **Iglesia de Los Jesuitas** is a Jesuit church that has 🔲**amazing views** from its towers. Located at one of the highest points in the city, the roof offers a panorama of all the towers and tiled roofs in the old city and the hills for miles around. It's breezy, so hold on to your hat. (Pl. Padre Juan de Mariana, 1, up C. Nuncio Viejo from the Cathedral, and then a left on Alfonso X El Sabio. ☎925 25 15 07. Open daily Apr.-Sept. 10am-6:45pm; Oct.-March 10am-5:45pm. €2.30.) For nightlife, head through the arch and to the left from Pl. de Zocodóver to **Calle Santa Fé,** which brims with beer and local youth. For upscale bars and clubs, try **Calle de la Sillería** and **Calle los Alfileritos,** west of Pl. de Zocodóver. To escape the raucous noise, check out the chill **Café Teatro Pícaro,** C. Cadenas, 6, where lights play on abstract art, and *batidos* (milkshakes €3, with Baileys €4) and mixed drinks abound. (☎925 22 13 01; www.picarocafeteatro.com. Mixed drinks €5. Beer €1.50-2.50. Open M-F 4pm-3am, Sa-Su 4pm-5am.)

CASTILLA Y LEÓN

Well before Fernando of Aragón and Isabel of Castilla were joined in world-shaking matrimony, Castilla was the political and military powerhouse of Spain. Castellano became the dominant language of the nation in the High Middle Ages. The aqueduct of Segovia, the Gothic cathedrals of León, and the sandstone of Salamanca continue to stand out as national images. Castilla's comrade in arms, León, though chagrined to be lumped with Castilla in a 1970s provincial reorganization, is very culturally similar to its co-province.

SEGOVIA   ☎921

Legend has it that the devil built Segovia's (pop. 56,000) famed aqueduct in an effort to win the soul of a Segovian water-seller named Juanilla. With or without Lucifer's help, Segovia's attractions draw their share of eager tourists.

🔲🔲 **TRANSPORTATION AND PRACTICAL INFORMATION. Trains** (RENFE; ☎902 24 02 02) run from Po. Obispo Quesada, rather far from town, to Madrid (2hr., 7-9 per day, €5.90). La Sepulvedana buses (☎921 42 77 07) run from Estación Municipal de Autobuses, Po. Ezequiel González 12, to Madrid (1hr., 2 per hr., €6.43) and Valladolid (2hr., 12 per day, €6.85). From the train station, bus #8 stops near the **Plaza Mayor,** the city's historic center and site of the regional **tourist office.** Maps are crucial in Segovia, so pick one up. (☎921 46 03 34. Open July-Sept. 15 M-Th and Su 9am-8pm, F-Sa 9am-9pm; Sept. 16-June 9am-2pm and

5-8pm.) Access the **Internet** for free at the **public library,** C. Juan Bravo 11. (☎921 46 35 33. Passport required. Limit 30min. Open Sept.-June M-F 9am-9pm, Sa 9am-2pm; July-Aug. M-F 9am-3pm, Sa 9am-2pm.) **Postal Code:** 40001.

▐▜▐▜ ACCOMMODATIONS AND FOOD. Reservations are a must for any of Segovia's hotels, especially those near major plazas. Arrive early to ensure space and expect to pay €21 or more for a single. *Pensiones* are significantly cheaper, with basic rooms and shared bathrooms. **Natura La Hosteria ❹,** C. Colón 5 and 7, is located just outside the Plaza Mayor with big and beautiful—though pricey—rooms, each decorated differently. (☎921 46 67 10; www.naturade-segovia.com. Free Wi-Fi. Prices vary, so call ahead. Generally, singles €35-40; doubles as low as €50-60, high as €70-80. MC/V.) **Hotel San Miguel ❸,** C. Infanta Isabel, 4 is a contrast to Segovia's stone and more "antique" lodgings. This hotel is full of bright, modern amenities. Huge full bath is sparkling, and big beds have downy, quilt-like patched comforters. The balcony has good views over the street. (☎921 46 36 57; www.sanmiguel-hotel.com. Rooms come with TV, A/C, and phone. Singles €35; doubles €60. MC/V.)

Sample Segovia's famed lamb, *cochinillo asado* (roast suckling pig), or *sopa castellana* (soup with bread, eggs, and garlic), but steer clear of expensive Pl. Mayor and Pl. del Azoguejo. For eclectic and scrumptious dishes (€4-11), try **▨Restaurante La Almuzara ❷,** C. Marqués del Arco 3, past the cathedral. (☎921 46 06 22. Salads €4-11. Soups €6.50-9. Lunch *menú* €10. Open Tu 8-11:30pm, W-Su 12:45-4pm and 8-11:30pm. MC/V.) At the casual but classy **Bar-Mesón Cueva de San Estéban ❸,** C. Vadeláguila 15, off Pl. Esteban and C. Escuderos, the owner knows his wines and the food is excellent. (☎921 46 09 82. Lunch *menú* M-F €9, Sa-Su €10. Meat dishes €12-20. Open daily 11am-midnight. MC/V.) Buy groceries at **Día,** C. Gobernador Fernández Jiménez, 3, off Av. de Fernández Ladreda. (Open M-Th 9:30am-2pm and 5:30-8:30pm, F-Sa 9am-9pm.)

◙ ▣ SIGHTS AND ENTERTAINMENT. The serpentine ▨**Roman aqueduct,** built in 50 BC and spanning 813m, commands the entrance to the Old Town. Some 20,000 blocks of granite were used in the construction—without a drop of mortar. This spectacular feat of engineering, restored by the monarchy in the 15th century, can transport 30L of water per second and was used until the late 1940s. With its spiraling towers and smooth, pointed turrets, Segovia's ▨**Alcázar,** a late-medieval castle and site of Isabel's coronation in 1474, would be at home in a fairy tale—it was reportedly a model for the castle in Disney's Cinderella. The mystifying message in the throne room, *tanto monta,* signifies that Fernando and Isabel had equal authority as sovereigns. The **Torre de Juan II** (80m), 152 steps up a nausea-inducing spiral staircase, provides a view of Segovia and the surrounding plains. (Pl. de la Reina Victoria Eugenia. ☎921 46 07 59. Alcázar open daily Apr.-Sept. 10am-7pm; Oct.-Mar. 10am-6pm. Tower closed Tu. Palace €4, seniors and students €2.50. Tower €2. English-language audio tour €3.) The 23 chapels of the **cathedral,** towering over Pl. Mayor, earned it the nickname "The Lady of all Cathedrals." The interior may look less impressive than the facade, but its vastness will make you feel truly small. (☎921 46 22 05. Open daily Apr.-Oct. 9am-6:30pm; Nov.-Mar. 9:30am-5:30pm. Mass M-Sa 10am, Su 11am and 12:30pm. €3, under 14 free.)

Though the city isn't particularly known for its sleepless nights, *segovianos* know how to party. Packed with bars and cafes, the **Plaza Mayor** is the center of it all. Head for **Calle Infanta Isabel,** appropriately nicknamed *calle de los bares* (street of the bars). Find drinks and plastic tchotchkes in the fun techno club **Toys,** C. Infanta Isabel 13. (☎609 65 41 42. Beer €1. Mixed drinks

€4.50-5.50. Open daily 10pm-4am.) Continuing in the doll vein is **Geographic Chic**, C. Infanta Isabel, 13. Small dressed mannequins line the windows and cherubs sit smilingly on the bar and light fixtures. A mixed crowd sips mixed drinks and dances for fun as the lights sweep the bar. (☎921 46 30 38. Beer €3. Cocktails €5. Open W-Sa 10:30pm-4am.) From June 23 to 29, Segovia holds a **fiesta** in honor of San Juan and San Pedro, with free open-air concerts on Pl. del Azoguejo and dances and fireworks on June 29.

SALAMANCA ☎923

Salamanca "la blanca" (pop. 163,000), city of royals, saints, and scholars, glows with the yellow stones of Spanish Plateresque architecture by day and a vivacious club scene by night. The prestigious Universidad de Salamanca, grouped in medieval times with Bologna, Oxford, and Paris as one of the "four leading lights of the world," continues to add youthful energy to the city.

▐▜ TRANSPORTATION AND PRACTICAL INFORMATION. Trains go from Po. de la Estación (☎923 24 02 02) to Madrid (2hr., 6-7 per day, €15) and Lisbon, POR (6hr., 1 per day, €47). **Buses** leave from the station (☎923 23 67 17) on Av. Filiberto Villalobos 71-85 for: Barcelona (11hr., 2 per day, €47); León (2hr., 4-7 per day, €13); Madrid (2hr., 16 per day, €12-17); Segovia (2hr., 2 per day, €10). Majestic **Plaza Mayor** is the center of Salamanca. From the train station, catch bus #1 (€0.80) to Gran Vía and ask to be let off at Pl. San Julián, a block from Pl. Mayor. The **tourist office** is at Pl. Mayor 32. (☎923 21 83 42. Open June-Sept. M-F 9am-2pm and 4:30-8pm, Sa 10am-8pm, Su 10am-2pm; Oct.-May M-F 9am-2pm and 4:30-6:30pm, Sa 10am-6:30pm, Su 10am-2pm.) *DGratis*, a free weekly newspaper about events in Salamanca, is available from newsstands, tourist offices, and around Pl. Mayor. Free **Internet** is available at the **public library**, C. Compañía 2, in Casa de las Conchas. (☎923 26 93 17. Limit 30min. Open July to mid-Sept. M-F 9am-3pm, Sa 9am-2pm; mid-Sept. to June M-F 9am-9pm, Sa 9am-2pm.) **Postal Code:** 37001.

▐▐ ACCOMMODATIONS AND FOOD. Reasonably priced *hostales* and *pensiones* cater to the floods of student visitors, especially off Pl. Mayor and C. Meléndez. **Hostal Las Vegas Centro ❷**, C. Meléndez 13, 1st fl., has friendly owners and spotless rooms with terrace and TV. (☎923 21 87 49; www.lasvegascentro. com. Singles €20, with bath €24; doubles €30. MC/V.) At nearby **Pensión Barez ❶**, C. Meléndez 19, 1st fl., clean rooms overlook the street. (☎923 21 74 95. Rooms €14. Cash only.) Many cafes and restaurants are in Pl. Mayor. Pork is the city's speciality, with dishes ranging from *chorizo* (spicy sausage) to *cochinillo* (suckling pig). Funky **Restaurante Delicatessen Café ❷**, C. Meléndez 25, serves a wide variety of *platos combinados* (€10.50-11) and a lunch *menú* (€11) in a colorful solarium. (☎923 28 03 09. Open daily 1:30-4pm and 9pm-midnight. MC/V.) *Salamantinos* crowd **El Patio Chico ❷**, C. Meléndez 13, but the hefty portions are worth the wait. (☎923 26 51 03. Entrees €5.50-17. *Menú* €14. Open daily 1-4pm and 8pm-midnight. MC/V.) At **El Ave Café ❷**, C. Libreros 24, enjoy your lunch (*menú* €11) on the terrace or take a peek at the colorful murals inside. (☎923 26 45 11. Open daily 8am-midnight. MC/V.) **Carrefour**, C. Toro 82, is a central supermarket. (☎923 21 22 08. Open M-Sa 9:30am-9:30pm.)

▐▐ SIGHTS AND NIGHTLIFE. From Pl. Mayor, follow R. Mayor, veer right onto T. Antigua, and left onto C. Libreros to reach █**La Universidad de Salamanca** (est. 1218), the city's focal point. Hidden in the delicate Plateresque filigree of the entryway is a tiny frog perched on a skull. According to legend, those who can spot him without assistance will be blessed with good luck. The old lecture halls inside are open to the public, but to get into the library you'll need to befriend a professor. The 15th-century classroom **Aula Fray Luis de León** has been left in its original state more or less. Located on the second floor atop a Plateresque staircase is the **Biblioteca Antigua,** one of Europe's oldest libraries. The staircase is thought to represent the ascent of the scholar through careless youth, love, and adventure on the perilous path to true knowledge. Don't miss the 800-year-old scrawlings on the walls of the **Capilla del Estudiante** and the benches of the **Sala Fray Luis de Leon.** Across the street and through the hall on the left corner of the patio is the **University Museum.** The reconstructed **Cielo de Salamanca,** the library's famous 15th-century ceiling fresco of the zodiac, is preserved here. (University ☎923 29 45 00, ext. 1225, museum ext 1150. Museum open Mon-Sa 10am-2pm and 4pm-8pm, Su 10am-2pm. University open M-F 9:30am-1:30pm and 4-7:30pm, Sa 9:30am-1:30pm and 4-7pm, Su 10am-1-:30pm. €4, students and seniors €2). It's not surprising it took 220 years to build the stunning **Catedral Nueva,** in Pl. de Anaya. Be sure to climb the tower to get a spectacular ◪**view** from above. (Open daily Apr.-Sept. 9am-8pm; Oct.-Mar. 9am-1pm and 4-6pm. Tower open daily 10am-8pm, last entry 7:45pm. Cathedral free. Tower €3; see www.ieronimus.com) According to *salamantinos,* Salamanca is the best place in Spain to party. Nightlife centers on **Plaza Mayor,** where troubadours serenade women, then spreads out to **Gran Vía, Calle Bordadores,** and side streets. **Calle Prior** and **Rúa Mayor** are also full of bars, while intense partying occurs off **Calle Varillas.** After a few shots (€1-2) at ◪**Bar La Chupitería,** Pl. de Monterrey, wander from club to club on C. Prior and C. Compañía.

SOUTHERN SPAIN

Southern Spain (Andalucía) is all that you expect of Spanish culture—flamenco, bullfighting, tall pitchers of sangria, and streets lined with orange trees. The Moors arrived in AD 711 and bequeathed to the region far more than flamenco music and gypsy ballads. The cities of Seville and Granada reached the pinnacle of Islamic arts, while Córdoba matured into the most culturally influential city in medieval Islam. Andalucía's *festivales, ferias,* and *carnavales* are world-famous for their extravagance.

SEVILLE (SEVILLA)   ☎954

Site of a Roman acropolis, capital of the Moorish empire, focal point of the Spanish Renaissance, and guardian of traditional Andalusian culture, romantic Seville (pop. 700,000) represents a fusion of cultures. Bullfighting, flamenco, and tapas are at their best here, and Seville's cathedral is among the most impressive in Spain. The city offers more than historical sights: its **Semana Santa** and **Feria de Abril** celebrations are among the most elaborate in Europe.

✈ INTERCITY TRANSPORTATION

Flights: All flights arrive at **Aeropuerto San Pablo,** Ctra. de Madrid (☎954 449 000; www.aena.es), 12km outside town. A taxi from the center costs about €25. **Los Amarillos** (☎954 989 184) runs a bus from outside the Prado de San Sebastián bus stop across from the university. (M-Sa every 15-30min. 5:15-12:15am; Su every 30min-1hr. 6:15am-11:15pm; €2.10. Also stops at the train station). **Iberia,** C. Guadaira, 8 (☎954

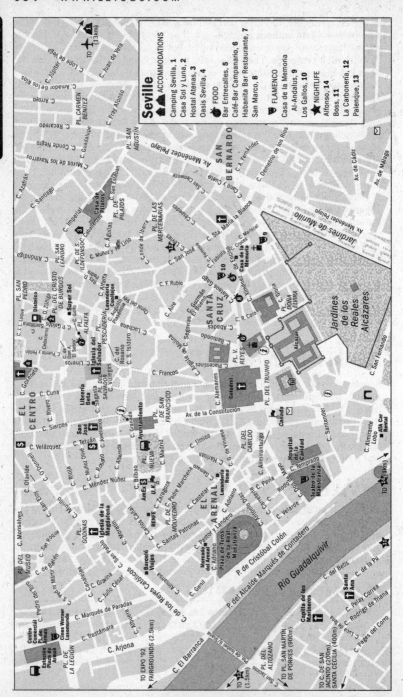

Seville

ACCOMMODATIONS
Camping Sevilla, **1**
Casa Sol y Luna, **2**
Hostal Atenas, **3**
Oasis Sevilla, **4**

FOOD
Bar Entrecalles, **5**
Café-Bar Campanario, **6**
Habanita Bar Restaurante, **7**
San Marco, **8**

FLAMENCO
Casa de la Memoria
Al-Andalus, **9**
Los Gallos, **10**

★ **NIGHTLIFE**
Alfonso, **14**
Boss, **11**
La Carbonería, **12**
Palenque, **13**

228 901, nationwide 902 400 500; open M-F 9am-1:30pm) runs daily flights to Barcelona (55min.) and Madrid (45min.).

Trains: Estación Santa Justa, Av. de Kansas City. (☎902 240 202. Info and reservations open daily 4:30am-12:30am.) Services include **luggage storage, car rental,** and **ATM.** In town, the RENFE office, C. Zaragoza, 29, posts prices and schedules on the windows and also handles bookings. (☎954 54 02 02. Open in summer 9:30am-2pm and 5:30-8pm, in winter M-F 9am-1:15pm and 4-7pm.) To get to Santa Cruz from the station, take bus C-2 and transfer to C-3 at the Jardines del Valle; it will drop you off on C. Menéndez Pelayo at the **Jardines de Murillo.** Turn right and walk 1 block past the gardens; C. Santa María la Blanca is on the left. Without the bus, it's a 15-20min. walk. To reach El Centro from the station, catch bus #32 to **Plaza de la Encarnación,** several blocks north of the cathedral.

Altaria and **Taigo** trains to: **Barcelona** (12½hr., 8:20am, €60); **Córdoba** (1hr., 8 per day 6:50am-9:35pm, €15); **Málaga** (2hr., 4-6 per day 6:05am-7:35pm, €35) and **Valencia** (9hr., 8:20am, €50). **AVE** trains to **Barcelona** (5½hr., 4pm, €134), **Córdoba** (45min., 12-18 per day 6:15am-9:45pm, €26-30), **Madrid** (2½hr., 12-18 per day 6:15am-9:45pm, €70-78), and **Zaragoza** (3½hr, 4pm, €104) **Regionales** trains to: **Almería** (5½hr., 4 per day 7am-5:40pm, €36); **Antequera** (2½hr., 6 per day 6:50am-7:35pm, €28); **Cádiz** (2hr., 11 per day 6:35am-9:35pm, €10); **Córdoba** (1½hr., 6 per day 7:50am-8:15pm, €8.60); **Granada** (3hr., 4 per day 7am-5:40pm, €23); **Huelva** (1hr.; 9:10am, 4:30, 8:40pm; €7.85); **Jaén** (2-3hr.; 1:25, 3, 7:52pm; €18-23); **Málaga** (2½hr., 5-6 per day 7:35am-8:10pm, €18).

Buses: Estación Prado de San Sebastián, C. Manuel Vázquez Sagastizábal (☎954 41 71 11), serves most of Andalucía and sits adjacent to its namesake. It's a five-minute walk (right on C. Diego Riaño, right on Av. Carlos V) to the Puerta de Jerez in Santa Cruz. (Open daily 5:30am-1am.) **Estación Plaza de Armas,** Av. Cristo de la Expiración (☎954 90 80 40), sends buses outside of Andalucía, including to many international destinations. (Open daily 5am-1:30am.) Bus C-4 connects the station to Prado de San Sebastián.

Estación Prado De San Sebastián: Alsina Graells (☎913 270 540; www.alsa.es). Open daily 6:30am-11pm. To: **Almería** (7hr.; 7, 8am, 5pm; €32); **Córdoba** (2-3hr., 10 per day 7:30am-10pm, €10); **Granada** (3hr., 10 per day 8am-11pm, €19-25); **Jaén** (4hr., 1:30pm, €19); **Málaga** (2-3hr., 9 per day 7am-7:30pm, €16); **Murcia** (7½hr;, 3 per day 8, 11am, 11pm; €38). **Los Amarillos** (☎902 210 317; www.touristbus.es). Open M-F 7:30am-2pm and 2:309pm, Sa-Su 7:30am-2pm and 2:30-8:30pm. To: **Arcos de la Frontera** (2½hr.; 8am, 2:30pm; €7); **Marbella** (3hr.; 8am, 4pm; €16); **Ronda** (2½hr., 8am, noon, 5pm; €11); **Sanlúcar de Barrameda** (2hr., 5-9 per day 8am-8pm, €7). **Transportes Comes** (☎902 199 208; www.tgcomes.es). Open daily 6:30am-10pm. To: **Algeciras** (3½hr., 4 per day 9:30am-7:30pm, €18); **Cádiz** (1hr., 9 per day 7am-10pm, €11.40); **Jerez de la Frontera** (1½hr., 7 per day 10:45am-10pm, €7.50); **Tarifa** (3hr., 4 per day 9:30am-7:30pm, €17).

Estación Plaza De Armas: ALSA (☎913 270 540; www.alsa.es). Open M-F 5:45am-10:30pm, Sa-Su 7:30am-10:45pm. To: **Cáceres** (4-4½hr., 7 per day 7am-8:30pm, €33); **León** (11hr.; 7, 11:30am, 8:30pm; €43); **Lisbon, POR** (6hr.; 3pm, midnight; €45); **Salamanca** (7hr., 6 per day 7am-8:30pm, €31); **Valencia** (9-11hr., 3 per day 9:30am, 4, 10pm, €50-57). **Damas** (☎954 908 040; www.damas-sa.es). Open daily 6am-10pm. To: **Badajoz** (3hr., 5 per day 6:45am-8pm, €13.25); **Faro, POR** (4hr.; 4 per day 7:30am, 4:15pm; €16); **Lagos, POR** (7hr.; 7:30am, 6:15pm; €20); **Huelva** (1hr., 16-20 per day 7:30am-9:30pm, €7). **Socibus** (☎902 229 292; www.socibus.es). Open daily 7:30-10:30am and 11-12:45am. To **Madrid** (6hr., 7 per day 8am-midnight, €19.40).

Public Transportation: TUSSAM (☎900 71 01 71; www.tussam.es). Most bus lines run daily every 10min. 6am-11:15pm and converge in Pl. Nueva, Pl. de la Encarnación, and at the cathedral. Night service departs from Pl. Nueva (every hr. M-Th and Su midnight-2am; F-Sa all night). C-3 and C-4 circle the center and #34 hits the HI-affiliated hostel, university, cathedral, and Pl. Nueva. €1.20. *Bonobús* (10 rides) €6. 30-day pass €30.

Taxis: TeleTaxi (☎954 622 222). **Radio Taxi** (☎954 580 000). Base rate €1.19 plus €0.83 per km; M-F after 9pm and all day Sa-Su €1.45 base plus €1.01 per km. Extra charge for luggage.

⚔ ⁊ ORIENTATION AND PRACTICAL INFORMATION

The **Río Guadalquivir** flows north to south through the city, bordered by Po. de Cristóbal, which becomes Po. de las Delicias by the municipal tourist office. Most of Sevilla's touristy areas, including **Santa Cruz** and **El Arenal,** are on the east bank. The historic *barrios* (neighborhoods) of **Triana, Santa Cecilia,** and **Los Remedios** lie on the western bank. **Avenida de la Constitución,** home of the *Andaluz* tourist office, runs along the cathedral. **El Centro,** a busy commercial pedestrian zone, starts at the intersection of Av. de la Constitución, **Plaza Nueva,** and **Plaza de San Francisco,** site of the *Ayuntamiento* (city hall). **Calle Tetuán** and **Calle Sierpes,** both popular shopping areas, run north from Pl. Nueva through El Centro.

Tourist Offices: Centro de Información de Sevilla Laredo, Pl. de San Francisco, 19 (☎954 592 915; www.turismo.sevilla.org). Main municipal office. English spoken. Open M-F 9am-7:30pm, Sa-Su 10am-2pm. **Naves del Barranco,** C. Aronja, 28 (☎954 221 714), near the bridge to Triana. Secondary municipal office. Open M-F 9am-7:30pm. **Turismo de la Provincia,** Pl. del Triunfo, 1-3 (☎954 210 005; www.turismodesevilla. org). Info on daytrips and specific themed itineraries. Open daily 10:30am-2:30pm and 3:30-7:30pm.**Turismo Andaluz,** Av. de la Constitución, 21B (☎954 221 404; www. andalucia.org). English spoken. Info on all of Andalucía. Free maps of the region. Open M-F 9am-7:30pm, Sa-Su 9:30am-3pm.

Budget Travel: Barceló Viajes, C. de los Reyes Católicos, 11 (☎954 226 131; www.barceloviajes.com). Open June-Sept. M-F 9:30am-1:30pm and 5-8:30pm, Sa 10am-1pm; Oct.-May M-F 9:30am-1:30pm and 4:30-7:30pm, Sa 10am-1pm.

Currency Exchange: Banco Santander Central Hispano, C. Tetuán, 10, and C. Martín Villa, 4 (☎902 24 24 24). Open M-F 8:30am-2pm, Sa 8:30am-1pm;. Apr.-Sept. closed Sa. Banks and *casas de cambio* (currency exchange) crowd Av. de la Constitución, El Centro, and the sights in Santa Cruz.

Luggage Storage: Estación Prado de San Sebastián. (€0.90 per day; open 6:30am-10pm); **Estación Plaza de Armas** (€3.50 per day); **train station** (€3.50 per day).

Laundromat: Lavandería Roma, C. Castelar, 2C (☎954 210 535). Wash, dry, and fold €6 per load. Open M-F 9:30am-2pm and 5:30-8:30pm, Sa 9am-2pm.

Police: Av. Paseo de las Delicias and Alameda de Hércules (☎091).

Medical Services: Cruz Roja (☎902 222 292). **Hospital Virgen Macarena,** Av. Dr. Fedriani, 56 (☎955 008 000).

Internet Access: It is substantially cheaper to use pre-paid minutes; most places offer internet *bonos,* which amount to wholesale bulk minutes (most come with a min. of 2hr. or more). Ask about *bonos* at the counter before using the computers. **Sevilla Internet Center,** Av. de la Constitucion at Almirantazgo (☎954 347 108; www.internetsevilla. com). €0.05 per min. Open daily 9am-10pm.

Post Office: Av. de la Constitución, 32 (☎954 21 64 76). **Lista de Correos** and fax. Have your mail addressed to the *Lista de Correos de la Constitución* (otherwise mail may end up at any of the Sevilla post offices). Open M-F 8:30am-8:30pm, Sa 9:30am2pm. **Postal Code:** 41080.

⌂ ACCOMMODATIONS

During *Semana Santa* and the *Feria de Abril,* vacant rooms vanish and prices double; reserve several months in advance. The tourist office has lists of *casas particulares* (private residences) that open for visitors on special occasions. Outside of these weeks, you should reserve a few days in advance and about a week ahead if you're staying for the weekend.

■ **Pensión Vergara,** C. Ximénez de Enciso, 11, 2nd fl. (☎954 215 668; www.pensionvergara.com). Above a souvenir shop at C. Mesón del Moro. Quirky, antique decor, colorful common spaces, and perfect location. Singles, doubles, triples, and quads, all with shared bath and A/C. No internet. €20 per person. Cash only. ❷

■ **Hostal Atenas,** C. Caballerizas 1 (☎954 21 80 47; www.hostal-atenas.com), off Pl. de Pilatos. Everything about this hostel is appealing, from the *mudéjar*-style arches and traditional patio to the cheery rooms. All have A/C and baths Internet €1 per 30min. Singles M-Th and Su €43, F-Sa €48; doubles €55/70; triples €70/79; quads €79/86. Prices fall €5-10 in winter. MC/V. ❹

■ **Oasis Sevilla,** reception at Pl. Encarnación, 29 1/2 (☎954 29 37 77; www.hostelsoasis.com), rooms above reception and at C. Alonso el Sabio, 1A. Young, international crowd packs this energetic hostel. Co-ed dorms are centrally located above the guests-only **Hiro** lounge. On C. Alonso doubles and 4- to 6-person dorms share bathrooms and fridges and are roomier and quieter. All rooms with A/C. Terrace pool, weekly tapas tours, and free Wi-Fi, internet, and breakfast (served 8-11am). Towels €1. Key deposit €5. Reserve early. Dorms €20; doubles €46. MC/V. ❷

Samay Sevilla Hostel, Menéndez Pelayo, 13 (☎955 100 160; www.samayhostels.com). The lively rooftop terrace at this 2-year-old backpackers' hostel may be the finest in Santa Cruz. Free daily walking tours, internet, and Wi-Fi. Laundry €8. Key deposit €5. 8-bed dorms €15-19, 6-bed €16-20, 4-bed €17-22. MC/V. ❷

Pensión Macarena, C. San Luis, 91 (☎954 37 01 41; www.hostalmacarena.es). Large yellow and green rooms with A/C surround a sunny inner atrium. Quiet, relaxed atmosphere and friendly staff. Singles €20; doubles €30, with bath and TV €40; triples €45/51. MC/V. ❷

▐ FOOD

Seville, which claims to be the birthplace of *tapas*, keeps its cuisine light. *Tapas* bars cluster around **Plaza San Martín** and along **Calle San Jacinto.** Popular venues for *el tapeo* (tapas barhopping) include **Barrio de Santa Cruz** and **El Arenal.** Find produce at **Mercado de la Encarnación,** near the bullring in Pl. de la Encarnación. (Open M-Sa 9am-2pm.) There is a supermarket below **El Corte Inglés,** in Pl. del Duque de la Victoria. (☎954 27 93 97. Open M-Sa 9am-10pm. AmEx/MC/V.)

■ **San Marco,** C. Mesón del Moro, 6 (☎954 564 390). Branches at C. del Betis, 68 (☎954 28 03 10) and C. Santo Domingo de la Calzada, 5 (☎954 583 343). Entrees and Italian desserts in vaulted basement rooms that once housed Arab baths. A full menu of creative salads (€4.30-9.25), pizza (€7.50-8.90), and meat and fish entrees (€9.60-16.50). Open daily 1-4:15pm and 8pm-12:15am. MC/V. ❸

■ **El Rinconcillo,** C. Gerona, 40 (☎954 223 183). Founded in 1670 in an abandoned convent, this *bodega* is the epitome of a local hangout, teeming with gray-haired men deep in conversation and locals stopping in for a quick glass of wine or a delicious tapas spread. The bartender tallies up your tab in chalk on the wooden counter. Tapas €1.80-3.20. *Raciones* €6-14.50. Open daily 1:30pm-1:30am. AmEx/MC/V. ❶

■ **Confitería La Campana,** C. Sierpes 1 and 3 (☎954 223 570). Founded in 1885, Sevilla's most famous cafe has twice made an appearance in Spanish short stories, and it continues to serve up *granizadas de limón* (lemon-flavored crushed ice), ice cream (€2-2.50), and an astounding variety of homemade pastries (€1.50-3.40). Open daily 8am-11pm. AmEx/MC/V. ❶

Bar Entrecalles, Ximenez de Enciso, 14 (☎617 86 77 52). Situated at the center of the tourist buzz, but the reggae music and relaxed atmosphere help maintain a local following. Tapas (only available inside, €2) and delicious gazpacho (meal-sized potion €6) are unusually generous. Open daily 1pm-2am. Kitchen closed 3:30-8pm. Cash only. ❶

THE LOCAL STORY

SEVILLE'S TRAGIC TALE

Among its many legacies, the *Judería* left Seville one of its most tragic legends: that of Susona, La Hermosa Hembra (vulgar for "beautiful woman").

During the 15th century, even as relations between Seville's Christian and Jewish populations were increasingly tense, Susona, the daughter of a Jewish merchant, fell in love with a Christian knight. Every night, she would sneak out the window, meet her lover by the army barracks, and make it back home before dawn unnoticed. One night, however, she overheard her father plotting a rebellion against the Christian government and, fearing that she would lose her lover forever, Susona warned him of the plot. The Christian army's retaliation was swift and merciless—Susona's entire family was slaughtered, and their bodies were left to scavengers. Susona's street thereafter bore the name C. Muerte.

Deeply remorseful, Susona confessed in Seville's Cathedral, received baptism, and retreated into a convent. When she died, she asked that her head be placed above her doorway as a symbol of redemption for all and, strangely, nobody touched it for over one-hundred years. While Susona's skull no longer can be seen on what is now C. Susona, a plaque still bears testimony to her tragic story.

Levíes Café-Bar, C. San José, 15 (☎954 215 308). The bar at this tapas restaurant predominates, pouring out deliciously liberal and refreshing glasses of *tinto de varano* (€1.45) and gazpacho (€3.30). Tapas €2.60-3.90. Entrees €6-12. Open M-F 7:30am2am, Sa-Su 11am-2am. ●

🔍 SIGHTS

While any visit to Seville should include the Catedral and Alcázar, there is much more to the city than Santa Cruz. Around these central icons are winding streets full of tapas joints, *artesanía*, and quirky finds. The **Plaza de Toros** is nestled on the riverbank to the east and serves as an ideal place to begin a scenic tour along the Guadalquivir. North of Santa Cruz, the bustling Centro, home to some of the city's finest museums, contrasts with the peaceful churches of La Macarena. Heading south toward the **Torre del Oro,** garden oases offer a breezy respite from the summer heat. There, the private gardens behind the Alcázar are flanked by the public **Jardines de Murillo,** near to the monumental **Plaza de España** and beautiful **Parque de María Luisa.**

🏛CATEDRAL

Entrance by Pl. de la Virgen de los Reyes. ☎954 21 49 71; www.catedralsevilla.com. Open M-Sa 11am-5pm, Su 2:30-6pm. Last entry 1hr. before closing. €7.50, seniors and students under 26 €2, under 16 free. Audio tour €3. Mass held in the Capilla Real M-Sa 8:30, 10:30am, noon; Su 8:30, 10:30, 11am, noon, and 1pm. Free.

Legend has it that the *reconquistadores* wanted to demonstrate their religious fervor by constructing a church so great that "those who come after us will take us for madmen." Sevilla's immense cathedral does appear to be the work of an extravagant madman—with 44 individual chapels, it is the third largest in the world, after St. Peter's Basilica in Rome and St. Paul's Cathedral in London, and it is the biggest Gothic edifice ever constructed.

In 1402, a 12th-century Almohad mosque was destroyed to clear space for the cathedral. All that remains is the **Patio de Los Naranjos,** where the faithful washed before prayer, the **Puerta del Perdón** entryway from C. Alemanes, and **La Giralda** minaret, built in 1198. The tower and its twins in Marrakesh and Rabat are the oldest and longest-surviving Almohad minarets in the world. The 35 ramps leading to the tower's top were installed to replace the stairs that once stood there, allowing a disabled *muezzín* to ride his horse up to issue the call to prayer. Climbing the ramps will leave you breathless, as will the views from the top—the entire city of Sevilla lies just on the other side of the iron bells. (Be warned that these bells sound every 15min., and they are very loud.)

The 42m central **nave,** decorated with 3 tons of gold leaf, is considered one of the greatest in the Christian world—take a good look at its four tiers via a well-placed mirror on the nave's floor. In the center of the cathedral, the Renaissance-style **Capilla Real** stands opposite choir stalls made of mahogany recycled from a 19th-century Austrian railway. The **retablo mayor,** one of the largest in the world, is an intricately wrought portrayal of saints and disciples. Nearby, the bronze **Sepulcro de Cristóbal Colón** (Columbus's tomb) is supported by four heralds that represent the ancient kingdoms of Spain united by Fernando and Isabel. The coffin holds Columbus' remains, brought back to Sevilla from Cuba in 1898. Farther on stands the **Sacristía Mayor,** which holds works by Ribera, Zurbarán, Goya, and Murillo, and a glittering Corpus Cristi icon.

■ALCÁZAR

Pl. del Triunfo, 7. ☎954 50 23 23. Open daily Apr.-Sept. 9:30am-7pm; Oct.-Mar. 9:30am5pm. Tours of private residence every 30min. Aug.-May 10am-1:30pm and 3:30-5:30pm; June-July 10am-1:30pm. Max. 15 people per tour, so buy tickets in advance. €7.50, students, over 65, and under 16 free. Tours €4.20. English audio tours €3.

The oldest European palace still used as a private residence for royals, Sevilla's Alcázar exudes extravagance. The palace, built by the Moors in the seventh century and embellished in the 17th century, is a mix of Moorish, Gothic, Renaissance, and Baroque architectural elements, but its intricacies are most prominently displayed in the *mudéjar* style of many of its many arches, tiles, and geometric ceiling designs. Fernando and Isabel, the Catholic monarchs of *reconquista* fame, are the palace's best known former residents; Carlos V lived here after marrying his cousin Isabel of Portugal in the **Salón Techo Carlos V.**

The Alcázar is a network of splendid patios and courtyards, around which court life revolved. From the moment you step through the **Patio de la Montería,** the melange of cultures is apparent; an Arabic inscription praising Allah is carved in Gothic script. Through the archway is the **Patio del Yeso,** an exquisite geometric space first used by Moorish governors. The center of public life at the Alcázar, however, was the **Patio de las Doncellas** (Patio of the Maids), a colonnaded quadrangle encircled by tiled archways. The **Patio de las Muñecas** (Patio of the Dolls), served as a private area for Moorish kings; the room had an escape path so that the king would not have to cross a wide-open space during an attack. The columns are thought to have come from the devastated **Madinat Al-Zahra,** built at the height of the caliph period. Look for the little faces at the bottom of one column for a hint at how the patio got its name.

The palace's interior is a sumptuous labyrinth where even the walls are works of art. In the **Sala de los Azulejos del Alcázar,** history's stain is literally visible—the room was the stage of a bloody duel between 14th-century King Pedro I and his half-brother Fadrique, and even today the traces of unlucky Fadrique's blood can be seen on the floor. On a more peaceful note, the golden-domed **Salón de los Embajadores** (Ambassadors' Room) is rumored to be the site where Fernando and Isabel welcomed Columbus back from the New World. Their son, Juan, was born in the red-and-blue tiled **Cuarto del Príncipe.** The private residences upstairs, the official home of the King and Queen on their visits to Sevilla, have been renovated and redecorated throughout the years, and most of the furniture today dates from the 18th and 19th centuries. These rooms are accessible only by 25min. guided tours.

■MUSEO PROVINCIAL DE BELLAS ARTES. This museum contains Spain's finest collection of works by painters of the Sevillana School, most notably Murillo, Valdés Leal, and Zurbarán, as well as El Greco and Dutch master Peter Brue-

ghel. Much of the art was cobbled together from convents in the mid-1800s, finding a stately home amid the traditional tiles and courtyards of this impressive building. Not to be missed are **Gallery V** (formerly a church, it's a splendid setting for Baroque art) and José Villegas Cordro's somber 1913 canvas *La muerte del maestro* upstairs. *(Pl. del Museo, 9. ☎ 954 786 500; www.museosdeandalucia. es. Open Tu-Sa 9am-8:30pm, Su 9am-2:30pm. €1.50, students and EU citizens free.)*

◗ NIGHTLIFE

Seville's reputation for hoopla is tried and true—most clubs don't get going until well after midnight, and the real fun often starts only after 3am. Popular bars can be found around **Calle Mateos Gago** near the cathedral, **Calle Adriano**, and **Calle del Betis** in Triana. Gay clubs cluster around **Plaza de Armas.**

▨ **La Carbonería,** C. Levies, 18 (☎954 22 99 45). A gigantic cellar bar frequented by students and young summer travelers. Agua de Sevilla pitchers €20 (M-W and Su €15). Sangria pitchers €8.50. Free live flamenco shows nightly at 11pm. Open daily 8pm-3 or 4am. Cash only.

▨ **Antique** (www.antiquetheatro.com), to the left of the Pte. de la Barqueta facing away from La Macarena. A monumental outdoor playground for Sevilla's rich and beautiful. Egyptian-stye columns preside over a lush outdoor dance space complete with VIP cabanas and a waterfall. Dress well and come before 2am to avoid a long line. Mixed drinks €8. No cover. Open in summer Tu-Su midnight-7am. MC/V.

▨ **Puerto de Cuba,** C. del Betis (www.riogrande-sevilla.com), immediately to the right of the Pte. de San Telmo as you cross into Triana. Right on the bank of the river, it's hard to believe this palmy oasis has no cover charge. Recline in a wicker couch or curl up in a pillow-strewn beached dingy. Th-Sa dance parties. Dressy casual will get you past the bouncers and to the bar (beer €3.50; mixed drinks from €6.50). Open only in summer daily 10:30pm-4am.

Terraza Chile, Po. de las Delicias at Av. de Chile. A 5min. walk from the Puente de San Telmo along the riverside Po. de las Delicias, away from the Torre del Oro. This popular, unpretentious bar-cafe transforms into a packed dance club Th-Sa, when loud salsa and pop bring together young *sevillanos*, foreign students, and tourists. Beer from €2; mixed drinks from €5. Open June-Sept. M-W 9am-3am, Th-Sa 9am-5am; Oct.-May M-Th 9am-1am, F-Sa 9am-4am. MC/V.

Ritual (www.todounritoalacopa.com), to the right of the Pte. de la Barqueta facing away from La Macarena. Dancers in shimmering outfits and silky tents hung with North African lamps lend this upscale outdoor lounge and dance club a desert-oasis feel. Well-dressed 20-somethings dance to American hip hop, Latin favorites, and lots of reggaeton. Wine and mixed drinks from €6. Typically 21+. No cover. Open in summer daily 10pm-late. AmEx/MC/V.

Noveccento, C. Julio Cesar, 10 (☎954 229 102; www.noveccento.com). A predominantly lesbian crowd sips mojitos (€6) and chills in this cozy, relaxed bar. Open in summer M-Th and Su 8pm-3am, F-Sa 8pm-4am; in winter M-Th and Su 5pm-3am, F-Sa 5pm-4am. Cash only.

◪ ENTERTAINMENT

The tourist office distributes *El Giraldillo* and its English counterpart, *The Tourist,* two free monthly magazines with listings on music, art exhibits, theater, dance, fairs, and film. It can also be found online at www.elgiraldillo.es.

FLAMENCO

Sevilla would not be Sevilla without flamenco. Born of a *gitano* (gypsy) musical tradition, flamenco consists of dance, guitar, and songs characterized by spontaneity and passion. Rhythmic clapping, intricate fretwork on the guitar, throaty wailing, and rapid foot-tapping accompany the swirling dancers.

Signs advertising *tablao* shows are everywhere, from souvenir shops to internet cafes, and the majority of flamenco *tablaos* in Sevilla cater to the tourist crowd rather than to true flamenco aficionados. Many *tablaos* are *tablao-restaurantes*, so you can eat while watching the show, but dinner tends to be very expensive. Less expensive alternatives are the impressive one-hour shows at the cultural center **Casa de la Memoria Al-Andalus,** C. Ximénez de Enciso, 28, in the middle of Santa Cruz. Ask at the tourist office or swing by their ticket office for a schedule of different themed performances, including traditional Sephardic Jewish concerts. (☎954 560 670; www.casadelamemoria.es. Shows nightly 9pm, in summer also 10:30pm; seating is very limited, so reserve your tickets a day or two ahead and up to four days in advance for weekend shows. €15, students €13, under 10 €9.)

La Carbonería, C. Levies, 18, fills with students and backpackers. **El Tamboril,** Pl. de Santa Cruz, hosts a primarily middle-aged tourist crowd for midnight singing and dancing. (☎954 561 590. Open daily June-Sept. 5pm-3am; Oct.-May noon-3am.) Bar-filled Calle del Betis, across the river, houses several other *tabernas:* **Lo Nuestro, El Rejoneo,** and **Taberna Flamenca Triana.**

BULLFIGHTING

Sevilla's bullring hosts bullfights from *Semana Santa* through October. The cheapest place to buy tickets is at the ring on Po. Alcalde Marqués de Contadero. When there's a good *cartel* (line-up), buy tickets at booths on **Calle Sierpes, Calle Velázquez,** and **Plaza de Toros.** Prices can run from €20 for a *grada de sol* (nosebleed seat in the sun) to €75+ for a *barrera de sombra* (front-row seat in the shade). The two main options are *corridas de toros* (traditional bullfights) or *novilladas* (fights with apprentice bullfighters and younger bulls). During July and August, *corridas* occasionally occur on Thursday at 9pm; check posters around town. (Pl. de Toros ticket office ☎954 50 13 82; www.plazadetorosdelamaestranza.com.)

✿ FESTIVALS

Sevilla swells with tourists during its fiestas, and with good reason: the parties are world-class. If you're in Spain during any major festivals, head straight to Sevilla—you won't regret it. Reserve a room a few months in advance, and expect to pay at least twice what you would normally.

▨ **Semana Santa,** from Palm Sunday to Easter Sunday. In each neighborhood, thousands of penitents in hooded cassocks guide *pasos* (huge, extravagantly-decorated floats) through the streets, illuminated by hundreds of candles; the climax is Good Friday, when the entire city turns out for a procession along the bridges and through the oldest neighborhoods. Book rooms well in advance. The tourist office stocks a helpful booklet on accommodations and food during the festivities.

▨ **Feria De Abril,** the final week in April. The city rewards itself for its Lenten piety with the *Feria de Abril,* held in the southern end of Los Remedios. Begun as part of a 19th-century revolt against foreign influence, the Feria has grown into a massive celebration of all things Andalucian, with circuses, bullfights, and flamenco. A spectacular array of flowers and lanterns decorates over 1000 kiosks, tents, and pavilions, known as *casetas,* which each have a small kitchen, bar, and dance floor. Most *casetas* are private, however, and the only way to get invited is by making friends with locals. The city holds bullfights daily during the festival; buy tickets in advance.

GRANADA

☎958

The splendors of the Alhambra, the magnificent palace that crowns the highest point of Granada (pop. 238,000), have fascinated both prince and pauper for centuries. Legend has it that in 1492, when the Moorish ruler Boabdil fled the city, the last Muslim stronghold in Spain, his mother berated him for casting a longing look back at the Alhambra. "You do well to weep as a woman," she told him, "for what you could not defend as a man." The Albaicín, an enchanting maze of Moorish houses, is Spain's best-preserved Arab quarter. Granada has grown into a university city infused with youthful energy.

▐ TRANSPORTATION

Trains: RENFE, Av. Andaluces (☎902 24 02 02. www.renfe.es). Take bus #3-6, 9, or 11 from Gran Vía to the Constitución (3 stops) and turn left onto Av. Andaluces. To: **Algeciras** (4-5hr., 3 per day 7:15am-5pm, €18.35); **Almería** (2hr., 4 per day 10:03am-9:06pm, €14.45); **Barcelona** (12hr.; 9:45pm; €52.10-57.40); **Madrid** (5-6hr.; 6:42am, 6pm; €61.80); **Sevilla** (4-5hr., 4 per day 8:18am-8:24pm, €21.65).

Buses: All major intercity bus routes start at the bus station (☎958 18 54 80) on the outskirts of Granada on **Ctra. de Madrid,** near C. Arzobispo Pedro de Castro. Take bus #3 or 33 from Gran Vía de Colón or a **taxi** (€6-7). Services reduced on Sundays.

ALSA (☎902 42 22 42 or 958 15 75 57; www.alsa.es) to: **Alicante** (6hr., 6 per day 2:31am-11:30pm, €26.69); **Barcelona** (14hr., 5 per day 2:31am-11:30pm, €65.96); **Valencia** (9hr., 5 per day 2:31am-11:30pm, €40.23); **Algeciras** (3hr., 6 per day 9am-8:15pm, €20.20); **Almería** (2hr., 8 per day 6:45am-7:30pm, €11.50); **Antequera** (1hr., 4 per day 9am-7pm, €7.20); **Cádiz** (5hr., 4 per day 3am-6:30pm, €29.52); **Córdoba** (3hr., 8 per day 7:30am-7pm, €12.04); **Madrid** (5-6hr., 15 per day 7am-1:30am, €15.66); **Málaga** (2hr., 16 per day 7am-9pm, €9.38); **Marbella** (2hr., 8 per day 8am-8:15pm, €14.35); **Sevill3** (3hr., 7 per day 8am-8pm, €18.57).

Public Transportation: Local buses (☎900 71 09 00). Pick up the bus map at the tourist office. Important buses include: "Bus Alhambra" #30 from Gran Vía de Cólon or Pl. Nueva to the Alhambra; #31 from Gran Vía or Pl. Nueva to the Albaicín; #10 from the bus station to the youth hostel, C. de Ronda, C. Recogidas, and C. Acera de Darro; #3 from the bus station to Av. de la Constitución, Gran Vía, and Pl. Isabel la Católica. €1.10, *bonobus* (9 tickets) €5.45.

✛ ⚦ ORIENTATION AND PRACTICAL INFORMATION

The center of Granada is small **Plaza Isabel la Católica,** at the intersection of the city's two main arteries, **Calle de los Reyes Católicos** and **Gran Vía de Colón.** Just off Gran Vía, you'll find the cathedral; farther down Gran Vía by Pl. de la Trinidad is the university area. Uphill from Pl. Isabel la Católica on C. Reyes Católicos sits **Plaza Nueva,** and the **Alhambra** rises on the hill above. From Pl. Nueva, **Calle Elvira,** lined with bars and eateries, runs parallel to Gran Vía. Downhill, the pedestrian streets off C. de los Reyes Católicos comprise the shopping district.

Tourist Offices: Junta de Andalucía, C. Santa Ana, 2 (☎958 57 52 02). Open M-F 9am-7:30pm, Sa 9:30am-3pm, Su 10am-2pm. Posts bus and train schedules and provides a list of accommodations. Use this office for information about all of Andalucía. **Oficina Provincial,** Pl. Mariana Pineda, 10 (☎958 24 71 28). Walk up to the left past plaza Isabel and make a right on Pineda. Walk until the square. English spoken. Great for all questions concerning Granada. Open M-F 9am-8pm, Sa 10am-7pm, Su 10am-3pm.

Currency Exchange: Banco Santander Central Hispano, Gran Vía, 3 (☎902 24 24 24). Open Apr.-Sept. M-F 8:30am-2pm.

Luggage Storage: 24hr. storage at the train and bus stations (€3). Frequently sold out.

English-Language Bookstore: Metro, C. Gracia, 31 (☎958 26 15 65), off Veronica de la Magdalena, off C. Recogidas, which begins where Reyes Católicos hits Puerta Real.. Vast foreign language section. Open M-F 10am-2pm and 56-8:30pm, Sa 11am-2pm.

Gay and Lesbian Resources: Información Homosexual Hotline (☎958 20 06 02).

Laundromat: Ç. de la Paz, 19., off Veronica de la Magdelena. Wash €8, dry €2 per 10min.; detergent included. Open M-F 10am-2pm and 5-8pm.

Police: C. Duquesa, 21 (☎091). English spoken.

Medical Services and Pharmacy: Hospital Universitario de San Cecilio, C. Dr. Olóriz, 16 (☎958 02 30 00). **Farmacia Gran Vía,** Gran Vía, 6 (☎958 22 29 90). Open M-F 9:30am-1:30pm and 5-8:30pm, Sa 9:30am-1:30pm and 5:30-9pm

Internet Access: Locutorio Cyber Alhambra, C. Joaquin Costa, 4 (☎958 22 43 96). €1.20 per hour; €5 *bono* for 6hr., €10 *bono* for 13hr. Open daily 9:30am-10:30pm. Second alley to left on Reyes Católicos walking away from Plaza Isabel.

Post Office: Pta. Real (☎958 22 48 35). *Lista de Correos* and fax service. Open M-F 8:30am-8:30pm, Sa 9:30am-2pm. **Postal Code:** 18009.

ACCOMMODATIONS

Hostels line Cuesta de Gomérez, Plaza Trinidad, and Gran Vía. Be sure to call ahead during Semana Santa (Apr. 3-12, 2009).

Funky Backpacker's, Cuesta de Rodrigo del Campo, 13 (☎958 22 14 62; funky@alternativeacc.com). From Pl. Nueva, go uphill on Cuchilleros 20m to find Cuesta de Rodrigo on the right. Sizable dorms surround a central atrium over the funky lobby. Take in the view of the Alhambra, mountains, and rooftops from the bar atop the hostel. The friendly staff hangs out with travelers. Outings to nearby thermal baths (€10), tapas bars and *flamenco* shows (€21). A/C, breakfast, and lockers included. Laundry (wash, dry and fold) €7. Free internet. Dinner €4.50-6. Dorms €16.50-17; doubles €40. MC/V. ●

Hostal Venecia, Cuesta de Gomérez, 2, 3rd fl. (☎958 22 39 87). Eccentrically decorated with bright colors and Granada paraphernalia, this small, homey hostel has the most character per square meter in town. Homemade herbal tea and conversation available any time of day. Reserve early, especially in summer, since the secret is out. Dorms €19; doubles €34; triples €45. MC/V. ●

Hospedaje Almohada, C. Postigo de Zárate, 4 (☎958 20 74 46; www.laalmohada.com). Follow C. Trinidad out of Pl. Trinidad to the T-intersection, then make a right and walk down the short street ahead. Look for double red doors with hand-shaped knockers. Lounge in the TV area, use the kitchen to cook your own meal, and peruse the communal music collection and travel guides. Laundry (wash and hang-dry) €5 for 8kg. Four-bed dorms €15; singles €19; doubles €35; triples €50. Cash only. ●

FOOD

North African cuisine and vegetarian options can be found around the Albaicín, while more typical *menús* await in Pl. Nueva and Pl. Trinidad. Picnickers can gather fresh fruit, vegetables, and meat for an outdoor feast at the indoor market on Pl. San Agustín. (Open M-Sa 9am-3pm.)

Bocadillería Baraka, C. Elvira, 20 (☎958 22 97 60). Stands out among many Middle Eastern eateries for being the cheapest and the tastiest. Proud that their meat is home prepared and never frozen, Baraka serves delicious traditional pitas (€2.50-4) and addictive homemade lemonade infused with *hierbabuena* (€1). Hedi, the owner, also organizes week long, all-inclusive excursions through Morocco (☎649 11 41 71). Open daily 1pm-2am. Cash only. ●

La Riviera, C. Cetti Meriem, 7 (☎958 22 79 69), off C. Elvira. The best place to score delicious, free *tapas*. You can't go wrong with the extensive list of traditional fare. Beer or *tinto de verano* €1.80. Open daily 12:30-4pm and 8pm-midnight. ●

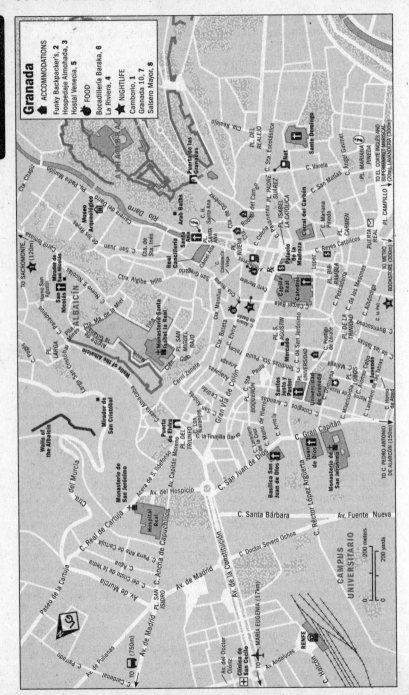

Granada

ACCOMMODATIONS
Funky Backpacker's, 2
Hospedaje Almohada, 3
Hostal Venecia, 5
FOOD
Bocadillería Baraka, 6
La Riviera, 4
NIGHTLIFE
Camborio, 1
Granada 10, 7
Salsero Mayor, 8

👁 SIGHTS

◼THE ALHAMBRA. From the streets of Granada, the Alhambra appears blocky and practical. But up close, the Alhambra is an elaborate and detailed work of architecture, one that unites water, light, wood, stucco, and ceramics to create a fortress-palace of aesthetic grandeur. The age-old saying holds true: *Si mueres sin ver la Alhambra, no has vivido.* (If you die without seeing the Alhambra, you have not lived.) Follow signs to the Palacio Nazaries to see the **◼Alcázar,** a 14th-century royal palace full of stalactite archways and sculpted fountains. The walls of the Patio del Cuarto Dorado are topped by the shielded windows of the harem. Off the far side of the patio, archways open onto the **Cuarto Dorado,** whose carved wooden ceiling is inlaid with ivory and mother-of-pearl. From the top of the patio, glimpse the 14th-century **Fachada de Serallo,** the palace's intricately carved facade. In the **Sala de los Abencerrajes,** Boabdil had the throats of 16 sons of the Abencerrajes family slit after one of them allegedly had amorous encounters with the sultana. Rust-colored stains in the basin are said to be traces of the massacre. (☎ *902 44 12 21; www.alhambra-patronato.es; reservations ☎ 902 22 44 60; www.alhambra-tickets.es. Open daily Apr.-Sept. 8:30am-8pm; Oct.-Mar. 8:30am-6pm. Also open June-Sept. Tu-Sa 10-11:30pm; Oct.-May F-Sa 8-9:30pm. Audio tours are worth the €5 and are available in English, French, German, Italian, and Spanish. €12, under 12 and the disabled free. €13 if purchased online. EU students with ID and EU seniors 65+ €9.)*

◼THE ALBAICÍN. A labyrinth of steep, narrow alleys, the Albaicín was the only Moorish neighborhood to escape the torches of the Reconquista. After the fall of the Alhambra, a small Muslim population remained here until their expulsion in the 17th century. Today, with North African cuisine, outdoor bazaars blasting Arabic music, teahouses, and the mosque near Pl. San Nicolás, the Albaicín attests to the persistence of Islamic culture in Andalucía. The best way to explore this maze is to proceed along Carrera del Darro off Pl. Santa Ana, climb the Cuesta del Chapiz on the left, then wander through the Muslim ramparts, cisterns, and gates. On Pl. Santa Ana, the 16th-century Real Cancillería, with its arcaded patio and stalactite ceiling, was the Christians' city hall. Farther uphill are the 11th-century Arab baths. *(Carrera del Darro, 31. ☎ 958 22 97 38. Call ☎ 958 22 56 03 to confirm hours. Free.)* The **◼mirador,** adjacent to Iglesia de San Nicolás, affords the city's best view of the Alhambra, especially in winter when snow adorns the Sierra Nevada behind it.

CAPILLA REAL AND CATHEDRAL. Downhill from the Alhambra, the **Capilla Real** (Royal Chapel), Fernando and Isabel's private chapel, exemplifies Christian Granada. Gothic masonry and meticulously rendered figurines, as well as La Reja, the gilded iron grille of Maestro Bartolomé, grace the couple's resting place. The Sacristía houses Isabel's private art collection and the royal jewels. (☎ *958 22 92 39. Capilla Real and Sacristía both open Apr.-Sept. M-Sa 10:30am-12:45pm and 4-7pm, Su 11am-12:45pm and 4-7pm; Oct.-May M-Sa 10:30am-12:45pm and 3:30-6:15pm, Su 11am-12:45pm and 3:30-6:15pm. Both sights €3.50.)* Behind the Capilla Real and the Sacristía is Granada's cathedral. After the Reconquista, construction of the cathedral began upon the smoldering embers of Granada's largest mosque. (☎ *958 22 29 59. Open Apr.-Sept. M-Sa 10:45am-1:30pm and 4-8pm, Su 4-8pm; Oct.-Mar. M-Sa 10:30am-1:30pm and 4-7pm, Su 11am-1:30pm and 4-7pm. €3.50.)*

🎵 NIGHTLIFE

Granada's policy of "free *tapas* with a drink" lures students and tourists to its many pubs and bars. Great *tapas* bars can be found off the side streets near Pl. Nueva. The most boisterous nightspots belong to **Calle Pedro Antonio de Alarcón,** between Pl. Albert Einstein and Ancha de Gracia, while hip new bars and clubs line **Calle Elvira.** Gay bars are around **Carrera del Darro.**

■ **Camborio,** Camino del Sacromonte, 48 (☎958 22 12 15), a quick taxi ride or 20min. walk uphill from Pl. Nueva; bus #34 stops at midnight. DJ-spun pop music echoes through dance floors to the rooftop patio above. Striking view of the Alhambra. Beer €4. Mixed drinks €5. Cover €6, includes 1 drink. Open Tu-Sa midnight-7am. Cash only.

■ **Salsero Mayor,** C. la Paz, 20 (☎958 52 27 41). An ageless group of locals and tourists alike flocks here for crowded nights of salsa, bachata, and merengue. Beer €2-3. Mixed drinks €5. Open M-Th and Su 10pm-3am, F-Sa 1pm-4am. Cash only.

Granada 10, C. Cárcel Baja 3 (☎958 22 40 01). Movie theater by evening (shows Sept.-June at 8 and 10pm), raging dance club by night. Flashy and opulent. No sneakers or sportswear. Open M-Th and Su 12:30-4am, F-Sa 12:30-6am. Cover €10. MC/V.

EASTERN SPAIN

Its rich soil and famous orange groves, fed by Moorish irrigation systems, have earned Eastern Spain the nickname *Huerta de España* (Spain's Orchard). Dunes, jagged promontories, and lagoons mark the coastline, while fountains grace landscaped public gardens in Valencia. The region has made a rapid transition from traditional to commercial, and continues to modernize.

VALENCIA ☎463

Valencia's white beaches, palm-lined avenues, and architectural treasures are noticeably less crowded than those of Spain's other major cities. Yet Valencia (pop. 807,000) possesses the energy of Madrid, the off-beat sophistication of Barcelona, and the warmth of Seville. Explore the life aquatic at L'Oceanogràfic or fulfill a quest for the Holy Grail at the stunning Catedral de Santa María.

⊏▶ TRANSPORTATION AND PRACTICAL INFORMATION. Trains arrive at Estación del Norte, C. Xàtiva 24 (☎463 52 02 02), and a slick new **metro** line runs from the Airport of Valencia to C. Colonor Xativa. **RENFE** (☎902 24 02 02) runs to: Alicante (2-3hr., 12 per day, €23.60-31.30); Barcelona (3hr., 8-16 per day, €29-37); Madrid (3hr., 12 per day, €20-39). **Buses** (☎463 46 62 66) go from Av. Menéndez Pidal 13 to: Alicante via the Costa Blanca (4hr., 10-30 per day, €16-18); Barcelona (4hr., 19 per day, €21); Madrid (4hr., 13 per day, €21-26); Seville (11hr., 3-4 per day, €43-50). Take bus #1 or 2 from the bus station. The comprehensive **tourist office,** C. de la Paz 48, which provides information on the city and the province of Valencia, has branches at the train station and at Pl. de la Reina. (☎463 98 64 22; www.valencia.es. Open M-F 9am-8pm, Sa 10am-8pm, Su 10am-2pm.) **Ono,** C. San Vicente Mártir 22, provides **Internet** daily until 1am. (☎463 28 19 02. €1-4 per hr., depending on the time of day.) The palatial **post office** is at Pl. del Ajuntament 24. (☎463 51 23 70. Open M-F 8:30am-8:30pm, Sa 9:30am-2pm.) **Postal Code:** divided into zones, 46000-46025.

⊏▷ ACCOMMODATIONS AND FOOD. For the best deals and proximity to restaurants, nightlife, and architectural marvels, try hostels around Plaça del Ajuntament, Plaça del Mercat, and Plaça de la Reina. From Pl. de la Reina, turn right on C. de la Paz to reach the chic and hopping ◨**Red Nest Youth Hostel ❷,** C. de la Paz 36, a great location for clubgoers. The hostel is spotless and smoothly operated, with a great international staff and funky, youthful decor. (☎463 42 71 68; www.nest-hostelsvalencia.net. Kitchen, dining area, and vending machines. Free luggage storage, Wi-Fi, linens, and towels (€5 deposit). Internet €1 per hr. 4-12 person dorms €18-22; doubles €41-47. AmEx/ MC/V.) **The Home Youth Hostel ❶**, C. Lonja 4, is across from the Mercado Central on a side street off Pl. Dr. Collado. A couch-laden lounge, four-person dorms, and a relaxed atmosphere make this 20-room complex one of Valencia's more intimate hostels. (☎463 91 62 29; www.likeathome.net. Fully equipped kitchen. Linens included. Internet €0.50 per 15min. Singles €21; doubles €40. MC/V.)

Valencia is renowned for its *paella*, served in mammoth skillets all over town. Stuff yourself with huge portions of *paella valenciana* in the intimate courtyard outside **El Rall ❸**, by the old Gothic silk exchange monument on C. Tundidores 2. (☎463 92 20 90. *Paella* €12-21 per person, min. 2 people. Open daily 1:30-3:30pm and 8:30-11:30pm. Reserve ahead. MC/V.) **Zumeria Naturalia ❶**, C. Del Mar 12, by the Pl. de la Reina, is a sherbet-hued gem offering more than 50 fruit drinks (with and without alcohol), *bocadillos* with new and different fillings, and crepes. (Open M-W 5pm-midnight, Th 5pm-1am, F-Sa 5pm-2am, Su 5-10:30pm. Cash only.) For groceries, stop by the **Mercado Central,** where fresh fish, meat, and fruit (including Valencia's famous oranges) are sold.

🔲 **SIGHTS.** Most sights line the **Río Turia** or cluster near **Pl. de la Reina, Pl. del Mercado,** and **Pl. de la Virgin.** EMT bus #5 is the only public bus that passes by most of Valencia's historic sites; for a guided tour, try the **Bus Turístico** from Pl. de la Reina (☎463 41 44 00; hop-on-hop-off day pass €12). The 13th-century 🔲**Catedral de Santa María** in Pl. de la Reina, which holds a chalice said to be the Holy Grail, is an impressive mix of Romanesque, Gothic, and Baroque architecture. Catch incredible views of Valencia's skyline atop the **Miguelete**, the cathedral tower. (☎463 91 01 89. Cathedral open daily 7:30am-1pm and 4:30-8:30pm. Closes earlier in winter. Tower open daily 10am-1pm and 4:30-7pm. €4 entrance fee, children and seniors €2.70. Includes audio guide.) Be sure to pass around back through the marbled **Plaza de la Virgin** and the **Basilica de la Virgin. El Palacio de los Marqueses de Dos Aguas,** C. Porta Querol 2, off C. de la Paz, is an architecturally stunning 14th-century building that recreates the home of a noble Valencian family. An incorporated ceramics museum includes works from as early as the 12th century, as well as rotating contemporary exhibits. (☎463 51 63 92; www.mnceramica.mcu.es. Open Tu-Sa 10am-2pm and 4-8pm. Tu-F €2.40, Students €1.20, Sa free.) Many museums are across the fortified bridges of what was once the Rio Turia—today, the riverbed is a lush green park that is perfect for bike rides, picnics, or walks. The blue-domed **Museu Provincial de Belles Artes,** C. Sant Pío V, displays stunning 14th- to 16th-century Valencian art and is home to El Greco's *San Juan Bautista*, Velázquez's self-portrait, and a number of works by Goya. (☎463 60 57 93; www.cult.gva.es/mbav. Open Tu-Sa 10am-8pm. Free.) Next door, pass through the eclectic **Jardines del Real,** taking in the many sculptures, fountains, and pleasant landscaping along the way.

🔲🔲 **ENTERTAINMENT AND NIGHTLIFE.** To reach Valencia's two most popular beaches, **Las Arenas** and **Malvarrosa,** take bus #20, #21, or #22. If you have time to spare, take an Autocares Herca **bus** from the corner of Gran Vía de Germanias and C. Sueca (☎463 49 12 50; 30min., 1 per hr. 7am-9pm, €1-1.10) to the pristine beach of **Salér.** On Pl. de la Virgin along C. Caballeros, bars and pubs kick into action around midnight. Most dance clubs here do not have a cover. 🔲**L'Umbracle Terraza,** Av. de Saler, 5, is a worthwhile exception to this rule: located in the garden that runs parallel to the Ciudad de las Artes y las Ciencias, this is the perfect setting to view Valencia's newest architectural gems in all their illuminated splendor. (☎963 31 97 45; www.umbracleterraza.com. €15 cover. Open Apr.-Sept. M-Sa, 11:30pm-late.) In the city center, sip *agua de Valencia* (orange

SEEING RED

On the last Wednesday of every August, tens of thousands of tourists descend upon the small town of Buñol, a town in Valencia, to participate in the world's largest food fight: La Tomatina. A tradition since 1944, this tomato battle serves as the culmination of a week-long festival. Although the sloppy free-for-all is followed by a celebration of the town's patron saints, the tomato fight has no significance beyond the primal desire to get dirty and throw food.

Festivities begin when an overgrown ham is placed on a greased pole in the center of town. Locals and tourists scramble up the slippery pole, climbing on top of one another to be the captor of the prized ham. Once a winner is announced, a cannon starts the marinara blood bath.

Throngs of tourists wearing clothes destined for the dumpster crowd around the open-bed trucks that haul 240,000 lb. of tomatoes into the plaza. Over the next 2hr., Buñol becomes an every-man-for-himself battle of oozy carnage. Revelers pelt one another with tomatoes until the entire crowd is covered in tomato guts.

The origins of this food fight are unclear: some say it began as a fight between friends, while others say the original tomatoes were directed at unsatisfactory civil dignitaries. Today, no one is safe from the wrath of tomatoes hurled at friends and foreigners alike.

juice, champagne, and vodka) at the outdoor terraces in Pl. Tossal. There you will find ⬛**Bolsería Café**, C. Bolsería 41, a cafe and club packed every night with the beautiful and chic. (☎463 91 89 03; www.bolseriavalencia.com. Beer €3, free *agua de Valencia* before 12:30am. Mixed drinks €6. 'Americana' party W, T. Brazilian theme Su. Open daily 7:30pm-3:30am. MC/V.) For more info, consult the entertainment supplement *La Cartelera* (€0.50), or the free *24/7 Valencia*, available at hostels and cafes. The most famous festival in Valencia is **Las Fallas** (Mar. 12-19), in which hundreds of colossal papier-mâché puppets are paraded down the street and burned at the end of the week in celebration of spring. The nearby town of Buñol hosts the world's largest food fight during **La Tomatina** (held annually in late August; see p. 698).

BARCELONA ☎93

Barcelona is a city that has grown young as it has grown old. In the 17 years since it hosted the Olympics, travelers have been drawn to this European hot-spot's beaches, clubs, and first-rate restaurants. Once home to Pablo Picasso and Joan Miró, the city has a strong art scene, which continues the tradition of the whimsical and daring *Modernisme* architectural movement. Barcelona is a gateway—not only to Catalan art and culture, but also to the Mediterranean and the Pyrenees—and its vibrant aura lingers long after you leave.

✈ INTERCITY TRANSPORTATION

Flights: Aeroport El Prat de Llobregat (BCN; ☎902 40 47 04; www.aena.es), 13km southwest of Barcelona. To get to Pl. Catalunya, take the **Aerobus** (☎934 15 60 20) in front of terminals A, B, or C (35-40min.; every 6-15min.; to Pl. Catalunya daily 6am-1am, to the airport 5:30am-12:15am; €4.05, round-trip €7.30).

Trains: Barcelona has 2 main train stations. **Estació Barcelona-Sants**, in Pl. Països Catalans (Ⓜ Sants Estació), is the main terminal for domestic and international traffic. **Estació de França**, on Av. Marquès de l'Argentera (Ⓜ Barceloneta), services regional destinations, including Tarragona and Zaragoza, and a limited number of international locations. Note that trains often stop before the main stations; check the schedule. **RENFE** (reservations and info ☎902 24 02 02, international 24 34 02) to: **Bilbao** (6½-9hr., 12:30 and 11pm, €41-60); **Madrid** (3hr.; from mid-June to mid-Sept. 14-21 per day, from mid-Sept. to mid-June 4-7 per day; €44); **Sevilla** (5½-12hr., 3 per day 8am-

10:05pm, €59-132); **Valencia** (3-4 hr., 14 per day, €34-41). International destinations include **Milan, ITA** (via **Figueres** and **Turin**) and **Montpellier, FRA,** with connections to Geneva, Paris, and the French Riviera. 20% discount on round-trip tickets.

Buses: Arrive at the **Barcelona Nord Estació d'Autobusos**, C. Alí-bei, 80 (☎902 26 06 06; www.barcelonanord.com). ⓂArc de Triomf or #54 bus. Info booth open 7am-9pm. Buses also depart from Estació Sants and the airport. **Sarfa** (☎902 30 20 25; www. sarfa.es). Bus stop and ticket office also at Ronda Sant Pere, 21 (☎933 02 62 23). To: **Cadaqués** (2¾hr.; M-F 2-4 per day 10:30am-7pm Sa-Su 2-4 per day 10:30am-8:45pm; €21); **Palafrugell** (2hr., 8-15 per day 8:15am-8:30pm, €16); **Tossa de Mar** via **Lloret de Mar** (1½hr., 7-13 per day 8am-8:30pm, €11). **Eurolines** (☎93 265 07 88; www.eurolines.es) goes to **Paris, FRA** via **Lyon** (15hr., M-Sa 9:30pm, €75-91); 10% discount under 26 or over 60. **ALSA/Enatcar** (☎902 42 22 42; www.alsa.es) goes to: **Alicante** (7-9hr., 8 per day, €41-46); **Bilbao** (7-8½hr., 4-7 per day, €42); **Madrid** (8hr., 18-21 per day 7am-1am, €29-41); **Sevilla** (15-20hr., 3 per day, €89); **Valencia** (4-5hr., 8 per day, €25-30); **Zaragoza** (4hr., 3-21 per day, €14-21).

Ferries: Transmediterránea (☎902 45 46 45; www.transmediterranea.es), in Terminal Drassanes, Moll Sant Bertran. **"Fast" ferry** (€51-69; round-trip €96-€103) June-Aug. to **Ibiza** (8-9hr., 1 per day Tu and Th-Su), **Mahón** (8½hr., M and W-Su 10:30pm), and **Palma de Mallorca** (8hr., 1-2 per day).

▓ ORIENTATION

Imagine yourself perched on Columbus's head at the **Monument a Colom** (on Passeig de Colom, along the shore), viewing the city with the sea at your back. From the harbor, the city slopes upward to the mountains. From the Monument a Colom, **La Rambla,** a pedestrian thoroughfare, runs from the harbor to **Plaça de Catalunya** (M: Catalunya), the city center. *Let's Go* uses "Las Ramblas" to refer to the general area and "La Rambla" in address listings. The **Ciutat Vella** (Old City) centers around Las Ramblas and includes the neighborhoods of Barri Gòtic, La Ribera, and El Raval. The **Barri Gòtic** is to the right (with your back to the ocean) of Las Ramblas, enclosed on the other side by Vía Laietana. East of V. Laietana lies the maze-like **La Ribera,** bordered by Parc de la Ciutadella and Estació de França. Beyond La Ribera—farther east outside the Ciutat Vella—are **Poble Nou** and **Port Olímpic.** To the west of Las Ramblas is **El Raval.** Farther west rises **Montjuïc,** with sprawling gardens, museums, the 1992 Olympic grounds, and a fortress. Directly behind the Monument a Colom is the **Port Vell** (old port) development, where a wavy bridge leads across to the ultra modern shopping and entertainment complexes Moll d'Espanya and Maremàgnum. North of the Ciutat Vella is **l'Eixample,** a gridded neighborhood created during the expansion of the 1860s, which sprawls from Pl. Catalunya toward the mountains. Gran Vía de les Corts Catalanes defines its lower edge, and the **Passeig de Gràcia,** l'Eixample's main avenue, bisects the neighborhood. **Avinguda Diagonal** marks the border between l'Eixample and the **Zona Alta** (Uptown), which includes **Pedralbes, Gràcia,** and other older neighborhoods in the foothills. The peak of **Tibidabo,** the northwest border of the city, offers the best view of Barcelona.

▐ LOCAL TRANSPORTATION

Public Transportation: ☎010. Passes *(abonos)* work for the Metro, bus, urban lines of FGC commuter trains, RENFE *cercanías,* Trams, and Nitbus. A *sencillo* ticket (1 ride)

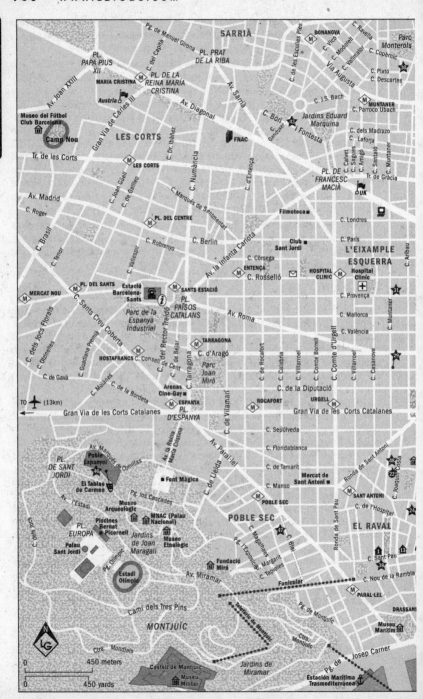

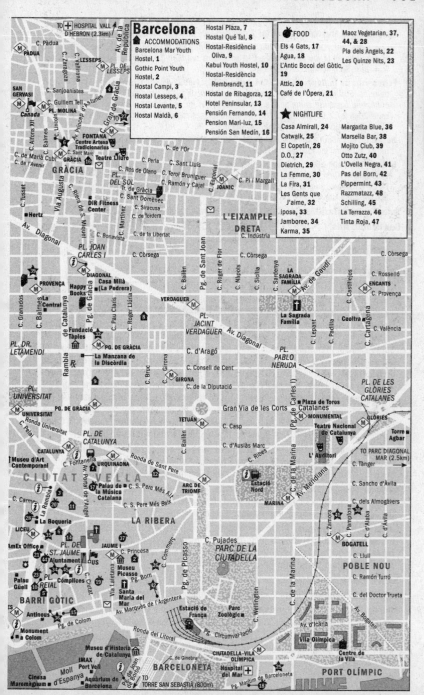

Barcelona

🏠 **ACCOMMODATIONS**

Barcelona Mar Youth Hostel, **1**
Gothic Point Youth Hostel, **2**
Hostal Campi, **3**
Hostal Lesseps, **4**
Hostal Levante, **5**
Hostal Maldà, **6**
Hostal Plaza, **7**
Hostal Qué Tal, **8**
Hostal-Residència Oliva, **9**
Kabul Youth Hostel, **10**
Hostal-Residència Rembrandt, **11**
Hostal de Ribagorza, **12**
Hotel Peninsular, **13**
Pensión Fernando, **14**
Pension Mari-luz, **15**
Pensión San Medín, **16**

🍎 **FOOD**

Els 4 Gats, **17**
Agua, **18**
L'Antic Bocoi del Gòtic, **19**
Attic, **20**
Café de l'Òpera, **21**
Maoz Vegetarian, **37, 44, & 28**
Pla dels Àngels, **22**
Les Quinze Nits, **23**

⭐ **NIGHTLIFE**

Casa Almirall, **24**
Catwalk, **25**
El Copetín, **26**
D.O., **27**
Dietrich, **29**
La Femme, **30**
La Fira, **31**
Les Gents que J'aime, **32**
iposa, **33**
Jamboree, **34**
Karma, **35**
Margarita Blue, **36**
Marsella Bar, **38**
Mojito Club, **39**
Otto Zutz, **40**
L'Ovella Negra, **41**
Pas del Born, **42**
Pippermint, **43**
Razzmatazz, **48**
Schilling, **45**
La Terrazza, **46**
Tinta Roja, **47**

costs €1.40. A **T-10 pass** (€7.70) is valid for 10 rides; a **T-Día pass** entitles you to unlimited bus and Metro travel for 1 day (€5.80) and the **T-mes** (€48) for 1 month.

Metro: ☎93 298 7000; www.tmb.net. Vending machines and ticket windows sell passes. Hold on to your ticket until you exit or risk a €40 fine. Trains run M-Th, Su and holidays 5am-midnight, F 5am-2am, Sa non-stop service. €1.40.

Ferrocarrils de la Generalitat de Catalunya (FGC): (☎932 05 15 15; www.fgc.es). Commuter trains to local destinations with main stations at Pl. de Catalunya and Pl. d'Espanya. The commuter line costs the same as the Metro (€1.40) as far as Tibidabo. After that, rates go up by zone: Zone 2 €2.10, Zone 3 €2.90, etc. Metro passes are valid on FGC trains. Info office at the Pl. de Catalunya station open M-F 7am-9pm.

Buses: Go just about anywhere, usually 5am-10pm. Most stops have maps posted. Buses run 4-6 per hr. in central locations. €1.40.

Nitbus: (www.emt-amb.cat/links/cat/cnitbus.htm). 18 different lines run every 20-30min. 10:30pm-4:30am, depending on the line; a few run until 5:30am. All buses depart from around Pl. de Catalunya, stop in front of most club complexes, and work their way through Ciutat Vella and the Zona Alta.

Taxis: Try **RadioTaxi033** (☎93 303 3033; www.radiotaxi033.com; AmEx/MC/V)

Car Rental: Avis, C. Corcega 293-295 (☎93 237 5680; www.avis.com). Also at airport (☎93 298 3600) and Estació Barcelona-Sants, Pl. dels Països Catalans. (☎93 330 4193. Open M-F 7:30am-10:30pm, Sa 8am-7pm, Su 9am-7pm.)

⑦ PRACTICAL INFORMATION

Tourist Offices: ☎90 730 1282; www.barcelonaturisme.com. In addition to several tourist offices, Barcelona has numerous mobile information kiosks. **Aeroport del Prat de Llobregat,** terminals A and B (☎93 478 0565). Info and last-minute accommodation booking. Open daily 9am-9pm. **Estació Barcelona-Sants,** Pl. Països Catalans. M: Sants-Estació. Info and last-minute accommodations booking. Open June 24-Nov. 24 daily 8am-8pm; Nov. 25-June 23 M-F 8am-8pm, Sa-Su 8am-2pm. **Oficina de Turisme de Catalunya,** Pg. de Gràcia 107 (☎93 238 4000; www.gencat.es/probert). M: Diagonal. Open M-Sa 10am-7pm, Su 10am-2pm. **Plaça de Catalunya,** Pl. de Catalunya 17S. M: Catalunya. The biggest, best, and busiest tourist office. Free **maps,** brochures on sights and public transportation, booking service for accommodations, gift shop, currency exchange, and box office. Open daily 9am-9pm. **Plaça de Sant Jaume,** C. Ciutat 2. M: Jaume I. Open M-F 9am-8pm, Sa 10am-8pm, Su and holidays 10am-2pm.

Currency Exchange: ATMs give the best rates; the next-best rates are available at banks. General banking hours are M-F 8:30am-2pm. Las Ramblas has many exchange stations open late, but the rates are not as good and a commission will be taken.

Luggage Storage: Estació Barcelona-Sants, Ⓜ Sants-Estació. Lockers €4.50 per day. Open daily 5:30am-11pm. **Estació Nord,** Ⓜ Arc de Triomf. Lockers €3.50-5 per day, 90-day limit. Also at the **El Prat Airport.** €5 per day.

Laundromat: Lavomatic, Pl. Joaquim Xirau, 1, a block off La Rambla and 1 block below C. Escudellers. Branch at C. Consolat del Mar, 43-45 (☎932 68 47 68), 1 block north of Pg. Colon and 2 blocks off Via Laietana. Wash €4.80. Dry €0.90 per 5min. Both open M-Sa 9am-9pm.

Tourist Police: La Rambla, 43 (☎932 56 24 30). Ⓜ Liceu. English spoken. Open 24hr.

Late-Night Pharmacy: Rotates; check any pharmacy window for the nearest on duty.

Medical Services: Medical Emergency: ☎061. **Hospital Clínic i Provincal,** C. Villarroel,170 (☎932 27 54 00). Ⓜ Hospital Clínic. Main entrance at C. Roselló and C. Casanova.

Internet: ▨ **Easy Internet Café,** La Rambla, 31 (☎933 01 7507; www.easyinternetcafe. com). Ⓜ Liceu. Fairly reasonable prices and over 200 terminals in a bright, modern center. €2.10 per hr., min. €2. 1-day unlimited pass €7; 1 week €15; 1 month €30. Open

8am-2:30am. **Branch** at Ronda Universitat, 35. Ⓜ️Catalunya. €2 per hour; 1-day pass €3; 1 week €7; 1 month €15. Open daily 8am-2:30am.

Navegaweb, La Rambla, 88-94 (☎933 17 90 26; navegabarcelona@terra.es). Ⓜ️Liceu. Good rates for international calls ($0.20 per min. to USA). Internet €2 per hr. Open M-Th 9am-midnight, F 9am-1am, Sa 9am-2am, Su 9am-midnight.

Bcnet, C. Barra de Ferro, 3 (☎932 68 15 07; www.bornet-bcn.com), down the street from the Museu Picasso. Ⓜ️Jaume I. €1 for 15min; €3 per hr.; 10hr. ticket €19. Open M-F 10am-11pm, Sa-Su noon-11pm.

Post Office: Pl. d'Antoni López (☎902 197 197). Ⓜ️Jaume I or Barceloneta. Fax and **Lista de Correos.** Open M-F 8:30am-9:30pm, Su noon-10pm. Dozens of branches; consult www.correos.es. **Postal Code:** 08001.

█ ACCOMMODATIONS

While there are plenty of accommodations in Barcelona, finding an affordable room can be difficult. To crash in touristy **Barri Gòtic** or **Las Ramblas** during the busier months (June-Sept. and Dec.), make reservations weeks, even months, ahead. Consider staying outside the tourist hub of *Ciutat Vella;* there are many affordable hostels in **l'Eixample** and **Gràcia** that tend to have more vacancies. The **Associació de Càmpings i C.V. de Barcelona,** Gran Via de les Corts Catalanes 608 (☎93 412 5955; www.campingsbcn.com), has more info.

LOWER BARRI GÒTIC

▨ **Hostal Levante,** Baixada de San Miquel, 2 (☎933 17 95 65; www.hostallevante.com). Ⓜ️Liceu. New rooms are large and tasteful, with light wood furnishings, exceptionally clean bathrooms, A/C, and fans; some have balconies. Ask for a newly renovated room. Apartments have kitchens, living rooms, and washing machines. Internet €1 per hr. Singles €35, with bath 45; doubles from €55/€65; 4-person apartments €30 per person. Credit card number required with reservation. MC/V. ❸

▨ **Pensión Mariluz,** C. Palau, 4 (☎933 17 34 63; www.pensionmariluz.com), 3rd fl. Ⓜ️Liceu or Jaume I. Gorgeous renovations turned this hostel into a warm, bright space around a classy old courtyard. Shared bathrooms are clean but a bit cramped. Offers short-term apartments nearby. A/C. Locker, sheets, and towels included. Free Wi-Fi in common area. Dorms €15-24; singles €30-41; doubles €40-60; triples €48-72; quads €65-90, with bath €94. MC/V. ❷

UPPER BARRI GÒTIC.

Hostal Maldà, C. Pi, 5 (☎933 17 30 02). Ⓜ️Liceu. Enter the small shopping center and follow the signs upstairs. Clean, no-frills rooms that would cost twice as much money at other places. All rooms have shared bath. Call for reservations. Singles €15; doubles €30; triples with shower €45. Cash only. ❶

Hostal-Residència Rembrandt, C. de la Portaferrissa, 23 (☎933 18 10 11; www.hostalrembrandt.com). Ⓜ️Liceu. Range of unique rooms. Cheapest are fairly standard but some have large baths, patios, and sitting areas. Breakfast €5. Reception 9am-11pm. Reservations require credit card or €50 deposit. Singles with shower around €30, with bath €40; doubles €50/65; triples €75/85. MC/V. ❷

LA RIBERA AND EL RAVAL.

▨ **Gothic Point Youth Hostel,** C. dels Vigatans, 5 (☎932 68 78 08; www.gothicpoint.com). Ⓜ️Jaume I. Jungle-gym rooms with A/C. Most beds come with curtains and personal lockers. Highly social, with lots of events, including a weekly DJ jam and free concerts. Rooftop terrace

SPAIN

and colorful lounge area with TV. Breakfast included. Lockers €3. Linens €2. Free internet. Refrigerator and kitchen access. Dorms €24. €1 credit card fee per night. AmEx/MC/V. ❶

⬛ **Hotel Peninsular,** C. de Sant Pau, 34 (☎934 12 36 99; www.hpeninsular.com). M: Liceu. This *Modernista* building has 78 rooms with green doors, phones, and A/C around a beautiful 4-story interior courtyard festooned with hanging plants. Breakfast included. Safety deposit boxes €2 per day with €20 deposit. Free internet and Wi-Fi. Check-out 11am. Singles €55; doubles €78; triples €95; quads €120; quints €140. MC/V. ❺

L'EIXAMPLE

⬛ **Sant Jordi Hostel Aragó,** C. Aragó, 268 (☎932 15 67 43; www.santjordihostels.com). ⓂPasseig de Gràcia. Walk 3 blocks up Pg. de Gràcia and make a left on C. Arago; it's on the left. Crash in this recently renovated hostel's sleek and homey common room and recuperate from a long day. They'll plan your night out for you if you so desire. Board games, DVDs, lockers, sheets, towels, TV, use of guitar all free. Laundry €5. Breakfast €3. Kitchen. Laundry €5. Internet and Wi-Fi. Parties and bar crawls organized regularly; call ahead. 4-bed dorms €14-17; 6-bed dorms €13-25. ❶

⬛ **Somnio Hostel,** C. Diputació 251. (☎932 72 53 08, www.somniohostels.com) ⓂPg. de Gràcia. Chic, clean, and neatly arranged rooms just blocks from Pl. de Catalunya. A/C throughout, free internet and Wi-Fi, TV in common area. Drinks available at the front desk. Breakfast €5. Single-sex dorms, complete with sheets and locker €25; singles €42; doubles €77, with bath €85. MC/V. ❷

⬛ **Hostal Residència Oliva,** Pg. de Gràcia, 32, 4th fl. (☎934 88 01 62; www.hostaloliva.com). ⓂPg. de Gràcia. Classy ambience—wooden bureaus, mirrors, and a light marble floor. Fragrant bouquets of flowers in the hallways are perhaps to be expected from a hostel that has been in operation since 1931. Rooms have TV, A/C, and Wi-Fi. Singles €38; doubles €66, with bath €85. Cash only. ❹

ZONA ALTA: GRÀCIA AND OUTER BARRIS

Pensión Norma, C. Gran de Gràcia, 87 (☎932 37 44 78). ⓂFontana. Meticulously kept rooms with sinks and wardrobes. The spacious shared bath is clean with speckled tile floors. Free Wi-Fi. Singles €27-32; doubles €38-47, with bath €55-60. MC/V. ❷

Hostal Lesseps, C. Gran de Gràcia, 239 (☎932 18 44 34; www.hostallesseps.com). ⓂLesseps. 16 spotless rooms, each with a high ceiling, classy velvet walls, small desk, TV, and bath. A/C €5. Cats and dogs allowed. Free internet and Wi-Fi. Singles €40; doubles €65; triples €75; quads €90. MC/V. ❹

🔲 FOOD

Port Vell and **Port Olímpic** are known for seafood. The restaurants on **Carrer Aragó** by Pg. de Gràcia have great lunchtime *menús*, and the **Passeig de Gràcia** has beautiful outdoor dining. Gràcia's **Plaça Sol** and the area around La Ribera's **Santa Maria del Mar** are the best *tapas* (or cheap, laid-back dinner) spots. For fruit, cheese, and wine, head to ⬛**La Boqueria** (Mercat de Sant Josep), off La Rambla outside M: Liceu. (Open M-Sa 8am-8pm.) Buy groceries at **Champion,** La Rambla 13. (M: Liceu. Open M-Sa 9am-10pm.)

BARRI GÒTIC

⬛ **Les Quinze Nits,** Pl. Reial, 6 (☎933 17 30 75; www.lesquinzenits.com). ⓂLiceu. Popular restaurant with lines halfway through the plaza every night; arrive early for excellent Catalan cuisine at unusually low prices. Sit in the classy interior or eat outside for no extra charge and keep an eye on your fellow tourists in Pl. Reial. Starters €4-7. Entrees €6-11. Wine €3. Sangria €4.70. Open daily 1-3:45pm and 8:30-11:30pm. AmEx/MC/V. ❷

🏠 **L'Antic Bocoi del Gòtic,** Baixada de Viladecols, 3 (☎933 10 50 67; www.bocoi.net). ⓂJaume I. Excellent salads (€7.20-9.20), *coques de recapte* (open-faced toasted sandwiches; €9), and cheese platters (€13-19) feature *jamón ibérico* and local produce. Look for the 1st-century Roman wall inside. Open M-Sa 8:30pm-midnight. Reserve in advance. AmEx/D/MC/V. ❸

🏠 **Attic,** La Rambla, 120 (☎933 02 48 66; www.angrup.com). ⓂLiceu. This chic restaurant promises high-class food at manageable prices. The modern, orange interior will feel like a refuge from touristy La Rambla. Mediterranean fusion cuisine, including fish (€10-14), meat (€8-15), and their specialty, ox burger (€11). Open daily 1-4:30pm and 7pm-12:30am. AmEx/MC/V. ❸

Arc Café, C. Carabassa, 19 (☎933 02 52 04; www.arccafe.com). ⓂDrassanes. This secluded, handsome cafe serves curries (€9.50-12) and salads (€4-7). Entrees €8-17. *Menú del mediodía* €9.60. Breakfast until 1pm. Thai dinner menu Th-F. Open M-Th 10am-1am, F 10am-3am, Sa 11am-3am, Su 11am-1am. MC/V. ❸

Juicy Jones, C. Cardenal Casañas, 7 (☎93 302 43 30; reservations 60 620 49 06). ⓂLiceu, L3. A vegan's haven, Juicy Jones is a refreshing touch of the psychedelic, with wildly decorated walls and a long bar spilling over with fresh fruit. The creative vegan *menú* (€8.50) features Spanish and Indian inspired dishes (after 1pm). They offer a full juice bar with every conceivable mixture of fresh juices and soy milkshakes (€3-5). Open daily 12:30pm-12am. Kitchen closes at 11:30pm. Cash only. ❷

Xaloc, C. de la Palla, 13-17 (☎933 01 19 90). ⓂLiceu. Classy local favorite. A clean look complements the butcher counter where pig legs hang from the ceiling. Expect simple plates with high-quality ingredients. Tapas €3-7. *Cocas* €4-6. Open M-F 9am-midnight, Sa-Su 10am-midnight. AmEx/MC/V. ❷

OTHER NEIGHBORHOODS

🏠 **La Llavor dels Origens,** C. d'Enric Granados, 9 (☎934 53 11 20; www.lallavordelsorigens.com); C. de la Vidrieria, 6-8 (☎933 10 75 31); Pg. del Born, 4 (☎932 95 66 90); and C. de Ramón y Cajal, 12 (☎932 13 60 31). A hip dining room with a new-school twist. Delectable entrees include beef-stuffed onion (€6.40) and rabbit with chocolate and almonds (€6.40). Soups, meat dishes, and some vegetarian dishes €4.30-7. Open daily 12:30pm-1am. AmEx/MC/V. ❷

🏠 **Petra,** C. dels Sombrerers, 13 (☎933 19 99 99). ⓂJaume I. Some of the best food in the area at shockingly low prices. Clever decor—stained-glass windows, menus printed on wine glasses, and light fixtures made from silverware—give the place a charming bohemian feel. Try the duck with brie and apple or the rigatoni with *foie gras* sauce and peach. Salads and pasta €5. Entrees €8. Open Tu-Th 1:30-4pm and 9-11:30pm, F-Sa 1:30-4pm and 9pm-midnight, Su 1:30-4pm. MC/V. ❷

🏠 **El Pebre Blau,** C. dels Banys Vells, 21 (☎933 19 13 08). ⓂJaume I. A *nouveau gourmet* restaurant serving Mediterranean and Middle Eastern fusion dishes under starry lanterns. Throw in a cheeky menu (available in English) and an attentive waitstaff for the win. Most dishes €10-18. Open daily 8pm-midnight. Reserve ahead, especially for weekend. MC/V. ❸.

Organic, C. Junta de Comerç, 11 (☎933 01 09 02; www.antoniaorganickitchen.com). This vegan-friendly eatery provides wholesome, healthy dishes—starting with the filtered water used to prepare the food. Vegan salad bar and lunch *menú* (M-F €10, Sa-Su €14) served under candlelight and exposed ceiling. Salad bar regulars include cheese-and-mushroom *croquetas* and cucumbers and yogurt. Dinner served a la carte. 2nd location in La Boqueria market also has a *menú* and *bocadillos;* takeout only. Open daily 12:30pm-midnight. MC/V. ❷

Rita Rouge, Pl. Gardunya (☎934 81 36 86; ritarouge@ritablue.com). M: Liceu. 2nd branch **Rita Blue**, Pl. Sant Augustí, 3 (☎933 42 40 86; www.ritablue.com). Savor a healthy, delicious, and high-quality lunch *menú* (€11; weekends €14) full of creative offerings and vegetarian choices on a shady, black-and-red terrace just behind La Boqueria, or come at night for a mixed drink (€6-8) on zebra-striped cushions or in the glittery bar's red and silver bucket seats. Entrees (€9.50-22) include chicken tandoori with yogurt and *basmati* rice. Salads and wok dishes €6-12. Open M-Sa noon-2am, Su 6pm-2am. ❸

👁 🏛 SIGHTS AND MUSEUMS

The **Ruta del Modernisme** pass is the cheapest and most flexible option for those with an interest in seeing Barcelona's major sights. Passes give holders a 25-30% discount on attractions including Palau de la Música Catalana, the Museu de Zoología, and tours of Hospital de la Santa Creu i Sant Pau. Purchase passes at the Pl. Catalunya tourist office or at the Modernisme Centre at Hospital Santa Creu i Sant Pau, C. Sant Antoni Maria Claret 167. (☎933 17 76 52; www.ruta-delmodernisme.com. Passes free with the purchase of a €12 guidebook, €5 per additional adult, adult accompanying someone under 18 free.)

LAS RAMBLAS

This pedestrian-only strip (roughly 1km long) is a cornucopia of street performers, fortune-tellers, human statues, pet and flower stands, and artists. The wide, tree-lined street, known in Catalan as Les Rambles, is actually six *ramblas* (promenades) that form one boulevard from the Pl. de Catalunya. According to legend, visitors who sample the water from the **Font de Canaletes** at the top of Las Ramblas will return to Barcelona. Pass the **Mirador de Colom** on your way out to Rambla del Mar for a beautiful view of the Mediterranean.

◪**GRAN TEATRE DEL LICEU.** After burning down for the second time in 1994, the Liceu was rebuilt and expanded; a tour of the building includes not just the original 1847 Sala de Espejos (Hall of Mirrors), but also the 1999 Foyer (a curvaceous bar/lecture hall/small theater). The five-level, 2292-seat theater is considered one of Europe's top stages, adorned with palatial ornamentation, gold facades, and sculptures. *(La Rambla, 51-59, by C. Sant Pau. ⓂLiceu, L3. ☎934 85 99 00; www.liceubarcelona.com. Box office open M-F 10am-1pm and 2-6pm or by ServiCaixa. Short 20min. non-guided visits daily 11:30am-1pm every 30min, €4. 1hr. tours 10am; €8.70, seniors and under 26 €6.70.)*

◪**LA BOQUERIA (MERCAT DE SANT JOSEP).** Just the place to pick up that hard-to-find animal part you've been looking for, La Boqueria is a traditional Catalan *mercat*—and the largest outdoor market in Spain—located in a giant, all-steel *Modernista* structure. Specialized vendors sell produce, fish, bread, wine, cheese, nuts, sweets and meat from a seemingly infinite number of independent stands. *(La Rambla, 89. ⓂLiceu. Open M-Sa 8am-8pm.)*

BARRI GÒTIC

◪**MUSEU D'HISTÒRIA DE LA CIUTAT.** Buried some 20m below a seemingly innocuous old plaza lies one of the two components to the Museu d'Història de la Ciutat: the subterranean excavations of the Roman city of Barcino. This 4000-square-meter **archaeological exhibit** displays incredibly well-preserved 1st- to 6th-century ruins. Built on top of those 4th-century walls, the second part, **Palau Reial Major,** served as the residence of the Catalan-Aragonese monarchs. When restoration on the building began, the Gothic **Saló de Tinell** (Throne Room) was discovered; it is supposedly the place where Fernando and Isabel received Columbus after his journey to America. *(Pl. del Rei. ⓂJaume I. ☎932 56 21 00; www.museuhistoria.bcn.cat. Wheelchair-accessible. Open Apr.-*

Sept. Tu-Sa 10am-8pm, Su 10am-3pm; Oct.-Mar. Tu-Sa 10am-2pm and 4-7pm, Su 10am-3pm. Free multilingual audio guides. Pamphlets available in English. Museum €6, students €4. Exhibition €1.80/1.10. Museum and exhibition €6.80/5.10. Under 16 free.)

■**ESGLÉSIA CATEDRAL DE LA SANTA CREU.** This cathedral is one of Barcelona's most recognizable monuments. The altar holds a cross designed by Frederic Marès in 1976, and the Crypt of Santa Eulàlia lies beneath. The museum in La Sala Capitular holds Bartolomé Bermejo's *Pietà*. *(Ⓜ Jaume I, L4. In Pl. Seu, up C. Bisbe from Pl. St. Jaume. Cathedral open daily 8:30am-12:30pm, 1-5pm, and 5:15-7:30pm. Museum open daily 10am-12:30pm, 1-5pm, and 5:15-7pm. Elevator to the roof open M-Sa 10am-12:30pm and 1-6pm. Services Su at noon and 6:30pm. From 1-5pm €5 (includes cathedral, elevator, and museum), otherwise free. Museum €2. Elevator €2.50.)*

LA RIBERA

■**PALAU DE LA MÚSICA CATALANA.** In 1891, the Orfeó Català Choir Society commissioned *Modernista* master Luis Domènech i Montaner to design this must-see concert venue. By day, the music hall is illuminated by tall stained-glass windows and an ornate stained-glass skylight, which gleam again after dark by electric light. Sculptures of wild horses and busts of the seven muses are on the walls flanking the stage. The **Sala de Luis Millet** has an up close view of the intricate *trencadis* pillars. *(C. del Palau de la Música, 4-6. ☎ 902 44 28 82; www.palaumusica. org. Ⓜ Jaume I, Urinaona. Mandatory 50min. tours in English every hr. Open daily Sept.-July 10am-3:30pm, Semana Santa and Aug. 10am-6pm. €12, students and seniors €11. Check website for scheduled performances. Concert tickets €8-175. Box office open 9am-9pm. MC/V.)*

■**MUSEU PICASSO.** Barcelona's most visited museum traces Picasso's artistic development with the world's most comprehensive collection of work from his formative Barcelona period. Picasso donated 1700 of the museum's 3600 works. *(C. de Montcada, 15-23. Ⓜ Jaume I, L4. From the metro, head down C. de la Princesa and turn right on C. de Montcada. ☎ 932 56 30 00; www.museupicasso.bcn.es. Open Tu-Su 10am-8pm. Last entry 30min. before closing. Wheelchair-accessible. €9, students and seniors €6, under 16 free. Special exhibits €5.80. Free Su after 3pm. 1st Su of each month free.)*

PARC DE LA CIUTADELLA. Host of the 1888 World's Fair, the park harbors several museums, well-labeled horticulture, the Cascada fountains, a pond, and a zoo. The sprawling lawns are filled with strolling families, students smoking and playing instruments, and affectionate couples. Buildings of note include Domènech i Montaner's *Modernista* **Castell dels Tres Dracs** (now the Museu de Zoología) and Josep Amergós's **Hivernacle**. The **Parc Zoològic** is home to several threatened and endangered species, including the Iberian wolf and the Sumatran tiger. *(Ⓜ Ciutadella or Marina. Park open daily 8am-11pm)*

EL RAVAL

MUSEU D'ART CONTEMPORANI (MACBA). The MACBA has received worldwide acclaim for its focus on post-avant-garde art and contemporary works. The main attractions are the highly innovative rotating exhibits and the *Nits de MACBA*, when the museum stays open until midnight for concerts and guided tours—tickets are cheap. *(Pl. Des Àngels, 1. M: Catalunya ☎ 934 12 08 10; www.macba.es. Open M and W-F 11am-8pm, Sa 10am-8pm, Su 10am-3pm. Tours in Catalan and English M and Th 6pm; Catalan and Spanish W and F 6pm, Su noon and 6pm. €7.50, students €6, under 14 free; temporary exhibitions €4. From mid-May to Sept. restaurant and bar service on 1st-fl. terrace. Restaurant and bar phone ☎ 672 20 73 89.)*

PALAU GÜELL. Gaudí's 1886 Palau Güell, the Modernist residence built for patron Eusebi Güell, has one of Barcelona's most spectacular interiors. Güell spared no expense on this house, considered to be the first example of Gaudí's revolutionary style. At the time of writing the Palau is closed for renovations until an undisclosed date. *(C. Nou de La Rambla, 3-5. M: Liceu. ☎ 933 17 39 74; www. palauguell.cat. Partial entrance only. Open Tu-Sa 10am-2:30pm. Free.)*

L'EIXAMPLE

■**LA SAGRADA FAMÍLIA.** Antoni Gaudí's masterpiece is far from finished, which makes La Sagrada Família the world's most visited construction site. Only 8 of the 18 planned towers have been completed and the church still lacks an "interior," yet millions of people make the touristic pilgrimage to witness its work-in-progress majesty. Of the three facades, only the **Nativity Facade** was finished under Gaudí. A new team of architects led by Jordi Bonet hopes to lay the last stone by 2026 (the 100th anniversary of Gaudí's death). The affiliated museum displays plans and computer models of the fully realized structure. *(C. Mallorca, 401. ☎ 932 08 04 14; www.sagradafamilia.org. Ⓜ Sagrada Família. Open daily Apr.-Sept. 9am-8pm, Oct.-Mar. 9am-6pm. Last elevator to the tower 15min. before close. Guided tours in English (€3) May-Oct. at 11am, 1, 3, 5pm; Nov.-Apr. at 11am and 1pm. €11, students €9, under 10 free. Elevator €2.50. Combined ticket with Casa-Museu Gaudí €13, students €11.)*

■**LA MANZANA DE LA DISCÒRDIA.** A short walk from Pl. de Catalunya, the odd-numbered side of Pg. de Gràcia between C. Aragó and C. Consell de Cent has been leaving passersby scratching their heads for a century. The Spanish nickname, which translates to the "block of discord," comes from the stylistic clashing of its three most extravagant buildings. Sprouting flowers, stained glass, and legendary doorway sculptures adorn **Casa Lleó i Morera,** #35, by Domènech i Montaner, on the far left corner of the block (admire from the outside; entrance is not permitted). Two buildings down, Puig i Cadafalch's geometric, Moorish-influenced facade makes **Casa Amatller,** #41, perhaps the most beautiful building on the block (guided tour with chocolate tasting M-F 4 per day 11am-6pm, Su at noon; €8). The real discord comes next door at **Casa Batlló,** #43, popularly believed to represent Catalonia's patron Sant Jordi (St. Jordi) slaying a dragon. The chimney plays the lance, the scaly roof is the dragon's back, and the bony balconies are the remains of his victims. The house was built using shapes from nature—the balconies ripple like the ocean. *(Pg. de Gràcia, 43. ☎ 932 16 03 06; www.casabatllo.cat. Open daily 9am-8pm. €17, students, BCN card €13. Cash only. Call for group discounts for more than 20 people. Free multilingual audio tour.)*

CASA MILÀ (LA PEDRERA). From the outside, this Gaudí creation looks like the sea—the undulating walls seem like waves and the iron balconies are reminiscent of seaweed. Chimneys resembling armored soldiers have views of every corner of Barcelona. The entrance fee entitles visitors to tour one well-equipped apartment, the roof, and the winding brick attic, now functioning as the **Espai Gaudí,** a multimedia presentation of Gaudí's life and works. The summer concert series transforms the roof into a jazz cabaret on weekend nights. *(Pg. de Gràcia, 92. ☎ 902 40 09 73; www.lapedreraeducacio.org. Open daily Mar.-Oct. 9am-8pm, last admission 7:30pm; Nov.-Feb. 9am-6:30pm. €9.50, students and seniors €5.50. Free audio tour. Concerts last weekend of June-July F-Sa 9pm-midnight. €12, glass of cava included.)*

MONTJUÏC

■**FUNDACIÓ MIRÓ.** An large collection of sculptures, drawings, and paintings from Miró's career, ranging from sketches to wall-sized canvases, engages visitors with the work of this Barcelona-born artist. His best-known pieces here include *El carnival de Arlequín, La masia,* and *L'or de l'Azuz.* The gallery also displays experimental work by young artists and pieces by Alexander Calder.

(Take the funicular from M: Paral·lel or catch the Park Montjuïc bus from Pl. Espanya. ☎ *934 43 94 70; www.fundaciomiro-bcn.org. Library open M and Sa 10am-2pm, Tu-F 10am-2pm and 3-6pm. Fundació open July-Sept. Tu-W and F-Sa 10am-8pm, Th 10am-9:30pm, Su and holidays 10am-2:30pm; Oct.-June Tu-W and F-Sa 10am-7pm, Th 10am-9:30pm, Su and holidays 10am-2:30pm. Last entry 15min. before closing. €8, students and seniors €6, under 13 €4. Temporary exhibitions €4/3/4. Headphones €4. Concert tickets €10.)*

◼ **MUSEU NACIONAL D'ART DE CATALUNYA (PALAU NACIONAL).** Designed by Enric Català and Pedro Cendoya for the 1929 International Exposition, the magnificent Palau Nacional has housed the Museu Nacional d'Art de Catalunya (MNAC) since 1934. Its main hall is a public event space, while the wings are home to the world's finest collection of Catalan Romanesque art and a wide variety of Gothic pieces. Highlights include Miró's *Gorg Bleu* stained glass, a gallery of Romanesque cathedral apses, and works by Joaquím Mir, a modernist painter known for color-saturated landscapes. The museum recently acquired the entire holdings of the Museu d'Art Modern, formerly located in the Parc de la Ciutadella, and is now the principal art museum of Catalonia. The **Fonts Luminoses** and the central **Font Màgica** are lit up by weekend laser shows. *(From M: Espanya, walk up Av. Reina María Cristina, away from the twin brick towers, and take the escalators to the top.* ☎ *936 22 03 76; www.mnac.es. Open Tu-Sa 10am-7pm, Su and holidays 10am-2:30pm. Wheelchair-accessible. €8.50, students and seniors €6, under 14 free. First Su of the month free. Audio tour included.)*

ZONA ALTA

◼ **PARC GÜELL.** This fantastical park was designed entirely by Gaudí but, in typical Gaudí fashion, was not completed until after his death. Gaudí intended Parc Güell to be a garden city, and its buildings and ceramic-mosaic stairways were designed to house the city's elite. However, only one house, now know as the **Casa-Museu Gaudí,** was built. Two staircases flank the park, leading to a towering *Modernista* pavilion originally designed as an open-air market but is now only occasionally used as a stage by street musicians. The longest park bench in the world, a multicolored serpentine wonder made of tile shards, decorates the top of the pavilion. *(Bus #24 from Pl. Catalunya stops at the upper entrance. Info center* ☎ *93 284 62 00. Park and info center open daily 9am-dusk. Free.)*

MUSEU DEL FÚTBOL CLUB BARCELONA. A close second to the Picasso Museum as Barcelona's most-visited museum, the FCB merits all the attention it gets from football fanatics. Fans will appreciate the storied history of the team. The high point is entering the stadium and taking in the 100,000-seat **Camp Nou.** *(Next to the stadium.* ☎ *93 496 3608. M: Collblanc. Enter through access gate 7 or 9. Open M-Sa 10am-6:15pm, Su and holidays 10am-2pm. €8.50, students and 13 or under €7. Museum and Camp Nou tour €13/10.40. Free parking.)*

🎭 ENTERTAINMENT

For tips on entertainment, nightlife, and food, pick up the *Guía del Ocio* (www.guiadelociobcn.es; €1) at any newsstand. The best shopping in the city is in the **Barri Gòtic,** but if you feel like dropping some extra cash, check out the posh **Passeig de Gràcia** in l'Eixample. Grab face paint to join fans of F.C. Barcelona (Barça) at the Camp Nou stadium for **fútbol.** (Box office C. Arístedes Maillol 12-18. ☎ 90 218 99 00. Tickets €30-60.) **Barceloneta** and **Poble Nou** feature specific sand for topless tanning and many places to rent sailboats and water-sports equipment. Head up to Montjuïc to take advantage of the **Olympic Facilities,** which are now open for public use, including **Piscines**

Bernat Picornell, a gorgeous pool complex. (Av. de l'Estadi 30-40. ☎93 423 4041. Open M-F 6:45am-midnight, Sa 7am-9pm, Su 6am-4pm.)

 MOONLIGHT MOVIES AT MONTJUIC. For a movie under the stars, head up the hill to Sala Montjuïc, an annual 5-week film series in the moat of Castell de Montjuïc. Bring a picnic and listen to live music before the show.

FESTIVALS

Check sight and museum hours during festival times, as well as during the Christmas season and *Semana Santa* (Holy Week). The **Festa de Sant Jordi** (St. George; Apr. 23, 2009) celebrates Catalunya's patron saint with a feast. Men give women roses, and women give men books. In the last two weeks of August, city folk jam at Gràcia's **Festa Mayor;** lights blaze in *plaças* and music plays all night. The three-day **Sónar** music festival comes to town in mid-June, attracting renowned DJs and electronica enthusiasts from all over the world. Other major music festivals include **Summercase** (indie and pop) and **Jazzaldia**. Check www.mondosonoro.com or pick up the *Mondo Sonoro* festival guide for more info. In July and August, the **Grec Festival** hosts dance performances, concerts, and film screenings. The **Festa Nacional de Catalunya** (Sept. 11) brings traditional costumes and dancing. **Festa de Sant Joan** takes place the night of June 23; ceaseless fireworks will prevent any attempts to sleep. The largest celebration in Barcelona is the **Festa de Mercè,** the weeks before and after September 24 when *barceloneses* revel with fireworks, *sardána* dancing, and concerts.

NIGHTLIFE

Barcelona's wild, varied nightlife treads the line between slick and kitschy. In many ways, the city is clubbing heaven—things don't get going until late (don't bother showing up at a club before 1am), and they continue until dawn. Yet for every full-blown dance club, there are 100 more relaxed bars, from Irish pubs to absinthe dens. Check the *Guía del Ocio* (www.guiadelocio.com) for the address of that place your hip *Barcelonese* friend just told you about.

 DON'T FEAR FLYERS. Many clubs hand out flyers, particularly in La Ribera. They are far from a tourist trap—travelers can save lots of money with free admission and drink passes.

☒ **Zeltas,** C. Casanova, 75 (☎934 50 84 69; www.zeltas.net). Complete with shimmering cloth hangings, feather boas, and low white couches, this exotic bar welcomes a classy clientele—usually gay—to sip a drink and enjoy the ambience. Wine €3. Beer €4.50. Mixed drinks €7. Open daily 10:30pm-3am. MC/V.

☒ **Tinta Roja,** C. Creus dels Molers, 17 (☎934 43 32 43; www.tintaroja.net). Located just off Av. Paral·lel in a newly pedestrian section of Poble Sec. Red tinted lights, red velvet chairs. The dance floor gets serious, especially during tango classes W 9-10:30pm, (call for details). Specialties include tropical mixed drinks (€7) and Argentine *yerba-mate* (€4.80) Open Th 9:30pm-2:30am, F-Sa 9:30pm-3am. Cash only.

☒ **Vinil,** C. Matilde, 2 (☎669 17 79 45; www.vinilus.blogspot.com). This bar's dim orange lighting, mismatched pillows, mellow background music, and screened daily movies make you never want to leave. Beer and wine €2.70. Mojitos and *caipirinhas* (the only mixed drinks served) €6. Open in summer M-Th 8pm-2am, F-Sa 8pm-3am; in winter M-Th and Su 8pm-2am, F-Sa 8pm-3am.

El Bosq de les Fades, Pg. de la Banca, 16 (☎933 17 26 49), near the Wax Museum. ⓂDrassanes. This spooky cafe-bar used to be the horror section of the Wax Museum and retains a fairytale look, with gnarled trees, gourd-lanterns, and a wishing well. Fills up early, so it's a good place to start the night. Beer €3. *Cava* €3. Tequila Sunrise €7.20. Open M-Th and Su 10am-1am, F-Sa 10am-2am. MC/V.

Barcelona Pipa Club, Pl. Reial, 3 (☎933 02 47 32; www.bpipaclub.com). ⓂLiceu, L3. Unmarked—look for the small plaque on the door to the left of Glaciar Bar, on your left as you enter the square from Las Ramblas, and ring the doorbell. Don't let the pseudo-secrecy deter you. A welcoming place for late-night drinks. The decor is 100% Sherlock Holmes, the music mostly jazz and fusion, and the people are a mix of local bartenders, artists, and tourists in the know. An impressive collection of pipes from around the world is housed in a side-room along with a small pool table (€1.50 a game). Live music (often jazz) F 11pm. Mixed drinks €7, beer €4. Open daily 11pm-4:30am. Cash only.

El Copetín, Pg. del Born, 19 (☎607 20 21 76). ⓂJaume I. Cuban rhythms invade this casual, dimly lit nightspot. Copetín fills up before some places open, making it a good place to start the night. When the bartenders break out the maracas and cowbell, be ready to get down. Mojitos €7. Open M-Th and Su 6pm-2:30am, F-Sa 6pm-3am. Cash only.

Ribborn, C. Antic de Sant Joan, 3 (☎933 10 71 48; www.ribborn.com). ⓂBarceloneta. Deep crimson light and an eclectic music selection, from jazz to funk to soul. Beer €2.50. Mixed drinks €7. Jazz piano W 9pm. Happy hour Tu-Sa 7-10pm. Open Tu-Su 7pm-3am. MC/V.

Les Gents que J'aime, C. València, 286, downstairs (☎932 15 68 79). ⓂPg. de Gràcia. You'll feel like Serge Gainsbourg at his hippest lounging in this dark, subterranean bar's velvet furniture. Background soul, funk, and jazz soothe patrons enjoying drinks like Les Gents (kiwi, lime, and pineapple juice; €7). Shotgun the chairs tucked beneath the staircase. Beer €4. Mixed drinks €6-7. Open daily 7pm-2:30am. AmEx/MC/V.

La Terrazza, Avda. Marquès de Comillas, s/n (☎932 72 49 80). On weekend summer nights, Poble Espanyol succumbs to the irrepressible revelry of La Terrazza, an outdoor dance club to one side of the village where you can sway along to techno with the masses. Get here after 2am and you may find yourself in a line of up to 100. Beer €6. Mixed drinks €9-10, although bars scattered in Poble Espanyol stay open late and serve cheaper alcohol. Cover €18, gets you into the village and club, plus 1 drink. Open June-Oct. Th midnight-5am, F-Sa midnight-6am. MC/V.

Absenta, C. Sant Carles, 36. ⓂBarceloneta. Walking down Pg. Joan de Borbó and take a left on C. Sant Carles. A green interior with vintage posters suits the star beverage at this absinthe bar, although most choose to sit out on the terrace during summer. Beer €2.50. Wine €2.80. Absinthe €4-7. Open M, W-Th, and Su 11am-2am, Tu 6pm-2am, F-Sa 11am-3am. Cash only.

Ke?, C. del Beluart, 54. (☎932 24 15 88) ⓂBarceloneta. Walking down Pg. Joan de Borbó, take a left on C. Sant Carles and another left at the plaza onto C. del Beluart. Decor meanders between tropical surf, the American west, and Popeye the Sailor. Hosts an equally eclectic crowd, from rowdy beachgoers to locals using the Wi-Fi on the back sofa over a beer (€2). Open daily 11:30am-2:30am. Cash only.

Cafe del Sol, Pl. del Sol, 16 (☎932 37 14 48). ⓂFontana. Walk down C. Gran de Gràcia, make a left on C. Ros de Olano and then a right on C. Cano/C.Leopoldo Alas. Locals pack the 8 tapas bars around Pl. del Sol every night and spill out into the plaza. This mainstay offers perfect tostadas (€3-5) and tapas (€1.70-5) as well as beer (€2-3), wine, and mixed drinks (€5-6). Come for lunch and take your tapas out into the plaza. Open M-Th and Su noon-2:30am, F and Sa noon-3am.

NAVARRA

From the unfathomable mayhem of Pamplona and the Running of the Bulls to the many hiking trails that wind up the peaks of the Pyrenees, there is seldom a dull moment in Navarra. Bordered by Basque Country and Aragón, the region is a mix of overlapping cultures and traditions.

PAMPLONA (IRUÑA)   ☎948

El encierro, la Fiesta de San Fermín, the Running of the Bulls, utter debauchery: call it what you will, the outrageous festival of the city's patron saint is the principal cause of the international notoriety Pamplona (pop. 200,000) enjoys. Since the city's immortalization in Ernest Hemingway's *The Sun Also Rises,* hordes of travelers have flocked to Pamplona for one week each July to witness the daily *corridas* and ensuing chaos. The city's monuments, museums, and parks merit exploration as well.

NOT JUST A LOAD OF BULL. Although Pamplona is generally safe, crime skyrockets during San Fermín. Beware of assaults and muggings and do not walk alone at night during the festival.

🖪🔁 TRANSPORTATION AND PRACTICAL INFORMATION. Trains (☎902 24 02 02) run from Estación RENFE. To travel the 2km take the #9 bus from the Po. Sarasate to the station, (20 minutes, €1, buses every 15 min., Av. de San Jorge, to Barcelona (6-8hr., 3 per day, from €36), Madrid (3hr., 4 per day, €52), and San Sebastián (1hr., 5 per day, €19). **Buses** leave from the bus station by the Ciudadela on C. Yangüas y Miranda for Barcelona (6-8hr., 4 per day, €26), Bilbao (2hr., 5-6 per day, €14), and Madrid (5hr., 6-10 per day, €28). From Pl. del Castillo, take C. San Nicolás, turn right on C. San Miguel, and walk through Pl. San Francisco to reach the **tourist office,** C. Hilarión Eslava. (☎948 42 04 20; www.turismo.navarra.es. Open during *San Fermín* daily 8am-8pm; July-Aug. M-Sa 9am-8pm, Su 10am-2pm; Sept.-June M-Sa 10am-2pm and 4-7pm, Su 10am-2pm.) **Luggage storage** is at the Escuelas de San Francisco in Pl. San Francisco during *San Fermín.* (€3.40 per day. Open 24hr. from July 4 at 8am to July 16 at 2pm.) The **biblioteca** has free Internet and Wi-Fi. (Open Sept.-June M-F 8:30am-8:45pm, Sa 8:30am-1:45pm, July-Aug. M-F 8:30am-2:45pm.) **Postal Code:** 31001.

🖪🔁 ACCOMMODATIONS AND FOOD. Smart San Ferministas book their rooms up to a year ahead; without a reservation, it's nearly impossible to find one. Expect to pay rates up to four times the normal price. Check the tourist office for a list of official accommodations with openings or the newspaper *Diario de Navarra* for *casas particulares* (private homes that rent rooms). Many roomless backpackers are forced to fluff up their sweatshirts and sleep rough. Stay in large groups, and if you can't store your backpack, sleep on top of it. Budget accommodations line **Calle San Gregorio** and **Calle San Nicolás** off Pl. del Castillo. Deep within the *casco antiguo* (Old Town), **Pensión Eslava ❶,** C. Hilarión Eslava 13, 2nd fl., is quieter and less crowded than other *pensiones.* Older rooms have a balcony and shared bath. (☎948 22 15 58. Singles €15; doubles €20-30, during San Fermín €100. Cash only.) Small **Horno de Aralar ❸,** C. San Nicolás 12, above the restaurant, has five spotless, bright rooms with bath and TV. (☎948 22 11 16. Singles €40; doubles €50; during San Fermín all rooms €200-300. MC/V.) Look for hearty *menús* at the cafe-bars above **Plaza de San**

Francisco and around **Paseo de Ronda.** Thoroughfares **Calle Navarrería** and **Paseo de Sarasate** are home to good *bocadillo* bars. **Café-Bar Iruña ❸**, Pl. del Castillo, the former casino made famous in Hemingway's *The Sun Also Rises*, is notable for its storied past and elegant interior. The *menú* (€13) is required if eating at a table, but the restaurant serves drinks and sandwiches at the bar. (☎948 22 20 64. Open M-Th 8am-11pm, F 8am-2am, Sa 9am-2am, Su 9am-11pm. MC/V.)

🔲🔳 **SIGHTS AND NIGHTLIFE.** Pamplona's rich architectural legacy is reason enough to visit during the 51 other weeks of the year. The restored 14th-century Gothic **Catedral de Santa María**, at the end of C. Navarrería is one of only four cathedrals of its kind in Europe. (☎948 22 29 90. Open M-F 10am-2pm and 4-7pm, Sa 10am-2pm. July 15-Sept. 15 M-F 10am-7pm, Sa 10am-2:30 pm. €4.40.) The walls of the pentagonal 🔳**Ciudadela** enclose free art exhibits, various summer concerts, and an amazing San Fermín fireworks display. Follow Po. de Sarasate to its end and go right on C. Navas de Tolosa, then take the next left onto C. Chinchilla and follow it to its end. (☎948 22 82 37. Open M-Sa 7:30am-9:30pm, Su 9am-9:30pm. Closed for San Fermín. Free.)

Central **Plaza del Castillo**, with outdoor seating galore, is the heart of Pamplona's social scene. A young crowd parties in the *casco antiguo*, particularly along the bar-studded **Calle San Nicolás, Calle Jarauta,** and **Calle San Gregorio.** The small plaza **Travesía de Bayona,** 600m past the Ciudela (follow Av. del Ejército as it turns into Av. de Bayona; the Travesía is just before Mo. de la Oliva branches off), has bars and *discotecas.* **Blue Shadow** (☎948 27 51 09) and **Tandem** (☎948 26 92 85), Tr. de Bayona 3 and 4, have good dancing and big crowds. (Beer €3.50. Mixed drinks €6. Both open Th-Sa 10pm-4am.)

⬛TIP

RUNNING SCARED. So, you're going to run, and nobody's going to stop you. But because nobody—except the angry, angry bulls—wants to see you get seriously injured, here are a few words of *San Fermín* wisdom:

1. Research the *encierro* before you run; the tourist office has a pamphlet that outlines the route and offers tips for the inexperienced. Running the entire 850m course is highly inadvisable; it would mean 2-8min. of evading 6 bulls moving at 24kph (15mph). Instead, pick a 50m stretch.

2. Don't stay up all night drinking and carousing. Experienced runners get lots of sleep the night before and arrive at the course around 6:30am.

3. Take a fashion tip from the locals: wear the traditional white-and-red outfit with closed-toe shoes. Ditch the baggy clothes, backpacks, and cameras.

4. Give up on getting near the bulls and concentrate on getting to the bullring in one piece. Though some whack the bulls with rolled newspapers, runners should never distract or touch the animals.

5. Never stop in doorways, alleys, or corners; you can be trapped and killed.

6. Run in a straight line; if you cut someone off, they can easily fall.

7. Be particularly wary of isolated bulls—they seek company in the crowds. In 2007, 13 runners were seriously injured by an isolated bull.

8. If you fall, stay down. Curl up into a fetal position, lock your hands behind your head, and do not get up until the clatter of hooves has passed.

🎆 **FIESTA DE SAN FERMÍN (JULY 4-15, 2009).** Visitors overcrowd the city as it delivers an eight-day frenzy of bullfights, concerts, dancing, fireworks, parades, parties, and wine in what is perhaps Europe's premier party. *Pamploneses,* clad in white with red sashes and bandanas, throw themselves into the merrymaking, displaying obscene levels of both physical stamina and alcohol tolerance. *El encierro*, or "The Running of the Bulls," is the highlight of *San Fermin*; the first *encierro* takes place on July 5 at 8am and is repeated at 8am every day for the next seven days. Hundreds of bleary-eyed, hungover, hyper-adrenalized runners flee from large bulls as bystanders cheer from balconies, barricades, doorways, and windows. Both the bulls and the mob are dangerous; terrified runners react without concern for those around them. To participate in the bullring excitement without the risk of the *encierro*, onlookers should arrive at 6:45am. To watch a **bullfight,** wait in the line that forms at the bullring around 7:30pm. As one fight ends, the next day's tickets go on sale. (Tickets from €10; check www.feriadeltoro.com for details.) Tickets are incredibly hard to get at face value, as over 90% belong to season holders. Once the running ends, insanity spills into the streets and explodes at night with singing, dancing in alleyways, parades, and a no-holds-barred party in **Plaza del Castillo.**

BASQUE COUNTRY (PAÍS VASCO)

The varied landscape of Spain's Basque Country combines energetic cities, lush hills, industrial wastelands, and fishing villages. Many believe that the strongly nationalistic Basques are the native people of Iberia, as their culture and language cannot be traced to any known source.

BILBAO (BILBO)   ☎944

The once gritty, industrial Bilbao (pop. 354,000) has risen to international cultural prominence since the creation of the shining **Guggenheim Museum.** However, this city, with its expansive parks, efficient transport, and grand architecture of all kinds, has plenty to offer beyond its oddly-shaped claim to fame.

▐ TRANSPORTATION. To reach the **airport** (**BIO;** ☎944 86 96 64), 25km from Bilbao, take the Bizkai bus (☎902 22 22 65) marked *Aeropuerto* from the Termibús terminal or Pl. Moyúa (line A-3247; 25min., 2 per hr., €1.10). RENFE **trains** (☎902 24 02 02) leave from **Estación de Abando,** Pl. Circular 2, for Barcelona (9-10hr., 2 per day, €39-51), Madrid (5-6hr., 2 per day, €40-45), and Salamanca (5hr., 2pm, €27). Trains run between Bilboa's Estación de Atxuri and San Sebastián (2hr., 17-18 per day). FEVE trains run from **Estación de Santander,** C. Bailén, 2 (☎944 25 06 15; www.feve.es) to: León (7hr., 2:30pm, €20.55) and Santander (3hr.; 8am, 1, 7:30pm; €7.25). Most **bus** companies leave from **Termibús,** C. Gurtubay 1 (☎944 39 52 05; M: San Mamés), for: Barcelona (7hr., 4 per day, €41); Madrid (4-5hr., 10-18 per day, €26); Pamplona (2hr., 4-6 per day, €13); San Sebastián (1hr., 1-2 per hr., €8.70). Within Bilbao, a **Creditrans pass** (purchased in denominations of €5, €10, or €15) allows access to Metro, BizkaiBus, Bilbobús, and EuskoTran, the new tram-train line, at a discounted rate.

▐▐ ORIENTATION AND PRACTICAL INFORMATION. The **Río de Bilbao** runs through the city, separating the historic *casco viejo* from the newer parts of town. The train stations are directly across the river to the west of the *casco viejo*. The city's major thoroughfare, **Gran Vía de Don Diego López de Haro,** connects three of Bilbao's main plazas. Heading east from Pl. de Sagrado Corazón, Gran Vía continues through the central **Pl. Moyúa** and ends at **Pl. Circular.** Past Pl. Circular, cross the Río de Bilbao on Puente del Arenal to arrive in **Plaza de Arriaga,** the entrance to the *casco viejo* and **Plaza Nueva.** The **tourist office** is at Pl. Ensanche 11. (☎944 79 57 60; www.bilbao.net/bilbaoturismo. Open M-F 9am-2pm, 4-7:30pm.), branches at Teatro Arriaga and near the Guggenheim. Free **Internet** at **Biblioteca Municipal,** C. Bidebarrieta, 4 (☎944 15 09 15; Open Sept.

16-May 31 M 2:30-8pm, Tu-F 8:30am-8:30pm, Sa 10am-1pm; July M-F 8:30am-7:30pm; Aug. M-F 8:30am-1:45pm; June Tu-F 8:30am-7:30pm, Sa 10am-2pm).

ACCOMMODATIONS AND FOOD. Plaza Arriaga and Calle Arenal have many budget accommodations, while upscale hotels are in the new city off Gran Vía. Rates climb during Semana Grande. **Pensión Méndez ❷**, C. Sta. María 13, 4th fl., provides cheery rooms with spacious balconies. (☎944 16 03 64. Singles €25; doubles €35; triples €50. MC/V.) **Hostal Méndez ❸**, on the first floor of the same building, is even more comfortable; rooms all have large windows, full bath, and TV. (Singles €38-40; doubles €50-55; triples €65-70. MC/V.) Restaurants and bars in the *casco viejo* offer a wide selection of local dishes, *pintxos* *(tapas)*, and *bocadillos*. The new city has even more variety. **Restaurante Peruano Ají Colorado ❸**, C. Barrenkale 5, specializes in traditional Andean *ceviche* (marinated raw fish; €10), and also serves Peruvian mountain dishes. (☎944 15 22 09. M-F lunch *menú* €12. Open M-Sa 1:30-4pm and 9-11pm, Su 1:30-4pm. MC/V.) **Restaurante Vegetariano Garibolo ❸**, C. Fernandez del Campo, 7, serves a vegetarian *menú* (€12) that lines locals up at lunchtime. (☎942 22 32 55; M-F 1-4pm, F-Sa 1-4pm and 9-11pm.)

SIGHTS AND NIGHTLIFE. Frank Gehry's **Museo Guggenheim Bilbao**, Av. Abandoibarra 2, is awe-inspiring. Lauded in the international press with every superlative imaginable, it has catapulted Bilbao straight into cultural stardom. The museum hosts rotating exhibits drawn from the Guggenheim Foundation's often eccentric collection; don't be surprised if you are asked to take your shoes off, lie on the floor, or even sing throughout your visit. (☎944 35 90 80; www.guggenheim-bilbao.es. Wheelchair-accessible. Admission includes English-language audioguide, as well as guided tours Tu-Su 11am, 12:30, 4:30, 6:30pm; sign up 30min. before tour at the info desk. Open July-Aug. daily 10am-8pm; Sept.-June Tu-Su 10am-8pm. €13, students €7.50, under 12 free.) The **Museo de Bellas Artes**, Pl. del Museo 2, has an impressive collection of 12th- to 20th-century art, including excellent 15th- to 17th-century Flemish paintings, canvases by Basque artists, and works by Mary Cassatt, El Greco, Gauguin, Goya, and Velázquez. Take C. Elcano to Pl. del Museo or bus #10 from Pte. del Arenal. (☎944 39 60 60, Open Tu-Sa 10am-8pm, Su 10am-2pm. €5.50, students and seniors €4, under 12 and W free.) The best view of Bilbao's landscape is from **Monte Artxanda**, between the *casco viejo* and the Guggenheim. (Funicular 3min.; 4 per hr. M-F, June-Sept. also Sa; €0.86. Wheelchair lift €0.30.)

Mellow **Alambique**, Alda. Urquijo 37, provides elegant seating and a chance for conversation under chandeliers and photos of old Bilbao. (☎944 43 41 88. Beer €2-3. Open M-Th 8am-2am, F-Sa 8am-3am, Su 5pm-3am.) The **Cotton Club**, C. Gregorio de la Revilla 25, decorated with over 30,000 bottle caps and featuring over 100 whiskeys, draws a huge crowd on weekend nights. (☎944 10 49 51. Beer €3. Mixed drinks €6. Rum €6. Open M-Th 5pm-3:30am, F-Sa 5pm-6am, Su 6:30pm-3:30am.)

DAYTRIP FROM BILBAO: GUERNICA. On April 26, 1937, at the behest of General Franco, the Nazi "Condor Legion" dropped 29,000kg of explosives on Guernica, obliterating 70% of the city in three hours. The atrocity, which killed nearly 2000 people, is immortalized in Pablo Picasso's masterpiece, *Guernica* (p. 675). The thought-provoking **Guernica Peace Museum**, Pl. Foru 1, features a variety of multimedia exhibits. From the train station, walk two blocks up C. Adolfo Urioste and turn right on C. Artekalea. (☎946 27 02 13. Open July-Aug. Tu-Sa 10am-8pm, Su 10am-3pm; Sept.-June Tu-Sa 10am-2pm and 4-7pm, Su 10am-2pm. English-language tours noon and 5pm. €4, students and seniors €2.) **El Árbol**, a 300-year-old oak trunk encased in stone columns, marks the former political center of the País Vasco. At its side stands the current **Árbol**, its youngest descendant. **Trains** (☎902 54 32 10; www.euskotren.es) head to Bilbao (45min., 1-2 per hr., €2.25). Bizkai Bus (☎902 22 22 65) runs frequent, convenient buses between Guernica and Bilbao's Estación Abando; **buses** leave from Hdo. Amezaga in front of the Bilbao RENFE station. *(Lines A-3514 and A-3515; 45min., 2-4 per hr., €2.25.)* To reach the **tourist office**, C. Artekale 8, from the train station, walk up C. Adolfo Urioste, turn right on C. Barrenkale, go left at the alleyway, and look for the signs. *(☎946 25 58 92; www.gernika-lumo.net. Open July-Aug. M-Sa 10am-7pm, Su 10am-2pm; Sept.-June M-Sa 10am-2pm and 4-7pm, Su 10am-2pm.)*

BALEARIC ISLANDS   ☎971

While all of the Islas Baleares are famous for their beautiful beaches and land-scapes, each island has its own character. While Mallorca absorbs the bulk of package-tour invaders, Ibiza has perhaps the best nightlife in Europe.

▛ TRANSPORTATION

Flying is the easiest way to reach the islands. Students with an ISIC can often get discounts from Iberia (☎902 40 05 00; www.iberia.com), which flies to Ibiza and Palma de Mallorca from Barcelona (40min., €80) and Madrid (1hr., €50). Air Europa (☎902 40 15 01; www.air-europa.com), Spanair (☎902 92 91 91; www.spanair.com), and Vueling (☎902 33 39 33; www.vueling.com) offer bud-get flights to and between the islands (€20-50). Ferries to the islands are less popular and take longer. Trasmediterránea (☎902 45 46 45; www.trasmedi-terranea.com) departs from Barcelona's Estació Marítima Moll and Valencia's Estació Marítima for Ibiza, Mallorca, and Menorca (€69-110). Fares between the islands run €28-82. Buquebus (☎902 41 42 42) has fast catamaran service between Barcelona and Palma de Mallorca (4hr., 2 per day, €11-150).

▛ IBIZA

Nowhere on Earth are decadence, opulence, and hedonism celebrated as reli-giously as on the glamorous island of Ibiza (pop. 100,000). A hippie enclave in the 1960s, Ibiza has entered a new age of debauchery and extravagance. Disco-goers, fashion gurus, movie stars, and party-hungry backpackers arrive to immerse themselves in the island's outrageous clubs and gorgeous beaches. Only one of Ibiza's beaches, **Figueretas**, is within walking distance of **Eivissa** (Ibiza City). Most, including the raucous and somewhat boozy **Platja d'en Bossa**, are a ferry or bus ride away. The best beach near the city is ▛**Playa de ses Salinas**, where you can groove to the music of club DJs or escape to nearby **Platja des Cavallet** for some (mostly nude) peace and quiet. (Bus #11 runs to Salinas from Av. d'Isidor Macabich.) Later, crowds migrate to the bars of **Carrer de Barcelona**. The island's giant ▛**discos** are world-famous—and outrageously expensive. Be on the lookout for publicity flyers, which list the week or night's events and often double as a coupon for a discounts. The **Discobus** runs to major hot spots (leaves Eivissa from Av. d'Isidor Macabich; hourly 12:30-6:30am, €1.75). ▛**Amne-sia**, on the road to the city of San Antoni, has a phenomenal sound system and psychedelic lights. (☎971 19 80 41. Drag performances and foam parties. Cover €20-50. Open daily midnight-8am.) World-famous **Pachá**, the only *discoteca* open year-round, is on Pg. Perimitral, a 15min. walk or 2min. cab ride from the port. (☎971 31 36 00; www.pacha.com. M "Release Yourself" night with up-and-coming DJs. Cover €35-60. Open daily midnight-7:30am.) Cap off your "night" at **Space,** on Platja d'en Bossa, which gets going around 8am and doesn't wind down until 5pm. (☎971 39 67 93; www.space-ibiza.es. Cover €30-60.)

Cheap *hostales* in town are rare, especially in summer; reserve well ahead. Rooms to rent in private homes (*casa de huéspedes*; look for the letters "CH" in doorways) are a much better deal, although they still run above €30 and can be difficult to contact. **Casa de Huespedes Vara de Rey,** Pg. Vara de Rey, 7, 3rd floor (☎971 30 13 76; www.hibiza.com), has relatively inexpensive prices given its prime location. (Singles with shared bathroom, €35; doubles, €70. Open all year. Reception open M-Sa, 9am-2pm, 7pm-10pm. MC/V.) **La Bodeguita Del Medio 1,** C. St. Cruz 15, has outdoor tables ideal for consuming beer (€3) and plates of *paella, tortillas* (€6.40), and *tapas.* (☎971 39 92 90. C/C accepted.) ⚑**Croissant Show,** Mercat Vell (☎971 31 76 65), on C. Antoni Palau is a bright cafe that serves creative sandwiches (€4.50-6), quiches, salads, pastries, and *platos del dia* (€7.50). Bleary-eyed punters come for "breakfast" after a hard night of clubbing. (Open daily 6am-2am. MC/V.) For groceries, try the **Spar** supermarket, near Pl. del Parque (open M-Sa 9am-9pm). **Tourist offices** are on Pg. Vara del Rey and at the airport. (☎971 30 19 00. Open June-Nov. M-F 9am-8pm, Sa 9am-7pm; schedule in winter subject to change.)

SWEDEN
(SVERIGE)

With the design world cooing over bright, blocky Swedish furniture and college students donning knock-off designs from H&M, Scandinavia's largest nation has earned a reputation abroad for its chic, mass-marketable style. At home, Sweden's struggle to balance a market economy with its generous social welfare system stems from its belief that all citizens should have access to education and health care. This neutral nation's zest for spending money on butter instead of guns has also shored up a strong sense of national unity, from Sámi reindeer herders in the Lappland forests to bankers in bustling Stockholm.

 DISCOVER SWEDEN: SUGGESTED ITINERARY

THREE DAYS. Spend them all in the capital city of **Stockholm** (p. 723), including one sunny afternoon out on the towns and beaches of the **Skärgård Archipelago** (p. 731). Take a daytrip, too, to historic **Lake Mälaren** in between Stockholm's 75 museums.

ESSENTIALS

FACTS AND FIGURES

OFFICIAL NAME: Kingdom of Sweden.

CAPITAL: Stockholm.

MAJOR CITIES: Gothenburg, Malmö.

POPULATION: 9,045,000.

TIME ZONE: GMT +1.

LANGUAGE: Swedish.

RELIGION: Lutheran (87%).

LAND AREA: 450,000 sq. km.

INCOME TAX: As high as 60% for top wage-earners. Ouch.

WHEN TO GO

The most popular months to visit Sweden are July and August, when temperatures average 20°C (68°F) in the south and 16°C (61°F) in the north. Travelers who arrive in May and early June can take advantage of low-season prices and enjoy the spring flowers, but some attractions don't open until late June. The 24 hours of daylight known as the **midnight sun** are best experienced between early June and mid-July. In winter, keep an eye out for the **Northern Lights** and bring heavy cold-weather gear; temperatures hover around -5°C (23°F).

DOCUMENTS AND FORMALITIES

EMBASSIES AND CONSULATES. Foreign embassies to Sweden are in Stockholm (p. 726). Swedish embassies and consulates abroad include: **Australia,** 5 Turrana St., Yarralumla, Canberra, ACT, 2600 (☎2 62 70 27 00; www.swedenabroad.com/

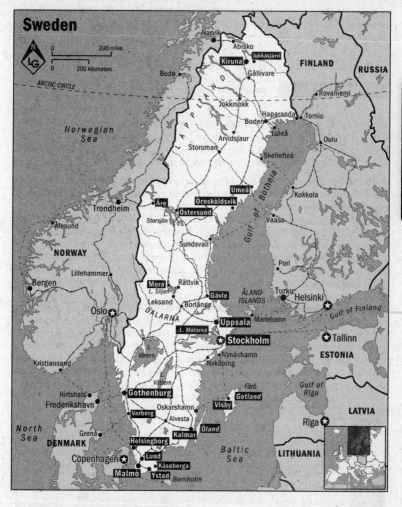

canberra); **Canada,** 377 Dalhousie St., Ottawa, ON, K1N 9N8 (☎613-244-8200; www. swedenabroad.com/ottawa); **Ireland,** 3rd Fl., Block E, Iveagh Court, Harcourt Rd., Dublin 2 (☎1 474 44 00; www.swedenabroad.com/dublin); **New Zealand,** Level 7, Molesworth House, 101 Molesworth St., Thorndon, Wellington 6011 (☎4 499 9895; www.swedenabroad.com/canberra); **UK,** 11 Montagu Pl., London, W1H 2AL (☎020 79 17 64 00; www.swedenabroad.com/london); **US,** 2900 K St., NW, Washington, D.C., 20007 (☎202-467-2600; www.swedenabroad.com/washington).

VISA AND ENTRY INFORMATION. EU citizens do not need a visa. Citizens of Australia, Canada, New Zealand, and the US do not need a visa for stays of up to 90 days, beginning upon entry into any of the countries in the EU's freedom-of-movement zone. For more info, see p. 13. For stays longer than 90 days, all non-EU citizens need visas (around US$90), available at Swedish consulates or online at www.swedenabroad.com. For US citizens, visas are usually issued a few weeks after application submission.

TOURIST SERVICES AND MONEY

EMERGENCY	Ambulance, Fire, and Police: ☎112.

TOURIST OFFICES. There are two types of tourist offices in Sweden: those marked with a yellow and blue "i" have both local and national information, while those marked with a green "i" have information only on the town they serve. The **Swedish Tourist Board** can be found online at www.visitsweden.com.

MONEY. Swedish voters rejected the adoption of the euro as the country's currency in September 2003. The Swedish unit of currency remains the **krona (kr)**, plural kronor. One krona is equal to 100 **öre,** with standard denominations of 50 öre, 1kr, 5kr, and 10kr in coins, and 20kr, 50kr, 100kr, 500kr, and 1000kr in notes. Many **ATMs** do not accept non-Swedish debit cards. **Banks** and post offices exchange currency; expect a 20-35kr commission for cash and 5-15kr for **traveler's checks. Forex** generally offers the best exchange rates and has ATMs that accept foreign debit cards. Note that many Swedish ATMs do not accept PINs longer than four digits; if your PIN is longer than this, entering the first four digits of your PIN should work. Although a service charge is usually added to the bill at restaurants, **tipping** is becoming more common and a 7-10% tip is now considered standard. For more info on money in Europe, see p. 16.

Sweden has a whopping 25% **value added tax (VAT),** a sales tax applied to most goods and services. The prices given in *Let's Go* include VAT. In the airport upon exiting the EU, non-EU citizens can claim a refund on the tax paid for goods purchased at participating stores. Some stores may have minimum expenditure requirements for refunds; make sure to ask for a refund form when you pay. For more info on qualifying for a VAT refund, see p. 19.

SWEDISH KRONOR (KR)		
AUS$1 = 5.54KR		10KR = AUS$1.81
CDN$1 = 6.00KR		10KR = CDN$1.67
EUR€1 = 9.39KR		10KR = EUR€1.07
NZ$1 = 4.54KR		10KR = NZ$2.20
UK£1 = 11.88KR		10KR = UK£0.84
US$1 = 6.37KR		10KR = US$1.57

TRANSPORTATION

BY PLANE. Most international flights land at **Arlanda Airport** in Stockholm (**ARN;** ☎797 6000; www.arlanda.com). Budget airlines, like **Ryanair,** fly out of **Västerås Airport (VST;** ☎21 805 600; www.stockholmvasteras.se) and **Skavsta Airport** (see p. 43 for more info), each located 1hr. from Stockholm. Other destinations in Sweden include **Gothenburg Airport (GSE)** and **Malmö-Sturup Airport (MMX).** The main carrier in Sweden, **SAS** (☎08 797 4000, UK 4420 8990 7159, US 800-221-2350; www.scandinavian.net), offers youth fares for those under 26 on some regional flights. For more info on traveling by plane in Europe, see p. 46.

BY TRAIN. Statens Järnväger (SJ), the state railway company, runs trains throughout southern Sweden, and offers a discount up to 30% for travelers under 26 (☎0771 75 75 75; www.sj.se/english). Seat reservations (28-55kr) are required on **InterCity** and high-speed **X2000** trains; they are included in the ticket price but not in rail passes. On other routes, check to see how full the train is; don't bother with reservations on empty trains. In northern Sweden, **Connex** runs trains from Stockholm through Umeå and Kiruna to Narvik, NOR (☎0771 26 00 00; https://bokning.connex.se/connexp/index_en.html). The 35min. trip over **Öresund Bridge** connecting Malmö to Copenhagen, DEN (70kr) is the fastest way to travel from continental Europe; reserve ahead. Timetables for all SJ and Connex trains are at www.resplus.se. **Eurail Passes** are valid on all of these trains. In the south, purple **Pågatågen** trains service local traffic between Helsingborg, Lund, Malmö, and Ystad; Eurail Passes are valid. For more info on traveling by train around Europe, see p. 46.

BY BUS. In the north, buses may be a better option than trains. **Swebus** (☎08 546 300 00; www.swebus.se) is the main carrier nationwide. **Swebus Express** (☎7712 182 18; www.swebusexpress.se) serves the region around Stockholm and Gothenburg. **Biljettservice** (p. 724), inside Stockholm's Cityterminalen, will reserve tickets for longer routes. Students and travelers under 26 get a 20% discount on express buses. Bicycles are not allowed on board.

BY FERRY. Ferries run from Stockholm (p. 724) to the Åland Islands, Gotland, Finland, and the Baltic states. Ystad sends several ferries a day to Bornholm, DEN. Ferries from Gothenburg serve Frederikshavn, DEN and Kiel, GER. Popular lines include **Tallinksilja** (☎08 20 21 40, international 358 60 01 57 00; www.tallinksilja.com/en), and the **Viking Line** (☎08 452 40 00, US 800-843-0602; www.vikingline.fi). On Tallinksilja, Eurail Pass holders ride for free or at reduced rates. On Viking ferries, a Eurail Pass plus a train ticket entitles holders to a free passenger fare. (Mention this discount when booking.) Additionally, Viking offers "early bird" discounts of 15-50% for those who book at least 30 days in advance within Finland or Sweden.

BY CAR. Sweden honors foreign drivers' licenses for up to one year for visitors over 18. Speed limits are 110kph on expressways, 50kph in densely populated areas, and 70-90kph elsewhere. Headlights must be used at all times. Swedish roads are uncrowded and in good condition, but take extra care in winter weather and beware of reindeer or elk in the road. Many gas stations are open until 10pm; after hours, look for cash-operated pumps marked *sedel automat*. For more info on car rental and driving in Europe, see p. 50.

BY BIKE AND THUMB. Bicycling is popular in Sweden. Paths are common, and both the **Sverigeleden** (National Route) and **Cykelspåret** (Bike Path) traverse the country. **Hitchhiking** is uncommon. *Let's Go* does not recommend hitchhiking.

KEEPING IN TOUCH

EMAIL AND THE INTERNET. There are a limited number of cybercafes in Stockholm and other big cities. Expect to pay about 20kr per hr. In smaller towns, Internet is available for free at most tourist offices marked with the yellow and blue "i" (p. 720), as well as for a small fee at most public libraries.

TELEPHONE. **Pay phones** take credit cards and often accept phone cards (Telefonkort); buy them at newsstands or other shops (60kr and 100kr). Whenever possible, use a calling card for **international phone calls,** as long-distance rates for national phone services are often very high. **Mobile phones** are an increasingly popular and economical option. Major mobile carriers include Telia, Tele2, Vodafone, and 3. International access codes for calling out of Sweden include: **AT&T Direct** (☎020 79 91 11); **Canada Direct** (☎020 79 90 15); **MCI** (☎0 200 895 438); **Sprint** (☎020 79 90 11); **Telecom New Zealand** (☎020 799 064). For more info on calling home from Europe, see p. 28.

PHONE CODES	**Country code: 46. International dialing prefix:** 00. For more info on how to place international calls, see **Inside Back Cover.**

MAIL. From Sweden, it costs approximately 5kr to send a postcard or letter domestically, 10kr within Europe, and 10.20kr to the rest of the world. For more info, visit www.posten.se. To receive mail in Sweden, have mail delivered **Poste Restante.** Mail will go to the main post office unless you specify a subsidiary by street address. Address mail to be held according to the following example: First name, Last Name, Poste Restante, Postal Code, City, SWEDEN. Bring a passport to pick up your mail; there may also be a small fee.

LANGUAGE. Although Sweden has no official language, Swedish is universally spoken. The region around Kiruna is home to a minority of Finnish speakers, as well as 7000 speakers of the Sámi languages. Most Swedes speak English fluently. For basic Swedish words and phrases, see **Phrasebook: Swedish,** p. 793.

ACCOMMODATIONS AND CAMPING

SWEDEN	❶	❷	❸	❹	❺
ACCOMMODATIONS	under 160kr	160-230kr	231-350kr	351-500kr	over 500kr

Youth hostels *(vandrarhem)* cost 120-200kr per night. The hostels run by the **Svenska Turistföreningen (STF)** and affiliated with HI are uniformly top-notch. Nonmembers should expect to pay 200-240kr per night; HI members receive a 45kr discount (☎08 463 21 00; www.svenskaturistforeningen.se). STF also manages **mountain huts** in the northern wilds (150-350kr). Many **campgrounds** (tent sites 80-110kr; www.camping.se) offer **cottages** *(stugor)* for 100-300kr per person. **International Camping Cards** aren't valid in Sweden; **Swedish Camping Cards**, available at all SCR campgrounds, are mandatory (one-year pass 90kr). The Swedish **right of public access** *(allemansrätten)* means travelers can camp for free in the countryside, as long as they are roughly 150m away from private homes. Tents may be pitched in one location usually for one or two days. Guidelines vary depending on the community. Visit www.allemansratten.se for more info.

FOOD AND DRINK

SWEDEN	❶	❷	❸	❹	❺
FOOD	under 50kr	50-75kr	76-100kr	101-160kr	over 160kr

Restaurant fare is usually expensive in Sweden, but **food halls** *(saluhallen)*, open-air markets, and **hot dog stands** *(varmkorv)* make budget eating easy enough. Many restaurants offer affordable **daily lunch specials** *(dagens rätt)* for 60-75kr. The Swedish palate has long been attuned to hearty meat-and-potatoes fare, but immigrant communities in Malmö and Stockholm have spiced things up for budget travelers. A league of five-star chefs in Gothenburg are tossing off increasingly imaginative riffs on herring and salmon. The Swedish love **drip coffee** (as opposed to espresso) and have institutionalized coffee breaks as a near-sacred rite of the workday. Aside from light beer containing less than 3.5% alcohol, alcohol can be purchased only at state-run **Systembolaget** liquor stores and in licensed bars and restaurants. You can buy light beer at 18, but otherwise it's 20+. Some classier bars and clubs have age restrictions as high as 25.

HOLIDAYS AND FESTIVALS

Holidays: New Year's Day (Jan. 1); Epiphany (Jan. 6); Good Friday (Apr. 10, 2009; Apr. 2, 2010); Easter (Apr. 12, 2009; Apr. 4, 2010); Ascension (May 21, 2009; May 13, 2010); May Day (May 1); Pentecost (May 31, 2009; May 23, 2010); Corpus Christi (June 14, 2009; June 6, 2010); National Day (June 6); Assumption (Aug. 15); All Saints' Day (Nov. 1); Christmas (Dec. 25); Boxing Day (Dec. 26).

Festivals: Valborgsmässoafton (Walpurgis Eve; Apr. 30) celebrates the arrival of spring with roaring bonfires in Dalarna and choral singing in Lund and Uppsala. Dalarna erects flowery maypoles in time for **Midsummer** (June 24), as young people flock to the islands of Gotland, Öland, and the Skärgård archipelago for all-night parties. Mid-July welcomes the **Stockholm Jazz Festival** (www.stockholmjazz.com) to the capital. Travelers with appetites should check out the crayfish parties in Aug. and eel parties in Sept.

BEYOND TOURISM

Summer employment is often easier to find than long-term work, since Sweden has fairly strict regulations governing the employment of foreigners. For more info on opportunities across Europe, see **Beyond Tourism**, p. 55.

The American-Scandinavian Foundation (AMSCAN), 58 Park Ave., New York, NY 10016, USA (☎212 879 9779; www.amscan.org/jobs). Internship and job opportunities throughout Scandinavia. Fellowships for study in Sweden for Americans.

Council of International Fellowship (CIF), Karlbergsvägen 80 nb. ög, SE-113 35 Stockholm (☎04 68 32 31 21; www.cif-sweden.org). Funds exchange programs for service professionals, including homestays in various Swedish cities.

Internationella Arbetslag, Tegelviksgatan 40, S-116 41 Stockholm, SWE (☎08 643 08 89; www.ial.se). Branch of Service Civil International (SCI; www.sciint.org) organizes a broad range of workcamps. Camp and SCI membership fees apply.

STOCKHOLM ☎08

The largest city in Scandinavia's biggest country, Stockholm (pop. 1,250,000) is the aptly self-titled "capital of the north." A focal point for culture and design, the elegant city exists by virtue of a latticework of bridges connecting its islands and peninsulas, uniting different neighborhoods with distinct personalities.

▌ TRANSPORTATION

Flights: Arlanda Airport (ARN; ☎08 797 6000; www.arlanda.com), 42km north of the city. **Flygbussarna** shuttles (☎08 600 1000; www.flygbussarna.se) run between Arlanda and Centralstationen in Stockholm (40min.; every 15min. Station to airport 4am-10pm, airport to station 4:50am-12:30am; 95kr, students, children, and seniors 65kr; MC/V), as do **Arlanda Express** trains (☎0202 222 24; www.arlandaexpress.com. 20min.; every 15min. 5am-midnight; 200kr, students 100kr). **Bus** #583 runs to the T-bana stop Märsta (10min., 20kr); take the T-bana to T-Centralen in downtown Stockholm (40min., 20kr). Flygbussarna also operates shuttles to **Västerås Airport (VST;**

☎21 80 56 00; www.stockholmvasteras.se) coordinating with Ryanair departures (1hr., 100kr). **Skavsta Airport** is a major budget airline hub for the region.

Regional Hubs: Stockholm Skavsta Airport (NYO; ☎155 28 04 00; www.skavsta.se), 100km south of Stockholm in the town of Nyköping, is a hub for budget airlines **Ryanair** and **Wizz Air. Flybussarna** (☎08 600 1000; www.flybussarna.se) operates frequent **buses** from Stockholm (1hr., 100-200kr), coordinated with Ryanair arrivals and departures. **SJ trains** (☎0771 75 75 75; www.sj.se) also run from Stockholm (1hr., 1-2 per hr., 90-160kr). Taxis and local buses (20kr) run from Nyköping station to the airport.

Trains: Centralstationen (☎08 410 626 00). T-bana: T-Centralen. To: **Copenhagen, DEN** (5hr., 7-14 per day, 1099kr, under 26 948kr); **Gothenburg** (3-5hr., every 1-2hr., 512-1110kr, under 26 437-955kr); and **Oslo, NOR** (6-8hr., 1-5 per day, 672kr, under 26 572kr). Book up to 90 days in advance for lower fares. Fewer trains on Sa.

Buses: Cityterminalen, upstairs on the north end of Centralstationen. **Terminal Service** (☎08 762 5997) goes to the airport (95kr, 65kr students) and Gotland ferries (70kr). **Biljettservice** (☎08 762 5979) makes reservations with Sweden's bus companies for longer routes. **Swebus** (☎0771 218 218; www.swebusexpress.se), one of the largest, runs to: **Copenhagen, DEN** (9hr., 2per day, 400-500kr); **Gothenburg** (7hr., 7 per day, 250-300kr); and **Malmö** (8hr., 3 per day, 400-500kr).

Ferries: Tallinksilja, Sveavägen 14 (☎08 440 5990; www.tallinksilja.com), sails to: **Helsinki, FIN** (17hr., 1 per day at 5pm, from 75kr); **Turku, FIN** (12hr., 2 per day, from 150kr); **Tallinn, EST** (16hr., 1 per day, from 470kr, low-season 260kr). T-bana: Gärdet, follow signs to Värtahamnen, or take the Tallinksilja bus (20kr) from Cityterminalen. 50% ScanRail discount on select fares. **Viking Line** (☎08 452 4000; www.vikingline.se) sails to: **Helsinki, FIN** (17hr., 1 per day, mid-June to mid-Aug. from 430kr, low-season 300kr); **Turku, FIN** (12hr., 2 per day, mid-June to mid-Aug. from 230kr, low-season 130kr). Office in Cityterminalen (open M-Th 8am-7pm, F 7:30am-6:30pm, Sa 8am-5pm). For more info on traveling by ferry in Scandinavia, see p. 52.

Public Transportation: T-bana (Tunnelbana, Stockholm's subway; stations marked with white circular sign with blue "T") runs M-Th and Su 5am-12:30am, F-Sa 5am-3am. **Night buses** run 12:30am-5:30am. Tickets 30kr; strip of 8 tickets 180kr, sold at Pressbyrån news agents; 1hr. unlimited transfer. The **SL Tourist Card** (*Turistkort*) is valid on all public transportation. 1-day 100kr; 3-day 200kr. Office in Centralstationen (☎08 600 1000). T-bana: T-Centralen. Open M-Sa 6:30am-11:15pm, Su 7am-11:15pm. MC/V.

Taxis: Many cabs have fixed prices to certain destinations; ask when you enter the cab. Expect to pay 440-475kr from Arlanda to Centralstationen. Major companies include **Taxi 020** (☎020 202 020), **Taxi Kurir** (☎08 30 00 00; www.taxikurir.se), and **Taxi Stockholm** (☎08 15 00 00; www.taxistockholm.se).

Bike Rental: Rent-a-Bike, Strandvägen, Kajplats 24 (☎08 660 7959). From 200kr per day. Open May-Sept. daily 10am-6pm. MC/V. **Djurgårdsbrons Sjöcafé,** Galärvarvsvägen 2 (☎08 660 5757). Bikes 250kr per day, canoes 300kr per day, in-line skates 200kr per day, kayaks 500kr per day. Open June-Aug. daily 9am-9pm. AmEx/MC/V.

✈ ⏱ ORIENTATION AND PRACTICAL INFORMATION

Stockholm spans a number of small islands (linked by bridges and the T-bana) at the junction of **Lake Mälaren** to the west and the **Baltic Sea** to the east. The large northern island is divided into two sections: **Norrmalm,** home to Centralstationen and the crowded shopping district around Drottningg., and **Östermalm,** which boasts the **Strandvägen** waterfront and upscale nightlife fanning out from Stureplan. The mainly residential western island, **Kungsholmen,** features beaches, waterside promenades, and the *Stadhuset* (city hall) on its eastern tip. The southern island of **Södermalm** retains a traditional feel in the midst of a budding cafe culture and club scene. Nearby **Långholmen** houses a nature

SWEDEN

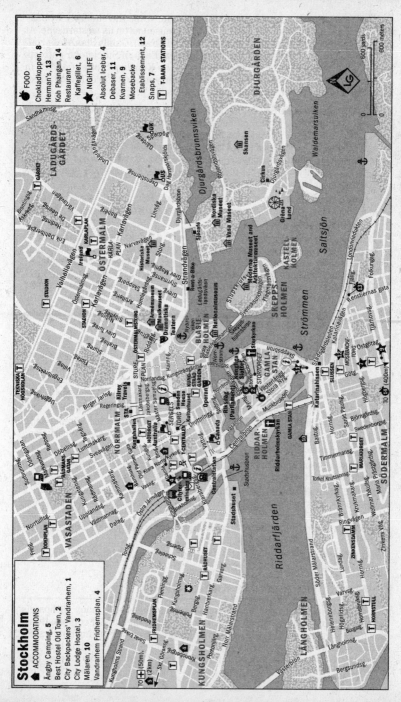

Stockholm

♠ ACCOMMODATIONS

Ängby Camping, 5
Best Hostel Old Town, 2
City Backpackers' Vandrarhem, 1
City Lodge Hostel, 3
Mälaren, 10
Vandrarhem Fridhemsplan, 4

🍴 FOOD

Chokladkoppen, 8
Herman's, 13
Koh Phangan, 14
Restaurant
Kaffegillet, 6

★ NIGHTLIFE

Absolut Icebar, 4
Debaser, 11
Kvarnen, 9
Mosebacke
Etablissement, 12
Snaps, 7

T T-BANA STATIONS

preserve and a prison-turned-hotel and museum, while the similarly woodsy eastern island **Djurgården** hosts several popular museums on its western side. At the center of these five islands is **Gamla Stan** (Old Town). Gamla Stan's less-trafficked neighbor (via Norrmalm) is **Skeppsholmen**. Each of Stockholm's streets begins with number "1" at the end closest to the Kungliga Slottet (p. 728) in Gamla Stan; the lower the numbers, the closer you are to Old Town. Street signs also contain that block's address numbers.

Tourist Offices: Sweden House (Sverigehuset), Hamng. 27 (☎08 508 285 08; www. stockholmtown.com), entrance off Kungsträdgården. From Centralstationen, walk up Klarabergsg. to Sergels Torg (look for the glass obelisk), bear right on Hamng., and turn right at the park. Agents sell the **SL card** and the **Stockholm Card** *(Stockholmskortet),* which includes public transportation and admission to 75 museums and attractions. 1-day 330kr; 2-day 460kr; 3-day 580kr. Internet 1kr per min. Open M-F 9am-7pm, Sa 10am-5pm, Su 10am-4pm. AmEx/MC/V.

Budget Travel: Kilroy Travels, Kungsg. 4 (☎0771 545 769; www.kilroytravels.se). Open M-F 10am-6pm. **STA Travel,** Kungsg. 30 (☎0771 61 10 10; www.statravel.se). Open M-F 10am-6pm. AmEx/MC/V.

Embassies: Australia, Sergels Torg 12, 11th fl. (☎08 613 2900; www.sweden.embassy. gov.au). Open M-F 8:30am-4:30pm. **Canada,** Tegelbacken 4, 7th fl. (☎08 453 3000; www.canadaemb.se). Open M-F 8:30am-noon and 1-5pm. **Ireland,** Östermalmsg. 97 (☎08 661 8005). Open M-F 10am-noon and 2:30-4pm. **UK,** Skarpög. 6-8 (☎08 671 3000; www.britishembassy.se). Open M-F 9am-5pm. **US,** Daghammarskjölds väg 31 (☎08 783 5300; www.usemb.se). Open M-Th 9-11am and 1-3pm, F 9-11am.

Currency Exchange: Forex, Centralstationen (☎08 411 6734). Branch at Cityterminalen (☎08 21 42 80). 25kr commission.

Luggage Storage: Lockers at Centralstationen and Cityterminalen (30-80kr per day).

GLBT Resources: The *Queer Extra (QX)* and the *QueerMap* give info about Stockholm's GLBT hot spots. Swedish-language version available at the Sweden House tourist office or online at www.qx.se. For an English-language version, visit www.qx.se/english.

24hr. Pharmacy: Look for green-and-white Apoteket signs. **Apoteket C. W. Scheele,** Klarabergsg. 64 (☎08 454 8130), at the overpass over Vasag. T-bana: T-Centralen.

Hospitals: Karolinska (☎517 740 93), north of Norrmalm near Solnavägen. T-Bana: Skt. Eriksplan. **Sankt Göran** (☎587 010 00), on Kungsholmen. T-Bana: Fridhemsplan.

Medical Services: 24hr. hotline ☎32 01 00.

Telephones: Almost all public phones require **Telia** phone cards; buy them at Pressbyrån newsstands in increments of 50 (50kr) or 120 (100kr) units.

Internet: Stadsbiblioteket, Odeng. 53, in the annex. T-bana: Odenplan. Sign up for 2 free 30min. slots daily or drop in for 15min. Bring your passport. Open M-Th 9am-9pm, F 9am-7pm, Sa-Su noon-4pm. **Dome House,** Sveavg. 108, has almost 80 terminals. 19kr per hr. Open 24hr. **Sidewalk Express** Internet stations are located inside malls and 7-Elevens throughout the city. 19kr per hr. Open 24hr. MC/V.

Post Office: 84 Klarabergsg. (☎23 22 20). Open M-F 7am-7pm. Stamps also available at press stands and souvenir shops.

ACCOMMODATIONS AND CAMPING

Reservations are necessary in the summer. In high-season, many HI hostels limit stays to five nights. Some non-HI hostels are hotel-hostel combinations. Specify that you want to stay in a dorm-style hostel, or risk paying hotel rates. Stockholm's **botels** (boat-hotels) often make for camaraderie, but they can be cramped—request a room with harbor views. There are also various **B&B**

booking services, including the **Bed and Breakfast Agency**. (☎08 643 8028; www.bba. nu. Open M 10am-noon and 1-5pm, Tu-W 9am-noon and 1-5pm.) The Sweden House **tourist office** can also help book rooms (5kr hostel booking fee, 75kr hotel booking fee). An SL or Stockholm Card is the cheapest way for campers to reach some of the more remote **campgrounds**. The right of **public access** (p. 722) does not apply within the city limits, although camping is allowed on most of the Skärgård archipelago (p. 731).

Best Hostel Old Town, Trångsund 12 (☎08 440 0004; www.besthostel.se). T-bana: Gamla Stan. With a great location in the Old Town and ample facilities, this hostel is a steal. Look out for their upcoming branch at Skeppsbron 22, which promises harbor views. 200kr per bed, 300kr per bed in twin room. Free Wi-Fi. Basic kitchen. Reception 7am-7pm, but arrivals at other times can be arranged. MC/V. ❷

City Backpackers' Vandrarhem, Upplandsg. 2A (☎08 20 69 20; www.citybackpackers. se). T-bana: T-centralen. Just north of the city center, this hostel features friendly service and free pasta, along with a relaxing courtyard for sharing travel tales. Linens 50kr. Laundry 50kr. Sauna 20kr, late-afternoon free. Free Internet and Wi-Fi. Reception 8am-2pm. Low-season dorms from 230kr; doubles 650kr. MC/V. ❷

City Lodge Hostel, Klara Norra Kyrkog. 15 (☎08 22 66 30; www.citylodge.se). T-bana: T-centralen. On a quiet street hidden in the rush of the city center, this hostel is a good place to rest. Breakfast 60kr. Linens 50kr. Towels 10kr. Laundry 50kr. Free Internet. Reception June-Aug. 8:30am-11pm, Sept.-May 8:30am-10pm. 18-bed dorms 195kr; 10-bed 225kr; doubles from 590kr. MC/V. ❷

Mälaren, Södermälarstrand, Kajplats 11 (☎08 644 4385; www.theredboat.com). T-bana: Gamla Stan. Just south of Gamla Stan, this bright red botel offers great views across the water from its compact dorms. Breakfast 65kr. Reception 8am-1am. Internet 10kr per 15min. Free Wi-Fi in reception area. Dorms 230kr; singles 450kr; doubles with bunk beds 590kr; quads 1040kr. MC/V. ❷

Vandrarhem Fridhemsplan (HI), S:t Eriksg. 20 (☎08 653 8800; www.fridhemsplan. se). T-bana: Fridhemsplan. This large hostel has modern decorations and a big kitchen. Breakfast buffet 60kr. Lockers 20kr. Linens 50kr. Laundry 50kr. Free Internet. Reception 24hr. Dorms 275kr; singles 500kr; doubles 650kr. 50kr HI discount. AmEx/MC/V. ❸

Ängby Camping, Blackebergsv. 24 (☎08 37 04 20; www.angbycamping.se), on Lake Mälaren. T-bana: Ängbyplan. Wooded campsite with swimming area. Cable TV 10kr. Stockholm Card vendor. Reception June-Aug. 8am-10pm; Sept.-May 5-8pm. 2-person tent sites 135kr; cabins 475-725kr. Electricity from 35kr. AmEx/MC/V. ❶

🖪 FOOD

Götgatan and **Folkunggatan** in Södermalm offer affordable cuisine from around the world, while pizza and kebabs are plentiful on Vasastaden's **Odengatan**. The **SoFo** (south of Folkunggatan) neighborhood offers many trendy cafe options. Grocery stores are easy to find around any T-bana station. Head to the outdoor fruit market at **Hötorget** for your Vitamin C fix (open M-Sa 7am-6pm), or to the **Kungshallen** food hall, Kungsg. 44, for a meal from one of the international food stands. (www.kungshallen.com. Open M-F 9am-11pm, Sa 11am-11pm, Su noon-11pm.) The **Östermalms Saluhall**, Nybrog. 31 (T-bana: Östermalmstorg), is a more traditional indoor market with fish, meat, cheese, fruit, and pastry stands, as well as more expensive restaurants serving Swedish dishes. (www. ostermalmshallen.se. Open M-Th 9:30am-6pm, F 9:30am-6:30pm, Sa 9:30am-4pm.) Take advantage of low lunch prices and track down *dagens rätt* (lunch specials; 50-80kr) to save money.

Herman's, Fjällg. 23A (☎08 643 9480). T-bana: Slussen. This small restaurant serves buffet style vegetarian fare with a grand view of the water. Lunch (88-140kr) and dinner (135-175kr) include dessert and drink combos. Open daily June-Aug. 11am-11pm, arrive by 9:30pm for full buffet; Sept.-May 11am-10pm. MC/V. ❹

Restaurant Kaffegillet, Trangsund 4 (☎08 21 39 95). T-bana: Gamla Stan. An excellent place to try classic Swedish cuisine. The reindeer roast (215kr) and the marinated herring with sour cream (135kr) are popular choices. Small dishes 105-115kr. Swedish Kitchen 145-235kr. Desserts 70-95kr. Salad and bread included. Open daily May-Sept. 9am-11pm; Oct.-Apr. 9am-6pm. AmEx/MC/V. ❹

Koh Phangan, Skåneg. 57 (☎08 642 5040). T-Bana: Skanstull. Dine on Thai food in this cozy restaurant modeled after a jungle treehouse, a welcoming sight in winter. Vegetarian entrees 139-159kr. Meat entrees 159-205kr. Seafood 180-265kr. Open M-Th 11am-11pm, F 11am-11:45pm, Sa 2-11:45pm, Su 2-11pm. AmEx/MC/V. ❺

Chokladkoppen, Stortorg. 18 (☎08 20 31 70). T-bana: Gamla Stan. Serves light meals (39-80kr) and generous desserts (23-48kr). The outdoor seating is a top people-watching spot on Stortorget. Open in summer M-Th and Su 9am-11pm, F-Sa 9am-midnight; low-season M-Th and Su 9am-10pm, F 9am-midnight. Cash only. ❷

🇬 SIGHTS

With over 75 museums, Stockholm gives visitors plenty to see. Break up your exploration of the city's inner neighborhoods with T-bana rides to more remote locations to get a sense of the capital's scope. The T-bana, spanning 110km, has been called the world's longest art exhibit—over the past 50 years, the city has commissioned more than 140 artists to decorate its stations. The blue line's art is particularly notable, but the murals and sculptures of T-Centralen remain the best-recognized example of T-bana artistry.

GAMLA STAN (OLD TOWN). Stockholm was once confined to the small island of Staden. Today, the island is the center of the city. The main pedestrian street is **Västerlånggatan,** but its maze of small side streets preserves the area's historic feel. *(Tours of the island are available May-Aug. M-Tu and Th 7:30pm. Sept.-Apr. Sa-Su 1:30pm. Meet at the obelisk in front of the southern entrance to the Royal Palace. 60kr. Cash only.)* Gamla Stan is dominated by the magnificent 1754 🔳**Kungliga Slottet** (Royal Palace), the winter home of the Swedish royal family. The **Royal Apartments** and the adjacent **Rikssalen** (State Hall) and **Slottskyrkan** (Royal Chapel) are all lavishly decorated in blue and gold, the colors of the Swedish flag. The **Skattkammaren** (Royal Treasury) houses a collection of jewel-encrusted crowns and other regal accoutrements. The statues in the **Gustav III Antikmuseum** are worth seeing, and the **Museum Tre Konor** offers an interesting look at the foundation of a 13th-century castle that once stood on the same site. *(Main ticket office and info area at the rear of the complex, near the Storkyrkan. ☎08 402 6130; www.royalcourt.se. Open Feb. to mid-May Tu-Su noon-4pm; mid-May to June 1st daily 10am-4pm; June 1st-Aug. daily 10am-5pm; Sept. 1st to mid-Sept. daily 10am-4pm; mid-Sept. to Dec. Tu-Su noon-3pm. Each attraction 90kr, students 35kr. Combination ticket 130/65kr. Guided tours 1 per hr. AmEx/MC/V.)* The **Livrustkammaren** (Armory) presents an extensive collection of royal clothes, weapons, and coaches. *(Slottsbacken 3. ☎08 519 555 44; www.livrustkammaren.se. Open June-Aug. daily 10am-5pm; Sept.-Apr. Tu-W and F-Su 11am-5pm, Th 11am-8pm. May daily 11am-5pm. 50kr, under 20 free. AmEx/MC/V.)* Across the street from the palace ticket office is the gilded **Storkyrkan** church. *(☎08 723 3016. Open M-Sa June-Aug. 9am-6pm; Sept.-May 9am-4pm. Church 25kr. 3 tower tours per day in summer. Cash only.)* Around the corner on **Stortorget,** the main square, the **Nobelmuseet** traces the history of the Nobel Prize and its laureates. *(☎08 534 818 00; www.nobelprize.org/nobelmuseum. Open mid-May to mid-Sept. M and W-Su 10am-5pm, Tu 10am-8pm; mid-Sept. to mid-May Tu 11am-8pm,*

W-Su 11am-5pm. 60kr, students 40kr. Guided English-language tours: M-F 11:15am and 3pm, Sa-Su 11:15am and 4pm. AmEx/MC/V.) For a quirkier attraction, look for **Mårten Trotzigs Gränd,** the narrowest lane in Stockholm.

KUNGSHOLMEN. The **Stadshuset** (City Hall) has been the seat of local government since the early 20th century. The required tour of the interior takes you through the council room and the enormous **Blue Hall,** where a 10,000-pipe organ greets Nobel Prize banquet attendees. In the stunning **Golden Hall,** 18 million shimmering tiles make up a golden Art Deco mosaic. The **tower** provides the best panoramic view of the city center. *(Hantverkarg. 1. T-bana: T-Centralen. ☎ 08 508 290 58; www.stockholm.se/stadshuset. Tower open daily May-Sept. 10am-4pm. Call the day of your visit to make sure the building is open to visitors. 20kr. Tours daily June-Aug. 1 per hr. 10am-4pm; Sept. 10am, noon, 2pm; Oct.-May 10am, noon. 60kr, students 50kr. AmEx/MC/V.)*

SKEPPSHOLMEN AND BLASIEHOLMEN. The collection at the ▨**Moderna Museet,** on the island of Skeppsholmen (SHEPS-hole-men), contains canvases by Dalí, Matisse, Munch, Picasso, Pollock, and Warhol. *(T-Bana: Kungsträdgården. Bus #65. ☎ 08 519 552 00; www.modernamuseet.se. 80kr, students 60kr, 18 and under free. Open Tu 10am-8pm, W-Su 10am-6pm. MC/V.)* In the same building, the **Arkitekturmuseet** displays the history of Swedish architecture and design using 3D models. *(T-Bana: Kungsträdgården. Bus #65. ☎ 08 587 270 00. Open Tu 10am-8pm, W-Su 10am-6pm. 50kr, under 19 free. F 4-6pm free. MC/V.)* Across the bridge on the Blasieholmen peninsula, the **Nationalmuseum,** Sweden's largest art museum, features pieces by Cézanne, El Greco, Monet, and Rembrandt. *(T-bana: Kungsträdgården. Bus #65. ☎ 08 519 544 10; www.nationalmuseum.se. Open Sept.-May Tu and Th 11am-8pm, W and F-Su 11am-5pm; June-Aug. Tu 11am-8pm, W-Su 11am-5pm. 100kr, students 80kr, under 19 free. AmEx/MC/V.)*

ÖSTERMALM. Among the dignified museums of this trendy area, the **Musikmuseet** is a quirky, fun stop. Don't miss the room in the basement where you can try a number of intriguing instruments. *(Sibylleg. 2. T-bana: Östermalmstorg, ☎ 08 519 554 90; www.stockholm.music.museum. Open Tu-Su July-Aug. 10am-5pm; Sept.-June noon-5pm. 40kr, students 20kr, under 19 free.)* Less than a block away, the **Armémuseum** chronicles Swedish military history. All signs are in Swedish, so be sure to pick up a language guide at the ticket desk. *(Riddarg. 13. T-bana: Östermalmstorg, exit Sibylleg. ☎ 08 519 563 00; www.armemuseum.se. Open Tu 11am-8pm, W-Su 11am-5pm. July-Aug. Tu 10am-8pm, W-Su 10am-5pm. 50kr, under 19 free.)* For a more complete account of Swedish history, head to the **Historiska Museet,** which plays host to famous collections of both Viking and ecclesiastical memorabilia. *(Narvav. 13-17. T-bana: Karlaplan. ☎ 08 519 556 00; www.historiska.se. Open May-Sept. daily 10am-5pm; Oct.-Apr. Tu-W and F-Su 11am-5pm, Th 11am-8pm. 50kr, students and seniors 40kr, under 19 free.)*

DJURGÅRDEN. This national park is a perfect summer picnic spot. The main attraction is the haunting ▨**Vasa Museet,** home to a massive warship that sank in Stockholm's harbor during its maiden voyage in 1628; it was salvaged, fantastically preserved, three centuries later. *(From the Galärvarvet bus stop, take bus #44, 47, or 69. ☎ 08 519 548 00; www.vasamuseet.se. Open June-Aug. daily 8:30am-6pm; Sept.-May W 10am-8pm, M-Tu and Th-Su 10am-5pm. 95kr, students 50kr. AmEx/MC/V.)* Next door, the **Nordiska Museet** explores Swedish cultural history from the 1500s to the present day. *(☎ 08 519 546 00; www.nordiskamuseet.se. Open June-Aug. daily 10am-5pm; Sept.-Aug. M-Tu and Th-F 10am-4pm, W 10am-8pm with free admission from 4pm, Sa-Su 11am-5pm. 60kr, special exhibits 60kr. AmEx/MC/V.)* The **Gröna Lund** amusement park features a handful of rides, including roller coasters. *(☎ 08 587 502 00; www.gronalund.se. Open daily late Apr. to late Aug., usually 11am-11pm; around Midsummer, open until 10pm; check website for detailed schedule. Prices vary throughout the year, from 65kr-120kr.)* A large portion of Djurgården is home to **Skansen,** an open-air museum established in 1891 that features 150 historical buildings, a small zoo, and an aquarium. Stroll along the hilly paths of the Old Town to find Sámi dwellings, schoolhouses, and an elk or two. Many festivals and events are held throughout the year—the Christmas market in early December is noteworthy. *(Take bus #44 or 47. ☎08 442 8000; www. skansen.se. Park and zoo open daily June-Aug. 10am-8pm; Sept.-May 10am-5pm. June-Aug. M and W-Su 90kr, Tu 110kr for concerts; Sept. 80kr; Oct.-May 60kr. AmEx/MC/V.)*

♫ 🎭 ENTERTAINMENT AND FESTIVALS

Stockholm's smaller performance venues are featured in the *What's On* pamphlet, available at the Sweden House tourist office. There are also a number of larger, more widely known performance spots. The stages of the national theater, **Dramatiska Teatern,** Nybroplan (☎08 667 0680; www.dramaten.se), feature performances of works by August Strindberg and others (60-300kr). Arrive an hour early to snatch up a 35% discount on last-minute tickets. A smaller stage behind the theater focuses on experimental material. The **Kulturhuset at Sergels Torg** (☎08 508 314 00; www.kulturhuset.se) houses art galleries, performance spaces, and cultural venues often free to the public. It also hosts **Lava** (☎08 508 314 44; www.lavaland.se; closed in July), a popular hangout with a stage, library, and cafe, that lends itself to poetry readings and other events geared toward a younger set. The **Operan,** Jakobs Torg 2, stages operas and ballets from late August through mid-June. (☎08 791 4400. Tickets 265-590kr. Student rush tickets available. AmEx/MC/V.) The imposing **Konserthuset,** Hötorg. 8, hosts the Stockholm Philharmonic and the Nobel Prize ceremony. (☎08 786 0200; www. konserthuset.se. 100-270kr. AmEx/MC/V.) Culture buffs on a budget should sample Stockholm's **Parkteatern** (☎08 506 202 99; www.stadsteatern.stockholm. se), a summer-long program of free outdoor theater, dance, and music in city parks. Call **Ticnet** (☎0771 707 070; www.ticnet.se) for tickets. The world-class 🎷**Stockholm Jazz Festival** (☎08 505 331 70; www.stockholmjazz.com) arrives in mid- to late July. Other festivals include GLBT **Stockholm Pride** (early Aug.; ☎08 33 59 55; www.stockholmpride.org), the November **Stockholm Film Festival,** (☎08 677 5000; www.filmfestival.se), and late August's **Strindberg Festival,** a celebration of Sweden's most famous morose playwright.

🍸 NIGHTLIFE

For a city with lasting summer sunlight, Stockholm knows a thing or two about nightlife. The scene varies by neighborhood, with particular social codes prevailing in each area. The posh **Stureplan** area in Östermalm (T-bana: Östermalmtorg) and **Kungsgatan** (T-bana: Hötorget) are where the beautiful people party until 5am. Expect long lines and note that many clubs honor strict guest lists. Across the river, **Södermalm's** (T-bana: Mariatorget) nightlife is less glitzy but more accessible and just as popular, with a diverse mix of bars and clubs along Götg. and around Medborgarpl. In the northern part of town, nightlife options line **Sveavägen** and the **Vasastaden** area (T-bana: Odenplan or Rådmansg.). Many bars and clubs set age limits as high as 25 to avoid crowds of drunk teenagers, but showing up early may help get you in, regardless of your age. Stockholm is compact enough to walk among all the islands, but night buses cover most of the city. The T-bana is generally safe until closing. Pick up *Queer Extra (QX)* and the *QueerMap* for gay nightlife tips.

🧊 **Absolut Icebar,** Vasaplan 2-4 (☎08 505 630 00; www.absoluticebar.com), in the Nordic Sea Hotel. T-bana: T-Centralen. Provided jacket and gloves keep you warm in the -5°C temperature of this bar, made completely out of natural ice. Make reservations at least 3 days ahead. Drop-in usually requires waiting. Cover 105-160kr with drink; under

18 60kr. Refills 85kr. Open June-Aug. M-W 12:45pm-midnight, Th-Sa 12:45pm-1am, Su 12:45pm-10pm; check website for details on Sept.-May hours. AmEx/MC/V.

Mosebacke Etablissement, Mosebacke Torg 3 (☎08 556 098 90). T-bana: Slussen. Take the Katarina lift (10kr) or climb the stairs to Söder Heights. Usually a large crowd inside at the bar and on the dance floor. Outside terrace is more relaxed with a great view and ample seating. Beer 48kr. Mixed drinks 74kr. 20+. Cover 80kr after 11pm. Open M-Th and Su 5pm-1am, F-Sa 5pm-2am. AmEx/MC/V.

Kvarnen, Tjärhovsg. 4 (☎08 643 0380; www.kvarnen.com). T-bana: Medborgarpl. Look for the red windmill. The mod cocktail lounge **H2O,** the energetic **Eld** dance club, and a 200-year-old **beer hall** coexist under the same roof. Beer 29-69kr. M-Th and Su 21+, F-Sa 23+. Open daily 5pm-3am. MC/V.

Debaser, Karl Johans Torg 1 (☎08 462 9860; www.debaser.se). T-bana: Slussen. Look for the plaza to your right as you cross the bridge from Södermalm to Gamla Stan. This popular rock club draws crowds with live music. 18+. Cover 60-120kr. Bar open daily 5pm-3am. Club open daily June-Aug. 10pm-3am; Sept.-May 8pm-3am. AmEx/MC/V.

Snaps, Götg. 48 (☎08 640 2868). T-bana: Medborgarpl. On the corner of Medborgarpl. Rock upstairs, house music outside, and an intimate basement dance floor that becomes more mainstream around midnight. Beer 70kr. Wine 90kr. Mixed drinks from 60kr. 23+. Cover F-Sa 60kr. Open M-W 5pm-1am, Th-Sa 5pm-3am. AmEx/MC/V.

▶ DAYTRIPS FROM STOCKHOLM

Stockholm is situated in the center of an archipelago, where the mainland gradually crumbles into the Baltic. The islands in either direction—east toward the Baltic or west toward Lake Mälaren—are a lovely escape from the city. **Ferries** leave from in front of the Grand Hotel on the **Stromkajen** docks between Gamla Stan and Skeppsholmen or the **Nybrohamnen** docks (T-bana: Kungsträdgården). Visit the **Excursion Shop** in Sweden House (p. 726) for more info.

STOCKHOLM ARCHIPELAGO (SKÄRGÅRD)

Vaxholm is accessible by ferry (1hr., late June to late Aug. 2 per hr., 65kr) or bus #670 from T-bana: Tekniska Hogskolan (45min., 1-4 per hr., 20kr). Waxholmsbolaget runs ferries to even the tiniest islands, including Sandhamn, year-round. All ferries depart from Vaxholm. (☎08 679 5830; www.waxholmsbolaget.se. June-Aug. 1 per hr.; Sept.-May 1 per 2hr. 65kr, ages 7-19 40kr, under 7 free. AmEx/MC/V.) Sweden House sells the Båtluffarkort card, good for unlimited Waxholmsbolaget rides. (5-day 300kr; 30-day 700kr.)

The wooded islands of the Stockholm archipelago become less developed as the chain of 24,000 islands coils out into the Baltic Sea. **Vaxholm** is the de facto capital of the archipelago. Its pristine **beaches,** Eriksö and Tenö in particular, and 16th-century **fortress** have spawned pricey waterside cafes, but the rest of the streets still maintain their charm. The **tourist office** is at Torget 1. (☎08 541 708 00; www.vaxholm.se.) Three hours from Stockholm, **Sandhamn** is quieter, although the white sands of Trouville Beach have many devotees. The island, with its active nightlife scene, is especially popular among a younger crowd. Hikers can escape from the masses by exploring coastal trails on the **Finnhamn** group and **Tjockö** to the north. Ask at Sweden House about **hostels.** They are usually booked up months in advance, but there are alternatives—the islands are a promising place to exercise the right of public access (p. 722).

LAKE MÄLAREN

Strömma Kanalbolaget ferries (☎08 587 140 00; www.strommakanalbolaget.com) depart Stockholm from the Stadshusbron docks next to the Stadshuset for Drottningholms Slott (45min.; 1-2 per hr.; round-trip 130kr, plus admission 210kr), and Björkö (July-Aug.

9:30am and 1pm, return 2:45 and 6:15pm; May and Sept. 9:30am, return 2:45pm. 195kr. Guided tour, museum admission, and round-trip ferry 265kr. MC/V.)

Drottningholms Slott (☎08 402 60 00; www.royalcourt.se) was built for the queens of Sweden in the late 17th century and has served as the royal family's residence since 1981, when they left Kungliga Slottet (p. 728). The interior and formal Baroque gardens are impressive, but the highlight is the 1766 **Court Theater,** where the artistic director uses 18th-century sets and stage equipment to mount provocative ballets, operas, and pantomime shows. The colorful **Chinese Pavillion** was built by King Adolf Fredrick as a surprise birthday present for his queen; how the large pavillion was kept secret enough to maintain the surprise remains a mystery. *(Drottningholms Slott open daily May-Aug. 10am-4:30pm; Sept. noon-3:30pm; Sa-Su Oct.-Apr. noon-3:30pm. Palace 90kr, students 35kr; palace and pavillion 110/55kr. Court Theater tickets start at 165kr. Drottningholms Slott English tours daily June-Aug. 1 per 2hr.; Sa-Su Oct.-May noon and 2pm. Court Theater 30min. guided tours 60/40kr. AmEx/MC/V.)* The island of **Björkö** on Lake Mälaren is home to **Birka,** Sweden's largest Viking-era settlement, dated to AD 750. Though little remains at the site, amateur excavations and modern Vikings bring the island to life in July and August.

SWITZERLAND
(SCHWEIZ, SUISSE, SVIZZERA)

While the stereotype of Switzerland as a country of bankers, chocolatiers, and watchmakers still exists, an energetic youth culture is reviving old images of a pastoral Swiss culture. The country's gorgeous lakes and formidable peaks entice outdoor enthusiasts from around the globe. Mountains dominate about two-thirds of the country: the Jura cover the northwest region, the Alps stretch across the lower half, and the eastern Rhaetian Alps border Austria. Only in Switzerland can one indulge in decadent chocolate as a cultural experience.

 DISCOVER SWITZERLAND: SUGGESTED ITINERARIES

THREE DAYS. Experience cosmopolitan Europe in **Zürich** (1 day). Head to **Luzern** (1 day; p. 746) for the perfect combination of city and country before jetting to **Geneva** (1 day; p. 747).

ONE WEEK. Begin in **Luzern** (1 day), which will fulfill your visions of a charming Swiss city. Then head to **Bern** (1 day; p. 738) and **Zürich** (2 days). Get a taste of French Switzerland in **Geneva** and **Lausanne** (2 days).

ESSENTIALS

FACTS AND FIGURES

OFFICIAL NAME: Swiss Confederation.

CAPITAL: Bern.

MAJOR CITIES: Basel, Geneva, Zürich.

POPULATION: 7,582,000

LAND AREA: 41,300 sq. km.

LANGUAGES: German (64%), French (20%), Italian (10%), Romansch (1%).

RELIGIONS: Roman Catholic (48%), Protestant (44%), other (8%).

TOTAL CHOCOLATE CONSUMED IN 2007: 93,501 tons.

WHEN TO GO

During ski season (Nov.-Mar.) prices double in eastern Switzerland and travelers must make reservations months ahead. The situation reverses in the summer, especially July and August, when the flatter, western half of Switzerland fills with vacationers and hikers enjoying low humidity and temperatures rarely exceeding 26°C (80°F). A good budget option is to travel during the shoulder season: May-June and September-October, when tourism lulls and the daytime temperature ranges from -2 to 7°C (46-59°F). Many mountain towns throughout Switzerland shut down completely in May and June, however, so call ahead.

DOCUMENTS AND FORMALITIES

EMBASSIES. Most foreign embassies in Switzerland are in Bern (p. p. 738). Swiss embassies abroad include: **Australia**, 7 Melbourne Ave., Forrest, Canberra, ACT, 2603 (☎02 6162 8400; www.eda.admin.ch/australia); **Canada**, 5 Marlbor-

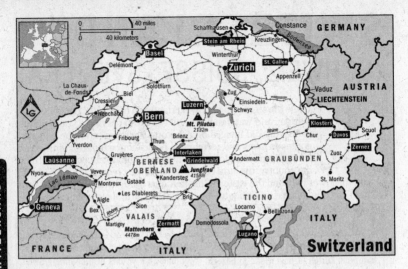

Switzerland

ough Ave., Ottawa, ON, K1N 8E6 (☎613-235-1837; www.eda.admin.ch/canada); **Ireland**, 6 Ailesbury Rd., Ballsbridge, Dublin, 4 (☎353 12 18 63 82; www.eda. admin.ch/dublin); **New Zealand**, 22 Panama St., Wellington (☎04 472 15 93; www. eda.admin.ch/wellington); **UK**, 16-18 Montagu Pl., London, W1H 2BQ (☎020 76 16 60 00; www.eda.admin.ch/london); **US**, 2900 Cathedral Ave., NW, Washington, D.C., 20008 (☎202-745-7900; www.eda.admin.ch/washington).

VISA AND ENTRY INFORMATION. EU citizens do not need a visa. Citizens of Australia, Canada, New Zealand, and the US do not need a visa for stays of up to 90 days. For stays longer than 90 days, all visitors need visas (around US$52), available at Swiss consulates. Travelers should anticipate a processing time of about six to eight weeks.

TOURIST SERVICES AND MONEY

EMERGENCY	Ambulance: ☎144. Fire: ☎118. Police: ☎117.

TOURIST OFFICES. Branches of the **Swiss National Tourist Office**, marked by a blue "i" sign, are present in nearly every town in Switzerland; most agents speak English. The official tourism website is www.myswitzerland.com.

scoop **THE INSIDE SCOOP.** If you're planning on spending a long time in Switzerland, consider the **Museum Pass** (30CHF). Available at some tourist offices and venues, it lets you into most major Swiss museums.

MONEY. The Swiss unit of currency is the **Swiss franc (CHF),** plural Swiss francs. One Swiss franc is equal to 100 centimes (called *Rappen* in German Switzerland), with standard denominations of 5, 10, 20, and 50 centimes and 1, 2, and 5CHF in coins; and 10, 20, 50, 100, 200, 500, and 1000CHF in notes. Widely accepted credit cards include American Express, MasterCard, and Visa. Euros (€) are also accepted at many museums and restaurants. Switzerland is not cheap; if you stay in hostels and prepare most of your own food, expect to spend 55-80CHF per day. Generally, it's less expensive to exchange money at home than in Switzerland. ATMs offer the best exchange rates. Although restaurant bills already include a 15% service charge, an additional tip of 1-2CHF for a modest meal or 5-10CHF for a more upscale dinner is expected. Give hotel porters and doormen about 1CHF per bag and airport porters 5CHF per bag.

Switzerland has a 7.6% **value added tax (VAT)**, a sales tax applied to goods and services. The prices given in *Let's Go* include VAT. In the airport upon exiting Switzerland, non-Swiss citizens can claim a refund on the tax paid for goods purchased at participating stores. In order to qualify for a refund in a store, you must spend at least 500CHF; make sure to ask for a refund form when you pay. For more info on qualifying for a VAT refund, see p. 19.

SWISS FRANC (CHF)		
AUS$1 = 0.95CHF		1CHF = AUS$1.05
CDN$1 = 1.03CHF		1CHF = CDN$0.97
EUR€1 = 1.61CHF		1CHF = EUR€0.62
NZ$1 = 0.78CHF		1CHF = NZ$1.28
UK£1 = 2.04CHF		1CHF = UK£0.49
US$1 = 1.09CHF		1CHF = US$0.92

TRANSPORTATION

BY PLANE. Major international airports are in **Bern** (BRN; ☎031 960 21 11; www.alpar.ch), **Geneva** (GVA; ☎022 717 71 11; www.gva.ch), and **Zürich** (ZRH; ☎043 816 22 11; www.zurich-airport.com). From London, **easyJet** (☎0871 244 23 66; www.easyjet.com) has flights to Geneva and Zürich. **Aer Lingus** (Ireland ☎0818 365 000, Switzerland 442 86 99 33, UK 0870 876 5000; www.aerlingus.com) sells tickets from Dublin, IRE to Geneva. For info on flying to Switzerland from other locations, see p. 46.

BY TRAIN. Federal (**SBB, CFF**) and private railways connect most towns with frequent trains. For times and prices, check online (www.sbb.ch). **Eurail, Europass,** and **Inter Rail** are all valid on federal trains. The **Swiss Pass,** sold worldwide, offers four, eight, 15, 22, or 30 consecutive days of unlimited rail travel (www.swisstravelsystem.com). It also doubles as a **Swiss Museum Pass,** allowing free entry to 400 museums. (2nd-class 4-day pass US$222, 8-day US$315, 15-day US$384, 22-day US$446, 1-month US$496.)

BY BUS. **PTT Post Buses,** a barrage of government-run yellow coaches, connect rural villages and towns that trains don't service. Swiss Passes are valid on many buses; Eurail passes are not. Even with the Swiss Pass, you might have to pay 5-10CHF extra if you're riding certain buses.

BY CAR. Roads, generally in good condition, may become dangerous at higher altitudes in the winter. The speed limit is 50kph in towns and cities, 80kph on open roads, and 120kph on highways. Be sure to drive under the speed limit; radar traps are frequent. Many small towns forbid cars; some require special permits or restrict driving hours. US and British citizens 18 and older with a valid driver's license may drive in Switzerland for up to one year following their arrival; for stays longer than one year, drivers should contact the **Service des automobiles et de la navigation** (SAN; ☎022 388 30 30; www.geneve.ch/san) about acquiring a Swiss permit. Custom posts sell windshield stickers (US$33) required for driving on Swiss roads. Call ☎140 for roadside assistance.

BY BIKE. Cycling is a splendid way to see the country. Find bikes to rent at large train stations. The **Touring Club Suisse,** (☎022 417 22 20; www.tcs.ch), is a good source for maps and route descriptions.

KEEPING IN TOUCH

PHONE CODES	**Country code: 41. International dialing prefix:** 00. For more information on how to place international calls, see **Inside Back Cover.**

EMAIL AND INTERNET. Most Swiss cities, as well as a number of smaller towns, have at least one Internet cafe with web access available for about 12-24CHF per hour. Hostels and restaurants frequently offer Internet access as well, but it seldom comes for free: rates can climb as high as 12CHF per hour.

TELEPHONE. Whenever possible, use a calling card for international phone calls, as long-distance rates are often exorbitant for national phone services. For info about using mobile phones abroad, see p. 29. Most pay phones in Switzerland accept only prepaid taxcards, which are available at kiosks, post offices, and train stations. Direct access numbers include: **AT&T Direct** (☎800 89 00 11); **Canada Direct** (☎800 55 83 30); **MCI WorldPhone** (☎800 89 02 22); **Sprint** (☎800 899 777); **Telecom New Zealand** (☎800 55 64 11).

MAIL. Airmail from Switzerland averages three to 15 days to North America, although times are unpredictable from smaller towns. Domestic letters take one to three days. Bright yellow logos mark Swiss national post offices, referred to as **Die Post** in German or **La Poste** in French. Letters from Switzerland cost 1.40CHF to mail to the US, 1.20CHF to mail to the UK, and 0.85CHF mailed domestically. To receive mail in Switzerland, have mail delivered **Poste Restante.** Mail will go to the main post office unless you specify a subsidiary by street address. Address mail to be held as follows: LAST NAME, First Name, *Postlagernde Briefe*, Postal Code, City, SWITZERLAND. Bring a passport to pick up your mail; there may be a small fee.

ACCOMMODATIONS AND CAMPING

SWITZERLAND	❶	❷	❸	❹	❺
ACCOMMODATIONS	under 30CHF	30-42CHF	43-65CHF	66-125CHF	over 125CHF

There are hostels (*Jugendherbergen* in German, *Auberges de Jeunesse* in French, *Ostelli* in Italian) in all cities in Switzerland as well as in most towns. **Schweizer Jugendherbergen** (SJH; www.youthhostel.ch) runs HI hostels throughout Switzerland. Non-HI members can stay in any HI hostel, where beds are usually 30-44CHF; members typically receive a 6CHF discount. The more informal **Swiss Backpackers** (SB) organization (☎062 892 2675; www.backpacker.ch) lists over 40 hostels aimed at young, foreign travelers interested in socializing. Most **Swiss campgrounds** are not idyllic refuges but large plots glutted with RVs. Prices average 12-20CHF per tent site per night and 6-9CHF per extra person. **Hotels** and **pensions** tend to charge at least 65-80CHF for a single room and 80-120CHF for a double. The cheapest have *Gasthof*, *Gästehaus*, or *Hotel-Garni* in the name. **Privatzimmer** (rooms in a family home) run about 30-60CHF per person. Breakfast is included at most hotels, pensions, and *Privatzimmer*.

HIKING AND SKIING. Nearly every town has **hiking trails:** Interlaken, Grindelwald, Luzern (p. 746), and Zermatt offer particularly good hiking opportunities. Trails are marked with either red-white-red markers (only sturdy boots and hiking poles needed) or blue-white-blue markers (mountaineering equipment needed). **Skiing** in Switzerland is less expensive than in North America, provided you avoid pricey resorts. **Ski passes** run 40-70CHF per day, 100-300CHF per week; a week of lift tickets, equipment rental, lessons, lodging, and demi-pension (breakfast plus one other meal) averages 475CHF. **Summer skiing** is available in a few towns.

FOOD AND DRINK

SWITZERLAND	❶	❷	❸	❹	❺
FOOD	under 9CHF	9-23CHF	24-32CHF	33-52CHF	over 52CHF

Switzerland is not for the lactose intolerant. The Swiss are serious about dairy products, from rich and varied **cheeses** to decadent **milk chocolate**—even the major Swiss soft drink, **Rivella,** contains dairy. Swiss dishes vary from region to region. Bernese **rösti,** a plateful of hash-brown potatoes (sometimes flavored with bacon or cheese), is prevalent in the German regions; cheese or meat **fondue** is popular in the French regions. Try Valaisian **raclette,** made by melting cheese over a fire, scraping it onto a baked potato, and garnishing it with meat or vegetables. Supermarkets **Migros** and **Co-op** double as cafeterias; stop in for a cheap meal and groceries. Water from the fountains that adorn cities and large towns is usually safe; filling your bottle with it will save you money. *Kein Trinkwasser* or *Eau non potable* signs indicate unclean water. Each canton has its own local beer, which is often cheaper than soda.

HOLIDAYS AND FESTIVALS

Holidays: New Year's Day (Jan. 1); Epiphany (Jan. 6); Good Friday (Apr. 10); Easter (Apr. 13); Ascension (May 21); Labor Day (May 1); Whit Monday (Jun. 1); Swiss National Day (Aug. 1); All Saints' Day (Nov. 1); Christmas (Dec. 25-26).

Festivals: Two raucous festivals are the *Fasnacht* (Mar. 2-4, 2009; www.fasnacht.ch) in Basel and the *Escalade*, celebrating the invading Duke of Savoy's 1602 defeat by Geneva (Dec. 11-13, 2009; www.compagniede1602.ch). Music festivals occur throughout the summer, including Open-Air St. Gallen (late June; ☎0900 500 700; www.openairsg.ch) and the Montreux Jazz Festival (July; ☎963 8282; www.montreux.ch/mjf).

BEYOND TOURISM

Although Switzerland's volunteer opportunities are limited, a number of ecotourism and rural development organizations allow you to give back to the country. Your best bet is to go through a placement service. Look for opportunities for short-term work on websites like www.emploi.ch. For more info on opportunities across Europe, see **Beyond Tourism,** see p. 55.

Bergwald Projekt/Mountain Forest Project, Hauptstr. 24, 7014 Trin (☎081 650 40 40; www.bergwaldprojekt.ch). Organizes week-long conservation projects in Austria, Germany, and Switzerland.

Workcamp Switzerland, Komturei Tobel, Postfach 7, 9555 Tobel (☎071 917 24 86; www.workcamp.ch). Offers 2-4 week sessions during which volunteers live in a group environment and work on a community service project.

BERN   ☎031

Bern (pop. 128,000) has been Switzerland's capital since 1848, but don't expect power politics or businessmen in suits—the Bernese prefer to focus on the more leisurely things in life, like strolling through the arcades of the *Altstadt* or meandering along the banks of the serpentine Aare River.

TRANSPORTATION AND PRACTICAL INFORMATION. Bern's small **airport** (BRN; ☎031 960 2111) is 20min. from the city. A **bus** runs from the train station 50min. before each flight (10min., 14CHF). **Trains** run from the station at Bahnhofpl. to: Geneva (2hr., 2 per hr., 45CHF); Luzern (1hr., 2 per hr., 35CHF); St. Gallen (2hr., every hr., 65CHF); Zürich (1hr., 4 per day, 46CHF); Berlin, GER (12hr., 1-2 per hr., 95CHF); Paris, FRA (6hr., 4-5 per day, 115CHF). Local Bernmobil **buses** (departing from the left of the train station) and **trams** (departing from the front of the station) run 5:45am-midnight. (☎321 86 41; www.bernmobil.ch. Single ride 3.80CHF, day pass 12CHF.) Buses depart from the back of the station and post office. **Free bikes** are available from Bern Rollt at two locations: on Hirscheng. near the train station and on Zeugausg. near Waisenhauspl. (☎079 652 2319; www.bernrollt.ch. Passport and 20CHF deposit. Open May-Oct. daily 7:30am-9:30pm.)

Most of old Bern lies to your left as you leave the train station, along the Aare River. Bern's main train station is an often confusing tangle of essential services and extraneous shops. Take extra caution in the parks around the Parliament (Bundeshaus), especially at night. The **tourist office** is on the street level of the station. (☎031 328 1212; www.berninfo.ch. Open June-Sept. daily 9am-8:30pm; Oct.-May M-Sa 9am-6:30pm, Su 10am-5pm.) The **post office,** Schanzenpost 1, is one block to the right from the train station. (Open M-F 7:30am-9pm, Sa 8am-4pm, Su 4-9pm.) **Postal Codes:** CH-3000 to CH-3030.

Embassies in Bern include: **Canada,** Kirchenfeldstr. 88 (☎031 357 3200; www. geo.international.gc.ca/canada-europa/switzerland); **Ireland,** Kirchenfeldstr. 68 (☎031 352 1442); **UK,** Thunstr. 50 (☎031 359 7700; www.britishembassy.gov.uk/switzerland); **US,** Jubilaumsstr. 93 (☎031 357 7011; bern.usembassy.gov). The **Australian** consulate is in Geneva (p. 749). **New Zealanders** should contact their embassy in Berlin, GER (p. 290).

ACCOMMODATIONS AND FOOD. If Bern's cheaper hostels are full, check the tourist office for a list of private rooms. **Backpackers Bern/Hotel Glocke ❷,** Rathausg. 75, in the middle of the *Altstadt*, has friendly owners and a large common room. From the train station, cross the tram lines and turn left on Spitalg., continuing onto Marktg. Turn left at Kornhauspl., then right on Rathausg. (☎031 311 3771; www.bernbackpackers.ch. Internet 1CHF per 10min. Reception 8am-noon and 3-10pm. Dorms 33CHF; singles 69CHF; doubles 82CHF, with bath 140CHF; quads 172CHF. AmEx/MC/V.) At **Jugendherberge (HI) ❷,** Weiherg. 4 near the river, guests receive free access to a public swimming pool. (☎031 311 6316; www.youthhostel.ch/bern. Dorms 33CHF; singles 55CHF; doubles 84-98CHF; quads 148CHF. 6CHF HI discount. AmEx/MC/V.)

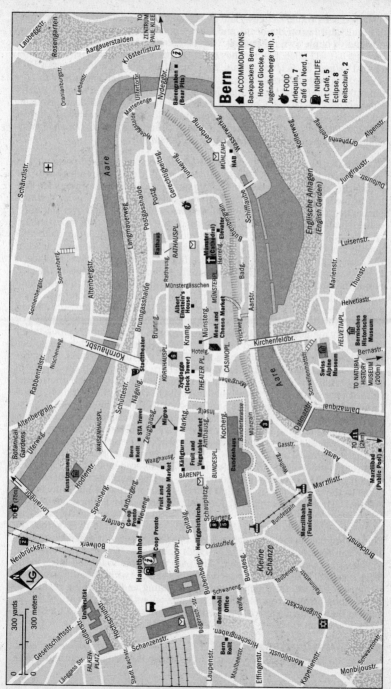

SWITZERLAND

Markets sell produce, cheese, and meats daily at Weinhauspl. and every Tuesday and Saturday on Bundespl. and Munstergasse from May through October. A friendly couple owns **Arlequin ❷**, Gerechtigkeitsg. 51, an 80s-inspired restaurant. (☎031 311 3946. Sandwiches 6-12CHF. Meat fondue 35CHF. Open Tu-W 11am-11:30pm, Th-F 11am-1:30am, Sa 11am-11pm. AmEx/MC/V; min. 20CHF.) A diverse crowd gathers under stage lights on the terrace at **Café du Nord ❸**, Lorrainestr. 2, and enjoys an all-organic menu. (☎031 332 2328. Pasta 19-25CHF. Meat entrees 22-32CHF. Open M-W 8am-11:30pm, Th-F 8am-1:30am, Sa 9am-1:30am, Su 4pm-11:30pm. Kitchen open M-Sa 11:30am-2pm and 6:30-10pm, Su 4:30-11:30pm. MC/V.) For groceries, head to **Migros**, Marktg. 46. (Open M 9am-6:30pm, Tu 8am-6:30pm, W-F 8am-9pm, Sa 7am-4pm.)

⑤ SIGHTS. Bern's historic center *(Altstadt)*, one of the best-preserved in Switzerland, is a UNESCO World Heritage sight. Covered arcades allow for wandering and window shopping, while the wide cobblestone streets are dotted by medieval wells topped with Renaissance statues. The Swiss national parliament meets in the massive **Bundeshaus,** which rises high over the Aare; water tumbles from fountains in front of the entrance. (www.parlament. ch. One 45min. tour per hr. M-Sa 9-11am and 2-4pm. English-language tour usually 2pm. Free.) From the Bundeshaus, Kocherg. and Herreng. lead to the 15th-century Protestant **Münster** (Cathedral); above the main entrance, a golden sculpture depicts the torments of hell. For a fantastic view of the city, climb the Münster's 100m spire. (Cathedral open Easter-Oct. Tu-Sa 10am-5pm, Su. 11:30am-5pm; Nov.-Easter Tu-Sa 10am-noon, Su 11:30am-2pm. Free. Audio guide 5CHF. Tower open Easter-Oct. M-Sa 10am-4:30pm, Su 11:30am-4:30pm; Nov.-Mar. M-F 2pm-3pm, Sa 2pm-5pm, Su 11:30am-1pm. 4CHF.) For some early medieval flair, check out the **Zytglogge**, a 12th-century clock tower on Kramg. that once marked the city's western boundary. Watch the golden figure use his hammer to ring the golden bell at the top every hour. Down the road is **Albert Einstein's house,** Kramg. 49, where he conceived the theory of general relativity in 1915. His small apartment is now filled with photos and letters. (☎031 312 0091; www.einstein-bern.ch. Open Apr.-Sept. daily 10am-5pm; Feb.-Mar. Tu-F 10am-5pm, Sa 10am-4pm. 6CHF, students 4.50CHF.) Several steep walkways lead from the Bundeshaus to the **Aare River.**

A recent addition to Bern's many museums is the **⬛Zentrum Paul Klee,** Monument im Fruchtland 3, which houses the world's largest collection of artwork by the renowned Paul Klee. (☎031 359 0101; www.zpk.org. Take bus #12 to Zentrum Paul Klee. Open Tu-Su 10am-5pm. 16CHF, students 14CHF.) Near Lorrainebrücke, the **Kunstmuseum,** Hodlerstr. 8-12, has paintings from the Middle Ages to the contemporary era and features a smattering of big 20th-century names: Giacometti, Kandinsky, Kirchner, Picasso, and Pollock. (☎031 328 0944; www.kunstmuseumbern.ch. Open Tu-Su 10am-5pm. 7CHF, students 5CHF. Special exhibits up to 18CHF.) At the east side of the river, across the Nydeggbrücke, lie the **Bärengraben** (Bear Pits), where gawking crowds observe three European brown bears—the city's namesake. (Open daily June-Sept. 9:30am-5pm; Oct.-May 10am-4pm.) The path up the hill to the left leads to the **⬛Rosengarten** (Rose Garden), which provides visitors with a breathtaking view of Bern's *Altstadt,* especially at sunset. Anything and everything relating to Bern's long history, from technological innovations to religious art, is on display in the jam-packed **Bernisches Historische Museum,** Helvetiapl. 5. (☎031 350 7711; www.bhm.ch. Open Tu-F 10am-5pm. 13CHF, students 8CHF.)

⬛⬛ ENTERTAINMENT AND NIGHTLIFE. Check out *Bewegungsmelder,* available at the tourist office, for events. July's **Gurten Festival** (www.gurtenfestival.

ch) draws young and energetic crowds and has attracted such luminaries as Bob Dylan and Elvis Costello, while jazz-lovers arrive in early May for the **International Jazz Festival** (www.jazzfestivalbern.ch). Bern's traditional folk festival is the **Onion Market**, which brings 50 tons of onions to the city (late Nov. 2009). The orange grove at **Stadtgärtnerei Elfenau** (tram #19, dir.: Elfenau, to Luternauweg) has free Sunday concerts in the summer. From mid-July to mid-August, **Orange-Cinema** (☎0800 07 80 78; www.orangecinema.ch) screens recent films outdoors; tickets are available from the tourist office in the train station.

Find new DJs at ■**Art Café**, Gurteng. 6, a cafe and club with huge windows overlooking the street. (☎031 318 2070. Open M-W 7am- 1:30am, Th-F 7am-3:30am, Sa 8am-3:30am, Su 10am-3:30am. Cash only.) The Art Café crowd wanders next door to dance to funky beats at **Eclipse**, which has the same owners. (☎031 882 0888; www.eclipse-bar.ch. Open M-W 7am- 1:30am, Th-F 7am-3am, Sa 9am-3am.) Many locals gather at **Gut Gelaunt**, Shauptplatzgasse 22, just around the corner, to relax outside and enjoy the special 12-14CHF alcoholic gelato sundaes. (☎031 312 8989; www.gutgelaunt.ch. Beer 4-6CHF, and wine 6-8CHF. Open noon-midnight.) To escape the fashionable folk that gather in the *Altstadt* at night, head to the **Reitschule**, Neubrückestr. 8, a graffiti-covered center for Bern's counterculture. (Open daily 8pm-late.)

ZÜRICH ☎044

Battalions of executives charge daily through Zürich, Switzerland's largest city (pop. 370,000) and the world's fourth-largest stock exchange—bringing with them enough money to keep upper-crust boutiques thriving. But only footsteps away from the flashy Bahnhofstr. shopping district is the old town and city's student quarter, home to cobblestoned pieces of history and an energetic counter-culture that has inspired generations of Swiss philosophers and artists.

▐ TRANSPORTATION

Flights: Zürich-Kloten Airport (ZRH; ☎044 816 2211; www.zurich-airport.com) is a major hub for Swiss International Airlines (☎084 885 2000; www.swiss.com). Daily connections to: **Frankfurt, GER; London, BRI; Paris, FRA.** Trains connect the airport to the Hauptbahnhof in the city center. 3-6 per hr., 6CHF; Eurail and SwissPass valid.

Trains: Run to: **Basel** (1hr., 2-3 per hr., 31CHF); **Bern** (1hr., 3-4 per hr., 46CHF); **Geneva** (3hr., 1-2 per hr., 88CHF); **Luzern** (1hr., 1-2 per hr., 23CHF); **St. Gallen** (30min.; 2-3 per hr.; 28CHF); **Milan, ITA** (4hr., 1 per 2hr., 72-87CHF); **Munich, GER** (5hr., 4-5 per day, 90CHF); **Paris, FRA** (5hr., 4 per day, 112-140CHF, under 26 86CHF).

Public Transportation: Trams criss-cross the city, originating at the *Hauptbahnhof*. Tickets valid for 1hr. cost 4CHF (press the blue button on automatic ticket machines); tickets (valid for 30min.) cost 2.40CHF (yellow button). Police fine riders without tickets 60CHF. If you plan to ride several times, buy a 24hr. **Tageskarte** (7.60CHF; green button), valid on trams, buses, and ferries. **Night buses** (5CHF ticket valid all night) run from the city center to outlying areas (F-Su).

Car Rental: The tourist office offers a 20% discount and free upgrade deal with **Europcar** (☎044 804 4646; www.europcar.ch). Prices from 155CHF per day with unlimited mileage. 20+. Branches at the airport (☎043 255 5656), Josefstr. 53 (☎044 271 5656), and Lindenstr. 33 (☎044 383 1747). Rent in the city; 40% tax is added at the airport.

Bike Rental: Bike loans from **Züri Rollt** (☎043 288 3400; www.zuerirollt.ch) are free for 6hr. during business hours; otherwise 5CHF per day, 20CHF per night. Pick up a bike from **Globus City**, the green hut on the edge of the garden between Bahnhofstr. and Löwenstr.; **Opernhaus**, by the opera house past Bellevuepl.; **Velogate**, across from

SWITZERLAND

SWITZERLAND

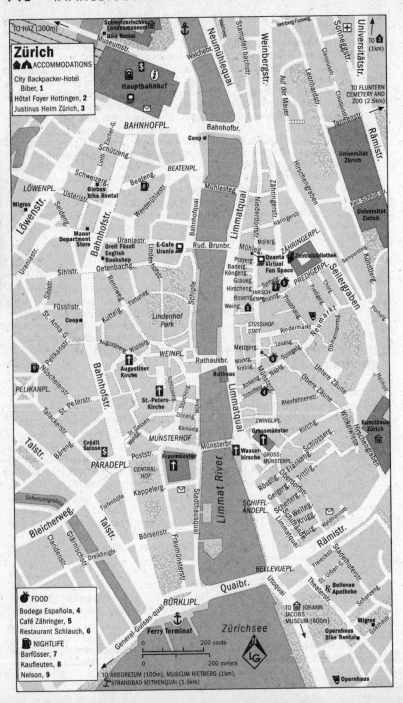

TO HAZ (300m)

Schweizerisches
Landesmuseum
Bike Rental
Museumstr.

Zürich

🏠 ACCOMMODATIONS

City Backpacker-Hotel
Biber, **1**
Hôtel Foyer Hottingen, **2**
Justinus Heim Zürich, **3**

Hauptbahnhof

BAHNHOFPL.

Bahnhofbr.

Coop

Schützeng.

Limmatbr.

BEATENPL.

Schweizerg.

LÖWENPL.

Beateng.

Globus
Bike Rental

Werdmühlestr.

Mühlesteg

Migros

Löwenstr.

Usterstr.

Seideng.

Bahnhofquai

Limmatquai

Zähringerstr.

Niederdorfstr.

Universität
Zürich

Karl-Schmid-str.

Universität
Zürich

Manor
Department
Store

Uraniastr.

Orell Füssli
English
Bookshop

E-Cafe
Urania

Rud. Brunbr.

Mühleg.

Preyerg.
Baderg.
Köngeng.
Graueg.
Hirscheng.
Rosengl.
Weing.

Quanta
Virtual
Fun Space

Zentralbibliothek

ZÄHRINGERPL.

PREDIGERPL.

HIRSCH-
ENGRABEN

Seilergraben

Oetenbachg.

Rennweg

Kuttelg.

Fortunag.

Lindenhof
Park

Schipfe

Sihlstr.

Füsslistr.

Coop

St.-Anna-G.

Pelikanstr.

Augustinerg.

Widderg.

STÜSSIHOF-
STATT.

Rindermarkt

Neumarkt

Metzgerg.

Leueng.

Obmannamtsg.

WEINPL.

Rathausbr.

Markt

Napfg.

Spiegelg.

Untere Zäune

Obere Zäune

Augustiner
Kirche

Rathaus

Ankeng.

Schöneng.

Bleufahnenstr.

PELIKANPL.

Nüschelerstr.

St. Peterstr.

St.-Peters-
Kirche

Schlüssesg.

Stüdacheg.

Zinneng.

Limmatquai

Münsterg.

ZWINGLIPL.

Grossmünster

Kirchg.

Schlosserg.

Kunsthaus
Zürich

Talstr.

Bäreng.

Crédit
Suisse

In Gassen
Woogg.

Kämbelg.

MÜNSTERHOF

Münsterbr.

Wasser-
kirche

GROSS-
MÜNSTERPL.

Talackerstr.

Poststr.

CENTRAL-
HOF

Fraumünster

Rössligl.

Oberdorfstr.

Geigerg.

Scheiterg.

Weiteg.

Oberfrankeng.

Trittlig.

Krugg.

PARADEPL.

Kappelerg.

SCHIFFL-
ÄNDEPL.

Limmatquai

Schanzengraben

Tiefenhöfe

Stadthausquai

Sorg.

Waldmannstr.

Rämistr.

Bleicherweg

Talstr.

Börsenstr.

Fraumünsterstr.

BELLEVUEPL.

Theaterstr.

Freieckstr.

St.-Urban-g.

Stadelhoferstr.

Schanzeng.

Bellevue
Apotheke

Claridenstr.

Glärnischstr.

Dreikönigstr.

BÜRKLIPL.

Quaibr.

Utoquai

Migros

Goethestr.

Limmat River

General-Guisan-quai

Ferry Terminal

Zürichsee

TO JOHANN
JACOBS
MUSEUM (800m)

Opernhaus
Bike Rental

Opernhaus

0   200 yards

0   200 meters

TO ARBORETUM (100m), MUSEUM RIETBERG (1km),
STRANDBAD MYTHENQUAI (1.5km)

Neumühlequai

Walchebr.

Stampfenbachstr.

Weinbergstr.

Weinberg Fussweg

Sonneggstr.

Universitätstr.

TO
(1km)

TO FLUNTERN
CEMETERY AND
ZOO (2.5km)

Clausiusstr.

Leonhardstr.

Tannenstr.

Rämistr.

Auf der Mauer

Hirschengraben

Sempersteig.

Künstlerg.

Florhofg.

Heimstr.

Froschaug.

Predigerg.

Chorg.

Winkelwiese

Hirschengraben

🍎 FOOD

Bodega Española, **4**
Café Zähringer, **5**
Restaurant Schlauch, **6**

🍴 NIGHTLIFE

Barfüsser, **7**
Kaufleuten, **8**
Nelson, **9**

Hauptbahnhof's tracks next to the Landesmuseum castle. Bikes must be returned to original rental station. Passport and 20CHF deposit. Open May-Oct. 7:30am-11:30pm.

🔷🔷 ORIENTATION AND PRACTICAL INFORMATION

Zürich is in north-central Switzerland, close to the German border and on some of the lowest land in the country. The **Limmat River** splits the city down the middle on its way to the **Zürichsee** (Lake Zürich). The **Hauptbahnhof** (train station) lies on the western bank and marks the beginning of **Bahnhofstraße,** the city's main shopping street. Two-thirds of the way down Bahnhofstr. lies **Paradeplatz,** the banking center of Zürich, which marks the beginning of the last stretch of the shopping street (reserved for those with trust funds). The eastern bank of the river is dominated by the university district, which stretches above the narrow **Niederdorfstraße** and pulses with bars, clubs, and restaurants.

Tourist Office: In the **Hauptbahnhof** (☎044 215 4000; www.zuerich.com). An electronic hotel reservation board is at the front of the station. Also sells the **ZürichCARD,** which is good for unlimited public transportation, free museum admission, and discounts on sights and tours (1-day 17CHF, 3-day 34CHF). Open May-Oct. M-Sa 8am-8:30pm, Su 8:30am-6:30pm; Nov.-Apr. M-Sa 8:30am-7pm, Su 9am-6:30pm.

Currency Exchange: On the main floor of the train station. Cash advances for MC/V with photo ID; min. 200CHF, max. 1000CHF. Open daily 6:30am-9:30pm. **Crédit Suisse,** at Paradepl. 5CHF commission. Open M-F 8:15am-5pm.

Luggage Storage: Middle level of *Hauptbahnhof*. 5-8CHF. Open daily 4:15am-1:30am.

GLBT Resources: Homosexuelle Arbeitsgruppe Zürich (HAZ), on the 3rd fl. of Sihlquai 67 (☎044 271 2250; www.haz.ch), has a library and meetings. Open W 2-6pm.

24hr. Pharmacy: Bellevue Apotheke, Theaterstr. 14, on Bellevuepl. (☎044 266 6222).

Internet: Quanta Virtual Fun Space (☎044 260 7266), at the corner of Mühleg. and Niederdorfstr. 3CHF per 15min., 5CHF per 30min. Open daily 9am-midnight.

Post Office: Sihlpost, Kasernestr. 95-97, behind the station. Open M-F 6:30am-10:30pm, Sa 6:30am-8pm, Su 10am-10:30pm. **Postal Code:** CH-8021.

🔷🔷 ACCOMMODATIONS AND CAMPING

Zürich's few budget accommodations are easily accessible by foot or public transportation. Reserve ahead, especially in summer.

▨ **Justinus Heim Zürich,** Freudenbergstr. 146 (☎044 361 3806; justinuszh@bluewin.ch). Take tram #9 or 10 (dir.: Bahnhof Oerlikon) to Seilbahn Rigiblick, then take the funicular to the top (open daily 5:20am-12:40am). This hillside hostel, which hosts students during the term period, is removed from the downtown bustle but is easily accessible. Beautiful view of the city. Breakfast included. Reception 8am-noon and 5-9pm. Singles 50CHF, with shower 65CHF; doubles 90-110CHF. Rates rise July-Aug. V. ❸

The City Backpacker-Hotel Biber, Niederdorfstr. 5 (☎044 251 9015; www.city-backpacker.ch). From the Hauptbahnhof, cross the bridge and Limmatquai, turn right onto Niederdorfst., and walk for 5min. With Niederdorfstr. nightlife right outside, you may not need your bunk bed. Linens and towels each 3CHF; blanket provided. Internet 6CHF per hr. Reception 8-11am and 3-10pm. Check-out 10am. Dorms 34CHF; singles 71CHF; doubles 98CHF; triples 135CHF; quads 176CHF. MC/V. ❷

Hôtel Foyer Hottingen, Hottingenstr. 31 (☎044 256 1919; www.foyer-hottingen.ch). Take tram #3 (dir.: Kluspl.) to Hottingerpl. Families and student backpackers fill this house a block from the Kunsthaus. Breakfast included. Reception 7am-11pm. Partitioned dorms (40CHF) provide privacy. Singles 85-95CHF, with bath 120-135CHF; doubles 120/160-170CHF; triples 145/190CHF; quads 180CHF. MC/V. ❷

☐ FOOD

Zürich's has over 1300 restaurants, offering a bite of everything. The cheapest meals are available at *Würstli* (sausage) stands for 5CHF. The **farmer's markets** at Bürklipl. (Tu and F 6-11am) and Rosenhof (Th 10am-8pm, Sa 10am-5pm) sell produce and flowers. Head to **Niederdorfstraße** for a variety of snack bars and cheaper restaurants interspersed among fancier establishments.

Café Zähringer, Zähringerpl. 11 (☎044 252 0500; www.cafe-zaehringer.ch). Enjoy mainly vegetarian and vegan fare in this colorful, student-friendly cafe. Try their *Kefirwasser*, a purple, fizzy drink made from dates and mushrooms fed with sugar (4CHF). Salads 7-13CHF. Pasta 4-14CHF. Stir-fry 18.50-26.50CHF. Breakfast specials 8.50-23CHF. Open M 6pm-midnight, Tu-Su 8am-midnight. Cash only. ❷

Restaurant Schlauch, Münstergasse 20 (☎044 251 2304). Enjoy the billiard tables at this affordable downtown eatery. Soups 5-8.50CHF. Salads 7-14CHF. Entrees 8-20CHF. Open Tu-Sa 11:30am-2pm and 6-9pm. AmEx/MC/V. ❷

Bodega Española, Münstergasse 15 (☎044 251 2310). Has been serving Catalán delights since 1874. Egg-and-potato tortilla dishes 16-18CHF. Tapas 4.80CHF. Open daily 10am-midnight. Kitchen open noon-2pm and 6-10pm. AmEx/MC/V. ❷

☉ SIGHTS

Bahnhofstraße leads into the city from the train station. The street is filled with shoppers during the day but falls dead quiet after 6pm and on weekends. At the Zürichsee end of Bahnhofstr., **Bürkliplatz** is a good place to begin walking along the lake shore. The *platz* itself hosts a Saturday **flea market** *(May-Oct. 6am-3pm)*. On the other side of the Limmat River, the pedestrian zone continues on Niederdorfstr. and Münsterg. Off Niederdorfstr., **Spiegelgasse** was once home to Goethe and Lenin. **Fraumünster, Grossmünster,** and **St. Peters Kirche** grace the Limmat River. For a view of Zürich from the water, as well as a chance to see some of the towns on the banks of the Zürichsee, ☐**boat tours** costing a fraction of those in other Swiss cities leave from the ferry terminal at Bürklipl. The shortest tour, A Kleine Rundfahrten, lasts 1hr. *(May-Sept. daily 11am-6:30pm., 7.80CHF.)*

FRAUMÜNSTER. Marc Chagall's stained glass windows depicting Biblical scenes add vibrancy to this otherwise austere 13th-century Gothic cathedral. A mural on the courtyard's archway depicts Felix and Regula (the decapitated patron saints of Zürich) with their heads in their hands. *(Off Paradepl. Open May-Nov. M-Sa 10am-6pm, Su 11:30am-6pm; Dec.-Apr. M-Sa 10am-4pm, Su 11:30am-4pm. Free.)*

GROSSMÜNSTER. Ulrich Zwingli kickstarted the Swiss German Reformation at Grossmünster in the 16th century. Today, the cathedral is Zürich's main landmark. Its defining twin towers are best viewed on the bridge near the Fraumünster. *(Towers open daily Mar.-Oct. 9:15am-5pm; Nov.-Feb. 10:15am-4:30pm. 2CHF.)* One of Zwingli's Bibles lies in a case near his pulpit. Downstairs in the cavernous 12th-century **crypt** is a menacing statue of Charlemagne and his 2m sword. *(Church open daily mid-Mar.-Oct. 9am-6pm; Nov.-mid-Mar. 10am-5pm. Free.)*

BEACHES. When the weather heats up, a visit to the beaches along the Zürichsee offers respite. The city has numerous free swimming spots, which are labeled on a map distributed by the tourist office. The convenient and popular **Arboretum** is about 10m down from the Quaibrücke. *(Tram #5 to Rentenanstalt and head to the water.)* Across the lake, **Zürichhorn** draws crowds with its peaceful gardens and a famous statue by Jean Tinguely. *(Tram #2 or 4 to Frolichst., then walk towards the lake.)* **Strandbad Mythenquai,** along the western shore, offers diving towers and a water trampoline. *(Tram #7 to Brunaustr. and walk 2min. in the same direction until you* *see a set of stairs. Look for signs. ☎044 201 0000. Check out www.sportamt.ch for info on water quality. Open daily May to early Sept. 9am-8pm. 6CHF, ages 16-20 4.50CHF.)*

🏛 MUSEUMS

🔲 MUSEUM RIETBERG. Rietberg presents an outstanding collection of Asian, African, and other non-European art, housed in three structures spread around the Rieter-Park. The basement of the new **Emerald Building** houses masterpieces from Asia and Africa; highlights include Chinese boddhisatvas and Japanese Noh masks. **Villa Wesendonck** (where Wagner wrote *Tristan and Isolde*) holds works from South Asia, Central America, and Oceania, while **Park-Villa Rieter** includes a small collection of Near Eastern art. *(Gablerstr. 15. Tram #7 to Museum Rietberg. ☎044 206 3131; www.rietberg.ch. Buy tickets in the Emerald building. All buildings open Apr.-Sept. Tu and F-Su 10am-5pm, W-Th 10am-8pm. 16CHF, students 12CHF. MC/V.)*

🔲 KUNSTHAUS ZÜRICH. The Kunsthaus, Europe's largest privately funded museum, houses a vast collection ranging from religious works by the Old Masters to 21st-century American Pop Art. Compositions by Chagall, Dalí, Gauguin, van Gogh, Munch, Picasso, Rembrandt, Renoir, and Rubens stretch from wall to wall in a patchwork of rich color while a Modern sculpture made of car tops adorns the entrance. *(Heimpl. 1. Take tram #3, 5, 8, or 9 to Kunsthaus. ☎044 253 8484; www.kunsthaus.ch. English-language audio tour and brochure. Open T and Sa-Su 10am-6pm, W-F 10am-8pm. 18CHF, students 12CHF. AmEx/MC/V.)*

🎵 🎭 ENTERTAINMENT AND NIGHTLIFE

Most English-language movies in Zürich are screened with French and German subtitles (marked "E/D/F"). Films generally cost 15CHF and up, but less on Mondays. From mid-July to mid-August, the **OrangeCinema,** an open-air cinema at Zürichhorn (tram #2 or 4 to Fröhlichstr.), attracts huge crowds to its lakefront screenings. In mid-August, the **Street Parade** brings together ravers from all over for the world's biggest techno party.

> **THAT EXPLAINS THE TASSELS.** Beware the deceptive and common title of "night club"—it's really just a euphemism for "strip club."

For information on after-dark happenings, check **ZüriTipp** (www.zueritipp.ch) or pick up a free copy of *ZürichGuide* or *ZürichEvents* from the tourist office. On **Niederdorfstraße,** the epicenter of Zürich's *Altstadt* nightlife, bars are packed to the brim almost every night. **Kreis 5,** once the industrial area of Zürich, has recently developed into party central, with ubiquitous clubs, bars, and lounges taking over former factories. Kreis 5 lies northwest of the *Hauptbahnhof,* with Hardstr. as its axis. To get there, take tram #4 (dir.: Werdholzi) or #13 (dir.: Albisgütli) to Escher-Wyss-Pl. and follow the crowds. Closer to the Old Town, **Langstraße,** reached by walking away from the river on the city's western side, is the reputed red-light district, with many bars and clubs (some sleazier than others). Beer in Zürich is pricey (from 6CHF), but an array of cheap bars have established themselves on Niederdorfstr. near Mühleg.

🔲 Kaufleuten, Pelikanstr. 18 (☎044 225 3322; www.kaufleuten.ch). For a memorable evening, visit this former theater transformed into trendy club. Cover 10-30CHF. Hours vary, but generally open M-Th and Su 11pm-2am, F-Sa 11pm-4am. MC/V.

Nelson, Beateng. 11 (☎044 212 6016). Locals, backpackers, and businessmen chug beer (9CHF per pint) at this large Irish pub. 20+. Open M-W 11:30am-2am, Th 11:30am-3am, F 11:30am-4:30am, Sa 3pm-4:30am, Su 3pm-2am. MC/V.

Barfüsser, Spitalg. 14 (☎044 251 4064), off Zähringerpl. Freely flowing mixed drinks (14-17CHF) and wine (6-9CHF) accompany delicious sushi at this gay bar. Open M-Th noon-1am, F-Sa noon-2am, Su 5pm-1am. AmEx/MC/V.

LUZERN (LUCERNE) ☎041

Luzern (pop. 58,000) rightfully welcomes busloads of tourists each day in the summer. The streets of the *Altstadt* lead down to the placid Vierwaldstättersee (Lake Lucerne); the covered bridges over the river are among the most photographed sights in Switzerland, and the sunrise over the famous Mt. Pilatus has hypnotized artists—including Goethe, Twain, and Wagner—for centuries.

TRANSPORTATION AND PRACTICAL INFORMATION. Trains leave the large Bahnhof for: Basel (1hr., 2 per hr., 31CHF); Bern via Olten (1hr., 2 per hr., 31CHF); Geneva (3hr., 1-2 per hr., 69CHF); Zürich (1hr., 2 per hr., 23CHF). **VBL buses** depart in front of the train station and provide extensive coverage of Luzern. **Boats** leave from across the road to destinations all over Lake Luzern; some offer themed cruises. (☎041 612 9090; www.lakelucerne.ch. Cruises 15-60CHF.) Route maps are available at the station **tourist office,** Banhofstr. 3, also accessible from the train station, which reserves rooms for free, and holds daily guided tours at 9:45am for 18CHF. (☎041 227 1717; www.luzern.org. Open May-Oct. M-F 8:30am-6:30pm, Sa-Su 9am-6:30pm; Nov.-Apr. M-F 8:30am-5:30pm, Sa 9am-1pm.) There are two **post offices** by the train station; the older building by the bridge is the main one.

ACCOMMODATIONS AND FOOD. Inexpensive beds are limited, so call ahead to reserve. Take Bus 19 to stop Jugendherberge to reach **Youth Hostel Luzern (HI) ❹,** AmRotsee Sedelstrasse 12. (☎041 420 8800; www.youthhostel.ch/luzern. Breakfast included. Internet 6CHF per hr. Reception 7-10am and 2pm-midnight. Dorms 40-41CHF. 6CHF HI discount. AmEx/V/MC.) To reach **Backpackers Lucerne ❷,** Alpenquai 42, turn right from the station onto Inseliquai and follow it for 20min. until it turns into Alpenquai. The hostel's distance from the center of town may be inconvenient, but it has a fun, communal vibe. (☎041 360 0420; www.backpackerslucerne.ch. Laundry 9CHF. Internet 10CHF per hr. Reception 7:30-10am and 4-11pm. Dorms 31CHF; doubles 70-76CHF. Bike rental 18CHF per day. Cash only.) Overlooking the river from the *Altstadt* is the **Tourist Hotel ❸,** St. Karliquai 12, which offers plain rooms and a prime location. From the station, walk along Bahnhofstr., cross the river at the second covered bridge, and make a left onto St. Karliquai. (☎041 410 2474; www.touristhotel.ch. Breakfast included. Dorms 38-45CHF; doubles 88-120CHF; triples 129-144CHF; quads 172-188CHF. AmEx/V.) Watch trains roll by while gorging on delicious Middle Eastern fare at **Erdem Kebab ❶,** down Zentralstr. from the Banhof. (Falafel 8CHF. Kebab 8-12CHF. Open M-Th 10am-midnight, F-Sa 11am-8pm. Cash only.) Markets along the river sell fresh food on Tuesday and Saturday mornings. There's also a **Coop** supermarket at the train station. (Open M-Sa 6:30am-9pm, Su 8am-9pm.)

SIGHTS AND ENTERTAINMENT. The *Altstadt*, across the river from the station, is famous for its frescoed houses; the best examples are on Hirschenpl. and Weinmarkt. The 14th-century **Kapellbrücke,** a wooden-roofed bridge, runs from the left of the train station to the *Altstadt* and is decorated with Swiss historical scenes. Farther down the river, the **Spreuerbrücke** is adorned by Kaspar Meglinger's eerie *Totentanz* (Dance of Death) paintings. On the hills above the river, the **Museggmauer** and its towers are all that remain of the medieval city's ramparts. Three of the towers are accessible to visitors and provide panoramic views of the city; one, the **Zyt,** features the inner workings of Luzern's oldest clock, a 16th-century doozy that chimes one minute before all other city clocks. From Mühlenpl., walk up Brugglig., then head uphill to the right on Museggstr. and follow the castle signs. (Open in summer daily 8am-7pm.) To the east is the magnificent **Löwendenkmal,** the dying lion of Luzern, carved into a cliff on Denkmalstr. to honor the Swiss soldiers who died defending King Louis XVI of France during the invasion of the Tuileries in 1792. Close by is the **Gletschergarten** (Glacier Garden), which showcases an odd but interesting collection including Ice Age formations, a 19th-century Swiss house, and a hall of mirrors. (☎041 410 4340; www.gletschergarten.ch. Open daily Apr.-Oct. 9am-6pm; Nov.-Mar. 10am-5pm. 12CHF, students 9.50.)

Europe's largest transportation museum, the ▓**Verkehrshaus der Schweiz** (Swiss Transport Museum), Lidostr. 5, has interactive displays on everything from early flying machines to cars. (☎041 370 4444; www.verkehrshaus.ch. Open daily Apr.-Oct. 10am-6pm; Nov.-Mar. 10am-5pm. 24CHF, students 22CHF, with Eurail Pass 14CHF.) The **Picasso Museum,** Am Rhyn Haus, Furreng. 21, displays some of Picasso's sketches and a large collection of photographs from his later years. (☎041 410 3533. Open daily Apr.-Oct. 10am-6pm; Nov.-Mar. 11am-1pm and 2-4pm. 8CHF, students 5CHF.)

Although Luzern's nightlife is more about relaxing than club-hopping, there are still many options for those looking to dance the night away. **The Loft,** Haldenstr. 21, hosts special DJs and theme nights. (☎041 410 9244; www. theloft.ch. Beer 9-11CHF. Open W 9pm-2am, Th-Su 10am-4am.) The mellow **Jazzkantine** club, Grabenstr. 8, is affiliated with the renowned **Lucerne School of Music.** (Sandwiches 6-8CHF. Open mid-Aug. to mid-July M-Sa 7am-1:30am, Su 4pm-1:30am. MC/V.) Luzern attracts big names for its two jazz festivals: **Blue Balls Festival** (last week of July) and **Blues Festival** (2nd week of Nov.)

FRENCH SWITZERLAND

The picturesque scenery and refined cities of French Switzerland have attracted herds of tourists for centuries, and there's no denying that the area's charm comes at a steep price. But the best experiences in French Switzerland are free: strolling down tree-lined avenues, soaking up endearing *vieilles villes*, and taking in the mountain vistas from across Lac Léman and Lac Neuchâtel.

GENEVA (GENÈVE)   ☎022

Geneva (pop. 186,000) began with a tomb, blossomed into a religious center, became the "Protestant Rome," and ultimately emerged as a center for world diplomacy. Today, thanks to the presence of dozens of multinational organizations, including the United Nations and the Red Cross, the city is easily the most worldly in Switzerland. But Geneva's heritage lingers; you can sense it in the street names paying homage to Genevese patriots of old and the ubiquitous presence of the cherished cuckoo clock.

▐ TRANSPORTATION

Flights: Cointrin Airport (GVA; ☎022 717 7111, flight info ☎022 717 7105) is a hub for **Swiss International Airlines** (☎0848 85 20 00) and also serves **Air France** (☎827 8787) and **British Airways** (☎0848 80 10 10). Several direct flights per day to **Amsterdam, NTH;**

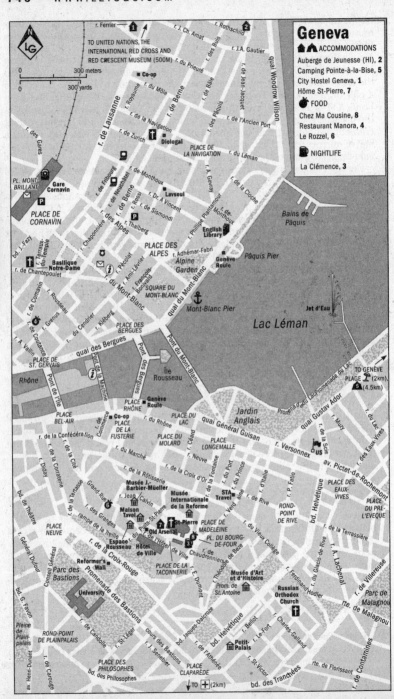

SWITZERLAND

N
LG

0   300 meters
0   300 yards

r. Ferrier

TO UNITED NATIONS, THE
INTERNATIONAL RED CROSS AND
RED CRESCENT MUSEUM (500M)

r. J. Ch. Amat
r. Rothschild
r. des Buis
r. J.A. Gautier
quai Woodrow Wilson

Geneva

ACCOMMODATIONS
Auberge de Jeunesse (HI), **2**
Camping Pointe-à-la-Bise, **5**
City Hostel Geneva, **1**
Hôme St-Pierre, **7**

FOOD
Chez Ma Cousine, **8**
Restaurant Manora, **4**
Le Rozzel, **6**

NIGHTLIFE
La Clémence, **3**

Co-op

r. du Prieuré
r. du Môle
r. Royaume
r. de la Navigation
r. de Zurich
r. de Lausanne
r. de Berne
r. de Bâle
r. de Jean-Jacquet
r. du Paquis
PLACE DE
LA NAVIGATION
Diologal
r. de l'Ancien Port
r. du Léman
r. des Gares
PL. MONT-
BRILLANT
Gare Cornavin
PLACE DE
CORNAVIN
r. J. Fazy
r. de Fribourg
r. de Neuchâtel
r. de Monthoux
Dr. A Vincent
Lavseul
r. de Berne
r. Rossi
r. de Sismondi
r. Thalberg
r. des Alpes
r. Chaponnière
PLACE DES
ALPES
r. Pécolat
r. Ami-Lévriet
r. du Mont-Blanc
r. de Monthoux
r. A. Gevray
r. de la Cloche
r. Philippe Plantamour
r. de Monthoux
r. Adhémar-Fabri
Genève Roule
English Library
Bains de Pâquis
Pâquis Pier
Basilique Notre-Dame
r. Terraux-du-Temple
r. de Chantepoulet
r. de Cornavin
r. Rousseau
r. A. Vallin
r. Grenus
r. du Cendrier
r. Kléber
r. de Coutance
PLACE DE
ST. GERVAIS
Rhône
quai des Bergues
Pont des Bergues
Pont de la Machine
Pont de l'Île
PLACE DES
BERGUES
Île Rousseau
Pont du Mont-Blanc
SQUARE DU
MONT-BLANC
quai du Mont-Blanc
Mont-Blanc Pier
Lac Léman
Jet d'Eau
TO GENÈVE PLAGE (2km),
(4.5km)
Promenade du Lac
quai Gustav Ador
Rhône
PLACE
BEL-AIR
r. de Commerce
Co-op
PLACE
RHÔNE
Genève Roule
r. du Rhône
r. de la Confédération
r. de la Cité
r. de la Corraterie
PLACE DE
LA FUSTERIE
r. du Marché
PLACE DU
MOLARD
PLACE DU
LAC
quai Général Guisan
Jardin Anglais
PLACE
LONGEMALLE
r. Neuve
r. de la Rôtisserie
r. de la Croix-d'Or
r. de la Fontaine
r. du Port
r. du Prince
r. d'Italie
r. de Rive
r. Versonnex
av. Pictet-de-Rochemont
PLACE DES
EAUX-VIVES
PLACE
DU PRÉ-
L'EVEQUE
Musée J.-Barbier-Mueller
Jean Calvin
Maison Tavel
Musée Internationale de la Reforme
STA Travel
Verdaine
r. du Vieux Collège
ROND-POINT
DE RIVE
PLACE
NEUVE
PLACE DE
MADELEINE
PL. DU BOURG-
DE-FOUR
St-Pierre
Old Arsenal
Espace Rousseau
Hôtel de Ville
Reformer's Wall
Parc des Bastions
University
Promenade des Bastions
r. de la Croix-Rouge
rampe de la Treille
r. des Granges
r. de Candolle
r. St-Léger
Parc de Malagnou
rte. de Malagnou
PLACE DE LA
TACONNERIE
r. Théodore de Bèze
r. de Chaudronniers
Prom. de
St. Antoine
Musée d'Art et d'Histoire
Russian Orthodox Church
r. Ferdinand-Hodler
r. du Glacis-de-Rive
r. de la Terrassière
r. de Villereuse
r. A. Lachenal
Pleine de Plain-palais
ROND-POINT
DE PLAINPALAIS
bd. des Philosophes
PLACE DES
PHILOSOPHES
cours des Bastions
r. Jaques-Dalcroze
PLACE
CLAPARÈDE
bd. des Tranchées
Petit-Palais
r. Le-Fort
Charles-Galland
r. St-Victor
rte. de Florissant
rte. de Contamines
TO (2km)

London, BRI; New York, USA; Paris, FRA; and **Rome, ITA.** Bus #10 runs to the Gare Cornavin (15min., 6-12 per hr., 3CHF), but the train trip is shorter (6min., 6 per hr., 3CHF).

Trains: Trains run 4:30am-1am. **Gare Cornavin,** pl. Cornavin, is the main station. To: **Basel** (2hr., 1 per 2hr., 69CHF); **Bern** (2hr., 2 per hr., 46CHF); **Lausanne** (40min., 3-4 per hr., 20.60CHF); **Zürich** (3hr., 1-2 per hr., 80CHF); **Nyon** (20 min., 8.20CHF); **St. Gallen** (4hr., 1-2 per hr., 95CHF). Ticket counter open M-F 5:15am-9:30pm, Sa-Su 5:30am-9:30pm. **Gare des Eaux-Vives** (☎022 736 1620), on av. de la Gare des Eaux-Vives (tram #12 to Amandoliers SNCF), connects to France's regional rail through **Annecy, FRA** (1hr., 6 per day, 15CHF) or **Chamonix, FRA** (2hr., 4 per day, 25CHF).

Public Transportation: Geneva has an efficient **bus and tram** network (☎022 308 3311; www.tpg.ch). Single tickets, which can be purchased in the train station, are valid for 1hr. within the "orange" city zone (which includes the airport) are 3CHF; rides of 3 stops or less 2CHF. **Day passes** (10CHF) and a **9hr. pass** (7CHF) are available for the canton of Geneva; day passes for the whole region 18CHF. MC/V. Stamp multi-use tickets before boarding at machines in the station. Buses run 5am-12:30am; **Noctambus** (F-Sa 12:30-3:45am, 3CHF) offers night service. Tram use is free with the **Geneva visitor card,** usually distributed by hotels and hostels—make sure to ask for one.

Taxis: Taxi-Phone (☎022 331 4133). 6.80CHF plus 3CHF per km. 30CHF from airport.

Bike Rental: Geneva has well-marked bike paths and special traffic signals. Behind the station, **Genève Roule,** pl. Montbrillant 17 (☎022 740 1343), has ■ **free bikes.** (Passport and 20CHF deposit. First 4 hours free, 1CHF per hour thereafter. Fines are 60CHF for lost free bike. Mountain bikes 17CHF per day. Touring bikes 28CHF per day. May-Oct. only.) Other locations at Bains des Pâquis, Plain de Plainpalis, Place de l'Octroi, and pl. du Rhône. Arrive before 9am, as bikes go quickly. Free **bike maps** available. Open daily May-Oct. 8am-9pm; Nov.-Apr. 8am-6pm. Cash only.

Hitchhiking: *Let's Go* does not recommend hitchhiking. Those headed to Germany or northern Switzerland take bus #4 to Jardin Botanique, where they try to catch a ride. Those headed to France take bus #4 to Palettes, then line D to St. Julien.

🔧🔋 ORIENTATION AND PRACTICAL INFORMATION

The twisting streets and quiet squares of the historic *vieille ville* (Old Town), centered on **Cathédrale de St-Pierre,** make up the heart of Geneva. Across the **Rhône River** to the north, five-star hotels give way to lakeside promenades, **International Hill,** and rolling parks. Across the **Arve River** to the south lies the village of **Carouge,** home to bars and clubs (take tram #12 or 13 to pl. du Marché).

Tourist Office: r. du Mont-Blanc 18 (☎022 909 7000; www.geneva-tourism.ch), in the Central Post Office Building. From Cornavin, walk 5min. toward the Pont du Mont-Blanc. Staff books hotel rooms for 5CHF, gives out free city **maps,** and leads English-language walking tours (daily 10am; 15CHF). Open M 10am-6pm, Tu-Su 9am-6pm.

Consulates: Australia, chemin des Fins 2 (☎022 799 9100). **Canada,** Laurenzerberg 2 (☎531 38 3000). **New Zealand,** chemin des Fins 2 (☎022 929 0350). **UK,** r. de Vermont 37 (☎022 918 2400). **US,** r. Versonnex 7 (☎022 840 5160).

Currency Exchange: The currency exchange inside the **Gare Cornavin** has good rates with no commission on traveler's checks, makes cash advances on credit cards, and arranges **Western Union** transfers. Open M-Sa 7am-8pm, Su 8am-5:50pm.

GLBT Resources: Dialogai, r. de la Navigation 11-13, entrance Rue d. Levant 5 (☎022 906 4040). From Gare Cornavin, turn left, walk 5min. down r. de Lausanne, and turn right onto r. de la Navigation. Open M 9am-10pm, Tu-Th 9am-6pm, F 9am-5pm.

Police: R. de Berne 6 (☎117). Open M-F 9am-noon and 3-6:30pm, Sa 9am-noon.

SWITZERLAND

Hospital: Geneva University Hospital, r. Micheli-du-Crest 24 (☎022 372 3311; www. hug-ge.ch). Bus #1 or 5 or tram #7, or Bus #35 from Place du Augustines. Door #2 is for emergency care; door #3 is for consultations.

Internet: Charly's Multimedia Check Point, r. de Fribourg 7 (☎022 901 1313; www. charlys.com). 4CHF per hr. Free Wi-Fi. Open M-Sa 9am-midnight, Su 1-11pm.

Post Office: Poste Centrale, r. du Mont-Blanc 18, 1 block from Gare Cornavin. Open M-F 7:30am-6pm, Sa 9am-4pm. **Postal Code:** CH-1200.

ACCOMMODATIONS AND CAMPING

The indispensable *Info Jeunes* lists about 30 budget options, and the tourist office publishes *Budget Hotels*, which stretches the definition of budget to 120CHF per person. Cheap beds are relatively scarce, so reserve ahead.

Hôme St-Pierre, Cour St-Pierre 4 (☎022 310 3707; info@homestpierre.ch). Take bus #5 to pl. Neuve, then walk up Rampe de la Treille, turn left onto R. Puits-St.-Pierre, then right on R. du Solil Levant. This 150-year-old "home" has comfortable beds and a great location beside the cathedral. Wi-Fi available. Reception M-Sa 9am-noon and 4-8pm, Su 9am-noon. Dorms 27CHF; singles 40CHF; doubles 60CHF. MC/V. ❶

City Hostel Geneva, r. Ferrier 2 (☎022 901 1500; www.cityhostel.ch). From the train station, head down r. de Lausanne. Take the 1st left on r. du Prieuré, which becomes r. Ferrier. Spotless, cozy rooms. Kitchens on each floor. Linens 3.50CHF. Internet 5CHF per hr. Reception 7:30am-noon and 1pm-midnight. 3-4 bed single-sex dorms 28.50CHF; singles 59-64CHF; doubles 72-86CHF. Reserve ahead in summer. MC/V. ❷

Auberge de Jeunesse (HI), r. Rothschild 30 (☎022 732 6260; www.youthhostel.ch/ geneva). Standard rooms, some of which have lake views. Chess lovers can duke it out on the life-size chess board outside. Breakfast included. Laundry 8CHF. Internet 4CHF per hr. Max. 6-night stay. Reception 6:30-10am and 2pm-midnight. Dorms 35CHF; doubles 85CHF, with shower 95CHF; quads 135CHF. 6CHF HI discount. AmEx/MC/V. ❷

Camping Pointe-à-la-Bise, chemin de la Bise (☎022 752 1296). Take bus #8 or tram #16 to Rive, then bus E north to Bise. Reception July-Aug. 8am-noon and 2-9pm; Apr.-June and Sept. 8am-noon and 4-8pm. Open Apr.-Sept. Reserve ahead. 7CHF per person, 12 CHF per tent; 4-person bungalows 98CHF. AmEx/MC/V. ❶

FOOD

Geneva has it all, from sushi to paella, but you may need a banker's salary to foot the bill. Pick up basics at *boulangeries*, *pâtisseries*, or supermarkets, which often have attached cafeterias. Try the **Coop** on the corner of r. du Commerce and r. du Rhône, in the Centre Rhône Fusterie, or the **Migros** in the basement of the Places des Cygnes shopping center on r. de Lausanne, down the street from the station. A variety of relatively cheap ethnic eateries center in the **Les Pâquis** area, bordered by r. de Lausanne and Gare Cornavin on one side and the quais Mont-Blanc and Wilson on the other. Around **place du Cirque** and **plaine de Plainpalais** are student-oriented tea rooms. To the south, the neighborhood of **Carouge** is known for its cozy pizzerias and funky brasseries.

Chez Ma Cousine, pl. du Bourg-de-Four 6 (☎022 310 9696; www.chezmacousine.ch), down the stairs behind the cathedral. This cheery cafe has perfected *poulet* with its half-chicken with salad and french fries special (14.90CHF) and a variety of chicken salads (14-15CHF). Open M-Sa 11am-11:30pm, Su 11am-10:30pm. AmEx/MC/V. ❷

Restaurant Manora, r. de Cornavin 4 (☎022 909 490), on the top floor of the Manor department store, near the train station. Offers a wide selection of entrees, fresh fruits and vegetables, and free water (a rarity in Switzerland). Entrees 5-12CHF. Open M-W 9am-7pm, Th 9am-9pm, F 9am-7:30pm, Sa 8:30am-6pm. AmEx/MC/V. ❶

Le Rozzel, Grand-Rue 18 (☎022 312 4272). Take bus #5 to pl. Neuve, then walk up the hill on r. Jean-Calvin to Grand-Rue. Pleasant outdoor seating on a winding street. Sweet and savory crepes 8-19CHF. Open M-Sa 10am-7pm, Su 10am-noon. MC/V. ❷

⬡ SIGHTS

The city's most interesting historical sights are located within walking distance from the *vieille ville* (Old Town). The tourist office has 2hr. English-language walking tours. (Mid-June to Sept. M, W, F-Sa 10am, Tu and Th at 6:30pm; Oct. to mid-June Sa 10am. 15CHF, students 10CHF.)

VIEILLE VILLE. From 1536 to 1564, Calvin preached at the **Cathédrale de St-Pierre,** which looms over the *vieille ville* from its hilltop location. Climb the north tower for an unparalleled view of the city, and the south tower for some interesting information about the bells. (*Cathedral open June-Sept. M-F 9:30-6:30, Sa 9:30am-5pm, Su 10am-6:30pm. Concert Sa 6pm; service Su 10am. Tower open June-Sept. M-F 9am-6pm, Sa 9am-4:30pm. Cathedral free, tower 4CHF.*) Ruins, including a Roman sanctuary and an AD 4th-century basilica, rest in an ▧**archaeological site** below the cathedral; you can even see the tomb around which the city was built. (*Open June-Sept. Tu-Su 10am-5pm; Oct.-May Tu-F 2-5pm, Sa-Su 1:30-5:30pm. Last entry 4:30. 8CHF, students 4CHF.*) For a dense presentation of Reformation 101, visit the **Musée International de la Réforme,** 4 r. du Cloître, housed on the site of the city's official acceptance of Protestantism in 1536. (*☎022 310 2431; www.musee-reforme.ch. Open Tu-Su 10am-5pm. 10CHF, students 7CHF.*) At the western end of the *vieille ville* sits the 12th-century **Maison Tavel,** r. de Puits Saint Pierre 6. The oldest privately owned home in Geneva contains a wonderful scale model of the city as well a wide selection of trinkets from everyday life throughout the years. (*☎022 418 3700; www.ville-ge.ch/mah. Open Tu-Su 10am-5pm. Free.*) Across the street is the **Hôtel de Ville** (Town Hall), where world leaders met on August 22, 1864 for the first Geneva Convention. The **Grand-Rue,** beginning at the Hôtel de Ville, is lined with medieval workshops and 18th-century mansions. Plaques commemorate famous residents like **Jean-Jacques Rousseau,** who was born at #40. Visit the ▧**Espace Rousseau** there for a short but informative audiovisual presentation of his life and work. (*☎022 310 1028; www.espace-rousseau.ch. Open Tu-Su 11am-5:30pm. 5CHF, students 3CHF.*) Below the cathedral, along r. de la Croix-Rouge, the **Parc des Bastions** stretches from pl. Neuve to pl. des Philosophes and includes **Le Mur des Réformateurs** (The Reformers' Wall), a sprawling collection of bas-relief figures depicting Protestant Reformers. The hulking **Musée d'Art et d'Histoire,** R. Charles-Galland 2, offers everything from prehistoric relics to contemporary art. (*☎022 418 2610; mah.ville-ge.ch. Open Tu-Su 10am-5pm. Free.*)

WATERFRONT. As you descend from the cathedral to the lake, medieval lanes give way to wide streets and chic boutiques. Down quai Gustave Ardor, the **Jet d'Eau,** Europe's highest fountain and Geneva's city symbol, spews a seven-ton plume of water 134m into the air. The **floral clock** in the **Jardin Anglais** pays homage to Geneva's watch industry. Possibly the city's most overrated attraction, it was once its most hazardous—the clock had to be cut back because tourists intent on taking the perfect photograph repeatedly backed into oncoming traffic. For a day on the waterfront, head up the south shore of the lake to Genève Plage, where there is a water slide and an enormous pool. (*☎022 736 2482; www.geneve-plage.ch. Open mid-May to mid-Sept. daily 10am-8pm. 7CHF, students 4.50CHF.*)

▧**INTERNATIONAL HILL.** North of the train station, the International Red Cross building contains the impressive **International Red Cross and Red Crescent Museum,** av. de la Paix 17. *(Bus #8, F, V or Z to Appia ☎ 022 748 9511; www.micr.org. Open M and W-Su 10am-5pm. 10CHF, students 5CHF. English-language audio tour 3CHF.)* Across the street, the European headquarters of the **United Nations**, av. de la Paix 14, is in the same building that once held the League of Nations. The constant traffic of international diplomats is entertainment in itself. *(☎ 022 917 4896; www.unog.ch. Mandatory 1hr. tour. English tours every hour. Open July-Aug. daily 10am-5pm; Apr.-June and Sept.-Oct. daily 10am-noon and 2-4pm; Nov.-Mar. M-F 10am-noon and 2-4pm. 10CHF, students 8CHF.)*

🎵 🎭 ENTERTAINMENT AND NIGHTLIFE

Genève Agenda, available at the tourist office, features event listings from major festivals to movies. In late June, the **Fête de la Musique** fills the city with nearly 500 free concerts of all styles. Parc de la Grange has free **jazz concerts.** Geneva hosts the biggest celebration of **American Independence Day** outside the US (July 4), and the **Fêtes de Genève** in early August fill the city with international music and fireworks. **L'Escalade** (Dec. 2009) commemorates the successful blockade of invading Savoyard troops.

Nightlife in Geneva is divided by neighborhood. **Place Bourg-de-Four,** below the cathedral in the *vieille ville,* attracts students to its charming terraces. **Place du Molard** has loud, somewhat upscale bars and clubs. For something more frenetic, head to **Les Pâquis,** near Gare Cornavin and pl. de la Navigation. As the city's red-light district, it has a wide array of rowdy, low-lit bars and some nightclubs. This neighborhood is also home to many of the city's gay bars. Carouge, across the Arve River, is a locus of student-friendly nightlife. In the *vieille ville,* generations of students have had their share of drinks at the intimate **La Clémence,** pl. du Bourg-de-Four 20. You can count on it to be open even when the rest of the city has shut down. Try the local 🍺Calvinus beer (7.40CHF) to do your part for Protestantism. *(Sandwiches 3.30-6.40CHF. Open M-Th 7am-12:30am, F-Sa 7am-1:30am. MC/V.)*

LAUSANNE   ☎ 021

The wonderfully unique museums, medieval *vieille ville,* and lazy Lac Léman waterfront of Lausanne (pop. 128,000) definitely make it worth a visit. The Gothic **Cathédrale,** with its intricate stained glass and old tombs stands as the centerpiece of the *vieille ville.* (Open May to mid-Sept. M-F 7am-7pm, Sa-Su 8am-7pm; mid-Sept. to Apr. M-F 7am-5:30pm, Sa-Su 8am-5:30pm.) Below the cathedral is the city hall, **Hôtel de Ville,** on pl. de la Palud, a meeting point for guided tours of the town. *(☎ 021 320 1261; www.lausanne.ch/visites. Tours May-Sept. M-Sa 10am and 2:30pm. 10CHF, students free.)* The 🏅**Musée Olympique,** quai d'Ouchy 1, is a high-tech shrine to modern Olympians; best of all is the extensive video collection, allowing visitors to relive almost any moment of the games. Take bus #2 to Ouchy, bus #8 to Musée Olympique, or bus #4 to Montchoisi. *(☎ 021 621 6511; www.olympic.org. Open Apr.-Oct. daily 9am-6pm; Nov.-Mar. Tu-Su 9am-6pm. 15CHF, students 10CHF.)* The fascinating 🎨**Collection de l'Art Brut,** av. Bergières 11, is filled with unusual sculptures, drawings, and paintings by fringe artists: schizophrenics, peasants, and criminals. Take bus #2 to Jomini or 3 to Beaulieu. The museum is behind the trees across from the Congress Center. *(☎ 021 315 2570; www.artbrut.ch. Open July-Aug. daily 11am-6pm; Sept.-June Tu-Su 11am-10pm. 8CHF, students 5CHF.)* The city's inhabitants descend to the lake on weekends and after work, making it one of the liveliest places in the city. In Ouchy, Lausanne's port, several booths along quai de Belgique rent **pedal boats** (13CHF per 30min., 20CHF per hr.) and offer **water skiing** or **wake boarding** (35CHF per 15min.) on Lac Léman. The gorgeous park also has a life-size chess board, a carousel (3CHF/ride), and a giant jungle gym for the young at heart. For more activity, Lausanne Roule loans **free bikes** beside pl. de la Riponne on R. du Tennel (☎021 533 0115. www.lausanneroule.ch. ID and 20CHF deposit. Open late Apr. to late Oct. daily 7:30am-9:30pm.)

◧**Lausanne Guesthouse and Backpacker ❷**, chemin des Epinettes 4, at the train tracks, manages to keep the noise out and makes the most of its location with lake views, an equipped kitchen, a cozy living room, and a rose garden with grills. Head left and downhill out of the station on W. Fraisse; take the first right on chemin des Epinettes. (☎021 601 8000; www.lausanne-guesthouse. ch. Bike rental 20CHF per day. Linens 5CHF. Laundry 5CHF. Internet 8CHF per hr. Wi-Fi free for the first 30min, 2CHF/hr thereafter. Kitchen closed from 1:30-2:30pm for cleaning. Reception daily 7:30am-noon and 3-10pm. Book ahead. Dorms 32CHF; singles 85CHF, with bath 94CHF; doubles 95/115CHF. 5% ISIC discount. MC/V.) Restaurants center around **Place St-François**, the *vieille ville*, and the lake front, while boulangeries sell sandwiches on practically every street. **Le Barbare ❶**, Escaliers du Marché 27, near the cathedral, has sandwiches (6.50CHF), omelettes (7.50-10CHF), and pizza (13-17CHF) for cheap. (☎021 312 2132. Open M-Sa 8:30am-midnight. AmEx/MC/V.)

Trains leave for: Basel (2hr., 1 per 2hr., 59CHF); Geneva (50min., 3-4 per hr., 20.60CHF); Montreux (20min., 3-4 per hr., 10.20CHF); Zürich (2½hr., 1-2 per hr., 67CHF); Paris, FRA (4hr., 4 per day, 146.20CHF). The **tourist office** by the Ouchy lakefront reserves rooms for 4CHF, and gives out free maps and water. (☎021 613 7373. Open daily 9am-7pm.) **Postal Code:** CH-1000.

TURKEY
(TÜRKİYE)

Turkey is a land rich with history and beauty. Home to some of the world's greatest civilizations, Turkey is at the intersection of two very different continents. İstanbul, on the land bridge that connects Europe and Asia, is the infinitely intricate and surprisingly seductive progeny of three thousand years of migrant history. Though resolutely secular by government decree, Turkish life is graced by the religious traditions of its 99% Muslim population. Tourists cram İstanbul and the glittering western coast, while Anatolia (the Asian portion of Turkey) remains a backpacker's paradise of alpine meadows, cliffside monasteries, and truly hospitable people.

ESSENTIALS

FACTS AND FIGURES

OFFICIAL NAME: Republic of Turkey.

FORM OF GOVERNMENT: Republican parliamentary democracy.

CAPITAL: Ankara.

MAJOR CITIES: İstanbul, Adana, Bursa, Gaziantep, İzmir.

POPULATION: 70,414,000.

TIME ZONE: GMT +2 or +3.

LANGUAGE: Turkish.

RELIGION: Muslim (99.8%).

LARGEST SKEWER OF KEBAB MEAT: Created by the Melike Döner Co. in Osmangazi-Bursa, Turkey on Nov. 6, 2005. Weighed in at 2698kg (5948 lb.).

WHEN TO GO

With mild winters and hot summers, there's no wrong time to travel to Turkey. While most tourists go in July and August, those visiting between April and June or September and October will enjoy temperate days, smaller crowds, and lower prices. The rainy season runs from November to February, so remember to bring appropriate gear if traveling during these months.

DOCUMENTS AND FORMALITIES

EMBASSIES AND CONSULATES. Foreign embassies to Turkey are in Ankara, though many nations also have consulates in İstanbul. Turkish embassies and consulates abroad include: **Australia,** 6 Moonah Pl., Yarralumla, Canberra, ACT 2600 (☎02 62 34 00 00; www.turkishembassy.org.au); **Canada,** 197 Wurtemburg St., Ottawa, ON, K1N 8L9 (☎613-789-4044; www.turkishembassy. com); **Ireland,** 11 Clyde Rd., Ballsbridge, Dublin 4 (☎353 668 52 40); **New Zealand,** 15-17 Murphy St., Level 8, Wellington 6011 (☎044 721 290; turkemşxtra. co.nz); **UK,** 43 Belgrave Sq., London SW1X 8PA (☎020 73 93 02 02; www. turkishembassylondon.org); **US,** 2525 Massachusetts Ave., N.W., Washington, D.C. 20008 (☎202-612-6700; www.turkishembassy.org).

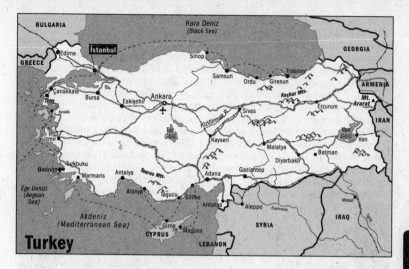

Turkey

VISA AND ENTRY INFORMATION.

Citizens of Canada and the US may obtain visas at entry points into Turkey for stays of less than three months (paid in cash). For longer stays, study, or work visas, and for citizens of Australia, New Zealand, and countries of the EU, it is necessary to obtain visas in advance (about US$20; Canadians, about US$60), available at Turkish consulates abroad. Travelers must apply at least one month in advance. For more info, visit www.mfa.gov.tr/mfa. If arriving by ferry, expect a port tax of at least €10.

ENTRANCE REQUIREMENTS.

Passport: Required for all travelers.

Visa: Required for citizens of Australia, Canada, some EU countries, the UK, and the US. Citizens of New Zealand do not need a visa to enter. Multiple-entry visas (€10-20), available at the border, are valid for up to 90 days.

Letter of Invitation: Not required.

Inoculations: Not required. Recommended up-to-date on DTaP (diphtheria, tetanus, and pertussis), hepatitis A, hepatitis B, MMR (measles, mumps, and rubella), polio booster, and typhoid.

Work Permit: Required for all foreigners planning to work in Turkey.

Driving Permit: Required for all those planning to drive.

TOURIST SERVICES

In big cities like İstanbul, many establishments that claim to be tourist offices are actually travel agencies. That said, **travel agencies** can often be more helpful for finding accommodations or booking transportation than the official Turkish **tourist offices.** Although it's best to shop around from agency to agency for a deal on tickets, be wary of exceptionally low prices—offices may tack on exorbitant hidden charges. The official tourism website (www.tourismturkey. org) has visa info, helpful links, and office locations.

MONEY

In response to rampant inflation and ever-confusing prices, Turkey revalued its currency in 2005, dropping 6 zeroes. One million Turkish Lira became 1 **Yeni**

Türk Lirası (New Turkish Lira; YTL). One New Turkish Lira equals 100 **New Kuruş,** with standard denominations of 5, 10, 25, and 50. 1YTL are available as both coins and bills, while denominations of 1, 5, 10, 20, 50 and 100YTL come only as banknotes. While Old Turkish Lira are no longer accepted as currency, Turkish Lira banknotes (bills) can be redeemed until 2016 at the Central Bank of the Republic of Turkey (CBRT) and at T.C. Ziraat Bank branches. Old Lira coins are no longer redeemable. **Banks** are generally open 8:30am-noon and 1:30-5:30pm. **Inflation** has decreased dramatically in recent years, dropping from 45% in 2003 to an all-time low of 7.7% in 2005 before rising again slightly. The best currency exchange rates can be found at state-run post and telephone offices (PTT). Many places in İstanbul and other major cities accept euro. Turkey has a **value added tax (VAT)** of 18% on general purchases and 8% on food. The prices in *Let's Go* include VAT. Spending more than 118YTL in one store entitles travelers to a tax refund upon leaving Turkey; look for "Tax-Free Shopping" stickers in shop windows or ask for a form inside. For more info on VAT refunds, see p. 20.

NEW TURKISH LIRA (YTL)		
	AUS$1 = 1.07YTL	1YTL = AUS$0.94
	CDN$1 = 1.12YTL	1YTL = CDN$0.90
	EUR€1 = 1.80YTL	1YTL = EUR€0.56
	NZ$1 = 0.84YTL	1YTL = NZ$1.20
	UK£1 = 2.28YTL	1YTL = UK£0.44
	US$1 = 1.17YTL	1YTL = US$0.85

HEALTH AND SAFETY

EMERGENCY | **Ambulance:** ☎112. **Fire:** ☎110. **Police:** ☎155.

Medical facilities in Turkey vary greatly. In İstanbul and Ankara, high-quality hospitals for foreigners and expats provide care for all but the most serious of conditions, and most have adequate medical supplies. Outside the cities, though, it is a different story; try to avoid rural hospitals. **Pharmacies** are easy to find in major cities and are generally well stocked and have at least one professional pharmacist, as they're mandated by the government. Don't drink **water** that hasn't been boiled or filtered, and watch out for ice in drinks. Most local dairy products are safe to eat.

Petty crime is common in urban centers, especially in crowded squares, the Grand Bazaar, and on public transportation. Common schemes include distracting travelers with a staged fight while they are being robbed; drugging travelers with tea, juice, or other drinks and then robbing them; or simply presenting travelers with outrageously expensive bills. Pay attention to your valuables, never accept drinks from a stranger, and always ask in advance for prices at bars and restaurants. Though **pirated goods** are sold on the street, it is illegal to buy them; doing so can result in fines. **Drug trafficking** leads to severe jail time. It is also illegal to show disrespect to Atatürk or to insult the state.

Foreign **women,** especially those traveling alone, attract significant attention in Turkey. Unwanted catcalls and other forms of verbal harassment are common, although physical harassment is rare. Regardless of the signals a foreign woman intends to send, her foreignness alone may suggest a liberal openness to amorous advances. Smiling, regarded in the West as a sign of confidence and friendliness, is sometimes associated in Turkey with sexual attraction. As

Adventure in Europe?
Do it by rail

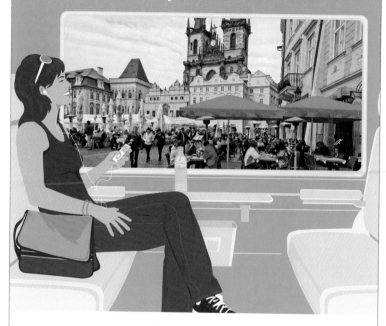

With a Eurail Global or Select Pass you zoom
fast from country to country, from city centre
to city centre. So you can soak up hip street
scenes. Shop till you drop. Explore the nightlife
and meet cool people.

**Why wait? Go to www.adventure-europe.com
or contact your local travel agent now!**

long as women expect plenty of attention and take common-sense precautions, however, even single travelers need not feel anxious.

Although **homosexuality** is legal in Turkey, religious and social norms keep most homosexual activity discreet. Homophobia can be a problem, especially in remote areas; expect authorities to be unsympathetic. Despite the close contact that Turks maintain with same-sex friends, public displays of affection between gay and lesbian travelers should be avoided. Turkey's urban centers have bars and informal cruising areas for men only, though they may not be very overt. **Lambda İstanbul,** a GLBT support group, lists guides to gay-friendly establishments on its website (www.qrd.org/qrd/www/world/europe/turkey/).

KEEPING IN TOUCH

PHONE CODES	**Country code: 90. International dialing prefix:** 00. From outside Turkey, dial int'l dialing prefix (see inside back cover) + 90 + city code + local number. Within Turkey, dial city code + local number.

EMAIL AND THE INTERNET. Like everything in Turkey, the availability of Internet services depends on where in the country you are. In İstanbul, Internet cafes are everywhere; in the east, they can be tough to find. Free Wi-Fi is available at hostels and cafes across the city.

TELEPHONES. Whenever possible, use a calling card for international phone calls, as long-distance rates for national phone services are often very high. **Mobile phones** are an increasingly popular and economical option. Major mobile carriers include **Turkcell, Telsim,** and **Avea.** Direct-dial access numbers for calling out of Turkey include: **AT&T Direct** (☎80 01 22 77); **British Telecom** (☎80 044 1177); **Canada Direct** (☎80 01 66 77). For info on calling from Europe, see p. 30.

MAIL. The postal system is quick and expensive in Turkey. Airmail should be marked *par avion,* and **Poste Restante** is available in most major cities.

ACCOMMODATIONS AND CAMPING

TURKEY	❶	❷	❸	❹	❺
ACCOMMODATIONS	under 20YTL	20-39YTL	40-59YTL	60-80YTL	over 80YTL

When it comes to lodging, Turkey is a budget traveler's paradise. **Hostels** are available in nearly every major city. **Pensions**—a step above hostels in both quality and price—are also generally available, as are **hotels** in every price range. **Camping** is very common throughout Turkey, especially on the Aegean coast; campgrounds are generally inexpensive (US$3-10) or free.

FOOD AND DRINK

TURKEY	❶	❷	❸	❹	❺
FOOD	under 8YTL	8-15YTL	16-20YTL	21-30YTL	over 30YTL

Turkish cuisine is as varied as Turkish culture. Strategically located on the land bridge between Europe and Asia, İstanbul is the culinary epicenter of the region, drawing from the dietary practices of many different cultures. Fish is a staple in Turkey, especially along the coast, where it is prepared with local spices according

TURKEY

to traditional recipes. When it comes to meat, lamb and chicken are Turkish favorites, and are typically prepared as ☒kebab—a term which means far more in Turkey than the dry meat cubes on a stick found in most Western restaurants. Despite its strong Muslim majority, Turkey produces good wines. More interesting, however, is the unofficial national drink: *rakı*. Translated as "lion's milk," *rakı* is Turkey's answer to French *pastis*, Italian *sambuca*, and Greek *ouzo*. An anise-flavored liquor, it turns milky white when mixed with water. The strong drink has inspired a Turkish saying: "you must drink the *rakı*, and not let the *rakı* drink you."

PEOPLE AND CULTURE

LANGUAGE. Turkish *(Türkçe)*, the official language of Turkey, is spoken by approximately 65 million people domestically and a few million more abroad. It is the most prominent member of the Turkic language family, which also includes Azerbaijani, Kazakh, Kyrgyz, Uighur, and Uzbek. Turkish was originally written in Arabic script and exhibited strong Arabic and Persian influences. In 1928, however, Atatürk reformed the language, purging foreign influences. This linguistic standardization was not absolute, and common Arabic and Persian words such as *merhaba* (hello) remain.

Visitors who speak little or no Turkish should not be intimidated. Though Turks appreciate attempts at conversing in their language, English is widely spoken wherever tourism is big business—mainly in the major coastal towns. Especially in İstanbul, a small phrasebook will help greatly. For in-depth study, consult *Teach Yourself Turkish* by Pollard and Pollard (New York, 2004; $17).

DEMOGRAPHICS. Over 99% of the Turkish population is **Muslim.** Jews and Orthodox Christians of Armenian, Greek, and Syrian backgrounds comprise the remainder. While Turkey does not have an official state religion, every Turkish citizen's national identification card states his or her faith. Although Atatürk's reforms aimed to secularize the nation, Islam continues to play a key role in the country's politics and culture.

CUSTOMS AND ETIQUETTE. Turks value **hospitality** and will frequently go out of their way to welcome travelers, commonly offering to buy visitors a meal or a cup of çay (tea). Try not to refuse tea unless you have very strong objections; accepting the offer provides a friendly, easy way to converse with locals. If you are invited to a Turkish house as a guest, it is customary to bring a small gift, often pastries or chocolates, and to remove your shoes before entering. A pair of slippers will usually be provided. Always treat elders with special respect. When chatting with Turks, do not speak with any disrespect or skepticism about **Atatürk,** as this is illegal, and avoid other sensitive subjects. In particular, avoid discussing the Kurdish issue, the PKK (the Kurdistan Workers' Party), Northern Cyprus, or Turkey's human rights record.

Many of Turkey's greatest architectural monuments, including **tombs** and **mosques,** have religious significance. Visitors are welcome but should show respect by dressing and acting appropriately. Shorts and skimpy clothing are forbidden inside mosques. Women must cover their arms, heads, and legs, and both sexes should take off their shoes and carry them inside. There are usually shoe racks in the back of the mosques; otherwise, caretakers will provide plastic bags for carrying shoes. Do not take flash photos, never photograph people in prayer, and avoid visits on Fridays (Islam's holy day). Also forgo visiting during prayer times, which are announced by the *müezzin's* call to prayer from the mosque's minarets. Donations are sometimes expected.

If **bargaining** is a fine art, then İstanbul is its cultural center. Never pay full price at the Grand Bazaar; start out by offering less than 50% of the asking price. For that matter, bargain just about everywhere—even when stores list prices, they'll usually take around 60-70%. If you're not asked to pay a service charge when paying by credit card, you're probably paying too much for your purchase. Tipping isn't required in Turkey: at bathhouses, hairdressers, hotels, and restaurants, a tip of 5-15% is common, but taxis and *dolmuş* drivers do not expect tips—just try to round up to the nearest YTL.

BODY VIBES. In Turkey, **body language** often matters as much as the spoken word. When a Turk raises his chin and clicks his tongue, he means *hayır* (no); this gesture is sometimes accompanied by a shutting of the eyes or the raising of eyebrows. A sideways shake of the head means *anlamadım* (I don't understand), and *evet* (yes) may be signaled by a sharp downward nod. If a Turk waves a hand up and down at you, palm toward the ground, he is signaling you to come, not bidding you farewell. In Turkey, the idle habit of snapping the fingers of one hand and then slapping the top of the other fist is considered obscene; so too is the hand gesture made by bringing thumb and forefinger together (the Western sign for "OK"). However, bringing all fingers toward the thumb is a compliment, generally meaning that something is "good." It is also considered rude to point your finger or the sole of your shoe toward someone. Though public displays of affection are considered inappropriate, Turks of both sexes greet each other with a kiss on both cheeks, and often touch or hug one another during conversation. Turks also tend to stand close to one another while talking.

DRESS. Wearing shorts will single you out as a tourist, as most Turks—particularly women—prefer pants or skirts. Women will probably find a **head scarf** or a bandana handy, perhaps essential, in more conservative regions. Even in İstanbul and the resort towns of the Aegean and Mediterranean coasts where casual, beachy dress is more widely accepted, revealing clothing sends a flirtatious message. More acceptable knee-length skirts and lightweight pants are also comfortable and practical, especially in summer. T-shirts are generally appropriate, though you should always cover your arms when entering mosques or traveling into the more religious regions of the country. Topless bathing is common in some areas along the Aegean and Mediterranean coasts but is severely inappropriate in a number of other regions.

BEYOND TOURISM

Finding work in Turkey is tough, as the government tries to restrict employment primarily to Turkish citizens. Foreigners seeking jobs must obtain a **work visa,** which in turn requires a **permit** issued by the Ministry of the Interior. An excellent option for work in Turkey is to **teach English.** Since English is the language of instruction at many Turkish universities, it's also possible to enroll directly as a special student, which might be less expensive than enrolling in an American university program. For more information on opportunities across Europe, see **Beyond Tourism, p. 59**.

Buğday Ekolojik Yaşam Kapısı İletişim Bilgileri, Kemankeş Cad. Akçe Sok. 14, Karaköy, İstanbul (☎212 252 5255; www.bugday.org/eng). Support sustainable agriculture by living or working on an *Ekolojik TaTuTa* (organic farm), or volunteer at the national organic farm association.

Gençtur Turizm ve Seyahat Ac. Ltd., İstiklal Cad. 212, Aznavur Pasajı, Kat: 5, Galatasaray, İstanbul 80080 (☎212 244 62 30; www.genctur.com). A tourism-travel agency that sets up various workshops, nannying jobs, volunteer camps, and year-round study tours.

Volunteers for Peace, 1034 Tiffany Rd., Belmont, VT 05730, USA (☎802-259-2759; www.vfp.org). Arranges placement in volunteer camps. Registration fee US$250.

TURKEY

İSTANBUL

İstanbul is the heart of Turkey. In this giant city that straddles Europe and Asia on two intercontinental bridges, the "East meets West" refrain of fusion restaurants, trendy boutiques, and yoga studios returns to its semantic roots. The huge, Western-style suburbs on the Asian side are evidence of rampant modernization, while across the Bosphorus the sprawling ancient city of mosques and bazaars—Old İstanbul—brims with cafes, bars, and people, day or night. As taxis rush by at mind-boggling speeds, shop owners sip tea with potential customers and tourists mingle with devout Muslims at the entrances to magnificent mosques. İstanbul is a turbulent city, full of history yet charged with a dynamism that makes it one of the most exciting cities in Europe—or Asia.

✖ INTERCITY TRANSPORTATION

Flights: Atatürk Havaalanı (IST; ☎663 6400), is 30km from the city. Buses (3 per hr. 6am-11pm) connect domestic and international terminals. To get to Sultanahmet from the airport, take the HAVAS bus or the metro to the Aksaray stop at the end of the line. From there catch a tram to Sultanahmet. A direct taxi to Sultanahmet costs 25YTL. Most hostels and hotels in Sultanahmet arrange airport shuttles several times a day.

Trains: Haydarpaşa Garı (☎21 63 36 04 75 or 336 2063), on the Asian side, sends trains to Anatolia. To get to the station, take the ferry from Karaköy pier #7 (every 20min. 6am-midnight), halfway between Galata Bridge and the Karaköy tourist office. Rail tickets for Anatolia can be bought in advance at the TCDD office upstairs or at any of the travel agencies in Sultanahmet; many of these offices also offer free transportation to the station. Trains go to **Ankara** (6-9hr., 6 per day, from 22YTL) and **Kars** (11-13hr., 1 per day, from 35YTL). Sirkeci Garı (☎527 0050 or 527 0051), in Eminönü, sends trains to Europe via **Athens, GCE** (24hr., 1 per day, 110YTL); **Bucharest, ROM** (17hr., 1 per day, 65YTL); and **Budapest, HUN** (40hr., 1 per day, 185YTL).

Buses: Modern, comfortable buses run to all major destinations in Turkey and are the cheapest and most convenient way to get around. If you arrange your tickets with any travel agency in Sultanahmet, a free ride is included from the agency to the bus station. To reach **Esenler Otobüs Terminal** (☎658 0036), take the tram to Yusufpaşa (1.30YTL); then, walk to the Aksaray Metro and take it to the *otogar* (bus station; 15min., 1.30YTL). Most companies have courtesy buses, called *servis*, that run to the *otogar* from Eminönü, Taksim, and other city points (free with bus ticket purchase). From İstanbul, buses travel to every city in Turkey. Buses run to: **Ankara** (8hr., 6-8 per day, 30YTL); **Antalya** (11hr., 2 per day, 40YTL); **Bodrum** (15hr., 2 per day, 45YTL); **İzmir** (10hr., 4 per day, 35YTL); **Kappadokia** (8hr., 2 per day, 30YTL). International buses run to: **Amman, JOR** (28hr., daily noon, 100YTL); **Athens, GCE** (19hr.; daily 10am; 130YTL, students 135YTL); **Damascus, SYR** (25hr., daily 1:30pm and 7:30pm, 50YTL); **Sofia, BUL** (15hr., daily 10am and 9pm, 65YTL); **Tehran, IRAN** (40hr., M-Sa 1:30pm, 70YTL). To get to Sultanahmet from the *otogar*, catch the metro to the Aksaray stop at the end of the line. From there, catch one of the trams that head to Sultanahmet.

TURKISH ROUTE-LETTE. Be wary of bus companies offering ludicrously low prices. Unlicensed companies have been known to offer discounts to Western European destinations and then ditch passengers somewhere en route. To ensure that you're on a legitimate bus, make sure to reserve your tickets with a travel agency in advance.

Ferries: Turkish Maritime Lines (reservations ☎252 1700, info 21 22 49 92 22), near pier #7 at Karaköy, to the left of the Haydarpaşa ferry terminal (blue awning marked

TURKEY

Denizcilik İşletmeleri). To **İzmir** (16hr., every 2 days, 65YTL) and other destinations on the coast. Many travel agencies don't know much about ferry connections, so you're better off going to the pier by the Galata Bridge, where you can pick up a free schedule. For more info, call ☎444 4436 or visit www.ido.com.tr. **To and from Greece:** One of the most popular routes into Turkey is from the Greek Dodecanese and Northern Aegean islands, whose proximity to the Turkish coast makes for an easy and inexpensive way into Asia. There are 5 main crossing points from Greece to Turkey: Rhodes to Marmaris, Kos to Bodrum, Samos to Kusadasi, Chios to Çeşme, and Lesvos to Ayvalik. Ferries run 1-2 times per day in summer, the ride takes under 2hr., and the tickets are usually €25-34, plus €10 port tax when entering Turkey and a €10-20 visa (see p. 13). If you are visiting a Greek island as a daytrip from Turkey, port taxes are usually waived.

■ ORIENTATION

Waterways divide İstanbul into three sections. The **Bosphorus Strait** (Boğaz) separates **Asya** (Asia) from **Avrupa** (Europe). The **Golden Horn,** a sizeable river originating just outside the city, splits Avrupa into northern and southern parts. Directions in İstanbul are usually further specified by neighborhood. On the European side, **Sultanahmet,** home to the major sights, is packed with tourists and has plenty of parks and benches and many monuments, shops, and cafes. In Sultanahmet, backpackers congregate in **Akbıyık Cad.,** while **Divan Yolu** is the main street. Walk away from **Aya Sofya** and the **Blue Mosque** to reach the **Grand Bazaar.** As you walk out of the covered Bazaar on the northern side, you'll reach more streets of outdoor markets that lead uphill to the massive **Suleymaniye Mosque** and the gardens of İstanbul's **University.** To the right, descend through the **Spice Bazaar** to reach the well-lit **Galata Bridge,** where street vendors and seafood restaurants keep the night lively. Across the two-level bridge, narrow, warehouse-filled streets lead to the panoramic **Galata Tower.** Past the tower is the broad main shopping drag **İstiklâl Cad.,** which takes you directly to **Taksim Square,** modern İstanbul's pulsing center. Sultanahmet and Taksim (on the European side), and **Kadıköy** (on the Asian side) are the most relevant for sightseers. Asya is primarily a residential area.

▐ TRANSPORTATION

PUBLIC TRANSPORTATION. AKBİL is an electronic ticket system that saves you 15-50% on fares for municipal ferries, buses, trams, water taxis, and subways (but not *dolmuş*). Cards (6YTL) are sold at tram stations or ticket offices and can be recharged in 1YTL increments at the white IETT public bus booths, marked **AKBİL satılır.**

Buses: Run 6am-midnight, arriving every 10min. at most stops, less frequently after 10:30pm. 1-2YTL. Hubs are Eminönü, Aksaray (Yusuf Paşa tram stop), Beyazıt, Taksim, Beşiktaş, and Üsküdar. Signs on the front of buses indicate destination, and signs on the right side list major stops. **Dolmuş** (shared taxi vans) are more comfortable but less frequent than buses. Most *dolmuş* gather on the side streets north of Taksim Sq.

Tram: The *Tramvay* runs from Eminönü to Zeytinburnu every 5min. Make sure to be on the right side of the street, as the carriage follows the traffic. Get tokens at any station and toss them in at the turnstile to board (1.30YTL). The old-fashioned carriages of the **historical tram** run 1km uphill from Tunnel (by the Galata Bridge) through İstiklâl Cad. and up to Taksim Sq. They're the same ones that made the trip in the early 20th century.

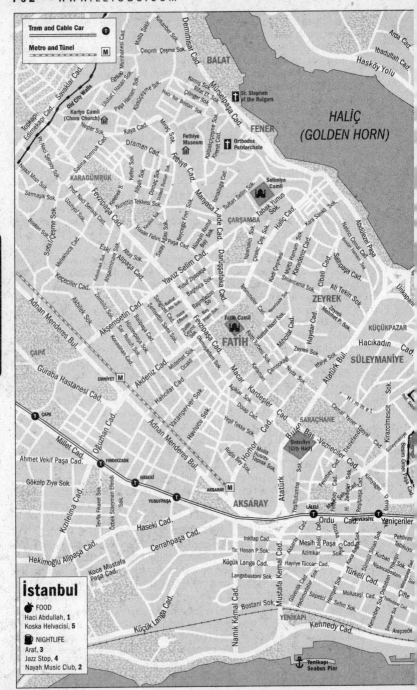

Tram and Cable Car — Ⓣ
Metro and Tünel — Ⓜ

BALAT

Dennishisar Cad.
Müselpaşa Cad.
Arda Cad.
Haskøy Yolu
İbadullah Sok.

St. Stephen of the Bulgars

Karlye Camii (Chora Church)

Fethiye Museum

FENER

HALİÇ (GOLDEN HORN)

Orthodox Patriarchate

KARAGÜMRÜK

Fevzipaşa Cad.

Selimiye Camii

Tabak Yunus

ÇARŞAMBA

ZEYREK

KÜÇÜKPAZAR

Ünkapanı

Hacıkadın Cad.

SÜLEYMANİYE

Yavuz Selim Cad.

Fatih Camii

FATİH

SARAÇHANE

Adnan Menderes Bul.

Guraba Hastanesi Cad.

ÇAPA

EMNİYET Ⓜ

ÇAPA Ⓣ

Millet Cad.

Akdeniz Cad.

Kardeşler Cad.

Büyük Baş
Belediye (City Hall)
Veznecileri Cad.

Ahmet Vekif Paşa Cad.

Gökalp Ziya Sok.

FINDIKZADE Ⓣ

HASEKİ Ⓣ

YUSUFPAŞA Ⓣ

AKSARAY Ⓜ

AKSARAY

ORDU Cad.

Atatürk

LÄLELİ

ÜNİVERSİTE

Yeniçeriler

Haseki Cad.

Cerrahpaşa Cad.

Hekimoğlu Alipaşa Cad.

Koca Mustafa Paşa Cad.

İnkılap Cad.

Mustafa Kemal Cad.

Türkeli Cad.

Küçük Langa Cad.

Langabastoni Sok.

Namık Kemal Cad.

Bostani Sok.

YENİKAPI

Kennedy Cad.

Yenikapı Seabus Pier

İstanbul

🍎 FOOD
Haci Abdullah, 1
Koska Helvacisi, 5

🌙 NIGHTLIFE
Araf, 3
Jazz Stop, 4
Nayah Music Club, 2

TURKEY

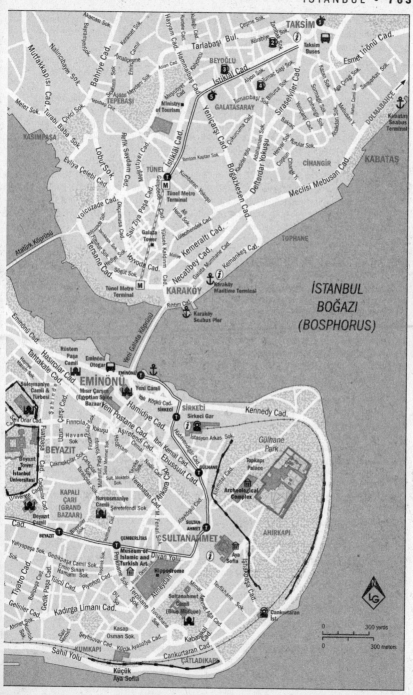

Metro: İstanbul operates two metro lines (☎568 9970): one from Aksaray to the Esenler Bus Terminal and the other from Taksim Sq. to 4th Levent. A funicular connects the tram stop Cabatas to Taksim Sq. The metro runs daily every 5min. 5:40am-11:15pm.

Commuter Rail: A slow commuter rail *(tren)* runs 6am-11pm between Sirkeci Gar and the far western suburbs, as well as the Asian side. The stop in Bostanci is near the ferry to the Princes Islands. Keep your ticket until the end of the journey.

Taxis: Taxi drivers are even more reckless and speed-crazed than other İstanbul drivers, but the city's more than 20,000 taxis offer an undoubtedly quick way to get around. Don't ask the driver to fix a price before getting in; instead, make sure he restarts the meter. Night fares, usually starting at midnight, are double. Rides from Sultanahmet to Taksim Sq. should be around 15YTL, and to the airport around 25YTL.

GETTING A FARE PRICE. While most İstanbul taxis are metered, some cabdrivers have a tendency to drive circles around the city before bringing you to your destination. Watch the roads and look out for signs pointing to where you're going. To avoid the risk altogether, take taxis only as far as the Galata Bridge, and walk from there to Sultanahmet or Taksim.

⚡ PRACTICAL INFORMATION

Tourist Office: 3 Divan Yolu (☎/fax 518 8754), at the north end of the Hippodrome in Sultanahmet. Open daily 9am-5pm. Branches in Taksim's Hilton Hotel Arcade on Cumhuriyet Cad., Sirkeci train station, Atatürk Airport, and Karaköy Maritime Station.

Budget Travel: İstanbul has many travel agencies; almost all speak English, and most hostels and hotels have started running their own travel services as well. Though most are trustworthy, there are some scams. Always check that the agency is licensed. If anything happens, make sure you have your agent's info and report it to the tourist police.

    Fez Travel, 15 Akbıyık Cad. (☎212 516 9024; www.feztravel.com). İstanbul's most efficient and well informed agency, Fez's English-speaking staff organizes everything from accommodations to ferries, flights, and buses, as well as their own backpacker-tailored tours of Turkey and Greece. STA-affiliated. Open daily 9am-7pm. MC/V.

    Hassle Free, 10 Akbıyık Cad. (☎212 458 9500; www.anzachouse.com), right next to New Backpackers. The name is self-explanatory, and the young, friendly staff provides great deals and tips. Books local buses or boat cruises of southern Turkey. Open daily 9am-11pm.

    Barefoot Travel, 1 Cetinkaya Sok. (☎212 517 0269; www.barefoot-travel.com), just off Akbıyık Cad. The English-speaking staff is helpful and offers good deals on airfare, as well as free maps of İstanbul and Turkey. Open daily in summer 8am-8pm; in winter 8am-6pm. AmEx/MC/V.

Consulates: Australia, 15 Asker Ocağ̇i Cad., Elmadag Sisli (☎212 257 7050; fax 212 243 1332). **Canada,** 373/5 İstiklâl Cad. (☎212 251 9838; fax 212 251 9888). **Ireland,** 26 Cumhuriyet Cad., Mobil Altı, Elmadağ̇ (☎212 246 6025). **NZ,** Inonu Caddesi No:48/3. (☎212 244 0272; fax 212 251 4004.) **UK,** 34 Meşrutiyet Cad., Beyoğlu/Tepebaşı (☎212 252 6436). **US,** 2 Kaplicalar Mevkii Sok., Istinye (☎212 335 9000).

Currency Exchange: *Bureaux de change* around the city are open M-F 8:30am-noon and 1:30-5pm. Most don't charge commission. **ATMs** generally accept all international cards. Most banks exchange **traveler's checks.** Exchanges in Sultanahmet have poor rates but are open late and on weekends. There is a yellow **PTT** kiosk between the Aya Sofya and the Blue Mosque that changes currency for no commission. **Western Union** offices are located in many banks throughout Sultanahmet and Taksim; they operate M-F 8:30am-noon and 1:30-5pm.

English-Language Bookstores: English-language books are all over the city. In Sultanahmet, *köşk* (kiosks) at the Blue Mosque, on Aya Sofya Meydanı, and on Divan Yolu sell international papers. **Galeri Kayseri,** 58 Divan Yolu (☎512 0456), caters to tourists with informational books on Turkish and Islamic history and literature, as well as a host of guidebooks. Open daily 9am-9pm. MC/V.

Laundromat: Star Laundry, 18 Akbıyık Cad., between New Backpackers and Hassle Free. Wash, dry, and iron 4YTL per kg. Min. 2kg. Ready in 3hr. Open daily 9am-8pm.

Tourist Police: In Sultanahmet, at the beginning of Yerebatan Cad. (24hr. hotline ☎527 4503 or 528 5369). Tourist police speak excellent English, and their mere presence causes hawkers to scatter. In an emergency, call from any phone.

Hospitals: American Hospital, Admiral Bristol Hastanesi, 20 Güzelbahçe Sok., Nişantaşı (☎231 4050), is applauded by locals and tourists. Has many English-speaking doctors. **German Hospital,** 119 Sıraselviler Cad., Taksim (☎293 2150), also has a multilingual staff and is conveniently located for Sultanahmet hostelers. **International Hospital,** 82 İstanbul Cad., Yesilköy (☎663 3000).

Internet: Internet in İstanbul is everywhere from hotels to barber shops, and connections are usually cheap and decently fast—notwithstanding the frequent power cuts. Most hostels have free Internet, though many impose a 15min. limit. Some hostels now offer Wi-Fi, as do more upscale hotels and eateries; signs are usually posted on the door. Rates at travel agencies are usually 1YTL per 15min., 3YTL per hr.

Post and Telephone Offices: Known as **PTTs.** All accept packages. **Main branch** in Sirkeci, 25 Büyük Postane Sok. Stamp and currency exchange services open daily 8:30am-midnight. 24hr. phones. Phone cards available for 5-10YTL. There is a yellow PTT kiosk in Sultanahmet between the Aya Sofya and the Blue Mosque, which exchanges currency and sells stamps. Open daily 9am-5pm.

PHONE CODES. The code is **212** on the European side and **216** on the Asian side. All numbers listed here begin with 212 unless otherwise specified. For more on how to place international calls, see **Inside Back Cover.**

ACCOMMODATIONS

Budget accommodations are concentrated in **Sultanahmet** (a.k.a. Türist Şeǵntral). As Turkey has become a backpacker's must, there has been an explosion of cheap places to stay, turning Akbıyık Cad. into a virtually uninterrupted line of hostels. The side streets around **Sirkeci** railway station and **Aksaray** have dozens of dirt-cheap, run-down hotels, while more expensive options are in more touristy districts. All accommodations listed below are in Sultanahmet and, despite their number, they fill up quickly in high-season. Though you will always find a bed somewhere, reserve ahead to get the hostel of your choice. Hotels in **Lâleli** are in İstanbul's center of prostitution and should be avoided. Rates can increase up to 20% in July and August.

Big Apple Hostel, 12 Bayram Fırını Sok. (☎517 7931; www.hostelbigapple.com), down the road from Akbıyık Cad., next to Barefoot Travel. On a quieter side street off of Akbıyık Cad., this hostel offers one of the most fun and relaxing atmospheres in İstanbul for both individuals and groups. Has a large downstairs common room and an upstairs terrace with beanbag chairs, beach loungers, and a swing, not to mention some of the friendliest staff around. Breakfast (8:30-10:30am), towels, and linens included. Internet. Dorms €10; singles €22; doubles €25. MC/V. ❷

Metropolis, 24 Terbıyık Sok. (☎212 518 1822; www.metropolishostel.com), removed from the hustle of Akbıyık, on a central yet quieter back street. This beautifully kept hostel has comfortable, stylish rooms, friendly staff, and a peaceful location. Guests get a 10% discount at the Metropolis Restaurant and Downunder Bar around the corner. Breakfast included. Free Internet. Single-sex dorms 23YTL; doubles 60YTL. MC/V. ❷

Bahaus Guesthouse, 11-13 Akbıyık Cad. (☎212 638 6534; www.travelinistanbul.com), across the street from Big Apple. Though its dorm rooms are simple, Bahaus's cozy Anatolian-themed closed terrace and couch-filled open terrace are comfortable and lively. Travelers rave about this place, and the rooms are usually full. Book in advance. Airport pickup available. Free Internet. Breakfast included. Dorms €9; doubles €44. MC/V. ❶

Sultan Hostel, 21 Akbıyık Cad. (☎212 9260; www.sultanhostel.com). Right in the middle of backpacker land, this happening hostel is İstanbul's most famous. Streetside, rooftop restaurant and comfortable, clean dorms make it a great place to meet new, fun, fellow travelers. Breakfast included. Free safes. Free Internet. Reserve ahead. Dorms with bathroom €14; doubles €19, with bathroom €22; quads €15/17. Rates per person, but rooms booked as a unit. MC/V. ❷

Sydney Hostel, 42 Akbıyık Cad. (☎212 518 6671; fax 518 6672), in the middle of Akbıyık. Calm, with cheerful sky-blue walls, modern rooms and bathrooms, and much-coveted in-room A/C. Rooftop terrace. Free safes. Free Internet. Breakfast included. Dorms €10; singles and doubles €35. V. ❶

Terrace Guesthouse, 39 Kutlugün Sok. (☎212 638 9733; www.terracehotelistanbul. com), behind Akbıyık Cad. Housed in a narrow carpet shop, this elegant hotel has beautifully decorated rooms for affordable prices. The 2 upstairs terraces have spectacular views. Breakfast included. Free Wi-Fi. Singles €60; doubles €70; triples €80. V. ❺

Zeugma Hostel, 35 Akbıyık Cad. (☎212 517 4040; www.zeugmahostel.net). This clean, 1-room hostel has a huge basement dorm with comfortable wooden bunks separated by colorful curtains, giving it a bedouin camp feel. Though there is no common space, the dorm has A/C and a quiet, relaxed vibe. Airport pick-up available. Linens included. Free Internet. Reception 24hr. Rooms €9-12, with breakfast €11-13. V. ❶

FOOD

İstanbul's restaurants often demonstrate the golden rule: if it's well advertised or easy to find, it's not worth a visit. Great meals can be found across the **Galata Bridge** and around **Taksim Square**. Small Bosphorus suburbs such as **Arnavutköy** and Sariyer (on the European side) and **Çengelköy** (on the Asian side) are the best places for fresh fish. For a cheaper meal, **İstiklâl Caddesi** has all the major Western chains, as well as quick and tasty Turkish fast food. Vendors in Ottoman dress sell *Vişne suyu* (sour cherry juice), and on any street you'll find dried fruit and nuts for sale, as well as the omnipresent stalls of sesame bagels (1YTL). The best open-air **market** is open daily in **Beşiktaş**, near Barbaros Cad., while at the Egyptian Spice Bazaar (*Mısır Çarşısı*) you can find almonds, fruit, and—of course—**kebab**, which range from shawarma-type meat to Western-style meat-on-a-stick.

▨ **Doy-Doy**, 13 Şifa Hammamı Sok. (☎517 1588). The best in Sultanahmet, 3-story Doy-Doy's rooftop tables are right under the Blue Mosque. On the lower levels are cushioned floors and plenty of *nargilas (hookahs)*. Try the *kebab* (5-10YTL) or shepherd salads with *cacik* (yogurt and cucumber; 4YTL). Open daily 8am-11pm. MC/V. ❷

▨ **Trabzon Lokantasi**, 10 Dervisler Sok, near Sirkeci. Tucked in an alleyway off the tram tracks, this small cafe-restaurant features real Turkish homecooking in cheap, plentiful servings, with several vegetarian options. The lentil soup (1.50YTL) is exceptional. Be sure to check out the colorful guestbook, filled with notes from visitors from around the world. Entrees 3-6YTL. Open 11am-11pm. Cash only. ❶

Muhammed Said Baklavaci, 88 Divan Yolu Cad. (☎212 526 9666; www.baklavacimuhammedsaid.com). Specializing in homemade *baklava* and Turkish delights, this small, locally-owned bakery is a wonderland of sweets. Prices are reasonable and the food is amazing. 1 kilo 20-29YTL. Open daily 9am-10pm. Cash only. ❸

Hacı Abdullah, 17 Sakizağacı Cad. (☎293 8561; www.haciabdullah.com.tr), down the street from Ağa Camii, in Taksim Sq. This family-style restaurant, going strong since 1888, features huge vases of preserved fruit, as well as high-tech bathrooms. Their homemade grapefruit juice is fantastic. Soups and salads 3-7YTL. Entrees 10-20YTL. No alcohol served. Open daily noon-11pm. Kitchen closes 10:30pm. MC/V. ❷

Koska Helvacısı, İstiklâl Cad. 238 (☎212 244 0877; www.koskahelvacisi.com.tr). This confectionery superstore, which celebrated its 100th anniversary in 2007, is a sugar-lover's dream. Fantastic take-out *baklava* trays (3YTL) and boxed assortments of sweets (6-20YTL) in all colors and flavors. Open daily 9am-11:30pm. V. ❷

SIGHTS

İstanbul's array of churches, mosques, palaces, and museums can keep an ardent tourist busy for weeks. Most first time travelers to İstanbul spend a lot of time in Sultanahmet, the area around the Aya Sofya south of and uphill from Sirkeci. Merchants crowd the district between the enormous Grand Bazaar, east of the university, and the less touristy Egyptian Spice Bazaar, just southeast of Eminönü. Soak in the city's sights and hop on one of the small boats near the Galata Bridge and go for a relaxing and panoramic ▧**Bosphorus tour.**

> **⭐TIP** **BARGAINING FOR BEGINNERS.** İstanbul bargaining doesn't end at carpets: it's acceptable to bargain for almost anything, including tours. For the best deals on boat trips, bargain with boat owners at the port. Trips shouldn't be more than 20YTL for a few hours down the Bosphorus.

▧**AYA SOFYA (HAGIA SOPHIA).** When Aya Sofya (Divine Wisdom) was built in AD 537, it was the biggest building in the world. Built as a church, it fell to the Ottomans in 1453 and was converted into a mosque; it remained such until 1932, when Atatürk declared it a museum. The nave is overshadowed by the gold-leaf mosaic dome, lined with hundreds of circular windows that make it seem as though the dome is floating on a bed of luminescent pearls. Throughout the building, Qur'anic inscriptions and mosaics of Mary and the angels intertwine in a fascinating symmetry. The gallery contains Byzantine mosaics uncovered from beneath a thick layer of Ottoman plaster, as well as the famed **sweating pillar,** sheathed in bronze. The pillar has a hole big enough to stick a finger in and collect the odd drop of water, believed to possess healing powers. *(Open daily 9am-7:30pm. Upper gallery open 9:30am-6:45pm. 10YTL.)*

▧**BLUE MOSQUE (SULTANAHMET CAMİİ).** Named for the beautiful blue İznik tiles covering the interior, the extravagant Blue Mosque and its six **minarets** were Sultan Ahmet's 1617 claim to fame. At the time of construction, only the mosque at Mecca had as many minarets, and the thought of rivaling that sacred edifice was considered heretical. The crafty Sultan circumvented this difficulty by financing the construction of a seventh minaret at Mecca. The interior was originally lit with candles, the chandelier structure intended to create the illusion of tiny starlights floating freely in the air. The small, square, single-domed structure in front of the Blue Mosque is **Sultanahmet'in Türbesi,** or Sultan Ahmet's Tomb, which contains the sultan's remains. The reliquary in the back contains strands of the Prophet Muhammad's beard. *(Open M-Th and Sa-Su 9am-12:30pm, 1:45-4:40pm and 5:40-6:30pm, F noon-2:20pm. The Blue Mosque is a working religious facility and closes to the public for prayer 5 times a day. Scarves are provided*

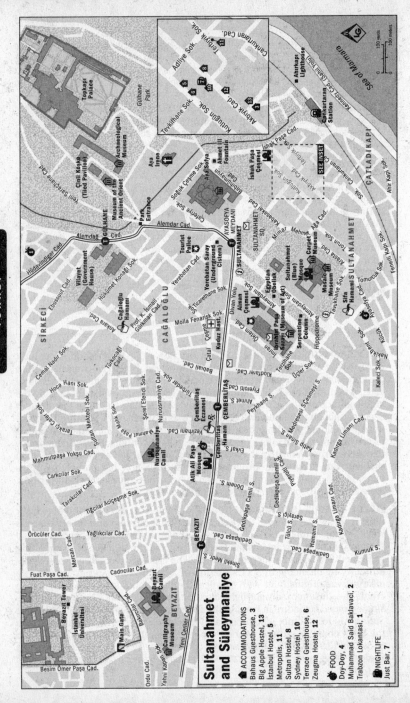

TURKEY

Sultanahmet and Süleymaniye

♦ ACCOMMODATIONS
Bahaus Guesthouse, **3**
Big Apple Hostel, **13**
Istanbul Hostel, **5**
Metropolis, **11**
Sultan Hostel, **8**
Sydney Hostel, **10**
Terrace Guesthouse, **6**
Zeugma Hostel, **12**

● FOOD
Doy-Doy, **4**
Muhammad Said Baklavaci, **2**
Trabzon Lokantasi, **1**

■ NIGHTLIFE
Just Bar, **7**

at the entrance; women should cover their knees, hair, and shoulders. Inside the mosque, behave respectfully and don't cross into the sections limited to prayer. Donations are welcome on the way out. See p. 758 for more details on appropriate mosque etiquette.)

TOPKAPI PALACE (TOPKAPI SARAYI). Towering from the high ground at the tip of the old city and hidden behind walls up to 12m high, Topkapı was the nerve center of the Ottoman Empire. Built by Mehmet the Conqueror in 1458-1465, the palace became an imperial residence during the reign of Süleyman the Magnificent. The palace is divided into a series of courtyards. The **first courtyard** was the popular center of the palace, where the general public could enter to watch executions and other displays of imperial might. The **second courtyard** leads to displays of wealth, including collections of porcelain, silver, gold, and torture instruments—not to mention crystal staircases. The Gate of Felicity leads to the **third courtyard,** which houses imperial clothing and the awesome 🖼**Palace Treasury.** The **fourth courtyard** is the pleasure center of the palace—it was among these pavilions, gardens, and fountains that the Ottomans really got their mojo working. The most interesting part of Topkapı is the 400-plus-room 🖼**harem.** Tours begin at the Blap. 758ck Eunuchs' Dormitory and continue into the chambers of the Valide Sultan, the sultan's mother and the harem's most powerful woman. Surrounding the room of the queen mum are the chambers of the concubines. If a particular woman attracted the sultan's affections or if the sultan spent a night with her, she would be promoted to "odalisque" status, which meant that she had to stay in İstanbul forever, but got nicer quarters in exchange for her undying ministrations. *(Palace open M and W-Su 9am-7pm. 10YTL. Harem open 10am-5pm. 10YTL. Audio tour of palace 5YTL. Harem can only be visited on guided tours, which leave every 30min. Lines for tours can be long; arrive early.)*

UNDERGROUND CISTERN (YEREBATAN SARAYI). This underground "palace" is a vast cavern whose shallow water reflects the images of its 336 supporting columns. The columns are all illuminated by colored ambient lighting, making the cistern slightly resemble a horror-movie set. Underground walkways originally linked the cistern to Topkapı Palace but were blocked to curb rampant trafficking in stolen goods and abducted women. At the far end of the cistern, two huge Medusa heads lie upside down in the water. Legend has it that looking at them directly turns people to stone. The cistern's overpriced cafe, in a dark corner, is a cross between creepy and romantic. *(The entrance lies 175m from the Aya Sofya in the small stone kiosk on the left side of Yerebatan Cad. Open daily 9am-6:30pm. 10YTL.)*

ARCHAEOLOGICAL MUSEUM COMPLEX. The Archaeological Museum Complex encompasses four distinct museums. The **Tiled Pavilion** explains more than you ever wanted to know about the omnipresent İznik tiles. The smaller, adjacent building is the 🖼**Ancient Orient Museum.** It houses an excellent collection of 3000-year-old stone artifacts from the ancient Middle East and the Treaty of Kadesh, the world's oldest known written treaty, drafted after a battle between Ramses II of Egypt and the Hittite King Muvatellish. The immense 🖼**Archaeology Museum** has one of the world's greatest collections of Classical and Hellenistic art but is surprisingly bereft of visitors. The highlight is the famous Alexander Sarcophagus. The superb **Museum of Turkish and Islamic Art** features a large collection of Islamic art, organized by period. *(150m downhill from the Topkapı Palace's 1st courtyard. All museums open Tu-Su 8:30am-5pm. 5YTL.)*

GRAND BAZAAR. Through banter, barter, and haggle, **Kapalı Çarşısı** (Grand Bazaar) operates on a scale unmatched by even the most frenetic of markets elsewhere in Europe. The largest, oldest covered bazaar in the world, the Grand Bazaar began in 1461 as a modest affair during the reign of Mehmet the Conqueror. Today, the enormous Kapalı Çarşısı combines the best and worst of shopping in Turkey to form the massive mercantile sprawl that starts at Çemberlitaş and covers the hill down to Eminönü, ending at the more authentic and less claustrophobic ◙Mısır Çarşısı (Egyptian Spice Bazaar) and the Golden Horn waterfront. Rule number one in bargaining: never settle for more than half the first price asked; the place is touristy and shop owners know their tricks. Most wares in the Grand Bazaar are available for less in the Spice Bazaar or in shops. And don't worry about getting lost—there are directional arrows from virtually any spot, so relax and enjoy the ride. *(From Sultanahmet, follow the tram tracks toward Aksaray until you see the Nuruosmanıye Camii on the right. Walk down Vezirhanı Cad. for one block, keeping the mosque on your left. Otherwise, follow the crowds. www.grandbazaar.com. Open M-Sa 9am-7pm.)*

SÜLEYMANİYE COMPLEX. To the north of İstanbul University stands the elegant **Süleymaniye Camii,** one of Ottoman architect Sinan's great masterpieces. This mosque is part of a larger **külliye** (complex), which includes **tombs,** an **imaret** (soup kitchen), and several **madrasas** (Islamic schools). After walking through the cemetery to see the **royal tombs** of Süleyman I and his wife, proceed inside the vast and perfectly proportioned mosque—the height of the dome (53m) is exactly twice the measurement of each side of the square base. The **stained-glass windows** are the sobering work of the master Sarhoş İbrahim (İbrahim the Drunkard). The İznik tile İnzanity all started here: the area around the **mihrab** showcases Sinan's first experiment in blue tiles. *(From Sultanahmet, take the tramvay to the Üniversite stop, walk across the square, and take Besim Ömer Paşa Cad. past the walls of the university to Süleymaniye Cad. Open daily except during prayer. Leave your shoes at the entrance. Women need to cover their shoulders; men and women should cover their heads. Scarves are available at the entrance.)*

⌂ HAMMAMS (TURKISH BATHS)

In the past, a man found in a women's bath was sentenced to death, but today customs have relaxed and it's not rare to find co-ed baths where both genders strip beyond their skivvies. Most baths have separate women's sections or hours, but only some have designated female attendants. If you'd rather have a masseuse of your same sex, make sure to ask at the entrance.

▨ **Cağaloğlu Hamamı,** on Yerebatan Cad. at Babiali Cad. (☎212 522 2424; www.cagalogluhamami.com.tr), near Cağaloğlu Sq. in Sultanahmet. Donated to İstanbul in 1741 by Sultan Mehmet I, this luxurious white-marble bath is one of the city's most illustrious. Self-service bath 20YTL, bath with scrub 30YTL, complete bath and massage 40YTL, luxury treatment with hand-knit Oriental washcloth 60YTL. Slippers, soap, and towels included. Open daily for women 8am-8pm, for men 8am-10pm. V.

Çemberlitaş Hamamı, 8 Vezirhan Cad. (☎212 522 7974; www.cemberlitashamami. com.tr). Just a soap-slide away from the Çemberlitaş tram stop. Built in 1584, the marble interiors make this place downright regal. Vigorous "towel service" after the bath; guests are welcome to lounge around the relaxing, hot marble rooms afterward. Open daily 6am-midnight. Am/Ex/MC/V.

◙ NIGHTLIFE

Locals and travelers alike pour into the streets to savor intense nightlife, which falls into three categories. The first includes male-only *çay* (tea) houses, backgammon parlors, and dancing shows. Women are not prohibited but are unwelcome and should avoid these places, which are often unsafe for male travelers as well. *Let's Go* does not endorse patronage of these establishments. The second category includes the local youth **cafe-bars, rock bars,** and **backpacker bars.** In

Sultanahmet, pubs are crammed within 10m of one another, usually on the rooftop or front tables of the hostels. They have standardized beer prices (5YTL) and are usually Australian-dominated; **Orient,** the most popular hostel bar, is open to all. **Clubs** and **discos** comprise the third nightlife category. Even taxi drivers can't keep up with the ever-fluctuating club scene. The Beşiktaş end of **Ortaköy** is a maze of upscale hangouts. The cheerful **Nevizade** is a virtually uninterrupted row of wine shops and *tapas* bars, parallel to İstiklâl Cad. İstanbul's local specialty is *balyoz* (sledgehammer/wrecking ball). Getting wrecked won't be difficult: *balyoz* consists of *rakı*, whiskey, vodka, and gin with orange juice.

■ **Just Bar,** 18 Akbıyık Cad. (☎01 23 45 67 89). This bar has become almost as much of a must-see as the Aya Sofya. Outdoor wooden pub tables, rock/funk/R&B music, and free-flowing beer make for a typical backpacker's night, every night. Beer 5YTL. Mixed drinks 7-10YTL. Open daily 11am-4am. It's hard to tell where Just Bar stops and **Cheers,** next door, begins. Cheers is equally popular, friendly, and laid-back. Beer 4-5YTL. Mixed drinks and shots 7-10YTL. Open daily noon-late. MC/V.

Jazz Stop, at the end of Büyük Parmakkapı Sok., in Taksim (☎292 5314). A mixed group of music lovers sit in this large underground tavern while live bands lay the funk, blues, and jazz on thick. The owner, the drummer from one of Turkey's oldest and most respected rock groups, occasionally takes part in the jams. A late-night hangout where the crowds don't build until 2 or 3am. Beer 5YTL. Mixed drinks 7-20YTL. Live music daily 2am. Cover F-Sa 10YTL; includes 1 drink. Open daily 7pm-6am. V.

Araf, İstiklâl Cad. and 32 Balo Sok. (☎244 8301), across from the entrance to Nevizade. Take the elevator to the 4th fl., then walk upstairs to reach this funky rooftop veranda with international music and freestyle dancing in a birthday-party atmosphere. No cover. Beer 4YTL. Mixed drinks 7-20YTL. Open daily 5pm-2am. Cash only.

Nayah Music Club, Kurabiye Sok. 23 (☎212 244 1183; www.myspace.com/nayahmusicclub), in Beyoglu. From İstiklâl Cad., take a right onto Mis Sok.; Nayah is one block down, on the corner with Kurabiye Sok. This reggae bar is small and relaxed, with rasta bartenders. Customers sit and groove to the music with subtle head bobs. Beer 4YTL. Mixed drinks 7-14YTL. Open M-Th 6pm-2am, F-Sa 6pm-4am. Cash only.

UKRAINE
(УКРАЇНА)

In late 2004, Ukraine's Orange Revolution brought international attention to the country. President Viktor Yushchenko and his administration have since enacted important reforms; however, a muddled Ukrainian political climate has slowed the rate of change. Today, Ukrainians are divided over their own identity: this internal struggle to reinvent and yet retain traditions can make Ukrainian culture confusing to navigate. Don't be surprised if a desk clerk and a website provide two different prices for a room, and don't expect anyone outside Kyiv to speak much English. Despite these inconveniences, Ukraine is captivating. Whole cities are under renovation, and the energy of revitalization spills over into the streets. If you can get past the almost complete lack of tourist infrastructure, Ukraine can be a beautiful and adventurous place to travel.

DISCOVER UKRAINE: SUGGESTED ITINERARIES

THREE DAYS. Stick to **Kyiv**, the epicenter of the Orange Revolution. Check out **Independence Square**, stop by **Shevchenko Park** to enjoy real Ukrainian fare at **O'Panas**, and ponder your mortality among the mummified monks of the **Kyiv-Cave Monastery** (p. 781).

ESSENTIALS

FACTS AND FIGURES

OFFICIAL NAME: Ukraine.

CAPITAL: Kyiv.

MAJOR CITIES: Lviv, Odessa, Sevastopol, Simferopol, Yalta.

POPULATION: 45,994,000.

LAND AREA: 603,700 sq. km.

TIME ZONE: GMT + 2.

LANGUAGE: Ukrainian.

RELIGIONS: Ukrainian Orthodox (29%), Orthodox (16%), other (55%).

THE HEART OF IT ALL: Some measurements have placed the geographic center of Europe in Dilove, UKR.

WHEN TO GO

Ukraine is a huge country with a diverse climate. Things heat up from June to August in Odessa and Crimea, which are just barely subtropical. It is best to reserve accommodations in advance at these times. Kyiv enjoys a moderate climate, while the more mountainous west remains cool even in summer. Winter tourism is popular in the Carpathians, but unless you're skiing, spring and summer are probably the best times to visit the country. Book accommodations early around the May 1 holiday.

DOCUMENTS AND FORMALITIES

EMBASSIES AND CONSULATES. Foreign embassies to Ukraine are in Kyiv (p. 779). Ukrainian embassies and consulates abroad include: **Australia,** Level 12, St. George Centre, 60 Marcus Clarke St., Canberra, ACT 2601 (☎02 62 30 57 89; www.ukremb.info); **Canada,** 310 Somerset St., West Ottawa, ON K2P 0J9 (☎613-230-2400; www.mfa.gov.ua/canada); **Ireland,** refer to UK embassy; **New Zealand,** 48, Ayton Drive, Glenfield, Auckland (☎94 01 94 93; http://ukraine.visahq.com/embassy/New-Zealand); **UK,** 60 Holland Park, London, W11 3SJ (☎020 77 27 63 12, visas ☎020 72 43 89 23; www.ukremb.org.uk); **US,** 3350 M St., NW, Washington, DC 20007 (☎202-333-0606; www.mfa.gov.ua/usa).

> **ENTRANCE REQUIREMENTS.**
> **Passport:** Required for all travelers.
> **Visa:** Not required for citizens of Canada, the EU, or the US, but mandatory for citizens of Australia and New Zealand.
> **Letter of Invitation:** Required for citizens of Australia and New Zealand.
> **Inoculations:** Recommended up-to-date on DTaP (diphtheria, tetanus, and pertussis), Hepatitis A, Hepatitis B, MMR (measles, mumps, and rubella), polio booster, rabies (if you'll be in rural areas for long periods of time), and typhoid.
> **Work Permit:** Required of all foreigners planning to work in Ukraine.
> **International Driving Permit:** Required for all those planning to drive.

VISA AND ENTRY INFORMATION. Ukraine's visa requirements have changed rapidly since 2005 as the new government works to encourage tourism. Visas are no longer required for American or Canadian citizens or citizens of the EU for stays of up to 90 days. All visas are valid for 90 days. Citizens of Australia and New Zealand require a **letter of invitation** (available from Ukrainian or Australian/New Zealand travel agencies) but citizens of Canada, the EU, and the US do not. Travelers should allow three weeks for processing. You can extend your visa in Ukraine, at the Ministry of Foreign Affairs, (Velyka Zhitomirska st., 2, Kyiv) or at the local **Office of Visas and Registration** (ОВИ; OVYR), often located at the police station. **Do not lose the paper given to you when entering the country to supplement your visa.** Make sure to carry your passport and visa at all times.

TOURIST SERVICES AND MONEY

EMERGENCY	Ambulance: ☎03. Fire: ☎01. Police: ☎02.

TOURIST OFFICES. Lviv's tourist office is helpful, but it is the only official tourist office in Ukraine. The remains of the Soviet giant **Intourist** have offices in hotels, but staff often doesn't speak English. The official tourist website, **www.traveltoukraine.org,** has a list of "reliable travel agents." Local travel agencies can be helpful, but are sometimes overly pushy.

MONEY. The Ukrainian unit of currency is the *hryvnya* (*hv*), and *Obmin Valyut* (Обмшн Валт) kiosks in most cities offer the best rates for currency exchange. **Traveler's checks** can be changed for a small commission in many cities. **ATMs** are everywhere. Most **banks** will give MasterCard and Visa **cash advances** for a high commission. The lobbies of upscale hotels usually exchange US dollars at

lousy rates. **Private money changers** lurk near kiosks, ready with brilliant schemes for scamming you, but exchanging money with them is illegal.

UKRANHIAN HRYVNIA (HV)	
AUS$1 = 3.85HV	1HV = AUS$0.26
CDN$1 = 4.58HV	1HV = CDN$0.22
EUR€1 = 6.47HV	1HV = EUR€0.15
NZ$1 = 3.23HV	1HV = NZ$0.31
UK£1 = 9.45HV	1HV = UK£0.11
US$1 = 5.05HV	1HV = US$0.20

HEALTH AND SAFETY

Hospital facilities in Ukraine are limited and do not meet American or Western European standards. Patients may be required to bring their own medical supplies (e.g., bandages). When in doubt, it is advisable to seek aid from your local embassy. Medical evacuations to Western Europe cost US$25,000 and upwards of US$50,000 to the US. **Pharmacies** (Аптеки; Apteky) are quite common and carry basic Western products. **Boil all water** or learn to love brushing your teeth with soda water. **Peel or wash fruits and vegetables** from open markets. Meat purchased at public markets should be checked carefully and cooked thoroughly; refrigeration is infrequent and insects run rampant. Avoid the tasty-looking hunks of meat for sale out of buckets on the Kyiv metro. Embassy officials declare that Chernobyl-related radiation poses minimal risk to short-term travelers. **Public restrooms** range from disgusting to frightening. **Pay toilets** (платн; *platni*) are cleaner and might provide toilet paper, but bring your own.

While Ukraine is politically stable, it is poor. Pickpocketing and wallet scams are the most common **crimes** against tourists; however, instances of armed robbery and assault have been reported. Do not accept drinks from strangers, as this could result in your being drugged. Credit card and ATM fraud are rampant; only use ATMs inside banks and hotels, and avoid using credit cards when possible. Also use caution when crossing the street—drivers do not stop for pedestrians. It's wise to register with your embassy once you get to Ukraine.

Women traveling alone may receive catcalls by men anywhere they go, but usually will be safe otherwise. Ukrainian women rarely go to restaurants alone, so expect to feel conspicuous if you do. Women may request to ride in female-only compartments during long train rides, though most do not. Although non-Caucasians may experience **discrimination,** the biggest problems stem from the militia, who frequently stop people who appear non-Slavic. **Homosexuality** is not yet accepted in Ukraine; it's best to be discreet.

TRANSPORTATION

BY PLANE. It is expensive to travel to Ukraine by plane, and few budget airlines fly in or out of the country. Ground transportation tends to be safer and more pleasant, but it can take a long time to traverse the great distances between cities. Most international flights land at **Borispol International Airport** (KPB, www.airport-borispol.kiev.ua, ☎490 47 77). Air Ukraine flies to Kyiv, Lviv, and Odessa from many European capitals. **Aerosvit, Air France, British Airways, SA, Delta, Lufthansa, LOT,** and **Malev** fly to Kyiv.

BY TRAIN. Trains run frequently and are the best way to travel. Ukraine's system is generally safe, although *Let's Go* discourages the use of **night trains** in the region. When coming from a non-ex-Soviet country, expect a 2hr. stop at the border. To purchase tickets, you must present a passport or student ID. Once on board, you must present both your ticket and ID to the *konduktor*. On most Ukrainian trains, there are three classes: плацкарт, or *platskart*, where you'll be crammed in with *babushki* (little old ladies) and baskets of strawberries; купе, or *kupe*, a clean, more private, four-person compartment; and first class, referred to as CB, or SV (for *Spalny Wagon*), which is twice as roomy and expensive as *kupe*. Unless you're determined to live like a local, pay the extra two dollars for *kupe*. Then again, women traveling alone may want to avoid the smaller, enclosed compartments of *kupe*; in that case, *platskart* may be the safer option. The *kasa* will sell you a kupe seat unless you specify otherwise. Except in larger cities, where platform numbers are posted on the electronic board, the only way to figure out which platform your train leaves from is by listening to the distorted announcement. In large cities, trains arrive well before they are scheduled to depart, so you'll have a few minutes to show your ticket to cashiers or fellow passengers and ask "plaht-FORM-ah?"

BY BUS, TAXI, AND THUMB. Buses cost about the same as trains, but are often much shabbier. For long distances, the train is usually more comfortable, although on some routes the bus proves considerably faster. One exception is **AutoLux** (АвтоЛкс, www.autolux.ua), which runs buses with A/C, snacks, and movies. Bus schedules are generally reliable, but low demand can cause cancellations. Buy tickets at the *kasa*; if they're sold out, try going directly to the driver, who might just magically find you a seat and pocket the money. Navigating the bus system can be tough for those who do not speak Ukrainian or Russian. **Taxi** drivers love to rip off foreigners, so negotiate the price beforehand. Few Ukrainians **hitchhike,** but those who do hold a sign with their destination or just wave an outstretched hand. *Let's Go* does not recommend hitchhiking.

DON'T MESS WITH TRANSNISTRIA. If you're planning a trip from Western Ukraine to the Crimea, make sure that your train or bus route doesn't pass through Moldova on the way. Much of eastern Moldova is part of the unrecognized breakaway territory of Transnistria; border guards in Transnistria have been known to demand bribes, confiscate expensive items like laptops and cameras, or simply throw unlucky travelers off of the train. To make sure this doesn't happen to you, check at the ticket counter before buying to make sure your ticket won't take you for an unpleasant ride.

KEEPING IN TOUCH

PHONE CODES — **Country code: 380. International dialing prefix:** 8, await a second tone, then 10. For more info on placing international calls, see **Inside Back Cover.**

TELEPHONE AND INTERNET. Telephone services are stumbling toward modernity. The easiest way to make **international calls** is with Utel. Buy an Utel **phonecard** (sold at most Utel phone locations) and dial the number of your international operator (counted as a local call). International access codes include: **AT&T Direct** (☎8 100 11); **Canada Direct** (☎8 100 17); and **MCI WorldPhone** (☎8 100 13). Alternatively, call at the **central telephone office**; estimate the length of your call and pay at the counter, and they'll direct you to a booth. Calling can be expensive, but you can purchase a 30min. international calling card for 15hv. Local calls from gray **payphones** generally cost 10-30hv. For an English-speaking operator, dial ☎8192. Cell phones are everywhere; to get one, stop at any kiosk or corner store. **Internet cafes** can be found in every major city and typically charge 4-12hv per hour of use. Major cities typically have 24hr. Internet cafes.

MAIL. Mail is cheap, reliable, and extremely user-friendly, taking about 8-10 days to reach North America. Sending a postcard or a letter of less than 20g internationally costs 0.66hv. Address **Poste Restante** (mail held at the post office for collection, до запитання; *do zapytannya*) as follows: First name LAST NAME, post office address, Postal Code, city, ГЛКФШТУ.

LANGUAGE. Traveling in Ukraine is much easier if you know some Ukrainian or Russian. Ukrainian is an East Slavic language written in the Cyrillic alphabet. For basic Russian words and phrases see **Phrasebook** (p. 792). In Kyiv, Odessa, and Crimea, Russian is more commonly spoken than Ukrainian (although all official signs are in Ukrainian). If you're trying to get by with Russian in western Ukraine, you may run into some difficulty: everyone understands Russian, but some people will answer in Ukrainian out of habit or nationalist sentiment. *Let's Go* provides city names in Ukrainian for Kyiv and western Ukraine, while Russian names are used for Crimea and Odessa.

ACCOMMODATIONS AND CAMPING

UKRAINE	❶	❷	❸	❹	❺
ACCOMMODATIONS	under 75hv	75-150hv	151-250hv	251-350hv	over 350hv

The **hostel** scene in Ukraine is quickly establishing itself, though hostels are uncommon outside Lviv, Kyiv, and Odessa. Budget accommodations are often in unrenovated Soviet-era buildings, though they are rapidly improving. More expensive lodgings aren't necessarily nicer. Not all hotels accept foreigners, and overcharging tourists is common. Though room prices in Kyiv are astronomical, singles run anywhere from 65-110hv in the rest of the country. Standard hotel rooms include TVs, phones, and refrigerators. You will be given a *vizitka* (hotel card) to show to the hall monitor (*dezhurnaya*) to get a key; return it each time you leave. Hot water doesn't necessarily come with a bath—ask before checking in. Private rooms are the best bargain and run 20-50hv. These can be arranged through overseas agencies or bargained for at the train station. Big cities have camping facilities—usually a remote spot with trailers. Camping outside designated areas is illegal, and enforcement is strict.

FOOD AND DRINK

UKRAINE	❶	❷	❸	❹	❺
FOOD	under 15hv	15-35hv	36-55hv	56-75hv	over 75hv

New, fancy restaurants accommodate tourists and the few Ukrainians who can afford them, while *stolovayas* (cafeterias)—remnants of Soviet times—serve cheap, hot food. Pierogi-like dumplings called *vavenyky* are ubiquitous and delicious. **Vegetarians** beware: meat has a tendency to show up in so-called "vegetarian" dishes. Finding **kosher** foods can be daunting, but it helps to eat non-meat items. Fruits and veggies are sold at markets; bring your own bag. State food stores are classified by content: *hastronom* (packaged goods); *moloko* (milk products); *ovochi-frukty* (fruits and vegetables); *myaso* (meat); *khlib* (bread); *kolbasy* (sausage); and *ryba* (fish). *Kvas* is a popular, barely-alcoholic, fermented bread drink. Grocery stores are often simply labeled *mahazyn* (store). Beer can be drunk publicly but hard liquor can't. The distinction is telling—"I drink beer," goes one Ukrainian saying, "and I also drink alcohol."

HOLIDAYS AND FESTIVALS

Holidays: Orthodox Christmas (Jan. 7); Orthodox New Year (Jan. 14); International Women's Day (Mar. 8); Easter (Apr. 19th, 2009; Apr. 4th, 2010); Labor Day (May 1-2); Victory Day (May 9); Holy Trinity Day (June 16); Constitution Day (June 28); Independence Day (Aug. 24).

Festivals: One of the most widely celebrated festivals is the **Donetsk Jazz Festival**, usually held in March. The **Chervona Ruta Festival,** which occurs in different Ukrainian cities each year, celebrating both modern Ukrainian pop and traditional music. The **Molodist Kyiv International Film Festival,** held in the last week of October, offers a platform for student films and up-and-coming film directors.

BEYOND TOURISM

For more info on opportunities across Europe, see **Beyond Tourism,** p. 55.

UKRAINE

Jewish Volunteer Corps, American Jewish World Service, 45 W. 36th St., New York City, NY 10018, USA (☎+1 212-792-2919, www.ajws.org). Places volunteers at summer camps and Jewish community centers in Russia Ukraine.

Odessa Language Center (☎+380 482 345 058; www.studyrus.com). Spend a few weeks or up to a year in Ukraine learning Russian and studying history and culture.

KYIV (КИЇВ)   ☎8044

Since becoming the capital of the Kyivan Rus empire over a millennium ago, Kyiv (pop. 2,700,000) has been a social and economic center for the region. No stranger to foreign control, the city was razed by the Nazi army only to be rebuilt with extravagant Stalinist pomp by the Soviets. Since Ukraine gained its independence from the USSR in 1991, Kyiv has reemerged as a proud capital and cultural center. One can find a legion of gilded towers and buildings reminiscent of mother Russia strewn along its hilly streets. However, the open squares, countless cafes, and shaded paths add a distinct western flavor to this Eastern European capital. The new government—elected beneath the international spotlight during the 2004 Orange Revolution—struggles to institute promised reforms as the cost of living rises.

▟ TRANSPORTATION

Flights: Boryspil International Airport (Бориспіль, **KBP**, ☎8044 281 7498) 30km southeast of the capital. Polit (Політ; ☎8044 296 7367), just right of the main entrance, sends **minibuses** called *marshrutkis* to Ploshcha Peremohi, the train station, and Boryspilska, the metro stop. Buy tickets on board (1-2 per hr., 17-22hv). Expect to be hassled by an army of **taxi** drivers upon exiting the airport. A taxi to the center costs 80-100hv. Negotiate with drivers near the Polit bus stop; those stationed outside customs will take you for a ride.

Trains: Kyiv-Pasazhyrskyy (Київ-Пасажирський), Vokzalna pl. (☎005 or 8044 465 4895). MR: Vokzalna (Вокзальна). Purchase tickets for **domestic trains** in the main hall. For international tickets, go to window #40 or 41 in the newest section of the train station, across the tracks. For the *elektrychka* **commuter rail** (електричка), go to Prymiskyy Vokzal (Примский Вокзал; Suburban Station), next to the Metro station. **Information windows** (довідка; dovidka) are located in each section of the train station; some stay open 24hr. However, assistance is entirely in Ukrainian or Russian. Look for a large departure board in the main hall that posts platform numbers and any last-minute changes. There is an **Advance Ticket Office** next to Hotel Express at Shevchenka 38. Train tickets are divided into 4 classes, and trains usually have beds rather than seats. 1st class seats hold 2 beds to a room, while 2nd class has 4 beds and shabbier conditions, but is considerably less expensive. Trains to: **Lviv** (10hr., 5-6 per day, 65-100hv); **Odessa** (11hr., 4-5 per day, 80-105hv); **Sevastopol** (20hr., 2 per day, 75-180hv); **Bratislava, SLK** (21hr., 1 per day, 700hv); **Budapest, HUN** (24hr., 1 per day, 800hv); **Moscow, RUS** (14-17hr., 12-15 per day, 350hv); **Prague, CZR** (35hr., 1 per day, 600hv); **Warsaw, POL** (19hr., 2 per day, 450hv). Check prices before purchasing train tickets, as train ticket prices in Ukraine change frequently.

Buses: Tsentralny Avtovokzal (Центральний Автовокзал), Moskovska pl. 3 (Московська; ☎8044 264 5774). MR: Libydska. Take trolley #1 or 11 from the Libydska metro station. Open 5am-10pm. Buses to: **Lviv** (7-12hr., 4 per day, 70hv); **Odessa** (8-10hr,, 9 per day, 75hv); **Moscow, RUS** (18hr., 1 per day, 150hv).

Public Transportation: 3 metro lines—blue (MB), green (MG), and red (MR)—cover the city center. Purchase tokens (житон; zhyton; 0.50hv) at the kasa (каса). "Вхід" (vkhid) indicates an entrance, "перехід" (perekhid) a walkway to another station, and "вихід y місто" (vykhid u misto) an exit onto the street. **Trolleys, buses,** and **marshrutki** (private vans) go where the metro doesn't. Bus tickets sold at kiosks or by the driver; punch your ticket using the manual lever on board or face a fine. *Marshrutki* tickets (1-3hv) are sold on board; pay attention and request stops from the driver. Public transport runs approx. 5:45am-12:15am. The *elektrychka* (електричка) **commuter rail** leaves from Prymiskyy Vokzal (Примский Вокзал), MR: Vokzalna.

Taxis: Taxis are everywhere. A ride to the center of town should cost about 20hv. Always agree on the price before getting in.

ORIENTATION AND PRACTICAL INFORMATION

Most attractions and services lie on the west bank of the Dniper River. Three metro stops from the train station is the main avenue, **vulitsa Khreshchatyk** (Хрещатик; MR line). The center of Kyiv is vul. Khreshchatyk's **Independence Square** (Майдан Незалежност; Maidan Nezalezhnosti; MB line), which is home to six fountains, an underground mall, and the 16m high **Independence Column.**

Tourist Offices: Kyiv lacks official tourist services. Various agencies at the airport offer vouchers, excursion packages, hotel arrangements, and other services. Travel agencies also organize **tours.** Carlson Wagonlit Travel, Khnoelnistkiy 33/34, 2nd fl. (☎8044 238 6156). Open daily 9am-9pm. Has branch at the US Embassy. For tours, accommodation, and **visa assistance,** go to Yana Travel Group, Saksahanskoho 42 (Саксаганського; ☎490 7373; www.yana.kiev.ua). Open M-F 10am-7pm, Sa 10am-5pm.

Embassies: Australia, Kominterna 18/137 (комінтерне; ☎8044 246 4223; fax 244 3597). Open M-Th 10am-1pm. **Canada,** Yaroslaviv Val. 31 (Ярославів; ☎8044 464 1144; fax 464 0598). Open M-F 8:30am-1pm and 2-5pm; visa section open M-Th. **Ireland,** 44 Shchorsa St. (☎8044 285 5902. Open M-Th 10am-1pm.) Citizens of **New Zealand** should refer to the Australian embassy. **UK,** Desyatynna 9 (Десятинна; ☎8044 490 3660; fax 8044 490 3662). Consular section at Glybochytska 4 (Глибоицька; ☎8044 494 3400; fax 8044 494 3418). Open M-Th 9am-1pm and 2pm-5:30pm, F 9am-1pm and 2pm-4pm. **US,** Yu. Kotsyubynskoho 10 (Коцбинського; ☎8044 490 4000; http://kyiv.usembassy.gov). Open M-F 9am-6pm. Consular section at Pymonenka 6 (Пимоненка; ☎8044 490 4422 or 8044 490 4445; fax 8044 490 4040). From the corner of Maidan Nezalezhnosti and Sofievska (Софієвска), take trolley #16 or 18 for 4 stops. Continue on bul. Artyoma (Артема) until it curves to the right, then take the 1st right, Pymonenka.

Medical Services: American Medical Center, Berdychivska 1 (Бердиерска; ☎8044 490 7600; www.amcenters.com). English-speaking doctors will take patients without documents or insurance. Open 24hr. MC/V.

Telephones: English operator (☎81 92.) **Telephone-Telegraph** (Телефон-Телеграф; telefon-telehraf) around the corner of the post office (enter on Khreshchatyk). The main post-office, located in independence square, also has **phone booths** where you can call destinations like the US for about $0.10/min. Open daily 8am-10pm. Buy cards for **public telephones** (тфксофон; taksofon) at any post office. Less widespread than Taksofon phones, **Utel** phones and cards are in the post office, train station, and hotels.

Internet: C-Club, Bessarabskaye pl. 1 (Бессарабскає; ☎8044 238 6446), in the underground mall (globus shopping center) between Bessarabskiy market and the Lenin statue has over 100 computers. 12hv per hr. 9am-8am. **Vault 13,** Bolshaya Vasilkovskaya 19. Also a bar, so feel free to surf the web with a gin and tonic in hand.

Post Office: Khreshchatyk 22 (☎8044 278 1167; www.poshta.kiev.ua). **Poste Restante** at counters #28 and 30. For packages, enter on Maidan Nezalezhnosti. Copy, fax, and photo services available. Open M-Sa 8am-9pm, Su 9am-7pm. **Postal Code:** 01001.

RADIOACTIVE TOURISM

The year 2006 marked the 20th anniversary of the world's worst nuclear accident. Controversy still exists about the overall effect of the explosion at Chernobyl. Independent studies contest the UN's estimate of 4000-9000 cancer deaths; some even suggest a staggering figure of 93,000.

Today, a new trade is beginning in the ghost-towns of Chernobyl: tourism. Although radiation levels remain extremely high in the "Dead Zone," several travel agencies have begun leading tours (which cost US$100-400), to look at the fateful reactor 4, visit towns in the Dead Zone, and check out radiation-filled tanks.

Despite the influx of tourism, Chernobyl is still not considered safe. Geiger counters have found over 50 times normal radiation. And to make matters worse, the ruins of reactor 4—still filled with nuclear material—are showing signs of breaking down, prompting Ukraine to propose the building of a new steel facility in 2008. Tour agencies press ahead, leading over 500 tourists every year, insising that the danger lies in long-term radiation, not in a one-day encounter. Others feel that the name "the Dead Zone" speaks for itself.

For info on tours, visit www. tourkiev.com/chernobyl.php, or call ☎ 405 35 00. Solo East Tours is located at Travneva St. 12.

ACCOMMODATIONS

Hotels in Kyiv tend to be expensive; the **Kyiv Post** (www.kyivpost.com) lists short-term apartment rentals, as do most English-language publications and websites about Kyiv. People at train stations offer cheaper rooms (from US$5), though English speakers are rare and the quality of rooms varies. Another way to find lodging is through the commission-free telephone service **Okean-9.** (☎8044 443 6167. Open M-F 9am-5pm, Sa 9am-3pm.)

International Youth Hostel Yaroslav (Ярослав), vul. Yaroslavska 10 (Ярославська; ☎8066 417 3189), in the historic Podil district; MB: Kontraktova Ploshcha. Enter through courtyard; it's the 1st door on the right. Press the numbers 4 and 7 simultaneously on the keypad to enter. 12-bed hostel with warm English-speaking staff. Free lockers for every bed, recently renovated 2nd floor. Spacious rooms. Kitchen. (Internet next door 9hv per hr. Doubles 250hv; 4- to 5-bed dorms 130hv, 120 with ISIC. MC/V.) ❸

International Hostel Tatarka, vul. Lukjanivska 77, (MB: Kontraktova Ploscha; ☎8044 417 3393) has large 5-bed rooms (some with balconies) and views of the city. Staff does not speak English, but if you can put together a few Ukrainian sentences this hostel is a real find. Bathrooms leave a little to be desired, however. Uphill from station, so from, consider a taxi (around 20hv). Rooms 80hv. Cash only. ❶

Youth Hostel Kiev, 52-A Artema #2, 5th floor. vul Artema. (MB: Lukjanivska; ☎8044 481 3838) Go past the new complex (which is also labeled 52-A) to the 2nd building with a garden in front. Calm, well-kept hostel with 30 beds, popular with families and groups. English speaking staff. Singles, doubles, triples available; all beds 125 hv. 24 hr reception. Laundry 10 hv. Towels, linen free. Cash only.) ❷

FOOD

Kyiv has a myriad of Western and Eastern restaraunts, with plenty of Chinese, Italian, and Russian restaraunts all over town. The most popular are traditional Ukrainian cafeteria-style eateries—these are usually quite cheap. When you go in, point at your food, get a big glass of beer, and enjoy.

O'Panas, (О'Панас), Tereshchenkivska vul. 10 (Терещенківська; ☎8044 235 2132), is located in the Taras Shevchenko Park. Serves local dishes in traditional Ukrainian decor. Known for delectable traditional Ukrainian pancakes; order them out of the front of the restaraunt. Entrees 40-120hv. Business lunch noon-3pm. Open M-F 8am-1am, Sa-Su 10am-1am. MC/V. ❸

🔳**Puzata Hata,** vul Sahaidachnoho 24 (Сагайдачного; ☎8044 391 4699; www.puzatahata.kiev.us) MB: Poshtova Poloscha. Food served in a beautiful 2-story restaraunt popular with youth and families alike. When coming in, go up the stairs, grab a tray, and point at the food you want. Soups and salads, to begin, followed by meat and potatoes, moving on to *piroshikis* and desserts. Pay by weight; the average hearty meal costs about 20-30hv. Open daily 8am-11pm. Cash only. ❶

Antresol, (Антресоль), bul. T. Shevchenka 2 (☎8044 235 8347), has a hip book-store-cafe downstairs and a restaurant upstairs. Large selection of coffee and good wine produces a relaxed ambiance, ideal for grabbing a book and enjoying a latte. English-language menu. Salads 25-50hv. Entrees 29-110hv. Tu and Su live piano 8-10pm. Open daily 9am-late. MC/V. ❸

👁 SIGHTS

🔳**KYIV-CAVE MONASTERY.** Also known as *Kyiv-Pechersk Lavra*, the Kyiv-Cave Monastery is Kyiv's oldest holy site, and a major pilgrimage site for Orthodox Christians. It houses the **Refectory Church,** the 12th-century **Holy Trinity Gate Church,** and caves where monks lie mummified (though they are hidden by decorative shrouds). The **Great Lavra Bell Tower** offers great views. *(Києво-Печерська Лавра; Kyivo-Pecherska Lavra. MR: Arsenalna; Арсенальна. ☎8044 255 1109. Turn left out of the metro and walk down vul. Sichnevoho Povstaniya to #25. Open daily May-Aug. 9am-7pm; Sept.-Apr. 9:30am-6pm. Upper lavra, which is state-run, will cost about 24hv. The lower section requires only the purchase of a candle as an entrance free. Monastery 10hv, students 5hv. Photography 12hv.)*

ST. SOPHIA CATHEDRAL. Once the religious center of Kyivan Rus, the 11th century St. Sophia Cathedral—with its ornamented facades and Byzantine mosaics—offers a look into the religious history of Ukraine. It was originally designed to rival Constantinople's Hagia Sofia. *(vul. Volodymyrska. MG: Zoloti Vorota or trolley #16 from Maidan Nezalezhnosti. Grounds open daily 10am-7pm. Museums open M-Tu and F-Su 10am-6pm, W 10am-5pm. Grounds 5hv. Museums 20hv, students 8hv. Bell tower 5/3hv.)*

VUL. KHRESHCHATYK. Kyiv's central road, vul. Khreshchatyk (Хрещатик), is where locals go to see and be seen. It begins at bul. T. Shevchenka and extends to **Independence Square** (Майдан Незалежности; Maidan Nezalezhnosti), which hosted a massive tent city during the Orange Revolution. **Khreshchatyk Park,** past the **Friendship of the Peoples Arch,** contains a monument to Prince Volodymyr, who converted the Kyivan Rus to Christianity. (MR: Khreshchatyk; Хрещатик.) Full of cafes and galleries, the cobblestone district of **Andriy's Descent** (Андрівский Узвз; Andriyivskyy uzviz) can be reached by walking down Desyatynna from Mikhaylivska Sq. *(MB: Poshtova Ploshcha; Поштова Площа.)*

MUSEUM OF ONE STREET. Bizarrely, this museum recounts the history of Kyiv's most famous street, Andriy's Descent. *(Andriyivskyy uzviz 2B. Open Tu-Su noon-6pm. 10hv. 45min. English-language tour 100hv.)*

ST. ANDREW'S CHURCH. At the corner of Volodymyrska and Andriyivskyy uzviz is the beautiful St. Andrew's Church. Its ornate exterior makes it one of Ukraine's most significant pieces of architecture. *(Open daily 10am-5pm.)*

THE CHERNOBYL MUSEUM. Artifacts and testimonies from the disaster's aftermath as well as a poster exhibit commemorating its 20th anniversary. *(1 Khoryvyj Pereulok Street. Open M-Sa 10am-6pm. Closed last M of each month. 8hv, with ISIC 4hv.)*

📷 📷 ENTERTAINMENT AND NIGHTLIFE

The last weekend in May brings the **Kyiv Days,** attracting thousands of spectators with art and music performances all over the city. During the rest of the year, the **National Philharmonic,** Volodymyrska 2, holds concerts most nights at 7pm. (☎8044 278 1697; www.filharmonia.com.ua. Kasa open Tu-Su noon-2pm and 3-7pm. 10-50hv.) While you're in town don't miss **Dynamo Kyiv,** Ukraine's top football team. (*Kasa* in front of stadium.) Check out *What's On* magazine (www.whatson-kiev.com) and the *Kyiv Post* (www.kyivpost.com) for nightlife listings. Kyiv's popular jazz club, 📷**Artclub 44,** vul. Khreshchatyk 44, has live music nightly starting at 10pm; it attracts a diverse crowd ranging from students to businessmen. (☎8044 279 4137. Cover 10-20hv. Open daily 11am-2 am.)

APPENDIX

CLIMATE

AVG. TEMP. (LOW/ HIGH), PRECIP.	JANUARY			APRIL			JULY			OCTOBER		
	°C	°F	mm	°C	°F	mm	°C	°F	mm	°C	°F	mm
Amsterdam	1/5	33/41	69	4/12	40/54	53	12/20	54/68	76	7/13	45/56	74
Athens	6/13	43/55	46	11/20	52/68	28	22/32	72/90	5	14/23	58/73	48
Berlin	-3/2	26/35	43	4/13	39/55	43	13/23	55/73	53	6/13	42/55	36
Budapest	-3/2	27/35	41	7/17	45/62	41	16/27	61/80	46	8/16	46/61	33
Copenhagen	-2/2	28/36	53	2/10	36/49	43	13/20	55/69	74	7/12	44/54	58
Dublin	3/8	37/46	69	4/12	40/53	51	12/19	53/66	51	8/14	46/57	71
İstanbul	3/8	37/47	99	8/17	46/62	48	18/28	65/82	20	12/19	53/67	71
Kraków	-7/-1	19/31	33	3/13	37/56	48	12/23	54/73	86	4/13	39/56	46
London	2/7	35/45	51	5/13	41/56	46	13/22	55/71	33	8/14	46/58	71
Madrid	0/11	32/51	46	6/17	42/63	46	16/32	61/90	10	8/20	47/68	46
Moscow	-10/-5	14/23	42	0/9	32/48	44	13/23	56/74	94	1/7	34/44	59
Paris	1/6	34/43	7	6/14	42/57	33	14/24	58/75	8	8/15	46/59	17
Prague	-4/1	24/34	20	2/12	36/54	36	12/22	54/72	66	4/12	39/54	31
Reykjavík	-3/2	27/35	86	1/5	33/41	56	8/13	47/55	51	2/7	36/44	89
Rome	2/12	35/53	84	7/19	44/66	69	17/31	62/88	23	10/22	50/72	107
Stockholm	-1/-5	23/30	38	1/8	34/47	31	13/22	56/71	71	5/9	41/49	51
Vienna	-3/2	27/36	38	5/14	41/57	51	15/25	59/77	64	6/14	43/57	41

MEASUREMENTS

Like the rest of the rational world, Europe uses the metric system. The basic unit of length is the meter (m), which is divided into 100 centimeters (cm) or 1000 millimeters (mm). One thousand meters make up one kilometer (km). Fluids are measured in liters (L), each divided into 1000 milliliters (mL). A liter of pure water weighs one kilogram (kg), the unit of mass that is divided into 1000 grams (g). One metric ton is 1000kg.

MEASUREMENT CONVERSIONS	
1 inch (in.) = 25.4mm	1 millimeter (mm) = 0.039 in.
1 foot (ft.) = 0.305m	1 meter (m) = 3.28 ft.
1 yard (yd.) = 0.914m	1 meter (m) = 1.094 yd.
1 mile (mi.) = 1.609km	1 kilometer (km) = 0.621 mi.
1 ounce (oz.) = 28.35g	1 gram (g) = 0.035 oz.
1 pound (lb.) = 0.454kg	1 kilogram (kg) = 2.205 lb.
1 fluid ounce (fl. oz.) = 29.57mL	1 milliliter (mL) = 0.034 fl. oz.
1 gallon (gal.) = 3.785L	1 liter (L) = 0.264 gal.

Britain uses the metric system, although its longtime conversion to the metric system is still in progress—road signs indicate distance in miles. Gallons in the US and those in Britain are not identical: one US gallon equals 0.83 Imperial gallons. Pub aficionados will note that an Imperial pint (20 oz.) is larger than its US counterpart (16 oz.).

LANGUAGE PHRASEBOOK

CYRILLIC ALPHABET

Ukraine uses a variation of the Russian Cyrillic alphabet.

CYRILLIC	ENGLISH	PRONOUNCED	CYRILLIC	ENGLISH	PRONOUNCED
А а	a	*ah* as in **Pr**a**gue**	Р р	r	*r* as in **r**evolution
Б б	b	*b* as in **B**osnia	С с	s	*s* as in **S**erbia
В в	v	*v* as in **V**olga	Т т	t	*t* as in **t**ank
Г г	g	*g* as in **G**lasnost	У у	u	*oo* as in B**u**dapest
Д д	d	*d* as in **d**ictatorship	Ф ф	f	*f* as in **f**ormer USSR
Е е	e	*yeh* as in **Ye**ltsin	Х х	kh	*kh* as in Ba**ch**
Ё ё	yo	*yo* as in **yo**!	Ц ц	ts	*ts* as in **ts**ar
Ж ж	zh, ž	*zh* as in mira**g**e	Ч ч	ch, \	*ch* as in Gorba**ch**ev
З з	z	*z* as in communi**s**m	Ш ш	sh, š	*sh* as in Bol**sh**evik
И и	i	*ee* as in Gr**ee**k	Щ щ	shch	*shch* in Khru**shch**ev
Й й	y	*y* as in Tolsto**y**	Ъ ъ	(hard sign)	(not pronounced)
К к	k	*k* as in **K**remlin	Ы ы	i	*i* as in s**i**lver
Л л	l	*l* as in **L**enin	Ь ь	(soft sign)	(not pronounced)
М м	m	*m* as in **M**oscow	Э э	e	*eh* as in **E**stonia
Н н	n	*n* as in **n**uclear	Ю ю	yu	*yoo* as in **U**kraine
О о	o	*o* as in Cr**o**atia	Я я	ya	*yah* as in **Ya**lta
П п	p	*p* as in **P**oland			

GREEK ALPHABET

SYMBOL	NAME	PRONOUNCED	SYMBOL	NAME	PRONOUNCED
Α α	alpha	*a* as in f**a**ther	Ν ν	nu	*n* as in **n**et
Β β	beta	*v* as in **v**elvet	Ξ ξ	xi	*x* as in mi**x**
Γ γ	gamma	*y* or *g* as in **yo**ga	Ο ο	omicron	*o* as in r**o**w
Δ δ	delta	*th* as in **th**ere	Π π	pi	*p* as in **p**eace
Ε ε	epsilon	*e* as in j**e**t	Ρ ρ	rho	*r* as in **r**oll
Ζ ζ	zeta	*z* as in **z**ebra	Σ σ/ς	sigma	*s* as in **s**ense
Η η	eta	*ee* as in qu**ee**n	Τ τ	tau	*t* as in **t**ent
Θ θ	theta	*th* as in **th**ree	Υ υ	upsilon	*ee* as in gr**ee**n
Ι ι	iota	*ee* as in tr**ee**	Φ φ	phi	*f* as in **f**og
Κ κ	kappa	*k* as in **k**ite	Χ χ	chi	*h* as in **h**orse
Λ λ	lambda	*l* as in **l**and	Ψ ψ	psi	*ps* as in oo**ps**
Μ μ	mu	*m* as in **m**oose	Ω ω	omega	*o* as in Let's **Go**

CROATIAN

ENGLISH	CROATIAN	PRONOUNCED	ENGLISH	CROATIAN	PRONOUNCED
Yes/No	Da/Ne	dah/neh	Train/Bus	Vlak/Autobus	vlahk/OW-toh-bus
Please	Molim	MOH-leem	Station	Kolodvor	KOH-loh-dvor
Thank you	Hvala lijepa	HVAH-la lee-yee-pah	Airport	Zračna Luka	ZRA-chna LU-kah
Good morning	Dobro jutro	DOH-broh YOO-tro	Ticket	Karta	KAHR-tah
Goodbye	Bog	Bog	Taxi	Taksi	TAH-ksee
Sorry/Excuse me	Oprostite	oh-PROH-stee-teh	Hotel	Hotel	HOH-tel
Help!	U pomoć!	OO poh-mohch	Bathroom	zahod	ZAH-hod

ENGLISH	CROATIAN	PRONOUNCED	ENGLISH	CROATIAN	PRONOUNCED
I'm lost.	Izgubljen sam.	eez-GUB-lye-n şahm	Open/Closed	Otvoreno/Zatvoreno	OHT-voh-reh-noh/ZAHT-voh-reh-noh
Police	Policija	po-LEE-tsee-ya	Left/Right	Lijevo/Desno	lee-YEH-voh/DEHS-noh
Embassy	Ambasada	ahm-bah-SAH-da	Bank	Banka	BAHN-kah
Passport	Putovnica	POO-toh-vnee-tsah	Exchange	Mjenjačnica	myehn-YAHCH-nee-tsah
Doctor/Hospital	Liječnik/Bolnica	lee-YECH-neek/BOHL-neet-sa	Grocery/Market	Trgovina	TER-goh-vee-nah
Pharmacy	Ljekarna	lye-KHAR-na	Post Office	Pošta	POSH-tah

ENGLISH	CROATIAN	PRONUNCIATION
Where is the...?	Gdje je...?	GDYE yeh
How much does this cost?	Koliko to košta?	KOH-lee-koh toh KOH-shtah
When is the next...?	Kada polazi sljedeći...?	ka-DA po-LA-zee SLYE-de-tchee
Do you have (a vacant room)?	Imate li (slobodne sobe)?	ee-MAH-teh lee (SLOH-boh-dneh SOH-beh)
Do you speak English?	Govorite li engleski?	GO-vohr-ee-teh lee ehn-GLEH-skee

				CROATIAN CARDINAL NUMBERS						
0	1	2	3	4	5	6	7	8	9	10
nula	jedan	dva	tri	četiri	pet	šest	sedam	osam	devet	sto

CZECH

ENGLISH	CZECH	PRONOUNCED	ENGLISH	CZECH	PRONOUNCED
Yes/No	Ano/Ne	AH-no/neh	Train/Bus	Vlak/Autobus	vlahk/OW-toh-boos
Please	Prosím	PROH-seem	Station	Nádraží	NA-drah-zhee
Thank you	Děkuji	DYEH-koo-yee	Airport	Letiště	LEH-teesh-tyeh
Hello	Dobrý den	DOH-bree den	Ticket	Lístek	LIS-tek
Goodbye	Nashledanou	NAS-kleh-dah-noh	Taxi	Taxi	TEHK-see
Sorry/Excuse me	Promiňte	PROH-meen-teh	Hotel	Hotel	HOH-tel
Help!	Pomoc!	POH-mots	Bathroom	WC	VEE-TSEE
I'm lost. (m/f)	Zabloudil(a) jsem.	ZAH-bloh-deel-(ah) sem	Open/Closed	Otevřeno/Zavřeno	O-te-zheno/ZAV-rzhen-o
Police	Policie	POH-leets-ee-yeh	Left/Right	Vlevo/Vpravo	VLE-voh/VPRAH-voh
Embassy	Velvyslanectví	VEHL-vee-slah-nehts-vee	Bank	Banka	BAN-ka
Passport	Cestovní pas	TSEH-stohv-nee pahs	Exchange	Směnárna	smyeh-NAR-na
Doctor	Lékař	LEK-arzh	Grocery	Potraviny	PO-tra-vee-nee
Pharmacy	Lékárna	LEE-khaar-nah	Post Office	Pošta	POSH-tah

ENGLISH	CZECH	PRONUNCIATION
Where is the...?	Kde je...?	gdeh yeh
How much does this cost?	Kolik to stojí?	KOH-lihk STOH-yee
When is the next...?	Kdy jede příští...?	gdi YEH-deh przh-EESH-tyee
Do you have (a vacant room)?	Máte (volný pokoj)?	MAA-teh (VOHL-nee POH-koy)
I would like...	Prosím...	PROH-seem

				CZECH CARDINAL NUMBERS						
0	1	2	3	4	5	6	7	8	9	10
nula	jeden	dva	tøi	ètyøi	pìt	šest	sedm	osm	devìt	deset

FINNISH

ENGLISH	FINNISH	PRONOUNCED	ENGLISH	FINNISH	PRONOUNCED
Yes/No	Kyllä/Ei	KEW-la/ay	Ticket	Lippu	LIP-ooh
Please	Olkaa hyvä	OHL-ka HEW-va	Train/Bus	Juna/Bussi	YU-nuh/BUS-see
Thank you	Kiitos	KEE-tohss	Boat	Vene	VEH-nay
Hello	Hei	hey	Departures	Lähtevät	lah-teh-VAHT
Goodbye	Näkemiin	NA-keh-meen	Market	Tori	TOH-ree
Sorry/Excuse me	Anteeksi	ON-take-see	Hotel	Hotelli	HO-tehl-lee
Help!	Apua!	AH-poo-ah	Hostel	Retkeilymaja	reht-kayl-oo-MAH-yuh
Police	Poliisi	POH-lee-see	Bathroom	Vessa	VEHS-sah
Embassy	Suurlähetystö	SOOHR-la-heh-toos-ter	Telephone	Puhelin	POO-heh-leen
I'm lost!	Olen kadoksissa!	OH-lehn cou-doc-sissa	Open/Closed	Avoinna/Suljettu	a-VOH-een-ah/sool-JET-too
Railway station	Rautatieasema	ROW-tah-tiah-ah-seh-ma	Hospital	Sairaala	SAIH-raah-lah
Bank	Pankki	PAHNK-kih	Left/Right	Vasen/Oikea	VAH-sen/OY-kay-uh
Currency exchange	Rahanvaihto-piste	RAA-han-vyeh-tow-pees-teh	Post Office	Posti	PAUS-teeh
Airport	lentokenttä	LEH-toh-kehnt-tah	Pharmacy	Apteekki	UHP-take-kee

ENGLISH	FINNISH	PRONUNCIATION
Where is the...?	Missä on..?	MEE-sah ohn
How do I get to...?	Miten pääsen...?	MEE-ten PA-sen
How much does this cost?	Paljonko se maksaa?	PAHL-yon-ko seh MOCK-sah
I'd like to buy...	Haluaisin ostaa...	HUH-loo-ay-sihn OS-tuh
Do you speak English?	Puhutteko englantia?	POO-hoot-teh-kaw ENG-lan-tee-ah
When is the next...?	Milloin on seuraava...?	MEEHL-loyhn OHN SEUH-raah-vah
I'm allergic to/I cannot eat...	En voi syödä...	ehn voy SEW-dah

FINNISH CARDINAL NUMBERS										
0	1	2	3	4	5	6	7	8	9	10
nolla	yksi	kaksi	kolme	neljä	viisi	kuusi	seitsemän	kahdeksan	yhdeksän	kymmenen

FRENCH

ENGLISH	FRENCH	PRONOUNCED	ENGLISH	FRENCH	PRONOUNCED
Hello	Bonjour	bohn-zhoor	Exchange	L'échange	lay-shanzh
Please	S'il vous plaît	see voo pley	Grocery	L'épicerie	lay-pees-ree
Thank you	Merci	mehr-see	Market	Le marché	leuh marzh-chay
Excuse me	Excusez-moi	ex-ku-zey mwah	Police	La police	la poh-lees
Yes/No	Oui/Non	wee/nohn	Embassy	L'ambassade	lahm-ba-sahd
Goodbye	Au revoir	oh ruh-vwahr	Passport	Le passeport	leuh pass-por
Help!	Au secours!	oh seh-coor	Post Office	La poste	la pohst
I'm lost.	Je suis perdu.	zhe swee pehr-doo	One-way	Le billet simple	leuh bee-ay samp
Train/Bus	Le train/Le bus	leuh tran/leuh boos	Round-trip	Le billet aller-retour	leuh bee-ay a-lay-re-toor
Station	La gare	la gahr	Ticket	Le billet	leuh bee-ay
Airport	L'aéroport	la-ehr-o-por	Single room	Une chambre simple	oon shahm-br samp
Hotel	L'hôtel	lo-tel	Double room	Une chambre pour deux	oon shahm-br poor duh

ENGLISH	FRENCH	PRONOUNCED	ENGLISH	FRENCH	PRONOUNCED
Hostel	L'auberge	lo-berzhe	With shower	Avec une douche	ah-vec une doosh
Bathroom	La salle de bain	la sal de bahn	Taxi	Le taxi	leuh tax-ee
Open/Closed	Ouvert/Fermé	oo-ver/fer-may	Ferry	Le bac	leuh bak
Doctor	Le médecin	leuh mehd-sen	Tourist office	Le bureau de tourisme	leuh byur-oh de toor-eesm
Hospital	L'hôpital	loh-pee-tal	Town hall	L'hôtel de ville	lo-tel de veel
Pharmacy	La pharmacie	la far-ma-see	Vegetarian	Végétarien	vay-jay-ta-ree-ehn
Left/Right	À gauche/À droite	a gohsh/a dwat	Kosher/Halal	Kascher/Halal	ka-shey/ha-lal
Straight	Tout droit	too dwa	Newsstand	Le tabac	leuh ta-bac

ENGLISH	FRENCH	PRONUNCIATION
Do you speak English?	Parlez-vous anglais?	par-leh voo ahn-gleh
Where is...?	Où se trouve...?	oo seh-trhoov
When is the next...?	À quelle heure part le prochain..?	ah kel ur par leuh pro-chan
How much does this cost?	Ça fait combien?	sah f com-bee-en?
Do you have rooms available?	Avez-vous des chambres disponibles?	av-eh voo deh shahm-br dees-pon-eeb-bl?
I would like...	Je voudrais...	zhe voo-dreh
I'm allergic to...	Je suis allergique à...	zhe swee al-ehr-zheek a
I love you.	Je t'aime.	zhe tem

FRENCH CARDINAL NUMBERS										
0	1	2	3	4	5	6	7	8	9	10
zéro	un	deux	trois	quatre	cinq	six	sept	huit	neuf	dix

GERMAN

ENGLISH	GERMAN	PRONOUNCED	ENGLISH	GERMAN	PRONOUNCED
Yes/No	Ja/Nein	yah/nein	Train/Bus	Zug/Bus	tsoog/boos
Please	Bitte	BIH-tuh	Station	Bahnhof	BAHN-hohf
Thank you	Danke	DAHNG-kuh	Airport	Flughafen	FLOOG-hah-fen
Hello	Hallo	HAH-lo	Taxi	Taxi	TAHK-see
Goodbye	Auf Wiedersehen	owf VEE-der-zehn	Ticket	Fahrkarte	FAR-kar-tuh
Excuse me	Entschuldigung	ent-SHOOL-dih-gung	Departure	Abfahrt	AHB-fart
Help!	Hilfe!	HIL-fuh	One-way	Einfache	AYHN-fah-kuh
I'm lost.	Ich habe mich verlaufen.	˚eesh HAH-buh meesh fer-LAU-fun	Round-trip	Hin und zurück	hin oond tsuh-RYOOK
Police	Polizei	poh-lee-TSAI	Reservation	Reservierung	reh-zer-VEER-ung
Embassy	Botschaft	BOAT-shahft	Ferry	Fährschiff	FAYHR-shiff
Passport	Reisepass	RYE-zeh-pahss	Bank	Bank	bahnk
Doctor/Hospital	Arzt/Kranken-haus	ahrtst/KRANK-en-house	Exchange	Wechseln	VEHK-zeln
Pharmacy	Apotheke	AH-po-TAY-kuh	Grocery	Lebensmittelge-schäft	LAY-bens-miht-tel-guh-SHEFT
Hotel/Hostel	Hotel/Jugend-herberge	ho-TEL/YOO-gend-air-BAIR-guh	Tourist office	Touristbüro	TU-reest-byur-oh
Single room	Einzelzimmer	EIN-tsel-tsihm-meh	Post Office	Postamt	POST-ahmt
Double room	Doppelzimmer	DOP-pel-tsihm-meh	Old Town/City Center	Altstadt	AHLT-shtat

ENGLISH	GERMAN	PRONOUNCED	ENGLISH	GERMAN	PRONOUNCED
Dorm	Schlafsaal	SHLAF-zahl	**Vegetarian**	Vegetarier	Feh-geh-TAYR-ee-er
With shower	Mit dusche	mitt DOO-shuh	**Vegan**	Veganer	FEH-gan-er
Bathroom	Badezimmer	BAH-deh-tsihm-meh	**Kosher/Halal**	Koscher/Halaal	KOH-shehr/hah-LAAL
Open/Closed	Geöffnet/Geschlossen	geh-UHF-net/geh-SHLOS-sen	**Nuts/Milk**	Nüsse/Milch	NYOO-seh/mihlsh
Left/Right	Links/Rechts	lihnks/rekhts	**Bridge**	Brücke	BRUKE-eh
Straight	Geradeaus	geh-RAH-de-OWS	**Castle**	Schloß	shloss
(To) Turn	Drehen	DREH-ehn	**Square**	Platz	plahtz

ENGLISH	GERMAN	PRONUNCIATION
Where is...?	Wo ist...?	vo ihst
How do I get to...?	Wie komme ich nach...?	vee KOM-muh eesh NAHKH
How much does that cost?	Wieviel kostet das?	VEE-feel KOS-tet das
Do you have...?	Haben Sie...?	HOB-en zee
I would like...	Ich möchte...	eesh MERSH-teh
I'm allergic to...	Ich bin zu...allergisch.	eesh bihn tsoo...ah-LEHR-gish
Do you speak English?	Sprechen sie Englisch?	SHPREK-en zee EHNG-lish
I'm waiting for my boyfriend/husband	Ich warte auf meinen Freund/Mann.	eesh VAHR-tuh owf MYN-en froynd/mahn

GERMAN CARDINAL NUMBERS										
0	1	2	3	4	5	6	7	8	9	10
null	eins	zwei	drei	vier	fünf	sechs	sieben	acht	neun	zehn

GREEK

For an introduction to the Greek alphabet, see p. 784.

ENGLISH	GREEK	PRONOUNCED	ENGLISH	GREEK	PRONOUNCED
Yes/No	Ναι/Οχι	neh/OH-hee	**Train/Bus**	Τραίνο/Λεωφορείο	TREH-no/leh-o-fo-REE-o
Please	Παρακαλώ	pah-rah-kah-LO	**Ferry**	Πλοίο	PLEE-o
Thank you	Ευχαριστώ	ef-hah-ree-STO	**Station**	Σταθμός	stath-MOS
Hello/Goodbye	Γειά σας	YAH-sas	**Airport**	Αεροδρόμιο	ah-e-ro-DHRO-mee-o
Sorry/Excuse me	Συγνόμη	sig-NO-mee	**Taxi**	Ταξί	tah-XEE
Help!	Βοήθειά!	vo-EE-thee-ah	**Hotel/Hostel**	Ξενοδοχείο	kse-no-dho-HEE-o
I'm lost.	Εχω χαθεί.	EH-O ha-THEE	**Rooms to let**	Δωμάτια	do-MA-tee-ah
Police	Αστυνομία	as-tee-no-MEE-a	**Bathroom**	Τουαλέττα	tou-ah-LET-ta
Embassy	Πρεσβεία	prez-VEE-ah	**Open/Closed**	Ανοικτό/Κλειστό	ah-nee-KTO/klee-STO
Passport	Διαβατήριο	dhee-ah-vah-TEE-ree-o	**Left/Right**	Αριστερά/Δεξία	aris-te-RA/de-XIA
Doctor	Γιατρός	yah-TROSE	**Bank**	Τράπεζα	TRAH-peh-zah
Pharmacy	Φαρμακείο	fahr-mah-KEE-o	**Exchange**	Ανταλλάσσω	an-da-LAS-so
Post Office	Ταχυδρομείο	ta-hi-dhro-MEE-o	**Market**	Αγορά	ah-go-RAH

ENGLISH	GREEK	PRONUNCIATION
Where is...?	Που είναι...?	poo-EE-neh
How much does this cost?	Πόσο κάνει?	PO-so KAH-nee
Do you have (a vacant room)?	Μήπως έχετε (ελεύθερα δωμάτια)?	mee-POSE EK-he-teh (e-LEF-the-ra dho-MA-tee-a)
Do you speak English?	Μιλατε αγγλικά?	mee-LAH-teh ahn-glee-KAH

				GREEK CARDINAL NUMBERS						
0	**1**	**2**	**3**	**4**	**5**	**6**	**7**	**8**	**9**	**10**
ουδέν	ενα	δυο	τρια	τεσσερα	πρια	εξι	επτα	οκτω	εννεα	δεκα

HUNGARIAN

ENGLISH	HUNGARIAN	PRONOUNCED	ENGLISH	HUNGARIAN	PRONOUNCED
Yes/No	Igen/Nem	EE-ghen/nehm	Train/Bus	Vonat/Autóbusz	VAW-noht/AU-OO-toh-boos
Please	Kérem	KEH-rehm	Train Station	Pályaudvar	pah-yoh-OOT-vahr
Thank you	Köszönöm	KUH-suh-nuhm	Airport	Repülőtér	rep-oo-loo-TAYR
Hello	Szervusz	SAYHR-voose	Ticket	Jegyet	YEHD-eht
Goodbye	Viszontlátásra	VEE-sohnt-laht-ah-shrah	Bus Station	Buszmegálló	boos-mehg-AH-loh
Excuse me	Elnézést	EHL-neh-zaysht	Hotel	Szálloda	SAH-law-dah
Help!	Segítség!	she-GHEET-sheg	Toilet	WC	VEH-tseh
I'm lost.	Eltévedtem.	el-TEH-ved-tem	Open/Closed	Nyitva/Zárva	NYEET-vah/ZAHR-vuh
Police	Rendőrség.	REN-dur-shayg	Left/Right	Bal/Jobb	bol/yowb
Embassy	Követséget	ker-vet-SHE-get	Bank	Bank	bohnk
Passport	Az útlevelemet	ahz oot-leh-veh-leh-meht	Exchange	Pénzaváltó	pehn-zah-VAHL-toh
Doctor/Hospital	Orvos/Kórház	OR-vosh/kohr-HAAZ	Grocery	Élelmiszerbolt	EH-lehl-meh-sehr-bawlt
Pharmacy	Gyógyszertár	DYAW-dyser-tar	Post Office	Posta	PAWSH-tuh

ENGLISH	HUNGARIAN	PRONUNCIATION
Where is...?	Hol van...?	haul vahn
How much does this cost?	Mennyibe kerül?	MEHN-yee-beh KEH-rool
When is the next...?	Mikor indul a következő...?	mee-KOR in-DUL ah ker-VET-ke-zoer
Do you have (a vacant room)?	Van üres (szoba)?	vahn ew-REHSH (SAH-bah)
Can I have...?	Kaphatok...?	KAH-foht-tohk
I do not eat...	Nem eszem...	nem EH-sem
Do you speak English?	Beszél angolul?	BESS-ayl AHN-gawl-ool

				HUNGARIAN CARDINAL NUMBERS						
0	**1**	**2**	**3**	**4**	**5**	**6**	**7**	**8**	**9**	**10**
nulla	egy	kettő	három	négy	öt	hat	hét	nyolc	kilenc	tíz

ITALIAN

ENGLISH	ITALIAN	PRONOUNCED	ENGLISH	ITALIAN	PRONOUNCED
Hello (informal/formal)	Ciao/Buongiorno	chow/bwohn-JOHR-noh	Bank	La banca	lah bahn-KAH
Please	Per favore/Per piacere	pehr fah-VOH-reh/pehr pyah-CHEH-reh	Supermarket	Il Supermercato	eel soo-pair-mehr-CAHT-oh
Thank you	Grazie	GRAHT-see-yeh	Exchange	Il cambio	eel CAHM-bee-oh
Sorry/Excuse me	Mi dispiace/Scusi	mee dees-PYAH-cheh/SKOO-zee	Police	La Polizia	lah po-LEET-ZEE-ah
Yes/No	Sì/No	see/no	Embassy	L'Ambasciata	lahm-bah-SHAH-tah
Help!	Aiuto!	ah-YOO-toh	Goodbye	Arrivederci/Arrivederla	ah-ree-veh-DAIR-chee/ah-ree-veh-DAIR-lah

ENGLISH	ITALIAN	PRONOUNCED	ENGLISH	ITALIAN	PRONOUNCED
I'm lost.	Sono perso.	SO-noh PERH-so	One-way	Solo andata	SO-lo ahn-DAH-tah
Train/Bus	Il treno/ l'autobus	eel TREH-no/ laow-toh-BOOS	Round-trip	Andata e ritorno	ahn-DAH-tah eh ree-TOHR-noh
Station	La stazione	lah staht-see-YOH-neh	Ticket	Il biglietto	eel beel-YEHT-toh
Airport	L'aeroporto	LAYR-o-PORT-o	Single room	Una camera singola	OO-nah CAH-meh-rah SEEN-goh-lah
Hotel/Hostel	L'albergo/ L'ostello	lal-BEHR-go/los-TEHL-loh	Left/Right	Sinistra/destra	see-NEE-strah/ DEH-strah
Bathroom	Un gabinetto/Un bagno	oon gah-bee-NEHT-toh/oon BAHN-yoh	Double room	Una camera doppia	OO-nah CAH-meh-rah DOH-pee-yah
Open/Closed	Aperto/Chiuso	ah-PAIR-toh/ KYOO-zoh	Tourist office	L'Ufficio Turistico	loof-FEETCH-o tur-EES-tee-koh
Doctor	Il medico	eel MEH-dee-koh	Ferry	Il traghetto	eel tra-GHEHT-toh
Hospital	L'ospedale	lohs-sped-DAL-e	Tip	La mancia	lah MAHN-cha
Vegetarian	Vegetariano	veh-jeh-tar-ee-AN-oh	Kosher/Halal	Kasher/Halal	KA-sher/HA-lal
Turn	Gira a	JEE-rah ah	Bill	Il conto	eel COHN-toh

ENGLISH	ITALIAN	PRONUNCIATION
Do you speak English?	Parla inglese?	PAHR-lah een-GLAY-zeh
Where is...?	Dov'è...?	doh-VEH
When is the next...?	A che ora è il prossimo...?	AH keh OH-rah eh eel pross-EE-moh
How much does this cost?	Quanto costa?	KWAN-toh CO-stah
Do you have rooms available?	Ha camere libere?	ah CAH-mer-reh LEE-ber-eh
I would like...	Vorrei...	VOH-re
Not even if you were the last man on Earth!	Neanche se tu fossi l'unico uomo sulla terra!	neh-AHN-keh seh too FOH-see LOO-nee-koh WOH-moh soo-LAH TEH-rah

ITALIAN CARDINAL NUMBERS										
0	1	2	3	4	5	6	7	8	9	10
zero	uno	due	tre	quattro	cinque	sei	sette	otto	nove	dieci

NORWEGIAN

ENGLISH	NORWEGIAN	PRONOUNCED	ENGLISH	NORWEGIAN	PRONOUNCED
Yes/No	Ja/Nei	yah/neh	Ticket	Billett	bee-LEHT
Please	Vær så snill	vah sho SNEEL	Train/Bus	Toget/Buss	TOR-guh/buhs
Thank you	Takk	tahk	Airport	Lufthavn	LUFT-hahn
Hello	Goddag	gud-DAHG	Departures	Avgang	AHV-gahng
Goodbye	Ha det bra	HAH deh BRAH	Market	Torget	TOHR-geh
Sorry/Excuse me	Unnskyld	UHRN-shuhrl (UHN-shuhl)	Hotel/Hostel	Hotell/Van-drerhjem	hoo-TEHL/VAN-drair-yaim
Help!	Hjelp!	yehlp	Pharmacy	Apotek	ah-pu-TAYK
Police	politiet	poh-lih-TEE-eh	Toilets	Toalettene	tuah-LEHT-tuh-nuh
Embassy	Ambassade	ahm-bah-SAH-duh	City center	Sentrum	SEHN-trum
I'm lost.	Jeg har gått meg bort	yai har goht mai boort	Open/Closed	Åpen/Stengt	OH-pen/Stengt
Bank	Bank	banhk	Left/Right	Venstre/Høyre	VEHN-stre/ HUHR-uh
Currency exchange	Vekslingskontor	VEHK-shlings-koon-toohr	Post Office	Postkontor	POST-koon-toohr

ENGLISH	NORWEGIAN	PRONUNCIATION
Where is...?	Hvor er...?	VORR ahr
How do I get to...?	Hvordan kommer jeg til...?	VOOR-dan KOH-mer yai teel
How much is...?	Hvor mye koster...?	voor MEE-uh KOH-ster
Do you speak English?	Snakker du engelsk?	SNA-koh dew EHNG-olsk

NORWEGIAN CARDINAL NUMBERS										
0	1	2	3	4	5	6	7	8	9	10
null	en	to	tre	fire	fem	seks	syv	åtte	ni	ti

POLISH

ENGLISH	POLISH	PRONOUNCED	ENGLISH	POLISH	PRONOUNCED
Yes/No	Tak/Nie	tahk/nyeh	Train/Bus	Pociąg/Autobus	POH-chawnk/ ow-TOH-booss
Please	Proszę	PROH-sheh	Train Station	Dworzec	DVOH-zhets
Thank you	Dziękuję	jen-KOO-yeh	Airport	Lotnisko	loht-NEE-skoh
Hello	Cześć	cheshch	Ticket	Bilet	BEE-leht
Goodbye	Do widzenia	doh veed-ZEHN-yah	Hostel	Schronisko młodzieżowe	sroh-NEE-skoh mwo-jeh-ZHO-veh
Sorry/Excuse me	Przepraszam	psheh-PRAH-shahm	Bathroom	Toaleta	toh-ah-LEH-tah
Help!	Pomocy!	poh-MOH-tsih	Open/Closed	Otwarty/ Zamknięty	ot-FAHR-tih/ zahmk-NYENT-ih
I'm lost.	Zgubiłem się.	zgoo-BEE-wem sheh	Left/Right	Lewo/Prawo	LEH-voh/PRAH-voh
Police	Policja	poh-LEETS-yah	Bank	Bank	bahnk
Embassy	Ambasada	am-ba-SA-da	Exchange	Kantor	KAHN-tor
Doctor/ Hospital	Lekarz/Szpital	LEH-kazh/ SHPEE-tal	Grocery/Market	Sklep spożywczy	sklehp spoh-ZHIV-chih
Pharmacy	Apteka	ahp-TEH-ka	Post Office	Poczta	POHCH-tah

ENGLISH	POLISH	PRONUNCIATION
Where is...?	Gdzie jest...?	g-JEH yest
How much does this cost?	Ile to kosztuje?	EE-leh toh kohsh-TOO-yeh
When is the next...?	O której jest następny...?	o KTOO-rey yest nas-TEMP-nee
Do you have (a vacant room)?	Czy są (jakieś wolne pokoje)?	chih SAWN (yah-kyesh VOHL-neh poh-KOY-eh)
I'd like to order...	Chciałbym zamówić...	kh-CHOW-bihm za-MOOV-eech
Do you (m/f) speak English?	Czy pan(i) mówi po angielsku?	chih PAHN(-ee) MOO-vee poh ahn-GYEL-skoo

POLISH CARDINAL NUMBERS										
0	1	2	3	4	5	6	7	8	9	10
zero	jeden	dwa	trzy	cztery	pięć	sześć	siedem	osiem	dziewięć	dziesięć

PORTUGUESE

ENGLISH	PORTUGUESE	PRONOUNCED	ENGLISH	PORTUGUESE	PRONOUNCED
Hello	Olá/Oi	oh-LAH/oy	Hotel	Pousada	poh-ZAH-dah
Please	Por favor	pohr fah-VOHR	Bathroom	Banheiro	bahn-YEH-roo
Thank you (m/f)	Obrigado/ Obrigada	oh-bree-GAH-doo/dah	Open/Closed	Aberto/Fechado	ah-BEHR-toh/ feh-CHAH-do
Sorry/ Excuse me	Desculpe	dish-KOOLP-eh	Doctor	Médico	MEH-dee-koo

APPENDIX

ENGLISH	PORTUGUESE	PRONOUNCED	ENGLISH	PORTUGUESE	PRONOUNCED
Yes/No	Sim/Não	seem/now	Pharmacy	Farmácia	far-MAH-see-ah
Goodbye	Adeus	ah-DEH-oosh	Left/Right	Esquerda/Direita	esh-KER-dah/dee-REH-tah
Help!	Socorro!	soh-KOO-roh	Bank	Banco	BAHN-koh
I'm lost.	Estou perdido.	ish-TOW per-DEE-doo	Exchange	Câmbio	CAHM-bee-yoo
Ticket	Bilhete	beel-YEHT	Market	Mercado	mer-KAH-doo
Train/Bus	Comboio/Autocarro	kom-BOY-yoo/OW-to-KAH-roo	Police	Polícia	po-LEE-see-ah
Station	Estação	eh-stah-SAO	Embassy	Embaixada	ehm-bai-SHAH-dah
Airport	Aeroporto	aye-ro-POR-too	Post Office	Correio	coh-REH-yoh

ENGLISH	PORTUGUESE	PRONUNCIATION
Do you speak English?	Fala inglês?	FAH-lah een-GLAYSH
Where is...?	Onde é...?	OHN-deh eh
How much does this cost?	Quanto custa?	KWAHN-too KOOSH-tah
Do you have rooms available?	Tem quartos disponíveis?	teng KWAHR-toosh dish-po-NEE-veysh
I want/would like...	Eu quero/gostaria de...	eh-oo KER-oh/gost-ar-EE-ah deh
Another round, please.	Mais uma rodada, por favor.	maish OO-mah roh-DAH-dah pohr fah-VOHR

PORTUGUESE CARDINAL NUMBERS										
0	1	2	3	4	5	6	7	8	9	10
zero	um	dois	três	quatro	cinco	seis	sete	oito	nove	dez

RUSSIAN

For the Cyrillic alphabet, see p. 784.

For the Cyrillic alphabet, see p. 784.

ENGLISH	RUSSIAN	PRONOUNCED	ENGLISH	RUSSIAN	PRONOUNCED
Yes/No	Да/нет	dah/nyet	Train/Bus	Поезд/автобус	POH-yihzt/av-TOH-boos
Please	Пожалуйста	pah-ZHAHL-uy-stah	Station	вокзал	vak-ZAL
Thank you	Спасибо	spa-SEE-bah	Airport	аэропрт	ai-roh-PORT
Hello	Здравствуйте	ZDRAHV-zvuht-yeh	Ticket	билет	bil-YET
Goodbye	До свидания	da svee-DAHN-yah	Hotel	гостиница	gahs-TEE-nee-tsah
Sorry/Excuse me	Извините	eez-vee-NEET-yeh	Dorm/Hostel	общежитие	ob-sheh-ZHEE-tee-yeh
Help!	Помогите!	pah-mah-GEE-tyeh	Bathroom	туалет	TOO-ah-lyet
I'm lost.	Я потерен.	ya po-TYE-ren	Open/Closed	открыт/закрыт	ot-KRIHT/za-KRIHT
Police	милиция	mee-LEE-tsee-ya	Left/Right	налево/направо	nah-LYEH-vah/nah-PRAH-vah
Embassy	посольство	pah-SOHL-stva	Bank	банк	bahnk
Passport	паспорт	PAS-pahrt	Exchange	обмен валюты	ab-MYEHN val-ee-YU-tee
Doctor/Hospital	Врач/больница	vrach/bol-NEE-tsa	Grocery/Market	гастроном/рынок	gah-stroh-NOM/REE-nohk
Pharmacy	аптека	ahp-TYE-kah	Post Office	Почта	POCH-ta

ENGLISH	RUSSIAN	PRONUNCIATION
Where is...?	Где...?	gdyeh
How much does this cost?	Сколько это стоит?	SKOHL-ka EH-ta STOY-iht
When is the next...?	Когда будет следущий...?	kog-DAH BOOD-yet SLYED-ooshee

Do you have a vacancy?	У вас етсь свободный номер?	oo vahs yehst svah-BOHD-neey NOH-myehr
I'd like (m/f)...	Я хотел(а) бы...	ya khah-TYEL(a) bwee
Do you speak English?	Вы говорите по-английски?	vy gah-vah-REE-tyeh pah ahn-GLEE-skee

RUSSIAN CARDINAL NUMBERS										
0	1	2	3	4	5	6	7	8	9	10
ноль	один	два	три	четыре	пять	шесть	семь	восемь	девять	десять

SPANISH

ENGLISH	SPANISH	PRONOUNCED	ENGLISH	SPANISH	PRONOUNCED
Hello	Hola	O-lah	Hotel/Hostel	Hotel/Hostal	oh-TEL/ohs-TAHL
Please	Por favor	pohr fah-VOHR	Bathroom	Baño	BAHN-yoh
Thank you	Gracias	GRAH-see-ahs	Open/Closed	Abierto(a)/ Cerrado(a)	ah-bee-EHR-toh/ sehr-RAH-doh
Sorry/Excuse me	Perdón	pehr-DOHN	Doctor	Médico	MEH-dee-koh
Yes/No	Sí/No	see/no	Pharmacy	Farmacia	far-MAH-see-ah
Goodbye	Adiós	ah-DYOYS	Left/Right	Izquierda/ Derecha	ihz-kee-EHR-da/ deh-REH-chah
Help!	¡Ayuda!	ay-YOOH-dah	Bank	Banco	BAHN-koh
I'm lost.	Estoy perdido (a).	ess-TOY pehr-DEE-doh (dah)	Exchange	Cambio	CAHM-bee-oh
Ticket	Boleto	boh-LEH-toh	Grocery	Supermercado	soo-pehr-mer-KAH-doh
Train/Bus	Tren/Autobús	trehn/ow-toh-BOOS	Police	Policía	poh-lee-SEE-ah
Station	Estación	es-tah-SYOHN	Embassy	Embajada	em-bah-HA-dah
Airport	Aeropuerto	ay-roh-PWER-toh	Post Office	Oficina de correos	oh-fee-SEE-nah deh coh-REH-ohs

ENGLISH	SPANISH	PRONUNCIATION
Do you speak English?	¿Habla inglés?	AH-blah een-GLEHS?
Where is...?	¿Dónde está?	DOHN-deh eh-STA?
How much does this cost?	¿Cuánto cuesta?	KWAN-toh KWEHS-tah?
Do you have rooms available?	¿Tiene habitaciones libres?	tee-YEH-neh ah-bee-tah-see-YOH-nehs LEE-brehs?
I want/would like...	Quiero/Me gustaría...	kee-YEH-roh/meh goo-tah-REE-ah

SPANISH CARDINAL NUMBERS										
0	1	2	3	4	5	6	7	8	9	10
cero	uno	dos	tres	cuatro	cinco	seis	siete	ocho	nueve	diez

SWEDISH

ENGLISH	SWEDISH	PRONOUNCED	ENGLISH	SWEDISH	PRONOUNCED
Yes/No	Ja/Nej	yah/nay	Ticket	Biljett	bihl-YEHT
Please	Va så snäll	VAH sahw snel	Train/Bus	Tåget/Buss	TOH-get/boos
Thank you	Tack	tahk	Ferry	Färjan	FAR-yuhn
Hello	Hej	hay	Departure	Avgångar	uhv-GONG-er
Goodbye	Hejdå	HAY-doh	Market	Torget	TOHR-yet
Excuse me	Ursäkta mig	oor-SHEHK-tuh MAY	Hotel/Hostel	Hotell/Vandrar-hem	hoo-TEHL/vun-DRAR-huhm
Help!	Hjälp!	yehlp	Pharmacy	Apotek	uh-poo-TEEK
Police	Polisen	poo-LEE-sehn	Toilets	Toaletten	too-uh-LEHT-en
Embassy	Ambassad	uhm-bah-SAHD	Post Office	Posten	POHS-tehn
I'm lost.	Jag har kommit bort.	yuh hahr KUM-met borht	Open/Closed	Öppen/Stängd	UH-pen/staingd

| Railway station | Järnvägssta-tionen | yairn-vas-gues-stah-SHO-nen | Hospital | Sjukhus | SHUHK-huhs |
| Currency exchange | Växel kontor | vai-xil KOON-toohr | Left/Right | Vänster/Höger | VAIN-ster/HUH-ger |

ENGLISH	SWEDISH	PRONUNCIATION
Where is...?	Var finns...?	vahr FIHNS
How much does this cost?	Hur mycket kostar det?	hurr MUEK-keh KOS-tuhr deh
I'd like to buy...	Jag skulle vilja köpa...	yuh SKOO-leh vihl-yuh CHEU-pah
Do you speak English?	Talar du engelska?	TAH-luhr du EHNG-ehl-skuh
I'm allergic to/I cannot eat...	Jag är allergisk mot/Jag kan inte ata...	yuh air ALLEHR-ghihsk moot/yuh kahn intuh aitah
Do you have rooms available?	Har Ni fria rum?	harh nih freeah ruhm

SWEDISH CARDINAL NUMBERS										
0	1	2	3	4	5	6	7	8	9	10
noll	ett	två	tre	fyra	fem	sex	sju	åtta	nio	tio

INDEX

MAP INDEX

MAP LEGEND

- Hospital
- Hotel/Hostel
- Camping
- Food
- Nightlife
- Museum
- Church
- Synagogue
- Theater
- Internet Café
- Bank
- Police
- Post Office
- Tourist Information
- Point of Interest
- Embassy/Consulate
- Telephone Office
- Airport
- Bus Station
- Train Station
- Ferry Landing

- Building
- Park: city, other
- Plaza/other area
- Beach
- Water
- Swamp
- Pedestrian Zone
- Steps
- Trail
- Ferry Route

- Thermal Bath
- Cave
- Waterfall
- Pass
- Peak
- Mountain Range
- Ranger Station
- Archaeological Site
- Monastery
- Border Crossing

ABBREVIATIONS:
- Lg.   Laguna, Lago
- M.N.   Monumento Naciona
- PL.   Plaza
- Pq.   Parque
- P.I.   Parque Internacional
- P.N.   Parque Nacional
- Q.   Quebrada
- R.   Rio
- R.B.   Reserva Biológica
- R.E.   Reserva Ecológica
- R.F.   Reserva Forestal
- R.F.S.   Refugio de Fauna Sil
- R.V.S.   Refugio de Vida Silve
- R.I.   Reserva Internaciona

The Let's Go compa always points NORTI

ABOUT LET'S GO

THE STUDENT TRAVEL GUIDE

Let's Go publishes the world's favorite student travel guides, written entirely by
Harvard students. Armed with pens, notebooks, and a few changes of clothes
stuffed into their backpacks, our student researchers go across continents,
through time zones, and above expectations to seek out invaluable travel experiences for our readers. Because we are a completely student-run company,
we have a unique perspective on how students travel, where they want to go,
and what they're looking to do when they get there. If your dream is to grab a
machete and forge through the jungles of Costa Rica, we can take you there. If
you'd rather bask in the Riviera sun at a beachside cafe, we'll set you a table. In
short, we write for readers who know that there's more to travel than tour buses.
To keep up, visit our website, www.letsgo.com, where you can sign up to blog,
post photos from your trips, and connect with the Let's Go community.

TRAVELING BEYOND TOURISM

We're on a mission to provide our readers with sharp, fresh coverage packed
with socially responsible opportunities to go beyond tourism. Each guide's
Beyond Tourism chapter shares ideas about responsible travel, study abroad,
and how to give back to the places you visit while on the road. To help you
gain a deeper connection with the places you travel, our fearless researchers
scour the globe to give you the heads-up on both world-renowned and off-the-
beaten-track opportunities. We've also opened our pages to respected writers
and scholars to hear their takes on the countries and regions we cover, and
asked travelers who have worked, studied, or volunteered abroad to contribute
first-person accounts of their experiences.

FIFTY YEARS OF WISDOM

Let's Go has been on the road for 50 years and counting. We've grown a lot since
publishing our first 20-page pamphlet to Europe in 1960, but five decades and
54 titles later our witty, candid guides are still researched and written entirely
by students on shoestring budgets who know that train strikes, stolen luggage,
food poisoning, and marriage proposals are all part of a day's work. This year,
for our 50th anniversary, we're publishing 26 titles—including 6 brand new
guides—brimming with editorial honesty, a commitment to students, and our
irreverent style. Here's to the next 50!

THE LET'S GO COMMUNITY

More than just a travel guide company, Let's Go is a community that reaches
from our headquarters in Cambridge, MA all across the globe. Our small staff of
dedicated student editors, writers, and tech nerds comes together because of
our shared passion for travel and our desire to help other travelers get the most
out of their experience. We love it when our readers become part of the Let's
Go community as well—when you travel, drop us a postcard (67 Mt. Auburn
St., Cambridge, MA 02138, USA), send us an e-mail (feedback@letsgo.com),
or sign up on our website (www.letsgo.com) to tell us about your adventures
and discoveries.

**For more information, updated travel coverage, and news from our researcher team,
visit us online at www.letsgo.com.**

Maps by Let's Go copyright © 2010 by Let's Go, Inc.

Distributed by Publishers Group West.
Printed in Canada by Friesens Corp.

ISBN-13: 978-1-59880-313-6
ISBN-10: 1-59880-313-1
Fiftieth edition
10 9 8 7 6 5 4 3 2 1

Let's Go Europe 2010 is written by Let's Go Publications, 67 Mount Auburn St., Cambridge, MA 02138, USA.

Let's Go® and the LG logo are trademarks of Let's Go, Inc.